❧ A SHAKESPEAREAN GENEALOGY ❧

THIS CHART REFLECTS SHAKESPEARE'S DRAMATIC REPRESENTATION OF ENGLISH HISTORY AND CONSEQUENTLY INCORPORATES SOME OF HIS MANY CHANGES TO THE HISTORICAL RECORD. MANY DESCENDANTS OF HENRY II AND EDWARD III, FOR EXAMPLE, ARE OMITTED. ON OCCASION, SHAKESPEARE COMBINED OR SIMPLY INVENTED HISTORICAL FIGURES. THESE CHANGES ARE EXPLAINED IN THE NOTES.

IN THE CHART, THE NAMES OF KINGS AND QUEENS ARE PRINTED IN CAPITALS, FOLLOWED BY THEIR BIRTH AND DEATH DATES. THE DATES OF THEIR REIGNS ARE PRINTED IN BOLDFACE, IN PARENTHESES. THE NAMES OF PEOPLE WHO ARE CHARACTERS IN THE PLAYS ARE UNDERLINED.

Henry
d. 1183

Edward, Prince of
Wales 1330–1376

— RICHARD II
1367–1400
(1377–99)

RICHARD I
1157–1199
(1189–99)

— Philip Faulconbridge*
(Richard Plantagenet)

William of
Hatfield

Lionel, Duke of
Clarence 1338–1368

— Philippa
m. Edmund
Mortimer, Earl
of March

John of Gaunt,
Duke of Lancaster
1340–1399
m. Blanche of
Lancaster
m. Constance of
Castile
m. Katherine
Swynford

— HENRY IV
1367–1413
(1399–1413)

HENRY II
1133–1189
(1154–89)
m. Eleanor
of Aquitaine
d. 1204

Geoffrey d. 1186
m. Constance
of Brittany

— Arthur
1187–1203

— Thomas Beaufort,
Duke of Exeter
1377–1427

— Henry Beaufort,
Bishop of Winchester
1375–1447

— John Beaufort,
Earl of Somerset
1372–1409

JOHN 1167–1216
(1199–1216)

— HENRY III
1207–1272
(1216–72)

— EDWARD I
1239–1307
(1272–1307)

— Joan Beaufort
m. Ralph Neville,
Earl of
Westmorland

EDWARD II
1284–1327
(1307–27)

EDWARD III
1312–1377
(1327–77)
m. Philippa of
Hainault

Edmund of Langley,
Duke of York
1341–1402

— Edward, Duke of
Aumerle d. 1415

— Richard, Earl
of Cambridge
d. 1415 m. Anne
Mortimer (above)

Thomas of
Woodstock, Duke of
Gloucester 1355–1397

— Anne

Eleanor
m. Alfonso VIII,
King of Castile

— Blanche d. 1252
m. Louis VIII
of France

William of
Windsor

*Philip Faulconbridge, the bastard son of Richard I, had no historical existence. Such a character appears in the play The Life and Death of King John and is referred to in passing in Holinshed's Chronicles.

† In the character of Edmund Mortimer, Shakespeare conflated two historical figures. The Edmund Mortimer who married Catrin, daughter of Owain Glyndŵr, was the grandson of Lionel, Duke of Clarence, and the younger brother of Roger Mortimer, Earl of March. He died in 1409. Shakespeare combined him with his nephew, the Edmund Mortimer recognized by Richard II as his heir, who died in 1424. This second Edmund was the son of Roger Mortimer, brother of Anne Mortimer, and uncle of Richard Plantagenet. In creating this character, Shakespeare eliminated the generation that includes Roger and the elder Edmund Mortimer, bringing the entire York family one step closer to the sons of Edward III.

‡The character of the Duke of Somerset combines Henry Beaufort with his younger brother Edmund (d. 1471), who succeeded him as duke.

Elizabeth Mortimer ("Kate") m. Henry Percy ("Hotspur") 1364–1403 — Henry, Earl of Northumberland 1394–1455

EDWARD IV 1442–1483 (1461–83) m. Elizabeth Woodville d. 1492

EDWARD V 1470–1483 (1483)

Richard, Duke of York 1472–1483

Elizabeth of York 1465–1503 m. HENRY VII (below)

Edmund, Earl of Rutland 1443–1460

Edmund Mortimer†

George, Duke of Clarence 1449–1478 m. Isabel Neville (below)

Anne Mortimer m. Richard, Earl of Cambridge (below)

Richard Plantagenet, Duke of York 1411–1460 m. Cicely Neville (below)

RICHARD III 1452–1485 (1483–85) m. Anne Neville (below)

— Edward, Prince of Wales

HENRY V 1387–1422 (1413–22) m. Catherine 1401–1437

HENRY VI 1421–1471 (1422–61) m. Margaret of Anjou d. 1482

Edward, Prince of Wales 1453–1471 m. Anne Neville (below)

Arthur m. Catherine of Aragon (below)

Thomas, Duke of Clarence d. 1421

Margaret m. James IV of Scotland

James V of Scotland
|
Mary, Queen of Scots
|
JAMES I 1566–1625 (1603–25)

John of Lancaster, Duke of Bedford 1389–1435

Humphrey, Duke of Gloucester 1391–1447 m. Eleanor Cobham d. 1454

John Beaufort, Duke of Somerset 1403–1444

Margaret Beaufort m. Edmund Tudor, Earl of Richmond

HENRY VII 1457–1509 (1485–1509) m. Elizabeth of York (above)

HENRY VIII 1491–1547 (1509–47) m. Catherine of Aragon

MARY I 1516–1558 (1553–58) m. Philip of Spain

Edmund Beaufort, Duke of Somerset 1406–1455

Henry Beaufort, Duke of Somerset 1436–1464‡

Isabel Neville d. 1476 m. George, Duke of Clarence (above)

m. Anne Boleyn

ELIZABETH I 1533–1603 (1558–1603)

Richard Neville, Earl of Warwick 1428–1471

m. Jane Seymour

EDWARD VI 1537–1553 (1547–53)

Richard Neville, Earl of Salisbury 1400–1460

John Neville, Marquess of Montague d. 1471

Anne Neville d. 1485 m. Edward, Prince of Wales (above)

m. Anne of Cleves

m. Katherine Howard

Cicely Neville m. Richard Plantagenet, Duke of York (above)

m. RICHARD III (above)

m. Katherine Parr

Mary m. Charles Brandon

Frances
|
Jane Grey 1537–1554

Humphrey, Duke of Buckingham 1402–1460

Humphrey Stafford d. 1455

Henry, Duke of Buckingham 1454?–1483

Edward, Duke of Buckingham 1478–1521

The Kings and Queens of England
1377–1625

RICHARD II, 1377–99 RICHARD was the eldest son of EDWARD THE BLACK PRINCE, himself the eldest son of KING EDWARD III, who ruled England from 1327 to 1377. When the BLACK PRINCE died in battle in France in 1376, RICHARD became the legitimate heir to the throne. He ruled from EDWARD's death in 1377 until he was deposed in 1399 by HENRY BOLINGBROKE, the eldest son of JOHN OF GAUNT, DUKE OF LANCASTER. Because he was the fourth son of EDWARD III, GAUNT and his Lancastrian descendants had weaker hereditary claims to the throne than did RICHARD. When deposed, RICHARD had no children to succeed him, but he recognized EDMUND MORTIMER, FIFTH EARL OF MARCH, as his heir presumptive. This MORTIMER was descended from LIONEL, DUKE OF CLARENCE, the third son of EDWARD III, and therefore also had stronger hereditary claims to the throne than did BOLINGBROKE. SHAKESPEARE combined this MORTIMER with his uncle EDMUND MORTIMER, who married OWAIN GLYNDŴR'S DAUGHTER.

HENRY IV, 1399–1413 HENRY BOLINGBROKE, eldest son of JOHN OF GAUNT, seized the throne from RICHARD II in 1399. When HENRY died in 1413, he was succeeded by his eldest son, PRINCE HAL, who became HENRY V.

HENRY V, 1413–22 HENRY V became king in 1413 and reigned until his death in 1422. He was succeeded by his son, HENRY VI.

HENRY VI, 1422–61 HENRY VI was less than one year old when he succeeded his father, HENRY V. In the young king's minority, his uncle HUMPHREY, DUKE OF GLOUCESTER, was named Lord Protector, and the kingdom was ruled by an aristocratic council. HENRY VI assumed personal authority in 1437. He was deposed in 1461 by his third cousin, who was crowned EDWARD IV. HENRY was murdered in 1471.

EDWARD IV, 1461–83 EDWARD, the eldest son of RICHARD, DUKE OF YORK, seized the throne from HENRY VI in 1461. His Yorkist claim to the throne derived from his grandmother, ANNE MORTIMER, who was descended from LIONEL, third son of EDWARD III, and was sister to that EDMUND MORTIMER recognized by RICHARD II as his heir presumptive; EDWARD IV's grandfather, RICHARD, EARL OF CAMBRIDGE, was the son of EDMUND OF LANGLEY, fifth son of EDWARD III. EDWARD IV reigned until his death in 1483. His heir was his eldest son (EDWARD), but the throne was usurped by his brother RICHARD, DUKE OF GLOUCESTER.

RICHARD III, 1483–85 RICHARD III was the younger brother of EDWARD IV. After the death of EDWARD IV in 1483, RICHARD prevented the coronation of EDWARD V with a claim of illegitimacy and succeeded to the throne himself. EDWARD and his younger brother, RICHARD, DUKE OF YORK, were murdered in the Tower of London. RICHARD III was killed at the Battle of Bosworth Field in 1485, and the kingdom fell to the victor, HENRY TUDOR, EARL OF RICHMOND.

HENRY VII, 1485–1509 HENRY TUDOR seized the throne from RICHARD III in 1485. He was descended from JOHN OF GAUNT by JOHN's third marriage, with KATHERINE SWYNFORD. He married ELIZABETH, daughter of EDWARD IV, uniting the houses of Lancaster and York. He died in 1509 and was succeeded by his son, HENRY VIII.

HENRY VIII, 1509–47 HENRY was the second son of HENRY VII. His older brother, ARTHUR, died in 1502. HENRY VIII's first wife was CATHERINE OF ARAGON, who bore his daughter MARY. His second wife, ANNE BOLEYN, was the mother of ELIZABETH. His third wife, JANE SEYMOUR, bore him a son, who succeeded to the throne as EDWARD VI after HENRY VIII died in 1547.

EDWARD VI, 1547–53 EDWARD VI was nine years old when he became king. From 1547 to 1549, the realm was governed by a Lord Protector, the DUKE OF SOMERSET; power then passed to JOHN DUDLEY, DUKE OF NORTHUMBERLAND. When EDWARD VI died in 1553, NORTHUMBERLAND attempted unsuccessfully to prevent the succession of MARY TUDOR by installing as queen his daughter-in-law, LADY JANE GREY, a great-granddaughter of HENRY VII.

MARY I, 1553–58 MARY, daughter of HENRY VIII and his first wife, CATHERINE OF ARAGON, came to the throne in 1553. She married KING PHILIP OF SPAIN but died childless. She was succeeded by her half-sister, ELIZABETH.

ELIZABETH I, 1558–1603 ELIZABETH, the daughter of HENRY VIII and his second wife, ANNE BOLEYN, became queen after the death of her half-sister, MARY, in 1558. She ruled until her death in 1603. She was succeeded by her cousin JAMES.

JAMES I, 1603–1625 JAMES VI OF SCOTLAND became JAMES I OF ENGLAND in 1603. His claim to the throne of England derived from his great-grandmother, MARGARET TUDOR, a daughter of HENRY VII who married JAMES IV OF SCOTLAND. James ruled England and Scotland until his death in 1625; he was succeeded by his son, CHARLES I.

THE NORTON SHAKESPEARE

BASED ON THE OXFORD EDITION

Histories

The original Oxford Text on which this
edition is based was prepared by

Stanley Wells
Gary Taylor
General Editors

John Jowett

William Montgomery

THE NORTON SHAKESPEARE

BASED ON THE OXFORD EDITION

Histories

Stephen Greenblatt, *General Editor*
HARVARD UNIVERSITY

Walter Cohen
CORNELL UNIVERSITY

Jean E. Howard
COLUMBIA UNIVERSITY

Katharine Eisaman Maus
UNIVERSITY OF VIRGINIA

*With an essay on the Shakespearean stage
by* Andrew Gurr

W · W · NORTON & COMPANY · NEW YORK · LONDON

Copyright © 1997 by W. W. Norton & Company, Inc.
Text and some commentaries copyright © 1986, 1988 by Oxford University Press.

The text of this book is composed in Electra with the display set in Centaur.
Composition by Binghamton Valley Composition.
Manufacturing by R. R. Donnelley & Sons.
Book design by Antonina Krass.

The Library of Congress has cataloged the one-volume edition as follows:
Shakespeare, William, 1564–1616.
The Norton Shakespeare / Stephen Greenblatt, general editor ;
Walter Cohen, Jean E. Howard, Katharine Eisaman Maus [editors] ;
with an essay on the Shakespearean stage by Andrew Gurr.
p.   cm.
"Based on the Oxford edition."
Includes bibliographical references and index.

ISBN 0-393-97087-6. — ISBN 0-393-04107-7

I. Greenblatt, Stephen Jay.   II. Cohen, Walter, 1949–   .
III. Howard, Jean E. (Jean Elizabeth), 1948–   .   IV. Maus,
Katharine Eisaman, 1955–   .   V. Title.
PR2754.G74   1997
822.3'3—DC21   97-7083
                                                                          CIP
                                                                          Rev.

Histories: ISBN 0-393-97671-8 (pbk.)

W. W. Norton & Company, Inc., 500 Fifth Avenue, New York, N.Y. 10110
www.wwnorton.com

W. W. Norton & Company Ltd., 10 Coptic Street, London WC1A 1PU

2 3 4 5 6 7 8 9 0

Contents

Histories

Appendices

Preface

Since Shakespeare's principal medium, the drama, was thoroughly collaborative, it seems appropriate that this edition of his works is itself the result of a sustained collaboration. Two lists of editors' names on the title-page spread hint at the collaboration that has brought to fruition *The Norton Shakespeare*. But the title page does not tell the full history of this project. The text on which *The Norton Shakespeare* is based was published in both modern-spelling and original-spelling versions by Oxford University Press, in 1986. Under the general editorship of Stanley Wells and Gary Taylor, the Oxford text was a thorough rethinking of the entire body of Shakespeare's works, the most far-reaching and innovative revision of the traditional canon in centuries. When many classroom instructors who wanted to introduce their students to the works of Shakespeare through a modern text expressed a need for the pedagogical apparatus they have come to expect in an edition oriented toward students, Norton negotiated with Oxford to assemble an editorial team of its own to prepare the necessary teaching materials around the existing Oxford text. Hence ensued a collaboration of two publishers and two editorial teams.

To what extent is this the *Norton Shakespeare* and to what extent the Oxford text? Since the Norton contributions appear here for the first time, the many pages that follow will provide the answer to the first part of the question. Introductions (both the General Introduction and those to individual plays and poems), footnotes, glosses, bibliographies, genealogies, annals, documents, and illustrations have all been the responsibility of the Norton team. We also asked Andrew Gurr of the University of Reading to contribute to this edition an essay on the London theater in Shakespeare's time, and we asked Donald W. Foster of Vassar College to introduce, edit, and gloss *A Funeral Elegy*, a poem, included here in an appendix, that raises important questions about the attribution of works to Shakespeare.

The textual notes and variants derive for the most part from the work of the Oxford team, especially as represented in *William Shakespeare: A Textual Companion* (Oxford University Press, 1987), a remarkably comprehensive explanation of editorial decisions that is herewith strongly recommended to instructors as a valuable companion to this volume. Some of the annotations spring from the never-published commentaries of the Oxford team, who have graciously allowed the Norton editors full use of them.

The Oxford text is widely available and already well-known to scholars. A few words here may help clarify the extent of our fidelity to that text and the nature of the collaboration that has brought about this volume. The Oxford editors have profited from the massive and sustained attention accorded their edition by Shakespeare scholars across the globe, and of course they have continued to participate actively in the ongoing scholarly discussion about the nature of Shakespeare's text. In the reprintings of the Oxford volumes and in various articles over the past years, the Oxford editors have made a number of refinements of the edition they originally published. Such changes have been incorporated silently here. A small number of other changes made by the Norton team, however, were not part of the Oxford editors' design and were only accepted by them after we reached, through lengthy consultation, a mutual understanding about the nature, purpose, and intended audience of this volume. In all such changes, our main concern was for the classroom; we wished to make fully and clearly available the scholarly innovation and freshness of the Oxford text, while at the same time making certain that this was a superbly useful teaching text. It is a pleasure here to record, on behalf of the Norton team, our gratitude for the personal and professional generosity of the Oxford editors in offering advice and entertaining arguments in our common goal of providing the best student Shakespeare for our times. The Norton changes to the Oxford text are various, but in only a few instances are they major. The following brief notes are sufficient to summarize all of these changes, which are also indicated in appropriate play introductions, footnotes, or textual notes.

1. The Oxford editors, along with other scholars, have strenuously argued—in both the Oxford text and elsewhere—that the now-familiar text of *King Lear*, so nearly omnipresent in our classrooms as to seem unquestionably authoritative but in reality dating from the work of Alexander Pope (1723) and Lewis Theobald (1733), represents a wrong-headed conflation of two distinct versions of the play: Shakespeare's original creation as printed in the 1608 Quarto and his substantial revision as printed in the First Folio (1623). The Oxford text, therefore, prints both *The History of King Lear* and *The Tragedy of King Lear*. Norton follows suit, but where Oxford presents these two texts sequentially, we print them on facing pages. While each version may be read independently, and to ensure this we have provided glosses and footnotes for each, the substantial points of difference between the two are immediately apparent and available for comparison. But even many who agree with the scholarly argument for the two texts of *Lear* nevertheless favor making available a conflated text, the text on which innumerable performances of the play have been based and on which a huge body of literary criticism has been written. With the reluctant acquiescence, therefore, of the Oxford editors, we have included a conflated *Lear*, a text that has no part in the Oxford canon and that has been edited by Barbara K. Lewalski of Harvard University rather than by Gary Taylor, the editor of the Oxford *Lears*.

The *Norton Shakespeare*, then, includes three separate texts of *King Lear*. The reader can compare them, understand the role of editors in constructing the texts we now call Shakespeare's, explore in considerable detail the kinds of decisions that playwrights, editors, and printers make and remake, witness first-hand the historical transformation of what might at first glance seem fixed and unchanging. The *Norton Shakespeare* offers extraordinary access to this supremely brilliant, difficult, compelling play.

2. *Hamlet* (along with several other plays, including *Richard II, Troilus and Cressida*, and *Othello*) offers similar grounds for objections to the traditional conflation, but both the economics of publishing and the realities of bookbinding—not to mention our recognition of the limited time in the typical undergraduate syllabus—preclude our offering three (or even four) *Hamlets* to match three *Lears*.

The Oxford text of *Hamlet* was based upon the Folio text, with an appended list of Additional Passages from the Second Quarto (Q2). These additional readings total more than two hundred lines, a significant number, among which are lines that have come to seem very much part of the play as widely received, even if we may doubt that they belong with all the others in any single one of Shakespeare's *Hamlets*. The Norton team, while following the Oxford text, has moved the Q2 passages from the appendix to the body of the play. But in doing so, we have not wanted once again to produce a conflated text. We have therefore indented the Q2 passages, printed them in a different typeface, and numbered them in such a way as to make clear their provenance. Those who wish to read the Folio version of *Hamlet* can thus simply skip over the indented Q2 passages, while at the same time it is possible for readers to see clearly the place that the Q2 passages occupy. We have adopted a similar strategy with several other plays: passages printed in Oxford in appendices are generally printed here in the play texts, though clearly demarcated and not conflated. In the case of *The Taming of the Shrew* and the related quarto text, *The Taming of a Shrew*, however, we have followed Oxford's procedure and left the quarto passages in an appendix, since we believe the texts reflect two distinct plays rather than a revision of one. We have similarly reproduced Oxford's brief appendices to *A Midsummer Night's Dream* and *Henry V*, enabling readers to consider alternative revisions of certain passages.

3. For reasons understood by every Shakespearean (and rehearsed at some length in this volume), the Oxford editors chose to restore the name "Sir John Oldcastle" to the character much better known as Falstaff in *1 Henry IV*. (They made comparable changes in the names of the characters known as Bardolph and Peto.) But for reasons understood by everyone who has presented this play to undergraduates or sampled the centuries of enthusiastic criticism, the Norton editors, with the Oxford editors' gracious agreement, have for this classroom edition opted for the familiar name "Falstaff " (and those of his boon companions), properly noting the change and its significance in the play's introduction.

4. The Oxford editors chose not to differentiate between those stage directions that appeared in the early editions up to and including the Folio and those that have been added by subsequent editors. Instead, in *A Textual Companion* they include separate lists of the original stage directions. These lists are not readily available to readers of the Norton text, whose editors opted instead to bracket all stage directions that derive from editions published after the Folio. Readers can thus easily see which stage directions derive from texts that may bear at least some relation to performances in Shakespeare's time, if not to Shakespeare's own authorship. The Norton policy is more fully explained in the General Introduction.

It has long been the dream of the publisher, W.W. Norton, to bring out a Shakespeare edition. The task proved to be a complex one, with many players. The initial efforts of the late John Benedict at Norton were followed, with the crucial encouragement of the firm's chairman, Donald S. Lamm, by the efforts of Barry Wade, who brought together with patience, tact, and goodwill the scholars who eventually carried the project to fruition. To our deep sadness and regret, Barry Wade did not live to see the completion of the work to which he devoted so much energy. He was succeeded in overseeing the project by Julia Reidhead, whose calm intelligence, common sense, and steady focus have been essential in enabling us to reach the end of the long road. We were blessed with the exceptionally thoughtful and scrupulous developmental editing of Marian Johnson and with the assistance of an extraordinary group of Norton staffers: head manuscript editor Susan Gaustad, who was assisted by copyeditor Alice Falk and project editor Kurt Wildermuth; editorial assistant Tara Parmiter, who, among many other things, coordinated the art program; production manager Diane O'Connor; in-house editor of the *Norton Shakespeare Workshop* CD-ROM Anna Karvellas; and proofreaders Carol Walker and Rich Rivellese.

The Norton Shakespeare editors have, in addition, had the valuable, indeed indispensable support of a host of undergraduate and graduate research assistants, colleagues, friends, and family. Even a partial listing of those to whom we owe our heartfelt thanks is very long, but we are all fortunate enough to live in congenial and supportive environments, and the edition has been part of our lives for a long time. We owe special thanks for sustained dedication and learning to our principal research assistants: Pat Cahill, Jody Greene, Nate Johnson, Jesse Liu, Joseph Nugent, Beth Quitslund, Henry Turner, and Michael Witmore. Particular thanks are due to Noah Heringman for his work on the texts assembled in the documents section and for the prefatory notes and comments on those texts; to Philip Schwyzer for preparing the genealogies and the glossary and for conceiving and preparing the Shakespearean Chronicle; and to Young Jean Lee for a variety of complex editorial tasks. In addition, we are deeply grateful to Jim, Kate, and Caleb Baker, Gen Beckman, Aimée Boutin, Dan Brayton, Laura Brown, Francesca Coppelli, Adam Feldman, Margaret Ferguson, William Flesch, Elizabeth Gardner, Ellen Greenblatt, Josh and Aaron Greenblatt, Mark Hazard, David Kastan, Dennis Kezar, Shawn Kirschner, Jeffrey Knapp, Baty Landis, Wendy Lesser, Laurie Maguire, Fred Everett Maus, Stephen

Orgel, Phyllis Rackin, James Shapiro, Debora Shuger, Melissa Wiley Stickney, Ramie Targoff, Elda Tsou, and the staff of the Wissenschaftskolleg zu Berlin. All of these companions, and many more besides, have helped us find in this long collective enterprise what the Dedicatory Epistle to the First Folio promises to its readers: delight. We make the same promise to the readers of our edition and invite them to continue the great Shakespearean collaboration.

Stephen Greenblatt
Walter Cohen
Jean E. Howard
Katharine Eisaman Maus

Acknowledgments

Among our many critics, advisers, and friends, the following were of special help in providing critiques of particular plays or of the project as a whole: Barry Adams (Cornell University), Richard Adams (California State University, Sacramento), Denise Albanes (George Mason University), Mark Anderson (SUNY Brockport), Herman Asarnow (University of Portland), John H. Astington (Erindale, University of Toronto), Jonathan Baldo (University of Rochester), Jonathan Bate, Leonard Barkan (New York University), John Baxter (Dalhousie University), D. A. Beecher (Carleton University), S. Berg (University of Alberta), Paula Berggren (CUNY), Edward Berry (University of Victoria), Walter Blanco (Lehman, CUNY), Thomas L. Blanton (Central Washington University), Al Braunmuller (UCLA), Stephen Brown (Trent University), Douglas Bruster (University of Chicago), Kate Buckley (Pontifical College, Josephinum), Joseph Candido (University of Arkansas), William Carroll (Boston University), Thomas Cartelli (Muhlenberg College), Sheila Cavanaugh (Emory University), Susan Cerasano (Colgate University), Gerald N. Chapman (University of Denver), Lois Chapman (South Suburban College), Maurice Charney (Rutgers University), Thomas Clayton (University of Minnesota), Peter J. Connelly (Grinnell College), Barbara Correll (Cornell University), Jonathan Crewe (Dartmouth College), Earl Dachslager (University of Houston), Roger Deakins (New York University), Kenneth L. Deal (Huntingdon College), Margreta de Grazia (University of Pennsylvania), H. Delisle (Bridgewater State University), Alan Dessen (University of North Carolina, Chapel Hill), Nirmal Singh Dhesi (Sonoma State University), William R. Drennan (University of Wisconsin, Center Baraboo), Heather Dubrow (University of Wisconsin), Sara Eaton (North Central College), Katherine Eggert (University of Colorado), Charles R. Forker (Indiana University), Donald Foster (Vassar College), Michael Frachmann (California State University, Bakersfield), Lisa Freinkel (University of Oregon), Charles Frey (University of Washington), Lloyd G. Gibbs (University of South Carolina), Dominique Goy-Blanquet (University of Amiens), Hugh Grady (Beaver College), Anthony Graham-White (University of Illinois, Chicago), Peter Greenfield (University of Puget Sound), R. Chris Hassel Jr. (Vanderbilt University), David Haley (University of Minnesota), Jay Halio (University of Delaware), Richard Helgerson (University of California, Santa Barbara), Richard Hillman (York University), Barbara Hodgdon (Drake University), Peter Holland (Cambridge University), Trevor Howard-Hill (University of South Carolina), Clark Hulse (University of Illinois, Chicago), Gabriele Bernhard Jackson (Temple University), Henry D. Janzen (University of Windsor), Barbara Kachur (University of Missouri, St. Louis), Coppelia Kahn (Brown University), Michael H. Keefer (Université Sainte Anne), Robert Knapp (Reed College), Mary Kramer (University of Lowell), James Lake (Louisiana State University, Shreveport), Ian Lancashire (New College, University of Toronto), Judiana Lawrence (St. John Fisher College), Alexander Leggatt (University College, University of Toronto), Ted Leinwand (University of Maryland, College Park), Carol Leventen (Adrian College), Murray J. Levith (Skidmore College), Barbara Lewalski (Harvard University), Cynthia Lewis (Davidson College), Arthur Little (UCLA), M. Loyola (University of Saskatchewan), J. M. Lyon (University of Bristol), Joyce MacDonald (University of Kentucky), Irene R. Makaryk (University of Ottawa), Eric Mallin (University of Texas, Austin), Leah Marcus (University of Texas, Austin), Arthur Marotti (Wayne State University), Cynthia Marshall (Rhodes College), Steven Marx (Cal Poly State University, San Luis Obispo), Margaret Maurer (Colgate University), M. A. McDonald (Belmont College), Nan Morrison (College of Charleston), Richard E. Morton (McMaster University), Steven Mullaney (University of Michigan), Ronnie Mulryne (University of Warwick), Carol Thomas Neely

(University of Illinois), Malcolm A. Nelson (SUNY Fredonia), Karen Newman (Brown University), M. Noble (Defiance College), John O'Connor (George Mason University), Gail Paster (George Washington University), Donald Peet (Indiana University), Lois Potter (University of Delaware), Phyllis Rackin (University of Pennsylvania), Constance Relihan (Auburn University), Neil Rhodes (University of St. Andrews), Jeremy Richard (University of Connecticut, Stamford), Gilbert Robinson (San Francisco State University), D. S. Rodes (UCLA), Mark Rose (University of California, Santa Barbara), David Rosen (University of Maine, Machias), Kiernan Ryan (Cambridge University), Peter Saccio (Dartmouth College), Nadine S. St. Louis (University of Wisconsin, Eau Claire), Naheeb Shaheen (Memphis State University), J. W. Shaw (University of Massachusetts), William P. Shaw (LeMoyne College), John W. Sider (Westmont College), Jim Siemon (Boston University), W. W. E. Slights (University of Saskatchewan), Molly Smith (Aberdeen University), Edward V. Stackpoole (University of San Francisco), Lisa Starks (East Texas State University), Michael J. Taylor (University of New Brunswick), Richard C. Tobias (University of Pittsburgh), Robert K. Turner (University of Wisconsin), Virginia Mason Vaughan (Clark University), Wendy Wall (Northwestern University), Robert N. Watson (UCLA), Valerie Wayne (University of Hawaii, Manoa), Herbert S. Weil, Jr. (University of Manitoba), Barry Weller (University of Utah), Paul Werstine (King's College), R. L. Widmann (University of Colorado, Boulder), Inga Wiehl (Yakina Valley Community College), Douglas B. Wilson (University of Denver).

Mr. WILLIAM

SHAKESPEARES

COMEDIES,
HISTORIES, &
TRAGEDIES.

Published according to the True Originall Copies.

Martin Droeshout sculpsit London.

L O N D O N
Printed by Isaac Iaggard, and Ed. Blount. 1623.

Engraving of Shakespeare by Martin Droeshout. Title page of the 1623 First Folio. (The Documents appendix, below, reproduces the front matter to the Folio, including Ben Jonson's poem "To the Reader.")

General Introduction

by

STEPHEN GREENBLATT

"He was not of an age, but for all time!"

The celebration of Shakespeare's genius, eloquently initiated by his friend and rival Ben Jonson, has over the centuries become an institutionalized rite of civility. The person who does not love Shakespeare has made, the rite implies, an incomplete adjustment not simply to a particular culture—English culture of the late sixteenth and early seventeenth centuries—but to "culture" as a whole, the dense network of constraints and entitlements, dreams and practices that links us to nature. Indeed, so absolute is Shakespeare's achievement that he has himself come to seem like great creating nature: the common bond of humankind, the principle of hope, the symbol of the imagination's power to transcend time-bound beliefs and assumptions, peculiar historical circumstances, and specific artistic conventions.

The near-worship Shakespeare inspires is one of the salient facts about his art. But we must at the same time acknowledge that this art is the product of peculiar historical circumstances and specific conventions, four centuries distant from our own. The acknowledgment is important because Shakespeare the working dramatist did not typically lay claim to the transcendent, visionary truths attributed to him by his most fervent admirers; his characters more modestly say, in the words of the magician Prospero, that their project was "to please" (*The Tempest*, Epilogue, line 13). The starting point, and perhaps the ending point as well, in any encounter with Shakespeare is simply to enjoy him, to savor his imaginative richness, to take pleasure in his infinite delight in language.

"If then you do not like him," Shakespeare's first editors wrote in 1623, "surely you are in some manifest danger not to understand him." Over the years, accommodations have been devised to make liking Shakespeare easier for everyone. When the stage sank to melodrama and light opera, Shakespeare—in suitably revised texts—was there. When the populace had a craving for hippodrama, plays performed entirely on horseback, *Hamlet* was dutifully rewritten and mounted. When audiences went mad for realism, live frogs croaked in productions of *A Midsummer Night's Dream*. When the stage was stripped bare and given over to stark exhibitions of sadistic cruelty, Shakespeare was our contemporary. And when the theater itself had lost some of its cultural centrality, Shakespeare moved effortlessly to Hollywood and the sound stages of the BBC.

This virtually universal appeal is one of the most astonishing features of the Shakespeare phenomenon: plays that were performed before glittering courts thrive in junior high school auditoriums; enemies set on destroying one another laugh at the same jokes and weep at the same catastrophes; some of the richest and most complex English verse ever written migrates with spectacular success into German and Italian, Hindi, Swahili, and Japanese. Is there a single, stable, continuous object that underlies all of these migrations and metamorphoses? Certainly not. The fantastic diffusion and long life of Shakespeare's works depends on their extraordinary malleability, their protean capacity to elude definition and escape secure possession. At the same time, they are not without identifiable shared features: across centuries and continents, family resemblances link many of the wildly diverse manifestations of plays such as *Romeo and Juliet*, *Hamlet*, and *Twelfth Night*. And if there is no clear limit or end point, there is a reasonably clear beginning, the

1

England of the late sixteenth and early seventeenth centuries, when the plays and poems collected in this volume made their first appearance.

An art virtually without end or limit but with an identifiable, localized, historical origin: Shakespeare's achievement defies the facile opposition between transcendent and time-bound. It is not necessary to choose between an account of Shakespeare as the scion of a particular culture and an account of him as a universal genius who created works that continually renew themselves across national and generational boundaries. On the contrary: crucial clues to understanding his art's remarkable power to soar beyond its originary time and place lie in the very soil from which that art sprang.

Shakespeare's World

Life and Death

Life expectation at birth in early modern England was exceedingly low by our standards: under thirty years old, compared with over seventy today. Infant mortality rates were extraordinarily high, and it is estimated that in the poorer parishes of London only about half the children survived to the age of fifteen, while the children of aristocrats fared only a little better. In such circumstances, some parents must have developed a certain detachment—one of Shakespeare's contemporaries writes of losing "some three or four children"—but there are many expressions of intense grief, so that we cannot assume that the frequency of death hardened people to loss or made it routine.

Still, the spectacle of death, along with that other great threshold experience, birth, must have been far more familiar to Shakespeare and his contemporaries than to ourselves. There was no equivalent in early modern England to our hospitals, and most births and deaths occurred at home. Physical means for the alleviation of pain and suffering were extremely limited—alcohol might dull the terror, but it was hardly an effective anesthetic—and medical treatment was generally both expensive and worthless, more likely to intensify suffering than to lead to a cure. This was a world without a concept of antiseptics, with little actual understanding of disease, with few effective ways of treating earaches or venereal disease, let alone the more terrible instances of what Shakespeare calls "the thousand natural shocks that flesh is heir to."

The worst of these shocks was the bubonic plague, which repeatedly ravaged England, and particularly English towns, until the third quarter of the seventeenth century. The plague was terrifyingly sudden in its onset, rapid in its spread, and almost invariably lethal. Physicians were helpless in the face of the epidemic, though they prescribed amulets, preservatives, and sweet-smelling substances (on the theory that the plague was carried by

Bill recording plague deaths in London, 1609.

noxious vapors). In the plague-ridden year of 1564, the year of Shakespeare's birth, some 254 people died in Stratford-upon-Avon, out of a total population of 800. The year before, some 20,000 Londoners are thought to have died; in 1593, almost 15,000; in 1603, 36,000, or over a sixth of the city's inhabitants. The social effects of these horrible visitations were severe: looting, violence, and despair, along with an intensification of the age's perennial poverty, unemployment, and food shortages. The London plague regulations of 1583, reissued with modifications in later epidemics, ordered that the infected and their households should be locked in their homes for a month; that the streets should be kept clean; that vagrants should be expelled; and that funerals and plays should be restricted or banned entirely.

The plague, then, had a direct and immediate impact on Shakespeare's own profession. City officials kept records of the weekly number of plague deaths; when these surpassed a certain number, the theaters were peremptorily closed. The basic idea was not only to prevent contagion but also to avoid making an angry God still angrier with the spectacle of idleness. While restricting public assemblies may in fact have slowed the epidemic, other public policies in times of plague, such as killing the cats and dogs, may have made matters worse (since the disease was spread not by these animals but by the fleas that bred on the black rats that infested the poorer neighborhoods). Moreover, the playing companies, driven out of London by the closing of the theaters, may have carried plague to the provincial towns.

Even in good times, when the plague was dormant and the weather favorable for farming, the food supply in England was precarious. A few successive bad harvests, such as occurred in the mid-1590s, could cause serious hardship, even starvation. Not surprisingly, the poor bore the brunt of the burden: inflation, low wages, and rent increases left large numbers of people with very little cushion against disaster. Further, at its best, the diet of most people seems to have been seriously deficient. The lower classes then, as throughout most of history, subsisted on one or two foodstuffs, usually low in protein. The upper classes disdained green vegetables and milk and gorged themselves on meat. Illnesses that we now trace to vitamin deficiencies were rampant. Some but not much relief from pain was provided by the beer that Elizabethans, including children, drank almost incessantly. (Home brewing aside, enough beer was sold in England for every man, woman, and child to have consumed forty gallons a year.)

Wealth

Despite rampant disease, the population of England in Shakespeare's lifetime was steadily growing, from approximately 3,060,000 in 1564 to 4,060,000 in 1600 and 4,510,000 in 1616. Though the death rate was more than twice what it is in England today, the birthrate was almost three times the current figure. London's population in particular soared, from 60,000 in 1520 to 120,000 in 1550, 200,000 in 1600, and 375,000 a half-century later, making it the largest and fastest-growing city not only in England but in all of Europe. Every year in the first half of the seventeenth century, about 10,000 people migrated to London from other parts of England—wages in London tended to be around 50 percent higher than in the rest of the country—and it is estimated that one in eight English people lived in London at some point in their lives. The economic viability of Shakespeare's profession was closely linked to this extraordinary demographic boom: between 1567 and 1642, a theater historian has calculated, the London playhouses were paid close to 50 million visits.

As these visits to the theater indicate, in the capital city and elsewhere a substantial number of English men and women, despite hardships that were never very distant, had money to spend. After the disorder and dynastic wars of the fifteenth century, England in the sixteenth and early seventeenth centuries was for the most part a nation at peace, and with peace came a measure of enterprise and prosperity: the landowning classes busied themselves building great houses, planting orchards and hop gardens, draining marshlands, bringing untilled "wastes" under cultivation. The artisans and laborers who actually accomplished these tasks, though they were generally paid very little, often managed to accumulate something, as did the small freeholding farmers, the yeomen, who are repeatedly celebrated in the period as the backbone of English national independence and well-being. William Harrison's *Description of Britaine* (1577) lovingly itemizes the yeoman's precious possessions: "fair garnish of pewter on his cupboard, with so much more odd vessel going about the house, three or four featherbeds, so many coverlets and carpets of tapestry, a silver salt[cellar], a bowl for wine (if not a whole nest) and a dozen of spoons." There are comparable accounts of the hard-earned acquisitions of the city dwellers—masters and apprentices in small workshops, shipbuilders, wool merchants, cloth makers, chandlers, tradesmen, shopkeepers, along with lawyers, apothecaries, schoolteachers, scriveners, and the like—whose pennies from time to time enriched the coffers of the players.

The chief source of England's wealth in the sixteenth century was its textile industry, an industry that depended on a steady supply of wool. In *The Winter's Tale*, Shakespeare provides a richly comic portrayal of a rural sheepshearing festival, but the increasingly intensive production of wool had in reality its grim side. When a character in Thomas More's *Utopia* (1516) complains that "the sheep are eating the people," he is referring to the practice of enclosure: throughout the sixteenth and early seventeenth centuries, many acres of croplands once farmed in common by rural communities were enclosed with fences by wealthy landowners and turned into pasturage. The ensuing misery, displacement, and food shortages led to repeated riots, some of them violent and bloody, along with a series of government proclamations, but the process of enclosure was not reversed.

The economic stakes were high, and not only for the domestic market. In 1565, woolen cloth alone made up more than three-fourths of England's exports. (The remainder consisted mostly of other textiles and raw wool, with some trade in lead, tin, grain, and skins.) The Merchant Adventurers Company carried cloth to distant ports on the Baltic and Mediterranean, establishing links with Russia and Morocco (each took about 2 percent of London's cloth in 1597–98). English lead and tin, as well as fabrics, were sold in Tuscany and Turkey, and merchants found a market for Newcastle coal on the island of Malta. In the latter half of the century, London, which handled more than 85 percent of all exports, regularly shipped abroad more than 100,000 woolen cloths a year, at a value of at least £750,000. This figure does not include the increasingly important and profitable trade in so-called New Draperies, including textiles that went by such exotic names as bombazines, callamancoes, damazellas, damizes, mockadoes, and virgenatoes. When the Earl of Kent in *King Lear* insults Oswald as a "filthy worsted-stocking knave" (2.2.14–15) or when the aristocratic Biron in *Love's Labour's Lost* declares that he will give up "taffeta phrases, silken terms precise, / Three-piled hyperboles" and woo henceforth "in russet yeas, and honest kersey noes" (5.2.406–07, 413), Shakespeare is assuming that a substantial portion of his audience will be alert to the social significance of fabric.

There is amusing confirmation of this alertness from an unexpected source: the report of a visit made to the Fortune playhouse in London in 1614 by a foreigner, Father Orazio Busino, the chaplain of the Venetian embassy. Father Busino neglected to mention the name of the play he saw, but like many foreigners, he was powerfully struck by the presence of gorgeously dressed women in the audience. In Venice, there was a special gallery for courtesans, but socially respectable women would not have been permitted to attend plays, as they could in England. In London, not only could middle- and upper-class women go to the theater, but they could also wear masks and mingle freely with male spectators and women of ill repute. The bemused cleric was uncertain about the ambiguous social situation in which he found himself:

> These theatres are frequented by a number of respectable and handsome ladies, who come freely and seat themselves among the men without the slightest hesitation. On the evening in question his Excellency and the Secretary were pleased to play me a trick by placing me amongst a bevy of young women. Scarcely was I seated ere a very elegant dame, but in a mask, came and placed herself beside me. . . . She asked me for my address both in French and English; and, on my turning a deaf ear, she determined

to honour me by showing me some fine diamonds on her fingers, repeatedly taking off not fewer than three gloves, which were worn one over the other. . . . This lady's bodice was of yellow satin richly embroidered, her petticoat of gold tissue with stripes, her robe of red velvet with a raised pile, lined with yellow muslin with broad stripes of pure gold. She wore an apron of point lace of various patterns: her head-tire was highly perfumed, and the collar of white satin beneath the delicately-wrought ruff struck me as extremely pretty.

Father Busino may have turned a deaf ear on this "elegant dame" but not a blind eye: his description of her dress is worthy of a fashion designer and conveys something of the virtual clothes cult that prevailed in England in the late sixteenth and early seventeenth centuries, a cult whose major shrine, outside the royal court, was the theater.

Imports, Patents, and Monopolies

England produced some luxury goods, but the clothing on the backs of the most fashionable theatergoers was likely to have come from abroad. By the late sixteenth century, the English were importing substantial quantities of silks, satins, velvets, embroidery, gold and silver lace, and other costly items to satisfy the extravagant tastes of the elite and of those who aspired to dress like the elite. The government tried to put a check on the sartorial ambitions of the upwardly mobile by passing sumptuary laws—that is, laws restricting to the ranks of the aristocracy the right to wear certain of the most precious fabrics. But the very existence of these laws, in practice almost impossible to enforce, only reveals the scope and significance of the perceived problem.

Sumptuary laws were in part a conservative attempt to protect the existing social order from upstarts. Social mobility was not widely viewed as a positive virtue, and moralists repeatedly urged people to stay in their place. Conspicuous consumption that was tolerated, even admired, in the aristocratic elite was denounced as sinful and monstrous in less exalted social circles. English authorities were also deeply concerned throughout the period about the effects of a taste for luxury goods on the balance of trade. One of the principal English imports was wine: the "sherris" whose virtues Falstaff extols in *2 Henry IV* came from Xeres in Spain; the malmsey in which poor Clarence is drowned in *Richard III* was probably made in Greece or in the Canary Islands (from whence came Sir Toby Belch's "cup of canary" in *Twelfth Night*); and the "flagon of rhenish" that Yorick in *Hamlet* had once poured on the Gravedigger's head came from the Rhine region of Germany. Other imports included canvas, linen, fish, olive oil, sugar, molasses, dates, oranges and lemons, figs, raisins, almonds, capers, indigo, ostrich feathers, and that increasingly popular drug tobacco.

Joint stock companies were established to import goods for the burgeoning English market. The Merchant Venturers of the City of Bristol (established in 1552) handled great shipments of Spanish sack, the light, dry wine that largely displaced the vintages of Bordeaux and Burgundy when trade with France was disrupted by war. The Muscovy Company (established in 1555) traded English cloth and manufactured goods for Russian furs, oil, and beeswax. The Venice Company and the Turkey Company—uniting in 1593 to form the wealthy Levant Company—brought silk and spices home from Aleppo and carpets from Constantinople. The East India Company (founded in 1600), with its agent at Bantam in Java, brought pepper, cloves, nutmeg, and other spices from east Asia, along with indigo, cotton textiles, sugar, and saltpeter from India. English privateers "imported" American products, especially sugar, fish, and hides, in huge quantities, along with more precious cargoes. In 1592, a privateering expedition principally funded by Sir Walter Ralegh captured a huge Portuguese carrack (sailing ship), the *Madre de Dios*, in the Azores and brought it back to Dartmouth. The ship, the largest that had ever entered any English port, held 536 tons of pepper, cloves, cinnamon, cochineal, mace, civet, musk, ambergris, and nutmeg, as well as jewels, gold, ebony, carpets, and silks. Before order could be established, the English seamen began to pillage this immensely rich prize, and witnesses said

Cannoneer. From *Edward Webbe, His Travailes* (1590).

they could smell the spices on all the streets around the harbor. Such piratical expeditions were rarely officially sanctioned by the state, but the queen had in fact privately invested £1,800, for which she received about £80,000.

In the years of war with Spain, 1586–1604, the goods captured by the privateers annually amounted to 10–15 percent of the total value of England's imports. But organized theft alone could not solve England's balance-of-trade problems. Statesmen were particularly worried that the nation's natural wealth was slipping away in exchange for unnecessary things. In his *Discourse of the Commonweal* (1549), the prominent humanist Sir Thomas Smith exclaims against the importation of such trifles as mirrors, paper, laces, gloves, pins, inkhorns, tennis balls, puppets, and playing cards. And more than a century later, the same fear that England was trading its riches for trifles and wasting away in idleness was expressed by the Bristol merchant John Cary. The solution, Cary argues in "An Essay on the State of England in Relation to Its Trade" (1695), is to expand productive domestic employment. "People are or may be the Wealth of a Nation," he writes, "yet it must be where you find Employment for them, else they are a Burden to it, as the Idle Drone is maintained by the Industry of the laborious Bee, so are all those who live by their Dependence on others, as Players, Ale-House Keepers, Common Fiddlers, and such like, but more particularly Beggars, who never set themselves to work."

Stage players, all too typically associated here with vagabonds and other idle drones, could have replied in their defense that they not only labored in their vocation but also exported their skills abroad: English acting companies routinely traveled overseas and performed as far away as Bohemia. But their labor was not regarded as a productive contribution to the national wealth, and plays were in truth no solution to the trade imbalances that worried authorities.

The government attempted to stem the flow of gold overseas by establishing a patent system initially designed to encourage skilled foreigners to settle in England by granting them exclusive rights to produce particular wares by a patented method. Patents were granted for such things as the making of hard white soap (1561), ovens and furnaces (1563), window glass (1567), sailcloths (1574), drinking glasses (1574), sulphur, brimstone, and oil (1577), armor and horse harness (1587), starch (1588), white writing paper made from rags (1589), aqua vitae and vinegar (1594), playing cards (1598), and mathematical instruments (1598).

Although their ostensible purpose was to increase the wealth of England, encourage technical innovation, and provide employment for the poor, the effect of patents was often the enrichment of a few and the hounding of poor competitors by wealthy monopolists, a group that soon extended well beyond foreign-born entrepreneurs to the favorites of the monarch who vied for the huge profits to be made. "If I had a monopoly out" on folly, the Fool in *King Lear* protests, glancing at the "lords and great men" around him, "they would have part on't." The passage appears only in the quarto version of the play (*History of King Lear* 4.135–36); it may have been cut for political reasons from the Folio. For the issue of monopolies provoked bitter criticism and parliamentary debate for decades. In 1601, Elizabeth was prevailed upon to revoke a number of the most hated monopolies, including aqua vitae and vinegar, bottles, brushes, fish livers, the coarse sailcloth known as poldavis and mildernix, pots, salt, and starch. The whole system was revoked during the reign of James I by an act of Parliament.

Haves and Have-Nots

When in the 1560s Elizabeth's ambassador to France, the humanist Sir Thomas Smith, wrote a description of England, he saw the commonwealth as divided into four sorts of people: "gentlemen, citizens, yeomen artificers, and laborers." At the forefront of the class of gentlemen was the monarch, followed by a very small group of nobles—dukes, marquesses, earls, viscounts, and barons—who either inherited their exalted titles, as the eldest male heirs of their families, or were granted them by the monarch. Under Elizabeth, this aristocratic peerage numbered between 50 and 60 individuals; James's promotions increased the number to nearer 130. Strictly speaking, Smith notes, the younger sons of the nobility were only entitled to be called "esquires," but in common speech they were also called "lords."

Below this tiny cadre of aristocrats in the social hierarchy of gentry were the knights, a title of honor conferred by the monarch, and below them were the "simple gentlemen." Who was a gentleman? According to Smith, "whoever studieth the laws of the realm, who studieth in the universities, who professeth liberal sciences, and to be short, who can live idly and without manual labor, and will bear the port, charge and countenance of a gentleman, he shall be called master . . . and shall be taken for a gentleman." To "live idly and without manual labor": where in Spain, for example, the crucial mark of a gentleman was "blood," in England it was "idleness," in the sense of sufficient income to afford an education and to maintain a social position without having to work with one's hands.

For Smith, the class of gentlemen was far and away the most important in the kingdom. Below were two groups that had at least some social standing and claim to authority: the citizens, or burgesses, those who held positions of importance and responsibility in their cities, and yeomen, farmers with land and a measure of economic independence. At the bottom of the social order was what Smith calls "the fourth sort of men which do not rule." The great mass of ordinary people have, Smith writes, "no voice nor authority in our commonwealth, and no account is made of them but only to be ruled." Still, even they can bear some responsibility, he notes, since they serve on juries and are named to such positions as churchwarden and constable.

In everyday practice, as modern social historians have observed, the English tended to divide the population not into four distinct classes but into two: a very small empowered group—the "richer" or "wiser" or "better" sort—and all the rest who were without much social standing or power, the "poorer" or "ruder" or "meaner" sort. References to the "middle sort of people" remain relatively rare until after Shakespeare's lifetime; these people are absorbed into the rulers or the ruled, depending on speaker and context.

The source of wealth for most of the ruling class, and the essential measure of social status, was land ownership, and changes to the social structure in the sixteenth and seventeenth centuries were largely driven by the land market. The property that passed into private hands as the Tudors and early Stuarts sold off confiscated monastic estates and then their own crown lands for ready cash amounted to nearly a quarter of all the land in England. At the same time, the buying and selling of private estates was on the rise throughout the period. Land was bought up not only by established landowners seeking to enlarge their estates but by successful merchants, manufacturers, and urban professionals; even if the taint of vulgar moneymaking lingered around such figures, their heirs would be taken for true gentlemen. The rate of turnover in land ownership was great; in many counties, well over half the gentle families in 1640 had appeared since the end of the fifteenth century. The class that Smith called "simple gentlemen" was expanding rapidly: in the fifteenth century, they had held no more than a quarter of the land in the country, but by the later seventeenth, they controlled almost half. Over the same period, the land held by the great aristocratic magnates held steady at 15–20 percent of the total.

Riot and Disorder

London was a violent place in the first half of Shakespeare's career. There were thirty-five riots in the city in the years 1581–1602, twelve of them in the volatile month of June

1595. These included protests against the deeply unpopular lord mayor Sir John Spencer, attempts to release prisoners, anti-alien riots, and incidents of "popular market regulation." There is an unforgettable depiction of a popular uprising in *Coriolanus*, along with many other glimpses in Shakespeare's works, including John Cade's grotesque rebellion in *The First Part of the Contention (2 Henry VI)*, the plebeian violence in *Julius Caesar*, and Laertes' "riotous head" in *Hamlet*.

The London rioters were mostly drawn from the large mass of poor and discontented apprentices who typically chose as their scapegoats foreigners, prostitutes, and gentlemen's servingmen. Theaters were very often the site of the social confrontations that sparked disorder. For two days running in June 1584, disputes between apprentices and gentlemen triggered riots outside the Curtain Theatre involving up to a thousand participants. On one occasion, a gentleman was said to have exclaimed that "the apprentice was but a rascal, and some there were little better than rogues that took upon them the name of gentlemen, and said the prentices were but the scum of the world." These occasions culminated in attacks by the apprentices on London's law schools, the Inns of Court.

The most notorious and predictable incidents of disorder came on Shrove Tuesday (the Tuesday before the beginning of Lent), a traditional day of misrule when apprentices ran riot. Shrove Tuesday disturbances involved attacks by mobs of young men on the brothels of the South Bank, in the vicinity of the Globe and other public theaters. The city authorities took precautions to keep these disturbances from getting completely out of control, but evidently did not regard them as serious threats to public order.

Of much greater concern throughout the Tudor and early Stuart years were the frequent incidents of rural rioting against the enclosure of commons and waste land by local landlords (and, in the royal forests, by the crown). This form of popular protest was at its height during Shakespeare's career: in the years 1590–1610, the frequency of anti-enclosure rioting doubled from what it had been earlier in Elizabeth's reign.

Although they often became violent, anti-enclosure riots were usually directed not against individuals but against property. Villagers—sometimes several hundred, often fewer than a dozen—gathered to tear down newly planted hedges. The event often took place in a carnival atmosphere, with songs and drinking, that did not prevent the participants from acting with a good deal of political canniness and forethought. Especially in the Jacobean period, it was common for participants to establish a common fund for legal defense before commencing their assault on the hedges. Women were frequently involved, and on a number of occasions wives alone participated in the destruction of the enclosure,

"The Peddler." From Jost Amman, *The Book of Trades* (1568).

since there was a widespread, though erroneous, belief that married women acting without the knowledge of their husbands were immune from prosecution. In fact, the powerful Court of Star Chamber consistently ruled that both the wives and their husbands should be punished.

Although Stratford was never the scene of serious rioting, enclosure controversies turned violent more than once in Shakespeare's lifetime. In January 1601, Shakespeare's friend Richard Quiney and others leveled the hedges of Sir Edward Greville, lord of Stratford manor. Quiney was elected bailiff of Stratford in September of that year but did not live to enjoy the office for long. He died from a blow to the head struck by one of Greville's men in a tavern brawl. Greville, responsible for the administration of justice, neglected to punish the murderer.

There was further violence in January 1615,

when William Combe's men threw to the ground two local aldermen who were filling in a ditch by which Combe was enclosing common fields near Stratford. The task of filling in the offending ditch was completed the next day by the women and children of Stratford. Combe's enclosure scheme was eventually stopped in the courts. Though he owned land whose value would have been affected by this controversy, Shakespeare took no active role in it, since he had previously come to a private settlement with the enclosers insuring him against personal loss.

Most incidents of rural rioting were small, localized affairs, and with good reason: when confined to the village community, riot was a misdemeanor; when it spread outward to include multiple communities, it became treason. The greatest of the anti-enclosure riots, those in which hundreds of individuals from a large area participated, commonly took place on the eve of full-scale regional rebellions. The largest of these disturbances, Kett's Rebellion, involved some 16,000 peasants, artisans, and townspeople who rose up in 1549 under the leadership of a Norfolk tanner and landowner, Robert Kett, to protest economic exploitation. The agrarian revolts in Shakespeare's lifetime were on a much smaller scale. In the abortive Oxfordshire Rebellion of 1596, a carpenter named Bartholomew Steere attempted to organize a rising against enclosing gentlemen. The optimistic Steere promised his followers that "it was but a month's work to overrun England" and informed them "that the commons long since in Spain did rise and kill all gentlemen . . . and since that time have lived merrily there." Steere expected several hundred men to join him on Enslow Hill on November 21, 1596, for the start of the rising; no more than twenty showed up. They were captured, imprisoned, and tortured. Several were executed, but Steere apparently died in prison.

Rebellions, most often triggered by hunger and oppression, continued into the reign of James I. The Midland Revolt of 1607, which may be reflected in *Coriolanus*, consisted of a string of agrarian risings in the counties of Northamptonshire, Warwickshire, and Leicestershire, involving assemblies of up to five thousand rebels in various places. The best-known of their leaders was John Reynolds, called "Captain Powch" because of the pouch he wore, whose magical contents were supposed to defend the rebels from harm. (According to the chronicler Edmund Howes, when Reynolds was captured and the pouch opened, it contained "only a piece of green cheese.") The rebels, who were called by themselves and others both "Levelers" and "Diggers," insisted that they had no quarrel with the king but only sought an end to injurious enclosures. But Robert Wilkinson, who preached a sermon against the leaders at their trial, credited them with the intention to "level all states as they leveled banks and ditches." Most of the rebels got off relatively lightly, but, along with other ringleaders, Captain Powch was executed.

The Legal Status of Women

Though England was ruled for over forty years by a powerful woman, the great majority of women in the kingdom had very restricted social, economic, and legal standing. To be sure, a tiny number of influential aristocratic women, such as the formidable Countess of Shrewsbury, Bess of Hardwick, wielded considerable power. But, these rare exceptions aside, women were denied any rightful claim to institutional authority or personal autonomy. When Sir Thomas Smith thinks of how he should describe his country's social order, he declares that "we do reject women, as those whom nature hath made to keep home and to nourish their family and children, and not to meddle with matters abroad, nor to bear office in a city or commonwealth." Then, with a kind of glance over his shoulder, he makes an exception of those few for whom "the blood is respected, not the age nor the sex": for example, the queen.

English women were not under the full range of crushing constraints that afflicted women in some countries in Europe. Foreign visitors were struck by their relative freedom, as shown, for example, by the fact that respectable women could venture unchaperoned into the streets and attend the theater. Single women, whether widowed or unmarried, could, if they were of full age, inherit and administer land, make a will, sign a contract, possess property, sue and be sued, without a male guardian or proxy. But married women had no such rights under the common law.

Early modern writings about women and the family constantly return to a political model of domination and submission, in which the father justly rules over wife and children as the monarch rules over the state. This conception of a woman's role conveniently ignores the fact that a *majority* of the adult women at any time in Shakespeare's England were not married. They were either widows or spinsters (a term that was not yet pejorative), and thus for the most part managing their own affairs. Even within marriage, women typically had more control over certain spheres than moralizing writers on the family cared to admit. For example, village wives oversaw the production of eggs, cheese, and beer, and sold these goods in the market.

Women were not in practice as bereft of economic power and property as, according to English common law, they should have been. Demographic studies indicate that the inheritance system called primogeniture, the orderly transmission of property from father to eldest male heir, was more often an unfulfilled wish than a reality. Some 40 percent of marriages failed to produce a son, and in such circumstances fathers often left their land to their daughters, rather than to brothers, nephews, or male cousins. In many families, the father died before his male heir was old enough to inherit property, leaving the land, at least temporarily, in the hands of the mother. And while they were less likely than their brothers to inherit land ("real property"), daughters normally inherited a substantial share of their father's personal property (cash and movables).

In fact, the legal restrictions upon women, though severe in Shakespeare's time, actually worsened in subsequent decades. The English common law, the system of law based on court decisions rather than on codified written laws, was significantly less egalitarian in its approach to wives and daughters than were alternative legal codes (manorial, civil, and ecclesiastical) still in place in the late sixteenth century. The eventual triumph of common law stripped women of many traditional rights, slowly driving them out of economically productive trades and businesses.

Limited though it was, the economic freedom of Elizabethan and Jacobean women far exceeded their political and social freedom—the opportunity to receive a grammar school or university education, to hold office in church or state, to have a voice in public debates, or even simply to speak their mind fully and openly in ordinary conversation. Women who asserted their views too vigorously risked being perceived as shrewish and labeled "scolds." Both urban and rural communities had a horror of scolds. In the Elizabethan period, such women came to be regarded as a threat to public order, to be dealt with by the local authorities. The preferred methods of correction included public humiliation—of the sort Katherine endures in *The Taming of the Shrew*—and such physical abuse as slapping, bridling, and soaking by means of a contraption called the "cucking stool" (or "ducking stool"). This latter punishment originated in the Middle Ages, but its use spread in the sixteenth century, when it became almost exclusively a punishment for women. From 1560 onward, cucking stools were built or renovated in many English provincial towns; between 1560 and 1600, the contraptions were installed by rivers or ponds in Norwich, Bridport, Shrewsbury, Kingston-upon-Thames, Marlborough, Devizes, Clitheroe, Thornbury, and Great Yarmouth.

Such punishment was usually intensified by a procession through the town to the sound of "rough music," the banging together of pots and pans. The same cruel festivity accompanied the "carting" or "riding" of those accused of being whores. In some parts of the country, villagers also took the law into their own hands, publicly shaming women who married men much younger than themselves or who beat or otherwise domineered over their husbands. One characteristic form of these charivaris, or rituals of shaming, was known in the West Country as the Skimmington Ride. Villagers would rouse the offending couple from bed with rough music and stage a raucous pageant in which a man, holding a distaff, would ride backward on a donkey, while his "wife" (another man dressed as a woman) struck him with a ladle. In these cases, the collective ridicule and indignation was evidently directed at least as much at the henpecked husband as at his transgressive wife.

Women and Print

Books published for a female audience surged in popularity in the late sixteenth century, reflecting an increase in female literacy. (It is striking how many of Shakespeare's women are shown reading.) This increase is probably linked to a Protestant longing for direct access to the Scriptures, and the new books marketed specifically for women included devotional manuals and works of religious instruction. But there were also practical guides to such subjects as female education (for example, Giovanni Bruto's *Necessary, Fit, and Convenient Education of a Young Gentlewoman*, 1598), midwifery (James Guillemeau's *Child-birth; or, the Happy Delivery of Women*, 1612), needlework (Federico di Vinciolo's *New and Singular Patterns and Works of Linen*, 1591), cooking (Thomas Dawson's *The Good Housewife's Jewel*, 1587), gardening (Pierre Erondelle, *The French Garden*, 1605), and married life (Patrick Hanney's *A Happy Husband; or, Directions for a Maid to Choose Her Mate*, 1619). As the authors' names suggest, many of these works were translations, and almost all were written by men.

Starting in the 1570s, writers and their publishers increasingly addressed works of recreational literature (romance, fiction, and poetry) partially or even exclusively to women. Some books, such as Robert Greene's *Mamillia, a Mirror or Looking-Glass for the Ladies of England* (1583), directly specified in the title their desired audience. Others, such as Sir Philip Sidney's influential and popular romance *Arcadia* (1590–93), solicited female readership in their dedicatory epistles. The ranks of Sidney's followers eventually included his own niece, Mary Wroth, whose romance *Urania* was published in 1621.

In the literature of Shakespeare's time, women readers were not only wooed but also frequently railed at, in a continuation of a popular polemical genre that had long inspired heated charges and countercharges. Both sides in the polemic generally agreed that it was the duty of women to be chaste, dutiful, shamefast, and silent; the argument was whether women fulfilled or fell short of this proper role. Ironically, then, a modern reader is more likely to find inspiring accounts of courageous women not in the books written in defense of female virtue but in attacks on those who refused to be silent and obedient.

The most famous English skirmish in this controversy took place in a rash of pamphlets at the end of Shakespeare's life. Joseph Swetnam's crude *Arraignment of Lewd, Idle, Froward, and Unconstant Women* (1615) provoked three fierce responses attributed to women: Rachel Speght's *A Muzzle for Melastomus*, Esther Sowernam's *Esther Hath Hang'd Haman*, and Constantia Munda's *Worming of a Mad Dog*, all 1617. There was also an anonymous play, *Swetnam the Woman-hater Arraigned by Women* (1618), in which Swetnam, depicted as a braggart and a lecher, is put on trial by women and made to recant his misogynistic lies.

Prior to the Swetnam controversy, only one English woman, "Jane Anger," had published a defense of women (*Jane Anger Her Protection for Women*, 1589). Learned women writers in the sixteenth century tended not to become involved in public debate but rather to undertake a project to which it was difficult for even obdurately chauvinistic males to object: the translation of devotional literature into English. Thomas More's daughter Margaret More Roper translated Erasmus (*A Devout Treatise upon the Pater Noster*, 1524); Francis Bacon's mother, Anne Cooke Bacon, translated Bishop John Jewel (*An Apology or Answer in Defence of the Church of England*, 1564); Anne Locke Prowse, a friend of John Knox, translated the *Sermons of John Calvin* in 1560; and Mary Sidney, the Countess of Pembroke, completed the metrical version of the Psalms that her brother Sir Philip Sidney had begun. Elizabeth Tudor (the future queen) herself translated, at the age of eleven, Marguerite de Navarre's *Le Miroir de l'âme pécheresse* (*The Glass of the Sinful Soul*, 1544). The translation was dedicated to her stepmother, Katherine Parr, herself the author of a frequently reprinted book of prayers.

There was in the sixteenth and early seventeenth centuries a social stigma attached to print. Far from celebrating publication, authors, and particularly female authors, often apologized for exposing themselves to the public gaze. Nonetheless, a number of women ventured beyond pious translations. Some, including Elizabeth Tyrwhitt, Anne Dowriche,

SWETNAM,
THE
VVoman-hater,
ARRAIGNED BY
WOMEN.

A new Comedie,
Acted at the *Red Bull*, by the late
Queenes Seruants.

LONDON,
Printed for *Richard Meighen*, and are to be sold at his Shops
at Saint *Clements* Church, ouer-againſt *Essex* Houſe, and
at *Westminster* Hall. 1620.

Title page of *Swetnam the Woman-Hater Arraigned by Women*
(1620), a play written in response to Joseph Swetnam's *The
Arraignment of Lewd, Idle, Froward and Unconstant Women*
(1615); the woodcut depicts the trial of Swetnam in Act 4.

Isabella Whitney, Mary Sidney, and Aemilia Lanyer, composed and published their own
poems. Aemilia Lanyer's *Salve Deus Rex Judaeorum*, published in 1611, is a poem in praise
of virtuous women, from Eve and the Virgin Mary to her noble patron, the Countess of
Cumberland. "A Description of Cookeham," appended to the poem, may be the first
English country house poem.

The first Tudor woman to translate a play was the learned Jane Lumley, who composed an English version of Euripides' *Iphigenia at Aulis* (c. 1550). The first known original play in English by a woman was by Elizabeth Cary, Viscountess Falkland, whose
Tragedy of Mariam, the Fair Queen of Jewry was published in 1613. This remarkable play,
which was not intended to be performed, includes speeches in defense of women's equality, though the most powerful of these is spoken by the villainous Salome, who schemes to
divorce her husband and marry her lover. Cary, who bore eleven children, herself had a
deeply troubled marriage, which effectively came to an end in 1625 when, defying her
husband's staunchly Protestant family, she openly converted to Catholicism. Her biography was written by one of her four daughters, all of whom became nuns.

Henry VIII and the English Reformation

There had long been serious ideological and institutional tensions in the religious life
of England, but officially, at least, England in the early sixteenth century had a single
religion, Catholicism, whose acknowledged head was the pope in Rome. In 1517, drawing

upon long-standing currents of dissent, Martin Luther, an Augustinian monk and professor of theology at the University of Wittenberg, challenged the authority of the pope and attacked several key doctrines of the Catholic Church. According to Luther, the Church, with its elaborate hierarchical structure centered in Rome, its rich monasteries and convents, and its enormous political influence, had become hopelessly corrupt, a conspiracy of venal priests who manipulated popular superstitions to enrich themselves and amass worldly power. Luther began by vehemently attacking the sale of indulgences—certificates promising the remission of punishments to be suffered in the afterlife by souls sent to purgatory to expiate their sins. These indulgences were a fraud, he argued; purgatory itself had no foundation in the Bible, which in his view was the only legitimate source of religious truth. Christians would be saved not by scrupulously following the ritual practices fostered by the Catholic Church—observing fast days, reciting the ancient Latin prayers, endowing chantries to say prayers for the dead, and so on—but by faith and faith alone.

This challenge, which came to be known as the Reformation, spread and gathered force, especially in northern Europe, where major leaders like the Swiss pastor Ulrich Zwingli and the French theologian John Calvin established institutional structures and elaborated various and sometimes conflicting doctrinal principles. Calvin, whose thought came to be particularly influential in England, emphasized the obligation of governments to implement God's will in the world. He advanced too the doctrine of predestination, by which, as he put it, "God adopts some to hope of life and sentences others to eternal death." God's "secret election" of the saved made Calvin uncomfortable, but his study of the Scriptures had led him to conclude that "only a small number, out of an incalculable multitude, should obtain salvation." It might seem that such a conclusion would lead to passivity or even despair, but for Calvin predestination was a mystery bound up with faith, confidence, and an active engagement in the fashioning of a Christian community.

The Reformation had a direct and powerful impact on those territories, especially in northern Europe, where it gained control. Monasteries were sacked, their possessions seized by princes or sold off to the highest bidder; the monks and nuns, expelled from their cloisters, were encouraged to break their vows of chastity and find spouses, as Luther and his wife, a former nun, had done. In the great cathedrals and in hundreds of smaller churches and chapels, the elaborate altarpieces, bejeweled crucifixes, crystal reliquaries holding the bones of saints, and venerated statues and paintings were attacked as "idols" and often defaced or destroyed. Protestant congregations continued, for the most part, to celebrate the most sacred Christian ritual, the Eucharist, or Lord's Supper, but they did so in a profoundly different spirit from that of the Catholic Church—more as commemoration than as miracle—and they now prayed not in the old liturgical Latin but in the vernacular.

The Reformation was at first vigorously resisted in England. Indeed, with the support of his ardently Catholic chancellor, Thomas More, Henry VIII personally wrote (or at least lent his name to) a vehement, often scatological attack on Luther's character and views, an attack for which the pope granted him the honorific title "Defender of the Faith." Protestant writings, including translations of the Scriptures into English, were seized by officials of the church and state and burned. Protestants who made their views known were persecuted, driven to flee the country, or arrested, put on trial, and burned at the stake. But the situation changed drastically and decisively when in 1527 Henry decided to seek a divorce from his first wife, Catherine of Aragon, in order to marry Anne Boleyn.

Catherine had given birth to six children, but since only a daughter, Mary, survived infancy, Henry did not have the son he craved. Then as now, the Catholic Church did not ordinarily grant divorce, but Henry's lawyers argued on technical grounds that the marriage was invalid (and therefore, by extension, that Mary was illegitimate and hence unable to inherit the throne). Matters of this kind were far less doctrinal than diplomatic: Catherine, the daughter of Ferdinand of Aragon and Isabella of Castile, had powerful allies in Rome, and the pope ruled against Henry's petition for a divorce. A series of momentous events followed, as England lurched away from the Church of Rome. In 1531, Henry charged the entire clergy of England with having usurped royal authority in the

"The Pope as Antichrist riding the Beast of the Apocalypse." From *Fierie Tryall of God's Saints* (1611; author unknown).

administration of canon law (the ecclesiastical law that governed faith, discipline, and morals, including such matters as divorce). Under extreme pressure, including the threat of mass confiscations and imprisonment, the Convocation of the Clergy begged for pardon, made a donation to the royal coffers of over £100,000, and admitted that the king was "supreme head of the English Church and clergy" (modified by the rider "as far as the law of Christ allows"). On May 15 of the next year, the convocation submitted to the demand that the king be the final arbiter of canon law; on the next day, Thomas More resigned his post.

In 1533, Henry's marriage to Catherine was officially declared null and void, and on June 1 Anne Boleyn was crowned queen (a coronation Shakespeare depicts in *All Is True*). The king was promptly excommunicated by the pope, Clement VII. In the following year, the parliamentary Act of Succession confirmed the effects of the divorce and required an oath from all adult male subjects confirming the new dynastic settlement. Thomas More and John Fisher, the Bishop of Rochester, were among the small number who refused. The Act of Supremacy, passed later in the year, formally declared the king to be "Supreme Head of the Church in England" and again required an oath to this effect. In 1535 and 1536, further acts made it treasonous to refuse the oath of royal supremacy or, as More had tried to do, to remain silent. The first victims were three Carthusian monks who rejected the oath—"How could the king, a layman," said one of them, "be Head of the Church of England?"—and in May 1535, they were duly hanged, drawn, and quartered. A few weeks later, Fisher and More were convicted and beheaded. Between 1536 and 1539, the monasteries were suppressed and their vast wealth seized by the crown.

Royal defiance of the authority of Rome was a key element in the Reformation but did not by itself constitute the establishment of Protestantism in England. On the contrary, in the same year that Fisher and More were martyred for their adherence to Roman Catholicism, twenty-five Protestants, members of a sect known as Anabaptists, were burned for heresy on a single day. Through most of his reign, Henry remained an equal-opportunity persecutor, ruthless to Catholics loyal to Rome and hostile to many of those who espoused Reformation ideas, though many of these ideas gradually established themselves on English soil.

Even when Henry was eager to do so, it proved impossible to eradicate Protestantism, as it would later prove impossible for his successors to eradicate Catholicism. In large part this tenacity arose from the passionate, often suicidal heroism of men and women who felt that their souls' salvation depended on the precise character of their Christianity. It arose too from a mid-fifteenth-century technological innovation that made it almost impossible to suppress unwelcome ideas: the printing press. Early Protestants quickly grasped that with a few clandestine presses they could defy the Catholic authorities and flood the country with their texts. "How many printing presses there be in the world," wrote the Protestant polemicist John Foxe, "so many blockhouses there be against the high castle" of the pope in Rome, "so that either the pope must abolish knowledge and printing or printing at length will root him out." By the century's end, it was the Catholics who were using the clandestine press to propagate their beliefs in the face of Protestant persecution.

The greatest insurrection of the Tudor age was not over food, taxation, or land but over religion. On Sunday October 1, 1536, stirred up by their vicar, the traditionalist parishioners of Louth in Lincolnshire, in the north of England, rose up in defiance of the ecclesiastical visitation sent to enforce royal supremacy. The rapidly spreading rebellion, which became known as the Pilgrimage of Grace, was led by the lawyer Robert Aske. The city of Lincoln fell to the rebels on October 6, and though it was soon retaken by royal forces, the rebels seized cities and fortifications throughout Yorkshire, Durham, Northumberland, Cumberland, Westmoreland, and northern Lancashire. Carlisle, Newcastle, and a few castles were all that were left to the king in the north. The Pilgrims soon numbered 40,000, led by some of the region's leading noblemen. The Duke of Norfolk, representing the crown, was forced to negotiate a truce, with a promise to support the rebels' demands that the king restore the monasteries, shore up the regional economy, suppress heresy, and dismiss his evil advisers.

The Pilgrims kept the peace for the rest of 1536, on the naive assumption that their demands would be met. But Henry moved suddenly early in 1537 to impose order and capture the ringleaders; 130 people, including lords, knights, heads of religious houses, and, of course, Robert Aske, were executed.

In 1549, two years after the death of Henry VIII, the west and the north of England were the sites of further unsuccessful risings for the restoration of Catholicism. The Western Rising is striking for its blend of Catholic universalism and intense regionalism among people who did not yet regard themselves as English. One of the rebels' articles, protesting against the imposition of the English Bible and religious service, declares, "We the Cornish men (whereof certain of us understand no English) utterly refuse this new English." The rebels besieged but failed to take the city of Exeter. As with almost all Tudor rebellions, the number of those executed in the aftermath of the failed rising was far greater than those killed in actual hostilities.

Henry VIII's Children: Edward, Mary, and Elizabeth

Upon Henry's death in 1547, his ten-year-old son, Edward VI, came to the throne, with his maternal uncle Edward Seymour named as Lord Protector and Duke of Somerset. Both Edward and his uncle were staunch Protestants, and reformers hastened to transform the English church accordingly. During Edward's reign, Archbishop Thomas Cranmer formulated the forty-two articles of religion that became the core of Anglican orthodoxy and wrote the first *Book of Common Prayer*, which was officially adopted in 1549 as the basis of English worship services.

Somerset fell from power in 1549 and was replaced as Lord Protector by John Dudley, later Duke of Northumberland. When Edward fell seriously ill, probably of tuberculosis, Northumberland persuaded him to sign a will depriving his half-sisters, Mary (the daughter of Catherine of Aragon) and Elizabeth (the daughter of Anne Boleyn), of their claim to royal succession. The Lord Protector was scheming to have his daughter-in-law the Protestant Lady Jane Grey, a granddaughter of Henry VII, ascend to the throne. But when Edward died in 1553, Mary marshaled support, quickly secured the crown from Lady Jane (who had been titular queen for nine days), and had Lady Jane executed, along with her husband and Northumberland.

Queen Mary immediately took steps to return her kingdom to Roman Catholicism. Though she was unable to get Parliament to agree to restore church lands seized under

The Family of Henry VIII: An Allegory of the Tudor Succession. By Lucas de Heere (c. 1572). Henry, in the middle, is flanked by Mary to his right, and Edward and Elizabeth to his left.

Henry VIII, she restored the Catholic Mass, once again affirmed the authority of the pope, and put down a rebellion that sought to depose her. Seconded by her ardently Catholic husband, Philip II, King of Spain, she initiated a series of religious persecutions that earned her (from her enemies) the name "Bloody Mary." Hundreds of Protestants took refuge abroad in cities such as Calvin's Geneva; almost three hundred less fortunate Protestants were condemned as heretics and burned at the stake.

Mary died childless in 1558, and her younger half-sister Elizabeth became queen. Elizabeth's succession had been by no means assured. For if Protestants regarded Henry VIII's marriage to Catherine as invalid and hence deemed Mary illegitimate, so Catholics regarded his marriage to Anne Boleyn as invalid and deemed Elizabeth illegitimate. Henry VIII himself seemed to support both views, since only three years after divorcing Catherine, he beheaded Anne Boleyn on charges of treason and adultery and urged Parliament to invalidate the marriage. Moreover, though during her sister's reign Elizabeth outwardly complied with the official Catholic religious observance, Mary and her advisers were deeply suspicious, and the young princess's life was in grave danger. Poised and circumspect, Elizabeth warily evaded the traps that were set for her. As she ascended the throne, her actions were scrutinized for some indication of the country's future course. During her coronation procession, when a girl in an allegorical pageant presented her with a Bible in English translation—banned under Mary's reign—Elizabeth kissed the book, held it up reverently, and laid it to her breast; when the abbot and monks of Westminster Abbey came to greet her in broad daylight with candles (a symbol of Catholic devotion) in their hands, she briskly dismissed them with the telling words "Away with those torches! we can see well enough." England had returned to the Reformation.

Many English men and women, of all classes, remained loyal to the old Catholic faith, but English authorities under Elizabeth moved steadily, if cautiously, toward ensuring at least an outward conformity to the official Protestant settlement. Recusants, those who refused to attend regular Sunday services in their parish churches, were fined heavily.

Anyone who wished to receive a university degree, to be ordained as a priest in the Church of England, or to be named as an officer of the state had to swear an oath to the royal supremacy. Commissioners were sent throughout the land to confirm that religious services were following the officially approved liturgy and to investigate any reported backsliding into Catholic practice or, alternatively, any attempts to introduce more radical reforms than the queen and her bishops had chosen to embrace. For the Protestant exiles who streamed back were eager not only to undo the damage Mary had done but to carry the Reformation much further. They sought to dismantle the church hierarchy, to purge the calendar of folk customs deemed pagan and the church service of ritual practices deemed superstitious, to dress the clergy in simple garb, and, at the extreme edge, to smash "idolatrous" statues, crucifixes, and altarpieces. Throughout her long reign, however, Elizabeth herself remained cautiously conservative and determined to hold in check religious zealotry.

In the space of a single lifetime, England had gone officially from Roman Catholicism, to Catholicism under the supreme headship of the English king, to a guarded Protestantism, to a more radical Protestantism, to a renewed and aggressive Roman Catholicism, and finally to Protestantism again. Each of these shifts was accompanied by danger, persecution, and death. It was enough to make some people wary. Or skeptical. Or extremely agile.

The English Bible

Luther had undertaken a fundamental critique of the Catholic Church's sacramental system, a critique founded on the twin principles of salvation by faith alone (*sola fide*) and the absolute primacy of the Bible (*sola scriptura*). *Sola fide* contrasted faith with "works," by which was meant primarily the whole elaborate system of rituals sanctified, conducted, or directed by the priests. Protestants proposed to modify or reinterpret many of these rituals or, as with the rituals associated with purgatory, to abolish them altogether. *Sola scriptura* required direct lay access to the Bible, which meant in practice the widespread availability of vernacular translations. The Roman Catholic Church had not always and everywhere opposed such translations, but it generally preferred that the populace encounter the Scriptures through the interpretations of the priests, trained to read the Latin translation known as the Vulgate. In times of great conflict, this preference for clerical mediation hardened into outright prohibition of vernacular translation and into persecution and book burning.

Zealous Protestants set out, in the teeth of fierce opposition, to put the Bible into the hands of the laity. A remarkable translation of the New Testament, by an English Lutheran named William Tyndale, was printed on the continent and smuggled into England in 1525; Tyndale's translation of the Pentateuch, the first five books of the Hebrew Bible, followed in 1530. Many copies of these translations were seized and burned, as was the translator himself, but the printing press made it extremely difficult for authorities to eradicate books for which there was a passionate demand. The English Bible was a force that could not be suppressed, and it became, in its various forms, the single most important book of the sixteenth century.

Tyndale's translation was completed by an associate, Miles Coverdale, whose rendering of the Psalms proved to be particularly influential. Their joint labor was the basis for the Great Bible (1539), the first authorized version of the Bible in English, a copy of which was ordered to be placed in every church in the kingdom. With the accession of Edward VI, many editions of the Bible followed, but the process was sharply reversed when Mary came to the throne in 1553. Along with people condemned as heretics, English Bibles were burned in great bonfires.

Marian persecution was indirectly responsible for what would become the most popular as well as most scholarly English Bible, the translation known as the Geneva Bible, prepared, with extensive, learned, and often fiercely polemical marginal notes, by English exiles in Calvin's Geneva and widely diffused in England after Elizabeth came to the throne. In addition, Elizabethan church authorities ordered a careful revision of the Great Bible, and this version, known as the Bishops' Bible, was the one read in the churches. The success of the Geneva Bible in particular prompted those Elizabethan Catholics who now in turn found themselves in exile to bring out a vernacular translation of their own in order to counter the Protestant readings and glosses. This Catholic translation, known as the Rheims Bible, may have been known to Shakespeare, but he seems to have been far better acquainted with the Geneva Bible, and he would also have repeatedly heard the Bishops' Bible read aloud. Scholars have identified over three hundred references to the Bible in Shakespeare's work; in one version or another, the Scriptures had a powerful impact on his imagination.

A Female Monarch in a Male World

In the last year of Mary's reign, 1558, the Scottish Calvinist minister John Knox thundered against what he called "the monstrous regiment of women." When the Protestant Elizabeth came to the throne the following year, Knox and his religious brethren were less inclined to denounce female rulers, but in England as elsewhere in Europe there remained a widespread conviction that women were unsuited to wield power over men. Many men seem to have regarded the capacity for rational thought as exclusively male; women, they assumed, were led only by their passions. While gentlemen mastered the arts of rhetoric and warfare, gentlewomen were expected to display the virtues of silence and good housekeeping. Among upper-class males, the will to dominate others was acceptable and indeed admired; the same will in women was condemned as a grotesque and dangerous aberration.

Apologists for the queen countered these prejudices by appealing to historical prece-

The Armada portrait: note Elizabeth's hand on the globe.

dent and legal theory. History offered inspiring examples of just female rulers, notably Deborah, the biblical prophetess who judged Israel. In the legal sphere, crown lawyers advanced the theory of "the king's two bodies." As England's crowned head, Elizabeth's person was mystically divided between her mortal "body natural" and the immortal "body politic." While the queen's natural body was inevitably subject to the failings of human flesh, the body politic was timeless and perfect. In political terms, therefore, Elizabeth's sex was a matter of no consequence, a thing indifferent.

Elizabeth, who had received a fine humanist education and an extended, dangerous lesson in the art of survival, made it immediately clear that she intended to rule in more than name only. She assembled a group of trustworthy advisers, foremost among them William Cecil (later named Lord Burghley), but she insisted on making many of the crucial decisions herself. Like many Renaissance monarchs, Elizabeth was drawn to the idea of royal absolutism, the theory that ultimate power was properly concentrated in her person and indeed that God had appointed her to be His deputy in the kingdom. Opposition to her rule, in this view, was not only a political act but also a kind of impiety, a blasphemous grudging against the will of God. Apologists for absolutism contended that God commands obedience even to manifestly wicked rulers whom He has sent to punish the sinfulness of humankind. Such arguments were routinely made in speeches and political tracts and from the pulpits of churches, where they were incorporated into the *Book of Homilies*, which clergymen were required to read out to their congregations.

In reality, Elizabeth's power was not absolute. The government had a network of spies, informers, and *agents provocateurs*, but it lacked a standing army, a national police force, an efficient system of communication, and an extensive bureaucracy. Above all, the queen had limited financial resources and needed to turn periodically to an independent and often recalcitrant Parliament, which by long tradition had the sole right to levy taxes and to grant subsidies. Members of the House of Commons were elected from their boroughs, not appointed by the monarch, and though the queen had considerable influence over their decisions, she could by no means dictate policy. Under these constraints, Elizabeth ruled through a combination of adroit political maneuvering and imperious command, all the while enhancing her authority in the eyes of both court and country by means of an extraordinary cult of love.

"We all loved her," Elizabeth's godson Sir John Harington wrote, with just a touch of irony, a few years after the queen's death, "for she said she loved us." Ambassadors, courtiers, and parliamentarians all submitted to Elizabeth's cult of love, in which the queen's gender was transformed from a potential liability into a significant asset. Those who approached her generally did so on their knees and were expected to address her with extravagant compliments fashioned from the period's most passionate love poetry; she in turn spoke, when it suited her to do so, in the language of love poetry. The court moved in an atmosphere of romance, with music, dancing, plays, and the elaborate, fancy-dress entertainments called masques. The queen adorned herself in gorgeous clothes and rich jewels. When she went on one of her summer "progresses," ceremonial journeys through her land, she looked like an exotic, sacred image in a religious cult of love, and her noble hosts virtually bankrupted themselves to lavish upon her the costliest pleasures. England's leading artists, such as the poet Edmund Spenser and the painter Nicholas Hilliard, enlisted themselves in the celebration of Elizabeth's mystery, likening her to the goddesses and queens of mythology: Diana, Astraea, Gloriana. Her cult drew its power from cultural discourses that ranged from the secular (her courtiers could pine for her as a cruel Petrarchan mistress) to the sacred (the veneration that under Catholicism had been due to the Virgin Mary could now be directed toward England's semidivine queen).

There was a sober, even grim aspect to these poetical fantasies: Elizabeth was brilliant at playing one dangerous faction off against another, now turning her gracious smiles on one favorite, now honoring his hated rival, now suddenly looking elsewhere and raising an obscure upstart to royal favor. And when she was disobeyed or when she felt that her prerogatives had been challenged, she was capable of an anger that, as Harington put it, "left no doubtings whose daughter she was." Thus when Sir Walter Ralegh, one of the queen's glittering favorites, married without her knowledge or consent, he found himself promptly imprisoned in the Tower of London. And when the Protestant polemicist John Stubbs ventured to publish a pamphlet stridently denouncing the queen's proposed marriage to the French Catholic Duke of Alençon, Stubbs and his publisher were arrested and had their right hands chopped off. (After receiving the blow, the now prudent Stubbs lifted his hat with his remaining hand and cried, "God save the Queen!")

The queen's marriage negotiations were a particularly fraught issue. When she came to the throne at twenty-five years old, speculation about a suitable match, already widespread, intensified and remained for decades at a fever pitch, for the stakes were high. If Elizabeth died childless, the Tudor line would come to an end. The nearest heir was her cousin Mary, Queen of Scots, a Catholic whose claim was supported by France and by the papacy and whose penchant for sexual and political intrigue confirmed the worst fears of English Protestants. The obvious way to avert the nightmare was for Elizabeth to marry and produce an heir, and the pressure upon her to do so was intense.

More than the royal succession hinged on the question of the queen's marriage; Elizabeth's perceived eligibility was a vital factor in the complex machinations of international diplomacy. A dynastic marriage between the Queen of England and a foreign ruler would forge an alliance powerful enough to alter the balance of power in Europe. The English court hosted a steady stream of ambassadors from kings and princes eager to win the hand of the royal maiden, and Elizabeth, who prided herself on speaking fluent French and Italian (and on reading Latin and Greek), played her romantic part with exemplary skill, sighing and spinning the negotiations out for months and even years. Most probably, she never meant to marry any of her numerous foreign (and domestic) suitors. Such a decisive act would have meant the end of her independence, as well as the end of the marriage game by which she played one power off against another. One day she would seem to be on the verge of accepting a proposal; the next, she would vow never to forsake her virginity. "She is a Princess," the French ambassador remarked, "who can act any part she pleases."

The Kingdom in Danger

Beset by Catholic and Protestant extremists, Elizabeth contrived to forge a moderate compromise that enabled her realm to avert the massacres and civil wars that poisoned France and other countries on the Continent. But menace was never far off, and there were constant fears of conspiracy, rebellion, and assassination. Many of the fears swirled around Mary, Queen of Scots, who had been driven from her own kingdom in 1568 by a powerful faction of rebellious nobles and had taken refuge in England. Her presence, under a kind of house arrest, was the source of intense anxiety and helped generate continual rumors of plots. Some of these plots were real enough, others imaginary, still others traps set in motion by the secret agents of the government's intelligence service under the direction of Sir Francis Walsingham. The situation worsened greatly after the St. Bartholomew's Day Massacre of Protestants (Huguenots) in France (1572), after Spanish imperial armies invaded the Netherlands in order to stamp out Protestant rebels, and after the assassination there of Europe's other major Protestant leader, William of Orange (1584).

The queen's life seemed to be in even greater danger after Pope Gregory XIII's proclamation in 1580 that the assassination of the great heretic Elizabeth (who had been excommunicated a decade before) would not constitute a mortal sin. The immediate effect of the proclamation was to make existence more difficult for English Catholics, most of whom were loyal to the queen but who fell under grave suspicion. Suspicion was intensified by the clandestine presence of English Jesuits, trained at seminaries abroad and smuggled back into England to serve the Roman Catholic cause. When Elizabeth's spymaster Walsingham unearthed an assassination plot in the correspondence between the Queen of Scots and the Catholic Anthony Babington, the wretched Mary's fate was sealed. After vacillating, a very reluctant Elizabeth signed the death warrant in February 1587, and her cousin was beheaded.

The long-anticipated military confrontation with Catholic Spain was now unavoidable.

Elizabeth learned that Philip II, her former brother-in-law and onetime suitor, was preparing to send an enormous fleet against her island realm. It was to sail to the Netherlands, where a Spanish army would be waiting to embark and invade England. Barring its way was England's small fleet of well-armed and highly maneuverable fighting vessels, backed up by ships from the merchant navy. The Invincible Armada reached English waters in July 1588, only to be routed in one of the most famous and decisive naval battles in European history. Then, in what many viewed as an act of God on behalf of Protestant England, the Spanish fleet was dispersed and all but destroyed by violent storms.

As England braced itself to withstand the invasion that never came, Elizabeth appeared in person to review a detachment of soldiers assembled at Tilbury. Dressed in a white gown and a silver breastplate, she declared that though some among her councillors had urged her not to appear before a large crowd of armed men, she would never fail to trust the loyalty of her faithful and loving subjects. Nor did she fear the Spanish armies. "I know I have the body of a weak and feeble woman," Elizabeth declared, "but I have the heart and stomach of a king, and of England too." In this celebrated speech, Elizabeth displayed many of her most memorable qualities: her self-consciously histrionic command of grand public occasion, her subtle blending of magniloquent rhetoric and the language of love, her strategic appropriation of traditionally masculine qualities, and her great personal courage. "We princes," she once remarked, "are set on stages in the sight and view of all the world."

The English and Otherness

Shakespeare's London had a large population of resident aliens, mainly artisans and merchants and their families, from Portugal, Italy, Spain, Germany, and above all France and the Netherlands. Many of these people were Protestant refugees, and they were accorded some legal and economic protection by the government. But they were not always welcome by the local populace. Throughout the sixteenth century, London was the site of repeated demonstrations and, on occasion, bloody riots against the communities of foreign artisans, who were accused of taking jobs away from Englishmen. There was widespread hostility as well toward the Welsh, the Scots, and especially the Irish, whom the English had for centuries been struggling unsuccessfully to subdue. The kings of England claimed to be rulers of Ireland, but in reality they effectively controlled only a small area known as the Pale, extending north from Dublin. The great majority of the Irish people remained stubbornly Catholic and, despite endlessly reiterated English repression, burning of villages, destruction of crops, and massacres, incorrigibly independent.

Shakespeare's *Henry V* (1598–99) seems to invite the audience to celebrate the conjoined heroism of English, Welsh, Scots, and Irish soldiers all fighting together as a "band of brothers" against the French. But such a way of imagining the national community must be set against the tensions and conflicting interests that often set these brothers at each other's throats. As Shakespeare's King Henry realizes, a feared or hated foreign enemy helps at least to mask these tensions, and indeed, in the face of the Spanish Armada, even the bitter gulf between Catholic and Protestant Englishmen seemed to narrow significantly. But the patriotic alliance was only temporary.

Another way of partially masking the sharp differences in language, belief, and custom among the peoples of the British Isles was to group these people together in contrast to the Jews. Medieval England's Jewish population, the recurrent object of persecution, extortion, and massacre, had been officially expelled by King Edward I in 1290, but Elizabethan England harbored a tiny number of Jews or Jewish converts to Christianity who were treated with suspicion and hostility. One of these was Elizabeth's own physician, Roderigo Lopez, who was tried in 1594 for an alleged plot to poison the queen. Convicted and condemned to the hideous execution reserved for traitors, Lopez went to his death, in the words of the Elizabethan historian William Camden, "affirming that he loved the Queen as well as he loved Jesus Christ; which coming from a man of the Jewish profession moved

A Jewish man depicted poisoning a well. From Pierre Boaistuau, *Certaine Secrete Wonders of Nature* (1569).

no small laughter in the standers-by." It is difficult to gauge the meaning here of the phrase "the Jewish profession," used to describe a man who never as far as we know professed Judaism, just as it is difficult to gauge the meaning of the crowd's cruel laughter.

Elizabethans appear to have been fascinated by Jews and Judaism but quite uncertain whether the terms referred to a people, a foreign nation, a set of strange practices, a living faith, a defunct religion, a villainous conspiracy, or a messianic inheritance. Protestant Reformers brooded deeply on the Hebraic origins of Christianity; government officials ordered the arrest of those "suspected to be Jews"; villagers paid pennies to itinerant fortune-tellers who claimed to be descended from Abraham or masters of cabalistic mysteries; and London playgoers, perhaps including some who laughed at Lopez on the scaffold, enjoyed the spectacle of the downfall of the wicked Barabas in Christopher Marlowe's *Jew of Malta* (c. 1592) and the forced conversion of Shylock in Shakespeare's *Merchant of Venice* (1596–97). Few if any of Shakespeare's contemporaries would have encountered on English soil Jews who openly practiced their religion, though England probably harbored a small number of so-called Marranos, Spanish or Portuguese Jews who had officially converted to Christianity but secretly continued to observe Jewish practices. Jews were not officially permitted to resettle in England until the middle of the seventeenth century, and even then their legal status was ambiguous.

Shakespeare's England also had a small African population whose skin color was the subject of pseudo-scientific speculation and theological debate. Some Elizabethans believed that Africans' blackness resulted from the climate of the regions in which they lived, where, as one traveler put it, they were "so scorched and vexed with the heat of the sun, that in many places they curse it when it riseth." Others held that blackness was a curse inherited from their forefather Chus, the son of Ham, who had, according to Genesis, wickedly exposed the nakedness of the drunken Noah. George Best, a proponent of this theory of inherited skin color, reported that "I myself have seen an Ethiopian as black as coal brought into England, who taking a fair English woman to wife, begat a son in all respects as black as the father was, although England were his native country, and an English woman his mother: whereby it seemeth this blackness proceedeth rather of some natural infection of that man."

As the word "infection" suggests, Elizabethans frequently regarded blackness as a physical defect, though the blacks who lived in England and Scotland throughout the sixteenth century were also treated as exotic curiosities. At his marriage to Anne of Denmark, James I entertained his bride and her family by commanding four naked black youths to dance before him in the snow. (The youths died of exposure shortly afterward.) In 1594, in the festivities celebrating the baptism of James's son, a "Black-Moor" entered pulling an elaborately decorated chariot that was, in the original plan, supposed to be drawn in by a lion. There was a black trumpeter in the courts of Henry VII and Henry VIII, while Elizabeth had at least two black servants, one an entertainer and the other a page. Africans became increasingly popular as servants in aristocratic and gentle households in the last decades of the sixteenth century.

Some of these Africans were almost certainly slaves, though the legal status of slavery in England was ambiguous. In Cartwright's Case (1569), the court ruled "that England was too Pure an Air for Slaves to breathe in," but there is evidence that black slaves were owned in Elizabethan and Jacobean England. Moreover, by the mid-sixteenth century, the English had become involved in the profitable trade that carried African slaves to the New World. In 1562, John Hawkins embarked on his first slaving voyage, transporting some three hundred blacks from the Guinea coast to Hispaniola, where they were sold for £10,000. Elizabeth is reported to have said of this venture that it was "detestable, and would call down the Vengeance of Heaven upon the Undertakers." Nevertheless, she invested in Hawkins's subsequent voyages and loaned him ships.

English men and women of the sixteenth century experienced an

Man with head beneath his shoulders. From a Spanish edition of Mandeville's *Travels.* See *Othello* 1.3.144–45: "and men whose heads / Do grow beneath their shoulders." Such men were occasionally reported by medieval travelers to the East.

unprecedented increase in knowledge of the world beyond their island, for a number of reasons. Religious persecution compelled both Catholics and Protestants to live abroad; wealthy gentlemen (and, in at least a few cases, ladies) traveled in France and Italy to view the famous cultural monuments; merchants published accounts of distant lands such as Turkey, Morocco, and Russia; and military and trading ventures took English ships to still more distant shores. In 1496, a Venetian tradesman living in Bristol, John Cabot, was granted a license by Henry VII to sail on a voyage of exploration; with his son Sebastian, he discovered Newfoundland and Nova Scotia. Remarkable feats of seamanship and reconnaissance soon followed: on his ship the *Golden Hind,* Sir Francis Drake circumnavigated the globe in 1579 and laid claim to California on behalf of the queen; a few years later, a ship commanded by Thomas Cavendish also completed a circumnavigation. Sir Martin Frobisher explored bleak Baffin Island in search of a Northwest Passage to the Orient; Sir John Davis explored the west coast of Greenland and discovered the Falkland Islands off the coast of Argentina; Sir Walter Ralegh ventured up the Orinoco Delta, in what is now Venezuela, in search of the mythical land of El Dorado. Accounts of these and other exploits were collected by a clergyman and promoter of empire, Richard Hakluyt, and published as *The Principal Navigations* (1589; expanded edition 1599).

"To seek new worlds for gold, for praise, for glory," as Ralegh characterized such enterprises, was not for the faint of heart: Drake, Cavendish, Frobisher, and Hawkins all died at sea, as did huge numbers of those who sailed under their command. Elizabethans sensible enough to stay at home could do more than read written accounts of their fellow countrymen's far-reaching voyages. Expeditions brought back native plants (including, most famously, tobacco), animals, cultural artifacts, and, on occasion, samples of the native

An Indian dance. From Thomas Hariot, A *Briefe and True Report of the New Found Land of Virginia* (1590).

peoples themselves, most often seized against their will. There were exhibitions in London of a kidnapped Eskimo with his kayak and of Virginians with their canoes. Most of these miserable captives, violently uprooted and vulnerable to European diseases, quickly perished, but even in death they were evidently valuable property: when the English will not give one small coin "to relieve a lame beggar," one of the characters in *The Tempest* wryly remarks, "they will lay out ten to see a dead Indian" (2.2.30–31).

Perhaps most nations learn to define what they are by defining what they are not. This negative self-definition is, in any case, what Elizabethans seemed constantly to be doing, in travel books, sermons, political speeches, civic pageants, public exhibitions, and theatrical spectacles of otherness. The extraordinary variety of these exercises (which include public executions and urban riots, as well as more benign forms of curiosity) suggests that the boundaries of national identity were by no means clear and unequivocal. Even peoples whom English writers routinely, viciously stigmatize as irreducibly alien—Italians, Indians, Turks, and Jews—have a surprising instability in the Elizabethan imagination and may appear for brief, intense moments as powerful models to be admired and emulated before they resume their place as emblems of despised otherness.

James I and the Union of the Crowns

Though under great pressure to do so, the aging Elizabeth steadfastly refused to name her successor. It became increasingly apparent, however, that it would be James Stuart, the son of Mary, Queen of Scots, and by the time Elizabeth's health began to fail, several of her principal advisers, including her chief minister, Robert Cecil, had been for several years in secret correspondence with him in Edinburgh. Crowned King James VI of Scotland in 1567 when he was but one year old, Mary's son had been raised as a Protestant by his powerful guardians, and in 1589 he married a Protestant princess, Anne of Denmark. When Elizabeth died on March 24, 1603, English officials reported that on her deathbed the queen had named James to succeed her.

Upon his accession, James—now styled James VI of Scotland and James I of England—made plain his intention to unite his two kingdoms. As he told Parliament in 1604, "What God hath conjoined then, let no man separate. I am the husband, and all of the whole isle is my lawful wife; I am the head and it is my body; I am the shepherd and it is my flock." But the flock was less perfectly united than James optimistically envisioned: English and Scottish were sharply distinct identities, as were Welsh and Cornish and other peoples who were incorporated, with varying degrees of willingness, into the realm.

Fearing that to change the name of the kingdom would invalidate all laws and institutions established under the name of England, a fear that was partly real and partly a cover for anti-Scots prejudice, Parliament balked at James's desire to be called "King of Great Britain" and resisted the unionist legislation that would have made Great Britain a legal reality. Though the English initially rejoiced at the peaceful transition from Elizabeth to her successor, there was a rising tide of resentment against James's advancement of Scots friends and his creation of new knighthoods. Lower down the social ladder, English and Scots occasionally clashed violently on the streets: in July 1603, James issued a proclamation against Scottish "insolencies," and in April 1604, he ordered the arrest of "swaggerers" waylaying Scots in London. The ensuing years did not bring the amity and docile obedience for which James hoped, and, though the navy now flew the Union Jack, combining the Scottish cross of St. Andrew and the English cross of St. George, the unification of the kingdoms remained throughout his reign an unfulfilled ambition.

Funeral procession of Queen Elizabeth. From a watercolor sketch by an unknown artist (1603).

The Jacobean Court

With James as with Elizabeth, the royal court was the center of diplomacy, ambition, intrigue, and an intense jockeying for social position. As always in monarchies, proximity to the king's person was a central mark of favor, so that access to the royal bedchamber was one of the highest aims of the powerful, scheming lords who followed James from his sprawling London palace at Whitehall to the hunting lodges and country estates to which he loved to retreat. A coveted office, in the Jacobean as in the Tudor court, was the Groom of the Stool, the person who supervised the disposal of the king's wastes. The officeholder was close to the king at one of his most exposed and vulnerable moments and enjoyed the further privilege of sleeping on a pallet at the foot of the royal bed and putting on the royal undershirt. Another, slightly less privileged official, the Gentleman of the Robes, dressed the king in his doublet and outer garments.

The royal life-style was increasingly expensive. Unlike Elizabeth, James had to maintain separate households for his queen and for the heir apparent, Prince Henry. (Upon Henry's death at the age of eighteen in 1612, his younger brother, Prince Charles, became heir, eventually succeeding his father in 1625.) James was also extremely generous to his friends, amassing his own huge debts in the course of paying off theirs. As early as 1605, he told his principal adviser that "it is a horror to me to think of the height of my place, the greatness of my debts, and the smallness of my means." This smallness notwithstanding, James continued to lavish gifts upon handsome favorites such as the Earl of Somerset, Robert Carr, and the Duke of Buckingham, George Villiers.

The attachment James formed for these favorites was highly romantic. "God so love me," the king wrote to Buckingham, "as I desire only to live in the world for your sake,

and that I had rather live banished in any part of the earth with you than live a sorrowful widow's life without you." Such sentiments, not surprisingly, gave rise to widespread rumors of homosexual activities at court. The rumors are certainly plausible, though the surviving evidence of same-sex relationships, at court or elsewhere, is extremely difficult to interpret. A statute of 1533 made "the detestable and abominable vice of buggery committed with mankind or beast" a felony punishable by death. (English law declined to recognize or criminalize lesbian acts.) The effect of the draconian laws against buggery and sodomy seems to have been to reduce actual prosecutions to the barest minimum: for the next hundred years, there are no known cases of trials resulting in a death sentence for homosexual activity alone. If the legal record is therefore unreliable as an index of the extent of homosexual relations, the literary record (including, most famously, the majority of Shakespeare's sonnets) is equally opaque. Any poetic avowal of male-male love may simply be a formal expression of affection based on clas-

James I. By Marc Gheeraerts II, court painter.

Two Young Men. By Crispin van den Broeck.

sical models, or, alternatively, it may be an expression of passionate physical and spiritual love. The interpretive difficulty is compounded by the absence in the period of any clear reference to a homosexual "identity," though there are many references to same-sex acts and feelings. What is clear is that male friendships at the court of James and elsewhere were suffused with a potential eroticism, at once delightful and threatening, that subsequent periods policed more anxiously.

In addition to the extravagant expenditures on his favorites, James was also the patron of ever more elaborate feasts and masques. Shakespeare's work provides a small glimpse of these in *The Tempest*, with its exotic banquet and its "majestic vision" of mythological goddesses and dancing nymphs and reapers, but the actual Jacobean court masques, designed by the great architect, painter, and engineer Inigo Jones, were spectacular, fantastic, technically ingenious, and staggeringly costly celebrations of regal magnificence. With their exquisite costumes and their elegant blend of music, dancing, and poetry, the masques, generally performed by the noble lords and ladies of the court, were deliberately ephemeral exercises in conspicuous expenditure and consumption: by tradition, at the end of the performance, the private audience would rush forward and tear to pieces the gorgeous scenery. And though masques were enormously sophisticated entertainments, often on rather esoteric allegorical themes, they could on occasion collapse into grotesque excess. In a letter of 1606, Sir John Harington describes a masque in honor of the visiting Danish king in which the participants, no doubt toasting their royal majesties, had had too much to drink. A lady playing the part of the Queen of Sheba attempted to present precious gifts, "but, forgetting the steps arising to the canopy, overset her caskets into his Danish Majesty's lap. . . . His Majesty then got up and would dance with the Queen of Sheba; but he fell down and humbled himself before her, and was carried to an inner chamber and laid on a bed." Meanwhile, Harington writes, the masque continued with a pageant of Faith, Hope, and Charity, but Charity could barely keep her balance, while Hope and Faith "were both sick and spewing in the lower hall." This was, we can hope, not a typical occasion.

While the English seem initially to have welcomed James's free-spending ways as a change from the parsimoniousness of Queen Elizabeth, they were dismayed by its consequences. Elizabeth had died owing £400,000. In 1608, the royal debt had risen to

£1,400,000 and was increasing by £140,000 a year. The money to pay off this debt, or at least to keep it under control, was raised by various means. These included customs farming (leasing the right to collect customs duties to private individuals); the highly unpopular impositions (duties on the import of nonnecessities, such as spices, silks, and currants); the sale of crown lands; the sale of baronetcies; and appeals to an increasingly grudging and recalcitrant Parliament. In 1614, Parliament demanded an end to impositions before it would relieve the king and was angrily dissolved without completing its business.

James's Religious Policy and the Persecution of Witches

Before his accession to the English throne, the king had made known his view of Puritans, the general name for a variety of Protestant sects that were agitating for a radical reform of the church, the overthrow of its conservative hierarchy of bishops, and the rejection of a large number of traditional rituals and practices. In a book he wrote, *Basilikon Doron* (1599), James denounced "brainsick and heady preachers" who were prepared "to let King, people, law and all be trod underfoot." Yet he was not entirely unwilling to consider religious reforms. In religion, as in foreign policy, he was above all concerned to maintain peace.

On his way south to claim the throne of England in 1603, James was presented with the Millenary Petition (signed by one thousand ministers), which urged him as "our physician" to heal the disease of lingering "popish" ceremonies. He responded by calling a conference on the ceremonies of the Church of England, which duly took place at Hampton Court Palace in January 1604. The delegates who spoke for reform were moderates, and there was little in the outcome to satisfy Puritans. Nevertheless, while the Church of England continued to cling to such remnants of the Catholic past as wedding rings, square caps, bishops, and Christmas, the conference did produce some reform in the area of

The "swimming" of a suspected witch.

ecclesiastical discipline. It also authorized a new English translation of the Bible, known as the King James Bible, which was printed in 1611, too late to have been extensively used by Shakespeare. Along with Shakespeare's works, the King James Bible has probably had the profoundest influence on the subsequent history of English literature.

Having arranged this compromise, James saw his main task as ensuring conformity. He promulgated the 1604 Canons (the first definitive code of canon law since the Reformation), which required all ministers to subscribe to three articles. The first affirmed royal supremacy; the second confirmed that there was nothing in the Book of Common Prayer "contrary to the Word of God" and required ministers to use only the authorized services; the third asserted that the central tenets of the Church of England were "agreeable to the Word of God." There were strong objections to the second and third articles from those of Puritan leanings inside and outside the House of Commons. In the end, many ministers refused to conform or subscribe to the articles, but only about ninety of them, or 1 percent of the clergy, were deprived of their livings. In its theology and composition, the Church of England was little changed from what it had been under Elizabeth. In hindsight, what is most striking are the ominous signs of growing religious divisions that would by the 1640s burst forth in civil war and the execution of James's son Charles.

James seems to have taken seriously the official claims to the sacredness of kingship, and he certainly took seriously his own theories of religion and politics, which he had printed for the edification of his people. He was convinced that Satan, perpetually warring against God and His representatives on earth, was continually plotting against him. James thought moreover that he possessed special insight into Satan's wicked agents, the witches, and in 1597, while King of Scotland, he published his *Demonology*, a learned exposition of their malign threat to his godly rule. Hundreds of witches, he believed, were involved in a 1590 conspiracy to kill him by raising storms at sea when he was sailing home from Denmark with his new bride.

In the 1590s, Scotland embarked on a virulent witch craze of the kind that had since the fifteenth century repeatedly afflicted France, Switzerland, and Germany, where many thousands of women (and a much smaller number of men) were caught in a nightmarish web of wild accusations. Tortured into lurid confessions of infant cannibalism, night flying, and sexual intercourse with the devil at huge, orgiastic "witches' Sabbaths," the victims had little chance to defend themselves and were routinely burned at the stake.

In England too there were witchcraft prosecutions, though on a much smaller scale and with significant differences in the nature of the accusations and the judicial procedures. Witch trials began in England in the 1540s; statutes against witchcraft were enacted in 1542, 1563, and 1604. English law did not allow judicial torture, stipulated lesser punishments in cases of "white magic," and mandated jury trials. Juries acquitted more than half of the defendants in witchcraft trials; in Essex, where the judicial records are particularly extensive, some 24 percent of those accused were executed, while the remainder of those convicted were pilloried and imprisoned or sentenced and reprieved. The accused were generally charged with *maleficium*, an evil deed—usually harming neighbors, causing destructive storms, or killing farm animals—but not with worshipping Satan.

After 1603, when James came to the English throne, he somewhat moderated his enthusiasm for the judicial murder of witches, for the most part defenseless, poor women resented by their neighbors. Though he did nothing to mitigate the ferocity of the ongoing witch-hunts in his native Scotland, he did not try to institute Scottish-style persecutions and trials in his new realm. This relative waning of persecutorial eagerness principally reflects the differences between England and Scotland, but it may also bespeak some small, nascent skepticism on James's part about the quality of evidence brought against the accused and about the reliability of the "confessions" extracted from them. It is sobering to reflect that plays like Shakespeare's *Macbeth* (1606), Thomas Middleton's *Witch* (before 1616), and Thomas Dekker, John Ford, and William Rowley's *Witch of Edmonton* (1621) seem to be less the allies of skepticism than the exploiters of fear.

The Playing Field

Cosmic Spectacles

The first permanent, freestanding public theaters in England date only from Shakespeare's own lifetime: a London playhouse, the Red Lion, is mentioned in 1567, and James Burbage's playhouse, The Theatre, was built in 1576. (The innovative use of these new stages, crucial to a full understanding of Shakespeare's achievement, is the subject of a separate essay in this volume, by the theater historian Andrew Gurr.) But it is quite misleading to identify English drama exclusively with these specially constructed playhouses, for in fact there was a rich and vital theatrical tradition in England stretching back for centuries. Many towns in late medieval England were the sites of annual festivals that mounted elaborate cycles of plays depicting the great biblical stories, from the creation of the world to Christ's Passion and its miraculous aftermath. Most of these plays have been lost, but the surviving cycles, such as those from York, are magnificent and complex works of art. They are sometimes called "mystery plays," either because they were performed by the guilds of various crafts (known as "mysteries") or, more likely, because they represented the mysteries of the faith. The cycles were most often performed on the annual feast day instituted in the early fourteenth century in honor of the Corpus Christi, the sacrament of the Lord's Supper, which is perhaps the greatest of these religious mysteries.

The feast of Corpus Christi, celebrated on the Thursday following Trinity Sunday, helped give the play cycles their extraordinary cultural resonance, but it also contributed to their downfall. For along with the specifically liturgical plays traditionally performed by religious confraternities and the "saints' plays, which depicted miraculous events in the lives of individual holy men and women, the mystery cycles were closely identified with the Catholic Church. Protestant authorities in the sixteenth century, eager to eradicate all remnants of popular Catholic piety, moved to suppress the annual procession of the Host, with its gorgeous banners, pageant carts, and cycle of visionary plays. In 1548, the Feast of Corpus Christi was abolished. Towns that continued to perform the mysteries were under increasing pressure to abandon them. It is sometimes said that the cycles were already dying out from neglect, but recent research has shown that many towns and their guilds were extremely reluctant to give them up. Desperate offers to strip away any traces of Catholic doctrine and to submit the play scripts to the authorities for their approval met with unbending opposition from the government. In 1576, the courts gave York permission to perform its cycle but only if

> in the said play no pageant be used or set forth wherein the Majesty of God the Father, God the Son, or God the Holy Ghost or the administration of either the Sacraments of baptism or of the Lord's Supper be counterfeited or represented, or anything played which tend to the maintenance of superstition and idolatry or which be contrary to the laws of God . . . or of the realm.

Such "permission" was tantamount to an outright ban. The local officials in the city of Norwich, proud of their St. George and the Dragon play, asked if they could at least parade the dragon costume through the streets, but even this modest request was refused. It is likely that as a young man Shakespeare had seen some of these plays: when Hamlet says of a noisy, strutting theatrical performance that it "out-Herods Herod," he is alluding to the famously bombastic role of Herod of Jewry in the mystery plays. But by the century's end, the cycles were no longer performed.

Early English theater was by no means restricted to these civic and religious festivals. Payments to professional and amateur performers appear in early records of towns and aristocratic households, though the terms—"ministralli," "histriones," "mimi," "lusores," and so forth—are not used with great consistency and make it difficult to distinguish among minstrels, jugglers, stage players, and other entertainers. Performers acted in town halls and the halls of guilds and aristocratic mansions, on scaffolds erected in town squares

Panorama of London, showing two theaters, both round and both flying flags: a flying flag indicated that a performance was in progress. The Globe is in the foreground, and the Beargarden or Hope is to the left.

and marketplaces, on pageant wagons in the streets, and in inn yards. By the fifteenth century, and probably earlier, there were organized companies of players traveling under noble patronage. Such companies earned a living providing amusement, while enhancing the prestige of the patron.

A description of a provincial performance in the late sixteenth century, written by one R. Willis, provides a glimpse of what seems to have been the usual procedure:

> In the City of Gloucester the manner is (as I think it is in other like corporations) that when the Players of Interludes come to town, they first attend the Mayor to inform him what nobleman's servant they are, and so to get licence for their public playing; and if the Mayor like the Actors, or would show respect to their Lord and Master, he appoints them to play their first play before himself and the Aldermen and common Council of the City and that is called the Mayor's play, where everyone that will come in without money, the Mayor giving the players a reward as he thinks fit to show respect unto them.

In addition to their take from this "first play," the players would almost certainly have supplemented their income by performing in halls and inn yards, where they could pass the hat after the performance or even on some occasions charge an admission fee. It was no doubt a precarious existence.

The "Interludes" mentioned in Willis's description of the Gloucester performances are likely plays that were, in effect, staged dialogues on religious, moral, and political themes. Such works could, like the mysteries, be associated with Catholicism, but they were also used in the sixteenth century to convey polemical Protestant messages, and they reached outside the religious sphere to address secular concerns as well. Henry Medwall's *Fulgens and Lucrece* (c. 1490–1501), for example, pits a wealthy but dissolute nobleman against a virtuous public servant of humble origins, while John Heywood's *Play of the Weather* (c. 1525–33) stages a debate among social rivals, including a gentleman, a merchant, a forest ranger, and two millers. The structure of such plays reflects the training in argumentation that students received in Tudor schools and, in particular, the sustained practice in examining all sides of a difficult question. Some of Shakespeare's amazing ability to look at critical issues from multiple perspectives may be traced back to this practice and the dramatic interludes it helped to inspire.

Another major form of theater that flourished in England in the fifteenth century and continued on into the sixteenth was the morality play. Like the mysteries, moralities addressed questions of the ultimate fate of the soul. They did so, however, not by rehearsing scriptural stories but by dramatizing allegories of spiritual struggle. Typically, a person named Human or Mankind or Youth is faced with a choice between a pious life in the company of such associates as Mercy, Discretion, and Good Deeds and a dissolute life among riotous companions like Lust or Mischief. Plays like *Mankind* (c. 1465–70) and *Everyman* (c. 1495) show how powerful these unpromising-sounding dramas could be, in part because of the extraordinary comic vitality of the evil character, or Vice, and in part because of the poignancy and terror of an individual's encounter with death. Shakespeare clearly grasped this power. The hunchbacked Duke of Gloucester in *Richard III* gleefully likens himself to "the formal Vice, Iniquity." And when Othello wavers between Desdemona and Iago (himself a Vice figure), his anguished dilemma echoes the fateful choice repeatedly faced by the troubled, vulnerable protagonists of the moralities.

If such plays sound a bit like sermons, it is because they were. Clerics and actors shared some of the same rhetorical skills. It would be misleading to regard churchgoing and playgoing as comparable entertainments, but in attacking the stage, ministers often seemed to regard the professional players as dangerous rivals. The players themselves were generally too discreet to rise to the challenge; it would have been foolhardy to present the theater as the church's direct competitor. Yet in its moral intensity and its command of impassioned language, the stage frequently emulates and outdoes the pulpit.

Music and Dance

Playacting took its place alongside other forms of public expression and entertainment as well. Perhaps the most important, from the perspective of the theater, were music and dance, since these were directly and repeatedly incorporated into plays. Many plays, comedies and tragedies alike, include occasions that call upon the characters to dance: hence Beatrice and Benedick join the other masked guests at the dance in *Much Ado About Nothing*; in *Twelfth Night*, the befuddled Sir Andrew, at the instigation of the drunken Sir Toby Belch, displays his skill, such as it is, in capering; Romeo and Juliet first see each other at the Capulet ball; the witches dance in a ring around the hideous caldron and perform an "antic round" to cheer Macbeth's spirits; and, in one of Shakespeare's strangest and most wonderful scenes, the drunken Antony in *Antony and Cleopatra* joins hands with Caesar, Enobarbus, Pompey, and others to dance "the Egyptian Bacchanals."

Moreover, virtually all plays in the period, including Shakespeare's, apparently ended with a dance. Brushing off the theatrical gore and changing their expressions from woe to pleasure, the actors in plays like *Hamlet* and *King Lear* would presumably have received the audience's applause and then bid for a second round of applause by performing a stately pavane or a lively jig. Indeed, jigs, with their comical leaping dance steps often accompanied by scurrilous ballads, became so popular that they drew not only large crowds but also official disapproval. A court order of 1612 complained about the "cut-purses and other lewd and ill-disposed persons" who flocked to the theater at the end of every play to be entertained by "lewd jigs, songs, and dances." The players were warned to suppress these disreputable entertainments on pain of imprisonment.

The displays of dancing onstage clearly reflected a widespread popular interest in dancing outside the walls of the playhouse as well. Renaissance intellectuals conjured up visions of the universe as a great cosmic dance, poets figured relations between men and women in terms of popular dance steps, stern moralists denounced dancing as an incitement to filthy lewdness, and, perhaps as significant, men of all classes evidently spent a great deal of time worrying about how shapely their legs looked in tights and how gracefully they could leap. Shakespeare assumes that his audience will be quite familiar with a variety of dances. "For, hear me, Hero," Beatrice tells her friend, "wooing, wedding, and repenting is as a Scotch jig, a measure, and a cinquepace" (2.1.60–61). Her speech dwells on the comparison a bit, teasing out its implications, but it still does not make much sense if you do not already know something about the dances and perhaps occasionally venture to perform them yourself.

Closely linked to dancing and even more central to the stage was music, both instrumental and vocal. In the early sixteenth century, the Reformation had been disastrous for sacred music: many church organs were destroyed, choir schools were closed, the glorious polyphonal liturgies sung in the monasteries were suppressed. But by the latter part of the century, new perspectives were reinvigorating English music. Latin masses were reset in English, and tunes were written for newly translated, metrical psalms. More important for the theater, styles of secular music were developed that emphasized music's link to humanist eloquence, its ability to heighten and to rival rhetorically powerful texts.

This link is particularly evident in vocal music, at which Elizabethan composers excelled. Renowned composers William Byrd, Thomas Morley, John Dowland, and others wrote a rich profusion of madrigals (part songs for two to eight voices unaccompanied) and ayres (songs for solo voice, generally accompanied by the lute). These works, along with hymns, popular ballads, rounds, catches, and other forms of song, enjoyed immense popularity, not only in the royal court, where musical skill was regarded as an important accomplishment, and in aristocratic households, where professional musicians were employed as entertainers, but also in less

Richard Tarlton. Tarlton was the lead comedian of the Queen's Company from 1583, the year of its founding, until 1588, when he died.

exalted social circles. In his *Plain and Easy Introduction to Practical Music* (1597), Morley tells a story of social humiliation at a failure to perform that suggests that a well-educated Elizabethan was expected to be able to sing at sight. Even if this is an exaggeration in the interest of book sales, there is evidence of impressively widespread musical literacy, reflected in a splendid array of music for the lute, viol, recorder, harp, and virginal, as well as the marvelous vocal music.

Whether it is the aristocratic Orsino luxuriating in the dying fall of an exquisite melody or bully Bottom craving "the tongs and the bones," Shakespeare's characters frequently call for music. They also repeatedly give voice to the age's conviction that there was a deep relation between musical harmony and the harmonies of the well-ordered individual and state. "The man that hath no music in himself," warns Lorenzo in *The Merchant of Venice*, "nor is not moved with concord of sweet sounds, / Is fit for treasons, stratagems, and spoils" (5.1.82–84). This conviction in turn reflects a still deeper link between musical harmony and the divinely created harmony of the cosmos. When Ulysses in *Troilus and Cressida* wishes to convey the image of universal chaos, he speaks of the untuning of a string (1.3.109).

The playing companies must have regularly employed trained musicians, and many actors (like the actor who in playing Pandarus in *Troilus and Cressida* is supposed to accompany himself on the lute) must have possessed musical skill. Unfortunately, we possess the original settings for very few of Shakespeare's songs, possibly because many of them may have been set to popular tunes of the time that everyone knew and no one bothered to write down.

Alternative Entertainments

Plays, music, and dancing were by no means the only shows in town. There were jousts, tournaments, royal entries, religious processions, pageants in honor of newly installed civic officials or ambassadors arriving from abroad; wedding masques, court masques, and costumed entertainments known as "disguisings" or "mummings"; juggling acts, fortune-tellers, exhibitions of swordsmanship, mountebanks, folk healers, storytellers, magic shows; bearbaiting, bullbaiting, cockfighting, and other blood sports; folk festivals such as Maying, the Feast of Fools, Carnival, and Whitsun Ales. For several years, Elizabethan Londoners were delighted by a trained animal—Banks's Horse—that could, it was thought, do arithmetic and answer questions. And there was always the grim but compelling spectacle of public shaming, mutilation, and execution.

Most English towns had stocks and whipping posts. Drunks, fraudulent merchants, adulterers, and quarrelers could be placed in carts or mounted backward on asses and paraded through the streets for crowds to jeer and throw refuse at. Women accused of being scolds could be publicly muzzled by an iron device called a "brank" or tied to a cucking stool and dunked in the river. Convicted criminals could have their ears cut off, their noses slit, their foreheads branded. Public beheadings (generally reserved for the elite) and hangings were common. In the worst cases, felons were sentenced to be "hanged by the neck, and being alive cut down, and your privy members to be cut off, and your bowels to be taken out of your belly and there burned, you being alive."

Shakespeare occasionally takes note of these alternative entertainments: at the end of *Macbeth*, for example, with his enemies closing in on him, the doomed tyrant declares, "They have tied me to a stake. I cannot fly, / But bear-like I must fight the course" (5.7.1–2). The audience is reminded then that it is witnessing the human equivalent of a popular spectacle—a bear chained to a stake and attacked by fierce dogs—that they could have paid to watch at an arena near the Globe. And when, a few moments later, Macduff enters carrying Macbeth's head, the audience is seeing the theatrical equivalent of the execution of criminals and traitors that they could have also watched in the flesh, as it were, nearby. In a different key, the audiences who paid to see *A Midsummer Night's Dream* or *The Winter's Tale* got to enjoy the comic spectacle of a Maying and a Whitsun Pastoral, while

An Elizabethan hanging.

the spectators of *The Tempest* could gawk at what the Folio list of characters calls a "salvage and deformed slave" and to enjoy an aristocratic magician's wedding masque in honor of his daughter.

The Enemies of the Stage

In 1624, a touring company of players arrived in Norwich and requested permission to perform. Permission was denied, but the municipal authorities, "in regard of the honorable respect which this City beareth to the right honorable the Lord Chamberlain," gave the players twenty shillings to get out of town. Throughout the sixteenth and early seventeenth centuries, there are many similar records of civic officials prohibiting performances and then, to appease a powerful patron, paying the actors to take their skills elsewhere. As early as the 1570s, there is evidence that the London authorities, while mindful of the players' influential protectors, were energetically trying to drive the theater out of the city.

Why should what we now regard as one of the undisputed glories of the age have aroused so much hostility? One answer, curiously enough, is traffic: plays drew large audiences—the public theaters could accommodate thousands—and residents objected to the crowds, the noise, and the crush of carriages. Other, more serious concerns were public health and crime. It was thought that numerous diseases, including the dreaded bubonic plague, were spread by noxious odors, and the packed playhouses were obvious breeding grounds for infection. (Patrons often tried to protect themselves by sniffing nosegays or stuffing cloves into their nostrils.) The large crowds drew pickpockets, cutpurses, and other scoundrels. On one memorable afternoon, a pickpocket was caught in the act and tied for the duration of the play to one of the posts that held up the canopy above the stage. The theater was, moreover, a well-known haunt of prostitutes, and, it was alleged, a place where innocent maids were seduced and respectable matrons corrupted. It was darkly rumored that "chambers and secret places" adjoined the theater galleries, and in any case, taverns, disreputable inns, and whorehouses were close at hand.

There were other charges as well. Plays were performed in the afternoon and therefore drew people, especially the young, away from their work. They were schools of idleness, luring apprentices from their trades, law students from their studies, housewives from their kitchens, and potentially pious souls from the sober meditations to which they might otherwise devote themselves. Wasting their time and money on disreputable shows, citizens exposed themselves to sexual provocation and outright political sedition. Even when the content of plays was morally exemplary—and, of course, few plays were so gratify-

Syphilis victim in tub. Frontispiece to the play *Cornelianum Dolium* (1638), possibly authored by Thomas Randolph. The tub inscription translates as "I sit on the throne of love, I suffer in the tub"; and the banner as "Farewell O sexual pleasures and lusts."

ingly high-minded—the theater itself, in the eyes of most mayors and aldermen, was inherently disorderly.

The attack on the stage by civic officials was echoed and intensified by many of the age's moralists and religious leaders, especially those associated with Puritanism. While English Protestants earlier in the sixteenth century had attempted to counter the Catholic mystery cycles and saints' plays by mounting their own doctrinally correct dramas, by the century's end a fairly widespread consensus, even among those mildly sympathetic toward the theater, held that the stage and the pulpit were in tension with one another. After 1591, a ban on Sunday performances was strictly enforced, and in 1606, Parliament passed an act imposing a fine of £10 on any person who shall "in any stage-play, interlude, show, May-game, or pageant, jestingly or profanely speak or use the holy name of God, or of Christ Jesus, or of the Holy Ghost, or of the Trinity (which are not to be spoken but with fear and reverence)." If changes in the printed texts are a reliable indication, the players seem to have complied at least to some degree with the ruling. The Folio (1623) text of *Richard III*, for example, omits the quarto's (1597) four uses of "zounds" (for "God's wounds"), along with a mention of "Christ's dear blood shed for our grievous sins"; "God's my judge" in *The Merchant of Venice* becomes "well I know"; "By Jesu" in *Henry V* becomes a very proper "I say"; and in all the plays, "God" is from time to time metamorphosed to "Jove."

But for some of the theater's more extreme critics, these modest expurgations were tiny bandages on a gaping wound. In his huge book *Histriomastix* (1633), William Prynne regurgitates a half-century of frenzied attacks on the "sinful, heathenish, lewd, ungodly Spectacles." In the eyes of Prynne and his fellow antitheatricalists, stage plays were part of a demonic tangle of obscene practices proliferating like a cancer in the body of society. It is "manifest to all men's judgments," he writes, that

> effeminate mixed dancing, dicing, stage-plays, lascivious pictures, wanton fashions, face-painting, health-drinking, long hair, love-locks, periwigs, women's curling, powdering and cutting of their hair, bonfires, New-year's gifts, May-games, amorous pastorals, lascivious effeminate music, excessive laughter, luxurious disorderly Christmas-keeping, mummeries . . . [are] wicked, unchristian pastimes.

Given the anxious emphasis on effeminacy, it is not surprising that denunciations of this kind obsessively focused on the use of boy actors to play the female parts. The enemies of the stage charged that theatrical transvestism excited illicit sexual desires, both heterosexual and homosexual.

Since cross-dressing violated a biblical prohibition (Deuteronomy 22:5), religious antitheatricalists attacked it as wicked regardless of its erotic charge; indeed, they often seemed to consider any act of impersonation as inherently wicked. In their view, the theater itself was Satan's domain. Thus a Cambridge scholar, John Greene, reports the sad fate of "a Christian woman" who went to the theater to see a play: "She entered in well and sound, but she returned and came forth possessed of the devil. Whereupon certain godly brethren demanded Satan how he durst be so bold, as to enter into her a Christian. Whereto he answered, that *he found her in his own house*, and therefore took possession of her as his own" (italic in original). When the "godly brethren" came to power in the mid-seventeenth century, with the overthrow of Charles I, they saw to it that the playhouses, temporarily shut down in 1642 at the onset of the Civil War, remained closed. The theater did not resume until the restoration of the monarchy in 1660.

Faced with enemies among civic officials and religious leaders, Elizabethan and Jacobean playing companies relied on the protection of their powerful patrons. As the liveried servants of aristocrats or of the monarch, the players could refute the charge that they were mere vagabonds, and they claimed, as a convenient legal fiction, that their public performances were necessary rehearsals in anticipation of those occasions when they would be called upon to entertain their noble masters. But harassment by the mayor and aldermen continued unabated, and the players were forced to build their theaters outside the immediate jurisdiction of the city authorities, either in the suburbs or in the areas known as the "liberties." A liberty was a piece of land within the City of London itself that was not directly subject to the authority of the lord mayor. The most significant of these from the point of view of the theater was the area near St. Paul's Cathedral called "the Blackfriars," where, until the dissolution of the monasteries in 1538, there had been a Dominican monastery. It was here that in 1608 Shakespeare's company, then called the King's Men, built the indoor playhouse in which they performed during the winter months, reserving the open-air Globe in the suburb of Southwark for their summer performances.

Censorship and Regulation

In addition to those authorities who campaigned to shut down the theater, there were others whose task was to oversee, regulate, and censor it. Given the outright hostility of the former, the latter may have seemed to the London players equivocal allies rather than enemies. After all, plays that passed the censor were at least licensed to be performed and hence conceded to have some limited legitimacy. In April 1559, at the very start of her reign, Queen Elizabeth drafted a proposal that for the first time envisaged a system for the prior review and regulation of plays throughout her kingdom:

> The Queen's Majesty doth straightly forbid all manner interludes to be played either openly or privately, except the same be notified beforehand, and licensed within any city or town corporate, by the mayor or other chief officers of the same, and within any shire, by such as shall be lieutenants for the Queen's Majesty in the same shire, or by two of the Justices of Peace inhabiting within that part of the shire where any shall be played. . . . And for instruction to every of the said officers, her Majesty doth likewise charge every of them, as they will answer: that they permit none to be played wherein either matters of religion or of the governance of the estate of the commonweal shall be handled or treated upon, but by men of authority, learning and wisdom, nor to be handled before any audience, but of grave and discreet persons.

This proposal, which may not have been formally enacted, makes an important distinction between those who are entitled to address sensitive issues of religion and politics—authors "of authority, learning and wisdom" addressing audiences "of grave and discreet persons"—and those who are forbidden to do so.

The London public theater, with its playwrights who were the sons of glovers, shoemakers, and bricklayers and its audiences in which the privileged classes mingled with rowdy apprentices, masked women, and servants, was clearly not a place to which the government wished to grant freedom of expression. In 1581, the Master of the Revels, an official in the lord chamberlain's department whose role had hitherto been to provide entertainment at court, was given an expanded commission. Sir Edmund Tilney, the functionary who held the office, was authorized

> to warn, command, and appoint in all places within this our Realm of England, as well within franchises and liberties as without, all and every player or players with their playmakers, either belonging to any nobleman or otherwise . . . to appear before him with all such plays, tragedies, comedies, or shows as they shall in readiness or mean to set forth, and them to recite before our said Servant or his sufficient deputy, whom we ordain, appoint, and authorize by these presents of all such shows, plays, players, and playmakers, together with their playing places, to order and reform, authorize and put down, as shall be thought meet or unmeet unto himself or his said deputy in that behalf.

What emerged from this commission was in effect a national system of regulation and censorship. One of its consequences was to restrict virtually all licensed theater to the handful of authorized London-based playing companies. These companies would have to submit their plays for official scrutiny, but in return they received implicit, and on occasion explicit, protection against the continued fierce opposition of the local authorities. Plays reviewed and allowed by the Master of the Revels had been deemed fit to be performed before the monarch; how could mere aldermen legitimately claim that such plays should be banned as seditious?

The key question, of course, is how carefully the Master of the Revels scrutinized the plays brought before him either to hear or, more often from the 1590s onward, to peruse. What was Tilney, who served in the office until his death in 1610, or his successor, Sir George Buc, who served from 1610 to 1621, looking for? What did they insist be cut before they would release what was known as the "allowed copy," the only version licensed for performance? Unfortunately, the office books of the Master of the Revels in Shakespeare's time have been lost; what survives is a handful of scripts on which Tilney, Buc, and their assistants jotted their instructions. These suggest that the readings were rather painstaking, with careful attention paid to possible religious, political, and diplomatic repercussions. References, directly or strongly implied, to any living Christian prince or any important English nobleman, gentleman, or government official were particularly sensitive and likely to be struck. Renaissance political life was highly personalized; people in power were exceptionally alert to insult and zealously patrolled the boundaries of their prestige and reputation.

Moreover, the censors knew that audiences and readers were quite adept at applying theatrical representations distanced in time and space to their own world. At a time of riots against resident foreigners, Tilney read *Sir Thomas More*, a play in which Shakespeare probably had a hand, and instructed the players to cut scenes that, though set in 1517, might have had an uncomfortable contemporary resonance. "Leave out the insurrection wholly," Tilney's note reads, "and the cause thereof and begin with Sir Thomas More at the Mayor's sessions, with a report afterwards of his good service done being sheriff of London upon a mutiny against the Lombards only by a short report and not otherwise at your own perils. E. Tilney." Of course, as Tilney knew perfectly well, most plays succeed precisely by mirroring, if only obliquely, their own times, but this particular reflection evidently seemed to him too dangerous or provocative.

The topical significance of a play depends in large measure on the particular moment in which it is performed, and on certain features of the performance—for example, a striking resemblance between one of the characters and a well-known public figure—that the script itself will not necessarily disclose to us at this great distance or even to the censor at the time. Hence the Master of the Revels noted angrily of one play performed in 1632 that "there were diverse personated so naturally, both of lords and others of the court, that I took it ill." Hence too a play that was deemed allowable when it was first written and performed could return, like a nightmare, to haunt a different place and time. The most famous instance of such a return involves Shakespeare, for on the day before the Earl of Essex's attempted coup against Queen Elizabeth in 1601, someone paid the Lord Chamberlain's Men (the name of Shakespeare's company at the time) forty shillings to revive their old play about the deposition and murder of Richard II. "I am Richard II," the queen declared. "Know ye not that?" However distressed she was by this performance, the queen significantly did not take out her wrath on the players: neither the playwright nor his company was punished, nor was the Master of the Revels criticized for allowing the play in the first place. It was Essex and several of his key supporters who lost their heads.

Evidence suggests that the Master of the Revels often regarded himself not as the strict censor of the theater but as its friendly guardian, charged with averting catastrophes. He was a bureaucrat concerned less with subversive ideas per se than with potential trouble. That is, there is no record of a dramatist being called to account for his heterodox beliefs; rather, plays were censored if they risked offending influential people, including important foreign allies, or if they threatened to cause public disorder by exacerbating religious or other controversies. The distinction is not a stable one, but it helps to explain the intellectual boldness, power, and freedom of a censored theater in a society in which the perceived enemies of the state were treated mercilessly. Shakespeare could have Lear articulate a searing indictment of social injustice—

Robes and furred gowns hide all. Plate sin with gold,
And the strong lance of justice hurtless breaks;
Arm it in rags, a pygmy's straw does pierce it.
(4.5.155–57)

—and evidently neither the Master of the Revels nor the courtiers in their robes and furred gowns protested. But when the Spanish ambassador complained about Thomas Middleton's anti-Spanish allegory *A Game at Chess*, performed at the Globe in 1624, the whole theater was shut down, the players were arrested, and the king professed to be furious at his official for licensing the play in the first place and allowing it to be performed for nine consecutive days.

In addition to the system for the licensing of plays for performance, there was also a system for the licensing of plays for publication. At the start of Shakespeare's career, such press licensing was the responsibility of the Court of High Commission, headed by the Archbishop of Canterbury and the Bishop of London. Their deputies, a panel of junior clerics, were supposed to review the manuscripts, granting licenses to those worthy of publication and rejecting any they deemed "heretical, seditious, or unseemly for Christian ears." Without a license, the Stationers' Company, the guild of the book trade, was not supposed to register a manuscript for publication. In practice, as various complaints and attempts to close loopholes attest, some playbooks were printed without a license. In 1607, the system was significantly revised when Sir George Buc began to license plays for the press. When Buc succeeded to the post of Master of the Revels in 1610, the powers to license plays for the stage and the page were vested in one man.

Theatrical Innovations

The theater continued to flourish under this system of regulation after Shakespeare's death; by the 1630s, as many as five playhouses were operating daily in London. When the theater reemerged after the eighteen-year hiatus imposed by Puritan rule, it quickly resumed its cultural importance, but not without a number of significant changes. Major innovations in staging resulted principally from continental influences on the English artists who accompanied the court of Charles II into exile in France, where they supplied it with masques and other theatrical entertainments.

The institutional conditions and business practices of the two companies chartered by Charles after the Restoration in 1660 also differed from those of Shakespeare's theater. In place of the more collective practice of Shakespeare's company, the Restoration theaters were controlled by celebrated actor-managers who not only assigned themselves starring roles, in both comedy and tragedy, but also assumed sole responsibility for many business decisions, including the setting of their colleagues' salaries. At the same time, the power of the actor-manager, great as it was, was limited by the new importance of outside capital. No longer was the theater, with all of its properties from script to costumes, owned by the "sharers," that is, by those actors who held shares in the joint-stock company. Instead, entrepreneurs would raise capital for increasingly fantastic sets and stage machinery that could cost as much as £3,000, an astronomical sum, for a single production. This investment in turn not only influenced the kinds of new plays written for the theater but helped to transform old plays that were revived, including Shakespeare's.

In his diary entry for August 24, 1661, Samuel Pepys notes that he has been "to the Opera, and there saw Hamlet, Prince of Denmark, done with scenes very well, but above all, Betterton did the prince's part beyond imagination." This is Thomas Betterton's first review, as it were, and it is typical of the enthusiasm he would inspire throughout his fifty-year career on the London stage. Pepys's brief and scattered remarks on the plays he voraciously attended in the 1660s are precious because they are among the few records from the period of concrete and immediate responses to theatrical performances. Modern readers might miss the significance of Pepys's phrase "done with scenes": this production of *Hamlet* was only the third play to use the movable sets first introduced to England by its producer, William Davenant. The central historical fact that makes the productions of this period so exciting is that public theater had been banned altogether for eighteen years until the Restoration of Charles II.

A brief discussion of theatrical developments in the Restoration period will enable us at least to glance longingly at a vast subject that lies outside the scope of this introduction: the rich performance history that extends from Shakespeare's time to our own, involving tens of thousands of productions and adaptations for theater, opera, Broadway musicals, and of course films. The scale of this history is vast in space as well as time: as early as 1607, there is a record of a *Hamlet* performed on board an English ship, HMS *Dragon*, off the coast of Sierra Leone, and troupes of English actors performed in the late sixteenth and early seventeenth centuries as far afield as Poland and Bohemia.

William Davenant, who claimed to be Shakespeare's bastard son, had become an expert on stage scenery while producing masques at the court of Charles I, and when the theaters reopened, he set to work on converting an indoor tennis court into a new kind of theater. He designed a broad open platform like that of the Elizabethan stage, but he replaced the relatively shallow space for "discoveries" (tableaux set up in an opening at the center of the stage, revealed by drawing back a curtain) and the "tiring-house" (the players' dressing room) behind this space with one expanded interior, framed by a proscenium arch, in which scenes could be displayed. These elaborately painted scenes could be moved on and off, using grooves on the floor. The perspectival effect for a spectator of one central painted panel with two "wings" on either side was that of three sides of a room. This effect anticipated that of the familiar "picture frame" stage, developed fully in the nineteenth century, and began a subtle shift in theater away from the elaborate verbal descriptions that are so central to Shakespeare and toward the evocative visual poetry of the set designer's art.

Another convention of Shakespeare's stage, the use of boy actors for female roles, gave way to the more complete illusion of women playing women's parts. The king issued a decree in 1662 forcefully permitting, if not requiring, the use of actresses. The royal decree is couched in the language of social and moral reform: the introduction of actresses will require the "reformation" of scurrilous and profane passages in plays, and this in turn will help forestall some of the objections that shut the theaters down in 1642. In reality, male theater audiences, composed of a narrower range of courtiers and aristocrats than in Shakespeare's time, met this intended reform with the assumption that the new actresses were fair game sexually; most actresses (with the partial exception of those who married male members of their troupes) were regarded as, or actually became, whores. But despite the social stigma, and the fact that their salaries were predictably lower than those of their male counterparts, the stage saw some formidable female stars by the 1680s.

The first recorded appearance of an actress was that of a Desdemona in December 1660. Betterton's Ophelia in 1661 was Mary Saunderson (c. 1637–1712), who became Mrs. Betterton a year later. The most famous Ophelia of the period was Susanna Mountfort, who appeared in that role for the first time at the age of fifteen in 1705. The performance by Mountfort that became legendary occurred in 1720, after a disappointment in love, or so it was said, had driven her mad. Hearing that *Hamlet* was being performed, Mountfort escaped from her keepers and reached the theater, where she concealed herself until the scene in which Ophelia enters in her state of insanity. At this point, Mountfort rushed onto the stage and, in the words of a contemporary, "was in truth Ophelia herself, to the amazement of the performers and the astonishment of the audience."

That the character Ophelia became increasingly and decisively identified with the mad scene owes something to this occurrence, but it is also a consequence of the text used for Restoration performances of *Hamlet*. Having received the performance rights to a good number of Shakespeare's plays, Davenant altered them for the stage in the 1660s, and many of these acting versions remained in use for generations. In the case of *Hamlet*, neither Davenant nor his successors did what they so often did with other plays by Shakespeare, that is, alter the plot radically and interpolate other material. But many of the lines were cut or "improved." The cuts included most of Ophelia's sane speeches, such as her spirited retort to Laertes' moralizing; what remained made her part almost entirely an emblem of "female love melancholy."

Thomas Betterton (1635–1710), the prototype of the actor-manager, who would be the dominant figure in Shakespeare interpretation and in the theater generally through the nineteenth century, made Hamlet his premier role. A contemporary who saw his last performance in the part (at the age of seventy-four, a rather old Prince of Denmark) wrote that to *read* Shakespeare's play was to encounter "dry, incoherent, & broken sentences," but that to see Betterton was to "prove" that the play was written "correctly." Spectators especially admired his reaction to the Ghost's appearance in the Queen's bedchamber: "his Countenance . . . thro' the violent and sudden Emotions of Amazement and Horror, turn[ed] instantly on the Sight of his fathers Spirit, as pale as his Neckcloath, when every Article of his Body seem's affected with a Tremor inexpressible."

Title page of Thomas Kyd's *Spanish Tragedy* (1615). The first known edition dates from 1592.

A piece of stage business in this scene, Betterton's upsetting his chair on the Ghost's entrance, became so thoroughly identified with the part that later productions were censured if the actor left it out. This business could very well have been handed down from Richard Burbage, the star of Shakespeare's original production, for Davenant, who had coached Betterton in the role, had known the performances of Joseph Taylor, who had succeeded Burbage in it. It is strangely gratifying to notice that Hamlets on stage and screen still occasionally upset their chairs.

Shakespeare's Life and Art

Playwrights, even hugely successful playwrights, were not ordinarily the objects of popular curiosity in early modern England, and few personal documents survive from Shakespeare's life of the kind that usually give the biographies of artists their appeal: no diary, no letters, private or public, no accounts of his childhood, almost no contemporary gossip, no scandals. Shakespeare's exact contemporary the great playwright Christopher Marlowe, lived a mere twenty-nine years—he was murdered in 1593—but he left behind tantalizing glimpses of himself in police documents, the memos of high-ranking government officials, and detailed denunciations by sinister double agents. Ben Jonson recorded his opinions and his reading in a remarkable published notebook, *Timber; or, Discoveries made upon men and matter*, and he also shared his views of the world (including some criticisms of his fellow playwright Shakespeare) with a Scottish poet, William Drummond of Hawthornden, who had the wit to jot them down for posterity. From Shakespeare, there is nothing comparable, not even a book with his name scribbled on the cover and a few marginal notes such as we have for Jonson, let alone working notebooks.

Yet Elizabethan England was a record-keeping society, and centuries of archival labor have turned up a substantial number of traces of its greatest playwright and his family. By themselves the traces would have relatively little interest, but in the light of Shakespeare's plays and poems, they have come to seem like precious relics and manage to achieve a considerable resonance.

Shakespeare's Family

William Shakespeare's grandfather Richard farmed land by the village of Snitterfield, near the small, pleasant market town of Stratford-upon-Avon, about ninety-six miles northwest of London. The playwright's father, John, moved in the mid-sixteenth century to Stratford, where he became a successful glover, landowner, moneylender, and dealer in wool and other agricultural goods. In or about 1557, he married Mary Arden, the daughter of a prosperous and well-connected farmer from the same area, Robert Arden of Wilmcote.

John Shakespeare was evidently highly esteemed by his fellow townspeople, for he held a series of important posts in local government. In 1556, he was appointed ale taster, an office reserved for "able persons and discreet," in 1558 was sworn in as a constable, and in 1561 was elected as one of the town's fourteen burgesses. As burgess, John served as one of the two chamberlains, responsible for administering borough property and revenues. In 1567, he was elected bailiff, Stratford's highest elective office and the equivalent of mayor. Though John Shakespeare signed all official documents with a cross or other sign, it is likely, though not certain, that he knew how to read and write. Mary, who also signed documents only with her mark, is less likely to have been literate.

According to the parish registers, which recorded baptisms and burials, the Shakespeares had eight children, four daughters and four sons, beginning with a daughter Joan born in 1558. A second daughter, Margaret, was born in December 1562 and died a few months later. William Shakespeare ("Gulielmus, filius Johannes Shakespeare"), their first son, was baptized on April 26, 1564. Since there was usually a few days' lapse between birth and baptism, it is conventional to celebrate Shakespeare's birthday on April 23, which happens to coincide with the feast of St. George, England's patron saint, and with the day of Shakespeare's death fifty-two years later.

William Shakespeare had three younger brothers, Gilbert, Richard, and Edmund, and

"Southeast Prospect of Stratford-upon-Avon, 1746." From *The Gentleman's Magazine* (December 1792).

two younger sisters, Joan and Anne. (It was often the custom to recycle a name, so the first-born Joan must have died before the birth in 1569 of another daughter christened Joan, the only one of the girls to survive childhood.) Gilbert, who died in his forty-fifth year in 1612, is described in legal records as a Stratford haberdasher; Edmund followed William to London and became a professional actor, though evidently of no particular repute. He was only twenty-eight when he died in 1607 and was given an expensive funeral, perhaps paid for by his successful older brother.

At the high point of his public career, John Shakespeare, the father of this substantial family, applied to the Herald's College for a coat of arms, which would have marked his (and his family's) elevation from the ranks of substantial middle-class citizenry to that of the gentry. But the application went nowhere, for soon after he initiated what would have been a costly petitioning process, John apparently fell on hard times. The decline must have begun when William was still living at home, a boy of twelve or thirteen. From 1576 onward, John Shakespeare stopped attending council meetings. He became caught up in costly lawsuits, started mortgaging his land, and incurred substantial debts. In 1586, he was finally replaced on the council; in 1592, he was one of nine Stratford men listed as absenting themselves from church out of fear of being arrested for debt.

The reason for the reversal in John Shakespeare's fortunes is unknown. Some have speculated that it may have stemmed from adherence to Catholicism, since those who remained loyal to the old faith were subject to increasingly vigorous and costly discrimination. But if John Shakespeare was a Catholic, as seems quite possible, it would not necessarily explain his decline, since other Catholics (and Puritans) in Elizabethan Stratford and elsewhere managed to hold on to their offices. In any case, his fall from prosperity and local power, whatever its cause, was not absolute. In 1601, the last year of his life, his name was included among those qualified to speak on behalf of Stratford's rights. And he was by that time entitled to bear a coat of arms, for in 1596, some twenty years after the application to the Herald's office had been initiated, it was successfully renewed. There is no record of who paid for the bureaucratic procedures that made the grant possible, but it is likely to have been John's oldest son William, by that time a highly successful London playwright.

Education

Stratford was a small provincial town, but it had long been the site of an excellent free school, originally established by the church in the thirteenth century. The main purpose of such schools in the Middle Ages had been to train prospective clerics; since many aristocrats could neither read nor write, literacy by itself conferred no special distinction and was not routinely viewed as desirable. But the situation began to change markedly in the sixteenth century. Protestantism placed a far greater emphasis upon lay literacy: for the sake of salvation, it was crucially important to be intimately acquainted with the Holy Book, and printing made that book readily available. Schools became less strictly bound up with training for the church and more linked to the general acquisition of "literature," in the sense both of literacy and of cultural knowledge. In keeping with this new emphasis on reading and with humanist educational reform, the school was reorganized during the reign of Edward VI (1547–53). School records from the period have not survived, but it is almost certain that William Shakespeare attended the King's New School, as it was renamed in Edward's honor.

Scholars have painstakingly reconstructed the curriculum of schools of this kind and have even turned up the names and rather impressive credentials of the schoolmasters who taught there when Shakespeare was a student. (Shakespeare's principal teacher was Thomas Jenkins, an Oxford graduate, who received £20 a year and a rent-free house.) A child's education in Elizabethan England began at age four or five with two years at what was called the "petty school," attached to the main grammar school. The little scholars carried a "hornbook," a sheet of paper or parchment framed in wood and covered, for protection, with a transparent layer of horn. On the paper was written the alphabet and the Lord's Prayer, which were reproduced as well in the slightly more advanced *ABC with the Catechism*, a combination primer and rudimentary religious guide.

The Cholmondeley sisters, c. 1600–1610. This striking image brings to mind Shakespeare's fascination with twinship, both identical (notably in *The Comedy of Errors*) and fraternal (in *Twelfth Night*).

After students demonstrated some ability to read, the boys could go on, at about age seven, to the grammar school. Shakespeare's images of the experience are not particularly cheerful. In his famous account of the Seven Ages of Man, Jaques in *As You Like It* describes

> the whining schoolboy with his satchel
> And shining morning face, creeping like snail
> Unwillingly to school.
>
> (2.7.144–46)

The schoolboy would have crept quite early: the day began at 6:00 A.M. in summer and 7:00 A.M. in winter and continued until 5:00 P.M., with very few breaks or holidays.

At the core of the curriculum was the study of Latin, the mastery of which was in effect a prolonged male puberty rite involving much discipline and pain as well as pleasure. A late sixteenth-century Dutchman (whose name fittingly was Batty) proposed that God had created the human buttocks so that they could be severely beaten without risking permanent injury. Such thoughts dominated the pedagogy of the age, so that even an able young scholar, as we might imagine Shakespeare to have been, could scarcely have escaped recurrent flogging.

Shakespeare evidently reaped some rewards for the miseries he probably endured: his works are laced with echoes of many of the great Latin texts taught in grammar schools. One of his earliest comedies, *The Comedy of Errors*, is a brilliant variation on a theme by the Roman playwright Plautus, whom Elizabethan schoolchildren often performed as well as read; and one of his earliest tragedies, *Titus Andronicus*, is heavily indebted to Seneca. These are among the most visible of the classical influences that are often more subtly and pervasively interfused in Shakespeare's works. He seems to have had a particular fondness for *Aesop's Fables*, Apuleius's *Golden Ass*, and above all Ovid's *Metamorphoses*. His learned contemporary Ben Jonson remarked that Shakespeare had "small Latin and less Greek," but from this distance what is striking is not the limits of Shakespeare's learning but rather the unpretentious ease, intelligence, and gusto with which he draws upon what he must have first encountered as laborious study.

Traces of a Life

In November 1582, William Shakespeare, at the age of eighteen, married twenty-six-year-old Anne Hathaway, who came from the village of Shottery near Stratford. Their first daughter, Susanna, was baptized six months later. This circumstance, along with the fact that Anne was eight years Will's senior, has given rise to a mountain of speculation, all the more lurid precisely because there is no further evidence. Shakespeare depicts in several plays situations in which marriage is precipitated by a pregnancy, but he also registers, in *Measure for Measure* (1.2.125ff.), the Elizabethan belief that a "true contract" of marriage could be legitimately made and then consummated simply by the mutual vows of the couple in the presence of witnesses.

On February 2, 1585, the twins Hamnet and Judith Shakespeare were baptized in Stratford. Hamnet died at the age of eleven, when his father was already living for much of the year in London as a successful playwright. These are Shakespeare's only known children, though the playwright and impressario William Davenant in the mid-seventeenth century claimed to be his bastard son. Since people did not ordinarily advertise their illegitimacy, the claim, though impossible to verify, at least suggests the unusual strength of the Shakespeare's posthumous reputation.

William Shakespeare's father, John, died in 1601; his mother died seven years later. They would have had the satisfaction of witnessing their eldest son's prosperity, and not only from a distance, for in 1597 William purchased New Place, the second largest house in Stratford. In 1607, the playwright's daughter Susanna married a successful and well-known physician, John Hall. The next year, the Halls had a daughter, Elizabeth, Shakespeare's first grandchild. In 1616, the year of Shakespeare's death, his daughter Judith married a vintner, Thomas Quiney, with whom she had three children. Shakespeare's widow, Anne, died in 1623, at the age of sixty-seven. His first-born, Susanna, died at the age of sixty-six in 1649, the year that King Charles I was beheaded by the parliamentary army. Judith lived through Cromwell's Protectorate and on to the Restoration of the monarchy; she died in February 1662, at the age of seventy-seven. By the end of the century, the line of Shakespeare's direct heirs was extinct.

Patient digging in the archives has turned up other traces of Shakespeare's life as a family man and a man of means: assessments, small fines, real estate deeds, minor actions in court to collect debts. In addition to his fine Stratford house and a large garden and cottage facing it, Shakespeare bought substantial parcels of land in the vicinity. When in *The Tempest* the wedding celebration conjures up a vision of "barns and garners never empty," Shakespeare could have been glancing at what the legal documents record as his own "tithes of corn, grain, blade, and hay" in the fields near Stratford. At some point after 1610, Shakespeare seems to have begun to shift his attention from the London stage to his Stratford properties, though the term "retirement" implies a more decisive and definitive break than appears to have been the case. By 1613, when the Globe Theatre burned down during a performance of *All Is True* (*Henry VIII*), Shakespeare was probably residing for the most part in Stratford, but he retained his financial interest in the rebuilt playhouse and probably continued to have some links to his theatrical colleagues. Still, by this point, his career as a playwright was substantially over. Legal documents from his last years show him concerned to protect his real estate interests in Stratford.

A half-century after Shakespeare's death, a Stratford vicar and physician, John Ward, noted in his diary that Shakespeare and his fellow poets Michael Drayton and Ben Jonson "had a merry meeting, and it seems drank too hard, for Shakespeare died of a fever there contracted." It is not inconceivable that Shakespeare's last illness was somehow linked, if only coincidentally, to the festivities on the occasion of the wedding in February 1616 of his daughter Judith (who was still alive when Ward made his diary entry). In any case, on March 25, 1616, Shakespeare revised his will, and on April 23 he died. Two days later, he was buried in the chancel of Holy Trinity Church beneath a stone bearing an epitaph he is said to have devised:

> Good friend for Jesus' sake forbear,
> To dig the dust enclosed here:
> Blest be the man that spares these stones,
> And curst be he that moves my bones.

The verses are hardly among Shakespeare's finest, but they seem to have been effective: though bones were routinely dug up to make room for others—a fate imagined with unforgettable intensity in the graveyard scene in *Hamlet*—his own remains were undisturbed. Like other vestiges of sixteenth- and early seventeenth-century Stratford, Shakespeare's grave has for centuries now been the object of a tourist industry that borders on a religious cult.

Shakespeare's will has been examined with an intensity befitting this cult; every provision and formulaic phrase, no matter how minor or conventional, has borne a heavy weight of interpretation, none more so than the bequest to his wife, Anne, of only "my second-best bed." Scholars have pointed out that Anne would in any case have been provided for by custom and that the terms are not necessarily a deliberate slight, but the absence of the customary words "my loving wife" or "my well-beloved wife" is difficult to ignore.

Portrait of the Playwright as Young Provincial

The great problem with the surviving traces of Shakespeare's life is not that they are few but that they are a bit dull. Christopher Marlowe was a double or triple agent, accused of brawling, sodomy, and atheism. Ben Jonson, who somehow clambered up from bricklayer's apprentice to classical scholar, served in the army in Flanders, killed a fellow actor in a duel, converted to Catholicism in prison in 1598, and returned to the Church of England in 1610. Provincial real estate investments and the second-best bed cannot compete with such adventurous lives. Indeed, the relative ordinariness of Shakespeare's social background and life has contributed to a persistent current of speculation that the glover's son from Stratford-upon-Avon was not in fact the author of the plays attributed to him.

The anti-Stratfordians, as those who deny Shakespeare's authorship are sometimes called, almost always propose as the real author someone who came from a higher social class and received a more prestigious education. Francis Bacon, the Earl of Oxford, the Earl of Southampton, even Queen Elizabeth, have been advanced, among many others, as glamorous candidates for the role of clandestine playwright. Several famous people, including Mark Twain and Sigmund Freud, have espoused these theories, though very few scholars have joined them. Since Shakespeare was quite well-known in his own time as the author of the plays that bear his name, there would need to have been an extraordinary conspiracy to conceal the identity of the real master who (the theory goes) disdained to appear in the vulgarity of print or on the public stage. Like many conspiracy theories, the extreme implausibility of this one only seems to increase the fervent conviction of its advocates.

To the charge that a middle-class author from a small town could not have imagined the lives of kings and nobles, one can respond by citing the exceptional qualities that Ben Jonson praised in Shakespeare: "excellent *Phantsie*; brave notions, and gentle expressions." Even in ordinary mortals, the human imagination is a strange faculty; in Shakespeare, it seems to have been uncannily powerful, working its mysterious, transforming effects on everything he encountered. It is possible to study this power in his reworking of books by Raphael Holinshed, Plutarch, Ovid, Plautus, Seneca, and others. But books were clearly not the only objects of Shakespeare's attention; like most artists, he drew upon the whole range of his life experiences.

To integrate some of the probable circumstances of Shakespeare's early years with the particular shape of the theatrical imagination associated with his name, let us indulge briefly in the biographical daydreams that modern scholarship is supposed to have rendered forever obsolete. The vignettes that follow are conjectural, but they may suggest ways in which his life as we know it found its way into his art.

1. THE GOWN OF OFFICE

Shakespeare was a very young boy—not quite four years old—when his father was chosen by the Stratford council as the town bailiff. The bailiff of an Elizabethan town was a significant position; he served the borough as a justice of the peace and performed a variety of other functions, including coroner and clerk of the market. He dealt routinely with an unusually wide spectrum of local society, for on the one hand he distributed alms and on the other he negotiated with the lord of the manor. More to the point, for our purposes, the office was attended with considerable ceremony. The bailiff and his deputy were entitled to appear in public in furred gowns, attended by sergeants bearing maces before them. On Rogation Days (three days of prayer for the harvest, before Ascension Day), they would solemnly pace out the parish boundaries, and they would similarly walk in processions on market and fair days. On Sundays, the sergeants would accompany the bailiff to church, where he would sit with his wife in a front pew, and he would have a comparable seat of honor at sermons in the Guild Chapel. On special occasions, there would also be plays in the Guildhall, at which the bailiff would be seated in the front row.

On a precocious child (or even, for that matter, on an ordinary child), the effect of this ceremony would be at least threefold. First, the ceremony would convey irresistibly the power of clothes (the ceremonial gown of office) and of symbols (the mace) to transform identity as if by magic. Second, it would invest the father with immense power, distinction, and importance, awakening what we may call a lifelong dream of high station. And third, pulling slightly against this dream, it would provoke an odd feeling that the father's clothes do not fit, a perception that the office is not the same as the man, and an intimate, first-hand knowledge that when the robes are put off, their wearer is inevitably glimpsed in a far different, less exalted light.

2. PROGRESSES AND ELECTIONS

This second biographical fantasy, slightly less plausible than the first but still quite likely, involves a somewhat older child witnessing two characteristic forms of Elizabethan political ceremony, both of which were well-known in the provinces. Queen Elizabeth was fond of going on what were known as "Progresses," triumphant ceremonial journeys around her kingdom. Let us imagine that the young Shakespeare—say, in 1574, when he was ten years old—went with his kinsfolk or friends to Warwick, some eight miles distant, to witness a Progress. He would thus have participated as a spectator in an elaborate cele-bration of charismatic power: the courtiers in their gorgeous clothes, the nervous local officials bedecked in velvets and silks, and at the center, carried in a special litter like a painted idol, the bejeweled queen. Let us imagine further that in addition to being struck by the overwhelming force of this charisma, the boy was struck too by the way this force depended paradoxically on a sense that the queen was after all quite human. Elizabeth was in fact fond of calling attention to this peculiar tension between near-divinization and human ordinariness. For example, on this occasion at Warwick (and what follows really happened), after the trembling Recorder, presumably a local civil official of high standing, had made his official welcoming speech, Elizabeth offered her hand to him to be kissed: "Come hither, little Recorder," she said. "It was told me that you would be afraid to look upon me or to speak boldly; but you were not so afraid of me as I was of you; and I now thank you for putting me in mind of my duty." Of course, the charm of this royal "confes-sion" of nervousness depends on its manifest implausibility: it is, in effect, a theatrical performance of humility by someone with immense confidence in her own histrionic power.

A royal Progress was not the only form of spectacular political activity that Shakespeare might well have seen in the 1570s; it is still more likely that he would have witnessed parliamentary elections, particularly since his father was qualified to vote. In 1571, 1572, 1575, and 1578, there were shire elections conducted in nearby Warwick, elections that would certainly have attracted well over a thousand voters. These were often memorable events: large crowds came together; there was usually heavy drinking and carnivalesque festivity; and at the same time, there was enacted, in a very different register from that of the monarchy, a ritual of empowerment. The people, those entitled to vote by virtue of meeting the property and residence requirements, chose their own representatives by giv-ing their votes—their voices—to candidates for office. Here, legislative sovereignty was conferred not by God but by the consent of the community, a consent marked by shouts and applause.

Recent cultural historians have been so fascinated by the evident links between the spectacles of the absolutist monarchy and the theater that they have largely ignored the significance of this alternative public arena, one that generated intense excitement throughout the country. A child who was a spectator at a parliamentary election in the 1570s might well have found the occasion enormously compelling. It is striking, in any case, how often the adult Shakespeare returns to scenes of acclamation and mass consent, and striking too how much the theater depends on the soliciting of popular voices.

3. EXORCISMS

A third and final Shakespearean fantasy is even more speculative than the second and involves a controversial discovery. It is a fact that in April 1757, the owner of Shakespeare's birthplace in Stratford decided to retile the roof. One of the workmen, described as of "very honest, sober, industrious character," found an old document between the rafters and the tiling. The document, six leaves stitched together, was a profession of faith in fourteen articles, conspicuously Catholic in form; it was, if genuine (for the original has disappeared), by John Shakespeare. The clear implication of this find, that the playwright was probably brought up in a Roman Catholic household in a time of official suspicion and persecution of recusancy, has found support in a recent biographical study by E. A. J. Honigmann. Honigmann has turned up a network of interlinked Catholic families in Lancashire with whom one "William Shakeshafte," possibly a young schoolmaster or player, was connected in the late 1570s or early 1580s.

Accepting for the moment that William Shakespeare was raised in the recusant faith of his father, let us imagine that one day in the early 1580s the young man attended a strange and extraordinary event: an exorcism conducted in secret in the house of a member of the Catholic gentry. These events, though illegal and potentially dangerous, were fairly common in the period and are known to have drawn substantial crowds. The rituals were generally conducted by Jesuits, living in hiding and under constant threat of torture and execution, and centered on the spectacular struggle between the sacred authority of the church and the obscene, blasphemous, and tenacious demons lodged deep within the demoniacs' tortured bodies. Elizabethan authorities were alarmed by the compelling power of exorcisms, which they regarded, not without some justification, as highly self-conscious Catholic propaganda. (The demons, speaking from within the possessed, had the disquieting habit of declaring their admiration for Martin Luther and John Calvin.) Official spokesmen repeatedly stigmatized the rituals as a form of illicit theater: a "play of sacred miracles," a "wonderful pageant," a "devil Theater."

Exorcism: Nicole Aubry, in the Cathedral at Laon, 1566.

The young Shakespeare, whether

true believer or skeptic or something in between ("So have I heard, and do in part believe it," says Hamlet's friend Horatio [1.1.146]), might have carried away from such an occasion several impressions: an awareness that strange, alien voices may speak from within ordinary, familiar bodies; a sense of the irresistible power of illusion; an intimation of immense, cosmic forces that may impinge upon human life; a belief in the possibility of making contact with these forces and compelling them to speak.

These imaginary portraits of the playwright as a young provincial introduce us to several of the root conditions of the Elizabethan theater. Biographical fantasies, though entirely speculative and playful, are useful in part because some people have found it difficult to conceive how Shakespeare, with his provincial roots and his restricted range of experience, could have so rapidly and completely mastered the central imaginative themes of his times. Moreover, it is sometimes difficult to grasp how seeming abstractions such as market society, monarchical state, and theological doctrine were actually experienced directly by peculiar, distinct individuals. Shakespeare's plays were social and collective events, but they also bore the stamp of a particular artist, one endowed with a remarkable capacity to craft lifelike illusions (what Jonson called "excellent *Phantsie*"), a daring willingness to articulate an original vision ("brave notions"), and a loving command, at once precise and generous, of language ("gentle expressions"). These plays are stitched together from shared cultural experiences, inherited dramatic devices, and the pungent vernacular of the day, but we should not lose sight of the extent to which they articulate an intensely personal vision, a bold shaping of the available materials. Four centuries of feverish biographical speculation, much of it foolish, bears witness to a basic intuition: the richness of these plays, their inexhaustible openness, is the consequence not only of the auspicious collective conditions of the culture but also of someone's exceptional skill, inventiveness, and courage at taking those conditions and making of them something rich and strange.

The Theater of the Nation

What precisely are the collective conditions highlighted by these vignettes? First, the growth of Stratford-upon-Avon, the bustling market town of which John Shakespeare was bailiff, is a small version of a momentous sixteenth-century development that made Shakespeare's career possible: the making of an urban "public." That development obviously depended on adequate numbers; the period experienced a rapid and still unexplained growth in population. With it came an expansion and elaboration of market relations: markets became less periodic, more continuous, and more abstract—centered, that is, not on the familiar materiality of goods but on the liquidity of capital and goods. In practical terms, this meant that it was possible to conceive of the theater not only as festive entertainment for special events—lord mayor's pageants, visiting princes, seasonal festivals, and the like—but as a permanent, year-round business venture. The venture relied on ticket sales—it was an innovation of this period to have money advanced in the expectation of pleasure rather than offered to servants afterward as a reward—and counted on habitual playgoing with a concomitant demand for new plays from competing theater companies: "But that's all one, our play is done," sings Feste at the end of *Twelfth Night* and adds a glance toward the next afternoon's proceeds: "And we'll strive to please you every day" (5.1.394–95).

Second, the royal Progress is an instance of what the anthropologist Clifford Geertz has called the Theater State, a state that manifests its power and meaning in exemplary public performances. Professional companies of players, like the one Shakespeare belonged to, understood well that they existed in relation to this Theater State and would, if they were fortunate, be called upon to serve it. Unlike Ben Jonson, Shakespeare did not, as far as we know, write royal entertainments on commission, but his plays were frequently performed before Queen Elizabeth and then before King James and Queen Anne, along with their courtiers and privileged guests. There are many fascinating glimpses of these performances, including a letter from Walter Cope to Robert Cecil, early in James's reign. "Burbage is come," Cope writes, referring to the leading actor of Shakespeare's company, "and says there is no new play that the queen hath not seen, but they have revived an old one, called *Love's Labours Lost*, which for wit and mirth he says will please her exceedingly. And this is appointed to be played tomorrow night at my Lord of Southampton's." Not only would such theatrical performances have given great pleasure — evidently, the queen had already exhausted the company's new offerings — but they conferred prestige upon those who commanded them and those in whose honor they were mounted.

Monarchical power in the period was deeply allied to spectacular manifestations of the ruler's glory and disciplinary authority. The symbology of power depended on regal magnificence, reward, punishment, and pardon, all of which were heavily theatricalized. Indeed, the conspicuous public display does not simply serve the interests of power; on many occasions in the period, power seemed to exist in order to make pageantry possible, as if the nation's identity were only fully realized in theatrical performance. It would be easy to exaggerate this perception: the subjects of Queen Elizabeth and King James were acutely aware of the distinction between shadow and substance. But they were fascinated by the political magic through which shadows could be taken for substantial realities, and the ruling elite was largely complicit in the formation and celebration of a charismatic absolutism. At the same time, the claims of the monarch who professes herself or himself to be not the representative of the nation but its embodiment were set against the counterclaims of the House of Commons. And this institution too, as we have glimpsed, had its own theatrical rituals, centered on the crowd whose shouts of approval, in heavily stage-managed elections, chose the individuals who would stand for the polity and participate in deliberations held in a hall whose resemblance to a theater did not escape contemporary notice.

Third, illicit exorcism points both to the theatricality of much religious ritual in the late Middle Ages and the Renaissance and to the heightened possibility of secularization. English Protestant authorities banned the medieval mystery plays, along with pilgrimages and other rituals associated with holy shrines and sacred images, but playing companies could satisfy at least some of the popular longings and appropriate aspects of the social energy no longer allowed a theological outlet. That is, official attacks on certain Catholic practices made it more possible for the public theater to appropriate and exploit their allure. Hence, for example, the plays that celebrated the solemn miracle of the Catholic Mass were banned, along with the most elaborate church vestments, but in *The Winter's Tale* Dion can speak in awe of what he witnessed at Apollo's temple:

> I shall report,
> For most it caught me, the celestial habits —
> Methinks I so should term them — and the reverence
> Of the grave wearers. O, the sacrifice —
> How ceremonious, solemn, and unearthly
> It was i'th' off'ring!
>
> (3.1.3–8)

And at the play's end, the statue of the innocent mother breathes, comes to life, and embraces her child.

The theater in Shakespeare's time, then, is intimately bound up with all three crucial cultural formations: the market society, the theater state, and the church. But it is important to note that the institution is not *identified* with any of them. The theater may be a market phenomenon, but it is repeatedly and bitterly attacked as the enemy of diligent, sober, productive economic activity. Civic authorities generally regarded the theater as a pestilential nuisance, a parasite on the body of the commonwealth, a temptation to students, apprentices, housewives, even respectable merchants to leave their serious business and lapse into idleness and waste. That waste, it might be argued, could be partially recuperated if it went for the glorification of a guild or the entertainment of an important dignitary, but the only group regularly profiting from the theater were the players and their disreputable associates.

For his part, Shakespeare made a handsome profit from the commodification of theatrical entertainment, but he seems never to have written "city comedy"—plays set in London and more or less explicitly concerned with market relations—and his characters express deep reservations about the power of money and commerce: "That smooth-faced gentleman, tickling commodity," Philip the Bastard observes in *King John*, "wins of all, / Of kings, of beggars, old men, young men, maids" (2.1.570–74). We could argue that the smooth-faced gentleman is none other than Shakespeare himself, for his drama famously mingles kings and clowns, princesses and panderers. But the mingling is set against a romantic current of social conservatism: in *Twelfth Night*, the aristocratic heiress Olivia falls in love with someone who appears far beneath her in wealth and social station, but it is revealed that he (and his sister Viola) are of noble blood; in *The Winter's Tale*, Leontes' daughter Perdita is raised as a shepherdess, but her noble nature shines through her humble upbringing, and she marries the Prince of Bohemia; the strange island maiden with whom Ferdinand, son of the King of Naples, falls madly in love in *The Tempest* turns out to be the daughter of the rightful Duke of Milan. Shakespeare pushes against this conservative logic in *All's Well That Ends Well*, but the noble young Bertram violently resists the unequal match thrust upon him by the King, and the play's mood is notoriously uneasy.

Similarly, Shakespeare's theater may have been patronized and protected by the monarchy—after 1603, his company received a royal patent and was known as the King's Men—but it was by no means identical in its interests or its ethos. To be sure, *Richard III* and *Macbeth* incorporate aspects of royal propaganda, but given the realities of censorship, Shakespeare's plays, and the period's drama as a whole, are surprisingly independent and complex in their political vision. There is, in any case, a certain inherent tension between kings and player kings: Elizabeth and James may both have likened themselves to actors onstage, but they were loath to admit their dependence on the applause and money, freely given or freely withheld, of the audience. The charismatic monarch insists that the sacredness of authority resides in the body of the ruler, not in a costume that may be worn and then discarded by an actor. Kings are not *representations* of power—or do not admit that they are—but claim to be the thing itself. The government institution that was actually based on the idea of representation, Parliament, had theatrical elements, as we have seen, but it significantly excluded any audience from its deliberations. And Shakespeare's oblique portraits of parliamentary representatives, the tribunes Sicinius Velutus and Junius Brutus in *Coriolanus*, are anything but flattering.

Finally, the theater drew significant energy from the liturgy and rituals of the late medieval church, but as Shakespeare's contemporaries widely remarked, the playhouse and the church were scarcely natural allies. Not only did the theater represent a potential competitor to worship services, and not only did ministers rail against prostitution and other vices associated with playgoing, but theatrical representation itself, even when ostensibly pious, seemed to many to empty out whatever it presented, turning substance into mere show. The theater could and did use the period's deep currents of religious feeling, but it had to do so carefully and with an awareness of conflicting interests.

Shakespeare Comes to London

How did Shakespeare decide to turn his prodigious talents to the stage? When did he make his way to London? How did he get his start? To these and similar questions we have a mountain of speculation but no secure answers. There is not a single surviving record of Shakespeare's existence from 1585, when his twins were baptized in Stratford church, until 1592, when a rival London playwright made an envious remark about him. In the late seventeenth century, the delightfully eccentric collector of gossip John Aubrey was informed that prior to moving to London the young Shakespeare had been a schoolteacher in the country. Aubrey also recorded a story that Shakespeare had been a rather unusual apprentice butcher: "When he killed a calf, he would do it in a high style, and make a speech."

These and other legends, including one that has Shakespeare whipped for poaching game, fill the void until the unmistakable reference in Robert Greene's *Groats-worth of Wit Bought with a Million of Repentaunce* (1592). An inspired hack writer with a university education, a penchant for self-dramatization, a taste for wild living, and a strong streak of resentment, Greene, in his early thirties, was dying in poverty when he penned his last farewell, piously urging his fellow dramatists Christopher Marlowe, Thomas Nashe, and George Peele to abandon the wicked stage before they were brought low, as he had been, by a new arrival: "For there is an upstart crow, beautified with our feathers, that with his 'Tiger's heart wrapped in player's hide' supposes he is as well able to bombast out a blank verse as the best of you, and, being an absolute *Johannes Factotum*, is in his own conceit the only Shake-scene in a country." If "Shake-scene" is not enough to identify the object of his attack, Greene parodies a line from Shakespeare's early play *Richard Duke of York (3 Henry VI)*: "O tiger's heart wrapped in a woman's hide!" (1.4.138). Greene is accusing Shakespeare of being an upstart, a plagiarist, an egomaniacal jack-of-all-trades—and, above all perhaps, a popular success.

By 1592, then, Shakespeare had already arrived on the highly competitive London theatrical scene. He was successful enough to be attacked by Greene and, a few months later, defended by Henry Chettle, another hack writer who had seen Greene's manuscript through the press (or, some scholars speculate, had written the attack himself and passed it off as the dying Greene's). Chettle expresses his regret that he did not suppress Greene's diatribe and spare Shakespeare "because myself have seen his demeanor no less civil than he excellent in the quality he professes." Besides, Chettle adds, "divers of worship have reported his uprightness of dealing, which argues his honesty and his facetious [polished] grace in writing that approves his art." "Divers of worship": not only was Shakespeare established as an accomplished writer and actor, but he evidently had aroused the attention and the approbation of several socially prominent people. In Elizabethan England, aristocratic patronage, with the money, protection, and prestige it alone could provide, was probably a professional writer's most important asset.

This patronage, or at least Shakespeare's quest for it, is most visible in the dedications in 1593 and 1594 of his narrative poems *Venus and Adonis* and *The Rape of Lucrece* to the young nobleman Henry Wriothesley, Earl of Southampton. It may be glimpsed as well, perhaps, in the sonnets, with their extraordinary adoration of the fair youth, though the identity of that youth has never been determined. What return Shakespeare got for his exquisite offerings is likewise unknown. We do know that among wits and gallants, the narrative poems won Shakespeare a fine reputation as an immensely stylish and accomplished poet. An amateur play performed at Cambridge University at the end of the sixteenth century, *The Return from Parnassus*, makes fun of this vogue, as a foolish character effusively declares, "I'll worship sweet Mr. Shakespeare, and to honour him will lay his *Venus and Adonis* under my pillow." Many readers at the time may have done so: the poem went through sixteen editions before 1640, more than any other work by Shakespeare.

Patronage was crucially important not only for individual artists but also for the actors, playwrights, and investors who pooled their resources to form professional theater companies. The public playhouses had enemies, especially among civic and religious authorities, who wished greatly to curb performances or to ban them altogether. An act of 1572 included players among those classified as vagabonds, threatening them therefore with the horrible punishments meted out to those regarded as economic parasites. The players' escape route was to be nominally enrolled as the servants of high-ranking noblemen. The legal fiction was that their public performances were a kind of rehearsal for the command performances before the patron or the monarch.

When Shakespeare came to London, presumably in the late 1580s, there were more than a dozen of these companies operating under the patronage of various aristocrats. We do not know for which of these companies, several of which had toured in Stratford, he originally worked, nor whether he began, as legend has it, as a prompter's assistant and then graduated to acting and playwriting. Shakespeare is listed among the actors in Ben Jonson's *Every Man in His Humour* (performed in 1598) and *Sejanus* (performed in 1603), but we do not know for certain what roles he played, nor are there records of any of his other performances. Tradition has it that he played Adam in *As You Like It* and the Ghost in *Hamlet*, but he was clearly not one of the leading actors of the day.

By the 1590s, the number of playing companies in London had been considerably reduced, in part through competition and in part through legislative restriction. (In 1572, knights and gentry lost the privilege of patronizing a troupe of actors; in 1598, justices of the peace lost the power to authorize performances.) By the early years of the seventeenth century, there were usually only three companies competing against one another in any season, along with two children's companies, which were often successful at drawing audiences away from the public playhouses. Shakespeare may initially have been associated with the Earl of Leicester's company or with the company of Ferdinando Stanley, Lord Strange; both groups included actors with whom Shakespeare was later linked. Or he may have belonged to the Earl of Pembroke's Men, since there is evidence that they performed *The Taming of a Shrew* and a version of *Richard Duke of York (3 Henry VI)*. At any event,

by 1594, Shakespeare was a member of the Lord Chamberlain's Men, for his name, along with those of Will Kempe and Richard Burbage, appears on a record of those "servants to the Lord Chamberlain" paid for performance at the royal palace at Greenwich on December 26 and 28. Shakespeare stayed with this company, which during the reign of King James received royal patronage and became the King's Men, for the rest of his career.

Many playwrights in Shakespeare's time worked freelance, moving from company to company as opportunities arose, collaborating on projects, adding scenes to old plays, scrambling from one enterprise to another. But certain playwrights, among them the most successful, wrote for a single company, often agreeing contractually to give that company exclusive rights to their theatrical works. Shakespeare seems to have followed such a pattern. For the Lord Chamberlain's Men, he wrote an average of two plays per year. His company initially performed in The Theatre, a playhouse built in 1576 by an entrepreneurial carpenter, James Burbage, the father of the actor Richard, who was to perform many of Shakespeare's greatest roles. When in 1597 their lease on this playhouse expired, the Lord Chamberlain's Men passed through a difficult and

Edward Alleyn (1566–1626). Artist unknown. Alleyn was the great tragic actor of the Lord Admiral's Men (the principal rival to Shakespeare's company). He was famous especially for playing the great Marlovian heroes.

legally perilous time, but they formed a joint-stock company, raising sufficient capital to lease a site and put up a splendid new playhouse in the suburb of Southwark, on the south bank of the Thames. This playhouse, the Globe, opened in 1599. Shakespeare is listed in the legal agreement as one of the principal investors, and when the company began to use Blackfriars as their indoor playhouse around 1609, he was a major shareholder in that theater as well. The Lord Chamberlain's Men, later the King's Men, dominated the theater scene, and the shares were quite valuable. Then as now, the theater was an extremely risky enterprise—most of those who wrote plays and performed in them made pathetically little money—but Shakespeare was a notable exception. The fine house in Stratford and the coat of arms he succeeded in acquiring were among the fruits of his multiple mastery, as actor, playwright, and investor of the London stage.

The Shakespearean Trajectory

Though Shakespeare's England was in many ways a record-keeping society, no reliable record survives that details the performances, year by year, in the London theaters. Every play had to be licensed by a government official, the Master of the Revels, but the records kept by the relevant officials from 1579 to 1621, Sir Edmund Tilney and Sir George Buc, have not survived. A major theatrical entrepreneur, Philip Henslowe, kept a careful account of his expenditures, including what he paid for the scripts he commissioned, but unfortunately Henslowe's main business was with the Rose and the Fortune theaters and not with the playhouses at which Shakespeare's company performed. A comparable ledger must have been kept by the shareholders of the Lord Chamberlain's Men, but it has not survived. Shakespeare himself apparently had no interest in preserving for posterity the sum of his writings, let alone in clarifying the chronology of his works or in specifying which plays he wrote alone and which with collaborators.

The principal source for Shakespeare's works is the 1623 Folio volume of *Mr. William Shakespeares Comedies, Histories, & Tragedies.* Most scholars believe that the editors were careful to include only those plays for which they knew Shakespeare to be the main author. Their edition does not, however, include any of Shakespeare's nondramatic poems, and it omits two plays in which Shakespeare is now thought to have had a significant hand, *Pericles, Prince of Tyre* and *The Two Noble Kinsmen,* along with his probable contribution to the multi-authored *Sir Thomas More.* (A number of other plays were attributed to Shakespeare, both before and after his death, but scholars have not generally accepted any of these into the established canon.) Moreover, the Folio edition does not print the plays in chronological order, nor does it attempt to establish a chronology. We do not know how much time would normally have

IF YOV KNOVV NOT ME,
You know no body.
OR,
The troubles of Queene ELIZABETH.

LONDON.
Printed by B.A. and T.F. for *Nathanaell Butter.* 1632.

Title page of *If You Know Not Me, You Know No Body; or, the Troubles of Queene Elizabeth* (1632).

elapsed between the writing of a play and its first performance, nor, with a few exceptions, do we know with any certainty the month or even the year of the first performance of any of Shakespeare's plays. The quarto editions of those plays that were published during Shakespeare's lifetime obviously establish a date by which we know a given play had been written, but they give us little more than an end point, because there was likely to be a substantial though indeterminate gap between the first performance of a play and its publication.

With enormous patience and ingenuity, however, scholars have gradually assembled a considerable archive of evidence, both external and internal, for dating the composition of the plays. Besides actual publication, the external evidence includes explicit reference to a play, a record of its performance, or (as in the case of Greene's attack on the "upstart crow") the quoting of a line, though all of these can be maddeningly ambiguous. The most important single piece of external evidence appears in 1598 in *Palladis Tamia*, a long book of jumbled reflections by Francis Meres that includes a survey of the contemporary literary scene. Meres finds that "the sweet, witty soul of Ovid lives in mellifluous and honey-tongued Shakespeare, witness his *Venus and Adonis*, his *Lucrece*, his sugered Sonnets among his private friends, etc." Meres goes on to list Shakespeare's accomplishments as a playwright as well:

> As Plautus and Seneca are accounted the best for Comedy and Tragedy among the Latins: so Shakespeare among the English is the most excellent in both kinds for the stage; for Comedy, witness his *Gentlemen of Verona*, his *Errors*, his *Love labors lost*, his *Love labours won*, his *Midsummers night dream*, & his *Merchant of Venice*: for Tragedy his *Richard the 2*, *Richard the 3*, *Henry the 4*, *King John*, *Titus Andronicus* and his *Romeo and Juliet*.

Meres thus provides a date by which twelve of Shakespeare's plays had definitely appeared (including one, *Love's Labour's Won*, that appears to have been lost). Unfortunately, Meres provides no clues about the order of appearance of these plays, and there are no other comparable lists.

Faced with the limitations of the external evidence, scholars have turned to a bewildering array of internal evidence, ranging from datable sources and topical allusions on the one hand to evolving stylistic features (ratio of verse to prose, percentage of rhyme to blank verse, colloquialisms, use of extended similes, and the like) on the other. Thus, for example, a cluster of plays with a high percentage of rhymed verse may follow closely upon Shakespeare's writing of the rhymed poems *Venus and Adonis* and *The Rape of Lucrece* and therefore be datable to 1594–95. Similarly, vocabulary overlap probably indicates proximity in composition, so if four or five plays share relatively "rare" vocabulary, it is likely that they were written in roughly the same period. Again, there seems to be a pattern in Shakespeare's use of colloquialisms, with a steady increase from *As You Like It* (1599–1600) to *Coriolanus* (1608), followed in the late romances by a retreat from the colloquial.

More sophisticated computer analysis should provide further guidance in the future, though the precise order of the plays, still very much in dispute, is never likely to be settled to universal satisfaction. Still, certain broad patterns are now widely accepted. These patterns can be readily grasped in the *Norton Shakespeare*, which presents the plays in the chronological order proposed by the Oxford editors.

Shakespeare began his career, probably in the early 1590s, by writing both comedies and history plays. The attack by Greene suggests that he made his mark with the series of theatrically vital but rather crude plays based on the foreign and domestic broils that erupted during the unhappy reign of the Lancastrian Henry VI. Modern readers and audiences are more likely to find the first sustained evidence of unusual power in *Richard III* (c. 1592), a play that combines a brilliantly conceived central character, a dazzling command of histrionic rhetoric, and an overarching moral vision of English history.

At virtually the same time that he was setting his stamp on the genre of the history play, Shakespeare was writing his first—or first surviving—comedies. Here, there are even fewer signs than in the histories of an apprenticeship: *The Comedy of Errors*, one of his early efforts in this genre, already displays a rare command of the resources of comedy: mistaken identity, madcap confusion, and the threat of disaster, giving way in the end to reconciliation, recovery, and love. Shakespeare's other comedies from the early 1590s, *The Taming of the Shrew, The Two Gentlemen of Verona*, and *Love's Labour's Lost*, are no less remarkable for their sophisticated variations on familiar comic themes, their inexhaustible rhetorical inventiveness, and their poignant intimation, in the midst of festive celebration, of loss.

Successful as are these early histories and comedies, and indicative of an extraordinary theatrical talent, Shakespeare's achievement in the later 1590s would still have been all but impossible to foresee. Starting with *A Midsummer Night's Dream* (c. 1595), Shakespeare wrote an unprecedented series of romantic comedies—*The Merchant of Venice, The Merry Wives of Windsor, Much Ado About Nothing, As You Like It*, and *Twelfth Night* (c. 1602)—whose poetic richness and emotional complexity remain unmatched. In the same period, he wrote a sequence of profoundly searching and ambitious history plays—*Richard II, 1* and *2 Henry IV*, and *Henry V*—which together explore the death throes of feudal England and the birth of the modern nation-state ruled by a charismatic monarch. Both the comedies and histories of this period are marked by their capaciousness, their ability to absorb characters who press up against the outermost boundaries of the genre: the comedy *Merchant of Venice* somehow contains the figure, at once nightmarish and poignant, of Shylock, while the *Henry IV* plays, with their somber vision of crisis in the family and the state, bring to the stage one of England's greatest comic characters, Falstaff.

If in the mid to late 1590s Shakespeare reached the summit of his art in two major genres, he also manifested a lively interest in a third. As early as 1593, he wrote the crudely violent tragedy *Titus Andronicus*, the first of several plays on themes from Roman history, and a year or two later, in *Richard II*, he created in the protagonist a figure who achieves by the play's close the stature of a tragic hero. In the same year that Shakespeare wrote the wonderfully farcical "Pyramus and Thisbe" scene in *A Midsummer Night's Dream*, he probably also wrote the deeply tragic realization of the same story in *Romeo and Juliet*. But once again, the lyric anguish of *Romeo and Juliet* and the tormented self-revelation of *Richard II*, extraordinary as they are, could not have led anyone to predict the next phase of Shakespeare's career, the great tragic dramas that poured forth in the early years of the seventeenth century: *Hamlet, Othello, King Lear, Macbeth, Antony and Cleopatra*, and *Coriolanus*. These plays, written from 1601 to 1607, seem to mark a major shift in sensibility, an existential and metaphysical darkening that many readers think must have originated in a deep personal anguish, perhaps caused by the death of Shakespeare's father, John, in 1601.

Whatever the truth of these speculations—and we have no direct, personal testimony either to support or to undermine them—there appears to have occurred in the same period a shift as well in Shakespeare's comic sensibility. The comedies written between 1601 and 1604, *Troilus and Cressida, All's Well That Ends Well*, and *Measure for Measure*, are sufficiently different from the earlier comedies—more biting in tone, more uneasy with comic conventions, more ruthlessly questioning of the values of the characters and the resolutions of the plots—to have led many twentieth-century scholars to classify them as "problem plays" or "dark comedies." This category has recently begun to fall out of favor, since Shakespeare criticism is perfectly happy to demonstrate that *all* of the plays are "problem plays." But there is another group of plays, among the last Shakespeare wrote, that continue to constitute a distinct category. *Pericles, Cymbeline, The Winter's Tale*, and *The Tempest*, written between 1608 and 1611, when the playwright had developed a remarkably fluid, dreamlike sense of plot and a poetic style that could veer, apparently effortlessly, from the tortured to the ineffably sweet, are known as the "romances." These plays share an interest in the moral and emotional life less of the adolescents who dominate the earlier comedies than of their parents. The romances are deeply concerned with patterns of loss and recovery, suffering and redemption, despair and renewal. They have seemed to many critics to constitute a deliberate conclusion to a career that began in histories and comedies and passed through the dark and tormented tragedies.

One effect of the practice of printing Shakespeare's plays in a reconstructed chronologi-cal order, as this edition does, is to produce a kind of authorial plot, a progress from youthful exuberance and a heroic grappling with history, through psychological anguish and radical doubt, to a mature serenity built upon an understanding of loss. The ordering of Shakespeare's "complete works" in this way reconstitutes the figure of the author as the beloved hero of his own, lived romance. There are numerous reasons to treat this romance with considerable skepticism: the precise order of the plays remains in dispute, the obses-sions of the earliest plays crisscross with those of the last, the drama is a collaborative art form, and the relation between authorial consciousness and theatrical representation is murky. Yet a longing to identify Shakespeare's personal trajectory, to chart his psychic and spiritual as well as professional progress, is all but irresistible.

The Fetishism of Dress

Whatever the personal resonance of Shakespeare's own life, his art is deeply enmeshed in the collective hopes, fears, and fantasies of his time. For example, throughout his plays, Shakespeare draws heavily upon his culture's investment in costume, symbols of authority, visible signs of status—the fetishism of dress he must have witnessed from early childhood. Disguise in his drama is often assumed to be incredibly effective: when Henry V borrows a cloak, when Portia dresses in a jurist's robes, when Viola puts on a young man's suit, it is as if each has become unrecognizable, as if identity resided in clothing. At the end of *Twelfth Night*, even though Viola's true identity has been disclosed, Orsino continues to call her Cesario; he will do so, he says, until she resumes her maid's garments, for only then will she be transformed into a woman:

> Cesario, come—
> For so you shall be while you are a man;
> But when in other habits you are seen,
> Orsino's mistress, and his fancy's queen.
> (5.1.372–75)

The pinnacle of this fetishism of costume is the royal crown, for whose identity-confer-ring power men are willing to die, but the principle is everywhere from the filthy blanket that transforms Edgar into Poor Tom to the coxcomb that is the badge of the licensed fool. Antonio, wishing to express his utter contempt, spits on Shylocks' "Jewish gaberdine," as if the clothing were the essence of the man; Kent, pouring insults on the loathsome Oswald, calls him a "filthy worsted-stocking knave"; and innocent Innogen, learning that her hus-band has ordered her murder, thinks of herself as an expensive cast-off dress, destined to be ripped at the seams:

> Poor I am stale, a garment out of fashion,
> And for I am richer than to hang by th' walls
> I must be ripped. To pieces with me!
> (*Cymbeline* 3.4.50–52)

What can be said, thought, felt, in this culture seems deeply dependent on the clothes one wears—clothes that one is, in effect, *permitted* or *compelled* to wear, since there is little freedom in dress. Shakespearean drama occasionally represents something like such freedom: after all, Viola in *Twelfth Night* chooses to put off her "maiden weeds," as does Rosalind, who declares, "We'll have a swashing and a martial outside" (*As You Like It* 1.3.114). But these choices are characteristically made under the pressure of desperate circumstances, here shipwreck and exile. Part of the charm of Shakespeare's heroines is their ability to transform distress into an opportunity for self-fashioning, but the plays often suggest that there is less autonomy than meets the eye. What looks like an escape from cultural determinism may be only a deeper form of constraint. We may take, as an allegori-cal emblem of this constraint, the transformation of the beggar Christopher Sly in the playful Induction to *The Taming of the Shrew* into a nobleman. The transformation seems to suggest that you are free to make of yourself whatever you choose to be—the play begins with the drunken Sly indignantly claiming the dignity of his pedigree ("Look in the Chronicles" [Induction 1.3–4])—but in fact he is only the subject of the mischievous lord's experiment, designed to demonstrate the interwovenness of clothing and identity. "What think you," the lord asks his huntsman,

> if he were conveyed to bed,
> Wrapped in sweet clothes, rings put upon his fingers,
> A most delicious banquet by his bed,
> And brave attendants near him when he wakes—
> Would not the beggar then forget himself?

To which the huntsman replies, in words that underscore the powerlessness of the drunken beggar, "Believe me, lord, I think he cannot choose" (Induction 1.33–38).

Petruccio's taming of Katherine is similarly constructed around an imposition of identity, an imposition closely bound up with the right to wear certain articles of clothing. When the haberdasher arrives with a fashionable lady's hat, Petruccio refuses it over his wife's vehement objections: "This doth fit the time, / And gentlewomen wear such caps as these." "When you are gentle," Petruccio replies, "you shall have one, too, / And not till then" (4.3.69–72). At the play's close, Petruccio demonstrates his authority by commanding his tamed wife to throw down her cap: "Off with that bauble, throw it underfoot" (5.2.126). Here as elsewhere in Shakespeare, acts of robing and disrobing are intensely charged, a charge that culminates in the trappings of monarchy. When Richard II, in a scene that was probably censored during the reign of Elizabeth from the stage as well as the printed text, is divested of his crown and scepter, he experiences the loss as the eradication of his name, the symbolic melting away of his identity:

> Alack the heavy day,
> That I have worn so many winters out
> And know not now what name to call myself!
> O, that I were a mockery king of snow,
> Standing before the sun of Bolingbroke
> To melt myself away in water-drops!
> (4.1.255–60)

When Lear tears off his regal "lendings" in order to reduce himself to the nakedness of the Bedlam beggar, he is expressing not only his radical loss of social identity but the breakdown of his psychic order as well, expressing therefore his reduction to the condition of the "poor bare forked animal" that is the primal condition of undifferentiated existence. And when Cleopatra determines to kill herself in order to escape public humiliation in Rome, she magnificently affirms her essential being by arraying herself as she had once done to encounter Antony:

> Show me, my women, like a queen. Go fetch
> My best attires. I am again for Cydnus
> To meet Mark Antony.
> (5.2.223–25)

Such scenes are a remarkable intensification of the everyday symbolic practice of Renaissance English culture, its characteristically deep and knowing commitment to illusion: "I know perfectly well that the woman in her crown and jewels and gorgeous gown is an aging, irascible, and fallible mortal—she herself virtually admits as much—yet I profess that she is the virgin queen, timelessly beautiful, wise, and just." Shakespeare understood how close this willed illusion was to the spirit of the theater, to the actors' ability to work on what the chorus in *Henry V* calls the "imaginary forces" of the audience.

But there is throughout Shakespeare's works a counterintuition that, while it does not exactly overturn this illusion, renders it poignant, vulnerable, fraught. The "masculine usurp'd attire" that is donned by Viola, Rosalind, Portia, Jessica, and other Shakespeare heroines alters what they can say and do, reveals important aspects of their character, and changes their destiny, but it is, all the same, not theirs and not all of who they are. They have, the plays insist, natures that are neither transformed nor altogether concealed by their dress: "Pray God defend me," exclaims the frightened Viola. "A little thing would make me tell them how much I lack of a man" (*Twelfth Night* 3.4.268–69).

The Paradoxes of Identity

The gap between costume and identity is not simply a matter of what women supposedly lack; virtually all of Shakespeare's major characters, men and women, convey the sense of both a *self-division* and an *inward expansion*. The belief in a complex inward realm beyond costumes and status is a striking inversion of the clothes cult: we know perfectly well that the characters have no inner lives apart from what we see on the stage, and yet we believe that they continue to exist when we do not see them, that they exist apart from their represented words and actions, that they have hidden dimensions. How is this conviction aroused and sustained? In part, it is the effect of what the characters themselves say: "My grief lies all within," Richard II tells Bolingbroke,

> And these external manner of laments
> Are merely shadows to the unseen grief
> That swells with silence in the tortured soul.
> (4.1.294–96)

Similarly, Hamlet, dismissing the significance of his outward garments, declares, "I have that within which passeth show— / These but the trappings and the suits of woe" (1.2.85–86). And the distinction between inward and outward is reinforced throughout this play and elsewhere by an unprecedented use of the aside and the soliloquy.

The soliloquy is a continual reminder in Shakespeare that the inner life is by no means transparent to one's surrounding world. Prince Hal seems open and easy with his mates in Eastcheap, but he has a hidden reservoir of disgust:

> I know you all, and will a while uphold
> The unyoked humour of your idleness.
> Yet herein will I imitate the sun,
> Who doth permit the base contagious clouds
> To smother up his beauty from the world,
> That when he please again to be himself,
> Being wanted he may be more wondered at
> By breaking through the foul and ugly mists
> Of vapours that did seem to strangle him.
> (*I Henry IV* 1.2.173–81)

"When he please again to be himself": the line implies that identity is a matter of free choice—you decide how much of yourself you wish to disclose—but Shakespeare employs other devices that suggest more elusive and intractable layers of inwardness. There is a peculiar, recurrent lack of fit between costume and character, in fools as in princes, that is not simply a matter of disguise and disclosure. If Hal's true identity is partially "smothered" in the tavern, it is not completely revealed either in his soldier's armor or in his royal robes, nor do his asides reach the bedrock of unimpeachable self-understanding.

Identity in Shakespeare repeatedly slips away from the characters themselves, as it does from Richard II after the deposition scene and from Lear after he has given away his land and from Macbeth after he has gained the crown. The slippage does not mean that they retreat into silence; rather, they embark on an experimental, difficult fashioning of themselves and the world, most often through role-playing. "I cannot do it," says the deposed and imprisoned Richard II. "Yet I'll hammer it out" (5.5.5). This could serve as the motto for many Shakespearean characters: Viola becomes Cesario, Rosalind calls herself Ganymede, Kent becomes Caius, Edgar presents himself as Poor Tom, Hamlet plays the madman that he has partly become, Hal pretends that he is his father and a highwayman and Hotspur and even himself. Even in comedy, these ventures into alternate identities are rarely matters of choice; in tragedy, they are always undertaken under pressure and compulsion. And often enough it is not a matter of role-playing at all, but of a drastic transformation whose extreme emblem is the harrowing madness of Lear and of Leontes.

There is a moment in *Richard II* in which the deposed King asks for a mirror and then, after musing on his reflection, throws it to the ground. The shattering of the glass serves to remind us not only of the fragility of identity in Shakespeare but of its characteristic appearance in fragmentary mirror images. The plays continually generate alternative reflections, identities that intersect with, underscore, echo, or otherwise set off that of the principal character. Hence, Desdemona and Iago are not only important figures in Othello's world, they also seem to embody partially realized aspects of himself; Falstaff and Hotspur play a comparable role in relation to Prince Hal, Fortinbras and Horatio in relation to Hamlet, Gloucester and the Fool in relation to Lear, and so forth. In many of these plays, the complementary and contrasting characters figure in subplots, subtly interwoven with the play's main plot and illuminating its concerns. The note so conspicuously sounded by Fortinbras at the close of *Hamlet*—what the hero might have been, "had he been put on"—is heard repeatedly in Shakespeare and contributes to the overwhelming intensity, poignancy, and complexity of the characters. This is a world in which outward appearance is everything and nothing, in which individuation is at once sharply etched and continually blurred, in which the victims of fate are haunted by the ghosts of the possible, in which everything is simultaneously as it must be and as it need not have been.

Are these antinomies signs of a struggle between contradictory and irreconcilable perspectives in Shakespeare? In certain plays—notably, *Measure for Measure, All's Well That Ends Well, Coriolanus*, and *Troilus and Cressida*—the tension seems both high and entirely unresolved. But Shakespearean contradictions are more often reminiscent of the capacious spirit of Montaigne, who refused any systematic order that would betray his sense of reality. Thus, individual characters are immensely important in Shakespeare—he is justly celebrated for his unmatched skill in the invention of particular dramatic identities, marked with distinct speech patterns, manifested in social status, and confirmed by costume and gesture—but the principle of individuation is not the rock on which his theatrical art is founded. After the masks are stripped away, the pretenses exposed, the claims of the ego shattered, there is a mysterious remainder; as the shamed but irrepressible Paroles declares in *All's Well That Ends Well*, "Simply the thing I am / Shall make me live" (4.3.309–10). Again and again the audience is made to sense a deeper energy, a source of power that at once discharges itself in individual characters and seems to sweep right through them.

The Poet of Nature

In *The Birth of Tragedy*, Nietzsche called a comparable source of energy that he found in Greek tragedy "Dionysos." But the god's name, conjuring up Bacchic frenzy, does not seem appropriate to Shakespeare. In the late seventeenth and eighteenth centuries, it was more plausibly called Nature: "The world must be peopled," says the delightful Benedick in *Much Ado About Nothing* (2.3.213–14), and there are frequent invocations elsewhere of the happy, generative power that brings couples together—

Jack shall have Jill,
Naught shall go ill,
the man shall have his mare again, and all shall be well.
(*A Midsummer Night's Dream* 3.3.45–47)

—and the melancholy, destructive power that brings all living things to the grave: "Golden lads and girls all must, / As chimney-sweepers, come to dust" (*Cymbeline* 4.2.263–64).

But the celebration of Shakespeare as a poet of nature—often coupled with an inane celebration of his supposedly "natural" (that is, untutored) genius—has its distinct limitations. For Shakespearean art brilliantly interrogates the "natural," refusing to take for granted precisely what the celebrants think is most secure. His comedies are endlessly inventive in showing that love is not simply natural: the playful hint of bestiality in the line quoted above, "the man shall have his mare again," (from a play in which the Queen of the Fairies falls in love with an ass-headed laborer), lightly unsettles the boundaries between the natural and the perverse. These boundaries are called into question throughout Shakespeare's work, from the cross-dressing and erotic crosscurrents that deliciously complicate the lives of the characters in *Twelfth Night* and *As You Like It* to the terrifying violence that wells up from the heart of the family in *King Lear* or from the sweet intimacy of sexual desire in *Othello*. Even the boundary between life and death is not secure, as the ghosts in *Julius Caesar*, *Hamlet*, and *Macbeth* attest, while the principle of natural death (given its most eloquent articulation by old Hamlet's murderer, Claudius!) is repeatedly tainted and disrupted.

Disrupted too is the idea of order that constantly makes its claim, most insistently in the history plays. Scholars have observed the presence in Shakespeare's works of the so-called Tudor myth—the ideological justification of the ruling dynasty as a restoration of national order after a cycle of tragic violence. The violence, Tudor apologists claimed, was divine punishment unleashed after the deposition of the anointed king, Richard II, for God will not tolerate violations of the sanctified order. Traces of this propaganda certainly exist in the histories—Shakespeare may, for all we know, have personally subscribed to its premises—but a closer scrutiny of his plays has disclosed so many ironic reservations and qualifications and subversions as to call into question any straightforward adherence to a political line. The plays manifest a profound fascination with the monarchy and with the ambitions of the aristocracy, but the fascination is never simply endorsement. There is always at least the hint of a slippage between the great figures, whether admirable or monstrous, who stand at the pinnacle of authority and the vast, miscellaneous mass of soldiers, scriveners, ostlers, poets, whores, gardeners, thieves, weavers, shepherds, country gentlemen, sturdy beggars, and the like who make up the commonwealth. And the idea of order, though eloquently articulated (most memorably by Ulysses in *Troilus and Cressida*), is always shadowed by a relentless spirit of irony.

The Play of Language

If neither the individual nor nature nor order will serve, can we find a single comprehensive name for the underlying force in Shakespeare's work? Certainly not. The work is too protean and capacious. But much of the energy that surges through this astonishing body of plays and poems is closely linked to the power of language. Shakespeare was the supreme product of a rhetorical culture, a culture steeped in the arts of persuasion and verbal expressiveness. In 1512, the great Dutch humanist Erasmus published a work called *De copia* that taught its readers how to cultivate "copiousness," verbal richness, in discourse. (Erasmus obligingly provides, as a sample, a list of 144 different ways of saying "Thank you for your letter.") Recommended modes of variation include putting the subject of an argument into fictional form, as well as the use of synonym, substitution, paraphrase, metaphor, metonymy, synecdoche, hyperbole, diminution, and a host of other figures of speech. To change emotional tone, he suggests trying *ironia, interrogatio, admiratio, dubitatio, abominatio*—the possibilities seem infinite.

In Renaissance England, certain syntactic forms or patterns of words known as "figures" (also called "schemes") were shaped and repeated in order to confer beauty or heighten expressive power. Figures were usually known by their Greek and Latin names, though in an Elizabethan rhetorical manual, *The Arte of English Poesie*, George Puttenham made a valiant if short-lived attempt to give them English equivalents, such as "*Hyperbole*, or the

Overreacher," "*Ironia*, or the Dry Mock," and "*Ploce*, or the Doubler." Those who received a grammar school education throughout Europe at almost any point between the Roman Empire and the eighteenth century probably knew by heart the names of up to one hundred such figures, just as they knew by heart their multiplication tables. According to one scholar's count, Shakespeare knew and made use of about two hundred.

As certain grotesquely inflated Renaissance texts attest, lessons from *De copia* and similar rhetorical guides could encourage mere prolixity and verbal self-display. But though he shared his culture's delight in rhetorical complexity, Shakespeare always understood how to swoop from baroque sophistication to breathtaking simplicity. Moreover, he grasped early in his career how to use figures of speech, tone, and rhythm not only to provide emphasis and elegant variety but also to articulate the inner lives of his characters. Take, for example, these lines from *Othello*, where, as scholars have noted, Shakespeare deftly combines four common rhetorical figures—*anaphora, parison, isocolon,* and *epistrophe*—to depict with painful vividness Othello's psychological torment:

> By the world,
> I think my wife be honest, and think she is not.
> I think that thou art just, and think thou art not.
> I'll have some proof.
>
> (3.3.388–91)

Anaphora is simply the repetition of a word at the beginning of a sequence of sentences or clauses ("I/I"). *Parison* is the correspondence of word to word within adjacent sentences or clauses, either by direct repetition ("think/think") or by the matching of noun with noun, verb with verb ("wife/thou"; "be/art"). *Isocolon* gives exactly the same length to corresponding clauses ("and think she is not/and think thou art not"), and *epistrophe* is the mirror image of *anaphora*, in that it is the repetition of a word at the end of a sequence of sentences or clauses ("not/not"). Do we need to know the Greek names for these figures in order to grasp the effectiveness of Othello's lines? Of course not. But Shakespeare and his contemporaries, convinced that rhetoric provided the most natural and powerful means by which feelings could be conveyed to readers and listeners, were trained in an analytical language that helped at once to promote and to account for this effectiveness. In his 1593 edition of *The Garden of Eloquence*, Henry Peacham remarks that *epistrophe* "serveth to leave a word of importance in the end of a sentence, that it may the longer hold the sound in the mind of the hearer," and in *Directions for Speech and Style* (c. 1599), John Hoskins notes that *anaphora* "beats upon one thing to cause the quicker feeling in the audience."

Shakespeare also shared with his contemporaries a keen understanding of the ways that rhetorical devices could be used not only to express powerful feelings but to hide them: after all, the artist who created Othello also created Iago, Richard III, and Lady Macbeth. He could deftly skewer the rhetorical affectations of Polonius in *Hamlet* or the pedant Holophernes in *Love's Labour's Lost*. He could deploy stylistic variations to mark the boundaries not of different individuals but of different social realms; in *A Midsummer Night's Dream*, for example, the blank verse of Duke Theseus is played off against the rhymed couplets of the well-born young lovers, and both in turn contrast with the prose spoken by the artisans. At the same time that he thus marks boundaries between both individuals and groups, Shakespeare shows a remarkable ability to establish unifying patterns of imagery that knit together the diverse strands of his plot and suggest subtle links among characters who may be scarcely aware of how much they share with one another.

One of the hidden links in Shakespeare's own works is the frequent use he makes of a somewhat unusual rhetorical figure called *hendiadys*. An example from the Roman poet Virgil is the phrase *pateris libamus et auro*, "we drink from cups and gold" (*Georgics* 2.192). Rather than serving as an adjective or a dependent noun, as in "golden cups" or "cups of gold," the word "gold" serves as a substantive joined to another substantive, "cups," by a conjunction, "and." Shakespeare uses the figure over three hundred times in all, and since it does not appear in ancient or medieval lists of tropes and schemes and is treated only briefly by English rhetoricians, he may have come upon it directly in Virgil. *Hendiadys* literally means "one through two," though Shakespeare's versions often make us quickly, perhaps only subliminally, aware of the complexity of what ordinarily passes for straightforward perceptions. When Othello, in his suicide speech, invokes the memory of "a malignant and a turbaned Turk," the figure of speech at once associates enmity with cultural difference and keeps them slightly apart. And when Macbeth speaks of his "strange and self-abuse," the *hendiadys* seems briefly to hold both "strange" and "self" up for scrutiny. It would be foolish to make too much of any single feature in Shakespeare's varied and diverse creative achievement, and yet this curious rhetorical scheme has something of the quality of a fingerprint.

But all of his immense rhetorical gifts, though rich, beautiful, and supremely useful, do not adequately convey Shakespeare's relation to language, which is less strictly functional than a total immersion in the arts of persuasion may imply. An Erasmian admiration for copiousness cannot fully explain Shakespeare's astonishing vocabulary of some 25,000 words. (His closest rival among the great English poets of the period was John Milton, with about 12,000 words, and most major writers, let alone ordinary people, have much smaller vocabularies.) This immense word hoard, it is worth noting, was not the result of scanning a dictionary; in the late sixteenth century, there were no English dictionaries of the kind to which we are now accustomed. Shakespeare seems to have absorbed new words from virtually every discursive realm he ever encountered, and he experimented boldly and tirelessly with them. These experiments were facilitated by the very fact that dictionaries as we know them did not exist and by a flexibility in grammar, orthography, and diction that the more orderly, regularized English of the later seventeenth and eighteenth centuries suppressed.

Owing in part to the number of dialects in London, pronunciation was variable, and there were many opportunities for phonetic association between words: the words "bear," "barn," "bier," "bourne," "born," and "barne" could all sound like one another. Homonyms were given greater scope by the fact that the same word could be spelled so many different ways—Christopher Marlowe's name appears in the records as Marlowe, Marloe, Marlen, Marlyne, Merlin, Marley, Marlye, Morley, and Morle—and by the fact that a word's grammatical function could easily shift, from noun to verb, verb to adjective, and so forth. Since grammar and punctuation did not insist on relations of coordination and subordination, loose, nonsyntactic sentences were common, and etymologies were used to forge surprising or playful relations between distant words.

It would seem inherently risky for a popular playwright to employ a vocabulary so far in excess of what most mortals could possibly possess, but Shakespeare evidently counted on his audience's linguistic curiosity and adventurousness, just as he counted on its general and broad-based rhetorical competence. He was also usually careful to provide a context that in effect explained or translated his more arcane terms. For example, when Macbeth reflects with horror on his murderous hands, he shudderingly imagines that even the sea could not wash away the blood; on the contrary, his bloodstained hand, he says, "will rather / The multitudinous seas incarnadine." The meaning of the unfamiliar word "incarnadine" is explained by the next line: "Making the green one red" (2.2.59–61).

What is most striking is not the abstruseness or novelty of Shakespeare's language but its extraordinary vitality, a quality that the playwright seemed to pursue with a kind of passionate recklessness. Perhaps Samuel Johnson was looking in the right direction when he complained that the "quibble," or pun, was "the fatal Cleopatra for which [Shakespeare] lost the world, and was content to lose it." For the power that continually discharges itself throughout the plays, at once constituting and unsettling everything it touches, is the polymorphous power of language, language that seems both costume and that which lies beneath the costume, personal identity and that which challenges the merely personal, nature and that which enables us to name nature and thereby distance ourselves from it.

Shakespeare's language has an overpowering exuberance and generosity that often resembles the experience of love. Consider, for example, Oberon's description in *A Mid-*

summer Night's Dream of the moment when he saw Cupid shoot his arrow at the fair vestal: "Thou rememb'rest," he asks Puck,

> Since once I sat upon a promontory
> And heard a mermaid on a dolphin's back
> Uttering such dulcet and harmonious breath
> That the rude sea grew civil at her song
> And certain stars shot madly from their spheres
> To hear the sea-maid's music?
>
> (2.1.149–54)

Here, Oberon's composition of place, lightly alluding to a classical emblem, is infused with a fantastically lush verbal brilliance. This brilliance, the result of masterful alliterative and rhythmical technique, seems gratuitous; that is, it does not advance the plot, but rather exhibits a capacity for display and self-delight that extends from the fairies to the playwright who has created them. The rich music of Oberon's words imitates the "dulcet and harmonious breath" he is intent on recalling, breath that has, in his account, an oddly contradictory effect: it is at once a principle of order, so that the rude sea is becalmed like a lower-class mob made civil by a skilled orator, and a principle of disorder, so that celestial bodies in their fixed spheres are thrown into mad confusion. And this contradictory effect, so intimately bound up with an inexplicable, supererogatory, and intensely erotic verbal magic, is the key to A *Midsummer Night's Dream*, with its exquisite blend of confusion and discipline, lunacy and hierarchical ceremony.

The fairies in this comedy seem to embody a pervasive sense found throughout Shakespeare's work that there is something uncanny about language, something that is not quite human, at least in the conventional and circumscribed sense of the human that dominates waking experience. In the comedies, this intuition is alarming but ultimately benign: Oberon and his followers trip through the great house at the play's close, blessing the bridebeds and warding off the nightmares that lurk in marriage and parenthood. But there is in Shakespeare an alternative, darker vision of the uncanniness of language, a vision also embodied in creatures that test the limits of the human—not the fairies of A *Midsummer Night's Dream* but the weird sisters of *Macbeth*. When in the tragedy's opening scene the witches chant, "Fair is foul, and foul is fair," they unsettle through the simplest and most radical act of linguistic equation (x is y) the fundamental antinomies through which a moral order is established. And when Macbeth appears onstage a few minutes later, his first words unconsciously echo what we have just heard from the witches' mouths: "So foul and fair a day I have not seen" (1.3.36). What is the meaning of this linguistic "unconscious"? On the face of things, Macbeth presumably means only that the day of fair victory is also a day of foul weather, but the fact that he echoes the witches (something that we hear but that he cannot know) intimates an occult link between them, even before their direct encounter. It is difficult, perhaps impossible, to specify exactly what this link signifies—generations of emboldened critics have tried without notable success—but we can at least affirm that its secret lair is in the play's language, like a half-buried pun whose full articulation will entail the murder of Duncan, the ravaging of his kingdom, and Macbeth's own destruction.

Macbeth is haunted by half-buried puns, equivocations, and ambiguous grammatical constructions known as amphibologies. They manifest themselves most obviously in the words of the witches, from the opening exchanges to the fraudulent assurances that deceive Macbeth at the close, but they are also present in his most intimate and private reflections, as in his tortured broodings about his proposed act of treason:

> If it were done when 'tis done, then 'twere well
> It were done quickly. If th'assassination
> Could trammel up the consequence, and catch
> With his surcease success: that but this blow

> Might be the be-all and the end-all, here,
> But here upon this bank and shoal of time,
> We'd jump the life to come.
>
> (1.7.1–7)

The dream is to reach a secure and decisive end, to catch as in a net (hence "trammel up") all of the slippery, unforeseen, and uncontrollable consequences of regicide, to hobble time as one might hobble a horse (another sense of "trammel up"), to stop the flow ("success") of events, to be, as Macbeth later puts it, "settled." But Macbeth's words themselves slip away from the closure he seeks; they slide into one another, trip over themselves, twist and double back and swerve into precisely the sickening uncertainties their speaker most wishes to avoid. And if we sense a barely discernible note of comedy in Macbeth's tortured language, a discordant playing with the senses of the word "done" and the hint of a childish tongue twister in the phrase "catch / With his surcease success," we are in touch with a dark pleasure to which Shakespeare was all his life addicted.

Look again at the couplet from *Cymbeline*: "Golden lads and girls all must, / As chimney-sweepers, come to dust."

The playwright who insinuated a pun into the solemn dirge is the same playwright whose tragic heroine in *Antony and Cleopatra*, pulling the bleeding body of her dying lover into the pyramid, says, "Our strength is all gone into heaviness" (4.16.34). He is the playwright whose Juliet, finding herself alone on the stage, says, "My dismal scene I needs must act alone" (*Romeo and Juliet* 4.3.19), and the playwright who can follow the long, wrenching periodic sentence that Othello speaks, just before he stabs himself, with the remark "O bloody period!" (5.2.366). The point is not merely the presence of puns in the midst of tragedy (as there are stabs of pain in the midst of Shakespearean comedy); it is rather the streak of wildness that they so deliberately disclose, the sublimely indecorous linguistic energy of which Shakespeare was at once the towering master and the most obedient, worshipful servant.

The Dream of the Master Text

Shakespeare and the Printed Book

Ben Jonson's famous tribute to Shakespeare—"He was not of an age, but for all time!"—comes in one of the dedicatory poems to the 1623 First Folio of *Mr. William Shakespeares Comedies, Histories, & Tragedies*. This large, handsome volume, the first collection of Shakespeare's plays, was not, as far as we know, the product of the playwright's own design. We do not even know if he would have approved of the Folio's division of each play into five acts or its organization of the plays into three loose generic categories, comedies, histories, and tragedies (to which modern editors have often added a fourth, the romances, to group together *Cymbeline, Pericles, The Winter's Tale*, and *The Tempest*). Published seven years after the playwright's death, the Folio was printed by the London printers William and Isaac Jaggard, who were joined in this expensive venture by Edward Blount, John Smethwicke, and William Apsley. It was edited by two of Shakespeare's old friends and fellow actors, John Heminges and Henry Condell, who claimed to be using "True Originall Copies" in the author's own hand. (None of these copies has survived, or, more cautiously, none has to date been found.) Eighteen plays included in the First Folio had already appeared individually in print in the small-format and relatively inexpensive texts called "quartos" (or, in one case, the still smaller format called "octavo"); to these, Heminges and Condell added eighteen others never before published: *All's Well That Ends Well, Antony and Cleopatra, As You Like It, The Comedy of Errors, Coriolanus, Cymbeline, All Is True (Henry VIII), Julius Caesar, King John, Macbeth, Measure for Measure, The Taming of the Shrew, The Tempest, Timon of Athens, Twelfth Night, The Two*

Sixteenth-century printing shop. Engraving by Jan van der Straet. From *Nova Reperta* (1580).

Gentlemen of Verona, The Winter's Tale, and *1 Henry VI*.* None of the plays included in the Folio has dropped out of the generally accepted canon of Shakespeare's works, and only two plays not included in the volume *(Pericles* and *The Two Noble Kinsmen)* have been allowed to join this select company, along with the nondramatic poems. Of the latter, *Venus and Adonis* (1593) and *The Rape of Lucrece* (1594) first appeared during Shakespeare's lifetime in quartos with dedications from the author to the Earl of Southampton. *Shakespeare's Sonnets* (1609) were apparently printed without his authorization, as were his poems in a collection called *The Passionate Pilgrim* (1599).

The plays were the property of the theatrical company in which Shakespeare was a shareholder. It was not normally in the interest of such companies to have their scripts circulating in print, at least while the plays were actively in repertory: players evidently feared competition from rival companies and thought that reading might dampen playgoing. Plays were generally sold only when the theaters were temporarily closed by plague, or when the company was in need of capital (four of Shakespeare's plays were published in 1600, presumably to raise money to pay the debts incurred in building the new Globe), or when a play had grown too old to revive profitably. There is no evidence that Shakespeare himself disagreed with this professional caution, no sign that he wished to see his plays in print. Unlike Ben Jonson, who took the radical step of rewriting his own plays for

---

*This sketch simplifies several complex questions such as the status of the 1594 Quarto called *The Taming of a Shrew*, sufficiently distinct from the similarly titled Folio text as to constitute for many editors a different play.

publication in the 1616 folio of his *Works*, Shakespeare evidently was not interested in constituting his plays as a canon. If in the sonnets he imagines his verse achieving a symbolic immortality, this dream apparently did not extend to his plays, at least through the medium of print.

Moreover, there is no evidence that Shakespeare had an interest in asserting authorial rights over his scripts, or that he or any other working English playwright had a public "standing," legal or otherwise, from which to do so. (Jonson was ridiculed for his presumption.) There is no indication whatever that he could, for example, veto changes in his scripts or block interpolated scenes or withdraw a play from production if a particular interpretation, addition, or revision did not please him. To be sure, in his advice to the players, Hamlet urges that those who play the clowns "speak no more than is set down for them," but—apart from the question of whether the Prince speaks for the playwright—the play-within-the-play in *Hamlet* is precisely an instance of a script altered to suit a particular occasion. It seems likely that Shakespeare would have routinely accepted the possibility of such alterations. Moreover, he would of necessity have routinely accepted the possibility, and in certain cases the virtual inevitability, of cuts in order to stage his plays in the two to two and one-half hours that was the normal performing time. There is an imaginative generosity in many of Shakespeare's scripts, as if he were deliberately offering his fellow actors more than they could use on any one occasion and hence giving them abundant materials with which to reconceive and revivify each play again and again, as they or their audiences liked it. The Elizabethan theater, like most theater in our own time, was a collaborative enterprise, and the collaboration almost certainly extended to decisions about selection, trimming, shifts of emphasis, and minor or major revision.

For many years, it was thought that Shakespeare himself did little or no revising. Some recent editors—above all the editors of the *Oxford Shakespeare*, whose texts the *Norton* presents—have argued persuasively that there are many signs of authorial revision, even wholesale rewriting. But there is no sign that Shakespeare sought through such revision to bring each of his plays to its "perfect," "final" form. On the contrary, many of the revisions seem to indicate that the scripts remained open texts, that the playwright and his company expected to add, cut, and rewrite as the occasion demanded.

Ralph Waldo Emerson once compared Shakespeare and his contemporary Francis Bacon in terms of the relative "finish" of their work. All of Bacon's work, wrote Emerson, "lies along the ground, a vast unfinished city." Each of Shakespeare's dramas, by contrast, "is perfect, hath an immortal integrity. To make Bacon's work complete, he must live to the end of the world." Recent scholarship suggests that Shakespeare was more like Bacon than Emerson thought. Neither the Folio nor the quarto texts of Shakespeare's plays bear the seal of final authorial intention, the mark of decisive closure that has served, at least ideally, as the guarantee of textual authenticity. We want to believe, as we read the text, "This is the play as Shakespeare himself wanted it read," but there is no license for such a reassuring sentiment. To be "not of an age, but for all time" means in Shakespeare's case not that the plays have achieved a static perfection, but that they are creatively, inexhaustibly unfinished.

That we have been so eager to link certain admired scripts to a single known playwright is closely related to changes in the status of artists in the Renaissance, changes that led to a heightened interest in the hand of the individual creator. Like medieval painting, medieval drama gives us few clues as to the particular individuals who fashioned the objects we admire. We know something about the places in which these objects were made, the circumstances that enabled their creation, the spaces in which they were placed, but relatively little about the particular artists themselves. It is easy to imagine a wealthy patron or a civic authority in the late Middle Ages commissioning a play on a particular subject (appropriate, for example, to a seasonal ritual, a religious observance, or a political festivity) and specifying the date, place, and length of the performance, the number of actors, even the costumes to be used, but it is more difficult to imagine him specifying a particular playwright and still less insisting that the entire play be written by this dramatist alone. Only with the Renaissance do we find a growing insistence on the name of the maker, the signature that heightens the value and even the meaning of the work by implying that it is the emanation of a single, distinct shaping consciousness.

In the case of Renaissance painting, we know that this signature does not necessarily mean that every stroke was made by the master. Some of the work, possibly the greater part of it, may have been done by assistants, with only the faces and a few finishing touches from the hand of the illustrious artist to whom the work is confidently attributed. As the skill of individual masters became more explicitly valued, contracts began to specify how much was to come from the brush of the principal painter. Consider, for example, the Italian painter Luca Signorelli's contract of 1499 for frescoes in Orvieto Cathedral:

> The said master Luca is bound and promises to paint [1] all the figures to be done on the said vault, and [2] especially the faces and all the parts of the figures from the middle of each figure upwards, and [3] that no painting should be done on it without Luca himself being present. . . . And it is agreed [4] that all the mixing of colours should be done by the said master Luca himself.

Such a contract at once reflects a serious cash interest in the characteristic achievement of a particular artist and a conviction that this achievement is compatible with the presence of other hands, provided those hands are subordinate, in the finished work. For paintings on a smaller scale, it was more possible to commission an exclusive performance. Thus the contract for a small altarpiece by Signorelli's great teacher, Piero della Francesca, specifies that "no painter may put his hand to the brush other than Piero himself."

There is no record of any comparable concern for exclusivity in the English theater. Unfortunately, the contracts that Shakespeare and his fellow dramatists almost certainly signed have not, with one significant exception, survived. But plays written for the professional theater are by their nature an even more explicitly collective art form than paintings; they depend for their full realization on the collaboration of others, and that collaboration may well extend to the fashioning of the script. It seems that some authors may simply have been responsible for providing plots that others then dramatized; still others were hired to "mend" old plays or to supply prologues, epilogues, or songs. A particular playwright's name came to be attached to a certain identifiable style—a characteristic set of plot devices, a marked rhetorical range, a tonality of character—but this name may refer in effect more to a certain product associated with a particular playing company than to the individual artist who may or may not have written most of the script. The one contract whose details do survive, that entered into by Richard Brome and the actors and owners of the Salisbury Court Theatre in 1635, does not stipulate that Brome's plays must be written by him alone or even that he must be responsible for a certain specifiable proportion of each script. Rather, it specifies that the playwright "should not nor would write any play or any part of a play to any other players or playhouse, but apply all his study and endeavors therein for the benefit of the said company of the said playhouse." The Salisbury Court players want rights to everything Brome writes for the stage; the issue is not that the plays associated with his name be exclusively *his* but rather that he be exclusively *theirs*.

Recent textual scholarship, then, has been moving steadily away from a conception of Shakespeare's plays as direct, unmediated emanations from the mind of the author and toward a conception of them as working scripts, composed and continually reshaped as part of a collaborative commercial enterprise in competition with other, similar enterprises. One consequence has been the progressive weakening of the idea of the solitary, inspired genius, in the sense fashioned by Romanticism and figured splendidly in the statue of Shakespeare in the public gardens in Germany's Weimar, the city of Goethe and Schiller: the poet, with his sensitive, expressive face and high domed forehead sitting alone and brooding, a skull at his feet, a long-stemmed rose in his crotch. In place of this projection of German Romanticism, we have now a playwright and sometime actor who is also (to his considerable financial advantage) a major shareholder in the company—the Lord Chamberlain's Men, later the King's Men—to which he loyally supplies for most of his career an average of two plays per year.

These developments are salutary insofar as they direct attention to the actual conditions in which the textual traces that the Folio calls Shakespeare's "Comedies, Histories, & Tragedies" came to be produced, reproduced, consumed, revised, and transmitted to future generations. They highlight elements that Shakespeare shared with his contemporaries, and they insistently remind us that we are encountering scripts written primarily for the stage and not for the study. They make us more attentive to such matters as business cycles, plague rolls, the cost of costumes, government censorship, and urban topography and less concerned with the elusive and enigmatic details of the poet's biography—his supposed youthful escapades and erotic yearnings and psychological crises.

All well and good. But the fact remains that in 1623, seven years after the playwright's death, Heminges and Condell thought they could sell copies of their expensive collection of Shakespeare's plays—"What euer you do," they urge their readers, "buy"—by insisting that their texts were "as he conceiued them." This means that potential readers in the early seventeenth century were already interested in Shakespeare's "conceits"—his "wit," his imagination, and his creative power—and were willing to assign a high value to the products of his particular, identifiable skill, one distinguishable from that of his company and of his rival playwrights. After all, Jonson's tribute praises Shakespeare not as the playwright of the incomparable King's Men but as the equal of Aeschylus, Sophocles, and Euripides. And if we now see Shakespeare's dramaturgy in the context of his contemporaries and of a collective artistic practice, readers continue to have little difficulty recognizing that most of the plays attached to his name tower over those of his rivals.

From Foul to Fair: The Making of the Printed Play

What exactly is a printed play by Shakespeare? Is it like a novel or a poem? Is it like the libretto or the score of an opera? Is it the trace of an absent event? Is it the blueprint of an imaginary structure that will never be completed? Is it a record of what transpired in the mind of a man long dead? We might say cautiously that it is a mechanically reproduced version of what Shakespeare wrote, but unfortunately, with the possible (and disputed) exception of a small fragment from a collaboratively written play called *Sir Thomas More*, virtually nothing Shakespeare actually wrote in his own hand survives. We might propose that it is a printed version of the script that an Elizabethan actor would have held in his hands during rehearsals, but here too no such script of a Shakespeare play survives; and besides, Elizabethan actors were evidently not given the whole play to read. To reduce the expense of copying and the risk of unauthorized reproduction, each actor received only his own part, along with the cue lines. (Shakespeare uses this fact to delicious comic effect in *A Midsummer Night's Dream* 3.1.80–88.) Nonetheless, the play certainly existed as a whole, either in the author's original manuscript or in the copy prepared for the government censor or for the company's prompter or stage manager, so we might imagine the text we hold in our hands as a printed copy of one of these manuscripts. But since no contemporary manuscript survives of any of Shakespeare's plays, we cannot verify this hypothesis. And even if we could, we would not have resolved the question of the precise relation of the printed text either to the playwright's imagination or to the theatrical performance by the company to which he belonged.

All of Shakespeare's plays must have begun their textual careers in the form of "foul papers," drafts presumably covered with revisions, crossings-out, and general "blotting." To be sure, Heminges and Condell remark that so great was the playwright's facility that they "have scarce received from him a blot in his papers." This was, however, a routine and conventional compliment in the period. The same claim, made for the playwright John Fletcher in an edition published in 1647, is clearly contradicted by the survival of Fletcher's far-from-unblotted manuscripts. It is safe to assume that, as Shakespeare was human, his manuscripts contained their share of second and third thoughts scribbled in the margins and between the lines. Once complete, this authorial draft would usually have to be written out again, either by the playwright or by a professional scribe employed by the theater company, as "fair copy."

In the hands of the theater company, the fair copy (or sometimes, it seems, the foul papers themselves) would be annotated and transformed into "the book of the play" or the "playbook" (what we would now call a "promptbook"). Shakespeare's authorial draft presumably contained a certain number of stage directions, though these may have been sketchy and inconsistent. The promptbook clarified these and added others, noted theatrical properties and sound effects, and on occasion cut the full text to meet the necessities of performance. The promptbook was presented to the Master of the Revels for licensing, and it incorporated any changes upon which the master insisted. As the editors of the Oxford Shakespeare put it, the difference between foul papers and promptbook is the difference between "the text in an as yet individual, private form" and "a socialized text."

But the fact remains that for Shakespeare's plays, we have neither foul papers nor fair copies nor promptbooks. We have only the earliest printed editions of these texts in numerous individual quartos and in the First Folio. (Quartos are so called because each sheet of paper was folded twice, making four leaves or eight pages front and back; folio sheets were folded once, making two leaves or four pages front and back.) From clues embedded in these "substantive" texts—substantive because (with the exception of *The Two Noble Kinsmen*) they date from Shakespeare's own lifetime or from the collected works edited by his associates using, or claiming to use, his own manuscripts—editors attempt to reconstruct each play's journey from manuscript to print. Different plays took very different journeys.

Of the thirty-six plays included in the First Folio, eighteen had previously appeared in quarto editions, some of these in more than one printing. Generations of editors have distinguished between "good quartos," presumably prepared from the author's own draft or from a scribal transcript of the play (fair copy), and "bad quartos." The latter category, first formulated as such by A. W. Pollard in 1909, includes, by widespread though not universal agreement, the 1594 version of *The First Part of the Contention (2 Henry VI)*, the 1595 *Richard Duke of York (3 Henry VI)*, the 1597 *Richard III*, the 1597 *Romeo and Juliet*, the 1600 *Henry V*, the 1602 *Merry Wives of Windsor*, the 1603 *Hamlet*, and *Pericles* (1609). Some editors also regard the 1591 *Troublesome Reign of King John*, the 1594 *Taming of a Shrew*, and the 1608 *King Lear* as bad quartos, but others have strenuously argued that these are distinct rather than faulty texts, and the whole concept of the bad quarto has come under increasingly critical scrutiny. The criteria for distinguishing between "good" and "bad" texts are imprecise, and the evaluative terms seem to raise as many questions as they answer. Nevertheless, the striking mistakes, omissions, repetitions, and anomalies in a number of the quartos require some explanation beyond the ordinary fallibility of scribes and printers.

The explanation most often proposed for suspect quartos is that they are the products of "memorial reconstruction." The hypothesis, first advanced in 1910 by W. W. Greg, is that a series of features found in what seem to be particularly flawed texts may be traced to the derivation of the copy from the memory of one or more of the actors. Elizabethan actors, Greg observed, often found themselves away from the London theaters, for example on tour in the provinces during plague periods, and may not on those occasions have had access to the promptbooks they would ordinarily have used. In such circumstances, those in the company who remembered a play may have written down or dictated the text, as best they could, perhaps adapting it for provincial performance. Moreover, unscrupulous actors may have sold such texts to enterprising printers eager to turn a quick profit.

Memorially reconstructed texts tend to be much shorter than those prepared from foul papers or fair copy; they frequently paraphrase or garble lines, drop or misplace speeches and whole scenes, and on occasion fill in the gaps with scraps from other plays. In several cases, scholars think they can detect which roles the rogue actors played, since these parts (and the scenes in which they appear) are reproduced with greater accuracy than the rest of the play. Typically, these roles are minor ones, since the leading parts would be played by actors with a greater stake in the overall financial interest of the company and hence less inclination to violate its policy. Thus, for example, editors speculate that the bad quarto of *Hamlet* (Q1) was provided by the actor playing Marcellus (and doubling as Lucianus). What is often impossible to determine is whether particular differences between a bad quarto and a good quarto or Folio text result from the actor's faulty memory or from changes introduced in performance, possibly with the playwright's own consent, or from both. Shakespearean bad quartos ceased to appear after 1609, perhaps as a result of greater scrutiny by the Master of the Revels, who after 1606 was responsible for licensing plays for publication as well as performance.

The syndicate that prepared the Folio had access to the manuscripts of the King's Men. In addition to the previously published editions of eighteen plays, they made use of scribal transcripts (fair copies), promptbooks, and (more rarely) foul papers. The indefatigable labors of generations of bibliographers, antiquaries, and textual scholars have recovered an extraordinary fund of information about the personnel, finances, organizational structure, and material practices of Elizabethan and Jacobean printing houses, including the names and idiosyncrasies of particular compositors who calculated the page length, set the type, and printed the sheets of the Folio. This impressive scholarship has for the most part intensified respect for the seriousness with which the Folio was prepared and printed, and where the Folio is defective, it has provided plausible readings from the quartos or proposed emendations to approximate what Shakespeare is likely to have written. But it has not succeeded, despite all its heroic efforts, in transforming the Folio, or any other text, into an unobstructed, clear window into Shakespeare's mind.

The dream of the master text is a dream of transparency. The words on the page should ideally give the reader unmediated access to the astonishing forge of imaginative power that was the mind of the dramatist. Those words welled up from the genius of the great artist, and if the world were not an imperfect place, they would have been set down exactly as he conceived them and transmitted to each of us as a precious inheritance. Such is the vision—at its core closely related to the preservation of the holy text in the great scriptural religions—that has driven many of the great editors who have for centuries produced successive editions of Shakespeare's works. The vision was not yet fully formed in the First Folio, for Heminges and Condell still felt obliged to apologize to their noble patrons for dedicating to them a collection of mere "trifles." But by the eighteenth century, there were no longer any ritual apologies for Shakespeare; instead, there was a growing recognition not only of the supreme artistic importance of his works but also of the uncertain, conflicting, and in some cases corrupt state of the surviving texts. Every conceivable step, it was thought, must be undertaken to correct mistakes, strip away corruptions, return the texts to their pure and unsullied form, and make this form perfectly accessible to readers.

Paradoxically, this feverishly renewed, demanding, and passionate editorial project has produced the very opposite of the transparency that was the dream of the master text. The careful weighing of alternative readings, the production of a textual apparatus, the writing of notes and glosses, the modernizing and regularizing of spelling and punctuation, the insertion of scene divisions, the complex calculation of the process of textual transmission from foul papers to print, the equally complex calculation of the effects that censorship, government regulation, and, above all, theatrical performance had on the surviving documents all make inescapably apparent the fact that we do not have and never will have any direct, unmediated access to Shakespeare's imagination. Every Shakespeare text, from the first that was published to the most recent, has been edited: it has come into print by means of a tangled social process and inevitably exists at some remove from the author.

Heminges and Condell, who knew the author and had access to at least some of his manuscripts, lament the fact that Shakespeare did not live "to have set forth and overseen his own writings." And even had he done so—or, alternatively, even if a cache of his manuscripts were discovered in a Warwickshire attic tomorrow—all of the editorial problems would not be solved, nor would all of the levels of mediation be swept away. Certainly the entire textual landscape would change. But the written word has strange powers: it seems to hold on to something of the very life of the person who has written it, but it also seems to pry that life loose from the writer, exposing it to vagaries of history and chance quite independent of those to which the writer was personally subject. Moreover, with the passing of centuries, the language itself and the whole frame of reference within which language and symbols are understood have decisively changed. The most learned modern scholar still lives at a huge experiential remove from Shakespeare's world and, even holding a precious copy of the First Folio in hand, cannot escape having to read across a vast chasm of time what is, after all, an edited text. The rest of us cannot so much as indulge in the fantasy of direct access: our eyes inevitably wander to the glosses and the explanatory notes.

The Oxford Shakespeare

The shattering of the dream of the master text is no cause for despair, nor should it lead us to throw our hands up and declare that one text is as good as another. What it does is to encourage the reader to be actively interested in the editorial principles that underlie the particular edition that he or she is using. It is said that the great artist Brueghel once told a nosy connoisseur who had come to his studio, "Keep your nose out of my paintings; the smell of the paint will poison you." In the case of Shakespeare, it is increasingly important to bring one's nose close to the page, as it were, and sniff the ink. More precisely, it is important to understand the rationale for the choices that the editors have made.

The text of the *Norton Shakespeare* is, with very few changes, that published in 1988 by the Oxford University Press. The *Oxford Shakespeare* was the extraordinary achievement of a team of editors, Stanley Wells, Gary Taylor, John Jowett, and William Montgomery, with Wells and Taylor serving as the general editors. The Oxford editors approached their task with a clear understanding that, as we have seen, all previous texts have been mediated by agents other than Shakespeare, but they regard this mediation not as a melancholy obstacle intervening between the reader and the "true" Shakespearean text but rather as a constitutive element of this text. The art of the playwright is thoroughly dependent on the craft of go-betweens.

Shakespeare's plays were not written to be circulated in manuscript or printed form among readers. They were written to be performed by the players and, as the preface to the quarto *Troilus and Cressida* indelicately puts it, "clapper-clawed with the palms of the vulgar." The public was thus never meant to be in a direct relationship with the author but in a "triangular relationship" in which the players gave voice and gesture to the author's words. As we have seen, Shakespeare was the master of the unfinished, the perpetually open. And even if we narrow our gaze and try to find only what Shakespeare himself might have regarded as a textual resting point, a place to stop and go on to another play, we have, the Oxford editors point out, a complex task. For whatever Shakespeare wrote was meant from the start to be supplemented by an invisible "para-text" consisting of words spoken by Shakespeare to the actors and by the actors to each other, concerning emphasis, stage business, tone, pacing, possible cuts, and so forth. To the extent that this para-text was ever written down, it was recorded in the promptbook. Therefore, in contrast to standard editorial practice, the Oxford editors prefer, when there is a choice, copy based on the promptbook to copy based on the author's own draft. They choose the text immersed in history, that is, in the theatrical embodiment for which it was intended by its author, over the text unstained by the messy, collaborative demands of the playhouse. The closest we can get to Shakespeare's "final" version of a play—understanding that for him as for us there is no true "finality" in a theatrical text—is the latest version of that play performed by his company during his professional life, that is, during the time in which he could still oversee and participate in any cuts and revisions.

This choice does not mean that the Oxford editors are turning away from the very idea of Shakespeare as author. On the contrary, Wells and Taylor are deeply committed to establishing a text that comes as close as possible to the plays as Shakespeare wrote them, but they are profoundly attentive to the fact that he wrote them as a member of a company of players, a company in which he was a shareholder and an actor as well as a writer. "Writing" for the theater, at least for Shakespeare, is not simply a matter of setting words to paper and letting the pages drift away; it is a social process as well as individual act. The Oxford editors acknowledge that some aspects of this social process may have been frustrating to Shakespeare: he may, for example, have been forced on occasion to cut lines and even whole scenes to which he was attached, or his fellow players may have insisted that they could not successfully perform what he had written, compelling him to make changes he did not welcome. But compromise and collaboration are part of what it means to be in the theater, and Wells and Taylor return again and again to the recognition that Shakespeare was, supremely, a man of the theater.

Is there a tension between the Oxford editors' preference for the performed, fully socialized text and their continued commitment to recovering the text as Shakespeare himself intended it? Yes. The tension is most visible in their determination to strip away textual changes arising from circumstances, such as government censorship, over which Shakespeare had no control. ("We have, wherever possible," they write, put "profanities back in Shakespeare's mouth.") It can be glimpsed as well in the editors' belief, almost a leap of faith, that there was little revision of Shakespeare's plays in his company's revivals between the time of his death and the publication of the Folio. But the tension is mainly a creative one, for it forces them (and therefore us) to attend to the playwright's unique imaginative power as well as his social and historical entanglements.

The Oxford editors took a radical stance on a second major issue: the question of authorial revision. Previous editors had generally accepted the fact that Shakespeare practiced revision within individual manuscripts, that is, while he was still in the act of writing a particular play, but they generally rejected the notion that he undertook substantial revisions from one version of a play to another (and hence from one manuscript to another). Wells and Taylor point out that six major works *(Hamlet, Othello, 2 Henry IV, King Lear, Richard II,* and *Troilus and Cressida)* survive in two independent substantive sources, both apparently authoritative, with hundreds of significant variant readings. Previous editors have generally sought to deny authority to one edition or another ("faced with two sheep," the Oxford editors observe wryly, "it is all too easy to insist that one *must* be a goat") or have conflated the two versions into a single text in an attempt to reconstruct the ideal, definitive, complete, and perfect version that they imagine Shakespeare must have reached for each of his plays. But if one doubts that Shakespeare ever conceived of his plays as closed, finished entities, if one recalls that he wrote them for the living repertory of the commercial playing company to which he belonged, then the whole concept of the single, authoritative text of each play loses its force. In a startling departure from the editorial tradition, the *Oxford Shakespeare* printed two distinct versions of *King Lear,* quarto and Folio, and the editors glanced longingly at the impractical but alluring possibility of including two texts of *Hamlet, Othello,* and *Troilus.*

The *Oxford Shakespeare* was published in both old-spelling and modern-spelling editions. The former, the first of its kind ever published, raised some reviewers' eyebrows because the project, a critical edition rather than a facsimile, required the modern editors to invent plausible Elizabethan spellings for their emendations and to add stage directions. The modern-spelling edition, which is the basis for Norton's text, is noteworthy for taking the principles of modernization further than they had generally been taken. Gone are such words as "murther," "mushrump," "vild," and "porpentine," which confer on many modern-spelling editions a certain cozy, Olde-English quaintness; Oxford replaces them with "murder," "mushroom," "vile," and "porcupine."

The inclusion of two texts of *King Lear* aroused considerable controversy when the *Oxford Shakespeare* first appeared, though by now the arguments for doing so have received widespread, though not unanimous, scholarly support. Other features remain controversial: "Ancients" Pistol and Iago have been modernized to "Ensigns"; *Henry VIII* has reverted to its performance title *All Is True;* demonic spirits in *Macbeth* sing lyrics written by Thomas Middleton. The inclusion of a poem not usually considered part of Shakespeare's canon, "Shall I die?" provoked an enormous wave of charge and countercharge. The white-hot intensity of the debates triggered by the *Oxford Shakespeare's* editorial choices casts an interesting light on the place of Shakespeare not only in the culture at large but in the psyches of millions of individuals: any alteration, however minor, in a deeply familiar and beloved text, even an alteration based on thoughtful and highly plausible scholarly principles, arouses genuine anxiety. The anxiety in this case was intensified not only by the boldness of certain crucial emendations but also by the fact that the editors' explanations, arguments, and justifications for all their decisions were printed in a separate, massive volume, *William Shakespeare: A Textual Companion*. This formidable, dense volume is an astonishing monument to the seriousness, scholarly rigor, and immense labor of the Oxford editors. Anyone who is interested in pursuing why Shakespeare's words appear as they do in the current edition, anyone who wishes insight into the editors' detailed reasons for making the thousands of decisions required by a project of this kind, should consult the *Textual Companion*.

The Norton Shakespeare

The primary task that the editors of the *Norton Shakespeare* set themselves was to present the modern-spelling Oxford *Complete Works* in a way that would make the text more accessible to modern readers. The *Oxford Shakespeare* prints little more than the text itself: along with one-page introductions to the individual works, it contains a short general introduction, a list of contemporary allusions to Shakespeare, and a brief glossary. But while it is possible to enjoy a Shakespeare play on stage or screen without any assistance beyond the actors' own art, many readers at least since the eighteenth century have found it far more difficult to understand and to savor the texts without some more substantial commentary.

In addition to writing introductions, textual notes, and brief bibliographies for each of the works, the Norton editors provide glosses and footnotes designed to facilitate comprehension. Such is the staggering richness of Shakespeare's language that it is tempting to gloss everything, but there is a law of diminishing returns: too much explanatory whispering at the margins makes it difficult to enjoy what the reader has come for in the first place. Our general policy is to gloss only those words that cannot be found in an ordinary dictionary or whose meanings have altered out of recognition. The glosses attempt to be simple and straightforward, giving multiple meanings for words only when the meanings are essential for making sense of the passages in which they appear. We try not to gloss the same word over and over—it becomes distracting to be told three times on a single page that "an" means "if"—but we also assume that the reader does not have a perfect memory, so after an interval we will gloss the same word again.

Marginal glosses generally refer to a single word or a short phrase. The footnotes paraphrase longer units or provide other kinds of information, such as complex plays on words, significant allusions, textual cruxes, historical and cultural contexts. Here too, however, we have tried to check the impulse to annotate so heavily that the reader is distracted from the pleasure of the text, and we have avoided notes that provide interpretation, as distinct from information.

Following each of the works, the Norton editors have provided lists of textual variants. These are variants from the control text only; that is, they do not record all of the variants in all of the substantive texts, nor do they record all of the myriad shifts of meaning that may arise from modernization of spelling and repunctuation. Readers who wish to pursue these interesting, if complex, topics are encouraged to consult the *Textual Companion*, along with the old-spelling *Oxford Shakespeare*, the Norton facsimile of the First Folio, and the quarto facsimiles published by the University of California Press. The *Norton Shakespeare* does provide a convenient list for each play of the different ways the same characters are designated in the speech prefixes in the substantive texts. These variants (for example, Lady Capulet in *Romeo and Juliet* is called, variously, "Lady, "Mother," "Wife," "Old Woman," etc.) often cast an interesting light on the ways a particular character is conceived. Variants as they appear in this edition, as well as their line numbers, are printed in boldface; each is followed by the corresponding reading in the control text, and sometimes the source from which the variant is taken. Further information on readings in substantive texts is given in brackets.

Stage directions pose a complex set of problems for the editors of a one-volume Shakespeare. The printing conventions for the stage directions in sixteenth- and seventeenth-century plays were different from those of our own time. Often all of the entrances for a particular scene are grouped together at the beginning, even though some of the characters clearly do not enter until later; placement in any case seems at times haphazard or simply incorrect. There are moments when the stage directions seem to provide stunning insight into the staging of the plays in Shakespeare's time, other moments when they are absent or misleading. It is difficult to gauge how much the stage directions in the substantive editions reflect Shakespeare's own words or at least decisions. It would seem that he was often relatively careless about them, understanding perhaps that these decisions in any precise sense would be the first to be made and unmade by different productions.

The Oxford editors, like virtually all modern editors, necessarily altered and supplemented the stage directions in their control texts. They decided to mark certain of the stage directions with a special sign to indicate a dubious action or placement, but they did not distinguish between the stage directions that came from the substantive texts and those added in later texts, from the seventeenth century to the present. They referred readers instead to the *Textual Companion*, which provides lists of the exact wording of the stage directions in the substantive texts.

The editors of the *Norton Shakespeare* share a sense of the limitations of the early stage directions and share as well some skepticism about how many of these should be attributed even indirectly to Shakespeare. Hence we do not routinely differentiate between quarto and Folio stage directions; we do so only when we think it is a significant point. But there is, it seems to us, a real interest in knowing which stage directions come from those editions of the plays published up to the 1623 Folio (and including *The Two Noble Kinsmen*, published shortly thereafter) and which were added when the editors were no longer in contact with Shakespeare's presence or his manuscripts. Therefore, we have placed brackets around all stage directions that were added after the First Folio. Unbracketed stage directions, then, all derive from editions up through the Folio.

The *Norton Shakespeare* has made several other significant departures from the Oxford text. The Oxford editors note that when *1 Henry IV* was first performed, probably in 1596, the character we know as Sir John Falstaff was called Sir John Oldcastle. But in the wake of protests from Oldcastle's descendants, one of whom, William Brooke, Seventh Lord Cobham, was Elizabeth I's lord chamberlain, Shakespeare changed the name to "Falstaff" (and probably for similar reasons changed the names of Falstaff's companions, Russell and Harvey, to "Bardolph" and "Peto"). Consistent with their decision not to honor changes that Shakespeare was *compelled* to make by censorship or other forms of pressure, the Oxford editors changed the names back to their initial form. But this decision is a problem for several reasons. It draws perhaps too sharp a distinction between those things that Shakespeare did under social pressure and those he did of his own accord. More seriously, it pulls against the principle of a text that represents the latest performance version of a play during Shakespeare's lifetime: after all, even the earliest quarto title page advertises "the humorous conceits of Sir John Falstaff." And, of course, it asks the reader to ignore completely and radically centuries of response—elaboration, fascination, and love—all focused passionately on Sir John Falstaff. The response is not a modern phenomenon: it began with Shakespeare, who developed the character as Sir John Falstaff in *2 Henry IV* and *The Merry Wives of Windsor*. Norton thus restores the more familiar names.

Another major departure from the Oxford text is Norton's printing of the so-called Additional Passages, especially in *Hamlet*. Consistent with their decision not to conflate quarto and Folio texts, the Oxford editors adhere to their control text for *Hamlet*, the Folio, and print those passages that appear only in the Second Quarto in an appendix at the end of the play. As explained at length in the Textual Note to the play, the Norton editors decided not to follow this course, but instead chose a different way of demarcating the quarto and Folio texts (inserting the quarto passages, indented, in the body of the text), one that makes it easier to see how the quarto passages functioned in a version of the play that Shakespeare also authored.

The *Norton Shakespeare* follows Oxford in printing separate quarto and Folio texts of *King Lear*. But we have departed from Oxford in printing these on facing pages, so that their differences can be readily weighed, and we have added a conflated version of *King*

Lear, so that readers will have the opportunity to assess for themselves the effects of the traditional editorial practice.

Finally, the *Norton Shakespeare* includes, among its appendices, a poem called "A Funeral Elegy," edited by Donald Foster, who has recently made a case for Shakespeare's authorship. An introduction presents some of the arguments for and against this attribution. We should add that there are several other texts that have been with some plausibility attributed at least in part to Shakespeare—among the most interesting, a play entitled *Edward III*—and that more may be found in the years to come. This should surprise no one who has read this General Introduction: with Shakespeare, the boundaries are and must remain forever open.

HISTORIES

HISTORIES

The First Part of the Contention of the Two Famous Houses of York and Lancaster (The Second Part of Henry VI)

When it was first printed in a quarto edition of 1594, the play known in the 1623 Folio as *The Second Part of Henry VI* bore the running title *The First Part of the Contention of the Two Famous Houses of York and Lancaster*. (For a discussion of the relation of these two versions of the play, see the Textual Note.) Unlike the Folio title, which centers attention on the King, Henry VI, the quarto title highlights the power struggles among the English nobility. Historically, the protracted broils depicted in this and the successive play were known as the Wars of the Roses because the House of York, which staked its claim to England's throne through Lionel Duke of Clarence, the third son of Edward III, took a white rose for its emblem, while the House of Lancaster, which claimed the throne through John of Gaunt, fourth son of Edward III, became identified with the red rose. While giving a war the name of a flower might suggest a trivial or symbolic struggle, Shakespeare's plays decisively refute such an idea. *The First Part of the Contention* graphically depicts the brutality let loose when commoners are set against nobles, the nobility is divided against itself, and the King is unable to assert his authority.

The date of the play is uncertain. The Oxford editors believe it was written before *1 Henry VI*, probably in 1591, making it one of Shakespeare's first works for the stage. In this play, he explores a difficult problem: what happens to the commonwealth when the legitimate King is too weak to rule effectively? Though the England of *The First Part of the Contention* is a dynastic monarchy, the hereditary King, Henry VI, crowned when nine months old, has never gained control of his realm. As his assertive French wife, Margaret of Anjou, exclaims in exasperation to the Duke of Suffolk, who had wooed her for Henry:

> I tell thee, Pole, when in the city Tours
> Thou rann'st a-tilt in honour of my love
> And stol'st away the ladies' hearts of France,
> I thought King Henry had resembled thee
> In courage, courtship, and proportion.
> But all his mind is bent to holiness,
> To number Ave-Maries on his beads.
>
> (1.3.54–60)

Margaret thought she would be marrying a chivalric hero, one adept at the arts of love and war; instead, she finds herself wed to an ineffective, pious man who elsewhere openly expresses his desire to live as a private person rather than as his country's King. Partly as a result of Henry's deficiencies, Margaret grows increasingly independent, conducting a love intrigue with Suffolk and eventually assuming the leadership of Henry's own army. Presented as a sexualized figure of gender disorder, Margaret fills the vacuum created by her husband's own weakness. In their relationship, traditional gender hierarchy is stood on its head.

Henry's temperament is disastrous not only for his marriage but also for the kingdom

Henry VI, depicted as a child, carried by the Earl of Warwick.

he is supposed to rule. Lacking a strong monarch to rein them in, Henry's nobles do indeed "contend" with one another, though for the first two acts Henry's weakness is counterbalanced by the strengths of Humphrey Duke of Gloucester, the man who had served since the King's youth as Lord Protector of the realm and who attempts to see that the common people receive justice and that the rivalries among the nobles are kept in check. Episodically structured, the play nonetheless reaches a decisive turning point when the Queen, Suffolk, York, and the Cardinal band together in Act 3 to bring down the good Duke. Once he is gone, no one can protect the King or the kingdom from the ambition of Richard Duke of York, the most powerful of the nobles who would supplant Henry. After York is given an army to fight against the Irish, he opportunistically uses that army to further his own designs on the throne. From Act 3 on, York and his minions dominate the action, countered primarily by the equally strong-willed Margaret. The play charts the rise and fall of many powerful figures. Gloucester's fall in Act 3 is followed in the second half of the play by the deaths of Winchester, Suffolk, Somerset, and other prominent nobles. York, however, does not fall but, like Margaret, moves with unnerving single-mindedness into the power vacuum created by the King's passivity.

This failure of monarchical leadership and the unrestrained personal ambition of many nobles have dire consequences for England. These are felt, in part, through the play's extraordinary emphasis on various forms of violence inflicted upon human bodies. Even as the metaphorical body of the kingdom is being rent apart in the course of the play, the suffering caused by this political cataclysm is registered first at the level of individual bodies: actual bodies that are hungry, frightened, wounded, hacked apart, and humiliated. Consider the pivotal death of Gloucester. In *The First Part of the Contention*, he is strangled onstage in his bed; in the Folio, his death occurs offstage. But in both texts, the corpse is eventually displayed to the audience while Warwick recites a grisly description of the state of the body. In contrast to the paleness of a man who has died peacefully, the good Duke's

> face is black and full of blood;
> His eyeballs further out than when he lived,
> Staring full ghastly like a strangled man;
> His hair upreared; his nostrils stretched with struggling;
> His hands abroad displayed, as one that grasped
> And tugged for life and was by strength subdued.
> Look on the sheets. His hair, you see, is sticking;
> His well-proportioned beard made rough and rugged,
> Like to the summer's corn by tempest lodged.
> It cannot be but he was murdered here.
> The least of all these signs were probable.
>
> (3.2.168–78)

This terrible inventory of the unnatural state of Gloucester's dead body highlights the marks of his futile struggle for life—the outstretched hands, the bulging eyes, the disordered hair and beard. Warwick's point is that these are *not* the signs of a soul weighed down by sin and unprepared for death, as is true of Cardinal Beaufort's death in the next scene; rather, Gloucester's disordered corpse testifies to the unnatural and unjust circumstances in which he died.

Many other bodies suffer indignity, pain, and death in this play. In Act 2, a poor man, Simpcox, tries to trick the King into believing both that he is lame and that he has by a miracle just been delivered from blindness. After Gloucester proves Simpcox's supposed blindness a hoax, he has him beaten until the imposter runs away, revealing his lameness to be a lie as well. In Act 4, Suffolk, captured on his flight to France, is beheaded offstage by his captors. His body is then taken to England, where Queen Margaret, in one of the most macabre scenes in Shakespeare, carries his severed head about the court, lamenting her lover's demise. Later in the same act, the rebels attacking London capture Lord Saye, a supporter of King Henry. After a catalog of his crimes has been enumerated, including the "crime" of literacy, Saye is also beheaded offstage, as is his son-in-law. Their heads are then stuck on poles and carried through the streets, grotesquely "kissing" at every corner. Eventually, Jack Cade, the chief rebel, is himself beheaded and his head carried to the King, after five days of living in the woods without food have rendered him too famished to fight effectively. This partial list of the forms of violence depicted in the play does not, moreover, take account of those slain in battle, such as Somerset, or of the disdain shown by Cade for defeated enemies such as Lord Stafford and his brother, whose corpses he strips of their armor and drags behind his horse toward London.

Some of this violence displays the monarch's sanctioned power to punish unruly or disobedient subjects. In Elizabethan England, traitors' heads were regularly displayed on London Bridge, and public executions were popular spectacles. In *The First Part of the Contention*, perhaps the most spectacular scene of public correction is that involving Eleanor Cobham. A proud and ambitious woman who hopes to see her husband displace Henry as King of England, Cobham dabbles in the forbidden arts of witchcraft and conjuration, soliciting prophecies about the fate of the King and two of his nobles, Suffolk and Somerset. Such prophecies were considered politically dangerous because they caused uncertainty and unrest among the common people and could be used to foment sedition. They had been specifically banned by Henry VIII, Edward VI, and Elizabeth. Like many famous prophecies, those delivered to Eleanor Cobham are ambiguous. For example, "The Duke yet lives that Henry shall depose, / But him outlive, and die a violent death" (1.4.29–30) can mean either that Henry shall depose a duke or that a duke shall depose Henry. Nor is it entirely clear who shall outlive whom and die a violent death. The ambiguity of such statements was exactly what rulers feared, since under the cover of a benign interpretation they could be used to predict and promote rebellion. For engaging in witchcraft and conjuration as well as for circulating such prophecies, Eleanor Cobham is first shamed—she must walk through London carrying a candle and wearing only a sheet, her crimes listed on a piece of paper pinned to her back—and then banished, and her confederates hanged and burned. The King here appears to be using sanctioned violence to punish dangerously seditious subjects.

Yet in much of the play, the state either fails to control violence or else uses it with questionable justice. Even Eleanor's case is more ambiguous than the above account suggests. She did undeniably dabble in witchcraft, yet she was urged on by people in the employ of Suffolk and the Cardinal, who wished through her acts to disgrace her innocent husband and dislodge him from power. Legally, Eleanor's punishment is just, yet it occurs in a context of chicanery and treachery that the King either does not or will not see until Gloucester, the chief prop of royal justice, has been removed. Between the discovery of Eleanor's witchcraft and her public shaming, the play shows the audience another troubling example of a ritual of justice. Earlier Peter Thump, an apprentice, had accused his master, Horner, of saying that the Duke of York—not Henry—was the rightful ruler of England. Thump had no proof but his own word, and Horner had no defense but denial. To resolve the issue, Gloucester, who has already detected Simpcox's hoax, orders a day of combat for the man and master: whoever wins the duel would be assumed to have spoken the truth. Such trials by combat were customary in adjudicating disputes among nobles. But the apprentice is terrified, having no experience with such contests or with the weapons commonly used in them: the sword or lance. As it is dramatized, the trial by combat becomes a parody of justice. Rather than fighting with swords, the two contestants appear with sandbags attached to poles, and Horner is so roaring drunk that he reels. It is under these conditions that the apprentice kills his master, and the King, who has now taken Gloucester's staff of office from him as the result of Eleanor's treason, seems satisfied that justice has prevailed. But the ludicrous nature of the drunken encounter threatens to empty such traditional rituals of their meaning and legitimacy.

With Gloucester's death, the King's fair and effective control of the machinery of justice and of violence is further compromised. Under the pressure of an enraged commons, Henry *does* banish Suffolk for his role in Gloucester's death, but the King cannot begin to contain the escalating stage violence. In the second half of the play, his loss of control is demonstrated by the spectacular rise to power of the lower-class rebel Jack Cade, one of York's minions. As he marches toward London, Cade boasts that the laws of England are to come from his mouth, and he arrogates to himself the right to kill whom he chooses. The murder of Lord Saye, the death of the clerk of Chartham, the desecration of Stafford's body—these are a mere sampling of events in a brutal career, and the play does not shrink from showing what is cruel and arbitrary in Cade's brief reign of terror. Critics often take Shakespeare's representation of Cade as confirming Elizabethan fears about the dangers of popular rule.

Yet interpreting Cade and his actions is a complicated business. Does Shakespeare create this character simply to discredit popular rebellion, or does he use Cade to articulate the legitimate grievances of the common people and employ Cade's brutality as a disquieting mirror of the brutality of the ruling classes? In thinking about these questions, we should remember that Cade is not synonymous with "the commons" in this play. In the opening acts, while he is still in power, Gloucester is presented as a champion of the people and promotes a commonwealth in which the kings and nobles care for the needs of the commoners and are responsive to their petitions. The people, in turn, seem confident that their views will be heard by those in power. For example, in 1.3, a group of three commoners wait with petitions for Gloucester: Peter Thump, who wishes to report his master's treasonous words about the Duke of York; one who says that Cardinal Beaufort's man has unlawfully seized his land, house, and wife from him; and another who protests that the Duke of Suffolk has enclosed the commons of Melford. (Enclosures—fencing in land once shared by many for growing food and grazing cattle—were a main cause of rural protest in the sixteenth and seventeenth centuries.) How these particular commoners behave as political agents registering grievances with those in power is highly revealing. First, the petitioners believe that they can get redress from the Lord Protector of the realm, the figure nearest the King himself. Second, they are using peaceful means to obtain their desires. Third, the entire scene assumes the loyalty of the common people to their King and his Lord Protector. Thump, in particular, is putting himself at personal risk to report an act of treason against Henry. These figures hardly constitute a mob or many-headed monster. Even when they become enraged by Gloucester's murder and demand the banishment of Suffolk, they couch their protest as a desire to protect the King rather than to seize power for themselves.

It is crucial to note, however, that in 1.3 the petitioners are largely thwarted in their appeal for justice because they mistake Suffolk for Gloucester. Suffolk and the Queen are interested in dealing with York's supposed treason only because they can use that accusation to prevent York from becoming Regent of France. They ignore the other petitions, one of which lodges a complaint against Suffolk himself. It is thus the nobles and not the commoners who fail to exercise their political duties responsibly. The King is timid and gullible and, surrounded by selfish nobles like Suffolk, disregards the welfare and the needs of the common people, who are presented in this scene as loyal and orderly actors in a hierarchical commonwealth.

Cade enters the picture only when the one noble—Gloucester—who cares about maintaining this paternal relationship between the commons and the King is about to be killed. At the end of 3.1, York, in soliloquy, reveals his intention to use the army levied against Ireland to further his own political ends; in addition, he will employ the Kentish-man Jack Cade as his stalking-horse in his move to seize the crown. Cade will pretend to be John Mortimer, a claimant to the throne through the Yorkist line, in order to test the waters for York's own bid for power. Cade is thus never an independent agent of the people; rather, he is the tool of an ambitious nobleman who employs him because he is stubborn, strong, and impervious to pain. York reports that in battle against the Irish, Cade

> fought so long till that his thighs with darts
> Were almost like a sharp-quilled porcupine;
> And in the end, being rescued, I have seen
> Him caper upright like a wild Morisco,
> Shaking the bloody darts as he his bells.
>
> (3.1.362–66)

Morris dancers tied bells to their legs, and these shook and jangled as they danced. The powerful image of the wounded Cade dancing depicts a man endowed with enormous spirit and physical strength. It is worth recalling that one of the most famous clowns of the 1590s, Will Kemp, who may have played the part of Cade, was himself a noted acrobat and dancer; in 1599, he left Shakespeare's company and did a celebrated morris dance from London to Norwich. Skilled and strong, Cade and Kemp suggest both what was feared and what was admired about hardhanded men, some of whom were employed in the London theater industry and some of whom would have been in the audience. In fact, the Cade scenes must have been powerfully charged, because out of this rebel's mouth—along with arbitrary brutality and pompous self-aggrandizement—issues a critique of social and economic inequality that, endowed with a long history, also spoke to living issues in the London of the 1590s.

Historically, Cade's rebellion occurred in 1450, but in portraying it, Shakespeare draws on accounts of many instances of popular social protest. For example, he takes from Raphael Holinshed's *Chronicles of England, Scotland, and Ireland* (1587) details from the Peasants' Rebellion of 1381, in which rebels such as Wat Tyler burned London Bridge

Will Kemp doing his morris dance. From Kemp's *Nine Days' Wonder* (1600).

and attacked the Savoy (John of Gaunt's house) and the Inns of Court, both places of privilege that became a focus for lower-class anger. Other popular uprisings occurred in 1517, when apprentices on Ill May Day attacked foreign workers in the City of London; in 1549 (Kett's Rebellion); and in London itself throughout the decade of the 1590s. Between 1581 and 1602, there were numerous outbreaks of disorder in London directed against various forms of economic hardship, some of which stemmed from disruptions and changes in the English cloth trade that disadvantaged English weavers. Protests also occurred against the high price of commodities such as butter and fish and against the granting of monopolies that put the sale of key goods, such as starch, in the hands of a small group. Apprentices were often involved in and blamed for these riots. Many of Cade's followers in *The First Part of the Contention* are artisans: weavers and butchers. Through Cade, their economic grievances find expression, along with the articulation of an alternative model of social and economic organization much more radically utopian than that implied in Gloucester's hierarchical paternalism.

This tradition of popular radicalism, whose roots went back at least to the fourteenth century, stressed that all men had been equally redeemed by Christ's blood and that there was as much nobility in the labor of an honest man as in the fine silks and the educated speech of a gentleman. A riddle common throughout Europe from the fourteenth century on—"When Adam delved and Eve span, who then was the gentleman?"—suggests the egalitarian purposes for which the Bible could be appropriated. The first man and woman, digging in the earth and spinning cloth, knew no distinctions of rank, simply the dignity of labor. Often, popular protest stressed the value of manual labor, as opposed to the idleness of the rich, and claimed the clouted shoe or hobnailed boot of the rural peasant and the leather apron of the urban laborer as valued emblems of their working lives.

The Cade scenes are filled with references to this egalitarian tradition. In 4.2, when the rebels first describe how Cade means to reform the commonwealth, they make clear that in their view working men, and only working men, should be magistrates and rulers. Referring to Scripture, the second rebel says: "Yet it is said 'Labour in thy vocation'; which is as much to say as 'Let the magistrates be labouring men'; and therefore should we be magistrates" (4.2.13–15). By contrast, the present nobility "scorn to go in leather aprons" (4.2.10) and have no respect for handicraftsmen. Part of Cade's success is that he is able to mobilize such artisan anger against the privileges of gentlemen, whether those be conferred by literacy or by inherited wealth. Much of Cade's violence is directed against those who can read and write, like the clerk of Chartham or Lord Saye. Literacy, whether defined as the ability to read or to read and write, was not nearly so widespread as it has since become. These skills were acquired by only a small part of the population, who thereby had certain advantages wherever the reading or writing of documents had importance, such as in courts of law. Cade would not only kill all the lawyers, but he would also punish all those who wrote on parchment, that is, those in control of written documents. He also promises that when he is in charge, bread will be cheap, beer of the highest quality, all material goods enjoyed in common, and all men dressed in a common livery.

It is hardly necessary to point out how often Cade contradicts himself in articulating his vision of a commonwealth of equals and how he undermines the utopian aspirations of the tradition of popular radicalism to which his words repeatedly refer. In his egalitarian commonwealth, Cade, of course, would be King, and from his mouth would come all the laws by which others would live. Women would have no rights in his commonwealth but would be fair game for rape. When a Sergeant complains to Cade that his wife has been ravished by one of Cade's men, Cade authorizes his man to cut out the Sergeant's tongue, cripple him, and then knock out his brains. Cade then invites his followers to enter London, where they will "lustily stand to it" and "take up these commodities following—item, a gown, a kirtle, a petticoat, and a smock" (4.7.134–36). The violence and arbitrary cruelty repeatedly displayed make Cade a frightening figure and one whom even his followers often recognize as a charlatan and a hypocrite.

Yet Cade's personal viciousness does not simply wipe away the power of the social critique to which he intermittently gives voice and which had a history extending far beyond this play. When Cade learns that Lord Saye has his horse covered with an elaborate

The houses of York and Lancaster depicted as two parts of a rose bush conjoined, by the marriage of Henry VII and Elizabeth of York, to form the Tudor dynasty. Title page to Edward Halle's *Union of the Two Noble and Illustre Famelies of Yorke and Lancastre* (1550 ed.).

cloth, he bluntly states a point of view that must have resonated with some in Shakespeare's audience: "Marry, thou ought'st not to let thy horse wear a cloak when honester men than thou go in their hose and doublets" (4.7.41–42). Moreover, Shakespeare gives plenty of evidence in the play that if many commoners feel anger and resentment toward the nobility, many nobility are in their turn full of contempt for the lower classes. Act 4, which is dominated by Cade, opens with the scene in which Suffolk is captured and questioned by the Captain of a ship. Furious that when he reveals himself as the Duke of Suffolk his captors do not free him immediately, Suffolk contemptuously attacks the Captain:

> Obscure and lousy swain, King Henry's blood,
> The honourable blood of Lancaster,
> Must not be shed by such a jady groom.
> (4.1.51–53)

The speech goes on in a similar vein for twelve more lines, making clear the truth of the second rebel's claim that the gentlemen of England do not have much respect for hard-handed men. Nor, after the grisly murder of Gloucester, can it be thought that only the common people have the capacity for lawless violence. In short, the play dramatizes many instances of class-based antagonisms rooted in the unequal distribution of wealth and cultural capital.

This complicated political drama seems unequivocally to confirm only one principle: the absence of a strong and just king leaves the commonwealth at risk, but at risk not solely from its most disenfranchised members. Cade, who offers the most radical critique of social inequality, is personally vilified and discredited within the play, as he probably had to be for the drama to be staged; but it is arguable that the larger context for his grim saturnalia of violence is the unspeakable selfishness of the English nobles. Many of them—York, Suffolk, Winchester—are everything Cade accuses the nobility of being. Moreover, though Cade is killed in this play, civil war does not vanish with his death, because the ambition and selfishness of these English nobles have not been contained. York still lives, and it will take Shakespeare another two plays to trace the destructive legacy of his ambition.

Some critics have suggested that given the venality of many of the nobles and the cruelty and hypocrisy of Cade, the play privileges the point of view of Alexander Iden, the landowning gentleman who kills Cade. Iden is well worth scrutiny. A property holder, a man who has built a brick wall around his garden, Iden also has charitable impulses. He "sends the poor well pleasèd from [his] gate" and at first does not want to fight with Cade, a "poor famished man" (4.9.21,41). Does Iden's garden represent an English Eden? Shakespeare sounds several evocative notes through the creation of this figure. Iden conjures up the virtues of rural England as opposed to the values of the corrupt court or the rampaging urban artisans. And he anticipates the emergence of the bourgeois property holder as the backbone of the nation. But Iden is not the dominant force in the political landscape of the play, nor, despite his seeming independence, are his loyalties in doubt. When he learns who the poor famished man really is, Iden is glad to have killed Cade; and when he delivers the rebel's head to King Henry, he receives a knighthood in return. The independent property holder is certainly the King's man and no friend to those who would level the social order and make property common. How deeply Shakespeare—the man from rural Stratford who eventually became a major property holder in that town—idealized Iden, or replicated his political stance, is a matter for debate.

JEAN E. HOWARD

TEXTUAL NOTE

The play commonly known as *2 Henry VI* existed in two versions in the early modern period. In 1594, a quarto version (Q) entitled *The First Part of the Contention of the Two Famous Houses of York and Lancaster* was published; it was followed in 1600 and 1619 by two other quartos based on the first. In 1623, a version of the play about a third longer than Q was included in the First Folio (F), where it was entitled *The Second Part of Henry VI*. The relationship between these two texts is one of the vexed issues in Shakespearean scholarship. In the 1920s, several scholars proposed that Q had been prepared by several actors who had performed in a London production of the play and had reconstructed as much of the script as they could remember. The stage directions in Q are unusually full, indicating the quarto's probable theatrical origins. It may derive, indirectly, from the promptbook prepared for either a London performance or a provincial tour.

Recently, some scholars have questioned whether memorial reconstruction (actors piecing together scripts from memory) provides an adequate explanation for the differences so often found among variant texts that survive for many early modern plays. In particular, Steven Urkowitz has argued that the 1594 Quarto of this play is not a product of memorial reconstruction but is Shakespeare's early version, which he later revised. Urkowitz maintains that both the 1594 and the 1623 texts were prepared by Shakespeare, though they differ from one another in important ways. He argues, for example, that Queen Margaret is a fiercer and more assertive figure in F than in Q. Urkowitz urges that each version of the play be studied on its own. Other textual editors argue that many people—actors, compositors, censors, scribes—may have had a hand in altering a play as it moved onto the stage or into print. Shakespeare may not himself have been responsible for all the differences we now perceive between quarto and Folio texts; nonetheless, the existing texts are distinct entities and should be examined separately rather than conflated into one amalgamated version.

The Oxford edition of the play adheres to the view, dominant since the 1920s, that the quarto is, indeed, a memorial reconstruction of some version of the Folio text, probably a version that had been abridged and otherwise revised on its way from the authorial "foul papers" on which F is based to the promptbook that lies behind Q. Therefore, while F serves as the primary control text, the Oxford edition, like most others, uses many of Q's stage directions to clarify playhouse practice. More controversially, the Oxford edition also assumes that in preparing the Folio text, the compositors who set type drew on the printed quarto versions in some places, probably because the manuscript serving as the basis of F was occasionally illegible or hard to use. At five points (indicated in the Textual Variants), the Oxford editors use Q rather than F as control text. At other points, they follow the quarto placement of particular events, interpolate material found only in Q, or replace Folio material with quarto material when they believe that the changes represent authorial revisions to the version of the Folio text on which Q was based. The Oxford editors also retain the title used for the 1594 Quarto on the grounds that it is more descriptive of the play's content than the blander *Second Part of Henry VI*, and because it is the title by which the play was probably known during Shakespeare's own lifetime.

The Oxford text differs, then, in many ways from modern texts based more exclusively on F. One striking change occurs at the beginning of 3.2: the Oxford edition follows Q in showing the actual murder of Gloucester onstage; F only shows the murderers running from the scene of the crime. The Oxford text also incorporates some quarto material about the Cade rebellion not found in F. These additions, lines 116–31 and 134–36 of 4.7, report the burning of London Bridge, the rape of a Sergeant's wife by one of Cade's men, and Cade's own boast that he will lead his men in sexual assaults upon the women of the city. Together, they darken further F's depiction of Cade's lawlessness. Another substantive change involves the Oxford editors' choice to print the quarto version of the final fight between York and Clifford (5.3.20–30) rather than the Folio version. The two differ markedly in tone; Q stresses the enmity of York and Clifford, F their mutual respect and chivalric honor. This edition prints both, providing the Folio version as an inset passage, and this juxtaposition affords an excellent opportunity to examine one of the important places where F and Q diverge.

The Oxford text in two places follows Q's ordering of particular incidents. In 1.4, a scene involving conjuration, F has a spirit deliver prophecies concerning the fate of several characters—the King, Suffolk, Somerset. York then breaks in upon the scene, seizes the written transcription of the prophecies, and reads them out a second time. The Oxford editors, however, follow Q: when York breaks into the scene of conjuration, he does *not* read the prophecies aloud, an act that seems theatrically redundant. Rather, they are read aloud by King Henry in the next scene (2.1.177–87), when the conjuring episode is reported to him. Similarly, in Act 5, the Oxford edition follows Q in having the final fight between Richard and Somerset occur as 5.2, right before Clifford's battle with York, rather than placing Somerset's death later as young Clifford is bearing off the body of his dead father. The quarto arrangement thus puts maximum emphasis on York's triumph over old Clifford, King Henry's champion.

The Oxford edition differs from most modern texts in one other interesting way. At the beginning of 4.2 in F, two minor characters are listed as Bevis and John Holland. Most editors assume that these are the names of actual players, George Bevis and John Holland, who at some time acted in the play, rather than of fictional characters, yet they use these names as speech prefixes. In the Oxford text, Bevis and Holland are designated, as in Q, simply as "rebels."

Scene numbers follow most modern editions, except that the Oxford edition makes one continuous scene of what are traditionally Scenes 7 and 8 of Act 4, Cade's attack on London and his encounter with Buckingham and Clifford. Oxford also divides Act 5 into five scenes rather than the usual three. Placing the fight between Richard and Somerset after Scene 1 requires setting that fight off as 5.2. In addition, the Oxford editors believe that the stage is cleared after the encounter in which York kills old Clifford, whose body is carried off by his son. Henry and Margaret's enusing flight from the battlefield is thus set off as a separate scene, 5.4.

SELECTED BIBLIOGRAPHY

Cartelli, Thomas. "Jack Cade in the Garden: Class Consciousness and Class Conflict in 2 *Henry VI." Enclosure Acts: Sexuality, Property, and Culture in Early Modern England.* Ed. Richard Burt and John Michael Archer. Ithaca, N.Y.: Cornell University Press, 1994. 48–64.

Greenblatt, Stephen. "Murdering Peasants: Status, Genre, and the Representation of Rebellion." *Representations,* no. 1 (1983): 1–29.

Helgerson, Richard. "Staging Exclusion." *Forms of Nationhood: The Elizabethan Writing of England.* Chicago: University of Chicago Press, 1992. 195–245.

Hobday, Charles. "Clouted Shoon and Leather Aprons: Shakespeare and the Egalitarian Tradition." *Renaissance and Modern Studies* 23 (1979): 63–78.

Knowles, Ronald. "The Farce of History: Miracle, Combat, and Rebellion in 2 *Henry VI." The Yearbook of English Studies* 21 (1991): 168–86.

Manning, Roger B. "Apprentice Riots in London." *Village Revolts: Social Protest and Popular Disturbances in England, 1509–1640.* Oxford: Clarendon Press, 1988. 187–219.

Patterson, Annabel. "The Peasant's Toe: Popular Culture and Popular Pressure." *Shakespeare and the Popular Voice.* Oxford: Basil Blackwell, 1989. 32–51.

Pugliatti, Paola. " 'More than history can pattern': The Jack Cade Rebellion in Shakespeare's *Henry VI, 2." Journal of Medieval and Renaissance Studies* 22 (1992): 451–78.

Urkowitz, Steven. " 'If I Mistake in These Foundations Which I Build Upon': Peter Alexander's Textual Analysis of *Henry VI Parts 2 and 3." ELR* 18 (1988): 230–56.

Wilson, Richard. " 'A Mingled Yarn': Shakespeare and the Cloth Workers." *Literature and History* 12 (1986): 164–80.

The First Part of the Contention of the Two Famous Houses of York and Lancaster (The Second Part of Henry VI)

Of the King's Party

KING HENRY VI
QUEEN MARGARET
William de la Pole, Marquis, later Duke, of SUFFOLK, the
  Queen's lover
Duke Humphrey of GLOUCESTER, the Lord Protector, the
  King's uncle
Dame Eleanor Cobham, the DUCHESS of Gloucester
CARDINAL BEAUFORT, Bishop of Winchester, Gloucester's uncle
  and the King's great-uncle
Duke of BUCKINGHAM
Duke of SOMERSET
Old Lord CLIFFORD
YOUNG CLIFFORD, his son

Of the Duke of York's Party

Duke of YORK
EDWARD, Earl of March ⎱
Crookback RICHARD   ⎰ his sons
Earl of SALISBURY
Earl of WARWICK, his son

The petitions and the combat

Two or three PETITIONERS
Thomas HORNER, an armourer
PETER Thump, his man
Three NEIGHBOURS, who drink to Horner
Three PRENTICES, who drink to Peter

The conjuration

Sir John HUME   ⎱
John SOUTHWELL   ⎰ priests
Margery Jordan, a WITCH
Roger BOLINGBROKE, a conjurer
ASNATH, a spirit

The false miracle

Simon SIMPCOX
SIMPCOX'S WIFE
The MAYOR of Saint Albans
Aldermen of Saint Albans
A BEADLE of Saint Albans
Townsmen of Saint Albans

Eleanor's penance

Gloucester's SERVANTS
Two SHERIFFS of London
Sir John STANLEY
HERALD

The murder of Gloucester

Two MURDERERS
COMMONS

The murder of Suffolk

CAPTAIN of a ship
MASTER of that ship
The Master's MATE
Walter WHITMORE
Two GENTLEMEN

The Cade Rebellion

Jack CADE, a Kentishman suborned by the Duke of York
Dick the BUTCHER ⎫
Smith the WEAVER │
A Sawyer   ⎬   Cade's followers
JOHN   │
REBELS   ⎭
Emmanuel, the CLERK of Chatham ⎫
Sir Humphrey STAFFORD   │
STAFFORD'S BROTHER   │
Lord SAYE   ⎬ those who die at the rebels' hands
Lord SCALES   │
Matthew Gough   │
A SERGEANT   ⎭
Three or four CITIZENS of London
Alexander IDEN, an esquire of Kent, who kills Cade

Others

VAUX, a messenger
A POST
MESSENGERS
A SOLDIER
Attendants, guards, servants, soldiers, falconers

1.1

Flourish° of trumpets, then hautboys.° Enter, at one   *Fanfare / oboes*
door, KING HENRY *and Humphrey Duke of* GLOUCESTER,
the Duke of SOMERSET, *the Duke of* BUCKINGHAM, CAR-
DINAL BEAUFORT, *and others. Enter, at the other door,*
the Duke of YORK, *and the Marquis of* SUFFOLK, *and*
QUEEN MARGARET, *and the Earl[s] of* SALISBURY *and*
WARWICK[1]
SUFFOLK [*kneeling before* KING HENRY]   As by your high imperial majesty
    I had in charge° at my depart° for France,   *was charged / departure*
    As Procurator° to your excellence,   *deputy*

_____

1.1 Location: The palace, London.
1. This stage direction, like many others, is modeled primarily upon that in Q. Many editors believe Q is based
indirectly on a promptbook and closely reflects playhouse

practice. In F, Salisbury, Warwick, Gloucester, and Beaufort enter with the King, while Somerset and Buckingham
enter with the Queen, Suffolk, and York.

To marry Princess Margaret for your grace,°   *on your behalf*

5 So, in the famous ancient city Tours,

In presence of the Kings of France and Sicil,[2]

The Dukes of Orléans, Calaber,° Bretagne, and Alençon,   *Calabria*

Seven earls, twelve barons, and twenty reverend bishops,

I have performed my task and was espoused,

10 And humbly now upon my bended knee,

In sight of England and her lordly peers,

Deliver up my title in the Queen

To your most gracious hands, that are the substance

Of that great shadow° I did represent—   *image (of royalty)*

15 The happiest° gift that ever marquis[3] gave,   *most fortunate; best*

The fairest queen that ever king received.

KING HENRY   Suffolk, arise. Welcome, Queen Margaret.

I can express no kinder° sign of love   *more natural*

Than this kind° kiss.   *affectionate*

      [*He kisses her*]

                     O Lord that lends me life,

20 Lend me a heart replete with thankfulness!

For thou hast given me in this beauteous face

A world of earthly blessings to my soul,

If sympathy° of love unite our thoughts.   *mutual feeling*

QUEEN MARGARET   Th'excess of love I bear unto your grace

25 Forbids me to be lavish of my tongue

Lest I should speak more than beseems a woman.

Let this suffice: my bliss is in your liking,°   *your affection for me*

And naught can make poor Margaret miserable

Unless the frown of mighty England's King.[4]

29.1   QUEEN MARGARET   *Great King of England, and my gracious lord,*

       The mutual conference° that my mind hath had—   *intimate talk*

       By day, by night; waking, and in my dreams;

       In courtly company, or at my beads°—   *while praying*

29.5   *With you, mine alder liefest° sovereign,*   *entirely most precious*

       Makes me the bolder to salute my king

       With ruder terms, such as my wit affords

       And overjoy of heart doth minister.

30 KING HENRY   Her sight did ravish, but her grace in speech,

Her words yclad° with wisdom's majesty,   *clad*

Makes me from wond'ring° fall to weeping joys,   *admiring*

Such is the fullness of my heart's content.

Lords, with one cheerful voice, welcome my love.

35 LORDS *kneel*[*ing*]   Long live Queen Margaret, England's happiness.

QUEEN MARGARET   We thank you all.

      Flourish. [*They all rise*]

SUFFOLK [*to* GLOUCESTER]   My Lord Protector, so it please your grace,

Here are the articles of contracted peace

Between our sovereign and the French King Charles,

40 For eighteen months concluded by consent.

GLOUCESTER (*reads*)   Imprimis:° it is agreed between the French   *First*

King Charles and William de la Pole, Marquis of Suffolk,

---

2. Sicily. Queen Margaret's father, René, the Duke of Anjou, was Sicily's king in name only.
3. A nobleman ranking below a duke and above an earl. In *1 Henry VI*, Suffolk holds the rank of earl; here he appears as a marquis; later in this scene, Henry will make

him a duke for his service as royal marriage broker.
4. Oxford adopts the 1594 Quarto version of the Queen's initial speech, lines 24–29; the F version, which follows as an indented passage (lines 29.1–29.8), may be the author's original draft.

ambassador for Henry, King of England, that the said Henry
shall espouse the Lady Margaret, daughter unto René, King
45 of Naples, Sicilia, and Jerusalem, and crown her Queen of
England, ere the thirtieth of May next ensuing.
　　Item:° it is further agreed between them that the duchy of　　　　*Likewise*
Anjou and the county of Maine shall be released and delivered
to the King her fa—
　　　　Duke Humphrey [GLOUCESTER] *lets* [*the paper*] *fall*⁵
KING HENRY　Uncle, how now?
50 GLOUCESTER　　　　　Pardon me, gracious lord.
Some sudden qualm° hath struck me at the heart　　　　　　　*illness; fear*
And dimmed mine eyes that I can read no further.
KING HENRY [*to* CARDINAL BEAUFORT]　Uncle of Winchester, I
　　pray read on.
CARDINAL BEAUFORT [*reads*]　Item: it is further agreed between
55 　them that the duchy of Anjou and the county of Maine shall
　be released and delivered to the King her father, and she sent
　over of° the King of England's own proper° cost and charges,　　*at / personal*
　without dowry.
KING HENRY　They please us well. [*To* SUFFOLK] Lord Marquis,
　　kneel down.
　　　　[SUFFOLK *kneels*]
60 We here create thee first Duke of Suffolk,
And gird thee with the sword.
　　　　[SUFFOLK *rises*]
　　　　　　　　　Cousin⁶ of York,
We here discharge your grace from being regent
I'th' parts° of France till term of eighteen months　　　　　*(English) regions*
Be full° expired. Thanks uncle Winchester,　　　　　　　　　*fully*
65 Gloucester, York, and Buckingham, Somerset,
Salisbury, and Warwick.
We thank you all for this great favour done
In entertainment° to my princely Queen.　　　　　　　　　*welcome*
Come, let us in, and with all speed provide
70 To see her coronation be performed.
　　　　Exeunt KING [HENRY], QUEEN [MARGARET], *and*
　　　　　　Suffolk. GLOUCESTER *stays all the rest*
GLOUCESTER　Brave peers of England, pillars of the state,
To you Duke Humphrey must unload his grief,
Your grief, the common grief of all the land.
What—did my brother Henry° spend his youth,　　　　　　　*Henry V*
75 His valour, coin, and people in the wars?
Did he so often lodge in open field
In winter's cold and summer's parching heat
To conquer France, his true inheritance?⁷
And did my brother Bedford toil his wits
80 To keep by policy° what Henry got?　　　　　　　　　　*political skill*
Have you yourselves, Somerset, Buckingham,
Brave York, Salisbury, and victorious Warwick,
Received deep scars in France and Normandy?
Or hath mine uncle Beaufort and myself,

---

5. In subsequent stage directions, "Humphrey" will often
be silently changed to "Gloucester." As with many directions, this one appears only in Q, not in F.
6. A form of address customarily used by English mon-

archs to nobles.
7. England laid claim to France throughout the fourteenth century, and Henry V won the title "heir of France"
with the Treaty of Troyes in 1420.

85 With all the learnèd Council of the realm,
Studied so long, sat in the Council House
Early and late, debating to and fro,
How France and Frenchmen might be kept in awe,°   *obedience*
And had his highness in his infancy
90 Crownèd in Paris in despite of foes?
And shall these labours and these honours die?
Shall Henry's conquest, Bedford's vigilance,
Your deeds of war, and all our counsel die?
O peers of England, shameful is this league,
95 Fatal this marriage, cancelling your fame,
Blotting your names from books of memory,
Razing the characters° of your renown,   *Erasing the records*
Defacing monuments of conquered France,
Undoing all, as° all had never been!   *as though*
100 CARDINAL BEAUFORT   Nephew, what means this passionate discourse,
This peroration° with such circumstance?[8]   *rhetorical speech*
For France, 'tis ours; and we will keep it still.°   *always*
GLOUCESTER   Ay, uncle, we will keep it if we can—
But now it is impossible we should.
105 Suffolk, the new-made duke that rules the roast,°   *roost*
Hath given the duchy of Anjou and Maine
Unto the poor King René, whose large style°   *exalted title*
Agrees not with the leanness of his purse.
SALISBURY   Now by the death of Him that died for all,[9]
110 These counties were the keys of Normandy—
But wherefore weeps Warwick, my valiant son?
WARWICK   For grief that they are past recovery.
For were there hope to conquer them again
My sword should shed hot blood, mine eyes no tears.
115 Anjou and Maine? Myself did win them both!
Those provinces these arms of mine did conquer—
And are the cities that I got with wounds
Delivered up again with peaceful words?
Mort Dieu![1]
120 YORK   For Suffolk's duke, may he be suffocate,°   *choked (a pun)*
That dims the honour of this warlike isle!
France should have torn and rent my very heart
Before I would have yielded to this league.
I never read but° England's kings have had   *I have always read that*
125 Large sums of gold and dowries with their wives—
And our King Henry gives away his own,
To match with° her that brings no vantages.°   *wed / profits (dowry)*
GLOUCESTER   A proper jest, and never heard before,
That Suffolk should demand a whole fifteenth[2]
130 For costs and charges in transporting her!
She should have stayed in France and starved in France
Before—
CARDINAL BEAUFORT   My lord of Gloucester, now ye grow too hot!
It was the pleasure of my lord the King.
135 GLOUCESTER   My lord of Winchester, I know your mind.
'Tis not my speeches that you do mislike,

8. Such long-winded formality; so many details.   1. God's death (French oath).
9. An oath equivalent to "by Christ's death."   2. A tax of one-fifteenth of the value of personal property.

But 'tis my presence that doth trouble ye.
Rancour will out. Proud prelate, in thy face
I see thy fury. If I longer stay
140   We shall begin our ancient bickerings—
But I'll be gone, and give thee leave to speak.
Lordings,° farewell, and say when I am gone,   *My lords*
I prophesied France will be lost ere long.   *Exit*
CARDINAL BEAUFORT   So, there goes our Protector in a rage.
145   'Tis known to you he is mine enemy;
Nay more, an enemy unto you all,
And no great friend, I fear me, to the King.
Consider, lords, he is the next of blood[3]
And heir apparent to the English crown.
150   Had Henry got an empire by his marriage,
And all the wealthy kingdoms of the west,[4]
There's reason he° should be displeased at it.   *(Gloucester)*
Look to it, lords—let not his smoothing° words   *flattering*
Bewitch your hearts. Be wise and circumspect.
155   What though the common people favour him,
Calling him 'Humphrey, the good Duke of Gloucester',
Clapping their hands and crying with loud voice
'Jesu maintain your royal excellence!'
With 'God preserve the good Duke Humphrey!'
160   I fear me, lords, for all this flattering gloss,°   *fair appearance*
He will be found a dangerous Protector.
BUCKINGHAM   Why should he then protect our sovereign,
He being of age[5] to govern of himself?
Cousin of Somerset, join you with me,
165   And all together, with the Duke of Suffolk,
We'll quickly hoist° Duke Humphrey from his seat.   *remove*
CARDINAL BEAUFORT   This weighty business will not brook° delay—   *permit*
I'll to the Duke of Suffolk presently.°   *Exit*   *immediately*
SOMERSET   Cousin of Buckingham, though Humphrey's pride
170   And greatness of his place be grief to us,
Yet let us watch the haughty Cardinal;
His insolence is more intolerable
Than all the princes in the land beside.
If Gloucester be displaced, he'll be Protector.
175 BUCKINGHAM   Or° thou or I, Somerset, will be Protector,   *Either*
Despite Duke Humphrey or the Cardinal.
                         Exeunt BUCKINGHAM *and* SOMERSET
SALISBURY   Pride went before, ambition follows him.[6]
While these do labour for their own preferment,°   *advancement*
Behoves it us to labour for the realm.
180   I never saw but Humphrey Duke of Gloucester
Did bear him like a noble gentleman.
Oft have I seen the haughty Cardinal,
More like a soldier than a man o'th' church,
As stout° and proud as° he were lord of all,   *arrogant / as if*

---

3. Because Henry VI did not yet have children, the heir to the throne was Gloucester, his father's brother.
4. An anachronistic reference to the European conquest of the Americas.
5. Henry VI being old enough. At the time represented in this scene, the historical king was twenty-four and

Gloucester was no longer Protector. Shakespeare here as elsewhere alters his sources.
6. A variation on the proverb "Pride goes before and shame comes after." Salisbury seems to refer to the Cardinal, who exited first, as "pride" and to Buckingham and Somerset as "ambition."

185   Swear like a ruffian, and demean° himself   *conduct*
             Unlike the ruler of a commonweal.
             Warwick, my son, the comfort of my age,
             Thy deeds, thy plainness,° and thy housekeeping°   *honesty / hospitality*
             Hath won thee greatest favour of the commons,
190   Excepting none but good Duke Humphrey.
             And, brother York,[7] thy acts in Ireland,
             In bringing them to civil discipline,°   *civilized order*
             Thy late exploits done in the heart of France,
             When thou wert Regent for our sovereign,
195   Have made thee feared and honoured of the people.
             The reverence of° mine age and Neville's name[8]   *respect for*
             Is of no little force if I command.
             Join we together for the public good,
             In what we can to bridle° and suppress   *restrain*
200   The pride of Suffolk and the Cardinal
             With Somerset's and Buckingham's ambition;
             And, as we may, cherish° Duke Humphrey's deeds   *encourage*
             While they do tend° the profit of the land.   *promote*
205 WARWICK   So God help Warwick, as he loves the land,
             And common profit of his country!
      YORK   And so says York, [*aside*] for he hath greatest cause.
      SALISBURY   Then let's away, and look unto the main.[9]
      WARWICK   Unto the main? O, father, Maine is lost!
210   That Maine which by main° force Warwick did win,   *overwhelming*
             And would have kept so long as breath did last!
             Main chance, father, you meant—but I meant Maine,
             Which I will win from France or else be slain.
                   Exeunt WARWICK *and* SALISBURY. *Manet*° YORK   *Remains*
      YORK   Anjou and Maine are given to the French,
             Paris is lost, the state of Normandy
215   Stands on a tickle° point now they are gone;   *an unstable*
             Suffolk concluded on the articles,
             The peers agreed, and Henry was well pleased
             To change two dukedoms for a duke's fair daughter.
             I cannot blame them all—what is't to them?
220   'Tis thine[1] they give away and not their own!
             Pirates may make cheap pennyworths of° their pillage,   *sell at a low price*
             And purchase friends, and give to courtesans,
             Still° revelling like lords till all be gone,   *Continually*
             Whileas the seely° owner of the goods   *While the helpless*
225   Weeps over them, and wrings his hapless° hands,   *unlucky*
             And shakes his head, and, trembling, stands aloof,
             While all is shared and all is borne away,
             Ready to starve and dare not touch his own.
             So York must sit and fret and bite his tongue,
230   While his own lands are bargained for and sold.
             Methinks the realms of England, France, and Ireland
             Bear that proportion° to my flesh and blood   *relation*
             As did the fatal brand Althaea burnt

---

7. York was actually Salisbury's brother-in-law, having married Salisbury's sister Cicely.
8. Neville was the family name of the Earl of Salisbury and of his son, Warwick.
9. And consider the principal matter at stake. A gambling term, with subsequent puns on the several meanings of "main," including wordplay on "Maine," a French province lost in Suffolk's treaty.
1. It is your own (York is addressing himself and referring to his claim to the throne).

Unto the prince's heart of Calydon.[2]
235   Anjou and Maine both given unto the French!
Cold° news for me—for I had hope of France,   *Unwelcome*
Even as I have of fertile England's soil.
A day will come when York shall claim his own,
And therefore I will take the Nevilles' parts,[3]
240   And make a show of love to proud Duke Humphrey,
And, when I spy advantage,° claim the crown,   *opportunity*
For that's the golden mark° I seek to hit.   *target*
Nor shall proud Lancaster[4] usurp my right,
Nor hold the sceptre in his childish fist,
245   Nor wear the diadem upon his head
Whose church-like humours° fits not for a crown.   *pious temperament*
Then, York, be still a while till time do serve.
Watch° thou, and wake when others be asleep,   *Stay awake*
To pry into the secrets of the state—
250   Till Henry, surfeit° in the joys of love   *sickened from excess*
With his new bride and England's dear-bought queen,
And Humphrey with the peers be fall'n at jars.°   *into contention*
Then will I raise aloft the milk-white rose,[5]
With whose sweet smell the air shall be perfumed,
255   And in my standard° bear the arms of York,   *military flag*
To grapple with the house of Lancaster;
And force perforce° I'll make him yield the crown,   *by violent coercion*
Whose bookish rule hath pulled fair England down.   *Exit*

1.2

Enter Duke Humphrey [of GLOUCESTER] *and his wife*
Eleanor [the DUCHESS]

DUCHESS   Why droops my lord, like over-ripened corn°   *grain*
Hanging the head at Ceres' plenteous load?[1]
Why doth the great Duke Humphrey knit his brows,
As frowning at the favours of the world?
5   Why are thine eyes fixed to the sullen earth,
Gazing on that which seems to dim thy sight?
What seest thou there? King Henry's diadem,
Enchased° with all the honours of the world?   *Adorned*
If so, gaze on, and grovel on thy face[2]
10   Until thy head be circled with the same.
Put forth thy hand, reach at the glorious gold.
What, is't too short? I'll lengthen it with mine;
And having both together heaved° it up,   *raised*
We'll both together lift our heads to heaven
15   And never more abase our sight so low
As to vouchsafe one glance unto the ground.
GLOUCESTER   O Nell, sweet Nell, if thou dost love thy lord,
Banish the canker° of ambitious thoughts!   *ulcer*
And may that hour when I imagine ill

2. Althaea, mother of Meleager, Prince of Calydon, was told by the Fates that her son would live only as long as a log burning in the fire at his birth. She snatched the log from the flames, but later, when Meleager killed her brothers, Althaea returned the log to the fire and Meleager's heart stopped beating. See Ovid, *Metamorphoses* 8.
3. And therefore will I ally myself with Salisbury and Warwick.

4. Henry VI was also Duke of Lancaster.
5. The emblem of the Yorkists; the red rose was the Lancastrian emblem.
1.2 Location: The Duke of Gloucester's house, London.
1. At the rich harvest of Ceres (the Roman goddess of agriculture and the harvest).
2. Crawl on the ground (perhaps to seek supernatural aid).

20   Against my king and nephew, virtuous Henry,
    Be my last breathing in this mortal world!
    My troublous dream this night° doth make me sad.   *this past night*
    DUCHESS   What dreamed my lord? Tell me and I'll requite it
    With sweet rehearsal° of my morning's dream.[3]   *recital*
25   GLOUCESTER   Methought this staff, mine office-badge° in court,   *symbol of my position*
    Was broke in twain—by whom I have forgot,
    But, as I think, it was by th' Cardinal—
    And on the pieces of the broken wand
    Were placed the heads of Edmund, Duke of Somerset,
30   And William de la Pole, first Duke of Suffolk.
    This was my dream—what it doth bode, God knows.
    DUCHESS   Tut, this was nothing but an argument°   *a proof*
    That he that breaks a stick of Gloucester's grove
    Shall lose his head for his presumption.
35   But list° to me, my Humphrey, my sweet duke: *listen*
    Methought I sat in seat of majesty
    In the cathedral church of Westminster,
    And in that chair° where kings and queens are crowned,   *throne*
    Where Henry and Dame Margaret kneeled to me,
40   And on my head did set the diadem.
    GLOUCESTER   Nay, Eleanor, then must I chide outright.
    Presumptuous dame! Ill-nurtured° Eleanor!   *Ill-bred*
    Art thou not second woman in the realm,
    And the Protector's wife beloved of him?
45   Hast thou not worldly pleasure at command
    Above the reach or compass of thy thought?
    And wilt thou still be hammering° treachery   *devising*
    To tumble down thy husband and thyself
    From top of honour to disgrace's feet?
50   Away from me, and let me hear no more!
    DUCHESS   What, what, my lord? Are you so choleric°   *hot tempered*
    With Eleanor for telling but her dream?
    Next time I'll keep my dreams unto myself
    And not be checked.°   *rebuked*
55   GLOUCESTER   Nay, be not angry; I am pleased again.
          Enter a MESSENGER
    MESSENGER   My Lord Protector, 'tis his highness' pleasure
    You do prepare to ride unto Saint Albans,
    Whereas° the King and Queen do mean to hawk.   *Where*
    GLOUCESTER   I go. Come, Nell, thou wilt ride with us?
60   DUCHESS   Yes, my good lord, I'll follow presently.°   *immediately*
          Exeunt GLOUCESTER [*and the* MESSENGER]
    Follow I must; I cannot go before
    While Gloucester bears this base° and humble mind.   *servile*
    Were I a man, a duke, and next of blood,
    I would remove these tedious stumbling blocks
65   And smooth my way upon their headless necks.
    And, being a woman, I will not be slack
    To play my part in fortune's pageant.[4]

---

3. Morning dreams were popularly believed to be true.
4. In Roman myth, the goddess Fortune symbolized the element of chance in human life and was often depicted with a rudder (as the pilot of destiny), wings, or a wheel. Here Fortune is imagined as directing a medieval play ("pageant") or leading a ceremonial procession.

[*Calling within*]   Where are you there? Sir John![5] Nay, fear not man.
We are alone. Here's none but thee and I.
    Enter Sir John HUME

70   HUME Jesus preserve your royal majesty.
    DUCHESS What sayst thou? 'Majesty'? I am but 'grace'.[6]
    HUME But by the grace of God and Hume's advice
    Your grace's title shall be multiplied.
    DUCHESS What sayst thou, man? Hast thou as yet conferred
75   With Margery Jordan, the cunning witch[7] of Eye,
    With Roger Bolingbroke, the conjuror?
    And will they undertake to do me good?
    HUME This they have promisèd: to show your highness
    A spirit raised from depth of underground
80   That shall make answer to such questions
    As by your Grace shall be propounded him.
    DUCHESS It is enough. I'll think upon the questions.
    When from Saint Albans we do make return,
    We'll see these things effected to the full.
85   Here, Hume [*giving him money*], take this reward. Make merry, man,
    With thy confederates in this weighty cause.   *Exit*
    HUME Hume must make merry with the Duchess' gold;
    Marry,[8] and shall. But how now, Sir John Hume?
    Seal up your lips, and give no words but mum;
90   The business asketh silent secrecy.
    Dame Eleanor gives gold to bring the witch.
    Gold cannot come amiss were she a devil.
    Yet have I gold flies from another coast[9]—
    I dare not say from the rich Cardinal
95   And from the great and new-made Duke of Suffolk,
    Yet I do find it so; for, to be plain,
    They, knowing Dame Eleanor's aspiring humour,°   *ambitious nature*
    Have hired me to undermine the Duchess,
    And buzz° these conjurations in her brain.   *whisper*
100 They say 'A crafty knave does need no broker',°   *middleman; agent*
    Yet am I Suffolk and the Cardinal's broker.
    Hume, if you take not heed you shall go near
    To call them both a pair of crafty knaves.
    Well, so it stands; and thus, I fear, at last
105 Hume's knavery will be the Duchess' wrack,°   *ruin*
    And her attainture° will be Humphrey's fall.   *conviction*
    Sort° how it will, I shall have gold for all.   *Exit*   *Turn out*

1.3

    Enter PETER, *the armourer's man,*° [*with*] *two or three*   *apprentice*
    [*other*] PETITIONERS
    FIRST PETITIONER My masters, let's stand close. My Lord Protec-
    tor will come this way by and by and then we may deliver our
    supplications in the quill.°   *as a group*
    SECOND PETITIONER Marry, the Lord protect him, for he's a good
5   man, Jesu bless him.

---

5. Priests were commonly addressed as "sir."
6. The appropriate title for a duchess.
7. Cunning women, sometimes prosecuted for witchcraft, were familiar village figures who made a living by
telling fortunes, healing sicknesses, making love potions,
and finding lost objects.
8. By the Virgin Mary (a mild oath).
9. I have gold that comes from another quarter.
1.3 Location: The palace, London.

Enter the Duke of SUFFOLK *and* QUEEN [MARGARET]

FIRST PETITIONER   Here a° comes, methinks, and the Queen   *he*
with him. I'll be the first, sure.¹

[*He goes to meet* SUFFOLK *and the* QUEEN]

SECOND PETITIONER   Come back, fool—this is the Duke of Suffolk and not my Lord Protector.

10 SUFFOLK [*to the* FIRST PETITIONER]   How now, fellow²—wouldst
anything with me?

FIRST PETITIONER   I pray, my lord, pardon me—I took ye for my
Lord Protector.

QUEEN MARGARET [*seeing his supplication, she reads*]   'To my
15 Lord Protector'—are your supplications to his lordship? Let me
see them.

[*She takes First Petitioner's supplication*]

What is thine?

FIRST PETITIONER   Mine is, an't° please your grace, against John   *if it*
Goodman, my lord Cardinal's man, for keeping my house and
20 lands and wife and all from me.

SUFFOLK   Thy wife too? That's some wrong indeed. [*To the* SEC-
OND PETITIONER]   What's yours?

[*He takes the supplication*]

What's here? [*Reads*] 'Against the Duke of Suffolk for enclosing
the commons³ of Melford'! [*To the* SECOND PETITIONER] How
25 now, Sir Knave?

SECOND PETITIONER   Alas, sir, I am but a poor petitioner of our
whole township.

PETER [*offering his petition*]   Against my master, Thomas Horner,
for saying that the Duke of York was rightful heir to the
30 crown

QUEEN MARGARET   What sayst thou? Did the Duke of York say
he was rightful heir to the crown?

PETER   That my master was? No, forsooth, my master said that
he was and that the King was an usurer.

35 QUEEN MARGARET   An usurper thou wouldst say.

PETER   Ay, forsooth—an usurper.

SUFFOLK [*calling within*]   Who is there?

Enter [*a*] *servant*

Take this fellow in and send for his master with a pursuivant°   *an officer*
presently. [*To* PETER] We'll hear more of your matter before
40 the King.   *Exit* [*the servant*] *with* [PETER] *the armourer's man*

QUEEN MARGARET [*to the* PETITIONERS]   And as for you that love
to be protected

Under the wings of our Protector's grace,

Begin your suits anew and sue to him.

[*She*] *tears the supplication*⁴

Away, base cullions!⁵ Suffolk, let them go.

45 ALL PETITIONERS   Come, let's be gone.   *Exeunt* PETITIONERS

QUEEN MARGARET   My lord of Suffolk, say, is this the guise?°   *custom*

---

1. In F, these lines are assigned to Peter, but lines 12–13
suggest they are spoken by the First Petitioner, who here
pushes himself forward to get the attention of the Queen
and Suffolk (whom he believes to be Gloucester).
2. A common form of address to a social inferior.
3. Fencing in for private use land once used by the entire
community. The practice of enclosure, which benefited
landowners while forcing into poverty the lower classes

who had farmed the land, was a chronic source of unrest
in many regions in early modern England.
4. In Q, Suffolk is the one who "tears the papers." This is
one of the places where F gives more initiative to Margaret than does Q.
5. Lowborn rascals. "Cullion" comes from the Italian
word *coglioni*, meaning "testicles."

Is this the fashions in the court of England?
Is this the government of Britain's isle,
And this the royalty of Albion's° king?   *England's*
50   What, shall King Henry be a pupil still
Under the surly Gloucester's governance?
Am I a queen in title and in style,°   *form of address*
And must be made a subject to a duke?
I tell thee, Pole, when in the city Tours
55   Thou rann'st a-tilt[6] in honour of my love
And stol'st away the ladies' hearts of France,
I thought King Henry had resembled thee
In courage, courtship,° and proportion.[7]   *courtly manners*
But all his mind is bent to holiness,
60   To number Ave-Maries on his beads.[8]
His champions are the prophets and apostles,[9]
His weapons holy saws° of sacred writ,   *sayings*
His study is his tilt-yard,° and his loves   *jousting arena*
Are brazen images of canonizèd saints.
65   I would the college of the cardinals
Would choose him Pope, and carry him to Rome,
And set the triple crown° upon his head—   *papal crown*
That were a state fit for his holiness.
SUFFOLK   Madam, be patient—as I was cause
70   Your highness came to England, so will I
In England work your grace's full content.
QUEEN MARGARET   Beside the haught° Protector have we Beaufort   *arrogant*
The imperious churchman, Somerset, Buckingham,
And grumbling York; and not the least of these
75   But can do more in England than the King.
SUFFOLK   And he of these that can do most of all
Cannot do more in England than the Nevilles:
Salisbury and Warwick are no simple peers.
QUEEN MARGARET   Not all these lords do vex me half so much
80   As that proud dame, the Lord Protector's wife.
She sweeps it through the court with troops of ladies
More like an empress than Duke Humphrey's wife.
Strangers in court do take her for the queen.
She bears a duke's revenues on her back,°   *wears costly clothing*
85   And in her heart she scorns our poverty.
Shall I not live to be avenged on her?
Contemptuous° base-born callet° as she is,   *Despicable / whore*
She vaunted 'mongst her minions° t'other day   *followers*
The very train of her worst-wearing° gown   *poorest*
90   Was better worth° than all my father's lands,   *worth more*
Till Suffolk gave two dukedoms° for his daughter. *(Maine and Anjou)*
SUFFOLK   Madam, myself have limed a bush[1] for her,
And placed a choir of such enticing birds
That she will light° to listen to their lays,°   *perch / songs*
95   And never mount to trouble you again.

---

6. You took part in a jousting tournament.
7. Physical grace; physique.
8. Referring to a Roman Catholic devotion in which a string of beads (a rosary) is used to keep track of prayers said in a particular sequence. Among the prayers are "Ave Maria," or "Hail Mary," addressed to the Virgin Mary.

9. A champion stood in for the King at jousts and tournaments. Margaret scornfully suggests that Henry VI makes holy men rather than real warriors his champions.
1. Have set a trap. Elizabethans caught birds by smearing bushes and twigs with a sticky substance known as birdlime.

So let her rest; and, madam, list to me,
For I am bold to counsel you in this:
Although we fancy not the Cardinal,
Yet must we join with him and with the lords
100 Till we have brought Duke Humphrey in disgrace.
As for the Duke of York, this late complaint[2]
Will make but little for his benefit.
So one by one we'll weed them all at last,
And you yourself shall steer the happy helm.

Sound a sennet.° Enter KING HENRY, [*with*] *the Duke of*   trumpet call
YORK *and the Duke of* SOMERSET *on both sides, whisper-*
ing with him. [*Also*] *enter Duke Humphrey* [*of*
GLOUCESTER], *Dame Eleanor the* DUCHESS [*of Glouces-*
ter], *the Duke of* BUCKINGHAM, *the Earl*[*s*] *of* SALISBURY
and WARWICK, *and* CARDINAL [BEAUFORT *Bishop*] *of*
Winchester

105 KING HENRY   For my part, noble lords, I care not which:
Or° Somerset or York, all's one to me.   Either
YORK   If York have ill demeaned° himself in France   conducted
Then let him be denied the regentship.
SOMERSET   If Somerset be unworthy of the place,
110 Let York be regent—I will yield to him.
WARWICK   Whether your grace be worthy, yea or no,
Dispute not that: York is the worthier.
CARDINAL BEAUFORT   Ambitious Warwick, let thy betters speak.
WARWICK   The Cardinal's not my better in the field.°   in battle
115 BUCKINGHAM   All in this presence are thy betters, Warwick.
WARWICK   Warwick may live to be the best of all.
SALISBURY   Peace, son; [*to* BUCKINGHAM] and show some reason,
Buckingham,
Why Somerset should be preferred in this.
QUEEN MARGARET   Because the King, forsooth, will have it so.
120 GLOUCESTER   Madam, the King is old enough himself
To give his censure.° These are no women's matters.   judgment
QUEEN MARGARET   If he be old enough, what needs your grace
To be Protector of his excellence?
GLOUCESTER   Madam, I am Protector of the realm,
125 And at his pleasure will resign my place.
SUFFOLK   Resign it then, and leave thine insolence.
Since thou wert king—as who is king but thou?—
The commonwealth hath daily run to wrack,
The Dauphin[3] hath prevailed beyond the seas,
130 And all the peers and nobles of the realm
Have been as bondmen to thy sovereignty.
CARDINAL BEAUFORT [*to* GLOUCESTER]   The commons hast thou
racked,° the clergy's bags   overtaxed
Are lank and lean with thy extortions.
SOMERSET [*to* GLOUCESTER]   Thy sumptuous buildings and thy
wife's attire
135 Have cost a mass of public treasury.
BUCKINGHAM [*to* GLOUCESTER]   Thy cruelty in execution

---

2. *This recent complaint.* Suffolk means that Peter's claim against his master casts doubt on York's loyalty to the King.
3. "Dauphin" was the title of the oldest son of the French King, but here it refers to the French King himself, Charles VII, and bears witness to the fact that England did not acknowledge Charles's right to the throne.

Upon offenders hath exceeded law
And left thee to the mercy of the law.
QUEEN MARGARET [*to* GLOUCESTER]   Thy sale of offices and
    towns in France—
140   If they were known, as the suspect° is great—   *suspicion*
Would make thee quickly hop without thy head.[4]
                          Exit GLOUCESTER
    QUEEN [MARGARET] *lets fall her fan*[5]
[*To the* DUCHESS] Give me my fan—what, minion,° can ye   *hussy*
    not?
    She gives the DUCHESS *a box on the ear*
I cry you mercy, madam! Was it you?
DUCHESS   Was't I? Yea, I it was, proud Frenchwoman!
145   Could I come near your beauty with my nails,
I'd set my ten commandments° in your face.   *(ten fingers)*
KING HENRY   Sweet aunt, be quiet—'twas against her will.° *unintentional*
DUCHESS   Against her will? Good King, look to't in time!
She'll pamper thee and dandle thee like a baby.
150   Though in this place most master[6] wear no breeches,
She shall not strike Dame Eleanor unrevenged!   *Exit*
BUCKINGHAM [*aside to* CARDINAL BEAUFORT]   Lord Cardinal, I
    will follow Eleanor
And listen after Humphrey how he proceeds.
She's tickled° now, her fury needs no spurs—   *vexed*
155   She'll gallop far enough to her destruction.   *Exit*
    Enter Duke Humphrey [*of* GLOUCESTER]
GLOUCESTER   Now, lords, my choler being overblown°   *dispelled*
With walking once about the quadrangle,
I come to talk of commonwealth affairs.
As for your spiteful false objections,
160   Prove them, and I lie open to the law.
But God in mercy so deal with my soul
As I in duty love my King and country.
But to the matter that we have in hand—
I say, my sovereign, York is meetest° man   *the most suitable*
165   To be your regent in the realm of France.
SUFFOLK   Before we make election,° give me leave   *a choice*
To show some reason of no little force
That York is most unmeet of any man.
YORK   I'll tell thee, Suffolk, why I am unmeet:
170   First, for° I cannot flatter thee in pride;   *because*
Next, if I be appointed for the place,
My lord of Somerset will keep me here
Without discharge,° money, or furniture,°   *payment / equipment*
Till France be won into the Dauphin's hands.
175   Last time I danced attendance on his will[7]
Till Paris was besieged, famished, and lost.
WARWICK   That can I witness, and a fouler fact°   *deed*
Did never traitor in the land commit.
SUFFOLK   Peace, headstrong Warwick.

---

4. Proverbial expression meaning to be beheaded.
5. In Q, the Queen lets fall a glove, not a fan.
6. The one most in control (the Queen).

7. I did as he wished. York refers to events depicted in *1
Henry VI*, specifically to Somerset's failure to supply him
with reinforcements during the wars in France.

180 WARWICK Image of pride, why should I hold my peace?
          Enter [guarded, HORNER *the] armourer and [*PETER*] his*
          man
  SUFFOLK Because here is a man accused of treason —
      Pray God the Duke of York excuse himself!
  YORK Doth anyone accuse York for a traitor?
  KING HENRY What mean'st thou, Suffolk? Tell me, what are these?
185 SUFFOLK Please it your majesty, this is the man
          [*He indicates* PETER]
      That doth accuse his master [*indicating* HORNER] of high treason.
      His words were these: that Richard Duke of York
      Was rightful heir unto the English crown,
      And that your majesty was an usurper.
190 KING HENRY [*to* HORNER] Say, man, were these thy words?
  HORNER An't shall please your majesty, I never said nor thought
      any such matter. God is my witness, I am falsely accused by
      the villain.
  PETER [*raising his hands*] By these ten bones,° my lords, he did   *(ten fingers)*
195   speak them to me in the garret one night as we were scouring
      my lord of York's armour.
  YORK Base dunghill villain and mechanical,°   *manual laborer*
      I'll have thy head for this thy traitor's speech!
      [*To* KING HENRY] I do beseech your royal majesty,
200   Let him have all the rigour of the law.
  HORNER Alas, my lord, hang me if ever I spake the words. My
      accuser is my prentice, and when I did correct him for his fault
      the other day, he did vow upon his knees he would be even
      with me. I have good witness of this, therefore, I beseech your
205   majesty, do not cast away° an honest man for a villain's accusa-   *destroy*
      tion.
  KING HENRY [*to* GLOUCESTER] Uncle, what shall we say to this in law?
  GLOUCESTER This doom,° my lord, if I may judge by case: *judgment*
      Let Somerset be regent o'er the French,
210   Because in York this breeds suspicion.[8]
      [*Indicating* HORNER *and* PETER] And let these have a day
          appointed them
      For single combat in convenient place,
      For he [*indicating* HORNER] hath witness of his servant's malice.
      This is the law, and this Duke Humphrey's doom.
215 KING HENRY Then be it so. [*To* SOMERSET] My lord of Somerset,
      We make you regent o'er the realm of France
      There to defend our rights 'gainst foreign foes.
  SOMERSET I humbly thank your royal majesty.
  HORNER And I accept the combat willingly.
220 PETER [*to* GLOUCESTER] Alas, my lord, I cannot fight; for God's
      sake, pity my case! The spite of man prevaileth against me. O
      Lord, have mercy upon me — I shall never be able to fight a
      blow! O Lord, my heart!
  GLOUCESTER Sirrah,[9] or° you must fight or else be hanged.   *either*
225 KING HENRY Away with them to prison, and the day
      Of combat be the last of the next month.
      Come, Somerset, we'll see thee sent away.   *Flourish. Exeunt*

---

8. Because this matter casts doubt on York's loyalty.   9. A common form of address to a social inferior.

1.4

Enter Margery Jordan, a WITCH; *Sir John* HUME [*and*
John SOUTHWELL, *two priests*]; *and Roger* BOLINGBROKE,
a conjuror[1]

HUME   Come, my masters, the Duchess, I tell you, expects performance of your promises.

BOLINGBROKE   Master Hume, we are therefore° provided. Will   *for that purpose*
her ladyship behold and hear our exorcisms?°   *conjuring of spirits*

5   HUME   Ay, what else? Fear you not her courage.

BOLINGBROKE   I have heard her reported to be a woman of an
invincible spirit. But it shall be convenient, Master Hume, that
you be by her, aloft, while we be busy below. And so, I pray
you, go in God's name and leave us.   *Exit* HUME

10   Mother Jordan, be you prostrate and grovel on the earth.
She lies down upon her face.
Enter Eleanor [*the* DUCHESS *of Gloucester*] *aloft*
John Southwell, read you and let us to our work.

DUCHESS   Well said, my masters, and welcome all. To this gear°   *business*
the sooner the better.
[*Enter* HUME *aloft*]

BOLINGBROKE   Patience, good lady—wizards know their times.

15   Deep night, dark night, the silent of the night,
The time of night when Troy was set on fire,[2]
The time when screech-owls cry and bandogs° howl,   *chained watchdogs*
And spirits walk, and ghosts break up° their graves—   *burst open*
That time best fits the work we have in hand.

20   Madam, sit you, and fear not. Whom we raise
We will make fast within a hallowed verge.°   *magic circle*
Here do the ceremonies belonging,[3] *and make the cir-*
cle. SOUTHWELL *reads 'Coniuro te',*[4] *&c. It thunders and*
lightens terribly, then the spirit [ASNATH][5] *riseth*

ASNATH   *Adsum.*°   *I am here*

WITCH   Asnath,
By the eternal God whose name and power

25   Thou tremblest at, answer that° I shall ask,   *what*
For till thou speak, thou shalt not pass from hence.

ASNATH   Ask what thou wilt, that° I had said and done.   *would that*

BOLINGBROKE [*reads*]   'First, of the King: what shall of him become?'

ASNATH   The Duke yet lives that Henry shall depose,

30   But him outlive, and die a violent death.[6]
[*As the spirit speaks,* SOUTHWELL *writes the answer*]

BOLINGBROKE [*reads*]   'Tell me what fate awaits the Duke of Suffolk.'

ASNATH   By water shall he die, and take his end.

1.4 Location: Gloucester's garden, London.
1. Neither Q nor F names John Southwell as one of the
two priests in this scene, but he is named in dialogue at
line 11. Q has Eleanor enter at the beginning of the
scene; F, as here, has her enter aloft a few lines into the
scene. After Hume's exit at line 9, he must reenter aloft at
some point to attend Eleanor. This entry is not marked,
but having Hume reenter after line 13 leaves enough
time for him to exit the stage at line 9 and make an
entrance above.
2. Virgil's *Aeneid*, Book 2, describes how the Greeks, having entered Troy through treachery, set fire to the ancient
city.
3. The rituals necessary (for conjuring spirits).

4. I conjure you (Latin), the beginning of a spell.
5. An anagram of "Sathan," a variant form of "Satan."
Demons were supposed to be invoked by anagrams.
6. *The . . . death:* like many prophecies, this one is ambiguous. The syntax of the first line can mean that there lives
a duke whom Henry shall depose or who shall depose
Henry. The duke is probably York, who in *Richard Duke*
of York (*3 Henry VI*) forces Henry to entail the crown to
York rather than to Henry's own son, thus symbolically
deposing him. York, however, dies a violent death after
the Battle of Wakefield, and Henry outlives him. But
Henry also dies a violent death, murdered in the Tower
of London by the Duke of York's son, Richard Duke of
Gloucester, who eventually becomes King Richard III.

BOLINGBROKE [*reads*] 'What shall betide the Duke of Somerset?'
ASNATH Let him shun castles. Safer shall he be
35 Upon the sandy plains than where castles mounted° stand. on mountains
Have done—for more I hardly can endure.
BOLINGBROKE Descend to darkness and the burning lake!
False° fiend, avoid!° Treacherous / be gone
Thunder and lightning. [The spirit] sinks down again[7]
38.1 BOLINGBROKE *Then down, I say, unto the damnèd pool*
Where Pluto[8] *in his fiery wagon° sits* chariot
Riding, amidst the singed and parchèd smokes,
The roads of Ditis by the River Styx.[9]
38.5 *There howl and burn for ever in those flames.*
Rise, Jordan, rise and stay° thy charming spells— halt
Zounds,° we are betrayed! By God's wounds (oath)
Enter the Duke[s] of YORK *and* BUCKINGHAM *with their
guard, [among them Sir Humphrey* STAFFORD] *and
break in*
YORK Lay hands upon these traitors and their trash.
[BOLINGBROKE, SOUTHWELL, *and Jordan are taken pris-
oner.* BUCKINGHAM *takes the writings from* BOLINGBROKE
and SOUTHWELL]
40 [*To Jordan*] Beldam,° I think we watched you at an inch.° Witch / closely
[*To the* DUCHESS] What, madam, are you there? The King
and common weal
Are deep indebted for this piece of pains.° your trouble
My lord Protector will, I doubt it not,
See you well guerdoned° for these good deserts. rewarded
45 DUCHESS Not half so bad as thine to England's king,
Injurious° Duke, that threatest where's no cause. Abusive
BUCKINGHAM True, madam, none at all—
[*He raises the writings*]
what call you this?
[*To his men*] Away with them. Let them be clapped up close° imprisoned securely
And kept asunder. [*To the* DUCHESS] You, madam, shall with us.
50 Stafford, take her to thee.
[*Exeunt* STAFFORD *and others to the* DUCHESS
and HUME *above*]
We'll see your trinkets here all forthcoming.[1]
All away!
Exeunt [below, Jordan, SOUTHWELL, *and*
BOLINGBROKE, *guarded, and, above,* HUME *and
the* DUCHESS *guarded by* STAFFORD *and others.*
YORK *and* BUCKINGHAM *remain*]
YORK Lord Buckingham, methinks you watched her well.
A pretty plot,° well chosen to build upon. trick; plot of ground
55 Now pray, my lord, let's see the devil's writ.
[BUCKINGHAM *gives him the writings*]
What have we here?
[*He*] *reads* [*the writings*]
Why, this is just° precisely

---

7. For lines 37–38, Q substitutes the following indented
passage (lines 38.1–38.7); it may record a revision made
in rehearsal to cover the spirit's descent.
8. In classical myth, the god of the infernal regions.

9. The river of Hades over which Charon ferried the
dead.
1. We'll see that your worthless goods (the conjuring par-
aphernalia) are produced as evidence against you.

Aio Aeacidam, Romanos vincere posse.[2]
These oracles are hardily° attained   with difficulty
And hardly understood. Come, come, my lord,
60   The King is now in progress towards Saint Albans;
With him the husband of this lovely lady.
Thither goes these news as fast as horse can carry them—
A sorry breakfast for my lord Protector.
BUCKINGHAM   Your grace shall give me leave, my lord of York,
65   To be the post° in hope of his reward.   messenger
YORK [*returning the writings to* BUCKINGHAM]   At your pleasure,
        my good lord.   *Exit* BUCKINGHAM
[*Calling within*] Who's within there, ho!
        Enter a SERVINGMAN
Invite my lords of Salisbury and Warwick
To sup with me tomorrow night. Away.   *Exeunt* [*severally*]°   separately

2.1

Enter KING [HENRY], QUEEN [MARGARET] *with her hawk
on her fist, Duke Humphrey* [*of* GLOUCESTER], CARDINAL
[BEAUFORT], *and* [*the Duke of*] SUFFOLK, *with falconers
hollering*

QUEEN MARGARET   Believe me, lords, for flying at the brook°   hawking for waterfowl
I saw not better sport these seven years' day;
Yet, by your leave, the wind was very high,
And, ten to one, old Joan had not gone out.[1]
5   KING HENRY [*to* GLOUCESTER]   But what a point,[2] my lord, your falcon made,
And what a pitch° she flew above the rest!   height
To see how God in all his creatures works!
Yea, man and birds are fain° of climbing high.   fond
SUFFOLK   No marvel, an it like° your majesty,   if it please
10   My Lord Protector's hawks do tower so well;
They know their master loves to be aloft,°   to rule over others
And bears his thoughts above his falcon's pitch.[3]
GLOUCESTER   My lord, 'tis but a base ignoble mind
That mounts no higher than a bird can soar.
15   CARDINAL BEAUFORT   I thought as much; he would be above the clouds.
GLOUCESTER   Ay, my lord Cardinal, how think you by that?
Were it not good your grace could fly to heaven?
KING HENRY   The treasury of everlasting joy.
CARDINAL BEAUFORT [*to* GLOUCESTER]   Thy heaven is on earth;
        thine eyes and thoughts
20   Beat on° a crown, the treasure of thy heart,   Think obsessively about
Pernicious Protector, dangerous peer,
That smooth'st it so with° King and common weal!   Who so flatters
GLOUCESTER   What, Cardinal? Is your priesthood grown peremptory?
Tantaene animis caelestibus irae?[4]
25   Churchmen so hot? Good uncle, hide such malice
With some holiness—can you do it?

---

2. I say that you, descendant of Aeacus, the Romans can
conquer. A famously ambiguous response by an oracle to
King Pyrrhus's question about whether he would conquer
Rome.
2.1 Location: St. Albans.
1. The hawk named "Old Joan" would probably not have
flown because of the high wind.

2. High position to which hawks fly to await prey.
3. Alluding to Gloucester's heraldic crest, which consisted of a falcon with a maiden's head. Suffolk is accusing Gloucester of overweening ambition.
4. Quoting Virgil's *Aeneid* I.11, "Can there be such
anger in heavenly minds?"

SUFFOLK   No malice, sir, no more than well becomes°   *is appropriate to*
   So good° a quarrel and so bad a peer.   *just*
GLOUCESTER   As who, my lord?
SUFFOLK   Why, as you, my lord—
30   An't like your lordly Lord's Protectorship.
GLOUCESTER   Why, Suffolk, England knows thine insolence.
QUEEN MARGARET   And thy ambition, Gloucester.
KING HENRY   I prithee peace,
   Good Queen, and whet not on° these furious peers—   *do not encourage*
   For blessèd are the peacemakers on earth.[5]
35 CARDINAL BEAUFORT   Let me be blessèd for the peace I make
   Against this proud Protector with my sword.
      [GLOUCESTER *and* CARDINAL BEAUFORT *speak privately*
      to one another]
GLOUCESTER   Faith, holy uncle, would't were come to that.
CARDINAL BEAUFORT   Marry, when thou dar'st.
GLOUCESTER   Dare? I tell thee, priest,
   Plantagenets[6] could never brook° the dare!   *tolerate*
40 CARDINAL BEAUFORT   I am Plantagenet as well as thou,
   And son to John of Gaunt.
GLOUCESTER   In bastardy.
CARDINAL BEAUFORT   I scorn thy words.
GLOUCESTER   Make up no factious numbers for the matter,[7]
45   In thine own person answer thy abuse.°   *insult; offense*
CARDINAL BEAUFORT   Ay, where thou dar'st not peep; an if° thou dar'st,   *an if = if*
   This evening on the east side of the grove.
KING HENRY   How now, my lords?
CARDINAL BEAUFORT [*aloud*]   Believe me, cousin Gloucester,
   Had not your man put up° the fowl so suddenly,   *raised; startled*
   We had had more sport. [*Aside to* GLOUCESTER] Come with thy
50   two-hand sword.
GLOUCESTER [*aloud*]   True, uncle.
   [*Aside to* CARDINAL BEAUFORT] Are ye advised?° The east side   *agreed*
   of the grove.
CARDINAL BEAUFORT [*aside to* GLOUCESTER]
   I am with you.
KING HENRY   Why, how now, uncle Gloucester?
GLOUCESTER   Talking of hawking, nothing else, my lord.
   [*Aside to the* CARDINAL] Now, by God's mother, priest, I'll shave
55   your crown[8] for this,
   Or all my fence° shall fail.   *skill in fencing*
CARDINAL BEAUFORT [*aside to* GLOUCESTER]
              Medice, teipsum[9]—
   Protector, see to't well; protect yourself.
KING HENRY   The winds grow high; so do your stomachs,° lords.   *tempers*
   How irksome is this music to my heart!

---

5. Quoting Christ's Sermon on the Mount (Matthew 5:9).
6. "Plantagenet" was a name given the kings descended from Geoffrey, Count of Anjou, and Matilda, daughter of Henry I, thought to derive from the Latin words for "a sprig of broom," which Geoffrey wore in his cap. Gloucester, a grandson of John of Gaunt, was a Plantagenet. John of Gaunt was Beaufort's father, but Beaufort's mother, Catherine Swynford, gave birth to him and his brothers before she married Gaunt; this explains why Gloucester calls Beaufort a bastard (line 42). Historically, the Beauforts, though eventually legitimated, were barred from any claim to the throne. The lines referring to Beaufort's bastardy, 38–43, appear only in Q and not in F.
7. Call in no supporters for this quarrel.
8. Alluding to a tonsure, or a shaved circular patch, often seen on the heads of religious men.
9. Physician, (heal) thyself (see Luke 4:23).

60 When such strings jar,[1] what hope of harmony?
    I pray, my lords, let me compound° this strife.   settle
                Enter one crying 'a miracle'
    GLOUCESTER What means this noise?
    Fellow, what miracle dost thou proclaim?
    ONE A miracle, a miracle!
65 SUFFOLK Come to the King—tell him what miracle.
    ONE [*to* KING HENRY] Forsooth, a blind man at Saint Alban's shrine[2]
    Within this half-hour hath received his sight—
    A man that ne'er saw in his life before.
    KING HENRY Now God be praised, that to believing souls
70 Gives light in darkness, comfort in despair!
                Enter the MAYOR *of Saint Albans and his brethren [alder-*
                *men] with music, bearing the man [*SIMPCOX] *between*
                two in a chair. [Enter SIMPCOX'S WIFE *and other towns-*
                men with them]
    CARDINAL BEAUFORT Here comes the townsmen on° procession   in
    To present your highness with the man.
                [*The townsmen kneel*]
    KING HENRY Great is his comfort in this earthly vale,
    Although by sight his sin be multiplied.[3]
    GLOUCESTER [*to the townsmen*] Stand by, my masters, bring him
75   near the King.
    His highness' pleasure is to talk with him.
                [*They rise and bear* SIMPCOX *before the* KING]
    KING HENRY [*to* SIMPCOX] Good fellow, tell us here the circumstance,
    That we for thee may glorify the Lord.
    What, hast thou been long blind and now restored?
    SIMPCOX Born blind, an't please your grace.
80 SIMPCOX'S WIFE   Ay, indeed, was he.
    SUFFOLK What woman is this?
    SIMPCOX'S WIFE His wife, an't like your worship.
    GLOUCESTER Hadst thou been his mother
    Thou couldst have better told.
    KING HENRY [*to* SIMPCOX]   Where wert thou born?
85 SIMPCOX At Berwick,[4] in the north, an't like your grace.
    KING HENRY Poor soul, God's goodness hath been great to thee.
    Let never day nor night unhallowed° pass,   unblessed
    But still° remember what the Lord hath done.   continually
    QUEEN MARGARET [*to* SIMPCOX] Tell me, good fellow, cam'st
        thou here by chance,
90 Or of devotion to this holy shrine?
    SIMPCOX God knows, of pure devotion, being called
    A hundred times and oftener, in my sleep,
    By good Saint Alban, who said, 'Simon, come;
    Come offer° at my shrine and I will help thee.'   make an offering
95 SIMPCOX'S WIFE Most true, forsooth, and many time and oft
    Myself have heard a voice to call him so.
    CARDINAL BEAUFORT [*to* SIMPCOX]
    What, art thou lame?
    SIMPCOX   Ay, God almighty help me.

---

1. When instruments such as these grow discordant.   3. Although his sight will lead him into more temptation.
2. A shrine to the first British martyr, who was beheaded   4. Town on the Scottish border, far from St. Albans.
by the Romans for giving sanctuary to Christians.

SUFFOLK   How cam'st thou so?

SIMPCOX   A° fall off of a tree.   *I*

SIMPCOX'S WIFE [*to* SUFFOLK]
   A plum tree,[5] master.

GLOUCESTER   How long hast thou been blind?

SIMPCOX   O, born so, master.

100 GLOUCESTER   What, and wouldst climb a tree?

SIMPCOX   But that° in all my life, when I was a youth.   *Only that once*

SIMPCOX'S WIFE [*to* GLOUCESTER]   Too true—and bought his
   climbing very dear.

GLOUCESTER [*to* SIMPCOX]   Mass,° thou loved'st plums well that   *By the mass (an oath)*
   wouldst venture so.

SIMPCOX   Alas, good master, my wife desired some damsons,°   *tiny plums; testicles*

105 And made me climb with danger of my life.

GLOUCESTER [*aside*]   A subtle knave, but yet it shall not serve.
   [*To* SIMPCOX] Let me see thine eyes: wink° now, now open them.   *close your eyes*
   In my opinion yet thou seest not well.

SIMPCOX   Yes, master, clear as day, I thank God and Saint Alban.

110 GLOUCESTER   Sayst thou me so? [*Pointing*] What colour is this cloak of?

SIMPCOX   Red, master; red as blood.

GLOUCESTER   Why, that's well said.
   [*Pointing*] And his cloak?

SIMPCOX   Why, that's green.

GLOUCESTER [*pointing*]   And what colour's
   His hose?

SIMPCOX   Yellow, master; yellow as gold.

GLOUCESTER   And what colour's my gown?

SIMPCOX   Black, sir; coal-black, as jet.°   *glossy black stone*

115 KING HENRY   Why, then, thou know'st what colour jet is of?

SUFFOLK   And yet I think jet did he never see.

GLOUCESTER   But cloaks and gowns before this day, a many.°   *a multitude*

SIMPCOX'S WIFE   Never before this day in all his life.

GLOUCESTER   Tell me, sirrah, what's my name?

120 SIMPCOX   Alas, master, I know not.

GLOUCESTER [*pointing*]   What's his name?

SIMPCOX   I know not.

GLOUCESTER [*pointing*]   Nor his?

125 SIMPCOX   No, truly, sir.

GLOUCESTER [*pointing*]   Nor his name?

SIMPCOX   No indeed, master.

GLOUCESTER   What's thine own name?

SIMPCOX   Simon[6] Simpcox, an it please you, master.

GLOUCESTER   Then, Simon, sit thou there the lying'st knave

130 In Christendom. If thou hadst been born blind
   Thou mightst as well have known our names as thus
   To name the several colours we do wear.
   Sight may distinguish colours, but suddenly
   To nominate° them all—it is impossible.   *name*

135 Saint Alban here hath done a miracle.
   Would you not think his cunning° to be great   *skill*
   That could restore this cripple to his legs again?

---

5. Slang for "female thighs and genitals."
6. Q and F both call the character "Sander Simpcox" at this point. At line 93 of F, however, Simpcox refers to himself as "Simon." It has been proposed that "Sander" was the name of an actor who played the part of Simpcox, that his name entered Q at this point, and that this portion of F derives from Q.

SIMPCOX   O master, that you could!

GLOUCESTER [*to the* MAYOR *and aldermen*]   My masters of Saint
      Albans, have you not
140   Beadles[7] in your town, and things called whips?

MAYOR   We have, my lord, an if it please your grace.

GLOUCESTER   Then send for one presently.°   *immediately*

MAYOR [*to a townsman*]   Sirrah, go fetch the beadle hither straight.

                                                             Exit one

GLOUCESTER   Bring me a stool.

      [*A stool is brought*]

      [*To* SIMPCOX]   Now, sirrah, if you mean
145   To save yourself from whipping, leap me° o'er   *for me*
      This stool and run away.

SIMPCOX   Alas, master,
      I am not able even to stand alone.
      You go about to torture me in vain.

                     Enter a BEADLE *with whips*

GLOUCESTER   Well, sirrah, we must have you find your legs.
150   [*To the* BEADLE] Whip him till he leap over that same stool.

BEADLE   I will, my lord.

      [*To* SIMPCOX] Come on, sirrah, off with your doublet quickly.

SIMPCOX   Alas, master, what shall I do? I am not able to stand.

      After the BEADLE *hath hit him once, he leaps over the*
      stool and runs away. [*Some of the townsmen*] *follow and*
      cry, 'A miracle! A miracle!'

KING HENRY   O God, seest thou this and bear'st so long?
155   QUEEN MARGARET   It made me laugh to see the villain run!

GLOUCESTER [*to the* BEADLE]   Follow the knave, and take this drab° away.   *slut*

SIMPCOX'S WIFE   Alas, sir, we did it for pure need.°   *out of utter poverty*

                     [*Exit the* BEADLE *with the* WIFE]

GLOUCESTER [*to the* MAYOR]   Let them be whipped through
      every market-town
      Till they come to Berwick, from whence they came.

            Exeunt [*the*] MAYOR [*and any remaining townsmen*]

160   CARDINAL BEAUFORT   Duke Humphrey has done a miracle today.

SUFFOLK   True: made the lame to leap and fly away.

GLOUCESTER   But you have done more miracles than I—
      You made, in a day, my lord, whole towns to fly.[8]

                     Enter the Duke of BUCKINGHAM

KING HENRY   What tidings with our cousin Buckingham?
165   BUCKINGHAM   Such as my heart doth tremble to unfold.
      A sort of naughty persons, lewdly bent,[9]
      Under the countenance and confederacy°   *protection and complicity*
      Of Lady Eleanor, the Protector's wife,
      The ringleader and head of all this rout,
170   Have practised° dangerously against your state,   *plotted*
      Dealing with witches and with conjurors,
      Whom we have apprehended in the fact,°   *in the very act*
      Raising up wicked spirits from under ground,
      Demanding of King Henry's life and death
175   And other° of your highness' Privy Council.   *other members*
      And here's the answer the devil did make to them.

---

7. Minor parish officials who administered punishment
to vagabonds and those guilty of petty offenses.
8. Referring to the French towns Suffolk gave away when
he arranged Henry's marriage to Margaret.
9. A gang of evil people, wickedly inclined.

[BUCKINGHAM *gives* KING HENRY *the writings*][1]

KING HENRY [*reads*]   'First of the King: what shall of him become?
　　The Duke yet lives that Henry shall depose,
　　But him outlive and die a violent death.'
180　God's will be done in all. Well, to the rest.
　　[*Reads*] 'Tell me what fate awaits the Duke of Suffolk?
　　By water shall he die, and take his end.'

SUFFOLK [*aside*]   By water must the Duke of Suffolk die?
　　It must be so, or else the devil doth lie.

185　KING HENRY [*reads*]   'What shall betide the Duke of Somerset?
　　Let him shun castles. Safer shall he be
　　Upon the sandy plains than where castles mounted stand.'

CARDINAL BEAUFORT [*to* GLOUCESTER]   And so, my Lord Protec-
　　tor, by this means
　　Your lady is forthcoming° yet at London.　　　　　　　　　　*in custody*
190　[*Aside to* GLOUCESTER] This news, I think, hath turned your
　　　　weapon's edge.°　　　　　　　　　　　　　　　　　*blunted your sword*
　　'Tis like, my lord, you will not keep your hour.[2]

GLOUCESTER   Ambitious churchman, leave° to afflict my heart.　　*cease*
　　Sorrow and grief have vanquished all my powers,
　　And, vanquished as I am, I yield to thee
195　Or to the meanest groom.°　　　　　　　　　　　　　*poorest servant*

KING HENRY   O God, what mischiefs work the wicked ones,
　　Heaping confusion on their own heads thereby!

QUEEN MARGARET   Gloucester, see here the tainture° of thy nest,　　*defilement*
　　And look thyself be faultless, thou wert best.

200　GLOUCESTER   Madam, for myself, to heaven I do appeal,
　　How I have loved my King and common weal;
　　And for my wife, I know not how it stands.
　　Sorry I am to hear what I have heard.
　　Noble she is, but if she have forgot
205　Honour and virtue and conversed° with such　　　　　　　　*consulted*
　　As, like to pitch, defile nobility,
　　I banish her my bed and company,[3]
　　And give her as a prey to law and shame
　　That hath dishonoured Gloucester's honest name.

210　KING HENRY   Well, for this night we will repose us here;
　　Tomorrow toward London back again,
　　To look into this business thoroughly,
　　And call these foul offenders to their answers,
　　And poise° the cause in justice' equal scales,　　　　　　　　*weigh*
215　Whose beam stands sure,[4] whose rightful cause prevails.
　　　　　　　　　　　　　　　　　　　　　　　Flourish. Exeunt

2.2

Enter the Duke of YORK *and the Earls of* SALISBURY *and*
WARWICK

YORK   Now, my good lords of Salisbury and Warwick,
　　Our simple supper ended, give me leave

---

1. Neither Q nor F directs Buckingham to hand Henry the prophecies, but he clearly must do so if, as in Q, Henry is to read them out at this point. Lines 177–87 follow the substance of York's reading of the prophecies in F's 1.4, but they have been reconstructed by the Oxford editors to fit their Q placement here. For details, see the Textual Variants.
2. Appointment (for the duel previously arranged be-
tween Gloucester and Cardinal Beaufort).
3. Echoing the language of church law, which permitted marital separation "from bed and board" in cases of adultery, heresy, and cruelty.
4. Whose bar (from which the two scales are suspended) is perfectly balanced and therefore allows accurate measurements.
2.2 The Duke of York's garden, London.

In this close walk° to satisfy myself   *secluded path*
In craving your opinion of my title,
5   Which is infallible, to England's crown.
SALISBURY   My lord, I long to hear it out at full.
WARWICK   Sweet York, begin, and if thy claim be good,
The Nevilles are thy subjects to command.
YORK   Then thus:
10   Edward the Third, my lords, had seven sons:
The first, Edward the Black Prince, Prince of Wales;
The second, William of Hatfield; and the third,
Lionel Duke of Clarence; next to whom
Was John of Gaunt, the Duke of Lancaster;
15   The fifth was Edmund Langley, Duke of York;
The sixth was Thomas of Woodstock, Duke of Gloucester;
William of Windsor was the seventh and last.
Edward the Black Prince died before his father
And left behind him Richard, his only son,
20   Who, after Edward the Third's death, reigned as king
Till Henry Bolingbroke, Duke of Lancaster,
The eldest son and heir of John of Gaunt,
Crowned by the name of Henry the Fourth,
Seized on the realm, deposed the rightful king,
25   Sent his poor queen to France from whence she came,
And him to Pomfret; where, as well you know,
Harmless Richard was murdered traitorously.
WARWICK [*to* SALISBURY]   Father, the Duke of York hath told the truth;
Thus got the house of Lancaster the crown.
30   YORK   Which now they hold by force and not by right;
For Richard, the first son's heir, being dead,
The issue of the next son should have reigned.
SALISBURY   But William of Hatfield died without an heir.
YORK   The third son, Duke of Clarence, from whose line
35   I claim the crown, had issue Phillipe, a daughter,
Who married Edmund Mortimer, Earl of March;[1]
Edmund had issue, Roger, Earl of March;
Roger had issue, Edmund, Anne and Eleanor.
SALISBURY   This Edmund, in the reign of Bolingbroke,
40   As I have read, laid claim unto the crown,
And, but for Owain Glyndŵr, had been king,
Who kept him in captivity till he died.
But to the rest.
YORK   His eldest sister, Anne,
My mother, being heir unto the crown,
45   Married Richard, Earl of Cambridge, who was son
To Edmund Langley, Edward the Third's fifth son.
By her I claim the kingdom: she was heir
To Roger, Earl of March, who was the son
Of Edmund Mortimer, who married Phillipe,
50   Sole daughter unto Lionel, Duke of Clarence.
So if the issue of the elder son

---

1. Like Raphael Holinshed and Edward Hall, whose
chronicles Shakespeare used as sources for this play,
Shakespeare conflates Edmund Mortimer, the fifth Earl
of March, who was named heir to the throne by Richard
II, with his uncle of the same name who was captured by
Glyndŵr, a Welsh lord Shakespeare was later to depict in
1 Henry IV as a rebel against the King. Though Shakespeare here says Glyndŵr kept Mortimer imprisoned until
he died, in *1 Henry IV* he follows the chronicles in having
Mortimer eventually marry Glyndŵr's daughter.

Succeed before the younger, I am king.

WARWICK   What plain proceedings is more plain than this?

Henry doth claim the crown from John of Gaunt,

55 The fourth son; York claims it from the third:

Till Lionel's issue fails, John's should not reign.

It fails not yet, but flourishes in thee

And in thy sons, fair slips of such a stock.[2]

Then, father Salisbury, kneel we together,

60 And in this private plot° be we the first   plot of ground

That shall salute our rightful sovereign

With honour of his birthright to the crown.

SALISBURY and WARWICK [kneeling]   Long live our sovereign

        Richard, England's king!

YORK   We thank you, lords;

        [SALISBURY and WARWICK rise]

                but I am not your king

65 Till I be crowned, and that° my sword be stained   until

With heart-blood of the house of Lancaster—

And that's not suddenly to be performed,

But with advice° and silent secrecy.   deliberation

Do you, as I do, in these dangerous days,

70 Wink at° the Duke of Suffolk's insolence,   Ignore

At Beaufort's pride, at Somerset's ambition,

At Buckingham, and all the crew of them,

Till they have snared the shepherd of the flock,

That virtuous prince, the good Duke Humphrey.

75 'Tis that they seek, and they, in seeking that,

Shall find their deaths, if York can prophesy.

SALISBURY   My lord, break off—we know your mind at full.

WARWICK   My heart assures me that the Earl of Warwick

Shall one day make the Duke of York a king.

80 YORK   And Neville, this I do assure myself—

Richard shall live to make the Earl of Warwick

The greatest man in England but the King.   *Exeunt*

2.3

Sound trumpets. Enter KING HENRY *and state,° with*   persons of rank
guard, to banish the DUCHESS: KING HENRY *and* QUEEN
[MARGARET], *Duke Humphrey* [*of* GLOUCESTER], *the*
Duke of SUFFOLK *and the Duke of* BUCKINGHAM, CARDI-
NAL [BEAUFORT], *and, led with officers, Dame Eleanor*
Cobham [*the* DUCHESS, *Margery Jordan the* WITCH,
John SOUTHWELL *and Sir John* HUME *the two priests,*
and Roger BOLINGBROKE *the conjuror*]; *then enter to*
them the Duke of YORK *and the Earls of* SALISBURY *and*
WARWICK[1]

KING HENRY [*to the* DUCHESS]   Stand forth, Dame Eleanor Cobham,

        Gloucester's wife.

        [*She comes forward*]

In sight of God and us your guilt is great;

Receive the sentence of the law for sins

---

2. Fair cuttings of such a tree.
2.3 Location: A London hall of justice.
1. F's stage direction simply reads "Sound Trumpets.

Enter the King and State, with Guard to banish the
Duchess." Q does not mention Jordan, the two priests, or
Bolingbroke, but F clearly requires them.

Such as by God's book are adjudged to death.[2]
[*To the* WITCH, SOUTHWELL, HUME, *and* BOLINGBROKE] You
5 four, from hence to prison back again;
From thence, unto the place of execution.
The witch in Smithfield[3] shall be burned to ashes,
And you three shall be strangled° on the gallows.   hanged
        [*Exeunt* WITCH, SOUTHWELL, HUME, *and*
                        BOLINGBROKE, *guarded*]
[*To the* DUCHESS] You, madam, for° you are more nobly born,   because
10 Despoilèd° of your honour in your life,   Deprived
Shall, after three days' open penance done,
Live in your country here in banishment
With Sir John Stanley in the Isle of Man.[4]
DUCHESS Welcome is banishment; welcome were my death.
15 GLOUCESTER Eleanor, the law, thou seest, hath judgèd thee;
I cannot justify° whom the law condemns.   excuse
                        Exit [*the* DUCHESS, *guarded*]
Mine eyes are full of tears, my heart of grief.
Ah, Humphrey, this dishonour in thine age
Will bring thy head with sorrow to the grave.
20 [*To* KING HENRY] I beseech your majesty, give me leave to go.
Sorrow would° solace, and mine age would ease.   desires
KING HENRY Stay, Humphrey Duke of Gloucester. Ere thou go,
Give up thy staff.[5] Henry will to himself
Protector be; and God shall be my hope,
25 My stay, my guide, and lantern to my feet.
And go in peace, Humphrey, no less beloved
Than when thou wert Protector to thy King.
QUEEN MARGARET I see no reason why a king of years°   who is of age
Should be to be° protected like a child.   need to be
30 God and King Henry govern England's helm!
Give up your staff, sir, and the King his° realm.   the king's
GLOUCESTER My staff? Here, noble Henry, is my staff.
As willingly do I the same resign
As erst° thy father Henry made it mine;   formerly
35 And even as willing at thy feet I leave it
As others would ambitiously receive it.
        [*He lays the staff at King Henry's feet*]
Farewell, good King. When I am dead and gone,
May honourable peace attend thy throne.   *Exit*
QUEEN MARGARET Why, now is Henry King and Margaret Queen,
40 And Humphrey Duke of Gloucester scarce himself,
That bears so shrewd a maim;[6] two pulls° at once —   pluckings; tugs
His lady banished and a limb° lopped off.   (his staff)
        [*She picks up the staff*]
This staff of honour raught,° there let it stand   seized
Where it best fits to be, in Henry's hand.
        [*She gives the staff to* KING HENRY]
45 SUFFOLK Thus droops this lofty pine and hangs his sprays;°   branches
Thus Eleanor's pride dies in her youngest days.°   in its youth

---

2. *Receive . . . death:* alluding to Exodus 22:18: "Thou
shalt not suffer a witch to live." At times throughout Elizabeth's reign, witch-hunts were conducted and laws against
witchcraft strictly enforced.
3. Famous as the site in London where heretics were

burned.
4. An island off England's northwest coast.
5. Emblem of his office as Protector.
6. Who endures so painful a mutilation.

YORK   Lords, let him go. Please it your majesty,
    This is the day appointed for the combat,
    And ready are the appellant° and defendant—   *challenger*
50   The armourer and his man—to enter the lists,°   *dueling area*
    So please your highness to behold the fight.
QUEEN MARGARET   Ay, good my lord, for purposely therefor
    Left I the court to see this quarrel tried.
KING HENRY   A° God's name, see the lists and all things fit;   *In*
55   Here let them end it, and God defend the right.
YORK   I never saw a fellow worse bestead,°   *prepared*
    Or more afraid to fight, than is the appellant,
    The servant of this armourer, my lords.
> *Enter at one door [HORNER] the armourer and his*
> NEIGHBOURS, *drinking to him so much that he is*
> *drunken; and he enters with a drum[mer] before him*
> *and [carrying] his staff with a sandbag fastened to it.*
> *[Enter] at the other door [PETER] his man, [also] with a*
> *drum[mer] and [a staff with] sandbag, and* PRENTICES
> *drinking to him*
FIRST NEIGHBOUR [*offering drink to* HORNER]   Here, neighbour
60   Horner, I drink to you in a cup of sack,° and fear not, neigh-   *sherry*
    bour, you shall do well enough.
SECOND NEIGHBOUR [*offering drink to* HORNER]   And here, neigh-
    bour, here's a cup of charneco.°   *port*
THIRD NEIGHBOUR [*offering drink to* HORNER]   Here's a pot of
65   good double° beer, neighbour, drink and be merry, and fear   *extra-strong*
    not your man.
HORNER [*accepting the offers of drink*]   Let it come,° i'faith I'll   *Pass it around*
    pledge you all, and a fig[7] for Peter.
FIRST PRENTICE [*offering drink to* PETER]   Here, Peter, I drink to
70   thee, and be not afeard.
SECOND PRENTICE [*offering drink to* PETER]   Here, Peter, here's
    a pint of claret wine for thee.
THIRD PRENTICE [*offering drink to* PETER]   And here's a quart for
    me, and be merry, Peter, and fear not thy master. Fight for
75   credit° of the prentices!   *the honor*
PETER [*refusing the offers of drink*]   I thank you all. Drink and
    pray for me, I pray you, for I think I have taken my last draught
    in this world. Here, Robin, an if° I die, I give thee my apron;   *an if = if*
    and, Will, thou shalt have my hammer; and here, Tom, take
80   all the money that I have. O Lord bless me, I pray God, for I
    am never able to deal with my master, he hath learned so much
    fence° already.   *fencing skill*
SALISBURY   Come, leave your drinking, and fall to blows.
    [*To* PETER] Sirrah, what's thy name?
85 PETER   Peter, forsooth.
SALISBURY   Peter? What more?
PETER   Thump.
SALISBURY   Thump! Then see that thou thump thy master well.
HORNER   Masters, I am come hither, as it were, upon my man's
90   instigation, to prove him a knave and myself an honest man;
    and touching the Duke of York, I will take my death° I never   *stake my life on it*

---

7. Slang for "vulva"; hence, an obscene insult. It was typi-   thrust between two closed fingers or into the mouth.
cally accompanied by a gesture in which the thumb was

meant him any ill, nor the King, nor the Queen; and therefore,
Peter, have at thee° with a downright blow.   *I come at thee*
YORK   Dispatch; this knave's tongue begins to double.°   *to slur his words*
        Sound trumpets [an] alarum to the combatants.[8] *They*
        fight and PETER *hits* [HORNER] *on the head and strikes*
        him down
95   HORNER   Hold, Peter, hold—I confess, I confess treason.
                                                               He dies
     YORK [*to an attendant, pointing to* HORNER]   Take away his weapon.
     [*To* PETER] Fellow, thank God and the good wine in thy mas-
     ter's wame.°   *belly*
     PETER *He kneels down*[9]   O God, have I overcome mine enemy
100   in this presence? O, Peter, thou hast prevailed in right.
     KING HENRY [*to attendants, pointing to* HORNER] Go, take hence
            that traitor from our sight,
        For by his death we do perceive his guilt.
        And God in justice hath revealed to us
        The truth and innocence of this poor fellow,
105   Which he° had thought to have murdered wrongfully.   *Whom he (Horner)*
        [*To* PETER] Come, fellow, follow us for thy reward.
            Sound a flourish. Exeunt [some carrying Horner's body]

2.4

Enter Duke Humphrey [of GLOUCESTER] *and his men in*
    mourning cloaks[1]
GLOUCESTER   Thus sometimes hath the brightest day a cloud;
        And after summer evermore succeeds°   *follows*
        Barren winter, with his wrathful nipping° cold;   *biting*
        So cares and joys abound as seasons fleet.°   *fly by*
5   Sirs, what's o'clock?
     SERVANT   Ten, my lord.
     GLOUCESTER   Ten is the hour that was appointed me
        To watch the coming of my punished Duchess;
        Uneath° may she endure the flinty streets,   *Scarcely*
10   To tread them with her tender-feeling feet.
        Sweet Nell, ill can thy noble mind abrook°   *endure*
        The abject° people gazing on thy face   *lowly born*
        With envious° looks, laughing at thy shame,   *spiteful*
        That erst did follow thy proud chariot wheels
15   When thou didst ride in triumph through the streets.
        But soft, I think she comes; and I'll prepare
        My tear-stained eyes to see her miseries.
            Enter the DUCHESS, *Dame Eleanor Cobham, barefoot,*
            [*with*] *a white sheet about her, written verses pinned on*
            her back,[2] [*and carrying a*] *wax candle in her hand;* [*she*
            is] *accompanied with the* [*two*] SHERIFFS *of London,*
            and Sir John STANLEY, *and officers with bills and hal-*
            berds[3]

8. In F, the line "Sound Trumpets, Alarum to the Combatants" is spoken by York as part of his prior speech.
9. Only Q records, "He [Peter] kneels down," just as Q,
and not F, indicates, "He [Horner] dies" (line 95).
2.4 Location: A London street.
1. Hooded black garments worn to funerals to express

sorrow.
2. Eleanor's offenses were presumably detailed in these
verses.
3. Both bills and halberds were long-handled weapons.
Bills had a curved blade, halberds an axe-like blade with
a spike at the back.

SERVANT [*to* GLOUCESTER]   So please your grace, we'll take her°   *rescue her by force*
    from the sheriffs.
GLOUCESTER   No, stir not for your lives, let her pass by.
20 DUCHESS   Come you, my lord, to see my open shame?
    Now thou dost penance too. Look how they gaze,
    See how the giddy multitude do point
    And nod their heads, and throw their eyes on thee.
    Ah, Gloucester, hide thee from their hateful° looks,   *full of hate*
25   And, in thy closet° pent up, rue my shame,   *private chamber*
    And ban° thine enemies—both mine and thine.   *curse*
GLOUCESTER   Be patient, gentle Nell; forget this grief.
DUCHESS   Ah, Gloucester, teach me to forget myself;
    For whilst I think I am thy married wife,
30   And thou a prince, Protector of this land,
    Methinks I should not thus be led along,
    Mailed up[4] in shame, with papers on my back,
    And followed with a rabble that rejoice
    To see my tears and hear my deep-fet groans.[5]
35   The ruthless flint doth cut my tender feet,
    And when I start,° the envious people laugh,   *flinch*
    And bid me be advisèd how I tread.
    Ah, Humphrey, can I bear this shameful yoke?
    Trowest° thou that e'er I'll look upon the world,   *Believeth*
40   Or count them happy that° enjoys the sun?   *who*
    No, dark shall be my light, and night my day;
    To think upon my pomp shall be my hell.
    Sometime I'll say I am Duke Humphrey's wife,
    And he a prince and ruler of the land;
45   Yet so he ruled, and such a prince he was,
    As he stood by whilst I, his forlorn Duchess,
    Was made a wonder and a pointing stock°   *an object of scorn*
    To every idle rascal° follower.   *lowborn*
    But be thou mild and blush not at my shame,
50   Nor stir at nothing till the axe of death
    Hang over thee, as sure it shortly will.
    For Suffolk, he that can do all in all
    With her° that hateth thee and hates us all,   *(Margaret)*
    And York, and impious Beaufort that false priest,
55   Have all limed bushes[6] to betray thy wings,
    And fly thou how thou canst, they'll tangle thee.
    But fear not thou until thy foot be snared,
    Nor never seek prevention of° thy foes.   *safeguards against*
GLOUCESTER   Ah, Nell, forbear; thou aimest all awry.
60   I must offend before I be attainted,°   *condemned for treason*
    And had I twenty times so many foes,
    And each of them had twenty times their power,
    All these could not procure me any scathe°   *harm*
    So long as I am loyal, true, and crimeless.
65   Wouldst have me rescue thee from this reproach?
    Why, yet thy scandal were not wiped away,

---

4. Enveloped: a term from falconry that describes the condition of a hawk wrapped in cloth so as to prevent its flying away.

5. Moans fetched from deep within me.

6. Coated bushes with birdlime (see note to 1.3.92).

But I in danger for the breach of law.
Thy greatest help is quiet, gentle Nell.
I pray thee sort° thy heart to patience.   adapt
70   These few days' wonder will be quickly worn.[7]
        Enter a HERALD
HERALD   I summon your grace to his majesty's parliament
holden° at Bury[8] the first of this next month.   to be held
GLOUCESTER   And my consent ne'er asked herein before?
This is close° dealing. Well, I will be there.   *Exit* HERALD   secret
75   My Nell, I take my leave; and, Master Sheriff,
Let not her penance exceed the King's commission.
FIRST SHERIFF   An't please your grace, here my commission stays,°   ends
And Sir John Stanley is appointed now
To take her with him to the Isle of Man.
80   GLOUCESTER   Must you, Sir John, protect° my lady here?   keep in custody
STANLEY   So am I given in charge, may't please your grace.
GLOUCESTER   Entreat° her not the worse in that° I pray   Treat / just because
You use her well. The world may laugh again,
And I may live to do you kindness if
85   You do it her. And so, Sir John, farewell.
        [GLOUCESTER *begins to leave*]
DUCHESS   What, gone, my lord, and bid me not farewell?
GLOUCESTER   Witness my tears—I cannot stay to speak.
        Exeunt GLOUCESTER *and his men*
DUCHESS   Art thou gone too? All comfort go with thee,
For none abides with me. My joy is death—
90   Death, at whose name I oft have been afeard,
Because I wished this world's eternity.°   immortality on earth
Stanley, I prithee go and take me hence.
I care not whither, for I beg no favour,
Only convey me where thou art commanded.
95   STANLEY   Why, madam, that is to the Isle of Man,
There to be used according to your state.°   rank; condition
DUCHESS   That's bad enough, for I am but reproach;°   in a state of shame
And shall I then be used reproachfully?
STANLEY   Like to a duchess and Duke Humphrey's lady,
100   According to that state you shall be used.
DUCHESS   Sheriff, farewell, and better than I fare,
Although thou hast been conduct° of my shame.   conductor
FIRST SHERIFF   It is my office; and, madam, pardon me.
DUCHESS   Ay, ay, farewell—thy office is discharged.   [*Exeunt* SHERIFFS]
105   Come, Stanley, shall we go?
STANLEY   Madam, your penance done, throw off this sheet,
And go we to attire you for our journey.
DUCHESS   My shame will not be shifted[9] with my sheet—
No, it will hang upon my richest robes
110   And show itself, attire me how I can.
Go, lead the way, I long to see my prison.   *Exeunt*

7. What was marveled at for a few days will soon be for-   9. Changed, with a pun on "shifted" as meaning "put on
gotten.   new undergarments."
8. Bury St. Edmunds, a town in Suffolk.

3.1

Sound a sennet. Enter to the parliament: enter two her-
alds before, then the Duke[s] of BUCKINGHAM *and* SUF-
FOLK, and then the Duke of YORK *and* CARDINAL
*[*BEAUFORT*], and then* KING *[*HENRY*] and* QUEEN *[*MARGA-
RET*], and then the Earl[s] of* SALISBURY *and* WARWICK
[with attendants]

KING HENRY   I muse° my lord of Gloucester is not come.   *am surprised*
'Tis not his wont° to be the hindmost man,   *habit*
Whate'er occasion keeps him from us now.

QUEEN MARGARET   Can you not see, or will ye not observe,
5 The strangeness of his altered countenance?
With what a majesty he bears himself?
How insolent of late he is become?
How proud, how peremptory, and unlike himself?
We know the time since° he was mild and affable, *We remember when*
10 And if we did but glance a far-off look,
Immediately he was upon his knee,
That all the court admired him for° submission.   *was amazed at his*
But meet him now, and be it in the morn
When everyone will give the time of day,°   *say good morning*
15 He knits his brow, and shows an angry eye,
And passeth by with stiff unbowèd knee,
Disdaining° duty that to us belongs.   *Not paying*
Small curs are not regarded when they grin,° *snarl, show the teeth*
But great men tremble when the lion roars—
20 And Humphrey is no little man in England.
First, note that he is near you in descent,
And, should you fall, he is the next will mount.° *mount the throne*
Meseemeth then it is no policy,°   *not prudent*
Respecting° what a rancorous mind he bears   *Considering*
25 And his advantage following your decease,
That he should come about your royal person,
Or be admitted to your highness' Council.
By flattery hath he won the commons' hearts,
And when he please to make commotion,°   *incite rebellion*
30 'Tis to be feared they all will follow him.
Now 'tis the spring, and weeds are shallow-rooted;
Suffer° them now, and they'll o'ergrow the garden, *Tolerate*
And choke the herbs for want of husbandry.
The reverent care I bear unto my lord
35 Made me collect° these dangers in the Duke.   *deduce*
If it be fond,° call it a woman's fear;   *foolish*
Which fear, if better reasons can supplant,
I will subscribe° and say I wronged the Duke.   *concur*
My lord of Suffolk, Buckingham, and York,
40 Reprove° my allegation if you can,   *Refute*
Or else conclude my words effectual.°   *decisive*

SUFFOLK   Well hath your highness seen into this Duke,
And had I first been put to speak my mind,
I think I should have told your grace's tale.
45 The Duchess by his subornation,°   *instigation*
Upon my life, began her devilish practices;

3.1 Location: A great hall, Bury St. Edmunds.

Or if he were not privy to those faults,°   *crimes*
Yet by reputing° of his high descent,   *boasting*
As next the King he was successive heir,
50   And such high vaunts° of his nobility,   *boasts*
Did instigate the bedlam[1] brainsick Duchess
By wicked means to frame° our sovereign's fall.   *devise*
Smooth runs the water where the brook is deep,
And in his simple show° he harbours treason.   *outward appearance*
55   The fox barks not when he would steal the lamb.
    [*To* KING HENRY] No, no, my sovereign, Gloucester is a man
Unsounded° yet, and full of deep deceit.   *Unfathomed*
CARDINAL BEAUFORT [*to* KING HENRY]   Did he not, contrary to
    form of law,
Devise strange° deaths for small offences done?   *cruel; illegal*
60   YORK [*to* KING HENRY]   And did he not, in his Protectorship,
Levy great sums of money through the realm
For soldiers' pay in France, and never sent it,
By means whereof the towns each day revolted?
BUCKINGHAM [*to* KING HENRY]   Tut, these are petty faults to°   *compared to*
    faults unknown,
65   Which time will bring to light in smooth Duke Humphrey.
KING HENRY   My lords, at once:° the care you have of us   *once and for all*
To mow down thorns that would annoy our foot
Is worthy praise, but shall I speak my conscience?
Our kinsman Gloucester is as innocent
70   From meaning treason to our royal person
As is the sucking lamb or harmless dove.
The Duke is virtuous, mild, and too well given
To dream on evil or to work my downfall.
QUEEN MARGARET   Ah, what's more dangerous than this fond
    affiance?°   *foolish confidence*
75   Seems he a dove? His feathers are but borrowed,
For he's disposèd as the hateful raven.
Is he a lamb? His skin is surely lent him,
For he's inclined as is the ravenous wolf.[2]
Who cannot steal a shape that means deceit?[3]
80   Take heed, my lord, the welfare of us all
Hangs on the cutting short that fraudful° man.   *treacherous*
    Enter the Duke of SOMERSET
SOMERSET [*kneeling before* KING HENRY]   All health unto my gra-
    cious sovereign.
KING HENRY   Welcome, Lord Somerset. What news from France?
SOMERSET   That all your interest in those territories
85   Is utterly bereft you—all is lost.
KING HENRY   Cold news, Lord Somerset; but God's will be done.
    [SOMERSET *rises*]
YORK [*aside*]   Cold news for me, for I had hope of France,
As firmly as I hope for fertile England.
Thus are my blossoms blasted° in the bud,   *withered*
90   And caterpillars eat my leaves away.

---

1. Insane (a shortened form of "Bethlehem Hospital," a notorious asylum maintained by the City of London).
2. *Is he . . . wolf*: alluding to the Sermon on the Mount, which warns of "false prophets, which come to you in sheep's clothing, but inwardly they are ravening wolves" (Matthew 7:15).
3. Who that intends to deceive cannot assume an appropriate disguise?

But I will remedy this gear° ere long,   *business*
Or sell my title for a glorious grave.
  Enter Duke Humphrey [of] GLOUCESTER
GLOUCESTER [*kneeling before* KING HENRY] All happiness unto
  my lord the King.
Pardon, my liege, that I have stayed° so long.   *delayed*

95 SUFFOLK Nay, Gloucester, know that thou art come too soon
Unless thou wert more loyal than thou art.
I do arrest thee of high treason here.
GLOUCESTER [*rising*] Well, Suffolk's Duke, thou shalt not see me blush,
Nor change my countenance for this arrest.

100 A heart unspotted is not easily daunted.
The purest spring is not so free from mud
As I am clear from treason to my sovereign.
Who can accuse me? Wherein am I guilty?
YORK 'Tis thought, my lord, that you took bribes of France,

105 And, being Protector, stayed° the soldiers' pay,   *withheld*
By means whereof his highness hath lost France.
GLOUCESTER Is it but thought so? What are they that think it?
I never robbed the soldiers of their pay,
Nor ever had one penny bribe from France.

110 So help me God, as I have watched the night,°   *stayed up all night*
Ay, night by night, in studying good for England,
That doit° that e'er I wrested from the King, *a coin of little value*
Or any groat° I hoarded to my use,   *a coin worth four pence*
Be brought against me at my trial day!

115 No: many a pound of mine own proper store,°   *personal fortune*
Because I would not tax the needy commons,
Have I dispursèd° to the garrisons,   *paid*
And never asked for restitution.
CARDINAL BEAUFORT It serves you well, my lord, to say so much.

120 GLOUCESTER I say no more than truth, so help me God.
YORK In your Protectorship you did devise
Strange tortures for offenders, never heard of,
That° England was defamed by° tyranny. *So that / was infamous for*
GLOUCESTER Why, 'tis well known that whiles I was Protector

125 Pity was all the fault that was in me,
For I should° melt at an offender's tears,   *would*
And lowly words were ransom for their fault.
Unless it were a bloody murderer,
Or foul felonious thief that fleeced poor passengers,° *travelers*

130 I never gave them condign° punishment.   *well-deserved*
Murder, indeed—that bloody sin—I tortured
Above the felon or what trespass else.[4]
SUFFOLK My lord, these faults are easy,° quickly answerèd, *slight*
But mightier crimes are laid unto your charge

135 Whereof you cannot easily purge yourself.
I do arrest you in his highness' name,
And here commit you to my good lord Cardinal
To keep until your further time of trial.
KING HENRY My lord of Gloucester, 'tis my special hope

140 That you will clear yourself from all suspense.°   *suspicion*
My conscience tells me you are innocent.

---

4. More than any other kind of crime.

GLOUCESTER Ah, gracious lord, these days are dangerous.
Virtue is choked with foul ambition,
And charity chased hence by rancour's hand.
145 Foul subornation⁵ is predominant,
And equity exiled° your highness' land.   *exiled from*
I know their complot° is to have my life,   *plot*
And if my death might make this island happy
And prove the period° of their tyranny,   *mark the end*
150 I would expend it with all willingness.
But mine is made the prologue to their play,
For thousands more that yet suspect no peril
Will not conclude their plotted tragedy.
Beaufort's red sparkling eyes blab his heart's malice,
155 And Suffolk's cloudy brow his stormy hate;
Sharp Buckingham unburdens with his tongue
The envious load that lies upon his heart;
And doggèd° York that reaches at the moon,   *currish; determined*
Whose overweening arm I have plucked back,
160 By false accuse° doth level° at my life.   *accusation / aim*
[*To* QUEEN MARGARET] And you, my sovereign lady, with the rest,
Causeless have laid disgraces on my head,
And with your best endeavour have stirred up
My liefest liege° to be mine enemy.   *dearest sovereign*
165 Ay, all of you have laid your heads together—
Myself had notice of your conventicles°—   *secret meetings*
And all to make away my guiltless life.
I shall not want° false witness to condemn me,   *lack*
Nor store of treasons to augment my guilt.
170 The ancient proverb will be well effected:
'A staff is quickly found to beat a dog'.
CARDINAL BEAUFORT [*to* KING HENRY] My liege, his railing is intolerable.
If those that care to keep your royal person
From treason's secret knife and traitor's rage
175 Be thus upbraided, chid, and rated at,°   *berated, scolded*
And the offender granted scope of speech,
'Twill make them cool in zeal unto your grace.
SUFFOLK [*to* KING HENRY] Hath he not twit° our sovereign lady here   *upbraided*
With ignominious words, though clerkly couched,°   *cleverly phrased*
180 As if she had subornèd some to swear
False allegations to o'erthrow his state?°   *high position*
QUEEN MARGARET But I can give the loser leave to chide.
GLOUCESTER Far truer spoke than meant. I lose indeed;
Beshrew° the winners, for they played me false!   *Curse*
185 And well such losers may have leave to speak.
BUCKINGHAM [*to* KING HENRY] He'll wrest the sense,° and hold   *distort the meaning*
us here all day.
Lord Cardinal, he is your prisoner.
CARDINAL BEAUFORT [*to some of his attendants*] Sirs, take away
the Duke and guard him sure.
GLOUCESTER Ah, thus King Henry throws away his crutch
190 Before his legs be firm to bear his body.
Thus is the shepherd beaten from thy side,
And wolves are gnarling° who shall gnaw thee first.   *snarling*

___

5. Instigating others to commit crimes, including perjury.

Ah, that my fear were false; ah, that it were!
For, good King Henry, thy decay° I fear.   *ruin*

Exit GLOUCESTER, [*guarded by*] *the Cardinal's men*

195 KING HENRY My lords, what to your wisdoms seemeth best
Do or undo, as if ourself were here.
QUEEN MARGARET What, will your highness leave the Parlia ment?
KING HENRY Ay, Margaret, my heart is drowned with grief,
Whose flood begins to flow within mine eyes,
200 My body round engirt with misery;
For what's more miserable than discontent?
Ah, uncle Humphrey, in thy face I see
The map of honour, truth, and loyalty;
And yet, good Humphrey, is the hour to come
205 That e'er I proved thee false, or feared thy faith.°   *doubted your loyalty*
What louring° star now envies thy estate,   *gloomy*
That these great lords and Margaret our Queen
Do seek subversion of thy harmless life?
Thou never didst them wrong, nor no man wrong.
210 And as the butcher takes away the calf,
And binds the wretch, and beats it when it strains,
Bearing it to the bloody slaughterhouse,
Even so remorseless have they borne him hence;
And as the dam° runs lowing up and down,   *mother*
215 Looking the way her harmless young one went,
And can do naught but wail her darling's loss;
Even so myself bewails good Gloucester's case
With sad unhelpful tears, and with dimmed eyes
Look after him, and cannot do him good,°   *give him help*
220 So mighty are his vowèd enemies.
His fortunes I will weep, and 'twixt each groan,
Say 'Who's a traitor? Gloucester, he is none'.

Exeunt KING, SALISBURY, *and* WARWICK

QUEEN MARGARET Free° lords, cold snow melts with the sun's hot beams. *Noble*
Henry my lord is cold in great affairs,
225 Too full of foolish pity; and Gloucester's show
Beguiles him as the mournful crocodile
With sorrow snares relenting passengers,[6]
Or as the snake rolled in a flow'ring bank
With shining chequered slough° doth sting a child   *skin*
230 That for the beauty thinks it excellent.
Believe me, lords, were none more wise than I—
And yet herein I judge mine own wit good—
This Gloucester should be quickly rid the world
To rid us from the fear we have of him.
235 CARDINAL BEAUFORT That he should die is worthy policy;
But yet we want a colour° for his death.   *pretext*
'Tis meet he be condemned by course of law.
SUFFOLK But, in my mind, that were no policy.
The King will labour still° to save his life,   *continually*
240 The commons haply° rise to save his life;   *perhaps*
And yet we have but trivial argument°   *evidence*
More than mistrust° that shows him worthy death. *Other than suspicion*

---

6. Compassionate travelers. Sixteenth-century natural historians claimed that crocodiles moaned and wept in order
to lure sympathetic humans to their death.

YORK   So that, by this, you would not have him die?

SUFFOLK   Ah, York, no man alive so fain as I.

245 YORK [*aside*] 'Tis York that hath more reason for his death.
[*Aloud*] But my lord Cardinal, and you my lord of Suffolk,
Say as you think, and speak it from your souls.
Were't not all one an empty° eagle were set   *a hungry*
To guard the chicken from a hungry kite,°   *bird of prey*
250 As place Duke Humphrey for the King's Protector?

QUEEN MARGARET   So the poor chicken should be sure of death.

SUFFOLK   Madam, 'tis true; and were't not madness then
To make the fox surveyor° of the fold,   *guardian*
Who being accused a crafty murderer,
255 His guilt should be but idly posted over°   *foolishly ignored*
Because his purpose is not executed?
No—let him die in that he is a fox,
By nature proved an enemy to the flock,
Before his chaps° be stained with crimson blood,   *jaws*
260 As Humphrey, proved by reasons, to my liege.[7]
And do not stand on quillets° how to slay him;   *subtle distinctions*
Be it by gins,° by snares, by subtlety,   *traps*
Sleeping or waking, 'tis no matter how,
So he be dead; for that is good conceit
265 Which mates° him first that first intends deceit.   *checkmates; kills*

QUEEN MARGARET   Thrice-noble Suffolk, 'tis resolutely spoke.

SUFFOLK   Not resolute, except° so much were done;   *unless*
For things are often spoke and seldom meant;
But that° my heart accordeth with my tongue,   *to show that*
270 Seeing the deed is meritorious,
And to preserve my sovereign from his foe,
Say but the word and I will be his priest.[8]

CARDINAL BEAUFORT   But I would have him dead, my lord of Suffolk,
Ere you can take due orders for a priest.[9]
275 Say you consent and censure° well the deed,   *approve*
And I'll provide his executioner;
I tender so the safety of my liege.

SUFFOLK   Here is my hand; the deed is worthy doing.

QUEEN MARGARET   And so say I.

280 YORK   And I. And now we three have spoke it,
It skills not greatly who impugns our doom.[1]
        Enter a POST

POST   Great lord, from Ireland am I come amain°   *in haste*
To signify that rebels there are up°   *up in arms*
And put the Englishmen unto the sword.
285 Send succours, lords, and stop the rage betime,°   *promptly*
Before the wound do grow uncurable;
For, being green,° there is great hope of help.   [*Exit*]   *fresh*

CARDINAL BEAUFORT   A breach that craves a quick expedient stop!
What counsel give you in this weighty cause?

290 YORK   That Somerset be sent as regent thither.
'Tis meet° that lucky ruler be employed—   *fit (said scornfully)*
Witness the fortune he hath had in France.

---

7. Just as Humphrey proved (to be a fox or enemy) to Henry.
8. I will kill him. Suffolk alludes to the priest's role in administering the sacrament of last rites to dying Christians.
9. Can become a priest; can arrange to have a priest there.
1. It doesn't matter who questions our decision.

SOMERSET   If York, with all his far-fet° policy,   *cunning*
    Had been the regent there instead of me,
295   He never would have stayed in France so long.
YORK   No, not to lose it all as thou hast done.
    I rather would have lost my life betimes
    Than bring a burden of dishonour home
    By staying there so long till all were lost.
300   Show me one scar charactered° on thy skin.   *inscribed*
    Men's flesh preserved so whole do seldom win.
QUEEN MARGARET   Nay, then, this spark will prove a raging fire
    If wind and fuel be brought to feed it with.
    No more, good York; sweet Somerset, be still.
305   Thy fortune, York, hadst thou been regent there,
    Might happily° have proved far worse than his.   *perhaps*
YORK   What, worse than naught? Nay, then a shame take all!
SOMERSET   And, in the number,° thee that wishest shame.   *among them*
CARDINAL BEAUFORT   My lord of York, try what your fortune is.
310   Th'uncivil kerns of Ireland² are in arms
    And temper clay° with blood of Englishmen.   *moisten the earth*
    To Ireland will you lead a band of men
    Collected choicely, from each county some,
    And try your hap° against the Irishmen?   *luck*
315 YORK   I will, my lord, so please his majesty.
SUFFOLK   Why, our authority is his consent,
    And what we do establish he confirms.
    Then, noble York, take thou this task in hand.
YORK   I am content. Provide me soldiers, lords,
320   Whiles I take order° for mine own affairs.   *arrange*
SUFFOLK   A charge, Lord York, that I will see performed.
    But now return we to the false Duke Humphrey.
CARDINAL BEAUFORT   No more of him—for I will deal with him
    That henceforth he shall trouble us no more.
325   And so, break off; the day is almost spent.
    Lord Suffolk, you and I must talk of that event.
YORK   My lord of Suffolk, within fourteen days
    At Bristol I expect my soldiers;
    For there I'll ship them all for Ireland.
330 SUFFOLK   I'll see it truly done, my lord of York.   *Exeunt. Manet* YORK³
330.1   YORK   *Let me have some bands of chosen soldiers,*
       And York shall try his fortune 'gainst those kerns.
      QUEEN MARGARET   *York, thou shalt. My lord of Buckingham,*
       Let it be your charge to muster up such soldiers
330.5   *As shall suffice him in these needful wars.*
      BUCKINGHAM   *Madam, I will, and levy such a band*
       As soon shall overcome those Irish rebels.
       But, York, where shall those soliders stay° for thee   *wait*
      YORK   *At Bristol I will expect them ten days hence.*
330.10   BUCKINGHAM   *Then thither shall they come, and so farewell*   Exit
      YORK   *Adieu, my lord of Buckingham.*

---

2. Barbaric Irish foot soldiers or rebels. Kerns were the most numerous, poorest, and most lightly armed of the Irish soldiers who fought against the English during Elizabeth's reign. Many Elizabethan writers described the Irish as an inferior, uncivilized "race" and used the term "kern" to signify all Irish opponents of England.
3. The entire debate on Duke Humphrey's death in 3.1 is handled differently by Q and F. Oxford retains F's version of the debate, but Q may represent authorial revision. The following indented Q lines (330.1–330.15), roughly corresponding to lines 310–30, are of particular interest because they supply Buckingham with speeches for this latter part of the scene.

QUEEN MARGARET *Suffolk, remember what you have to do—*
And you, Lord Cardinal—concerning Duke Humphrey.
'Twere good that you did see to it in time.

330.15 *Come, let us go, that it may be performed.* *Exeunt all. Manet* YORK

YORK Now, York, or never, steel thy fearful thoughts,
And change misdoubt° to resolution.   *fear*
Be that thou hop'st to be, or what thou art
Resign to death; it is not worth th'enjoying.

335 Let pale-faced fear keep° with the mean-born° man   *dwell / lowborn*
And find no harbour in a royal heart.
Faster than springtime showers comes thought on thought,
And not a thought but thinks on dignity.°   *high estate (kingship)*
My brain, more busy than the labouring spider,

340 Weaves tedious° snares to trap mine enemies.   *laborious*
Well, nobles, well: 'tis politicly done
To send me packing with an host of men.
I fear me° you but warm the starvèd° snake,   *I am afraid / frozen*
Who, cherished in your breasts, will sting your hearts.

345 'Twas men I lacked, and you will give them me.
I take it kindly. Yet be well assured
You put sharp weapons in a madman's hands.
Whiles I in Ireland nurse a mighty band,
I will stir up in England some black storm

350 Shall blow ten thousand souls to heaven or hell,
And this fell° tempest shall not cease to rage   *ferocious*
Until the golden circuit° on my head   *crown*
Like to the glorious sun's transparent beams
Do calm the fury of this mad-bred flaw.[4]

355 And for a minister° of my intent,   *an agent*
I have seduced a headstrong Kentishman,
John Cade of Ashford,
To make commotion,° as full well he can,   *rebellion*
Under the title of John Mortimer.[5]

360 In Ireland have I seen this stubborn Cade
Oppose himself against a troop of kerns,
And fought so long till that his thighs with darts[6]
Were almost like a sharp-quilled porcupine;
And in the end, being rescued, I have seen

365 Him caper° upright like a wild Morisco,[7]   *leap*
Shaking the bloody darts as he° his bells.   *as would the dancer*
Full often like a shag-haired[8] crafty kern
Hath he conversèd with the enemy
And, undiscovered, come to me again

370 And given me notice of their villainies.
This devil here shall be my substitute,
For that° John Mortimer, which now is dead,   *Because*
In face, in gait, in speech, he doth resemble.

---

4. This storm ("flaw") created by madness.
5. The Mortimers are the family line by which York claims the crown. See York's account of his claim in 2.2.10–52.
6. Light spears or arrows, the weapons for which kerns were known.
7. A Moor who converted to Christianity; a morris dancer. Deriving from the Spanish word for "Moor," the morris dance was originally a Spanish dance that reen-acted Christian battles with Moors. From the fifteenth century, it was associated with English popular festivals and was usually performed by men with bells attached to their legs who carried sticks and wore costumes from English folklore.
8. Alluding to the popular notion that the Irish grew "glibs," or long thick bangs, in order to disguise them-selves and escape punishment for their crimes.

By this I shall perceive the commons' mind,
375   How they affect° the house and claim of York.   *like*
  Say he be taken, racked,⁹ and torturèd—
  I know no pain they can inflict upon him
  Will make him say I moved him to those arms.
  Say that he thrive, as 'tis great like° he will—   *very likely*
380   Why then from Ireland come I with my strength
  And reap the harvest which that coistrel° sowed.   *base fellow*
  For Humphrey being dead, as he shall be,
  And Henry put apart, the next for me.   *Exit*

3.2

The curtains [are] drawn [apart, revealing] Duke Hum-
phrey [of GLOUCESTER] *in his bed [with] two men lying*
*on his breast, smothering him in his bed*¹
FIRST MURDERER [*to the* SECOND MURDERER]   Run to my lord of
    Suffolk—let him know
We have dispatched the Duke as he commanded.
SECOND MURDERER   O that it were to do!² What have we done?
  Didst ever hear a man so penitent?
    Enter the Duke of SUFFOLK
5   FIRST MURDERER   Here comes my lord.
SUFFOLK   Now, sirs, have you dispatched this thing?
FIRST MURDERER   Ay, my good lord, he's dead.
SUFFOLK   Why, that's well said. Go, get you to my house.
  I will reward you for this venturous° deed.   *dangerous*
10   The King and all the peers are here at hand.
  Have you laid fair° the bed? Is all things well,   *rearranged*
  According as I gave directions?
FIRST MURDERER   'Tis, my good lord.
SUFFOLK   Then draw the curtains close; away, be gone!
    Exeunt [the] MURDERERS [*drawing the curtains as they leave*]
    Sound trumpets, then enter KING [HENRY] *and* QUEEN
    [MARGARET], CARDINAL [BEAUFORT], *the Duke of* SOMER-
    SET, [*and*] *attendants*
15   KING HENRY [*to* SUFFOLK]   Go call our uncle to our presence straight.°   *immediately*
  Say we intend to try his grace today
  If° he be guilty, as 'tis publishèd.   *To find whether*
SUFFOLK   I'll call him presently,° my noble lord.   *Exit*   *at once*
KING HENRY   Lords, take your places; and, I pray you all,
20   Proceed no straiter° 'gainst our uncle Gloucester   *more severely*
  Than from true evidence, of good esteem,°   *worthy of belief*
  He be approved in practice culpable.°   *determined guilty*
QUEEN MARGARET   God forbid any malice should prevail
  That faultless may condemn a noble man!³
25   Pray God he may acquit him° of suspicion!   *himself*
KING HENRY   I thank thee, Meg. These words content me much.
    Enter SUFFOLK
  How now? Why look'st thou pale? Why tremblest thou?

---

9. Tortured by having one's limbs fastened to a frame
that stretched the body.
3.2 Location: Gloucester's bedchamber and an adjoining
room of state, Bury St. Edmunds.
1. F's stage direction reads, "Enter two or three running
over the Stage, from the Murder of Duke Humfrey." Q,
by contrast, indicates that the actual smothering of
Gloucester is shown onstage.
2. Would that it were still to be done (so that it could
remain undone).
3. That may condemn a noble man who is blameless.

Where is our uncle? What's the matter, Suffolk?
SUFFOLK   Dead in his bed, my lord—Gloucester is dead.
30 QUEEN MARGARET   Marry, God forfend!°   forbid
CARDINAL BEAUFORT   God's secret judgement. I did dream tonight°   last night
     The Duke was dumb and could not speak a word.
               KING HENRY falls [to the ground]⁴
QUEEN MARGARET   How fares my lord? Help, lords—the King is dead!
SOMERSET   Rear° up his body; wring him by the nose.⁵   Raise
35 QUEEN MARGARET   Run, go, help, help! O Henry, ope thine eyes!
SUFFOLK   He doth revive again. Madam, be patient.
KING HENRY   O heavenly God!
QUEEN MARGARET   How fares my gracious lord?
SUFFOLK   Comfort, my sovereign; gracious Henry, comfort.
KING HENRY   What, doth my lord of Suffolk comfort me?
40   Came he right now° to sing a raven's note⁶   a moment ago
     Whose dismal tune bereft° my vital powers;   robbed me of
     And thinks he that the chirping of a wren,
     By crying comfort from a hollow° breast   an insincere
     Can chase away the first-conceivèd° sound?   previously perceived
45   Hide not thy poison with such sugared words.
               [He begins to rise. SUFFOLK offers to assist him]
     Lay not thy hands on me—forbear, I say!
     Their touch affrights me as a serpent's sting.
     Thou baleful messenger, out of my sight!
     Upon thy eyeballs murderous tyranny
50   Sits in grim majesty to fright the world.
     Look not upon me, for thine eyes are wounding—
     Yet do not go away. Come, basilisk,⁷
     And kill the innocent gazer with thy sight.
     For in the shade° of death I shall find joy;   shadow
55   In life, but double death, now Gloucester's dead.
QUEEN MARGARET   Why do you rate° my lord of Suffolk thus?   chide
     Although the Duke was enemy to him,
     Yet he most Christian-like laments his death.
     And for myself, foe as he was to me,
60   Might liquid tears, or heart-offending° groans,   heart-wounding
     Or blood-consuming⁸ sighs recall his life,
     I would be blind with weeping, sick with groans,
     Look pale as primrose with blood-drinking sighs,
     And all to have the noble Duke alive.
65   What know I how the world may deem° of me?   judge
     For it is known we were but hollow friends,
     It may be judged I made the Duke away.
     So shall my name with slander's tongue be wounded
     And princes' courts be filled with my reproach.
70   This get I by his death. Ay me, unhappy,
     To be a queen, and crowned with infamy.
KING HENRY   Ah, woe is me for Gloucester, wretched man!
QUEEN MARGARET   Be woe° for me, more wretched than he is.   woeful, sorry
     What, dost thou turn away and hide thy face?

4. In Q, the stage direction reads, "The King falls in a   7. A mythical reptile, hatched from a cock's egg, whose
sound" (swoon). F reads, "King sounds."   look was supposed to be fatal.
5. This was thought to revive circulation and restore con-   8. It was popularly believed that each sigh or groan drew
sciousness.   a drop of blood from the heart.
6. According to popular superstition, an omen of death.

75 I am no loathsome leper—look on me!
What, art thou, like the adder, waxen deaf?[9]
Be poisonous too and kill thy forlorn queen.
Is all thy comfort shut in Gloucester's tomb?
Why, then Queen Margaret was ne'er thy joy.
80 Erect his statuë and worship it,
And make my image but an alehouse sign.[1]
Was I for this nigh wrecked upon the sea,
And twice by awkward° winds from England's bank°   *unfavorable / shore*
Drove back again unto my native clime?
85 What boded this, but° well forewarning winds   *but that*
Did seem to say, 'Seek not a scorpion's nest,
Nor set no footing on this unkind shore'.
What did I then, but cursed the gentle gusts
And he that loosed them forth their brazen caves,[2]
90 And bid them blow towards England's blessèd shore,
Or turn our stern upon a dreadful rock.
Yet Aeolus would not be a murderer,
But left that hateful office unto thee.
The pretty vaulting° sea refused to drown me,   *bounding*
95 Knowing that thou wouldst have me drowned on shore
With tears as salt as sea through thy unkindness.
The splitting rocks cow'red in the sinking sands,[3]
And would not dash me with their ragged sides,
Because thy flinty heart, more hard than they,
100 Might in thy palace perish° Margaret.   *destroy*
As far as I could ken° thy chalky cliffs,   *see*
When from thy shore the tempest beat us back,
I stood upon the hatches° in the storm,   *deck*
And when the dusky sky began to rob
105 My earnest-gaping° sight of thy land's view,   *earnestly peering*
I took a costly jewel from my neck—
A heart it was, bound in with diamonds—
And threw it towards thy land. The sea received it,
And so I wished thy body might my heart.
110 And even with this I lost fair England's view,
And bid mine eyes be packing° with my heart,   *be gone*
And called them blind and dusky spectacles°   *instruments of sight*
For losing ken of Albion's° wishèd coast.   *England's*
How often have I tempted Suffolk's tongue—
115 The agent of thy foul inconstancy—
To sit and witch° me, as Ascanius[4] did,   *bewitch*
When he to madding° Dido would unfold   *going mad (with love)*
His father's acts, commenced in burning Troy!
Am I not witched like her? Or thou not false like him?
120 Ay me, I can no more.° Die, Margaret,   *my strength fails*
For Henry weeps that thou dost live so long.
  Noise within. Enter the Earls of WARWICK *and* SALIS-
  BURY, [*with*] *many* COMMONS

9. Alluding to the belief that adders stopped up their ears to resist attempts to charm them.
1. Inns and shops in Elizabethan London were usually distinguished by signs bearing images rather than words.
2. Referring to Aeolus, whom Zeus appointed ruler of the winds, which he kept in caves. *brazen:* strong (as brass).
3. Rocks that ordinarily break ships into pieces crouched down fearfully in the sands where ships usually sink.
4. In Book 1 of the *Aeneid*, Venus sends Cupid in the form of Ascanius, son of Aeneas, to bewitch Dido, Queen of Carthage, and inflame her with love for Aeneas.

WARWICK [*to* KING HENRY]   It is reported, mighty sovereign,
    That good Duke Humphrey traitorously is murdered
    By Suffolk and the Cardinal Beaufort's means.
125   The commons, like an angry hive of bees
    That want° their leader, scatter up and down   *lack*
    And care not who they sting in his revenge.
    Myself have calmed their spleenful° mutiny,   *angry*
    Until they hear the order° of his death.   *manner*
130 KING HENRY   That he is dead, good Warwick, 'tis too true.
    But how he died God knows, not Henry.
    Enter his chamber, view his breathless corpse,
    And comment then upon° his sudden death.   *And then explain*
    WARWICK   That shall I do, my liege.—Stay, Salisbury,
135   With the rude multitude till I return.

Exeunt [WARWICK *at one door,*] SALISBURY [*and*
COMMONS *at another*][5]

KING HENRY   O thou that judgest all things, stay° my thoughts, *restrain*
    My thoughts that labour to persuade my soul
    Some violent hands were laid on Humphrey's life.
    If my suspect° be false, forgive me God,   *suspicion*
140   For judgement only doth belong to thee.
    Fain would I go to chafe his paly° lips   *pale*
    With twenty thousand kisses, and to drain°   *rain, let fall*
    Upon his face an ocean of salt tears,
    To tell my love unto his dumb, deaf trunk,°   *body*
145   And with my fingers feel his hand unfeeling.°   *which lacks feeling*
    But all in vain are these mean obsequies,°   *funeral rites*

[*Enter*] WARWICK [*who*] *draws* [*apart*] *the curtains and
shows* GLOUCESTER [*dead*] *in his bed. Bed put forth*

    And to survey his dead and earthy image,
    What were it but to make my sorrow greater?
    WARWICK   Come hither, gracious sovereign, view this body.
150 KING HENRY   That is to see how deep my grave is made:
    For with his soul fled all my worldly solace,
    For seeing him I see my life° in death.   *that my life will end*
    WARWICK   As surely as my soul intends to live
    With that dread King° that took our state° upon Him *(Christ) / condition*
155   To free us from his Father's wrathful curse,
    I do believe that violent hands were laid
    Upon the life of this thrice-famèd° Duke.   *very famous*
    SUFFOLK   A dreadful oath, sworn with a solemn tongue!
    What instance° gives Lord Warwick for his vow?   *evidence*
160 WARWICK   See how the blood is settled in his face.
    Oft have I seen a timely-parted ghost[6]
    Of ashy semblance, meagre, pale, and bloodless,
    Being all descended to the labouring heart;[7]
    Who, in the conflict that it holds with death,
165   Attracts the same° for aidance° 'gainst the enemy; *(the blood) / aid*
    Which, with the heart, there cools, and ne'er returneth
    To blush and beautify the cheek again.

5. Q has Salisbury exit at this point, while the dialogue
in F and Q indicates that Warwick also leaves the stage.
He must return to reveal Gloucester's corpse at line 146.
Some editors have suggested that Salisbury stays onstage
with the Commons here, but at line 243 he is directed to
enter, and it appears that the Commons are also then offstage. Both must have exited at some point.
6. The corpse of someone who died a natural death.
7. The blood having all drained into the palpitating heart.

But see, his face is black and full of blood;
His eyeballs further out than when he lived,
170 Staring full ghastly like a strangled man;
His hair upreared; his nostrils stretched with struggling;
His hands abroad displayed,° as one that grasped   *spread wide*
And tugged for life and was by strength subdued.
Look on the sheets. His hair, you see, is sticking;
175 His well-proportioned beard made rough and rugged,
Like to the summer's corn by tempest lodged.°   *beaten down*
It cannot be but he was murdered here.
The least of all these signs were probable.°   *sufficient proof*
SUFFOLK   Why, Warwick, who should do the Duke to death?
180 Myself and Beaufort had him in protection,
And we, I hope, sir, are no murderers.
WARWICK   But both of you were vowed Duke Humphrey's foes,
[*To* CARDINAL BEAUFORT] And you, forsooth, had the good
   Duke to keep.°   *guard*
'Tis like you would not feast him like a friend;
185 And 'tis well seen he found an enemy.
QUEEN MARGARET   Then you, belike,° suspect these noblemen   *perchance*
As guilty of Duke Humphrey's timeless° death?   *untimely*
WARWICK   Who finds the heifer dead and bleeding fresh,
And sees fast° by a butcher with an axe,   *near*
190 But will suspect 'twas he that made the slaughter?
Who finds the partridge in the puttock's° nest   *kite's (bird of prey)*
But may imagine how the bird was dead,°   *killed*
Although the kite soar with unbloodied beak?
Even so suspicious is this tragedy.
195 QUEEN MARGARET   Are you the butcher, Suffolk? Where's your knife?
Is Beaufort termed a kite? Where are his talons?
SUFFOLK   I wear no knife to slaughter sleeping men.
But here's a vengeful sword, rusted with ease,°   *lack of use*
That shall be scourèd in his rancorous heart
200 That° slanders me with murder's crimson badge.   *Who*
Say, if thou dar'st, proud Lord of Warwickshire,
That I am faulty in Duke Humphrey's death.
                Exit CARDINAL [BEAUFORT *assisted by* SOMERSET]
WARWICK   What dares not Warwick, if false Suffolk dare him?
QUEEN MARGARET   He dares not calm his contumelious° spirit,   *insolent*
205 Nor cease to be an arrogant controller,°   *critic; slanderer*
Though Suffolk dare him twenty thousand times.
WARWICK   Madam, be still, with reverence may I say,
For every word you speak in his behalf
Is slander to your royal dignity.
210 SUFFOLK   Blunt-witted lord, ignoble in demeanour!
If ever lady wronged her lord so much,
Thy mother took into her blameful bed
Some stern° untutored churl, and noble stock   *rough*
Was graffed with crabtree slip, whose fruit thou art,[8]
215 And never of the Nevilles' noble race.
WARWICK   But that the guilt of murder bucklers° thee   *shields*

---

8. *noble . . . art*: into the trunk of a great tree was inserted a cutting, or "slip," from an inferior, wild one, and you are the result. The analogy puns on "stock" as meaning "an aristocratic line of descent" and implies that the pedi- gree has been tainted. "Noble stock" may also refer to the trunk of a noblewoman's body into which a worthless "slip," such as the penis of a lowborn man, has been inserted.

	And I should rob the deathsman° of his fee,	*executioner*
	Quitting° thee thereby of ten thousand shames,	*Freeing*
	And that my sovereign's presence makes me mild,⁹	
220	I would, false murd'rous coward, on thy knee	
	Make thee beg pardon for thy passèd° speech,	*just uttered*
	And say it was thy mother that thou meant'st—	
	That thou thyself wast born in bastardy!	
	And after all this fearful homage° done,	*cowardly submission*
225	Give thee thy hire° and send thy soul to hell,	*reward*
	Pernicious blood-sucker of sleeping men!	

SUFFOLK   Thou shalt be waking while I shed thy blood,
    If from this presence° thou dar'st go with me.   *the King's presence*
WARWICK   Away, even now, or I will drag thee hence.
230   Unworthy though thou art, I'll cope° with thee,   *fight*
    And do some service to Duke Humphrey's ghost.
                    Exeunt SUFFOLK *and* WARWICK
KING HENRY   What stronger breastplate than a heart untainted?
    Thrice is he armed that hath his quarrel just;
    And he but naked, though locked up in steel,°   *armored*
235   Whose conscience with injustice is corrupted.
COMMONS (*within*)   Down with Suffolk! Down with Suffolk!¹
QUEEN MARGARET   What noise is this?
                    Enter SUFFOLK *and* WARWICK *with their weapons drawn*
KING HENRY   Why, how now, lords? Your wrathful weapons drawn
    Here in our presence? Dare you be so bold?
240   Why, what tumultuous clamour have we here?
SUFFOLK   The trait'rous Warwick with the men of Bury
    Set all upon me, mighty sovereign!
COMMONS [*within*]   Down with Suffolk! Down with Suffolk!
                    Enter from [*the* COMMONS] *the Earl of* SALISBURY
SALISBURY [*to the* COMMONS, *within*]   Sirs, stand apart. The
    King shall know your mind.
245   [*To* KING HENRY] Dread lord, the commons send you word by me
    Unless Lord Suffolk straight be done to death,
    Or banishèd° fair England's territories,   *banished from*
    They will by violence tear him from your palace
    And torture him with grievous ling'ring death.
250   They say, by him the good Duke Humphrey died;
    They say, in him they fear your highness' death;
    And mere° instinct of love and loyalty,   *pure*
    Free from a stubborn opposite° intent,   *antagonistic*
    As being thought to contradict your liking,²
255   Makes them thus forward in° his banishment.   *insistent upon*
    They say, in care of your most royal person,
    That if your highness should intend to sleep,
    And charge that no man should disturb your rest
    In pain of your dislike, or pain of death,
260   Yet, notwithstanding such a strait° edict,   *strict*
    Were there a serpent seen with forkèd tongue,
    That slily glided towards your majesty,

---

9. It was illegal to draw weapons in the king's presence.
1. In Q, this line is printed inside a longer stage direction: "Exit Warwick and Suffolk, and then all the Commons within, cries, down with Suffolk, down with

Suffolk. And then enter again, the Duke of Suffolk and
Warwick, with their weapons drawn."
2. That might be thought to contradict your wishes.

It were but necessary you were waked,

Lest, being suffered° in that harmful slumber,   *permitted to remain*

265 The mortal worm° might make the sleep eternal.   *deadly serpent*

And therefore do they cry, though you forbid,

That they will guard you, whe'er° you will or no,   *whether*

From such fell° serpents as false Suffolk is,   *cruel*

With whose envenomèd and fatal sting

270 Your loving uncle, twenty times his worth,

They say, is shamefully bereft of life.

COMMONS (*within*) An answer from the King, my lord of Salisbury!

SUFFOLK 'Tis like° the commons, rude unpolished hinds,°   *probable / boors*

Could send such message to their sovereign.

275 But you, my lord, were glad to be employed,

To show how quaint° an orator you are.   *skilled*

But all the honour Salisbury hath won

Is that he was the Lord Ambassador

Sent from a sort° of tinkers to the King.   *gang*

280 COMMONS (*within*) An answer from the King, or we will all break in!

KING HENRY Go, Salisbury, and tell them all from me

I thank them for their tender loving care,

And had I not been 'cited° so by them,   *urged*

Yet did I purpose as they do entreat;

285 For sure my thoughts do hourly prophesy

Mischance unto my state by Suffolk's means.

And therefore by His° majesty I swear,   *(God's)*

Whose far unworthy deputy I am,

He shall not breathe° infection in this air   *breathe out; spread*

290 But three days longer, on the pain of death.   *Exit* SALISBURY

QUEEN MARGARET [*kneeling*] O Henry, let me plead for gentle° Suffolk.   *noble*

KING HENRY Ungentle Queen, to call him gentle Suffolk.

No more, I say! If thou dost plead for him

Thou wilt but add increase unto my wrath.

295 Had I but said, I would have kept my word;

But when I swear, it is irrevocable.

[*To* SUFFOLK] If after three days' space thou here beest found

On any ground that I am ruler of,

The world shall not be ransom for thy life.

300 Come, Warwick; come, good Warwick, go with me.

I have great matters to impart to thee.

   Exeunt KING [HENRY] *and* WARWICK [*with attendants*

   who draw the curtains as they leave]. Manent° *Remain*

   [MARGARET] *and* SUFFOLK

QUEEN MARGARET [*rising*] Mischance and sorrow go along with you!

Heart's discontent and sour affliction

Be playfellows to keep you company!

305 There's two of you, the devil make a third,

And threefold vengeance tend upon your steps!

SUFFOLK Cease, gentle Queen, these execrations,

And let thy Suffolk take his heavy° leave.   *sorrowful*

QUEEN MARGARET Fie, coward woman³ and soft-hearted wretch!

310 Hast thou not spirit to curse thine enemies?

---

3. In calling Suffolk a woman, Margaret questions his manhood. The pun in the next line on "spirit" as meaning "semen" as well as "courage" continues Margaret's assault on Suffolk's masculinity.

SUFFOLK   A plague upon them! Wherefore° should I curse them?   *Why*
   Could curses kill, as doth the mandrake's groan,[4]
   I would invent as bitter searching° terms,   *piercing*
   As curst, as harsh, and horrible to hear,
315   Delivered strongly through my fixèd° teeth,   *clenched*
   With full as many signs of deadly hate,
   As lean-faced envy[5] in her loathsome cave.
   My tongue should stumble in mine earnest words;
   Mine eyes should sparkle like the beaten flint;
320   My hair be fixed on end, as one distraught;
   Ay, every joint should seem to curse and ban.°   *curse*
   And, even now, my burdened heart would break
   Should I not curse them. Poison be their drink!
   Gall,° worse than gall, the daintiest that they taste!   *Bile (a bitter fluid)*
325   Their sweetest shade a grove of cypress trees![6]
   Their chiefest prospect° murd'ring basilisks![7]   *view*
   Their softest touch as smart° as lizards' stings!   *sharp*
   Their music frightful as the serpent's hiss,
   And boding screech-owls make the consort° full!   *group of musicians*
330   All the foul terrors in dark-seated hell—
QUEEN MARGARET   Enough, sweet Suffolk, thou torment'st thyself,
   And these dread curses, like the sun 'gainst glass,
   Or like an overchargèd gun, recoil
   And turn the force of them upon thyself.
335 SUFFOLK   You bade me ban, and will you bid me leave?°   *stop*
   Now by this ground that I am banished from,
   Well could I curse away a winter's night,
   Though standing naked on a mountain top,
   Where biting cold would never let grass grow,
340   And think it but a minute spent in sport.
QUEEN MARGARET   O let me entreat thee cease. Give me thy hand,
   That I may dew it with my mournful tears;
   Nor let the rain of heaven wet this place
   To wash away my woeful monuments.°   *signs of grief (tears)*
       [*She kisses his palm*]
345   O, could this kiss be printed in thy hand
   That thou mightst think upon these lips by the seal,°   *imprint*
   Through whom° a thousand sighs are breathed for thee!   *which (her lips)*
   So get thee gone, that I may know my grief.
   'Tis but surmised whiles thou art standing by,
350   As one that surfeits° thinking on a want.°   *gorges / famine*
   I will repeal thee,° or, be well assured,   *win your recall*
   Adventure to be banishèd° myself.   *Risk banishment*
   And banishèd I am, if but from thee.
   Go, speak not to me; even now be gone!
355   O, go not yet. Even thus two friends condemned
   Embrace, and kiss, and take ten thousand leaves,
   Loather a hundred times to part than die.

---

4. It was popularly believed that the mandrake—an herb whose root was thought to resemble a man and to grow wherever the semen of a man executed for murder had fallen—killed humans with its dreadful scream when it was uprooted.

5. Envy was traditionally described as an emaciated woman. See Ovid, *Metamorphoses* 2.949ff.

6. From ancient times, trees associated with death. Frequently planted in graveyards, their wood was used for coffins.

7. See note to line 52 above.

Yet now farewell, and farewell life with thee.
SUFFOLK   Thus is poor Suffolk ten times banishèd—
360   Once by the King, and three times thrice by thee.
        'Tis not the land I care for, wert thou thence,
        A wilderness is populous enough,
        So Suffolk had thy heavenly company.
        For where thou art, there is the world itself,
365   With every several° pleasure in the world;   distinct
        And where thou art not, desolation.
        I can no more. Live thou to joy° thy life;   enjoy
        Myself no joy in naught but that thou liv'st.
              Enter VAUX
QUEEN MARGARET   Whither goes Vaux so fast? What news, I prithee?
370 VAUX   To signify unto his majesty
        That Cardinal Beaufort is at point of death.
        For suddenly a grievous sickness took him
        That makes him gasp, and stare, and catch the air,
        Blaspheming God and cursing men on earth.
375   Sometime he talks as if Duke Humphrey's ghost
        Were by his side; sometime he calls the King,
        And whispers to his pillow as to him
        The secrets of his over-chargèd° soul;   overburdened
        And I am sent to tell his majesty
380   That even now he cries aloud for him.
QUEEN MARGARET   Go tell this heavy message to the King.   *Exit* VAUX
        Ay me! What is this world? What news are these?
        But wherefore grieve I at an hour's poor loss[8]
        Omitting° Suffolk's exile, my soul's treasure?   Ignoring
385   Why only, Suffolk, mourn I not for thee,
        And with the southern clouds[9] contend in tears—
        Theirs for the earth's increase, mine for my sorrow's?
        Now get thee hence. The King, thou know'st, is coming.
        If thou be found by° me, thou art but dead.   near
390 SUFFOLK   If I depart from thee, I cannot live.
        And in thy sight to die, what were it else
        But like a pleasant slumber in thy lap?[1]
        Here could I breathe my soul into the air,
        As mild and gentle as the cradle babe
395   Dying with mother's dug° between his lips;   nipple
        Where, from° thy sight, I should be raging mad,   out of
        And cry out for thee to close up mine eyes,
        To have thee with thy lips to stop my mouth,
        So shouldst thou either turn° my flying soul   return to me
400   Or I should breathe it, so, into thy body—
              [*He kisseth her*]
        And then it lived in sweet Elysium.[2]
        By thee to die were but to die in jest;[3]
        From thee to die were torture more than death.
        O, let me stay, befall what may befall!

8. Alluding to the Cardinal's old age and suggesting that   2. In classical mythology, the paradise where blessed souls
he has in any case but a short time (an hour) to live.   dwelled.
9. It was generally thought that rain came from the south.   3. To die near you or by means of you is not really to
1. Punning on "die in thy lap" as meaning "have an   die (with a continuing pun on "die" as meaning "attain
orgasm while in your embrace."   orgasm").

405 QUEEN MARGARET Away. Though parting be a fretful corrosive,°   *painful remedy*
    It is applièd to a deathful° wound.   *deadly*
    To France, sweet Suffolk. Let me hear from thee.
    For wheresoe'er thou art in this world's Globe
    I'll have an Iris[4] that shall find thee out.
410 SUFFOLK I go.
QUEEN MARGARET And take my heart with thee.
    She kisseth him
SUFFOLK A jewel, locked into the woefull'st cask°   *casket*
    That ever did contain a thing of worth.
    Even as a splitted barque,° so sunder° we—   *boat / part*
    This way fall I to death.
415 QUEEN MARGARET   This way for me.   *Exeunt [severally]*

3.3

Enter KING [HENRY *and the Earls of*] SALISBURY *and*
WARWICK. *Then the curtains be drawn [revealing]* CARDI-
NAL [BEAUFORT] *in his bed raving and staring as if he*
were mad

KING HENRY [*to* CARDINAL BEAUFORT] How fares my lord? Speak, Beaufort,
    to thy sovereign.
CARDINAL BEAUFORT If thou beest death, I'll give thee England's treasure
    Enough to purchase such another island,
    So° thou wilt let me live and feel no pain.   *If*
5 KING HENRY Ah, what a sign it is of evil life
    Where death's approach is seen so terrible.
WARWICK Beaufort, it is thy sovereign speaks to thee.
CARDINAL BEAUFORT Bring me unto my trial when you will.
    Died he° not in his bed? Where should he die?   *(Gloucester)*
10   Can I make men live whe'er° they will or no?   *whether*
    O, torture me no more—I will confess.
    Alive again? Then show me where he is.
    I'll give a thousand pound to look upon him.
    He hath no eyes! The dust hath blinded them.
15   Comb down his hair—look, look: it stands upright,
    Like lime twigs[1] set to catch my wingèd soul.
    Give me some drink, and bid the apothecary
    Bring the strong poison that I bought of him.
KING HENRY O Thou eternal mover of the heavens,°   *(God)*
20   Look with a gentle eye upon this wretch.
    O, beat away the busy meddling fiend
    That lays strong siege unto this wretch's soul,
    And from his bosom purge this black despair.
WARWICK See how the pangs of death do make him grin.°   *bare his teeth*
25 SALISBURY Disturb him not; let him pass peaceably.
KING HENRY Peace to his soul, if God's good pleasure be.
    Lord Card'nal, if thou think'st on heaven's bliss,
    Hold up thy hand, make signal of thy hope.
        CARDINAL [BEAUFORT] *dies*
    He dies and makes no sign. O God, forgive him.
30 WARWICK So bad a death argues a monstrous life.
KING HENRY Forbear to judge, for we are sinners all.

---

4. Iris was the messenger of the gods, particularly of Juno.   1. Twigs smeared with birdlime. See note to 1.3.92.
3.3 Location: The Cardinal's bedchamber, London.

Close up his eyes and draw the curtain close,
And let us all to meditation.°   *prayer*

Exeunt [drawing the curtains. The bed is removed]

4.1

Alarums within, and the chambers° be discharged like as   *small cannon*
it were a fight at sea. And then enter the CAPTAIN *of the*
ship, the MASTER, *the Master's* MATE, *Walter* WHITMORE,[1]
and others. [With them, as their prisoners,] the Duke of
SUFFOLK, *disguised [and two* GENTLEMEN]

CAPTAIN   The gaudy, blabbing, and remorseful day[2]
Is crept into the bosom of the sea;
And now loud-howling wolves arouse the jades[3]
That drag the tragic melancholy night;
5   Who, with their drowsy, slow, and flagging wings
Clip° dead men's graves, and from their misty jaws   *Embrace*
Breathe foul contagious darkness in the air.
Therefore bring forth the soldiers of our prize,°   *captured ship*
For whilst our pinnace° anchors in the downs,°   *small ship / anchorage*
10   Here shall they make their ransom on the sand,
Or with their blood stain this discoloured shore.[4]
Master, [*pointing to the* FIRST GENTLEMAN] this prisoner freely give I thee,
[*To the* MATE] And thou, that art his mate, make boot of this.[5]
[*He points to the* SECOND GENTLEMAN]
[*To Walter* WHITMORE] The other [*pointing to* SUFFOLK], Walter
Whitmore, is thy share.
FIRST GENTLEMAN [*to the* MASTER]   What is my ransom, Master,
15   let me know.
MASTER   A thousand crowns, or else lay down your head.
MATE [*to the* SECOND GENTLEMAN] And so much shall you give,
or off goes yours.
CAPTAIN [*to both the* GENTLEMEN]   What, think you much to pay
two thousand crowns,
And bear the name and port° of gentlemen?   *demeanor*
20   WHITMORE   Cut both the villains' throats! [*To* SUFFOLK] For die you shall.
The lives of those which we have lost in fight
[   ][6]
Be counterpoised° with such a petty sum.   *Be compensated*
FIRST GENTLEMAN [*to the* MASTER]   I'll give it, sir, and therefore
spare my life.
SECOND GENTLEMAN [*to the* MATE]   And so will I, and write
25   home for it straight.
WHITMORE [*to* SUFFOLK]   I lost mine eye in laying the prize
aboard,°   *boarding the ship*
And therefore to revenge it, shalt thou die—
And so should these, if I might have my will.
CAPTAIN   Be not so rash; take ransom; let him live.
30   SUFFOLK   Look on my George[7]—I am a gentleman.

4.1 Location: At sea off the Kentish coast.
1. Q's stage direction reads, "Water Whickmore," anticipating the later play on "Walter" and "Water."
2. The garish, telltale (revealing secrets of the dark), and
guilty day.
3. Referring contemptuously to the dragons ("jades")
that, according to classical myth, drew night's chariot.
4. Or discolor this shore with their blood.

5. Make a profit from (the ransom of) this second prisoner.
6. A line appears to be missing from F at this point, probably one indicating that the ransom demanded can never
compensate for the lives lost in battle.
7. Alluding to the image of St. George and the dragon on
the insignia of the Order of the Garter, the highest order
of English knighthood.

Rate° me at what thou wilt, thou shalt be paid.   *Value*
WHITMORE   And so am I; my name is Walter[8] Whitmore.
        [SUFFOLK] *starteth*
How now—why starts thou? What doth thee affright?
SUFFOLK   Thy name affrights me, in whose sound is death.
35   A cunning man did calculate my birth,[9]
And told me that by 'water' I should die.
Yet let not this make thee be bloody-minded;
Thy name is Gualtier,[1] being rightly sounded.
WHITMORE   Gualtier or Walter—which it is I care not.
40   Never yet did base dishonour blur our name
But with our sword we wiped away the blot.
Therefore, when merchant-like I sell revenge,
Broke be my sword, my arms° torn and defaced,   *coat of arms*
And I proclaimed a coward through the world.
45   SUFFOLK   Stay, Whitmore; for thy prisoner is a prince,
The Duke of Suffolk, William de la Pole.
WHITMORE   The Duke of Suffolk muffled up in rags?
SUFFOLK   Ay, but these rags are no part of the Duke.
Jove sometime went disguised, and why not I?
50   CAPTAIN   But Jove was never slain as thou shalt be.
SUFFOLK   Obscure and lousy° swain, King Henry's blood,[2]   *lice-infested*
The honourable blood of Lancaster,
Must not be shed by such a jady groom.[3]
Hast thou not kissed thy hand° and held my stirrup?   *(a gesture of servility)*
55   Bare-headed plodded by my foot-cloth mule[4]
And thought thee happy when I shook° my head?   *nodded*
How often hast thou waited at my cup,
Fed from my trencher,° kneeled down at the board°   *platter / table*
When I have feasted with Queen Margaret?
60   Remember it, and let it make thee crestfall'n,[5]
Ay, and allay this thy abortive° pride,   *monstrous*
How in our voiding lobby° hast thou stood   *antechamber*
And duly waited for my coming forth?
This hand of mine hath writ° in thy behalf,   *written testimonials*
65   And therefore shall it charm° thy riotous tongue.   *silence*
WHITMORE   Speak, Captain—shall I stab the forlorn swain?°   *wretched peasant*
CAPTAIN   First let my words stab him as he hath me.
SUFFOLK   Base slave, thy words are blunt° and so art thou.   *harmless*
CAPTAIN   Convey him hence and, on our longboat's side,
Strike off his head.
70   SUFFOLK   Thou dar'st not for thy own.
CAPTAIN Pole—
SUFFOLK   Pole?[6]
CAPTAIN   Ay, kennel,° puddle, sink,° whose filth   *open gutter / cesspool*
        and dirt
Troubles the silver spring where England drinks,

---

8. "Walter" was usually pronounced "water." The spirit Asnath, conjured by Roger Bolingbroke, had predicted that Suffolk should die by "water" (see 1.4.32).
9. An astrologer cast my horoscope.
1. French for "Walter."
2. A dubious claim: Suffolk's mother was a distant cousin to Henry VI.
3. Servant in charge of horses; contemptible fellow.
4. The animal used to bear the large, richly ornamented

cloth displayed in royal processions.
5. Humble; deprived of a "crest" (coat of arms).
6. The fact that Suffolk's family name could be pronounced "pool" leads to the punning insults that follow. Lines 71–72 are garbled in F (see Textual Variants). Oxford's reconstruction assumes that abbreviations for "Suffolk" and "Lieutenant" were misread as "Sir" and "Lord" by those who set type from the Folio manuscript.

Now will I dam up this thy yawning mouth
For swallowing the treasure of the realm.
75 Thy lips that kissed the Queen shall sweep the ground,
And thou that smiledst at good Duke Humphrey's death
Against the senseless° winds shalt grin in vain,   *unfeeling*
Who in contempt shall hiss at thee again.
And wedded be thou to the hags of hell,
80 For daring to affy° a mighty lord   *betroth*
Unto the daughter of a worthless king,
Having neither subject, wealth, nor diadem.
By devilish policy art thou grown great,
And like ambitious Sylla,[7] overgorged
85 With gobbets° of thy mother's° bleeding heart.   *chunks / (England's)*
By thee Anjou and Maine were sold to France,
The false revolting° Normans, thorough° thee,   *rebellious / because of*
Disdain to call us lord, and Picardy
Hath slain their governors, surprised our forts,
90 And sent the ragged soldiers, wounded, home.
The princely Warwick, and the Nevilles all,
Whose dreadful swords were never drawn in vain,
As hating thee, are rising up in arms;
And now the house of York, thrust from the crown,
95 By shameful murder of a guiltless king[8]
And lofty, proud, encroaching tyranny,
Burns with revenging fire, whose hopeful colours
Advance° our half-faced sun,[9] striving to shine,   *Display*
Under the which is writ, '*Invitis nubibus*'.°   *In spite of clouds*
100 The commons here in Kent are up in arms,
And, to conclude, reproach and beggary
Is crept into the palace of our King,
And all by thee. [*To* WHITMORE] Away, convey him hence.
SUFFOLK   O that I were a god, to shoot forth thunder
105 Upon these paltry, servile, abject drudges.
Small things make base men proud. This villain here,
Being captain of a pinnace, threatens more
Than Bargulus, the strong Illyrian pirate.[1]
Drones° suck not eagles' blood, but rob beehives.   *Beetles; parasites*
110 It is impossible that I should die
By such a lowly vassal as thyself.
Thy words move rage, and not remorse in me.
CAPTAIN   But my deeds, Suffolk, soon shall stay thy rage.
SUFFOLK   I go of message° from the Queen to France—   *as messenger*
115 I charge thee, waft° me safely cross the Channel!   *convey*
CAPTAIN   Walter—
WHITMORE   Come, Suffolk, I must waft thee to thy death.
SUFFOLK   *Paene gelidus timor occupat artus*[2] —
It is thee I fear.
120 WHITMORE   Thou shalt have cause to fear before I leave thee.
What, are ye daunted now? Now will ye stoop?

---

7. The Roman dictator Sulla, notorious for drawing up
lists of enemies whom he executed or banished.
8. Alluding to the deposition and murder of Richard II,
which allowed the Lancastrian branch of the royal family
to seize the throne. Shakespeare dramatizes these events
in *Richard II*.
9. A sun emerging above clouds was the badge of Edward

III and his successor, Richard II.
1. An ancient pirate alluded to in Cicero's *De officiis* (*On
Public Duties*), a text much used in Elizabethan schools.
2. Cold fear seizes my limbs almost entirely (perhaps
alluding to Virgil, *Aeneid* 7.446; Lucan, *Pharsalia* 1.246;
or both).

FIRST GENTLEMAN [*to* SUFFOLK] My gracious lord, entreat
    him—speak him fair.
SUFFOLK Suffolk's imperial tongue is stern and rough,
    Used to command, untaught to plead for favour.
125   Far be it we should honour such as these
    With humble suit. No, rather let my head
    Stoop to the block than these knees bow to any
    Save to the God of heaven and to my king;
    And sooner dance upon a bloody pole[3]
130   Than stand uncovered to the vulgar groom.
    True nobility is exempt from fear;
    More can I bear than you dare execute.
CAPTAIN Hale° him away, and let him talk no more.   *Drag*
SUFFOLK Come, 'soldiers', show what cruelty ye can,
135   That this my death may never be forgot.
    Great men oft die by vile Besonians;[4]
    A Roman sworder and banditto° slave   *cutthroat and lawless*
    Murdered sweet Tully; Brutus' bastard hand[5]
    Stabbed Julius Caesar; savage islanders
140   Pompey the Great;[6] and Suffolk dies by pirates.
                       Exit WHITMORE *with* SUFFOLK
CAPTAIN And as for these whose ransom we have set,
    It is our pleasure one of them depart.
    [*To the* SECOND GENTLEMAN] Therefore, come you with us
      and [*to his men, pointing to the* FIRST GENTLEMAN] let
      him go.
                Exeunt. Manet the FIRST GENTLEMAN
        Enter WHITMORE *with* [*Suffolk's head and*] *body*
WHITMORE There let his head and lifeless body lie,
145   Until the Queen his mistress bury it.   *Exit*
FIRST GENTLEMAN O barbarous and bloody spectacle!
    His body will I bear unto the King.
    If he revenge it not, yet will his friends;
    So will the Queen, that living held him dear.
             [*Exit with Suffolk's head and body*]

4.2

Enter two REBELS *with long staves*[1]
FIRST REBEL Come and get thee a sword, though made of a
    lath;[2] they have been up° these two days.   *in revolt*
SECOND REBEL They have the more need to sleep now then.
FIRST REBEL I tell thee, Jack Cade the clothier[3] means to dress
5   the commonwealth, and turn it,[4] and set a new nap upon it.[5]

---

3. Punning on his name ("Pole") and on Elizabethan slang for "head" ("poll"), Suffolk alludes to the fact that heads of executed criminals were set upon poles in public places. Londoners would often pass by such poles as they crossed the bridge on their way to the theaters in Southwark.
4. Base fellows. From the Spanish word *bisoño*, meaning "recruit": foot soldiers were usually poor commoners.
5. Brutus, who helped murder Caesar, was rumored to have been his illegitimate son. *Tully*: the Roman orator Cicero, who was in fact murdered by Roman soldiers.
6. Alluding either to Plutarch's claim that the Egyptians who murdered this Roman general were led by one born

on the island of Chios or to the tradition that Pompey was murdered on the island of Lesbos.
4.2 Location: Blackheath, Kent.
1. Staves are mentioned only in the Q stage directions and dialogue and may reflect performance.
2. A strip of wood commonly used as a sword or dagger by the Vice figure in English morality plays.
3. Clothiers, or textile workers, were involved in a number of uprisings throughout the sixteenth century.
4. Turn it inside out (as a way of renewing old cloth), with a secondary sense of inverting the social hierarchy.
5. Improve its surface texture, probably by brushing the outer fibers ("nap") of the cloth; reform it.

SECOND REBEL   So he had need, for 'tis threadbare. Well, I say it
was never merry world in England since gentlemen came up.°   *came into fashion*
FIRST REBEL   O, miserable age! Virtue is not regarded in handicraftsmen.°   *artisans*
10   SECOND REBEL   The nobility think scorn to go in leather aprons.°   *(workers' attire)*
FIRST REBEL   Nay more, the King's Council are no good
workmen.
SECOND REBEL   True; and yet it is said 'Labour in thy vocation';
which is as much to say as 'Let the magistrates be labouring
15   men'; and therefore should we be magistrates.
FIRST REBEL   Thou hast hit it; for there's no better sign of a
brave° mind than a hard° hand.   *fine / calloused*
SECOND REBEL   I see them! I see them! There's Best's son, the
tanner of Wingham—
20   FIRST REBEL   He shall have the skins of our enemies to make
dog's leather⁶ of.
SECOND REBEL   And Dick the butcher—
FIRST REBEL   Then is sin struck down like an ox, and iniquity's
throat cut like a calf.
25   SECOND REBEL   And Smith the weaver—
FIRST REBEL   Argo,⁷ their thread of life is spun.
SECOND REBEL   Come, come, let's fall in with them.
       Enter Jack CADE, *Dick [the]* BUTCHER, *Smith the*
       WEAVER, *a sawyer, [and a drummer,] with infinite num-*
       bers, [all] with long staves
CADE   We, John Cade, so termed of° our supposed father—   *named for*
BUTCHER [*to his fellows*]   Or rather of stealing a cade° of herrings.   *barrel*
30   CADE   For our enemies shall fall before us,⁸ inspired with the
spirit of putting down kings and princes—command silence!
BUTCHER   Silence!
CADE   My father was a Mortimer—
BUTCHER [*to his fellows*]   He was an honest man and a good
35   bricklayer.⁹
CADE   My mother a Plantagenet—
BUTCHER [*to his fellows*]   I knew her well, she was a midwife.
CADE   My wife descended of the Lacys¹—
BUTCHER [*to his fellows*]   She was indeed a pedlar's daughter and
40   sold many laces.
WEAVER [*to his fellows*]   But now of late, not able to travel with
her furred pack,² she washes bucks³ here at home.
CADE   Therefore am I of an honourable house.
BUTCHER [*to his fellows*]   Ay, by my faith, the field is honourable,
45   and there was he born, under a hedge; for his father had never
a house but the cage.°   *prison*
CADE   Valiant I am—
WEAVER [*to his fellows*]   A° must needs, for beggary is valiant.⁴   *He*
CADE   I am able to endure much—

---

6. Inferior leather used in glove making.
7. A variant form of *ergo*, Latin for "therefore."
8. Borrowing biblical language and punning on the Latin *cadere*, meaning "fall."
9. Punning on "Mortimer" and "mortarer" (meaning "builder").
1. The family name of the earls of Lincoln.
2. Not able to travel with her peddler's pack made of

skins with the hair turned outward; not able to make a living ("travail") with her sexual organs.
3. She washes laundry; she absolves ("washes") cuckolds (husbands with horns, like bucks) of their shame by helping them get even with their unfaithful wives.
4. Worthy of praise; sturdy. The Weaver is referring ironically to the fact that Elizabethan poor laws made it illegal to give alms to able-bodied, or "valiant," beggars.

50 BUTCHER [*to his fellows*] No question of that, for I have seen
   him whipped[5] three market days together.
   CADE I fear neither sword nor fire.
   WEAVER [*to his fellows*] He need not fear the sword, for his coat
   is of proof.[6]
55 BUTCHER [*to his fellows*] But methinks he should stand in fear
   of fire, being burned i'th' hand for stealing of sheep.[7]
   CADE Be brave, then, for your captain is brave and vows reformation. There shall be in England seven halfpenny loaves sold
   for a penny, the three-hooped pot shall have ten hoops,[8] and I
60 will make it felony to drink small° beer. All the realm shall be   *weak*
   in° common, and in Cheapside[9] shall my palfrey° go to grass.   *held in / saddle horse*
   And when I am king, as king I will be—
   ALL CADE'S FOLLOWERS God save your majesty!
   CADE I thank you good people!—there shall be no money. All
65 shall eat and drink on my score,° and I will apparel them all in   *at my expense*
   one livery that they may agree like brothers, and worship me
   their lord.
   BUTCHER The first thing we do let's kill all the lawyers.
   CADE Nay, that I mean to do. Is not this a lamentable thing that
70 of the skin of an innocent lamb should be made parchment?
   That parchment, being scribbled o'er, should undo a man?
   Some say the bee stings, but I say 'tis the bee's wax.° For I did   *sealing wax*
   but seal[1] once to a thing, and I was never mine own man since.
   How now? Who's there?
       Enter [some bringing forth] the CLERK *of Chatham*
75 WEAVER The Clerk of Chatham—he can write and read and
   cast account.°   *do arithmetic*
   CADE O, monstrous!
   WEAVER We took him setting of boys' copies.[2]
   CADE Here's a villain.
80 WEAVER He's a book in his pocket with red letters[3] in't.
   CADE Nay, then he is a conjuror!
   BUTCHER Nay, he can make obligations° and write court hand.[4]   *bonds*
   CADE I am sorry for't. The man is a proper° man, of mine hon-   *handsome*
   our. Unless I find him guilty, he shall not die. Come hither,
85 sirrah, I must examine thee. What is thy name?
   CLERK Emmanuel.
   BUTCHER They use to write that on the top of letters[5]—'twill go
   hard with you.
   CADE Let me alone. [*To the* CLERK] Dost thou use to write thy
90 name? Or hast thou a mark[6] to thyself like an honest plain-
   dealing man?
   CLERK Sir, I thank God I have been so well brought up that I
   can write my name.
   ALL CADE'S FOLLOWERS He hath confessed—away with him! He's
95 a villain and a traitor.

5. The usual punishment for vagabonds.
6. Impenetrable (from dirt?); well-worn.
7. Thieves were branded on one hand with a "T" for
"thief."
8. "Hoops," or regularly spaced bands on pots, were used
for measuring. Cade means that for the price of a three-
hooped pot (about a quart), one will receive over three
times that amount.
9. Elizabethan London's chief commercial district.

1. Sign and seal (a legal document).
2. Preparing writing exercises for schoolboys. Village
clerks often doubled as schoolmasters.
3. Alluding to the red printing in almanacs and primers.
4. The script used for legal documents.
5. The name, which means "God is with us," commonly
appeared on legal documents.
6. Those who were illiterate often "signed" documents
by using distinctive marks.

CADE Away with him, I say, hang him with his pen and inkhorn
about his neck.   *Exit one with the* CLERK
          Enter [a MESSENGER*]*[7]
MESSENGER Where's our general?
CADE Here I am, thou particular[8] fellow.
100 MESSENGER Fly, fly, fly! Sir Humphrey Stafford and his brother
are hard by with the King's forces.
CADE Stand, villain, stand—or I'll fell thee down. He shall be
encountered with a man as good as himself. He is but a knight,
is a?
105 MESSENGER No.[9]
CADE To equal him I will make myself a knight presently.
          [*He kneels and knights himself*]
Rise up, Sir John Mortimer.
          [*He rises*]
Now have at him!
          Enter Sir Humphrey STAFFORD *and his brother, with [a]*
          drum[mer] and soldiers
STAFFORD [*to Cade's followers*] Rebellious hinds,° the filth and   peasants
scum of Kent,
110 Marked for the gallows, lay your weapons down;
Home to your cottages, forsake this groom.
The King is merciful, if you revolt.°   turn against Cade
STAFFORD'S BROTHER [*to Cade's followers*] But angry, wrathful,
and inclined to blood,
If you go forward. Therefore, yield or die.
115 CADE [*to his followers*] As for these silken-coated slaves, I pass° not.   care
It is to you, good people, that I speak,
Over whom, in time to come, I hope to reign—
For I am rightful heir unto the crown.
STAFFORD Villain, thy father was a plasterer
120 And thou thyself a shearman,[1] art thou not?
CADE And Adam was a gardener.
STAFFORD'S BROTHER   And what of that?
CADE Marry, this: Edmund Mortimer, Earl of March,
Married the Duke of Clarence' daughter, did he not?
STAFFORD Ay, sir.
125 CADE By her he had two children at one birth.
STAFFORD'S BROTHER That's false.
CADE Ay, there's the question—but I say 'tis true.
The elder of them, being put to nurse,
Was by a beggar-woman stol'n away,
130 And, ignorant of his birth and parentage,
Became a bricklayer when he came to age.
His son am I—deny it an° you can.   if
BUTCHER Nay, 'tis too true—therefore he shall be king.
WEAVER Sir, he made a chimney in my father's house, and the
135 bricks are alive at this day to testify. Therefore deny it not.
STAFFORD [*to Cade's followers*] And will you credit this base drudge's words
That speaks he knows not what?
ALL CADE'S FOLLOWERS Ay, marry, will we—therefore get ye gone.

---

7. Q calls this figure "Tom," F "Michael."
8. Private (as opposed to "general" in the previous line).
9. No, nothing but a knight. The Messenger is replying
to the negative implied in the prior sentence: "He is nothing but a knight, is he?"
1. One who cuts the nap from cloth during its manufacture.

STAFFORD'S BROTHER   Jack Cade, the Duke of York hath taught you this.

140 CADE [*aside*]   He lies, for I invented it myself.
[*Aloud*] Go to, sirrah² —tell the King from me that for his
father's sake, Henry the Fifth, in whose time boys went to span-
counter° for French crowns,³ I am content he shall reign; but   *played a game of toss*
I'll be Protector over him.

145 BUTCHER   And, furthermore, we'll have the Lord Saye's head for
selling the dukedom of Maine.

CADE   And good reason, for thereby is England maimed, and
fain to go with a staff, but that my puissance° holds it up. Fel-   *power*
low-kings, I tell you that that Lord Saye hath gelded the com-
150 monwealth, and made it an eunuch, and, more than that, he
can speak French, and therefore he is a traitor!

STAFFORD   O gross and miserable ignorance!

CADE   Nay, answer if you can: the Frenchmen are our enemies;
go to, then, I ask but this—can he that speaks with the tongue
155 of an enemy be a good counsellor or no?

ALL CADE'S FOLLOWERS   No, no—and therefore we'll have his head!

STAFFORD'S BROTHER [*to* STAFFORD]   Well, seeing gentle words
will not prevail,
Assail them with the army of the King.

STAFFORD   Herald, away, and throughout every town
160 Proclaim them traitors that are up with Cade;
That those which fly before the battle ends
May, even in their wives' and children's sight,
Be hanged up for° example at their doors.   *to make an*
And you that be the King's friends, follow me!
Exeunt [the] STAFFORD[S] *and his men [their soldiers]*

165 CADE   And you that love the commons, follow me!
Now show yourselves men—'tis for liberty.
We will not leave one lord, one gentleman—
Spare none but such as go in clouted shoon,°   *hobnailed shoes*
For they are thrifty honest men, and such
170 As would, but that they dare not, take our parts.

BUTCHER   They are all in order, and march toward us.

CADE   But then are we in order when we are
Most out of order.° Come, march forward!   *rebellious*
Exeunt

4.3

Alarums to the fight; [excursions,]° wherein both the   *skirmishes*
STAFFORDS *are slain. Enter Jack* CADE, [*Dick the*
BUTCHER,] *and the rest*

CADE   Where's Dick, the butcher of Ashford?

BUTCHER   Here, sir.

CADE   They fell before thee like sheep and oxen, and thou
behaved'st thyself as if thou hadst been in thine own slaughter-
5 house. Therefore, thus will I reward thee—the Lent shall be as
long again as it is. Thou shalt have licence to kill for a hundred,
lacking one.¹

---

2. Term used to address inferiors.
3. Alluding to Henry V's conquest of France. "French
crowns" might refer to French coins, kings, kingdoms, or
the bald heads that were symptomatic of the venereal diseases blamed on the French.

4.3 Location: Scene continues.
1. Butchers were not permitted to slaughter meat during
Lent (the forty-day period before Easter during which
Christians were to avoid eating flesh) except by special
license to provide food for the ill. Cade promises the

BUTCHER   I desire no more.

CADE   And to speak truth, thou deserv'st no less.

[*He apparels himself in the Staffords' armour*]

10   This monument of the victory will I bear, and the bodies shall
be dragged at my horse heels till I do come to London, where
we will have the Mayor's sword borne before us.

BUTCHER   If we mean to thrive and do good, break open the jails
and let out the prisoners.

15   CADE   Fear not° that, I warrant thee. Come, let's march towards   *Don't worry about*
London.   *Exeunt* [*dragging the Staffords' bodies*]

4.4

Enter KING [HENRY] *reading a supplication,* QUEEN
[MARGARET] *with Suffolk's head, the Duke of* BUCKING-
HAM, *and the Lord* SAYE, *with others*

QUEEN MARGARET [*aside*]   Oft have I heard that grief softens the mind,
And makes it fearful and degenerate;
Think, therefore, on revenge, and cease to weep.
But who can cease to weep and look on this?

5   Here may his head lie on my throbbing breast,
But where's the body that I should embrace?

BUCKINGHAM [*to* KING HENRY]   What answer makes your grace to
the rebels' supplication?

KING HENRY   I'll send some holy bishop to entreat,
For God forbid so many simple souls

10   Should perish by the sword. And I myself,
Rather than bloody war shall cut them short,
Will parley° with Jack Cade their general.   *speak*
But stay, I'll read it over once again.
[*He*] read[s]

QUEEN MARGARET [*to Suffolk's head*]   Ah, barbarous villains!
Hath this lovely face

15   Ruled like a wandering planet over me,[1]
And could it not enforce them to relent,
That were unworthy to behold the same?

KING HENRY   Lord Saye, Jack Cade hath sworn to have thy head.

SAYE   Ay, but I hope your highness shall have his.

KING HENRY [*to* QUEEN MARGARET]   How now, madam? Still

20   lamenting and mourning
Suffolk's death?
I fear me, love, if that I had been dead,
Thou wouldest not have mourned so much for me.

QUEEN MARGARET   No, my love, I should not mourn, but die for thee.

Enter a MESSENGER [*in haste*]

25   KING HENRY   How now? What news? Why com'st thou in such haste?

MESSENGER   The rebels are in Southwark[2]—fly, my lord!
Jack Cade proclaims himself Lord Mortimer,
Descended from the Duke of Clarence' house,
And calls your grace usurper, openly,

30   And vows to crown himself in Westminster.

Butcher that he will have such a license and that Lent
will be twice as long as it is now. *Thou . . . one:* You can
kill ninety-nine animals, or serve ninety-nine customers.
4.4 Location: The palace, London.
1. It was popularly believed that influences from the stars

("wandering planets") determined the fate of those born
under them.
2. A suburb of London (in Shakespeare's time, the site of
brothels and theaters).

His army is a ragged multitude
Of hinds and peasants, rude and merciless.
Sir Humphrey Stafford and his brother's death
Hath given them heart and courage to proceed.
35 All scholars, lawyers, courtiers, gentlemen,
They call false caterpillars° and intend their death.   *treacherous parasites*
KING HENRY   O, graceless° men; they know not what they do.   *sinful*
BUCKINGHAM   My gracious lord, retire to Kenilworth°   *(a royal castle)*
Until a power be raised to put them down.
40 QUEEN MARGARET   Ah, were the Duke of Suffolk now alive
These Kentish rebels would be soon appeased!°   *made peaceful*
KING HENRY   Lord Saye, the trait'rous rabble hateth thee—
Therefore away with us to Kenilworth.
SAYE   So might your grace's person be in danger.
45 The sight of me is odious in their eyes,
And therefore in this city will I stay
And live alone as secret as I may.
            Enter another MESSENGER
SECOND MESSENGER [*to* KING HENRY]   Jack Cade hath almost gotten
         London Bridge;
The citizens fly and forsake their houses;
50 The rascal people, thirsting after prey,
Join with the traitor; and they jointly swear
To spoil° the city and your royal court.   *plunder*
BUCKINGHAM [*to* KING HENRY]   Then linger not, my lord; away, take horse!
KING HENRY   Come, Margaret. God, our hope, will succour us.
55 QUEEN MARGARET [*aside*]   My hope is gone, now Suffolk is deceased.
KING HENRY [*to* SAYE]   Farewell, my lord. Trust not the Kentish rebels.
BUCKINGHAM [*to* SAYE]   Trust nobody, for fear you be betrayed.
SAYE   The trust I have is in mine innocence,
And therefore am I bold and resolute.
            Exeunt [SAYE *at one door, the rest at another*]

4.5

Enter the Lord SCALES *upon the Tower, walking. Enter*
three or four CITIZENS *below*[1]
SCALES   How now? Is Jack Cade slain?
FIRST CITIZEN   No, my lord Scales, nor likely to be slain, for he
and his men have won the bridge, killing all those that did
withstand them. The Lord Mayor craveth aid of your honour
5 from the Tower to defend the city from the rebels.
SCALES   Such aid as I can spare you shall command,
But I am troubled here with them myself.
The rebels have essayed° to win the Tower.   *attempted*
Get you to Smithfield,[2] there to gather head,°   *raise forces*
10 And thither will I send you Matthew Gough.
Fight for your king, your country, and your lives!
And so, farewell, for I must hence again.
            Exeunt [SCALES *above, the* CITIZENS *below*]

4.5 Location: The Tower, London.
1. Q1's stage direction indicates that three or four citizens enter here; F's stage direction indicates two or three.
Oxford explains the discrepancy by arguing that Q3,
which omits all mention of citizens entering, was the text
consulted when this portion of F was being typeset.
Because the dialogue makes clear that citizens do enter
here, those preparing F improvised a stage direction.
2. Area just outside London's walls and to the northwest.

4.6

Enter Jack Cade, [the WEAVER, *the* BUTCHER,] *and the rest. [*CADE] *strikes his sword on London Stone*[1]

CADE   Now is Mortimer lord of this city. And, here sitting upon London Stone, I charge and command that, of the city's cost, the Pissing Conduit[2] run nothing but claret wine this first year of our reign. And now henceforward it shall be treason for any

5   that calls me otherwise than Lord Mortimer.

Enter a SOLDIER, *running*

SOLDIER   Jack Cade, Jack Cade!

CADE   Zounds, knock him down there!

They kill him

BUTCHER   If this fellow be wise, he'll never call ye Jack Cade more; I think he hath a very fair warning.

[He takes a paper from the soldier's body and reads it]

10   My lord, there's an army gathered together in Smithfield.

CADE   Come then, let's go fight with them—but first, go on and set London Bridge afire, and, if you can, burn down the Tower too. Come, let's away.   *Exeunt*

4.7

Alarums. [Excursions, wherein] Matthew GOUGH *is slain, and all the rest [of his men] with him. Then enter Jack* CADE *with his company [among them the* BUTCHER, *the* WEAVER, *and* JOHN, *a rebel]*

CADE   So, sirs, now go some and pull down the Savoy;[1] others to th' Inns of Court[2]—down with them all.

BUTCHER   I have a suit unto your lordship.

CADE   Be it a lordship, thou shalt have it for that word.

5   BUTCHER   Only that the laws of England may come out of your mouth.

JOHN *[aside to his fellows]*   Mass, 'twill be sore° law then, for he was thrust in the mouth with a spear, and 'tis not whole yet.   harsh

WEAVER *[aside to* JOHN]   Nay, John, it will be stinking law, for

10   his breath stinks with eating toasted cheese.

CADE   I have thought upon it—it shall be so. Away! Burn all the records of the realm. My mouth shall be the Parliament of England.

JOHN *[aside to his fellows]*   Then we are like to have biting° stat-   severe

15   utes unless his teeth be pulled out.

CADE   And henceforward all things shall be in common.

Enter a MESSENGER

MESSENGER   My lord, a prize, a prize! Here's the Lord Saye which sold the towns in France. He that made us pay one-and-twenty fifteens and one shilling to the pound the last subsidy.[3]

Enter a rebel with the Lord SAYE[4]

20   CADE   Well, he shall be beheaded for it ten times. [*To* SAYE] Ah,

---

4.6 Location: Cannon Street, London.
1. An ancient stone found in Cannon Street and famous as a London landmark.
2. The nickname for Little Conduit, a fountain used by lower-class Londoners as a water supply.
4.7 Location: Smithfield, London.
1. An anachronistic reference to the London residence of the Duke of Lancaster, which was burned down during a 1381 uprising and not rebuilt until 1505.

2. The buildings where London's lawyers were trained and lived.
3. He who made us pay very high personal property taxes in the last tax assessment. A "fifteen" was a levy of one-fifteenth of the property value; "twenty-one fifteens" would be a tax in excess of the value of the property itself.
4. F and Q both read, "Enter George." As elsewhere, the Oxford editors change what is assumed to be an actor's name to the generic "a rebel."

thou say, thou serge—nay, thou buckram lord![5] Now art thou
within point-blank° of our jurisdiction regal. What canst thou   *within reach*
answer to my majesty for giving up of Normandy unto Moun-
sieur Basimecu,[6] the Dauphin of France? Be it known unto
25   thee by these presence,[7] even the presence of Lord Mortimer,
that I am the besom° that must sweep the court clean of such   *broom*
filth as thou art. Thou hast most traitorously corrupted the
youth of the realm in erecting a grammar school; and, whereas
before, our forefathers had no other books but the score and
30   the tally,[8] thou hast caused printing to be used and, contrary to
the King his° crown and dignity, thou hast built a paper-mill.[9]   *the King's*
It will be proved to thy face that thou hast men about thee that
usually talk of a noun and a verb and such abominable words
as no Christian ear can endure to hear. Thou hast appointed
35   justices of peace to call poor men before them about matters
they were not able to answer. Moreover, thou hast put them in
prison, and, because they could not read,[1] thou hast hanged
them when indeed only for that cause° they have been most   *for that reason alone*
worthy to live. Thou dost ride on a foot-cloth, dost thou not?

40   SAYE   What of that?

    CADE   Marry, thou ought'st not to let thy horse wear a cloak
when honester men than thou go in° their hose and doublets.   *wear only*

    BUTCHER   And work in their shirts, too; as myself, for example,
that am a butcher.

45   SAYE   You men of Kent.

    BUTCHER   What say you of Kent?

    SAYE   Nothing but this—'tis *bona terra, mala gens*.[2]

    CADE   *Bonum terrum*—zounds, what's that?

    BUTCHER   He speaks French.

50   FIRST REBEL   No, 'tis Dutch.

    SECOND REBEL   No, 'tis Out-talian, I know it well enough.

    SAYE   Hear me but speak, and bear me where you will.
Kent, in the commentaries Caesar writ,
Is termed the civil'st° place of all this isle;   *most civilized*
55   Sweet is the country, because full of riches;
The people liberal,° valiant, active, wealthy;   *generous*
Which makes me hope you are not void of pity.
I sold not Maine, I lost not Normandy;
Yet to recover them would lose my life.
60   Justice with favour° have I always done,   *leniency*
Prayers and tears have moved me—gifts could never.
When have I aught° exacted at your hands,   *anything*
But to maintain the King, the realm, and you?
Large gifts have I bestowed on learnèd clerks°   *scholars*
65   Because my book preferred me to[3] the King,
And seeing ignorance is the curse of God,

5. Say was an expensive silk fabric, serge a durable
woolen fabric often worn by the lower classes, and buckram a coarse linen also worn by the poor.
6. Punning on *baise mon cul*, French for "kiss my ass."
7. "These presents" was a legal term meaning "the present document," a phrase that begins many legal writings
of the period. Cade, however, means "in the presence of
the King, who declares the law."
8. A rudimentary device for keeping track of financial
transactions. Sticks were marked, or "scored," split into
two pieces, and then divided between the debtor and

creditor. Each half was called a "tally."
9. Printing presses and paper mills were not in fact established in England until late in the fifteenth century.
Under Elizabeth, they were subject to strict regulation.
1. Read Latin. By demonstrating reading knowledge of
Latin, a person charged with a crime in early modern
England could plead "benefit of clergy" and thereby be
excused from hanging.
2. A good land, a bad people.
3. Because my own education brought me to the attention of the King (and improved my social position).

Knowledge the wing wherewith we fly to heaven.
Unless you be possessed with devilish spirits,
You cannot but forbear to murder me.
70 This tongue hath parleyed unto° foreign kings   *negotiated with*
For your behoof°—   *behalf*
CADE   Tut, when struck'st thou one blow in the field?°   *battlefield*
SAYE   Great men have reaching hands.[4] Oft have I struck
Those that I never saw, and struck them dead.
75 REBEL   O monstrous coward! What, to come behind folks?
SAYE   These cheeks are pale for watching for your good—
CADE   Give him a box o'th' ear, and that will make 'em red
again.
          [*One of the rebels strikes* SAYE]
SAYE   Long sitting° to determine poor men's causes   *(as a judge)*
80 Hath made me full of sickness and diseases.
CADE   Ye shall have a hempen caudle,[5] then, and the health
o'th' hatchet.°   *executioner's axe*
BUTCHER [*to* SAYE]   Why dost thou quiver, man?
SAYE   The palsy, and not fear, provokes me.
85 CADE   Nay, he nods at us as who should say 'I'll be even with
you'. I'll see if his head will stand steadier on a pole or no. Take
him away, and behead him.
SAYE   Tell me wherein have I offended most?
Have I affected wealth or honour? Speak.
90 Are my chests filled up with extorted gold?
Is my apparel sumptuous to behold?
Whom have I injured, that ye seek my death?
These hands are free from guiltless bloodshedding,
This breast from harbouring foul deceitful thoughts.
95 O let me live!
CADE [*aside*]   I feel remorse in myself with his words, but I'll
bridle it. He shall die an it be but for pleading so well for his
life. [*Aloud*] Away with him—he has a familiar° under his   *demon*
tongue; he speaks not a God's name. Go, take him away, I say,
100 to the Standard[6] in Cheapside, and strike off his head presently;° and then go to Mile End Green—break into his son-in-   *immediately*
law's house, Sir James Cromer, and strike off his head, and
bring them both upon two poles hither.
ALL CADE'S FOLLOWERS   It shall be done!
105 SAYE   Ah, countrymen, if, when you make your prayers,
God should be so obdurate as yourselves,
How would it fare with your departed souls?
And therefore yet relent and save my life!
CADE   Away with him, and do as I command ye!
           Exeunt [*the* BUTCHER *and*] *one or two*
           with the Lord SAYE
110 The proudest peer in the realm shall not wear a head on his
shoulders unless he pay me tribute. There shall not a maid be
married but she shall pay to me her maidenhead,[7] ere they

---

4. A variation on the classical proverb "Kings have long hands," suggesting that monarchs and influential people such as Lord Saye have influence that causes much to happen even when they are not present.
5. Caudel was a warm gruel, but "a hempen caudel" was a slang term for "hangman's noose."

6. A water conduit in Cheapside often used as a place of execution.
7. Alluding to a supposed feudal practice by which a lord had the right to sleep with the bride of any of his vassals on the night of her wedding.

have it. Married men shall hold of me *in capite*.[8] And we
charge and command that their wives be as free° as heart can   *sexually available*
115 wish or tongue can tell.
     Enter a REBEL
REBEL O captain, London Bridge is afire!
CADE Run to Billingsgate and fetch pitch and flax and quench
     it.
     Enter the BUTCHER *and a* SERGEANT
SERGEANT Justice, justice, I pray you, sir, let me have justice of
120 this fellow here.
CADE Why, what has he done?
SERGEANT Alas, sir, he has ravished° my wife.   *raped*
BUTCHER [*to* CADE] Why, my lord, he would have 'rested° me   *arrested*
     and I went and entered my action in his wife's proper house.[9]
125 CADE Dick, follow thy suit in her common place.[1] [*To the* SER-
     GEANT] You whoreson° villain, you are a sergeant—you'll take   *bastard*
     any man by the throat for twelve pence, and 'rest a man when
     he's at dinner, and have him to prison ere the meat be out of
     his mouth. [*To the* BUTCHER] Go, Dick, take him hence:
130 cut out his tongue for cogging,° hough° him for running, and,   *deception / cripple*
     to conclude, brain him with his own mace.°   *staff of office*
     Exit [*the* BUTCHER] *with the* SERGEANT
REBEL My lord, when shall we go to Cheapside and take up
     commodities upon our bills?[2]
CADE Marry, presently. He that will lustily stand to it[3] shall go
135 with me and take up these commodities following—item, a
     gown, a kirtle, a petticoat, and a smock.[4]
ALL CADE'S FOLLOWERS O brave!
     Enter two with the Lord Saye's head and Sir James
     Cromer's upon two poles
CADE But is not this braver? Let them kiss one another, for they
     loved well when they were alive.
     [*The two heads are made to kiss*]
140 Now part them again, lest they consult about the giving up of
     some more towns in France. Soldiers, defer the spoil° of the   *destruction; plunder*
     city until night. For with these borne before us instead of maces
     will we ride through the streets, and at every corner have them
     kiss. Away!
     Exeunt [*two with the heads. The others begin to follow*]
145 Up Fish Street! Down Saint Magnus' Corner![5] Kill and knock
     down! Throw them into Thames!
     Sound a parley
     What noise is this? Dare any be so bold to sound retreat or
     parley when I command them kill?
     Enter the Duke of BUCKINGHAM *and old Lord* CLIFFORD
BUCKINGHAM Ay, here they be that dare and will disturb thee!
150 Know, Cade, we come ambassadors from the King
     Unto the commons, whom thou hast misled,

---

8. A Latin phrase indicating property held by grant
directly from the king, with a pun on *caput* (Latin for
"head") as slang for "maidenhead."
9. Stated my case in his wife's own house; had sex in his
wife's own body.
1. Pursue your sexual desire in her vagina; pursue your
legal suit in her meetinghouse.
2. And acquire goods on credit or by means of our weap-

ons ("bills"); and rape women, punning on "commodity"
as meaning "female sexual organs" and "bills" as meaning
"penises."
3. Apply himself manfully; have an erection.
4. Slang terms for "female sexual organs."
5. Place at the north end of London Bridge opposite
Southwark.

And here pronounce free pardon to them all
That will forsake thee and go home in peace.
CLIFFORD   What say ye, countrymen, will ye relent
155   And yield to mercy whilst 'tis offered you,
Or let a rebel lead you to your deaths?
Who loves the King and will embrace his pardon,
Fling up his cap and say 'God save his majesty'.
Who hateth him and honours not his father,
160   Henry the Fifth, that made all France to quake,
Shake he his weapon at us,° and pass by.   *Defy us*
They [fling up their caps and] forsake CADE
ALL CADE'S FOLLOWERS   God save the King! God save the King!
CADE   What, Buckingham and Clifford, are ye so brave?° [*To the*   *arrogant*
rabble] And you, base peasants, do ye believe him? Will you
165   needs be hanged with your pardons about your necks? Hath
my sword, therefore, broke through London gates that you
should leave me at the White Hart[6] in Southwark? I thought
ye would never have given out° these arms till you had recov-   *abandoned*
ered your ancient freedom. But you are all recreants and das-
170   tards,° and delight to live in slavery to the nobility. Let them   *traitors and cowards*
break your backs with burdens, take your houses over your
heads, ravish your wives and daughters before your faces. For
me, I will make shift for one,° and so God's curse light upon   *take care of myself*
you all.
175   ALL CADE'S FOLLOWERS   We'll follow Cade! We'll follow Cade!
They run to CADE *again*
CLIFFORD   Is Cade the son of Henry the Fifth
That thus you do exclaim you'll go with him?
Will he conduct you through the heart of France
And make the meanest° of you earls and dukes?   *lowest born*
180   Alas, he hath no home, no place to fly to,
Nor knows he how to live but by the spoil—
Unless by robbing of your friends and us.
Were't not a shame that whilst you live at jar°   *at odds*
The fearful° French, whom you late vanquishèd,   *timid*
185   Should make a start° o'er seas and vanquish you?   *rouse themselves*
Methinks already in this civil broil
I see them lording it in London streets,
Crying '*Villiago!*'[7] unto all they meet.
Better ten thousand base-born Cades miscarry°   *meet disaster*
190   Than you should stoop unto a Frenchman's mercy.
To France! To France! And get what you have lost!
Spare England, for it is your native coast.
Henry hath money; you are strong and manly;
God on our side, doubt not of victory.
195   ALL CADE'S FOLLOWERS   A Clifford!° A Clifford! We'll follow the   *To Clifford*
King and Clifford!
[*They forsake* CADE]
CADE [*aside*]   Was ever feather so lightly blown to and fro as this
multitude? The name of Henry the Fifth hales° them to an   *draws*
hundred mischiefs, and makes them leave me desolate. I see
200   them lay their heads together to surprise° me. My sword make   *capture*

6. An inn, with a pun on the coward's "white heart"   7. A variation on the Italian word for "coward."
(because drained of its blood or spirit).

way for me, for here is no staying. [*Aloud*] In despite of the
devils and hell, have through° the very middest of you! And   *here I come through*
heavens and honour be witness that no want of resolution in
me, but only my followers' base and ignominious treasons,
205   makes me betake me to my heels.
                    He runs through them with his staff, and flies away
BUCKINGHAM   What, is he fled? Go, some, and follow him,
And he that brings his head unto the King
Shall have a thousand crowns for his reward.
                    Exeunt some of them [after CADE]
[*To the remaining rebels*] Follow me, soldiers, we'll devise a mean°   *way*
210   To reconcile you all unto the King.   *Exeunt*

<h2 style="text-align:center">4.8</h2>

Sound trumpets. Enter KING HENRY, QUEEN [MARGA-
RET], *and* [*the Duke of*] SOMERSET *on the terrace*
KING HENRY   Was ever King that joyed° an earthly throne   *enjoyed*
And could command no more content than I?
No sooner was I crept out of my cradle
But I was made a king at nine months old.
5   Was never subject longed to be a king
As I do long and wish to be a subject.
            Enter the Duke of BUCKINGHAM *and* [*Lord*] CLIFFORD
            [*on the terrace*]
BUCKINGHAM [*to* KING HENRY]   Health and glad tidings to your majesty.
KING HENRY   Why, Buckingham, is the traitor Cade surprised?
Or is he but retired to make him strong?
            Enter [*below*] *multitudes with halters*[1] *about their*
            necks
10   CLIFFORD   He is fled, my lord, and all his powers do yield,
And humbly thus with halters on their necks
Expect° your highness' doom° of life or death.   *Await / sentence*
KING HENRY   Then, heaven, set ope° thy everlasting gates   *open*
To entertain my vows of thanks and praise.
15   [*To the multitudes below*] Soldiers, this day have you redeemed your lives,
And showed how well you love your prince and country.
Continue still° in this so good a mind,   *always*
And Henry, though he be infortunate,°   *unlucky*
Assure yourselves will never be unkind.
20   And so, with thanks and pardon to you all,
I do dismiss you to your several countries.°   *different regions*
ALL CADE'S FORMER FOLLOWERS   God save the King! God save
the King!   [*Exeunt multitudes below*]
            Enter a MESSENGER [*on the terrace*]
MESSENGER [*to* KING HENRY]   Please it your grace to be advertisèd°   *informed*
25   The Duke of York is newly come from Ireland,
And with a puissant and a mighty power
Of galloglasses and stout Irish kerns[2]
Is marching hitherward in proud array,
And still proclaimeth, as he comes along,
30   His arms are only to remove from thee

4.8 Location: Kenilworth Castle.
1. Cade's followers wore nooses as a sign of their submission.

2. See note to 3.1.310. *galloglasses*: professional Irish
mercenary soldiers who were usually armed with axes and
rode on horseback.

The Duke of Somerset, whom he terms a traitor.

KING HENRY   Thus stands my state,° 'twixt Cade and York distressed,   *condition*
    Like to a ship that, having scaped a tempest,
    Is straightway calmed° and boarded with a pirate.   *becalmed*
35   But now is Cade driven back, his men dispersed,
    And now is York in arms to second° him.   *support*
    I pray thee, Buckingham, go and meet him,
    And ask him what's the reason of these arms.
    Tell him I'll send Duke Edmund° to the Tower;   *Somerset*
40   And, Somerset, we will commit thee thither,
    Until his army be dismissed from him.
SOMERSET   My lord, I'll yield myself to prison willingly,
    Or unto death, to do my country good.
KING HENRY [*to* BUCKINGHAM]   In any case, be not too rough in terms,°   *language*
45   For he is fierce and cannot brook° hard language.   *endure*
BUCKINGHAM   I will, my lord, and doubt not so to deal
    As all things shall redound unto your good.
KING HENRY   Come, wife, let's in and learn to govern better;
    For yet° may England curse my wretched reign.   *up until now*

                        Flourish. Exeunt

4.9

Enter Jack CADE[1]

CADE   Fie on ambitions; fie on myself that have a sword and yet
    am ready to famish. These five days have I hid me in these
    woods and durst not peep out, for all the country is laid° for   *set with traps*
    me. But now am I so hungry that if I might have a lease of my
5   life for a thousand years, I could stay° no longer. Wherefore   *delay*
    o'er a brick wall have I climbed into this garden to see if I can
    eat grass or pick a sallet° another while, which is not amiss to   *salad*
    cool a man's stomach° this hot weather. And I think this word   *hunger; anger*
    'sallet' was born to do me good; for many a time, but for a
10   sallet,° my brain-pan had been cleft with a brown bill;[2] and   *helmet*
    many a time, when I have been dry, and bravely marching, it
    hath served me instead of a quart pot to drink in; and now the
    word 'sallet' must serve me to feed on.
        [*He*] *lies down picking of herbs and eating them. Enter*
        [*Sir*] *Alexander* IDEN *and* [*five of*] *his men*
IDEN   Lord, who would live turmoilèd° in the court   *harried*
15   And may enjoy such quiet walks as these?
    This small inheritance my father left me
    Contenteth me, and worth a monarchy.
    I seek not to wax great by others' waning,
    Or gather wealth I care not with what envy;
20   Sufficeth that° I have maintains my state,   *that what*
    And sends the poor well pleasèd° from my gate.   *(with their alms)*
        [CADE *rises to his knees*]
CADE [*aside*]   Zounds, here's the lord of the soil come to seize
    me for a stray° for entering his fee-simple[3] without leave. [*To*   *trespasser*

4.9 Location: Alexander Iden's garden, in Kent.
1. Q's stage direction indicates that Jack Cade enters at one door and Alexander Iden and his men at another. Q's version of this scene is shorter than F's and makes clear what F only implies: that Iden is accompanied by attendants. The presence of these figures makes Cade's offer to fight Iden seem the more courageous. In Q, Iden enters

unarmed, orders one of his men to fetch his sword, and chivalrously orders them to stand aside while he fights Cade. In F, Iden presumably enters armed.
2. A long-handled weapon with an axe-like blade. The brown color is from blood or varnish.
3. Property that belonged forever to its owner and his or her heirs; on it, stray animals could legally be seized.

IDEN] A villain, thou wilt betray me and get a thousand crowns
of the king by carrying my head to him; but I'll make thee eat
iron like an ostrich[4] and swallow my sword like a great pin, ere
thou and I part.

CADE Why, rude companion,° whatsoe'er thou be,   *lowborn fellow*
I know thee not. Why then should I betray thee?
Is't not enough to break into my garden,
And, like a thief, to come to rob my grounds,
Climbing my walls in spite of me the owner,
But thou wilt brave° me with these saucy terms?   *taunt*

CADE Brave thee? Ay, by the best blood that ever was broached°—   *shed*
and beard° thee too! Look on me well—I have eat no meat   *defy*
these five days, yet come thou and thy five men, an if I do not
leave you all as dead as a doornail I pray God I may never eat
grass more.

IDEN Nay, it shall ne'er be said while England stands
That Alexander Iden, an esquire of Kent,
Took odds° to combat a poor famished man.   *advantage*
Oppose thy steadfast gazing eyes to mine—
See if thou canst outface me with thy looks.
Set limb to limb, and thou art far the lesser—
Thy hand is but a finger to my fist,
Thy leg a stick comparèd with this truncheon.°   *thick staff (his leg)*
My foot shall fight with all the strength thou hast,
And if mine arm be heavèd in the air,
Thy grave is digged already in the earth.
As for words, whose greatness answers words,[5]
Let this my sword report what speech forbears.
[*To his men*] Stand you all aside.

CADE By my valour, the most complete° champion that ever I   *accomplished*
heard. [*To his sword*] Steel, if thou turn the edge° or cut not   *fail to cut*
out the burly-boned clown in chines° of beef ere thou sleep in   *roasts*
thy sheath, I beseech God on my knees thou mayst be turned
to hobnails.
           [CADE *stands.*] *Here they fight, and* CADE *falls down*
O, I am slain! Famine and no other hath slain me! Let ten
thousand devils come against me, and give me but the ten
meals I have lost, and I'd defy them all. Wither, garden, and be
henceforth a burying place to all that do dwell in this house,
because the unconquered soul of Cade is fled.

IDEN Is't Cade that I have slain, that monstrous traitor?
Sword, I will hallow thee for this thy deed
And hang thee o'er my tomb when I am dead.
Ne'er shall this blood be wipèd from thy point
But thou shalt wear it as a herald's coat
To emblaze the honour that thy master got.[6]

CADE Iden, farewell, and be proud of thy victory. Tell Kent from
me she hath lost her best man, and exhort all the world to be
cowards. For I, that never feared any, am vanquished by famine, not by valour.   *He dies*

IDEN How much thou wrong'st me, heaven be my judge.

---

4. It was popularly believed that ostriches ate iron.
5. This line may be corrupt. It may mean "As for words,
I whose might more than matches your words."

6. *But . . . got:* Just as a device on a herald's coat proclaims his lord's identity and status, so the blood on Iden's
sword proclaims the fame he has won for killing Cade.

Die, damnèd wretch, the curse of her that bore thee!
75 And [*stabbing him again*] as I thrust thy body in with my sword,[7]
So wish I I might thrust thy soul to hell.
Hence will I drag thee headlong° by the heels   *head downward*
Unto a dunghill, which shall be thy grave,
And there cut off thy most ungracious head,
80 Which I will bear in triumph to the King,
Leaving thy trunk for crows to feed upon.

Exeunt [with the body]

5.1

Enter the Duke of YORK *and his army of Irish with [a]*
drum[mer] and soldiers [bearing] colours

YORK   From Ireland thus comes York to claim his right,
And pluck the crown from feeble Henry's head.
Ring, bells, aloud; burn, bonfires, clear and bright,
To entertain° great England's lawful king.   *welcome*
5 Ah, *sancta maiestas!*° Who would not buy thee dear?   *sacred majesty*
Let them obey that knows not how to rule;
This hand was made to handle naught but gold.
I cannot give due action to my words,
Except° a sword or sceptre balance it.   *Unless*
10 A sceptre shall it have, have I° a sword,   *as sure as I have*
On which I'll toss the fleur-de-lis of France.[1]

Enter the Duke of BUCKINGHAM

[*Aside*] Whom have we here? Buckingham to disturb me?
The King hath sent him sure—I must dissemble.
BUCKINGHAM   York, if thou meanest well, I greet thee well.
15 YORK   Humphrey of Buckingham, I accept thy greeting.
Art thou a messenger, or come of pleasure?
BUCKINGHAM   A messenger from Henry, our dread liege,
To know the reason of these arms° in peace;   *armed men*
Or why thou, being a subject as I am,
20 Against thy oath and true allegiance sworn,
Should raise so great a power without his leave,
Or dare to bring thy force so near the court?
YORK [*aside*]   Scarce can I speak, my choler is so great.
O, I could hew up rocks and fight with flint,
25 I am so angry at these abject terms;°   *insulting words*
And now, like Ajax Telamonius,[2]
On sheep or oxen could I spend my fury.
I am far better born than is the King,
More like a king, more kingly in my thoughts;
30 But I must make fair weather° yet a while,   *pretend to be mild*
Till Henry be more weak and I more strong.
[*Aloud*] Buckingham, I prithee pardon me,
That I have given no answer all this while;
My mind was troubled with deep melancholy.
35 The cause why I have brought this army hither
Is to remove proud Somerset from the King,
Seditious to his grace and to the state.

---

7. As I thrust my sword into your body.
5.1 Location: The remainder of the play takes place in
an open field between St. Albans and London.
1. On which I'll impale the national emblem of France,

the lily flower.
2. A Greek hero of the Trojan War who went mad and
slaughtered a flock of sheep, taking them to be his Greek
enemies.

BUCKINGHAM   That is too much presumption on thy part;
    But if thy arms be to no other end,
40   The King hath yielded unto thy demand:
    The Duke of Somerset is in the Tower.
YORK   Upon thine honour, is he prisoner?
BUCKINGHAM   Upon mine honour, he is prisoner.
YORK   Then, Buckingham, I do dismiss my powers.
45   Soldiers, I thank you all; disperse yourselves;
    Meet me tomorrow in Saint George's field.[3]
    You shall have pay and everything you wish.   *Exeunt soldiers*
    [*To* BUCKINGHAM] And let my sovereign, virtuous Henry,
    Command° my eldest son—nay, all my sons—   *Demand*
50   As pledges of my fealty and love.
    I'll send them all as willing as I live.
    Lands, goods, horse, armour, anything I have
    Is his to use, so° Somerset may die.   *provided that*
BUCKINGHAM   York, I commend this kind° submission.   *natural; proper*
55   We twain will go into his highness' tent.
        Enter KING HENRY *and attendants*
KING HENRY   Buckingham, doth York intend no harm to us,
    That thus he marcheth with thee arm in arm?
YORK   In all submission and humility
    York doth present himself unto your highness.
60 KING HENRY   Then what intends these forces thou dost bring?
YORK   To heave the traitor Somerset from hence,
    And fight against that monstrous rebel Cade,
    Who since I heard to be discomfited.°   *defeated*
        Enter IDEN *with Cade's head*
IDEN   If one so rude° and of so mean condition°   *uncultivated / low rank*
65   May pass into the presence of a king,
    [*Kneeling*] Lo, I present your grace a traitor's head,
    The head of Cade, whom I in combat slew.
KING HENRY   The head of Cade? Great God, how just art thou!
    O let me view his visage, being dead,
70   That living wrought me such exceeding trouble.
    Tell me, my friend, art thou the man that slew him?
IDEN [*rising*]   Iwis,° an't like° your majesty.   *Truly / if it please*
KING HENRY   How art thou called? And what is thy degree?°   *rank*
IDEN   Alexander Iden, that's my name;
75   A poor esquire[4] of Kent that loves his king.
BUCKINGHAM [*to* KING HENRY]   So please it you, my lord, 'twere not amiss
    He were created knight for his good service.
KING HENRY   Iden, kneel down.
        [IDEN *kneels and* KING HENRY *knights him*]
                    Rise up a knight.
        [IDEN *rises*]
    We give thee for reward a thousand marks,
80   And will° that thou henceforth attend on us.   *command*
IDEN   May Iden live to merit such a bounty,
    And never live but true unto his liege.   *Exit*
        Enter QUEEN [MARGARET] *and the Duke of* SOMERSET
KING HENRY   See, Buckingham, Somerset comes wi'th' Queen.

---

3. One of the main drill grounds for Elizabethan militia,   4. A member of the gentry ranking just below a knight.
located south of the Thames.

Go bid her hide him quickly from the Duke.
85 QUEEN MARGARET   For thousand Yorks he shall not hide his head,
But boldly stand and front° him to his face.   *confront*
YORK   How now? Is Somerset at liberty?
Then, York, unloose thy long imprisoned thoughts,
And let thy tongue be equal with thy heart.
90 Shall I endure the sight of Somerset?
False King, why hast thou broken faith with me,
Knowing how hardly I can brook abuse?[5]
'King' did I call thee? No, thou art not king;
Not fit to govern and rule multitudes,
95 Which dar'st not—no, nor canst not—rule a traitor.
That head of thine doth not become a crown;
Thy hand is made to grasp a palmer's° staff,   *pilgrim's*
And not to grace an aweful° princely sceptre.   *awe-inspiring*
That gold must round engird these brows of mine,
100 Whose smile and frown, like to Achilles' spear,
Is able with the change to kill and cure.[6]
Here is a hand to hold a sceptre up,
And with the same to act° controlling laws.   *enact*
Give place! By heaven, thou shalt rule no more
105 O'er him whom heaven created for thy ruler.
SOMERSET   O monstrous traitor! I arrest thee, York,
Of capital treason 'gainst the King and crown.
Obey, audacious traitor; kneel for grace.
YORK [*to an attendant*]   Sirrah, call in my sons to be my bail.
                                                     [*Exit attendant*]
110 I know, ere they will have me go to ward,°   *into custody*
They'll pawn° their swords for my enfranchisement.°   *pledge / freedom*
QUEEN MARGARET [*to* BUCKINGHAM]   Call hither Clifford; bid
        him come amain,°   *at once*
To say if that the bastard boys of York
Shall be the surety for their traitor father.   [*Exit* BUCKINGHAM]
115 YORK   O blood-bespotted Neapolitan,[7]
Outcast of Naples, England's bloody scourge!
The sons of York, thy betters in their birth,
Shall be their father's bail, and bane° to those   *destruction*
That for my surety will refuse the boys.
        Enter at one door York's sons EDWARD *and crookback*
        RICHARD *with [a] drum[mer] and soldiers*[8]
120 See where they come. I'll warrant they'll make it good.
        Enter at the other door CLIFFORD *and his son, with [a]*
        drum[mer] and soldiers
QUEEN MARGARET   And here comes Clifford to deny their bail.
CLIFFORD [*kneeling before* KING HENRY]   Health and all happi-
        ness to my lord the King.
        [*He rises*]
YORK   I thank thee, Clifford. Say, what news with thee?
Nay, do not fright us with an angry look—
125 We are thy sovereign, Clifford; kneel again.

5. Knowing with what difficulty I can tolerate deception.
6. Telephus, wounded by Achilles' spear, was cured by rust from that same spear.
7. Margaret's father claimed the throne of Naples. Elizabethan writers typically associated Italy with sexual vice,

criminality, and the evils of Roman Catholicism.
8. This spectacular double entry of York's sons, followed by Clifford and his son, each accompanied by drummer and soldiers, is indicated only in Q. F's stage directions read, "Enter Edward and Richard" and "Enter Clifford."

For thy mistaking so, we pardon thee.
CLIFFORD   This is my king, York; I do not mistake.
But thou mistakes me much to think I do.
[*To* KING HENRY] To Bedlam[9] with him! Is the man grown mad?
130 KING HENRY   Ay, Clifford, a bedlam° and ambitious humour°   mad / disposition
Makes him oppose himself against his king.
CLIFFORD   He is a traitor; let him to the Tower,
And chop away that factious pate° of his.   rebellious head
QUEEN MARGARET   He is arrested, but will not obey.
135 His sons, he says, shall give their words for him.
YORK [*to* EDWARD *and* RICHARD]   Will you not, sons?
EDWARD   Ay, noble father, if our words will serve.
RICHARD   And if words will not, then our weapons shall.
CLIFFORD   Why, what a brood of traitors have we here!
140 YORK   Look in a glass,° and call thy image so.   mirror
I am thy king, and thou a false-heart traitor.
Call hither to the stake my two brave bears,
That with the very shaking of their chains,
They may astonish these fell-lurking° curs.[1]   savagely waiting
145 [*To an attendant*] Bid Salisbury and Warwick come to me.
                                        [*Exit attendant*]
        Enter the Earls of WARWICK *and* SALISBURY *with* [*a*]
        drum[mer] and soldiers
CLIFFORD   Are these thy bears? We'll bait thy bears to death,
And manacle the bearherd° in their chains,   bear keeper (York)
If thou dar'st bring them to the baiting place.°   bear pit
RICHARD   Oft have I seen a hot o'erweening° cur   overconfident
150 Run back and bite,° because he was withheld;   (his keeper)
Who, being suffered with° the bear's fell° paw,   injured by / savage
Hath clapped his tail between his legs and cried;
And such a piece of service will you do,
If you oppose yourselves° to match Lord Warwick.   undertake
155 CLIFFORD   Hence, heap of wrath, foul indigested lump,
As crooked in thy manners as thy shape![2]
YORK   Nay, we shall heat you thoroughly anon.°   soon
CLIFFORD   Take heed, lest by your heat you burn yourselves.
KING HENRY   Why, Warwick, hath thy knee forgot to bow?
160 Old Salisbury, shame to thy silver hair,
Thou mad misleader of thy brainsick son!
What, wilt thou on thy deathbed play the ruffian,
And seek for sorrow with thy spectacles?°   eyes; eyeglasses
O, where is faith? O, where is loyalty?
165 If it be banished from the frosty head,
Where shall it find a harbour in the earth?
Wilt thou go dig a grave to find out° war,   in seeking out
And shame thine honourable age with blood?
Why, art thou old and want'st° experience?   lack
170 Or wherefore dost abuse it if thou hast it?
For shame in duty bend thy knee to me,

---

9. The shortened name of a London lunatic asylum. See
note to 3.1.51.
1. York refers to the Elizabethan sport of bearbaiting, in
which a tame bear was chained to a stake and set upon
with dogs. Warwick's family crest depicted a bear chained
to a staff. See below, lines 200–1.

2. *foul . . . shape*: alluding to the fact that Richard of
Gloucester was deformed from birth (he was a hunchback) and to the notion that bears are born as formless
lumps and licked into shape by their mothers. *indigested*:
ill-formed.

That bows unto the grave with mickle° age.   *much*
SALISBURY My lord, I have considered with myself
  The title of this most renownèd Duke,
175 And in my conscience do repute his grace
  The rightful heir to England's royal seat.
KING HENRY Hast thou not sworn allegiance unto me?
SALISBURY I have.
KING HENRY Canst thou dispense with heaven for³ such an oath?
180 SALISBURY It is great sin to swear unto a sin,
  But greater sin to keep a sinful oath.
  Who can be bound by any solemn vow
  To do a murd'rous deed, to rob a man,
  To force a spotless virgin's chastity,
185 To reave° the orphan of his patrimony,   *bereave*
  To wring the widow from her customed right,⁴
  And have no other reason for this wrong
  But that he was bound by a solemn oath?
QUEEN MARGARET A subtle traitor needs no sophister.°   *expert in false reasoning*
KING HENRY [*to an attendant*] Call Buckingham, and bid him
190   arm himself.   [*Exit attendant*]
YORK [*to* KING HENRY] Call Buckingham and all the friends thou hast,
  I am resolved for death or dignity.°   *(the crown)*
CLIFFORD The first, I warrant thee, if dreams prove true.
WARWICK You were best to go to bed and dream again,
195 To keep you from the tempest of the field.
CLIFFORD I am resolved to bear a greater storm
  Than any thou canst conjure up today—
  And that I'll write upon thy burgonet°   *helmet*
  Might I but know thee by thy household badge.°   *family crest*
200 WARWICK Now by my father's badge, old Neville's crest,⁵
  The rampant bear chained to the ragged° staff,   *jagged*
  This day I'll wear aloft° my burgonet,   *on top of*
  As on a mountain top the cedar shows
  That keeps his leaves in spite of any storm,
205 Even to affright thee with the view thereof.
CLIFFORD And from thy burgonet I'll rend thy bear,
  And tread it under foot with all contempt,
  Despite the bearherd that protects the bear.
YOUNG CLIFFORD And so to arms, victorious father,
210 To quell the rebels and their complices.°   *accomplices*
RICHARD Fie, charity, for shame! Speak not in spite—
  For you shall sup with Jesu Christ tonight.
YOUNG CLIFFORD Foul stigmatic,⁶ that's more than thou canst tell.
RICHARD If not in heaven, you'll surely sup in hell.
                                 Exeunt [*severally*]

---

3. Can you win dispensation from heaven for breaking.
4. Her traditional right to a portion of her husband's estate.
5. The Neville badge was actually a bull. Warwick inherited the badge of a bear from his father-in-law, Richard Beauchamps.
6. One branded with the mark of crime, as Richard is "branded" with deformity.

5.2

*[An alehouse sign: a castle.] Alarums to the battle. Then
enter the Duke of* SOMERSET *and* RICHARD *fighting.* RICH-
ARD *kills* [SOMERSET] *under the sign*

RICHARD So lie thou there—
For underneath an alehouse' paltry sign,
The Castle in Saint Albans, Somerset
Hath made the wizard famous in his death.[1]
5   Sword, hold thy temper;[2] heart, be wrathfull still—
Priests pray for enemies, but princes kill.

Exit [with Somerset's body. The sign is removed]

5.3

Alarum again. Enter the Earl of WARWICK

WARWICK Clifford of Cumberland, 'tis Warwick calls!
An if thou dost not hide thee from the bear,
Now, when the angry trumpet sounds alarum,
And dead° men's cries do fill the empty air,   *dying*
5   Clifford I say, come forth and fight with me!
Proud northern lord, Clifford of Cumberland,
Warwick is hoarse with calling thee to arms!

CLIFFORD *[within]* Warwick, stand still; and stir not till I come.

Enter [the Duke of] YORK

WARWICK How now, my noble lord? What, all afoot?°   *not on horseback*
10 YORK The deadly-handed Clifford slew my steed.
But match to match I have encountered him,
And made a prey for carrion kites and crows
Even of the bonny beast he loved so well.

Enter [Lord] CLIFFORD

WARWICK *[to* CLIFFORD*]* Of one or both of us the time is come.
15 YORK Hold, Warwick—seek thee out some other chase,°   *game*
For I myself must hunt this deer to death.

WARWICK Then nobly, York; 'tis for a crown thou fight'st.
[To CLIFFORD*]* As I intend, Clifford, to thrive today,
It grieves my soul to leave thee unassailed.   *Exit*

20 YORK Clifford, since we are singled here alone,
Be this the day of doom to one of us.
For know my heart hath sworn immortal hate
To thee and all the house of Lancaster.

CLIFFORD And here I stand and pitch my foot to thine,
25 Vowing not to stir till thou or I be slain.
For never shall my heart be safe at rest
Till I have spoiled° the hateful house of York.   *stripped of honor*

Alarums. They fight. YORK *kills* CLIFFORD

YORK Now, Lancaster, sit sure—thy sinews shrink.°   *powers fail*
Come, fearful° Henry, grovelling on thy face—   *timid*
30 Yield up thy crown unto the prince of York.[1]   *Exit*

30.1   CLIFFORD *What seest thou in me, York? Why dost thou pause?*
     YORK *With thy brave bearing° should I be in love,*   *fine appearance*
     But that thou art so fast mine enemy.

5.2 Location: Scene continues.
1. Somerset's death under the sign of the Castle Inn confirms the spirit's warning that he shun castles (see 1.4.34–36). *in his:* by his (Somerset's).
2. Retain the resiliency of steel.

5.3 Location: Scene continues.
1. Oxford adopts Q's version of the confrontation between Clifford and York at lines 20–30; the F version, an edited text of which follows in the indented passage (lines 30.1–30.12), may be the author's original draft.

CLIFFORD *Nor should thy prowess want° praise and esteem,*   lack
30.5   *But that 'tis shown ignobly and in treason.*
YORK *So let it help me now against thy sword,*
      As I in justice and true right express it.
CLIFFORD *My soul and body on the action,° both.*   fight
YORK *A dreadful lay.° Address° thee instantly.*   wager / Prepare
30.10 CLIFFORD *La fin couronne les oeuvres.*[2]
          Alarums. They fight. YORK *kills* CLIFFORD
      YORK *Thus war hath given thee peace, for thou art still.*
      Peace with his soul, heaven, if it be thy will.   Exit
      Alarums, then enter YOUNG CLIFFORD
YOUNG CLIFFORD Shame and confusion, all is on the rout!°   in disorderly retreat
Fear frames° disorder, and disorder wounds   gives rise to
Where it should guard. O, war, thou son of hell,
Whom angry heavens do make their minister,
35 Throw in the frozen° bosoms of our part°   cowardly / faction
Hot coals of vengeance! Let no soldier fly!
He that is truly dedicate° to war   dedicated
Hath no self-love; nor he that loves himself
Hath not essentially, but by circumstance,°   merely by accident
The name of valour.
          [*He sees his father's body*]
40   O, let the vile world end,
And the premisèd° flames of the last day   foreordained
Knit earth and heaven together.
Now let the general trumpet blow his blast,[3]
Particularities° and petty sounds   Individual affairs
45 To cease! Wast thou ordainèd, dear father,
To lose thy youth in peace, and to achieve
The silver livery of advisèd° age,   wise
And in thy reverence and thy chair-days,° thus   old age
To die in ruffian battle? Even at this sight
50 My heart is turned to stone, and while 'tis mine
It shall be stony. York not our old men spares;
No more will I their babes. Tears virginal
Shall be to me even as the dew to fire,[4]
And beauty that the tyrant oft reclaims°   calms the tyrant
55 Shall to my flaming wrath be oil and flax.
Henceforth I will not have to do with pity.
Meet I an infant of the house of York,
Into as many gobbets° will I cut it   lumps of flesh
As wild Medea young Absyrtus did.[5]
60 In cruelty will I seek out my fame.
Come, thou new ruin of old Clifford's house,
          He takes [*his father's body*] *up on his back*
As did Aeneas old Anchises bear,[6]
So bear I thee upon my manly shoulders.
But then Aeneas bare a living load,
65 Nothing so heavy as these woes of mine.   [*Exit with the body*]

2. The end crowns the works (French).
3. Young Clifford is evoking doomsday, when a trumpet will summon everyone to judgment (see 1 Corinthians 15:52).
4. Dew was popularly believed to make fire burn more fiercely.
5. According to classical myth, as Medea fled over the sea with her lover, Jason, she murdered her brother Absyrtus and scattered bits of his body on the waves so that her father would stop to collect the fragments and be delayed in his pursuit of her.
6. In Virgil's *Aeneid* 2.707–29, Aeneas carries his aged father, Anchises, on his back in their escape from the burning city of Troy.

5.4

Alarums again. Then enter three or four bearing the
Duke of BUCKINGHAM *wounded to his tent. Alarums still.*
Enter KING [HENRY], QUEEN [MARGARET], *and others*

QUEEN MARGARET   Away, my lord! You are slow. For shame, away!
KING HENRY   Can we outrun the heavens?° Good Margaret, stay.   *escape our fate*
QUEEN MARGARET   What are you made of? You'll nor° fight nor fly.   *neither*
   Now is it manhood, wisdom, and defence,
5 To give the enemy way, and to secure us°   *save ourselves*
   By what° we can, which° can no more but fly.   *whatever means / who*
     Alarum afar off
   If you be ta'en, we then should see the bottom
   Of all our fortunes; but if we haply scape°—   *by chance escape*
   As well we may if not° through your neglect—   *if we don't fail*
10 We shall to London get where you are loved,
   And where this breach now in our fortunes made
   May readily be stopped.
     Enter [YOUNG] CLIFFORD
YOUNG CLIFFORD [*to* KING HENRY]   But that my heart's on future
     mischief set,
   I would speak blasphemy ere° bid you fly;   *before I would*
15 But fly you must; uncurable discomfit°   *irreversible defeat*
   Reigns in the hearts of all our present parts.°   *remaining forces*
   Away for your relief, and we will live
   To see their day and them our fortune give.[1]
   Away, my lord, away!   *Exeunt*

5.5

Alarum. Retreat. Enter the Duke of YORK, [*his sons*
EDWARD *and*] RICHARD, *and soldiers,* [*including a*]
drum[*mer*] *and* [*some bearing*] *colours*

YORK [*to* EDWARD *and* RICHARD]   How now, boys! Fortunate this
     fight hath been,
   I hope, to us and ours for England's good
   And our great honour, that so long we lost
   Whilst faint-heart Henry did usurp our rights.
5 Of Salisbury, who can report of him?
   That winter° lion who in rage forgets   *aged*
   Agèd contusions and all brush of time,[1]
   And, like a gallant in the brow° of youth,   *prime*
   Repairs° him with occasion.° This happy day   *Revives / action*
10 Is not itself, nor have we won one foot
   If Salisbury be lost.
RICHARD   My noble father,
   Three times today I holp° him to his horse;   *helped*
   Three times bestrid him;[2] thrice I led him off,
   Persuaded him from any further act;
15 But still° where danger was, still there I met him,   *always*
   And like rich hangings in a homely° house,   *humble*
   So was his will in his old feeble body.
     Enter [*the Earls of*] SALISBURY *and* WARWICK

5.4 Location: Scene continues.
1. we . . . give: we will survive to see a day of victory like
theirs and to make them suffer misfortunes like ours.

5.5 Location: Scene continues.
1. Bruises of old age and all assaults of time.
2. Stood over the fallen Salisbury to protect him.

EDWARD [*to* YORK] See, noble father, where they both do come —
　　The only props unto the house of York!
20　SALISBURY　Now, by my sword, well hast thou fought today;
　　By th' mass, so did we all. I thank you, Richard.
　　God knows how long it is I have to live,
　　And it hath pleased him that three times today
　　You have defended me from imminent death.
25　Well, lords, we have not got that which we have[3] —
　　'Tis not enough our foes are this time fled,
　　Being opposites of such repairing nature.[4]
　　YORK　I know our safety is to follow them,
　　For, as I hear, the King is fled to London,
30　To call a present court of Parliament.
　　Let us pursue him ere the writs° go forth.　　　　　　　*summons to Parliament*
　　What says Lord Warwick, shall we after them?
　　WARWICK　After them? Nay, before them if we can!
　　Now by my hand, lords, 'twas a glorious day!
35　Saint Albans battle won by famous York
　　Shall be eternized° in all age to come.　　　　　　　　　*immortalized*
　　Sound drums and trumpets, and to London all,
　　And more such days as these to us befall!　　[*Flourish.*] *Exeunt*

TEXTUAL VARIANTS

Control text: F, primarily, and Q1 for some passages: 1.1.54–70; 2.1.70 s.d.; 2.1.116–53 s.d.; 4.5 initial s.d.–4.6 initial s.d.; and most of 2.3, from s.d. following line 58 to initial s.d. in 2.4. In these five passages, readings taken from F are treated as variants of Q1 and marked as such. In addition, this edition prints some material from Q not in F but that derives, the Oxford editors believe, from a revised version of the Folio text. These passages are also marked in the variants because they are alterations to the control text. For discussion of the status of this text, see the Textual Note; for a much fuller collation and discussion of Q and F variants, see Oxford's *William Shakespeare: A Textual Companion*.

F: The Folio of 1623
Q1: The Quarto of 1594
Q2: The Quarto of 1600
Q3: The Quarto of 1619

s.p. KING HENRY [F's use of *King* has been changed throughout.]
s.p. QUEEN MARGARET [F's use of *Queen* has been changed throughout.]
s.p. CARDINAL BEAUFORT [F's use of *Cardinal* and *Winchester* has been standardized throughout.]
s.p. GLOUCESTER [F's use of *Gloucester* and *Humphrey* has been standardized throughout.]
s.p. DUCHESS [F's use of *Elianor* and *Duchess* has been standardized throughout.]
s.p. HORNER [F's use of *Armorer* has been changed throughout.]
s.p. BOLINGBROKE [F's spelling, *Bullingbrooke*, has been changed throughout.]
s.p. ASNATH [F's use of *Spirit* (in 1.4) has been changed.]

---

3. We have not secured what we have won.
4. Since they are enemies who can quickly recover what they have lost.

s.p. SIMPCOX'S WIFE [F's use of *Wife* (in 2.1) has been changed.]

s.p. CAPTAIN [F's use of *Lieutenant* (in 4.1) has been changed to Q's *Captain*.]

s.p. WHITMORE [F's use of *Whitmore* and *Walter* (in 4.1) has been standardized.]

s.p. FIRST REBEL [F's use of *Bevis* has been changed throughout.]

s.p. SECOND REBEL [F's use of *Holland* has been changed throughout.]

s.p. MESSENGER [F's use of *Michael* (in 4.2) has been changed.]

s.p. STAFFORD'S BROTHER [F's use of *Brother* (in 4.2) has been changed.]

s.p. WEAVER [F's use of *Smith* and *Weaver* has been standardized throughout.]

s.p. BUTCHER [F's use of *Dicke* and *Butcher* has been standardized throughout.]

s.p. REBEL [Q's use of *Robin* has been changed at 4.7.116 (Q is control text for this section).]

s.p. CLIFFORD [F's use of *Clifford* and *Old Clifford* has been standardized throughout.]

s.p. YOUNG CLIFFORD [F's use of *Clifford* and *Young Clifford* has been standardized throughout.]

Title: *The first part of the contention of the two famous / Houses, of Yorke and Lancaster* [Q running title] THE / First part of the Con- / tention betwixt the two famous Houses of Yorke / and Lancaster, with the death of the good / Duke Humphrey: / And the banishment and death of the Duke of / *Suffolke,* and the Tragicall end of the proud Cardinall / of *Winchester,* with the notable Rebellion / of *Jacke Cade:* / And the Duke of Yorkes first claime unto / the Crowne [Q title page] The second Part of Henry the Sixt, / with the death of the Good Duke / HUMFREY [F head title]

1.1.24–29 Th' . . . King [Q, not in F; for F's version of this speech, see inset passage in text.] **24 excess of** excessive **28 naught** nothing **35 s.p. LORDS** *kneel*[*ing*] *All kneel.* **44 René** Raynard [Q] Reignier [F] **47 it is further agreed between them** [Q; not in F] **49 fa–** [Q] *father* **54–70** [Q is control text for these lines.] **55 duchy of Anjou and the county of** Duches of *Anioy* and of **56 delivered** delivered over **63 I'th** [F] in the **89 had** hath **141 But I'll . . . speak.** [Q; not in F] **166 hoist** hoyse **175 Protector** [Q] Protectors **189 thee** [Q] the **196–97 The reverence . . . command.** [Q; not in F] **207 Then let's away** Then lets make hast away **250 surfeit in the** surfetting in **255 in** [Q] in in

1.2.19 hour thought **22 dream** dreames **38 are** [Q] wer **75 Jordan** *Jordane* **cunning witch of Eye** cunning witch [F]

1.3.6 s.p. FIRST PETITIONER *Peter* **33 master** Mistresse **34–36 usurer . . . usurper** [Q] Usurper **45 s.p. ALL PETITIONERS** *All* **72 haught** haughtie **94 their** the **104 helm** [Q] Helme. *Exit.* **146 I'd** [Q] I could [F] **149 pamper** hamper **154 fury** Fume **208 judge by case** judge **215 s.p. KING HENRY** Then . . . of Somerset [Q; not in F] **216–17 We make . . . foes.** We make your grace Regent over the French, / And to defend our rights gainst forraine foes, / And so do good unto the Realme of *France* [Q; not in F] **226 be** shall be

1.4.23 Asnath Asmath **31 Tell me what fate awaits** [Q2, Q3] what fates await **33 betide** [Q] befall **37–38** [For Q's version of these lines, see inset passage in text.] **42 deep** deeply **56–57 What have . . . posse.** [In F, York reads the prophecies aloud at this point; Q transposes this reading to the next scene and assigns it to King Henry at 2.1.177–87]. **56 s.d.** [*He*] **reads** [*the writings*] Reades. / The Duke yet lives, that Henry shall depose: / But him out-live, and dye a violent death. **57 Aeacidam** AEacida **posse** posso. / Well, to the rest: / Tell me what fate awaits the Duke of Suffolke? / By Water shall he dye, and take his end. / What shall betide the Duke of Somerset? / Let him shunne Castles, Safer shall he be upon the sandie Plaines, / Then where Castles mounted stand **58–59 These oracles are hardily attained / And hardly understood. Come, come, my lord,** Come, come, my Lords, These oracles are hardily attained / And hardly understood.

2.1.26 some such **37–43 s.p. GLOUCESTER . . . words.** [Q; not in F] **46 an if** And if **53 s.p. CARDINAL BEAUFORT** [F makes the line a continuation of Gloucester's prior speech.] **65 tell** and tell **74 sight** his sight **109 Alban** Albones **114 And . . . sir;** [Q]

What Coulour is my Gowne of? / *Simpc⟨oxe⟩*. Black forsooth, **116–53** [Q is control text for this section.] **117 before** [F] ere **a many** [F] many, a one **118 s.p. SIMPCOX'S WIFE** . . . **life.** [F; not in Q] **119 Tell** [F] But tell **128 Simon** Sander **Simpcox** [F; not in Q] **129 Simon** Sander **thou** [not in Q] **131 our** all our **133 distinguish** distinguish of **135 Saint** My Lords, Saint **Alban** [F] Albones **136 Would** and would **138 that** [F] I would **141 We have, my lord, an if it please your grace.** Yes, my Lord, if it please your Grace. **144 Bring** Now fetch **stool** stoole hither by and by **145 o'er** over **147 am not able even to** am not able to **149 sirrah** Sir **150 Whip** Sirrah Beadle, whip **177– 87** [Following Q, the Oxford editors move the reading of the prophecies from 1.4.56 to this location.] **176 And here's** . . . **them.** [Q; not in F] **177 s.p. KING HENRY** [Q] *Yorke*. **First . . . of him become?** become of him? [Q; not in F] **178–79 The Duke . . . death.** [after Q; not in F here] **180 God's will be done in all.** [Q; not in F] **Well, to the rest** [after F] **181–82 Tell . . . end.** [after Q; not in F here] **183–184 s.p. SUFFOLK . . . lie.** [Q; not in F] **185 s.p. KING HENRY** [Q; F assigns to York] **185–87 What . . . stand.** [after Q; not in F here]

2.2.6 out at full at full **26 well** all **28 Duke of York** Duke **41 Owain Glyndŵr** *Owen Glendour* **45 was** son was **46 son** Sonnes *Sonne* **56 John's** his **77 off** we off

2.3.3 sins sinne **19 grave** ground **30 helm** Realme **34 erst** [Q1, Q2] ere **35 willing** [Q] willingly **2.3.58–2.4.0** [In these lines, Q is control text for 2.3.58–75, 2.3.83–88, and 2.3.101–2.4.0] **78 an** if and if **88 well** [F; not in Q] **98 wame** way **99 enemy** Enemies

2.4.18 sheriffs [Q] Sherife **77, 103 s.p. FIRST SHERIFF** *Sh⟨erife⟩*, *Sherife*

3.1.78 wolf Wolves **98 Suffolk's Duke** [Q] *Suffolke* **137 my good** [Q] my **211 strains** strayes **264 conceit** deceit **319–30** [For the Q version of these lines, see inset passage in the text.] **330.2 'gainst** against **348 nurse** nourish **363 porcupine** Porpentine **381 coistrel** [Q] rascall [F]

3.2.14 Then draw the curtains close; away, be gone! Away, be gone **26 Meg** Nell **75 leper** Leaper **79 Queen Margaret** Dame *Elianor* **ne'er** neere **82 wrecked** wrack'd **83, 85 winds** [Q] winde **100 Margaret** *Elianor* **107 heart** Hart **116 witch** watch **120 Margaret** *Elinor* **223 born** borne **236 s.p. COMMONS . . . Suffolk! Down with Suffolk!** [Q; not in F; F s.d. reads A *noyse within*.] **243 s.p. COMMONS . . . the commons** [after Q; not in F] **272 s.p. COMMONS (*within*)** (*Commons within*.) **280 s.p. COMMONS (*within*)** *Within*. **310 enemies** [Q] enemy **312 Could** [Q] Would **320 My** mine **on** an **distraught** distract **334 turn** turnes **336 this** [Q] the **346 upon these lips** upon these **395 his** [Q] it's **402 By thee to die** [Q] To dye by thee

3.3.10 whe'er where

4.1.6 Clip Cleape **20 s.p. WHITMORE Cut** Cut **22** [line assumed missing] **33 thee** death **49 Jove sometime went disguised, and why not I?** [Q; not in F] **51 s.p. SUF-FOLK (*Suf.*)** [Q; not in F] **52 The** [Q] *Suf⟨folke⟩*. The **53 jady** [Q] iaded **71 s.p. CAP-TAIN . . . Ay** Lieu. Poole, Sir *Poole?* Lord, / I **77 shalt** [Q] shall **85 mother's bleeding** Mother-bleeding **93 are** and **113 s.p. CAPTAIN . . . rage.** [not in F] **114 s.p. SUFFOLK** [not in F] **116 s.p. CAPTAIN Walter—** s.p. WHITMORE Come *Lieu⟨tenant⟩*. Water: W. Come **118** *Paene* Pine **121 daunted** danted **134 s.p. SUFFOLK Come** Come **135 That** *Suf⟨folke⟩*. That

4.2.30 fall fail **75 Chatham** [Q] Chartam **80 He's** Ha's **87 that** [Q] it **90 an** a **132 an** [Q] if **135 testify** [Q1, Q2] testifie it **147 maimed** main'd

4.3.6 Thou [Q1, Q2] and thou **6 licence** a License

4.4.20 lamenting and mourning lamenting and mourning for **38 Kenilworth** Kill-ingworth **42 trait'rous rabble hateth** Traitors hateth **48 almost** [Q; not in F] **57 be betrayed** betraid

4.5–4.6.0 [Q is control text for these lines.] **2 lord Scales** Lord **2–3 he and his men** they **3–4 did withstand** withstand **8 essayed** [F] attempted **9 Get you to Smithfield, there to gather head** But get you to Smythfield, and gather head **10 will I** I will

4.6.5 otherwise [Q] other **7 Zounds** [Q; not in F] **10 My** *Dicke*. My **11 go on** [Q] go **12 afire** [Q1, Q3] on fire

4.7.21 serge Surge **24 Dauphin** Dolphine **39 on** [Q] in **43 their shirts** their shirt **48–51 *Bonum* . . . well enough.** [Q] Away with him, away with him, he speaks Latine. **63 But** Kent **81 caudle** Candle **81–82 the health o'** the help of **100 to the Standard in Cheapside** [Q; not in F] **101 go to Mile End Green** [Q; not in F] **113 Married men** [Q] Men **115 s.d.–131 s.d.** *Enter . . . Sergeant* [Q; not in F] **117 quench** [Q3] squench **124 went and** went and and **proper** paper **131 brain** Brave **134–36 He that . . . smock.** [Q; not in F] **147 What noise is this?** What noise is this heare? **156 rebel** rabble

4.8.27 stout Irish stout **34 calmed** calme

4.9.6 oe'r on **18 waning** warning **22 Zounds** Sounes [Q; not in F] **52 Stand you all aside.** [Q; not in F] **56 God** [Q] love **74 bore** bare

5.1.10 sword soule **72 Iwis** I was **83 wi'th'** with th' **109 Sirrah** Wold'st have me kneele? First let me ask of thee, / If they can brooke I bow a knee to man: / Sirrah **sons** [Q] sonne **111 for** of **147 bearheard** Berard **192 or** and **195 you** [Q] thee **199 household** [Q] housed **205 to** [Q] io [or possibly "so"]

5.2.0–6 *Alarums* . . . *Somerset's body.* [After F; F places this passage following 5.3.65.]

5.3.8 s.p. CLIFFORD Warwick . . . come. [Q; not in F] **20–30 s.p. YORK** Clifford . . . York. [Q; not in F. For the F version of this encounter, see inset passage in the text.] **20 Clifford** Now Clifford **22 know** now **25 not** never **30.10 oeuvres** *eumenes*

5.5.1–4 How now, . . . rights. [Q; not in F] **5.5.17 s.d.–19** *Enter . . . York* [Q] But Noble as he is, looke where he comes. / s.d. Enter Salisbury **37 drums** Drumme

Richard Duke of York
(3 Henry VI)

There are two Richards in the play known in its octavo version as *The True Tragedy of Richard Duke of York and the Good King Henry the Sixth (3 Henry VI)*. As the play begins, the title character, Richard of York, is leading an attempt to seize the English throne from Henry VI, the Lancastrian king. This Richard is killed at the end of the first act, and it is his tragic death to which the play's title refers. He, however, has four sons: Edward, Edmund (known as the Earl of Rutland), George, and Richard. This second Richard, who eventually acquires the title Duke of Gloucester, is a hunchback; and much of the play chronicles his attempts to continue his father's efforts to seize the English throne. Near the end of the play, this second Richard meditates on his condition:

> Then, since the heavens have shaped my body so,
> Let hell make crooked my mind to answer it.
> I had no father, I am like no father;
> I have no brother, I am like no brother;
> And this word, 'love', which greybeards call divine,
> Be resident in other men like one another
> And not in me — I am myself alone.
>
> (5.6.78–84)

This chilling pronouncement places Richard outside kinship networks, even though his two older brothers, Edward and George, are very much alive; and it exempts him from ordinary bonds of human affection.

Claiming to know nothing of love, Richard blames his isolation on his deformity. He is not "like" other men, not like his brothers, because heaven has shaped his body crookedly. This is a convenient explanation for villainy and alienation. But the play's exploration of deformity and its relationship to the breakdown of social order and emotional bonds is more complex than Richard here allows. Is Richard's hunchback the cause of his villainy or merely its outward sign? Are his villainy and deformity unique or simply the most tangible manifestation of a social deformity that reaches far beyond this single character? Richard's hump invites such questions, but the answers must be sought by broadly surveying the dramatic world in which Richard is placed.

Richard Duke of York is one of the most ambitious of Shakespeare's history plays simply in terms of the historical matter it covers. It is in part a continuation of *The First Part of the Contention of the Two Famous Houses of York and Lancaster (2 Henry VI)*, the play in which Shakespeare began to dramatize the Wars of the Roses between the Lancastrian descendants of Edward III, who took the red rose for their symbol, and his Yorkist descendants, who claimed the white. *Richard Duke of York* depicts many of the most significant military encounters of that war, stretching from the Battle of Wakefield (1460), in which the Duke of York was captured and killed by the Lancastrian forces of Henry VI, to the Battle of Tewkesbury in 1471, in which Edward, the eldest son of Richard Duke of York, decisively defeated the Lancastrian army. It is after the latter battle, and Richard Duke of Gloucester's subsequent murder of Henry VI in the Tower of London, that the hunchbacked Richard speaks his chilling lines about having no father and no brother.

As with all his history plays, Shakespeare's *Richard Duke of York* takes many liberties with its historical sources, in this case Raphael Holinshed's *Chronicles of England, Scotland, and Ireland* (1587 edition) and Edward Hall's *Union of the Two Noble and Illustre*

[Illustrious] Families of Lancaster and York (1548). Many historical events are simply omitted or conflated with other events, and aspects of the historical record are altered for dramatic or thematic purposes. For example, at the time of the Battle of Wakefield, at which Richard Duke of York was killed, his son Richard was only seven years old. But in Shakespeare's play, he is a grown man who himself participates in the battle and after it vows revenge for his father's death. Moreover, that death is handled with grim originality. In Hall, Clifford decapitates York, then puts a paper crown on his severed head and presents it on a pole to Margaret, Henry VI's warlike queen. In Holinshed, Clifford verbally torments York before beheading him. But in none of the sources does Margaret dominate the scene as she does in Shakespeare's play. In *Richard Duke of York*, she taunts York ferociously and—a detail found in none of the sources—to wipe his tears gives him a handkerchief that has been dipped in the blood of Rutland, York's twelve-year-old son, who had been butchered by Clifford earlier in the same battle. Eventually both Margaret and Clifford stab York, and Margaret orders his head displayed on the gates of the city of York. This act is

[typ]ical of Margaret's audacity throughout the play. [Th]e only character to appear in all four of Shake-[spe]are's first histories (*The First Part of the Con-tion [2 Henry VI]*, *Richard Duke of York [3 Henry [VI]*, *1 Henry VI*, and *Richard III*), Margaret domi-[nat]es much of the action of this one. Fiercely protec-[tive] of her son's rights and skilled as both general and [dip]lomat, she is unmatched as a publicly powerful [figu]re by any of the female characters in Shake-[spe]are's later histories.

The scene in which Margaret tortures York and [he] excoriates her as an Amazonian whore must have [bee]n riveting theater. In September of 1592, Robert [Gr]eene, a rival playwright, published *Greene's [Gr]oats-worth of Wit*, in which he makes fun of [Sh]akespeare by parodying a line from this scene. [Ric]hard at one point exclaims of Margaret, "O tiger's [hea]rt wrapped in a woman's hide!" (1.4.138). [Gre]ene writes of Shakespeare that "there is an [up]start Crow, beautified with our feathers, that with [his] *Tiger's heart wrapt in a Player's hide*, supposes he [is] well able to bombast out a blank verse as the [bes]t of you: and being an absolute *Johannes fac [tot]um* [jack-of-all-trades], is in his own conceit the [on]ly Shakes-scene in a country." Greene, who had [u]niversity education, was clearly angry at and jeal-[ous] of Shakespeare, who did not. He accuses Shake-[spe]are either of appropriating Greene's work or of [act]ing in Greene's dramas ("beautified with our [fea]thers") and of thinking too well of himself and [his] many theatrical skills. But particularly striking is [Gr]eene's own appropriation of Richard's line about [Ma]rgaret to apply to Shakespeare. Implicitly, [Gr]eene suggests that there is something as unnatural [and] presumptuous in Shakespeare's theatrical ambi-[tio]n as in the cruelty and ambition of Henry's man-[nish] Queen. At the same time, this appropriative gesture pays tribute, however grudging, to Shake-speare's skill as a writer of memorable dialogue. Affronted by Shakespeare's success, Greene none-

Seventeenth-century ornamental halberd from southern Germany.

theless grants his rival the homage of parody. The lines have another value as well. Though *Richard Duke of York* was first printed in a shortened octavo version in 1595, Greene's comments suggest that some version of the play had been staged or was circulating in manuscript by late summer of 1592 (see Textual Note).

This early play, then, may have brought Shakespeare contemporary notoriety. It certainly shows his boldness in adopting chronicle history to fit the requirements of the theater. And while some critics have seen *Richard Duke of York* as flawed, evidencing Shakespeare's weariness with his dramatization of the Wars of the Roses or his inability to shape so much matter into coherent form, theatrical productions of this play attest to its viability on the stage. The vicious energies of hate and ambition that propel the play make its enactment an intense and exhausting experience. The vigorous stage battles, the soaring rhetorical duels between the contending factions, the centrality of the ruthless Margaret, the emergence of the alienated Richard Duke of Gloucester as the brooding antihero— these are elements that, particularly in the post–World War II period, have led to many memorable productions, productions that emphasize a once-civil world spiraling vertiginously toward chaos.

But the play is also more than the sum of its memorable parts. When Richard asserts, "I am myself alone," his chosen isolation follows from the play's carefully orchestrated dramatization of the breakdown of social order, particularly as epitomized in the breakdown of family ties. From its inception, the Wars of the Roses, a continuing civil war, was also a family feud in that it pitted the Lancastrian and Yorkist descendants of Edward III against one another. But in the prior play, *The First Part of the Contention*, members of each family line and their followers typically remained loyal to their faction. Family lineage was a source of pride and identity. One sees this also in *1 Henry VI* in the idealized relationship between the English hero Lord Talbot and his son John. John aspires in all respects to emulate his father, and the two of them die together in battle defending England and the honor of their family name. In *Richard Duke of York*, by contrast, family bonds are hideously fragile; and when they break, chaos ensues. Unflinching in its depiction of emotional and physical violence, the play examines the forms of monstrous individualism that emerge when the social identities provided by networks of kinship and feudal loyalty no longer exert their hold. In effect, *Richard Duke of York* depicts the radical separation of self from defining social networks as a species of monstrosity.

The signal event in the play's treatment of the sundering of family bonds is King Henry's startling offer, at the beginning of Act 1, to entail the crown to Richard Duke of York in exchange for Henry's right to hold the throne during his lifetime. Henry has a son, Prince Edward, and his act negates his son's right to the throne. It also transforms the crown of England from a symbol of lineal succession into an alienable property. The immediate consequence is that Henry's supporters turn from him in disgust and his wife, Queen Margaret, proclaims:

> I here divorce myself
> Both from thy table, Henry, and thy bed,
> Until that act of Parliament be repealed
> Whereby my son is disinherited.
>
> (1.1.248–51)

Suddenly, Edward is *her* son, not Henry's; and soon thereafter she is raising an army to lead against the Yorkists. Many in the play describe Margaret's acts as unnatural, yet they follow from Henry's feckless negation of his role as guarantor of his son's succession. It was a truism of the early modern gender system that unmanly men, unnatural in their weakness, opened the door to a corresponding anomaly, the manlike woman. Margaret is represented as such a figure, taking Henry's place both at the head of his army and also as champion of young Edward's lineal rights. In both roles, the Queen is highly effective for much of the play. Though demonized, Margaret embodies strengths that contradict the patriarchal view that women are inherently weaker than men and therefore less suited to have dominion either in the state or in the household.

Edward IV. Probably painted during his reign (1442–1483); artist unknown.

Occasionally, especially in his early plays, Shakespeare wrote what Hereward T. Price called "mirror scenes," that is, scenes that are separate from the main line of plot development but that symbolically encapsulate, or mirror, some of the play's chief thematic concerns. In *Richard Duke of York*, 2.5 is such a scene. Having given command of his army to Clifford and Margaret, Henry sits contemplatively upon a molehill while the Battle of Towton proceeds without him. Voicing his longing for the simplicity of a pastoral life, Henry suddenly sees a soldier carry onstage a man he has killed. It turns out to be the soldier's father, who was forced to serve with the Yorkist forces, while the son had been impressed into King Henry's service. The King then observes a second soldier carry onstage a man *he* has killed. It turns out to be the soldier's son. The scene schematically underscores one of the play's primary emblems of social disintegration: namely, the severing of bonds between father and son, son and father, leaving nothing to replace these bonds but individual rapaciousness. In both instances, the killers of the dead men have brought the bodies onstage to search them for money—"some store of crowns" (2.5.57) and "gold" (80). The ironic power of the scene is heightened, of course, because its central events are witnessed and lamented by King Henry, who has already disinherited his own son and as King is the symbolic fountainhead from which the familial disorder before him flows.

But the most interesting variation on the theme of dissevered families is embodied in the persons of Richard Duke of York and his four sons: Edward, George, Richard, and Rutland. At the beginning of the play, the Yorks constitute an unusually integrated unit. Richard's sons support their father and urge him to seize the crown. Before he is captured at the Battle of Wakefield, Richard praises his offspring, assuming that in the battle "they have demeaned themselves / Like men born to renown by life or death" (1.4.7–8). At Wakefield, one of Richard's sons, the young Rutland, is killed. Just before the remaining three sons learn that their father has also died as a consequence of that battle, they praise him, as he has praised them. No one is more gracious than young Richard, who says, "Methinks 'tis prize enough to be his son" (2.1.20). At that moment, three suns appear in the heavens, each distinct, and then these suns join together. The pun on "suns/sons" seems to lead Edward to interpret this odd spectacle to mean that the three sons of Richard,

> Each one already blazing by our meeds,
> Should notwithstanding join our lights together
> And over-shine the earth as this the world.
> (2.1.36–38)

He then pledges to have three suns emblazoned on his shield.

Like all portents, the exact significance of this one is unclear. To Edward, it seems to imply the unwavering unity of the three sons of York. Yet Richard, who is to be as devastated as any of them by the news of their father's death, treats Edward's assertion that he will wear three suns on his shields as the occasion for a joke that distances him from his brother. "Nay, bear three daughters—by your leave I speak it— / You love the breeder better than the male" (2.1.41–42). With the death of the powerful patriarch, Richard Duke of York, fraternal rivalry quickly replaces fraternal unity, and broken allegiances multiply. When Edward insists on marrying a commoner, the widow Lady Elizabeth Gray, Warwick, who is Edward's strongest supporter and who has been sent to France to secure a French bride for Edward, turns against him in disgust. George temporarily abandons his brother, marries Warwick's daughter, and joins the Lancastrian cause. Richard, always outwardly loyal, privately vows to hack his way to the throne and displace both of his brothers in the process.

"My ashes, as the phoenix, may bring forth / A bird that will revenge upon you all" (1.4.36–37). From Geffrey Whitney, *A Choice of Emblemes* (1586).

With ties of kinship and loyalty broken, nothing remains but the sheer exertion of individual will. Richard emerges as both the most fascinating and the most horrific character in the second half of the play because his will is indomitable and his desires unchecked by any moral constraints. The audience probably registers this fact most decisively during the bravura soliloquy that Richard speaks after he and George have watched—and obscenely commented upon—Edward's wooing of Lady Gray. Soliloquies, in which a character speaks to himself but is overheard by the theater audience, help create the illusion of interiority and inner subjectivity. Perhaps goaded by jealousy at the sight of Edward's successful wooing of Lady Gray, Richard in his soliloquy both reveals his frustrations and desires and hardheadedly maps a future course. In quick succession, he contemplates the number of people who before him have claims on the throne; resigns himself to seek instead the pleasures of courtship and love; despairs, since his deformed body prevents him from being loved; resolves therefore to seek the crown at any cost; and vows to change himself into any imaginable persona necessary to achieve his end. The soliloquy is long (3.2.124–96) and relentless. Richard tracks his argument like a bloodhound, registering his predicament with memorably vivid language.

> And yet I know not how to get the crown,
> For many lives stand between me and home.
> And I—like one lost in a thorny wood,
> That rends the thorns and is rent with the thorns,
> Seeking a way and straying from the way,
> Not knowing how to find the open air,
> But toiling desperately to find it out—
> Torment myself to catch the English crown.
> (3.2.172–79)

Struggle and frustration are evident in the repetitions of this passage. Seeking, straying, toiling, Richard is in constant motion, throwing himself against impossible barriers. The crown eludes him, yet he goes on. He is by turns attractive and frightening.

Many prototypes are drawn upon to create this distinctive character. His "individuality" does not emerge from nowhere but depends on Shakespeare's skillful appropriation of prior dramatic resources. Richard's characterization owes much, for example, to the striving, overreaching stage heroes created by Shakespeare's early rival Christopher Marlowe. Like Marlowe's Tamburlaine, Richard makes his heaven "to dream upon the crown" (3.2.168) and stops at nothing to achieve that goal. In part, he is also fashioned after the Vice figure from the medieval religious drama. The Vice was the character—often witty and quite disconcertingly entertaining—who embodied the principle of evil and tried to compel others to sin. Richard's witty asides, as much as his aggression and lack of scruple, reveal his kinship to the Vice. Perhaps this character's strongest association, however, is with the figure of the stage Machiavel, whom Richard himself evokes at the end of his soliloquy. The historical Niccolò Machiavelli was an Italian political philosopher whose influential book *The Prince* pragmatically rather than moralistically detailed the tactics and principles that made for successful government in the modern world. In the popular imagination, he came to stand for the hypocrisy and political cunning associated with Protestant England's symbolic enemy Catholic Italy.

Sharing affinities with each of these figures but not fully modeled on any of them, Richard functions in Shakespeare's play to suggest what emerges when one no longer acknowledges the primacy of the identities constructed by the words "son" and "brother." In a society that defined people in terms of their place within family structures and social hierarchies, to separate oneself from those structures and hierarchies risked being read as monstrous and unnatural. Richard is riveting precisely because he seems so autonomous and so indifferent to the bonds and loyalties—to family and to king—that supposedly hold his society together and constrain the actions of its members. Though not the only one in the play whose ambition corrodes ties of blood and allegiance, Richard most fully epitomizes ambition's deforming effects. One way to read Richard's crooked back is as a physical sign of his unnatural inner being. Yet it is also true that to Richard his crooked body is the cause of (or at least the excuse for) his behavior. In modern psychological terms, he is compensating for a handicap in the only way he can. But it is a measure of Shakespeare's distance from us that such a reading of Richard's deformity is countered by another that emphasizes the moral significance of physical signs and is deeply ambivalent about the very idea of the socially autonomous individual.

Marriage is one way to incorporate individuals into social structures, but in *Richard Duke of York* the breakdown of social bonds is both caused and symbolized by its disorderly marriages. In the feudal world depicted in most of Shakespeare's early history plays, marriages in noble or monarchical families were primarily premised not on love but on dynastic convenience. Wives were to be chosen for the dowry or the territory or the alliances they brought with them. To marry for love was viewed as dangerous because it introduced irrational passion into what was supposed to be a rational choice and threatened the husband's control of himself and of his spouse. In marrying the widow Lady Gray, Edward makes such a passion-driven marriage and thereby nearly loses control of the kingdom. By his actions, he forfeits Warwick's loyalty and temporarily that of his brother George. King Henry had also made an irrational match in marrying the dowerless Margaret (see *The First Part of the Contention* 1.1). In *Richard Duke of York*, this initial lack of control finds its consequence in Henry's inability to govern Margaret and in the increasingly topsy-turvy nature of their marriage. She is the monstrous Amazon whose disregard of her husband's putative authority marks her as unnatural, even as it exposes the fragility of masculine claims to natural sovereignty.

The end of the play, however, refocuses on the marriage of Edward and Lady Gray to bring a tenuous and highly ironized sense of resolution to the play's action. In the final scene, King Edward admires the son to which his wife, now Queen Elizabeth, has given birth and invites his brothers Richard and Clarence to do the same. The ambience is domestic in a modern way. This is a marriage of affection more than utility. Edward calls the babe "Ned" (5.7.16) and his wife "Bess" (15), the nicknames suggesting intimacy. But if Edward thinks this cosy domesticity, so pleasing to him but so politically ill-advised, can reestablish the Yorkist dynasty and center it on him and his descendants, the presence of Richard signals otherwise. Leaning down to kiss the babe, Richard says, "And that I love the tree from whence thou sprang'st, / Witness the loving kiss I give the fruit" (31–32). The tree he refers to is, of course, the family of York, the family tree from which he himself springs. But then, in an aside, he adds: "To say the truth, so Judas kissed his master, / And cried 'All hail!' whenas he meant all harm" (33–34). For Richard to cast himself as the betrayer of Christ bodes badly for the happy family: Edward, Ned, and Bess. To late-twentieth-century audiences and theatergoers, the King's doting attention to his wife and son may make him seem quite modern and quite human. Yet viewed historically and in its dramatic context, the King's behavior also signals his weakness, his propensity to let his affections overrule his reason. Fixated on his Ned and his Bess, he seems oblivious to the threat posed by his alienated, thoroughly undomestic brother.

Richard Duke of York ends, then, with a scene that underscores the tenuousness of Edward's purchase on power and threatens a renewal of civil war and family strife. The play's imaginative landscape is dominated by those willful, monstrous individuals such as Richard and Margaret who thrive amid the chaos of a disintegrating society. Few can oppose them, most especially not "the good King Henry," a man disastrously unsuited to play a monarch's part. Hovering on the periphery of this play's action and killed before its final scene, Henry is gradually transformed into a mere observer of the public world around him. Saintly and detached, he comes to represent the antithesis of Richard's surging, self-centered ambition, finally serving almost as choric commentator and as prophet. He predicts, for example, that Henry Earl of Richmond (later Henry VII) will be England's savior (4.7.68–76), and he predicts that many will come to curse the hunchbacked Richard (later Richard III, 5.6.37–43). But hope for release from Richard's evil lies far in the future, and Henry's increasing saintliness neither erases his responsibility for civil war nor solves the immediate problem of secular rule. Neither saints nor monsters are particularly suited to govern other men, and Edward, who is neither, appears unable to control, or even properly to decipher, his brother. *Richard Duke of York* feels so very grim because its compelling depiction of the unraveling of England's social fabric suggests little about how that fabric can once again be rewoven.

JEAN E. HOWARD

TEXTUAL NOTE

In 1595, *The True Tragedy of Richard Duke of York and the Good King Henry the Sixth* was published in an octavo volume, and the same text appeared in quarto format in 1600. In 1602, control of the play fell to Thomas Pavier, who in 1619 issued another, edited, quarto version. Both of these quartos are based on the Octavo of 1595 (O) and have no independent textual authority. In 1623, a play approximately one thousand lines longer than any of these early texts appeared in Shakespeare's First Folio (F) under the title *The Third Part of Henry the Sixt*. While some scholars believe that the 1595 Octavo text is an early draft of the play included in the First Folio, the Oxford editors follow the majority of editors since the 1920s in assuming that the octavo is a memorial reconstruction of an abridged and revised version of the Folio text. (For a discussion of theories of memorial reconstruction, see the Textual Note to *The First Part of the Contention [2 Henry VI].*) Consequently, the control text for *Richard Duke of York* is F, though the Oxford editors have retained the title used in the octavo text on the theory that that was the title by which the play was probably known during Shakespeare's lifetime. They assume that the manuscript used for setting the Folio copy was the author's "foul papers," which had not been marked up for theatrical performance, because F contains a number of vague and unspecific stage directions, though also a high proportion of musical cues. Interestingly, several speeches bear actor's names (Gabriel, Sinklo, Humfrey) rather than characters' (Messenger [1.2.49] and First Gamekeeper and Second Gamekeeper [3.1]). The octavo text, however, is believed to have been based on the promptbook for a theatrical production and contains important stage directions and perhaps some authorial revisions that occurred between the play's foul-papers stage and the promptbook. In some cases, when octavo staging seems preferable to that suggested in F, this edition has rearranged dialogue or speech assignments to accord with such staging. These changes are marked in the notes and Textual Variants.

The Oxford text employs the standard act and scene divisions into which the play was divided in the eighteenth century, with two exceptions. A new scene is marked at 4.3.27, indicating that the stage is cleared between the time Edward's guards fly from his tent and Edward is subsequently brought onstage as a captive. And at the very end of Act 4, Scene 10 is introduced to separate Henry's conversation with Warwick about Edward's return from the Low Countries from his subsequent conversation with Exeter before he is surprised and seized by Edward and Richard Duke of Gloucester.

SELECTED BIBLIOGRAPHY

Bergeron, David. "The Play-Within-the-Play in 3 *Henry VI.*" *Tennessee Studies in Literature* 22 (1977): 37–47.

Berman, Ronald. "Fathers and Sons in the *Henry VI* Plays." *Shakespeare Quarterly* 13 (1962): 487–97.

Carroll, D. Allen. "Greene's 'Upstart Crow' Passage: A Survey of Commentary." *Research Opportunities in Renaissance Drama* 28 (1985): 111–27.

Champion, Larry. "Developmental Structure in Shakespeare's Early Histories: The Perspective of 3 *Henry VI.*" *Studies in Philology* 76 (1979): 218–38.

Hodgdon, Barbara. *The End Crowns All: Closure and Contradiction in Shakespeare's History.* Princeton: Princeton University Press, 1991. 44–99.

Kahn, Coppélia. " 'The Shadow of the Male': Masculine Identity in the History Plays." *Man's Estate: Masculine Identity in Shakespeare.* Berkeley: University of California Press, 1981. 47–81.

Leggatt, Alexander. *"Henry VI." Shakespeare's Political Drama.* London: Routledge, 1988. 1–31.

Sen Gupta, S. C. *Shakespeare's Historical Plays.* New York: Oxford University Press, 1964. 78–87.

Tillyard, E. M. W. "The Third Part of Henry VI." *Shakespeare's History Plays.* London: Chatto and Windus, 1944. 188–98.

Williamson, Marilyn L. " 'When Men Are Rul'd by Women': Shakespeare's First Tetralogy." *Shakespeare Studies* 19 (1987): 41–59.

The True Tragedy of Richard Duke of York and the Good King Henry the Sixth

THE PERSONS OF THE PLAY

Of the King's Party

KING HENRY VI
QUEEN MARGARET
PRINCE EDWARD, their son
Duke of SOMERSET
Duke of EXETER
Earl of NORTHUMBERLAND
Earl of WESTMORLAND
Lord CLIFFORD
Lord Stafford
SOMERVILLE
Henry, young Earl of Richmond
A SOLDIER who has killed his father
A HUNTSMAN who guards King Edward

The Divided House of Neville

Earl of WARWICK, first of York's party, later of Lancaster's
Marquis of MONTAGUE, his brother, of York's party
Earl of OXFORD, their brother-in-law, of Lancaster's party
Lord HASTINGS, their brother-in-law, of York's party

Of the Duke of York's Party

Richard Plantagenet, Duke of YORK
EDWARD, Earl of March, his son, later Duke of York and
    KING EDWARD IV
LADY GRAY, a widow, later Edward's wife and queen
Earl RIVERS, her brother
GEORGE, Edward's brother, later Duke OF CLARENCE
RICHARD, Edward's brother, later Duke OF GLOUCESTER
Earl of RUTLAND, Edward's brother
Rutland's TUTOR, a chaplain
SIR JOHN Mortimer, York's uncle
Sir Hugh Mortimer, his brother
Duke of NORFOLK
Sir William Stanley
Earl of Pembroke
Sir John MONTGOMERY
A NOBLEMAN
TWO GAMEKEEPERS
Three WATCHMEN, who guard King Edward's tent
LIEUTENANT of the Tower

The French

KING LOUIS
LADY BONA, his sister-in-law
Lord Bourbon, the French High Admiral

Others

A SOLDIER who has killed his son
A SECOND SOLDIER who has killed his father
Mayor of Coventry
MAYOR of York
Aldermen of York
Soldiers, messengers, and attendants

1.1

[*A chair of state.*][1] *Alarum.° Enter Richard Plantagenet,*   Call to arms
Duke of YORK, [*his two sons*] EDWARD, *Earl of March,*
[*and*] *Crookback°* RICHARD, *the Duke of* NORFOLK, [*the*]   hunchback
Marquis [*of*] MONTAGUE, [*and*] *the Earl of* WARWICK,
with drum[*mers*] *and soldiers.* [*They all wear*] *white*
roses[2] *in their hats*

WARWICK   I wonder how the King escaped our hands?
YORK   While we pursued the horsemen of the north,
   He slyly stole away and left his men;
   Whereat the great lord of Northumberland,
5   Whose warlike ears could never brook retreat,[3]
   Cheered up the drooping army; and himself,
   Lord Clifford, and Lord Stafford, all abreast,
   Charged our main battle's° front, and, breaking in,   army's
   Were by the swords of common soldiers slain.[4]
10 EDWARD   Lord Stafford's father, Duke of Buckingham,
   Is either slain or wounded dangerous.°   dangerously
   I cleft his beaver° with a downright° blow.   helmet visor / vertical
   That this is true, father, behold his blood.
   [*He shows a bloody sword*]
MONTAGUE [*to* YORK]   And, brother,[5] here's the Earl of Wiltshire's blood,
   [*He shows a bloody sword*]
15   Whom I encountered as the battles joined.
RICHARD [*to Somerset's head, which he shows*]
   Speak thou for me, and tell them what I did.
YORK   Richard hath best deserved of all my sons.
   [*To the head*] But is your grace dead, my lord of Somerset?
NORFOLK   Such hap have all the line of John of Gaunt.[6]
20 RICHARD   Thus do I hope to shake King Henry's head.
   [*He holds aloft the head, then throws it down*]

1.1 Location: The Parliament House, London.
1. Although neither O nor F indicates a chair or a raised platform ("a state"), Warwick's lines at 22–26, King Henry's at 50–51, and the stage direction at 32 ("They go up") all suggest that both stage properties are required here.
2. Emblem of the Yorkists. This play depicts part of what is called the Wars of the Roses between the Yorkists, who wore the white rose, and the Lancastrians, who wore the red rose. For Shakespeare's dramatization of the origin of this convention, see *1 Henry VI* 2.4. In O, when the Lancastrian faction enters at line 49 below, they wear red roses. Both here and at line 49, F's stage directions make no mention of roses. O concludes this direction "with Drum and Soldiers, with white Roses in their hats," leaving ambiguous whether the roses are worn by the soldiers

alone or by the entire party.
3. Could never endure hearing the trumpet call signaling retreat.
4. Shakespeare names York (rather than a common soldier) as the person who killed Clifford at several points later in the play. *The First Part of the Contention (2 Henry VI)* dramatizes this death in 5.3.
5. The historical Montague was York's nephew. He was also, as Shakespeare suggests elsewhere in this play, Warwick's brother.
6. May all the descendants of John of Gaunt have the same fate. John of Gaunt held the title Duke of Lancaster; Somerset was his grandson, and Henry VI his great-grandson. The Yorkists contended that John of Gaunt's son Henry IV had usurped Richard II's crown.

WARWICK   And so do I, victorious prince of York.
Before I see thee seated in that throne
Which now the house of Lancaster usurps,
I vow by heaven these eyes shall never close.
25   This is the palace of the fearful° King,   *frightened*
And this [*pointing to the chair of state*], the regal seat—possess it, York,
For this is thine, and not King Henry's heirs'.
YORK   Assist me then, sweet Warwick, and I will,
For hither we have broken in by force.
30   NORFOLK   We'll all assist you—he that flies shall die.
YORK   Thanks, gentle° Norfolk. Stay by me, my lords   *noble*
And soldiers—stay, and lodge by me this night.
         They go up [upon the state]
WARWICK   And when the King comes, offer him no violence
Unless he seek to thrust you out perforce.°   *by force*
         [*The soldiers withdraw*][7]
35   YORK   The Queen this day here holds her Parliament,
But little thinks we shall be of her council;
By words or blows here let us win our right.
RICHARD   Armed as we are, let's stay within this house.
WARWICK   'The Bloody Parliament' shall this be called,
40   Unless Plantagenet, Duke of York, be king,
And bashful Henry deposed, whose cowardice
Hath made us bywords° to our enemies.   *objects of scorn*
YORK   Then leave me not, my lords. Be resolute—
I mean to take possession of my right.
45   WARWICK   Neither the King nor he that loves him best—
The proudest he that holds up° Lancaster—   *supports*
Dares stir a wing if Warwick shake his bells.[8]
I'll plant Plantagenet,[9] root him up who dares.
Resolve thee, Richard—claim the English crown.
         [YORK *sits in the chair.*]
         Flourish.° Enter KING HENRY, [*Lord*] CLIFFORD, *the Earl*   *Trumpet fanfare*
         of NORTHUMBERLAND, *the Earl of* WESTMORLAND, *the*
         Duke of EXETER, *and the rest.* [*They all wear*] *red roses*
         in their hats
50   KING HENRY   My lords, look where the sturdy° rebel sits—   *stubborn*
Even in the chair of state! Belike he means,
Backed by the power of Warwick, that false peer,
To aspire unto the crown and reign as king.
Earl of Northumberland, he slew thy father—
55   And thine, Lord Clifford—and you both have vowed revenge
On him, his sons, his favourites, and his friends.
NORTHUMBERLAND   If I be not, heavens be revenged on me.
CLIFFORD   The hope thereof makes Clifford mourn in steel.[1]
WESTMORLAND   What, shall we suffer this? Let's pluck him down.
60   My heart for anger burns—I cannot brook it.
KING HENRY   Be patient, gentle Earl of Westmorland.
CLIFFORD   Patience is for poltroons,° such as he [*indicating* YORK].   *cowards*

---

7. Neither F nor O indicates when the soldiers leave the
stage, but we can assume that they do leave, as they are
given a reentrance at line 170.
8. If Warwick makes a move. Elizabethans attached bells
to the legs of falcons in order to further frighten the falcon's prey; Warwick is comparing himself to such a
threatening bird.

9. Richard Duke of York was also called Richard Plantagenet. The Plantagenets were the medieval dynasty that
began to rule England in 1154, when Henry II assumed
the throne. The Yorkist and Lancastrian families were
both descended from this dynasty.
1. In armor (rather than the black cloaks that were conventionally worn by mourners).

He durst not sit there had your father lived.
My gracious lord, here in the Parliament
65 Let us assail the family of York.
NORTHUMBERLAND Well hast thou spoken, cousin,° be it so.   *kinsman*
KING HENRY Ah, know you not the city° favours them,   *(London)*
And they have troops of soldiers at their beck?°   *absolute command*
EXETER But when the Duke is slain, they'll quickly fly.
70 KING HENRY Far be the thought of this from Henry's heart,
To make a shambles° of the Parliament House.   *slaughterhouse*
Cousin of Exeter, frowns, words, and threats
Shall be the war that Henry means to use.
[*To* YORK] Thou factious° Duke of York, descend my throne   *rebellious*
75 And kneel for grace and mercy at my feet.
I am thy sovereign.
YORK   I am thine.
EXETER For shame, come down—he made thee Duke of York.
YORK It was mine inheritance, as the earldom² was.
EXETER Thy father was a traitor to the crown.³
80 WARWICK Exeter, thou art a traitor to the crown
In following this usurping Henry.
CLIFFORD Whom should he follow but his natural king?
WARWICK True, Clifford, and that's Richard Duke of York.
KING HENRY [*to* YORK] And shall I stand and thou sit in my throne?
85 YORK It must and shall be so—content thyself.
WARWICK [*to* KING HENRY] Be Duke of Lancaster, let him be king.
WESTMORLAND He is both king and Duke of Lancaster—
And that, the Lord of Westmorland shall maintain.
WARWICK And Warwick shall disprove it. You forget
90 That we are those which chased you from the field,
And slew your fathers, and, with colours° spread,   *flags*
Marched through the city to the palace gates.
NORTHUMBERLAND Yes, Warwick, I remember it to my grief,
And, by his soul, thou and thy house shall rue it.
95 WESTMORLAND [*to* YORK] Plantagenet, of thee, and these thy sons,
Thy kinsmen, and thy friends, I'll have more lives
Than drops of blood were in my father's veins.
CLIFFORD [*to* WARWICK] Urge it no more, lest that, instead of words,
I send thee, Warwick, such a messenger
100 As shall revenge his death before I stir.
WARWICK [*to* YORK] Poor Clifford, how I scorn his worthless threats.
YORK [*to* KING HENRY] Will you we° show our title to the crown?   *Do you wish us to*
If not, our swords shall plead it in the field.
KING HENRY What title hast thou, traitor, to the crown?
105 Thy father was, as thou art, Duke of York;⁴
Thy grandfather, Roger Mortimer, Earl of March.
I am the son of Henry the Fifth,
Who made the Dauphin⁵ and the French to stoop
And seized upon their towns and provinces.
110 WARWICK Talk not of France, sith° thou hast lost it all.   *since*

---

2. The earldom of March, which York inherited from his
mother and through which he claimed the throne.
3. York's father, the Earl of Cambridge, was executed for
treason (see *Henry V* 2.2).

4. In fact, the historical York's father was not Duke of
York. York inherited that title from his uncle (Edward).
5. Title of the oldest son of the French king.

KING HENRY The Lord Protector[6] lost it, and not I.
  When I was crowned, I was but nine months old.
RICHARD You are old enough now, and yet,° methinks, you lose.   *and even now*
  [*To* YORK] Father, tear the crown from the usurper's head.
115 EDWARD [*to* YORK] Sweet father, do so—set it on your head.
MONTAGUE [*to* YORK] Good brother, as thou lov'st and honour'st arms,
  Let's fight it out and not stand cavilling thus.
RICHARD Sound drums and trumpets, and the King will fly.
YORK Sons, peace!
NORTHUMBERLAND[7] Peace, thou—and give King Henry leave°   *permission*
120   to speak.
KING HENRY Ah, York, why seekest thou to depose me?
  Are we not both Plantagenets by birth,
  And from two brothers lineally descent?
  Suppose by right and equity thou be king—

    KING HENRY *Peace, thou—and give King Henry leave to*
124.1   *speak.*
    WARWICK *Plantagenet shall speak first—hear him, lords,*
    And be you silent and attentive too,
    For he that interrrupts him shall not live.
    KING HENRY [*to* YORK] *Think'st thou that I will leave my*
124.5   *kingly throne,*
125 Think'st thou that I will leave my Kingly throne,
  Wherein my grandsire and my father sat?
  No—first shall war unpeople this my realm;
  Ay, and their colours, often borne in France,
  And now in England to our heart's great sorrow,
130 Shall be my winding-sheet.° Why faint you,[8] lords?   *burial shroud*
  My title's good, and better far than his.
WARWICK Prove it, Henry, and thou shalt be king.
KING HENRY Henry the Fourth by conquest got the crown.
YORK 'Twas by rebellion against his king.°   *(Richard II)*
135 KING HENRY [*aside*] I know not what to say—my title's weak.
  [*To* YORK] Tell me, may not a king adopt an heir?
YORK What then?
KING HENRY An if° he may, then am I lawful king—   *An if = If*
  For Richard, in the view of many lords,
140 Resigned the crown to Henry the Fourth,
  Whose heir my father was, and I am his.
YORK He rose against him,° being° his sovereign,   *(Richard) / who was*
  And made him to resign his crown perforce.
WARWICK Suppose, my lords, he did it unconstrained—
145 Think you 'twere prejudicial to his crown?°   *his claim to the throne*
EXETER No, for he could not so resign his crown
  But° that the next heir should succeed and reign.   *Without ensuring*
KING HENRY Art thou against us, Duke of Exeter?

---

6. Humphrey, Duke of Gloucester, was Lord Protector during Henry VI's youth and, as such, had oversight of the King and kingdom. His downfall is dramatized in *The First Part of the Contention (2 Henry VI)*.
7. For lines 120–25, Oxford follows O. F assigns line 120 to King Henry, then gives three lines to Warwick and has Henry begin again at 125, omitting the octavo passage here printed as 121–24. For the F version, see the inset passage that follows (lines 124.1–124.5). Critics such as

Steven Urkowitz have argued that the difference here between O and F indicates two different views of Henry's character, and they treat O and F as completely separate texts, with O composed first. Here as elsewhere, Oxford takes these O lines as an authorial revision that occurred sometime between the play's foul-paper stage and the subsequent promptbook.
8. Why do you lose heart?

EXETER His° is the right, and therefore pardon me.   *(York's)*

150 YORK Why whisper you, my lords, and answer not?

EXETER [*to* KING HENRY] My conscience tells me he is lawful king.

KING HENRY [*aside*] All will revolt from me and turn to him.

NORTHUMBERLAND [*to* YORK] Plantagenet, for all the claim thou lay'st,
    Think not that Henry shall be so deposed.

155 WARWICK Deposed he shall be, in despite° of all.   *spite*

NORTHUMBERLAND Thou art deceived— 'tis not thy southern power
    Of Essex, Norfolk, Suffolk, nor of Kent,
    Which makes thee thus presumptuous and proud,
    Can set the Duke up° in despite of me.   *(on the throne)*

160 CLIFFORD King Henry, be thy title right or wrong,
    Lord Clifford vows to fight in thy defence.
    May that ground gape and swallow me alive
    Where I shall kneel to him that slew my father.

KING HENRY O, Clifford, how thy words revive my heart!

165 YORK Henry of Lancaster, resign thy crown.
    What mutter you, or what conspire you, lords?

WARWICK Do right unto this princely Duke of York,
    Or I will fill the house with armèd men
    And over the chair of state, where now he sits,

170   Write up his title with usurping blood.[9]
        He stamps with his foot and the soldiers
        show themselves

KING HENRY My lord of Warwick, hear me but one word—
    Let me for this my lifetime reign as king.

YORK Confirm the crown to me and to mine heirs,
    And thou shalt reign in quiet while thou liv'st.

175 KING HENRY I am content. Richard Plantagenet,
    Enjoy the kingdom after my decease.

CLIFFORD What wrong is this unto the prince your son?

WARWICK What good is this to England and himself?

WESTMORLAND Base, fearful, and despairing Henry.

180 CLIFFORD How hast thou injured both thyself and us?

WESTMORLAND I cannot stay to hear these articles.°   *terms of agreement*

NORTHUMBERLAND Nor I.

CLIFFORD Come, cousin, let us tell the Queen these news.

WESTMORLAND [*to* KING HENRY] Farewell, faint-hearted and
        degenerate king,

185 In whose cold blood no spark of honour bides.°   *lives*
                      Exit [with his soldiers][1]

NORTHUMBERLAND [*to* KING HENRY] Be thou a prey unto the
        house of York,
    And die in bands° for this unmanly deed.   *fetters*
                      Exit [with his soldiers]

CLIFFORD [*to* KING HENRY] In dreadful war mayst thou be overcome,
    Or live in peace, abandoned and despised.
                      Exit [with his soldiers]

190 WARWICK [*to* KING HENRY] Turn this way, Henry, and regard them not.

EXETER [*to* KING HENRY] They seek revenge and therefore will not yield.

---

9. With the blood of Henry, whom Warwick considers a usurper.

1. F gives no exit for Westmorland, Northumberland, or Clifford; O marks a separate exit for each, as here. Each man is probably followed out by his soldiers.

KING HENRY   Ah, Exeter.
WARWICK   Why should you sigh, my lord?
KING HENRY   Not for myself, Lord Warwick, but my son,
    Whom I unnaturally shall disinherit.
195   But be it as it may. [*To* YORK] I here entail°   *bequeath*
    The crown to thee and to thine heirs for ever,
    Conditionally, that here thou take thine oath
    To cease this civil war, and whilst I live
    To honour me as thy king and sovereign,
200   And nor by treason nor hostility
    To seek to put me down and reign thyself.
YORK   This oath I willingly take and will perform.
WARWICK   Long live King Henry. [*To* YORK] Plantagenet, embrace him.
        [YORK *descends.* HENRY *and* YORK *embrace*]
KING HENRY [*to* YORK]   And long live thou, and these thy forward° sons.   *precocious*
205   YORK   Now York and Lancaster are reconciled.
EXETER   Accursed be he that seeks to make them foes.
        Sennet.[2] *Here* [York's train] *comes down* [from the state][3]
YORK [*to* KING HENRY]   Farewell, my gracious lord, I'll to my castle.
                Exeunt YORK *and his sons* [EDWARD *and*
                            RICHARD, *with soldiers*]
WARWICK   And I'll keep London with my soldiers.
                                Exit [*with soldiers*]
NORFOLK   And I to Norfolk with my followers.
                                Exit [*with soldiers*]
210   MONTAGUE   And I unto the sea from whence I came.
                                Exit [*with soldiers*]
KING HENRY   And I with grief and sorrow to the court.
        [KING HENRY *and* EXETER *turn to leave.*]
        Enter QUEEN [MARGARET] *and* PRINCE [EDWARD]
EXETER   Here comes the Queen, whose looks bewray° her anger.   *reveal*
    I'll steal away.
KING HENRY   Exeter, so will I.
QUEEN MARGARET   Nay, go not from me—I will follow thee.
215   KING HENRY   Be patient, gentle Queen, and I will stay.
QUEEN MARGARET   Who can be patient in such extremes?
    Ah, wretched man, would I had died a maid
    And never seen thee, never borne thee son,
    Seeing thou hast proved so unnatural a father.
220   Hath he deserved to lose his birthright thus?
    Hadst thou but loved him half so well as I,
    Or felt that pain° which I did for him once,   *(labor pains)*
    Or nourished him as I did with my blood,
    Thou wouldst have left thy dearest heart-blood there
225   Rather than have made that savage Duke thine heir
    And disinherited thine only son.
PRINCE EDWARD   Father, you cannot disinherit me.
    If you be king, why should not I succeed?
KING HENRY   Pardon me, Margaret; pardon me, sweet son—
230   The Earl of Warwick and the Duke enforced me.
QUEEN MARGARET   Enforced thee? Art thou king, and wilt be forced?

2. Trumpet notes signaling a procession.
3. F's "Here they come down" again indicates that a state is required for the scene.

I shame° to hear thee speak! Ah, timorous wretch,   *am ashamed*
Thou hast undone thyself, thy son, and me,
And giv'n unto the house of York such head[4]
235   As thou shalt reign but by their sufferance.
To entail him and his heirs unto the crown—
What is it, but to make thy sepulchre
And creep into it far before thy time?
Warwick is Chancellor and the Lord of Calais;
240   Stern Falconbridge commands the narrow seas;°   *(Straits of Dover)*
The Duke° is made Protector of the Realm;   *(York)*
And yet shalt thou be safe? Such safety finds
The trembling lamb environèd° with wolves.   *surrounded*
Had I been there, which am a seely° woman,   *helpless*
245   The soldiers should have tossed me on their pikes°   *axe-like weapons*
Before I would have granted° to that act.   *assented*
But thou preferr'st thy life before thine honour.
And seeing thou dost, I here divorce myself
Both from thy table, Henry, and thy bed,[5]
250   Until that act of Parliament be repealed
Whereby my son is disinherited.
The northern lords that have forsworn thy colours
Will follow mine, if once they see them spread—
And spread they shall be, to thy foul disgrace
255   And the utter ruin of the house of York.
Thus do I leave thee. [*To* PRINCE EDWARD] Come, son, let's away.
Our army is ready—come, we'll after them.
KING HENRY   Stay, gentle Margaret, and hear me speak.
QUEEN MARGARET   Thou hast spoke too much already.
[*To* PRINCE EDWARD]   Get thee gone.
260   KING HENRY   Gentle son Edward, thou wilt stay with me?
QUEEN MARGARET   Ay, to be murdered by his enemies.
PRINCE EDWARD [*to* KING HENRY]   When I return with victory
     from the field,
I'll see your grace. Till then, I'll follow her.
QUEEN MARGARET   Come, son, away—we may not linger thus.
[*Exit with* PRINCE EDWARD][6]
265   KING HENRY   Poor Queen, how love to me and to her son
Hath made her break out into terms of rage.
Revenged may she be on that hateful Duke,
Whose haughty spirit, wingèd with desire,
Will coast° my crown, and, like an empty° eagle,   *attack / a hungry*
270   Tire° on the flesh of me and of my son.   *Feed ravenously*
The loss of those three lords torments my heart.
I'll write unto them and entreat them fair.°   *courteously*
Come, cousin, you shall be the messenger.
EXETER   And I, I hope, shall reconcile them all.
                         Flourish. Exeunt[7]

---

4. Such freedom to act. To give a horse its head means to loosen its reins and let it go where it will.
5. *I here . . . bed*: echoing the language of church law, which permitted marital separation "from bed and board" in cases of adultery, heresy, and cruelty.
6. O omits the Queen's last line and has her exit at line 261, Prince Edward at 263.
7. F marks a single exit for Exeter here and places the "Flourish" before Richard's entrance in the next line.

1.2

Enter RICHARD, EDWARD [*Earl of March*], *and* [*the Marquis of*] MONTAGUE

RICHARD Brother, though I be youngest give me leave.° ⟶ *allow me (to speak)*
EDWARD No, I can better play the orator.
MONTAGUE But I have reasons strong and forcible.

Enter the Duke of YORK

YORK Why, how now, sons and brother—at a strife?
5   What is your quarrel? How began it first?
EDWARD No quarrel, but a slight contention.
YORK About what?
RICHARD About that which concerns your grace and us—
    The crown of England, father, which is yours.
10 YORK Mine, boy? Not till King Henry be dead.
RICHARD Your right depends not on his life or death.
EDWARD Now you are heir—therefore enjoy it now.
    By giving the house of Lancaster leave to breathe,° ⟶ *permission to rest*
    It will outrun you, father, in the end.
15 YORK I took an oath that he should quietly reign.
EDWARD But for a kingdom any oath may be broken.
    I would break a thousand oaths to reign one year.
RICHARD [*to* YORK] No—God forbid your grace should be forsworn.
YORK I shall be if I claim by open war.
20 RICHARD I'll prove the contrary, if you'll hear me speak.
YORK Thou canst not, son—it is impossible.
RICHARD An oath is of no moment° being not took ⟶ *consequence*
    Before a true and lawful magistrate
    That hath authority over him that swears.
25 Henry had none, but did usurp the place.
    Then, seeing 'twas he that made you to depose,° ⟶ *swear an oath*
    Your oath, my lord, is vain and frivolous.
    Therefore to arms—and, father, do but think
    How sweet a thing it is to wear a crown,
30 Within whose circuit° is Elysium[1] ⟶ *circumference*
    And all that poets feign° of bliss and joy. ⟶ *imagine*
    Why do we linger thus? I cannot rest
    Until the white rose that I wear be dyed
    Even in the luke-warm blood of Henry's heart.
35 YORK Richard, enough! I will be king or die.
    [*To* MONTAGUE] Brother, thou shalt to London presently° ⟶ *at once*
    And whet on Warwick to this enterprise.
    Thou, Richard, shalt to the Duke of Norfolk
    And tell him privily° of our intent. ⟶ *secretly*
40 You, Edward, shall to Edmund Brook, Lord Cobham,
    With whom the Kentishmen will willingly rise.° ⟶ *rebel; take arms*
    In them I trust, for they are soldiers
    Witty, courteous, liberal, full of spirit.
    While you are thus employed, what resteth more° ⟶ *what else remains*
45 But that I seek occasion how to rise,
    And yet the King not privy to my drift,° ⟶ *aware of my intent*
    Nor any of the house of Lancaster.

Enter a MESSENGER

1.2 Location: York's castle, Sandal (in Yorkshire).
1. In classical myth, the paradise where blessed souls dwelled.

But stay, what news? Why com'st thou in such post?°   *haste*
MESSENGER   The Queen, with all the northern earls and lords,
50   Intend here to besiege you in your castle.
She is hard by with twenty thousand men,
And therefore fortify your hold,° my lord.   *castle*
YORK   Ay, with my sword. What—think'st thou that we fear them?
Edward and Richard, you shall stay with me;
55   My brother Montague shall post to London.
Let noble Warwick, Cobham, and the rest,
Whom we have left protectors of the King,
With powerful policy° strengthen themselves,   *cunning*
And trust not simple Henry nor his oaths.
60   MONTAGUE   Brother, I go—I'll win them, fear it not.
And thus most humbly I do take my leave.   *Exit*
    Enter SIR JOHN *Mortimer and his brother Sir Hugh*
YORK   Sir John and Sir Hugh Mortimer, mine uncles,
You are come to Sandal in a happy° hour.   *fortunate*
The army of the Queen mean to besiege us.
65   SIR JOHN   She shall not need, we'll meet her in the field.
YORK   What, with five thousand men?
RICHARD   Ay, with five hundred, father, for a need.°   *if necessary*
A woman's general—what should we fear?
    A march [*sounds*] *afar off*
EDWARD   I hear their drums. Let's set our men in order,
70   And issue forth and bid them battle straight.°   *at once*
YORK [*to* SIR JOHN *and Sir Hugh*]   Five men to twenty—though
    the odds be great,
I doubt not, uncles, of our victory.
Many a battle have I won in France
Whenas° the enemy hath been ten to one—   *When*
75   Why should I not now have the like success?   *Exeunt*

1.3

    Alarums, and then enter the young Earl of RUTLAND *and*
    his TUTOR [*a chaplain*]
RUTLAND   Ah, whither shall I fly to scape° their hands?   *escape*
    Enter [*Lord*] CLIFFORD [*with soldiers*]
Ah, tutor, look where bloody Clifford comes.
CLIFFORD [*to the* TUTOR]   Chaplain, away—thy priesthood saves thy life.
As for the brat of this accursèd duke,
5   Whose father slew my father—he shall die.
TUTOR   And I, my lord, will bear him company.
CLIFFORD   Soldiers, away with him.
TUTOR   Ah, Clifford, murder not this innocent child
Lest thou be hated both of° God and man.   *Exit* [*guarded*]   *by*
    [RUTLAND *falls to the ground*]
10   CLIFFORD   How now—is he dead already?
Or is it fear that makes him close his eyes?
I'll open them.
RUTLAND [*reviving*]   So looks the pent-up° lion o'er the wretch   *caged*
That trembles under his devouring paws,
15   And so he walks, insulting° o'er his prey,   *scornfully triumphing*
And so he comes to rend his limbs asunder.

1.3 Location: A battlefield between Sandal and Wakefield.

Ah, gentle Clifford, kill me with thy sword
And not with such a cruel threat'ning look.
Sweet Clifford, hear me speak before I die.
20 I am too mean° a subject for thy wrath.   *lowly*
Be thou revenged on men, and let me live.
CLIFFORD   In vain thou speak'st, poor boy. My father's blood
Hath stopped the passage where thy words should enter.
RUTLAND   Then let my father's blood open it again.
25 He is a man, and, Clifford, cope° with him.   *fight*
CLIFFORD   Had I thy brethren here, their lives and thine
Were not revenge sufficient for me.
No—if I digged up thy forefathers' graves,
And hung their rotten coffins up in chains,
30 It could not slake° mine ire nor ease my heart.   *lessen*
The sight of any of the house of York
Is as a fury to torment my soul.
And till I root out their accursèd line,
And leave not one alive, I live in hell.
35 Therefore—
RUTLAND   O, let me pray before I take my death.
[*Kneeling*] To thee I pray: sweet Clifford, pity me.
CLIFFORD   Such pity as my rapier's point affords.
RUTLAND   I never did thee harm—why wilt thou slay me?
CLIFFORD   Thy father hath.
40 RUTLAND   But 'twas ere I was born.
Thou hast one son—for his sake pity me,
Lest in revenge thereof, sith° God is just,   *since*
He be as miserably slain as I.
Ah, let me live in prison all my days,
45 And when I give occasion of offence,
Then let me die, for now thou hast no cause.
CLIFFORD   No cause? Thy father slew my father, therefore die.
        [*He stabs him*]
RUTLAND   *Dii faciant laudis summa sit ista tuae.*[1]   [*He dies*]
CLIFFORD   Plantagenet—I come, Plantagenet!
50 And this thy son's blood cleaving to my blade
Shall rust upon my weapon till thy blood,
Congealed with this, do make me wipe off both.
                Exit [*with Rutland's body and soldiers*][2]

1.4

Alarum. Enter Richard Duke of YORK
YORK   The army of the Queen hath got° the field;   *won*
My uncles[1] both are slain in rescuing me;
And all my followers to the eager foe
Turn back,° and fly like ships before the wind,   *Turn their backs*
5 Or lambs pursued by hunger-starvèd wolves.
My sons—God knows what hath bechancèd° them.   *happened to*
But this I know—they have demeaned° themselves   *conducted*
Like men born to renown by life or death.

---

1. "The gods grant that this may be the height of your
glory" (Ovid, *Heroides* 2.66).
2. Although no F or O stage direction indicates whether
any soldiers are present during this scene, Clifford's command at line 7 makes it clear that some, at least, escort
the tutor offstage. Some may remain to exit here. Oxford

notes that "the question, unresolvable, is an important
one, for it asks, essentially, whether Clifford's murder of
Rutland is witnessed by anyone."
1.4 Location: Scene continues.
1. Sir John and Sir Hugh Mortimer.

Three times did Richard make a lane to me,
10 And thrice cried, 'Courage, father, fight it out!'
And full as oft came Edward to my side,
With purple falchion° painted to the hilt *curved sword*
In blood of those that had encountered him.
And when the hardiest warriors did retire,
15 Richard cried, 'Charge and give no foot of ground!'
[   ]²
And cried 'A crown or else a glorious tomb!
A sceptre or an earthly sepulchre!'
With this, we charged again—but out, alas—
20 We bodged° again, as I have seen a swan *gave way*
With bootless° labour swim against the tide *fruitless*
And spend her strength with over-matching° waves. *against too powerful*
     A short alarum within
Ah, hark—the fatal followers do pursue,
And I am faint and cannot fly their fury;
25 And were I strong, I would not shun their fury.
The sands° are numbered that makes up my life. *(of the hourglass)*
Here must I stay, and here my life must end.
     Enter QUEEN [MARGARET, *Lord*] CLIFFORD, [*the Earl of*]
     NORTHUMBERLAND, [*and*] *the young* PRINCE [EDWARD,
     with] *soldiers*
Come bloody Clifford, rough Northumberland—
I dare your quenchless fury to more rage!
30 I am your butt,° and I abide your shot. *target (in archery)*
NORTHUMBERLAND   Yield to our mercy, proud Plantagenet.
CLIFFORD   Ay, to such mercy as his ruthless arm,
With downright payment,³ showed unto my father.
Now Phaëton hath tumbled from his car,⁴
35 And made an evening at the noontide prick.⁵
YORK   My ashes, as the phoenix,⁶ may bring forth
A bird° that will revenge upon you all, *child*
And in that hope I throw mine eyes to heaven,
Scorning whate'er you can afflict me with.
40 Why come you not? What—multitudes, and fear?
CLIFFORD   So cowards fight when they can fly no further;
So doves do peck the falcon's piercing talons;
So desperate thieves, all hopeless of their lives,
Breathe out invectives 'gainst the officers.
45 YORK   O, Clifford, but bethink thee once again,
And in thy thought o'errun° my former time, *review*
And, if thou canst for blushing, view this face
And bite thy tongue, that slanders him with cowardice
Whose frown hath made thee faint and fly ere this.
50 CLIFFORD   I will not bandy with thee word for word,
But buckle° with thee blows twice two for one. *join in close combat*

---

2. It has been conjectured that this missing line referred to Edward, who, like his brother Richard, may have cried out encouragement to York's forces.
3. Alluding to the "downright," or vertical, sword stroke that York used to kill Clifford's father in *The First Part of the Contention.*
4. Phaeton, in classical myth, was the son of Phoebus (the sun god) and nearly set the world on fire when he attempted to drive his father's chariot ("car," the sun).

Zeus hurled a thunderbolt, and Phaeton fell blazing to his death. This is one of the play's many allusions to the fact that the sun was an emblem of the house of York. See note to 2.1.40.
5. The noon mark on a sundial.
6. A mythological bird that periodically built an elaborate funeral pyre, set itself on fire, and was reborn from its own ashes.

[*He draws his sword*]

QUEEN MARGARET   Hold, valiant Clifford: for a thousand causes
    I would prolong a while the traitor's life.
    Wrath makes him deaf—speak thou, Northumberland.
55 NORTHUMBERLAND   Hold, Clifford—do not honour him so much
    To prick thy finger though to wound his heart.
    What valour were it when a cur doth grin°   *show its teeth*
    For one to thrust his hand between his teeth
    When he might spurn° him with his foot away?   *kick*
60 It is war's prize to take all vantages,°   *opportunities*
    And ten to one is no impeach of valour.[7]
       [*They*] *fight and take* [YORK]
CLIFFORD   Ay, ay, so strives the woodcock with the gin.[8]
NORTHUMBERLAND   So doth the cony° struggle in the net.   *rabbit*
YORK   So triumph thieves upon their conquered booty,
65 So true° men yield, with robbers so o'ermatched.   *honest*
NORTHUMBERLAND [*to the* QUEEN]   What would your grace have
       done unto him now?
QUEEN MARGARET   Brave warriors, Clifford and Northumberland,
    Come make him stand upon this molehill here,
    That wrought° at mountains with outstrechèd arms   *reached*
70 Yet parted but° the shadow with his hand.   *only*
    [*To* YORK] What—was it you that would be England's king?
    Was't you that revelled in our Parliament,
    And made a preachment° of your high descent?   *sermon*
    Where are your mess of° sons to back you now?   *group of four*
75 The wanton Edward and the lusty George?
    And where's that valiant crookback prodigy,°   *marvel; monster*
    Dickie, your boy, that with his grumbling voice
    Was wont to cheer his dad in mutinies?
    Or with the rest where is your darling Rutland?
80 Look, York, I stained this napkin° with the blood   *handkerchief*
    That valiant Clifford with his rapier's point
    Made issue from the bosom of thy boy.
    And if thine eyes can water for his death,
    I give thee this to dry thy cheeks withal.°   *with*
85 Alas, poor York, but that I hate thee deadly
    I should lament thy miserable state.
    I prithee, grieve, to make me merry, York.
    What—hath thy fiery heart so parched thine entrails° *inner organs*
    That not a tear can fall for Rutland's death?
90 Why art thou patient, man? Thou shouldst be mad,
    And I, to make thee mad, do mock thee thus.
    Stamp, rave, and fret, that I may sing and dance.
    Thou wouldst be fee'd,° I see, to make me sport.   *paid*
    York cannot speak unless he wear a crown.
95 [*To her men*] A crown for York, and, lords, bow low to him.
    Hold you his hands whilst I do set it on.
       [*She puts a paper crown on York's head*]
    Ay, marry, sir, now looks he like a king,
    Ay, this is he that took King Henry's chair,
    And this is he was his adopted heir.

---

7. And for ten to fight with one does not call our bravery
into question.

8. Trap. *woodcock*: a bird reputed to lack brains and thus
easily caught in traps.

100   But how is it that great Plantagenet
       Is crowned so soon and broke his solemn oath?
       As I bethink me, you should not be king
       Till our King Henry had shook hands with death.
       And will you pale° your head in Henry's glory,   *enclose*
105   And rob his temples of the diadem
       Now, in his life, against your holy oath?
       O 'tis a fault too, too, unpardonable.
       Off with the crown,
                     [*She knocks it from his head*]
                            and with the crown his head,
       And whilst we breathe,° take time to do him dead.°   *rest / kill him*
110 CLIFFORD   That is my office for my father's sake.
     QUEEN MARGARET   Nay, stay—let's hear the orisons° he makes.   *prayers*
     YORK   She-wolf of France, but worse than wolves of France,
       Whose tongue more poisons than the adder's tooth—
       How ill-beseeming° is it in thy sex   *unbecoming*
115   To triumph like an Amazonian trull[9]
       Upon their woes whom fortune captivates!°   *subdues*
       But that° thy face is visor-like,[1] unchanging,   *Were it not that*
       Made impudent with use of evil deeds,
       I would essay,° proud Queen, to make thee blush.   *attempt*
120   To tell thee whence thou cam'st, of whom derived,
       Were shame enough to shame thee— wert thou not shameless.
       Thy father bears the type° of King of Naples,   *title*
       Of both the Sicils,[2] and Jerusalem—
       Yet not so wealthy as an English yeoman.[3]
125   Hath that poor monarch taught thee to insult?
       It needs not, nor it boots° thee not, proud Queen,   *profits*
       Unless the adage must be verified
       That beggars mounted run their horse to death.
       'Tis beauty that doth oft make women proud—
130   But, God he knows, thy share thereof is small;
       'Tis virtue that doth make them most admired—
       The contrary doth make thee wondered at;
       'Tis government° that makes them seem divine—   *self-control*
       The want thereof makes thee abominable.
135   Thou art as opposite to every good
       As the antipodes[4] are unto us,
       Or as the south to the septentrion.[5]
       O tiger's heart wrapped in a woman's hide!
       How couldst thou drain the life-blood of the child
140   To bid the father wipe his eyes withal,
       And yet be seen to bear a woman's face?
       Women are soft, mild, pitiful,° and flexible—   *full of pity*
       Thou stern, obdurate, flinty, rough, remorseless.
       Bidd'st thou me rage? Why, now thou hast thy wish.
145   Wouldst have me weep? Why, now thou hast thy will.
       For raging wind blows up incessant showers,

9. In the manner of an Amazonian whore. Amazons were   2. Naples and Sicily (known as the Kingdom of the Two
a tribe of mythical warrior women who governed them-   Sicilies).
selves and lived separate from men.   3. Landowner below the rank of gentleman.
1. Masklike; fixed in expression like the front piece of a 4. People living on the opposite side of the world.
helmet. Perhaps alluding to the practice of prostitutes   5. North. The word refers to the seven stars that make up
who wore masks.   the Great Bear constellation.

And when the rage allays° the rain begins.   *abates*
These tears are my sweet Rutland's obsequies,
And every drop cries vengeance for his death
150   'Gainst thee, fell° Clifford, and thee, false Frenchwoman.   *cruel*
NORTHUMBERLAND Beshrew° me, but his passions move me so   *Curse*
    That hardly can I check my eyes from tears.
   YORK That face of his the hungry cannibals
    Would not have touched, would not have stained with blood—
155   But you are more inhuman, more inexorable,
    O, ten times more than tigers of Hyrcania.[6]
    See, ruthless Queen, a hapless° father's tears.   *an unlucky*
    This cloth thou dipped'st in blood of my sweet boy,
    And I with tears do wash the blood away.
160   Keep thou the napkin and go boast of this,
    And if thou tell'st the heavy° story right,   *sorrowful*
    Upon my soul the hearers will shed tears,
    Yea, even my foes will shed fast-falling tears
    And say, 'Alas, it was a piteous deed'.
165   There, take the crown—and with the crown, my curse:
    And in thy need such comfort come to thee
    As now I reap at thy too cruel hand.
    Hard-hearted Clifford, take me from the world.
    My soul to heaven, my blood upon your heads.
170 NORTHUMBERLAND Had he been slaughter-man to all my kin,
    I should not, for my life, but weep with him,
    To see how inly° sorrow gripes his soul.   *inward*
    QUEEN MARGARET What—weeping-ripe,° my lord Northumberland?   *ready to weep*
    Think but upon the wrong he did us all,
175   And that will quickly dry thy melting tears.
    CLIFFORD Here's for my oath, here's for my father's death.
      [*He stabs* YORK]
    QUEEN MARGARET And here's to right our gentle-hearted King.
      [*She stabs* YORK]
   YORK Open thy gate of mercy, gracious God—
    My soul flies through these wounds to seek out thee.
                           [*He dies*]
180 QUEEN MARGARET Off with his head and set it on York gates,
    So York may overlook the town of York.
            Flourish. Exeunt [*with York's body*]

2.1

  [*A*] *march. Enter* EDWARD [*Earl of March*] *and* RICHARD,
  with [*a*] *drum*[*mer*] *and soldiers*
  EDWARD I wonder how our princely father scaped,
    Or whether he be scaped away or no
    From Clifford's and Northumberland's pursuit.
    Had he been ta'en we should have heard the news;
5   Had he been slain we should have heard the news;
    Or had he scaped, methinks we should have heard
    The happy tidings of his good escape.
    How fares my brother? Why is he so sad?
   RICHARD I cannot joy until I be resolved

---

6. Region in ancient Persia known for the cruelty of its
tigers (see *Aeneid* 4.366–67).

2.1 Location: Fields near the border, or marches,
between Wales and England.

10 Where our right valiant father is become.°   *has betaken himself*
    I saw him in the battle range about,
    And watched him how he singled Clifford forth.
    Methought he bore him in the thickest troop,
    As doth a lion in a herd of neat;°   *cattle*
15 Or as a bear encompassed round with dogs,
    Who having pinched° a few and made them cry,   *bitten*
    The rest stand all aloof and bark at him.
    So fared our father with his enemies;
    So fled his enemies my warlike father.
20 Methinks 'tis prize enough to be his son.
         Three suns appear in the air[1]
    See how the morning opes her golden gates
    And takes her farewell of the glorious sun.
    How well resembles it the prime of youth,
    Trimmed° like a younker° prancing to his love!   *Dressed up / young man*
25 EDWARD   Dazzle mine eyes, or do I see three suns?
    RICHARD   Three glorious suns, each one a perfect sun;
    Not separated with the racking° clouds,   *drifting*
    But severed in a pale clear-shining sky.
       [*The three suns begin to join*]
    See, see—they join, embrace, and seem to kiss,
30 As if they vowed some league inviolable.
    Now are they but one lamp, one light, one sun.
    In this the heaven figures° some event.   *prefigures*
    EDWARD   'Tis wondrous strange, the like yet never heard of.
    I think it cites° us, brother, to the field,   *urges*
35 That we, the sons of brave Plantagenet,
    Each one already blazing by our meeds,°   *merits*
    Should notwithstanding join our lights together
    And over-shine the earth as this° the world.   *this phenomenon*
    Whate'er it bodes, henceforward will I bear
40 Upon my target three fair-shining suns.[2]
    RICHARD   Nay, bear three daughters— by your leave I speak it—
    You love the breeder° better than the male.   *child-bearer; woman*
         Enter one blowing[3]
    But what art thou whose heavy looks foretell
    Some dreadful story hanging on thy tongue?
45 MESSENGER   Ah, one that was a woeful looker-on
    Whenas° the noble Duke of York was slain—   *When*
    Your princely father and my loving lord.
    EDWARD   O, speak no more, for I have heard too much.
    RICHARD   Say how he died, for I will hear it all.
50 MESSENGER   Environèd° he was with many foes,   *Surrounded*
    And stood against them as the hope of Troy[4]
    Against the Greeks that would have entered Troy.
    But Hercules[5] himself must yield to odds;

---

1. This stage direction appears in O, which may have been based on a theatrical promptbook (see Textual Note). It suggests that the acting company who performed the play had some kind of artificial "suns" they used as properties for this scene.
2. As elsewhere, Shakespeare here slightly changes his sources. In Holinshed's chronicles, Edward chose the sun as his badge because he had seen three suns join in one before the Battle of Mortimer's Cross, which he won. *tar-*

get: shield.
3. Blowing a horn as messengers did to announce themselves.
4. *hope of Troy*: Hector, a mighty warrior in Homer's *Iliad*, who defended the city of Troy against Greek invaders.
5. A mythic hero of enormous physical strength and courage.

And many strokes, though with a little axe,
55 Hews down and fells the hardest-timbered oak.
By many hands your father was subdued,
But only slaughtered by the ireful arm
Of unrelenting Clifford and the Queen,
Who crowned the gracious Duke in high despite,°   *in great contempt*
60 Laughed in his face, and when with grief he wept,
The ruthless Queen gave him to dry his cheeks
A napkin steepèd in the harmless blood
Of sweet young Rutland, by rough Clifford slain;
And after many scorns, many foul taunts,
65 They took his head, and on the gates of York
They set the same; and there it doth remain,
The saddest spectacle that e'er I viewed.
EDWARD   Sweet Duke of York, our prop to lean upon,
Now thou art gone, we have no staff, no stay.°   *support*
70 O Clifford, boist'rous° Clifford—thou hast slain   *savage*
The flower of Europe for his chivalry,
And treacherously hast thou vanquished him—
For hand to hand he would have vanquished thee.
Now my soul's palace° is become a prison.   *(my body)*
75 Ah, would she° break from hence that this my body   *(my soul)*
Might in the ground be closèd up in rest.
For never henceforth shall I joy again—
Never, O never, shall I see more joy.
RICHARD   I cannot weep, for all my body's moisture
80 Scarce serves to quench my furnace-burning heart;
Nor can my tongue unload my heart's great burden,
For selfsame wind° that I should speak withal   *breath*
Is kindling coals that fires all my breast,
And burns me up with flames that tears would quench.
85 To weep is to make less the depth of grief;
Tears, then, for babes—blows and revenge for me!
Richard, I bear thy name; I'll venge° thy death   *revenge*
Or die renownèd by attempting it.
EDWARD   His name that valiant Duke hath left with thee,
90 His dukedom and his chair[6] with me is left.
RICHARD   Nay, if thou be that princely eagle's bird,
Show thy descent by gazing 'gainst the sun:[7]
For 'chair and dukedom', 'throne and kingdom' say—
Either that is thine or else thou wert not his.
    March. Enter the Earl of WARWICK *[and the] Marquis*
    [of] MONTAGUE, *with drum[mers], [an] ensign, and sol-*
    diers
95 WARWICK   How now, fair lords? What fare?° What news abroad?   *success*
RICHARD   Great lord of Warwick, if we should recount
Our baleful° news, and at each word's deliverance   *deadly*
Stab poniards° in our flesh till all were told,   *daggers*
The words would add more anguish than the wounds.
100 O valiant lord, the Duke of York is slain.
EDWARD   O Warwick, Warwick! That Plantagenet,

---

6. Seat of his authority as Duke.
7. Eagles, described by Elizabethans as the king of birds, were supposed to be able to gaze unblinkingly at the sun.

Which held thee dearly as his soul's redemption,
Is by the stern Lord Clifford done to death.
WARWICK   Ten days ago I drowned these news in tears.
105   And now, to add more measure to your woes,
I come to tell you things sith° then befall'n.   *since*
After the bloody fray at Wakefield fought,
Where your brave father breathed his latest° gasp,   *last*
Tidings, as swiftly as the posts° could run,   *messengers*
110   Were brought me of your loss and his depart.°   *death*
I then in London, keeper of the King,
Mustered my soldiers, gathered flocks of friends,
And, very well appointed° as I thought,   *equipped*
Marched toward Saint Albans to intercept the Queen,
115   Bearing the King in my behalf along—
For by my scouts I was advisèd°   *informed*
That she was coming with a full intent
To dash our late° decree in Parliament   *recent*
Touching King Henry's oath and your succession.
120   Short tale to make, we at Saint Albans met,
Our battles° joined, and both sides fiercely fought;   *armies*
But whether 'twas the coldness of the King,
Who looked full gently on his warlike queen,
That robbed my soldiers of their heated spleen,°   *fiery passion*
125   Or whether 'twas report of her success,
Or more than common fear of Clifford's rigour—
Who thunders to his captains blood and death—
I cannot judge; but, to conclude with truth,
Their weapons like to lightning came and went;
130   Our soldiers', like the night-owl's lazy flight,
Or like an idle thresher with a flail,[8]
Fell gently down, as if they struck their friends.
I cheered them up with justice of our cause,
With promise of high pay, and great rewards.
135   But all in vain. They had no heart to fight,
And we in them no hope to win the day.
So that we fled—the King unto the Queen,
Lord George your brother, Norfolk, and myself
In haste, post-haste, are come to join with you.
140   For in the Marches° here we heard you were,   *Welsh borders*
Making another head° to fight again.   *Raising another army*
EDWARD   Where is the Duke of Norfolk, gentle Warwick?
And when came George from Burgundy to England?
WARWICK   Some six miles off the Duke is with his soldiers;
145   And for your brother—he was lately sent
From your kind aunt, Duchess of Burgundy,[9]
With aid of soldiers to this needful war.
RICHARD   'Twas odd belike[1] when valiant Warwick fled.
Oft have I heard his praises in pursuit,°   *(of enemies)*
150   But ne'er till now his scandal of retire.[2]
WARWICK   Nor now my scandal, Richard, dost thou hear—

---

8. Threshers beat grain from wheat with specially designed sticks, or "flails."
9. According to the chronicles, both George and Richard were sent for safety to the court of Philip of Burgundy; his wife, the Duchess of Burgundy Warwick mentions, was a granddaughter of John of Gaunt.
1. The odds must have been much against him.
2. Defamation or condemnation of him for retreating (from his enemies).

For thou shalt know this strong right hand of mine
Can pluck the diadem from faint° Henry's head   *weak*
And wring the aweful° sceptre from his fist,   *awe-inspiring*
155 Were he as famous and as bold in war
As he is famed for mildness, peace, and prayer.
RICHARD   I know it well, Lord Warwick—blame me not.
'Tis love I bear thy glories make me speak.
But in this troublous time what's to be done?
160 Shall we go throw away our coats of steel,
And wrap our bodies in black mourning gowns,
Numb'ring our Ave-Maries with our beads?³
Or shall we on the helmets of our foes
Tell our devotion⁴ with revengeful arms?
165 If for the last, say 'ay', and to it, lords.
WARWICK   Why, therefore Warwick came to seek you out,
And therefore comes my brother Montague.
Attend me, lords. The proud insulting Queen,
With Clifford and the haught° Northumberland,   *haughty*
170 And of their feather many more proud birds,
Have wrought° the easy-melting King like wax.   *worked on*
[*To* EDWARD] He swore consent to your succession,
His oath enrollèd° in the Parliament.   *officially recorded*
And now to London all the crew are gone,
175 To frustrate both his oath and what beside
May make against° the house of Lancaster.   *be unfavorable to*
Their power, I think, is thirty thousand strong.
Now, if the help of Norfolk and myself,
With all the friends that thou, brave Earl of March,⁵
180 Amongst the loving Welshmen canst procure,
Will but amount to five-and-twenty thousand,
Why, *via*,° to London will we march,   *onward*
And once again bestride our foaming steeds,
And once again cry 'Charge!' upon our foes—
185 But never once again turn back and fly.
RICHARD   Ay, now methinks I hear great Warwick speak.
Ne'er may he live to see a sunshine day
That cries 'Retire!' if Warwick bid him stay.
EDWARD   Lord Warwick, on thy shoulder will I lean,
190 And when thou fail'st—as God forbid the hour—
Must Edward fall, which peril heaven forfend!°   *forbid*
WARWICK   No longer Earl of March, but Duke of York;
The next degree° is England's royal throne—   *step*
For King of England shalt thou be proclaimed
195 In every borough as we pass along,
And he that throws not up his cap for joy,
Shall for the fault make forfeit of his head.
King Edward, valiant Richard, Montague—
Stay we no longer dreaming of renown,
200 But sound the trumpets and about our task.
RICHARD   Then, Clifford, were thy heart as hard as steel,

---

3. Rosary beads are used in Roman Catholic devotion for keeping track of the prayers one has said, including "Ave Maria's" ("Hail Mary's"), prayers addressed to the Virgin Mary.
4. Proclaim the object of our devotion (York), with a pun on "telling" as meaning "counting," which is what one does when saying the rosary.
5. The title by which Edward and his father before him laid claim to the throne of England. See line 192 and note to 1.1.78.

As thou hast shown it flinty by thy deeds,
I come to pierce it or to give thee mine.
EDWARD   Then strike up drums—God and Saint George°   patron saint of England
for us!
        Enter a MESSENGER
205 WARWICK   How now? What news?
MESSENGER   The Duke of Norfolk sends you word by me
The Queen is coming with a puissant° host,   powerful
And craves your company for speedy counsel.
WARWICK   Why then it sorts.° Brave warriors, let's away.   is fitting
                            [*March.*] *Exeunt*

                            2.2
[*York's head is thrust out, above.*]¹
Flourish. Enter KING [HENRY], QUEEN [MARGARET],
[*Lord*] CLIFFORD, [*the Earl of*] NORTHUMBERLAND, *and
young* PRINCE EDWARD, *with* [*a*] *drum*[*mer*] *and trum-
pet*[*er*]*s*
QUEEN MARGARET   Welcome, my lord, to this brave town of York.
Yonder's the head of that arch-enemy
That sought to be encompassed with your crown.
Doth not the object cheer your heart, my lord?
5 KING HENRY   Ay, as the rocks cheer them that fear their wreck.
To see this sight, it irks my very soul.
Withhold revenge, dear God—'tis not my fault,
Nor wittingly have I infringed my vow.
CLIFFORD   My gracious liege,° this too much lenity   sovereign
10 And harmful pity must be laid aside.
To whom do lions cast their gentle looks?
Not to the beast that would usurp their den.
Whose hand is that the forest bear doth lick?
Not his that spoils° her young before her face.   takes as prey
15 Who scapes the lurking serpent's mortal sting?
Not he that sets his foot upon her back.
The smallest worm will turn, being trodden on,
And doves will peck in safeguard of their brood.
Ambitious York did level° at thy crown,   aim
20 Thou smiling while he knit his angry brows.
He, but a duke, would have his son a king,
And raise° his issue° like a loving sire;   raise in rank / offspring
Thou, being a king, blest with a goodly son,
Didst yield consent to disinherit him,
25 Which argued thee a most unloving father.
Unreasonable creatures° feed their young,   Animals
And though man's face be fearful to their eyes,
Yet, in protection of their tender ones,
Who hath not seen them, even with those wings
30 Which sometime they have used with fearful flight,
Make war with him that climbed unto their nest,
Offering their own lives in their young's defence?
For shame, my liege, make them your precedent!

2.2 Location: Before the walls of York.
1. Neither F nor O indicates in stage directions that
York's head is displayed above the stage, but Queen Margaret's words in lines 2–4 and King Henry's response suggest that it remains visible, perhaps (as Oxford proposes)
until 2.6.110.

Were it not pity that this goodly boy
35   Should lose his birthright by his father's fault,
And long hereafter say unto his child
'What my great-grandfather and grandsire got
My careless father fondly° gave away'?   *foolishly*
Ah, what a shame were this! Look on the boy,
40   And let his manly face, which promiseth
Successful fortune, steel thy melting heart
To hold thine own and leave thine own with him.
KING HENRY   Full well hath Clifford played the orator,
Inferring° arguments of mighty force.   *Offering*
45   But, Clifford, tell me—didst thou never hear
That things ill got had ever bad success?°   *outcome*
And happy always was it for that son
Whose father for his hoarding went to hell?
I'll leave my son my virtuous deeds behind,
50   And would my father had left me no more.
For all the rest is held at such a rate°   *cost*
As brings a thousandfold more care to keep
Than in possession any jot of pleasure.
Ah, cousin York, would thy best friends did know
55   How it doth grieve me that thy head is here.
QUEEN MARGARET   My lord, cheer up your spirits—our foes are nigh,
And this soft courage makes your followers faint.°   *lose heart*
You promised knighthood to our forward° son.   *precocious*
Unsheathe your sword and dub² him presently.°   *at once*
60   Edward, kneel down.
      [PRINCE EDWARD *kneels*]
KING HENRY   Edward Plantagenet, arise a knight—
And learn this lesson: draw thy sword in right.
PRINCE EDWARD [*rising*]   My gracious father, by your kingly leave,
I'll draw it as apparent° to the crown,   *heir*
65   And in that quarrel° use it to the death.   *cause*
CLIFFORD   Why, that is spoken like a toward° prince.   *bold*
      Enter a MESSENGER
MESSENGER   Royal commanders, be in readiness—
For with a band of thirty thousand men
Comes Warwick backing of° the Duke of York;   *supporting*
70   And in the towns, as they do march along,
Proclaims him king, and many fly to him.
Darraign your battle,° for they are at hand.   *Deploy your troops*
CLIFFORD [*to* KING HENRY]   I would your highness would depart
    the field—
The Queen hath best success when you are absent.
QUEEN MARGARET [*to* KING HENRY]   Ay, good my lord, and
75   leave us to our fortune.
KING HENRY   Why, that's my fortune too—therefore I'll stay.
NORTHUMBERLAND   Be it with resolution then to fight.
PRINCE EDWARD [*to* KING HENRY]   My royal father, cheer these
    noble lords
And hearten those that fight in your defence.
80   Unsheathe your sword, good father; cry 'Saint George!'

---

2. Confer the rank of knight by the ceremony of striking the shoulder with a sword.

March. Enter EDWARD [*Duke of York, the Earl of*] WAR-
WICK, RICHARD, [GEORGE,³ *the Duke of*] NORFOLK, [*the
Marquis of*] MONTAGUE, *and soldiers*

EDWARD   Now, perjured Henry, wilt thou kneel for grace,
   And set thy diadem upon my head—
   Or bide° the mortal° fortune of the field?   *wait for / fatal*
QUEEN MARGARET   Go rate° thy minions,° proud insulting boy!   *chide / favorites*
85   Becomes it thee to be thus bold in terms
   Before thy sovereign and thy lawful king?
EDWARD   I am his king, and he should bow his knee.
   I was adopted heir by his consent.
GEORGE [*to* QUEEN MARGARET]   Since when his oath is broke—
   for, as I hear,
90   You that are king, though he do wear the crown,
   Have caused him by new act of Parliament
   To blot our brother out, and put his own son in.
CLIFFORD   And reason too—
   Who should succeed the father but the son?
95   RICHARD   Are you there, butcher? O, I cannot speak!
CLIFFORD   Ay, crookback, here I stand to answer thee,
   Or any he the proudest of thy sort.°   *gang*
RICHARD   'Twas you that killed young Rutland, was it not?
CLIFFORD   Ay, and old York, and yet not satisfied.
100   RICHARD   For God's sake, lords, give signal to the fight.
WARWICK   What sayst thou, Henry, wilt thou yield the crown?
QUEEN MARGARET   Why, how now, long-tongued Warwick, dare
   you speak?
   When you and I met at Saint Albans last,
   Your legs did better service than your hands.
105   WARWICK   Then 'twas my turn to fly—and now 'tis thine.
CLIFFORD   You said so much before, and yet you fled.
WARWICK   'Twas not your valour, Clifford, drove me thence.
NORTHUMBERLAND   No, nor your manhood that durst make you stay.
RICHARD   Northumberland, I hold thee reverently.°   *in respect*
110   Break off the parley, for scarce I can refrain
   The execution of my big-swoll'n heart⁴
   Upon that Clifford, that cruel child-killer.
CLIFFORD   I slew thy father—call'st thou him a child?
RICHARD   Ay, like a dastard° and a treacherous coward,   *base coward*
115   As thou didst kill our tender brother Rutland.
   But ere sun set I'll make thee curse the deed.
KING HENRY   Have done with words, my lords, and hear me speak.
QUEEN MARGARET   Defy them, then, or else hold close thy lips.
KING HENRY   I prithee give no limits to my tongue—
120   I am a king, and privileged to speak.
CLIFFORD   My liege, the wound that bred this meeting here
   Cannot be cured by words—therefore be still.
RICHARD   Then, executioner, unsheathe thy sword.
   By him that made us all, I am resolved
125   That Clifford's manhood lies upon his tongue.°   *exists only in words*
EDWARD   Say, Henry, shall I have my right or no?

---

3. Here and elsewhere, F's stage directions read "Clar-   4. From acting passionately. Passions were supposed to
ence" rather than "George." The Duke of Clarence is the   cause the heart to swell.
title he eventually assumes.

A thousand men have broke their fasts today
That ne'er shall dine unless thou yield the crown.
WARWICK [*to* KING HENRY] If thou deny,° their blood upon thy head;   *refuse*
130 For York in justice puts his armour on.
PRINCE EDWARD   If that be right which Warwick says is right,
There is no wrong, but everything is right.
RICHARD   Whoever got° thee, there thy mother stands—   *sired*
For, well I wot,° thou hast thy mother's tongue.   *know*
135 QUEEN MARGARET   But thou art neither like thy sire nor dam,
But like a foul misshapen stigmatic,[5]
Marked by the destinies[6] to be avoided,
As venom° toads or lizards' dreadful stings.   *poisonous*
RICHARD   Iron of Naples, hid with English gilt,[7]
140 Whose father bears the title of a king—
As if a channel° should be called the sea—   *gutter*
Sham'st thou not, knowing whence thou art extraught,°   *descended*
To let thy tongue detect° thy base-born heart?   *reveal*
EDWARD   A wisp of straw[8] were° worth a thousand crowns   *would be*
145 To make this shameless callet° know herself.   *whore*
Helen of Greece was fairer far than thou,
Although thy husband may be Menelaus;[9]
And ne'er was Agamemnon's brother° wronged   *(Menelaus)*
By that false woman, as this king by thee.
150 His father° revelled in the heart of France,   *(Henry V)*
And tamed the King, and made the Dauphin[1] stoop;
And had he matched° according to his state,°   *(Henry VI) wed / rank*
He might have kept that glory to this day.
But when he took a beggar to his bed,
155 And graced thy poor sire with his bridal day,[2]
Even then that sunshine brewed a shower for him
That washed his father's fortunes forth of° France,   *out of*
And heaped sedition on his crown at home.
For what hath broached this tumult but thy pride?
160 Hadst thou been meek, our title° still had slept,   *claim to the throne*
And we, in pity of the gentle King,
Had slipped° our claim until another age.   *postponed*
GEORGE [*to* QUEEN MARGARET]   But when we saw our sunshine
    made thy spring,
And that thy summer bred us no increase,°   *harvest*
165 We set the axe to thy usurping root.
And though the edge hath something° hit ourselves,   *to some extent*
Yet know thou, since we have begun to strike,
We'll never leave till we have hewn thee down,
Or bathed thy growing with our heated bloods.
170 EDWARD [*to* QUEEN MARGARET]   And in this resolution I defy thee,

5. A deformed person; a criminal marked by means of an iron brand for his or her crime.
6. The Fates, three goddesses in classical mythology thought to determine the course of a person's life.
7. You cheap product of Naples, hiding under the gold veneer of an English marriage. Since Naples is synonymous in many Elizabethan texts with prostitution and venereal disease, "iron" may also refer to the metal noses allegedly worn by wealthy people to disguise the disfiguring effects of syphilis.
8. Being made to wear or hold straw was a practice by which women were marked as scolds in public shaming rituals.
9. The Trojan War was said to have begun because the Greek Helen, the most beautiful woman in the world, betrayed her husband, Menelaus, and eloped with the Trojan warrior Paris.
1. The French King's oldest son, later Charles VII of France.
2. And brought honor to your impoverished father by marrying you.

Not willing any longer conference
Since thou deniest the gentle King to speak.
Sound trumpets—let our bloody colours wave!
And either victory, or else a grave!
175　QUEEN MARGARET　Stay, Edward.
EDWARD　No, wrangling woman, we'll no longer stay—
These words will cost ten thousand lives this day.
　　　　　　　　[*Flourish. March.*] *Exeunt* [EDWARD *and his men*
　　　　　　　　at one door and QUEEN MARGARET *and her men*
　　　　　　　　　　　　　　　at another door][3]

2.3

Alarum. Excursions.° *Enter* [*the Earl of*] WARWICK[1]　　　*Skirmishes*
WARWICK　Forespent° with toil, as runners with a race,　　　*Exhausted*
I lay me down a little while to breathe;°　　　　　　　　　　*rest*
For strokes received, and many blows repaid,
Have robbed my strong-knit° sinews of their strength,　　　*powerful*
5　And, spite of spite,° needs must I rest a while.　　　*come what may*
　　　Enter EDWARD [*the Duke of York*] *running*
EDWARD　Smile, gentle heaven, or strike, ungentle° death!　　*ignoble*
For this world frowns, and Edward's sun[2] is clouded.
WARWICK　How now, my lord, what hap?° What hope of good?　　*fortune*
　　　Enter GEORGE [*running*]
GEORGE　Our hap is loss, our hope but sad despair;
10　Our ranks are broke, and ruin follows us.
What counsel give you? Whither shall we fly?
EDWARD　Bootless° is flight—they follow us with wings,　　　*Useless*
And weak we are, and cannot shun pursuit.
　　　Enter RICHARD, *running*
RICHARD　Ah, Warwick, why hast thou withdrawn thyself?
15　Thy brother's[3] blood the thirsty earth hath drunk,
Broached° with the steely point of Clifford's lance.　　　*Set flowing*
And in the very pangs of death he cried,
Like to a dismal clangour heard from far,
'Warwick, revenge—brother, revenge my death!'
20　So, underneath the belly of their steeds
That stained their fetlocks in his smoking° blood,　　　*steaming*
The noble gentleman gave up the ghost.
WARWICK　Then let the earth be drunken with our blood.
I'll kill my horse, because I will not fly.
25　Why stand we like soft-hearted women here,
Wailing our losses, whiles the foe doth rage;
And look upon,° as if the tragedy　　　　　　　　　　　　　*on*
Were played in jest by counterfeiting actors?
[*Kneeling*]　Here, on my knee, I vow to God above
30　I'll never pause again, never stand still,
Till either death hath closed these eyes of mine
Or fortune given me measure of revenge.
EDWARD [*kneeling*]　O, Warwick, I do bend my knee with thine,

---

3. Oxford proposes that Edward and Margaret and their men exit at separate stage doors to indicate symbolically their enmity. F and O read simply "Exeunt omnes."
2.3 Location: The remaining scenes in Act 2 take place in the fields near York.
1. While Shakespeare does not specify the locale, the events in this and the following three scenes resemble those associated with a battle waged at Towton in Yorkshire in 1461.
2. Good fortune, alluding to the sun as Edward's emblem.
3. Warwick's half-brother, the Bastard of Salisbury.

And in this vow do chain my soul to thine.
35 And, ere my knee rise from the earth's cold face,
I throw my hands, mine eyes, my heart to Thee,°   *(God)*
Thou setter up and plucker down of kings,[4]
Beseeching Thee, if with Thy will it stands°   *agrees*
That to my foes this body must be prey,
40 Yet that Thy brazen gates of heaven may ope
And give sweet passage to my sinful soul.
    [*They rise*]
Now, lords, take leave until we meet again,
Where'er it be, in heaven or in earth.
RICHARD   Brother, give me thy hand; and, gentle° Warwick,   *noble*
45 Let me embrace thee in my weary arms.
I, that did never weep, now melt with woe
That winter should cut off our springtime so.
WARWICK   Away, away! Once more, sweet lords, farewell.
GEORGE   Yet let us all together to our troops,
50 And give them leave° to fly that will not stay;   *permission*
And call them pillars that will stand to° us;   *by*
And, if we thrive, promise them such rewards
As victors wear at the Olympian games.[5]
This may plant courage in their quailing breasts,
55 For yet is hope of life and victory.
Forslow° no longer—make we hence amain.°   *Exeunt*   *Delay / speedily*

2.4

Alarums. Excursions. Enter RICHARD *at one door and*
[*Lord*] CLIFFORD *at the other*
RICHARD   Now, Clifford, I have singled thee alone.[1]
Suppose this arm is for the Duke of York,
And this for Rutland, both bound to revenge,
Wert thou environed° with a brazen wall.   *surrounded*
5 CLIFFORD   Now, Richard, I am with thee here alone.
This is the hand that stabbed thy father York,
And this the hand that slew thy brother Rutland,
And here's the heart that triumphs in their death
And cheers these hands that slew thy sire and brother
10 To execute the like upon thyself—
And so, have at thee!
    They fight. [*The Earl of*] WARWICK *comes and rescues*
    RICHARD. [*Lord*] CLIFFORD *flies*
RICHARD   Nay, Warwick, single out some other chase°—   *prey*
For I myself will hunt this wolf to death.   *Exeunt*

2.5

Alarum. Enter KING HENRY
KING HENRY   This battle fares like to the morning's war,[1]
When dying clouds contend with growing light,

---

4. Echoing a biblical description of God in Daniel 2:21.
See also 3.3.157, where Margaret calls Warwick the "set-
ter-up and puller-down of kings."
5. The Olympian Games in ancient Greece were festivals that included athletic contests. Victors were presented with garlands of olive leaves.

2.4
1. I have isolated you from the herd (a hunting term).
2.5
1. In O, King Henry's ensuing fifty-four-line soliloquy as
found in F is reduced to thirteen lines, perhaps shortened
for performance.

What time° the shepherd, blowing of° his nails,   *When / on*
  Can neither call it perfect day nor night.
5 Now sways it this way like a mighty sea
  Forced by the tide to combat with the wind,
Now sways it that way like the selfsame sea
  Forced to retire by fury of the wind.
Sometime the flood prevails, and then the wind;
10 Now one the better, then another best—
Both tugging to be victors, breast to breast,
  Yet neither conqueror nor conquerèd.
So is the equal poise° of this fell° war.   *balance / deadly*
  Here on this molehill will I sit me down.
15 To whom God will, there be the victory.
For Margaret my queen, and Clifford, too,
  Have chid me from the battle, swearing both
They prosper best of all when I am thence.
  Would I were dead, if God's good will were so—
20 For what is in this world but grief and woe?
O God! Methinks it were a happy life
  To be no better than a homely swain.°   *simple shepherd*
To sit upon a hill, as I do now;
  To carve out dials quaintly,° point by point,   *sundials artfully*
25 Thereby to see the minutes how they run:
How many makes the hour full complete,
  How many hours brings about° the day,   *completes*
How many days will finish up the year,
  How many years a mortal man may live.
30 When this is known, then to divide the times:
So many hours must I tend my flock,
  So many hours must I take my rest,
So many hours must I contemplate,
  So many hours must I sport myself,
35 So many days my ewes have been with young,
So many weeks ere the poor fools will ean,°   *give birth*
  So many years ere I shall shear the fleece.
So minutes, hours, days, weeks, months, and years,
  Passed over to the end they° were created,   *for which they*
40 Would bring white hairs unto a quiet grave.
Ah, what a life were this! How sweet! How lovely!
  Gives not the hawthorn bush a sweeter shade
To shepherds looking on their seely° sheep   *innocent*
  Than doth a rich embroidered canopy
45 To kings that fear their subjects' treachery?
O yes, it doth—a thousandfold it doth.
  And to conclude, the shepherd's homely curds,
His cold thin drink out of his leather bottle,
  His wonted° sleep under a fresh tree's shade,   *customary*
50 All which secure and sweetly he enjoys,
Is far beyond a prince's delicates,°   *delicacies*
  His viands° sparkling in a golden cup,   *food*
His body couchèd in a curious° bed,   *an ornate*
  When care, mistrust, and treason waits on him.

     Alarum. Enter at one door a SOLDIER *with a dead man*
     in his arms. [KING HENRY *stands apart*][2]

2. Here Oxford adopts a combination of F and O staging. F indicates a simultaneous entrance, at two different

55	SOLDIER Ill blows the wind that profits nobody.	
	This man, whom hand to hand I slew in fight,	
	May be possessèd with some store of crowns;°	*coins*
	And I, that haply° take them from him now,	*by chance*
	May yet ere night yield both my life and them	
60	To some man else, as this dead man doth me.	
	[*He removes the dead man's helmet*]	
	Who's this? O God! It is my father's face	
	Whom in this conflict I, unwares, have killed.	
	O, heavy times, begetting such events!	
	From London by the King was I pressed forth;[3]	
65	My father, being the Earl of Warwick's man,°	*servant*
	Came on the part° of York, pressed by his master;	*side*
	And I, who at his hands received my life,	
	Have by my hands of life bereavèd him.	
	Pardon me, God, I knew not what I did;	
70	And pardon, father, for I knew not thee.	
	My tears shall wipe away these bloody marks,	
	And no more words till they have flowed their fill.	
	[*He weeps*]	
	KING HENRY O piteous spectacle! O bloody times!	
	Whiles lions war and battle for their dens,	
75	Poor harmless lambs abide their enmity.	
	Weep, wretched man, I'll aid thee tear for tear;	
	And let our hearts and eyes, like civil war,	
	Be blind with tears, and break, o'erchargèd° with grief.	*overburdened*
	Enter at another door another SOLDIER *with a dead man*	
	[*in his arms*]	
	SECOND SOLDIER Thou that so stoutly hath resisted me,	
80	Give me thy gold, if thou hast any gold—	
	For I have bought it with an hundred blows.	
	[*He removes the dead man's helmet*]	
	But let me see: is this our foeman's° face?	*enemy's*
	Ah, no, no, no—it is mine only son!	
	Ah, boy, if any life be left in thee,	
85	Throw up thine eye! [*Weeping*] See, see, what showers arise,	
	Blown with the windy tempest of my heart,	
	Upon thy wounds, that kills mine eye and heart!	
	O, pity, God, this miserable age!	
	What stratagems,° how fell,° how butcherly,	*violent acts / cruel*
90	Erroneous,° mutinous, and unnatural,	*Criminal*
	This deadly quarrel daily doth beget!	
	O boy, thy father gave thee life too soon,	
	And hath bereft thee of thy life too late!°	*recently*
	KING HENRY Woe above woe! Grief more than common grief!	
95	O that my death would stay° these ruthful° deeds!	*stop / pitiful*
	O, pity, pity, gentle heaven, pity!	
	The red rose and the white are on his face,	
	The fatal colours of our striving houses;	

---

doors, of a "Son that hath kill'd his Father" and a "Father that hath kill'd his Son." O, as here, designates both figures as simply "a soldier with a dead man in his arms" and "another soldier with a dead man" and gives them entrances at lines 54 and 78, respectively, but without mention of two doors. In O, the relationship between the living and the dead is revealed through the dialogue only.
3. Forcibly enlisted. Because England had no standing army until the latter half of the seventeenth century, many soldiers in Elizabethan England were conscripts.

The one his purple blood right well resembles,
100 The other his pale cheeks, methinks, presenteth.
Wither one rose, and let the other flourish—
If you contend, a thousand lives must wither.
FIRST SOLDIER   How will my mother for a father's death
Take on with° me, and ne'er be satisfied!   *Rage against*
105 SECOND SOLDIER   How will my wife for slaughter of my son
Shed seas of tears, and ne'er be satisfied!
KING HENRY   How will the country for these woeful chances°   *events*
Misthink° the King, and not be satisfied!   *Think ill of*
FIRST SOLDIER   Was ever son so rued a father's death?
110 SECOND SOLDIER   Was ever father so bemoaned his son?
KING HENRY   Was ever king so grieved for subjects' woe?
Much is your sorrow, mine ten times so much.
FIRST SOLDIER [*to his father's body*]   I'll bear thee hence where
I may weep my fill.
         Exit [at one door] with [the body of] his father
SECOND SOLDIER [*to his son's body*]   These arms of mine shall
be thy winding sheet;°   *shroud*
115 My heart, sweet boy, shall be thy sepulchre,
For from my heart thine image ne'er shall go.
My sighing breast shall be thy funeral bell,
And so obsequious° will thy father be,   *dutiful in mourning*
E'en for the loss of thee, having no more,
120 As Priam⁴ was for all his valiant sons.
I'll bear thee hence, and let them fight that will—
For I have murdered where I should not kill.
         Exit [at another door] with [the body of] his son
KING HENRY   Sad-hearted men, much overgone° with care,   *overcome*
Here sits a king more woeful than you are.
         Alarums. Excursions. Enter PRINCE EDWARD⁵
125 PRINCE EDWARD   Fly, father, fly—for all your friends are fled,
And Warwick rages like a chafèd° bull!   *an angered*
Away—for death doth hold us in pursuit!
         Enter QUEEN [MARGARET]
QUEEN MARGARET   Mount you, my lord—towards Berwick⁶ post
amain.°   *ride speedily*
Edward and Richard, like a brace° of greyhounds   *pair*
130 Having the fearful flying hare in sight,
With fiery eyes sparkling for very wrath,
And bloody steel grasped in their ireful hands,
Are at our backs—and therefore hence amain.°   *at full speed*
         Enter EXETER
EXETER   Away—for vengeance comes along with them!
135 Nay—stay not to expostulate°—make speed—   *argue*
Or else come after. I'll away before.
KING HENRY   Nay, take me with thee, good sweet Exeter.
Not that I fear to stay, but love to go
Whither the Queen intends. Forward, away.   *Exeunt*

4. King of Troy during the Trojan War. His fifty sons, of whom Hector was one, were killed defending the city.
5. F indicates a single entrance for "the Queen, the Prince, and Exeter" at line 124, and they speak in the order Prince-Queen-Exeter; O has Margaret enter first, then Prince Edward, and finally Exeter. Oxford follows O and divides the entrances, but places them in F's order of speech.
6. Berwick-on-Tweed, a village near Scotland in Northumberland.

2.6

A loud alarum. Enter [Lord] CLIFFORD, *wounded with*
an arrow in his neck

CLIFFORD   Here burns my candle out—ay, here it dies,
  Which, whiles it lasted, gave King Henry light.
  O Lancaster, I fear thy overthrow
  More than my body's parting with my soul!
5 My love and fear° glued many friends to thee—   *Love and fear of me*
  And, now I fall, thy tough commixture¹ melts,
  Impairing Henry, strength'ning misproud° York.   *arrogant*
  The common people swarm like summer flies,
  And whither fly the gnats but to the sun?²
10 And who shines now but Henry's enemies?
  O Phoebus, hadst thou never given consent
  That Phaëton³ should check° thy fiery steeds,   *manage*
  Thy burning car° never had scorched the earth!   *chariot*
  And, Henry, hadst thou swayed° as kings should do,   *ruled*
15 Or as thy father and his father did,
  Giving no ground unto the house of York,
  They never then had sprung like summer flies;
  I and ten thousand in this luckless realm
  Had left no mourning widows for our death;
20 And thou this day hadst kept thy chair° in peace.   *throne*
  For what doth cherish° weeds, but gentle air?   *nurture*
  And what makes robbers bold, but too much lenity?
  Bootless are plaints,° and cureless are my wounds;   *Useless are pleas*
  No way to fly, nor strength to hold out flight;
25 The foe is merciless and will not pity,
  For at their hands I have deserved no pity.
  The air hath got into my deadly wounds,
  And much effuse° of blood doth make me faint.   *effusion*
  Come York and Richard, Warwick and the rest—
30 I stabbed your fathers' bosoms; split my breast.
     [*He faints.*]
     Alarum and retreat. Enter EDWARD [*Duke of York, his*
     brothers] GEORGE *and* RICHARD, [*the Earl of*] WARWICK,
     [*the Marquis of*] MONTAGUE, *and soldiers*⁴

EDWARD   Now breathe we, lords—good fortune bids us pause,
  And smooth the frowns of war with peaceful looks.
  Some troops pursue the bloody-minded Queen,
  That led calm Henry, though he were a king,
35 As doth a sail filled with a fretting° gust   *blowing fitfully*
  Command an argosy° to stem° the waves.   *a merchant ship / resist*
  But think you, lords, that Clifford fled with them?
WARWICK   No—'tis impossible he should escape;
  For, though before his face I speak the words,
40 Your brother Richard marked him for the grave.
  And whereso'er he is, he's surely dead.
     CLIFFORD *groans*

2.6
1. The compound of love and fear that I commanded.
2. Alluding to the sun as Edward's emblem. See note to
2.1.40.
3. The son of Phoebus, god of the sun. See note to
1.4.34.
4. In F, the order of names in the stage direction ends

with "Montague and Clarence" (George) placed after
"Soldiers." The peculiarity of listing these noble figures
last may suggest that they were added as an afterthought.
Montague does not speak during the scene. Neither he
nor George is indicated in O's stage directions, in which
George speaks the same lines as in F.

EDWARD   Whose soul is that which takes her heavy leave?[5]
RICHARD   A deadly groan, like life and death's departing.
EDWARD [*to* RICHARD]   See who it is.
          [RICHARD *goes to* CLIFFORD]
                                                  And now the battle's ended,
45   If friend or foe, let him be gently used.
RICHARD   Revoke that doom° of mercy, for 'tis Clifford;   *sentence*
     Who not contented that he lopped the branch
     In hewing Rutland when his leaves put forth,
     But set his murd'ring knife unto the root
50   From whence that tender spray° did sweetly spring—   *shoot*
     I mean our princely father, Duke of York.
WARWICK   From off the gates of York fetch down the head,
     Your father's head, which Clifford placèd there.
     Instead whereof let this supply the room[6]—
55   Measure for measure[7] must be answerèd.°   *given in return*
EDWARD   Bring forth that fatal screech-owl to our house,[8]
     That nothing sung but death to us and ours.
          [CLIFFORD *is dragged forward*]
     Now death shall stop his dismal threat'ning sound
     And his ill-boding° tongue no more shall speak.   *doom-promising*
60   WARWICK   I think his understanding is bereft.°   *destroyed*
     Speak, Clifford, dost thou know who speaks to thee?
     Dark cloudy death o'ershades his beams of life,
     And he nor° sees nor hears us what we say.   *neither*
RICHARD   O, would he did—and so perhaps he doth.
65   'Tis but his policy to counterfeit,
     Because he would avoid such bitter taunts
     Which in the time of death he gave our father.
GEORGE   If so thou think'st, vex him with eager° words.   *bitter*
RICHARD   Clifford, ask mercy and obtain no grace.
70   EDWARD   Clifford, repent in bootless penitence.
WARWICK   Clifford, devise excuses for thy faults.
GEORGE   While we devise fell° tortures for thy faults.   *cruel*
RICHARD   Thou didst love York, and I am son to York.
EDWARD   Thou pitied'st Rutland—I will pity thee.
75   GEORGE   Where's Captain Margaret to fence° you now?   *protect*
WARWICK   They mock thee, Clifford—swear as thou wast wont.
RICHARD   What, not an oath? Nay, then, the world goes hard
     When Clifford cannot spare his friends an oath.
     I know by that he's dead—and, by my soul,
80   If this right hand would buy but two hours' life
     That I, in all despite, might rail at him,
     This hand° should chop it off, and with the issuing blood   *(his left hand)*
     Stifle° the villain whose unstanchèd° thirst   *Choke / insatiable*
     York and young Rutland could not satisfy.
85   WARWICK   Ay, but he's dead. Off with the traitor's head,
     And rear it in the place your father's stands.
     And now to London with triumphant march,
     There to be crownèd England's royal king;

---

5. In F, lines 42 and 43 and half of line 44 are assigned
to Richard. O divides them as here. Oxford, as elsewhere,
argues that this is an instance of authorial revision
between foul papers and promptbook.
6. Let Clifford's head take its place.

7. Alluding to the strict rule of justice described in Mark
4:24: "With what measure ye mete, it shall be measured
unto you."
8. Bring forth that creature ominous to our house.

From whence shall Warwick cut the sea to France,
90   And ask the Lady Bona[9] for thy queen.
So shalt thou sinew° both these lands together.   *tie firmly*
And, having France thy friend, thou shalt not dread
The scattered foe that hopes to rise again,
For though they cannot greatly sting to hurt,
95   Yet look to have them buzz to offend thine ears.
First will I see the coronation,
And then to Brittany I'll cross the sea
To effect this marriage, so it please my lord.
EDWARD   Even as thou wilt, sweet Warwick, let it be.
100   For in thy shoulder° do I build my seat,   *with your support*
And never will I undertake the thing
Wherein thy counsel and consent is wanting.
Richard, I will create thee Duke of Gloucester,
And George, of Clarence; Warwick, as ourself,
105   Shall do and undo as him pleaseth best.
RICHARD   Let me be Duke of Clarence, George of Gloucester—
For Gloucester's dukedom is too ominous.[1]
WARWICK   Tut, that's a foolish observation—
Richard, be Duke of Gloucester. Now to London
110   To see these honours in possession.
                                    Exeunt. [York's head is removed]

3.1

                Enter two [GAME]KEEPERS, with crossbows in their hands
FIRST GAMEKEEPER   Under this thick-grown brake° we'll shroud   *thicket*
                ourselves,
For through this laund° anon the deer will come,   *clearing*
And in this covert will we make our stand,
Culling the principal° of all the deer.   *Selecting the best*
5   SECOND GAMEKEEPER   I'll stay above the hill, so both may shoot.
FIRST GAMEKEEPER   That cannot be—the noise of thy crossbow
Will scare the herd, and so my shoot is lost.
Here stand we both, and aim we at the best.°   *as well as we can*
And, for° the time shall not seem tedious,   *so that*
10   I'll tell thee what befell me on a day
In this self place where now we mean to stand.
FIRST GAMEKEEPER   Here comes a man—let's stay till he be past.
                [*They stand apart.*]
                Enter KING HENRY, disguised, with a prayer-book
KING HENRY   From Scotland am I stolen, even of° pure love,   *out of*
To greet mine own land with my wishful° sight.   *longing*
15   No, Harry, Harry—'tis no land of thine.
Thy place is filled, thy sceptre wrung from thee,
Thy balm washed off wherewith thou wast anointed.
No bending knee will call thee Caesar° now,   *emperor*
No humble suitors press to speak for right,°   *beg for justice*
20   No, not a man comes for redress of° thee—   *from*
For how can I help them and not myself?

---

9. The sister-in-law of King Louis XI of France and
daughter of Louis, Duke of Savoy.
1. Referring to the fact that three previous dukes of

Gloucester had suffered violent deaths.
3.1 Location: A forest in northern England near the Scottish border.

FIRST GAMEKEEPER [*to the* SECOND GAMEKEEPER] Ay, here's a
    deer whose skin's a keeper's fee:[1]
  This is the quondam° king—let's seize upon him.   *former*
KING HENRY Let me embrace thee, sour adversity,
25   For wise men say it is the wisest course.
SECOND GAMEKEEPER [*to the* FIRST GAMEKEEPER] Why linger
    we? Let us lay hands upon him.
FIRST GAMEKEEPER [*to the* SECOND GAMEKEEPER] Forbear
    awhile—we'll hear a little more.
KING HENRY My queen and son are gone to France for aid,
    And, as I hear, the great commanding Warwick
30   Is thither gone to crave the French King's sister
    To wife for Edward. If this news be true,
    Poor Queen and son, your labour is but lost—
    For Warwick is a subtle orator,
    And Louis a prince soon won with moving words.
35   By this account, then, Margaret may win him—
    For she's a woman to be pitied much.
    Her sighs will make a batt'ry° in his breast,   *a breach*
    Her tears will pierce into a marble heart,
    The tiger will be mild whiles she doth mourn,
40   And Nero[2] will be tainted° with remorse   *touched*
    To hear and see her plaints,° her brinish° tears.   *pleas / salty*
    Ay, but she's come to beg; Warwick to give.
    She on his left side, craving aid for Henry;
    He on his right, asking a wife for Edward.
45   She weeps and says her Henry is deposed,
    He smiles and says his Edward is installed;
    That she, poor wretch, for grief can speak no more,
    Whiles Warwick tells his title,[3] smooths the wrong,
    Inferreth° arguments of mighty strength,   *Presents*
50   And in conclusion wins the King from her
    With promise of his sister and what else
    To strengthen and support King Edward's place.
    O, Margaret, thus 'twill be; and thou, poor soul,
    Art then forsaken, as thou went'st forlorn.
SECOND GAMEKEEPER [*coming forward*] Say, what art thou that
55   talk'st of kings and queens?
KING HENRY More than I seem, and less than I was born to:
    A man at least, for less I should not be;
    And men may talk of kings, and why not I?
SECOND GAMEKEEPER Ay, but thou talk'st as if thou wert a king.
60 KING HENRY Why, so I am, in mind—and that's enough.
SECOND GAMEKEEPER But if thou be a king, where is thy crown?
KING HENRY My crown is in my heart, not on my head;
    Not decked with diamonds and Indian stones,
    Nor to be seen. My crown is called content—
65   A crown it is that seldom kings enjoy.
SECOND GAMEKEEPER Well, if you be a king crowned with content,
    Your crown content and you must be contented
    To go along with us—for, as we think,
    You are the king King Edward hath deposed,

---

1. Traditionally, hunters presented the horns and skin of   2. A notoriously cruel Roman emperor.
a captured deer to the park's gamekeeper.   3. While Warwick asserts Edward's claim to the throne.

70 And we his subjects sworn in all allegiance
Will apprehend you as his enemy.
KING HENRY But did you never swear and break an oath?
SECOND GAMEKEEPER No—never such an oath, nor will not now.
KING HENRY Where did you dwell when I was King of England?
75 SECOND GAMEKEEPER Here in this country, where we now remain.
KING HENRY I was anointed king at nine months old,
My father and my grandfather were kings,
And you were sworn true subjects unto me—
And tell me, then, have you not broke your oaths?
80 FIRST GAMEKEEPER No, for we were subjects but° while you were king.   *only*
KING HENRY Why, am I dead? Do I not breathe a man?
Ah, simple men, you know not what you swear.
Look as I blow this feather from my face,
And as the air blows it to me again,
85 Obeying with° my wind when I do blow,   *Submitting to*
And yielding to another when it blows,
Commanded always by the greater gust—
Such is the lightness° of you common men.   *fickleness*
But do not break your oaths, for of that sin
90 My mild entreaty shall not make you guilty.
Go where you will, the King shall be commanded;
And be you kings, command, and I'll obey.
FIRST GAMEKEEPER We are true subjects to the King, King Edward.
KING HENRY So would you be again to Henry,
95 If he were seated as King Edward is.
FIRST GAMEKEEPER We charge you, in God's name and in the King's,
To go with us unto the officers.
KING HENRY In God's name, lead; your king's name be obeyed;
And what God will, that let your king perform;
100 And what he will I humbly yield unto.   *Exeunt*

3.2

Enter KING EDWARD, [RICHARD *Duke* OF] GLOUCESTER,
[GEORGE *Duke* OF] CLARENCE, *and the* LADY GRAY

KING EDWARD Brother of Gloucester, at Saint Albans field
This lady's husband, Sir Richard Gray, was slain,
His lands then seized on by the conqueror.
Her suit is now to repossess those lands,
5 Which we in justice cannot well deny,
Because in quarrel of the house of York
The worthy gentleman did lose his life.
RICHARD OF GLOUCESTER Your highness shall do well to grant her suit—
It were dishonour to deny it her.
10 KING EDWARD It were no less; but yet I'll make a pause.
RICHARD OF GLOUCESTER [*aside to* GEORGE] Yea, is it so?
I see the lady hath a thing° to grant   *favor; genitals*
Before the King will grant her humble suit.
GEORGE OF CLARENCE [*aside to* RICHARD] He knows the game;
how true he keeps the wind![1]

3.2 Location: The palace, London.
1. "The game" suggests the "sport" of hunting animals or of pursuing sex partners, as well as the objects of both pursuits. Hounds "keep the wind" by keeping the prey against the wind so that it does not catch the scent of the hunter and run away. Clarence implies that Edward pursues Lady Gray with similar skill. The following lines are full of sexual wordplay that Clarence and Richard clearly intend, but that Lady Gray probably does not.

15 RICHARD OF GLOUCESTER [*aside to* GEORGE] Silence.

KING EDWARD [*to* LADY GRAY] Widow, we will consider of your suit;
  And come some other time to know our mind.

LADY GRAY Right gracious lord, I cannot brook° delay. *tolerate*
  May it please your highness to resolve me now,

20 And what your pleasure° is shall satisfy me. *will; sexual desire*

RICHARD OF GLOUCESTER [*aside to* GEORGE] Ay, widow? Then
  I'll warrant° you all your lands *guarantee*
  An if° what pleases him shall pleasure you. *An if = If*
  Fight closer, or, good faith, you'll catch a blow.[2]

GEORGE OF CLARENCE [*aside to* RICHARD] I fear° her not unless *fear for*
  she chance to fall.[3]

RICHARD OF GLOUCESTER [*aside to* GEORGE] God forbid that!

25 For he'll take vantages.° *opportunities*

KING EDWARD [*to* LADY GRAY] How many children hast thou,
  widow? Tell me.

GEORGE OF CLARENCE [*aside to* RICHARD] I think he means to
  beg a child of her.[4]

RICHARD OF GLOUCESTER [*aside to* GEORGE] Nay, whip me
  then—he'll rather give her two.

LADY GRAY [*to* KING EDWARD] Three, my most gracious lord.

RICHARD OF GLOUCESTER [*aside*] You shall have four, an° you'll *if*

30 be ruled by him.

KING EDWARD [*to* LADY GRAY] 'Twere pity they should lose their
  father's lands.

LADY GRAY Be pitiful, dread lord, and grant it them.

KING EDWARD [*to* RICHARD *and* GEORGE] Lords, give us leave°— *leave us alone*
  I'll try this widow's wit.

RICHARD OF GLOUCESTER [*aside to* GEORGE] Ay, good leave
  have you; for you will have leave,

35 Till youth take leave and leave you to the crutch.[5]
  [RICHARD *and* GEORGE *stand apart*]

KING EDWARD [*to* LADY GRAY] Now tell me, madam, do you
  love your children?

LADY GRAY Ay, full as dearly as I love myself.

KING EDWARD And would you not do much to do them good?

LADY GRAY To do them good I would sustain some harm.

40 KING EDWARD Then get your husband's lands, to do them good.

LADY GRAY Therefore I came unto your majesty.

KING EDWARD I'll tell you how these lands are to be got.

LADY GRAY So shall you bind me to your highness' service.

KING EDWARD What service wilt thou do me, if I give them?

45 LADY GRAY What you command, that rests in me to do.

KING EDWARD But you will take exceptions to my boon.° *request*

LADY GRAY No, gracious lord, except° I cannot do it. *unless*

KING EDWARD Ay, but thou canst do what I mean to ask.

LADY GRAY Why, then, I will do what your grace commands.

RICHARD OF GLOUCESTER [*to* GEORGE] He plies her hard, and

50 much rain wears the marble.

---

2. Fight nearer to avoid his thrusts. Conflating sexual slang and the language of dueling, Richard puns on "blow" as meaning both "hit" and "sexual thrust."
3. Stumble; submit to sex.
4. To ask her to bear him a child; to petition for guardianship of one of her children. English monarchs generated income by gaining control of wealthy orphans from the Court of Wards and arranging their marriages in ways profitable to the monarch.
5. Ay . . . *crutch*: Yes, we will leave you alone, for you will take liberties (with Lady Gray) until your youth departs and leaves you walking on crutches (too old for love). The multiple puns in these lines include "crutch" as a play on "crotch."

GEORGE OF CLARENCE   As red as fire! Nay, then her wax must melt.

LADY GRAY [*to* KING EDWARD]   Why stops my lord? Shall I not hear my task?

KING EDWARD   An easy task—'tis but to love a king.

LADY GRAY   That's soon performed, because I am a subject.

55 KING EDWARD   Why, then, thy husband's lands I freely give thee.

LADY GRAY [*curtsies*]   I take my leave, with many thousand thanks.

RICHARD OF GLOUCESTER [*to* GEORGE]   The match is made—
she seals it with a curtsy.

KING EDWARD [*to* LADY GRAY]   But stay thee—'tis the fruits of
love I mean.

LADY GRAY   The fruits of love *I* mean, my loving liege.

60 KING EDWARD   Ay, but I fear me in another sense.
What love think'st thou I sue so much to get?

LADY GRAY   My love till death, my humble thanks, my prayers—
That love which virtue begs and virtue grants.

KING EDWARD   No, by my troth, I did not mean such love.

65 LADY GRAY   Why, then, you mean not as I thought you did.

KING EDWARD   But now you partly may perceive my mind.

LADY GRAY   My mind will never grant what I perceive
Your highness aims at, if I aim aright.°   *guess correctly*

KING EDWARD   To tell thee plain, I aim to lie with thee.

70 LADY GRAY   To tell *you* plain, I had rather lie in prison.

KING EDWARD   Why, then, thou shalt not have thy husband's lands.

LADY GRAY   Why, then, mine honesty° shall be my dower;   *chastity*
For by that loss I will not purchase them.

KING EDWARD   Therein thou wrong'st thy children mightily.

75 LADY GRAY   Herein your highness wrongs both them and me.
But, mighty lord, this merry inclination
Accords not with the sadness° of my suit.   *seriousness*
Please you dismiss me either with ay or no.

KING EDWARD   Ay, if thou wilt say 'ay' to my request;

80 No, if thou dost say 'no' to my demand.

LADY GRAY   Then, no, my lord—my suit is at an end.

RICHARD OF GLOUCESTER [*to* GEORGE]   The widow likes him
not—she knits her brows.

GEORGE OF CLARENCE   He is the bluntest wooer in Christendom.

KING EDWARD [*aside*]   Her looks doth argue° her replete with modesty;   *prove*

85 Her words doth show her wit incomparable;
All her perfections challenge° sovereignty.   *lay claim to*
One way or other, she is for a king;
And she shall be my love or else my queen.
[*To* LADY GRAY] Say that King Edward take thee for his queen?

90 LADY GRAY   'Tis better said than done, my gracious lord.
I am a subject fit to jest withal,
But far unfit to be a sovereign.

KING EDWARD   Sweet widow, by my state° I swear to thee   *kingship*
I speak no more than what my soul intends,

95 And that is to enjoy thee for my love.

LADY GRAY   And that is more than I will yield unto.
I know I am too mean to be your queen,
And yet too good to be your concubine.

KING EDWARD   You cavil,° widow—I did mean my queen.   *object frivolously*

100 LADY GRAY   'Twill grieve your grace my sons should call you father.

KING EDWARD   No more than when my daughters call thee mother.
Thou art a widow and thou hast some children;

And, by God's mother, I, being but a bachelor,
Have other some.° Why, 'tis a happy thing   *some others*
105 To be the father unto many sons.
Answer no more, for thou shalt be my queen.
RICHARD OF GLOUCESTER [*to* GEORGE]   The ghostly father° now   *priest*
      hath done his shrift.⁶
GEORGE OF CLARENCE   When he was made a shriver, 'twas for shift.⁷
KING EDWARD [*to* RICHARD *and* GEORGE]   Brothers, you muse°   *wonder*
      what chat we two have had.
            [RICHARD *and* GEORGE *come forward*]
110 RICHARD OF GLOUCESTER   The widow likes it not, for she looks very sad.
KING EDWARD   You'd think it strange if I should marry her.
GEORGE OF CLARENCE   To who, my lord?
KING EDWARD   Why, Clarence, to myself.
RICHARD OF GLOUCESTER   That would be ten days' wonder at the least.
GEORGE OF CLARENCE   That's a day longer than a wonder lasts.⁸
115 RICHARD OF GLOUCESTER   By so much is the wonder in extremes.°   *exceedingly great*
KING EDWARD   Well, jest on, brothers—I can tell you both
      Her suit is granted for her husband's lands.
            Enter a NOBLEMAN
NOBLEMAN   My gracious lord, Henry your foe is taken
      And brought as prisoner to your palace gate.
120 KING EDWARD   See that he be conveyed unto the Tower—
      [*To* RICHARD *and* GEORGE] And go we, brothers, to the man that took him,
      To question of his apprehension.
      [*To* LADY GRAY] Widow, go you along. [*To* RICHARD *and*
            GEORGE] Lords, use her honourably.
                              Exeunt. Manet° RICHARD   *Remains*
RICHARD OF GLOUCESTER   Ay, Edward will use women honourably.
125 Would he were wasted, marrow, bones, and all,⁹
      That from his loins no hopeful branch may spring
      To cross° me from the golden time I look for.   *keep*
      And yet, between my soul's desire and me—
      The lustful Edward's title burièd°—   *eliminated*
130 Is Clarence, Henry, and his son young Edward,
      And all the unlooked-for° issue of their bodies,   *unforseen*
      To take their rooms° ere I can place myself.   *places*
      A cold premeditation° for my purpose.   *A discouraging prospect*
      Why, then, I do but dream on sovereignty
135 Like one that stands upon a promontory
      And spies a far-off shore where he would tread,
      Wishing his foot were equal with his eye,¹
      And chides the sea that sunders him from thence,
      Saying he'll lade° it dry to have his way—   *empty*
140 So do I wish° the crown being so far off,   *wish for*
      And so I chide the means that keeps me from it,
      And so I say I'll cut the causes off,
      Flattering me with impossibilities.
      My eye's too quick, my heart o'erweens° too much,   *presumes*
145 Unless my hand and strength could equal them.

---

6. Has heard her confession and given absolution.
7. It was for a purpose; it was in order to gain access to her undergarments ("shift").
8. Referring to the proverbial expression "nine day's wonder," something that for a short while causes a sensation.

9. Would he were destroyed by disease. Elizabethan medical theory held that syphilis attacked the bones, affected male "mettle," or semen, and caused sterility.
1. Wishing he were able to attain what his eye sees.

Well, say there is no kingdom then for Richard—
What other pleasure can the world afford?
I'll make my heaven in a lady's lap,
And deck my body in gay ornaments,
150 And 'witch° sweet ladies with my words and looks.　　　　　*bewitch*
O, miserable thought! And more unlikely
Than to accomplish° twenty golden crowns.　　　　　*obtain*
Why, love forswore° me in my mother's womb,　　　　　*abandoned*
And, for° I should not deal in her soft laws,　　　　　*so that*
155 She did corrupt frail nature with some bribe
To shrink mine arm up like a withered shrub,
To make an envious° mountain on my back—　　　　　*a detested*
Where sits deformity to mock my body—
To shape my legs of an unequal size,
160 To disproportion me in every part,
Like to a chaos,° or an unlicked bear whelp[2]　　　　　*formless mass*
That carries no impression like the dam.[3]
And am I then a man to be beloved?
O, monstrous fault, to harbour such a thought!
165 Then, since this earth affords no joy to me
But to command, to check,° to o'erbear° such　　　　　*rebuke / dominate*
As are of better person° than myself,　　　　　*appearance*
I'll make my heaven to dream upon the crown,
And whiles I live, t'account this world but hell,
170 Until my misshaped trunk that bears this head
Be round impalèd° with a glorious crown.　　　　　*enclosed*
And yet I know not how to get the crown,
For many lives stand between me and home.°　　　　　*(my goal)*
And I—like one lost in a thorny wood,
175 That rends the thorns and is rent with the thorns,
Seeking a way and straying from the way,
Not knowing how to find the open air,
But toiling desperately to find it out—
Torment myself to catch the English crown.
180 And from that torment I will free myself,
Or hew my way out with a bloody axe.
Why, I can smile, and murder whiles I smile,
And cry 'Content!' to that which grieves my heart,
And wet my cheeks with artificial tears,
185 And frame my face to all occasions.
I'll drown more sailors than the mermaid[4] shall;
I'll slay more gazers than the basilisk;[5]
I'll play the orator as well as Nestor,[6]
Deceive more slyly than Ulysses[7] could,
190 And, like a Sinon,[8] take another Troy.
I can add colours to the chameleon,[9]

2. Alluding to the popular belief that bears were born as formless lumps and licked into shape by their mothers.
3. That does not resemble its mother.
4. A fabulous monster, resembling a woman, who sang sweet songs to lure sailors onto the rocks and to their death.
5. A mythical reptile, hatched from a cock's egg, whose look was supposed to be fatal.
6. The Greek king and aged counselor present at the siege of Troy, famous for his skill in speech.
7. The Greek warrior famous for his cunning, hero of Homer's *Odyssey*.
8. Like a treacherous man. According to Virgil, Sinon's lies convinced the Trojans to accept as a gift the wooden horse in which the Greek soldiers who later sacked Troy were concealed.
9. A reptile able to change the color of its skin in order to blend into its surroundings.

Change shapes with Proteus[1] for advantages,
And set the murderous Machiavel[2] to school.
Can I do this, and cannot get a crown?
195　Tut, were it farther off, I'll pluck it down.　　　　　　　*Exit*

3.3

[*Two chairs of state.*][1] *Flourish. Enter* KING LOUIS [*of
France*], *his sister the* LADY BONA, [*Lord*] *Bourbon his
admiral,* PRINCE EDWARD, QUEEN MARGARET, *and the
Earl of* OXFORD. LOUIS [*goes up upon the state,*] *sits,
and riseth up again*

KING LOUIS　Fair Queen of England, worthy Margaret,
　　Sit down with us. It ill befits thy state
　　And birth that thou shouldst stand while Louis doth sit.
QUEEN MARGARET　No, mighty King of France, now Margaret
5　　Must strike her sail° and learn a while to serve　　　　*humble herself*
　　Where kings command. I was, I must confess,
　　Great Albion's° queen in former golden days,　　　　　*England's*
　　But now mischance hath trod my title down,
　　And with dishonour laid me on the ground,
10　　Where I must take like seat unto my fortune[2]
　　And to my humble state conform myself.
KING LOUIS　Why, say, fair Queen, whence springs this deep despair?
QUEEN MARGARET　From such a cause as fills mine eyes with tears
　　And stops my tongue, while heart is drowned in cares.
15　KING LOUIS　Whate'er it be, be thou still like thyself,
　　And sit thee by our side.
　　　　　　　Seats her by him
　　　　　　　　　　Yield not thy neck
　　To fortune's yoke, but let thy dauntless mind
　　Still ride in triumph over all mischance.
　　Be plain, Queen Margaret, and tell thy grief.
20　　It shall be eased if France° can yield relief.　　　　*the King of France*
QUEEN MARGARET　Those gracious words revive my drooping
　　　　thoughts,
　　And give my tongue-tied sorrows leave to speak.
　　Now, therefore, be it known to noble Louis
　　That Henry, sole possessor of my love,
25　　Is of° a king become a banished man,　　　　　　　*Instead of*
　　And forced to live in Scotland a forlorn,°　　　　　*an outcast*
　　While proud ambitious Edward, Duke of York,
　　Usurps the regal title and the seat
　　Of England's true-anointed lawful King.
30　　This is the cause that I, poor Margaret,
　　With this my son, Prince Edward, Henry's heir,
　　Am come to crave thy just and lawful aid.
　　An if thou fail us all our hope is done.
　　Scotland hath will to help, but cannot help;
35　　Our people and our peers are both misled,

---

1. A minor sea god who was able to assume different shapes at will.
2. Niccolò Machiavelli (1469–1527), an Italian political philosopher popularly known in England as a depraved advocate of political cunning and ruthlessness.
3.3 Location: The King's palace, France.

1. Louis's request for Margaret to "sit down with us" at line 2 suggests that at least two chairs of state are required, possibly three (including one for Lady Bona).
2. Where I must take a position in keeping with my fortune.

Our treasure seized, our soldiers put to flight,
And, as thou seest, ourselves in heavy plight.
KING LOUIS Renownèd Queen, with patience calm the storm,
    While we bethink a means to break it off.
40 QUEEN MARGARET The more we stay,° the stronger grows our foe.   *delay*
KING LOUIS The more I stay, the more I'll succour thee.
QUEEN MARGARET O, but impatience waiteth on° true sorrow.   *attends*
    Enter [the Earl of] WARWICK
    And see where comes the breeder of my sorrow.
KING LOUIS What's he approacheth boldly to our presence?
45 QUEEN MARGARET Our Earl of Warwick, Edward's greatest friend.
KING LOUIS Welcome, brave Warwick. What brings thee to France?
    He descends. She ariseth
QUEEN MARGARET [*aside*] Ay, now begins a second storm to rise,
    For this is he that moves both wind and tide.
WARWICK [*to* KING LOUIS] From worthy Edward, King of Albion,
50   My lord and sovereign, and thy vowèd friend,
    I come in kindness and unfeignèd love,
    First, to do greetings to thy royal person,
    And then, to crave a league of amity,°   *friendship*
    And lastly, to confirm that amity
55   With nuptial knot, if thou vouchsafe to grant
    That virtuous Lady Bona, thy fair sister,
    To England's King in lawful marriage.
QUEEN MARGARET [*aside*] If that go forward, Henry's hope is done.
WARWICK (*to* [LADY] BONA) And, gracious madam, in our King's behalf
60   I am commanded, with your leave and favour,
    Humbly to kiss your hand, and with my tongue
    To tell the passion of my sovereign's heart,
    Where fame, late ent'ring at his heedful ears,
    Hath placed thy beauty's image and thy virtue.
65 QUEEN MARGARET King Louis and Lady Bona, hear me speak
    Before you answer Warwick. His demand
    Springs not from Edward's well-meant honest love,
    But from deceit, bred by necessity.
    For how can tyrants safely govern home
70   Unless abroad they purchase° great alliance?   *obtain*
    To prove him tyrant this reason may suffice —
    That Henry liveth still; but were he dead,
    Yet here Prince Edward stands, King Henry's son.
    Look, therefore, Louis, that by this league and marriage
75   Thou draw not on thy danger and dishonour,
    For though usurpers sway the rule° a while,   *wield power*
    Yet heav'ns are just and time suppresseth wrongs.
WARWICK Injurious° Margaret.   *Insulting*
PRINCE EDWARD   And why not 'Queen'?
WARWICK Because thy father Henry did usurp,
80   And thou no more art prince than she is queen.
OXFORD Then Warwick disannuls° great John of Gaunt,   *cancels*
    Which did subdue the greatest part of Spain;
    And, after John of Gaunt, Henry the Fourth,
    Whose wisdom was a mirror to the wisest;
85   And, after that wise prince, Henry the Fifth,
    Who by his prowess conquerèd all France.
    From these our Henry lineally descends.

WARWICK Oxford, how haps it in this smooth discourse
    You told not how Henry the Sixth hath lost
90   All that which Henry the Fifth had gotten?
    Methinks these peers of France should smile at that.
    But for the rest, you tell a pedigree
    Of threescore and two years[3]—a silly° time   *trifling*
    To make prescription for a kingdom's worth.[4]
95 OXFORD Why, Warwick, canst thou speak against thy liege,
    Whom thou obeyedest thirty and six years,
    And not bewray° thy treason with a blush?   *reveal*
WARWICK Can Oxford, that did ever fence the right,°   *defend justice*
    Now buckler° falsehood with a pedigree?   *shield*
100   For shame—leave Henry, and call Edward king.
OXFORD Call him my king by whose injurious doom°   *insulting judgment*
    My elder brother, the Lord Aubrey Vere,[5]
    Was done to death? And more than so, my father,
    Even in the downfall° of his mellowed years,   *decline*
105   When nature brought him to the door of death?
    No, Warwick, no—while life upholds this arm,
    This arm upholds the house of Lancaster.
WARWICK And I the house of York.
KING LOUIS Queen Margaret, Prince Edward, and Oxford,
110   Vouchsafe, at our request, to stand aside
    While I use further conference° with Warwick.   *talk further*
    [QUEEN MARGARET *comes down from the state and, with*
    PRINCE EDWARD *and* OXFORD, *stands apart*][6]
QUEEN MARGARET Heavens grant that Warwick's words bewitch him not.
KING LOUIS Now, Warwick, tell me even upon thy conscience,
    Is Edward your true king? For I were loath
115   To link with him that were not lawful chosen.
WARWICK Thereon I pawn my credit and mine honour.
KING LOUIS But is he gracious in the people's eye?
WARWICK The more that[7] Henry was unfortunate.
KING LOUIS Then further, all dissembling set aside,
120   Tell me for truth the measure of his love
    Unto our sister Bona.
WARWICK   Such it seems
    As may beseem° a monarch like himself.   *befit*
    Myself have often heard him say and swear
    That this his love was an eternal plant,
125   Whereof the root was fixed in virtue's ground,
    The leaves and fruit maintained with beauty's sun,
    Exempt from envy, but not from disdain,[8]
    Unless the Lady Bona quit° his pain.°   *end / (by loving him)*
KING LOUIS [*to* LADY BONA] Now, sister, let us hear your firm resolve.
130 LADY BONA Your grant, or your denial, shall be mine.
    (*To* WARWICK) Yet I confess that often ere this day,
    When I have heard your king's desert° recounted,   *merit*
    Mine ear hath tempted judgement to desire.

---

3. Meaning the sixty-two years between 1399, when Henry IV deposed Richard II, and 1461, when Henry VI was deposed by Edward.
4. To make a claim based on custom for something as valuable as a kingdom.
5. Eldest son of the twelfth Earl of Oxford, John de Vere.

Both were executed for treason by the Yorkists in 1462.
6. F's stage direction reads "They stand aloof."
7. The more (gracious) because.
8. Exempt from malice, but not exempt from (being hurt by) her disdain for him.

KING LOUIS [*to* WARWICK]   Then, Warwick, thus— our sister
    shall be Edward's.
135 And now, forthwith, shall articles be drawn
    Touching the jointure° that your king must make,   *marriage settlement*
    Which with her dowry shall be counterpoised.°   *equally balanced*
    [*To* QUEEN MARGARET] Draw near, Queen Margaret, and be
    a witness
    That Bona shall be wife to the English king.
    [QUEEN MARGARET, PRINCE EDWARD, *and* OXFORD *come*
    forward]
140 PRINCE EDWARD   To Edward, but not to the English king.
QUEEN MARGARET   Deceitful Warwick—it was thy device
    By this alliance to make void my suit!
    Before thy coming Louis was Henry's friend.
KING LOUIS   And still is friend to him and Margaret.
145 But if your title to the crown be weak,
    As may appear by Edward's good success,
    Then 'tis but reason that I be released
    From giving aid which late° I promisèd.   *recently*
    Yet shall you have all kindness at my hand
150 That your estate requires and mine can yield.
WARWICK [*to* QUEEN MARGARET]   Henry now lives in Scotland at his ease,
    Where having nothing, nothing can he lose.
    And as for you yourself, our quondam° queen,   *former*
    You have a father able to maintain you,
155 And better 'twere you troubled him than France.
QUEEN MARGARET   Peace, impudent and shameless Warwick, peace!
    Proud setter-up and puller-down of kings!
    I will not hence till, with my talk and tears,
    Both full of truth, I make King Louis behold
160 Thy sly conveyance° and thy lord's false love,   *deceit*
    POST° *blowing a horn within*   *Messenger*
    For both of you are birds of selfsame feather.
KING LOUIS   Warwick, this is some post to us or thee.
    Enter the POST
POST (*to* WARWICK)   My lord ambassador, these letters are for you,
    Sent from your brother Marquis Montague;
165 (*To* LOUIS) These from our King unto your majesty;
    (*To* [QUEEN] MARGARET) And, madam, these for you, from
    whom I know not.
    They all read their letters
OXFORD [*to* PRINCE EDWARD]   I like it well that our fair Queen and mistress
    Smiles at her news, while Warwick frowns at his.
PRINCE EDWARD   Nay, mark how Louis stamps as he were nettled.
170 I hope all's for the best.
KING LOUIS   Warwick, what are thy news? And yours, fair Queen?
QUEEN MARGARET   Mine, such as fill my heart with unhoped joys.
WARWICK   Mine, full of sorrow and heart's discontent.
KING LOUIS   What! Has your king married the Lady Gray?
175 And now to soothe° your forgery° and his,   *smooth over / deceit*
    Sends me a paper to persuade me patience?
    Is this th'alliance that he seeks with France?
    Dare he presume to scorn us in this manner?
QUEEN MARGARET   I told your majesty as much before—
180 This proveth Edward's love and Warwick's honesty.

WARWICK King Louis, I here protest in sight of heaven
  And by the hope I have of heavenly bliss,
  That I am clear from this misdeed of Edward's,
  No more my king, for he dishonours me,
185 But most himself, if he could see his shame.
  Did I forget that by the house of York
  My father came untimely to his death?[9]
  Did I let pass th'abuse done to my niece?[1]
  Did I impale him° with the regal crown?   *encircle his head*
190 Did I put Henry from his native right?
  And am I guerdoned° at the last with shame?   *rewarded*
  Shame on himself, for my desert is honour.
  And to repair my honour, lost for him,
  I here renounce him and return to Henry.
195 [*To* QUEEN MARGARET] My noble Queen, let former grudges pass,
  And henceforth I am thy true servitor.°   *servant*
  I will revenge his wrong to Lady Bona
  And replant Henry in his former state.
QUEEN MARGARET Warwick, these words have turned my hate to love,
200 And I forgive and quite forget old faults,
  And joy that thou becom'st King Henry's friend.
WARWICK So much his friend, ay, his unfeignèd friend,
  That if King Louis vouchsafe to furnish us
  With some few bands of chosen soldiers,
205 I'll undertake to land them on our coast
  And force the tyrant from his seat by war.
  'Tis not his new-made bride shall succour him.
  And as for Clarence, as my letters tell me,
  He's very likely now to fall from° him   *desert*
210 For matching° more for wanton lust than honour, *marrying*
  Or than for strength and safety of our country.
LADY BONA [*to* KING LOUIS] Dear brother, how shall Bona be revenged,
  But by thy help to this distressèd Queen?
QUEEN MARGARET [*to* KING LOUIS] Renownèd Prince, how shall
    poor Henry live
215 Unless thou rescue him from foul despair?
LADY BONA [*to* KING LOUIS] My quarrel and this English Queen's are one.
WARWICK And mine, fair Lady Bona, joins with yours.
KING LOUIS And mine with hers, and thine, and Margaret's.
  Therefore at last I firmly am resolved:
220 You shall have aid.
QUEEN MARGARET Let me give humble thanks for all at once.
KING LOUIS [*to the* POST] Then, England's messenger, return in post° *haste*
  And tell false Edward, thy supposèd king,
  That Louis of France is sending over masquers[2]
225 To revel it with him and his new bride.
  Thou seest what's passed, go fear° thy king withal.° *frighten / with it*
LADY BONA [*to the* POST] Tell him, in hope he'll prove a widower shortly,
  I'll wear the willow garland[3] for his sake.

---

9. Actually, Warwick's father, the Earl of Salisbury of *The First Part of the Contention*, was executed by the Lancastrians. Perhaps Warwick means that his father would not have died in the Yorkist cause had the Yorkists never tried to seize the throne.
1. The chronicles report that while visiting Warwick's house, Edward attempted to sexually assault his host's daughter or niece.
2. The actors in courtly revels and entertainments that were often staged to celebrate the marriages of members of the Elizabethan aristocracy.
3. Token of a forsaken lover.

QUEEN MARGARET [*to the* POST]   Tell him my mourning weeds°   *apparel*
    are laid aside,
230   And I am ready to put armour on.
WARWICK [*to the* POST]   Tell him from me that he hath done me wrong,
    And therefore I'll uncrown him ere't be long.
    [*Giving money*] There's thy reward—be gone.   *Exit* POST
KING LOUIS   But, Warwick, thou and Oxford, with five thousand men,
235   Shall cross the seas and bid false Edward battle;
    And, as occasion serves, this noble Queen
    And Prince shall follow with a fresh supply.
    Yet, ere thou go, but answer me one doubt:
    What pledge have we of thy firm loyalty?
240   WARWICK   This shall assure my constant loyalty:
    That if our Queen and this young Prince agree,
    I'll join mine eldest daughter⁴ and my joy
    To him forthwith in holy wedlock bands.
QUEEN MARGARET   Yes, I agree, and thank you for your motion.°   *proposal*
245   [*To* PRINCE EDWARD] Son Edward, she is fair and virtuous,
    Therefore delay not. Give thy hand to Warwick,
    And with thy hand thy faith irrevocable
    That only Warwick's daughter shall be thine.
PRINCE EDWARD   Yes, I accept her, for she well deserves it,
250   And here to pledge my vow I give my hand.
    He gives his hand to WARWICK
KING LOUIS   Why stay we now? These soldiers shall be levied,
    And thou, Lord Bourbon, our high admiral,
    Shall waft° them over with our royal fleet.   *convey by water*
    I long till Edward fall by war's mischance
255   For mocking marriage with a dame of France.
    Exeunt. Manet WARWICK
WARWICK   I came from Edward as ambassador,
    But I return his sworn and mortal foe.
    Matter of marriage was the charge he gave me,
    But dreadful war shall answer his demand.
260   Had he none else to make a stale° but me?   *laughingstock*
    Then none but I shall turn his jest to sorrow.
    I was the chief that raised him to the crown,
    And I'll be chief to bring him down again.
    Not that I pity Henry's misery,
265   But seek revenge on Edward's mockery.   *Exit*

4.1

Enter RICHARD [*Duke* OF GLOUCESTER, GEORGE *Duke*
OF] CLARENCE, [*the Duke of*] SOMERSET, *and* [*the*
Marquis of] MONTAGUE
RICHARD OF GLOUCESTER   Now tell me, brother Clarence, what think you
    Of this new marriage with the Lady Gray?
    Hath not our brother made a worthy choice?
GEORGE OF CLARENCE   Alas, you know 'tis far from hence to France;
5   How could he stay° till Warwick made return?   *wait*
SOMERSET   My lords, forbear this talk—here comes the King.

---

4. The historical Edward was betrothed (but never married) to Warwick's second daughter, Anne. She eventually married Richard Duke of York (later Richard III). War-wick's eldest daughter married George of Clarence.
4.1 Location: The palace, London.

Flourish. Enter KING EDWARD, *the* LADY GRAY [*his*]
Queen, [*the Earl of*] *Pembroke,* [*and the Lords*] *Stafford*
[*and*] HASTINGS. *Four stand on one side* [*of the King*],
and four on the other

RICHARD OF GLOUCESTER   And his well-chosen bride.

GEORGE OF CLARENCE   I mind° to tell him plainly what I think.   *intend*

KING EDWARD   Now, brother of Clarence, how like you our choice,
10   That you stand pensive, as half-malcontent?°   *partly discontented*

GEORGE OF CLARENCE   As well as Louis of France, or the Earl
    of Warwick,
    Which° are so weak of courage and in judgement   *Who*
    That they'll take no offence at our abuse.°   *insult*

KING EDWARD   Suppose they take offence without a cause—
15   They are but Louis and Warwick; I am Edward,
    Your king and Warwick's, and must have my will.°   *way; sexual desire*

RICHARD OF GLOUCESTER   And you shall have your will,
        because our king.
    Yet hasty marriage seldom proveth well.

KING EDWARD   Yea, brother Richard, are you offended too?

RICHARD OF GLOUCESTER   Not I, no—God forbid that I should
20   wish them severed
    Whom God hath joined together. Ay, and 'twere pity
    To sunder them that yoke° so well together.   *who are coupled*

KING EDWARD   Setting your scorns and your mislike° aside,   *displeasure*
    Tell me some reason why the Lady Gray
25   Should not become my wife and England's queen.
    And you too, Somerset and Montague,
    Speak freely what you think.

GEORGE OF CLARENCE   Then this is my opinion: that King Louis
    Becomes your enemy for mocking him
30   About the marriage of the Lady Bona.

RICHARD OF GLOUCESTER   And Warwick, doing what you gave in charge,
    Is now dishonourèd by this new marriage.

KING EDWARD   What if both Louis and Warwick be appeased
    By such invention° as I can devise?   *scheme*

35 MONTAGUE   Yet, to have joined with France in such alliance
    Would more have strengthened this our commonwealth
    'Gainst foreign storms than any home-bred marriage.

HASTINGS   Why, knows not Montague that of itself
    England is safe, if true within itself?

40 MONTAGUE   But the safer when 'tis backed with France.

HASTINGS   'Tis better using France than trusting France.
    Let us be backed with God and with the seas
    Which he hath giv'n for fence impregnable,
    And with their helps only° defend ourselves.   *alone*
45   In them and in ourselves our safety lies.

GEORGE OF CLARENCE   For this one speech Lord Hastings well deserves
    To have the heir of the Lord Hungerford.[1]

KING EDWARD   Ay, what of that? It was my will and grant—
    And for this once my will shall stand for law.

RICHARD OF GLOUCESTER   And yet, methinks, your grace hath
50   not done well

---

1. To marry a rich heiress. Clarence is objecting to the Queen's upstart relatives, such as Hastings, being given wealthy
marriage partners.

To give the heir and daughter of Lord Scales
Unto the brother° of your loving bride.   *(Lord Anthony Rivers)*
She better would have fitted me or Clarence,
But in° your bride you bury° brotherhood.   *because of / forget*
55 GEORGE OF CLARENCE Or else you would not have bestowed the heir
Of the Lord Bonville on your new wife's son,°   *(Sir Thomas Gray)*
And leave your brothers to go speed elsewhere.
KING EDWARD Alas, poor Clarence, is it for a wife
That thou art malcontent? I will provide thee.
GEORGE OF CLARENCE In choosing for yourself you showed
60   your judgement,
Which being shallow, you shall give me leave
To play the broker° in mine own behalf,   *marriage broker*
And to that end I shortly mind to leave you.
KING EDWARD Leave me, or tarry. Edward will be king,
65 And not be tied unto his brother's will.
LADY GRAY My lords, before it pleased his majesty
To raise my state to title of a queen,
Do me but right, and you must all confess
That I was not ignoble of descent—
70 And meaner° than myself have had like fortune.[2]   *people of lower rank*
But as this title honours me and mine,
So your dislikes, to whom I would be pleasing,
Doth cloud my joys with danger° and with sorrow.   *apprehension*
KING EDWARD My love, forbear to fawn upon° their frowns.   *be abject before*
75 What danger or what sorrow can befall thee
So long as Edward is thy constant friend,
And their true sovereign, whom they must obey?
Nay, whom they shall obey, and love thee too—
Unless they seek for hatred at my hands,
80 Which if they do, yet will I keep thee safe,
And they shall feel the vengeance of my wrath.
RICHARD OF GLOUCESTER [*aside*] I hear, yet say not much, but
     think the more.
          Enter [*the*] POST [*from France*]
KING EDWARD Now, messenger, what letters or what news from France?
POST My sovereign liege, no letters and few words,
85 But such as I, without your special pardon,
Dare not relate.
KING EDWARD Go to, we pardon thee. Therefore, in brief,
Tell me their words as near as thou canst guess° them.   *approximate*
What answer makes King Louis unto our letters?
90 POST At my depart these were his very words:
'Go tell false Edward, thy supposèd king,
That Louis of France is sending over masquers
To revel it with him and his new bride.'
KING EDWARD Is Louis so brave? Belike° he thinks me Henry.   *Perhaps*
95 But what said Lady Bona to my marriage?
POST These were her words, uttered with mild disdain:
'Tell him in hope he'll prove a widower shortly,
I'll wear the willow garland for his sake.'
KING EDWARD I blame not her, she could say little less;

2. In fact, the historical Lady Gray was the first commoner to become Queen of England.

100 She had the wrong. But what said Henry's queen?
For I have heard that she was there in place.
POST 'Tell him', quoth she, 'my mourning weeds are done,
And I am ready to put armour on.'
KING EDWARD Belike she minds to play the Amazon.[3]
105 But what said Warwick to these injuries?
POST He, more incensed against your majesty
Than all the rest, discharged me with these words:
'Tell him from me that he hath done me wrong,
And therefore I'll uncrown him ere't be long.'
110 KING EDWARD Ha! Durst the traitor breathe out so proud words?
Well, I will arm me, being thus forewarned.
They shall have wars and pay for their presumption.
But say, is Warwick friends with Margaret?
POST Ay, gracious sovereign, they are so linked in friendship
115 That young Prince Edward marries Warwick's daughter.
GEORGE OF CLARENCE Belike the elder; Clarence will have the younger.
Now, brother King, farewell, and sit you fast,
For I will hence to Warwick's other daughter,
That, though I want° a kingdom, yet in marriage   lack
120 I may not prove inferior to yourself.
You that love me and Warwick, follow me.
                              Exit CLARENCE, *and* SOMERSET *follows*
RICHARD OF GLOUCESTER   Not I—[*aside*] my thoughts aim at a
          further matter.
I stay not for the love of Edward, but the crown.
KING EDWARD   Clarence and Somerset both gone to Warwick?
125 Yet am I armed against the worst can happen,
And haste is needful in this desp'rate case.
Pembroke and Stafford, you in our behalf
Go levy men and make prepare° for war.   preparation
They are already, or quickly will be, landed.
130 Myself in person will straight follow you.
                              Exeunt Pembroke and Stafford
But ere I go, Hastings and Montague,
Resolve my doubt. You twain, of all the rest,
Are near'st to Warwick by blood and by alliance.
Tell me if you love Warwick more than me.
135 If it be so, then both depart to him—
I rather wish you foes than hollow° friends.   false
But if you mind to hold your true obedience,
Give me assurance with some friendly vow
That I may never have you in suspect.°   under suspicion
140 MONTAGUE   So God help Montague as he proves true.
HASTINGS   And Hastings as he favours Edward's cause.
KING EDWARD   Now, brother Richard, will you stand by us?
RICHARD OF GLOUCESTER   Ay, in despite of all that shall withstand you.
KING EDWARD   Why, so. Then am I sure of victory.
145 Now, therefore, let us hence and lose no hour
Till we meet Warwick with his foreign power.°   *Exeunt*   army

3. Legendary warrior woman. See note to 1.4.115.

4.2

Enter [the Earls of] WARWICK *and* OXFORD *in England,*
with French soldiers

WARWICK   Trust me, my lord, all hitherto° goes well.   *thus far*
The common sort by numbers swarm to us.
Enter [the Dukes of] CLARENCE *and* SOMERSET
But see where Somerset and Clarence comes.
Speak suddenly, my lords, are we all friends?

5   GEORGE OF CLARENCE   Fear not that, my lord.
WARWICK   Then, gentle Clarence, welcome unto Warwick—
And welcome, Somerset. I hold it cowardice
To rest mistrustful where a noble heart
Hath pawned° an open hand in sign of love,   *pledged*

10   Else might I think that Clarence, Edward's brother,
Were but a feignèd friend to our proceedings.
But come, sweet Clarence, my daughter shall be thine.
And now what rests° but, in night's coverture,°   *remains / shadow*
Thy brother being carelessly encamped,

15   His soldiers lurking° in the towns about,   *idling*
And but attended by a simple guard,
We may surprise and take him at our pleasure?
Our scouts have found the adventure very easy;
That, as Ulysses and stout Diomed

20   With sleight° and manhood° stole to Rhesus' tents   *stealth / bravery*
And brought from thence the Thracian fatal steeds,[1]
So we, well covered with the night's black mantle,
At unawares° may beat down Edward's guard   *Suddenly*
And seize himself—I say not 'slaughter him',

25   For I intend but only to surprise° him.   *capture*
You that will follow me to this attempt,
Applaud the name of Henry with your leader.
They all cry 'Henry'
Why, then, let's on our way in silent sort,°   *manner*
For Warwick and his friends, God and Saint George!°   *patron saint of England*
Exeunt

4.3

Enter three WATCHMEN, *to guard the King's [Edward's]*
tent

FIRST WATCHMAN   Come on, my masters, each man take his stand.°   *post*
The King by this is set him down° to sleep.   *settled (in a chair)*
SECOND WATCHMAN   What, will he not to bed?
FIRST WATCHMAN   Why, no—for he hath made a solemn vow

5   Never to lie and take his natural rest
Till Warwick or himself be quite suppressed.°   *vanquished*
SECOND WATCHMAN   Tomorrow then belike shall be the day,
If Warwick be so near as men report.
THIRD WATCHMAN   But say, I pray, what nobleman is that

10   That with the King here resteth in his tent?

4.2 Location: Fields near Warwick.
1. The Greek warriors Ulysses and Diomedes captured
the horses of the Thracian prince Rhesus in a night raid,
after an oracle predicted that Troy would not fall to the
Greeks as long as the horses of Rhesus grazed on the
plains of Troy (see *The Iliad*, Book 10). *fatal:* fateful.
4.3 Location: King Edward's camp near Warwick.

FIRST WATCHMAN   'Tis the Lord Hastings, the King's chiefest friend.
THIRD WATCHMAN   O, is it so? But why commands the King
    That his chief followers lodge in towns about him,
    While he himself keeps° in the cold field?   lodges
15 SECOND WATCHMAN   'Tis the more honour, because more dangerous.
THIRD WATCHMAN   Ay, but give me worship° and quietness—   dignity
    I like it better than a dangerous honour.
    If Warwick knew in what estate° he° stands,   condition / (Edward)
    'Tis to be doubted° he would waken him.   feared
20 FIRST WATCHMAN   Unless our halberds¹ did shut up° his passage.   bar
SECOND WATCHMAN   Ay, wherefore else guard we his royal tent
    But to defend his person from night-foes?

> *Enter [the Earl of]* WARWICK, [GEORGE *Duke* OF] CLAR-
> ENCE, *[the Earl of]* OXFORD, *[and the Duke of]* SOMER-
> SET, *and French soldiers. Silent all*

WARWICK   This is his tent—and see where stand his guard.
    Courage, my masters—honour now or never!
25 But follow me, and Edward shall be ours.
FIRST WATCHMAN   Who goes there?
SECOND WATCHMAN   Stay or thou diest.

> WARWICK *and the rest all cry 'Warwick, Warwick!'*
> *and set upon the guard, who fly, crying 'Arm, arm!'*
> WARWICK *and the rest follow them*

4.4

> *[With] the drum[mer] playing and trumpet[er] sound-*
> *ing, enter [the Earl of]* WARWICK, *[the Duke of]* SOMER-
> SET, *and the rest bringing the* KING [EDWARD] *out in his*
> *gown, sitting in a chair.* RICHARD [*Duke* OF GLOUCES-
> TER] *and [Lord]* HASTINGS *flies over the stage*

SOMERSET   What are they that fly there?
WARWICK   Richard and Hastings—let them go. Here is the Duke.
KING EDWARD   'The Duke'! Why, Warwick, when we parted,
    Thou calledst me king.
WARWICK   Ay, but the case is altered.¹
5   When you disgraced me in my embassade,°   diplomatic mission
    Then I degraded you from being king,
    And come now to create you Duke of York.
    Alas, how should you govern any kingdom
    That know not how to use ambassadors,
10 Nor how to be contented with one wife,
    Nor how to use your brothers brotherly,
    Nor how to study for the people's welfare,
    Nor how to shroud° yourself from enemies?   conceal
KING EDWARD [*seeing* GEORGE]   Yea, brother of Clarence, art
        thou here too?
15 Nay, then, I see that Edward needs must down.°   must fall
    Yet, Warwick, in despite of all mischance,
    Of thee thyself and all thy complices,
    Edward will always bear himself as king.

---

1. Long-handled weapons with axe-like blades.   4.4 Location: Scene continues.
                                                       1. Proverbial for "things have changed."

Though fortune's malice overthrow my state,°   *sovereignty*
20   My mind exceeds the compass of her wheel.[2]
WARWICK   Then, for his° mind, be Edward England's king.   *in his (Edward's)*
     [WARWICK] *takes off [Edward's] crown*
But Henry now shall wear the English crown,
And be true king indeed, thou but the shadow.
My lord of Somerset, at my request,
25   See that, forthwith, Duke Edward be conveyed
Unto my brother, Archbishop of York.
When I have fought with Pembroke and his fellows,
I'll follow you, and tell what answer
Louis and the Lady Bona send to him.
30   Now for a while farewell, good Duke of York.
     They [begin to] lead [EDWARD] *out forcibly*
KING EDWARD   What fates impose, that men must needs abide.°   *endure*
It boots not to resist both wind and tide.[3]
                       Exeunt some with EDWARD
OXFORD   What now remains, my lords, for us to do
But march to London with our soldiers?
35   WARWICK   Ay, that's the first thing that we have to do—
To free King Henry from imprisonment
And see him seated in the regal throne.   *Exeunt*

4.5

Enter [Earl] RIVERS *and [his sister,]* LADY GRAY
[Edward's queen]
RIVERS   Madam, what makes you in this sudden change?[1]
LADY GRAY   Why, brother Rivers, are you yet to learn
What late misfortune is befall'n King Edward?
RIVERS   What? Loss of some pitched battle against Warwick?
5   LADY GRAY   No, but the loss of his own royal person.
RIVERS   Then is my sovereign slain?
LADY GRAY   Ay, almost slain—for he is taken prisoner,
Either betrayed by falsehood of his guard
Or by his foe surprised at unawares,
10   And, as I further have to understand,
Is new committed to the Bishop of York,
Fell° Warwick's brother, and by that° our foe.   *Cruel / therefore*
RIVERS   These news, I must confess, are full of grief.
Yet, gracious madam, bear it as you may.
15   Warwick may lose, that now hath won the day.
LADY GRAY   Till then fair hope must hinder life's decay,
And I the rather° wean me from despair   *I am the more obliged to*
For love of Edward's offspring in my womb.
This is it that makes me bridle° passion   *control*
20   And bear with mildness my misfortune's cross.
Ay, ay, for this I draw in many a tear
And stop the rising of blood-sucking[2] sighs,
Lest with my sighs or tears I blast° or drown   *blight*
King Edward's fruit, true heir to th'English crown.

---

2. My thoughts escape the control of fortune. The goddess Fortune was often depicted turning a wheel on which human destinies both rose and fell, sometimes coming full circle.
3. Compare with 3.3.48, where Margaret says that War-

wick "moves both wind and tide." *boots:* profits.
4.5 Location: The palace, London.
1. What is the reason for this sudden change of mind?
2. It was popularly believed that each sigh consumed a drop of blood from the heart.

25 RIVERS   But, madam, where is Warwick then become?°   *gone*
LADY GRAY   I am informèd that he comes towards London
 To set the crown once more on Henry's head.
 Guess thou the rest—King Edward's friends must down.
 But to prevent the tyrant's violence—
30 For trust not him that hath once broken faith—
 I'll hence forthwith unto the sanctuary,³
 To save at least the heir of Edward's right.
 There shall I rest secure from force and fraud.
 Come, therefore, let us fly while we may fly.
35 If Warwick take us, we are sure to die.   *Exeunt*

4.6
Enter RICHARD [*Duke* OF GLOUCESTER], *Lord* HASTINGS,
and Sir William Stanley [*with soldiers*]

RICHARD OF GLOUCESTER   Now my lord Hastings and Sir William Stanley,
 Leave off to wonder why I drew you hither
 Into this chiefest thicket of the park.°   *hunting grounds*
 Thus stands the case: you know our King, my brother,
5 Is prisoner to the Bishop here, at whose hands
 He hath good usage and great liberty,
 And, often but attended with weak guard,
 Comes hunting this way to disport° himself.   *amuse*
 I have advertised° him by secret means   *informed*
10 That if about this hour he make this way
 Under the colour° of his usual game,°   *pretext / hunting*
 He shall here find his friends with horse and men
 To set him free from his captivity.
  Enter KING EDWARD *and a* HUNTSMAN *with him*
HUNTSMAN   This way, my lord—for this way lies the game.
15 KING EDWARD   Nay, this way, man—see where the huntsmen stand.
 Now, brother of Gloucester, Lord Hastings, and the rest,
 Stand you thus close° to steal the Bishop's deer?   *concealed*
RICHARD OF GLOUCESTER   Brother, the time and case requireth haste.
 Your horse stands ready at the park corner.
20 KING EDWARD   But whither shall we then?
HASTINGS   To Lynn,¹ my lord,
 And shipped from thence to Flanders.
RICHARD OF GLOUCESTER [*aside*]   Well guessed, believe me—
 for that was my meaning.
KING EDWARD   Stanley, I will requite thy forwardness.°   *reward your zeal*
25 RICHARD OF GLOUCESTER   But wherefore stay we? 'Tis no time to talk.
KING EDWARD   Huntsman, what sayst thou? Wilt thou go along?
HUNTSMAN   Better do so than tarry and be hanged.
RICHARD OF GLOUCESTER   Come then, away—let's have no more ado.
KING EDWARD   Bishop, farewell—shield thee from Warwick's frown,
30 And pray that I may repossess the crown.   *Exeunt*

---

3. Place that by law conferred immunity from arrest.   ground, Yorkshire.
4.6 Location: The Archbishop of York's park or hunting   1. King's Lynn, a town on the Norfolk coast.

4.7

Flourish. Enter [the Earl of] WARWICK *and [*GEORGE
Duke OF] CLARENCE *with the crown. Then [enter]* KING
HENRY, *[the Earl of]* OXFORD, *[the Duke of]* SOMERSET,
[with] young Henry Earl of Richmond, [the Marquis of]
MONTAGUE, *and [the]* LIEUTENANT *[of the Tower]*

KING HENRY   Master Lieutenant, now that God and friends
Have shaken Edward from the regal seat
And turned my captive state to liberty,
My fear to hope, my sorrows unto joys,
At our enlargement° what are thy due fees?[1]   *release*
LIEUTENANT   Subjects may challenge° nothing of their sovereigns—   *demand*
But if an humble prayer may prevail,
I then crave pardon of your majesty.
KING HENRY   For what, Lieutenant? For well using me?
Nay, be thou sure I'll well requite thy kindness,
For that it made my prisonment a pleasure—
Ay, such a pleasure as encagèd birds
Conceive when, after many moody thoughts,
At last by notes of household harmony
They quite forget their loss of liberty.
But, Warwick, after God, thou sett'st me free,
And chiefly therefore I thank God and thee.
He was the author, thou the instrument.
Therefore, that I may conquer fortune's spite
By living low,° where fortune cannot hurt me,   *humbly*
And that the people of this blessèd land
May not be punished with my thwarting stars,[2]
Warwick, although my head still wear the crown,
I here resign my government to thee,
For thou art fortunate in all thy deeds.
WARWICK   Your grace hath still° been famed for virtuous,   *always*
And now may seem as wise as virtuous
By spying and avoiding fortune's malice,
For few men rightly temper with the stars.[3]
Yet in this one thing let me blame your grace:
For choosing me when Clarence is in place.
GEORGE OF CLARENCE   No, Warwick, thou art worthy of the sway,°   *rule*
To whom the heav'ns in thy nativity[4]
Adjudged an olive branch and laurel crown,[5]
As likely to be blest in peace and war.
And therefore I yield thee my free consent.
WARWICK   And I choose Clarence only° for Protector.[6]   *alone*
KING HENRY   Warwick and Clarence, give me both your hands.
Now join your hands, and with your hands your hearts,
That no dissension hinder government.
I make you both Protectors of this land,
While I myself will lead a private life

4.7 Location: The Tower, London.
1. Wealthy prisoners paid fees for special food and services.
2. My bad luck. Stars were believed to emit influences
that might either favor or thwart the actions of individuals.
3. Because not many men correctly conform to or come

to terms with their fate.
4. The precise position of the stars at one's birth was held
to determine the course of one's life.
5. Symbols of peace and victory, respectively.
6. The title of an individual given charge of the kingdom
while the monarch is absent, incapacitated, or a youth.

And in devotion spend my latter days,
To sin's rebuke and my creator's praise.

45 WARWICK   What answers Clarence to his sovereign's will?
GEORGE OF CLARENCE   That he consents, if Warwick yield consent,
For on thy fortune I repose myself.
WARWICK   Why, then, though loath, yet must I be content.
We'll yoke together, like a double shadow
50 To Henry's body, and supply° his place—   take
I mean in bearing weight of government—
While he enjoys the honour and his ease.
And, Clarence, now then it is more than needful
Forthwith that Edward be pronounced a traitor,
55 And all his lands and goods be confiscate.
GEORGE OF CLARENCE   What else? And that succession be determined.
WARWICK   Ay, therein Clarence shall not want his part.[7]
KING HENRY   But with the first of all your chief affairs,
Let me entreat—for I command no more—
60 That Margaret your queen and my son Edward
Be sent for, to return from France with speed.
For, till I see them here, by doubtful fear
My joy of liberty is half eclipsed.
GEORGE OF CLARENCE   It shall be done, my sovereign, with all speed.
65 KING HENRY   My lord of Somerset, what youth is that
Of whom you seem to have so tender care?
SOMERSET   My liege, it is young Henry, Earl of Richmond.[8]
KING HENRY   Come hither, England's hope.
   [KING HENRY] lays his hand on [Richmond's] head
                                                        If secret powers
Suggest but truth to my divining° thoughts,   prophesying
70 This pretty lad will prove our country's bliss.
His looks are full of peaceful majesty,
His head by nature framed to wear a crown,
His hand to wield a sceptre, and himself
Likely in time to bless a regal throne.
75 Make much of him, my lords, for this is he
Must help you more than you are hurt by me.
         Enter a POST
WARWICK   What news, my friend?
POST   That Edward is escapèd from your brother°   (the Archbishop of York)
And fled, as he hears since, to Burgundy.
80 WARWICK   Unsavoury news—but how made he escape?
POST   He was conveyed by Richard Duke of Gloucester
And the Lord Hastings, who attended him
In secret ambush on the forest side
And from the Bishop's huntsmen rescued him—
85 For hunting was his daily exercise.
WARWICK   My brother was too careless of his charge.
   [To KING HENRY]   But let us hence, my sovereign, to provide
A salve for any sore that may betide.°   occur
         Exeunt. Manent° SOMERSET, RICHMOND, and OXFORD   Remain
SOMERSET [to OXFORD]   My lord, I like not of this flight of Edward's,

---

7. George of Clarence would be next in line to the throne if the Lancastrian claim were dismissed and Edward pronounced a traitor. *want:* lack.
8. Somerset's nephew was the future Henry VII, the founder of the Tudor dynasty. The Wars of the Roses, represented in this play and in *The First Part of the Contention*, ended upon his accession to the throne, depicted at the end of *Richard III*.

90 For doubtless Burgundy will yield him help,
And we shall have more wars before't be long.
As Henry's late presaging prophecy
Did glad my heart with hope of this young Richmond,
So doth my heart misgive me, in these conflicts,
95 What may befall him, to his harm and ours.
Therefore, Lord Oxford, to prevent the worst,
Forthwith we'll send him hence to Brittany,
Till storms be past of civil enmity.
OXFORD   Ay, for if Edward repossess the crown,
100 'Tis like that Richmond with the rest shall down.°   fall
SOMERSET   It shall be so—he shall to Brittany.
Come, therefore, let's about it speedily.   *Exeunt*

4.8

Flourish. Enter [KING] EDWARD, RICHARD [*Duke* OF
GLOUCESTER], *and* [*Lord*] HASTINGS, *with a troop of Hollanders*

KING EDWARD   Now, brother Richard, Lord Hastings, and the rest,
Yet thus far fortune maketh us amends,
And says that once more I shall interchange
My wanèd° state for Henry's regal crown.   diminished
5 Well have we passed and now repassed the seas
And brought desirèd help from Burgundy.
What then remains, we being thus arrived
From Ravenspurgh¹ haven before the gates of York,
But that we enter, as into our dukedom?
[HASTINGS *knocks at the gates of York*]
10 RICHARD OF GLOUCESTER   The gates made fast? Brother, I like not this.
For many men that stumble at the threshold
Are well foretold that danger lurks within.
KING EDWARD   Tush, man, abodements° must not now affright us.   omens
By fair or foul means we must enter in,
15 For hither will our friends repair to us.
HASTINGS   My liege, I'll knock once more to summon them.
[*He knocks.*]
Enter, on the walls, the MAYOR *of York, and his Brethren*
[*aldermen*]
MAYOR   My lords, we were forewarnèd of your coming,
And shut the gates for safety of ourselves—
For now we owe allegiance unto Henry.
20 KING EDWARD   But, Master Mayor, if Henry be your king,
Yet Edward at the least is Duke of York.
MAYOR   True, my good lord, I know you for no less.
KING EDWARD   Why, and I challenge nothing but my dukedom,
As being well content with that alone.
RICHARD OF GLOUCESTER [*aside*]   But when the fox hath once
25   got in his nose,
He'll soon find means to make the body follow.
HASTINGS   Why, Master Mayor, why stand you in a doubt?
Open the gates—we are King Henry's friends.
MAYOR   Ay, say you so? The gates shall then be opened.

4.8 Location: Outside the walls of York.   1. Town on the coast of Yorkshire.

[They] descend[2]

30   RICHARD OF GLOUCESTER   A wise stout° captain, and soon persuaded.   *valiant*

HASTINGS   The good old man would fain° that all were well,   *wish*

  So 'twere not long of him;[3] but being entered,

  I doubt not, I, but we shall soon persuade

  Both him and all his brothers unto reason.

Enter [below] the MAYOR *and two aldermen*

35   KING EDWARD   So, Master Mayor, these gates must not be shut

  But in the night or in the time of war.

  What—fear not, man, but yield me up the keys,

    *[*KING EDWARD*] takes [some] keys [from the* MAYOR*]*

  For Edward will defend the town and thee,

  And all those friends that deign° to follow me.   *are willing*

March. Enter Sir John MONTGOMERY *with [a] drum[mer]*

and soldiers

40   RICHARD OF GLOUCESTER   Brother, this is Sir John Montgomery,

  Our trusty friend, unless I be deceived.

KING EDWARD   Welcome, Sir John—but why come you in arms?

MONTGOMERY   To help King Edward in his time of storm,

  As every loyal subject ought to do.

45   KING EDWARD   Thanks, good Montgomery, but we now forget

  Our title to the crown, and only claim

  Our dukedom till God please to send the rest.

MONTGOMERY   Then fare you well, for I will hence again.

  I came to serve a king and not a duke.

50   Drummer, strike up, and let us march away.

The drum[mer] begins to [sound a] march

KING EDWARD   Nay, stay, Sir John, a while, and we'll debate

  By what safe means the crown may be recovered.

MONTGOMERY   What talk you of debating? In few words,

  If you'll not here proclaim yourself our king

55   I'll leave you to your fortune and be gone

  To keep them back that come to succour you.

  Why shall we fight, if you pretend° no title?   *claim*

RICHARD OF GLOUCESTER *[to* KING EDWARD*]*   Why, brother,

    wherefore stand you on nice points?[4]

KING EDWARD   When we grow stronger, then we'll make our claim.

60   Till then 'tis wisdom to conceal our meaning.

HASTINGS   Away with scrupulous wit!° Now arms must rule.   *reasoning*

RICHARD OF GLOUCESTER   And fearless minds climb soonest unto crowns.

  Brother, we will proclaim you out of hand,

  The bruit° thereof will bring you many friends.   *news*

65   KING EDWARD   Then be it as you will, for 'tis my right,

  And Henry but usurps the diadem.

MONTGOMERY   Ay, now my sovereign speaketh like himself,

  And now will I be Edward's champion.

HASTINGS   Sound trumpet, Edward shall be here proclaimed.

    [To MONTGOMERY*]*[5]

70   Come, fellow soldier, make thou proclamation.

Flourish

MONTGOMERY   Edward the Fourth, by the grace of God King of

---

2. F's stage direction reads "He descends," as if only the Mayor comes down from the walls.
3. So long as he is not held responsible.
4. Why do you dwell on such overly precise distinctions?

5. F assigns lines 71–72 to a "Soul⟨dier⟩" and 73–74 to Montgomery; O omits line 70 and the following stage direction and assigns all the lines to Montgomery.

England and France, and Lord of Ireland—
And whosoe'er gainsays° King Edward's right,   *denies*
By this I challenge him to single fight.
    [*He*] *throws down his gauntlet*[6]
75 ALL Long live Edward the Fourth!
KING EDWARD Thanks, brave Montgomery, and thanks unto you all.
If fortune serve me I'll requite° this kindness.   *repay*
Now, for this night, let's harbour here in York;
And when the morning sun shall raise his car°   *chariot*
80 Above the border of this horizon,
We'll forward towards Warwick and his mates.
For well I wot° that Henry is no soldier.   *know*
Ah, froward° Clarence, how evil it beseems thee   *perverse*
To flatter Henry and forsake thy brother!
85 Yet, as we may, we'll meet both thee and Warwick.
Come on, brave soldiers—doubt not of the day
And, that once gotten, doubt not of large pay.   *Exeunt*

4.9

Flourish. Enter KING [HENRY, *the Earl of*] WARWICK,
[*the Marquis of*] MONTAGUE, [GEORGE *Duke of*] CLAR-
ENCE, *and* [*the Earl of*] OXFORD[1]
WARWICK What counsel, lords? Edward from Belgia,°   *the Low Countries*
With hasty° Germans and blunt° Hollanders,   *rash / merciless*
Hath passed in safety through the narrow seas,
And with his troops doth march amain° to London,   *at full speed*
5 And many giddy people flock to him.
KING HENRY Let's levy men and beat him back again.
GEORGE OF CLARENCE A little fire is quickly trodden out,
  Which, being suffered, rivers cannot quench.
WARWICK In Warwickshire I have true-hearted friends,
10 Not mutinous in peace, yet bold in war.
Those will I muster up. And thou, son° Clarence,   *son-in-law*
Shalt stir in Suffolk, Norfolk, and in Kent,
The knights and gentlemen to come with thee.
Thou, brother Montague, in Buckingham,
15 Northampton, and in Leicestershire shalt find
Men well inclined to hear what thou command'st.
And thou, brave Oxford, wondrous well beloved
In Oxfordshire, shalt muster up thy friends.
My sovereign, with the loving citizens,
20 Like to his island girt in with the ocean,
Or modest Dian[2] circled with her nymphs,
Shall rest in London till we come to him.
Fair lords, take leave and stand not to reply.
Farewell, my sovereign.
25 KING HENRY Farewell, my Hector,[3] and my Troy's true hope.

---

6. Throwing down a gauntlet, or glove, was a medieval rite of chivalry. To pick it up was to accept a challenge to duel.
4.9 Location: The Bishop of London's palace.
1. F includes Somerset at this entrance and does not mark a scene division here or at line 32. Somerset has no lines in this scene. Oxford omits him until the stage direction at 5.1.71, begins a new scene (4.10) after 4.9.32, and places Exeter's entrance there.

2. The goddess of the moon, of hunting, and of chastity, often depicted presiding over a circle of virginal nymphs in the forest. Queen Elizabeth was sometimes represented as Diana.
3. The greatest warrior of Troy, killed when the Greeks conquered the city (see note to 2.1.51). By one legendary account, London was founded as a second Troy by Brutus (or Brute), a Trojan who conquered Albion and renamed it Britain.

GEORGE OF CLARENCE In sign of truth, I kiss your highness' hand.
> [He kisses King Henry's hand]

KING HENRY Well-minded Clarence, be thou fortunate.

MONTAGUE Comfort, my lord, and so I take my leave.
> [He kisses King Henry's hand]

OXFORD And thus I seal my truth° and bid adieu.   affirm my loyalty
> [He kisses King Henry's hand]

30 KING HENRY Sweet Oxford, and my loving Montague,
And all at once,° once more a happy farewell.   [Exit]   together

WARWICK Farewell, sweet lords—let's meet at Coventry.
> Exeunt [severally]°   separately

4.10

[Enter KING HENRY and the Duke of EXETER]

KING HENRY Here at the palace will I rest a while.
Cousin of Exeter, what thinks your lordship?
Methinks the power that Edward hath in field
Should not be able to encounter mine.

5 EXETER The doubt° is that he will seduce the rest.   fear

KING HENRY That's not my fear. My meed° hath got° me fame.   merit / won
I have not stopped mine ears to their demands,
Nor posted off° their suits with slow delays.   postponed
My pity hath been balm to heal their wounds,
10 My mildness hath allayed their swelling griefs,
My mercy dried their water-flowing tears.
I have not been desirous of their wealth,
Nor much oppressed them with great subsidies,°   taxes
Nor forward of° revenge, though they much erred.   eager for
15 Then why should they love Edward more than me?
No, Exeter, these graces challenge grace;°   claim favor
And when the lion fawns upon the lamb,
The lamb will never cease to follow him.
> Shout within 'A Lancaster'[, 'A York']¹

EXETER Hark, hark, my lord—what shouts are these?
> Enter [KING] EDWARD and [RICHARD Duke OF GLOUCES-
> TER, with] soldiers

20 KING EDWARD Seize on the shame-faced° Henry—bear him hence,   timid
And once again proclaim us King of England.
You are the fount that makes small brooks to flow.
Now stops thy spring—my sea shall suck them dry,
And swell so much the higher by their ebb.
25 Hence with him to the Tower—let him not speak.
> Exeunt [some] with KING HENRY [and EXETER]

And lords, towards Coventry bend we our course,
Where peremptory° Warwick now remains.   overbearing
The sun shines hot, and, if we use delay,
Cold biting winter mars our hoped-for hay.°   expected harvest
30 RICHARD OF GLOUCESTER Away betimes,° before his forces join,   quickly
And take the great-grown traitor unawares.
Brave warriors, march amain towards Coventry.   Exeunt

4.10 Location: Scene continues.
1. F indicates "A Lancaster, A Lancaster"; Oxford's

emendation suggests offstage conflict between the two
armies.

5.1

Enter [the Earl of] WARWICK, *the Mayor of Coventry,*
two MESSENGERS, *and others upon the walls*[1]

WARWICK   Where is the post that came from valiant Oxford?
[*The* FIRST MESSENGER *steps forward*]
How far hence is thy lord, mine honest fellow?
FIRST MESSENGER   By this° at Dunsmore,[2] marching hitherward.   *By now*
WARWICK   How far off is our brother Montague?
5   Where is the post that came from Montague?
[*The* SECOND MESSENGER *steps forward*]
SECOND MESSENGER   By this at Da'ntry,[3] with a puissant° troop.   *powerful*
Enter SOMERVILLE [*to them, above*]
WARWICK   Say, Somerville—what says my loving son?
And, by thy guess, how nigh is Clarence now?
SOMERVILLE   At Southam[4] I did leave him with his forces,
10   And do expect him here some two hours hence.
[*A march afar off*]
WARWICK   Then Clarence is at hand—I hear his drum.
SOMERVILLE   It is not his, my lord. Here Southam lies.[5]
The drum your honour hears marcheth from Warwick.
WARWICK   Who should that be? Belike,° unlooked-for friends.   *Perhaps*
15   SOMERVILLE   They are at hand, and you shall quickly know.
Flourish. Enter [below KING*]* EDWARD, [*and*] RICHARD
[*Duke* OF GLOUCESTER, *with*] *soldiers*
KING EDWARD   Go, trumpet, to the walls, and sound a parley.[6]
[*Sound a parley*]
RICHARD OF GLOUCESTER   See how the surly Warwick mans the wall.
WARWICK   O, unbid° spite—is sportful° Edward come?   *unwelcome / lecherous*
Where slept our scouts, or how are they seduced,
20   That we could hear no news of his repair?°   *approach*
KING EDWARD   Now, Warwick, wilt thou ope the city gates,
Speak gentle words, and humbly bend thy knee,
Call Edward king, and at his hands beg mercy?
And he shall pardon thee these outrages.
25   WARWICK   Nay, rather, wilt thou draw thy forces hence,
Confess who set thee up and plucked thee down,
Call Warwick patron, and be penitent?
And thou shalt still remain the Duke of York.
RICHARD OF GLOUCESTER   I thought at least he would have said 'the King'.
30   Or did he make the jest against his will?
WARWICK   Is not a dukedom, sir, a goodly gift?
RICHARD OF GLOUCESTER   Ay, by my faith, for a poor earl[7] to give.
I'll do thee service for so good a gift.
WARWICK   'Twas I that gave the kingdom to thy brother.
35   KING EDWARD   Why then, 'tis mine, if but by Warwick's gift.
WARWICK   Thou art no Atlas[8] for so great a weight;

5.1 Location: Before the walls of Coventry.
1. This entire scene was probably played with Warwick's party in the gallery above the main stage and King Edward and Richard of Gloucester below, looking upward in lines 16–17 and throughout. In stage directions following lines 59, 67, and 72, first Oxford, then the Marquis of Montague, and then the Duke of Somerset enter. They may enter above to Warwick or, more probably, enter below, cross the stage, and then exit through a stage door as if "into the city" and thus out of view. F gives each an entrance but no exit; O marks both an entrance and an exit for each.
2. Dunsmore Heath, between Coventry and Daventry.
3. Daventry, a Northamptonshire town about twenty miles southeast of Coventry.
4. A town about ten miles southeast of Coventry.
5. Southam is in this direction.
6. A trumpet signal requesting a conference between warring troops.
7. Dukes are higher in rank than earls.
8. A giant who bore the weight of the heavens on his shoulders.

And, weakling, Warwick takes his gift again;
And Henry is my king, Warwick his subject.

KING EDWARD   But Warwick's king is Edward's prisoner,

40   And, gallant Warwick, do but answer this:
What is the body when the head is off?

RICHARD OF GLOUCESTER   Alas, that Warwick had no more forecast,°   *anticipated*
But whiles he thought to steal the single ten,[9]
The king was slyly fingered° from the deck.   *stolen*

45   [*To* WARWICK]   You left poor Henry at the Bishop's palace,
And ten to one you'll meet him in the Tower.

KING EDWARD   'Tis even so—[*to* WARWICK] yet you are Warwick still.

RICHARD OF GLOUCESTER   Come, Warwick, take the time°—   *seize the moment*
    kneel down, kneel down.
Nay, when? Strike now, or else the iron cools.[1]

50 WARWICK   I had rather chop this hand off at a blow,
And with the other fling it at thy face,
Than bear so low a sail° to strike to thee.   *be so humble as*

KING EDWARD   Sail how thou canst, have wind and tide thy friend,
This hand, fast wound about thy coal-black hair,

55   Shall, whiles thy head is warm and new cut off,
Write in the dust this sentence with thy blood:
'Wind-changing° Warwick now can change no more'.   *Fickle*

Enter [the Earl of] OXFORD, *with [a]* drum[mer] *and sol-*
    diers [bearing] colours°   *flags*

WARWICK   O cheerful colours! See where Oxford comes.

OXFORD   Oxford, Oxford, for Lancaster!

    [OXFORD *and his men pass over the stage and*
         exeunt into the city]

RICHARD OF GLOUCESTER [*to* KING EDWARD]   The gates are

60   open—let us enter too.

KING EDWARD   So other foes may set upon our backs?
Stand we in good array, for they no doubt
Will issue out again and bid us battle.
If not, the city being but of small defence,

65   We'll quickly rouse[2] the traitors in the same.

WARWICK [*to* OXFORD, *within*]   O, welcome, Oxford—for we want° thy help.   *need*

Enter [the Marquis of] MONTAGUE *with [a]* drum[mer]
    and soldiers [bearing] colours

MONTAGUE   Montague, Montague, for Lancaster!

    [MONTAGUE *and his men pass over the stage and*
         exeunt into the city]

RICHARD OF GLOUCESTER   Thou and thy brother both shall bye°   *atone for*
    this treason
Even with the dearest blood your bodies bear.

70 KING EDWARD   The harder matched, the greater victory.
My mind presageth happy gain and conquest.

Enter [the Duke of] SOMERSET *with [a]* drum[mer] *and*
    soldiers [bearing] colours

SOMERSET   Somerset, Somerset, for Lancaster!

    [SOMERSET *and his men pass over the stage and exeunt into the city*]

---

9. Alluding to the conventions of card games in which
the ten is valuable, but less so than the king. *single*: mere.
1. Referring to the proverb "Strike while the iron is hot,"
with a pun on "strike" as meaning "to lower a sail" or "to

yield."
2. A hunting term meaning "to surprise creatures in their
lair."

RICHARD OF GLOUCESTER   Two of thy name, both dukes of Somerset,
   Have sold their lives unto the house of York—
75 And thou shalt be the third, an° this sword hold.³   *if*
     Enter [GEORGE *Duke* OF] CLARENCE *with* [*a*] *drum*[*mer*]
     and soldiers [*bearing*] *colours*
WARWICK   And lo, where George of Clarence sweeps along,
   Of force enough to bid his brother battle;
   With whom an upright zeal to right° prevails   *for justice*
   More than the nature of a brother's love.
80 GEORGE OF CLARENCE   Clarence, Clarence, for Lancaster!
KING EDWARD   *Et tu, Brute*⁴—wilt thou stab Caesar too?
   [*To a trumpeter*] A parley, sirra,⁵ to George of Clarence.
     Sound a parley. RICHARD [OF GLOUCESTER] *and*
     [GEORGE OF] CLARENCE *whisper together*
WARWICK   Come, Clarence, come—thou wilt if Warwick call.
GEORGE OF CLARENCE   Father of Warwick, know you what this means?
     [*He*] *takes his red rose out of his hat and throws it at* WARWICK
85 Look—here I throw my infamy at thee!
   I will not ruinate my father's house,
   Who gave his blood to lime° the stones together,   *cement*
   And set up Lancaster. Why, trowest thou,° Warwick,   *do you believe*
   That Clarence is so harsh, so blunt,° unnatural,   *uncivilized*
90 To bend the fatal instruments of war
   Against his brother and his lawful king?
   Perhaps thou wilt object° my holy oath.   *invoke*
   To keep that oath were more impiety
   Than Jephthah, when he sacrificed his daughter.⁶
95 I am so sorry for my trespass made
   That, to deserve well at my brothers' hands,
   I here proclaim myself thy mortal foe,
   With resolution, wheresoe'er I meet thee—
   As I will meet thee, if thou stir abroad°—   *(outside Coventry)*
100 To plague thee for thy foul misleading me.
   And so, proud-hearted Warwick, I defy thee,
   And to my brothers turn my blushing cheeks.
   [*To* KING EDWARD] Pardon me, Edward—I will make amends.
   [*To* RICHARD] And, Richard, do not frown upon my faults,
105 For I will henceforth be no more unconstant.
KING EDWARD   Now welcome more, and ten times more beloved,
   Than if thou never hadst deserved our hate.
RICHARD OF GLOUCESTER [*to* GEORGE]   Welcome, good Clar-
   ence—this is brother-like.
WARWICK [*to* GEORGE]   O, passing° traitor—perjured and unjust!   *unsurpassed*
110 KING EDWARD   What, Warwick, wilt thou leave the town and fight?
   Or shall we beat the stones about thine ears?
WARWICK [*aside*]   Alas, I am not cooped° here for defence.   *shut up*

---

3. Richard addresses Edmund, the fourth Duke of Somerset. The defection of his older brother Henry, the third
Duke, from Edward's cause is described in 4.1 and 4.2.
Richard threw the head of their father, the second Duke,
across the stage in the play's first scene.
4. "You, too, Brutus": Julius Caesar's exclamation when
he realized that his friend was one of the conspirators to
his murder.

5. Fellow: a customary form of address to a social inferior.
6. Alluding to the biblical story in which Jephthah, an
Israelite leader, kills his daughter in fulfillment of a vow.
He swore that if he were victorious in battle, he would
sacrifice to God whoever first met him from his house
when he returned from the battlefield (see Judges 11).

[*To* KING EDWARD] I will away towards Barnet[7] presently,
And bid thee battle, Edward, if thou dar'st.
115 KING EDWARD   Yes, Warwick—Edward dares, and leads the way.
Lords, to the field—Saint George and victory!
         Exeunt [*below* KING EDWARD *and his company*].
         March. [*The Earl of*] WARWICK *and his company*
                          [*descend and*] *follow*

                            5.2
         Alarum and excursions. Enter [KING] EDWARD *bringing*
         forth [*the Earl of*] WARWICK, *wounded*
KING EDWARD   So lie thou there. Die thou, and die our fear—
For Warwick was a bug° that feared° us all.   *goblin / frightened*
Now, Montague, sit fast°—I seek for thee   *be on guard*
That Warwick's bones may keep thine company.   *Exit*
5 WARWICK   Ah, who is nigh? Come to me, friend or foe,
And tell me who is victor, York or Warwick?
Why ask I that? My mangled body shows,
My blood, my want of strength, my sick heart shows,
That I must yield my body to the earth
10 And by my fall the conquest to my foe.
Thus yields the cedar[1] to the axe's edge,
Whose arms gave shelter to the princely eagle,[2]
Under whose shade the ramping lion[3] slept,
Whose top-branch over-peered° Jove's spreading tree[4]   *rose above*
15 And kept low shrubs from winter's powerful wind.
These eyes, that now are dimmed with death's black veil,
Have been as piercing as the midday sun
To search the secret treasons of the world.
The wrinkles in my brows, now filled with blood,
20 Were likened oft to kingly sepulchres—
For who lived king, but I could dig his grave?
And who durst smile when Warwick bent his brow?
Lo now my glory smeared in dust and blood.
My parks,° my walks, my manors that I had,   *hunting grounds*
25 Even now forsake me, and of all my lands
Is nothing left me but my body's length.
Why, what is pomp, rule, reign, but earth and dust?
And, live we how we can, yet die we must.
         Enter [*the Earl of*] OXFORD *and* [*the Duke of*]
         SOMERSET
SOMERSET   Ah, Warwick, Warwick—wert thou as we are,
30 We might recover all our loss again.
The Queen from France hath brought a puissant power.°   *powerful army*
Even now we heard the news. Ah, couldst thou fly!
WARWICK   Why, then I would not fly. Ah, Montague,
If thou be there, sweet brother, take my hand,

---

7. Shakespeare treats this town, which is about ten miles
north of London and seventy-five miles southeast of Coventry, as though it were near Coventry.
5.2 Location: Near Barnet.
1. Often regarded as the king of evergreens and thus a
symbol of sovereignty.
2. Probably referring to Richard Duke of York. In 2.1.91,
his son Richard refers to the Duke of York as a "princely

eagle." The eagle was often described as the king of birds.
3. Under whose protection Henry VI rested. A reference
both to the lion as king of the animal world and to the
Lancastrian coat of arms, which showed three lions rampant, or reared on their hind legs.
4. Jove's tree, according to Virgil, was the oak, the king
of deciduous trees.

35 And with thy lips keep in my soul a while.[5]
Thou lov'st me not—for, brother, if thou didst,
Thy tears would wash this cold congealèd blood
That glues my lips and will not let me speak.
Come quickly, Montague, or I am dead.
40 SOMERSET Ah, Warwick—Montague hath breathed his last,
And to the latest gasp cried out for Warwick,
And said 'Commend me to my valiant brother.'
And more he would have said, and more he spoke,
Which sounded like a canon in a vault,
45 That mote° not be distinguished; but at last   *might*
I well might hear, delivered with a groan,
'O, farewell, Warwick.'
WARWICK Sweet rest his soul. Fly, lords, and save yourselves—
For Warwick bids you all farewell, to meet in heaven. *He dies*
50 OXFORD Away, away—to meet the Queen's great power!
Here they bear away [*Warwick's*] *body. Exeunt*

5.3

Flourish. Enter KING EDWARD *in triumph, with* RICHARD
[*Duke* OF GLOUCESTER, GEORGE *Duke* OF] CLARENCE,
and soldiers

KING EDWARD Thus far our fortune keeps an upward course,
And we are graced with wreaths of victory.
But in the midst of this bright-shining day
I spy a black suspicious threatening cloud
5 That will encounter with our glorious sun
Ere he attain his easeful western bed.
I mean, my lords, those powers that the Queen
Hath raised in Gallia° have arrived our coast,   *France*
And, as we hear, march on to fight with us.
10 GEORGE OF CLARENCE A little gale will soon disperse that cloud,
And blow it to the source from whence it came.
Thy very beams will dry those vapours up,
For every cloud engenders not a storm.
RICHARD OF GLOUCESTER The Queen is valued° thirty thou-   *estimated to be*
    sand strong,
15 And Somerset, with Oxford, fled to her.
If she have time to breathe,° be well assured,   *gather her strength*
Her faction will be full as strong as ours.
KING EDWARD We are advertised° by our loving friends   *informed*
That they do hold their course toward Tewkesbury.[1]
20 We, having now the best at Barnet field,
Will thither straight, for willingness rids way[2]—
And, as we march, our strength will be augmented
In every county as we go along.
Strike up the drum, cry 'Courage!'; and away.
[Flourish. March.] Exeunt

5. Kiss me. Many Elizabethans believed the soul escaped
through the mouth at death.
5.3 Location: Scene continues.

1. A town in Gloucestershire.
2. For eagerness to travel makes the journey seem
shorter.

5.4

Flourish. March. Enter QUEEN [MARGARET], PRINCE
EDWARD, [*the Duke of*] SOMERSET, [*the Earl of*]
OXFORD, *and soldiers*

QUEEN MARGARET   Great lords, wise men ne'er sit and wail their loss,
  But cheerly° seek how to redress their harms.   cheerfully
  What though the mast be now blown overboard,
  The cable broke, the holding-anchor[1] lost,
5 And half our sailors swallowed in the flood?
  Yet lives our pilot° still. Is't meet that he   (Henry)
  Should leave the helm and, like a fearful lad,
  With tearful eyes add water to the sea,
  And give more strength to that which hath too much,
10 Whiles, in his moan,° the ship splits on the rock   state of grief
  Which industry and courage might have saved?
  Ah, what a shame; ah, what a fault were this.
  Say Warwick was our anchor—what of that?
  And Montague our top-mast—what of him?
15 Our slaughtered friends the tackles[2]—what of these?
  Why, is not Oxford here another anchor?
  And Somerset another goodly mast?
  The friends of France our shrouds[3] and tacklings?
  And, though unskilful, why not Ned° and I   (her son Edward)
20 For once allowed the skilful pilot's charge?°   responsibility
  We will not from the helm to sit and weep,
  But keep our course, though the rough wind say no,
  From shelves° and rocks that threaten us with wreck.   sandbanks
  As good to chide the waves as speak them fair.
25 And what is Edward but a ruthless sea?
  What Clarence but a quicksand of deceit?
  And Richard but a raggèd° fatal rock?   jagged
  All these the enemies to our poor barque.°   ship
  Say you can swim—alas, 'tis but a while;
30 Tread on the sand—why, there you quickly sink;
  Bestride the rock—the tide will wash you off,
  Or else you famish. That's a threefold death.
  This speak I, lords, to let you understand,
  If° case some one of you would fly from us,   In
35 That there's no hoped-for mercy with the brothers York
  More than with ruthless waves, with sands, and rocks.
  Why, courage then—what cannot be avoided
  'Twere childish weakness to lament or fear.
PRINCE EDWARD   Methinks a woman of this valiant spirit
40 Should, if a coward heard her speak these words,
  Infuse his breast with magnanimity°   great courage
  And make him, naked,° foil° a man at arms.   unarmed / defeat
  I speak not this as doubting any here—
  For did I but suspect a fearful man,
45 He should have leave to go away betimes,°   at once
  Lest in our need he might infect another
  And make him of like spirit to himself.

5.4 Location: Fields near Tewkesbury.
1. The anchor meant to stabilize the ship by taking hold
of the sea bottom.

2. Ropes and pulleys used for raising and lowering sails.
3. Ropes that brace and support the mast.

If any such be here—as God forbid—
Let him depart before we need his help.

50 OXFORD   Women and children of so high a courage,
And warriors faint°—why, 'twere perpetual shame!   *fainthearted*
O brave young Prince, thy famous grandfather°   *(Henry V)*
Doth live again in thee! Long mayst thou live
To bear his image and renew his glories!

55 SOMERSET   And he that will not fight for such a hope,
Go home to bed, and like the owl by day,
If he arise, be mocked and wondered at.

QUEEN MARGARET   Thanks, gentle Somerset; sweet Oxford, thanks.

PRINCE EDWARD   And take his thanks that yet° hath nothing else.   *who as yet*
          Enter a MESSENGER

60 MESSENGER   Prepare you, lords, for Edward is at hand
Ready to fight—therefore be resolute.

OXFORD   I thought no less. It is his policy
To haste thus fast to find us unprovided.°   *unprepared*

SOMERSET   But he's deceived; we are in readiness.

65 QUEEN MARGARET   This cheers my heart, to see your forwardness.

OXFORD   Here pitch our battle°—hence we will not budge.   *deploy our army*
          Flourish and march. Enter KING EDWARD, RICHARD
          [*Duke* OF GLOUCESTER], *and* [GEORGE *Duke* OF] CLAR-
          ENCE, [*with*] *soldiers*

KING EDWARD [*to his followers*]   Brave followers, yonder stands
          the thorny wood
Which, by the heavens' assistance and your strength,
Must by the roots be hewn up yet ere night.

70 I need not add more fuel to your fire,
For well I wot° ye blaze to burn them out.   *know*
Give signal to the fight, and to it, lords.

QUEEN MARGARET [*to her followers*]   Lords, knights, and gentle-
          men—what I should say
My tears gainsay;° for every word I speak   *hinder*

75 Ye see I drink the water of my eye.
Therefore, no more but this: Henry your sovereign
Is prisoner to the foe, his state usurped,
His realm a slaughter-house, his subjects slain,
His statutes cancelled, and his treasure spent—

80 And yonder is the wolf that makes this spoil.
You fight in justice; then in God's name, lords,
Be valiant, and give signal to the fight.
          Alarum, retreat, excursions. Exeunt

5.5

          Flourish. Enter [KING] EDWARD, RICHARD [DUKE OF
          GLOUCESTER, *and* GEORGE *Duke* OF] CLARENCE, [*with*]
          QUEEN [MARGARET, *the Earl of*] OXFORD, [*and the Duke
          of*] SOMERSET [*guarded*]

KING EDWARD   Now here a period of° tumultuous broils.   *an end to*
Away with Oxford to Hames Castle[1] straight;
For Somerset, off with his guilty head.
Go bear them hence—I will not hear them speak.

5.5 Location: Scene continues.   1. Hammes Castle, near Calais.

5 OXFORD   For my part, I'll not trouble thee with words.
                                                    Exit [guarded]
SOMERSET   Nor I, but stoop with patience to my fortune.
                                                    Exit [guarded]
QUEEN MARGARET   So part we sadly in this troublous world
   To meet with joy in sweet Jerusalem.[2]
KING EDWARD   Is proclamation made that who finds Edward
10 Shall have a high reward and he his life?
RICHARD OF GLOUCESTER   It is, and lo where youthful Edward comes.
        Enter PRINCE [EDWARD, *guarded*]
KING EDWARD   Bring forth the gallant—let us hear him speak.
   What, can so young a thorn begin to prick?
   Edward, what satisfaction° canst thou make   amends
15 For bearing arms, for stirring up my subjects,
   And all the trouble thou hast turned me to?
PRINCE EDWARD   Speak like a subject, proud ambitious York.[3]
17.1   ALL THE LANCASTER PARTY   *Saint George for Lancaster!*
              Alarums to the battle. [The house of] York flies, then
              the chambers° [are] discharged. Then enter KING   small cannon
              [EDWARD, GEORGE OF] CLARENCE, *and* [RICHARD OF]
              GLOUCESTER, *and [their followers; they] make a great*
              shout, and cry 'For York! For York!' Then QUEEN [MAR-
              GARET], PRINCE [EDWARD], OXFORD *and* SOMERSET
              [*are all] taken [prisoner. Flourish,] and enter all*
              again
        KING EDWARD   *Now here a period of° tumultuous broils*   an end to
              Away with Oxford to Hames Castle straight;
              For Somerset, off with his guilty head.
17.5   *Go, bear them hence—I will not hear them speak.*
        OXFORD   *For my part, I'll not trouble thee with words.*
                                                    Exit [guarded]
        SOMERSET   *Nor I, but stoop with patience to my death.*
                                                    Exit [guarded]
        KING EDWARD [*to* PRINCE EDWARD]   *Edward, what satisfaction°*   amends
              canst thou make
              For stirring up my subjects to rebellion?
17.10 PRINCE EDWARD   *Speak like a subject, proud ambitious York.*
   Suppose that I am now my father's mouth—
   Resign thy chair, and where I stand, kneel thou,
20 Whilst I propose the self-same words to thee,
   Which, traitor, thou wouldst have me answer to.
QUEEN MARGARET   Ah, that thy father had been so resolved.
RICHARD OF GLOUCESTER   That you might still have worn the petticoat
   And ne'er have stolen the breech° from Lancaster.   trousers
25 PRINCE EDWARD   Let Aesop[4] fable in a winter's night—
   His currish riddles sorts not with this place.[5]
RICHARD OF GLOUCESTER   By heaven, brat, I'll plague ye for that word.
QUEEN MARGARET   Ay, thou wast born to be a plague to men.
RICHARD OF GLOUCESTER   For God's sake take away this captive scold.
30 PRINCE EDWARD   Nay, take away this scolding crookback° rather.   hunchback

---

2. Referring to heaven, which is described as the new   4. An ancient storyteller famous for his fables about ani-
Jerusalem in the Book of Revelation.   mals. Like Richard, he reputedly was physically
3. O abridges 5.4.82–5.5.17 and may reflect authorial   deformed. *fable:* tell tales.
revision. An edited text of the abridged passage is given as   5. His mean and cynical comments are not welcome
the inset passage that follows (lines 17.1–17.10).   here.

KING EDWARD   Peace, wilful boy, or I will charm° your tongue.   *silence with a charm*
GEORGE OF CLARENCE [*to* PRINCE EDWARD]   Untutored lad,
    thou art too malapert.°   *saucy*
PRINCE EDWARD   I know my duty—you are all undutiful.
    Lascivious Edward, and thou, perjured George,
35   And thou, misshapen Dick—I tell ye all
    I am your better, traitors as ye are,
    And thou usurp'st my father's right and mine.
KING EDWARD   Take that, the likeness of this railer° here.   *scold (Margaret)*
    [KING EDWARD] *stabs* [PRINCE EDWARD]
RICHARD OF GLOUCESTER   Sprawl'st thou?[6] Take that, to end thy agony.
    RICHARD *stabs* [PRINCE EDWARD]
40 GEORGE OF CLARENCE   And there's for twitting me with perjury.
    [GEORGE] *stabs* [PRINCE EDWARD, *who dies*]
QUEEN MARGARET   O, kill me too!
RICHARD OF GLOUCESTER   Marry,[7] and shall.
    [*He*] *offers to kill her*
KING EDWARD   Hold, Richard, hold—for we have done too much.
RICHARD OF GLOUCESTER   Why should she live to fill the world with words?
    [QUEEN MARGARET *faints*]
KING EDWARD   What—doth she swoon? Use means for her recovery.
RICHARD OF GLOUCESTER [*aside to* GEORGE]   Clarence, excuse
45   me to the King my brother.
    I'll hence to London on a serious matter.
    Ere ye come there, be sure° to hear some news.   *expect*
GEORGE OF CLARENCE [*aside to* RICHARD]   What? What?
RICHARD OF GLOUCESTER [*aside to* GEORGE]   The Tower, the Tower.
                                Exit
50 QUEEN MARGARET   O Ned, sweet Ned—speak to thy mother, boy.
    Canst thou not speak? O traitors, murderers!
    They that stabbed Caesar shed no blood at all,
    Did not offend, nor were not worthy blame,
    If this foul deed were by to equal it.°   *to compare with it*
55   He was a man—this, in respect,° a child;   *in comparison*
    And men ne'er spend their fury on a child.
    What's worse than murderer that I may name it?
    No, no, my heart will burst an if I speak;
    And I will speak that so my heart may burst.
60   Butchers and villains! Bloody cannibals!
    How sweet a plant have you untimely cropped!
    You have no children, butchers; if you had,
    The thought of them would have stirred up remorse.
    But if you ever chance to have a child,
65   Look in his youth to have him so cut off
    As, deathsmen, you have rid° this sweet young Prince!   *killed*
KING EDWARD   Away with her—go, bear her hence perforce.
QUEEN MARGARET   Nay, never bear me hence—dispatch° me here.   *kill*
    Here sheathe thy sword—I'll pardon thee my death.
70   What? Wilt thou not? Then, Clarence, do it thou.
GEORGE OF CLARENCE   By heaven, I will not do thee so much ease.
QUEEN MARGARET   Good Clarence, do; sweet Clarence, do thou do it.
GEORGE OF CLARENCE   Didst thou not hear me swear I would not do it?
QUEEN MARGARET   Ay, but thou usest° to forswear thyself.   *are accustomed*

---

6. Do you convulse in the agonies of death?   7. A mild oath invoking the name of the Virgin Mary.

75   'Twas sin before, but now 'tis charity.
        What, wilt thou not? Where is that devil's butcher,
        Hard-favoured° Richard? Richard, where art thou?   Ugly
        Thou art not here. Murder is thy alms-deed°—   act of charity
        Petitioners for blood thou ne'er putt'st back.°   you never turn away
80 KING EDWARD   Away, I say—I charge ye, bear her hence.
    QUEEN MARGARET   So come to you and yours as to this Prince!
                                                    Exit [*guarded*]
    KING EDWARD   Where's Richard gone?
    GEORGE OF CLARENCE   To London all in post° [—*aside*] and as I guess,   haste
        To make a bloody supper in the Tower.
85 KING EDWARD   He's sudden if a thing comes in his head.
        Now march we hence. Discharge the common sort°   ordinary soldiers
        With pay and thanks, and let's away to London,
        And see our gentle Queen how well she fares.
        By this° I hope she hath a son for me.   *Exeunt*   By now

5.6

    Enter on the walls [KING] HENRY VI, [*reading a book,*]
        RICHARD [*Duke* OF GLOUCESTER, *and*] *the* LIEUTENANT
        [*of the Tower*][1]
    RICHARD OF GLOUCESTER   Good day, my lord. What, at your book so hard?
    KING HENRY   Ay, my good lord—'my lord', I should say, rather.
        'Tis sin to flatter; 'good' was little better.°   (than flattery)
        'Good Gloucester' and 'good devil' were alike,
5   And both preposterous°—therefore not 'good lord'.   unnatural
    RICHARD OF GLOUCESTER [*to the* LIEUTENANT]   Sirrah,° leave us   Fellow
        to ourselves. We must confer.   [*Exit* LIEUTENANT]
    KING HENRY   So flies the reckless° shepherd from the wolf;   careless
        So first the harmless sheep doth yield his fleece,
        And next his throat unto the butcher's knife.
10   What scene of death hath Roscius[2] now to act?
    RICHARD OF GLOUCESTER   Suspicion always haunts the guilty mind;
        The thief doth fear each bush an officer.
    KING HENRY   The bird that hath been limèd[3] in a bush
        With trembling wings misdoubteth° every bush.   fears
15   And I, the hapless male° to one sweet bird,°   father / child
        Have now the fatal object in my eye
        Where my poor young was limed, was caught and killed.
    RICHARD OF GLOUCESTER   Why, what a peevish° fool was that of Crete,   silly
        That taught his son the office of a fowl![4]
20   And yet, for all his wings, the fool was drowned.
    KING HENRY   I, Daedalus; my poor boy, Icarus;
        Thy father, Minos,[5] that denied our course;
        The sun that seared the wings of my sweet boy,
        Thy brother Edward;[6] and thyself, the sea,

5.6 Location: The Tower, London.
1. The precise setting is ambiguous. F's stage directions indicate that the scene takes place "on the Walls," O's that it occurs "in the Tower." Richard's first line makes clear that Henry is reading, which may mean he is in an inner chamber. His murder could be staged in a small alcove at the back of the main stage, on the walls (up in the gallery), or in full view on the main stage.
2. An ancient Roman actor (actually best-known as a comedian) whom many Elizabethans cited as the archetype of a great tragedian.

3. Caught with birdlime, a sticky substance smeared on twigs.
4. Alluding to the myth of Daedalus, who, in order to escape imprisonment in Crete, designed wings made of wax and feathers for himself and his son Icarus. When Icarus flew too near the sun, the wax melted, and he fell to his death in the sea.
5. The king of Crete who imprisoned Daedalus and Icarus.
6. Referring to the sun insignia associated with Edward.

25   Whose envious gulf did swallow up his life.
      Ah, kill me with thy weapon, not with words!
      My breast can better brook° thy dagger's point   *tolerate*
      Than can my ears that tragic history.
      But wherefore dost thou come? Is't for my life?
30   RICHARD OF GLOUCESTER Think'st thou I am an executioner?
      KING HENRY A persecutor I am sure thou art;
      If murdering innocents be executing,
      Why, then thou art an executioner.
      RICHARD OF GLOUCESTER Thy son I killed for his presumption.
35   KING HENRY Hadst thou been killed when first thou didst presume,
      Thou hadst not lived to kill a son of mine.
      And thus I prophesy: that many a thousand
      Which now mistrust no parcel of my fear,[7]
      And many an old man's sigh, and many a widow's,
40   And many an orphan's water-standing° eye—   *flooded with tears*
      Men for their sons', wives for their husbands',
      Orphans for their parents' timeless° death—   *untimely*
      Shall rue the hour that ever thou wast born.
      The owl shrieked at thy birth—an evil sign;
45   The night-crow[8] cried, aboding° luckless time;   *foretelling*
      Dogs howled, and hideous tempests shook down trees;
      The raven rooked her° on the chimney's top;   *crouched*
      And chatt'ring pies° in dismal discords sung.   *magpies*
      Thy mother felt more than a mother's pain,
50   And yet brought forth less than a mother's hope—
      To wit, an indigested° and deformèd lump,   *a shapeless*
      Not like the fruit of such a goodly tree.
      Teeth hadst thou in thy head when thou wast born,
      To signify thou cam'st to bite the world;
55   And if the rest be true which I have heard
      Thou cam'st—
      RICHARD I'll hear no more. Die, prophet, in thy speech,
              He stabs him
      For this, amongst the rest, was I ordained.
      KING HENRY Ay, and for much more slaughter after this.
60   O, God forgive my sins, and pardon thee.   *He dies*
      RICHARD OF GLOUCESTER What—will the aspiring blood of Lancaster
      Sink in the ground? I thought it would have mounted.
      See how my sword weeps for the poor King's death.
      O, may such purple° tears be alway shed   *blood-red*
65   From those that wish the downfall of our house!
      If any spark of life be yet remaining,
      Down, down to hell, and say I sent thee thither—
              [*He*] *stabs him again*
      I that have neither pity, love, nor fear.
      Indeed, 'tis true that Henry told me of,
70   For I have often heard my mother say
      I came into the world with my legs forward.
      Had I not reason, think ye, to make haste,
      And seek their ruin that usurped our right?
      The midwife wondered and the women cried
75   'O, Jesus bless us, he is born with teeth!'—

---

7. Who do not share any of my fears.   8. A mythical bird supposed to be an evil omen.

And so I was, which plainly signified
That I should snarl and bite and play the dog.
Then, since the heavens have shaped my body so,
Let hell make crooked my mind to answer° it.   match
80 I had no father, I am like no father;
I have no brother, I am like no brother;
And this word, 'love', which greybeards call divine,
Be resident in men like one another
And not in me—I am myself alone.
85 Clarence, beware; thou kept'st me from the light—
But I will sort° a pitchy° day for thee.   arrange / dark
For I will buzz abroad such prophecies
That Edward shall be fearful of his life,
And then, to purge his fear, I'll be thy death.
90 Henry and his son are gone; thou, Clarence, art next;
And by one and one I will dispatch the rest,
Counting myself but bad till I be best.
I'll throw thy body in another room
And triumph, Henry, in thy day of doom. *Exit [with the body]*

5.7

[A chair of state.] Flourish. Enter KING EDWARD, *[*LADY
GRAY *his] Queen, [*GEORGE *Duke* OF] CLARENCE, RICH-
ARD *[Duke* OF GLOUCESTER, *the Lord]* HASTINGS, *a
nurse, [carrying the infant] Prince [Edward], and attendants*

KING EDWARD   Once more we sit in England's royal throne,
Repurchased with the blood of enemies.
What valiant foemen, like to autumn's corn,
Have we mowed down in tops° of all their pride!   at the peak
5 Three dukes of Somerset, threefold renowned
For hardy and undoubted° champions;   fearless
Two Cliffords, as the father and the son;
And two Northumberlands—two braver men
Ne'er spurred their coursers° at the trumpet's sound.   warhorses
10 With them, the two brave bears, Warwick and Montague,[1]
That in their chains fettered the kingly lion
And made the forest tremble when they roared.
Thus have we swept suspicion° from our seat°   worry / throne
And made our footstool of security.
15 *[To* LADY GRAY*]* Come hither, Bess, and let me kiss my boy.
[The nurse brings forth the infant prince. KING EDWARD
kisses him]
Young Ned, for thee, thine uncles and myself
Have in our armours watched° the winter's night,   stayed awake during
Went all afoot in summer's scalding heat,
That thou mightst repossess the crown in peace;
20 And of our labours thou shalt reap the gain.
RICHARD OF GLOUCESTER *[aside]* I'll blast° his harvest, an your   wither
head were laid;[2]
For yet I am not looked on° in the world.   noticed

5.7 Location: The palace, London.
1. The coat of arms of these brothers included the image

of a bear chained to a staff.
2. Once your head is laid in the grave.

This shoulder was ordained so thick to heave;
And heave it shall some weight or break my back.
25 Work thou the way, and thou shalt execute.[3]
KING EDWARD   Clarence and Gloucester, love my lovely queen;
And kiss your princely nephew, brothers, both.
GEORGE OF CLARENCE   The duty that I owe unto your majesty
I seal upon the lips of this sweet babe.
[*He kisses the infant prince*]
30 LADY GRAY   Thanks, noble Clarence—worthy brother, thanks.
RICHARD OF GLOUCESTER   And that I love the tree° from   *(family of York)*
whence thou sprang'st,
Witness the loving kiss I give the fruit.
[*He kisses the infant prince*]
[*Aside*] To say the truth, so Judas kissed his master,
And cried 'All hail!' whenas he meant all harm.[4]
35 KING EDWARD   Now am I seated as my soul delights,
Having my country's peace and brothers' loves.
GEORGE OF CLARENCE   What will your grace have done with Margaret?
René her father, to the King of France
Hath pawned the Sicils° and Jerusalem,   *Naples and Sicily*
40 And hither have they sent it° for her ransom.   *(the money raised)*
KING EDWARD   Away with her, and waft her° hence to France.   *convey her by water*
And now what rests° but that we spend the time   *remains*
With stately triumphs,° mirthful comic shows,   *festivals*
Such as befits the pleasure of the court?
45 Sound drums and trumpets—farewell, sour annoy!°   *bitter troubles*
For here, I hope, begins our lasting joy.   [*Flourish.*] *Exeunt*

TEXTUAL VARIANTS

Control text: F

F: The Folio of 1623
O: The Octavo of 1595
Q2: The Quarto of 1600
Q3: The Quarto of 1619
Fa, Fb: Successive states of F incorporating various print-shop corrections and changes

s.p. YORK [F's *Plantagenet* and *York* have been standardized throughout.]
s.p. KING HENRY [F's *Henry* has been changed throughout.]
s.p. QUEEN MARGARET [F's *Queen* and *Margaret* have been changed throughout.]
s.p. PRINCE EDWARD [F's *Prince* and *Prince Edward* have been standardized throughout.]
s.p. GEORGE/GEORGE OF CLARENCE [F's *Clarence* has been changed to "George" (1.1–3.1) and to "George of Clarence" once he is granted the title Duke of Clarence.]
s.p. RICHARD OF GLOUCESTER [F's *Richard* has been changed after 3.1 once he is granted the title Duke of Gloucester.]
s.p. KING EDWARD [F's *King* and *King Edward* have been standardized from 3.2 to the end of the play.]
s.p. LADY GRAY [F's *Widow*, *Lady Gray*, and *Gray* have been standardized throughout.]

---

3. Devise a way, (my head), and you, (shoulder and hand), shall carry it out.
4. Judas identified Jesus to the officers eager to arrest him by greeting him with a kiss and the salutation "All hail." *whenas*: when.

s.p. **KING LOUIS** [F's *Lewis* has been changed throughout.]
s.p. **LADY BONA** [F's *Bona* has been changed throughout.]
s.p. **MESSENGER** [F's *Gabriel* has been changed at 1.2.49.]
s.p. **SOLDIER** [F's *Son* has been changed throughout 2.5.]
s.p. **SECOND SOLDIER** [F's *Father* has been changed throughout 2.5.]
s.p. **FIRST GAMEKEEPER** [F's *Sinklo* has been changed throughout 3.1]
s.p. **SECOND GAMEKEEPER** [F's *Humfrey* has been changed throughout 3.1.]

Title: The true Tragedie of Richard Duke / *of Yorke, and the good King* / Henry the Sixt
   [O head title] The true Tragedie of Richard / *Duke of Yorke, and the death of* / good
   King Henrie the Sixt, / *with the whole contention betweene* / the two Houses Lancaster /
   and Yorke, as it was sundrie times / acted by the Right Honoura- / ble the Earle of Pem-
   / brooke his servants. [O title page] The third Part of Henry the Sixt, / with the death of
   the Duke of / YORKE [F]

1.1.19 hap hope   69 s.p. **EXETER** [O] *Westm⟨orland⟩*   78 **mine** [O, Q2] my   83 **and that's**
   [Q3] that's   105 **Thy** [O] My   120–24 s.p. **NORTHUMBERLAND . . . king** [O; for F, see
   inset passage in text.]   121 **York** *Plantagenet*   122 **both** both both   138 **An** And   171 **me**
   [O; not in F]   197 **thine** [O, Q2] an   200 **nor** neyther   255 **the utter ruin** vtter
   ruine   260 **with** [O; not in F]   262 **from** [O] to   269 **coast** cost
1.2.40 **to Edmund Brook** [O] vnto my   65 s.p. **SIR JOHN** *John*   72 **uncles** Vnckle
1.4.51 **buckle** [O] buckler   82 **thy** [O] the   138 **tiger's** Tygres   151 **passions move** [O]
   passions moues
2.1.113 **And, very well appointed as I thought,** [O; not in F]   127 **captains** [O] Cap-
   tiues   131 **an idle** [O] a lazie   144 **his** [O] the
2.2.92 **our brother out** [O] out me   133 s.p. **RICHARD** [O] *War⟨wicke⟩*   172 **deniest** [O]
   denied'st
2.5.38 **weeks** [not in F]   119 **E'en** Men
2.6.6 **commixture** [O] Commixtures   8 **The common people swarm like summer flies,**
   [O; not in F]   42 s.p. **EDWARD** [O] *Rich⟨ard⟩*   43 s.p. **RICHARD A** [O] A   44 s.p.
   EDWARD . . . See [O] See   44 **And** [O] *Ed⟨ward⟩* And   60 **his** [O] is   80 **buy but** [O]
   buy
3.1.17 **wast** was   24 **thee** the   **sour adversity** sower Aduesaries   30 **Is I:**   55 **thou that** [O]
   thou   96 **in the** the the
3.2.3 **lands** [O] Land   28 **whip me then** [O] then whip me   30 **an** [O, Q2] if   32 **them**
   [O] then   119 **as** [O] your   123 **honourably** [O] honourable
3.3.11 **state** Seat   33 **An** And   124 **eternal** [O] externall   156 **Warwick, peace** War-
   wicke   202 **ay** I   228 **I'll** [O] I
4.1.17 **you** [not in F]   28 **my** [O, Q2] mine   91 **thy** [O] the   133 **near'st** [O, Q2] neere
4.2.2 **sort** people   12 **come** welcome   15 **towns** Towne
4.6.4 **stands** stand   8 **Comes** Come
4.7.11 **prisonment** imprisonment   55 **be confiscate** confiscate
4.8.67–74 **Ay . . . fight.** [O omits line 4.8.70 and the following stage direction and assigns
   the remainder of these lines to Montgomery. F divides them among Montgomery, Hastings, and a soldier.]   71 s.p. **MONTGOMERY** [O] *Soul⟨dier⟩*   72 **Ireland** [O] *Ireland, &
   c.*   73 **And** [O] *Mount⟨gomerie⟩* And
4.9.12 **stir** stirre vp
5.1.68 **bye** buy   75 **an** [O, Q2] if   78 **an** in   80–83 s.p. **GEORGE OF CLARENCE . . . WAR-**
   WICKE [O; not in F]   94 **Jephthah** Iephah   102 **brothers** [O] Brother
5.4.27 **raggèd** raged   35 **York** [not in F]   82 s.d.–5.5.17 **Alarum . . . ambitious York.** [For
   the O version, see inset passage in the text.]
5.5.17.1 s.p. **ALL THE LANCASTER PARTY** *All*   17.2 **Now** [F] Lo   17.5 **Go, bear them hence**
   [F] Awaie   17.8 **Edward** [F] Now *Edward*   49 **The** [O; not in F]   76–77 **butcher,** /
   Hard-favoured Richard? [O] butcher *Richard?*
5.6.46 **tempests** [O] Tempest   80 **I had no father, I am like no father;** [O; not in F]   85

kept'st kept'st **90–91 Henry . . . the rest,** [O, Q2] King *Henry,* and the Prince his Son are gone, / *Clarence* thy turne is next, and then the rest **90 art** [F; not in O]

5.7.5 renowned [O] Renowne **21 an** [O, Q2] if **25 and** [Fb] add [Fa] **thou** [O] that **27 kiss** [Fb] 'tis [Fa] **30 s.p. LADY GRAY** *Cla⟨rence⟩* **Thanks** [O] Thanke **42 rests** [Fb] tests [Fa]

The First Part of Henry the Sixth

1 Henry VI is a play punctuated by battles. Set in the fifteenth century, it depicts England's attempts to retain a military and political foothold in France. Orléans, Rouen, Angiers, Bordeaux—the English and French clash at each place, spilling vast amounts of blood to gain undisputed claim to the territories of France. In this struggle, England has one incomparable hero, the valiant Lord Talbot, who fights with such ferocity that the French flee the very sound of his name. In 1592, probably just a few months after the play was first performed, Thomas Nashe, one of Shakespeare's contemporaries (and himself a playwright who may have had a hand in the composition of the play—see Textual Note), wrote: "How would it have joyed brave Talbot (the terror of the French) to think that after he had lain two hundred yeares in his tomb, he should triumph again on the stage, and have his bones new embalmed with the tears of ten thousand spectators at least (at several times), who, in the Tragedian that represents his person, imagine they behold him fresh bleeding?" This comment—which imagines the long-dead Talbot cheered by the thought of having his mighty victories and lamentable death played again and again—forms part of Nashe's extended defense of stage plays. While many Elizabethan writers attacked the theater as a place of idleness where lies and lewd stories were circulated, Nashe and others used plays like *1 Henry* VI to argue for the value of the stage, partly because of its role in preserving the memory of England's glorious heroes. As Nashe says, "For the subject of them (for the most part) it is borrowed out of our English Chronicles, wherein our forefathers' valiant acts (that have lain long buried in rusty brass and worm-eaten books) are revived, and they themselves raised from the grave of oblivion, and brought to plead their aged honors in open presence." For Nashe, Talbot is one of those worthy forefathers, pleased to be resurrected in the person of an English actor.

Shakespeare was instrumental in creating the vogue in the 1590s for stage plays based on events from the reigns of England's former monarchs. The division of the 1623 First Folio into histories, comedies, and tragedies indicates that the plays dealing with English history were perceived as a distinct and important group of works. From the beginning of his career until 1599, when *Henry V* was first acted, Shakespeare wrote or contributed to the writing of at least eight plays based loosely on the reigns of English kings from Richard II, who was deposed in 1399, to Henry VII, who assumed the English throne in 1485 after the Battle of Bosworth Field; in addition, there was one play on the reign of King John (1199–1216). Some of these plays chronicle the English wars in France. And some depict the lengthy struggle, known as the War of the Roses, between two branches of England's royal family for possession of the English throne: on one side of this struggle were the Lancastrians, who wore the red rose as their badge; on the other side were the York-ists, who wore the white. Both groups claimed descent from King Edward III. (For charts showing the genealogies of the Lancastrians and the Yorkists, see the endpapers at back.) The Battle of Bosworth Field ended this civil strife when Henry Tudor, a de-scendant of John of Gaunt, Duke of Lancaster, defeated Richard III, the last of the York-ist kings, and then married Elizabeth of York, the daughter of an earlier Yorkist king, Edward IV. Henry Tudor thus united the red rose and the white, and the Tudors ruled England until 1603, when Elizabeth I, granddaughter of Henry VII, died without issue. It was during the final years of Elizabeth's reign that Shakespeare wrote his history plays.

Many have speculated about why these plays about England's past became so popular. Nashe gives us a clue when he emphasizes their role in celebrating martial heroes and in creating for the common people a collective memory of their national past. In the sixteenth century, many chronicle histories of England were written, such as Edward Hall's *Union of the Two Noble and Illustre Famelies of Lancastre and Yorke* (1548) and Raphael Holinshed's *Chronicles of England, Scotland, and Ireland*; the second edition of Holinshed, published in 1587, was used extensively by Shakespeare in composing his history plays. These prose chronicles, in fact, may have been some of the "worm-eaten" books from which Nashe imagined Talbot being revived for a more pleasurable life on the stage. The theater, unlike obscure and musty texts, made a version of English history accessible even to those who could not read. For a penny, a common person could go to the theater, stand in the pit, and thrill to the exploits of Talbot, the terror of the French. Dramatized history thus served a nation-building function. It gave ordinary people a sense of England's past, celebrated its heroes, and vilified its enemies.

In the early 1590s, there were good reasons why arousing patriotic sentiment might have been popular. In 1588, England had, with the help of bad weather, repulsed an attack by the Spanish Armada, an invasion fleet sent by Europe's most powerful Catholic power, Spain. This victory had encouraged many Britons in their feeling that England should play a more active role in supporting the Protestant powers of Europe against their Catholic enemies. In 1591–92, Elizabeth had with some reluctance sent her charismatic nobleman the Earl of Essex into France to aid Henry Navarre and the French Protestant faction. In this campaign, Essex participated in a struggle for control of the city of Rouen. We can date *1 Henry VI* to sometime in 1592 both because Nashe's comments on Talbot were published that year and because the play seems to refer to this French campaign. It depicts fifteenth-century Englishmen invading French soil—and attacking Rouen—at the very moment an English army was once again before the city's walls. Many in England might thus have seen in Talbot an image of their contemporary champion the dashing Earl of Essex.

Shakespeare was involved in writing two more plays on the reign of Henry VI; in the First Folio, these were entitled, respectively, *The Second Part of Henry the Sixth* and *The Third Part of Henry the Sixth*. These two plays, however, were also published in earlier octavo or quarto versions, where they bore the titles *The First Part of the Contention of the Two Famous Houses of York and Lancaster* and *The True Tragedy of Richard Duke of York and the Good King Henry the Sixth*. No one knows for certain whether these plays were written before or after *1 Henry VI*. The Oxford editors believe they precede *Part 1*, though the evidence is not conclusive. Whatever the exact order of composition, these three plays represent Shakespeare's earliest efforts in the history genre. They were quickly followed by *Richard III*, about the Yorkist monarchs Edward IV and Richard III, who pushed their way to the throne after Henry VI and his son had been killed. This completed Shakespeare's treatment of the reign of Henry VI and of the bloody civil war that erupted during it. Only later in the decade did Shakespeare dramatize the events leading up to Henry VI's kingship. These later history plays—*Richard II*, *1* and *2 Henry IV*, and *Henry V*—take us from the late fourteenth century to the moment with which the present play begins: Henry V's death in 1422.

Today, when Shakespeare's plays are far more popular than prose histories, many people assume that the history of England in the late fourteenth and fifteenth centuries is accurately and adequately depicted in his dramas. This is a mistake. In composing *1 Henry VI*, the author or authors drew on the 1587 edition of Holinshed's chronicles, Edward Hall's history of the War of the Roses, and a number of other historical works, but literally dozens of changes, both large and small, were made in these source materials to give dramatic shape to their sprawling succession of battles, deaths, and diplomatic stratagems. For example, *1 Henry VI* opens with the funeral of Henry V, the great Lancastrian King who won much of France for England. In the midst of this scene comes news that many of the French territories captured by Henry V have already been lost. In actuality, these French towns did not fall until years after Henry's death. But the alteration heightens the sense of crisis attendant upon the great warrior's death. English interests are imperiled; a vigorous military King has been succeeded on the throne by a mere child and his squabbling advisers. Indeed, Henry VI was only nine months old when his father died. Again, the play changes the facts so that Henry, while not old enough to govern without the aid of a Lord Protector, is certainly not an infant when the play opens and is ready to marry when it ends.

Much else was changed. Talbot's capture of Rouen, though unhistorical, may have been added to indicate the desired outcome of Essex's adventures in France. Other events Shakespeare or his collaborators made up from whole cloth: for example, the striking scene in the Temple Garden when the followers of York and Somerset pluck red and white roses to indicate whose side they choose in a quarrel over a point in law. The bloody conflict that was to result in the fall of kings and the death of thousands of nobles and common soldiers is thus given a moment of origin, traced back to an obscure event that—in the unstable conditions of Henry's tenuous reign—flares into a conflagration of blood and death. In some cases, Shakespeare simply repeats the historical confusion of his sources. In this play, for

King Henry VI. Artist and date unknown.

example, the Edmund Mortimer who had a claim to the throne is conflated with his cousin John Mortimer, who was imprisoned in the Tower for many years for supporting his kinsman's royal ambitions. Sir John Fastolf is treated as a cowardly knight, when in actuality he was a distinguished officer of Henry's in the French wars. Both of these inaccuracies were probably repetitions of what Shakespeare or his possible collaborators would have found in texts available to them.

Indisputably, the play depicts events neither exactly as they were presented in the chronicles nor as a modern historian might present them. In turning historical materials into effective drama, Shakespeare or his collaborators gave one of many possible shapes to the welter of events recorded in the various sources. Much ink has been spilled trying to figure out what Shakespeare's "philosophy of history" could have been. Did he, for example, subscribe to the view expressed in Edward Hall's history that the turmoil of the fifteenth century was God's punishment for Henry IV's crime in deposing a rightful king, Richard II—a crime for which England paid in blood for over a hundred years? Or did he take a more secular view of history, in which events unfold as they do because of human choices and actions rather than because of God's intervention? One must read the plays to decide about these questions, and the answers may differ from play to play. As an early and possibly a collaborative work, 1 Henry VI does not necessarily elaborate any consistent philosophy of history. However, unlike some of Shakespeare's other history plays, this one contains very little language suggesting that an angry God is punishing England for Henry IV's earlier deposition of Richard II. Rather, events seem to unfold as a direct consequence of human decisions and human rivalries, though the appearance of demons to Joan in Act 5 tacitly acknowledges a supernatural realm with which she, at least, has made a desperate bargain.

1 Henry VI is structured by juxtaposing two conflicts. In the foreground is the struggle between the French and English forces in France. The English, led by Talbot, clash repeatedly with the army of Charles, the French Dauphin. He, in turn, is given aid throughout much of the play by a remarkable figure: the martial maid, Joan of Arc. But a counterpoint to the struggle between French and English emerges by way of the feuding the play depicts among the English nobility. These two lines of action impinge on one

another, as the internal squabbling among the English leaders keeps them from giving proper support to their soldiers in the field, eventually allowing Joan and Charles to kill Talbot before the walls of Bordeaux.

If the play has a message to deliver to the English, it would seem to be that petty rivalries and divisions among the English nobility can destroy England from within. As the boy King says to his quarreling nobles, Gloucester and Winchester,

> Believe me, lords, my tender years can tell
> Civil dissension is a viperous worm
> That gnaws the bowels of the commonwealth.
> (3.1.72–74)

The play seldom lets the audience forget about this worm. As early as the first scene, Winchester, whose status as bishop and then later as cardinal connects him to the Church of Rome, quarrels with Gloucester, who has been appointed the Protector of the Realm — that is, the one who effectively holds royal power while the King is still a child. Secular and religious authority clash, and the division this causes in the fabric of the commonwealth finds visual embodiment in the several arguments and stage fights that break out between Winchester's tawny-clothed followers and Gloucester's blue-coated serving men. This striking visual juxtaposition makes apparent how the cankerworm of civil dissension divides the realm into warring factions. The red and white roses worn by the followers, respectively, of Somerset and York serve the same purpose, dividing England into two parties just when a united front is needed to sustain the French wars. Young Henry, though aware of the danger of civil dissension, can do little to stop it. On the one hand, he empowers Richard of York by returning to him the lands and titles taken from his father, the Earl of Cambridge, who had been accused of treason; and on the other hand, he decides to wear the red rose of the House of Lancaster. Striving, perhaps, for evenhandedness, he inadvertently encourages the factionalism he would suppress.

Yet to modern readers, perhaps the most interesting part of the play is not its demonstration of the dangers of civil dissension but its handling of the opposition between Talbot, terror of the French, and Joan, scourge of the English. In contrast to the rivalrous and selfish nobles who surround the young Henry, Talbot is the epitome of the unselfish heroism Nashe found so compelling. Like a good feudal lord, he lives to serve his King in battle, an arena in which he repeatedly confirms his noble lineage and demonstrates his masculinity. Captured by the French when stabbed in the back by "a base Walloon" (an inhabitant of a French-speaking province now in Belgium), he nonetheless so terrifies his captors that they keep a guard of armed bowmen around him even when he sleeps. Talbot embodies the play's nostalgia for an idealized feudal world in which the values of valor and loyalty are shared by a community of men and passed on by them to their sons. In this regard, the play quite possibly spoke to a longing on the part of some of Elizabeth's subjects to be ruled once more by a king, not by an aging female monarch. When 1 Henry VI was written, Elizabeth, no longer young and with no heir, was entering the fourth decade of her long reign. The play seems to tap into a yearning for a return to masculine rule and martial values.

In France, Talbot is surrounded by other great English warriors: most notably Salisbury, who dies at the siege of Orléans, and Bedford, who, though sick and dying, insists on being carried in a chair to the battlefield at Rouen in order to give courage to his men. Perhaps most touchingly, at Bordeaux, where the warring English nobles refuse to send him aid, Talbot is joined on the battlefield by his son John, a fledgling warrior come to learn from his father the skills and the values of the warrior class he aspires to join. Urged to flee, he refuses, certain that flight would prove him both effeminate and baseborn. Instead, he is initiated into the rites of manhood by shedding blood and sustaining wounds in what can only be described as an erotics of battle. Having rescued him from the Bastard of Orléans, his father says:

> When from the Dauphin's crest thy sword struck fire
> It warmed thy father's heart with proud desire
> Of bold-faced victory. Then leaden age,
> Quickened with youthful spleen and warlike rage,
> Beat down Alençon, Orléans, Burgundy,
> And from the pride of Gallia rescued thee.
> The ireful Bastard Orléans, that drew blood
> From thee, my boy, and had the maidenhood
> Of thy first fight, I soon encounterèd,
> And interchanging blows, I quickly shed
> Some of his bastard blood.
>
> (4.6.10–20)

Young Talbot, shedding blood in his first battle, is compared to a young girl who bleeds during her first experience of intercourse. The cut and thrust of battle is thus imaged as a sexual encounter in which the goal is to penetrate the body and shed the blood of one's enemy. Young Talbot's willingness to participate in such struggles, no matter how inevitable his ultimate defeat, signifies the purity of his lineage and blood. Bound together by a code of chivalric values and by the rites of blood, Talbot, his son, and Bedford, Salisbury, and those who fight with them upon the fields of France embody the heroism Nashe suggested would stir the hearts of English theatergoers. By play's end, however, all these warriors are dead. With young Talbot's premature slaughter on the plains of Bordeaux, the bright flame of English chivalry flickers out. England passes into the hands of mere politicians and rivalrous churchmen who, if they fight, fight not for king and country but for their own particular interests.

The English in this play are defeated in part because of their failure to live up to and support their own best ideals as embodied in the figure of Talbot. Their defeat, however, also owes much to Talbot's chief antagonist, Joan of Arc, a magnetic and complicated figure. Depending on the vantage point from which she is viewed, Joan is a holy maid sent by God to aid her country, a servant of the devil, or a deceitful whore. When the Bastard of Orléans first introduces Joan to the Dauphin, he calls her a holy maid and a prophet, and after she both sees through the Dauphin's trick to substitute René for himself and defeats the Dauphin in single combat, he proclaims her an Amazon (one of the legendary race of women warriors) and a Deborah (an Old Testament prophet and judge who accompanied an Israelite army against their Canaanite oppressors). These comparisons suggest how highly the French at first value their female champion. For a time, Joan seems possessed of uncanny powers. Not only does she recognize the Dauphin without ever having seen him before, but, perhaps more remarkably, she seems to suck away the great Talbot's strength, leaving him confused and ashamed before the walls of Orléans.

The English respond to this powerful but disarmingly down-to-earth peasant girl by calling her a witch and a whore. Much of their language concerning Joan is filled with bawdy double meanings, beginning with their play on the word *pucelle*, meaning "maid" in French, but sounding like "puzzel," Eng-

Fifteenth-century Franco-Flemish portrait of Joan of Arc.

lish slang for "whore." From the first time he meets her in battle, Talbot assumes that Joan's powers can come only from witchcraft, rather than from a heavenly or merely human source. Joan's circumstances invite this kind of denigration. She is an unmarried woman who has turned soldier and assumed the garments of a man. In the early modern period, to dress like a man was often read as a violation of woman's assigned place in the gender hierarchy and an indication of the cross-dresser's uncontrolled will and appetites. Such women were easily assumed to be sexually transgressive, as well as vulnerable to the temptations of the devil.

Even Elizabeth, the unmarried queen, was subject to endless rumors concerning her sexuality. Some whispered that she had had bastard children with the Earl of Leicester, some that her hymen was so thick that no man could penetrate her. The virgin and the whore, the heaven-sent exception and the unnatural monster—the one could easily be turned into the other. While it seems implausible that Joan was constructed explicitly to remind spectators of the English queen, nonetheless the shepherd girl serves as a lightning rod to capture some of the ambivalent emotions attached to the queen and to the idea of powerful public women more generally. Occasionally Joan is portrayed in language echoing that used of Elizabeth. Charles, for example, calls her Astraea's daughter—that is, daughter of the goddess of justice—a title often applied to Elizabeth. Several critics have argued that Joan's battlefield exploits recall the stories circulated about Elizabeth in 1588, when she was said to have appeared in armor before her troops at Tilbury as they prepared to go into battle against the Spanish. Having the body of a woman but the role and the clothing of a man, each of these women could incite reverence but also demonization. Anomalies, they could be read as criminals or fiends rather than as miraculous exceptions to their cultures' expectations concerning virtuous women.

The Joan of this play is constructed of contradictions, and it is perhaps a mistake to try to assign a single meaning to her character. At times, she demonstrates Amazonian strength; at other times, she betrays the sharp tongue and pragmatic realism of a shepherd girl. She refuses, for example, to take responsibility for Talbot's recapture of Rouen, telling Charles the fault lies with the carelessness of the French guard. She can speak home truths to friends and foes alike. When the English herald delivers an extended eulogy over the body of Talbot on the plains of Bordeaux, Joan interrupts him: "Him that thou magnifi'st with all these titles / Stinking and flyblown lies here at our feet" (4.7.75–76). Elsewhere, having persuaded Burgundy to leave his alliance with Talbot and rejoin the French side, she remarks with irony: "Done like a Frenchman—[aside] turn and turn again" (3.7.85). The greatest shift in the presentation of Joan, however, occurs in Act 5, when she unexpectedly dwindles into a frightened and ineffectual practitioner of witchcraft. Summoning demons, she offers to let them suck her blood in return for doing her bidding. They refuse, leaving her vainly attempting to save herself from burning by pleading pregnancy. This diminished Joan of the last act—who, when directly depicted as a witch, is presented as an impotent one—seems deployed in part to bring the play to a closure acceptable to English pride. Talbot may have been defeated, but Joan is not allowed to win the war or even to live.

Joan's connection with witchcraft also capitalizes on the widespread interest in the phenomenon in the early 1590s. In 1591, accounts had reached England of the Scottish King James's prosecution of witches; and some had dared to hint that Elizabeth herself had used witchcraft to defeat the Spanish Armada. Several English treatises had been published in the 1580s debating whether witches were indeed the servants of the devil or were simply people, usually old women, scapegoated by their communities or deluded into thinking they had powers they actually lacked. The play, of course, doesn't settle the matter, giving us a Joan whose success against the English could have either a supernatural cause or a more mundane origin in her own strength, cleverness, and ability to inspire others. And while she does summon demons in the last act, they fail to aid her.

But Joan is not the only woman in 1 Henry VI. There are two others, the Countess of Auvergne and Margaret of Anjou, both French and both allied to Joan in the threat they pose to English manhood. While this play insistently calls attention to the dangers of civil dissension among the English nobility, it also repeatedly stresses the dangers posed to men by powerful women, though it overtly displaces that threat onto the women of another country. No English women appear in *1 Henry VI*, but three French women threaten English men. Joan almost ousts the English from France. The Countess of Auvergne attempts to imprison Talbot in her castle. Margaret conquers men's hearts by her great beauty, causing Henry VI to accept Margaret as his bride, though dowerless, despite his promise to marry another woman. However, Suffolk, the King's retainer, has already fallen prey to her charms, setting up the possibility that, Joan gone, yet another French woman will cause civil dissension in England.

"Thou Icarus; thy life to me is sweet" (4.6.55). From Geffrey Whitney, *A Choice of Emblemes* (1586).

In the warrior culture idealized in the person of Talbot, women would not seem to figure very importantly, except perhaps as they give birth to sons who will continue the lineage and the values of the fathers. But *1 Henry VI* depicts a more complicated reality. It shows, for example, how a potential wife, like Margaret, can incite uncontrollable desires in men and so become much more than a vehicle for reproduction or a pawn in a dynastic settlement. It also shows that some men, like the French of this play, seem unable to be martial heroes without the extraordinary and exceptional help of a woman. And it acknowledges that sometimes fathers don't beget sons worthy of the paternal name, as seems to be the case with Henry VI. Sometimes women must fill the void left by masculine failings; occasionally, as with Elizabeth I, a woman must even become king. *1 Henry VI* puts all of these complex and contradictory knowledges in play. While it creates heroes for men weary of feminine rule, in the process it also acknowledges the potential weaknesses of men, the occasional failures of the patriarchal gender system to function as it should, and the sometimes surprising and terrifying powers of women. As it turns out, Nashe painted too simple a picture of the history plays. They are not only about the valiant acts of "our forefathers" but also about the failings of less admirable Englishmen and indeed about the actions of women, some of whom, though foreign, seem to have spoken to anxieties generated very close to home.

JEAN E. HOWARD

TEXTUAL NOTE

The only text of *1 Henry VI* is found in the First Folio (F) of 1623. Using several types of stylistic and metrical evidence, the Oxford editors have returned to an existing editorial tradition of assigning authorship to several dramatists. Much of Act 1, they believe, was written by Thomas Nashe; Shakespeare is assigned only 2.4, the scene in the Temple Garden in which the followers of York and Somerset pluck the white roses and the red, and 4.2 through 4.7.32, the battle scenes at Bordeaux in which Talbot and his son meet their death after being denied aid by the quarreling English nobles. Other contemporary textual critics, who attribute the entire play to Shakespeare, feel that the kinds of textual evidence used to adduce multiple authorship are unreliable for work produced so early in

Shakespeare's career and discern no marked differences between the quality of this and other plays attributed to him in the early 1590s.

Act and scene divisions are incomplete in the Folio text and may not be theatrical in origin. The Oxford editors have divided the text in Acts 1, 3, and 5 into more scenes than are found in most modern editions. Generally, additional scenes are marked at points during a battle when the stage appears momentarily to be clear of all characters, the traditional indication in the Renaissance theater that one scene has ended and another begun. Thus, during the battle for Orléans, what are traditionally designated as 1.2 and 1.4 are each divided into two shorter scenes (1.2–1.3 and 1.5–1.6); during the struggle for Rouen, the scene traditionally designated as 3.2 is divided into five parts (3.2–3.6); and during the battle for Angiers, 5.3 is divided in this text into three scenes (5.3–5.5).

In addition, the Oxford editors have disposed of what has long been a confusion in F concerning whether Winchester is a cardinal for the whole duration of the play or is elevated to cardinal in Act 5. In Act 1, he is referred to both as a bishop and as a cardinal. The Oxford editors have taken the liberty of deleting or altering all Act 1 references to Winchester as a cardinal. Thus, for example, at 1.4.41, the Oxford text refers to Winchester's "purple robes," while F refers to his "scarlet robes," the color traditionally worn by cardinals.

SELECTED BIBLIOGRAPHY

Berman, Ronald. "Fathers and Sons in the *Henry VI* Plays." *Shakespeare Quarterly* 13 (1962): 487–97.

Brockbank, J. P. "The Frame of Disorder—*Henry VI*." *Early Shakespeare*. Ed. John Russell Brown and Bernard Harris. Stratford-upon-Avon Studies 3. London: Edward Arnold, 1961. 73–99.

Burckhardt, Sigurd. " 'I Am But Shadow of Myself': Ceremony and Design in *I Henry VI*." *Modern Language Quarterly* 28 (1967): 139–58.

Jackson, Gabriele Bernhard. "Topical Ideology: Witches, Amazons, and Shakespeare's Joan of Arc." *English Literary Renaissance* 18 (1988): 40–65.

Lee, Patricia-Ann. "Reflections of Power: Margaret of Anjou and the Dark Side of Queenship." *Renaissance Quarterly* 39 (1986): 183–217.

Marcus, Leah. *Puzzling Shakespeare: Local Reading and Its Discontents*. Berkeley: University of California Press, 1988. 51–105.

Rackin, Phyllis. *Stages of History: Shakespeare's English Chronicles*. Ithaca: Cornell University Press, 1990. 146–200.

Riggs, David. *Shakespeare's Heroical Histories: Henry VI and Its Literary Tradition*. Cambridge: Harvard University Press, 1971. 93–139.

Saccio, Peter. *Shakespeare's English Kings: History, Chronicle, and Drama*. New York: Oxford University Press, 1977. 90–113.

Taylor, Gary. "Shakespeare and Others: The Authorship of *Henry the Sixth, Part I*." *Medieval and Renaissance Drama in England* 7 (1995) : 145–205.

The First Part of Henry the Sixth

The Persons of the Play

The English

KING HENRY VI
Duke of GLOUCESTER, Lord Protector, uncle of King Henry
Duke of BEDFORD, Regent of France
Duke of EXETER
Bishop of WINCHESTER (later Cardinal), uncle of King Henry
Duke of SOMERSET
RICHARD PLANTAGENET, later DUKE OF YORK, and Regent of
    France
Earl of WARWICK
Earl of SALISBURY
Earl of SUFFOLK
Lord TALBOT
JOHN Talbot
Edmund MORTIMER
Sir William GLASDALE
Sir Thomas GARGRAVE
Sir John FASTOLF
Sir William LUCY
WOODVILLE, Lieutenant of the Tower of London
MAYOR of London
VERNON
BASSET
A LAWYER
A LEGATE and ambassadors
Messengers, warders and keepers of the Tower of London,
    servingmen, officers, captains, soldiers, heralds, watch

The French

CHARLES, Dauphin of France
RENÉ, Duke of Anjou, King of Naples
MARGARET, his daughter
Duke of ALENÇON
BASTARD of Orléans
Duke of BURGUNDY, uncle of King Henry
GENERAL of the French garrison at Bordeaux
COUNTESS of Auvergne
MASTER GUNNER of Orléans
A BOY, his son
JOAN la Pucelle
A SHEPHERD, father of Joan
Porter, French sergeant, French sentinels, French scout,
    French herald, the Governor of Paris, fiends, and soldiers

1.1

Dead march.° Enter the funeral of King Henry the Fifth,   *Funeral march*
attended on by the Duke of BEDFORD *(Regent of*
France), the Duke of GLOUCESTER *(Protector), the Duke*
of EXETER, [*the Earl of*] WARWICK, *the Bishop of* WIN-
CHESTER, *and the Duke of* SOMERSET

BEDFORD   Hung be the heavens with black![1] Yield, day, to night!
Comets, importing° change of times and states,   *foretelling*
Brandish your crystal tresses[2] in the sky,
And with them scourge the bad revolting° stars   *rebellious*
5   That have consented unto Henry's death—
King Henry the Fifth, too famous to live long.[3]
England ne'er lost a king of so much worth.
GLOUCESTER   England ne'er had a king until his time.
Virtue° he had, deserving to command.   *Merit; power*
10 His brandished sword did blind men with his° beams.   *its*
His arms spread wider than a dragon's wings.
His sparkling eyes, replete with wrathful fire,
More dazzled and drove back his enemies
Than midday sun, fierce bent against their faces.
15 What should I say? His deeds exceed all speech.
He ne'er lift up his hand but conquerèd.[4]
EXETER   We mourn in black; why mourn we not in blood?°   *by shedding blood*
Henry is dead, and never shall revive.
Upon a wooden coffin we attend,
20 And death's dishonourable victory
We with our stately presence glorify,
Like captives bound to a triumphant car.°   *chariot*
What, shall we curse the planets of mishap,
That plotted thus our glory's overthrow?
25 Or shall we think the subtle-witted French
Conjurers and sorcerers, that, afraid of him,
By magic verses have contrived his end?
WINCHESTER   He was a king blest of the King of Kings.[5]
Unto the French, the dreadful judgement day
30 So dreadful will not be as was his sight.
The battles of the Lord of Hosts[6] he fought.
The Church's prayers made him so prosperous.°   *successful*
GLOUCESTER   The Church? Where is it? Had not churchmen prayed,[7]
His thread of life had not so soon decayed.°   *grown weak*
35 None do you like but an effeminate prince,
Whom like a schoolboy you may overawe.
WINCHESTER   Gloucester, whate'er we like, thou art Protector,[8]
And lookest to command the Prince and realm.
Thy wife is proud: she holdeth thee in awe,°   *overawes or rules you*

1.1 Location: Westminster Abbey, England.
1. Alluding to the theatrical practice, when a tragedy was
to be performed, of hanging black draperies from the
"heavens," or roof projecting over the stage.
2. Flash your bright hair (the tails of the comets).
3. Henry V, the English conqueror of France who is the
subject of a later play by Shakespeare, lived from 1387
until 1422. The assertion that he was too famous to live
long may refer to the popular belief that jealous fate (the
stars of line 4) prematurely cut down those whose fame
became too great.

4. He never lifted up his hand (in battle) without conquering.
5. The name for God in biblical descriptions of the Last
Judgment (see Revelation 19:16).
6. Another biblical name for God (see Psalms 24:10,
Isaiah 13:13).
7. Punning on "preyed" and implying that Winchester
conspired against the King.
8. Ruler of the kingdom during the King's youth. (Henry
VI was an infant when his father died.)

40   More than God or religious churchmen may.

GLOUCESTER Name not religion, for thou lov'st the flesh,
    And ne'er throughout the year to church thou go'st,
    Except it be to pray against thy foes.

BEDFORD Cease, cease these jars,° and rest your minds in peace.   *discords*

45   Let's to the altar. Heralds, wait on us.°   *attend us*
       [*Exeunt* WARWICK, SOMERSET, *and heralds with coffin*]⁹
    Instead of gold, we'll offer up our arms—
    Since arms avail not, now that Henry's dead.
    Posterity, await for° wretched years,   *expect*
    When, at their mothers' moistened eyes, babes shall suck,¹

50   Our isle be made a marish° of salt tears,   *marsh*
    And none but women left to wail the dead.
    Henry the Fifth, thy ghost I invocate:
    Prosper this realm; keep it from civil broils;°   *wars*
    Combat with adverse planets in the heavens.

55   A far more glorious star thy soul will make
    Than Julius Caesar² or bright—
       Enter a MESSENGER

MESSENGER My honourable lords, health to you all.
    Sad tidings bring I to you out of France,
    Of loss, of slaughter, and discomfiture.

60   Guyenne, Compiègne, Rouen, Rheims, Orléans,
    Paris, Gisors, Poitiers are all quite lost.

BEDFORD What sayst thou, man, before dead Henry's corpse?
    Speak softly, or the loss of those great towns
    Will make him burst his lead° and rise from death.   *lead lining of coffin*

65 GLOUCESTER [*to the* MESSENGER] Is Paris lost? Is Rouen yielded up?
    If Henry were recalled to life again,
    These news would cause him once more yield the ghost.°   *to die*

EXETER [*to the* MESSENGER] How were they lost? What
    treachery was used?

MESSENGER No treachery, but want° of men and money.   *lack*

70   Amongst the soldiers this is mutterèd:
    That here you maintain several factions,
    And whilst a field° should be dispatched and fought,   *an army; battle*
    You are disputing of° your generals.   *about*
    One would have ling'ring wars, with little cost;

75   Another would fly swift, but wanteth wings;
    A third thinks, without expense at all,
    By guileful fair words peace may be obtained.
    Awake, awake, English nobility!
    Let not sloth dim your honours new-begot.

80   Cropped° are the flower-de-luces³ in your arms;   *Plucked*
    Of England's coat,° one half is cut away.   [*Exit*]   *coat of arms*

---

9. F does not indicate when the funeral procession exits.
If it exits now rather than at the end of the scene, then
Henry's coffin is not onstage when the messengers from
France arrive; but the actors carrying the coffin would
have more time to prepare for their parts in the battle
scene in 1.2.
1. When babies are fed only with their mother's tears.
2. According to Roman tradition, Caesar's soul was
turned into a shining star (Ovid's *Metamorphoses*) or
comet (Suetonius) after his murder.

3. English name for the French national emblem, the
fleur-de-lis (lily flower), which appeared in the English
coat of arms and signified the English claim to the
French throne. By the Treaty of Troyes (1420), Henry V
was named heir to the French King Charles VI, but
Henry died shortly before Charles; at Charles's death, the
French throne passed to his son, the Dauphin, leading to
the renewed struggles between the French and English
depicted here.

EXETER   Were our tears wanting to this funeral,
These tidings would call forth her° flowing tides.   *(England's)*
BEDFORD   Me they concern; Regent[4] I am of France.
85   Give me my steelèd coat. I'll fight for France.
Away with these disgraceful wailing robes!
[*He removes his mourning robe*]
Wounds will I lend the French, instead of eyes,
To weep[5] their intermissive° miseries.   *temporarily interrupted*
Enter to them another MESSENGER [*with letters*]
SECOND MESSENGER   Lords, view these letters, full of bad mischance.
90   France is revolted from the English quite,
Except some petty towns of no import.
The Dauphin[6] Charles is crownèd king in Rheims;
The Bastard of Orléans[7] with him is joined;
René, Duke of Anjou, doth take his part;
95   The Duke of Alençon flyeth to his side.   *Exit*
EXETER   The Dauphin crownèd King? All fly to him?
O whither shall *we* fly from this reproach?
GLOUCESTER   We will not fly, but to our enemies' throats.
Bedford, if thou be slack, I'll fight it out.
100   BEDFORD   Gloucester, why doubt'st thou of my forwardness?
An army have I mustered in my thoughts,
Wherewith already France is overrun.
Enter another MESSENGER
THIRD MESSENGER   My gracious lords, to add to your laments,
Wherewith you now bedew King Henry's hearse,
105   I must inform you of a dismal° fight   *disastrous*
Betwixt the stout° Lord Talbot[8] and the French.   *brave*
WINCHESTER   What, wherein Talbot overcame—is't so?
THIRD MESSENGER   O no, wherein Lord Talbot was o'erthrown.
The circumstance I'll tell you more at large.°   *in greater detail*
110   The tenth of August last, this dreadful° lord,   *fear-inspiring*
Retiring from the siege of Orléans,
Having full scarce° six thousand in his troop,   *barely*
By three-and-twenty thousand of the French
Was round encompassèd and set upon.
115   No leisure had he to enrank° his men.   *to set in battle lines*
He wanted pikes[9] to set before his archers—
Instead whereof, sharp stakes plucked out of hedges
They pitchèd in the ground confusèdly,
To keep the horsemen off from breaking in.
120   More than three hours the fight continuèd,
Where valiant Talbot above human thought
Enacted wonders with his sword and lance.
Hundreds he sent to hell, and none durst stand° him;   *face*
Here, there, and everywhere, enraged he slew.
125   The French exclaimed the devil was in arms:

4. Ruler in the King's absence.
5. *Wounds . . . weep:* I will give the French wounds, so that they will weep blood (from the wounds, instead of tears from the eyes).
6. Charles VII (1403–1461) held the title of Dauphin (heir to the French throne) until he became King in 1422. Historically, his coronation at Rheims did not occur until 1429.
7. Jean, Count of Dunois (1403–1468), illegitimate son

of the Duke of Orléans and nephew of King Charles VI.
8. John Talbot, first Earl of Shrewsbury (1388–1453) and perhaps the most celebrated English military hero of his day, was captured by the French at the Battle of Patay, the "dismal fight" described here.
9. He lacked ironbound stakes (normally set in the ground in front of archers to protect against attacking cavalry).

All the whole army stood agazed on° him.   *astonished at*
His soldiers, spying his undaunted spirit,
'A° Talbot! A Talbot!' cried out amain,°   *To / strongly*
And rushed into the bowels of the battle.
130   Here had the conquest fully been sealed up,
If Sir John Fastolf¹ had not played the coward.
He, being in the vanguard placed behind,²
With purpose to relieve and follow them,
Cowardly fled, not having struck one stroke.
135   Hence grew the general wrack° and massacre.   *destruction*
Enclosèd were they with° their enemies.   *by*
A base Walloon,³ to win the Dauphin's grace,
Thrust Talbot with a spear into the back—
Whom all France, with their chief assembled strength,
140   Durst not presume to look once in the face.
BEDFORD   Is Talbot slain then? I will slay myself,
For living idly here in pomp and ease
Whilst such a worthy leader, wanting aid,
Unto his dastard foemen° is betrayed.   *enemies*
145   THIRD MESSENGER   O no, he lives, but is took prisoner,
And Lord Scales with him, and Lord Hungerford;
Most of the rest slaughtered, or took likewise.
BEDFORD   His ransom there is none but I shall pay.
I'll hale the Dauphin headlong from his throne;
150   His crown shall be the ransom of my friend.
Four of their lords I'll change° for one of ours.   *exchange (kill)*
Farewell, my masters; to my task will I.
Bonfires in France forthwith I am to make,
To keep our great Saint George's feast⁴ withal.
155   Ten thousand soldiers with me I will take,
Whose bloody deeds shall make all Europe quake.
THIRD MESSENGER   So you had need. Fore Orléans, besieged,
The English army is grown weak and faint.
The Earl of Salisbury craveth supply,°   *reinforcements*
160   And hardly keeps his men from mutiny,
Since they, so few, watch such a multitude.   *[Exit]*
EXETER   Remember, lords, your oaths to Henry sworn:
Either to quell the Dauphin utterly,
Or bring him in obedience to your yoke.
165   BEDFORD   I do remember it, and here take my leave
To go about my preparation.   *Exit*
GLOUCESTER   I'll to the Tower⁵ with all the haste I can,
To view th'artillery and munition,
And then I will proclaim young Henry king.   *Exit*
170   EXETER   To Eltham⁶ will I, where the young King is,
Being ordained his special governor,
And for his safety there I'll best devise.   *Exit*

---

1. Shakespeare follows a doubtful historical tradition here. Though in some chronicles depicted as a coward, Sir John Fastolf (1378?–1459) was actually a distinguished soldier and officer of Henry V in the French wars. For this character's relationship with the cowardly knight Falstaff in (*1* and *2*) *Henry IV*, see the Introduction to *1 Henry IV*.
2. He being stationed in the rear of the vanguard.
3. Inhabitant of a French-speaking province in what is now southern Belgium.
4. The feast day of St. George, England's patron saint, April 23, was traditionally celebrated with bonfires. Bedford suggests he will celebrate it every day with military victories over the French.
5. The Tower of London, which served as both a royal residence and an arsenal.
6. Another royal residence, located south of London.

WINCHESTER   Each hath his place and function to attend;
I am left out; for me, nothing remains.
175   But long I will not be Jack-out-of-office.[7]
The King from Eltham I intend to steal,
And sit at chiefest stern° of public weal.   *Exit*   *(as steersman)*

1.2

Sound a flourish.° Enter CHARLES [*the Dauphin, the*   *fanfare of trumpets*
Duke of] ALENÇON, *and* RENÉ [*Duke of Anjou*],
marching with drum[mer] and soldiers

CHARLES   Mars his true moving—even as in the heavens,
So in the earth—to this day is not known.[1]
Late° did he shine upon the English side;   *Recently*
Now we are victors: upon us he smiles.
5   What towns of any moment° but we have?   *importance*
At pleasure here we lie near Orléans
Otherwhiles° the famished English, like pale ghosts,   *Occasionally*
Faintly besiege us one hour in a month.
ALENÇON   They want their porrage° and their fat bull beeves.   *porridge; stew*
10   Either they must be dieted° like mules,   *fed*
And have their provender tied to their mouths,
Or piteous they will look, like drownèd mice.
RENÉ   Let's raise the siege. Why live we idly here?
Talbot is taken, whom we wont° to fear.   *were accustomed*
15   Remaineth none but mad-brained Salisbury,
And he may well in fretting spend his gall:°   *exhaust his anger*
Nor° men nor money hath he to make war.   *Neither*
CHARLES   Sound, sound, alarum!° We will rush on them.   *(the call to arms)*
Now for the honour of the forlorn[2] French,
20   Him I forgive my death that killeth me
When he sees me go back one foot or flee.   *Exeunt*

1.3

Here alarum. They [*the French*] *are beaten back by the*
English with great loss. Enter CHARLES [*the Dauphin,*
the Duke of] ALENÇON, *and* RENÉ [*Duke of Anjou*]

CHARLES   Who ever saw the like? What men have I?
Dogs, cowards, dastards! I would ne'er have fled,
But that they left me 'midst my enemies.
RENÉ   Salisbury is a desperate homicide.
5   He fighteth as one weary of his life.
The other lords, like lions wanting food,
Do rush upon us as their hungry prey.°   *prey to their hunger*
ALENÇON   Froissart,[1] a countryman of ours, records
England all Olivers and Rolands[2] bred
10   During the time Edward the Third did reign.
More truly now may this be verified,
For none but Samsons and Goliases[3]
It sendeth forth to skirmish. One to ten?

---

7. Proverbial for someone who had been dismissed from a job.
1.2 Location: Near Orléans, France.
1. The precise nature of the planet Mars's orbit was a subject of debate until Johannes Kepler described it in 1609. Mars, the god of war, was known for his unpredictability.

2. Performing their duty at the risk of death.
1.3 Location: Near Orléans.
1. Jean Froissart, author of a history of medieval France and England.
2. The most famous of Charlemagne's knights.
3. The biblical warriors Samson and Goliath were noted for their exceptional strength.

Lean raw-boned rascals,° who would e'er suppose   *thin, inferior deer*
15   They had such courage and audacity?
      CHARLES   Let's leave this town, for they are hare-brained slaves,
            And hunger will enforce them to be more eager.°   *fierce*
            Of old I know them: rather with their teeth
            The walls they'll tear down, than forsake the siege.
20   RENÉ   I think by some odd gimmers⁴ or device
            Their arms are set, like clocks, still to strike on,
            Else ne'er could they hold out so as they do.
            By my consent we'll even let them alone.
      ALENÇON   Be it so.
                  Enter the BASTARD *of Orléans*
25   BASTARD   Where's the Prince Dauphin? I have news for him.
      CHARLES   Bastard of Orléans, thrice welcome to us.
      BASTARD   Methinks your looks are sad, your cheer appalled.°   *countenance made pale*
            Hath the late overthrow wrought this offence?
            Be not dismayed, for succour is at hand.
30   A holy maid hither with me I bring,
            Which, by a vision sent to her from heaven,
            Ordainèd is to raise this tedious siege
            And drive the English forth° the bounds of France.   *out of*
            The spirit of deep prophecy she hath,
35   Exceeding the nine sibyls of old Rome.⁵
            What's past and what's to come she can descry.
            Speak: shall I call her in? Believe my words,
            For they are certain and unfallible.
      CHARLES   Go call her in.   [*Exit* BASTARD]⁶
                        But first, to try her skill,
40   René stand thou as Dauphin in my place.
            Question her proudly; let thy looks be stern.
            By this means shall we sound° what skill she hath.   *test*
                  Enter [the BASTARD *of Orléans with]* JOAN *[la]* Pucelle⁷
                  [armed]
      RENÉ [*as Charles*]   Fair maid, is't thou wilt do these wondrous feats?
      JOAN   René, is't thou that thinkest to beguile me?
45   Where is the Dauphin? [*To* CHARLES] Come, come from behind.
            I know thee well, though never seen before.
            Be not amazed. There's nothing hid from me.
            In private will I talk with thee apart.
            Stand back you lords, and give us leave awhile.
                  [RENÉ, ALENÇON *and* BASTARD *stand apart*]
      RENÉ [*to* ALENÇON *and* BASTARD]   She takes upon her bravely, at
50   first dash.⁸
      JOAN   Dauphin, I am by birth a shepherd's daughter,
            My wit untrained in any kind of art.
            Heaven and our Lady gracious° hath it pleased   *(the Virgin Mary)*
            To shine on my contemptible estate.
55   Lo, whilst I waited on my tender lambs,
            And to sun's parching heat displayed my cheeks,

4. Gimmals, mechanical parts for transmitting motion (as in clockwork).
5. Sibyls were women in antiquity possessing the power of prophecy, perhaps "nine" here because of confusion with the nine prophetic books offered to Tarquin, the ruler of Rome, by the Cumaean Sibyl.
6. F does not indicate who brings in Joan, but it seems likely that it is the Bastard himself rather than a servant.
7. French for "the maid," or "the virgin." Joan of Arc (1412–1431) was celebrated by the French as the "Maid of Orléans" after she fought in the battle depicted here. A formidable warrior, she eventually became a prisoner of the English and was burned alive for heresy.
8. She plays her part well from the start.

God's mother deignèd to appear to me,
And in a vision, full of majesty,
Willed me to leave my base vocation
60 And free my country from calamity.
Her aid she promised, and assured success.
In complete glory she revealed herself—
And whereas I was black and swart° before,   °dark, swarthy
With those clear rays which she infused° on me   °shed
65 That beauty am I blest with, which you may see.
Ask me what question thou canst possible,
And I will answer unpremeditated.
My courage try by combat, if thou dar'st,
And thou shalt find that I exceed my sex.
70 Resolve on° this: thou shalt be fortunate,   °Be sure of
If thou receive me for thy warlike mate.°   °co-worker; lover
CHARLES Thou hast astonished me with thy high terms.°   °lofty phrases
Only this proof° I'll of thy valour make: °test
In single combat thou shalt buckle° with me.   °contend; make love
75 An if° thou vanquishest, thy words are true;   °An if = If
Otherwise, I renounce all confidence.
JOAN I am prepared. Here is my keen-edged sword,
Decked with five flower-de-luces on each side—
The which at Touraine, in Saint Katherine's churchyard,
80 Out of a great deal of old iron I chose forth.
CHARLES Then come a° God's name. I fear no woman.   °in
JOAN And while I live, I'll ne'er fly from a man.
     Here they fight and JOAN [*la*] *Pucelle overcomes*
CHARLES Stay, stay thy hands! Thou art an Amazon,[9]
And fightest with the sword of Deborah.[1]
85 JOAN Christ's mother helps me, else I were too weak.
CHARLES Whoe'er helps thee, 'tis thou that must help me.
Impatiently I burn with thy desire.°   °with desire for you
My heart and hands thou hast at once subdued.
Excellent Pucelle if thy name be so,
90 Let me thy servant,° and not sovereign be.   °lover
'Tis the French Dauphin sueth to thee thus.
JOAN I must not yield to any rites of love,
For my profession's sacred from above.
When I have chasèd all thy foes from hence,
95 Then will I think upon a recompense.
CHARLES Meantime, look gracious on thy prostrate thrall.
RENÉ [*to the other lords apart*] My lord, methinks, is very long in talk.
ALENÇON Doubtless he shrives this woman to her smock,[2]
Else ne'er could he so long protract his speech.
100 RENÉ Shall we disturb him, since he keeps no mean?°   °moderation
ALENÇON He may mean more than we poor men do know.
These women are shrewd tempters with their tongues.
RENÉ [*to* CHARLES] My lord, where are you? What devise° you on?   °decide
Shall we give o'er Orléans, or no?
105 JOAN Why, no, I say. Distrustful recreants,°   °cowards

---

9. One of the tribe of legendary female warriors claimed by Herodotus to live in Scythia.
1. An Old Testament prophet and judge who accompanied Barak as he led a victorious Israelite army against the Canaanites (see Judges 4–5).
2. Hears her confession completely; examines her intimately (to her "smock," or undergarments).

Fight till the last gasp; I'll be your guard.
CHARLES   What she says, I'll confirm. We'll fight it out.
JOAN   Assigned am I to be the English scourge.[3]
    This night the siege assurèdly I'll raise.
110   Expect Saint Martin's summer, halcyon's days,[4]
    Since I have entered into these wars.
    Glory is like a circle in the water,
    Which never ceaseth to enlarge itself
    Till, by broad spreading, it disperse to naught.
115   With Henry's death, the English circle ends.
    Dispersèd are the glories it included.
    Now am I like that proud insulting° ship   *exultant*
    Which Caesar and his fortune bore at once.[5]
CHARLES   Was Mohammed inspirèd with a dove?[6]
120   Thou with an eagle[7] art inspirèd then.
    Helen,[8] the mother of great Constantine,
    Nor yet Saint Philip's daughters[9] were like thee.
    Bright star of Venus,° fall'n down on the earth,   *Roman goddess of love*
    How may I reverently worship thee enough?
125 ALENÇON   Leave off delays, and let us raise the siege.
RENÉ   Woman, do what thou canst to save our honours.
    Drive them from Orléans, and be immortalized.
CHARLES   Presently° we'll try. Come, let's away about it.   *Immediately*
    No prophet will I trust, if she prove false.   *Exeunt*

1.4

Enter [the Duke of] GLOUCESTER, with his SERVINGMEN
[in blue coats][1]
GLOUCESTER   I am come to survey the Tower this day.
    Since Henry's death, I fear there is conveyance.°   *dishonesty*
    Where be these warders,° that they wait not here?   *guards*
    [A SERVINGMAN *knocketh on the gates*]
    Open the gates: 'tis Gloucester that calls.
FIRST WARDER [*within the Tower*]   Who's there that knocketh so
5   imperiously?
GLOUCESTER'S FIRST MAN   It is the noble Duke of Gloucester.
SECOND WARDER [*within the Tower*]   Whoe'er he be, you may
    not be let in.
GLOUCESTER'S FIRST MAN   Villains,° answer you so the Lord Pro-   *Scoundrels; peasants*
    tector?
FIRST WARDER [*within the Tower*]   The Lord protect him, so we
    answer him.
10 We do no otherwise than we are willed.°   *commanded*
GLOUCESTER   Who willèd you? Or whose will stands, but mine?

---

3. An individual sent by God to punish sin.
4. A period of unseasonable calm (the sea was thought to grow calm in December so that halcyons, or kingfishers, could build their nests upon it). *Saint Martin's summer:* Indian summer (St. Martin's Day falls on November 11).
5. According to Plutarch, an anxious sea captain was calmed when Caesar told him that his ship contained both Caesar and Caesar's natural good fortune.
6. Mohammed was the prophet and founder of Islam. Some Elizabethans claimed he was a fraud who fooled followers into thinking he was divinely inspired by training a dove to take seeds from his ear. Christians saw the dove as an incarnation of the Holy Spirit.
7. Attribute of the apostle St. John and hence a symbol of divine inspiration; also an aggressive enemy of the dove.
8. St. Helena, the mother of the emperor who made Christianity the official religion of the Roman Empire, was said to have been led by a vision to discover Jesus' cross and sepulcher.
9. Four virgins noted in the New Testament (Acts 21:9) for their powers of prophecy.
1.4. Location: The Tower of London.
1. The typical attire of Elizabethan servants.

There's none Protector of the realm but I.
[*To* SERVINGMEN] Break up the gates. I'll be your warrantize.°   *surety; authorization*
Shall I be flouted thus by dunghill grooms?
    Gloucester's men rush at the Tower gates
WOODVILLE[2] [*within the Tower*][3] What noise is this? What trai-
15   tors have we here?
GLOUCESTER   Lieutenant, is it you whose voice I hear?
Open the gates! Here's Gloucester, that would enter.
WOODVILLE [*within the Tower*] Have patience, noble duke: I
    may not open.
My lord of Winchester forbids.
20 From him I have express commandëment
That thou, nor none of thine, shall be let in.
GLOUCESTER   Faint-hearted Woodville! Prizest him fore me?—
Arrogant Winchester, that haughty prelate,
Whom Henry, our late sovereign, ne'er could brook?°   *tolerate*
25 Thou art no friend to God or to the King.
Open the gates, or I'll shut thee out shortly.
SERVINGMEN   Open the gates unto the Lord Protector,
Or we'll burst them open, if that you come not quickly.
    Enter, to the [*Lord*] *Protector at the Tower gates,* [*the*
    Bishop of] WINCHESTER *and his men in tawny coats*[4]
WINCHESTER   How now, ambitious vizier![5] What means this?
GLOUCESTER   Peeled° priest, dost thou command me to be shut   *Shaven; tonsured*
30   out?
WINCHESTER   I do, thou most usurping proditor,°   *traitor*
And not 'Protector', of the King or realm.
GLOUCESTER   Stand back, thou manifest conspirator.
Thou that contrived'st to murder our dead lord,
35 Thou that giv'st whores indulgences to sin,[6]
If thou proceed in this thy insolence—
WINCHESTER   Nay, stand thou back! I will not budge a foot.
This be Damascus,[7] be thou cursèd Cain,
To slay thy brother Abel, if thou wilt.
40 GLOUCESTER   I will not slay thee, but I'll drive thee back.
Thy purple robes, as a child's bearing-cloth,°   *christening gown*
I'll use to carry thee out of this place.
WINCHESTER   Do what thou dar'st, I beard° thee to thy face.   *defy*
GLOUCESTER   What, am I dared and bearded to my face?
45 Draw, men, for all this privilegèd place.[8]
    [*All draw their swords*]
Blue coats to tawny coats!—Priest, beware your beard.
I mean to tug it, and to cuff you soundly.
Under my feet I'll stamp thy bishop's mitre.

---

2. Richard Woodville (died c. 1441) was a loyal follower of the Lancastrian King Henry VI. His granddaughter Elizabeth married the Yorkist King Edward IV in 1464, a marriage Shakespeare depicts in *Richard III*.
3. The original stage direction at 1.4.14 reads: "Gloucester's men rush at the Tower gates, and Woodville the Lieutenant speaks within." The First and Second Warders most likely also speak here from within the Tower, but it is unclear whether they speak from the upper stage or from behind some stage device suggesting a grate or window.
4. Typically worn by attendants of important churchmen.
5. A high state official in the Turkish Empire, which

Elizabethans frequently denounced as barbaric.
6. In 1426, Gloucester charged Winchester with attempting to have King Henry V ("our dead lord") killed. He here also accuses Winchester of encouraging prostitution, referring to the revenues that the Bishop of Winchester collected from the brothels on the south bank of the Thames (where, in Shakespeare's time, many theaters were also located).
7. Damascus, in Syria, was believed to have been built on the spot where Adam and Eve's son Cain murdered his brother Abel (see Genesis 4).
8. It was illegal to draw swords near "privileged" sites, including royal residences. *for all this*: though this is a.

In spite of Pope, or dignities of church,
50 Here by the cheeks I'll drag thee up and down.
WINCHESTER Gloucester, thou wilt answer this before the Pope.
GLOUCESTER Winchester goose! I cry, 'A rope, a rope!'⁹
[To his SERVINGMEN] Now beat them hence. Why do you let them stay?
[To WINCHESTER] Thee I'll chase hence, thou wolf in sheep's array.
55 Out, tawny coats! Out, cloakèd hypocrite!
*Here Gloucester's men beat out the Bishop's men.*¹ *Enter*
in the hurly-burly the MAYOR *of London and his Officers*
MAYOR Fie, lords!—that you, being supreme magistrates,
Thus contumeliously° should break the peace.   *contemptuously*
GLOUCESTER Peace, mayor, thou know'st little of my wrongs.
Here's Beaufort—that regards nor° God nor king—   *neither*
60 Hath here distrained° the Tower to his use.   *seized*
WINCHESTER [*to* MAYOR] Here's Gloucester—a foe to citizens,
One that still motions° war, and never peace,   *who always advocates*
O'ercharging your free purses² with large fines°—   *taxes*
That seeks to overthrow religion,
65 Because he is Protector of the realm,
And would have armour here out of the Tower
To crown himself king and suppress the Prince.
GLOUCESTER I will not answer thee with words but blows.
Here they [*the factions*] *skirmish again*
MAYOR Naught rests° for me, in this tumultuous strife,   *is left*
70 But to make open proclamation.
Come, officer, as loud as e'er thou canst, cry.
OFFICER All manner of men, assembled here in arms this day
against God's peace and the King's, we charge and command
you in his highness' name to repair to your several dwelling
75 places, and not to wear, handle, or use any sword, weapon, or
dagger henceforward, upon pain of death.
[*The skirmishes cease*]
GLOUCESTER Bishop, I'll be no breaker of the law.
But we shall meet and break our minds° at large.   *express our views*
WINCHESTER Gloucester, we'll meet to thy cost, be sure.
80 Thy heart-blood I will have for this day's work.
MAYOR I'll call for clubs,³ if you will not away.
[*Aside*] This bishop is more haughty than the devil.
GLOUCESTER Mayor, farewell. Thou dost but what thou mayst.
WINCHESTER Abominable Gloucester, guard thy head,
85 For I intend to have it ere long.
Exeunt [*both factions severally*]°   *separately*
MAYOR [*to* OFFICERS] See the coast cleared, and then we will depart.—
Good God, these nobles should such stomachs° bear!   *angry tempers*
I myself fight not once in forty year.   *Exeunt*

9. A call for a hangman's noose. *Winchester goose:* slang expression for a swelling in the groin caused by venereal disease; a prostitute or a victim of venereal disease.
1. F's stage direction reads "Cardinal's men." Here, as elsewhere, the Oxford editors have removed the confusion about when Winchester is made a cardinal by assuming him to be a bishop until Act 5.
2. Overburdening your generous purses.
3. I'll shout for London apprentices to bring their clubs and quell this riot. "Prentices and clubs" was a common rallying cry.

1.5

Enter the MASTER GUNNER *of Orléans and his* BOY

MASTER GUNNER   Sirrah,[1] thou know'st how Orléans is besieged,
And how the English have the suburbs won.
BOY   Father, I know, and oft have shot at them;
Howe'er, unfortunate, I missed my aim.
5 MASTER GUNNER   But now thou shalt not. Be thou ruled by me.
Chief Master Gunner am I of this town;
Something I must do to procure me grace.°   honor
The Prince's spials° have informèd me   spies
How the English, in the suburbs close entrenched,
10 Wont,° through a secret grate of iron bars   Are accustomed
In yonder tower, to overpeer the city,
And thence discover how with most advantage
They may vex us with shot or with assault.
To intercept this inconvenience,°   harm
15 A piece of ordnance 'gainst° it I have placed,   directed toward
And even these three days have I watched, if I could see them.
Now do thou watch, for I can stay no longer.
If thou spy'st any, run and bring me word,
And thou shalt find me at the governor's.
20 BOY   Father, I warrant you, take you no care°—   don't worry
Exit [MASTER GUNNER *at one door*]
I'll never trouble you, if I may spy them.
Exit [*at the other door*]

1.6

Enter [*the Earl of*] SALISBURY *and* [*Lord*] TALBOT
[*above*] *on the turrets with others* [*among them Sir
Thomas* GARGRAVE *and Sir William* GLASDALE]

SALISBURY   Talbot, my life, my joy, again returned?
How wert thou handled, being prisoner?
Or by what means got'st thou to be released?
Discourse, I prithee, on this turret's top.
5 TALBOT   The Duke of Bedford had a prisoner,
Called the brave Lord Ponton de Santrailles;
For him was I exchanged and ransomèd.
But with a baser man-of-arms° by far   soldier of lower rank
Once in contempt they would have bartered me—
10 Which I, disdaining, scorned, and cravèd death
Rather than I would be so pilled esteemed.°   so cheaply valued
In fine,° redeemed I was, as I desired.   In short
But O, the treacherous Fastolf wounds my heart,
Whom with my bare fists I would execute
15 If I now had him brought into my power.
SALISBURY   Yet tell'st thou not how thou wert entertained.°   treated
TALBOT   With scoffs and scorns and contumelious taunts.
In open market place produced they me,
To be a public spectacle to all.
20 'Here', said they, 'is the terror of the French,
The scarecrow that affrights our children so.'
Then broke I from the officers that led me
And with my nails digged stones out of the ground

1.5 Location: Orléans.
1. Normally used to address social inferiors, but here

used to address the Master Gunner's young son.
1.6 Location: Tower before the walls of Orléans.

To hurl at the beholders of my shame.
25   My grisly countenance made others fly.
None durst come near, for fear of sudden death.
In iron walls they deemed me not secure:
So great fear of my name 'mongst them were spread
That they supposed I could rend bars of steel
30   And spurn° in pieces posts of adamant.[1]   *kick*
Wherefore a guard of chosen shot° I had   *selected marksmen*
That walked about me every minute while;°   *constantly*
And if I did but stir out of my bed,
Ready they were to shoot me to the heart.
The BOY [*passes over the stage*] *with a linstock*[2]
35   SALISBURY   I grieve to hear what torments you endured.
But we will be revenged sufficiently.
Now it is supper time in Orléans.
Here, through this grate, I count each one,
And view the Frenchmen how they fortify.
40   Let us look in: the sight will much delight thee.—
Sir Thomas Gargrave and Sir William Glasdale,
Let me have your express° opinions   *precise*
Where is best place to make our batt'ry next.
[*They look through the grate*]
GARGRAVE   I think at the north gate, for there stands Lou.°   *fortress of St. Lou*
45   GLASDALE   And I here, at the bulwark of the Bridge.
TALBOT   For aught I see, this city must be famishèd°   *starved out*
Or with light skirmishes enfeeblèd.
Here they° *shoot* [*off chambers within*] *and* SALISBURY   *(the French)*
[*and* GARGRAVE] *fall down*
SALISBURY   O Lord have mercy on us, wretched sinners!
GARGRAVE   O Lord have mercy on me, woeful man!
50   TALBOT   What chance is this that suddenly hath crossed us?
Speak, Salisbury—at least, if thou canst, speak.
How far'st thou, mirror° of all martial men?   *best example*
One of thy eyes and thy cheek's side struck off?
Accursèd tower! Accursèd fatal hand
55   That hath contrived this woeful tragedy!
In thirteen battles Salisbury o'ercame;
Henry the Fifth he first trained to the wars;
Whilst any trump did sound or drum struck up
His sword did ne'er leave striking in the field.
60   Yet liv'st thou, Salisbury? Though thy speech doth fail,
One eye thou hast to look to heaven for grace.
The sun with one eye vieweth all the world.
Heaven, be thou gracious to none alive
If Salisbury wants° mercy at thy hands.—   *lacks*
65   Sir Thomas Gargrave, hast thou any life?
Speak unto Talbot. Nay, look up to him.—
Bear hence his body; I will help to bury it.
[*Exit one with Gargrave's body*]
Salisbury, cheer thy spirit with this comfort:
Thou shalt not die whiles°—   *until*

---

1. A legendary stony substance said to be impregnable.
2. F's stage direction reads: "Enter the Boy with a linstock." He probably does not stay onstage, however, but
passes from one side to the other on his way to light the
charge that will strike down Salisbury and Gargrave. *linstock:* a stick used to hold a lighted match or torch for
firing cannon.

70   He beckons with his hand, and smiles on me,
     As who should say, 'When I am dead and gone,
     Remember to avenge me on the French.'
     Plantagenet, I will—and like thee, Nero,[3]
     Play on the lute, beholding the towns burn.
75   Wretched shall France be only in° my name.   *at the mere sound of*
     Here an alarum, and it thunders and lightens
     What stir is this? What tumult's in the heavens?
     Whence cometh this alarum and the noise?
     Enter a MESSENGER
MESSENGER   My lord, my lord, the French have gathered head.°   *assembled an army*
     The Dauphin, with one Joan la Pucelle joined,
80   A holy prophetess new risen up,
     Is come with a great power° to raise the siege.   *army*
     Here SALISBURY *lifteth himself up and groans*
TALBOT   Hear, hear, how dying Salisbury doth groan!
     It irks his heart he cannot be revenged.
     Frenchmen, I'll be a Salisbury to you.
85   *Pucelle* or pucelle,[4] Dauphin or dog-fish,[5]
     Your hearts I'll stamp out with my horse's heels
     And make a quagmire of your mingled brains.—
     Convey me° Salisbury into his tent,   *for me*
     And then we'll try what these dastard Frenchmen dare.
     Alarum. Exeunt [carrying SALISBURY]

1.7

     Here an alarum again, and [Lord] TALBOT *pursueth the*
     Dauphin and driveth him. Then enter JOAN *[la] Pucelle*
     driving Englishmen before her [and exeunt]. Then enter
     [Lord] TALBOT
TALBOT   Where is my strength, my valour, and my force?
     Our English troops retire; I cannot stay them.
     A woman clad in armour chaseth men.
     *Enter [*JOAN *la] Pucelle*
     Here, here she comes. *[To* JOAN] I'll have a bout[1] with thee.
5   Devil or devil's dam,° I'll conjure thee.   *mother*
     Blood will I draw on thee—thou art a witch[2]—
     And straightway give thy soul to him thou serv'st.
JOAN   Come, come, 'tis only I that must disgrace thee.
     Here they fight
TALBOT   Heavens, can you suffer hell so to prevail?
10   My breast I'll burst with straining of my courage°   *vital energy*
     And from my shoulders crack my arms asunder
     But I will° chastise this high-minded° strumpet.   *If I do not / arrogant*
     They fight again
JOAN   Talbot, farewell. Thy hour is not yet come.
     I must go victual° Orléans forthwith.   *supply with provisions*

---

3. Talbot here compares himself with Nero, the emperor who played music while he watched Rome burn. Salisbury was a descendant of the Plantagenet dynasty, which ruled England from 1154 to 1485.
4. Talbot puns on the French word for "virgin" (*pucelle*), which sounds like the English slang for "slut" ("puzzel").
5. Punning on the Elizabethan spelling of "dauphin" as

"dolphin": hence the taunt that the Dauphin is a "dog-fish."
1.7 Location: In and before Orléans.
1. Fight; sexual encounter. Much of the speech to and about Joan has sexual overtones.
2. Whoever drew blood from a witch was supposed to be protected from her magic.

*A short alarum, then [the French pass over the stage
and] enter the town with soldiers*

15 O'ertake me if thou canst. I scorn thy strength.
    Go, go, cheer up thy hungry-starvèd° men.   *starving to death*
    Help Salisbury to make his testament.
    This day is ours, as many more shall be.   *Exit [into the town]*
    TALBOT My thoughts are whirlèd like a potter's wheel.
20 I know not where I am nor what I do.
    A witch by fear, not force, like Hannibal³
    Drives back our troops and conquers as she lists.
    So bees with smoke and doves with noisome° stench   *noxious*
    Are from their hives and houses driven away.
25 They called us, for our fierceness, English dogs;
    Now, like to whelps, we crying run away.
        A short alarum. [Enter English soldiers]
    Hark, countrymen: either renew the fight
    Or tear the lions out of England's coat.°   *coat of arms*
    Renounce your style;° give sheep in lions' stead.⁴   *distinguishing mark*
30 Sheep run not half so treacherous° from the wolf,   *cowardly*
    Or horse or oxen from the leopard,
    As you fly from your oft-subduèd slaves.
        Alarum. Here another skirmish
    It will not be. Retire into your trenches.
    You all consented unto Salisbury's death,
35 For none would strike a stroke in his revenge.°   *in revenge of his death*
    Pucelle is entered into Orléans
    In spite of us or aught that we could do.   *[Exeunt Soldiers]*
    O would I were to die with Salisbury!
    The shame hereof will make me hide my head.
        Exit. Alarum. Retreat⁵

1.8

*Flourish. Enter on the walls [JOAN la] Pucelle, [CHARLES
the] Dauphin, RENÉ [Duke of Anjou, the Duke of]
ALENÇON and [French] Soldiers [with colours]*

JOAN Advance° our waving colours on the walls;   *Raise*
    Rescued is Orléans from the English.
    Thus Joan la Pucelle hath performed her word.
    CHARLES Divinest creature, Astraea's¹ daughter,
5   How shall I honour thee for this success?
    Thy promises are like Adonis' garden,²
    That one day bloomed and fruitful were the next.
    France, triumph in thy glorious prophetess!
    Recovered is the town of Orléans.
10 More blessèd hap° did ne'er befall our state.   *event*
    RENÉ Why ring not out the bells aloud throughout the town?
    Dauphin, command the citizens make bonfires
    And feast and banquet in the open streets

3. The Carthaginian military leader who once put to
flight his Roman enemies by tying firebrands to the horns
of two thousand oxen.
4. Display (on your coat of arms) sheep instead of lions.
5. A trumpet call to signal a retreat.
1.8 Location: Scene continues.

1. Goddess of justice; she lived on earth during the
Golden Age but fled to the heavens during the corruption
of the Iron Age. Queen Elizabeth I was often compared
to Astraea.
2. A mythical garden noted for its fertility and described
by Spenser in *The Faerie Queene*.

To celebrate the joy that God hath given us.
15 ALENÇON   All France will be replete with mirth and joy
When they shall hear how we have played the men.°   *acted like men*
CHARLES   'Tis Joan, not we, by whom the day is won—
For which I will divide my crown with her,
And all the priests and friars in my realm
20 Shall in procession sing her endless praise.
A statelier pyramid to her I'll rear
Than Rhodope's[3] of Memphis ever was.
In memory of her, when she is dead
Her ashes, in an urn more precious
25 Than the rich-jewelled coffer of Darius,[4]
Transported shall be at high festivals
Before the kings and queens of France.
No longer on Saint Denis° will we cry,   *patron saint of France*
But Joan la Pucelle shall be France's saint.
30 Come in, and let us banquet royally
After this golden day of victory.

Flourish. Exeunt

2.1

*Enter [on the walls] a [French] SERGEANT of a band,
with two SENTINELS*

SERGEANT   Sirs, take your places and be vigilant.
If any noise or soldier you perceive
Near to the walls, by some apparent° sign   *obvious*
Let us have knowledge at the court of guard.°   *guardroom*
A SENTINEL   Sergeant, you shall.   [*Exit* SERGEANT]
5   Thus are poor servitors,
When others sleep upon their quiet beds,
Constrained to watch in darkness, rain, and cold.

*Enter [Lord] TALBOT, [the Dukes of] BEDFORD and BUR-
GUNDY [and soldiers], with scaling ladders, their drums
beating a dead march[1]*

TALBOT   Lord regent, and redoubted° Burgundy—   *distinguished*
By whose approach the regions of Artois,
10 Wallon, and Picardy are friends to us[2]—
This happy night the Frenchmen are secure,°   *overconfident*
Having all day caroused and banqueted.
Embrace we then this opportunity,
As fitting best to quittance° their deceit,   *repay*
15 Contrived by art° and baleful sorcery.   *craftiness*
BEDFORD   Coward of France![3] How much he wrongs his fame,°   *reputation*
Despairing of his own arms' fortitude,
To join with witches and the help of hell.
BURGUNDY   Traitors have never other company.
20 But what's that 'Pucelle' whom they term so pure?
TALBOT   A maid, they say.
BEDFORD   A maid? And be so martial?

---

3. A Greek courtesan who married the King of Memphis
(city in Egypt) and reputedly built the third pyramid.
4. A jeweled treasure chest that Alexander allegedly won
from the Persian King Darius and used to store the works
of Homer.
2.1 Location: In and before Orléans.
1. Either a funeral march for Salisbury or the muffled

march that signifies a secret attack.
2. *By . . . us:* during Henry V's reign, the Duke of Burgundy became an English ally and won support for the
English from the French and Netherlandish regions to
which Talbot refers.
3. The Dauphin.

BURGUNDY Pray God she prove not masculine ere long.[4]
   If underneath the standard of the French[5]
   She carry armour[6] as she hath begun—
25 TALBOT Well, let them practise and converse[7] with spirits.
   God is our fortress, in whose conquering name
   Let us resolve to scale their flinty bulwarks.
BEDFORD Ascend, brave Talbot. We will follow thee.
TALBOT Not all together. Better far, I guess,
30   That we do make our entrance several ways—
   That, if it chance the one of us do fail,
   The other yet may rise against their force.[8]
BEDFORD Agreed. I'll to yon corner.
BURGUNDY   And I to this.
            [*Exeunt severally* BEDFORD *and* BURGUNDY
                       with some soldiers][9]
TALBOT And here will Talbot mount, or make his grave.
35   Now, Salisbury, for thee, and for the right
   Of English Henry, shall this night appear
   How much in duty I am bound to both.
        [TALBOT *and his soldiers scale the walls*]
SENTINELS Arm! Arm! The enemy doth make assault!
ENGLISH SOLDIERS Saint George! A Talbot![1]   [*Exeunt above.*]
    [*Alarum.*] *The French* [*soldiers*] *leap o'er the walls in
    their shirts* [*and exeunt*]. *Enter several ways* [*the*] BAS-
    TARD [*of Orléans, the Duke of*] ALENÇON, [*and*] RENÉ
    [*Duke of Anjou*], *half ready and half unready*[2]
40 ALENÇON How now, my lords? What, all unready so?
BASTARD Unready? Ay, and glad we scaped so well.
RENÉ 'Twas time, I trow,° to wake and leave our beds,   *believe*
   Hearing alarums at our chamber doors.
ALENÇON Of all exploits since first I followed arms
45   Ne'er heard I of a warlike enterprise
   More venturous or desperate than this.
BASTARD I think this Talbot be a fiend of hell.
RENÉ If not of hell, the heavens sure favour him.
ALENÇON Here cometh Charles. I marvel how he sped.°   *fared*
    Enter CHARLES [*the Dauphin*] *and* JOAN [*la Pucelle*]
50 BASTARD Tut, holy Joan[3] was his defensive guard.
CHARLES [*to* JOAN] Is this thy cunning,° thou deceitful dame?   *skill; sorcery*
   Didst thou at first, to flatter us withal,
   Make us partakers of a little gain
   That now our loss might be ten times so much?
55 JOAN Wherefore is Charles impatient with his friend?
   At all times will you have my power alike?
   Sleeping or waking must I still prevail,

---

4. She does not turn out to be a man; she does not turn out to be carrying a male child. The following lines are full of sexual innuendoes.
5. French ensign; French penis.
6. Wear armor; bear the weight of an armed man (in intercourse).
7. Scheme and talk; have sex and be intimate.
8. May scale the walls despite French resistance.
9. The staging of this scene is complex. Bedford and Burgundy may stay onstage and attack different parts of the tiring-house wall, or, as here, they may exit in several directions and fight offstage.
1. To Talbot. This cry is included in the actual stage

directions in F, but here it is assigned to nameless "English soldiers" (see also line 79).
2. In this complicated piece of stage business, Talbot's men ascend ladders to the upper stage, which represents the walls of Rouen. They there surprise French soldiers, some of whom leap down from the upper to the lower stage as if fleeing from Rouen. On the lower stage, the fleeing and defeated French nobles debate their plight. *half ready and half unready*: half dressed and half undressed.
3. A reference to her sexual availability; "hole" was slang for "vagina."

Or will you blame and lay the fault on me? —
Improvident° soldiers, had your watch been good,   *Negligent*
60   This sudden mischief never could have fall'n.
CHARLES   Duke of Alençon, this was your default,
That, being captain of the watch tonight,
Did look no better to that weighty charge.
ALENÇON   Had all your quarters been as safely kept
65   As that whereof I had the government,
We had not been thus shamefully surprised.
BASTARD   Mine was secure.
RENÉ   And so was mine, my lord.
CHARLES   And for myself, most part of all this night
Within her° quarter and mine own precinct   *(Joan's)*
70   I was employed in passing to and fro
About relieving of the sentinels.
Then how or which way should they first break in?
JOAN   Question, my lords, no further of the case,
How or which way. 'Tis sure they found some place
75   But weakly guarded, where the breach was made.
And now there rests° no other shift° but this —   *remains / device*
To gather our soldiers, scattered and dispersed,
And lay new platforms° to endamage them.   *plots, schemes*
            Alarum. Enter a[n ENGLISH] SOLDIER
ENGLISH SOLDIER   A Talbot! A Talbot!
            They [the French] fly, leaving their clothes behind
80   ENGLISH SOLDIER   I'll be so bold to take what they have left.
The cry of 'Talbot' serves me for a sword,
For I have loaden me with many spoils,
Using no other weapon but his name.   *Exit [with spoils]*

                                    2.2
            Enter [Lord] TALBOT, [the Dukes of] BEDFORD [and]
                BURGUNDY [a CAPTAIN, and soldiers]
BEDFORD   The day begins to break and night is fled,
Whose pitchy mantle overveiled the earth.
Here sound retreat and cease our hot pursuit.
            Retreat [is sounded]
TALBOT   Bring forth the body of old Salisbury
5   And here advance it° in the market place,   *raise it up (on a bier)*
The middle centre of this cursèd town.   *[Exit one or more]*
Now have I paid my vow unto his soul:
For every drop of blood was° drawn from him   *that was*
There hath at least five Frenchmen died tonight.
10   And that hereafter ages may behold
What ruin happened in revenge of him,
Within their chiefest temple I'll erect
A tomb, wherein his corpse shall be interred —
Upon the which, that everyone may read,
15   Shall be engraved the sack of Orléans,
The treacherous manner of his mournful death,
And what a terror he had been to France.
But, lords, in all our bloody massacre
I muse° we met not with the Dauphin's grace,   *wonder*
20   His new-come champion, virtuous[1] Joan of Arc,

2.2 Location: Within Orléans.   1. Full of virtue or manly courage; chaste (said ironically).

Nor any of his false confederates.

BEDFORD 'Tis thought, Lord Talbot, when the fight began,
Roused on the sudden from their drowsy beds,
They did amongst the troops of armèd men
25 Leap o'er the walls for refuge in the field.

BURGUNDY Myself, as far as I could well discern
For smoke and dusky vapours of the night,
Am sure I scared the Dauphin and his trull,°   whore
When arm-in-arm they both came swiftly running,
30 Like to a pair of loving turtle-doves
That could not live asunder day or night.
After that things are set in order here,
We'll follow them with all the power we have.

Enter a MESSENGER

MESSENGER All hail, my lords! Which of this princely train
35 Call ye the warlike Talbot, for his acts
So much applauded through the realm of France?

TALBOT Here is the Talbot. Who would speak with him?

MESSENGER The virtuous lady, Countess of Auvergne,
With modesty admiring thy renown,
40 By me entreats, great lord, thou wouldst vouchsafe
To visit her poor castle where she lies,°   dwells
That she may boast she hath beheld the man
Whose glory fills the world with loud report.°   acclaim; din of war

BURGUNDY Is it even so? Nay, then I see our wars
45 Will turn unto a peaceful comic sport,
When ladies crave to be encountered with.
You may not, my lord, despise her gentle suit.°   well-bred request

TALBOT Ne'er trust me then, for when a world of men
Could not prevail with all their oratory,
50 Yet hath a woman's kindness overruled. —
And therefore tell her I return great thanks,
And in submission will attend on her. —
Will not your honours bear me company?

BEDFORD No, truly, 'tis more than manners will.°   etiquette allows
55 And I have heard it said, 'Unbidden guests
Are often welcomest when they are gone'.

TALBOT Well then, alone—since there's no remedy—
I mean to prove° this lady's courtesy.   test
Come hither, captain.

[He] whispers

You perceive my mind?
60 CAPTAIN I do, my lord, and mean° accordingly.   intend to act

Exeunt [severally]

2.3

Enter [the] COUNTESS *[of Auvergne and her* PORTER*]*

COUNTESS Porter, remember what I gave in charge,°   I commanded
And when you have done so, bring the keys to me.

PORTER Madam, I will.   *Exit*

COUNTESS The plot is laid. If all things fall out right,
5 I shall as famous be by this exploit
As Scythian Tomyris[1] by Cyrus' death.

2.3. Location: The Countess's castle, Auvergne.
1. Asian queen who, in revenge for her son's death, killed

the Persian King Cyrus and kept his head in a wineskin
filled with human blood.

Great is the rumour° of this dreadful° knight, *fame / fear-inspiring*
And his achievements of no less account.
Fain° would mine eyes be witness with mine ears, *Gladly*
10   To give their censure° of these rare° reports. *opinion / remarkable*
Enter MESSENGER *and [Lord]* TALBOT
MESSENGER   Madam, according as your ladyship desired,
By message craved, so is Lord Talbot come.
COUNTESS   And he is welcome. What, is this the man?
MESSENGER   Madam, it is.
COUNTESS   Is this the scourge² of France?
15   Is this the Talbot, so much feared abroad
That with his name the mothers still their babes?
I see report is fabulous and false.
I thought I should have seen some Hercules,³
A second Hector,⁴ for his grim aspect° *appearance*
20   And large proportion of his strong-knit limbs.
Alas, this is a child, a seely° dwarf. *feeble*
It cannot be this weak and writhled° shrimp *wrinkled*
Should strike such terror to his enemies.
TALBOT   Madam, I have been bold to trouble you.
25   But since your ladyship is not at leisure,
I'll sort some other time to visit you.
          [*He is going*]
COUNTESS [*to* MESSENGER]   What means he now? Go ask him
          whither he goes.
MESSENGER   Stay, my Lord Talbot, for my lady craves
To know the cause of your abrupt departure.
30   TALBOT   Marry,⁵ for that° she's in a wrong belief, *because*
I go to certify her Talbot's here.
Enter PORTER *with keys*
COUNTESS   If thou be he, then art thou prisoner.
TALBOT   Prisoner? To whom?
COUNTESS   To me, bloodthirsty lord;
And for that cause I trained° thee to my house. *enticed*
35   Long time thy shadow° hath been thrall° to me, *image / slave*
For in my gallery thy picture hangs;
But now the substance shall endure the like,
And I will chain these legs and arms of thine
That hast by tyranny these many years
40   Wasted our country, slain our citizens,
And sent our sons and husbands captive°— *into captivity*
TALBOT   Ha, ha, ha!
COUNTESS   Laughest thou, wretch? Thy mirth shall turn to moan.
TALBOT   I laugh to see your ladyship so fond° *foolish*
45   To think that you have aught but Talbot's shadow
Whereon to practise your severity.
COUNTESS   Why? Art not thou the man?
TALBOT   I am indeed.
COUNTESS   Then have I substance too.
50   TALBOT   No, no, I am but shadow of myself.
You are deceived; my substance is not here.

---

2. Individual sent by God to punish sin. Joan describes herself as "the English scourge" at 1.3.108.
3. Mythical hero famous for his immense strength.
4. Greatest of the Trojan warriors, celebrated in Homer's Iliad.
5. By the Virgin Mary, a mild oath.

For what you see is but the smallest part
And least proportion of humanity.[6]
I tell you, madam, were the whole frame[7] here,
55 It is of such a spacious lofty pitch°   height
Your roof were not sufficient to contain't.
COUNTESS   This is a riddling merchant for the nonce.[8]
He will be here, and yet he is not here.
How can these contrarieties agree?
60 TALBOT   That will I show you presently.°   immediately
        [He] winds° his horn. [Within,] drums strike up; a peal   blows
        of ordnance. Enter [English] soldiers
How say you, madam? Are you now persuaded
That Talbot is but shadow of himself?
These are his substance, sinews, arms, and strength,
With which he yoketh your rebellious necks,
65 Razeth your cities and subverts° your towns,   overthrows
And in a moment makes them desolate.
COUNTESS   Victorious Talbot, pardon my abuse.°   error; deception
I find thou art no less than fame hath bruited,°   proclaimed
And more than may be gathered by thy shape.
70 Let my presumption not provoke thy wrath,
For I am sorry that with reverence
I did not entertain° thee as thou art.   receive
TALBOT   Be not dismayed, fair lady, nor misconster°   misconstrue
The mind of Talbot, as you did mistake
75 The outward composition of his body.
What you have done hath not offended me;
Nor other satisfaction do I crave
But only, with your patience,° that we may   permission
Taste of your wine and see what cates° you have: delicacies
80 For soldiers' stomachs always serve them well.
COUNTESS   With all my heart; and think me honourèd
To feast so great a warrior in my house.   Exeunt

2.4

[A rose brier.] Enter RICHARD PLANTAGENET, [the Earl
of] WARWICK, [the Duke of] SOMERSET, [William de la]
Pole [the Earl of SUFFOLK], and others [VERNON, and a
LAWYER]
RICHARD PLANTAGENET   Great lords and gentlemen, what
        means this silence?
Dare no man answer in a case of truth?
SUFFOLK   Within the Temple hall we were° too loud.   would have been
The garden here is more convenient.
5 RICHARD PLANTAGENET   Then say at once if I maintained the truth;
Or else was wrangling Somerset in th'error?
SUFFOLK   Faith, I have been a truant in the law,
And never yet could frame° my will to it,   adapt
And therefore frame the law unto my will.
10 SOMERSET   Judge you, my lord of Warwick, then between us.
WARWICK   Between two hawks, which flies the higher pitch,°   height

---

6. Smallest part of the whole man (and, by implication, of the whole army that constitutes Talbot's military presence).
7. The entire structure of my body (and of my army).

8. This is a dealer in riddles as occasion requires.
2.4 Location: The Temple Garden, near the Middle and Inner Temple, two buildings that housed the London law schools known as the Inns of Court.

Between two dogs, which hath the deeper mouth,°   *voice*
Between two blades, which bears the better temper,[1]
Between two horses, which doth bear him best,
15   Between two girls, which hath the merriest eye,
I have perhaps some shallow spirit of judgement;
But in these nice° sharp quillets° of the law,   *precise / distinctions*
Good faith, I am no wiser than a daw.[2]
RICHARD PLANTAGENET   Tut, tut, here is a mannerly forbearance.
20   The truth appears so naked on my side
That any purblind° eye may find it out.   *half-blind*
SOMERSET   And on my side it is so well apparelled,
So clear, so shining, and so evident,
That it will glimmer through a blind man's eye.
25   RICHARD PLANTAGENET   Since you are tongue-tied and so loath to speak,
In dumb significants° proclaim your thoughts.   *silent gestures*
Let him that is a true-born gentleman
And stands upon the honour of his birth,
If he suppose that I have pleaded truth,[3]
30   From off this briar pluck a white rose[4] with me.
       [*He plucks a white rose*]
SOMERSET   Let him that is no coward nor no flatterer,
But dare maintain the party° of the truth,   *side*
Pluck a red rose[5] from off this thorn with me.
       [*He plucks a red rose*]
WARWICK   I love no colours,° and without all colour   *hues; pretenses*
35   Of base insinuating flattery
I pluck this white rose with Plantagenet.
SUFFOLK   I pluck this red rose with young Somerset,
And say withal° I think he held the right.   *besides*
VERNON   Stay, lords and gentlemen, and pluck no more
40   Till you conclude that he upon whose side
The fewest roses from the tree are cropped
Shall yield° the other in the right opinion.   *concede*
SOMERSET   Good Master Vernon, it is well objected.°   *urged*
If I have fewest, I subscribe° in silence.   *submit*
45   RICHARD PLANTAGENET   And I.
VERNON   Then for the truth and plainness of the case
I pluck this pale and maiden blossom here,
Giving my verdict on the white rose' side.
SOMERSET   Prick not your finger as you pluck it off,
50   Lest, bleeding, you do paint the white rose red,
And fall on my side so against your will.
VERNON   If I, my lord, for my opinion° bleed,   *conviction*
Opinion° shall be surgeon to my hurt   *Reputation*
And keep me on the side where still I am.
55   SOMERSET   Well, well, come on! Who else?
LAWYER   Unless my study and my books be false,

---

1. *the better temper*: this refers to the degree of hardness attained by a steel swordblade when it is tempered (that is, heated to a required temperature and then plunged into cold liquid).
2. Jackdaw (a proverbially stupid bird).
3. Presented the case for truth according to proper procedures. (This scene contains many legal terms.)
4. Badge of the House of York. In the mid-fifteenth cen-

tury, two branches of the Plantagenet dynasty, the Yorkists and the Lancastrians, fought what was termed the War of the Roses over who would hold the English throne. Shakespeare invented this scene to provide a point of origin for the quarrel that grew into the civil wars he depicted in his plays on the reigns of Henry VI, Edward IV, and Richard III.
5. Badge of the House of Lancaster.

The argument you held was wrong in law;
In sign whereof I pluck a white rose too.
RICHARD PLANTAGENET   Now Somerset, where is your argument?
60   SOMERSET   Here in my scabbard, meditating that°   *thinking of what*
Shall dye your white rose in a bloody red.
RICHARD PLANTAGENET   Meantime your cheeks do counterfeit° our roses,   *imitate*
For pale they look with fear, as witnessing
The truth on our side.
SOMERSET   No, Plantagenet,
65   'Tis not for fear, but anger, that thy cheeks
Blush for pure shame to counterfeit our roses,
And yet thy tongue will not confess thy error.
RICHARD PLANTAGENET   Hath not thy rose a canker,° Somerset?   *cankerworm; grub*
SOMERSET   Hath not thy rose a thorn, Plantagenet?
70   RICHARD PLANTAGENET   Ay, sharp and piercing, to maintain his° truth,   *its*
Whiles thy consuming canker eats his falsehood.
SOMERSET   Well, I'll find friends to wear my bleeding roses,
That shall maintain what I have said is true,
Where false Plantagenet dare not be seen.
75   RICHARD PLANTAGENET   Now, by this maiden blossom in my hand,
I scorn thee and thy fashion,° peevish boy.   *sort*
SUFFOLK   Turn not thy scorns this way, Plantagenet.
RICHARD PLANTAGENET   Proud Pole,[6] I will, and scorn both him and thee.
SUFFOLK   I'll turn my part thereof into thy throat.[7]
80   SOMERSET   Away, away, good William de la Pole.
We grace° the yeoman[8] by conversing with him.   *do honor to*
WARWICK   Now, by God's will, thou wrong'st him, Somerset.
His grandfather was Lionel Duke of Clarence,
Third son to the third Edward, King of England.[9]
85   Spring crestless° yeomen from so deep a root?   *without a coat of arms*
RICHARD PLANTAGENET   He bears him on the place's privilege,[1]
Or durst not for his craven° heart say thus.   *cowardly*
SOMERSET   By him that made me, I'll maintain my words
On any plot of ground in Christendom.
90   Was not thy father, Richard Earl of Cambridge,
For treason executed in our late king's days?
And by his treason stand'st not thou attainted,[2]
Corrupted, and exempt° from ancient gentry?   *excluded*
His trespass yet lives guilty in thy blood,
95   And till thou be restored[3] thou art a yeoman.
RICHARD PLANTAGENET   My father was attachèd, not attainted;[4]
Condemned to die for treason, but no traitor—
And that I'll prove on better men than Somerset,
Were growing time once ripened to my will.[5]
100   For your partaker° Pole, and you yourself,   *As for your ally*

6. The Duke of Suffolk's family name.
7. I'll throw the slanders back into your throat.
8. A man, below the rank of gentleman, holding a small estate. (Richard Plantagenet lost his lands and titles when Henry V executed his father, Richard, Earl of Cambridge, for treason.)
9. Clarence was actually Richard's great-great-grandfather on his mother's side. Edmund, Duke of York, fifth son of Edward III, was his paternal grandfather; thus Richard could trace his descent from Edward III through both his mother and his father.
1. He takes advantage of the safety provided by a privi-
leged place. Quarreling with drawn weapons was prohibited in some precincts, but the Temple, though originally founded as a religious house, was not one of them.
2. Condemned for treason. One so convicted lost his estate and property. His blood was declared "corrupted" (see line 93), so he could neither inherit nor transmit property and titles.
3. Are given back your lands and titles.
4. Was arrested, not convicted. Plantagenet implies that his father's execution was illegal because there was no parliamentary bill of attainder.
5. If the unfolding of time brings me my desire.

I'll note you in my book of memory,
To scourge you for this apprehension.°   *opinion*
Look to it well, and say you are well warned.
SOMERSET   Ah, thou shalt find us ready for thee still,
105   And know us by these colours for thy foes,
For these my friends, in spite of° thee, shall wear.   *in contempt of*
RICHARD PLANTAGENET   And, by my soul, this pale and angry rose,
As cognizance° of my blood-drinking hate,   *an emblem*
Will I forever, and my faction, wear
110   Until it wither with me to my grave,
Or flourish to the height of my degree.°   *noble rank*
SUFFOLK   Go forward, and be choked with thy ambition.
And so farewell until I meet thee next.   *Exit*
SOMERSET   Have with thee,° Pole.—Farewell, ambitious Richard.   *Let us go*
                                                            Exit
115   RICHARD PLANTAGENET   How I am braved,° and must perforce endure it!   *insulted*
WARWICK   This blot that they object° against your house   *allege*
Shall be wiped out in the next parliament,
Called for the truce of° Winchester and Gloucester.   *to make peace between*
An if° thou be not then created York,   *An if = If*
120   I will not live to be accounted Warwick.
Meantime, in signal of my love to thee,
Against proud Somerset and William Pole,
Will I upon thy party wear this rose.
And here I prophesy: this brawl today,
125   Grown to this faction° in the Temple garden,   *conflict*
Shall send, between the red rose and the white,
A thousand souls to death and deadly night.
RICHARD PLANTAGENET   Good Master Vernon, I am bound to you,
That you on my behalf would pluck a flower.
130   VERNON   In your behalf still will I wear the same.
LAWYER   And so will I.
RICHARD PLANTAGENET   Thanks, gentles.
Come, let us four to dinner. I dare say
This quarrel will drink blood another day.
                        Exeunt. [The rose brier is removed]

2.5

Enter [Edmund] MORTIMER, *brought in a chair [by his*
KEEPERS]¹
MORTIMER   Kind keepers of my weak decaying age,
Let dying Mortimer here rest himself.
Even like a man new-halèd° from the rack,²   *newly dragged*
So fare my limbs with long imprisonment;
5   And these grey locks, the pursuivants° of death,   *heralds*
Argue the end of Edmund Mortimer,³

2.5 Location: A cell in the Tower of London.
1. F's stage direction reads: "Enter Mortimer, brought in
in a Chair and Jailors."
2. Instrument of torture on which the victim's body was
stretched.
3. As in the sources that Shakespeare probably used, several historical Mortimers are conflated here. In 1385,
Richard II declared Roger Mortimer, 4th Earl of March,
his heir. When Roger died in battle in 1398, his claim
passed to Edmund Mortimer, 5th Earl of March and
uncle of Richard Plantagenet, who in turn inherited the
Mortimer claim to the throne. It was Edmund's cousin
Sir John Mortimer, however, who lay imprisoned in the
Tower until 1424, when he was executed for advocating
Edmund's claim to the throne.

Nestor-like⁴ agèd in an age of care.
These eyes, like lamps whose wasting oil is spent,
Wax dim, as drawing to their exigent;°   *end*
10   Weak shoulders, overborne with burdening grief,
And pithless° arms, like to a withered vine   *strengthless*
That droops his° sapless branches to the ground.   *its*
Yet are these feet—whose strengthless stay° is numb,   *support*
Unable to support this lump of clay—
15   Swift-wingèd with desire to get a grave,
As witting° I no other comfort have.   *knowing*
But tell me, keeper, will my nephew come?
KEEPER   Richard Plantagenet, my lord, will come.
We sent unto the Temple, unto his chamber,
20   And answer was returned that he will come.
MORTIMER   Enough. My soul shall then be satisfied.
Poor gentleman, his wrong° doth equal mine.   *(wrong done to him)*
Since Henry Monmouth° first began to reign—   *(Henry V)*
Before whose glory I was great in arms—
25   This loathsome sequestration° have I had;   *imprisonment*
And even since then hath Richard been obscured,
Deprived of honour and inheritance.
But now the arbitrator of despairs,
Just Death, kind umpire of men's miseries,
30   With sweet enlargement° doth dismiss me hence.   *release*
I would his° troubles likewise were expired,   *(Richard's)*
That so he might recover what was lost.
          Enter RICHARD [PLANTAGENET]
KEEPER   My lord, your loving nephew now is come.
MORTIMER   Richard Plantagenet, my friend, is he come?
35   RICHARD PLANTAGENET   Ay, noble uncle, thus ignobly used:
Your nephew, late° despisèd Richard, comes.   *recently*
MORTIMER [*to* KEEPERS]   Direct mine arms I may embrace his neck
And in his bosom spend my latter° gasp.   *final*
O tell me when my lips do touch his cheeks,
40   That I may kindly give one fainting kiss.
          [*He embraces* RICHARD]
And now declare, sweet stem from York's great stock,°   *trunk*
Why didst thou say of late thou wert despised?
RICHARD PLANTAGENET   First lean thine agèd back against mine arm,
And in that ease I'll tell thee my dis-ease.°   *trouble*
45   This day in argument upon a case
Some words there grew 'twixt Somerset and me;
Among which terms he used his lavish tongue
And did upbraid me with my father's death;
Which obloquy° set bars before my tongue,   *disgrace*
50   Else with the like I had requited him.
Therefore, good uncle, for my father's sake,
In honour of a true Plantagenet,
And for alliance'° sake, declare the cause   *kinship's*
My father, Earl of Cambridge, lost his head.
55   MORTIMER   That cause, fair nephew, that imprisoned me,
And hath detained me all my flow'ring youth
Within a loathsome dungeon, there to pine,

---

4. Like Nestor, the agèd Homeric hero and adviser famous for his wisdom.

Was cursèd instrument of his decease.

RICHARD PLANTAGENET Discover° more at large what cause that was,   *Explain*
60   For I am ignorant and cannot guess.

MORTIMER I will, if that my fading breath permit
And death approach not ere my tale be done.
Henry the Fourth, grandfather to this King,
Deposed his nephew° Richard, Edward's son,   *kinsman (here, cousin)*
65   The first begotten and the lawful heir
Of Edward king, the third of that descent;
During whose° reign the Percies of the north,   *(Henry IV's)*
Finding his usurpation most unjust,
Endeavoured my advancement to the throne.
70   The reason moved° these warlike lords to this   *that moved*
Was for that°—young King Richard thus removed,   *Was because*
Leaving no heir begotten of his body—
I was the next° by birth and parentage,   *(in line for the throne)*
For by my mother I derivèd° am   *descended*
75   From Lionel Duke of Clarence, the third son
To King Edward the Third—whereas the King
From John of Gaunt doth bring his pedigree,
Being but fourth of that heroic line.
But mark: as in this haughty° great attempt   *lofty*
80   They labourèd to plant the rightful heir,
I lost my liberty, and they their lives.
Long after this, when Henry the Fifth,
Succeeding his father Bolingbroke, did reign,
Thy father, Earl of Cambridge then, derived
85   From famous Edmund Langley, Duke of York,
Marrying my sister that thy mother was,
Again, in pity of my hard distress,
Levied an army, weening° to redeem   *intending*
And have installed me in the diadem;°   *crown*
90   But, as the rest, so fell that noble earl,
And was beheaded. Thus the Mortimers,
In whom the title rested, were suppressed.

RICHARD PLANTAGENET Of which, my lord, your honour is the last.

MORTIMER True, and thou seest that I no issue have,
95   And that my fainting words do warrant° death.   *promise*
Thou art my heir. The rest I wish thee gather°—   *infer*
But yet be wary in thy studious° care.   *diligent*

RICHARD PLANTAGENET Thy grave admonishments prevail with me.
But yet methinks my father's execution
100   Was nothing less than bloody tyranny.

MORTIMER With silence, nephew, be thou politic.°   *prudent*
Strong-fixèd is the house of Lancaster,
And like a mountain, not to be removed.
But now thy uncle is removing° hence,   *departing*
105   As princes do their courts, when they are cloyed°   *sickened*
With long continuance in a settled place.

RICHARD PLANTAGENET O uncle, would some part of my young years
Might but redeem the passage of your age.

MORTIMER Thou dost then wrong me, as that slaughterer doth
110   Which giveth many wounds when one will kill.
Mourn not, except° thou sorrow for my good.   *unless*
Only give order for my funeral.

And so farewell, and fair be all thy hopes,
And prosperous be thy life in peace and war. *Dies*
115 RICHARD PLANTAGENET   And peace, no war, befall thy parting soul.
In prison hast thou spent a pilgrimage,
And like a hermit overpassed° thy days. *spent*
Well, I will lock his counsel in my breast,
And what I do imagine, let that rest.
120 Keepers, convey him hence, and I myself
Will see his burial better than his life.⁵
Exeunt [KEEPERS *with Mortimer's body*]
Here dies the dusky torch of Mortimer,
Choked with° ambition of the meaner sort.⁶ *by*
And for° those wrongs, those bitter injuries, *And as for*
125 Which Somerset hath offered to my house,
I doubt not but with honour to redress.
And therefore haste I to the Parliament,
Either to be restorèd to my blood,° *inherited rights*
Or make mine ill th'advantage of my good.⁷ *Exit*

3.1

Flourish. Enter [*young*] KING [HENRY],¹ [*the Dukes of*]
EXETER, [*and*] GLOUCESTER, [*the Bishop of*] WINCHES-
TER, [*the Duke of*] SOMERSET, [*and the Earl of*] SUF-
FOLK, [*with red roses, the Earl of*] WARWICK, [*and*]
RICHARD PLANTAGENET [*with white roses*].² GLOUCES-
TER *offers to put up a bill;° WINCHESTER snatches it,* *written statement*
tears it

WINCHESTER   Com'st thou with deep premeditated lines?
With written pamphlets studiously devised?
Humphrey of Gloucester, if thou canst accuse,
Or aught intend'st to lay unto my charge,
5   Do it without invention,° suddenly, *premeditated design*
As I with sudden and extemporal speech
Purpose to answer what thou canst object.° *lay to my charge*
GLOUCESTER   Presumptuous priest, this place° commands my patience, *(Parliament)*
Or thou shouldst find thou hast dishonoured me.
10   Think not, although in writing I preferred° *set out*
The manner of thy vile outrageous crimes,
That therefore I have forged, or am not able
Verbatim° to rehearse the method of my pen.³ *Orally*
No, prelate, such is thy audacious wickedness,
15   Thy lewd,° pestiferous,° and dissentious pranks, *base / deadly*
As very° infants prattle of thy pride. *That even*
Thou art a most pernicious usurer,⁴
Froward° by nature, enemy to peace, *Perverse*

---

5. *better than his life*: more sumptuous than the life he
led (in prison).
6. *meaner sort*: people of lower rank (referring to Bolingbroke and his line).
7. Or turn the injuries I have suffered to my advantage.
3.1 Location: The Parliament House, London.
1. The historical Henry VI was five years old at the time
of this Parliament. In this scene, Shakespeare refers to the
King's "tender years" but does not specify his age.
2. F does not mention that roses are worn in this scene,

but in 2.4 the rival factions promised to wear them forever. This edition indicates their presence throughout the
ensuing action.
3. To recount the order of the argument I wrote.
4. Alluding to the fact that Winchester's wealth was partly
derived from his use of a papal bull and partly from the
Southwark brothels (see 1.4.35 and note). In *Measure for
Measure*, Shakespeare refers to prostitution as one of the
"two usuries" (3.1.6). Moneylending bred interest; prostitution bred both illicit offspring and financial profit.

Lascivious, wanton, more than well beseems
20 A man of thy profession and degree.°   *rank*
And for° thy treachery, what's more manifest?—   *And as for*
In that thou laid'st a trap to take my life,
As well at London Bridge as at the Tower.
Beside, I fear me, if thy thoughts were sifted,°   *closely examined*
25 The King thy sovereign is not quite exempt
From envious malice of thy swelling heart.
WINCHESTER   Gloucester, I do defy thee.—Lords, vouchsafe
To give me hearing what I shall reply.
If I were covetous, ambitious, or perverse,
30 As he will have me, how am I so poor?
Or how haps it I seek not to advance
Or raise myself, but keep my wonted° calling?   *customary*
And for dissension, who preferreth peace
More than I do?—except I be provoked.
35 No, my good lords, it is not that offends;
It is not that that hath incensed the Duke.
It is because no one should sway° but he,   *rule*
No one but he should be about the King—
And that engenders thunder in his breast
40 And makes him roar these accusations forth.
But he shall know I am as good—
GLOUCESTER   As good?—
Thou bastard of my grandfather.[5]
WINCHESTER   Ay, lordly sir; for what are you, I pray,
45 But one imperious° in another's throne?   *ruling*
GLOUCESTER   Am I not Protector, saucy priest?
WINCHESTER   And am not I a prelate of the Church?
GLOUCESTER   Yes—as an outlaw in a castle keeps°   *dwells*
And useth it to patronage° his theft.   *protect*
WINCHESTER   Unreverent Gloucester.
50 GLOUCESTER   Thou art reverend
Touching° thy spiritual function, not thy life.   *With regard to*
WINCHESTER   Rome shall remedy this.
GLOUCESTER[6]   Roam thither then.
WARWICK [*to* WINCHESTER]   My lord, it were your duty to forbear.
SOMERSET   Ay, so° the bishop be not overborne:°   *as long as / overruled*
55 Methinks my lord° should be religious,°   *(Gloucester) / pious*
And know the office° that belongs to such.°   *duty / (prelates)*
WARWICK   Methinks his lordship° should be humbler.   *(Winchester)*
It fitteth not a prelate so to plead.°   *wrangle*
SOMERSET   Yes, when his holy state is touched so near.°   *affected so directly*
60 WARWICK   State holy or unhallowed, what of that?
Is not his grace Protector to the King?
RICHARD PLANTAGENET [*aside*]   Plantagenet, I see, must hold his tongue,
Lest it be said, 'Speak, sirrah,[7] when you should;
Must your bold verdict intertalk° with lords?'   *bold opinion converse*
65 Else would I have a fling at Winchester.
KING HENRY   Uncles of Gloucester and of Winchester,
The special watchmen of our English weal,°   *well-being; state*

---

5. Winchester was born an illegitimate son of Gloucester's grandfather, John of Gaunt, though later he was
made legitimate by an act of Parliament.
6. F assigns this line to Warwick, but giving it to Gloucester further heightens the antipathy between Winchester
and the Lord Protector.
7. Term used to address social inferiors.

    I would prevail, if prayers might prevail,
    To join your hearts in love and amity.
70   O what a scandal is it to our crown
    That two such noble peers as ye should jar!°   *quarrel*
    Believe me, lords, my tender years can tell
    Civil dissension is a viperous worm
    That gnaws the bowels of the commonwealth.
       A noise within
75 SERVINGMEN [*within*]   Down with the tawny coats!⁸
  KING HENRY   What tumult's this?
  WARWICK   An uproar, I dare warrant,
    Begun through malice of the Bishop's men.
       A noise again
  SERVINGMEN [*within*]   Stones, stones!
       Enter [the] MAYOR [*of London*]
  MAYOR   O my good lords, and virtuous Henry,
80   Pity the city of London, pity us!
    The Bishop and the Duke of Gloucester's men,
    Forbidden late° to carry any weapon,   *lately*
    Have filled their pockets full of pebble stones
    And, banding themselves in contrary parts,°   *opposing parties*
85   Do pelt so fast at one another's pate
    That many have their giddy brains knocked out.
    Our windows are broke down in every street,
    And we for fear compelled to shut our shops.
       Enter in skirmish, with bloody pates[, Winchester's SERV-
         INGMEN *in tawny coats and Gloucester's in blue coats*]
  KING HENRY   We charge you, on allegiance to ourself,
90   To hold your slaught'ring hands and keep the peace.
       [*The skirmish ceases*]
    Pray, Uncle Gloucester, mitigate this strife.
  FIRST SERVINGMAN   Nay, if we be forbidden stones, we'll fall to
    it with our teeth.
  SECOND SERVINGMAN   Do what ye dare, we are as resolute.
       Skirmish again
95 GLOUCESTER   You of my household, leave this peevish broil,°   *this foolish fight*
    And set this unaccustomed° fight aside.   *unusual; disorderly*
  THIRD SERVINGMAN   My lord, we know your grace to be a man
    Just and upright and, for your royal birth,
    Inferior to none but to his majesty;
100   And ere that° we will suffer such a prince,   *And before*
    So kind a father of the commonweal,
    To be disgracèd° by an inkhorn mate,°   *insulted / scribbler*
    We and our wives and children all will fight
    And have our bodies slaughtered by thy foes.
105 FIRST SERVINGMAN   Ay, and the very parings of our nails
    Shall pitch a field⁹ when we are dead.
       [*They*] *begin* [*to skirmish*] *again*
  GLOUCESTER   Stay, stay, I say!
    An if you love me as you say you do,
    Let me persuade you to forbear a while.

---

8. Again, this line is included as part of the stage directions in F and is here plausibly assigned to "Servingmen." The same is true at line 78, where F's stage direction reads: "A noise again, Stones, Stones."

9. Shall fortify a battlefield (usually with defensive wood or iron stakes).

KING HENRY   O how this discord doth afflict my soul!
110   Can you, my lord of Winchester, behold
      My sighs and tears, and will not once relent?
      Who should be pitiful° if you be not?   *merciful*
      Or who should study to prefer° a peace,   *propose*
      If holy churchmen take delight in broils?
115 WARWICK   Yield, my lord Protector; yield, Winchester—
      Except you mean with obstinate repulse°   *refusal*
      To slay your sovereign and destroy the realm.
      You see what mischief—and what murder, too—
      Hath been enacted through your enmity.
120   Then be at peace, except° ye thirst for blood.   *unless*
   WINCHESTER   He shall submit, or I will never yield.
   GLOUCESTER   Compassion on the King commands me stoop,
      Or I would see his heart out ere the priest
      Should ever get that privilege of° me.   *advantage over*
125 WARWICK   Behold, my lord of Winchester, the Duke
      Hath banished moody° discontented fury,   *sullen*
      As by his smoothèd brows it doth appear.
      Why look you still so stern and tragical?
   GLOUCESTER   Here, Winchester, I offer thee my hand.
130 KING HENRY [*to* WINCHESTER]   Fie, Uncle Beaufort! I have heard you preach
      That malice was a great and grievous sin;
      And will not you maintain the thing you teach,
      But prove a chief offender in the same?
   WARWICK   Sweet King! The Bishop hath a kindly gird.°   *a gentle rebuke*
135   For shame, my lord of Winchester, relent.
      What, shall a child instruct you what to do?
   WINCHESTER   Well, Duke of Gloucester, I will yield to thee
      Love for thy love, and hand for hand I give.
   GLOUCESTER [*aside*]   Ay, but I fear me with a hollow° heart.   *an insincere*
140   [*To the others*] See here, my friends and loving countrymen,
      This token serveth for a flag of truce
      Betwixt ourselves and all our followers.
      So help me God, as I dissemble not.
   WINCHESTER   So help me God [*aside*] as I intend it not.
145 KING HENRY   O loving uncle, kind Duke of Gloucester,
      How joyful am I made by this contract!
      [*To* SERVINGMEN] Away, my masters, trouble us no more,
      But join in friendship as your lords have done.
   FIRST SERVINGMAN   Content. I'll to the surgeon's.
150 SECOND SERVINGMAN   And so will I.
   THIRD SERVINGMAN   And I will see what physic° the tavern   *medicine*
      affords.
                Exeunt [*the* MAYOR *and* SERVINGMEN]
   WARWICK   Accept this scroll, most gracious sovereign,
      Which in the right of Richard Plantagenet
155   We do exhibit to your majesty.
   GLOUCESTER   Well urged, my lord of Warwick—for, sweet prince,
      An if your grace mark every circumstance,
      You have great reason to do Richard right,
      Especially for those occasions°   *reasons*
160   At Eltham Place I told your majesty.
   KING HENRY   And those occasions, uncle, were of force.—
      Therefore, my loving lords, our pleasure is

That Richard be restorèd to his blood.
WARWICK Let Richard be restorèd to his blood.
165 So shall his father's wrongs be recompensed.
WINCHESTER As will the rest, so willeth Winchester.
KING HENRY If Richard will be true,° not that alone   *loyal*
      But all the whole inheritance I give
      That doth belong unto the house of York,
170 From whence you spring by lineal descent.[1]
RICHARD PLANTAGENET Thy humble servant vows obedience
      And humble service till the point of death.
KING HENRY Stoop then, and set your knee against my foot.
      [RICHARD *kneels*]
      And in reguerdon° of that duty done,   *reward*
175 I gird thee with the valiant sword of York.
      Rise, Richard, like a true Plantagenet,
      And rise created princely Duke of York.
RICHARD DUKE OF YORK [*rising*] And so thrive Richard, as thy
            foes may fall;
      And as my duty springs, so perish they
180 That grudge one thought° against your majesty.   *hold any grudges*
ALL BUT RICHARD AND SOMERSET Welcome, high prince, the
            mighty Duke of York!
SOMERSET [*aside*] Perish, base prince, ignoble Duke of York!
GLOUCESTER Now will it best avail your majesty
      To cross the seas and to be crowned in France.
185 The presence of a king engenders love
      Amongst his subjects and his loyal friends,
      As it disanimates° his enemies.   *discourages*
KING HENRY When Gloucester says the word, King Henry goes,
      For friendly counsel cuts off many foes.
190 GLOUCESTER Your ships already are in readiness.
            Sennet.[2] *Exeunt. Manet*° EXETER   *Remains*
EXETER Ay, we may march in England or in France,
      Not seeing what is likely to ensue.
      This late° dissension grown betwixt the peers   *recent*
      Burns under feignèd ashes of forged love,
195 And will at last break out into a flame.
      As festered members° rot but by degree   *parts of the body*
      Till bones and flesh and sinews fall away,
      So will this base and envious discord breed.
      And now I fear that fatal prophecy
200 Which, in the time of Henry named the Fifth,
      Was in the mouth of every sucking babe:
      That 'Henry born at Monmouth° should win all,   *(Henry V)*
      And Henry born at Windsor° should lose all' —   *(Henry VI)*
      Which is so plain that Exeter doth wish
205 His days may finish, ere that hapless time.   *Exit*

---

1. *But . . . descent*: the King restores Richard not only to   also to the dukedom of York (inherited from his uncle).
the earldom of Cambridge (inherited from his father) but   2. Trumpet notes that accompany a procession.

3.2

Enter [JOAN la] Pucelle, disguised, with four [French]
SOLDIERS *with sacks upon their backs*

JOAN   These are the city gates, the gates of Rouen,
   Through which our policy° must make a breach.   *trickery*
   Take heed. Be wary how you place your words.
   Talk like the vulgar° sort of market men   *common*
5   That come to gather money for their corn.°   *grain*
   If we have entrance, as I hope we shall,
   And that° we find the slothful watch but weak,   *if*
   I'll by a sign give notice to our friends,
   That Charles the Dauphin may encounter them.
10 A SOLDIER   Our sacks shall be a mean° to sack the city,   *means*
   And we be lords and rulers over Rouen.
   Therefore we'll knock.
       [They] knock
WATCH [*within*]   *Qui là?*°   *Who is there*
JOAN   *Paysans, la pauvre gens de France:*[1]
   Poor market folks that come to sell their corn.
15 WATCH [*opening the gates*]   Enter, go in. The market bell is rung.
JOAN [*aside*]   Now, Rouen, I'll shake thy bulwarks to the ground.
                                Exeunt

3.3

Enter CHARLES *[the Dauphin, the]* BASTARD *[of Orléans,*
the Duke of] ALENÇON[, RENÉ *Duke of Anjou, and*
French soldiers]

CHARLES   Saint Denis bless this happy stratagem,
   And once again we'll sleep secure in Rouen.
BASTARD   Here entered Pucelle and her practisants.°   *conspirators*
   Now she is there, how will she specify
5   'Here is the best and safest passage in'?
RENÉ   By thrusting out a torch from yonder tower—
   Which, once discerned, shows that her meaning is:
   No way to that, for weakness, which she entered.[1]
       *Enter [*JOAN la*] Pucelle on the top, thrusting out a torch*
       burning
JOAN   Behold, this is the happy wedding torch
10   That joineth Rouen unto her countrymen,
   But burning fatal to the Talbonites.°   *followers of Talbot*
BASTARD   See, noble Charles, the beacon of our friend.
   The burning torch in yonder turret stands.
CHARLES   Now shine it° like a comet of revenge,   *may it shine*
15   A prophet to the fall of all our foes!
RENÉ   Defer no time; delays have dangerous ends.
   Enter and cry, 'The Dauphin!', presently,°   *at once*
   And then do execution on the watch.°   *Alarum. [Exeunt]*   *then kill the guards*

3.4

An alarum. [Enter Lord] TALBOT *in an excursion*°   *a skirmish*
TALBOT   France, thou shalt rue this treason with thy tears,
   If Talbot but survive thy treachery.

3.2 Location: In and around Rouen, France.
1. Peasants, the poor folk of France.
3.3 Location: Scene continues.

1. No entrance is as weakly guarded as the one she
entered.
3.4 Location: Scene continues.

Pucelle, that witch, that damnèd sorceress,
Hath wrought this hellish mischief unawares,°   *unexpectedly*
5   That hardly we escaped the pride of France.¹   *Exit*

3.5

An alarum. Excursions. [The Duke of] BEDFORD
brought in sick, in a chair. Enter [Lord] TALBOT and
[the Duke of] BURGUNDY, without; within,¹ [JOAN la]
Pucelle, CHARLES [the Dauphin, the] BASTARD [of
Orléans, the Duke of ALENÇON], and RENÉ [Duke of
Anjou] on the walls

JOAN   Good morrow gallants. Want ye corn for bread?
I think the Duke of Burgundy will fast
Before he'll buy again at such a rate.
'Twas full of darnel.° Do you like the taste?   *weeds*
5   BURGUNDY   Scoff on, vile fiend and shameless courtesan.
I trust ere long to choke thee with thine own,°   *your own bread*
And make thee curse the harvest of that corn.
CHARLES   Your grace may starve, perhaps, before that time.
BEDFORD   O let no words, but deeds, revenge this treason.
10   JOAN   What will you do, good graybeard? Break a lance
And run a-tilt at° death within a chair?   *joust with*
TALBOT   Foul fiend of France, and hag of all despite,°   *most despicable*
Encompassed with thy lustful paramours,
Becomes it thee to taunt his valiant age
15   And twit with cowardice a man half dead?
Damsel, I'll have a bout° with you again,   *fight; sexual struggle*
Or else let Talbot perish with this shame.
JOAN   Are ye so hot,° sir? —Yet, Pucelle, hold thy peace.   *angry; lustful*
If Talbot do but thunder, rain will follow.
They [the English] whisper together in counsel
20   God speed the parliament; who shall be the Speaker?
TALBOT   Dare ye come forth and meet us in the field?
JOAN   Belike your lordship takes us then for fools,
To try if that our own be ours or no.
TALBOT   I speak not to that railing Hecate²
25   But unto thee, Alençon, and the rest.
Will ye, like soldiers, come and fight it out?
ALENÇON   Seignieur, no.
TALBOT   Seignieur, hang! Base muleteers° of   *Lowborn mule drivers*
    France,
Like peasant footboys do they keep° the walls   *stay near*
And dare not take up arms like gentlemen.
30   JOAN   Away, captains, let's get us from the walls,
For Talbot means no goodness by his looks.
Goodbye, my lord. We came but to tell you
That we are here.   *Exeunt [French] from the walls*
TALBOT   And there will we be, too, ere it be long,
35   Or else reproach be Talbot's greatest fame.
Vow Burgundy, by honour of thy house,
Pricked on° by public wrongs sustained in France,   *Urged on*
Either to get the town again or die.

---

1. That only with difficulty we escaped the princely
power of France.
3.5 Location: Scene continues.
1. The stage directions suggest that Talbot's party is on

the main stage; Joan's party may appear on the upper
stage gallery.
2. In classical myth, the goddess of night and the underworld and the patron of witchcraft.

And I—as sure as English Henry lives,
40 And as his father here was conqueror;[3]
As sure as in this late° betrayèd town   *recently*
Great Cœur-de-lion's heart was burièd[4]—
So sure I swear to get the town or die.
BURGUNDY   My vows are equal partners with thy vows.
45 TALBOT   But ere we go, regard this dying prince,
The valiant Duke of Bedford. [*To* BEDFORD] Come, my lord,
We will bestow you in some better place,
Fitter for sickness and for crazy° age.   *feeble*
BEDFORD   Lord Talbot, do not so dishonour me.
50 Here will I sit before the walls of Rouen,
And will be partner of your weal or woe.
BURGUNDY   Courageous Bedford, let us now persuade you.
BEDFORD   Not to be gone from hence; for once I read
That stout Pendragon,[5] in his litter sick,
55 Came to the field and vanquishèd his foes.
Methinks I should revive the soldiers' hearts,
Because I ever found them as myself.
TALBOT   Undaunted spirit in a dying breast!
Then be it so; heavens keep old Bedford safe.
60 And now no more ado, brave Burgundy,
But gather we our forces out of hand,°   *at once*
And set upon our boasting enemy.   *Exit* [*with* BURGUNDY]
An alarum. Excursions. Enter Sir John FASTOLF *and a*
CAPTAIN
CAPTAIN   Whither away, Sir John Fastolf, in such haste?
FASTOLF   Whither away? To save myself by flight.
65 We are like to have the overthrow° again.   *to be defeated*
CAPTAIN   What, will you fly, and leave Lord Talbot?
FASTOLF   Ay, all the Talbots in the world, to save my life.   *Exit*
CAPTAIN   Cowardly knight, ill fortune follow thee!   *Exit*
Retreat. Excursions. [JOAN *la*] *Pucelle,* ALENÇON, *and*
CHARLES *fly*
BEDFORD   Now, quiet soul, depart when heaven please,
70 For I have seen our enemies' overthrow.
What is the trust or strength of foolish man?
They that of late were daring with their scoffs
Are glad and fain° by flight to save themselves.   *eager*
BEDFORD *dies, and is carried in by two in his chair*

3.6

An alarum. Enter [*Lord*] TALBOT, [*the Duke of*] BUR-
GUNDY, *and the rest* [*of the English soldiers*]
TALBOT   Lost and recovered in a day again!
This is a double honour, Burgundy;
Yet heavens have glory for this victory!
BURGUNDY   Warlike and martial Talbot, Burgundy
5 Enshrines thee in his heart, and there erects
Thy noble deeds as valour's monuments.

---

3. Henry V had captured Rouen in 1419.
4. According to Holinshed's *Chronicles*, Richard Coeur-
de-Lion (the Lion-Hearted), who ruled England from
1189 to 1199, willed that his heart be buried in Rouen as
a sign of his love for the city.

5. Uther Pendragon, the father of King Arthur. This story
is told in Geoffrey of Monmouth's history of Britain (*His-
toria Regnum Britanniae*). **stout**: brave.
3.6 Location: Scene continues.

TALBOT Thanks, gentle° Duke. But where is Pucelle now?   *noble*
I think her old familiar° is asleep.   *attendant demon*
Now where's the Bastard's braves,° and Charles his gleeks?°   *boasts / Charles's jests*
10 What, all amort?° Rouen hangs her head for grief   *dispirited*
That such a valiant company are fled.
Now will we take some order° in the town,   *establish order*
Placing therein some expert officers,
And then depart to Paris, to the King,
15 For there young Henry with his nobles lie.°   *lives*
BURGUNDY What wills Lord Talbot pleaseth Burgundy.
TALBOT But yet, before we go, let's not forget
The noble Duke of Bedford late deceased,
But see his exequies° fulfilled in Rouen.   *funeral rites*
20 A braver soldier never couchèd° lance;   *leveled (for attack)*
A gentler heart did never sway in court.
But kings and mightiest potentates must die,
For that's the end of human misery.   *Exeunt*

3.7

Enter CHARLES [*the Dauphin, the*] BASTARD [*of Orléans,*
the Duke of] ALENÇON, [JOAN *la*] *Pucelle* [*and French*
soldiers]

JOAN Dismay not, princes, at this accident,
Nor grieve that Rouen is so recoverèd.
Care° is no cure, but rather corrosive,°   *Sorrow / destructive*
For things that are not to be remedied.
5 Let frantic° Talbot triumph for a while,   *mad*
And like a peacock sweep along his tail;
We'll pull his plumes and take away his train,°   *peacock's tail; army*
If Dauphin and the rest will be but ruled.
CHARLES We have been guided by thee hitherto,
10 And of thy cunning had no diffidence.°   *doubt*
One sudden foil° shall never breed distrust.   *defeat*
BASTARD [*to* JOAN] Search out thy wit for secret policies,°   *stratagems*
And we will make thee famous through the world.
ALENÇON [*to* JOAN] We'll set thy statue in some holy place
15 And have thee reverenced like a blessèd saint.
Employ thee then, sweet virgin, for our good.
JOAN Then thus it must be; this doth Joan devise:
By fair persuasions mixed with sugared words
We will entice the Duke of Burgundy
20 To leave the Talbot and to follow us.
CHARLES Ay, marry, sweeting,° if we could do that   *(a lover's nickname)*
France were no place for Henry's warriors,
Nor should that nation boast it so with us,
But be extirpèd° from our provinces.   *rooted out*
25 ALENÇON For ever should they be expulsed from France
And not have title of an earldom here.
JOAN Your honours shall perceive how I will work
To bring this matter to the wishèd end.
    Drum sounds afar off
Hark, by the sound of drum you may perceive
30 Their powers are marching unto Paris-ward.°   *toward Paris*

3.7 Location: Plains near Rouen.

Here sound an English march
There goes the Talbot, with his colours spread,°   *flags unfurled*
And all the troops of English after him.
    [*Here sound a*] *French march*
Now in the rearward comes the Duke and his;
Fortune in favour° makes him lag behind.   *as a favor to us*
35   Summon a parley.[1] We will talk with him.
    Trumpets sound a parley
CHARLES [*calling*]   A parley with the Duke of Burgundy.
    [*Enter the Duke of* BURGUNDY]
BURGUNDY   Who craves a parley with the Burgundy?
JOAN   The princely Charles of France, thy countryman.
BURGUNDY   What sayst thou, Charles?—for I am marching hence.
40   CHARLES   Speak, Pucelle, and enchant him with thy words.
    JOAN   Brave Burgundy, undoubted° hope of France,   *certain*
    Stay. Let thy humble handmaid speak to thee.
BURGUNDY   Speak on, but be not over-tedious.
JOAN   Look on thy country, look on fertile France,
45   And see the cities and the towns defaced
    By wasting ruin of the cruel foe.
    As looks the mother on her lowly babe
    When death doth close his tender-dying° eyes,   *young-dying*
    See, see the pining malady of France;
50   Behold the wounds, the most unnatural wounds,
    Which thou thyself hast given her woeful breast.
    O turn thy edgèd sword another way,
    Strike those that hurt, and hurt not those that help.
    One drop of blood drawn from thy country's bosom
55   Should grieve thee more than streams of foreign gore.
    Return thee, therefore, with a flood of tears,
    And wash away thy country's stainèd spots.[2]
BURGUNDY [*aside*]   Either she hath bewitched me with her words,
    Or nature makes me suddenly relent.
60   JOAN   Besides, all French and France exclaims on° thee,   *denounces*
    Doubting thy birth and lawful progeny.°   *ancestry*
    Who join'st thou with but with a lordly nation
    That will not trust thee but for profit's sake?
    When Talbot hath set footing once in France
65   And fashioned thee that instrument of ill,
    Who then but English Henry will be lord,
    And thou be thrust out like a fugitive?
    Call we to mind, and mark but this for proof:
    Was not the Duke of Orléans thy foe?
70   And was he not in England prisoner?
    But when they heard he was thine enemy
    They set him free, without his ransom paid,
    In spite of Burgundy and all his friends.[3]
    See, then, thou fight'st against thy countrymen,
75   And join'st with them will be thy slaughtermen.
    Come, come, return; return, thou wandering lord,
    Charles and the rest will take thee in their arms.

---

1. Sound a trumpet to request a conference.
2. And wash away the spots of blood that defile your country.
3. The historical Orléans was not released by the English until five years after Burgundy abandoned the English alliance.

BURGUNDY [*aside*] I am vanquishèd.[4] These haughty° words of hers   *lofty*
      Have battered me like roaring cannon-shot
80   And made me almost yield upon my knees.
      [*To the others*] Forgive me, country, and sweet countrymen;
      And lords, accept this hearty kind embrace.
      My forces and my power of men are yours.
      So farewell, Talbot. I'll no longer trust thee.
85 JOAN   Done like a Frenchman—[*aside*] turn and turn again.
    CHARLES   Welcome, brave Duke. Thy friendship makes us fresh.
    BASTARD   And doth beget new courage in our breasts.
    ALENÇON   Pucelle hath bravely played her part in this,
      And doth deserve a coronet of gold.
90 CHARLES   Now let us on, my lords, and join our powers,
      And seek how we may prejudice° the foe.   *Exeunt*   *hurt*

3.8

      [*Flourish.*] *Enter* KING [HENRY, *the Duke of*] GLOUCES-
      TER, [*the Bishop of*] WINCHESTER, [*the Duke of*] EXE-
      TER; [RICHARD DUKE OF] YORK, [*the Earl of*] WARWICK,
      [*and* VERNON *with white roses; the Earl of*] SUFFOLK,
      [*the Duke of*] SOMERSET [*and* BASSET *with red roses*]. *To
      them, with his soldiers,* [*enter Lord*] TALBOT
    TALBOT   My gracious prince and honourable peers,
      Hearing of your arrival in this realm
      I have a while given truce unto my wars
      To do my duty° to my sovereign;   *give homage*
5   In sign whereof, this arm that hath reclaimed
      To your obedience fifty fortresses,
      Twelve cities, and seven walled towns of strength,
      Beside five hundred prisoners of esteem,°   *noble rank*
      Lets fall his sword before your highness' feet,
10   And with submissive loyalty of heart
      Ascribes the glory of his conquest got
      First to my God, and next unto your grace.
            [*He kneels*][1]
    KING HENRY   Is this the Lord Talbot, uncle Gloucester,
      That hath so long been resident in France?
15 GLOUCESTER   Yes, if it please your majesty, my liege.
    KING HENRY [*to* TALBOT]   Welcome, brave captain and victorious lord.
      When I was young—as yet I am not old—
      I do remember how my father said
      A stouter champion never handled sword.
20   Long since we were resolvèd° of your truth,°   *convinced / loyalty*
      Your faithful service and your toil in war,
      Yet never have you tasted our reward,
      Or been reguerdoned° with so much as thanks,   *rewarded*
      Because till now we never saw your face.
      Therefore stand up,
            [TALBOT *rises*]
25   and for these good deserts
      We here create you Earl of Shrewsbury;

---

4. The historical Burgundy did not return to the French
side until four years after Joan's death.
3.8 Location: The palace, Paris.

1. F does not indicate when Talbot kneels, but he must
do so: at line 25, he is urged to "stand up."

And in our coronation take your place.[2]

Sennet. Exeunt. Manent° VERNON *and* BASSET   *Remain*

VERNON   Now sir, to you that were so hot° at sea,   *angry*
    Disgracing of these colours° that I wear   *this badge (the rose)*
30   In honour of my noble lord of York,
    Dar'st thou maintain the former words thou spak'st?

BASSET   Yes, sir, as well as you dare patronage°   *defend*
    The envious barking of your saucy tongue
    Against my lord the Duke of Somerset.

35 VERNON   Sirrah, thy lord I honour as he is.

BASSET   Why, what is he? — as good a man as York.

VERNON   Hark ye, not so. In witness, take ye that.
    [VERNON] *strikes him*

BASSET   Villain, thou know'st the law of arms[3] is such
    That whoso draws a sword 'tis present° death,   *immediate*
40   Or else this blow should broach° thy dearest blood.   *tap (as a wine vat)*
    But I'll unto his majesty and crave
    I may have liberty° to venge this wrong,   *permission*
    When thou shalt see I'll meet thee to thy cost.

VERNON   Well, miscreant,° I'll be there as soon as you,   *villain*
45   And after meet you sooner than you would.°   *Exeunt*   *would wish*

4.1

[*Flourish.*] *Enter* KING [HENRY, *the Duke of*] GLOUCES-
TER, [*the Bishop of*] WINCHESTER, [*the Duke of*] EXE-
TER, [RICHARD DUKE OF] YORK, [*and the Earl of*]
WARWICK, [*with white roses; the Earl of*] SUFFOLK, [*and
the Duke of*] SOMERSET, [*with red roses; Lord*] TALBOT,
and [*the*] Governor [*of Paris*]

GLOUCESTER   Lord Bishop, set the crown upon his head.

WINCHESTER   God save King Henry, of that name the sixth!
    [WINCHESTER *crowns the* KING]

GLOUCESTER   Now, Governor of Paris, take your oath
    That you elect° no other king but him;   *acknowledge*
5   Esteem none friends but such as are his friends,
    And none your foes but such as shall pretend°   *propose*
    Malicious practices against his state.
    This shall ye do, so help you righteous God.
    Enter [*Sir John*] FASTOLF [*with a letter*]

FASTOLF   My gracious sovereign, as I rode from Calais
10   To haste unto your coronation
    A letter was delivered to my hands,
    [*He presents the letter*]
    Writ to your grace from th' Duke of Burgundy.

TALBOT   Shame to the Duke of Burgundy and thee!
    I vowed, base knight, when I did meet thee next,
15   To tear the Garter[1] from thy craven's° leg,   *coward's*
    [*He tears it off*]
    Which I have done because unworthily
    Thou wast installèd in that high degree. —

---

2. The historical Talbot was created Earl of Shrewsbury in 1442, more than ten years after Henry's coronation.
3. The law that forbade fighting near a royal residence (see also 1.4.45 and 2.4.86).

4.1 Location: The palace, Paris.
1. A ribbon, worn below the left knee, signifying membership in the Order of the Garter, the highest rank of English knighthood.

Pardon me, princely Henry and the rest.
This dastard° at the battle of Patay   *coward*
20   When but in all° I was six thousand strong,   *When all told*
And that the French were almost ten to one,
Before we met, or that a stroke was given,
Like to a trusty° squire did run away;   *faithful (here ironic)*
In which assault we lost twelve hundred men.
25   Myself and divers gentlemen beside
Were there surprised and taken prisoners.
Then judge, great lords, if I have done amiss,
Or whether that such cowards ought to wear
This ornament of knighthood: yea or no?
30   GLOUCESTER   To say the truth, this fact° was infamous   *deed*
And ill beseeming any common man,
Much more a knight, a captain and a leader.
TALBOT   When first this order was ordained, my lords,
Knights of the Garter were of noble birth,
35   Valiant and virtuous, full of haughty° courage,   *lofty*
Such as were grown to credit° by the wars;   *fame*
Not fearing death nor shrinking for distress,
But always resolute in most extremes.°   *in greatest extremities*
He then that is not furnished in this sort°   *not endowed like this*
40   Doth but usurp the sacred name of knight,
Profaning this most honourable order,
And should—if I were worthy to be judge—
Be quite degraded,° like a hedge-born swain²   *reduced in rank*
That doth presume to boast of gentle° blood.   *noble*
KING HENRY [*to* FASTOLF]   Stain to thy countrymen, thou hear'st
45   thy doom.°   *sentence*
Be packing, therefore, thou that wast a knight.
Henceforth we banish thee on pain of death.   [*Exit* FASTOLF]
And now, my Lord Protector, view the letter
Sent from our uncle, Duke of Burgundy.³
GLOUCESTER   What means his grace that he hath changed his
50   style?°   *form of address*
No more but plain and bluntly 'To the King'?
Hath he forgot he is his sovereign?
Or doth this churlish superscription°   *rude address*
Pretend° some alteration in good will?   *Indicate*
55   What's here? 'I have upon especial cause,
Moved with compassion of my country's wrack°   *destruction*
Together with the pitiful complaints
Of such as your oppression feeds upon,
Forsaken your pernicious faction
60   And joined with Charles, the rightful King of France.'
O monstrous treachery! Can this be so?
That in alliance, amity, and oaths
There should be found such false dissembling guile?
KING HENRY   What? Doth my uncle Burgundy revolt?
65   GLOUCESTER   He doth, my lord, and is become your foe.
KING HENRY   Is that the worst this letter doth contain?
GLOUCESTER   It is the worst, and all, my lord, he writes.

2. a lowly or illegitimate country bumpkin.
3. Henry VI's uncle, the Duke of Bedford, married Burgundy's sister Anne.

KING HENRY   Why then, Lord Talbot there shall talk with him
And give him chastisement for this abuse.
70   [*To* TALBOT] How say you, my lord? Are you not content?
TALBOT   Content, my liege? Yes. But that I am prevented,°   *anticipated*
I should have begged I might have been employed.
KING HENRY   Then gather strength and march unto him straight.°   *at once*
Let him perceive how ill we brook° his treason,   *tolerate*
75   And what offence it is to flout his friends.
TALBOT   I go, my lord, in heart desiring still°   *always*
You may behold confusion of your foes.   [*Exit*]
    Enter VERNON [*wearing a white rose,*] *and* BASSET [*wear-*
    ing a red rose]
VERNON [*to* KING HENRY]   Grant me the combat,° gracious sover-   *permission to duel*
    eign.
BASSET [*to* KING HENRY]   And me, my lord; grant me the combat, too.
RICHARD DUKE OF YORK [*to* KING HENRY, *pointing to* VERNON]
80   This is my servant;° hear him, noble Prince.   *follower*
SOMERSET [*to* KING HENRY, *pointing to* BASSET]   And this is mine,
    sweet Henry; favour him.
KING HENRY   Be patient, lords, and give them leave to speak.
Say, gentlemen, what makes you thus exclaim,
And wherefore crave you combat, or with whom?
85   VERNON   With him, my lord; for he hath done me wrong.
BASSET   And I with him; for he hath done me wrong.
KING HENRY   What is that wrong whereof you both complain?
First let me know, and then I'll answer you.
BASSET   Crossing the sea from England into France,
90   This fellow here with envious carping tongue
Upbraided me about the rose I wear,
Saying the sanguine° colour of the leaves°   *blood-red / petals*
Did represent my master's blushing cheeks
When stubbornly he did repugn° the truth   *reject*
95   About a certain question[4] in the law
Argued betwixt the Duke of York and him,
With other vile and ignominious terms;
In confutation of which rude reproach,
And in defence of my lord's worthiness,
100 I crave the benefit of law of arms.[5]
VERNON   And that is my petition, noble lord;
For though he seem with forgèd quaint conceit°   *false cunning words*
To set a gloss° upon his bold intent,   *good appearance*
Yet know, my lord, I was provoked by him,
105 And he first took exceptions at this badge,
Pronouncing that the paleness of this flower
Bewrayed° the faintness of my master's heart.   *Revealed*
RICHARD DUKE OF YORK   Will not this malice, Somerset, be left?°   *put aside*
SOMERSET   Your private grudge, my lord of York, will out,
110 Though ne'er so cunningly you smother it.
KING HENRY   Good Lord, what madness rules in brainsick men
When for so slight and frivolous a cause

---

4. The "certain question" apparently concerns the question of York's succession to the throne and the attainder
of his father. See 2.4 and 2.5.45–129.
5. The right to decide the matter in a duel.

Such factious emulations° shall arise?   *divisive jealousies*
Good cousins both of York and Somerset,
115   Quiet yourselves, I pray, and be at peace.
RICHARD DUKE OF YORK   Let this dissension first be tried by fight,
And then your highness shall command a peace.
SOMERSET   The quarrel toucheth none but us alone;
Betwixt ourselves let us decide it then.
120   RICHARD DUKE OF YORK   There is my pledge.[6] Accept it, Somerset.
VERNON [*to* KING HENRY]   Nay, let it rest where it began at first.[7]
BASSET [*to* KING HENRY]   Confirm it so, mine honourable lord.
GLOUCESTER   Confirm it so? Confounded be your strife,
And perish ye with your audacious prate!°   *prattling*
125   Presumptuous vassals, are you not ashamed
With this immodest clamorous outrage
To trouble and disturb the King and us?
And you, my lords, methinks you do not well
To bear with their perverse objections,°   *accusations*
130   Much less to take occasion° from their mouths   *the opportunity*
To raise a mutiny betwixt yourselves.
Let me persuade you take a better course.
EXETER   It grieves his highness. Good my lords, be friends.
KING HENRY   Come hither, you that would be combatants.
135   Henceforth I charge you, as you love our favour,
Quite to forget this quarrel and the cause.
And you, my lords, remember where we are—
In France, amongst a fickle wavering nation.
If they perceive dissension in our looks,
140   And that within ourselves we disagree,
How will their grudging stomachs° be provoked   *resentful tempers*
To wilful disobedience, and rebel!
Beside, what infamy will there arise
When foreign princes shall be certified°   *informed*
145   That for a toy,° a thing of no regard,   *trifle*
King Henry's peers and chief nobility
Destroyed themselves and lost the realm of France!
O, think upon the conquest of my father,
My tender years, and let us not forgo
150   That for a trifle that was bought with blood.[8]
Let me be umpire in this doubtful° strife.   *uncertain*
I see no reason, if I wear this rose,
     [*He takes a red rose*]
That anyone should therefore be suspicious
I more incline to Somerset than York.
155   Both are my kinsmen, and I love them both.
As well they may upbraid me with my crown
Because, forsooth, the King of Scots is crowned.
But your discretions better can persuade
Than I am able to instruct or teach,
160   And therefore, as we hither came in peace,
So let us still continue peace and love.
Cousin of York, we institute° your grace   *appoint*

---

6. A glove or gauntlet thrown down in a duel.
7. Let the quarrel remain with me and Basset, who began
it.

8. *let . . . blood:* let us not lose for a trifle what was bought
with blood (that is, let us not lose France).

To be our regent in these parts of France;
And good my lord of Somerset, unite
165 Your troops of horsemen with his bands of foot,°   *infantry*
And like true subjects, sons of your progenitors,
Go cheerfully together and digest°   *dissipate*
Your angry choler on your enemies.
Ourself, my Lord Protector, and the rest,
170 After some respite, will return to Calais,
From thence to England, where I hope ere long
To be presented by your victories
With Charles, Alençon, and that traitorous rout.°   *rabble*
    [*Flourish.*] *Exeunt. Manent* YORK, WARWICK,
                 VERNON, [*and*] EXETER
WARWICK   My lord of York, I promise you, the King
175 Prettily, methought, did play the orator.
RICHARD DUKE OF YORK   And so he did; but yet I like it not
In that he wears the badge of Somerset.
WARWICK   Tush, that was but his fancy; blame him not.
I dare presume, sweet Prince, he thought no harm.
180 RICHARD DUKE OF YORK   An if I wist° he did—but let it rest.   *If I knew for certain*
Other affairs must now be managèd.   *Exeunt. Manet* EXETER
EXETER   Well didst thou, Richard, to suppress thy voice;
For had the passions of thy heart burst out
I fear we should have seen deciphered° there   *revealed*
185 More rancorous spite, more furious raging broils,
Than yet can be imagined or supposed.
But howsoe'er, no simple man that sees
This jarring discord of nobility,
This shouldering of each other in the court,
190 This factious bandying° of their favourites,°   *quarreling / followers*
But that° it doth presage some ill event.°   *But sees that / outcome*
'Tis much when sceptres are in children's hands,
But more when envy breeds unkind° division: *unnatural*
There comes the ruin, there begins confusion.   *Exit*

4.2

Enter [Lord] TALBOT *with [a] trump[eter] and drum[mer
and soldiers] before Bordeaux*
TALBOT   Go to the gates of Bordeaux, trumpeter.
Summon their general unto the wall.
    [*The trumpeter*] *sounds [a parley]. Enter [French]* GEN-
    ERAL, *aloft*
English John Talbot, captain, calls you forth,
Servant in arms to Harry King of England;
5 And thus he would:° open your city gates,   *desires*
Be humble to us, call my sovereign yours
And do him homage as obedient subjects,
And I'll withdraw me and my bloody power.
But if you frown upon this proffered peace,
10 You tempt the fury of my three attendants—
Lean famine, quartering° steel, and climbing fire—   *dismembering*
Who in a moment even° with the earth   *level*

4.2 Location: Before Bordeaux.

Shall lay your stately and air-braving° towers   *air-defying; lofty*
    If you forsake the offer of their love.
15 GENERAL   Thou ominous and fearful owl[1] of death,
    Our nation's terror and their bloody scourge,
    The period° of thy tyranny approacheth.   *end*
    On us thou canst not enter but by death,
    For I protest we are well fortified
20   And strong enough to issue out and fight.
    If thou retire, the Dauphin well appointed°   *equipped*
    Stands with the snares of war to tangle thee.
    On either hand thee° there are squadrons pitched[2]   *On both sides of you*
    To wall thee from the liberty of flight,
25   And no way canst thou turn thee for redress
    But death doth front thee with apparent spoil,[3]
    And pale destruction meets thee in the face.
    Ten thousand French have ta'en the sacrament[4]
    To fire their dangerous artillery
30   Upon no Christian soul but English Talbot.
    Lo, there thou stand'st, a breathing valiant man
    Of an invincible unconquered spirit.
    This is the latest° glory of thy praise,   *final*
    That I thy enemy due° thee withal,   *endow*
35   For ere the glass° that now begins to run   *hourglass*
    Finish the process of his° sandy hour,   *progress of its*
    These eyes that see thee now well colourèd°   *in good health*
    Shall see thee withered, bloody, pale, and dead.
        Drum afar off
    Hark, hark, the Dauphin's drum, a warning bell,
40   Sings heavy music to thy timorous soul,
    And mine shall ring thy dire departure out.[5]   *Exit*
  TALBOT   He fables not. I hear the enemy.
    Out, some light horsemen, and peruse their wings.°   *survey their flanks*
      [Exit one or more]
    O negligent and heedless° discipline,   *careless*
45   How are we parked° and bounded in a pale!°—   *enclosed / fenced area*
    A little herd of England's timorous deer
    Mazed with[6] a yelping kennel of French curs.
    If we be English deer, be then in blood,°   *vigorous*
    Not rascal-like[7] to fall down with a pinch,°   *nip (from hounds)*
50   But rather, moody-mad° and desperate stags,   *enraged*
    Turn on the bloody hounds with heads of steel
    And make the cowards stand aloof at bay.
    Sell every man his life as dear as mine
    And they shall find dear° deer of us, my friends.   *costly*
55   God and Saint George, Talbot and England's right,
    Prosper our colours in this dangerous fight!   *[Exeunt]*

---

1. The owl's cry was thought to portend evil or death (see Ovid's *Metamorphoses* 10.521–52).
2. Arranged on the field for battle.
3. But death confronts you with obvious destruction.
4. Have received the Christian sacrament of holy communion (as a way of confirming their oaths).

5. And my drum—the alarm signal given when the general's army is to "issue out and fight" (line 20) against Talbot—shall signal your death.
6. Bewildered by; trapped in a maze with.
7. Not like lean, worthless deer.

4.3

Enter a MESSENGER *that meets [the* DUKE OF] YORK.
*Enter [*RICHARD DUKE OF] YORK *with [a] trumpet[er]
and many soldiers*

RICHARD DUKE OF YORK   Are not the speedy scouts returned again
That dogged° the mighty army of the Dauphin?   *tracked*
MESSENGER   They are returned, my lord, and give it out
That he is marched to Bordeaux with his power
5   To fight with Talbot. As he marched along,
By your espials° were discoverèd   *spies*
Two mightier troops than that the Dauphin led,
Which joined with him and made their march for Bordeaux.
RICHARD DUKE OF YORK   A plague upon that villain Somerset
10   That thus delays my promisèd supply
Of horsemen that were levied for this siege!
Renownèd Talbot doth expect my aid,
And I am louted° by a traitor villain   *made a fool of*
And cannot help the noble chevalier.
15   God comfort him in this necessity;
If he miscarry,° farewell wars in France!   *come to harm*
Enter another messenger [Sir William LUCY]
LUCY[1]   Thou princely leader of our English strength,
Never so needful on the earth of France,
Spur to the rescue of the noble Talbot,
20   Who now is girdled with a waste° of iron   *vast expanse; belt*
And hemmed about with grim destruction.
To Bordeaux, warlike Duke; to Bordeaux, York,
Else farewell Talbot, France, and England's honour.
RICHARD DUKE OF YORK   O God, that Somerset, who in proud heart
25   Doth stop my cornets,° were in Talbot's place!   *troops of cavalry*
So should we save a valiant gentleman
By forfeiting a traitor and a coward.
Mad ire and wrathful fury makes me weep,
That thus we die while remiss° traitors sleep.   *idle; negligent*
30 LUCY   O, send some succour to the distressed lord.
RICHARD DUKE OF YORK   He dies, we lose; I break my warlike word;
We mourn, France smiles; we lose, they daily get,
All 'long° of this vile traitor Somerset.   *because*
LUCY   Then God take mercy on brave Talbot's soul,
35   And on his son young John, who two hours since
I met in travel toward his warlike father.
This seven years did not Talbot see his son,
And now they meet where both their lives are done.
RICHARD DUKE OF YORK   Alas, what joy shall noble Talbot have
40   To bid his young son welcome to his grave?
Away—vexation almost stops my breath
That sundered friends greet in the hour of death.
Lucy, farewell. No more my fortune can°   *can do*
But curse the cause I cannot aid the man.
45   Maine, Blois, Poitiers, and Tours are won away
'Long all° of Somerset and his delay.   *Exeunt [all but* LUCY]   *All because*

4.3 Location: An unspecified field in France.
1. In F, this and the subsequent three speeches assigned
to Lucy are spoken by "Second Messenger" and "Messenger." However, at line 43, York addresses the speaker as
"Lucy."

LUCY   Thus while the vulture of sedition
    Feeds in the bosom of such great commanders,
    Sleeping neglection° doth betray to loss   *Careless disregard*
50   The conquest of our scarce-cold conqueror,[2]
    That ever-living man of memory[3]
    Henry the Fifth. Whiles they each other cross,
    Lives, honours, lands, and all hurry to loss.   *[Exit]*[4]

4.4

Enter [the Duke of] SOMERSET with his army

SOMERSET *[to a CAPTAIN]*   It is too late, I cannot send them now.
    This expedition was by York and Talbot
    Too rashly plotted. All our general force
    Might with a sally of the very town
5   Be buckled with.[1] The over-daring Talbot
    Hath sullied all his gloss of former honour
    By this unheedful, desperate, wild adventure.
    York set him on to fight and die in shame
    That, Talbot dead, great York might bear the name.°   *claim preeminence*
    [Enter LUCY]
10   CAPTAIN   Here is Sir William Lucy, who with me
    Set from our o'ermatched forces forth for aid.
SOMERSET   How now, Sir William, whither were you sent?
LUCY   Whither, my lord? From bought and sold[2] Lord Talbot,
    Who, ringed about with bold adversity,
15   Cries out for noble York and Somerset
    To beat assailing death from his weak legions;
    And whiles the honourable captain there
    Drops bloody sweat from his war-wearied limbs
    And, unadvantaged,° ling'ring looks for rescue,   *disadvantaged*
20   You his false hopes, the trust of England's honour,
    Keep off aloof with worthless emulation.°   *rivalry*
    Let not your private discord keep away
    The levied succours° that should lend him aid,   *reinforcements*
    While he, renownèd noble gentleman,
25   Yield up his life unto a world of° odds.   *immense*
    Orléans the Bastard, Charles, and Burgundy,
    Alençon, René, compass him about,
    And Talbot perisheth by your default.
SOMERSET   York set him on; York should have sent him aid.
30   LUCY   And York as fast upon your grace exclaims,
    Swearing that you withhold his levied horse
    Collected for this expedition.
SOMERSET   York lies. He might have sent° and had the horse.   *sent for*
    I owe him little duty and less love,
35   And take foul scorn° to fawn on him by sending.   *find it disgraceful*
LUCY   The fraud of England, not the force of France,
    Hath now entrapped the noble-minded Talbot.

---

2. The conquest made by our recently dead conqueror. (The events of this scene actually took place thirty-one years after the death of the historical Henry V.)
3. That man who will live forever in memory.
4. F does not mark Lucy's exit at this point. Conceivably, he stays onstage as Somerset enters to him.
4.4 Location: Scene continues.
1. *All . . . with:* Our entire army might be engaged by an attack simply from the French garrison in the town (without taking into account the other French forces coming as reinforcements).
2. *bought and sold:* a proverbial expression meaning "betrayed," perhaps alluding to the biblical account of Christ's betrayal by his disciple Judas for forty pieces of silver.

Never to England shall he bear his life,
But dies betrayed to fortune by your strife.
40 SOMERSET Come, go. I will dispatch the horsemen straight.
Within six hours they will be at his aid.
LUCY Too late comes rescue. He is ta'en or slain,
For fly he could not if he would have fled,
And fly would Talbot never, though he might.
45 SOMERSET If he be dead, brave Talbot, then adieu.
LUCY His fame lives in the world, his shame in you.

Exeunt [severally]

4.5

Enter [Lord] TALBOT *and his son [*JOHN]
TALBOT O young John Talbot, I did send for thee
To tutor thee in stratagems of war,
That Talbot's name might be in thee revived
When sapless° age and weak unable limbs   *withered*
5   Should bring thy father to his drooping chair.[1]
But O—malignant and ill-boding stars!—
Now thou art come unto a feast of death,
A terrible and unavoided° danger.   *unavoidable*
Therefore, dear boy, mount on my swiftest horse,
10 And I'll direct thee how thou shalt escape
By sudden flight. Come, dally not, be gone.
JOHN Is my name Talbot, and am I your son,
And shall I fly? O, if you love my mother,
Dishonour not her honourable name
15 To make a bastard and a slave of me.
The world will say he is not Talbot's blood
That basely fled when noble Talbot stood.
TALBOT Fly to revenge my death if I be slain.
JOHN He that flies so will ne'er return again.
20 TALBOT If we both stay, we both are sure to die.
JOHN Then let me stay and, father, do you fly.
Your loss is great; so your regard° should be.   *concern for yourself*
My worth unknown, no loss is known in me.
Upon my death the French can little boast;
25 In yours they will: in you all hopes are lost.
Flight cannot stain the honour you have won,
But mine it will, that no exploit have done.
You fled for vantage,° everyone will swear,   *military advantage*
But if I bow, they'll say it was for fear.
30 There is no hope that ever I will stay
If the first hour I shrink and run away.
Here on my knee I beg mortality°   *death*
Rather than life preserved with infamy.
TALBOT Shall all thy mother's hopes lie in one tomb?
35 JOHN Ay, rather than I'll shame my mother's womb.
TALBOT Upon my blessing I command thee go.
JOHN To fight I will, but not to fly the foe.
TALBOT Part of thy father may be saved in thee.

4.5. Location: Battlefield near Bordeaux.
1. Chair where he sits wearily, as his strength and life decline.

JOHN   No part of him but will be shamed in me.

40   TALBOT   Thou never hadst renown, nor canst not lose it.

JOHN   Yes, your renownèd name—shall flight abuse it?

TALBOT   Thy father's charge° shall clear thee from that stain.   *order*

JOHN   You cannot witness for me, being slain.°   *if you are slain*

If death be so apparent,° then both fly.   *appear so likely*

45   TALBOT   And leave my followers here to fight and die?

My age° was never tainted with such shame.   *life*

JOHN   And shall my youth be guilty of such blame?

No more can I be severed from your side

Than can yourself your self in twain divide.

50   Stay, go, do what you will: the like do I,

For live I will not if my father die.

TALBOT   Then here I take my leave of thee, fair son,

Born to eclipse° thy life this afternoon.   *extinguish*

Come, side by side together live and die,

55   And soul with soul from France to heaven fly.   *Exeunt*

4.6

*Alarum. Excursions, wherein [Lord] Talbot's son [JOHN]
is hemmed about [by French soldiers] and* TALBOT *res-
cues him. [The English drive off the French]*

TALBOT   Saint George° and victory! Fight, soldiers, fight!   *patron saint of England*

The Regent[1] hath with Talbot broke his word,

And left us to the rage of France his° sword.   *(France's)*

Where is John Talbot? [*To* JOHN] Pause and take thy breath.

5   I gave thee life, and rescued thee from death.

JOHN   O twice my father, twice am I thy son:

The life thou gav'st me first was lost and done

Till with thy warlike sword, despite of fate,

To my determined° time thou gav'st new date.°   *exactly defined / limit*

10   TALBOT   When from the Dauphin's crest thy sword struck fire

It warmed thy father's heart with proud desire

Of bold-faced victory. Then leaden age,

Quickened with youthful spleen° and warlike rage,   *courage*

Beat down Alençon, Orléans, Burgundy,

15   And from the pride of Gallia° rescued thee.   *France*

The ireful Bastard Orléans, that drew blood

From thee, my boy, and had the maidenhood

Of thy first fight,[2] I soon encounterèd,

And interchanging blows, I quickly shed

20   Some of his bastard blood, and in disgrace°   *disdain*

Bespoke him thus: 'Contaminated, base,

And misbegotten blood I spill of thine,

Mean° and right poor, for that pure blood of mine   *Base*

Which thou didst force from Talbot, my brave boy.'

25   Here, purposing° the Bastard to destroy,   *as I was intending*

Came in strong rescue. Speak thy father's care:

Art thou not weary, John? How dost thou fare?

Wilt thou yet leave the battle, boy, and fly,

4.6 Location: Scene continues.
1. York, who was appointed regent at 4.1.162–63.
2. *that drew . . . fight*: an allusion to the notion that a

woman bleeds during her first experience of heterosexual
intercourse. So young Talbot has bled during his first
battle.

Now thou art sealed° the son of chivalry?   *confirmed*
30   Fly to revenge my death when I am dead;
The help of one stands me in little stead.°   *does me little good*
O, too much folly is it, well I wot,°   *knew*
To hazard all our lives in one small boat.
If I today die not with Frenchmen's rage,
35   Tomorrow I shall die with mickle° age.   *great*
By me they nothing gain, and if I stay
'Tis but the short'ning of my life one day.
In thee thy mother dies, our household's name,
My death's revenge, thy youth, and England's fame.
40   All these and more we hazard by thy stay;
All these are saved if thou wilt fly away.
JOHN   The sword of Orléans hath not made me smart;°   *suffer*
These words of yours draw life-blood from my heart.
On that advantage,³ bought with such a shame,
45   To save a paltry life and slay bright fame,
Before young Talbot from old Talbot fly
The coward horse that bears me fall° and die;   *may it fall*
And like me° to the peasant boys of France,   *compare me*
To be shame's scorn and subject of mischance!⁴
50   Surely, by all the glory you have won,
An if I fly I am not Talbot's son.
Then talk no more of flight; it is no boot.°   *use; profit*
If son to Talbot, die at Talbot's foot.
TALBOT   Then follow thou thy desp'rate sire of Crete,
55   Thou Icarus;⁵ thy life to me is sweet.
If thou wilt fight, fight by thy father's side,
And commendable proved, let's die in pride.   *Exeunt*

4.7

Alarum. Excursions. Enter old [Lord] TALBOT *led [by a*
SERVANT]
TALBOT   Where is my other life? Mine own is gone.
O where's young Talbot, where is valiant John?
Triumphant death smeared with captivity,°   *the blood of captives*
Young Talbot's valour makes me smile at thee.
5   When he perceived me shrink° and on my knee,   *weaken*
His bloody sword he brandished over me,
And like a hungry lion did commence
Rough deeds of rage and stern impatience.
But when my angry guardant° stood alone,   *protector*
10   Tend'ring° my ruin and assailed of none,   *Concerned for*
Dizzy-eyed fury and great rage of heart
Suddenly made him from my side to start
Into the clust'ring battle° of the French,   *crowded ranks*
And in that sea of blood my boy did drench°   *drown*
15   His over-mounting spirit; and there died
My Icarus, my blossom, in his pride.
    Enter [English soldiers] with John Talbot['s body], borne
SERVANT   O my dear lord, lo where your son is borne.
TALBOT   Thou antic° death, which laugh'st us here to scorn,   *grotesquely grinning*

---

3. For the sake of that advantage (of safety).
4. To be an ashamed object of scorn and a victim of misfortune.
5. According to classical myth, Icarus and his father,

Daedalus, tried to escape imprisonment in Crete using
artificial wings of feathers and wax. Daedalus succeeded,
but Icarus flew too close to the sun and died.
4.7 Location: Scene continues.

Anon° from thy insulting tyranny,	*Soon*
20 Coupled in bonds of perpetuity,	
Two Talbots wingèd through the lither° sky	*yielding*
In thy despite shall scape mortality.	
[*To* JOHN] O thou whose wounds become hard-favoured death,[1]	
Speak to thy father ere thou yield thy breath.	
25 Brave° death by speaking, whether he will or no;	*Defy*
Imagine him a Frenchman and thy foe.—	
Poor boy, he smiles, methinks, as who° should say	*as one who*
'Had death been French, then death had died today'.	
Come, come, and lay him in his father's arms.	

> [*Soldiers lay* JOHN *in Talbot's arms*]

| 30   My spirit can no longer bear these harms. |
| Soldiers, adieu. I have what I would have, |
| Now my old arms are young John Talbot's grave. |

> [*He*] *dies.* [*Alarum. Exeunt soldiers leaving the bodies*]
> *Enter* CHARLES [*the Dauphin, the dukes of*] ALENÇON
> [*and*] BURGUNDY, [*the*] BASTARD [*of Orléans*], *and* [JOAN
> *la*] *Pucelle*

CHARLES   Had York and Somerset brought rescue in,
We should have found a bloody day of this.

35   BASTARD   How the young whelp of Talbot's,[2] raging wood,°   *mad*
Did flesh his puny sword[3] in Frenchmen's blood!

JOAN   Once I encountered[4] him, and thus I said:
'Thou maiden[5] youth, be vanquished by a maid.'
But with a proud, majestical high scorn

40   He answered thus: 'Young Talbot was not born
To be the pillage of a giglot° wench.'   *plunder of a wanton*
So rushing in the bowels° of the French,   *center*
He left me proudly, as unworthy fight.

BURGUNDY   Doubtless he would have made a noble knight.

45   See where he lies inhearsèd° in the arms   *(as in a coffin)*
Of the most bloody nurser of his harms.[6]

BASTARD   Hew them to pieces, hack their bones asunder,
Whose life was England's glory, Gallia's° wonder.   *France's*

CHARLES   O no, forbear; for that which we have fled

50   During the life, let us not wrong it dead.

> *Enter* [*Sir William*] LUCY [*with a French herald*]

LUCY   Herald, conduct me to the Dauphin's tent
To know who hath obtained the glory of the day.

CHARLES   On what submissive message art thou sent?

LUCY   Submission, Dauphin? 'Tis a mere° French word.   *pure*

55   We English warriors wot° not what it means.   *know*
I come to know what prisoners thou hast ta'en,
And to survey the bodies of the dead.

CHARLES   For prisoners ask'st thou? Hell our prison is.[7]
But tell me whom thou seek'st.

60   LUCY   But where's the great Alcides[8] of the field,

---

1. Whose wounds make ugly death attractive.
2. The young puppy of Talbot's (John Talbot). The Bastard is punning on "talbot" as the name for a kind of hunting dog.
3. Plunged in his inexperienced sword for the first time, with a sexual wordplay: plunged in his inexperienced or diminutive penis for the first time.
4. Another bawdy pun: "encounter" may mean "to meet sexually."
5. Virginal; inexperienced in battle.
6. Person who taught him to harm his enemies; person who caused his injuries.
7. Charles implies that the French have killed their enemies (sent them to hell) rather than taking prisoners.
8. Hercules (a descendant of Alcaeus), the hero of classical myth famous for performing difficult feats of strength and bravery.

Valiant Lord Talbot, Earl of Shrewsbury,
Created for his rare success in arms
Great Earl of Wexford, Waterford, and Valence,
Lord Talbot of Goodrich and Urchinfield,
65 Lord Strange of Blackmere, Lord Verdun of Alton,
Lord Cromwell of Wingfield, Lord Furnival of Sheffield,
The thrice victorious lord of Falconbridge,
Knight of the noble order of Saint George,
Worthy[9] Saint Michael and the Golden Fleece,
70 Great *Maréchal*° to Henry the Sixth   *commander-in-chief*
Of all his wars within the realm of France?
JOAN   Here's a silly, stately style° indeed.   *list of titles*
The Turk,° that two-and-fifty kingdoms hath,   *Sultan of Turkey*
Writes not so tedious a style as this.
75 Him that thou magnifi'st with all these titles
Stinking and flyblown° lies here at our feet.   *putrified*
LUCY   Is Talbot slain, the Frenchmen's only scourge,
Your kingdom's terror and black Nemesis?[1]
O, were mine eye-balls into bullets turned,
80 That I in rage might shoot them at your faces!
O, that I could but call these dead to life! —
It were enough to fright the realm of France.
Were but his picture left amongst you here
It would amaze° the proudest of you all.   *terrify*
85 Give me their bodies, that I may bear them hence
And give them burial as beseems° their worth.   *as is appropriate to*
JOAN [*to* CHARLES]   I think this upstart is old Talbot's ghost,
He speaks with such a proud commanding spirit.
For God's sake let him have them. To keep them here
90 They would but stink and putrefy the air.
CHARLES   Go, take their bodies hence.
LUCY   I'll bear them hence, but from their ashes shall be reared
A phoenix[2] that shall make all France afeard.
CHARLES   So we be rid of them, do with them what thou wilt.
        [*Exeunt* LUCY *and herald with the bodies*]
95 And now to Paris in this conquering vein.
All will be ours, now bloody Talbot's slain.   *Exeunt*

5.1

Sennet. Enter KING [HENRY, *the Dukes of*] GLOUCESTER,
and EXETER [*and others*]

KING HENRY [*to* GLOUCESTER]   Have you perused the letters from the Pope,
The Emperor, and the Earl of Armagnac?
GLOUCESTER   I have, my lord, and their intent is this:
They humbly sue unto your excellence
5   To have a godly peace concluded of
Between the realms of England and of France.
KING HENRY   How doth your grace affect their motion?°   *like their proposal*
GLOUCESTER   Well, my good lord, and as the only means
To stop effusion° of our Christian blood   *spilling*
10 And 'stablish quietness on every side.

---

9. Worthy of; equal in value to. The Order of St. Michael was a French chivalric order established in 1469, after the events of the play occurred.
1. The Greek goddess of avenging justice.

2. A legendary bird that was said to live five hundred years, burn itself to ashes, and then be reborn from the ashes.
5.1 Location: The palace, London.

KING HENRY   Ay, marry, uncle; for I always thought
It was both impious and unnatural
That such immanity° and bloody strife   *barbarity*
Should reign among professors of one faith.
15 GLOUCESTER   Beside, my lord, the sooner to effect
And surer bind this knot of amity,
The Earl of Armagnac, near knit° to Charles—   *closely related*
A man of great authority in France—
Proffers his only daughter to your grace
20 In marriage, with a large and sumptuous dowry.
KING HENRY   Marriage, uncle? Alas, my years are young,
And fitter is my study and my books
Than wanton dalliance with a paramour.
Yet call th'ambassadors,   *[Exit one or more]*
and as you please,
25 So let them have their answers every one.
I shall be well content with any choice
Tends° to God's glory and my country's weal.°   *That tends / welfare*
        Enter [the Bishop of] WINCHESTER, [now in cardinal's
        habit,] and three ambassadors [one a Papal LEGATE]
EXETER *[aside]*   What, is my lord of Winchester installed
And called unto a cardinal's degree?
30 Then I perceive that will be verified
Henry the Fifth did sometime° prophesy: *at one time*
'If once he come to be a cardinal,
He'll make his cap° co-equal with the crown.'   *(a cardinal's red hat)*
KING HENRY   My lords ambassadors, your several suits
35 Have been considered and debated on.
Your purpose is both good and reasonable,
And therefore are we certainly resolved
To draw° conditions of a friendly peace,   *draft*
Which by my lord of Winchester we mean
40 Shall be transported presently to France.
GLOUCESTER *[to ambassadors]*   And for the proffer of my lord your master,
I have informed his highness so at large°   *in full*
As,° liking of the lady's virtuous gifts,   *That*
Her beauty, and the value of her dower,
45 He doth intend she shall be England's queen.
KING HENRY *[to ambassadors]*   In argument° and proof of which   *As evidence*
        contract
Bear her this jewel, pledge of my affection.
[To GLOUCESTER] And so, my lord Protector, see them guarded
And safely brought to Dover, wherein shipped,°   *where once embarked*
50 Commit them to the fortune of the sea.
        Exeunt [severally all but WINCHESTER and LEGATE]
WINCHESTER   Stay, my lord legate; you shall first receive
The sum of money which I promisèd
Should be delivered to his holiness
For clothing me in these grave ornaments.°   *solemn robes of office*
55 LEGATE   I will attend upon your lordship's leisure.   *[Exit]*[1]
WINCHESTER   Now Winchester will not submit, I trow,°   *trust*
Or be inferior to the proudest peer.

---

1. The legate may leave at this point, but there is no exit   chester makes his final speech and then exit with the
marked in F. He may simply step to the side while Win-   prelate.

Humphrey of Gloucester, thou shalt well perceive
That nor° in birth or for authority   *neither*
60 The Bishop will be overborne° by thee.   *overruled*
I'll either make thee stoop and bend thy knee,
Or sack this country with a mutiny.°   *Exit*   *an open revolt*

5.2

Enter CHARLES [*the Dauphin reading a letter, the Dukes
of*] BURGUNDY [*and*] ALENÇON, [*the*] BASTARD [*of
Orléans*], RENÉ [*Duke of Anjou*], *and* JOAN [*la Pucelle*]
CHARLES   These news, my lords, may cheer our drooping spirits.
'Tis said the stout° Parisians do revolt   *valiant*
And turn again unto the warlike French.
ALENÇON   Then march to Paris, royal Charles of France,
5   And keep not back your powers in dalliance.°   *idleness*
JOAN   Peace be amongst them if they turn to us;
Else, ruin combat with their palaces![1]
        Enter [*a*] SCOUT
SCOUT   Success unto our valiant general,
And happiness to his accomplices.°   *allies*
10 CHARLES   What tidings send our scouts? I prithee speak.
SCOUT   The English army, that divided was
Into two parties, is now conjoined in one,[2]
And means to give you battle presently.°   *immediately*
CHARLES   Somewhat too sudden, sirs, the warning is;
15 But we will presently provide for them.
BURGUNDY   I trust the ghost of Talbot is not there.
JOAN   Now he is gone, my lord, you need not fear.[3]
Of all base passions, fear is most accursed.
Command the conquest, Charles, it shall be thine;
20 Let Henry fret and all the world repine.°   *complain*
CHARLES   Then on, my lords; and France be fortunate!   *Exeunt*

5.3

Alarum. Excursions. Enter JOAN [*la*] *Pucelle*
JOAN   The Regent° conquers, and the Frenchmen fly.   *(Richard Duke of York)*
Now help, ye charming° spells and periapts,°   *magic / amulets*
And ye choice spirits that admonish° me   *forewarn*
And give me signs of future accidents.°   *events*
        Thunder
5   You speedy helpers, that are substitutes°   *deputies*
Under the lordly monarch of the north,[1]
Appear, and aid me in this enterprise.
        Enter Fiends
This speed and quick appearance argues° proof   *offers*
Of your accustomed° diligence to me.   *customary*
10 Now, ye familiar spirits[2] that are culled
Out of the powerful regions under earth,
Help me this once, that France may get the field.°   *win the battle*
        They walk and speak not

5.2 Location: Plains in Anjou, France.
1. Otherwise, let ruin destroy their palaces.
2. In other words, York and Suffolk have joined forces.
3. F assigns this line to Burgundy.
5.3 Location: Before Angiers, France.

1. The devil and his demons were frequently associated with the north.
2. Attendant spirits that could be summoned by a witch; often they inhabited the bodies of animals.

O, hold me not with silence overlong!
Where I was wont to feed you with my blood,[3]
15 I'll lop a member° off and give it you   *limb*
   In earnest° of a further benefit,   *As an advance payment*
   So you do condescend to help me now.
      They hang their heads
   No hope to have redress? My body shall
   Pay recompense if you will grant my suit.
      They shake their heads
20 Cannot my body nor blood-sacrifice
   Entreat you to your wonted furtherance?°   *usual assistance*
   Then take my soul—my body, soul, and all—
   Before that England give the French the foil.°   *defeat*
      They depart
   See, they forsake me. Now the time is come
25 That France must vail her lofty-plumèd crest[4]
   And let her head fall into England's lap.
   My ancient° incantations are too weak,   *former*
   And hell too strong for me to buckle° with.   *fight, do combat*
   Now, France, thy glory droopeth to the dust.   *Exit*

5.4

Excursions. [The Dukes of] BURGUNDY *and* YORK *fight
hand to hand. [The] French fly. [*JOAN *la Pucelle is
taken]*

RICHARD DUKE OF YORK   Damsel of France, I think I have you fast.
   Unchain your spirits now with spelling° charms,   *conjuring*
   And try if they can gain your liberty.
   A goodly prize, fit for the devil's grace![1]
5 *[To his soldiers]* See how the ugly witch doth bend her brows,°   *scowls*
   As if with Circe[2] she would change my shape.
JOAN   Changed to a worser shape thou canst not be.
RICHARD DUKE OF YORK   O, Charles the Dauphin is a proper° man.   *handsome*
   No shape but his can please your dainty° eye.   *fastidious*
10 JOAN   A plaguing mischief light on Charles and thee,
   And may ye both be suddenly surprised
   By bloody hands in° sleeping on your beds!   *while*
RICHARD DUKE OF YORK   Fell banning° hag, enchantress, hold   *Fierce cursing*
      thy tongue.
JOAN   I prithee give me leave to curse awhile.
RICHARD DUKE OF YORK   Curse, miscreant,° when thou comest   *heretic*
15   to the stake.   *Exeunt*

5.5

Alarum. Enter [the Earl of] SUFFOLK *with* MARGARET *in
his hand*°   *led by the hand*

SUFFOLK   Be what thou wilt, thou art my prisoner.
      [He] gazes on her
   O fairest beauty, do not fear nor fly,
   For I will touch thee but with reverent hands,

---

3. Witches were thought to have extra nipples with
which they fed their familiars, or attendant spirits.
4. Must lower her high-feathered helmet.
5.4 Location: Scene continues.
1. Fit for his grace, the devil (said sarcastically).

2. According to Greek myth, a witch who seduced Odys-
seus and turned his men into swine (see Homer, *Odyssey*
10).
5.5 Location: Scene continues.

And lay them gently on thy tender side.
5 I kiss these fingers for eternal peace.
Who art thou? Say, that I may honour thee.
MARGARET   Margaret my name, and daughter to a king,
The King of Naples,[1] whosoe'er thou art.
SUFFOLK   An earl I am, and Suffolk am I called.
10 Be not offended, nature's miracle,
Thou art allotted° to be ta'en by me.   destined
So doth the swan his downy cygnets save,°   young swans protect
Keeping them prisoner underneath his wings.
Yet if this servile usage° once offend,   treatment as a slave
15 Go, and be free again, as Suffolk's friend.
          She is going
O stay! [*Aside*] I have no power to let her pass.
My hand would free her, but my heart says no.
As plays the sun upon the glassy stream,
Twinkling another counterfeited° beam,   reflected
20 So seems this gorgeous beauty to mine eyes.
Fain would I woo her, yet I dare not speak.
I'll call for pen and ink, and write my mind.
Fie, de la Pole,[2] disable° not thyself!   disparage
Hast not a tongue? Is she not here to hear?
25 Wilt thou be daunted at a woman's sight?[3]
Ay, beauty's princely majesty is such
Confounds° the tongue, and makes the senses rough.°   *That it confuses* / dull
MARGARET   Say, Earl of Suffolk—if thy name be so—
What ransom must I pay before I pass?
30 For I perceive I am thy prisoner.
SUFFOLK [*aside*]   How canst thou tell she will deny° thy suit   refuse
Before thou make a trial of her love?
MARGARET   Why speak'st thou not? What ransom must I pay?
SUFFOLK [*aside*]   She's beautiful, and therefore to be wooed;
35 She is a woman, therefore to be won.
MARGARET   Wilt thou accept of ransom, yea or no?
SUFFOLK [*aside*]   Fond° man, remember that thou hast a wife;   Foolish
Then how can Margaret be thy paramour?°   mistress
MARGARET [*aside*]   I were best to leave him, for he will not hear.
40 SUFFOLK [*aside*]   There° all is marred; there lies a cooling card.[4]   By that fact
MARGARET [*aside*]   He talks at random; sure the man is mad.
SUFFOLK [*aside*]   And yet a dispensation[5] may be had.
MARGARET   And yet I would that you would answer me.
SUFFOLK [*aside*]   I'll win this Lady Margaret. For whom?
45 Why, for my king—tush, that's a wooden[6] thing.
MARGARET [*aside*]   He talks of wood. It is some carpenter.
SUFFOLK [*aside*]   Yet so my fancy° may be satisfied,   love
And peace establishèd between these realms.
But there remains a scruple° in that too,   an objection
50 For though her father be the King of Naples,
Duke of Anjou and Maine, yet is he poor,
And our nobility will scorn the match.

---

1. That is, the René of earlier scenes, Duke of Anjou and
also titular King of Naples and Sicily.
2. Suffolk's family name.
3. At the sight of a woman; at a woman's gaze.
4. An obstacle; literally, a card that, when played, dashes

the hopes of one's opponent.
5. Special permission from the pope to dissolve a marriage.
6. Stupid (referring either to King Henry or to his own
scheme to woo Margaret).

MARGARET   Hear ye, captain? Are you not at leisure?
SUFFOLK [*aside*]   It shall be so, disdain they ne'er so much.
55   Henry is youthful, and will quickly yield.
        [*To* MARGARET] Madam, I have a secret to reveal.
MARGARET [*aside*]   What though I be enthralled,° he seems a knight   taken captive
        And will not any way dishonour me.
SUFFOLK   Lady, vouchsafe to listen° what I say.   listen to
60 MARGARET [*aside*]   Perhaps I shall be rescued by the French,
        And then I need not crave his courtesy.
SUFFOLK   Sweet madam, give me hearing in a cause.
MARGARET [*aside*]   Tush, women have been captivate[7] ere now.
SUFFOLK   Lady, wherefore talk you so?
65 MARGARET   I cry you mercy, 'tis but *quid* for *quo*.°   tit for tat
SUFFOLK   Say, gentle Princess, would you not suppose
        Your bondage happy to be° made a queen?   if you were to be
MARGARET   To be a queen in bondage is more vile
        Than is a slave in base servility,°   slavery
        For princes should be free.
70 SUFFOLK   And so shall you,
        If happy England's royal king be free.
MARGARET   Why, what concerns his freedom unto me?
SUFFOLK   I'll undertake to make thee Henry's queen,
        To put a golden sceptre in thy hand,
75   And set a precious crown upon thy head,
        If thou wilt condescend° to be my—   agree
MARGARET   What?
SUFFOLK   His love.
MARGARET   I am unworthy to be Henry's wife.
SUFFOLK   No, gentle madam, I unworthy am
80   To woo so fair a dame to be his wife
        [*Aside*] And have no portion° in the choice myself.—   share
        How say you, madam; are ye so content?
MARGARET   An if my father please, I am content.
SUFFOLK   Then call our captains and our colours forth,
        [*Enter captains, colours, and trumpeters*]
85   And, madam, at your father's castle walls
        We'll crave a parley to confer with him.
                Sound [*a parley*]. *Enter* RENÉ [*Duke of Anjou*] *on the
                walls*
        See, René, see thy daughter prisoner.
RENÉ   To whom?
SUFFOLK   To me.
RENÉ   Suffolk, what remedy?
        I am a soldier, and unapt° to weep   unsuited
90   Or to exclaim on° fortune's fickleness.   complain of
SUFFOLK   Yes, there is remedy enough, my lord.
        Assent, and for thy honour give consent
        Thy daughter shall be wedded to my king,
        Whom I with pain have wooed and won thereto;
95   And this her easy-held° imprisonment   easily endured
        Hath gained thy daughter princely liberty.
RENÉ   Speaks Suffolk as he thinks?

7. Have been taken prisoner; have fallen in love against their will.

SUFFOLK   Fair Margaret knows
    That Suffolk doth not flatter, face° or feign.   *deceive*
    RENÉ   Upon thy princely warrant° I descend   *guarantee*
100   To give thee answer of thy just demand.
    SUFFOLK   And here I will expect° thy coming.   *await*
                              [*Exit* RENÉ *above*]
        Trumpets sound. Enter RENÉ
    RENÉ   Welcome, brave Earl, into our territories.
    Command in Anjou what your honour pleases.
    SUFFOLK   Thanks, René, happy for° so sweet a child,   *fortunate in having*
105   Fit to be made companion with a king.
    What answer makes your grace unto my suit?
    RENÉ   Since thou dost deign to woo her little worth
    To be the princely bride of such a lord,
    Upon condition I may quietly
110   Enjoy mine own, the countries Maine and Anjou,
    Free from oppression or the stroke of war,
    My daughter shall be Henry's, if he please.
    SUFFOLK   That is her ransom. I deliver her,
    And those two counties° I will undertake   *domains of a count*
115   Your grace shall well and quietly enjoy.
    RENÉ   And I again° in Henry's royal name,   *in return*
    As deputy unto that gracious king,
    Give thee her hand for sign of plighted faith.°   *a marriage pledge*
    SUFFOLK   René of France, I give thee kingly thanks,
120   Because this is in traffic° of a king.   *business*
    [*Aside*] And yet methinks I could be well content
    To be mine own attorney in this case.[8]
    [*To* RENÉ] I'll over then to England with this news,
    And make this marriage to be solemnized.
125   So farewell, René; set this diamond safe
    In golden palaces, as it becomes.°   *as befits it*
    RENÉ   I do embrace thee as I would embrace
    The Christian prince King Henry, were he here.
    MARGARET [*to* SUFFOLK]   Farewell, my lord. Good wishes, praise,
        and prayers
130   Shall Suffolk ever have of Margaret.
        She is going
    SUFFOLK   Farewell, sweet madam; but hark you, Margaret—
    No princely commendations° to my king?   *greetings*
    MARGARET   Such commendations as becomes a maid,
    A virgin, and his servant, say to him.
135   SUFFOLK   Words sweetly placed, and modestly directed.
        [*She is going*]
    But madam, I must trouble you again—
    No loving token to his majesty?
    MARGARET   Yes, my good lord: a pure unspotted heart,
    Never yet taint° with love, I send the King.   *tinged*
140   SUFFOLK   And this withal.°   *in addition*
        [*He*] kiss[*es*] *her*
    MARGARET   That for thyself; I will not so presume
    To send such peevish° tokens to a king.   *trifling*
                    [*Exeunt* RENÉ *and* MARGARET]

---

8. To act on my own behalf in this instance, with a pun on "case" as slang for "vagina."

SUFFOLK [*aside*]   O, wert thou for myself! — but Suffolk, stay.
　　Thou mayst not wander in that labyrinth.[9]
145　There Minotaurs and ugly treasons lurk.
　　Solicit° Henry with her wondrous praise.　　　　　　　　　　　*Entice*
　　Bethink thee on her virtues that surmount,
　　Mad° natural graces that extinguish° art.　　　　　*Extravagant / eclipse*
　　Repeat their semblance[1] often on the seas,
150　That when thou com'st to kneel at Henry's feet
　　Thou mayst bereave° him of his wits with wonder.　*Exeunt*　　*dispossess*

5.6

Enter [RICHARD DUKE OF] YORK, [*the Earl of*] WARWICK,
[*and a*] SHEPHERD

RICHARD DUKE OF YORK　Bring forth that sorceress condemned to burn.
　　[*Enter* JOAN *la Pucelle guarded*][1]
SHEPHERD　Ah, Joan, this kills thy father's heart outright.
　　Have I sought° every country far and near,　　　　　　　　*searched*
　　And now it is my chance to find thee out°　　　　　　　　*discover you*
5　Must I behold thy timeless° cruel death?　　　　　　　　　　*untimely*
　　Ah Joan, sweet daughter Joan, I'll die with thee.
JOAN　Decrepit miser,° base ignoble wretch,　　　　　　　　　*wretch*
　　I am descended of a gentler° blood.　　　　　　　*more aristocratic*
　　Thou art no father nor no friend° of mine.　　　　　　　　*kinsman*
10　SHEPHERD　Out, out! — My lords, an't please you, 'tis not so.
　　I did beget her, all the parish knows.
　　Her mother liveth yet, can testify
　　She was the first fruit of my bach'lorship.[2]
WARWICK [*to* JOAN]　Graceless,° wilt thou deny thy parentage?　*Depraved person*
RICHARD DUKE OF YORK　This argues° what her kind of life hath　*testifies to*
15　　　been —
　　Wicked and vile; and so her death concludes.°　　　　　*confirms; ends*
SHEPHERD　Fie, Joan, that thou wilt be so obstacle.[3]
　　God knows thou art a collop° of my flesh,　　　　　　　　*slice*
　　And for thy sake have I shed many a tear.
20　Deny me not, I prithee, gentle Joan.
JOAN　Peasant, avaunt! [*To the English*] You have suborned[4] this man
　　Of purpose to obscure my noble birth.
SHEPHERD [*to the English*]　'Tis true I gave a noble[5] to the priest
　　The morn that I was wedded to her mother.
25　[*To* JOAN] Kneel down, and take my blessing, good my girl.
　　Wilt thou not stoop? Now cursèd be the time
　　Of thy nativity. I would the milk
　　Thy mother gave thee when thou sucked'st her breast
　　Had been a little ratsbane° for thy sake.　　　　　　　　*rat poison*
30　Or else, when thou didst keep° my lambs afield,　　　　　　*tend*
　　I wish some ravenous wolf had eaten thee.
　　Dost thou deny thy father, cursèd drab?°　　　　　　　　　*whore*
　　[*To the English*] O burn her, burn her! Hanging is too good.　*Exit*

---

9. A maze built by Daedalus for King Minos of Crete,
who kept in it the Minotaur (a monster born from Queen
Pasiphaë's sexual encounter with a bull).
1. Recall the image or description of her virtues.
5.6 Location: Camp of the Duke of York, France.
1. In F, Joan is included in the list of those who enter at
the beginning of this scene, but it makes sense to have
her enter after York commands that she be brought forth.
2. The first child I had as an unmarried man.
3. Obstinate. This use of "obstacle" suggests the shepherd's country dialect.
4. Hired to give false evidence.
5. English gold coin, worth about one-third of a pound.

RICHARD DUKE OF YORK [to guards]   Take her away, for she hath
     lived too long,
35   To fill the world with vicious qualities.
JOAN   First let me tell you whom you have condemned:
    Not one begotten of a shepherd swain,
    But issued from the progeny of kings;
    Virtuous and holy, chosen from above
40   By inspiration of celestial grace
    To work exceeding° miracles on earth.   *exceptional*
    I never had to do with wicked spirits;
    But you that are polluted with your lusts,
    Stained with the guiltless blood of innocents,
45   Corrupt and tainted with a thousand vices—
    Because you want° the grace that others have,   *lack*
    You judge it straight° a thing impossible   *immediately*
    To compass° wonders but by help of devils.   *accomplish*
    No, misconceivèd[6] Joan of Arc hath been
50   A virgin from her tender infancy,
    Chaste and immaculate in very thought,
    Whose maiden-blood thus rigorously effused°   *cruelly shed*
    Will cry for vengeance at the gates of heaven.
RICHARD DUKE OF YORK   Ay, ay, [to guards] away with her to execution.
55 WARWICK [to guards]   And hark ye, sirs: because she is a maid,
    Spare for no faggots. Let there be enough.
    Place barrels of pitch upon the fatal stake,
    That so her torture may be shortenèd.[7]
JOAN   Will nothing turn° your unrelenting hearts?   *change*
60   Then Joan, discover° thine infirmity,   *reveal*
    That warranteth by law to be thy privilege:[8]
    I am with child, ye bloody homicides.
    Murder not then the fruit within my womb,
    Although ye hale° me to a violent death.   *drag*
65 RICHARD DUKE OF YORK   Now heaven forfend—the holy maid with child?
WARWICK [to JOAN]   The greatest miracle that e'er ye wrought.
    Is all your strict preciseness° come to this?   *propriety*
RICHARD DUKE OF YORK   She and the Dauphin have been
     ingling.°   *having sex; dallying*
    I did imagine° what would be her refuge.°   *wonder / last defense*
70 WARWICK   Well, go to, we will have no bastards live,
    Especially since Charles must father it.
JOAN   You are deceived. My child is none of his.
    It was Alençon[9] that enjoyed my love.
RICHARD DUKE OF YORK   Alençon, that notorious Machiavel?[1]
75   It dies an if it had a thousand lives.
JOAN   O give me leave, I have deluded you.
    'Twas neither Charles nor yet the Duke I named,
    But René King of Naples that prevailed.
WARWICK   A married man?—That's most intolerable.

---

6. Misunderstood, with a pun on "misconceived" as
"miscreated in the womb."
7. The orders for wood and pitch are meant to ensure
either that Joan will die quickly as a result of asphyxiation
from the smoke, rather than from the flames themselves,
or that she will die swiftly from the intensity of the fire.
8. The legal right of a pregnant woman to postpone her
execution until after she has given birth.
9. Henry Alençon, Duke of Anjou, who was notorious for
his part in the Saint Bartholomew's Day Massacre of
French Protestants in 1572.
1. Scheming politician. Niccolò Machiavelli (1469–
1527), author of *The Prince*, became associated with principles of cunning statecraft.

80 RICHARD DUKE OF YORK   Why, here's a girl; I think she knows not well—
     There were so many—whom she may accuse.
   WARWICK   It's sign she hath been liberal° and free.   *generous; promiscuous*
   RICHARD DUKE OF YORK   And yet forsooth she is a virgin pure!
     [*To* JOAN] Strumpet, thy words condemn thy brat and thee.
85   Use no entreaty, for it is in vain.
   JOAN   Then lead me hence; with whom I leave my curse.
     May never glorious sun reflex° his beams   *throw*
     Upon the country where you make abode,
     But darkness and the gloomy shade of death
90   Environ you till mischief° and despair   *misfortune*
     Drive you to break your necks or hang yourselves.
        Enter [the Bishop of WINCHESTER, *now] Cardinal*
   RICHARD DUKE OF YORK   [*to* JOAN]   Break thou in pieces, and
        consume° to ashes,   *burn away*
     Thou foul accursèd minister of hell.   [*Exit* JOAN, *guarded*]
   WINCHESTER   Lord Regent, I do greet your excellence
95   With letters of commission from the King.
     For know, my lords, the states of Christendom,
     Moved with remorse of° these outrageous broils,   *pity for*
     Have earnestly implored a general peace
     Betwixt our nation and the aspiring French,
100 And here at hand the Dauphin and his train
     Approacheth to confer about some matter.
   RICHARD DUKE OF YORK   Is all our travail° turned to this effect?   *labor*
     After the slaughter of so many peers,
     So many captains, gentlemen, and soldiers
105 That in this quarrel have been overthrown
     And sold their bodies for their country's benefit,
     Shall we at last conclude effeminate peace?
     Have we not lost most part of all the towns
     By treason, falsehood, and by treachery,
110 Our great progenitors had conquerèd?
     O Warwick, Warwick, I foresee with grief
     The utter loss of all the realm of France!
   WARWICK   Be patient, York. If we conclude a peace
     It shall be with such strict and severe covenants
115 As° little shall the Frenchmen gain thereby.   *That*
        Enter CHARLES [*the Dauphin, the Duke of*] ALENÇON,
        [*the*] BASTARD [*of Orléans, and*] RENÉ [*Duke of Anjou*]
   CHARLES   Since, lords of England, it is thus agreed
     That peaceful truce shall be proclaimed in France,
     We come to be informèd by yourselves
     What the conditions of that league° must be.   *treaty*
120 RICHARD DUKE OF YORK   Speak, Winchester; for boiling choler° chokes   *anger*
     The hollow passage of my poisoned voice
     By sight of these our baleful° enemies.   *deadly*
   WINCHESTER   Charles and the rest, it is enacted thus:
     That, in regard° King Henry gives consent,   *since*
125 Of mere° compassion and of lenity,°   *Out of pure / mildness*
     To ease your country of distressful war
     And suffer° you to breathe in fruitful peace,   *allow*
     You shall become true liegemen² to his crown.

2. Those bound to serve a feudal lord; faithful subjects.

And, Charles, upon condition thou wilt swear
130 To pay him tribute and submit thyself,
Thou shalt be placed as viceroy under him,
And still enjoy thy regal dignity.
ALENÇON Must he be then as shadow of himself? —
Adorn his temples with a coronet,³
135 And yet in substance and authority
Retain but privilege of a private man?
This proffer is absurd and reasonless.
CHARLES 'Tis known already that I am possessed
With more than half the Gallian° territories,   French
140 And therein reverenced for their lawful king.
Shall I, for lucre° of the rest° unvanquished,   gain / rest that are
Detract so much from that prerogative
As to be called but° viceroy of the whole?   merely
No, lord ambassador, I'll rather keep
145 That which I have than, coveting for more,
Be cast° from possibility of all.   excluded
RICHARD DUKE OF YORK Insulting Charles, hast thou by secret means
Used intercession to obtain a league
And, now the matter grows to compromise,°   toward resolution
150 Stand'st thou aloof upon comparison?⁴
Either accept the title thou usurp'st,
Of benefit° proceeding from our king   As a benefaction
And not of any challenge of desert,⁵
Or we will plague thee with incessant wars.
155 RENÉ [aside to CHARLES] My lord, you do not well in obstinacy
To cavil⁶ in the course of this contract.
If once it be neglected,° ten to one   disregarded
We shall not find like opportunity.
ALENÇON [aside to CHARLES] To say the truth, it is your policy°   astute course
160 To save your subjects from such massacre
And ruthless slaughters as are daily seen
By our proceeding in hostility;
And therefore take this compact of a truce,
Although you break it when your pleasure serves.
165 WARWICK How sayst thou, Charles? Shall our condition stand?
CHARLES It shall,
Only reserved° you claim no interest   With the reservation
In any of our towns of garrison.°   fortified towns
RICHARD DUKE OF YORK Then swear allegiance to his majesty,
170 As thou art knight, never to disobey
Nor be rebellious to the crown of England,
Thou nor thy nobles, to the crown of England.
    [They swear]
So, now dismiss your army when ye please.
Hang up your ensigns, let your drums be still;
175 For here we entertain a solemn peace.   Exeunt

---

3. Small crown worn by nobles.
4. Do you hold off in order to quibble about the terms?
5. And not by any claim of inherent right.
6. To raise frivolous objections.

5.7

Enter [the Earl of] SUFFOLK, in conference with KING
[HENRY, and the Dukes of] GLOUCESTER and EXETER

KING HENRY [*to* SUFFOLK]   Your wondrous rare description, noble Earl,
    Of beauteous Margaret hath astonished me.
    Her virtues gracèd with external gifts
    Do breed love's settled° passions in my heart,   *unchanging*
5   And like as rigour° of tempestuous gusts   *violent force*
    Provokes° the mightiest hulk° against the tide,   *Drives / ship*
    So am I driven by breath of her renown°   *word of her fame*
    Either to suffer shipwreck or arrive
    Where I may have fruition of her love.
10 SUFFOLK   Tush, my good lord, this superficial tale
    Is but a preface of her worthy praise.°   *the praise she deserves*
    The chief perfections of that lovely dame,
    Had I sufficient skill to utter them,
    Would make a volume of enticing lines
15   Able to ravish any dull conceit;°   *imagination*
    And, which is more, she is not so divine,
    So full° replete with choice of all delights,   *fully*
    But with as humble lowliness of mind
    She is content to be at your command—
20   Command, I mean, of virtuous chaste intents,
    To love and honour Henry as her lord.
    KING HENRY   And otherwise will Henry ne'er presume.
    [*To* GLOUCESTER] Therefore, my lord Protector, give consent
    That Marg'ret may be England's royal queen.
25 GLOUCESTER   So should I give consent to flatter sin.
    You know, my lord, your highness is betrothed
    Unto another lady of esteem.[1]
    How shall we then dispense with that contract
    And not deface your honour with reproach?
30 SUFFOLK   As doth a ruler with unlawful oaths,
    Or one that, at a triumph[2] having vowed
    To try his strength, forsaketh yet the lists[3]
    By reason of his adversary's odds.
    A poor earl's daughter is unequal odds,
35   And therefore may be broke[4] without offence.
    GLOUCESTER   Why, what, I pray, is Margaret more than that?
    Her father is no better than an earl,
    Although in glorious titles he excel.
    SUFFOLK   Yes, my lord; her father is a king,
40   The King of Naples and Jerusalem,
    And of such great authority in France
    As his alliance will confirm our peace
    And keep the Frenchmen in allegiance.
    GLOUCESTER   And so the Earl of Armagnac may do,
45   Because he is near kinsman unto Charles.
    EXETER   Beside, his wealth doth warrant° a liberal dower,   *guarantee*
    Where René sooner will receive than give.
    SUFFOLK   A dower, my lords? Disgrace not so your King

5.7 Location: The palace, London.
1. The daughter of the Earl of Armagnac (see 5.1.15–20).
2. Tournament or combat between two opponents on horseback and armed with lances.

3. *forsaketh yet the lists:* nevertheless leaves the tournament grounds.
4. That is, the marriage pledge may be broken.

That he should be so abject, base, and poor
50 To choose for wealth and not for perfect love.
Henry is able to enrich his queen,
And not to seek a queen to make him rich.
So worthless peasants bargain for their wives,
As market men for oxen, sheep, or horse.
55 Marriage is a matter of more worth
Than to be dealt in by attorneyship.°   *proxy*
Not whom *we* will but whom his grace affects°   *desires*
Must be companion of his nuptial bed.
And therefore, lords, since he affects her most,
60 That most of all these reasons bindeth us:
In our opinions she should be preferred.
For what is wedlock forcèd° but a hell,   *enforced marriage*
An age of discord and continual strife,
Whereas the contrary bringeth bliss,
65 And is a pattern° of celestial peace.   *an example*
Whom should we match with Henry, being a king,
But Margaret, that is daughter to a king?
Her peerless feature° joinèd with her birth°   *form / high rank*
Approves her° fit for none but for a king.   *Confirms that she is*
70 Her valiant courage and undaunted spirit,
More than in women commonly is seen,
Will answer our hope in issue of a king.[5]
For Henry, son unto a conqueror,
Is likely to beget more conquerors
75 If with a lady of so high resolve°   *determination*
As is fair Margaret he be linked in love.
Then yield, my lords, and here conclude with me:
That Margaret shall be queen, and none but she.
KING HENRY   Whether it be through force of your report,
80 My noble lord of Suffolk, or for that°   *or because*
My tender youth was never yet attaint°   *infected*
With any passion of inflaming love,
I cannot tell; but this I am assured:
I feel such sharp dissension in my breast,
85 Such fierce alarums° both of hope and fear,   *alarms*
As I am sick with working of my thoughts.
Take therefore shipping; post,° my lord, to France;   *hasten*
Agree to any covenants, and procure
That Lady Margaret do vouchsafe° to come   *promise*
90 To cross the seas to England and be crowned
King Henry's faithful and anointed queen.
For your expenses and sufficient charge,°   *money to spend*
Among the people gather up a tenth.[6]
Be gone, I say; for till you do return
95 I rest perplexèd° with a thousand cares.   *I remain troubled*
[*To* GLOUCESTER] And you, good uncle, banish all offence.°   *hostility*
If you do censure me by what you were,[7]
Not what you are, I know it will excuse
This sudden execution of my will.
100 And so conduct me where from° company   *away from*

5. Will satisfy our hopes by bringing forth a king.
6. A tax of 10 percent on income or property.
7. If you judge me by how you behaved when you were young.

I may revolve and ruminate my grief.[8]   *Exit [with* EXETER]
GLOUCESTER   Ay, grief, I fear me, both at first and last.   *Exit*
SUFFOLK   Thus Suffolk hath prevailed, and thus he goes
As did the youthful Paris[9] once to Greece,
105 With hope to find the like event° in love,   *the same outcome*
But prosper better than the Trojan did.
Margaret shall now be queen and rule the King;
But I will rule both her, the King, and realm.   *Exit*

TEXTUAL VARIANTS

Control text: F

F: The Folio of 1623

s.p. KING HENRY [F's use of *King* has been changed throughout.]
s.p. JOAN [F's use of *Joan, Pucelle,* and *Puzzel* (see note 4 to 1.6.85) has been standardized throughout.]
s.p. CHARLES [F's use of *Dolphin (Dauphin)* and *Charles* has been standardized throughout.]
s.p. RICHARD PLANTAGENET / RICHARD DUKE OF YORK [F's use of *York* and *Richard* has been standardized to "Richard Plantagenet" until 3.1.175–77, when he regains his title; thereafter, "Richard Duke of York" is used.]
s.p. WINCHESTER [F's use of *Winchester* and *Cardinal* has been standardized throughout.]
s.p. FASTOLF [F's use of *Falstaff* has been changed throughout (see note to 1.1.131).]
s.p. RENÉ [F's use of *Reigneir* and *Reignier* has been changed throughout.]
s.p. GLASDALE [F's spelling, *Glansdale,* has been changed throughout.]
s.p. ALENÇON [F's spelling, *Alanson,* has been changed throughout.]

1.1.50 marish Nourish   **60 Rouen, Rheims,** Rheimes,   **62 corpse** Coarse   **89 s.p.** SECOND MESSENGER *Mess.*   **94 René** *Reynold*   **103 s.p.** THIRD MESSENGER *Mes.*   **131 Fastolf** *Falstaffe*   **132 vanguard** Vauward   **157 Fore Orléans** for Orleance is   **176 steal** send
1.2.21 flee fly
1.3.9 bred breed   **78 five** fine   **92 rites** rights   **110 halcyon's** *Halcyons*
1.4.5 knocketh knocks   **19 My lord** The Cardinall   **29 vizier** *Vmphier*   **36 If** Ile canuas thee in thy broad Cardinalls Hat, If   **41 purple** Scarlet   **48 I'll** I   **bishop's mitre** Cardinalls Hat   **55 cloakèd** Scarlet   **72 s.p.** OFFICER [not in F]   **77 Bishop** Cardinall   **82 bishop is** Cardinall's
1.5.8 Prince's spials Princes espyals   **10 Wont** Went
1.6.5 Duke Earle   **11 pilled** pil'd   **41 Glasdale** *Glansdale*   **44 Lou** Lords   **67 Bear . . . bury it** [F places after 1.6.64]   **73 like thee, Nero,** like thee,   **79 la Pucelle** *de Puzel*   **85 Pucelle or pucelle** *Puzel* or *Pussel*   **Dauphin** Dolphin
1.7.3 men them   **29 style** Soyle
1.8.3 la Pucelle *de Puzel*   **21 pyramid** Pyramis   **22 of** or   **29 la Pucelle** *de Puzel*
2.1.5 s.p. A SENTINEL *Sent.*   **29 all together** altogether   **38 s.p.** SENTINELS *Sent.*
2.2.6 centre Centure   **20 Arc** Acre
2.3.21 seely silly
2.4.41 from the tree are cropped are cropt from the Tree   **57 law** you   **117 wiped** whipt   **132 gentles** gentle

---

8. I may return again and again in my mind to my grief.
9. According to Greek myth, Paris went to Greece from Troy and abducted Helen, the wife of Menelaus. This act was said to have brought about the Trojan War, in which Paris was killed.

2.5.3 rack Wrack **6–7 Argue . . . Mortimer, / Nestor-like . . . care.** *Nestor*-like . . . Care, / Argue . . . *Mortimer.* **44 dis-ease** Disease **71 King** [not in F] **75 the third** third **76 the King** hee **129 mine ill** my will

3.1.52 s.p. GLOUCESTER *Warw(icke).* **53 s.p. WARWICK** [not in F, where this line and the prior three words, here assigned to Gloucester, are given to Warwick] **54 so** see **64 intertalk** enter talke **83 pebble** peeble **167 alone** all alone **175 gird** gyrt **203 should lose** loose

3.2.13 *Qui* Che

3.5.32 Goodbye God b'uy

4.1.14 thee the **19 Patay** *Poictiers* **48 my** [not in F] **180 I wist** I wish

4.2.3 captain Captaines **calls** call **15 s.p. GENERAL** *Cap.* **29 fire** ryue **34 due** dew

4.3.17 s.p. LUCY 2. *Mes.* **30 s.p. LUCY** *Mes.* **34 s.p. LUCY** *Mes.* **47 s.p. LUCY** *Mes.*

4.4.16 legions Regions **19 unadvantaged** in aduantage **26 and** [not in F] **27 René** *Reignard* **31 horse** hoast

4.5.39 shamed shame

4.7.70 Maréchal Marshall **89 have them** haue him **94 with them** with him

5.1.59 nor neither

5.2.17–18 s.p. JOAN Now . . . fear. / Of Now . . . feare. / *Pucel.* Of

5.3.8 speed and quick speedy and quicke

5.4.15 comest comst

5.5.4–5 And . . . side. / I . . . peace, I . . . peace, / And . . . side. **12 his** her **18 stream** streames **24 here to hear** heere **41 random** randon **92 Assent** Consent **110 countries** Country **135 modestly** modestie

5.6.10 an't and **37 one** me, **49 Arc** *Aire* **68 ingling** iugling **70 we will** we'll

5.7.60 That [not in F]

Richard III

Among the very few anecdotes about Shakespeare that date from his own lifetime is a ribald story recorded in 1602 in the diary of a London law student, John Manningham:

> Upon a time when Burbage played Richard III there was a citizen grew so far in liking with him, that before she went from the play she appointed him to come that night unto her by the name of Richard III. Shakespeare, overhearing their conclusion, went before, was entertained and at his game ere Burbage came. The message being brought that Richard III was at the door, Shakespeare caused return to be made that William the Conqueror was before Richard III.

Like most stories about celebrities, this one probably says more about those who circulated it than about those it describes. But it does at least suggest that Richard Burbage, the famous actor who first played Richard III (as well as such parts as Romeo and Hamlet), had not by virtue of his villainous role lost all of his glamour. Indeed it is striking that Richard—the "elvish-marked, abortive, rooting hog" (1.3.225), the "poisonous bunch-backed toad" (1.3.244), the heartless cur sent, as he himself puts it, "deformed" and "unfinished" (1.1.20) into the world—has seemed weirdly and compellingly attractive to generations of playgoers. From the start, the play seems to have aroused intense interest: first performed in 1592 or 1593, *Richard III* was published in quarto no fewer than five times during Shakespeare's lifetime.

What can account for this attraction? It is not an obvious feature in the chronicle histories upon which Shakespeare relied, nor does Richard seem to have a comparable allure in another play, of unknown authorship, that dates from the same period, *The True Tragedy of Richard III*. In these works, Richard figures as the pitiless, treacherous villain of what has been called the "Tudor Myth"—that is, the officially sanctioned account of the origin and legitimacy of the Tudor dynasty. That dynasty was founded by Henry, Earl of Richmond, who defeated Richard III at the Battle of Bosworth Field (1485), reigned until his death in 1509 as Henry VII, and was the grandfather of Queen Elizabeth (1533–1603). It is hardly surprising that the new regime, whose claim to the throne was somewhat shaky, would wish to discredit the old. Modern historians emphasize Richard's solid administrative skills; Tudor apologists depict Richard, the last Yorkist king, not merely as venal or unscrupulous but as a monster of evil, a creature whose moral viciousness was vividly stamped on his twisted body.

The principal literary source for this spectacularly partisan depiction was not a piece of simple propaganda but an unusually subtle and complex *History of King Richard the Third* (c. 1513) by the great humanist Thomas More. Later sixteenth-century historians, notably Edward Hall in *The Union of the Noble and Illustre Famelies of Lancastre and Yorke* (1548) and Raphael Holinshed in *The Chronicles of England, Scotland, and Ireland* (1577, revised in 1587), followed closely in More's wake, repeating many of the details that Shakespeare in turn borrowed: Richard's habit of gnawing his lip, for example, or his restlessness, or the rumor that he was born with teeth. More and his followers deftly interwove three distinct explanatory accounts of Richard's behavior: political, psychological, and metaphysical. As a politician (a word with nasty connotations in the Renaissance), Richard is a particularly cunning player in a corrupt world, a Stalin-like schemer plotting to seize power and destroy all real or potential rivals. Psychologically, he is a strange blend of courage, wit, skillful dissembling, and fathomless malice. And on the metaphysical plane, he is a horrible instrument of God's wrath, a virtual devil incarnate.

Most sixteenth-century historians and chroniclers were, by our standards, far more interested in conveying moral meanings than in impartially recounting facts. Shakespeare allowed himself an even greater latitude, freely reshaping and condensing his historical materials in order to heighten dramatic effect and to intensify the political, psychological, and metaphysical dimensions of his villainous antihero. The play compresses events that in reality occurred over a long period of time, so that, for example, Richard's murderous plot against his brother Clarence (1478) is cleverly twined around his cynical courtship of Lady Anne (1472), which is in turn depicted as occurring during the funeral procession of King Henry (1471). The historical Lady Anne had only been betrothed to King Henry's son Edward, but Shakespeare writes as if she had actually been married to him; likewise, he folds Richmond's unsuccessful attempt to invade England in 1483 into his successful invasion of 1485, and he has old Queen Margaret, who was not even in England during most of the events the play depicts, haunting the royal court like a bitter, half-crazed Greek tragic chorus.

Manipulating the insecurities, factional rivalries, and ambitions of everyone around him, Shakespeare's Richard is a consummate portrait of what sixteenth-century Englishmen termed a "machiavel": that is, a person who acts on the immoral advice allegedly offered by the Florentine humanist Niccolò Machiavelli in *The Prince* (written in 1513, first printed in 1532). According to the period's lurid and grossly distorted account of this advice, Machiavelli had counseled princes to lie, cheat, and murder under the cover of hypocritical professions of virtue and piety. "I count Religion but a childish Toy," declares the character called Machevil, who speaks the prologue to Marlowe's *Jew of Malta* (c. 1590). Shakespeare's Richard, at first terrified by the apparition of the ghosts in Act 5, rallies to express comparable sentiments: "Conscience is but a word that cowards use, / Devised at first to keep the strong in awe" (5.6.39–40). These are sentiments that, for the most part, Richard keeps to himself—or, rather, shares only with the audience in a succession of gleeful asides—for he is highly skilled at assuming the pose of religious faith. Aided by his fellow hypocrite Buckingham, Richard appears in a memorable scene, prayer book in hand, miming "devotion and right Christian zeal" (3.7.103) while cynically stage-managing the supposedly popular call for his coronation.

Richard III. Portrait by unknown artist (c. 1590).

Shakespeare's vision of Richard as a consummate role-player goes back to a brilliant sketch of the same character in one of the three earlier plays he had written on fifteenth-century English history. Taken together, these plays—*The First Part of Henry the Sixth, The First Part of the Contention of the Two Famous Houses of York and Lancaster* (2 Henry VI), and *The True Tragedy of Richard Duke of York and the Good King Henry the Sixth* (3 Henry VI)—depict the chaotic, violent factional struggles unleashed by the weakness of the well-meaning but inept Henry VI. These struggles, known as the Wars of the Roses, pitted two noble houses, the Lancastrians and the Yorkists, against each other. At the close of *Richard Duke of York* (3 Henry VI), the Yorkist faction, led by the Duke of York's three surviving sons (Edward, George, and Richard), has triumphed. The last Lancastrian king, Henry VI, has been murdered by Richard, Duke of

Gloucester, and Richard's eldest brother has been crowned King Edward V. But a shadow is cast across this decisive Yorkist victory by the ruthless and unsatisfied ambition of Richard.

Though it can stand (and be performed) entirely on its own, *Richard III* may be regarded as the fourth part of a tetralogy, for it picks up directly from the turbulent events depicted in *Richard Duke of York* and, more particularly, from the project Richard announces in a long soliloquy. He declares that since nature has seen fit to deform his body and so exclude him from sensual pleasures, he will instead pursue the crown. "I can add colours to the chameleon," he boasts, "change shapes with Proteus for advantages, / And set the murderous Machiavel to school" (*Richard Duke of York* 3.2.191–93). Here Shakespeare is beginning to psychologize the machiavel, to provide inner motives for his violent ambition and his compulsive shape changing. *Richard III* continues and intensifies this process: as his opening soliloquy suggests, Richard feels that from birth he has been cruelly cheated by dissembling nature. Deprived of the normal satisfactions of nurturing and kindness—it is as if his mother's womb itself had rejected him—he tries to find compensatory satisfaction in cruelty and dissembling of his own. He seeks not only vengeance against an unloving world but also the pleasure of cherishing himself. Yet at the end, in a vigorous if crude moment of self-analysis, he discovers that even self-love eludes him: "I love myself. Wherefore? . . . O no, alas, I rather hate myself" (5.5.141–43).

Richard's self-hatred is psychologically revealing—evidently, he has internalized the loathing that he inspires in virtually everyone around him—but it is not simply generated from within: there is, the play's characters continually imply, a divinely sanctioned, objective moral order independent of both individuals and society, and by the fixed norms of this order Richard *is* hateful. It is possible for villains like Richard or the murderers of Clarence to close their ears to the admonitions of conscience, but all human actions are part of a larger design and will ultimately be judged by a heavenly power. From this higher perspective, Richard's deformity is less the *cause* of his evil nature than its *sign*. Similarly, the ghosts in Act 5 are not merely psychological projections but metaphysical emissaries. The dead do not simply rot and disappear, nor do they survive only in the memories and dreams of the living: they are an ineradicable presence, a part of the structure of reality, an uncanny age group capable of blessing and cursing. Richard tries to shake off their condemnation, as earlier he had jauntily deflected Margaret's elaborate curse, but their words bring beads of sweat to his trembling flesh. For while he may tell himself that his victims' words are merely the impotent weapons of the powerless, he cannot escape the play's pervasive sense that there is something eerie and disturbing about curses, as if through incantatory verbal ritual they magically touch the hidden order of things.

Despite Richard's disruptive mockery and unceremonious violence, an atmosphere of ritual lingers over much of *Richard III*, tinging the rhetorically elaborate expressions of grief and anger, solemnizing formal ceremonies, and shaping the percep-

Henry VII. Portrait by Michael Sittow (1505).

"For they account his head upon the bridge" (3.2.67). London Bridge adorned with the heads of traitors. From Claes Jansz Vischer, *Londinum florentissima Britanniae urbs* (1625).

tions of the guilt-ridden characters. Though the play gives us historical figures with psychological motivations and political stratagems, often we seem less in the secular world of disenchanted politics than in the world of classical tragedy or medieval rite. Thus, for example, Clarence's terrible nightmare just before his murder recalls the hell of the Roman playwright Seneca and, still more, the hell of fourteenth-century Christian painting, with its howling fiends and damned souls. Clarence is haunted by the sense of an unappeasable God preparing to punish him for his crimes, and his dream discloses what he does not yet consciously know: that the agent of divine retribution is his own brother, Richard.

This ritual process—the inexorable working out of retributive justice or nemesis through the agency of Richard—is best conveyed perhaps by the chorus of grief-crazed women, above all by old Queen Margaret, who identifies Richard as "hell's black intelligencer" (4.4.71), or secret agent. In a series of stiff antiphonal laments (4.4.35ff.), Margaret (the widow of the slain Henry VI), Queen Elizabeth (the widow of Edward IV), and the Duchess of York (the widowed mother of Edward and his brothers, including Richard) tease out the strict eye-for-an-eye logic of the action. And at one startling moment, Richard himself comes close to acknowledging his role within this scheme: he likens himself to "the formal Vice, Iniquity" (3.1.82).

The character called the Vice is an inheritance of the medieval morality play: the busy enemy of mankind, the Vice was at once the agent of hell and the tool of divine providence, a master plotter and a puppet in a play that is not of his own making. Yet this fixed place in the divine plan did not preclude his acquiring an extraordinary theatrical power and resourcefulness, qualities that Shakespeare would later exploit in characters as different (and as magnificent) as Falstaff and Iago. Shakespeare constructs Richard out of many elements in the Vice tradition: a jaunty use of asides, a delight in sharing his schemes with the audience, a grotesque appearance, a penchant for disguise, a manic energy and humor, and a wickedly engaging ability to defer though not finally to escape well-deserved punishment. Richard's own allusion to the Vice calls attention to yet another element, a skill in playing with the doubleness of words and exploiting the slipperiness of language: "Thus like the formal Vice, Iniquity, / I moralize two meanings in one word" (3.1.82–83). *Richard III* puts the demonic master of this vicious skill on display and, in the end, stages his destruction: in a sense, the ritual that lingers over the play is an exorcism.

But, of course, *Richard III* is not in fact a ritual, and Shakespeare's subtle blending of psychological, metaphysical, and political perspectives carefully suspends any determination of their relative significance in the history he portrays. This suspension helps make the play work, but it also marks the limits of its achievement, since each of the perspectives subverts the others. The psychological development of Richard is arrested by the intimation that psychology is itself the tool of a supernatural scheme; the supernatural is subverted (at least until the ghost scene) by the Machiavellian subordination of religion to power politics; but power politics is itself undermined by the suggestion that individuals act in the grip not of rational calculation but of psychological pressures and passions over which they have little or no control.

That these perspectives do not simply cancel each other out is the result of the extraordinary theatrical force of Richard himself. Only *Hamlet*, of all Shakespeare's plays, is comparably dominated by a single character, and only *Macbeth* is comparably structured around an evil hero. (The villains Richard most anticipates—Philip the Bastard in *King John*, Don John in *Much Ado About Nothing*, Iago in *Othello*, and Edmund in *King Lear*—are all at varying degrees of distance from the main protagonist.) Without for a moment concealing from the audience Richard's appalling, monstrous evil, Shakespeare makes his villain immensely captivating. In large part, his allure derives from what Keats called the "gusto" of Shakespeare's evil characters: "Your eyes drop millstones when fools' eyes fall tears," says Richard to the murderers; "I like you, lads" (1.3.351–52). The startling frankness of this villainy has a comic charge, a charge renewed in the open wickedness of his plans for unsuspecting Hastings—"Chop off his head" (3.1.190)—or for the innocent young princes: "I wish the bastards dead" (4.2.19). There is gusto in Richard's slyness as well as in his frankness, a slyness that also is often comic: "So wise so young, they say, do never live long" (3.1.79).

The allure of such moments seems to be bound up with the allure of the theater itself, with its capacity for emotional intensification, surprise, deception, and heightened energy. The religious enemies of the theater in Shakespeare's age charged that this energy was essentially erotic—the playhouse, they complained, aroused sexual desire—and before dismissing their charges as preposterous, we might recall the comic anecdote from John Manningham's diary with which this introduction began. Shakespeare himself in *Richard III* seems to play with the seductive power of theatrical performance in the bizarre scene in which Richard successfully courts Lady Anne over the body of her father-in-law, the King, whom he has murdered: "Was ever woman in this humour wooed? / Was ever woman in this humour won?" (1.2.215–16). Richard's wooing has nothing to do with tenderness, affection, sympathy, or even sexual attraction; we witness an aggressive male assault upon Lady Anne's rooted, eloquently expressed, and eminently justified fear and loathing. Here, as elsewhere, Richard gets what he wants because he possesses greater power to control the scenario: more than Anne, more than anyone, he knows how to initiate action, conceal motives, threaten, intimidate, and hurt. He has killed Anne's husband as well as her father-in-law; he will, when she has served his purpose, kill Anne too. Anne knows this well enough—"Ill rest betide the chamber where thou liest" (1.2.112)— but she virtually invents uncertainties to mask the calculating murderousness she herself has perceived with cold clarity: "I would I knew thy heart," she muses, seconds after she has thoroughly inventoried Richard's villainous heart (1.2.180).

Anne is shallow, corruptible, naively ambitious, and, above all, frightened—all qualities that help to account for her spectacular surrender—but the scene's theatrical power rests less upon a depiction of her character than upon the spectacle of Richard's restless aggression transformed during the rapid-fire exchange of one-liners (called in rhetoric *stichomythia*) into a perverse form of sexual provocation and of Anne's verbal violence transformed, in spite of itself, into an erotic response. In light of this transformation, the misshapen Richard's celebration of his sexual attractiveness—

> I do mistake my person all this while.
> Upon my life she finds, although I cannot,
> Myself to be a marv'lous proper man—

is not wholly ironic, even if he himself thinks it is (1.2.239–50).

Eros has not been excluded from Richard's career; it has found a new and compelling form in his energetic, witty, and murderous chafing against the obstacles in his path. These obstacles are not simply set in opposition to his desire; rather they virtually constitute it, for it is the extent of his distance from power that generates Richard's craving for it. His politics, and hence the sexuality implied by that politics, is transgressive; it thrives on the violation of social and natural bonds. His is the psychology of the rapist, and the character in Shakespeare closest to Richard III is the rapist Tarquin (in *The Rape of Lucrece*), whose lust is excited precisely by the barriers he is forced to overcome. This chafing structure is why the violent verbal assaults upon Richard, most intense from the women in the play, seem only to intensify his political and erotic energies. It is perhaps also why Richard seems to lose much of his erotic power as soon as he has established himself on the throne. When the obstacles in his path to the crown have been removed, when there is no legitimate authority to transgress, the erotic quality of his ambition immediately begins to wane.

The play has allowed Richard to be a perverse erotic champion—a role probably possible only in this highly theatrical vision of history—but the desire he embodies cannot be integrated into any viable social or natural order; nor does it constitute a coherent, stable inner life. By the play's end, he seems a hollow man, a set of theatrical masks that project grotesque shadows upon the world. Fittingly, when "shadows," in the form of those he has murdered, return to produce terror in him—"Cold fearful drops stand on my trembling flesh" (5.5.135)—he can only express his fear in histrionic terms, staging a miniature dialogue with himself and then imagining his conscience as the audience, with its thousand tongues condemning him for a villain.

Richard's manifest theatricality is only the extreme form of a theatricality diffused throughout the play. Virtually all of the speeches—lamentation, cursing, debate, persuasion—are cast as self-conscious performances: "What means this scene of rude impatience?" asks the Duchess of York; Queen Elizabeth replies, "To mark an act of tragic violence" (2.2.38–39). Moreover, there is a pervasive sense that the characters exist as figures in someone else's play: through most of the performance, they are figures, without knowing it, in Richard's play, but Richard himself is a figure in another play, larger than himself. That larger play is at once the drama of history, scripted (as Tudor ideology claimed) by God, and the historical drama, scripted by Shakespeare. If the script obliges all of the characters to display the power of divine providence, it obliges them at the same time to display the power of the theater. For if the stage pays homage to the state, it also makes the state into a histrionic spectacle on the public stage. *Richard III* manages to imply that the whole vast enterprise of Tudor power exists to make this play, and the theater in which it is performed, possible.

STEPHEN GREENBLATT

TEXTUAL NOTE

Richard III first appeared in quarto (Q1) in 1597, without the playwright's name but with a very full title page:

> THE TRAGEDY OF King Richard the third. Containing, His treacherous Plots against his brother Clarence: the pittiefull murther of his iunocent nephewes: his tyrannicall vsurpation: with the whole course of his detested life, and most deserued death. As it hath beene lately Acted by the Right honourable the Lord Chamberlaine his seruants AT LONDON Printed by Valentine Sims, for Andrew Wise, dwelling in Paules Chu[r]chyard, at the Signe of the Angell. 1597.

The play proved to be a popular one: so much so that five more quarto versions came out before the appearance of the First Folio (F) in 1623. These quarto editions (Q2–Q6) can claim no textual authority, because of their means of composition; each was based on the text of the one immediately preceding it. Each not only carried forward, therefore, the accumulated errors of its predecessors but added some of its own. The main editorial questions revolve, then, about the authority of, and the relationship between, Q1 and F.

Certainly the quarto text influenced F. But the hundreds of differences between the two suggest that a further source, an independent manuscript, was also used in the construction of F. The Oxford editor Gary Taylor believes that this manuscript was probably a transcript, presumably done by a scribe, of Shakespeare's "foul papers," that is, a version of the play in Shakespeare's own hand, with whatever additions, corrections, and revisions he may have inserted in the course of its composition.

It appears that neither Q nor F derives directly from Shakespeare's own manuscript. It has, however, been proposed that Q, the shorter text, might represent a first draft of the play. Gary Taylor rejects this hypothesis. In his view, Q is a "bad" quarto, that is, one reconstructed from memory of the play as performed. If so, it is a surprisingly thorough reconstruction, carried out, probably, not by one or two renegade players of minor roles but by Shakespeare's company itself, or rather by those members to hand when the reconstructed text was being written down. Some part of the company on tour in the provinces, for example, could have found itself without a prompt copy of *Richard III*. A text hurriedly assembled in such circumstances might be substantially complete, except for gaps in the minor roles, which would have been played by hired men. Such gaps, showing up as omissions and textual variants, do in fact occur in the Q version of the play and therefore lend support to Taylor's theory. Given that the passages Q omits tend to slow down the dramatic action, and that its only substantial additional passage is a particularly impressive one (the "clock" dialogue, 4.2.101–20), it seems to follow that Q is a later text—one more theatrically attuned, one trimmed of some superfluous bulk. Hence, Oxford adopts a substantial number of the Q variants.

Other omissions appear to show the effects of censorship. The exclamation "Zounds" ("by His wounds") appears four times in Q but not in F, as does a reference to "Christ's dear blood shed for our grievous sins." The name "God," however, appears frequently in both texts. Political rather than purely religious concerns seem to have caused a further omission. Hastings's lines at the conclusion of 3.4, in which he prophesies "the fearful'st time" in a coming "miserable England," could well be seen as unsettling to an audience that laid great store by prophecy. These lines do not appear in F. But what of the inclusion only in Q of the "clock" dialogue mentioned above? In fact, this seeming anomaly (it is the only major passage not in F) adds weight to the early F hypothesis. The very singular nature of this passage leads Oxford to see it as "an inspired afterthought." No political considerations, far less theatrical ones, could justify its deletion. We might also note that in what was an already very long play, Shakespeare might have been more inclined to deletion than to addition.

F, we can see, is closer to its sources, Hall and Holinshed, and is manifestly the superior text. Many passages are better crafted in meter and meaning than their Q counterparts. F, then, is the control text for substantive readings. Recalling, however, that the Q reconstruction would have taken place at a time when Shakespeare himself was active in the company and may have had a hand in revision for the stage, an unusually large number of departures from the control text have been retained. The reader is thus presented, we hope, with the play in its most fully realized theatrical form.

In this edition, F passages that were omitted from Q and relegated in the *Oxford Shakespeare* to an appendix are printed inset and in italics.

SELECTED BIBLIOGRAPHY

Carroll, William. " 'The Form of Law': Ritual and Succession in *Richard III*." *True Rites and Maimed Rites*. Ed. Linda Woodbridge and Edward Berry. Urbana: University of Illinois Press, 1992. 203–19.

Clemen, Wolfgang H. *A Commentary on Shakespeare's "Richard III."* London: Methuen, 1968.

Garber, Marjorie. "Descanting on Deformity: Richard III and the Shape of History." *The*

Historical Renaissance: New Essays on Tudor and Stuart Literature and Culture. Ed. Heather Dubrow and Richard Strier. Chicago: University of Chicago Press, 1988. 79–103.

Hunter, Robert G. *Shakespeare and the Mystery of God's Judgments.* Athens: University of Georgia Press, 1976.

Jones, Emrys. *The Origins of Shakespeare.* Oxford: Oxford University Press, 1977.

Ornstein, Robert. *A Kingdom for a Stage: The Achievement of Shakespeare's History Plays.* Cambridge: Harvard University Press, 1972.

Ribner, Irving. *The English History Play in the Age of Shakespeare.* Princeton: Barnes and Noble, 1957.

Rossiter, A. P. *Angel with Horns and Other Shakespeare Lectures.* New York: Theater Arts Books, 1961.

Tillyard, E. M. W. *Shakespeare's History Plays.* New York: Macmillan, 1946.

Wheeler, Richard P. "History, Character, and Conscience in *Richard III.*" *Comparative Drama* 5 (1971–72): 301–21.

The Tragedy of
King Richard the Third

THE PERSONS OF THE PLAY

KING EDWARD IV
DUCHESS OF YORK, his mother
PRINCE EDWARD
Richard, the young Duke of YORK } his sons
George, Duke of CLARENCE
RICHARD, Duke of GLOUCESTER, later KING RICHARD } his brothers
Clarence's SON
Clarence's DAUGHTER
QUEEN ELIZABETH, King Edward's wife
Anthony Woodeville, Earl RIVERS, her brother
Marquis of DORSET
Lord GRAY } her sons
Sir Thomas VAUGHAN
GHOST OF KING HENRY VI
QUEEN MARGARET, his widow
GHOST OF PRINCE EDWARD, his son
LADY ANNE, Prince Edward's widow
William, LORD HASTINGS, Lord Chamberlain
Lord STANLEY, Earl of Derby, his friend
HENRY EARL OF RICHMOND, later KING HENRY VII, Stanley's son-in-law
Earl of OXFORD
Sir James BLUNT } Richmond's followers
Sir Walter HERBERT
Duke of BUCKINGHAM
Duke of NORFOLK
Sir Richard RATCLIFFE
Sir William CATESBY } Richard Gloucester's followers
Sir James TYRRELL
Two MURDERERS
A PAGE
CARDINAL
BISHOP OF ELY
John, a PRIEST
SIR CHRISTOPHER, a Priest
Sir Robert BRACKENBURY, Lieutenant of the Tower of London
Lord MAYOR of London
A SCRIVENER
Hastings, a PURSUIVANT
SHERIFF
Aldermen and Citizens
Attendants, two bishops, messengers, soldiers

1.1

Enter RICHARD *Duke of* GLOUCESTER[1]

RICHARD GLOUCESTER   Now is the winter of our discontent
Made glorious summer by this son of York;[2]
And all the clouds that loured° upon our house°   glowered / family
In the deep bosom of the ocean buried.
5 Now are our brows bound with victorious wreaths,
Our bruisèd arms° hung up for monuments,°   armor / memorials
Our stern alarums° changed to merry meetings,   call to arms
Our dreadful marches to delightful measures.°   dances
Grim-visaged war hath smoothed his wrinkled front,°   forehead
10 And now—instead of mounting barbèd° steeds   armored
To fright the souls of fearful adversaries—
He capers[3] nimbly in a lady's chamber
To the lascivious pleasing of a lute.
But I, that am not shaped for sportive° tricks   amorous
15 Nor made to court an amorous looking-glass,
I that am rudely stamped[4] and want° love's majesty   lack
To strut before a wanton ambling° nymph,   strolling
I that am curtailed of this fair proportion,°   shape
Cheated of feature° by dissembling nature,   good appearance
20 Deformed, unfinished, sent before my time
Into this breathing world scarce half made up—
And that so lamely and unfashionable°   badly formed
That dogs bark at me as I halt° by them—   limp
Why, I in this weak piping[5] time of peace
25 Have no delight to pass away the time,
Unless to spy my shadow in the sun
And descant on° mine own deformity.   remark upon
And therefore since I cannot prove° a lover   prove to be
To entertain these fair well-spoken days,
30 I am determinèd to prove a villain
And hate the idle pleasures of these days.
Plots have I laid, inductions[6] dangerous,
By drunken prophecies, libels and dreams
To set my brother Clarence[7] and the King
35 In deadly hate the one against the other.
And if King Edward be as true and just
As I am subtle false and treacherous,
This day should Clarence closely be mewed up°   caged (like a hawk)
About a prophecy which says that 'G'[8]
40 Of Edward's heirs the murderer shall be.

Enter [George Duke of] CLARENCE, *guarded, and [Sir Robert]* BRACKENBURY

Dive, thoughts, down to my soul: here Clarence comes.
Brother, good day. What means this armèd guard
That waits upon your grace?

1.1 Location: A street in London.
1. Pronounced "Gloster."
2. *son of York:* Edward IV, son of Richard, Duke of York; with wordplay on Edward's emblem, a sun in splendor.
3. In court dances, men often made "capers," or showy leaps; also suggests a sexual escapade.
4. Roughly, imperfectly shaped (alluding to the stamping of a coin with an image).
5. Characterized by the music of a peaceful shepherd's

flute: shrill-voiced, like women or children.
6. Initial moves, prologues.
7. George, Duke of Clarence, Richard, Duke of Gloucester, and King Edward IV were brothers; Clarence, being older than Richard, would become King if Edward and his heirs died.
8. Which Edward interprets as "George"; but which could—and does—mean "Gloucester."

CLARENCE His majesty,
Tend'ring° my person's safety, hath appointed *Caring about*
45 This conduct° to convey me to the Tower.[9] *escort*
RICHARD GLOUCESTER Upon what cause?
CLARENCE Because my name is George.
RICHARD GLOUCESTER Alack, my lord, that fault is none of yours.
He should for that commit your godfathers.[1]
Belike° his majesty hath some intent *Probably*
50 That you should be new-christened in the Tower.
But what's the matter, Clarence? May I know?
CLARENCE Yea, Richard, when I know—for I protest
As yet I do not. But as I can learn
He hearkens after prophecies and dreams,
55 And from the cross-row° plucks the letter 'G' *alphabet*
And says a wizard told him that by 'G'
His issue° disinherited should be. *children*
And for my name of George begins with 'G',
It follows in his thought that I am he.
60 These, as I learn, and suchlike toys° as these, *trifles*
Hath moved his highness to commit° me now. *arrest*
RICHARD GLOUCESTER Why, this it is when men are ruled by women.
'Tis not the King that sends you to the Tower;
My Lady Gray,[2] his wife—Clarence, 'tis she
65 That tempts him to this harsh extremity.
Was it not she, and that good man of worship[3]
Anthony Woodeville her brother there,
That made him send Lord Hastings to the Tower,
From whence this present day he is delivered?
70 We are not safe, Clarence; we are not safe.
CLARENCE By heaven, I think there is no man secure
But the Queen's kindred, and night-walking heralds° *secret go-betweens*
That trudge betwixt the King and Mrs Shore.[4]
Heard ye not what an humble suppliant
75 Lord Hastings was for his delivery?
RICHARD GLOUCESTER Humbly complaining to her deity[5]
Got my Lord Chamberlain[6] his liberty.
I'll tell you what: I think it is our way,° *strategy*
If we will keep in favour with the King,
80 To be her men and wear her livery.[7]
The jealous, o'erworn widow[8] and herself,° *(Jane Shore)*
Since that our brother dubbed them[9] gentlewomen,
Are mighty gossips° in our monarchy. *busybodies*
BRACKENBURY I beseech your graces both to pardon me.
85 His majesty hath straitly given in charge° *has strictly ordered*

9. Tower of London, used to house noble prisoners as well as (in Elizabethan England) traitors and political agitators.
1. The godfather was responsible for the naming of a newborn child.
2. A sarcastic reference to the Queen, widow of Sir John Gray before her marriage to the King. Her maiden name was Elizabeth Woodeville.
3. Honor (here, a sarcastic phrase, more appropriate to a solid, middle-class citizen than to the Queen's brother, Anthony Woodeville, who succeeded his father as Earl Rivers).
4. Jane Shore, wife of a London goldsmith. Her liaison

with Edward was notorious. Mrs.: Mistress (here in both the polite and the abusive sense).
5. Jane Shore (ironically, by analogy with "her majesty").
6. Hastings. According to Shakespeare's sources, Jane Shore became his mistress when her affair with the King ended.
7. Servants ("men") in noble households wore the colors of the family.
8. The Queen, a widow before she married Edward IV. o'erworn: faded.
9. Invested them with the status of (usually used of knights). Richard grossly exaggerates the lowly status of the Queen's family before her marriage.

That no man shall have private conference,
Of what degree soever,[1] with your brother.
RICHARD GLOUCESTER   Even so. An't° please your worship, Brackenbury,   *If it*
You may partake of anything we say.

90   We speak no treason, man. We say the King
Is wise and virtuous, and his noble Queen
Well struck° in years, fair, and not jealous.   *advanced*
We say that Shore's wife hath a pretty foot,
A cherry lip,

95   A bonny eye, a passing° pleasing tongue,   *an exceedingly*
And that the Queen's kin are made gentlefolks.
How say you, sir? Can you deny all this?
BRACKENBURY   With this, my lord, myself have naught° to do.   *nothing*
RICHARD GLOUCESTER   Naught[2] to do with Mrs Shore? I tell thee, fellow:

100   He that doth naught with her—excepting one—
Were best to do it secretly alone.
BRACKENBURY   What one, my lord?
RICHARD GLOUCESTER   Her husband, knave. Wouldst thou betray me?
BRACKENBURY   I beseech your grace to pardon me, and do withal°   *moreover*

105   Forbear your conference with the noble Duke.
CLARENCE   We know thy charge, Brackenbury, and will obey.
RICHARD GLOUCESTER   We are the Queen's abjects,° and must obey.   *base subjects*
Brother, farewell. I will unto the King,
And whatsoe'er you will employ me in—

110   Were it to call King Edward's widow° 'sister'—   *(Queen Elizabeth)*
I will perform it to enfranchise° you.   *free*
Meantime, this deep disgrace in brotherhood
Touches me dearer[3] than you can imagine.
CLARENCE   I know it pleaseth neither of us well.

115   RICHARD GLOUCESTER   Well, your imprisonment shall not be long.
I will deliver you or lie for you.[4]
Meantime, have patience.
CLARENCE   I must perforce.° Farewell.   *of necessity*
         Exeunt CLARENCE[, BRACKENBURY, *and guard, to the Tower*]
RICHARD GLOUCESTER   Go tread the path that thou shalt ne'er return.
Simple plain Clarence, I do love thee so

120   That I will shortly send thy soul to heaven,
If heaven will take the present at° our hands.   *from*
But who comes here? The new-delivered° Hastings?   *newly released*
         Enter LORD HASTINGS [*from the Tower*]
LORD HASTINGS   Good time of day unto my gracious lord.
RICHARD GLOUCESTER   As much unto my good Lord Chamberlain.

125   Well are you welcome to the open air.
How hath your lordship brooked° imprisonment?   *tolerated*
LORD HASTINGS   With patience, noble lord, as prisoners must.
But I shall live, my lord, to give them thanks
That were the cause of my imprisonment.

130   RICHARD GLOUCESTER   No doubt, no doubt—and so shall Clarence too,
For they that were your enemies are his,
And have prevailed as much on him as you.

---

1. *no . . . soever:* that is, despite Richard's high rank
("degree"), he must not speak with the prisoner.
2. Wickedness; here, specifically sexual intercourse.
3. Wounds me more, but also (as a hidden meaning),

implicates me more.
4. In prison, in place of Clarence (with a pun on "lie" as
"tell falsehoods about"). "Deliver" and "lie for" rhyme.

LORD HASTINGS   More pity that the eagles should be mewed
While kites° and buzzards prey at liberty.   *scavenger birds*
135   RICHARD GLOUCESTER   What news abroad?°   *circulating*
LORD HASTINGS   No news so bad abroad as this at home:
The King is sickly, weak, and melancholy,
And his physicians fear° him mightily.   *fear for*
RICHARD GLOUCESTER   Now by Saint Paul, that news is bad indeed.
140   O he hath kept an evil diet° long,   *way of life*
And overmuch consumed his royal person.⁵
'Tis very grievous to be thought upon.
Where is he? In his bed?
LORD HASTINGS   He is.
RICHARD GLOUCESTER   Go you before and I will follow you.
                                        Exit HASTINGS
145   He cannot live, I hope, and must not die
Till George be packed with post-haste° up to heaven.   *by express*
I'll in to urge his hatred more to Clarence,
With lies well steeled° with weighty arguments.   *made strong*
And if I fail not in my deep intent,
150   Clarence hath not another day to live—
Which done, God take King Edward to his mercy
And leave the world for me to bustle in.
For then I'll marry Warwick's youngest daughter.⁶
What though I killed her husband and her father?⁷
155   The readiest way to make the wench amends
Is to become her husband and her father,
The which will I: not all so much for love,
As for another secret close intent,°   *private purpose*
By marrying her, which I must reach unto.
160   But yet I run before my horse to market.
Clarence still breathes, Edward still lives and reigns;
When they are gone, then must I count my gains.   *Exit*

1.2

*Enter [gentlemen, bearing] the corpse of [King] Henry
VI [in an open coffin], with halberdiers¹ to guard it,*
LADY ANNE *being the mourner*
LADY ANNE   Set down, set down your honourable load,
If honour may be shrouded in a hearse,°   *an open coffin*
Whilst I a while obsequiously° lament   *mournfully*
Th'untimely fall of virtuous Lancaster.²
      [They set the coffin down]
5   Poor key-cold³ figure of a holy king,
Pale ashes of the house of Lancaster,
Thou bloodless remnant of that royal blood:
Be it lawful that I invocate thy ghost⁴
To hear the lamentations of poor Anne,
10   Wife to thy Edward, to thy slaughtered son,

5. And has been weakened by extravagant living.
6. Lady Anne Neville, who had been betrothed (but not married) to Edward, Prince of Wales, the son of King Henry VI. Shakespeare, however, writes of Anne as Edward's widow.
7. *her father*: Henry VI (father-in-law).
1.2 Location: A street in London.
1. Men carrying halberds (a spearlike weapon with a blade as well as a point).
2. Henry VI, of the house of Lancaster, was deposed and murdered by the Yorkists; the dynastic quarrel dates from the deposition of Richard II and is dramatized in Shakespeare's three *Henry VI* plays.
3. Proverbial for "cold as death."
4. Conjuring of spirits was generally condemned. *invocate*: invoke.

Stabbed by the selfsame hand that made these wounds.
Lo, in these windows[5] that let forth thy life,
I pour the helpless° balm of my poor eyes.   *useless*
O cursèd be the hand that made these holes,
15   Cursèd the blood that let this blood from hence,
Cursèd the heart that had the heart to do it.
More direful hap betide° that hated wretch   *fate befall*
That makes us wretched by the death of thee
Than I can wish to wolves, to spiders, toads,
20   Or any creeping venomed thing that lives.
If ever he have child, abortive° be it,   *incompletely formed*
Prodigious,° and untimely brought to light,   *Monstrous*
Whose ugly and unnatural aspect°   *appearance*
May fright the hopeful mother at the view,
25   And that be heir to his unhappiness.[6]
If ever he have wife, let her be made
More miserable by the death of him
Than I am made by my young lord and thee.[7] —
Come now towards Chertsey° with your holy load,   *monastery near London*
30   Taken from Paul's[8] to be interrèd there,
      [*The gentlemen lift the coffin*]
And still as° you are weary of this weight   *Whenever*
Rest you, whiles I lament King Henry's corpse.
      Enter RICHARD *Duke of* GLOUCESTER
RICHARD GLOUCESTER [*to the gentlemen*]   Stay, you that bear
      the corpse, and set it down.
LADY ANNE   What black magician conjures up this fiend
35   To stop devoted charitable deeds?
RICHARD GLOUCESTER [*to the gentlemen*]   Villains,° set down   *Scoundrels; peasants*
      the corpse, or by Saint Paul
I'll make a corpse of him that disobeys.
HALBERDIER   My lord, stand back and let the coffin pass.
RICHARD GLOUCESTER   Unmannered dog, stand thou when I command.
40   Advance[9] thy halberd higher than my breast,
Or by Saint Paul I'll strike thee to my foot
And spurn° upon thee, beggar, for thy boldness.   *kick*
      [*They set the coffin down*]
LADY ANNE [*to gentlemen and halberdiers*]   What, do you tremble?
      Are you all afraid?
Alas, I blame you not, for you are mortal,
45   And mortal eyes cannot endure the devil. —
Avaunt,° thou dreadful minister of hell.   *Be gone*
Thou hadst but power over his mortal body;
His soul thou canst not have; therefore be gone.
RICHARD GLOUCESTER   Sweet saint, for charity be not so cursed.°   *bad-tempered*
50   LADY ANNE   Foul devil, for God's sake hence and trouble us not,
For thou hast made the happy earth thy hell,
Filled it with cursing cries and deep exclaims.
If thou delight to view thy heinous deeds,
Behold this pattern° of thy butcheries. —   *example*
55   O gentlemen, see, see! Dead Henry's wounds

---

5. Stab wounds (possibly referring to the custom of opening the windows to let a dying soul pass).
6. Evil nature; ill fortune.

7. By the deaths of Prince Edward and King Henry VI.
8. St. Paul's, cathedral of the City of London.
9. Raise upright (rather than hold it pointing at Richard).

Ope their congealèd mouths and bleed afresh.[1] —
Blush, blush, thou lump of foul deformity,
For 'tis thy presence that ex-hales° this blood   *calls forth*
From cold and empty veins where no blood dwells.
60 Thy deed, inhuman and unnatural,
Provokes this deluge supernatural.[2]
O God, which this blood mad'st, revenge his death.
O earth, which this blood drink'st, revenge his death.
Either heav'n with lightning strike the murd'rer dead,
65 Or earth gape open wide and eat him quick°   *alive*
As thou dost swallow up this good king's blood,
Which his hell-governed arm hath butcherèd.
RICHARD GLOUCESTER Lady, you know no rules of charity,
Which renders good for bad, blessings for curses.
70 LADY ANNE Villain, thou know'st no law of God nor man.
No beast so fierce but knows some touch of pity.
RICHARD GLOUCESTER But I know none, and therefore am no beast.
LADY ANNE O wonderful, when devils tell the truth![3]
RICHARD GLOUCESTER More wonderful, when angels are so angry.
75 Vouchsafe,° divine perfection of a woman,   *Grant*
Of these supposèd crimes to give me leave
By circumstance° but to acquit myself.   *detailed argument*
LADY ANNE Vouchsafe, diffused infection[4] of a man,
Of these known evils but to give me leave
80 By circumstance t'accuse thy cursèd self.
RICHARD GLOUCESTER Fairer than tongue can name thee, let me have
Some patient leisure to excuse myself.
LADY ANNE Fouler than heart can think thee, thou canst make
No excuse current° but to hang thyself.   *valid*
85 RICHARD GLOUCESTER By such despair I should accuse myself.
LADY ANNE And by despairing shalt thou stand excused,
For doing worthy vengeance on thyself
That didst unworthy slaughter upon others.
RICHARD GLOUCESTER Say that I slew them not.
LADY ANNE   Then say they were not slain.
90 But dead they are—and, devilish slave, by thee.
RICHARD GLOUCESTER I did not kill your husband.
LADY ANNE   Why, then he is alive.
RICHARD GLOUCESTER Nay, he is dead, and slain by Edward's hand.
LADY ANNE In thy foul throat thou liest. Queen Margaret saw
Thy murd'rous falchion° smoking in his blood,[5]   *curved sword*
95 The which thou once didst bend against° her breast,   *turn toward*
But that thy brothers beat aside the point.
RICHARD GLOUCESTER I was provokèd by her sland'rous tongue,
That laid their guilt upon my guiltless shoulders.
LADY ANNE Thou wast provokèd by thy bloody mind,
100 That never dream'st on aught° but butcheries.   *anything*
Didst thou not kill this king?
RICHARD GLOUCESTER   I grant ye.

---

1. A murdered victim's wounds were supposed to bleed again in the presence of the murderer.
2. Q, F: most unnatural. The emendation underscores Anne's call (in the next line) for divine intervention.
3. That is, Richard is a devil, not man or beast.

4. Misshapen, but also an infection whose harmful effects are dispersed widely.
5. In *Richard Duke of York* (*3 Henry VI*) 5.5, King Edward stabbed the Prince first, and Richard followed.

LADY ANNE   Dost grant me, hedgehog?[6] Then God grant me, too,
Thou mayst be damnèd for that wicked deed.
O he was gentle, mild, and virtuous.
105 RICHARD GLOUCESTER   The better for the King of Heaven that hath him.
LADY ANNE   He *is* in heaven, where thou shalt never come.
RICHARD GLOUCESTER   Let him thank me that holp° to send him thither,   *helped*
For he was fitter for that place than earth.
LADY ANNE   And thou unfit for any place but hell.
110 RICHARD GLOUCESTER   Yes, one place else, if you will hear me name it.
LADY ANNE   Some dungeon.
RICHARD GLOUCESTER   Your bedchamber.
LADY ANNE   Ill rest betide° the chamber where thou liest.   *befall*
RICHARD GLOUCESTER   So will it, madam, till I lie with you.
LADY ANNE   I hope so.
RICHARD GLOUCESTER   I know so. But gentle Lady Anne,
115 To leave this keen encounter of our wits
And fall something into a slower method,[7]
Is not the causer of the timeless° deaths   *untimely*
Of these Plantagenets, Henry and Edward,
As blameful as the executioner?
120 LADY ANNE   Thou wast the cause of that accursed effect.
RICHARD GLOUCESTER   Your beauty was the cause of that effect—
Your beauty that did haunt me in my sleep
To undertake the death of all the world
So I might live one hour in your sweet bosom.
125 LADY ANNE   If I thought that, I tell thee, homicide,°   *murderer*
These nails should rend that beauty from my cheeks.
RICHARD GLOUCESTER   These eyes could not endure sweet beauty's wreck.
You should not blemish it if I stood by.
As all the world is cheerèd by the sun,
130 So I by that: it is my day, my life.
LADY ANNE   Black night o'ershade thy day, and death thy life.
RICHARD GLOUCESTER   Curse not thyself, fair creature: thou art both.
LADY ANNE   I would I were, to be revenged on thee.[8]
RICHARD GLOUCESTER   It is a quarrel most unnatural,
135 To be revenged on him that loveth you.
LADY ANNE   It is a quarrel just and reasonable,
To be revenged on him that killed my husband.
RICHARD GLOUCESTER   He that bereft thee, lady, of thy husband,
Did it to help thee to a better husband.
140 LADY ANNE   His better doth not breathe upon the earth.
RICHARD GLOUCESTER   He lives that loves thee better than he° could.   *(Edward)*
LADY ANNE   Name him.
RICHARD GLOUCESTER   Plantagenet.
LADY ANNE   Why, that was he.
RICHARD GLOUCESTER   The selfsame name, but one of better nature.
LADY ANNE   Where is he?
RICHARD GLOUCESTER   Here.
    She spits at him
    Why dost thou spit at me?
145 LADY ANNE   Would it were mortal poison for thy sake.

---

6. Term of abuse applied to someone who pays no attention to others' feelings; alluding to Richard's hunchback
and his heraldic badge, the boar.

7. And argue somewhat less hastily.
8. That is, if Anne were Richard's day and his life, she
could end both and thus be revenged on him.

RICHARD GLOUCESTER   Never came poison from so sweet a place.

LADY ANNE   Never hung poison on a fouler toad.[9]

    Out of my sight! Thou dost infect mine eyes.

RICHARD GLOUCESTER   Thine eyes, sweet lady, have infected mine.

150   LADY ANNE   Would° they were basilisks[1] to strike thee dead.   *I wish that*

RICHARD GLOUCESTER   I would they were, that I might die at once,°   *once and for all*

    For now they kill me with a living death.

    Those eyes of thine from mine have drawn salt tears,

    Shamed their aspects° with store of childish drops.[2]   *appearance*

154.1   *These eyes, which never shed remorseful tear—*

       No, when my father York and Edward[3] wept

       To hear the piteous moan that Rutland[4] made

       When black-faced° Clifford shook his sword at him;   *threatening*

154.5   *Nor when thy warlike father° like a child*   *(Warwick)*

       Told the sad story of my father's death

       And twenty times made pause to sob and weep,

       That all the standers-by had wet their cheeks

       Like trees bedashed with rain. In that sad time

154.10   *My manly eyes did scorn an humble tear,*

       And what these sorrows could not thence exhale°   *draw out*

       Thy beauty hath, and made them blind with weeping.

155   I never sued° to friend nor enemy;   *petitioned*

    My tongue could never learn sweet smoothing° word;   *flattering*

    But now thy beauty is proposed my fee,°   *recompense*

    My proud heart sues and prompts my tongue to speak.

        She looks scornfully at him

    Teach not thy lip such scorn, for it was made

160   For kissing, lady, not for such contempt.

    If thy revengeful heart cannot forgive,

       [He kneels and offers her his sword]

    Lo, here I lend thee this sharp-pointed sword,

    Which if thou please to hide in this true breast

    And let the soul forth that adoreth thee,

165   I lay it naked to the deadly stroke

    And humbly beg the death upon my knee.

       He lays his breast open;° she offers° at [it] with his sword   *bare / thrusts*

    Nay, do not pause, for I did kill King Henry;

    But 'twas thy beauty that provokèd me.

    Nay, now dispatch: 'twas I that stabbed young Edward;

170   But 'twas thy heavenly face that set me on.

       She lets fall the sword

    Take up the sword again, or take up me.

LADY ANNE   Arise, dissembler.

       [He rises]

                  Though I wish thy death,

    I will not be thy executioner.

RICHARD GLOUCESTER   Then bid me kill myself, and I will do it.

LADY ANNE   I have already.

175   RICHARD GLOUCESTER   That was in thy rage.

    Speak it again, and even with the word

---

9. Toads were popularly regarded as "ugly and venomous" (*As You Like It* 2.1.13).

1. Legendary monsters, supposed to kill with a glance.

2. The indented passage that follows, 154.1–154.12, appears only in F.

3. His brother, now the King.

4. Historically, Rutland was Richard's older brother. Shakespeare unhistorically makes him a child. His death is dramatized in *Richard Duke of York* 1.3–2.1.

This hand—which for thy love did kill thy love—
Shall, for thy love, kill a far truer love.
To both their deaths shalt thou be accessary.

180 LADY ANNE   I would I knew thy heart.

RICHARD GLOUCESTER   'Tis figured in my tongue.

LADY ANNE   I fear me both are false.

RICHARD GLOUCESTER   Then never man was true.

LADY ANNE   Well, well, put up your sword.

185 RICHARD GLOUCESTER   Say then my peace is made.

LADY ANNE   That shalt thou know hereafter.

RICHARD GLOUCESTER   But shall I live in hope?

LADY ANNE   All men, I hope, live so.

RICHARD GLOUCESTER   Vouchsafe° to wear this ring.   *Consent*

190 LADY ANNE   To take is not to give.⁵

RICHARD GLOUCESTER   Look how my ring encompasseth° thy finger;   *encircles*
Even so thy breast encloseth my poor heart.
Wear both of them, for both of them are thine.
And if thy poor devoted servant° may   *lover*
195 But beg one favour at thy gracious hand,
Thou dost confirm his happiness for ever.

LADY ANNE   What is it?

RICHARD GLOUCESTER   That it may please you leave these sad designs°   *affairs*
To him that hath most cause to be a mourner,
200 And presently° repair to Crosby House,⁶   *at once*
Where—after I have solemnly interred
At Chertsey monast'ry this noble king,
And wet his grave with my repentant tears—
I will with all expedient° duty see you.   *prompt*
205 For divers unknown° reasons, I beseech you   *various secret*
Grant me this boon.°   *favor*

LADY ANNE   With all my heart—and much it joys me, too,
To see you are become so penitent.
Tressell and Berkeley, go along with me.

RICHARD GLOUCESTER   Bid me farewell.

210 LADY ANNE   'Tis more than you deserve.⁷
But since you teach me how to flatter you,
Imagine I have said farewell already.   *Exeunt two with* ANNE

RICHARD GLOUCESTER   Sirs, take up the corpse.

GENTLEMAN   Towards Chertsey, noble lord?

RICHARD GLOUCESTER   No, to Blackfriars; there attend° my coming.   *await*
                    Exeunt [with] corpse. Manet° GLOUCESTER   *Remains*
215 Was ever woman in this humour° wooed?   *mood; manner*
Was ever woman in this humour won?
I'll have her, but I will not keep her long.
What, I that killed her husband and his father,
To take her in her heart's extremest hate,
220 With curses in her mouth, tears in her eyes,
The bleeding witness of my hatred by,
Having God, her conscience, and these bars° against me,   *obstacles*
And I no friends to back my suit withal
But the plain devil and dissembling looks—
225 And yet to win her, all the world to nothing?° Ha!   *against such odds*

---

5. To take your ring is not to give myself.
6. One of Richard's London residences.

7. That is, to fare well is more than you deserve.

Hath she forgot already that brave prince,
Edward her lord, whom I some three months since
Stabbed in my angry mood at Tewkesbury?
A sweeter and a lovelier gentleman,
230 Framed in the prodigality of nature,[8]
Young, valiant, wise, and no doubt right royal,
The spacious world cannot again afford° —   *provide*
And will she yet abase° her eyes on me,   *lower, humble*
That cropped the golden prime[9] of this sweet prince
235 And made her widow to a woeful bed?
On me, whose all not equals Edward's moiety?°   *half*
On me, that halts° and am misshapen thus?   *limp*
My dukedom to a beggarly *denier*,[1]
I do mistake my person all this while.
240 Upon my life she finds, although I cannot,
Myself to be a marv'lous proper° man.   *handsome*
I'll be at charges for° a looking-glass   *I'll buy*
And entertain° a score or two of tailors   *hire*
To study fashions to adorn my body.
245 Since I am crept in° favour with myself,   *into*
I will maintain it with some little cost.
But first I'll turn yon fellow in his grave,
And then return lamenting to my love.
Shine out, fair sun, till I have bought a glass,
250 That I may see my shadow as I pass.   *Exit*

1.3

Enter QUEEN [ELIZABETH], *Lord* RIVERS, [*Marquis* DORSET],
and Lord GRAY

RIVERS [*to* ELIZABETH]   Have patience, madam. There's no doubt his majesty
Will soon recover his accustomed health.
GRAY [*to* ELIZABETH]   In that you brook it ill,° it makes him worse.   *take it badly*
Therefore, for God's sake entertain good comfort,
5   And cheer his grace with quick° and merry eyes.   *lively*
QUEEN ELIZABETH   If he were dead, what would betide on° me?   *befall*
RIVERS[1]   No other harm but loss of such a lord.
QUEEN ELIZABETH   The loss of such a lord includes all harms.
GRAY   The heavens have blessed you with a goodly son
10   To be your comforter when he is gone.
QUEEN ELIZABETH   Ah, he is young, and his minority
Is put unto the trust of Richard Gloucester,
A man that loves not me — nor none of you.
RIVERS   Is it concluded° he shall be Protector?   *officially decreed*
15   QUEEN ELIZABETH   It is determined,° not concluded yet;   *decided*
But so it must be, if the King miscarry.°   *die*

Enter [the Duke of] BUCKINGHAM *and [Lord* STANLEY
Earl of] Derby

GRAY   Here come the Lords of Buckingham and Derby.
BUCKINGHAM [*to* ELIZABETH]   Good time of day unto your royal grace.
STANLEY [*to* ELIZABETH]   God make your majesty joyful, as you have been.

---

8. Made when nature in its gift giving was being lavish.
9. Springtime (Richard "cropped," or harvested, Edward's life prematurely).
1. French coin, one-twelfth of a sou (extremely little). *to:*

against (as in betting).
1.3 Location: The royal palace of Westminster.
1. F: Gray. Rivers's role in the conversation is far fuller in Q than in F (see lines 30, 54).

20 QUEEN ELIZABETH The Countess Richmond,[2] good my lord of Derby,
    To your good prayer will scarcely say 'Amen'.
    Yet, Derby—notwithstanding she's your wife,
    And loves not me—be you, good lord, assured
    I hate not you for her proud arrogance.
25 STANLEY I do beseech you, either not believe
    The envious° slanders of her false accusers   *malicious*
    Or, if she be accused on true report,
    Bear with her weakness, which I think proceeds
    From wayward° sickness, and no grounded malice.   *not easily treated*
30 RIVERS Saw you the King today, my lord of Derby?
    STANLEY But° now the Duke of Buckingham and I   *Just*
    Are come from visiting his majesty.
    QUEEN ELIZABETH With likelihood of his amendment,° lords?   *recovery*
    BUCKINGHAM Madam, good hope: his grace speaks cheerfully.
35 QUEEN ELIZABETH God grant him health. Did you confer with him?
    BUCKINGHAM Ay, madam. He desires to make atonement°   *reconciliation*
    Between the Duke of Gloucester and your brothers,
    And between them and my Lord Chamberlain,°   *(Hastings)*
    And sent to warn° them to his royal presence.   *summon*
40 QUEEN ELIZABETH Would all were well! But that will never be.
    I fear our happiness is at the height.[3]

        Enter RICHARD [*Duke of*] GLOUCESTER [*and* LORD
            HASTINGS]

    RICHARD GLOUCESTER They do me wrong, and I will not endure it.
    Who are they that complain unto the King
    That I forsooth am stern and love them not?
45 By holy Paul, they love his grace but lightly
    That fill his ears with such dissentious rumours.
    Because I cannot flatter and look fair,
    Smile in men's faces, smooth,° deceive, and cog,°   *flatter / cheat*
    Duck with French nods[4] and apish° courtesy,   *imitative; clumsy*
50 I must be held a rancorous enemy.
    Cannot a plain man live and think no harm,
    But thus his simple truth must be abused
    With° silken, sly, insinuating jacks?°   *By / nobodies*
    RIVERS To whom in all this presence° speaks your grace?   *present company*
55 RICHARD GLOUCESTER To thee, that hast nor honesty nor grace.
    When have I injured thee? When done thee wrong?
    Or thee? Or thee? Or any of your faction?
    A plague upon you all! His royal grace—
    Whom God preserve better than you would wish—
60 Cannot be quiet scarce a breathing while[5]
    But you must trouble him with lewd complaints.
    QUEEN ELIZABETH Brother of Gloucester, you mistake the matter.
    The King—on his own royal disposition,°   *inclination*
    And not provoked by any suitor else—
65 Aiming belike° at your interior hatred,   *Guessing probably*
    That in your outward action shows itself
    Against my children, brothers, and myself,

---

2. Lady Margaret Beaufort, Lord Stanley's wife, was (by
an earlier marriage) the mother of Henry Tudor, Earl of
Richmond, who at play's end succeeds Richard and
becomes Henry VII. As a descendant of the house of Lancaster, she was unlikely to have friendly feelings toward
the Yorkist King Edward IV or his family.
3. At its highest point on Fortune's proverbial wheel, and
thus about to decline.
4. *French nods*: elaborate bows.
5. Long enough to catch his breath.

Makes[6] him to send, that he may learn the ground
Of your ill will, and thereby to remove it.

70 RICHARD GLOUCESTER   I cannot tell. The world is grown so bad
That wrens make prey where eagles dare not perch.
Since every jack became a gentleman,
There's many a gentle person made a jack.

QUEEN ELIZABETH   Come, come, we know your meaning, brother Gloucester.
75 You envy my advancement, and my friends'.
God grant we never may have need of you.

RICHARD GLOUCESTER   Meantime, God grants that I have need of you.
Our brother° is imprisoned by your means,   (Clarence)
Myself disgraced, and the nobility
80 Held in contempt, while great promotions
Are daily given to ennoble those
That scarce some two days since were worth a noble.[7]

QUEEN ELIZABETH   By him° that raised me to this care-full height   (God)
From that contented hap° which I enjoyed,   fortune, lot
85 I never did incense his majesty
Against the Duke of Clarence, but have been
An earnest advocate to plead for him.
My lord, you do me shameful injury
Falsely to draw me in these vile suspects.°   suspicions

90 RICHARD GLOUCESTER   You may deny that you were not the mean°   instigation
Of my Lord Hastings' late imprisonment.

RIVERS   She may, my lord, for—

RICHARD GLOUCESTER   She may, Lord Rivers; why, who knows not so?
She may do more, sir, than denying that.
95 She may help you to many fair preferments,°   lucrative positions
And then deny her aiding hand therein,
And lay those honours on[8] your high desert.
What may she not? She may—ay, marry,[9] may she.

RIVERS   What 'marry, may she'?

100 RICHARD GLOUCESTER   What marry, may she? Marry with a king:
A bachelor, and a handsome stripling,° too.   young man
Iwis your grandam had a worser match.[1]

QUEEN ELIZABETH   My lord of Gloucester, I have too long borne
Your blunt upbraidings and your bitter scoffs.
105 By heaven, I will acquaint his majesty
Of those gross taunts that oft I have endured.
I had rather be a country servant-maid
Than a great queen, with this condition:
To be so baited,° scorned, and stormèd at.   provoked
            Enter old QUEEN MARGARET[2] [*unseen behind them*]
110 Small joy have I in being England's queen.

QUEEN MARGARET [*aside*]   And lessened be that small, God I beseech him.
Thy honour, state,° and seat° is due to me.   rank / throne

RICHARD GLOUCESTER [*to* ELIZABETH]   What? Threat you me
        with telling of the King?
Tell him, and spare not. Look what° I have said,   Whatever

---

6. The grammatical subject is still "the King."
7. Gold coin, worth one-third of a pound sterling.
8. And attribute those honors to.
9. Indeed (originally, an oath on the Virgin Mary), with pun in next line on "wed."
1. Your mother (and the Queen's) was born of a less dis-

tinguished union. Iwis: Assuredly (already archaic).
2. Historically, Margaret—widow of the Lancastrian King Henry VI—was held prisoner in England for five years after her husband's defeat at the Battle of Tewkesbury and then exiled to France.

115 I will avouch't in presence of the King.
I dare adventure to be° sent to th' Tower.   *I risk being*
'Tis time to speak; my pains³ are quite forgot.
QUEEN MARGARET [*aside*]   Out, devil! I remember them too well.
Thou killed'st my husband Henry in the Tower,
120 And Edward, my poor son, at Tewkesbury.
RICHARD GLOUCESTER [*to* ELIZABETH]   Ere you were queen—
    ay, or your husband king—
I was a packhorse° in his great affairs,   *beast of burden*
A weeder-out of his proud adversaries,
A liberal rewarder of his friends.
125 To royalize his blood, I spent mine own.
QUEEN MARGARET [*aside*]   Ay, and much better blood than his or thine.
RICHARD GLOUCESTER [*to* ELIZABETH]   In all which time you
    and your husband Gray
Were factious° for the house of Lancaster;   *partisan*
And Rivers, so were you.—Was not your husband
130 In Margaret's battle° at Saint Albans slain?⁴   *army*
Let me put in your minds, if you forget,
What you have been ere this, and what you are;
Withal,° what I have been, and what I am.   *In addition, also*
QUEEN MARGARET [*aside*]   A murd'rous villain, and so still thou art.
135 RICHARD GLOUCESTER   Poor Clarence did forsake his father⁵ Warwick—
Ay, and forswore himself, which Jesu pardon—
QUEEN MARGARET [*aside*]   Which God revenge!
RICHARD GLOUCESTER   To fight on Edward's party° for the crown,   *side*
And for his meed,° poor lord, he is mewed up.   *reward*
140 I would to God my heart were flint like Edward's,
Or Edward's soft and pitiful like mine.
I am too childish-foolish for this world.
QUEEN MARGARET [*aside*]   Hie° thee to hell for shame, and leave this world,   *Hurry*
Thou cacodemon;° there thy kingdom is.   *evil spirit*
145 RIVERS   My lord of Gloucester, in those busy days
Which here you urge° to prove us enemies,   *recall*
We followed then our lord, our sovereign king.
So should we you, if you should be our king.
RICHARD GLOUCESTER   If I should be? I had rather be a pedlar.
150 Far be it from my heart, the thought thereof.
QUEEN ELIZABETH   As little joy, my lord, as you suppose
You should enjoy, were you this country's king,
As little joy may you suppose in me,
That I enjoy being the queen thereof.
155 QUEEN MARGARET [*aside*]   Ah, little joy enjoys the queen thereof,
For I am she, and altogether joyless.
I can no longer hold me patient.
    [*She comes forward*]
Hear me, you wrangling pirates, that fall out
In sharing that which you have pilled° from me.   *pillaged*
160 Which of you trembles not that looks on me?
If not that I am Queen, you bow like subjects;

---

3. Efforts, trouble (on the King's behalf).
4. Queen Elizabeth's first husband, Sir John Gray, died fighting for the Lancastrian faction.
5. Father-in-law. Clarence married Warwick's daughter

Isabella, sister of this play's Lady Anne, and for a time defied his brothers by supporting the Lancastrian faction. He "forswore himself" (line 136) by returning to fight for the Yorkist faction.

Yet that by you deposed, you quake like rebels.[6]
[*To* RICHARD] Ah, gentle villain,[7] do not turn away.
RICHARD GLOUCESTER   Foul wrinkled witch, what mak'st thou°   *what are you doing*
    in my sight?
165 QUEEN MARGARET   But repetition° of what thou hast marred: *recounting*
    That will I make before I let thee go.[8]
165.1   RICHARD GLOUCESTER   *Wert thou not banishèd on pain of death?*
    QUEEN MARGARET   *I was, but I do find more pain in banishment*
    Than death can yield me here by my abode.
A husband and a son thou ow'st to me,
[*To* ELIZABETH] And thou a kingdom; [*to the rest*] all of you allegiance.
This sorrow that I have by right is yours,
170 And all the pleasures you usurp are mine.
RICHARD GLOUCESTER   The curse my noble father laid on thee—
    When thou didst crown his warlike brows with paper,
    And with thy scorns° drew'st rivers from his eyes,   *mocking speeches*
    And then, to dry them, gav'st the duke a clout°   *rag; handkerchief*
175 Steeped in the faultless° blood of pretty Rutland[9]—   *innocent*
    His curses then, from bitterness of soul
    Denounced against thee, are all fall'n upon thee,
    And God, not we, hath plagued thy bloody deed.
QUEEN ELIZABETH [*to* MARGARET]   So just is God to right the innocent.
LORD HASTINGS [*to* MARGARET]   O 'twas the foulest deed to slay
180   that babe,°   *(Rutland)*
    And the most merciless that e'er was heard of.
RIVERS [*to* MARGARET]   Tyrants themselves wept when it was reported.
DORSET [*to* MARGARET]   No man but prophesied revenge for it.
BUCKINGHAM [*to* MARGARET]   Northumberland, then present, wept to see it.
185 QUEEN MARGARET   What? Were you snarling all before I came,
    Ready to catch each other by the throat,
    And turn you all your hatred now on me?
    Did York's dread curse prevail so much with heaven
    That Henry's death, my lovely Edward's death,
190 Their kingdom's loss, my woeful banishment,
    Should all but answer for° that peevish brat?   *Should merely equal*
    Can curses pierce the clouds and enter heaven?
    Why then, give way, dull clouds, to my quick° curses!   *lively*
    Though not by war, by surfeit° die your king,   *high living*
195 As ours by murder to make him a king.
[*To* ELIZABETH] Edward thy son, that now is Prince of Wales,
    For Edward my son, that was Prince of Wales,
    Die in his youth by like° untimely violence.   *similarly*
    Thyself, a queen, for me that was a queen,
200 Outlive thy glory like my wretched self.
    Long mayst thou live—to wail thy children's death,
    And see another, as I see thee now,
    Decked° in thy rights, as thou art 'stalled° in mine.   *Dressed / installed*
    Long die thy happy days before thy death,
205 And after many lengthened hours of grief
    Die, neither mother, wife, nor England's queen.—

6. *If . . . rebels:* Even if you do not bow because I am Queen, at least you tremble like rebels because you deposed me.
7. Well-born peasant; kindly scoundrel.
8. The indented passage that follows, 165.1–165.3, appears only in F.
9. This is dramatized in *Richard Duke of York* 1.4.80–96, in which Margaret crowns the Duke of York with a paper crown and waves a handkerchief dipped in his son Rutland's blood in front of his eyes.

Rivers and Dorset, you were standers-by,
And so wast thou, Lord Hastings,[1] when my son
Was stabbed with bloody daggers. God I pray him,
210 That none of you may live his natural age,
But by some unlooked° accident cut off.   *unlooked-for*
RICHARD GLOUCESTER   Have done thy charm,° thou hateful,   *spell; curse*
   withered hag.
QUEEN MARGARET   And leave out thee? Stay, dog, for thou shalt hear me.
  If heaven have any grievous plague in store
215 Exceeding those that I can wish upon thee,
O let them keep it till thy sins be ripe,
And then hurl down their indignation
On thee, the troubler of the poor world's peace.
The worm of conscience still begnaw thy soul.
220 Thy friends suspect for° traitors while thou liv'st,   *to be*
And take deep traitors for thy dearest friends.
No sleep close up that deadly eye of thine,
Unless it be while some tormenting dream
Affrights thee with a hell of ugly devils.
225 Thou elvish-marked, abortive, rooting hog,[2]
Thou that wast sealed° in thy nativity   *stamped*
The slave of nature[3] and the son of hell,
Thou slander of thy heavy° mother's womb,   *sorrowful*
Thou loathèd issue of thy father's loins,
230 Thou rag of honour, thou detested—
RICHARD GLOUCESTER   Margaret.
QUEEN MARGARET   Richard.
RICHARD GLOUCESTER   Ha?
QUEEN MARGARET   I call thee not.
RICHARD GLOUCESTER   I cry thee mercy° then, for I did think   *I beg your pardon*
  That thou hadst called me all these bitter names.
235 QUEEN MARGARET   Why so I did, but looked for no reply.
O let me make the period° to my curse.   *full stop; finish*
RICHARD GLOUCESTER   'Tis done by me, and ends in 'Margaret'.
QUEEN ELIZABETH [*to* MARGARET]   Thus have you breathed your
  curse against yourself.
QUEEN MARGARET   Poor painted Queen, vain flourish[4] of my fortune,
240 Why strew'st thou sugar on that bottled° spider   *bottle-shaped; swollen*
Whose deadly web ensnareth thee about?
Fool, fool, thou whet'st a knife to kill thyself.
The day will come that thou shalt wish for me
To help thee curse this poisonous bunch-backed° toad.   *hunchbacked*
245 LORD HASTINGS   False-boding° woman, end thy frantic curse,   *Falsely prophesying*
Lest to thy harm thou move our patience.
QUEEN MARGARET   Foul shame upon you, you have all moved mine.
RIVERS   Were you well served, you would be taught your duty.
QUEEN MARGARET   To serve me well you all should do me duty.°   *show me deference*
250 Teach me to be your queen, and you my subjects:
O serve me well, and teach yourselves that duty.
DORSET   Dispute not with her: she is lunatic.

---

1. Rivers, Dorset, and Hastings were not present at Prince Edward's murder at Tewkesbury as dramatized in *Richard Duke of York* 5.5, but they are in the chronicles that served as Shakespeare's sources; the Prince, in fact, was slain by unknown combatants during the battle.

2. Richard's emblem was the white boar. *elvish-marked*: deformed by evil fairies. *abortive*: misshapen.
3. Because he was deformed from birth.
4. *painted*: counterfeit, with play on "use of cosmetics." *vain flourish*: empty, meaningless decoration.

QUEEN MARGARET Peace, master Marquis, you are malapert.° *impertinent*
   Your fire-new stamp of honour is scarce current.⁵
255   O that your young nobility could judge
   What 'twere to lose it and be miserable.
   They that stand high have many blasts to shake them,
   And if they fall they dash themselves to pieces.
RICHARD GLOUCESTER Good counsel, marry!—Learn it, learn it, Marquis.
260 DORSET It touches you, my lord, as much as me.
RICHARD GLOUCESTER Ay, and much more; but I was born so high.
   Our eyrie⁶ buildeth in the cedar's top,
   And dallies with the wind, and scorns the sun.
QUEEN MARGARET And turns the sun to shade. Alas, alas!
265 Witness my son, now in the shade of death,
   Whose bright outshining beams thy cloudy wrath
   Hath in eternal darkness folded up.
   Your eyrie buildeth in our eyrie's nest.—
   O God that seest it, do not suffer it;
270 As it was won with blood, lost be it so.
RICHARD GLOUCESTER Peace, peace! For shame, if not for charity.
QUEEN MARGARET Urge neither charity nor shame to me.
   Uncharitably with me have you dealt,
   And shamefully my hopes by you are butchered.
275 My charity is outrage; life, my shame;° *my life is one of shame*
   And in that shame still live my sorrow's rage.
BUCKINGHAM Have done, have done.
QUEEN MARGARET O princely Buckingham, I'll kiss thy hand
   In sign of league and amity with thee.
280 Now fair befall° thee and thy noble house! *good fortune to*
   Thy garments are not spotted with our blood,
   Nor thou within the compass° of my curse. *scope*
BUCKINGHAM Nor no one here, for curses never pass
   The lips of those that breathe them in the air.⁷
285 QUEEN MARGARET I will not think but they ascend the sky
   And there awake God's gentle sleeping peace.
   O Buckingham, take heed of yonder dog.
      [*She points at* RICHARD]
   Look when he fawns, he bites; and when he bites,
   His venom tooth will rankle⁸ to the death.
290 Have naught to do with him; beware of him;
   Sin, death, and hell have set their marks on him,
   And all their ministers attend on him.
RICHARD GLOUCESTER What doth she say, my lord of Buckingham?
BUCKINGHAM Nothing that I respect, my gracious lord.
295 QUEEN MARGARET What, dost thou scorn me for my gentle counsel,
   And soothe the devil that I warn thee from?
   O but remember this another day,
   When he shall split thy very heart with sorrow,
   And say, 'Poor Margaret was a prophetess'.—
300 Live each of you the subjects to his hate,
   And he to yours, and all of you to God's. *Exit*
HASTINGS My hair doth stand on end to hear her curses.

---

5. Your recently acquired title is not yet secure (as newly minted coins that have not yet achieved common currency).
6. Eagle's brood (the sons of York).
7. *curses . . . air:* it is as if curses were never spoken or afflict only the curser.
8. Will cause a wound that will fester.

RIVERS   And so doth mine. I muse why she's at liberty.

RICHARD GLOUCESTER   I cannot blame her, by God's holy mother.
305 She hath had too much wrong, and I repent
My part thereof that I have done to her.

QUEEN ELIZABETH   I never did her any, to my knowledge.

RICHARD GLOUCESTER   Yet you have all the vantage of her wrong.⁹
I was too hot° to do somebody good,   *eager*
310 That° is too cold° in thinking of it now.   *Who / ungrateful*
Marry, as for Clarence, he is well repaid:
He is franked up to fatting¹ for his pains.
God pardon them that are the cause thereof.

RIVERS   A virtuous and a Christian-like conclusion,
315 To pray for them that have done scathe° to us.   *harm*

RICHARD GLOUCESTER   So do I ever—*(speaks to himself)* being well advised:
For had I cursed now, I had cursed myself.

                    Enter [Sir William] CATESBY

CATESBY   Madam, his majesty doth call for you,
And for your grace, and you my gracious lords.

320 QUEEN ELIZABETH   Catesby, I come.—Lords, will you go with me?

RIVERS   We wait upon your grace.   *Exeunt. Manet* RICHARD

RICHARD GLOUCESTER   I do the wrong, and first begin to brawl.°   *complain, protest*
The secret mischiefs that I set abroach°   *set in motion*
I lay unto the grievous charge of² others.
325 Clarence, whom I indeed have cast in darkness,
I do beweep to many simple gulls°—   *credulous fools*
Namely to Derby, Hastings, Buckingham—
And tell them, "Tis the Queen and her allies
That stir the King against the Duke my brother'.
330 Now they believe it, and withal whet me
To be revenged on Rivers, Dorset, Gray;
But then I sigh, and with a piece of scripture
Tell them that God bids us do good for evil;
And thus I clothe my naked villainy
335 With odd old ends,° stol'n forth of Holy Writ,   *old bits and pieces*
And seem a saint when most I play the devil.

                    Enter two MURDERERS

But soft, here come my executioners.—
How now, my hardy, stout, resolvèd° mates!   *resolute*
Are you now going to dispatch this thing?

340 A MURDERER   We are, my lord, and come to have the warrant,
That we may be admitted where he is.

RICHARD GLOUCESTER   Well thought upon; I have it here about me.

          [*He gives them the warrant*]

When you have done, repair° to Crosby Place.   *return*
But sirs, be sudden° in the execution,   *swift*
345 Withal obdurate; do not hear him plead,
For Clarence is well spoken, and perhaps
May move your hearts to pity, if you mark° him.   *listen to*

A MURDERER   Tut, tut, my lord, we will not stand to prate.
Talkers are no good doers. Be assured,
350 We go to use our hands, and not our tongues.

---

9. All the benefits acquired as a result of the wrongs she   2. I make into a serious accusation against.
has suffered.
1. He is penned up to fatten (for slaughter, like a pig).

RICHARD GLOUCESTER   Your eyes drop millstones when fools'
    eyes fall° tears.   *let fall*
  I like you, lads. About your business straight.°   *straightaway*
  Go, go, dispatch.
MURDERERS   We will, my noble lord.
    Exeunt [RICHARD *at one door, the* MURDERERS *at another*]

1.4

Enter [*George Duke of*] CLARENCE [*and Sir Robert*
BRACKENBURY[1]]
BRACKENBURY   Why looks your grace so heavily° today?   *melancholy*
CLARENCE   O I have passed a miserable night,
  So full of fearful dreams, of ugly sights,
  That as I am a Christian faithful man,
5 I would not spend another such a night
  Though 'twere to buy a world of happy days,
  So full of dismal terror was the time.
BRACKENBURY   What was your dream, my lord? I pray you, tell me.
CLARENCE   Methoughts that I had broken from the Tower,
10 And was embarked to cross to Burgundy,
  And in my company my brother Gloucester,
  Who from my cabin tempted me to walk
  Upon the hatches;[2] there we looked toward England,
  And cited up° a thousand heavy times   *recalled*
15 During the wars of York and Lancaster
  That had befall'n us. As we paced along
  Upon the giddy footing of the hatches,
  Methought that Gloucester stumbled, and in falling
  Struck me—that sought to stay° him—overboard   *steady*
20 Into the tumbling billows of the main.
  O Lord! Methought what pain it was to drown,
  What dreadful noise of waters in my ears,
  What sights of ugly death within my eyes.
  Methoughts I saw a thousand fearful wrecks,
25 Ten thousand men that fishes gnawed upon,
  Wedges of gold, great ouches,[3] heaps of pearl,
  Inestimable° stones, unvalued° jewels,   *Countless / invaluable*
  All scattered in the bottom of the sea.
  Some lay in dead men's skulls; and in those holes
30 Where eyes did once inhabit, there were crept—
  As 'twere in scorn of eyes—reflecting gems,
  Which wooed the slimy bottom of the deep
  And mocked the dead bones that lay scattered by.
BRACKENBURY   Had you such leisure in the time of death,
35 To gaze upon these secrets of the deep?
CLARENCE   Methought I had, and often did I strive
  To yield the ghost,° but still° the envious° flood   *To die / always / malicious*
  Stopped-in° my soul and would not let it forth   *Stopped up*
  To find the empty, vast, and wand'ring air,
40 But smothered it within my panting bulk,°   *body*
  Who° almost burst to belch it in the sea.   *Which*

1.4 Location: In the Tower of London.
1. F gives this part to an anonymous keeper, Brackenbury not entering until line 72.
2. Planks laid across the hold of a ship, forming a temporary deck.
3. Gold or silver brooches set with jewels. Q, F: anchors.

BRACKENBURY   Awaked you not in this sore agony?
CLARENCE   No, no, my dream was lengthened after life.[4]
    O then began the tempest to my soul!
45   I passed, methought, the melancholy flood,[5]
    With that sour ferryman which poets write of,
    Unto the kingdom of perpetual night.
    The first that there did greet my stranger soul
    Was my great father-in-law, renownèd Warwick,
50   Who cried aloud, 'What scourge° for perjury   *punishment*
    Can this dark monarchy afford false Clarence?'
    And so he vanished. Then came wand'ring by
    A shadow[6] like an angel, with bright hair,
    Dabbled in blood, and he shrieked out aloud,
55   'Clarence is come: false, fleeting,° perjured Clarence,   *fickle*
    That stabbed me in the field by Tewkesbury.
    Seize on him, furies![7] Take him unto torment!'
    With that, methoughts a legion of foul fiends
    Environed° me, and howlèd in mine ears   *Surrounded*
60   Such hideous cries that with the very noise
    I trembling waked, and for a season after
    Could not believe but that I was in hell,
    Such terrible impression made my dream.
BRACKENBURY   No marvel, lord, though° it affrighted you;   *that*
65   I am afraid, methinks, to hear you tell it.
CLARENCE   Ah, Brackenbury, I have done these things,
    That now give evidence against my soul,
    For Edward's sake; and see how he requites me.[8]
68.1   *O God! If my deep prayers cannot appease thee*
      But thou wilt be avenged on my misdeeds,
      Yet execute thy wrath in me alone.
      O spare my guiltless wife and my poor children.
    Keeper, I pray thee, sit by me awhile.
70   My soul is heavy, and I fain would° sleep.   *I desire to*
BRACKENBURY   I will, my lord. God give your grace good rest.
      [CLARENCE *sleeps*]
    Sorrow breaks seasons and reposing hours,[9]
    Makes the night morning and the noontide night.
    Princes have but their titles for their glories,
75   An outward honour for an inward toil,
    And for unfelt imaginations[1]
    They often feel a world of restless cares;
    So that, between their titles and low name,
    There's nothing differs but the outward fame.
      Enter two MURDERERS
80 FIRST MURDERER   Ho, who's here?
BRACKENBURY   What wouldst thou, fellow? And how cam'st thou hither?
SECOND MURDERER   I would speak with Clarence, and I came
    hither on my legs.

---

4. My dream also depicted my fate after death.
5. The river Styx, across which Charon (the "sour ferryman" of the next line) ferried souls to Hades, the classical hell.
6. Shade, ghost (Edward, Prince of Wales—son of Henry VI, and Clarence's brother-in-law—whom Clarence helped to murder; see *Richard Duke of York* 5.5.40).
7. In Greek myth, female spirits who enacted vengeance

for blood crimes against relatives.
8. The indented passage that follows, 68.1–68.4, appears only in F. *requites*: repays.
9. Sorrow disrupts life's normal rhythms and disregards the hours appropriate to sleep.
1. *for unfelt imaginations*: "for the sake of imaginary and unreal gratifications" (Dr. Johnson).

BRACKENBURY   What, so brief?

85 FIRST MURDERER   'Tis better, sir, than to be tedious. [*To* SECOND
MURDERER] Let him see our commission,° and talk no more.   *authorization*
   [BRACKENBURY] *reads*
BRACKENBURY   I am in this commanded to deliver
   The noble Duke of Clarence to your hands.
   I will not reason what is meant hereby,
90   Because I will be° guiltless of the meaning.   *wish to be*
   There lies the Duke asleep, and there the keys.
   [*He throws down the keys*]
   I'll to the King and signify to him
   That thus I have resigned to you my charge.°   *responsibility*
FIRST MURDERER   You may, sir; 'tis a point of wisdom. Fare you
95 well.   *Exit* [BRACKENBURY]
SECOND MURDERER   What, shall I stab him as he sleeps?
FIRST MURDERER   No. He'll say 'twas done cowardly, when he
   wakes.
SECOND MURDERER   Why, he shall never wake until the great
100 judgement day.
FIRST MURDERER   Why, then he'll say we stabbed him sleeping.
SECOND MURDERER   The urging of that word 'judgement' hath
   bred a kind of remorse in me.
FIRST MURDERER   What, art thou afraid?
105 SECOND MURDERER   Not to kill him, having a warrant, but to be
   damned for killing him, from the which no warrant can defend
   me.
FIRST MURDERER   I thought thou hadst been resolute.
SECOND MURDERER   So I am—to let him live.
110 FIRST MURDERER   I'll back to the Duke of Gloucester and tell
   him so.
SECOND MURDERER   Nay, I pray thee. Stay a little. I hope this
   passionate humour° of mine will change. It was wont to hold   *compassionate mood*
   me but while one tells° twenty.   *counts*
   [*He counts to twenty*]
115 FIRST MURDERER   How dost thou feel thyself now?
SECOND MURDERER   Some certain dregs of conscience are yet
   within me.
FIRST MURDERER   Remember our reward, when the deed's done.
SECOND MURDERER   'Swounds,° he dies. I had forgot the reward.   *By God's wounds*
120 FIRST MURDERER   Where's thy conscience now?
SECOND MURDERER   O, in the Duke of Gloucester's purse.
FIRST MURDERER   When he opens his purse to give us our
   reward, thy conscience flies out.
SECOND MURDERER   'Tis no matter. Let it go. There's few or
125 none will entertain° it.   *host; employ*
FIRST MURDERER   What if it come to thee again?
SECOND MURDERER   I'll not meddle with it. It makes a man a
   coward. A man cannot steal but it accuseth him. A man cannot
   swear but it checks him. A man cannot lie with his neighbour's
130 wife but it detects° him. 'Tis a blushing, shamefaced spirit, that
   mutinies in a man's bosom. It fills a man full of obstacles. It
   made me once restore a purse of gold that by chance I found.
   It beggars any man that keeps it. It is turned out of towns and
   cities for a dangerous thing, and every man that means to live
135 well endeavours to trust to himself and live without it.

FIRST MURDERER 'Swounds, 'tis even now at my elbow, persuading me not to kill the Duke.

SECOND MURDERER Take the devil in thy mind, and believe
him° not: he would insinuate with thee but to make thee sigh.[2]   *(conscience)*

140 FIRST MURDERER I am strong framed; he cannot prevail with
me.

SECOND MURDERER Spoke like a tall° man that respects thy rep-   *valiant*
utation. Come, shall we fall to work?

FIRST MURDERER Take him on the costard with the hilts of thy

145 sword, and then throw him into the malmsey butt[3] in the next
room.

SECOND MURDERER O excellent device!—and make a sop[4] of
him.

FIRST MURDERER Soft,° he wakes.   *Hush*

150 SECOND MURDERER Strike!

FIRST MURDERER No, we'll reason with him.

CLARENCE Where art thou, keeper? Give me a cup of wine.

SECOND MURDERER You shall have wine enough, my lord, anon.

CLARENCE In God's name, what art thou?

FIRST MURDERER A man, as you are.

155 CLARENCE But not as I am, royal.

FIRST MURDERER Nor you as we are, loyal.

CLARENCE Thy voice is thunder, but thy looks are humble.

FIRST MURDERER My voice is now the King's;[5] my looks, mine own.

CLARENCE How darkly and how deadly dost thou speak.

160 Your eyes do menace me. Why look you pale?
Who sent you hither? Wherefore do you come?

SECOND MURDERER To, to, to—

CLARENCE To murder me.

BOTH MURDERERS Ay, ay.

CLARENCE You scarcely have the hearts to tell me so,
And therefore cannot have the hearts to do it.

165 Wherein, my friends, have I offended you?

FIRST MURDERER Offended us you have not, but the King.

CLARENCE I shall be reconciled to him again.

SECOND MURDERER Never, my lord; therefore prepare to die.

CLARENCE Are you drawn forth° among a world of men   *selected from*

170 To slay the innocent? What is my offence?
Where is the evidence that doth accuse me?
What lawful quest° have given their verdict up   *jury*
Unto the frowning judge, or who pronounced
The bitter sentence of poor Clarence' death?

175 Before I be convict by course of law,
To threaten me with death is most unlawful.
I charge you, as you hope to have redemption
By Christ's dear blood, shed for our grievous sins,
That you depart and lay no hands on me.

180 The deed you undertake is damnable.

FIRST MURDERER What we will do, we do upon command.

SECOND MURDERER And he that hath commanded is our king.

CLARENCE Erroneous vassals,° the great King of Kings   *Misguided subjects*

---

2. *he . . . sigh:* he (conscience) would ingratiate himself
with you simply to cause you grief.
3. Wine barrel (malmsey is a strong, sweet wine). *costard:*
head (literally, a large apple).
4. Piece of bread or wafer soaked in wine.
5. I am now acting on the King's command.

Hath in the table of his law° commanded   *the Ten Commandments*
185   That thou shalt do no murder. Will you then
Spurn at his edict, and fulfil a man's?
Take heed, for he holds vengeance in his hand
To hurl upon their heads that break his law.
SECOND MURDERER   And that same vengeance doth he hurl on thee,
190   For false forswearing, and for murder too.
Thou didst receive the sacrament[6] to fight
In quarrel of ° the house of Lancaster.   *On the side of*
FIRST MURDERER   And, like a traitor to the name of God,
Didst break that vow, and with thy treacherous blade
195   Unripped'st the bowels of thy sov'reign's son.[7]
SECOND MURDERER   Whom thou wast sworn to cherish and defend.
FIRST MURDERER   How canst thou urge God's dreadful law to us,
When thou hast broke it in such dear degree?
CLARENCE   Alas, for whose sake did I that ill deed?
200   For Edward, for my brother, for his sake.
He sends ye not to murder me for this,
For in that sin he is as deep as I.
If God will be avengèd for the deed,
O know you yet, he doth it publicly.
205   Take not the quarrel from his pow'rful arm;
He needs no indirect or lawless course
To cut off those that have offended him.
FIRST MURDERER   Who made thee then a bloody minister°   *agent*
When gallant springing° brave Plantagenet,°   *sprightly / (Edward)*
210   That princely novice,° was struck dead by thee?   *youth*
CLARENCE   My brother's love,° the devil, and my rage.   *My love for my brother*
FIRST MURDERER   Thy brother's love, our duty, and thy faults
Provoke us hither now to slaughter thee.
CLARENCE   If you do love my brother, hate not me.
215   I am his brother, and I love him well.
If you are hired for meed,° go back again,   *reward*
And I will send you to my brother Gloucester,
Who shall reward you better for my life
Than Edward will for tidings of my death.
220 SECOND MURDERER   You are deceived. Your brother Gloucester hates you.
CLARENCE   O no, he loves me, and he holds me dear.
Go you to him from me.
FIRST MURDERER   Ay, so we will.
CLARENCE   Tell him, when that our princely father York
Blessed his three sons with his victorious arm,
225   And charged us from his soul to love each other,
He little thought of this divided friendship.
Bid Gloucester think of this, and he will weep.
FIRST MURDERER   Ay, millstones, as he lessoned° us to weep.   *taught*
CLARENCE   O do not slander him, for he is kind.[8]
230 FIRST MURDERER   As snow in harvest. Come, you deceive yourself.
'Tis he that sends us to destroy you here.
CLARENCE   It cannot be, for he bewept my fortune,

6. Take communion and in doing so swear by the body of God.
7. That is, Prince Edward, son of the then sovereign, Henry VI.
8. He is full of natural feelings (and hence a loving brother).

And hugged me in his arms, and swore with sobs
That he would labour° my delivery.   *work for*
235 FIRST MURDERER Why, so he doth, when he delivers you
From this earth's thraldom to the joys of heaven.
SECOND MURDERER Make peace with God, for you must die, my lord.
CLARENCE Have you that holy feeling in your souls
To counsel me to make my peace with God,
240 And are you yet to your own souls so blind
That you will war with God by murd'ring me?
O sirs, consider: they that set you on
To do this deed will hate you for the deed.
SECOND MURDERER [*to* FIRST] What shall we do?
CLARENCE   Relent, and save your souls.
245 FIRST MURDERER Relent? No. 'Tis cowardly and womanish.
CLARENCE Not to relent is beastly, savage, devilish. —
My friend, I spy some pity in thy looks.
O if thine eye be not a flatterer,°   *deceiver (of Clarence)*
Come thou on my side, and entreat for me.
250 A begging prince, what beggar pities not?
Which of you, if you were a prince's son,
Being pent° from liberty as I am now,   *restrained*
If two such murderers as yourselves came to you,
Would not entreat for life? As you would beg
255 Were you in my distress—
SECOND MURDERER Look behind you, my lord!
FIRST MURDERER (*He stabs* [CLARENCE]) Take that, and that! If
        all this will not serve,
I'll drown you in the malmsey butt within.
                              Exit [*with Clarence's body*]
SECOND MURDERER A bloody deed, and desperately dispatched!
260 How fain,° like Pilate, would I wash my hands   *gladly*
Of this most grievous, guilty murder done.
              Enter FIRST MURDERER
FIRST MURDERER How now? What mean'st thou, that thou help'st me not?
By heaven, the Duke shall know how slack you have been.
SECOND MURDERER I would he knew that I had saved his brother.
265 Take thou the fee, and tell him what I say,
For I repent me that the Duke is slain.   *Exit*
FIRST MURDERER So do not I. Go, coward as thou art. —
Well, I'll go hide the body in some hole
Till that the Duke give order for his burial.
270 And, when I have my meed, I will away,
For this will out,⁹ and then I must not stay.   *Exit*

2.1

Flourish.° Enter KING [EDWARD], *sick,* QUEEN [ELIZA-   *Trumpet call*
BETH], *Lord Marquis* DORSET, [*Lord*] RIVERS, [LORD]
HASTINGS, [*Sir William*] CATESBY, [*the Duke of*] BUCK-
INGHAM [*and Lord* GRAY]
KING EDWARD Why, so! Now have I done a good day's work.
You peers, continue this united league.
I every day expect an embassage
From my redeemer to redeem me hence,

---

9. "Murder will out" was proverbial.   2.1 Location: The palace, London.

5   And more in peace my soul shall part to heaven
       Since I have made my friends at peace on earth.
       Hastings and Rivers, take each other's hand.
       Dissemble not¹ your hatred; swear your love.
       RIVERS   By heaven, my soul is purged from grudging hate,
10   And with my hand I seal my true heart's love.
          [*He takes Hastings' hand*]
       LORD HASTINGS   So thrive I,° as I truly swear the like.   *May I prosper*
       KING EDWARD   Take heed you dally° not before your king,   *trifle*
       Lest he that is the supreme King of Kings
       Confound° your hidden falsehood, and award°   *Defeat / cause*
15   Either of you to be the other's end.²
       LORD HASTINGS   So prosper I, as I swear perfect love.
       RIVERS   And I, as I love Hastings with my heart.
       KING EDWARD [*to* ELIZABETH]   Madam, yourself is not exempt from this,
       Nor your son Dorset;—Buckingham, nor you.
20   You have been factious one against the other.
       Wife, love Lord Hastings, let him kiss your hand—
       And what you do, do it unfeignedly.
       QUEEN ELIZABETH [*giving* HASTINGS *her hand to kiss*]   There,
          Hastings. I will never more remember
       Our former hatred: so thrive I, and mine.°   *my family*
25   KING EDWARD   Dorset, embrace him. Hastings, love Lord Marquis.
       DORSET   This interchange of love, I here protest,
       Upon my part shall be inviolable.
       LORD HASTINGS   And so swear I.
          [*They embrace*]
       KING EDWARD   Now, princely Buckingham, seal thou this league
30   With thy embracements to my wife's allies,
       And make me happy in your unity.
       BUCKINGHAM [*to* ELIZABETH]   Whenever Buckingham doth turn his hate
       Upon your grace, but° with all duteous love   *nor*
       Doth cherish you and yours, God punish me
35   With hate in those where I expect most love.
       When I have most need to employ a friend,
       And most assurèd that he is a friend,
       Deep,° hollow, treacherous, and full of guile   *Crafty*
       Be he unto me. This do I beg of heaven,
40   When I am cold in love to you or yours.
          [*They*] *embrace*
       KING EDWARD   A pleasing cordial,° princely Buckingham,   *health-giving drink*
       Is this thy vow unto my sickly heart.
       There wanteth now our brother Gloucester here,
       To make the blessèd period° of this peace.   *conclusion*
          Enter [*Sir Richard*] RATCLIFFE *and* [RICHARD *Duke of*]
          GLOUCESTER
45   BUCKINGHAM   And in good time,
       Here comes Sir Richard Ratcliffe and the Duke.
       RICHARD GLOUCESTER   Good morrow to my sovereign King and Queen.—
       And princely peers, a happy time of day.
       KING EDWARD   Happy indeed, as we have spent the day.
50   Brother, we have done deeds of charity,
       Made peace of enmity, fair love of hate,

---

1. Do not merely disguise.   2. Each of you to cause the death of the other.

Between these swelling wrong-incensèd[3] peers.
RICHARD GLOUCESTER A blessèd labour, my most sovereign lord.
Among this princely heap° if any here,   *company*
55 By false intelligence° or wrong surmise,   *information*
Hold me a foe,
If I unwittingly or in my rage
Have aught committed that is hardly borne°   *is deeply resented*
By any in this presence, I desire
60 To reconcile me to his friendly peace.
'Tis death to me to be at enmity.
I hate it, and desire all good men's love.—
First, madam, I entreat true peace of you,
Which I will purchase with my duteous service.—
65 Of you, my noble cousin Buckingham,
If ever any grudge were lodged between us.—
Of you, Lord Rivers, and Lord Gray of you,
That all without desert° have frowned on me.—   *entirely without cause*
Dukes, earls, lords, gentlemen, indeed of all!
70 I do not know that Englishman alive
With whom my soul is any jot at odds
More than the infant that is born tonight.
I thank my God for my humility.
QUEEN ELIZABETH A holy day shall this be kept hereafter.
75 I would to God all strifes were well compounded.°—   *resolved*
My sovereign lord, I do beseech your highness
To take our brother Clarence to your grace.
RICHARD GLOUCESTER Why, madam, have I offered love for this,
To be so flouted° in this royal presence?   *mocked*
80 Who knows not that the gentle Duke is dead?
                They all start
You do him injury to scorn his corpse.[4]
RIVERS[5] Who knows not he is dead? Who knows he is?
QUEEN ELIZABETH All-seeing heaven, what a world is this?
BUCKINGHAM Look I so pale, Lord Dorset, as the rest?
85 DORSET Ay, my good lord, and no one in the presence°   *(of the King)*
But his red colour hath forsook his cheeks.
KING EDWARD Is Clarence dead? The order was reversed.
RICHARD GLOUCESTER But he, poor man, by your first order died,
And that a wingèd Mercury[6] did bear;
90 Some tardy cripple bore the countermand,
That came too lag° to see him burièd.   *late*
God grant that some, less noble and less loyal,
Nearer in bloody thoughts, but not in blood,[7]
Deserve not worse than wretched Clarence did,
95 And yet go current from suspicion.[8]
                Enter [Lord STANLEY] Earl of Derby
STANLEY [kneeling] A boon,° my sovereign, for my service done.   *favor*
KING EDWARD I pray thee, peace! My soul is full of sorrow.
STANLEY I will not rise, unless your highness hear me.

---

3. *swelling*: inflated with anger and pride. *wrong-incensèd*: mistakenly provoked; provoked by wrongs, injuries.
4. *to scorn his corpse*: by (supposedly) speaking ironically of him.
5. F assigns this line to King Edward.

6. The speedy messenger of the gods in classical mythology.
7. That is, nearer to bloody plots than was the innocent Clarence, but not so near the King in blood (another dig at the Queen's upstart relatives).
8. And yet are accepted at face value without suspicion.

KING EDWARD   Then say at once, what is it thou requests?
100 STANLEY   The forfeit, sovereign, of my servant's life,[9]
    Who slew today a riotous gentleman,
    Lately attendant on the Duke of Norfolk.
KING EDWARD   Have I a tongue to doom° my brother's death,   *order*
    And shall that tongue give pardon to a slave?
105 My brother slew no man; his fault was thought;
    And yet his punishment was bitter death.
    Who sued to me for him? Who in my wrath
    Kneeled at my feet, and bid me be advised?°   *consider carefully*
    Who spoke of brotherhood? Who spoke of love?
110 Who told me how the poor soul did forsake
    The mighty Warwick and did fight for me?
    Who told me, in the field at Tewkesbury,
    When Oxford had me down, he rescued me,
    And said, 'Dear brother, live, and be a king'?
115 Who told me, when we both lay in the field,
    Frozen almost to death, how he did lap° me   *wrap*
    Even in his garments, and did give himself
    All thin° and naked to the numb-cold night?   *thinly clad*
    All this from my remembrance brutish wrath
120 Sinfully plucked, and not a man of you
    Had so much grace to put it in my mind.
    But when your carters° or your waiting vassals   *cart drivers*
    Have done a drunken slaughter, and defaced
    The precious image of our dear redeemer,
125 You straight° are on your knees for 'Pardon, pardon!'—   *straightaway*
    And I, unjustly too, must grant it you.
    But, for my brother, not a man would speak,
    Nor I, ungracious, speak unto myself
    For him, poor soul. The proudest of you all
130 Have been beholden to him in his life,
    Yet none of you would once beg for his life.
    O God, I fear thy justice will take hold
    On me—and you, and mine, and yours, for this.—
    Come, Hastings, help me to my closet.°   *private (bed)room*
135 Ah, poor Clarence!   *Exeunt some with* KING *and* QUEEN
RICHARD GLOUCESTER   This is the fruits of rashness. Marked you not
    How that the guilty kindred of the Queen
    Looked pale, when they did hear of Clarence' death?
    O, they did urge it still unto the King.
140 God will revenge it. Come, lords, will you go
    To comfort Edward with our company?
BUCKINGHAM   We wait upon your grace.   *Exeunt*

2.2

Enter the old DUCHESS OF YORK *with the two children of*
Clarence[1]

BOY   Good grannam, tell us, is our father dead?
DUCHESS OF YORK   No, boy.
GIRL   Why do you weep so oft, and beat your breast,

---

9. That is, the release of his servant from a sentence of
death.
2.2 Location: The palace, London.

1. Edward and Margaret Plantagenet (not to be confused
with King Edward, Prince Edward, or Queen Margaret).

And cry, 'O Clarence, my unhappy son'?
5   BOY   Why do you look on us and shake your head,
And call us orphans, wretches, castaways,
If that our noble father were alive?
DUCHESS OF YORK   My pretty cousins,° you mistake me both.   kinsmen
I do lament the sickness of the King,
10   As loath to lose him, not your father's death.
It were lost sorrow to wail one that's lost.
BOY   Then you conclude, my grannam, he is dead.
The King mine uncle is to blame for this.
God will revenge it—whom I will importune°   beg
15   With earnest prayers, all to that effect.
GIRL   And so will I.
DUCHESS OF YORK   Peace, children, peace! The King doth love you well.
Incapable° and shallow innocents,   Uncomprehending
You cannot guess who caused your father's death.
20   BOY   Grannam, we can. For my good uncle Gloucester
Told me the King, provoked to it by the Queen,
Devised impeachments° to imprison him,   charges
And when my uncle told me so he wept,
And pitied me, and kindly kissed my cheek,
25   Bade me rely on him as on my father,
And he would love me dearly as his child.
DUCHESS OF YORK   Ah, that deceit should steal such gentle shapes,°   appearances
And with a virtuous visor° hide deep vice!   mask
He is my son, ay, and therein my shame;
30   Yet from my dugs° he drew not this deceit.   breasts
BOY   Think you my uncle did dissemble, grannam?
DUCHESS OF YORK   Ay, boy.
BOY   I cannot think it. Hark, what noise is this?
        Enter QUEEN [ELIZABETH] *with her hair about her ears*[2]
QUEEN ELIZABETH   Ah, who shall hinder me to wail and weep?
35   To chide my fortune, and torment myself?
I'll join with black despair against my soul,
And to myself become an enemy.
DUCHESS OF YORK   What means this scene of rude° impatience?   violent
QUEEN ELIZABETH   To mark an act of tragic violence.
40   Edward, my lord, thy son, our king, is dead.[3]
Why grow the branches when the root is gone?
Why wither not the leaves that want° their sap?   lack
If you will live, lament; if die, be brief,
That our swift-wingèd souls may catch the King's,
45   Or like obedient subjects follow him
To his new kingdom of ne'er-changing night.
DUCHESS OF YORK   Ah, so much interest° have I in thy sorrow   right to share
As I had title[4] in thy noble husband.
I have bewept a worthy husband's[5] death,
50   And lived with looking on his images.°   likenesses (his sons)
But now two mirrors[6] of his princely semblance

---

2. Disheveled hair was a conventional expression of grief on the Elizabethan stage. F adds "Rivers and Dorset after her" and gives them lines to speak later in the scene.
3. Shakespeare is telescoping events. Edward actually died some five years after Clarence.
4. Legal right (as Edward's mother, the Duchess of York has a right to mourn).
5. The Duke of York (whose death is dramatized in *Richard Duke of York*).
6. Clarence and King Edward.

Are cracked in pieces by malignant death,   *(Richard)*
And I for comfort have but one false glass,°
That grieves me when I see my shame in him.
55   Thou art a widow, yet thou art a mother,
And hast the comfort of thy children left.
But death hath snatched my husband from mine arms
And plucked two crutches from my feeble hands,
Clarence and Edward. O what cause have I,
60   Thine being but a moiety° of my moan,   *half*
To overgo° thy woes, and drown thy cries?   *exceed*
    BOY [*to* ELIZABETH]   Ah, aunt, you wept not for our father's death.
How can we aid you with our kindred tears?°   *tears of relatives*
    DAUGHTER [*to* ELIZABETH]   Our fatherless distress was left unmoaned;
65   Your widow-dolour° likewise be unwept.   *widow's grief*
    QUEEN ELIZABETH   Give me no help in lamentation.
I am not barren to bring forth complaints.[7]
All springs reduce[8] their currents to mine eyes,
That I, being governed by the wat'ry moon,
70   May send forth plenteous tears to drown the world.
Ah, for my husband, for my dear Lord Edward!
    CHILDREN   Ah, for our father, for our dear Lord Clarence!
    DUCHESS OF YORK   Alas, for both, both mine, Edward and Clarence!
    QUEEN ELIZABETH   What stay° had I but Edward, and he's gone?   *support*
75   CHILDREN   What stay had we but Clarence, and he's gone?
    DUCHESS OF YORK   What stays had I but they, and they are gone?
    QUEEN ELIZABETH   Was never widow had so dear° a loss!   *grievous*
    CHILDREN   Were never orphans had so dear a loss!
    DUCHESS OF YORK   Was never mother had so dear a loss!
80   Alas, I am the mother of these griefs.
Their woes are parcelled;° mine is general.   *inclusive*
She for an Edward weeps, and so do I;
I for a Clarence weep, so doth not she.
These babes for Clarence weep, and so do I;
85   I for an Edward weep, so do not they.
Alas, you three on me, threefold distressed,
Pour all your tears. I am your sorrow's nurse,
And I will pamper° it with lamentation.[9]   *(over)feed*
88.1   DORSET   *Comfort, dear mother. God is much displeased*
        That you take with unthankfulness his doing.
        In common worldly things 'tis called ungrateful
        With dull unwillingness to pay a debt
88.5   *Which with a bounteous hand was kindly lent;*
        Much more to be thus opposite with° heaven   *in opposition to*
        For it requires° the royal debt it lent you.   *calls back*
     RIVERS   *Madam, bethink you like a careful mother*
        Of the young Prince your son. Send straight for him;
88.10   *Let him be crowned. In him your comfort lives.*
        Drown desperate sorrow in dead Edward's grave
        And plant your joys in living Edward's throne.

---

7. I can deliver my own lamentations.
8. Lead back (as to the sea, which is governed by the moon).
9. The indented passage that follows, 88.1–88.12, appears only in F.

Enter RICHARD [*Duke of*] GLOUCESTER, *the* [*Duke of*]
BUCKINGHAM, [*Lord* STANLEY *Earl of*] *Derby,* [LORD]
HASTINGS, *and* [*Sir Richard*] RATCLIFFE

RICHARD GLOUCESTER [*to* ELIZABETH]   Sister, have comfort. All of us have cause
90   To wail the dimming of our shining star,
But none can help our harms by wailing them. —
Madam, my mother, I do cry you mercy.°   *I beg your pardon*
I did not see your grace. Humbly on my knee
I crave your blessing.
95   DUCHESS OF YORK   God bless thee, and put meekness in thy breast,
Love, charity, obedience, and true duty.
RICHARD GLOUCESTER   Amen. [*Aside*] 'And make me die a good old man.'
That is the butt-end° of a mother's blessing;   *conclusion*
I marvel that her grace did leave it out.
100   BUCKINGHAM   You cloudy° princes and heart-sorrowing peers   *sad; raining (tears)*
That bear this heavy mutual load of moan,°   *lamentation*
Now cheer each other in each other's love.
Though we have spent our harvest of this king,
We are to reap the harvest of his son.
105   The broken rancour[1] of your high-swoll'n hearts
But lately° splinted, knit, and joined together,   *Only recently*
Must gently be preserved, cherished, and kept.
Meeseemeth° good that, with some little train,°   *I think it / entourage*
Forthwith from Ludlow[2] the young Prince be fet°   *fetched*
110   Hither to London to be crowned our king.[3]
110.1   RIVERS   *Why with some little train, my lord of Buckingham?*
BUCKINGHAM   *Marry, my lord, lest by a multitude*°   *large entourage*
The new-healed wound of malice should break out,
Which would be so much the more dangerous
110.5   *By how much the estate is green and yet ungoverned.*[4]
Where every horse bears his commanding rein[5]
And may direct his course as please himself°   *as he pleases*
As well the fear of harm as harm apparent°   *as actual harm*
In my opinion ought to be prevented.
110.10   RICHARD GLOUCESTER   *I hope the King made peace with all of us,*
And the compact is firm and time in me.
RIVERS   *And so in me, and so I think in all.*
Yet since it is but green, it should be put
To no apparent likelihood of breach,
110.15   *Which haply° by much company might be urged.*   *perhaps*
Therefore I say, with noble Buckingham,
That it is meet° so few should fetch the Prince.   *fitting*
HASTINGS   *And so say I.*
RICHARD GLOUCESTER   Then be it so, and go we to determine
Who they shall be that straight shall post° to Ludlow. —   *ride speedily*
Madam, and you my sister, will you go
To give your censures° in this weighty business?   *opinions*
115   QUEEN ELIZABETH *and* DUCHESS OF YORK   With all our hearts.
Exeunt. Manent RICHARD *and* BUCKINGHAM

1. Bitterness that caused you to be divided (unnaturally, like a broken limb).
2. Royal castle in Shropshire, near the Welsh border, where Prince Edward, as Prince of Wales, was staying.
3. The indented passage that follows, 110.1–110.18,

appears only in F.
4. *By . . . ungoverned:* Considering that the government is newly established and not yet in full control.
5. *bears . . . rein:* takes charge of the rein that should restrain him.

BUCKINGHAM   My lord, whoever journeys to the Prince,
For God's sake let not us two stay at home,
For by the way I'll sort° occasion,   *find*
As index° to the story we late° talked of,   *prologue / lately*
120   To part the Queen's proud kindred from the Prince.
RICHARD GLOUCESTER   My other self, my counsel's consistory,°   *council chamber*
My oracle, my prophet, my dear cousin!
I, as a child, will go by thy direction.
Towards Ludlow then, for we'll not stay behind.   *Exeunt*

2.3

Enter one CITIZEN *at one door and another at the other*

FIRST CITIZEN   Good morrow, neighbour. Whither away so fast?
SECOND CITIZEN   I promise° you, I scarcely know myself.   *assure*
Hear you the news abroad?
FIRST CITIZEN   Yes, that the King is dead.
SECOND CITIZEN   Ill news, by'r Lady;° seldom comes the better.[1]   *by the Virgin Mary*
5   I fear, I fear, 'twill prove a giddy° world.   *mad*
Enter another CITIZEN
THIRD CITIZEN   Neighbours, God speed.
FIRST CITIZEN   Give you good morrow, sir.
THIRD CITIZEN   Doth the news hold of good King Edward's death?
SECOND CITIZEN   Ay, sir, it is too true. God help the while.
THIRD CITIZEN   Then, masters,° look to see a troublous world.   *sirs*
10   FIRST CITIZEN   No, no, by God's good grace his son shall reign.
THIRD CITIZEN   Woe to that land that's governed by a child.
SECOND CITIZEN   In him there is a hope of government,
Which in his nonage council under him,[2]
And in his full and ripened years himself,
15   No doubt shall then, and till then, govern well.
FIRST CITIZEN   So stood the state when Henry the Sixth
Was crowned in Paris but at nine months old.
THIRD CITIZEN   Stood the state so? No, no, good friends, God wot.°   *knows*
For then this land was famously enriched
20   With politic,° grave counsel;° then the King   *astute / advisers*
Had virtuous uncles to protect his grace.
FIRST CITIZEN   Why, so hath this, both by his father and mother.
THIRD CITIZEN   Better it were they all came by his father,
Or by his father there were none at all.
25   For emulation° who shall now be near'st[3]   *competition*
Will touch us all too near, if God prevent not.
O full of danger is the Duke of Gloucester,
And the Queen's sons and brothers haught° and proud.   *haughty*
And were they° to be ruled, and not to rule,   *(both factions)*
30   This sickly land might solace° as before.   *prosper*
FIRST CITIZEN   Come, come, we fear the worst. All will be well.
THIRD CITIZEN   When clouds are seen, wise men put on their cloaks;
When great leaves fall, then winter is at hand;
When the sun sets, who doth not look for night?
35   Untimely storms make men expect a dearth.

2.3 Location: A street in London.
1. Things rarely change for the better (proverbial).
2. The Privy Council governing in his name during the
years of his minority.
3. Most influential with the King.

All may be well, but if God sort° it so   ordain
'Tis more than we deserve, or I expect.
SECOND CITIZEN   Truly the hearts of men are full of fear.
You cannot reason° almost with a man   converse
40   That looks not heavily and full of dread.
THIRD CITIZEN   Before the days of change still is it so.
By a divine instinct men's minds mistrust
Ensuing danger, as by proof° we see   experience
The water swell before a boist'rous storm.
45   But leave it all to God. Whither away?
SECOND CITIZEN   Marry, we were sent for to the justices.
THIRD CITIZEN   And so was I. I'll bear you company.   *Exeunt*

2.4

Enter [Lord] CARDINAL, *young [Duke of]* YORK, QUEEN
*[*ELIZABETH*], and the [old]* DUCHESS OF YORK
CARDINAL   Last night, I hear, they lay them at Northampton.
At Stony Stratford¹ they do rest tonight.
Tomorrow, or next day, they will be here.
DUCHESS OF YORK   I long with all my heart to see the Prince.
5   I hope he is much grown since last I saw him.
QUEEN ELIZABETH   But I hear, no. They say my son of York
Has almost overta'en him in his growth.
YORK   Ay, mother, but I would not have it so.
DUCHESS OF YORK   Why, my young cousin, it is good to grow.
10   YORK   Grandam, one night as we did sit at supper,
My uncle Rivers talked how I did grow
More than my brother. 'Ay', quoth my nuncle° Gloucester,   uncle (colloquial)
'Small herbs have grace; gross weeds do grow apace'.°   rapidly
And since, methinks I would not grow so fast,
15   Because sweet flow'rs are slow, and weeds make haste.
DUCHESS OF YORK   Good faith, good faith, the saying did not hold°   hold true
In him that did object° the same to thee.   argue
He was the wretched'st thing when he was young,
So long a-growing, and so leisurely,
20   That if his rule were true he should be gracious.
CARDINAL   Why, so no doubt he is, my gracious madam.
DUCHESS OF YORK   I hope he is, but yet let mothers doubt.
YORK   Now, by my troth, if I had been remembered,
I could have given my uncle's grace a flout²
25   To touch his growth, nearer than he touched° mine.   hit
DUCHESS OF YORK   How, my young York? I pray thee, let me hear it.
YORK   Marry, they say my uncle grew so fast
That he could gnaw a crust at two hours old.
'Twas full two years ere I could get a tooth.
30   Grannam, this would have been a biting jest.
DUCHESS OF YORK   I pray thee, pretty York, who told thee this?
YORK   Grannam, his nurse.
DUCHESS OF YORK   His nurse? Why, she was dead ere thou wast born.
YORK   If 'twere not she, I cannot tell who told me.
35   QUEEN ELIZABETH   A parlous° boy! Go to,³ you are too shrewd.°   mischievous / sharp

---

2.4 Location: The palace, London.
1. Town in Buckinghamshire (south of Northampton). F
reverses the order of the towns.
2. *if . . . flout*: if I had been told this, I could have taunted
my noble uncle.
3. Expression of disapproval.

CARDINAL   Good madam, be not angry with the child.
QUEEN ELIZABETH   Pitchers have ears.[4]

Enter [Marquis] DORSET

CARDINAL   Here comes your son, Lord Dorset.
What news, Lord Marquis?
DORSET   Such news, my lord,
As grieves me to report.
QUEEN ELIZABETH   How doth the Prince?
DORSET   Well, madam, and in health.
40 DUCHESS OF YORK   What is thy news then?
DORSET   Lord Rivers and Lord Gray are sent to Pomfret,[5]
And with them Thomas Vaughan, prisoners.
DUCHESS OF YORK   Who hath committed them?
DORSET   The mighty dukes,
Gloucester and Buckingham.
CARDINAL   For what offence?
45 DORSET   The sum of all I can,° I have disclosed.   *know*
Why or for what the nobles were committed
Is all unknown to me, my gracious lord.
QUEEN ELIZABETH   Ay me! I see the ruin of our house.
The tiger now hath seized the gentle hind.°   *doe*
50 Insulting tyranny begins to jet°   *encroach; strut*
Upon the innocent and aweless[6] throne.
Welcome destruction, blood, and massacre!
I see, as in a map, the end of all.
DUCHESS OF YORK   Accursèd and unquiet wrangling days,
55 How many of you have mine eyes beheld?
My husband lost his life to get the crown,
And often up and down my sons were tossed,
For me to joy and weep their gain and loss.
And being seated,° and domestic broils°   *enthroned / disorders*
60 Clean overblown,° themselves the conquerors   *Completely ended*
Make war upon themselves, brother to brother,
Blood to blood, self against self. O preposterous
And frantic outrage, end thy damnèd spleen,°   *malice*
Or let me die, to look on death no more.
65 QUEEN ELIZABETH [*to* YORK]   Come, come, my boy, we will to sanctuary.[7]—
Madam, farewell.
DUCHESS OF YORK   Stay, I will go with you.
QUEEN ELIZABETH   You have no cause.
CARDINAL [*to* ELIZABETH]   My gracious lady, go,
And thither bear your treasure and your goods.
For my part, I'll resign° unto your grace   *hand over*
70 The seal[8] I keep, and so betide° to me   *and so may it happen*
As well I tender° you and all of yours.   *care for*
Go, I'll conduct you to the sanctuary.   *Exeunt*

---

4. Proverbially said of children who overhear remarks made by adults: "Little pitchers have big ears."
5. Modern Pontefract, in west Yorkshire, site of the castle where Richard II was murdered.
6. Not able to command respect (because the King is so young).
7. Anyone, including criminals, could claim the protec-

tion of the church ("sanctuary") and thus immunity from civil law, initially for forty days. The Queen sought sanctuary at Westminster Abbey.
8. An engraved stamp, signifying the authority of the bearer, used to authenticate legal documents; here, the Great Seal of England.

3.1[1]

The Trumpets sound. Enter young PRINCE [EDWARD],
the Dukes of GLOUCESTER *and* BUCKINGHAM, *Lord* CAR-
DINAL, *with others [including Lord* STANLEY *Earl of*
Derby and Sir William CATESBY]

BUCKINGHAM Welcome, sweet Prince, to London, to your chamber.[2]

RICHARD GLOUCESTER [*to* PRINCE EDWARD] Welcome, dear
    cousin, my thoughts' sovereign.°   *ruler of my thoughts*
    The weary way hath made you melancholy.

PRINCE EDWARD No, uncle, but our crosses[3] on the way

5   Have made it tedious, wearisome, and heavy.
    I want° more uncles here to welcome me.   *lack; desire*

RICHARD GLOUCESTER Sweet Prince, the untainted virtue of your years
    Hath not yet dived into the world's deceit,
    Nor more can you distinguish of a man

10   Than of his outward show, which God he knows
    Seldom or never jumpeth° with the heart.   *coincides*
    Those uncles[4] which you want were dangerous.
    Your grace attended to their sugared words,
    But looked not on the poison of their hearts.

15   God keep you from them, and from such false friends.

PRINCE EDWARD God keep me from false friends; but they were none.

Enter Lord MAYOR [*and his train*]

RICHARD GLOUCESTER My lord, the Mayor of London comes to greet you.

MAYOR [*kneeling to* PRINCE EDWARD] God bless your grace with
    health and happy days.

PRINCE EDWARD I thank you, good my lord, and thank you all.—

20   I thought my mother and my brother York
    Would long ere this have met us on the way.
    Fie, what a slug° is Hastings, that he hastes not   *sluggard*
    To tell us whether they will come or no.

Enter LORD HASTINGS

BUCKINGHAM In happy time here comes the sweating lord.

PRINCE EDWARD [*to* HASTINGS] Welcome, my lord. What, will

25   our mother come?

LORD HASTINGS On what occasion° God he knows, not I,   *For what reason*
    The Queen your mother, and your brother York,
    Have taken sanctuary. The tender° Prince   *young; affectionate*
    Would fain have° come with me to meet your grace, *Would have liked to*

30   But by his mother was perforce° withheld.   *forcibly*

BUCKINGHAM Fie, what an indirect and peevish° course   *perverse*
    Is this of hers!—Lord Cardinal, will your grace
    Persuade the Queen to send the Duke of York
    Unto his princely brother presently?°—   *immediately*

35   If she deny, Lord Hastings, go with him,
    And from her jealous° arms pluck him perforce. *suspicious, mistrustful*

CARDINAL My lord of Buckingham, if my weak oratory
    Can from his mother win the Duke of York,

3.1 Location: A street in London.
1. Either because of defects in the original manuscript or because of blunders in the printing house, the text of this scene, up to line 148, is exceptionally corrupt and has been editorially reconstructed.
2. Capital (London was known as *camera regis*, "the King's chamber").

3. Referring to the arrests of his uncle and half-brothers on the journey.
4. Of the two arrested, only Rivers, being Elizabeth's brother, was Prince Edward's real uncle; Gray, a son by Elizabeth's previous marriage, was therefore actually half-brother to the Prince.

Anon° expect him. But if she be obdurate   *Very soon*
40   To mild entreaties, God in heaven forbid
We should infringe the sacred privilege
Of blessèd sanctuary. Not for all this land
Would I be guilty of so deep a sin.
BUCKINGHAM   You are too senseless-obstinate, my lord,
45   Too ceremonious° and traditional.   *rule-bound*
Weigh it not with the grossness° of this age.   *coarseness*
You break not sanctuary in seizing him.
The benefit thereof is always granted
To those whose dealings have deserved the place,
50   And those who have the wit to claim the place.
This prince hath neither claimed it nor deserved it,
And therefore, in my mind, he cannot have it.
Then taking him from thence that 'longs not there,[5]
You break thereby no privilege nor charter.
55   Oft have I heard of 'sanctuary men',[6]
But 'sanctuary children' ne'er till now.
CARDINAL   My lord, you shall o'errule my mind for once. —
Come on, Lord Hastings, will you go with me?
LORD HASTINGS   I come, my lord.
60   PRINCE EDWARD   Good lords, make all the speedy haste you may. —
Exeunt CARDINAL *and* HASTINGS
Say, uncle Gloucester, if our brother come,
Where shall we sojourn° till our coronation?   *stay*
RICHARD GLOUCESTER   Where it seems best unto your royal self.
If I may counsel you, some day or two
65   Your highness shall repose you at the Tower,[7]
Then where you please and shall be thought most fit
For your best health and recreation.
PRINCE EDWARD   I do not like the Tower of any place.° —   *of all places*
Did Julius Caesar build that place, my lord?
70   BUCKINGHAM   He did, my gracious lord, begin that place,
Which since succeeding ages have re-edified.°   *built further*
PRINCE EDWARD   Is it upon record, or else reported[8]
Successively from age to age, he built it?
BUCKINGHAM   Upon record, my gracious liege.
75   PRINCE EDWARD   But say, my lord, it were not registered,°   *documented*
Methinks the truth should live from age to age,
As 'twere retailed° to all posterity   *related orally*
Even to the general all-ending day.°   *Day of Judgment*
RICHARD GLOUCESTER [*aside*]   So wise so young, they say, do
never live long.
80   PRINCE EDWARD   What say you, uncle?
RICHARD GLOUCESTER   I say, 'Without characters° fame lives long'.   *writing*
[*Aside*] Thus like the formal Vice, Iniquity,[9]
I moralize two meanings in one word.[1]
PRINCE EDWARD   That Julius Caesar was a famous man:

---

5. Taking the Prince from a place he has not claimed as sanctuary.
6. Criminals seeking to avoid prosecution.
7. It was customary for kings of England (before James II) to spend the night before their coronation in the Tower, it being a royal palace and one of the strongest fortresses in the country. But Edward fears its other aspect, as a prison.

8. Is it on written record or otherwise told orally.
9. The conventional Vice figure, called Iniquity, who in sixteenth-century morality plays symbolized all of the vices.
1. As the Vice often did, Richard makes the same phrase have a double meaning.

85   With what his valour did t'enrich his wit,
        His wit set down to make his valour live.[2]
        Death made no conquest of this conqueror,
        For yet he lives in fame though not in life.
        I'll tell you what, my cousin Buckingham.
90 BUCKINGHAM What, my good lord?
    PRINCE EDWARD An if° I live until I be a man,   An if = If
        I'll win our ancient right[3] in France again,
        Or die a soldier, as I lived a king.
    RICHARD GLOUCESTER [aside] Short summers lightly have a
        forward spring.[4]
            Enter young [Duke of] YORK, [LORD] HASTINGS, and
            [Lord] CARDINAL
95 BUCKINGHAM Now in good time, here comes the Duke of York.
    PRINCE EDWARD Richard of York, how fares our loving brother?
    YORK Well, my dread[5] lord—so must I call you now.
    PRINCE EDWARD Ay, brother, to our grief, as it is yours.
        Too late° he died that might have kept that title,   recently
100   Which by his death hath lost much majesty.
    RICHARD GLOUCESTER How fares our noble cousin, Lord of York?
    YORK I thank you, gentle uncle, well. O, my lord,
        You said that idle° weeds are fast in growth;   useless
        The Prince, my brother, hath outgrown me far.
    RICHARD GLOUCESTER He hath, my lord.
105 YORK   And therefore is he idle?
    RICHARD GLOUCESTER O my fair cousin, I must not say so.
    YORK He is more beholden to you then than I.
    RICHARD GLOUCESTER He may command me as my sovereign,
        But you have power in me as a kinsman.
110 YORK I pray you, uncle, render me this dagger.
    RICHARD GLOUCESTER My dagger, little cousin? With all my heart.
    PRINCE EDWARD A beggar, brother?
    YORK Of my kind uncle that I know will give,
        It being but a toy° which is no grief to give.   trifle
115 RICHARD GLOUCESTER A greater gift than that I'll give my cousin.
    YORK A greater gift? O, that's the sword to it.[6]
    RICHARD GLOUCESTER Ay, gentle cousin, were it light enough.
    YORK O, then I see you will part but° with light° gifts.   only / trivial
        In weightier things you'll say a beggar nay.
120 RICHARD GLOUCESTER It is too heavy for your grace to wear.
    YORK I'd weigh it lightly, were it heavier.[7]
    RICHARD GLOUCESTER What, would you have my weapon, little lord?
    YORK I would, that I might thank you as you call me.
    RICHARD GLOUCESTER How?
125 YORK Little.
    PRINCE EDWARD My lord of York will still be cross° in talk.—   perverse; quarrelsome
        Uncle, your grace knows how to bear with him.
    YORK You mean to bear me, not to bear with me.—
        Uncle, my brother mocks both you and me.

---

2. With . . . live: The same valorous deeds that enlivened
Caesar's writing were themselves made immortal by his
retelling of them.
3. Right to the throne (claimed by Henry V and his son
Henry VI).
4. Proverbial: Those who die young ("forward") are often

("lightly") precocious.
5. Held in awe (a common formula for addressing a
king).
6. to it: that is, to the dagger (the sword is to the dagger
as the greater gift is to the lesser).
7. I'd consider it of little value, even if it were heavier.

130 Because that I am little like an ape,
He thinks that you should bear me on your shoulders.[8]
BUCKINGHAM   With what a sharp, prodigal wit[9] he reasons.
To mitigate the scorn he gives his uncle,
He prettily and aptly taunts himself.
135 So cunning and so young is wonderful.°   *a cause of wonder*
RICHARD GLOUCESTER [*to* PRINCE EDWARD]   My lord, will't
        please you pass along?
Myself and my good cousin Buckingham
Will° to your mother to entreat of her   *Will go*
To meet you at the Tower and welcome you.
140 YORK [*to* PRINCE EDWARD]   What, will you go unto the Tower, my lord?
PRINCE EDWARD   My Lord Protector needs will have it so.
YORK   I shall not sleep in quiet at the Tower.
RICHARD GLOUCESTER   Why, what should you fear there?
YORK   Marry, my uncle Clarence' angry ghost.
145   My grannam told me he was murdered there.
PRINCE EDWARD   I fear no uncles dead.
RICHARD GLOUCESTER   Nor none that live, I hope.
PRINCE EDWARD   An if they[1] live, I hope I need not fear.
[*To* YORK] But come, my lord, and with a heavy heart,
Thinking on them, go we unto the Tower.
A sennet.[2]
        Exeunt. Manent RICHARD, BUCKINGHAM, *and* CATESBY
BUCKINGHAM [*to* RICHARD]   Think you, my lord, this little prating°   *chattering*
150   York
Was not incensèd° by his subtle mother   *incited*
To taunt and scorn you thus opprobriously?
RICHARD GLOUCESTER   No doubt, no doubt. O, 'tis a parlous° boy,   *shrewd*
Bold, quick, ingenious, forward, capable.
155 He is all the mother's, from the top to toe.
BUCKINGHAM   Well, let them rest.—Come hither, Catesby. Thou art sworn
As deeply° to effect what we intend   *cunningly*
As closely° to conceal what we impart.   *secretly*
Thou know'st our reasons, urged upon the way.[3]
160 What think'st thou? Is it not an easy matter
To make Lord William Hastings of our mind,[4]
For the instalment° of this noble duke   *enthroning*
In the seat royal of this famous isle?
CATESBY   He for his father's sake so loves the Prince[5]
165 That he will not be won to aught against him.
BUCKINGHAM   What think'st thou then of Stanley?° Will not he?   *(Earl of Derby)*
CATESBY   He will do all-in-all as Hastings doth.
BUCKINGHAM   Well then, no more but this. Go, gentle Catesby,
And, as it were far off, sound thou Lord Hastings
170 How he doth stand affected to our purpose.[6]
170.1   *And summon him tomorrow to the Tower*
        To sit about° the coronation.   *To discuss in council*
If thou dost find him tractable° to us,   *compliant*

---

8. Alluding to Richard's hunchback, which is compared to the saddle worn by jesters who carried monkeys about at carnivals and fairs.
9. A nimble wit (intelligence); a wit both sharp and prodigal (abundant or excessive).
1. Richard meant himself; Edward refers to Rivers and Gray.

2. Trumpet notes to signal a procession.
3. On the journey from London to Ludlow.
4. To have Hastings share in our opinion.
5. Hastings loves the Prince as the son of the beloved King Edward.
6. The following indented passage, 170.1–170.2, appears only in F. *stand affected to:* regard, like.

Encourage him, and tell him all our reasons.
If he be leaden, icy, cold, unwilling,
Be thou so too, and so break off your talk,
175 And give us notice of his inclination,
For we tomorrow hold divided counsels,[7]
Wherein thyself shalt highly° be employed.   *importantly*
RICHARD GLOUCESTER   Commend me to Lord William.° Tell   *(Hastings)*
    him, Catesby,
His ancient knot[8] of dangerous adversaries
180 Tomorrow are let blood° at Pomfret Castle,   *are executed*
And bid my lord, for joy of this good news,
Give Mrs Shore[9] one gentle kiss the more.
BUCKINGHAM   Good Catesby, go effect this business soundly.°   *thoroughly; well*
CATESBY   My good lords both, with all the heed I can.
185 RICHARD GLOUCESTER   Shall we hear from you, Catesby, ere we sleep?
CATESBY   You shall, my lord.
RICHARD GLOUCESTER   At Crosby House,° there shall you find   *(Richard's residence)*
    us both.   *Exit* CATESBY
BUCKINGHAM   My lord, what shall we do if we perceive
Lord Hastings will not yield to our complots?°   *plots*
190 RICHARD GLOUCESTER   Chop off his head. Something we will determine.
And look when° I am king, claim thou of me   *And as soon as*
The earldom of Hereford, and all the movables[1]
Whereof the King my brother was possessed.
BUCKINGHAM   I'll claim that promise at your grace's hand.
195 RICHARD GLOUCESTER   And look° to have it yielded with all kindness.   *And expect*
Come, let us sup betimes,° that afterwards   *early*
We may digest our complots in some form.[2]   *Exeunt*

3.2
Enter a MESSENGER *to the door of* LORD HASTINGS
MESSENGER [*knocking*]   My lord, my lord!
LORD HASTINGS [*within*]   Who knocks?
MESSENGER   One from Lord Stanley.
    Enter LORD HASTINGS
LORD HASTINGS   What is't o'clock?
MESSENGER   Upon the stroke of four.
LORD HASTINGS   Cannot my Lord Stanley sleep these tedious nights?
MESSENGER   So it appears by that I have to say.
5 First he commends him to your noble self.
LORD HASTINGS   What then?
MESSENGER   Then certifies° your lordship that this night   *assures*
He dreamt the boar had razèd off his helm.[1]
Besides, he says there are two councils kept,
10 And that may be determined at the one
Which may make you and him to rue at° th'other.   *regret*
Therefore he sends to know your lordship's pleasure,
If you will presently° take horse with him,   *immediately*

---

7. There will be two separate council meetings, one public to plan the Prince's coronation, the other private to plot Richard's seizing of the crown.
8. Conspiracy, with additional meaning of "tumor," picked up in the next line in the image of bloodletting as medical treatment.
9. After Edward's death, Jane Shore (see 1.1.71–77) became Hastings's mistress.

1. Personal as opposed to real property: furnishings, rather than land.
2. We may break plans down into an orderly system (with pun on "digest").
3.2 Location: Outside Lord Hastings's house, in London.
1. He dreamed the boar (Richard's emblem) had sheared off his helmet (figuratively, cut off his head).

And with all speed post with him toward the north
15 To shun the danger that his soul divines.°   *prophesies*
  LORD HASTINGS   Go, fellow, go, return unto thy lord.
  Bid him not fear the separated councils.
  His honour and myself are at the one,
  And at the other is my good friend Catesby,
20 Where nothing can proceed that toucheth° us   *concerns; harms*
  Whereof I shall not have intelligence.°   *secret information*
  Tell him his fears are shallow, without instance.°   *evidence*
  And for his dreams, I wonder he's so simple,°   *childish*
  To trust the mock'ry of unquiet slumbers.
25 To fly the boar before the boar pursues
  Were to incense the boar to follow us,
  And make pursuit where he did mean° no chase.   *intend*
  Go, bid thy master rise, and come to me,
  And we will both together to the Tower,
30 Where he shall see the boar will use us kindly.[2]
  MESSENGER   I'll go, my lord, and tell him what you say.   *Exit*
      Enter CATESBY
  CATESBY   Many good morrows to my noble lord.
  LORD HASTINGS   Good morrow, Catesby. You are early stirring.
  What news, what news, in this our tott'ring state?
35 CATESBY   It is a reeling° world indeed, my lord,   *an unstable*
  And I believe will never stand upright
  Till Richard wear the garland of the realm.
  LORD HASTINGS   How? 'Wear the garland'? Dost thou mean the crown?
  CATESBY   Ay, my good lord.
40 LORD HASTINGS   I'll have this crown° of mine cut from my shoulders   *head*
  Before I'll see the crown so foul misplaced.
  But canst thou guess that he doth aim at it?
  CATESBY   Ay, on my life, and hopes to find you forward°   *a strong supporter*
  Upon his party° for the gain thereof—   *On his side*
45 And thereupon he sends you this good news:
  That this same very day your enemies,
  The kindred of the Queen, must die at Pomfret.
  LORD HASTINGS   Indeed I am no mourner for that news,
  Because they have been still my adversaries.
50 But that I'll give my voice on Richard's side
  To bar my master's heirs in true descent,
  God knows I will not do it, to the death.[3]
  CATESBY   God keep your lordship in that gracious mind!
  LORD HASTINGS   But I shall laugh at this a twelvemonth hence:
55 That they which brought me in my master's hate,[4]
  I live to look upon their tragedy.
  Well, Catesby, ere a fortnight make me older,
  I'll send some packing that yet think not on't.
  CATESBY   'Tis a vile thing to die, my gracious lord,
60 When men are unprepared, and look not for it.
  LORD HASTINGS   O monstrous, monstrous! And so falls it out
  With Rivers, Vaughan, Gray—and so 'twill do
  With some men else, that think themselves as safe

2. Gently (but also, with unintended irony, characteristically).
3. Even at the risk of death.

4. That those (Rivers, Vaughan, and Gray) who turned
King Edward against me.

As thou and I, who as thou know'st are dear
65 To princely Richard and to Buckingham.
CATESBY The Princes both make high account of° you—   *highly esteem*
    [*Aside*] For they account° his head upon the bridge.[5]   *expect*
LORD HASTINGS I know they do, and I have well deserved it.
        Enter Lord STANLEY
    Come on, come on, where is your boar-spear,[6] man?
70 Fear you the boar, and go so unprovided?[7]
STANLEY My lord, good morrow.—Good morrow, Catesby.—
    You may jest on, but by the Holy Rood°   *Cross*
    I do not like these several° councils, I.   *separate*
LORD HASTINGS My lord, I hold my life as dear as you do yours,
75 And never in my days, I do protest,
    Was it so precious to me as 'tis now.
    Think you, but° that I know our state secure,   *if it were not*
    I would be so triumphant as I am?
STANLEY The lords at Pomfret, when they rode from London,
80 Were jocund,° and supposed their states were sure,°   *merry / secure*
    And they indeed had no cause to mistrust;
    But yet you see how soon the day o'ercast.°   *became overcast*
    This sudden stab of rancour I misdoubt.[8]
    Pray God, I say, I prove a needless coward.
85 What, shall we toward the Tower? The day is spent.[9]
LORD HASTINGS Come, come, have with you!° Wot° you what,   *I'll go with you / Know*
    my lord?
    Today the lords you talked of are beheaded.
STANLEY They for their truth° might better wear their heads   *honesty*
    Than some that have accused them wear their hats.°   *retain their offices*
90 But come, my lord, let us away.
        Enter a PURSUIVANT [*named*] *Hastings*[1]
LORD HASTINGS Go on before; I'll follow presently.
        Exeunt STANLEY *and* CATESBY
    Well met, Hastings. How goes the world with thee?
PURSUIVANT The better that your lordship please° to ask.   *is pleased*
LORD HASTINGS I tell thee, man, 'tis better with me now
95 Than when I met thee last, where now we meet.
    Then was I going prisoner to the Tower,
    By the suggestion° of the Queen's allies;   *incitement*
    But now, I tell thee—keep it to thyself—
    This day those enemies are put to death,
100 And I in better state than e'er I was.
PURSUIVANT God hold it[2] to your honour's good content.
LORD HASTINGS Gramercy,° Hastings. There, drink that for me.   *Many thanks*
        He throws him his purse
PURSUIVANT God save your lordship.   *Exit*
        Enter a PRIEST

---

5. London Bridge (where the heads of traitors were displayed high on poles).
6. Specialized hunting spear with a cross-bar to prevent the impaled boar's tusks from wounding the hunter.
7. Do you fear the boar, and (yet) go unprepared?
8. I mistrust such sudden attacks (as those that befell Rivers, Vaughan, and Gray).
9. It's getting late (in the morning). The scene had opened at 4:00 A.M.

1. F omits his name (taken from Holinshed's *Chronicles*), here and in the dialogue. The name may be important in calling attention to the significance of Lord Hastings's own name: the word means either "someone who hurries" (here, to his destruction) or "a fruit that ripens early or before its time." *pursuivant:* state messenger with authority to execute warrants (particularly of treason). Figuratively, a pursuivant was any summoner or messenger.
2. May God maintain your prosperity.

PRIEST Well met, my lord. I am glad to see your honour.
105 LORD HASTINGS I thank thee, good Sir[3] John, with all my heart.
I am in your debt for your last exercise.°   *sermon*
Come the next sabbath, and I will content you.[4]
He whispers in his ear.
Enter BUCKINGHAM
BUCKINGHAM What, talking with a priest, Lord Chamberlain?
Your friends at Pomfret, they do need the priest;
110 Your honour hath no shriving work[5] in hand.
LORD HASTINGS Good faith, and when I met this holy man
The men you talk of came into my mind.
What, go you toward the Tower?
BUCKINGHAM I do, my lord, but long I cannot stay there;
115 I shall return before your lordship thence.
LORD HASTINGS Nay, like enough, for I stay dinner[6] there.
BUCKINGHAM [*aside*] And supper° too, although thou[7] know'st it not.   *evening meal*
Come, will you go?
LORD HASTINGS   I'll wait upon° your lordship.   *Exeunt*   *attend; go with*

3.3

Enter Sir Richard RATCLIFFE *with halberdiers carrying
Lords* RIVERS, GRAY, *and [Sir Thomas]* VAUGHAN *to
death at Pomfret*[1]
RIVERS Sir Richard Ratcliffe, let me tell thee this:
Today shalt thou behold a subject die
For truth, for duty, and for loyalty.
GRAY [*to* RATCLIFFE] God bless the Prince from all the pack of you!
5 A knot° you are of damnèd bloodsuckers.   *group*
VAUGHAN [*to* RATCLIFFE] You live, that shall cry woe for° this   *shall regret*
hereafter.
RATCLIFFE Dispatch.° The limit of your lives is out.   *Be quick*
RIVERS O Pomfret, Pomfret! O thou bloody prison,
Fatal and ominous to noble peers!
10 Within the guilty closure° of thy walls,   *enclosure*
Richard the Second here was hacked to death,
And, for more slander to thy dismal seat,[2]
We give to thee our guiltless blood to drink.
GRAY Now Margaret's curse is fall'n upon our heads,
15 For standing by when Richard stabbed her son.
RIVERS Then cursed she Hastings; then cursed she Buckingham;
Then cursed she Richard. O remember, God,
To hear her prayer for them as now for us.
And for° my sister and her princely sons,   *as for*
20 Be satisfied, dear God, with our true blood,
Which, as thou know'st, unjustly must be spilt.
RATCLIFFE Make haste: the hour of death is expiate.°   *fully come*
RIVERS Come, Gray; come, Vaughan; let us here embrace.
Farewell, until we meet again in heaven.   *Exeunt*

---

3. Courteous title of respect for clergymen.
4. I will pay your "debt" with a donation.
5. Confession and absolution (here, before execution).
6. I stay for dinner (eaten at about 11:00 A.M.).
7. Here, used contemptuously, as opposed to the formal "you" in line 118.

3.3 Location: Pontefract Castle.
1. Q has an extra opening line for this scene:
    RATCLIFFE Come, bring forth the prisoners.
2. And, in order to increase the notoriety of this gloomy place.

3.4

Enter [the Duke of] BUCKINGHAM, [Lord STANLEY Earl of] Derby, [LORD] HASTINGS, BISHOP OF ELY, [the Duke of] NORFOLK, [Sir William CATESBY,]¹ with others at a table

LORD HASTINGS   Now, noble peers, the cause why we are met
  Is to determine of° the coronation.   *decide upon*
  In God's name, speak: when is the royal day?
BUCKINGHAM   Is all things ready for that solemn time?
5   STANLEY   It is, and wants but nomination.°   *naming the day*
BISHOP OF ELY   Tomorrow, then, I judge a happy° day.   *suitable*
BUCKINGHAM   Who knows the Lord Protector's mind herein?
  Who is most inward° with the noble Duke?   *intimate*
BISHOP OF ELY   Your grace, methinks, should soonest know his mind.
10   BUCKINGHAM   We know each other's faces. For° our hearts,   *As for*
  He knows no more of mine than I of yours,
  Or I of his, my lord, than you of mine. —
  Lord Hastings, you and he are near in love.
LORD HASTINGS   I thank his grace; I know he loves me well.
15   But for his purpose in the coronation,
  I have not sounded him,° nor he delivered   *sounded him out*
  His gracious pleasure any way therein.
  But you, my honourable lords, may name the time,
  And in the Duke's behalf I'll give my voice,°   *vote*
20   Which I presume he'll take in gentle part.°   *he'll graciously approve*
    Enter [RICHARD Duke of] GLOUCESTER
BISHOP OF ELY   In happy time, here comes the Duke himself.
RICHARD GLOUCESTER   My noble lords, and cousins all, good morrow.
  I have been long a sleeper, but I trust
  My absence doth neglect no great design²
25   Which by my presence might have been concluded.
BUCKINGHAM   Had not you come upon your cue, my lord,
  William Lord Hastings had pronounced your part—
  I mean, your voice, for crowning of the King.
RICHARD GLOUCESTER   Than my Lord Hastings no man might be bolder.³
30   His lordship knows me well, and loves me well. —
  My lord of Ely, when I was last in Holborn⁴
  I saw good strawberries in your garden there.
  I do beseech you send for some of them.
BISHOP OF ELY   Marry, and will, my lord, with all my heart. *Exit*
35   RICHARD GLOUCESTER   Cousin of Buckingham, a word with you.
  [*Aside*] Catesby hath sounded Hastings in° our business,   *in respect to*
  And finds the testy gentleman so hot
  That he will lose his head ere give consent
  His 'master's child'—as worshipful° he terms it—   *reverentially*
40   Shall lose the royalty° of England's throne.   *sovereignty*
BUCKINGHAM   Withdraw yourself a while; I'll go with you.
    Exeunt [RICHARD and BUCKINGHAM]⁵
STANLEY   We have not yet set down this day of triumph.

3.4 Location: The Tower of London.
1. F has Ratcliffe and Lovell (Sir Thomas Lovell; see 4.4.449) instead of Catesby.
2. My absence delays no important project.
3. No one could more confidently speak for me than Lord Hastings; but also, no one could be more presumptuous.
4. The Bishop of Ely's official London residence.
5. Q keeps Buckingham on, and changes "I'll go with you" to "I'll follow you."

Tomorrow, in my judgement, is too sudden,
For I myself am not so well provided°   *well equipped*
45 As else I would be, were the day prolonged.°   *further off*
       Enter BISHOP OF ELY
BISHOP OF ELY   Where is my lord, the Duke of Gloucester?
I have sent for these strawberries.
LORD HASTINGS   His grace looks cheerfully and smooth° this morning.   *untroubled*
There's some conceit° or other likes° him well,   *thought / pleases*
50 When that he bids good morrow with such spirit.
I think there's never a man in Christendom
Can lesser hide his love or hate than he,
For by his face straight° shall you know his heart.   *immediately*
STANLEY   What of his heart perceive you in his face
55 By any likelihood° he showed today?   *appearance*
LORD HASTINGS   Marry, that with no man here he is offended —
For were he, he had shown it in his looks.
STANLEY   I pray God he be not.
       Enter RICHARD[6] *and* BUCKINGHAM
RICHARD GLOUCESTER   I pray you all, tell me what they deserve
60 That do conspire my death with devilish plots
Of damnèd witchcraft, and that have prevailed
Upon my body with their hellish charms?
LORD HASTINGS   The tender love I bear your grace, my lord,
Makes me most forward in this princely presence
65 To doom th'offenders, whatsoe'er they be.
I say, my lord, they have deservèd death.
RICHARD GLOUCESTER   Then be your eyes the witness of their evil:
See how I am bewitched. Behold, mine arm
Is like a blasted sapling withered up.
70 And this is° Edward's wife, that monstrous witch,   *this is the work of*
Consorted° with that harlot, strumpet Shore,   *In league with*
That by their witchcraft thus have markèd me.
LORD HASTINGS   If they have done this deed, my noble lord —
RICHARD GLOUCESTER   'If'? Thou protector of this damnèd strumpet,
75 Talk'st thou to me of 'ifs'? Thou art a traitor. —
Off with his head. Now, by Saint Paul I swear,
I will not dine until I see the same.
Some see it done.
The rest that love me, rise and follow me.
       Exeunt. Manent CATESBY[7] *with* HASTINGS
80 LORD HASTINGS   Woe, woe for England! Not a whit for me,
For I, too fond,° might have prevented this.   *foolish*
Stanley did dream the boar did raze our helms,
But I did scorn it and disdain to fly.
Three times today my footcloth horse[8] did stumble,
85 And started when he looked upon the Tower,
As° loath to bear me to the slaughterhouse.   *As though*
O now I need the priest that spake to me.
I now repent I told the pursuivant,
As too triumphing,° how mine enemies   *exulting*

6. According to Holinshed, "He returned into the cham-   7. F calls for Ratcliffe and Lovell.
ber . . . with a wonderful sour, angry countenance, knit-   8. Horse draped with a richly ornamented covering
ting the brows, frowning and fretting, and gnawing on his   reaching almost to the ground.
lips."

90　Today at Pomfret bloodily were butchered,
　　And I myself secure in grace and favour.
　　O Margaret, Margaret! Now thy heavy curse
　　Is lighted on poor Hastings' wretched head.
　　CATESBY　Come, come, dispatch: the Duke would be at dinner.
95　Make a short shrift;° he longs to see your head.　　　　*confession (to a priest)*
　　LORD HASTINGS　O momentary grace of mortal men,
　　Which we more hunt for than the grace of God.
　　Who builds his hope in th'air of your good looks⁹
　　Lives like a drunken sailor on a mast,
100　Ready with every nod¹ to tumble down
　　Into the fatal bowels of the deep.²
　　CATESBY　Come, come, dispatch. 'Tis bootless to exclaim.°　　*pointless to protest*
　　LORD HASTINGS　O bloody Richard! Miserable England!
　　I prophesy the fearful'st time to thee
105　That ever wretched age hath looked upon.—
　　Come lead me to the block; bear him my head.
　　They smile at me, who shortly shall be dead.　　　　*Exeunt*

3.5

Enter RICHARD *Duke of* GLOUCESTER *and* [*the Duke of*]
　BUCKINGHAM in rotten° armour, marvellous ill-favoured°　　*rusty / ugly*
RICHARD GLOUCESTER　Come, cousin, canst thou quake and change thy
　　colour?
　　Murder thy breath in middle of a word?
　　And then again begin, and stop again,
　　As if thou wert distraught and mad with terror?
5　BUCKINGHAM　Tut, I can counterfeit the deep tragedian,
　　Tremble and start at wagging of a straw,¹
　　Speak, and look back, and pry° on every side,　　　　*peer*
　　Intending° deep suspicion; ghastly looks　　　　*Suggesting*
　　Are at my service, like enforcèd smiles,
10　And both are ready in their offices²
　　At any time to grace my stratagems.
　　　Enter the [*Lord*] MAYOR
RICHARD GLOUCESTER [*aside to* BUCKINGHAM]　Here comes the Mayor.
BUCKINGHAM [*aside to* RICHARD]　Let me alone to entertain him.—Lord Mayor—
RICHARD GLOUCESTER [*calling as to one within*]　Look to the drawbridge there!
15　BUCKINGHAM　Hark, a drum!
RICHARD GLOUCESTER [*calling as to one within*]　Catesby, o'erlook°　　*look (out) over*
　　the walls!
BUCKINGHAM　Lord Mayor, the reason we have sent—
RICHARD GLOUCESTER　Look back, defend thee! Here are enemies.
BUCKINGHAM　God and our innocence defend and guard us.
　　　Enter [*Sir William*] CATESBY³ *with Hastings' head*
20　RICHARD GLOUCESTER　O, O, be quiet! It is Catesby.
CATESBY　Here is the head of that ignoble traitor,
　　The dangerous and unsuspected Hastings.
RICHARD GLOUCESTER　So dear I loved the man that I must weep.

---

9. *Who . . . looks:* Anyone who puts his faith in your
seemingly favorable glances.
1. Complex play on words: Ready as he dozes off; as the
ship rolls; as the monarch, whose "good looks" upheld
him, condemns him with a silent nod.
2. Lines 102–7 appear only in F. Censorship or the fear
of censorship may well be why Hastings's ominous predic-

tion was omitted from Q.
3.5 Location: The Tower of London.
1. Act startled by the least movement or gesture.
2. Both are eager to perform their functions.
3. F calls for Ratcliffe and Lovell, and brings on Catesby
earlier, with the Mayor.

I took him for the plainest° harmless creature   *most manifestly*
25   That breathed upon the earth, a Christian,
Made him my book° wherein my soul recorded   *diary*
The history of all her secret thoughts.
So smooth he daubed his vice with show of virtue
That, his apparent open guilt omitted—
30   I mean, his conversation⁴ with Shore's wife—
He lived from all attainture of suspect.⁵

BUCKINGHAM   The covert'st sheltered° traitor that ever lived.   *The most hidden*
[*To the* MAYOR] Would you imagine, or almost believe—
Were't not that, by great preservation,⁶
35   We live to tell it—that the subtle traitor
This day had plotted in the Council house
To murder me and my good lord of Gloucester?

MAYOR   Had he done so?

RICHARD GLOUCESTER   What, think you we are Turks or infidels,
40   Or that we would against the form of law
Proceed thus rashly in the villain's death
But that the extreme peril of the case,
The peace of England, and our persons' safety,
Enforced us to this execution?

45 MAYOR   Now fair befall you, he deserved his death,
And your good graces both have well proceeded,°   *acted*
To warn false traitors from the like° attempts.   *similar*
I never looked for better at his hands
After he once fell in with Mrs Shore.

50 RICHARD GLOUCESTER⁷   Yet had not we determined he should die,
Until your lordship came to see his end,
Which now the loving haste of these our friends°—   *(Catesby and Buckingham)*
Something against our meanings°—have prevented;   *intentions*
Because, my lord, we would have had you hear
55   The traitor speak, and timorously confess
The manner and the purpose of his treason,
That you might well have signified the same
Unto the citizens, who haply° may   *perhaps*
Misconster us in him,⁸ and wail his death.

60 MAYOR   But, my good lord, your graces' word shall serve
As well as° I had seen and heard him speak.   *As well as = As if*
And do not doubt, right noble princes both,
But° I'll acquaint our duteous citizens   *That*
With all your just proceedings in this cause.°   *action*

65 RICHARD GLOUCESTER   And to that end we wished your lordship here,
T'avoid the censures of the carping° world.   *overcritical*

BUCKINGHAM   Which, since you come too late of our intent,°   *for what we intended*
Yet witness° what you hear we did intend,   *bear witness to*
And so, my good Lord Mayor, we bid farewell.   *Exit* MAYOR

70 RICHARD GLOUCESTER   Go after; after, cousin Buckingham!
The Mayor towards Guildhall⁹ hies him in all post;°   *haste*
There, at your meetest vantage of the time,¹
Infer° the bastardy of Edward's children.   *Allege*
Tell them how Edward put to death a citizen

---

4. Intercourse (in both senses).   Buckingham.
5. He lived free from all taint of suspicion.   8. Misunderstand our treatment of him.
6. By the most fortunate preservation (of our lives).   9. Center of municipal government in London.
7. F assigns this speech and the two preceding lines to   1. At your most appropriate and advantageous moment.

75   Only for saying he would make his son
     'Heir to the Crown' — meaning indeed, his house,°   *tavern*
     Which by the sign thereof was termèd so.
     Moreover, urge his hateful luxury°   *lasciviousness*
     And bestial appetite in change of lust,[2]
80   Which stretched unto their servants, daughters, wives,
     Even where° his raging eye, or savage heart,   *Wherever*
     Without control, listed° to make a prey.   *desired*
     Nay, for a need, thus far come near my person:[3]
     Tell them, when that my mother went with child
85   Of that insatiate Edward,[4] noble York,
     My princely father, then had wars in France,
     And by true computation of the time
     Found that the issue° was not his begot —   *offspring*
     Which well appearèd in his lineaments,°   *features*
90   Being nothing like the noble Duke my father.
     Yet touch this sparingly, as 'twere far off,
     Because, my lord, you know my mother lives.
     BUCKINGHAM   Doubt not, my lord, I'll play the orator
     As if the golden fee[5] for which I plead
95   Were for myself. And so, my lord, adieu.   [*He starts to go*]
     RICHARD GLOUCESTER   If you thrive well, bring them to Baynard's Castle,[6]
     Where you shall find me well accompanied
     With reverend fathers and well-learnèd bishops.
     BUCKINGHAM   I go, and towards three or four o'clock
100 Look for the news that the Guildhall affords.[7]   *Exit*
100.1   KING RICHARD   *Go, Lovell, with all speed to Doctor Shaw;*
         [*To* RATCLIFFE] *Go thou to Friar Penker.*[8] *Bid them both*
         Meet me within this hour at Baynard's Castle.
                         [*Exeunt* LOVELL *and* RATCLIFFE]
     RICHARD GLOUCESTER   Now will I in, to take some privy order[9]
     To draw the brats of Clarence[1] out of sight,
     And to give notice that no manner[2] person
     Have any° time recourse unto the Princes.   *Exeunt*   *at any*

3.6

     Enter a SCRIVENER° *with a paper in his hand*   *scribe*
     SCRIVENER   Here is the indictment of the good Lord Hastings,
     Which in a set hand fairly is engrossed,[1]
     That it may be today read o'er in Paul's[2] —
     And mark how well the sequel° hangs together: *sequence of events*
5   Eleven hours I have spent to write it over,
     For yesternight by Catesby was it sent me;
     The precedent° was full as long a-doing;   *rough draft*
     And yet, within these five hours, Hastings lived,

2. In continually shifting the object of his lust.
3. *for . . . person*: if necessary, impugn even to this extent my own honor (by implying that his mother was unfaithful).
4. *went . . . Edward*: was pregnant with dissolute Edward. *insatiate*: impossible to satisfy.
5. The crown (punning on "lawyer's fee").
6. Richard's stronghold, between Blackfriars and London Bridge.
7. The indented passage that follows, 100.1–100.3, appears only in F.
8. Dr. Shaw, brother to the Lord Mayor, and Friar Pen-

kins, provincial of the Augustinian Order, were prominent clerics who made public speeches supporting Richard's claim to the throne.
9. To make some secret arrangements.
1. The two children seen in 2.2.
2. No kind of (in other words, of whatever status or importance).
3.6 Location: Somewhere in London.
1. Which is written in official script (as opposed to a draft copy) and in the format of a legal document.
2. St. Paul's Cathedral, which served as a secular as well as sacred gathering place.

Untainted,° unexamined, free, at liberty.   *Unaccused*
10 Here's a good world the while! Who is so gross°   *stupid*
That cannot see this palpable device?°   *obvious stratagem*
Yet who so bold but says he sees it not?
Bad is the world, and all will come to naught,°   *wickedness; nothing*
When such ill dealing must be seen in thought.[3]   *Exit*

3.7

Enter RICHARD [*Duke of*] GLOUCESTER *at one door and*
[*the Duke of*] BUCKINGHAM *at another*

RICHARD GLOUCESTER How now, how now! What say the citizens?
BUCKINGHAM Now, by the holy mother of our Lord,
The citizens are mum, say not a word.
RICHARD GLOUCESTER Touched you° the bastardy of Edward's   *Did you touch on*
children?
5 BUCKINGHAM I did, with his contract with Lady Lucy,[1]
And his contract by deputy[2] in France,
Th'insatiate greediness of his desire,
And his enforcement° of the city wives,   *violation*
His tyranny for trifles, his own bastardy—
10 As being got° your father then in France,   *conceived*
And his resemblance,° being not like the Duke.   *appearance*
Withal, I did infer your lineaments°—   *lineage*
Being the right idea° of your father   *true image*
Both in your face[3] and nobleness of mind;
15 Laid open all your victories in Scotland,[4]
Your discipline in war, wisdom in peace,
Your bounty, virtue, fair humility—
Indeed, left nothing fitting for your purpose
Untouched or slightly handled° in discourse.   *lightly mentioned*
20 And when mine oratory grew toward end,
I bid them that did love their country's good
Cry 'God save Richard, England's royal king!'
RICHARD GLOUCESTER And did they so?
BUCKINGHAM No, so God help me. They spake not a word,
25 But, like dumb statues or breathing stones,
Stared each on other and looked deadly pale—
Which, when I saw, I reprehended them,
And asked the Mayor, what meant this wilful silence?
His answer was, the people were not used
30 To be spoke to but by the Recorder.°   *(a city official)*
Then he was urged to tell my tale again:
'Thus saith the Duke . . . thus hath the Duke inferred'°—   *asserted*
But nothing spoke in warrant from himself.°   *on his own authority*
When he had done, some followers of mine own,
35 At lower end of the Hall, hurled up their caps,

---

3. Must be perceived but not spoken of.
3.7 Location: Baynard's Castle.
1. Lady Elizabeth Lucy bore Edward a child. If, as Buckingham alleges, there had been a formal engagement between them, Edward's subsequent marriage to Elizabeth Gray would have been ruled invalid. His children by that marriage would have been bastards and hence ineligible to inherit the throne.
2. The Earl of Warwick, as deputy, had contracted with Louis IX of France for the marriage of Edward to Bona of

Savoy, the French queen's sister (see *Richard Duke of York* 3.3).
3. Q, F: forme. The Oxford editors observe that since Richard is prominently deformed, "form" is inappropriate; in the chronicles, it is Richard's *face* that is compared with his father's.
4. In 1482, as leader of an English expeditionary force against the Scots, Richard had advanced all the way to Edinburgh.

And some ten voices cried 'God save King Richard!'
And thus I took the vantage of° those few: *opportunity presented by*
'Thanks, gentle citizens and friends', quoth I;
'This general applause and cheerful shout
40   Argues your wisdoms and your love to Richard' —
And even here brake off and came away.
RICHARD GLOUCESTER   What tongueless blocks were they!
      Would they not speak?
BUCKINGHAM[5]   No, by my troth, my lord.
RICHARD GLOUCESTER   Will not the Mayor then, and his brethren, come?
45   BUCKINGHAM   The Mayor is here at hand. Intend° some fear;   *Pretend*
Be not you spoke with, but by mighty suit;[6]
And look you get a prayer book in your hand,
And stand between two churchmen, good my lord,
For on that ground I'll build a holy descant.[7]
50   And be not easily won to our request.
Play the maid's part:[8] still answer 'nay' — and take it.
RICHARD GLOUCESTER   I go. An if you plead as well for them
As I can say nay to thee for myself,
No doubt we'll bring it to a happy issue.
      [*One knocks within*]
55   BUCKINGHAM   Go, go, up to the leads![9] The Lord Mayor knocks.—
                                    Exit [RICHARD]
      Enter the [*Lord*] MAYOR, [*aldermen,*] *and citizens*
Welcome, my lord. I dance attendance° here.   *am kept waiting*
I think the Duke will not be spoke withal.
      Enter CATESBY
Now Catesby, what says your lord to my request?
CATESBY   He doth entreat your grace, my noble lord,
60   To visit him tomorrow, or next day.
He is within with two right reverend fathers,
Divinely bent to meditation,
And in no worldly suits would he be moved,
To draw him from his holy exercise.
65   BUCKINGHAM   Return, good Catesby, to the gracious Duke.
Tell him myself, the Mayor, and aldermen,
In deep designs, in matter of great moment,
No less importing than[1] our general good,
Are come to have some conference with his grace.
70   CATESBY   I'll signify so much unto him straight.   *Exit*
BUCKINGHAM   Ah ha! My lord, this prince is not an Edward.
He is not lolling on a lewd day-bed,
But on his knees at meditation;
Not dallying with a brace° of courtesans,   *pair*
75   But meditating with two deep° divines;   *profoundly learned*
Not sleeping to engross° his idle body,   *fatten*
But praying to enrich his watchful° soul.   *vigilant*
Happy were England would this virtuous prince
Take on his grace the sovereignty thereof.
80   But, sure I fear, we shall not win him to it.

---

5. F omits this line.
6. Do not let them speak with you unless they beg you.
7. Comment; improvised musical variation, usually the highest part. *ground*: basis; musical theme or air, often the bass line.
8. Keep refusing, but at the same time take whatever is offered (proverbial, with sexual innuendo).
9. Flat roof covered with lead.
1. Of no less significance than.

MAYOR Marry, God defend° his grace should say us nay.   *forbid*

BUCKINGHAM I fear he will. Here Catesby comes again.

      Enter CATESBY

Now Catesby, what says his grace?

CATESBY He wonders to what end you have assembled

85 Such troops of citizens to come to him,

His grace not being warned thereof before.

He fears, my lord, you mean no good to him.

BUCKINGHAM Sorry I am my noble cousin should

Suspect me that I mean no good to him.

90 By heaven, we come to him in perfect love,

And so once more return and tell his grace.   *Exit* CATESBY

When holy and devout religious men

Are at their beads,° 'tis much to draw them thence.   *prayers*

So sweet is zealous contemplation.

      Enter RICHARD *aloft, between two bishops. [Enter*

      CATESBY *below]*

95 MAYOR See where his grace stands 'tween two clergymen.

BUCKINGHAM Two props of virtue for a Christian prince,

To stay him from the fall of vanity;[2]

And see, a book of prayer in his hand—

True ornaments to know[3] a holy man.—

100 Famous Plantagenet, most gracious prince,

Lend favourable ear to our request,

And pardon us the interruption

Of thy devotion and right Christian zeal.

RICHARD GLOUCESTER My lord, there needs no such apology.

105 I do beseech your grace to pardon me,

Who, earnest in the service of my God,

Deferred the visitation of my friends.

But leaving this, what is your grace's pleasure?

BUCKINGHAM Even that, I hope, which pleaseth God above,

110 And all good men of this ungoverned isle.

RICHARD GLOUCESTER I do suspect I have done some offence

That seems disgracious° in the city's eye,   *displeasing*

And that you come to reprehend my ignorance.

BUCKINGHAM You have, my lord. Would it might please your grace

115 On our entreaties to amend your fault.

RICHARD GLOUCESTER Else wherefore breathe I in a Christian land?[4]

BUCKINGHAM Know then, it is your fault that you resign

The supreme seat, the throne majestical,

The sceptred office of your ancestors,

120 Your state of fortune[5] and your due of birth,

The lineal glory of your royal house,

To the corruption of a blemished stock,[6]

Whiles in the mildness of your sleepy° thoughts—   *contemplative*

Which here we waken to our country's good—

125 The noble isle doth want her proper° limbs: *lack her own*

Her face defaced with scars of infamy,

Her royal stock graft with ignoble plants

And almost shouldered in° the swallowing gulf   *shoved into*

2. To prevent him from falling into the sin of vanity.
3. *True . . . know:* Prayer books (and also, perhaps, the clergymen) by which to recognize.
4. How could I, a good Christian, do otherwise?

5. The position that fortune has given you.
6. Edward's "family tree" is degraded by bastardy and immorality.

Of dark forgetfulness and deep oblivion,
130　Which to recure° we heartily solicit　　　　　　　　　　　　　　*restore*
　　　Your gracious self to take on you the charge
　　　And kingly government of this your land—
　　　Not as Protector, steward, substitute,
　　　Or lowly factor° for another's gain,　　　　　　　　　　　　　　*agent*
135　But as successively,° from blood to blood,　　　　　　　*in order of succession*
　　　Your right of birth, your empery,° your own.　　　　　*absolute dominion*
　　　For this, consorted° with the citizens,　　　　　　　　　　　　*together*
　　　Your very worshipful° and loving friends,　　　　　　　　　　*respectful*
　　　And by their vehement instigation,
140　In this just cause come I to move your grace.
　　　RICHARD GLOUCESTER　I cannot tell if to depart in silence
　　　Or bitterly to speak in your reproof
　　　Best fitteth my degree° or your condition.[7]　　　　　　　　　*rank*
143.1　　　*If not to answer, you might haply° think*　　　　　　　　*perhaps*
　　　　　Tongue-tied ambition, not replying, yielded°　　　　　*agreed*
　　　　　To bear the golden yoke of sovereignty,
　　　　　Which fondly° you would here impose on me.　　　　　*foolishly*
143.5　　　*If to reprove you for this suit of yours,*
　　　　　So seasoned° with your faithful love to me,　　　　*made palatable*
　　　　　Then on the other side I checked° my friends.　　　　*rebuked*
　　　　　Therefore to speak, and to avoid the first,
　　　　　And then in speaking not to incur the last,
143.10　　*Definitively thus I answer you.*
　　　Your love deserves my thanks; but my desert,
145　Unmeritable,° shuns your high request.　　　　　　　　　　　*Undeserving*
　　　First, if all obstacles were cut away
　　　And that my path were even° to the crown,　　　　　　　　　　*smooth*
　　　As the ripe revenue and due of birth,
　　　Yet so much is my poverty of spirit,
150　So mighty and so many my defects,
　　　That I would rather hide me from my greatness—
　　　Being a barque to brook° no mighty sea—　　　　　*a boat to endure*
　　　Than in my greatness covet to be hid,[8]
　　　And in the vapour of my glory smothered.
155　But God be thanked, there is no need of me,
　　　And much I need° to help you, were there need.　　　　　*lack (ability)*
　　　The royal tree hath left us royal fruit,
　　　Which, mellowed by the stealing hours of time,
　　　Will well become the seat of majesty
160　And make, no doubt, us happy by his reign.
　　　On him I lay that° you would lay on me,　　　　　　　　　　　*what*
　　　The right and fortune of his happy° stars,　　　　　　　　*auspicious*
　　　Which God defend that I should wring from him.
　　　BUCKINGHAM　My lord, this argues conscience in your grace,
165　But the respects thereof are nice and trivial,[9]
　　　All circumstances well considerèd.
　　　You say that Edward is your brother's son;
　　　So say we, too—but not by Edward's wife.
　　　For first was he contract° to Lady Lucy—　　　　　　　　　*betrothed*

---

7. Social rank. The indented passage that follows, 143.1–　　　9. But the reasons you advance are nit-picking (thus,
143.10, appears only in F.　　　　　　　　　　　　　　　　　　overscrupulous).
8. Than desire to be enveloped by my greatness.

170 Your mother lives a witness to his vow[1] —
And afterward, by substitute,° betrothed   *proxy*
To Bona, sister to the King of France.
These both put off, a poor petitioner,
A care-crazed mother to a many sons,
175 A beauty-waning and distressèd widow
Even in the afternoon of her best days,
Made prize and purchase° of his wanton eye,   *booty*
Seduced the pitch and height of his degree[2]
To base declension° and loathed bigamy.   *degradation*
180 By her in his unlawful bed he got
This Edward, whom our manners° call the Prince.   *we in politeness*
More bitterly could I expostulate,
Save that for reverence to some alive[3]
I give a sparing limit to my tongue.
185 Then, good my lord, take to your royal self
This proffered benefit° of dignity—   *bestowal*
If not to bless us and the land withal,
Yet to draw forth° your noble ancestry   *to rescue*
From the corruption of abusing times,
190 Unto a lineal, true-derivèd course.
MAYOR [*to* RICHARD]   Do, good my lord; your citizens entreat you.
BUCKINGHAM [*to* RICHARD]   Refuse not, mighty lord, this proffered love.
CATESBY [*to* RICHARD]   O make them joyful: grant their lawful suit.
RICHARD GLOUCESTER   Alas, why would you heap this care on me?
195 I am unfit for state and majesty.
I do beseech you, take it not amiss.
I cannot, nor I will not, yield to you.
BUCKINGHAM   If you refuse it—as, in love and zeal,
Loath to depose the child, your brother's son,
200 As well we know your tenderness of heart
And gentle, kind, effeminate remorse,[4]
Which we have noted in you to your kindred,
And equally indeed to all estates°—   *social classes*
Yet know, whe'er° you accept our suit or no,   *whether*
205 Your brother's son shall never reign our king,
But we will plant some other in the throne,
To the disgrace and downfall of your house.
And in this resolution here we leave you.—
Come, citizens. 'Swounds,° I'll entreat no more.   *By God's wounds*
210 RICHARD GLOUCESTER   O do not swear, my lord of Buckingham.
                    Exeunt [BUCKINGHAM *and some others*]
CATESBY   Call him again, sweet prince. Accept their suit.
ANOTHER[5]   If you deny them, all the land will rue° it.   *suffer for*
RICHARD GLOUCESTER   Will you enforce° me to a world of cares? *condemn*
Call them again.   [*Exit one or more*]
I am not made of stone,
215 But penetrable to your kind entreats,°   *entreaties*
Albeit against my conscience and my soul.

1. Buckingham draws attention to the Duchess of York's objection to her son Edward's marriage to Elizabeth Gray; Edward's supposed betrothals (see notes to lines 5–6), along with the fact of Elizabeth's widowhood, are put forward as evidence that the marriage should be considered bigamous and hence the offspring illegitimate.
2. Drew him down from the eminence appropriate to his noble rank.
3. Richard's own mother, the Duchess of York.
4. And natural, tender pity (feelings thought of at that time as primarily feminine).
5. One of the remaining citizens, city officials, or bishops. In F, Catesby speaks this line.

Enter BUCKINGHAM *and the rest*

Cousin of Buckingham, and sage, grave men,
Since you will buckle fortune on my back,
To° bear her burden, whe'er I will or no,   *To make me*
220   I must have patience to endure the load.
But if black scandal or foul-faced reproach
Attend the sequel of your imposition,°   *what you impose on me*
Your mere° enforcement shall acquittance° me   *outright / acquit*
From all the impure blots and stains thereof;
225   For God doth know, and you may partly see,
How far I am from the desire of this.
MAYOR   God bless your grace! We see it, and will say it.
RICHARD GLOUCESTER   In saying so, you shall but say the truth.
BUCKINGHAM   Then I salute you with this royal title:
230   Long live kind Richard, England's worthy king!
ALL BUT RICHARD[6]   Amen.
BUCKINGHAM   Tomorrow may it please you to be crowned?
RICHARD GLOUCESTER   Even when you please, for you will have it so.
BUCKINGHAM   Tomorrow then, we will attend your grace.
235   And so, most joyfully, we take our leave.
RICHARD GLOUCESTER   [*to the bishops*]   Come, let us to our holy work again.—
Farewell, my cousin. Farewell, gentle friends.
Exeunt [RICHARD *and bishops above, the rest below*]

4.1

Enter QUEEN [ELIZABETH], *the* [*old*] DUCHESS OF YORK,
and Marquis DORSET *at one door;* [LADY] ANNE *Duchess
of Gloucester* [*with Clarence's daughter*] *at another door*

DUCHESS OF YORK   Who meets us here? My niece° Plantagenet,   *granddaughter*
Led in° the hand of her kind aunt of Gloucester?   *by*
Now for° my life, she's wand'ring to the Tower,   *upon*
On pure heart's love, to greet the tender° Prince.—   *young*
Daughter,° well met.   *Daughter-in-law*
5   LADY ANNE   God give your graces both
A happy and a joyful time of day.
QUEEN ELIZABETH   As much to you, good sister.° Whither away?   *sister-in-law*
LADY ANNE   No farther than the Tower, and—as I guess—
Upon the like devotion° as yourselves: *devout duty*
10   To gratulate° the gentle princes there.   *greet*
QUEEN ELIZABETH   Kind sister, thanks. We'll enter all together—
Enter [*from the Tower* BRACKENBURY] *the Lieutenant*
And in good time, here the Lieutenant comes.
Master Lieutenant, pray you by your leave,
How doth the Prince, and my young son of York?
15   BRACKENBURY   Right well, dear madam. By your patience,
I may not suffer° you to visit them.   *permit*
The King hath strictly charged the contrary.
QUEEN ELIZABETH   The King? Who's that?
BRACKENBURY   I mean, the Lord Protector.
QUEEN ELIZABETH   The Lord protect him from that kingly title.[1]
20   Hath he set bounds° between their love and me?   *barriers*

---

6. Q assigns this word to the Mayor only.   1. May God prevent Richard from acquiring the title of
4.1 Location: Before the Tower.   King.

I am their mother; who shall bar me from them?

DUCHESS OF YORK   I am their father's mother; I will see them.

LADY ANNE   Their aunt I am in law, in love their mother;
Then bring me to their sights. I'll bear thy blame,

25   And take thy office from thee on my peril.[2]

BRACKENBURY   No, madam, no; I may not leave it° so.   *give up my office*
I am bound by oath, and therefore pardon me.   *Exit*

    Enter Lord STANLEY [*Earl of Derby*]

STANLEY   Let me but meet you ladies one hour hence,
And I'll salute your grace of York as mother

30   And reverend looker-on° of two fair queens.[3]   *beholder*
[*To* ANNE] Come, madam, you must straight to Westminster,[4]
There to be crownèd Richard's royal queen.

QUEEN ELIZABETH   Ah, cut my lace asunder,[5] that my pent heart
May have some scope to beat, or else I swoon

35   With this dead-killing news.

LADY ANNE   Despiteful tidings! O unpleasing news!

DORSET [*to* ANNE]   Be of good cheer.—Mother, how fares your grace?

QUEEN ELIZABETH   O Dorset, speak not to me. Get thee gone.
Death and destruction dogs thee at thy heels.

40   Thy mother's name is ominous to children.[6]
If thou wilt outstrip death, go cross the seas,
And live with Richmond from[7] the reach of hell.
Go, hie thee! Hie thee from this slaughterhouse,
Lest thou increase the number of the dead,

45   And make me die the thrall° of Margaret's curses: *slave*
'Nor mother, wife, nor counted° England's Queen'.   *regarded as*

STANLEY   Full of wise care is this your counsel, madam.
[*To* DORSET] Take all the swift advantage of the hours.
You shall have letters from me to my son°   *stepson (Richmond)*

50   In your behalf, to meet you on the way.
Be not ta'en tardy by unwise delay.

DUCHESS OF YORK   O ill-dispersing° wind of misery!   *misfortune-scattering*
O my accursèd womb, the bed° of death!   *birthplace*
A cockatrice[8] hast thou hatched to the world,

55   Whose unavoided eye is murderous.

STANLEY [*to* ANNE]   Come, madam, come. I in all haste was sent.

LADY ANNE   And I in all unwillingness will go.
O would to God that the inclusive verge°   *enclosing rim*
Of golden metal that must round° my brow   *encircle*

60   Were red-hot steel, to sear me to the brains.
Anointed let me be with deadly venom,[9]
And die ere men can say 'God save the Queen'.

QUEEN ELIZABETH   Go, go, poor soul. I envy not thy glory.
To feed my humour,° wish thyself no harm.   *To humor me*

65 LADY ANNE   No? Why? When he that is my husband now
Came to me as I followed Henry's corpse,
When scarce the blood was well washed from his hands,

---

2. And take on the responsibilities of your position at my own risk.
3. Elizabeth, widow of Edward IV, and Anne, wife of Richard III.
4. To Westminster Abbey, where English monarchs are traditionally crowned.
5. Elizabethan women wore tightly laced bodices.

6. The fact that you are my son places you in danger.
7. Away from. Henry Tudor, Earl of Richmond, had fled to Brittany in 1472, when Edward IV secured his grasp on the throne.
8. Basilisk (see note to 1.2.150).
9. Instead of the holy oil used in the ceremony of coronation.

Which issued from my other angel husband
And that dear saint which then I weeping followed—
70 O when, I say, I looked on Richard's face,
This was my wish: 'Be thou', quoth I, 'accursed
For making me, so young, so old a widow,[1]
And when thou wedd'st, let sorrow haunt thy bed;
And be thy wife—if any be so mad—
75 More miserable made by the life of thee
Than thou hast made me by my dear lord's death.'
Lo, ere I can repeat this curse again,
Within so small a time, my woman's heart
Grossly° grew captive to his honey words   *Stupidly*
80 And proved the subject of mine own soul's curse,
Which hitherto hath held mine eyes from rest—
For never yet one hour in his bed
Did I enjoy the golden dew of sleep,
But with his timorous° dreams was still° awaked.   *fearful / continually*
85 Besides, he hates me for° my father Warwick,   *because of*
And will, no doubt, shortly be rid of me.
QUEEN ELIZABETH   Poor heart, adieu. I pity thy complaining.°   *lamenting*
LADY ANNE   No more than with my soul I mourn for yours.
DORSET   Farewell, thou woeful welcomer of glory.
90 LADY ANNE   Adieu, poor soul, that tak'st thy leave of it.
DUCHESS OF YORK [*to* DORSET] Go thou to Richmond, and good fortune guide thee.
        [*To* ANNE, STANLEY, *and Clarence's daughter*] Go thou to Richard, and good angels
            tend thee.
        [*To* ELIZABETH] Go thou to sanctuary, and good thoughts possess thee.
        I to my grave, where peace and rest lie with me.
95 Eighty odd years of sorrow have I seen,
And each hour's joy racked with a week of teen.[2]   [*Exit*]
96.1   QUEEN ELIZABETH   *Stay: yet look back with me unto the Tower.—*
              Pity, you ancient stones, those tender babes,
              Whom envy° hath immured within your walls,   *malice*
              Rough cradle for such little pretty ones,
96.5   *Rude ragged nurse, old sullen playfellow*
              For tender princes: use my babies well.
              So foolish sorrow bids your stones farewell.   Exeunt

4.2

        Sound a sennet. Enter [KING] RICHARD *in pomp,* [*the*
        Duke of] BUCKINGHAM, [*Sir William*] CATESBY, *other*
        nobles[1] [*and a* PAGE]
KING RICHARD   Stand all apart.°—Cousin of Buckingham.   *aside*
BUCKINGHAM   My gracious sovereign?
KING RICHARD   Give me thy hand.
        Sound [*a sennet*]. *Here he ascendeth the throne*
        Thus high by thy advice
5 And thy assistance is King Richard seated.
But shall we wear these glories for a day?
Or shall they last, and we rejoice in them?
BUCKINGHAM   Still° live they, and for ever let them last.   *Perpetually*

---

1. Doomed to a long life of widowhood.
2. Grief. The indented passage that follows, 96.1–96.7, appears only in F; the other characters remain onstage.

4.2 Location: The palace, London.
1. In F, specifically Ratcliffe and Lovell.

KING RICHARD   Ah, Buckingham, now do I play the touch,[2]
10   To try if thou be current° gold indeed.   *real, genuine*
       Young Edward lives. Think now what I would speak.
BUCKINGHAM   Say on, my loving lord.
KING RICHARD   Why, Buckingham, I say I would be king.
BUCKINGHAM   Why, so you are, my thrice-renownèd liege.
15 KING RICHARD   Ha? Am I king? 'Tis so. But Edward lives.
BUCKINGHAM   True, noble prince.
KING RICHARD   O bitter consequence,°   *conclusion; retort*
       That Edward still should live 'true noble prince'.
       Cousin, thou wast not wont to be° so dull.   *you once were not*
       Shall I be plain? I wish the bastards dead,
20   And I would have it immediately performed.
       What sayst thou now? Speak suddenly,° be brief.   *at once*
BUCKINGHAM   Your grace may do your pleasure.
KING RICHARD   Tut, tut, thou art all ice. Thy kindness freezes.
       Say, have I thy consent that they shall die?
25 BUCKINGHAM   Give me some little breath, some pause, dear lord,
       Before I positively speak in this.
       I will resolve° you herein presently.°   *Exit*   *answer / shortly*
CATESBY [*to another, aside*]   The King is angry. See, he gnaws his lip.
KING RICHARD [*aside*]   I will converse with iron-witted fools
30   And unrespective° boys. None are for me   *unobservant*
       That look into me with considerate° eyes.   *critical*
       High-reaching° Buckingham grows circumspect.—   *Ambitious*
       Boy.
PAGE   My lord?
35 KING RICHARD   Know'st thou not any whom corrupting gold
       Will tempt unto a close° exploit of death?   *secret*
PAGE   I know a discontented gentleman
       Whose humble means match not his haughty spirit.
       Gold were as good as twenty orators,
40   And will no doubt tempt him to anything.
KING RICHARD   What is his name?
PAGE   His name, my lord, is Tyrrell.
KING RICHARD   I partly know the man. Go call him hither, boy.
                                                              Exit [PAGE]
       [*Aside*] The deep-revolving,° witty° Buckingham   *deeply scheming / clever*
       No more shall be the neighbour to my counsels.
45   Hath he so long held out° with me untired,   *kept up*
       And stops he now for breath? Well, be it so.
              Enter [*Lord*] STANLEY [*Earl of*] *Derby*
       How now, Lord Stanley? What's the news?
STANLEY   Know, my loving lord,
       The Marquis Dorset, as I hear, is fled
50   To Richmond, in those parts beyond the seas
       Where he abides.
KING RICHARD   Come hither, Catesby. [*Aside to* CATESBY] Rumour it abroad
       That Anne, my wife, is very grievous sick.
       I will take order for her keeping close.[3]
55   Enquire me out some mean-born gentleman,
       Whom I will marry straight to Clarence' daughter.

---

2. Touchstone: a means of testing gold.   3. I will arrange to have her kept out of sight.

The boy[4] is foolish,° and I fear not him.   *simpleminded*
Look how thou dream'st. I say again, give out
That Anne, my queen, is sick, and like to die.
60   About it, for it stands me much upon°   *is very important to me*
To stop all hopes whose growth may damage me.
                                                        [*Exit* CATESBY]
        [*Aside*] I must be married to my brother's daughter,[5]
        Or else my kingdom stands on brittle glass.
        Murder her brothers, and then marry her?
65   Uncertain way of gain, but I am in
        So far in blood that sin will pluck on° sin.   *incite*
        Tear-falling pity dwells not in this eye.—
                    Enter [*Sir James*] TYRRELL; [*he kneels*]
        Is thy name Tyrrell?
TYRRELL   James Tyrrell, and your most obedient subject.
KING RICHARD   Art thou indeed?
70   TYRRELL   Prove° me, my gracious lord.   *Test*
KING RICHARD   Dar'st thou resolve to kill a friend of mine?
TYRRELL   Please you,° but I had rather kill two enemies.   *If you wish*
KING RICHARD   Why there thou hast it: two deep enemies,
        Foes to my rest, and my sweet sleep's disturbers,
75   Are they that I would have thee deal upon.°   *set to work upon*
        Tyrrell, I mean those bastards in the Tower.
TYRRELL   Let me have open means to come[6] to them,
        And soon I'll rid you from the fear of them.
KING RICHARD   Thou sing'st sweet music. Hark, come hither, Tyrrell.
80   Go, by this token. Rise, and lend thine ear.
                    [RICHARD] *whispers in his ear*
        'Tis no more but so.° Say it is done,   *That's all*
        And I will love thee, and prefer° thee for it.   *promote*
TYRRELL   I will dispatch it straight.
KING RICHARD   Shall we hear from thee, Tyrrell, ere we sleep?[7]
                    Enter BUCKINGHAM
85   TYRRELL   Ye shall, my lord.   *Exit*
BUCKINGHAM   My lord, I have considered in my mind
        The late request that you did sound me in.
KING RICHARD   Well, let that rest. Dorset is fled to Richmond.
BUCKINGHAM   I hear the news, my lord.
90   KING RICHARD   Stanley, he° is your wife's son. Well, look to it.   *(Richmond)*
BUCKINGHAM   My lord, I claim the gift, my due by promise,
        For which your honour and your faith is pawned:
        Th'earldom of Hereford, and the movables
        Which you have promisèd I shall possess.
95   KING RICHARD   Stanley, look to your wife. If she convey
        Letters to Richmond, you shall answer it.°   *for it*
BUCKINGHAM   What says your highness to my just request?
KING RICHARD   I do remember me, Henry the Sixth
        Did prophesy that Richmond should be king,
100   When Richmond was a little peevish boy.
        A king . . . perhaps . . . perhaps.[8]
BUCKINGHAM   My lord?

4. Clarence's eldest son, Edward, Earl of Warwick.   6. Let me have free access.
5. To Edward's daughter, Elizabeth of York, who was   7. F omits this and the following line.
later to unite the two houses by becoming queen to the   8. The passage that follows, 101–119, appears only in Q.
Lancastrian Henry VII, formerly the Earl of Richmond.

KING RICHARD   How chance the prophet could not at that time
    Have told me, I being by, that I should kill him?
BUCKINGHAM   My lord, your promise for the earldom.
105 KING RICHARD   Richmond? When last I was at Exeter,
    The Mayor in courtesy showed me the castle,
    And called it 'Ruge-mount'⁹—at which name I started,
    Because a bard of Ireland¹ told me once
    I should not live long after I saw 'Richmond'.
110 BUCKINGHAM   My lord?
KING RICHARD   Ay? What's o'clock?
BUCKINGHAM   I am thus bold to put your grace in mind
    Of what you promised me.
KING RICHARD   But what's o'clock?
BUCKINGHAM   Upon the stroke of ten.
115 KING RICHARD   Well, let it strike!
BUCKINGHAM   Why 'let it strike'?
KING RICHARD   Because that, like a jack,² thou keep'st the stroke
    Betwixt thy begging and my meditation.
    I am not in the giving vein today.
120 BUCKINGHAM   Why then resolve me,° whe'er you will or no?   *answer me resolutely*
KING RICHARD   Thou troublest me. I am not in the vein.°   *mood*
        Exit [RICHARD, *followed by all but* BUCKINGHAM]
BUCKINGHAM   And is it thus? Repays he my deep° service   *i.e., rendered at great risk*
    With such contempt? Made I him king for this?
    O let me think on Hastings, and be gone
125   To Brecon,° while my fearful head is on.   *manor house in Wales*
                        Exit [*at another door*]

4.3

Enter Sir [*James*] TYRRELL
TYRRELL   The tyrannous and bloody act is done—
    The most arch° deed of piteous massacre   *preeminent*
    That ever yet this land was guilty of.
    Dighton and Forrest,¹ whom I did suborn°   *induce*
5   To do this piece of ruthless butchery,
    Albeit they were fleshed² villains, bloody dogs,
    Melted with tenderness and mild compassion,
    Wept like two children in their deaths' sad story.³
    'O thus', quoth Dighton, 'lay the gentle babes';
10   'Thus, thus', quoth Forrest, 'girdling° one another   *embracing*
    Within their alabaster° innocent arms.   *marble-white*
    Their lips were four red roses on a stalk,
    And in their summer beauty kissed each other.
    A book of prayers on their pillow lay,
15   'Which once', quoth Forrest, 'almost changed my mind.
    But O, the devil'—there the villain stopped,
    When° Dighton thus told on, 'We smotherèd   *At which point*
    The most replenishèd° sweet work of nature,   *complete*

---

9. Redhill (but punning on "Richmond").
1. Celtic bards, or poets, were also considered prophets.
2. A Jack was the mechanical figure who appeared to strike the hours in early clocks. By clockwork reiterations of his suit, Richard suggests, Buckingham is behaving like an annoying beggar and interfering with Richard's "meditation."
4.3 Location: The palace, London.

1. For the murder of the princes, Tyrrell recruited his servant, John Dighton, along with Myles Forrest and two others.
2. Experienced in killing; applied to hounds that had been fed part of their first kill in order to give them a taste for blood.
3. Wept in telling the sad story of the princes' deaths.

That from the prime° creation e'er she framed.'　　　　　　　　　　*first*
20　Hence both are gone,° with conscience and remorse.　　　　　*overcome*
They could not speak, and so I left them both,
To bear this tidings to the bloody king.

Enter KING RICHARD

And here he comes.—All health, my sovereign lord.
KING RICHARD　Kind Tyrrell, am I happy in thy news?
25　TYRRELL　If to have done the thing you gave in charge
Beget your happiness,[4] be happy then,
For it is done.
KING RICHARD　　But didst thou see them dead?
TYRRELL　I did, my lord.
KING RICHARD　　　　　And buried, gentle Tyrrell?
TYRRELL　The chaplain of the Tower hath buried them;
30　But where, to say the truth, I do not know.
KING RICHARD　Come to me, Tyrrell, soon, at after-supper,°　　*dessert*
When thou shalt tell the process° of their death.　　　　　　*story*
Meantime, but think how I may do thee good,
And be inheritor of thy desire.[5]
Farewell till then.
35　TYRRELL　　　　　I humbly take my leave.　　　*Exit*
KING RICHARD　The son of Clarence have I pent° up close.　　*locked*
His daughter meanly have I matched in marriage.[6]
The sons of Edward sleep in Abraham's bosom,[7]
And Anne, my wife, hath bid this world goodnight.
40　Now, for° I know the Breton[8] Richmond aims　　　　　　*because*
At young Elizabeth, my brother's daughter,
And by that knot° looks proudly o'er the crown,　　　*marriage, alliance*
To her go I, a jolly thriving wooer[9]—

Enter [Sir Richard] RATCLIFFE[1] [*running*]

RATCLIFFE　My lord.
45　KING RICHARD　Good news or bad, that thou com'st in so bluntly?
RATCLIFFE　Bad news, my lord. Ely° is fled to Richmond,　　*(Bishop of Ely)*
And Buckingham, backed with the hardy Welshmen,
Is in the field, and still his power increaseth.
KING RICHARD　Ely with Richmond troubles me more near°　*deeply*
50　Than Buckingham and his rash-levied strength.°　　*hastily raised army*
Come, I have learned that fearful commenting
Is leaden servitor[2] to dull delay.
Delay leads impotent and snail-paced beggary.°　　　　　　　*ruin*
Then fiery expedition° be my wing:　　　　　　　　　　　　*speed*
55　Jove's Mercury,[3] an herald for a king.
Go, muster men. My counsel is my shield.[4]
We must be brief, when traitors brave the field.[5]　　　*Exeunt*

---

4. *If . . . happiness:* If it pleases you to have accomplished
what you ordered done.
5. *but . . . desire:* you have only to think what you want of
me, and you will possess it.
6. I have married her off to a poor man.
7. In heaven (see Luke 16:22–23).
8. Person from Brittany; Richmond spent fourteen years
in exile there before returning to England to face Richard
III in 1485.
9. It was widely rumored that Anne was poisoned in
order to facilitate a plan by Richard to marry Elizabeth,

sister to the missing princes; modern historians believe
that these allegations are probably untrue. The charges
regarding Clarence's son and daughter (lines 36–37) are
certainly untrue.
1. Q calls for Catesby.
2. *fearful . . . servitor:* frightened talk is the sluggish attendant.
3. The swift messenger of the gods.
4. *My . . . shield:* I do not talk, but arm myself to fight.
counsel: adviser.
5. When traitors defy (us on) the battlefield.

4.4

Enter old QUEEN MARGARET

QUEEN MARGARET   So now prosperity begins to mellow°   *ripen*
And drop into the rotten mouth of death.
Here in these confines slyly have I lurked
To watch the waning of mine enemies.
5   A dire induction° am I witness to,   *prologue (as to a play)*
And will to France, hoping the consequence°   *conclusion (as of a play)*
Will prove as bitter, black, and tragical.

Enter the [old] DUCHESS OF YORK *and* QUEEN [ELIZABETH]

Withdraw thee, wretched Margaret. Who comes here?
QUEEN ELIZABETH   Ah, my poor princes! Ah, my tender babes!
10   My unblown° flowers, new-appearing sweets!°   *unopened / blooms*
If yet your gentle souls fly in the air,
And be not fixed in doom perpetual,[1]
Hover about me with your airy wings
And hear your mother's lamentation.
15   QUEEN MARGARET [*aside*]   Hover about her, say that right for right
Hath dimmed your infant morn to agèd night.[2]
DUCHESS OF YORK[3]   So many miseries have crazed° my voice   *cracked*
That my woe-wearied tongue is still and mute.
Edward Plantagenet, why art thou dead?
20   QUEEN MARGARET [*aside*]   Plantagenet doth quit° Plantagenet;   *pay for (the deeds of)*
Edward for Edward pays a dying debt.[4]
QUEEN ELIZABETH   Wilt thou, O God, fly from such gentle lambs
And throw them in the entrails of the wolf?
When° didst thou sleep, when such a deed was done?   *Whenever (up until now)*
25   QUEEN MARGARET [*aside*]   When holy Harry[5] died, and my sweet son.
DUCHESS OF YORK   Dead life, blind sight, poor mortal living ghost,[6]
Woe's scene, world's shame, grave's due by life usurped,[7]
Brief abstract° and record of tedious days,   *epitome; summary*
Rest thy unrest on England's lawful earth,
30   Unlawfully made drunk with innocents' blood.
[*They sit*]
QUEEN ELIZABETH   Ah that thou[8] wouldst as soon afford a grave
As thou canst yield a melancholy seat.
Then would I hide my bones, not rest them here.
Ah, who hath any cause to mourn but we?
35   QUEEN MARGARET [*coming forward*]   If ancient sorrow be most reverend,
Give mine the benefit of seniory,[9]
And let my griefs frown on the upper hand.[1]
If sorrow can admit society,
Tell o'er° your woes again by viewing mine.   *Count; narrate*
40   I had an Edward, till a Richard killed him;
I had a husband, till a Richard killed him.

4.4 Location: Before the palace.
1. *fixed in doom perpetual:* assigned by an irrevocable sentence to your final place of punishment or reward.
2. *right for . . . night:* even-handed justice has destroyed the bright hopes of your young lives.
3. Q places this after line 34 (making it the last speech before Margaret's intervention) and omits lines 20–21.
4. A debt for which payment is death. *Edward for Edward:* Prince Edward (Elizabeth's son) for Prince Edward (Margaret's son, whose murder is dramatized in *Richard Duke of York*).

5. Henry VI (Margaret's husband).
6. *mortal living ghost:* a dead person doomed to exist among the living.
7. *graves . . . usurped:* person who ought to be dead, unlawfully alive.
8. Here, Elizabeth is addressing the earth directly.
9. Seniority; Q1–5 have "signorie," F "signeurie," which suggests that Margaret may mean "sovereignty" or "lordship" ("seigniory").
1. *frown . . . hand:* have precedence in mourning.

[*To* ELIZABETH] Thou hadst an Edward, till a Richard killed him;
Thou hadst a Richard,[2] till a Richard killed him.
DUCHESS OF YORK [*rising*] I had a Richard too, and thou didst kill him;
45 I had a Rutland too,[3] thou holpst to kill him.
QUEEN MARGARET   Thou hadst a Clarence too, and Richard killed him.
From forth the kennel of thy womb hath crept
A hell-hound that doth hunt us all to death:
That dog that had his teeth before his eyes,[4]
50 To worry° lambs and lap their gentle blood;   *tear apart*
That foul defacer of God's handiwork,
That reigns in gallèd eyes of weeping souls;[5]
That excellent grand tyrant of the earth
Thy womb let loose to chase us to our graves.
55 O upright, just, and true-disposing God,
How do I thank thee that this charnel[6] cur
Preys on the issue° of his mother's body,   *offspring*
And makes her pewfellow° with others' moan.   *companion at church*
DUCHESS OF YORK   O Harry's wife, triumph not in my woes.
60 God witness with me, I have wept for thine.
QUEEN MARGARET   Bear with me. I am hungry for revenge,
And now I cloy me° with beholding it.   *gorge myself*
Thy Edward, he is dead, that killed my Edward;
Thy other Edward dead, to quite° my Edward;   *requite*
65 Young York, he is but boot,[7] because both they
Matched not the high perfection of my loss;
Thy Clarence, he is dead, that stabbed my Edward,
And the beholders of this frantic° play—   *insane*
Th'adulterate Hastings, Rivers, Vaughan, Gray—
70 Untimely smothered° in their dusky graves.   *buried*
Richard yet lives, hell's black intelligencer,°   *spy*
Only reserved their factor[8] to buy souls
And send them thither; but at hand, at hand
Ensues his piteous and unpitied end.
75 Earth gapes, hell burns, fiends roar, saints pray,
To have him suddenly conveyed from hence.
Cancel his bond of life, dear God, I plead,
That I may live and say, 'The dog is dead'.
QUEEN ELIZABETH   O thou didst prophesy the time would come
80 That I should wish for thee to help me curse
That bottled spider, that foul bunch-backed toad.
QUEEN MARGARET   I called thee then 'vain flourish of my fortune';
I called thee then, poor shadow,° 'painted queen'[9]—   *semblance*
The presentation of but what I was,
85 The flattering index° of a direful pageant,°   *prologue / play*
One heaved a-high to be hurled down below,
A mother only mocked with two fair babes,
A dream of what thou wast, a garish flag

---

2. Edward and Richard were Queen Elizabeth's two sons
(smothered in the Tower).
3. Her husband (Richard, Duke of York) and youngest
son; both deaths are dramatized in Act 1 of *Richard Duke
of York*.
4. His enemies rumored that the savage Richard was
born with teeth.
5. *That reigns . . . souls*: Who rules over the sore eyes

(from crying) of persons he has harmed.
6. Of the charnel house or tomb. Q, F print "carnal."
7. He is thrown in simply to make the bargain even.
8. *Only . . . factor*: Retained (or preserved from death)
only in order to serve as hell's agent. *their*: the demonic
inhabitants of hell.
9. See 1.3.239.

To be the aim of every dangerous shot,[1]
90 A sign° of dignity, a breath, a bubble,   *mere symbol*
A queen in jest, only to fill the scene.
Where is thy husband now? Where be thy brothers?
Where are thy two sons? Wherein dost thou joy?
Who sues, and kneels, and says 'God save the Queen'?
95 Where be the bending° peers that flattered thee?   *bowing; yielding*
Where be the thronging troops that followed thee?
Decline[2] all this, and see what now thou art:
For happy wife, a most distressèd widow;
For joyful mother, one that wails the name;
100 For queen, a very caitiff,° crowned with care;   *wretch*
For one being sued to, one that humbly sues;
For she that scorned at me, now scorned of° me;   *by*
For she being feared of all, now fearing one;
For she commanding all, obeyed of none.
105 Thus hath the course of justice whirled about,
And left thee but a very prey to time,
Having no more but thought of what thou wert
To torture thee the more, being what thou art.
Thou didst usurp my place, and dost thou not
110 Usurp° the just proportion of my sorrow?   *burdensome*
Now thy proud neck bears half my burdened yoke—
From which, even here, I slip my weary head,
And leave the burden of it all on thee.
Farewell, York's wife, and queen of sad mischance.
115 These English woes shall make me smile in France.
QUEEN ELIZABETH [*rising*]   O thou, well skilled in curses, stay a while,
And teach me how to curse mine enemies.
QUEEN MARGARET   Forbear to sleep the nights, and fast the days;
Compare dead happiness with living woe;
120 Think that thy babes were sweeter than they were,
And he that slew them fouler than he is.
Bett'ring° thy loss makes the bad causer worse.   *Magnifying*
Revolving° this will teach thee how to curse.   *Musing on*
QUEEN ELIZABETH   My words are dull. O quicken° them with   *enliven; sharpen*
thine!
QUEEN MARGARET   Thy woes will make them sharp and pierce
125 like mine.   *Exit*
DUCHESS OF YORK   Why should calamity be full of words?
QUEEN ELIZABETH   Windy attorneys to their client woes,[3]
Airy recorders of intestate joys,[4]
Poor breathing° orators of miseries.   *speaking*
130 Let them have scope. Though what they will impart
Help nothing else, yet do they ease the heart.
DUCHESS OF YORK   If so, then be not tongue-tied; go with me,
And in the breath of bitter words let's smother
My damnèd son, that thy two sweet sons smothered.
[*A march within*]
135 The trumpet sounds. Be copious in exclaims.°   *exclamation*

1. *garish . . . shot*: bearer of a brightly colored standard who draws the enemy fire.
2. Recite in order with the proper endings (as a noun in Latin grammar).
3. Words are long-winded pleaders for the sufferings that have hired them.
4. Words record joys that have died without bequeathing anything.

Enter KING RICHARD *and his train marching with*
drummers and trumpeters

KING RICHARD   Who intercepts me in my expedition?°   *haste; march*
DUCHESS OF YORK   O, she that might have intercepted thee,
  By strangling thee in her accursèd womb,
  From all the slaughters, wretch, that thou hast done.
140   QUEEN ELIZABETH   Hid'st thou that forehead with a golden crown,
  Where should be branded—if that right were right—
  The slaughter of the prince that owed° that crown,   *rightfully owned*
  And the dire death of my poor sons and brothers?
  Tell me, thou villain-slave, where are my children?
145   DUCHESS OF YORK   Thou toad, thou toad, where is thy brother Clarence?
  And little Ned Plantagenet his son?
  QUEEN ELIZABETH   Where is the gentle Rivers, Vaughan, Gray?
  DUCHESS OF YORK   Where is kind Hastings?
  KING RICHARD [*to his train*]   A flourish, trumpets! Strike
    alarum,° drums!   *Call to arms*
150   Let not the heavens hear these tell-tale women
  Rail on the Lord's anointed. Strike, I say!
    Flourish. Alarums
  [*To the women*] Either be patient and entreat me fair,°   *treat me courteously*
  Or with the clamorous report° of war   *noise*
  Thus will I drown your exclamations.
155   DUCHESS OF YORK   Art thou my son?
  KING RICHARD   Ay, I thank God, my father, and yourself.
  DUCHESS OF YORK   Then patiently hear my impatience.
  KING RICHARD   Madam, I have a touch of your condition,°   *temperament*
  That cannot brook the accent° of reproof.   *abide the language*
  DUCHESS OF YORK   O let me speak!
160   KING RICHARD   Do, then; but I'll not hear.
  DUCHESS OF YORK   I will be mild and gentle in my words.
  KING RICHARD   And brief, good mother, for I am in haste.
  DUCHESS OF YORK   Art thou so hasty? I have stayed° for thee,   *waited*
  God knows, in torment and in agony—
165   KING RICHARD   And came I not at last to comfort you?
  DUCHESS OF YORK   No, by the Holy Rood,° thou know'st it well.   *Cross*
  Thou cam'st on earth to make the earth my hell.
  A grievous burden was thy birth to me;
  Tetchy° and wayward was thy infancy;   *Irritable*
170   Thy schooldays frightful,° desp'rate, wild, and furious;   *frightening*
  Thy prime° of manhood daring, bold, and venturous;   *beginning*
  Thy age confirmed,° proud, subtle, sly, and bloody;   *settled maturity*
  More mild, but yet more harmful; kind in hatred.[5]
  What comfortable hour canst thou name
175   That ever graced me[6] in thy company?
  KING RICHARD   Faith, none but Humphrey Hewer,[7] that called your grace
  To breakfast once, forth° of my company.   *out*
  If I be so disgracious° in your eye,   *unpleasing*
  Let me march on, and not offend you, madam.—
  Strike up the drum.
180   DUCHESS OF YORK   I pray thee, hear me speak.

---

5. Concealing hatred under cover of kindness.
6. Gave me pleasure; but Richard interprets as "called
me by the title 'your grace.'"
7. A proper name, based on "ewer" (a servant who waits

at table), but also suggesting "huer" (someone who makes
a hue or cry) and playing on "hour" (line 174). Proverbially, "to dine with Duke Humphrey" was not to dine at
all.

KING RICHARD   You speak too bitterly.
DUCHESS OF YORK   Hear me a word,
   For I shall never speak to thee again.
KING RICHARD   So.
DUCHESS OF YORK   Either thou wilt die by God's just ordinance
185   Ere from this war thou turn° a conqueror,   *return*
   Or I with grief and extreme age shall perish,
   And never more behold thy face again.
   Therefore take with thee my most heavy curse,
   Which in the day of battle tire thee more
190   Than all the complete armour that thou wear'st.
   My prayers on the adverse party° fight,   *opposite side*
   And there the little souls of Edward's children
   Whisper° the spirits of thine enemies,   *Whisper to*
   And promise them success and victory.
195   Bloody thou art, bloody will be thy end;
   Shame serves° thy life, and doth thy death attend.   *Exit*   *accompanies*
QUEEN ELIZABETH   Though far more cause, yet much less spirit to curse
   Abides in me; I say 'Amen' to all.
KING RICHARD   Stay, madam. I must talk a word with you.
200 QUEEN ELIZABETH   I have no more sons of the royal blood
   For thee to slaughter. For my daughters, Richard,
   They shall be praying nuns, not weeping queens,
   And therefore level not to hit their lives.[8]
KING RICHARD   You have a daughter called Elizabeth,
205   Virtuous and fair, royal and gracious.
QUEEN ELIZABETH   And must she die for this? O let her live,
   And I'll corrupt her manners,° stain her beauty,   *morals*
   Slander myself as false to Edward's bed,
   Throw over her the veil of infamy.
210   So° she may live unscarred of bleeding slaughter,   *Provided that*
   I will confess she was not Edward's daughter.
KING RICHARD   Wrong not her birth. She is a royal princess.
QUEEN ELIZABETH   To save her life I'll say she is not so.
KING RICHARD   Her life is safest only in her birth.[9]
215 QUEEN ELIZABETH   And only in that safety died her brothers.
KING RICHARD   Lo, at their births good stars were opposite.°   *adverse*
QUEEN ELIZABETH   No, to their lives ill friends were contrary.°   *opposed*
KING RICHARD   All unavoided° is the doom° of destiny—   *unavoidable / sentence*
QUEEN ELIZABETH   True, when avoided grace[1] makes destiny.
220   My babes were destined to a fairer death,
   If grace had blessed thee with a fairer life.[2]
221.1   KING RICHARD   *You speak as if that I had slain my cousins.*
     QUEEN ELIZABETH   *Cousins indeed, and by their uncle cozened°*   *cheated*
     Of comfort, kingdom, kindred, freedom, life.
     Whose hand soever lanced their tender hearts,
221.5   *Thy head all indirectly gave direction.[3]*
     No doubt the murd'rous knife was dull and blunt
     Till it was whetted on thy stone-hard heart
     To revel in the entrails of my lambs.
     But that still° use of grief makes wild grief tame,   *Except that continual*

---

8. And therefore do not take aim to kill them.
9. Her life is safe only because of her high birth.
1. When a man who has rejected God's grace (that is, Richard).

2. The indented passage that follows, 221.1–221.14, appears only in F.
3. *Whose . . . direction:* No matter who killed them, it was you, though indirectly, who caused it.

221.10
> My tongue should to thy ears not name my boys
> Till that my nails were anchored in thine eyes—
> And I in such a desp'rate bay[4] of death,
> Like a poor barque° of sails and tackling reft,°   *boat / deprived*
> Rush all to pieces on thy rocky bosom.

KING RICHARD   Madam, so thrive I in my enterprise
And dangerous success of bloody wars,
As I intend more good to you and yours

225 Than ever you or yours by me were harmed.[5]

QUEEN ELIZABETH   What good is covered with the face of heaven,[6]
To be discovered, that can do me good?

KING RICHARD   Th'advancement of your children, gentle lady.

QUEEN ELIZABETH   Up to some scaffold, there to lose their heads.

230 KING RICHARD   Unto the dignity and height of fortune,
The high imperial type° of this earth's glory.   *symbol*

QUEEN ELIZABETH   Flatter my sorrow with report of it.
Tell me what state, what dignity, what honour,
Canst thou demise° to any child of mine?   *transmit*

235 KING RICHARD   Even all I have—ay, and myself and all,
Will I withal endow a child of thine,
So° in the Lethe[7] of thy angry soul   *If*
Thou drown the sad remembrance of those wrongs,
Which thou supposest I have done to thee.

240 QUEEN ELIZABETH   Be brief, lest that the process° of thy kindness   *story*
Last longer telling° than thy kindness' date.°   *in the telling / duration*

KING RICHARD   Then know that, from my soul,[8] I love thy daughter.

QUEEN ELIZABETH   My daughter's mother thinks that with her soul.

KING RICHARD   What do you think?

245 QUEEN ELIZABETH   That thou dost love my daughter *from* thy soul;
So *from* thy soul's love didst thou love her brothers,
And *from* my heart's love I do thank thee for it.

KING RICHARD   Be not so hasty to confound° my meaning.   *deliberately misconstrue*
I mean, that *with* my soul I love thy daughter,

250 And do intend to make her queen of England.

QUEEN ELIZABETH   Well then, who dost thou mean shall be her king?

KING RICHARD   Even he that makes her queen. Who else should be?

QUEEN ELIZABETH   What, thou?

KING RICHARD   Even so. How think you of it?

QUEEN ELIZABETH   How canst thou woo her?

KING RICHARD   That would I learn of you,

255 As one being best acquainted with her humour.°   *temperament*

QUEEN ELIZABETH   And wilt thou learn of me?

KING RICHARD   Madam, with all my heart.

QUEEN ELIZABETH   Send to her, by the man that slew her brothers,
A pair of bleeding hearts; thereon engrave
'Edward' and 'York'; then haply° will she weep.   *perhaps*

260 Therefore present to her—as sometimes° Margaret   *once*
Did to thy father, steeped in Rutland's blood[9]—
A handkerchief which, say to her, did drain

---

4. Inlet; the situation of a cornered animal when it turns
to face its hunters.
5. *Madam . . . harmed:* (I pray) that the success of my
upcoming battles be as certain as is my intention to do to
you more good in the future than I have done you harm
in the past. *success:* consequence.

6. What good is there on earth.
7. A river in the underworld whose waters induced forgetfulness.
8. With all my soul (but Queen Elizabeth takes it as "separated from," "at variance with").
9. Dramatized in *Richard Duke of York* 1.4.

The purple sap° from her sweet brother's body, blood
And bid her wipe her weeping eyes withal.° with it
265 If this inducement move her not to love,
Send her a letter of thy noble deeds.
Tell her thou mad'st away her uncle Clarence,
Her uncle Rivers—ay, and for her sake
Mad'st quick conveyance with° her good aunt Anne. Got rid of
270 KING RICHARD   You mock me, madam. This is not the way
To win your daughter.
QUEEN ELIZABETH   There is no other way,
Unless thou couldst put on some other shape,
And not be Richard, that hath done all this.[1]
273.1   KING RICHARD   *Say that I did all this for love of her.*
        QUEEN ELIZABETH   *Nay, then indeed she cannot choose but hate thee,*
        Having bought love with such a bloody spoil.° slaughter
        KING RICHARD   *Look what° is done cannot be now amended.* Whatever
273.5   *Men shall deal° unadvisedly sometimes,* act
        Which after-hours gives leisure to repent.
        If I did take the kingdom from your sons,
        To make amends I'll give it to your daughter.
        If I have killed the issue of your womb,
273.10   *To quicken your increase[2] I will beget*
        Mine issue of your blood upon your daughter.
        A grandam's name is little less in love
        Than is the doting title of a mother.
        They are as children but one step below,
273.15   *Even of your mettall,° of your very blood:* spirit
        Of all one pain, save for a night of groans
        Endured of her for whom you bid like sorrow.[3]
        Your children were vexation to your youth,
        But mine shall be a comfort to your age.
273.20   *The loss you have is but a son being king,*
        And by that loss your daughter is made queen.
        I cannot make you what amends I would,
        Therefore accept such kindness as I can.° can give
        Dorset your son, that with a fearful soul
273.25   *Leads discontented steps in foreign soil,*
        This fair alliance quickly shall call home
        To high promotions and great dignity.
        The king that calls your beauteous daughter wife,
        Familiarly shall call thy Dorset brother.
273.30   *Again shall you be mother to a king,*
        And all the ruins of distressful times
        Repaired with double riches of content.
        What? We have many goodly days to see.
        The liquid drops of tears that you have shed
273.35   *Shall come again, transformed to orient° pearl,* shining
        Advantaging° their loan with interest Augmenting
        Of ten times double gain of happiness.
        Go then, my mother, to thy daughter go.
        Make bold her bashful years with your experience.

---

1. The indented passage that follows, 273.1–273.55,
appears only in F.
2. To give (new) life to your offspring.

3. *Of all . . . sorrow:* Originating from a single bout of
labor (Elizabeth's), with the addition of just one more
night of pain by the daughter you bore.

273.40
> *Prepare her ears to hear a wooer's tale.*
> *Put in her tender heart th'aspiring flame*
> *Of golden sovereignty. Acquaint the Princess*
> *With the sweet silent hours of marriage joys.*
> *And when this arm of mine hath chastisèd*

273.45
> *The petty rebel, dull-brained Buckingham,*
> *Bound with triumphant garlands will I come*
> *And lead thy daughter to a conqueror's bed—*
> *To whom I will retail° my conquest won,*   *relate*
> *And she shall be sole victoress: Caesar's Caesar.*

273.50 QUEEN ELIZABETH *What were I best to say? Her father's brother*
> *Would° be her lord?° Or shall I say her uncle?*   *Wishes to / husband*
> *Or he that slew her brothers and her uncles?*
> *Under what title shall I woo for thee,*
> *That God, the law, my honour, and her love*

273.55
> *Can make seem pleasing to her tender years?*

KING RICHARD   Infer° fair England's peace by this alliance.   *Give as a reason*

275 QUEEN ELIZABETH   Which she shall purchase with still-lasting° war.   *perpetual*

KING RICHARD   Tell her the King, that may command, entreats.

QUEEN ELIZABETH   That at her hands which the King's King° forbids.   *(God)*

KING RICHARD   Say she shall be a high and mighty queen.

QUEEN ELIZABETH   To vail° the title,° as her mother doth.   *yield / (of Queen)*

280 KING RICHARD   Say I will love her everlastingly.

QUEEN ELIZABETH   But how long shall that title 'ever' last?

KING RICHARD   Sweetly in force unto her fair life's end.

QUEEN ELIZABETH   But how long fairly° shall her sweet life last?   *without foul play*

KING RICHARD   As long as heaven and nature lengthens it.

285 QUEEN ELIZABETH   As long as hell and Richard likes of it.

KING RICHARD   Say I, her sovereign, am her subject love.

QUEEN ELIZABETH   But she, your subject, loathes such sovereignty.

KING RICHARD   Be eloquent in my behalf to her.

QUEEN ELIZABETH   An honest tale speeds° best being plainly told.   *succeeds*

290 KING RICHARD   Then plainly to her tell my loving tale.

QUEEN ELIZABETH   Plain and not honest is too harsh a style.[4]

KING RICHARD   Your reasons are too shallow and too quick.[5]

QUEEN ELIZABETH   O no, my reasons are too deep and dead—
Too deep and dead, poor infants, in their graves.

295 KING RICHARD   Harp not on that string, madam. That is past.

QUEEN ELIZABETH   Harp on it still shall I, till heart-strings break.

KING RICHARD   Now by my George, my garter,[6] and my crown—

QUEEN ELIZABETH   Profaned, dishonoured, and the third usurped.

KING RICHARD   I swear—

QUEEN ELIZABETH   By nothing, for this is no oath.

300 Thy George, profaned, hath lost his° holy honour;   *its*
Thy garter, blemished, pawned his lordly virtue;
Thy crown, usurped, disgraced his kingly glory.
If something thou wouldst swear to be believed,
Swear then by something that thou hast not wronged.

KING RICHARD   Then by myself—

305 QUEEN ELIZABETH   Thy self is self-misused.

KING RICHARD   Now by the world—

---

4. The plain style (as in the proverb "Truth is plain"), unless it is truth telling, will be too harsh; lies need elaborate decoration.

5. Rash, ill-considered; but Elizabeth's response plays on "quick" as "alive."

6. A garter and a jeweled pendant with the figure of St. George were parts of the insignia of the Order of the Garter, the highest order of knighthood.

QUEEN ELIZABETH	'Tis full of thy foul wrongs.	
KING RICHARD	My father's death—	
QUEEN ELIZABETH	Thy life hath that dishonoured.	
KING RICHARD	Why then, by God—	
QUEEN ELIZABETH	God's wrong is most of all.	

QUEEN ELIZABETH   God's wrong is most of all.
If thou didst fear to break an oath with him,
310 The unity the King my husband made[7]
Thou hadst not broken, nor my brothers died.
If thou hadst feared to break an oath by him,
Th'imperial metal circling now thy head
Had graced the tender temples of my child,
315 And both the princes had been breathing here,
Which now—two tender bedfellows for dust—
Thy broken faith hath made the prey for worms.
What canst thou swear by now?

KING RICHARD   The time to come.

QUEEN ELIZABETH   That thou hast wrongèd in the time o'erpast,
320 For I myself have many tears to wash
Hereafter time,° for time past wronged by thee.   *The future*
The children live, whose fathers thou hast slaughtered—
Ungoverned youth,[8] to wail it in their age.°   *when they grow older*
The parents live, whose children thou hast butchered—
325 Old barren plants, to wail it with° their age.   *along with*
Swear not by time to come, for that thou hast
Misused ere used, by times ill-used o'erpast.[9]

KING RICHARD   As I intend[1] to prosper and repent,
So thrive I in my dangerous affairs
330 Of hostile arms—myself myself confound,°   *may I ruin myself*
Heaven and fortune bar me happy hours,
Day yield me not thy light nor night thy rest;
Be opposite, all planets of good luck,
To my proceeding—if, with dear heart's love,
335 Immaculate devotion, holy thoughts,
I tender° not thy beauteous, princely daughter.   *love*
In her consists my happiness and thine.
Without her follows—to myself and thee,
Herself, the land, and many a Christian soul—
340 Death, desolation, ruin, and decay.
It cannot be avoided but by this;
It will not be avoided but by this.
Therefore, good-mother°—I must call you so—   *mother-in-law*
Be the attorney of my love to her.
345 Plead what I will be, not what I have been;
Not my deserts, but what I will deserve.
Urge the necessity and state of times,°   *state of affairs*
And be not peevish-fond° in great designs.   *foolishly obstinate*

QUEEN ELIZABETH   Shall I be tempted of the devil thus?
350 KING RICHARD   Ay, if the devil tempt you to do good.

QUEEN ELIZABETH   Shall I forget myself to be myself?[2]

KING RICHARD   Ay, if yourself's remembrance wrong yourself.

---

7. The "reconciliation" staged in 2.1 between Queen
Elizabeth and her enemies.
8. Youth without a father's guidance.
9. *thou . . . o'erpast:* you have, by the continuing effects
of your past crimes, misused the future even before it

comes to pass.
1. *As I intend:* the formulation has the force of "I swear
that as I intend."
2. Am I to overlook all wrongs done me in order to
become Queen Mother (as I already have been)?

QUEEN ELIZABETH   Yet thou didst kill my children.
KING RICHARD   But in your daughter's womb I bury them,
355   Where, in that nest of spicery,³ they will breed
    Selves of themselves, to your recomfiture.°   *consolation*
QUEEN ELIZABETH   Shall I go win my daughter to thy will?
KING RICHARD   And be a happy mother by the deed.
QUEEN ELIZABETH   I go. Write to me very shortly,
360   And you shall understand from me her mind.
KING RICHARD   Bear her my true love's kiss,
        [*He kisses her*]   and so farewell—
                               Exit [ELIZABETH]
    Relenting fool, and shallow, changing woman.
        Enter [*Sir Richard*] RATCLIFFE
    How now, what news?
RATCLIFFE   Most mighty sovereign, on the western coast
365   Rideth a puissant° navy. To our shores   *mighty*
    Throng many doubtful, hollow-hearted friends,
    Unarmed and unresolved, to beat them back.
    'Tis thought that Richmond is their° admiral,   *(the navy's)*
    And there they hull,° expecting but the aid   *drift; wait*
370   Of Buckingham to welcome them ashore.
KING RICHARD   Some light-foot° friend post° to the Duke of   *swift-footed / hasten*
        Norfolk.
    Ratcliffe thyself, or Catesby—where is he?⁴
CATESBY   Here, my good lord.
KING RICHARD   Catesby, fly to the Duke.
CATESBY   I will, my lord, with all convenient haste.
375 KING RICHARD   Ratcliffe, come hither. Post to Salisbury;
    When thou com'st thither—[*to* CATESBY] dull, unmindful villain,
    Why stay'st thou here, and goest not to the Duke?
CATESBY   First, mighty liege, tell me your highness' pleasure:
    What from your grace I shall deliver to him?
380 KING RICHARD   O true, good Catesby. Bid him levy straight
    The greatest strength and power that he can make,°   *raise*
    And meet me suddenly° at Salisbury.   *without delay*
CATESBY   I go.   *Exit*
RATCLIFFE   What, may it please you, shall I do at Salisbury?
385 KING RICHARD   Why, what wouldst thou do there before I go?
RATCLIFFE   Your highness told me I should post before.
KING RICHARD   My mind is changed.
        Enter Lord STANLEY
                       Stanley, what news with you?
STANLEY   None, good my liege, to please you with the hearing,
    Nor none so bad but well may be reported.
390 KING RICHARD   Hoyday,° a riddle! Neither good nor bad.   *(an exclamation)*
    Why need'st thou run so many mile about
    When thou mayst tell thy tale the nearest° way?   *most direct*
    Once more, what news?
STANLEY   Richmond is on the seas.
KING RICHARD   There let him sink, and be the seas on him.
395   White-livered° renegade, what doth he there?   *Cowardly*

---

3. Fragrant spices—in contrast to the stench of other burial places; the spices on the phoenix's pyre. *nest:* place where eggs are hatched, but also specifically the nest or pyre on which the legendary phoenix burned itself and then rose from its own ashes.
4. Parts of lines 373–74 appear only in F.

STANLEY   I know not, mighty sovereign, but by guess.

KING RICHARD   Well, as you guess?

STANLEY   Stirred up by Dorset, Buckingham, and Ely,
    He makes for England, here to claim the crown.

400 KING RICHARD   Is the chair° empty? Is the sword unswayed?   *throne*
    Is the King dead? The empire° unpossessed?   *state*
    What heir of York is there alive but we?
    And who is England's king but great York's heir?
    Then tell me, what makes he° upon the seas?   *what is he doing*

405 STANLEY   Unless for that, my liege, I cannot guess.

KING RICHARD   Unless for that° he comes to be your liege,   *because*
    You cannot guess wherefore the Welshman⁵ comes.
    Thou wilt revolt and fly to him, I fear.

STANLEY   No, my good lord, therefore mistrust me not.

410 KING RICHARD   Where is thy power then? To beat him back,
    Where be thy tenants and thy followers?
    Are they not now upon the western shore,
    Safe-conducting the rebels from their ships?

STANLEY   No, my good lord, my friends are in the north.

415 KING RICHARD   Cold friends to me. What do they in the north,
    When they should serve their sovereign in the west?

STANLEY   They have not been commanded, mighty King.
    Pleaseth° your majesty to give me leave,   *If it please*
    I'll muster up my friends and meet your grace
420   Where and what time your majesty shall please.

KING RICHARD   Ay, ay, thou wouldst be gone to join with Richmond.
    But I'll not trust thee.

STANLEY   Most mighty sovereign,
    You have no cause to hold my friendship doubtful.
    I never was, nor never will be, false.

425 KING RICHARD   Go then and muster men—but leave behind
    Your son George Stanley. Look your heart be firm,
    Or else his head's assurance is but frail.

STANLEY   So deal with him as I prove true to you.   *Exit*
    Enter a MESSENGER

MESSENGER   My gracious sovereign, now in Devonshire,
430   As I by friends am well advertisèd,°   *well informed*
    Sir Edward Courtenay and the haughty prelate,
    Bishop of Exeter, his elder brother,
    With many more confederates are in arms.
    Enter another MESSENGER

SECOND MESSENGER   In Kent, my liege, the Guildfords are in arms,
435   And every hour more competitors°   *associates*
    Flock to the rebels, and their power grows strong.
    Enter another MESSENGER

THIRD MESSENGER   My lord, the army of great Buckingham—

KING RICHARD   Out on ye, owls!⁶ Nothing but songs of death?
    He striketh him
    There, take thou that, till thou bring better news.

440 THIRD MESSENGER   The news I have to tell your majesty
    Is that, by sudden flood and fall of water,°   *rain*
    Buckingham's army is dispersed and scattered,
    And he himself wandered away alone,

---

5. Richmond's grandfather, Owen Tudor, was Welsh.   6. The cry of the owl was thought to portend evil.

No man knows whither.

KING RICHARD   I cry thee mercy.°—   *I beg your pardon*

445   Ratcliffe, reward him for the blow I gave him.—

Hath any well-advisèd° friend proclaimed   *foresighted*

Reward to him that brings the traitor in?

THIRD MESSENGER   Such proclamation hath been made, my lord.

Enter another MESSENGER

FOURTH MESSENGER   Sir Thomas Lovell and Lord Marquis Dorset—

450   'Tis said, my liege—in Yorkshire are in arms.

But this good comfort bring I to your highness:

The Breton navy is dispersed by tempest.

Richmond in Dorsetshire sent out a boat

Unto the shore, to ask those on the banks

455   If they were his assistants,° yea or no?   *allies*

Who answered him they came from Buckingham

Upon his party.° He, mistrusting them,   *faction*

Hoist sail and made his course again for Bretagne.°   *Brittany*

KING RICHARD   March on, march on, since we are up in arms,

460   If not to fight with foreign enemies,

Yet to beat down these rebels here at home.

Enter CATESBY

CATESBY   My liege, the Duke of Buckingham is taken.

That is the best news. That the Earl of Richmond

Is with a mighty power landed at Milford[7]

465   Is colder tidings, yet they must be told.

KING RICHARD   Away, towards Salisbury! While we reason° here,   *talk*

A royal battle might be won and lost.

Someone take order Buckingham be brought

To Salisbury. The rest march on with me.   *Flourish. Exeunt*

4.5

Enter [Lord STANLEY *Earl of] Derby and* SIR CHRISTO-
PHER *[a priest]*

STANLEY   Sir Christopher, tell Richmond this from me:

That in the sty of this most deadly boar

My son George Stanley is franked up in hold.[1]

If I revolt, off goes young George's head.

5   The fear of that holds off my present aid.

But tell me, where is princely Richmond now?

SIR CHRISTOPHER   At Pembroke, or at Ha'rfordwest[2] in Wales.

STANLEY   What men of name° resort to him?   *rank*

SIR CHRISTOPHER   Sir Walter Herbert, a renownèd soldier,

10   Sir Gilbert Talbot, Sir William Stanley,[3]

Oxford, redoubted° Pembroke,[4] Sir James Blunt,   *dreaded*

And Rhys-ap-Thomas with a valiant crew,

And many other of great name and worth—

And towards London do they bend their power,°   *lead their troops*

15   If by the way they be not fought withal.

STANLEY   Well, hie° thee to thy lord. Commend me to him.   *hasten*

---

7. Milford Haven, a large, deep natural harbor on the Welsh coast, far enough from centers of population to be ideal for an invading army. The events of Richmond's successful invasion at Milford in 1485 are telescoped, in the mouths of the four messengers, with those of his unsuccessful rebellion against Richard two years earlier.
4.5 Location: A private place, perhaps Derby's house.

1. Is shut up (in a sty) in custody.
2. Haverford West, town at northern end of Milford Haven. Pembroke was the county town of Pembrokeshire, situated on Milford Haven.
3. Lord Stanley, the Earl of Derby's brother.
4. Jasper Tudor, Richmond's uncle.

Tell him the Queen hath heartily consented
He should espouse Elizabeth her daughter.
My letter will resolve him of my mind.[5]
20 Farewell.   *Exeunt [severally]*

5.1

*Enter [the Duke of] BUCKINGHAM with halberdiers, led
[by a SHERIFF] to execution*

BUCKINGHAM Will not King Richard let me speak with him?
SHERIFF No, my good lord, therefore be patient.
BUCKINGHAM Hastings, and Edward's children, Gray and Rivers,
Holy King Henry and thy fair son Edward,
5   Vaughan, and all that have miscarrièd°   *died*
By underhand, corrupted, foul injustice:
If that your moody, discontented souls[1]
Do through the clouds behold this present hour,
Even for revenge mock my destruction.
10 This is All-Souls' day,[2] fellow, is it not?
SHERIFF It is.
BUCKINGHAM Why then All-Souls' day is my body's doomsday.
This is the day which, in King Edward's time,
I wished might fall on me,[3] when I was found
15 False to his children and his wife's allies.°   *kinsmen*
This is the day wherein I wished to fall
By the false faith of him whom most I trusted.
This, this All-Souls' day to my fearful soul
Is the determined respite of my wrongs.[4]
20 That high all-seer which I dallied with
Hath turned my feignèd prayer on my head,
And given in earnest what I begged in jest.
Thus doth he force the swords of wicked men
To turn their own points in their masters' bosoms.
25 Thus Margaret's curse falls heavy on my neck.
'When he', quoth she, 'shall split thy heart with sorrow,
Remember Margaret was a prophetess.'[5]
Come lead me, officers, to the block of shame.
Wrong hath but wrong, and blame the due of blame.   *Exeunt*

5.2

*Enter [HENRY EARL OF] RICHMOND [with a letter, the
Earl of] OXFORD, [Sir James] BLUNT, [Sir Walter] HER-
BERT, and others, with drum and colours*

HENRY EARL OF RICHMOND Fellows in arms, and my most loving friends,
Bruised underneath the yoke of tyranny,
Thus far into the bowels° of the land   *center*

---

5. Will make my intentions clear to him.
5.1 Location: Salisbury.
1. Because they are unable to rest in peace until their
violent deaths have been avenged. *moody:* angry.
2. November 2, the day on which the Roman Catholic
Church intercedes for all Christian souls, and on which
spirits were supposed to walk (as in the following scenes
at Shrewsbury).

3. See Buckingham's prophetic speech in 2.1.32–40.
4. Is the preordained ending of my wrongdoing (but
alluding to the more usual significance of All Souls' Day,
"preordained final rest from suffering"). *respite:* day to
which something is postponed.
5. See 1.3.298–99.
5.2 Location: Near Tamworth in Staffordshire.

Have we marched on without impediment,
5   And here receive we from our father[1] Stanley
Lines of fair comfort and encouragement.
The wretched, bloody, and usurping boar,
That spoils your summer fields and fruitful vines,
Swills your warm blood like wash,° and makes his trough   *pig fodder*
10 In your inbowelled° bosoms, this foul swine   *disemboweled*
Lies now even in the centry° of this isle,   *center; sentry post*
Near to the town of Leicester, as we learn.
From Tamworth thither is but one day's march.
In God's name, cheerly° on, courageous friends,   *cheerfully*
15 To reap the harvest of perpetual peace
By this one bloody trial of sharp war.
OXFORD   Every man's conscience is a thousand swords
To fight against this guilty homicide.°   *murderer*
HERBERT   I doubt not but his friends will turn to us.
20 BLUNT   He hath no friends but what are friends for fear,
Which in his dearest° need will fly from him.   *most extreme*
HENRY EARL OF RICHMOND   All for our vantage.° Then, in God's   *advantage*
name, march.
True hope is swift, and flies with swallows' wings;
Kings it makes gods, and meaner° creatures kings.   *baser*
                              Exeunt [marching]

5.3

Enter KING RICHARD *in arms, with [the Duke of]* NOR-
FOLK, *[Sir Richard]* RATCLIFFE, *Sir William* [CATESBY,
and others][1]

KING RICHARD   Here pitch our tent, even here in Bosworth field.
   [Soldiers begin to pitch a tent]
Why, how now, Catesby? Why look you so sad?
CATESBY   My heart is ten times lighter than my looks.
KING RICHARD   My lord of Norfolk.
NORFOLK   Here, most gracious liege.
5   KING RICHARD   Norfolk, we must have knocks.° Ha, must we not?   *blows*
NORFOLK   We must both give and take, my loving lord.
KING RICHARD   Up with my tent! Here will I lie tonight.
But where tomorrow? Well, all's one for that.°   *it makes no difference*
Who hath descried° the number of the traitors?   *discerned*
10 NORFOLK   Six or seven thousand is their utmost power.
KING RICHARD   Why, our battalia° trebles that account.°   *army / number*
Besides, the King's name is a tower of strength,
Which they upon the adverse faction want.°   *lack*
·Up with the tent! Come, noble gentlemen,
15 Let us survey the vantage of the ground.[2]
Call for some men of sound direction.°   *military judgment*
Let's lack no discipline, make no delay—
For, lords, tomorrow is a busy day.   *Exeunt [at one door]*

---

1. Stepfather (Richmond was the son of Edmund Tudor
and Margaret Beaufort; Lord Stanley, Earl of Derby, was
his mother's third husband). *our*: royal plural.
5.3 Location: The rest of the play takes place on Bosworth
Field.

1. Instead of Catesby, the F stage direction has the Earl
of Surrey, who speaks with Richard at line 3.
2. *vantage of the ground*: military advantages offered by
the spot chosen for battle.

5.4

Enter [at another door HENRY EARL OF *] RICHMOND, [Sir*
James BLUNT,*] Sir William Brandon, [the Earl of]*
OXFORD, *[Marquis]* DORSET *[and others]*[1]

HENRY EARL OF RICHMOND   The weary sun hath made a golden set,
  And by the bright track of his fiery car°   *chariot (of Phoebus)*
  Gives token of a goodly day tomorrow.
  Sir William Brandon, you shall bear my standard.
5 The Earl of Pembroke keeps° his regiment;   *stays with*
  Good Captain Blunt, bear my good night to him,
  And by the second hour in the morning
  Desire the Earl to see me in my tent.
  Yet one thing more, good Captain, do for me:
10 Where is Lord Stanley quartered, do you know?
BLUNT   Unless I have mista'en his colours much,
  Which well I am assured I have not done,
  His regiment lies half a mile, at least,
  South from the mighty power of the King.
15 HENRY EARL OF RICHMOND   If without peril it be possible,
  Sweet Blunt, make some good means to speak with him,
  And give him from me this most needful note.
BLUNT   Upon my life, my lord, I'll undertake it.
  And so God give you quiet rest tonight.
HENRY EARL OF RICHMOND   Good night, good Captain Blunt.
                                            [*Exit* BLUNT]
20   Come, gentlemen.
  Give me some ink and paper in my tent.
  I'll draw the form and model° of our battle,   *plan*
  Limit° each leader to his several charge,°   *Appoint / separate duty*
  And part° in just proportion our small power.   *divide*
25 Let us consult upon tomorrow's business.
  Into my tent: the dew is raw and cold.
                        They withdraw into the tent

5.5

[A table brought in.] Enter KING RICHARD, *[Sir Richard]*
RATCLIFFE, *[the Duke of]* NORFOLK, *[Sir William]*
CATESBY *[and others]*

KING RICHARD   What is't o'clock?
CATESBY   It's supper-time, my lord. It's nine o'clock.
KING RICHARD   I will not sup tonight. Give me some ink and paper.
  What, is my beaver easier° than it was?   *my helmet visor looser*
5 And all my armour laid into my tent?
CATESBY   It is, my liege, and all things are in readiness.
KING RICHARD   Good Norfolk, hie thee° to thy charge.   *hasten*
  Use careful watch; choose trusty sentinels.
NORFOLK   I go, my lord.
10 KING RICHARD   Stir with the lark tomorrow, gentle Norfolk.
NORFOLK   I warrant° you, my lord.   *Exit*   *assure, guarantee*
KING RICHARD   Catesby.
CATESBY   My lord?

5.4
1. Although Q and F are silent on the question of how
many tents are onstage at the end of this scene, most editors direct these attendants to pitch another for Richmond

during the following dialogue. Oxford and Dorset are
specified in F but not in Q, which calls only for "the
lords."
5.5

KING RICHARD   Send out a pursuivant-at-arms°   *one who attends a herald*
 To Stanley's regiment. Bid him bring his power°   *forces*
 Before sun-rising, lest his son George fall
15 Into the blind cave of eternal night.   [*Exit* CATESBY]
 Fill me a bowl of wine. Give me a watch.[1]
 Saddle white Surrey[2] for the field tomorrow.
 Look that my staves be sound, and not too heavy.
 Ratcliffe.
20 RATCLIFFE   My lord?
 KING RICHARD   Saw'st thou the melancholy Lord Northumberland?
 RATCLIFFE   Thomas the Earl of Surrey and himself,
 Much about cockshut° time, from troop to troop   *twilight*
 Went through the army, cheering up the soldiers.
25 KING RICHARD   So, I am satisfied. Give me some wine.
 I have not that alacrity of spirit,
 Nor cheer of mind, that I was wont to have.
   [*The wine is brought*]
 Set it down. Is ink and paper ready?
 RATCLIFFE   It is, my lord.
 KING RICHARD   Leave me. Bid my guard watch.
30 About the mid of night come to my tent,
 Ratcliffe, and help to arm me. Leave me, I say.
   Exit RATCLIFFE [*with others.* RICHARD *writes, and later sleeps*]
   Enter [*Lord* STANLEY *Earl of*] *Derby to* [HENRY EARL
   OF] RICHMOND [*and the lords*] *in his tent*
 STANLEY   Fortune and victory sit on thy helm!°   *helmet*
 HENRY EARL OF RICHMOND   All comfort that the dark night can afford
 Be to thy person, noble father-in-law.°   *stepfather*
35 Tell me, how fares our loving mother?
 STANLEY   I, by attorney,° bless thee from thy mother,   *by proxy*
 Who prays continually for Richmond's good.
 So much for that. The silent hours steal on,
 And flaky° darkness breaks within the east.   *streaked with light*
40 In brief—for so the season° bids us be—   *time of day*
 Prepare thy battle early in the morning,
 And put thy fortune to th'arbitrement
 Of bloody strokes and mortal-sharing[3] war.
 I, as I may—that which I would, I cannot—
45 With best advantage will deceive the time,[4]
 And aid thee in this doubtful shock° of arms.   *this uncertain clash*
 But on thy side I may not be too forward—
 Lest, being seen, thy brother,° tender° George,   *stepbrother / young*
 Be executed in his father's sight.
50 Farewell. The leisure° and the fearful time   *time available*
 Cuts off the ceremonious vows of love
 And ample interchange of sweet discourse,
 Which so long sundered friends should dwell upon.
 God give us leisure for these rights of love.
55 Once more, adieu. Be valiant, and speed well.

1. Probably a watch light (a slow-burning candle, to write by); possibly a special guard (see line 29).
2. The chroniclers report that Richard was mounted on a "great white course," but the name is Shakespeare's.
3. Apportioning to mortals their lot; shearing or cutting down mortals. Q has "mortal staring," giving the commonplace image of war as both evil looking and able to cause damage with its glance (as a basilisk).
4. *as . . . time:* as best I can—for I cannot fight openly on your side—I will mislead Richard.

HENRY EARL OF RICHMOND   Good lords, conduct him to his regiment.
I'll strive with° troubled thoughts to take a nap,   *despite*
Lest leaden slumber peise° me down tomorrow,   *weigh*
When I should mount with wings of victory.
60 Once more, good night, kind lords and gentlemen.
Exeunt [STANLEY *and the lords*]. *Manet* RICHMOND
[RICHMOND *kneels*]
O thou, whose captain I account myself,
Look on my forces with a gracious eye.
Put in their hands thy bruising irons° of wrath,   *swords*
That they may crush down with a heavy fall
65 Th'usurping helmets of our adversaries.
Make us thy ministers of chastisement,
That we may praise thee in the victory.
To thee I do commend my watchful° soul,   *alert*
Ere I let fall the windows° of mine eyes.   *eyelids*
70 Sleeping and waking, O defend me still!   [*He*] *sleeps*
Enter the GHOST OF *young* PRINCE EDWARD [*above*]⁵
GHOST OF PRINCE EDWARD (*to* RICHARD)   Let me sit heavy on
thy soul tomorrow,
Prince Edward, son to Henry the Sixth.⁶
Think how thou stabbedst me in my prime of youth
At Tewkesbury. Despair, therefore, and die.
75 (*To* RICHMOND)Be cheerful, Richmond, for the wrongèd souls
Of butchered princes fight in thy behalf.
King Henry's issue,° Richmond, comforts thee.   [*Exit*]⁷   *offspring*
Enter [*above*] *the* GHOST OF [KING] HENRY VI
GHOST OF KING HENRY (*to* RICHARD)   When I was mortal, my
anointed° body   (*with sacred oil*)
By thee was punchèd full of deadly holes.
80 Think on the Tower⁸ and me. Despair and die.
Harry the Sixth bids thee despair and die.
(*To* RICHMOND) Virtuous and holy, be thou conqueror.
Harry that prophesied⁹ thou shouldst be king
Comforts thee in thy sleep. Live and flourish!   [*Exit*]
Enter [*above*] *the* GHOST OF [*George Duke of*] CLARENCE
85 GHOST OF CLARENCE [*to* RICHARD]   Let me sit heavy on thy soul tomorrow,
I that was washed to death with fulsome° wine,   *sickening*
Poor Clarence, by thy guile betrayed to death.
Tomorrow in the battle think on me,
And fall° thy edgeless sword. Despair and die.   *drop*
90 (*To* RICHMOND) Thou offspring of the house of Lancaster,
The wrongèd heirs of York do pray for thee.
Good angels guard thy battle.° Live and flourish!   [*Exit*]   *army*
Enter [*above*] *the* GHOSTS OF [*Lords*] RIVERS, GRAY, *and*
[*Sir Thomas*] VAUGHAN
GHOST OF RIVERS [*to* RICHARD]   Let me sit heavy on thy soul tomorrow,
Rivers that died at Pomfret. Despair and die.
95 GHOST OF GRAY [*to* RICHARD]   Think upon Gray, and let thy soul despair.

5. Q, F do not specify how or where the ghosts enter.
6. Line not present in Q, F; it is added here because Edward is the one character not seen previously, and it is possible that information originally intended as dialogue ended up as the stage direction when the text was printed.
7. Exits not given in Q, F. The ghosts could exeunt together at the end.
8. Where Henry VI was supposedly murdered.
9. See *Richard Duke of York* 4.7, in which King Henry (sometimes "Harry"), declaring the young Richmond "England's hope," foresees Richmond's accession to the throne and the beginning of what was to become the Tudor dynasty.

GHOST OF VAUGHAN [*to* RICHARD]   Think upon Vaughan, and with guilty fear
    Let fall thy pointless lance. Despair and die.
ALL THREE (*to* RICHMOND)   Awake, and think our wrongs in Richard's bosom
    Will conquer him. Awake, and win the day!   [*Exeunt* GHOSTS]
        Enter [*above*] *the* GHOSTS OF THE *two young* PRINCES
GHOSTS OF THE PRINCES (*to* RICHARD)   Dream on thy cousins,[1]
100   smothered in the Tower.
    Let us be lead within thy bosom, Richard,
    And weigh thee down to ruin, shame, and death.
    Thy nephews' souls bid thee despair and die.
    (*To* RICHMOND) Sleep, Richmond, sleep in peace and wake in joy.
105   Good angels guard thee from the boar's annoy.
    Live, and beget a happy race of kings!
    Edward's unhappy sons do bid thee flourish.   [*Exeunt* GHOSTS]
        Enter [*above*] *the* GHOST OF *Lord* HASTINGS[2]
GHOST OF HASTINGS [*to* RICHARD]   Bloody and guilty, guiltily awake,
    And in a bloody battle end thy days.
110   Think on Lord Hastings, then despair and die.
    (*To* RICHMOND) Quiet, untroubled soul, awake, awake!
    Arm, fight, and conquer for fair England's sake.   [*Exit*]
        Enter [*above*] *the* GHOST OF LADY ANNE
GHOST OF LADY ANNE (*to* RICHARD)   Richard, thy wife, that wretched Anne thy wife,
    That never slept a quiet hour with thee,
115   Now fills thy sleep with perturbations.
    Tomorrow in the battle think on me,
    And fall thy edgeless sword. Despair and die.
    (*To* RICHMOND) Thou quiet soul, sleep thou a quiet sleep.
    Dream of success and happy victory.
120   Thy adversary's wife doth pray for thee.   [*Exit*]
        Enter [*above*] *the* GHOST [OF *the Duke*] *of* BUCKINGHAM
GHOST OF BUCKINGHAM (*to* RICHARD)   The first was I that helped thee to the crown;
    The last was I that felt thy tyranny.
    O in the battle think on Buckingham,
    And die in terror of thy guiltiness!
125   Dream on, dream on, of bloody deeds and death;
    Fainting,° despair; despairing, yield thy breath.   *Losing heart*
    (*To* RICHMOND) I died for hope[3] ere I could lend thee aid.
    But cheer thy heart, and be thou not dismayed.
    God and good angels fight on Richmond's side,
130   And Richard falls in height of all his pride.   [*Exit*]
        RICHARD *starteth up out of a dream*
KING RICHARD   Give me another horse! Bind up my wounds!
    Have mercy, Jesu!—Soft, I did but dream.
    O coward conscience, how dost thou afflict me?
    The lights burn blue.[4] It is now dead midnight.
135   Cold fearful drops stand on my trembling flesh.
    What do I fear? Myself? There's none else by.
    Richard loves Richard; that is, I am I.
    Is there a murderer here? No. Yes, I am.
    Then fly! What, from myself? Great reason. Why?

---

1. Nephews ("cousins" was a term used for any kinsmen).   3. I died hoping I could aid you.
2. Q has him enter before the princes, as he had died   4. Thought to indicate the presence of ghosts.
before them.

140 Lest I revenge. Myself upon myself?
    Alack, I love myself. Wherefore?° For any good   *Why*
    That I myself have done unto myself?
    O no, alas, I rather hate myself
    For hateful deeds committed by myself.
145 I am a villain. Yet I lie: I am not.
    Fool, of thyself speak well.—Fool, do not flatter.
    My conscience hath a thousand several° tongues,   *separate*
    And every tongue brings in a several tale,
    And every tale condemns me for a villain.
150 Perjury, perjury, in the high'st degree![5]
    Murder, stern murder, in the dir'st degree!
    All several sins, all used in each degree,
    Throng to the bar,° crying all, 'Guilty, guilty!'   *(of the court)*
    I shall despair.[6] There is no creature loves me,
155 And if I die no soul will pity me.
    Nay, wherefore should they?—Since that I myself
    Find in myself no pity to myself.
    Methought the souls of all that I had murdered
    Came to my tent, and every one did threat
160 Tomorrow's vengeance on the head of Richard.
            Enter RATCLIFFE
    RATCLIFFE   My lord?
    KING RICHARD   'Swounds, who is there?
    RATCLIFFE   My lord, 'tis I. The early village cock
      Hath twice done salutation to the morn.
165   Your friends are up, and buckle on their armour.
    KING RICHARD   O Ratcliffe, I have dreamed a fearful dream.
      What thinkest thou, will all our friends prove true?
    RATCLIFFE   No doubt, my lord.
    KING RICHARD   Ratcliffe, I fear, I fear.
    RATCLIFFE   Nay, good my lord, be not afraid of shadows.°   *illusions; ghosts*
170 KING RICHARD   By the Apostle Paul, shadows tonight
      Have struck more terror to the soul of Richard
      Than can the substance of ten thousand soldiers
      Armèd in proof° and led by shallow Richmond.   *impenetrable armor*
      'Tis not yet near day. Come, go with me.
175   Under our tents I'll play the eavesdropper,
      To see if any mean to shrink from me.
            Exeunt RICHARD *and* RATCLIFFE
            Enter the lords to [HENRY EARL OF] RICHMOND, *sitting*
            in his tent
    LORDS   Good morrow, Richmond.
    HENRY EARL OF RICHMOND   Cry mercy,° lords and watchful   *Beg your pardon*
            gentlemen,
      That you have ta'en a tardy sluggard here.
180 A LORD   How have you slept, my lord?
    HENRY EARL OF RICHMOND   The sweetest sleep and fairest
            boding° dreams   *most propitious*
      That ever entered in a drowsy head
      Have I since your departure had, my lords.

---

5. Every kind of sin, from least to most wicked.
6. Despair was considered the only unforgivable sin; see 1.2.85–88.

Methought their souls whose bodies Richard murdered
185 Came to my tent and cried on⁷ victory.
I promise you, my soul is very jocund°   *joyful*
In the remembrance of so fair a dream.
How far into the morning is it, lords?
A LORD   Upon the stroke of four.
190 HENRY EARL OF RICHMOND   Why then, 'tis time to arm, and give direction.
    His oration to his soldiers
Much that I could say, loving countrymen,
The leisure° and enforcement of the time   *time available*
Forbids to dwell on. Yet remember this:
God and our good cause fight upon our side.
195 The prayers of holy saints and wrongèd souls,
Like high-reared bulwarks, stand before our forces.
Richard except,° those whom we fight against   *excepted*
Had rather have us win than him they follow.
For what is he they follow? Truly, friends,
200 A bloody tyrant and a homicide;
One raised in blood, and one in blood established;⁸
One that made means° to come by what he hath,   *that contrived*
And slaughtered those that were the means to help him;
A base, foul stone, made precious by the foil⁹
205 Of England's chair, where he is falsely set;¹
One that hath ever been God's enemy.
Then if you fight against God's enemy,
God will, in justice, ward° you as his soldiers.   *guard*
If you do sweat to put a tyrant down,
210 You sleep in peace, the tyrant being slain.
If you do fight against your country's foes,
Your country's foison° pays your pains the hire.   *abundance*
If you do fight in safeguard of your wives,
Your wives shall welcome home the conquerors.
215 If you do free your children from the sword,
Your children's children quites° it in your age.   *requites*
Then, in the name of God and all these rights,
Advance° your standards! Draw your willing swords!   *Raise*
For me, the ransom of this bold attempt
220 Shall be my cold corpse on the earth's cold face;²
But if I thrive,° to gain of my attempt,   *succeed*
The least of you shall share his part thereof.
Sound, drums and trumpets, bold and cheerfully!
God and Saint George!° Richmond and victory!   *patron saint of England*
    [*Exeunt to the sound of drums and trumpets*]

5.6

Enter KING RICHARD, [*Sir Richard*] RATCLIFFE, [*Sir Wil-
liam*] CATESBY [*and others*]
KING RICHARD   What said Northumberland, as touching° Richmond?   *regarding*
RATCLIFFE   That he was never trainèd up in arms.

---

7. And called out (a hunting term); here, urged me on to.
8. *One raised . . . established:* One who has come to the throne by bloodshed and has held it through further bloodshed.
9. Metal leaf was often placed under a jewel as a part of its setting, in order to increase its radiance.
1. Of the throne of England, on which he is wrongly placed; with a pun on "being set like a jewel."
2. *the ransom . . . face:* the only ransom I will give them is my dead body.
5.6

KING RICHARD He said the truth. And what said Surrey then?

RATCLIFFE He smiled and said, 'The better for our purpose.'

5 KING RICHARD He was in the right, and so indeed it is.

      Clock strikes

Tell the clock there.[1] Give me a calendar.°   *an almanac*

Who saw the sun today?

      [*A book is brought*]

RATCLIFFE   Not I, my lord.

KING RICHARD Then he disdains to shine, for by the book°   *(the almanac)*

He should have braved° the east an hour ago.   *made resplendent*

10 A black day will it be to somebody.

Ratcliffe.

RATCLIFFE My lord?

KING RICHARD   The sun will not be seen today.

The sky doth frown and lour° upon our army.   *glower*

I would these dewy tears were from the ground.

15 Not shine today—why, what is that to me

More than to Richmond? For the selfsame heaven

That frowns on me looks sadly upon him.

      Enter [*the Duke of*] NORFOLK

NORFOLK Arm, arm, my lord! The foe vaunts° in the field.   *flaunts his strength*

KING RICHARD Come, bustle, bustle! Caparison° my horse.   *Put the trappings on*

      [RICHARD *arms*]

20 Call up Lord Stanley, bid him bring his power.°   [*Exit one*]   *forces*

I will lead forth my soldiers to the plain,

And thus my battle° shall be orderèd.   *army*

My forward° shall be drawn out all in length,   *front rank*

Consisting equally of horse and foot,

25 Our archers placèd strongly in the midst.

John Duke of Norfolk, Thomas Earl of Surrey,

Shall have the leading of this multitude.

They thus directed,° we ourself will follow   *positioned*

In the main battle, whose puissance° on both sides   *power*

30 Shall be well wingèd° with our chiefest horse.°   *flanked / best cavalry*

This, and Saint George to boot![2] What think'st thou, Norfolk?

NORFOLK A good direction, warlike sovereign.

      He showeth him a paper

This paper found I on my tent this morning.

      [*He reads*]

'Jackie of Norfolk be not too bold,

35 For Dickon thy master is bought and sold.'[3]

KING RICHARD A thing devisèd by the enemy.—

Go, gentlemen, each man unto his charge.

Let not our babbling dreams affright our souls.

Conscience is but a word that cowards use,

40 Devised at first to keep the strong in awe.

Our strong arms be our conscience; swords, our law.

March on, join° bravely! Let us to't, pell mell—   *join battle*

If not to heaven, then hand in hand to hell.

      His oration to his army

What shall I say, more than I have inferred?°   *said*

45 Remember whom you are to cope withal:°   *with*

---

1. Count the clock's strokes.
2. *and . . . boot:* with the aid of our patron saint as a
bonus.
3. Is betrayed. *Dickon:* Dick (that is, Richard).

A sort° of vagabonds, rascals and runaways,   *gang*
A scum of Bretons and base lackey° peasants,   *lowly*
Whom their o'ercloyèd° country vomits forth   *nauseously overfull*
To desperate ventures and assured destruction.
50   You sleeping safe, they bring to you unrest;
You having lands and blessed with beauteous wives,
They would distrain° the one, distain° the other.   *confiscate / dishonor*
And who doth lead them, but a paltry fellow?
Long kept in Bretagne at our mother's[4] cost;
55   A milksop; one that never in his life
Felt so much cold as over shoes in snow.[5]
Let's whip[6] these stragglers o'er the seas again,
Lash hence these overweening rags of France,
These famished beggars, weary of their lives,
60   Who—but for° dreaming on this fond° exploit—   *were it not for / foolish*
For want of means,° poor rats, had hanged themselves.   *livelihood*
If we be conquered, let *men* conquer us,
And not these bastard Bretons, whom our fathers
Have in their own land beaten, bobbed,° and thumped,   *pounded*
65   And in record left them the heirs of shame.[7]
Shall these enjoy our lands? Lie with our wives?
Ravish our daughters?
     Drum afar off
                         Hark, I hear their drum.
Fight, gentlemen of England! Fight, bold yeomen!
Draw, archers, draw your arrows to the head!
70   Spur your proud horses hard, and ride in blood!
Amaze the welkin° with your broken staves!°   *sky / lance shafts*
     Enter a MESSENGER
What says Lord Stanley? Will he bring his power?
MESSENGER   My lord, he doth deny° to come.   *refuse*
KING RICHARD   Off with young George's head!
75   NORFOLK   My lord, the enemy is past the marsh.
After the battle let George Stanley die.
KING RICHARD   A thousand hearts are great within my bosom.
Advance our standards! Set upon our foes!
Our ancient word° of courage, fair Saint George,   *battle cry*
80   Inspire us with the spleen° of fiery dragons.   *anger*
Upon them! Victory sits on our helms!°   *Exeunt*   *helmets*

5.7

Alarum. Excursions. Enter [Sir William] CATESBY
CATESBY [*calling*][1]   Rescue, my lord of Norfolk! Rescue, rescue!
[*To a soldier*][2] The King enacts more wonders than a man,[3]
Daring an opposite° to every danger.   *to oppose himself*
His horse is slain, and all on foot he fights,
5   Seeking for Richmond in the throat of death.
[*Calling*] Rescue, fair lord, or else the day is lost!

---

4. Apparently from a misprint in Holinshed, which
should have read "brother's" (that is, Richard's brother-in-
law, Charles, Duke of Burgundy, who supported Richmond in exile).
5. *as . . . snow:* as one does who walks in snow that covers
the tops of his shoes.
6. English vagabonds were whipped out of the parish by
a local official.

7. And gave them a shameful record in history.
5.7
1. Some editors bring Norfolk onstage, although the Q,
F stage directions do not call for him.
2. Several could here come onstage during the excursions.
3. More wonders than seems possible for a man.

Alarums. Enter [KING] RICHARD

KING RICHARD A horse! A horse! My kingdom for a horse!

CATESBY Withdraw, my lord. I'll help you to a horse.

KING RICHARD Slave, I have set my life upon a cast,[4]

10 And I will stand the hazard of the die.
I think there be six Richmonds[5] in the field.
Five have I slain today, instead of him.
A horse! A horse! My kingdom for a horse!   [*Exeunt*]

5.8

Alarum. Enter [KING] RICHARD [*at one door*] *and*
[HENRY EARL OF] RICHMOND [*at another*]. *They fight.*
RICHARD *is slain.* [*Exit* RICHMOND.] *Retreat*[1] *and flour-*
ish. Enter [HENRY EARL OF] RICHMOND *and* [*Lord* STAN-
LEY *Earl of*] *Derby, with divers other lords* [*and soldiers*]

HENRY EARL OF RICHMOND God and your arms be praised, victorious friends!
The day is ours. The bloody dog is dead.

STANLEY [*bearing the crown*] Courageous Richmond, well hast
thou acquit° thee.   *acquitted; conducted*
Lo, here this long usurpèd royalty[2]

5 From the dead temples of this bloody wretch
Have I plucked off, to grace thy brows withal.°   *with*
Wear it, enjoy it, and make much of it.
[*He sets the crown on Henry's head*]

KING HENRY VII Great God of heaven, say 'Amen' to all.
But tell me—young George Stanley, is he living?

10 STANLEY He is, my lord, and safe in Leicester town,
Whither, if it please you, we may now withdraw us.

KING HENRY VII What men of name are slain on either side?

STANLEY [*reads*] John Duke of Norfolk, Robert Brackenbury,
Walter Lord Ferrers, and Sir William Brandon.

15 KING HENRY VII Inter their bodies as becomes their births.°   *befits their rank*
Proclaim a pardon to the soldiers fled
That in submission will return to us,
And then—as we have ta'en the sacrament[3]—
We will unite the white rose and the red.[4]

20 Smile, heaven, upon this fair conjunction,°   *union*
That long have frowned upon their enmity.
What traitor hears me and says not 'Amen'?
England hath long been mad, and scarred herself;
The brother blindly shed the brother's blood;

25 The father rashly slaughtered his own son;
The son, compelled, been butcher to the sire;
All that divided York and Lancaster,
United in their dire division.[5]
O now let Richmond and Elizabeth,

30 The true succeeders of each royal house,
By God's fair ordinance° conjoin together,   *decree*

---

4. A throw of the die in line 10 (one of a pair of dice).
5. In addition to Richmond, five other men dressed and armed to resemble him (a common safety measure).
5.8
1. A trumpet signal for (Richard's) men to retire.
2. Emblem of sovereignty; here, the crown.
3. Referring to the oath, taken by Richmond in the cathedral at Rheims, that he would marry Princess Elizabeth

as soon as he was crowned.
4. The badges of the Yorkist and Lancastrian factions. The marriage of Richmond (Lancastrian) and Princess Elizabeth (Yorkist) brought to an end the so-called Wars of the Roses, dramatized in the three *Henry VI* plays.
5. Joined by hatred, having nothing in common but mutual antagonism.

And let their heirs—God, if his will be so—
Enrich the time to come with smooth-faced peace,
With smiling plenty, and fair prosperous days.
35 Abate° the edge of traitors, gracious Lord,   *Blunt*
That would reduce° these bloody days again   *bring back*
And make poor England weep forth streams of blood.
Let them not live to taste this land's increase,
That would with treason wound this fair land's peace.
40 Now civil wounds are stopped; peace lives again.
That she may long live here, God say 'Amen'.
                               [*Flourish.*] *Exeunt*

TEXTUAL VARIANTS

Control text: F (except for 3.1.0–148 and 5.5.4–end, for which the copy text is Q1)

F: The Folio of 1623
Q1: The Quarto of 1597
Q2: The Quarto of 1598
Q3: The Quarto of 1602
Q4: The Quarto of 1605
Q5: The Quarto of 1612
Q6: The Quarto of 1622

1.1–3.1 and 3.1.148–5.5.4

s.p. RICHARD GLOUCESTER [F's use of *Richard* and *Gloucester* has been standardized until 4.2.]

s.p. KING RICHARD [F's use of *King* and *Richard* has been standardized after 4.2.]

s.p. BRACKENBURY [F's use of *Brackenbury* and *Lieutenant* has been standardized throughout.]

s.p. LORD HASTINGS [F's use of *Hastings* has been changed throughout.]

s.p. LADY ANNE [F's use of *Anne* has been changed throughout.]

s.p. HALBERDIER [F uses *Gentleman.*]

s.p. QUEEN ELIZABETH [F's use of *Queen* has been standardized throughout.]

s.p. STANLEY [F's use of *Stanley* and *Derby* has been standardized throughout.]

s.p. QUEEN MARGARET [F's use of *Queen Margaret* and *Margaret* has been standardized throughout.]

s.p. A MURDERER, MURDERERS [F's use of *Villain* has been standardized throughout.]

s.p. FIRST MURDERER [F's use of *1 Murderer* and *1* has been standardized throughout.]

s.p. SECOND MURDERER [F's use of *2 Murderer* and *2* has been standardized throughout.]

s.p. KING EDWARD [F's use of *King* has been standardized throughout.]

s.p. BOY [F's use of *Boy* and *Edward* has been standardized until 3.1.]

s.p. DUCHESS OF YORK [F's use of *Duchess of York* and *Duchess* has been standardized throughout.]

s.p. GIRL [F's use of *Daughter* has been standardized throughout.]

s.p. FIRST CITIZEN [F's use of *1 Citizen* and *1* has been standardized throughout.]

s.p. SECOND CITIZEN [F's use of *2 Citizen* and *2* has been standardized throughout.]

s.p. THIRD CITIZEN [F's use of *3* has been standardized throughout.]

s.p. CARDINAL [F's use of *Archbishop* and *Cardinal* has been standardized throughout.]

s.p. MAYOR [F's use of *Lord Mayor* and *Mayor* has been standardized throughout.]

s.p. BISHOP OF ELY [F's use of *Ely* has been standardized throughout.]

s.p. ALL BUT RICHARD [F's use of *All* has been standardized throughout.]

s.p. SECOND MESSENGER, THIRD MESSENGER, FOURTH MESSENGER [F only uses *Messenger.*]

s.p. SIR CHRISTOPHER [F's use of *Christopher* has been standardized throughout.]
s.p. HENRY EARL OF RICHMOND [F's use of *Richmond* has been standardized throughout.]

3.1.0–148 and 5.5.4–end
s.p. KING RICHARD [Q's use of *King Richard* and *Richard* has been standardized throughout.]
s.p. PRINCE EDWARD [Q's use of *Prince* has been standardized throughout.]
s.p. GHOST OF PRINCE EDWARD, GHOST OF KING HENRY, GHOST OF CLARENCE, GHOSTS OF THE PRINCES, GHOST OF HASTINGS [Q's use of *Ghost* has been standardized throughout.]
s.p. GHOST OF GRAY [Q's use of *Gray* has been standardized throughout.]
s.p. GHOST OF VAUGHAN [Q's use of *Vaughan* has been standardized throughout.]

Title: *The Tragedy of King Richard the Third*] THE TRAGEDY OF / King Richard the third. / Containing, / His treacherous Plots against his brother Clarence: / the pittiefull murther of his innocent nephewes: / his tyrannicall vsurpation: with the whole course / of his detested life, and most deserued death. [Q title page] The Tragedy of Richard the Third: / with the Landing of Earle Richmond, and the / Battell at Bosworth Field. [F head title]

1.1.26 spy [Q] see 49 Belike O belike 52 for [Q] but 67 Woodeville Woodeulle 73 Mrs Mistresse 74 ye [Q] you 75 for his for her 88 An't and 92 jealous [Q] iealious 96 kin kindred 104 I [Q] I do do withal withal 113 dearer deeper 116 or [Q] or else 125 the [Q1] this 134 prey [Q] play 139 Paul [Q] Iohn 146 haste horse
1.2.15 Cursèd ... hence, [F places the line after 1.2.16.] 39 stand [Q] Stand'st 56 Ope Open 60 deed Deeds 61 supernatural most vnnaturall 70 no [Q] nor 78 a [Q; not in F] 80 t'accuse to curse 92 hand [Q] hands 101 ye [Q1] yee 120 of that accursed effect and most accurst effect 126 rend [Q] rent 127 sweet [Q] yᵗ 154 drops. [Q; F here adds twelve lines; see indented passage.] Shamed [Q, F (text)] For [F (catchword)] 189 s.p. RICHARD GLOUCESTER [Q; not in F] 190 s.p. LADY ANNE ... give. [Q; not in F] 213 s.p. RICHARD GLOUCESTER ... corpse. [Q; not in F] 214 Blackfriars white Friers 238 *denier* denier
1.3.6 If ... me? [Q; F gives the line twice, spanning a page break.] 7 s.p. RIVERS [Q] If he were dead, what would betide me on / Gray. [F (text)] Gray. [F (catchword)] 17 come [Q1] comes Lords [Q] Lord 30 s.p. RIVERS [Q] Qu⟨een Elizabeth⟩. 33 With [Q1] What 43 are they [Q] is it complain complaines 54 s.p. RIVERS [Q] Gray. whom [Q1] who 68–69 that ... it that he may learne the ground 114 Tell ... said, [Q; not in F] 118 remember [Q] do remember 153 may you [Q] you may 155 Ah A 160 of [Q] off 166 go. [Q; F here adds three lines; see indented passage.] 197 my [Q] our 270 was [Q] is 271 s.p. RICHARD GLOUCESTER Buc⟨kingham⟩. 290 naught not 302 s.p. HASTINGS [Q] Buc⟨kingham⟩. 307 s.p. QUEEN ELIZABETH [Q] Mar⟨garet⟩. 319 you my gracious lords yours my gracious Lord 325 whom [Q] who
1.4.19 sought thought 22 waters [Q1] water 22–23 my ... my [Q1] mine ... mine 25 Ten [Q] A 26 ouches anchors 29 those [Q] the 32 Which [Q] That 50 cried [Q] spake 58 methoughts [Q1] me thought 66 Brackenbury [Q] Keeper, Keeper 68 me. [Q; F here adds four lines; see indented passage.] 69 Keeper, I pray thee Keeper, I prythee 90 of [Q] from 96 I [Q1] we 112 pray thee [Q] prythee 119 'Swounds [Q] Come 136 'Swounds [Q; not in F] 177 to have redemption [Q] for any goodnesse 178 By ... sins, [Q; not in F] 201 ye [Q] you 225 And ... other, [Q; not in F] 227 of [Q1] on 230 As Right as 251–55 Which distress— [F places the lines after 1.4.244.] 257 serve [Q] do 261 guilty murder done [Q] murther
2.1.5 in [Q] to 7 Hastings and Rivers Dorset and *Riuers* 19 your [Q] you 50 Brother [Q] Gloster 57 unwittingly [Q] vnwillingly 59 By [Q] To 67 Of you ... of you [Q] Of you and you, Lord *Riuers* and of Dorset 68 me.— [Q] me: / Of you Lord *Wooduill*

and Lord *Scales*, of you, 70 **Englishman** [Q] Englishmen 82 **s.p. RIVERS** [Q] *King* 85 **one** [Q] man 93 **but** [Q] and 97 **pray thee** [Q] prethee 105 **slew** [Q] kill'd 108 **at** [Q] and 131 **once** [Q] onee

2.2.3 **you** [Q; not in F] 13 **this** [Q] it 26 **his** [Q] a 27 **shapes** [Q] shape 39 **mark** make 47 **I** [Q; not in F] 83 **weep** [Q] weepes 84–85 **and . . . weep** [Q; not in F] 88 **lamentation.** [F here adds twelve lines; see indented passage.] 105 **hearts** [Q] hates 106 **splinted** [Q, F] splinterd 110 **king.** [Q; F here adds eighteen lines; see indented passage.] 112 **Ludlow** [Q] London 114 **weighty** [Q; not in F] 115 **s.p. QUEEN . . . YORK** [not in F] **With . . . hearts.** [Q; not in F] 117 **God's sake** [Q] God sake 124 **Ludlow** [Q] London

2.3.35 **make** [Q] makes 43 **Ensuing** [Q, F (catchword)] Pursuing [F (text)]

2.4.1 **hear** [Q1] heard **them** [not in F] 1–2 **Northampton. / at Stony Stratford** [Q] Stony Stratford, / And at Northampton 9 **young** [Q] good 12 **nuncle** Vnkle 13 **gross** great 21 **s.p. CARDINAL Why** [Q] *Yor⟨k⟩. And* 26 **pray thee** [Q] prythee 36 **s.p. CARDINAL** [Q] *Dut.* (Duchess of York) 37 **your son, Lord Dorset** a Messenger 38 **Lord Marquis** [Q; not in F] **s.p. DORSET** [Q; throughout scene] *Mes⟨senger⟩.* 40 **then** [Q; not in F] 42 **And with them** and with them, / Sir 48 **our** [Q] my 50 **jet** [Q] Iutt 64 **death** [Q] earth

3.1.0 [Right after this stage direction, F loses its independent authority until c. 3.1.148. Q1 is the control text in this interim; F is here a direct reprint of Q3, which contains errors that need to be corrected by reference to Q1.] 22 **hastes** comes 24 **In happy time** And in good time 39 **Anon expect him** Anone expect him here 41 **sacred** holy 46 **not** but 52 **my mind, he** mine opinion 53 **'longs** is 54 **You . . . charter** You breake no priuiledge nor charter there 59 **I come** I go 74 **liege.** Lo: 85 **t'enrich** enrich 87 **made** makes 88 **yet** now 90 **good** gratious 101 **noble cousin** Cosen noble 102 **uncle, well** Vnckle 107 **He . . . you then** Then he . . . you 109 **as** as in 110 **render** giue 111 **With all** [Q3–6, F] withall 113–14 **give, / It being but** giue, / And being but 121 **I'd** I 132 **sharp, prodigal** sharpe, prouided 136 **My . . . along** [Q, F; none of the many attempts to pad out this line carries any conviction.] 143 **there** [not in Q] 148 **and** [F, not in Q] 149 **we** I 153 **parlous** perillous 161 **Lord William** William Lo: 166 **Will not** [F; F regains its full authority at this line.] Will 170 **purpose.** [Q; for F, see indented passage.] 174 **your** [Q] the 188 **My** Now my

3.2.1 **from Lord** from the lo: 3 **my Lord Stanley** Stanley 17 **councils** [Q] Councell 74 **you do** [Q; not in F] 87 **talked** [Q1] talke 91 **follow presently** [Q] talke with this good fellow 92 **Well met, Hastings** [Q] How now, Sirrha? 95 **I met thee** [Q] thou met'st me 102 **Hastings** [Q] fellow 103 **God save your lordship** [Q] I thanke your

3.3.14 **heads,** [Q] Heads / When shee exclaim'd on *Hastings*, you, and I 16–17 **Hastings . . . Richard** [Q] *Richard . . . Hastings*

3.4.4 **that** [Q] the **solemn** royall 9 **methinks** [Q] we thinke 26 **not you** [Q] you not 39 **worshipful** [Q] worshipfully 55 **likelihood** [Q] liuelyhood 58 **s.p. STANLEY I . . . not.** [not in F] 65 **whatsoe'er** [Q] whosoe're 68 **See** [Q] Looke 78 **Some see it done** [Q] *Louell* and *Ratcliffe*, looke that it be done 82 **raze** [Q] rowse 83 **But** [Q] And 94 **s.p. CATESBY** *Ra⟨tcliffe⟩.* 98 **th'air** aire 102 **s.p. CATESBY** *Lou⟨ell⟩.*

3.5.4 **wert** [Q] were 6 **Tremble . . . straw,** [F places the line after 3.5.7.] 12 **s.p. RICHARD GLOUCESTER . . . Mayor** [Q] But what, is *Catesby* gone? / *Rich⟨ard⟩.* He is, and see he brings the Maior along 13 **Let . . . him.** [Q; not in F] 19 **innocence** [Q1] innocencie 20 **O . . . Catesby** [Q] Be patient, they are friends: *Ratcliffe,* and *Louell.* 21 **s.p. CATESBY** [Q] *Louell.* 31 **attainture** attainder 32 **The** Well, well, he was the 48 **I** [Q] *Buck⟨ingham⟩. I* 50 **s.p. RICHARD GLOUCESTER** [Q4; not in F] 54 **we** [Q] I **hear** heard 56 **treason** [Q] Treasons 60 **word** [Q] words 64 **cause** [Q1] case 82 **listed** [Q] lusted 101 **Now** [Q; for F, see indented passage.] **in** [Q] goe 103 **notice** [Q] order

3.6.13 **naught** [Q1] nought

3.7.7 **insatiate** [Q] vnsatiate 14 **face** forme 20 **mine** [Q1] my 40 **wisdoms** [Q] wisdome 43–44 **s.p. BUCKINGHAM No . . . lord. / s.p. RICHARD GLOUCESTER** [Q; not in F] 49 **build** [Q] make 50 **request** [Q] requests 54 **we'll** [Q] we 72 **lolling** [Q, F]

lulling **day-bed** [Q] Loue-Bed **101 request** [Q] requests **125 her** [Q] his **126 Her** [Q] His **127 Her** His **143 condition.** [Q; F here adds ten lines; see indented passage.] **160 no doubt, us** [Q] no doubt vs **203 equally** [Q, F] egallie **209 'Swounds, I'll** [Q] we will **210 s.p. RICHARD GLOUCESTER** O . . . Buckingham. [Q; not in F] **212 s.p. ANOTHER** [Q; not in F] **214 stone** stones **215 entreats** [Q] entreaties **230 kind** King **237 cousin** [Q] Cousins
4.1.46 counted England's Englands counted **57 in** [Q] with **75 made** [not in F] **96 racked** [Q, F] wrackt **teen.** [Q; F here adds seven lines; see indented passage.]
4.2.14 liege [Q] Lord **20 immediately** suddenlie **50 those parts beyond the seas** [Q] the parts **55 born** [Q] poore **73 there** [Q] then **81 'Tis** [Q] There is **84–85 s.p. KING RICHARD** Shall . . . lord. [Q; not in F] **90 to** [Q] vnto **101 perhaps.** [Q; not in F] **101–19 s.p. BUCKINGHAM** . . . today. [Q; not in F] **120 Why . . . no?** [Q] May it please you to resolue me in my suit.
4.3.4 whom [Q] who **5 ruthless** [Q1] ruthfull **8 two** [Q] to **15 once** [Q] one **31 at** [Q] and **39 goodnight** [Q] good night **40 Breton** [Q, F] Brittaine **42 o'er** [Q] on **45 Good news or bad** [Q] Good or bad newes **46 Ely** [Q] *Mourton* **53 leads** [Q] leds **55 an** and
4.4.10 unblown [Q] vnblowed **30 innocents'** [Q] innocent **36 seniory** [Q] signeurie **39 Tell . . . mine.** [Q; not in F] **45 holpst** hop'st **56 charnel** [Q, F] carnal **64 Thy** [Q] The **quite** [Q6] quit **77 plead** pray **93 are** [Q1] be **100 For queen . . . care** [Q; F places the line after 4.4.101.] **107 wert** [Q1] wast **112 weary** [Q1] wearied **118 nights . . . days** [Q1] night . . . day **127 client** [Q1] Clients **128 recorders** succeeders **intestate** [Q] intestine **141 Where** [Q] Where't **175 in** [Q] with **176 Hewer** *Hower* **180 pray thee** prythee **188 heavy** [Q] greeuous **216 births** [Q] Birth **221 life.** [Q; F here adds fourteen lines; see indented passage.] **225 or** [Q1–5] and **243 that** it **254 would I** [Q1] I would **260 sometimes** [Q1] sometime **270 is** [Q; not in F] **273 this.** [Q; F here adds fifty-five lines; see indented passage.] **286 love** [Q] low **295 s.p. KING RICHARD** . . . past. [Q1; F places the line after 4.4.296.] **296 s.p. QUEEN ELIZABETH** [Q1; not in F] **297 s.p. KING RICHARD** [Q; not in F] **300 holy** [Q] Lordly **301 lordly** knightlie **307 that** [Q] it **308 God . . . God's** [Q] Heauen . . . Heanens **323 in** [Q1] with **327 o'erpast** [Q] repast **343 good** [Q] deare **348 peevishfond** [Q] peeuish found **356 recomfiture** [Q] recomforture **375 Ratcliffe** *Catesby* **391 mile** [Q] miles **395 renegade** [Q, F] runnagate **398 Ely** [Q] *Morton* **421 Ay, ay** [Q] I **431 Courtenay** [Q, F] Courtney **434 Guildfords** [Q, F] Guilfords **441 flood . . . water** [Q] Floods . . . Waters **445 Ratcliffe . . . gave him** [Q] There is my Purse, to cure that Blow of thine **452 Breton** [Q, F] Brittaine **458 Bretagne** [Q, F] Brittaine **465 tidings,** [Q1] Newes, but
4.5.2 this [Q] the **5 aid** [Q] ayde. / So get thee gone: commend me to thy Lord **17–18 Tell . . . daughter.** [Q; F places the lines after 4.5.5.] **17 Tell him** [Q] Withall say, that
5.2.8 spoils spoild **11 Lies** [Q] Is **12 Near** [Q] Ne're **17 swords** [Q] men
5.3.2 Why, how now, Catesby [Q] My Lord of Surrey **3 s.p. CATESBY** [Q] Sur⟨rey⟩.
5.4.4 standard. [Q; F places 5.4.21–24 here and adds, "My Lord of Oxford, you Sir *William Brandon*, / And your Sir *Walter Herbert* stay with me."] **21–24 Give . . . power.** [Q, F places the lines after 5.4.4.]
5.5.3 [Q1 is the control text for the remainder of the play, though a handful of Folio variants are considered or adopted, as derived from the damaged final leaves of the manuscript.] **8 sentinels** [F] centinell **10 s.p. KING RICHARD** Stir [F, Q (text)] Sturr [Q (catchword)] **11 s.p. CATESBY** Rat⟨cliffe⟩. **19 Ratcliffe** [Q6, F (italic)] Ratliffe **25 some** a boule of **29 Leave me. Bid my guard watch.** Bid my guard watch, leaue me. **30–31 About . . . tent,** / Ratcliffe, and Ratliffe about . . . tent / And **32 sit** [Q2] set **43 mortal-sharing** mortal staring **53 sundered** [Q3] sundried **72 tomorrow,** / Prince . . . Sixth. to morrow. **84 Comforts** Doth comfort **85 sit** [Q2] set **on** [Q5] in **93 s.p. GHOST OF RIVERS** [Q3] *King* **on** [Q5] in **97 pointless** [not in Q] **99 Will** [Q2] Wel **100 s.p. GHOSTS OF THE PRINCES** [F] *Ghost.* **110 Hastings, then** Hastings **137 am** [Q2] and **140 Myself** What my selfe **156 Nay** [F] And **163 My** Rat-

cliffe, my 167 **all our friends prove** our friends proue all 168 **Ratcliffe** O
Ratcliffe 177 s.p. LORDS [Q3–6] Lo⟨rds⟩. 180 s.p. A LORD [Q] Lo⟨rd⟩. 189 s.p. A LORD
[Q] Lo⟨rd⟩. 191 **Much that I could say** More than I haue said 193 **on** vpon 196
forces faces 199 **friends** gentlemen 212 **foison** fat **pays** shall paie 219–20 **this . . .
my** my . . . this 221 **to the** 223 **bold and** boldlie, and

5.6.12 **not** [Q2] nor 25 **placèd strongly** shall be placed 27 **multitude** foote and
horse 28 **ourself** [not in Q] 29 **both sides** either side 31 **boot!** [Q3] bootes 32 s.p.
NORFOLK **A good** [F, Q (text)] A good [Q (catchword)] 33 **paper** [not in Q] 34 **Jackie**
[Q, F] Iocky **too** so 37 **each** euery 47 **Bretons** [Q, F] Brittains 49 **ventures** aduen-
tures 52 **distain** restraine 54 **Bretagne** [Q, F] Brittaine 55 **milksop** [Q6, F] milke-
sopt 74 **young** his sonne

5.8.8–9 s.p. KING . . . **But** [F, Q (text)] But [Q (catchword)] 9 **young George Stanley, is
he** is yong George Stanley 13 s.p. STANLEY [F] Der⟨by⟩. [not in Q] 14 **Ferrers**
Ferris 15 **becomes** become 27 **that** this 28 **United** Deuided 32 **his** thy 37 **forth** in

Richard II

In the first scene of *Richard II*, two armed noblemen face each other before the royal throne. They hurl insults at one another, their deadly antagonism barely held in check by the formality of the occasion. This is an "appeal for treason," a kind of trial already archaic in Shakespeare's time, in which plaintiff and defendant present their cases in their own persons before the King, who instantly dispenses justice. The structure of the situation suggests what the men themselves insist upon: that one lies and one tells the truth, that one is a traitor and one a true subject. But even while we are implicitly asked to judge between rival claims, we have no way of knowing what has happened or whom to trust.

In the ensuing scenes, we learn that Bolingbroke and Mowbray are fighting about the murder of Thomas of Woodstock, the uncle of King Richard II. Apparently Bolingbroke knows that Richard secretly ordered Woodstock's death. Since he cannot say so, he picks Richard's agent Mowbray as his target, for Woodstock had been in Mowbray's safekeeping. Meanwhile, Mowbray, likewise unable to blame the true culprit openly, is outraged at being called a traitor when it was his allegiance to Richard that led him to acquiesce in the killing.

This is a far more tangled situation than the simple yes-or-no structure of the appeal for treason or, several scenes later, the "trial by combat" could allow anyone to acknowledge. Moreover, the King's participation in the crime upon which he is supposed to be passing judgment obviously compromises his impartiality. The institution of the appeal for treason is premised on the assumptions that, as Richard himself states emphatically, the King has no part in his subjects' quarrels and that it is in his best interests to have the truth revealed. Here, neither assumption is correct. The ceremonies of royal authority so colorfully staged in the first few scenes turn out to be inconclusive, postponing rather than confronting real sources of discord.

As the play continues, we come to realize that the confusion of the first few scenes, a confusion Shakespeare forces his audience momentarily to share, results from an intractable problem in a system of monarchical government. Since the King's subjects are obliged to obey him, it is not clear how, short of direct divine intervention, his follies or vices may be checked. To admit that subjects have a right to judge or even to remove their King threatens the stability of the realm, since any subject, discontented for any reason, might incite a revolt. But to allow the King to have his own way no matter what opens the way to tyranny.

The proper extent of a monarch's power was a crucial, and unresolved, political issue in sixteenth- and early-seventeenth-century England, when first the Tudors and then the Stuarts struggled to extend their traditional prerogatives. A few decades after Shakespeare's death, disagreement about the nature of royal authority would provoke the English Civil War. In the 1590s, when Shakespeare was writing his history plays, the lines of stress upon which the country would eventually fracture were already apparent, even though the disasters to come would not have seemed inevitable.

When Shakespeare wrote about the medieval reign of *Richard II*, in other words, he saw the conflicts of that reign through the lens of the late sixteenth century. His meticulous re-creation of antiquated judicial processes did not conceal from audiences in his own time the contemporary relevance of the play. In all sixteenth-century texts and perhaps in performance, the lines in which Richard gives up his crown were omitted: many scholars theorize that this episode was considered too inflammatory to print or stage. When the Earl of Essex rebelled against Elizabeth I in 1601, some of his supporters cited Richard's reign as providing a historical precedent for the deposition of a monarch. They paid Shakespeare's company to perform a play about Richard's reign—almost certainly Shakespeare's play—in an attempt to rally supporters to their cause. "I am Richard II," snapped the furious queen. "Know you not that?"

To acknowledge the contemporary relevance of Richard's reign is not to claim that Shakespeare wrote his play purely as a means of commenting obliquely on the policies of Elizabeth I. Rather, the urgent contemporary task of defining a nation-state led Shakespeare to an extended historical inquiry into the institution of the English monarchy, an inquiry of which *Richard II* is a part. By looking at points at which the normal order of royal succession is challenged, Shakespeare illuminates interesting inconsistencies in Renaissance theories of kingship and political authority. Several years earlier, he had written the three *Henry VI* plays and *Richard III*, which while not originally conceived as a series eventually constituted what critics call the "first tetralogy": a group of plays that together present a continuous chronicle of the long Wars of the Roses in the fifteenth century. Soon after finishing *Richard III*, Shakespeare began writing another group of history plays, the "second tetralogy," which backtrack in time to treat the origins of the conflicts he had already brought to the stage.

As he had for his earlier history plays, Shakespeare turned to Raphael Holinshed's *Chronicles of England, Scotland, and Ireland* (1587). There he found in the reign of Richard II a remote cause of the war to be waged many years hence. Richard II was grandson of Edward III, whose formidable precedent haunts all the plays of the second tetralogy. King Edward had five sons who survived to adulthood, but his eldest, Edward the Black Prince, predeceased him. The Black Prince left a son of his own, however, the future Richard II, to whom the throne descended after Edward III's death. At the time of his accession, Richard was ten years old, and during his adolescence his powerful uncles, the younger brothers of the Black Prince, administered his kingdom on his behalf. After Richard reached young adulthood and began to rule in his own name, he found it difficult to gain the respect of his uncles, experienced middle-aged men who had become accustomed to command. His own rashness and ineffectuality only compounded his troubles. Shakespeare's play opens upon the young Richard, already complicit in the murder of one of his uncles; the remaining uncles, who scorn Richard's maladroit rule but realize they owe allegiance to him; and Richard's cousins Bolingbroke and Northumberland, who are more willing than their elders to act on the recognition of the ruler's weakness.

Early in the play, Richard reacts to Bolingbroke's veiled challenge by exiling him; shortly thereafter, he confiscates Bolingbroke's estate. When, exasperated, Bolingbroke invades England and successfully seizes the crown from his cousin, his action neatly ruptures two traditional sources of royal authority. Unquestionably, Bolingbroke is the more astute tactician, the more effective leader. Richard, however, is equally undoubtedly the rightful heir of Edward III, and as such has been anointed King in a sacred coronation ceremony. Thus one character has all the advantages con-

Richardus ii. From John Rastell, *The Pastyme of People* (1529).

"Like perspectives, which, rightly gazed upon,/Show nothing but confusion; eyed awry,/Distinguish form" (*Richard II* 2.2.18–20). The most famous Renaissance example of such a "perspective" or anamorphic picture is Hans Holbein's *The Ambassadors* (1533); when the painting is viewed from the side ("awry"), the elongated object in the foreground reveals itself to be a skull.

sidered from a material and practical point of view, while the other derives his claim to authority from the more abstract principle of divinely sanctioned hereditary right.

Shakespeare imagines the division between the two men not merely as a political issue but as a question of character. A vivid sense of Bolingbroke's personality emerges in his confrontation with Mowbray. Mowbray harps on Bolingbroke's lies, laments the damage Bolingbroke's accusation has done to his reputation, and experiences Bolingbroke's verbal accusation as a physical attack: he is "pierced to the soul with slander's venomed spear" (1.1.171). Bolingbroke, by contrast, trusts not words but physical strength: "What my tongue speaks my right-drawn sword may prove," he stoutly declares (1.1.46). Tellingly, his word "right" conflates his proficiency as a warrior with the uprightness of his cause, suggesting that he does not care to recognize the potential difference. Likewise, Bolingbroke repeatedly speaks of making his words *good*, by which he means backing them up by force. As a corollary, he is suspicious or dismissive of anything that seems merely imaginary, verbal, or abstract. When his father, Gaunt, encourages him to reconcile himself to his exile by renaming it an educational tour or a pleasure junket, Bolingbroke replies:

> O, who can hold a fire in his hand
> By thinking on the frosty Caucasus,
> Or cloy the hungry edge of appetite
> By bare imagination of a feast?
> (1.3.257–60)

As the play proceeds, this insistence on material facts rather than words or imagination comes to seem entirely characteristic of a man who has no legal claim on the throne, but who takes it because he is able to do so.

Unlike Bolingbroke, Richard is an inept manager of practical affairs. In the first act, most of his powerful kinfolk let him literally get away with murder; but in the second act, it becomes clear that they will not tolerate his infringement of property rights. To the upper aristocracy, this encroachment is worse than homicide, because it directly threatens the social structure upon which their status depends. Inherited property distinguishes noblemen from "men of no name": in fact, noble names are derived from property, the lands of Lancaster, Gloucester, York, Northumberland, and so forth. In *Richard II*, both social disruptions and identity crises are marked by a struggle over such titles and the power they signify. Bolingbroke, returning to England, insists on being called "Lancaster," not "Hereford"; Northumberland presumptuously forgets to call Richard "King"; Richard himself laments, upon his deposition, that "I must nothing be . . . I have no name, no title" (4.1.191, 245).

Although technically aristocrats did not own their land outright but held it in trust from the sovereign, by Richard's time Magna Carta protected the right of property holders to pass their lands to their heirs. Only a conviction for treason could forfeit the family claim. Ironically, at the moment Richard commandeers the Lancastrian estates, Bolingbroke is apparently on the verge of invading England with an armed force, so he is actually a traitor and Richard could eventually have appropriated his property in a perfectly legal manner. But Richard's characteristic neglect of proper procedure makes Bolingbroke's return seem a response to dispossession and thus turns the nobility toward the rebel cause.

Richard does not imagine that he must earn the respect of the people he governs, or balance his budget, or follow laws. He does not believe that his authority depends on the consent of the governed or on the effective manipulation of material resources. Whereas Bolingbroke thinks of power as emanating from "below"—from the King's subjects, from the deployment of material resources—Richard thinks of it as descending from "above," from the God whose representative on earth he was born to be. His assertion in 3.2.50–53 is entirely characteristic:

> Not all the water in the rough rude sea
> Can wash the balm from an anointed king.
> The breath of worldly men cannot depose
> The deputy elected by the Lord.

Later in the same scene, deserted by all but a few supporters, he exclaims: "Is not the King's name forty thousand names? / Arm, arm, my name!" (3.2.81–82). What Richard needs now, of course, is not names but soldiers, but he deliberately refuses to acknowledge the difference.

Richard's drastic impracticalities derive from his conviction that the God who put him on the throne is immanent in the created universe and vigilant in defense of His deputy. Richard is not unique in this conviction: the assumption that God intervenes continuously in human affairs in order to guarantee just outcomes underlies the ritual of the trial by combat as it is staged in 1.3. The way spirit informs and controls the material world can render "dead matter" sympathetic to human beings. "This earth shall have a feeling," Richard claims (3.2.24). Thus he is confident that the earth will put toads in the way of traitors, and that angels will rush to save a king in trouble. Medieval histories are full of such narratives: the ground opens up and swallows an atheist; lightning strikes a perjurer dead.

By Shakespeare's time, the trial by combat had been discredited and the conception of the world to which Richard adheres was beginning to seem obsolete. Advanced thinkers were increasingly discarding anthropocentric ways of thinking and conceiving of the material world as something alien to human consciousness, ruled by purely physical laws of cause and effect. This change in mentality affected historians, who were subjecting long-accepted myths to critical scrutiny; scientists, who began to place a new value on empirical experimentation; and theologians, who were becoming more skeptical of the continuation of miracles in post-biblical times. Political theorists like Machiavelli pragmatically insisted on describing political power as it really was exercised, and not as God or moral scruples might dictate that it ought to be exercised. The pragmatic Bolingbroke, then, is associated with a new, effective, but not necessarily moral or satisfying way of thinking about the manipulation of men and matter.

Richard's assumptions about the world and his place in it turn out to be wrong. His naïveté about the relationship of language and power, spirit and matter, leaves him vulnerable to Bolingbroke's assault. Bolingbroke's supplanting of Richard, then, might be seen not merely as a personal or even a political victory, but as the uprooting of one worldview by another. Whether this displacement represents an advance or a deterioration is, however, another question. The second part of the play, in which Bolingbroke emerges victorious, reexamines the nature of the conflict between the two men and the principles they represent.

In a pivotal scene in Act 3, Bolingbroke, Northumberland, and York approach the castle in which Richard has sequestered himself. When Richard finally emerges on the battlements, Bolingbroke exclaims:

> See, see, King Richard doth himself appear,
> As doth the blushing discontented sun
> From out the fiery portal of the east
> When he perceives the envious clouds are bent
> To dim his glory and to stain the track
> Of his bright passage to the occident.
> (3.3.61–66)

Bolingbroke is untypically eloquent here, but interestingly, his extended simile works against his own interests. The comparison between King and sun, a traditional figure of speech, implies that the King is both unique and indispensable. Rebels are not rival suns; they are transient clouds that the mighty King will eventually burn away. Even while he mutinies against Richard's misgovernment, Bolingbroke seems unable to escape a conservative conception of monarchy in which rebellion is a form of envy doomed to failure.

Bolingbroke's linguistic slip suggests that it may be easier to amass an army and seize the throne than to put aside one's inherited convictions about the nature of royal authority. Bolingbroke does not have an alternative vocabulary in which to justify his own behavior. Thus, throughout the play, it is hard to be sure whether he is cunningly concealing his true motives or simply incapable of articulating them even to himself. In the opening scenes, although Richard recognizes Bolingbroke's challenge to his authority, Bolingbroke himself seems a bit obtuse about his own purposes, as if his accusation of Mowbray were merely an effect of his sturdy loyalty to Richard. Likewise, it is unclear whether he initially realizes that his return from exile commits him not merely to regaining the Lancastrian estates but to a more thorough attack on Richard's sovereignty. Bolingbroke never appears before us, alone or in company, to ponder his own conduct and motives. In this regard, he differs not only from the obsessively self-reflective Richard but from other Shakespearean usurpers: Richard III, Macbeth, Hamlet's Claudius.

In Act 4, however unable he may be to justify the grounds of his own authority, Bolingbroke—now King Henry IV—astutely recognizes that he must convince his subjects that he is legitimately entitled to the crown. Henry needs, somehow, to transfer to himself that mysterious sense of royal sanctity in which Richard initially places so much confidence, and to which Henry has no plausible claim. Henry and his followers thus attempt to paper over his gross procedural breach with procedural punctiliousness. Richard cannot be summarily imprisoned or executed; rather, he must seem voluntarily and publicly to resign his sovereignty to Henry.

Unfortunately for Henry, he is not good at managing such rituals, while Richard is in his element. In 4.1, Richard masterfully seizes the symbolic initiative from the apparent victors. "Now mark me how I will undo myself," he announces.

> I give this heavy weight from off my head,
> And this unwieldy sceptre from my hand,

The pride of kingly sway from out my heart.
With mine own tears I wash away my balm,
With mine own hands I give away my crown,
With mine own tongue deny my sacred state,
With mine own breath release all duteous oaths.
All pomp and majesty I do forswear.
My manors, rents, revenues I forgo.
My acts, decrees, and statutes I deny.

(lines 194–203)

Richard's actions and words here are meant to recall a coronation ceremony, in which the King is invested with the crown and scepter as his insignia of office, anointed with balm as a sign that he is God's chosen, promised the allegiance of his subjects, given formal title to the royal domains. One of the main points of this ceremony is its permanence: it cannot be undone. By referring to this ritual at the moment of his deposition, Richard implies that giving up the crown is an impossible act, a kind of absurdity. Moreover, reversing the ceremonies—taking off the crown rather than putting it on, relinquishing rather than accepting the scepter—suggests a special scandal. In medieval and early modern Europe, as among some fundamentalist religious groups today, reversing beneficent ceremonies supposedly evoked their diabolical opposites. One called up devils by reciting Scripture passages backward, or bound oneself to Satan by performing an inversion of baptismal rites. Richard's enthusiastic self-dramatization of his plight does not quell doubts about the legitimacy of the usurpation, but encourages those doubts. Immediately after Richard departs, his friends begin to conspire on his behalf; and although their plot is eventually crushed, Henry's reign will never be quiet thereafter.

As the play proceeds, the view of politics associated with Bolingbroke, a view that initially seems hardheaded and realistic, begins to seem not very practical after all. An acceptable social order requires more than the brute force Henry deploys so expertly. It requires a common set of ideas and practices, a common language and attitude, a set of rituals—all the immaterial abstractions Henry had originally been inclined to disregard.

Just as Shakespeare, over the course of the play, alters our view of the political dilemma represented by the rebellion, so he manipulates our outlook on its main characters. As soon as Richard has lost his throne, we need no longer evaluate him in terms of his effectiveness as a ruler. Immediately his talents seem more obvious, his faults less reprehensible. Richard's extraordinary poetic and introspective gifts allow him to analyze his own situation with a delicacy and insight of which Bolingbroke is entirely incapable. He is acutely aware of the figure he cuts to the only audience that matters to him, himself; in fact, his self-destructive behavior might be seen as an unconscious quest for the expressive opportunities provided only by misery. Always preoccupied with analogies between kingship and godhead, Richard identifies more and more as the play continues with the suffering Christ, consoling himself with the comparison and deriving from it a certain sad grandeur. Obviously Richard's particular strengths are intrinsically connected to his weaknesses, but that does not mean that those strengths are negligible. They are especially hard to ignore in a *play*, in which poetic language, symbolic thought, and the effective deployment of spectacle are central concerns.

Richard's case encourages us to reflect on the way the political emphases of the history play constrain our evaluation of him. In *Richard II*, Shakespeare uses female characters to suggest the possibility of an alternative perspective on the events he depicts. In the second scene, the Duchess of Gloucester urges Gaunt to revenge Thomas of Woodstock, her husband and his brother. Gaunt refuses: in his view, the subject's duty to his monarch must outweigh his obligation to his kin. Their conversation reminds us that England's political crisis is also a familial disaster, and that construing it as one rather than the other has important consequences.

Throughout the play, the men, like Gaunt, tend to subordinate domestic concerns to civic ones, family bonds to the all-important relationship between King and subject. The

Death of Phaeton. From Antonio Tempesta, Ovid's "Metamorphoses" (1606).

women, like the Duchess of Gloucester, do the opposite. Although the historical Richard was married to a ten-year-old queen, Shakespeare makes Isabella a mature young woman and invents touching, wholly nonfactual scenes in which she intuitively senses her husband's trouble, then discovers the usurpation in a garden and suffers through an imposed parting from her husband. The pathos of these scenes derives from the Queen's utter helplessness. She is imagined as Richard's wife, a domestic function, not England's Queen, a public one. All her responses are thus founded on her singleminded loyalty to the marital tie, as sharply distinguished from the bonds of politics. "Banish us both, and send the King with me," she begs Northumberland, when he informs them that she will be exiled and her husband kept under house arrest in England. "That were some love, but little policy," Northumberland replies (5.1.83, 84). The last thing Bolingbroke needs is a legitimate child of Richard's to confuse his claims on the throne even more. But the Queen fails to grasp Northumberland's meaning, because she does not understand "policy"—that is, politics. It is not her sphere.

The difference between civic and domestic domains also appears in the scenes immediately following, which stage a dispute between the Duke and Duchess of York over their son, Aumerle. Here again Shakespeare altered his sources, unhistorically making Aumerle an only child and the Duchess his natural mother. Having discovered that Aumerle is involved in a plot to kill the new Henry IV and reinstate Richard, York feels bound to inform Henry of the treason. He puts what he sees as his civic duty above the ties of blood. The Duchess is outraged. "Wilt thou not hide the trespass of thine own?" she asks. "Have we more sons? Or are we like to have?" (5.2.89–90). For her, the familial relationship takes precedence over the public one.

This dividing of the "public" male role from the "private" female role is hardly a

Shakespearean invention. But Shakespeare puts that division of perspective to thematic use in *Richard II*. In 2.2, when Isabella has a presentiment of ruin, Bushy tries to console her in an elaborate speech about perspective glasses and "anamorphic" paintings. These two Renaissance inventions encourage speculation about the difference between the "right" or "centered" way of seeing and an oblique outlook from which shapes look very different. Of course, Isabella's inexplicable presentiment of disaster turns out to be more apt than her male companions' optimism. Perhaps the women's different perspective implies that the history play's focus on traditionally masculine political concerns may exclude whole realms of human experience.

In the fifth act, Richard—weeping, enclosed, suffering, and excluded from authority— finds himself in the position the play has defined as a feminine one. Politically marginalized, he nonetheless dominates the closing moments of the play, first by his powerful soliloquizing and later by his courageous defiance of his murderers. In some respects, the final scenes of *Richard II* recall its opening. What seems to be a simple opposition turns out to be far more complex, as categories of expedience and impracticality, power and weakness, right and wrong, mutate and change places. Once again, the apparent conclusion of a conflict merely postpones its resolution. The *Henry IV* plays will stage the aftermath.

KATHARINE EISAMAN MAUS

TEXTUAL NOTE

The first printed version of *Richard II* was a quarto published in 1597 (Q1). The quality of the text is good, and most scholars have assumed that it was printed either directly from Shakespeare's manuscript or (because the stage directions are very brief) from a transcript of Shakespeare's manuscript not designed to provide the basis for theatrical performance. Two more quartos, printed in 1598 (Q2 and Q3), mention Shakespeare as the author of the play on their title pages. In 1608, a fourth quarto appeared (Q4), and in 1615, a fifth (Q5); each quarto seems based on the one that had appeared before it. However, Q4 was the first to print the "new additions of the parliament scene, and the deposing of King Richard," scenes not present in the earlier quartos.

The First Folio of 1623 (F) text was probably printed with reference to a promptbook, because it has much more detailed stage directions than the quarto texts. Editors disagree, however, over whether this promptbook text was based on Shakespeare's manuscript or on a corrected copy of Q1 or Q3. F includes a version of the abdication scene that is different, and better, than the one in Q4 and Q5. F omits some lines that are present in Q1, and there are also a number of single-word divergences between the two texts. In cases where only a single line is missing, the deletion may represent a compositor's error, so the Oxford editors have followed Q1. In cases where more substantial passages have been excluded, the editors assume that Shakespeare himself was responsible; these passages are indented in the text.

The most important difference between Q1 and F is F's inclusion of the deposition scene. Some scholars have argued that Elizabeth's censors considered the passage too provocative to stage and insisted that it be deleted; after Elizabeth's death, it was possible to reinstate the offending material. Others argue that Shakespeare revised the play during the first decade of the seventeenth century and wrote the deposition scene at that time.

The Oxford editors have generally based their text on Q1, except for the deposition scene, where they have followed F. They have, however, assimilated many of F's more complete stage directions and many of its single-word variants from Q1, when in the editors' opinion those variants represent Shakespeare's revisions to his own text rather than compositorial corruptions.

SELECTED BIBLIOGRAPHY

Berger, Harry. "Textual Dramaturgy: Representing the Limits of Theatre in *Richard II*." *Theatre Journal* 39 (1987): 135–55.

Calderwood, James. "*Richard II* and the Fall of Speech." *Shakespearean Metadrama*. Minneapolis: University of Minnesota Press, 1979. 149–86.

Doran, Madeline. "Imagery in *Richard II* and *Henry IV*." *Modern Language Review* 37 (1942): 113–22.

Gaudet, Paul. "The 'Parasitical Counselors' in Shakespeare's *Richard II*: A Problem in Dramatic Interpretation." *Shakespeare Quarterly* 33 (1982): 142–54.

Hamilton, Donna. "The State of Law in *Richard II*." *Shakespeare Quarterly* 34 (1983): 5–17.

Kantorowicz, E. H. *The King's Two Bodies: A Study in Medieval Political Theology*. Chapter 2. Princeton: Princeton University Press, 1957.

Kastan, David. "Proud Majesty Made a Subject: Shakespeare and the Spectacle of Rule." *Shakespeare Quarterly* 37 (1986): 459–75.

McMillin, Scott. "*Richard II*: Eyes of Sorrow, Eyes of Desire." *Shakespeare Quarterly* 35 (1984): 40–52.

Moore, Jeanie Grant. "Queen of Sorrow, King of Grief: Reflections and Perspectives in *Richard II*." *In Another Country: Feminist Perspectives on Renaissance Drama*. Ed. Dorothea Kehler and Susan Baker. Metuchen, N.J.: Scarecrow Press, 1991. 19–35.

Saccio, Peter. *Shakespeare's English Kings: History, Chronicle, and Drama*. Chapter 2. New York: Oxford University Press, 1977.

Tillyard, E. M. W. *Shakespeare's History Plays*. London: Chatto and Windus, 1938. 244–63.

The Tragedy of King Richard
the Second

THE PERSONS OF THE PLAY

KING RICHARD II
The QUEEN, his wife
JOHN OF GAUNT, Duke of Lancaster, Richard's uncle
Harry BOLINGBROKE, Duke of Hereford, John of Gaunt's son,
    later KING HENRY IV
DUCHESS OF GLOUCESTER, widow of Gaunt's and York's brother
Duke of YORK, King Richard's uncle
DUCHESS OF YORK
Duke of AUMERLE, their son
Thomas MOWBRAY, Duke of Norfolk
GREEN ⎫
BAGOT ⎬ followers of King Richard
BUSHY ⎭
Percy, Earl of NORTHUMBERLAND ⎫
HARRY PERCY, his son ⎪
Lord ROSS ⎬ of Bolingbroke's party
Lord WILLOUGHBY ⎭
Earl of SALISBURY ⎫
BISHOP OF CARLISLE ⎬ of King Richard's party
Sir Stephen SCROPE ⎭
Lord BERKELEY
Lord FITZWALTER
Duke of SURREY
ABBOT OF WESTMINSTER
Sir Piers EXTON
LORD MARSHAL
HERALDS
CAPTAIN of the Welsh army
LADIES attending the Queen
GARDENER
Gardener's MEN
Exton's MEN
KEEPER of the prison at Pomfret
GROOM of King Richard's stable
Lords, soldiers, attendants

1.1

Enter KING RICHARD, JOHN OF GAUNT, *with [the* LORD
MARSHAL,] *other nobles, and attendants*
KING RICHARD   Old John of Gaunt,[1] time-honoured Lancaster,
    Hast thou according to thy oath and bond
    Brought hither Henry Hereford, thy bold son,
    Here to make good the boist'rous late appeal,°   *violent recent accusation*

1.1 Location: Windsor Castle.
1. Named after his birthplace, Ghent (in Flanders); his title was Duke of Lancaster. He was fifty-eight years old.

5   Which then our leisure² would not let us hear,
       Against the Duke of Norfolk, Thomas Mowbray?
JOHN OF GAUNT   I have, my liege.
KING RICHARD   Tell me moreover, hast thou sounded° him   *inquired of*
       If he appeal the Duke on ancient malice³
10   Or worthily, as a good subject should,
       On some known ground of treachery in him?
JOHN OF GAUNT   As near as I could sift° him on that argument,°   *discover from / topic*
       On some apparent° danger seen in him   *manifest*
       Aimed at your highness, no inveterate malice.
KING RICHARD   Then call them to our presence.
                                          [*Exit one or more*]
15   Face to face
       And frowning brow to brow, ourselves will hear
       The accuser and the accusèd freely speak.
       High-stomached° are they both and full of ire;   *Haughty*
       In rage, deaf as the sea, hasty as fire.
            Enter BOLINGBROKE [*Duke of Hereford*], *and* MOWBRAY
            [*Duke of Norfolk*]
20 BOLINGBROKE   Many years of happy days befall
       My gracious sovereign, my most loving liege!
MOWBRAY   Each day still better others' happiness,⁴
       Until the heavens, envying earth's good hap,°   *fortune*
       Add an immortal title to your crown!
25 KING RICHARD   We thank you both. Yet one but flatters us,
       As well appeareth by the cause you come,
       Namely, to appeal each other of high treason.
       Cousin of Hereford, what dost thou object°   *charge*
       Against the Duke of Norfolk, Thomas Mowbray?
30 BOLINGBROKE   First—heaven be the record to my speech—
       In the devotion of a subject's love,
       Tend'ring° the precious safety of my Prince,   *Having care for*
       And free from other misbegotten hate,
       Come I appellant° to this princely presence.   *as accuser*
35   Now, Thomas Mowbray, do I turn to thee;
       And mark my greeting° well, for what I speak   *address*
       My body shall make good upon this earth,
       Or my divine° soul answer it in heaven.   *immortal*
       Thou art a traitor and a miscreant,
40   Too good° to be so, and too bad to live,   *wellborn*
       Since the more fair and crystal is the sky,
       The uglier seem the clouds that in it fly.
       Once more, the more to aggravate the note,°   *emphasize the reproach*
       With a foul traitor's name stuff I thy throat,
45   And wish, so please my sovereign, ere I move
       What my tongue speaks my right-drawn sword may prove.
MOWBRAY   Let not my cold words here accuse my zeal.°   *cast doubt on my loyalty*
       'Tis not the trial of a woman's war,
       The bitter clamour of two eager° tongues,   *sharp*
50   Can arbitrate⁵ this cause betwixt us twain.
       The blood is hot that must be cooled for this.
       Yet can I not of such tame patience boast

---

2. That is, lack of leisure. Richard uses the royal "we."   4. May each day be better than the last.
3. Out of long-standing enmity.   5. Judge (without implying compromise).

As to be hushed and naught at all to say.
First, the fair reverence of your highness curbs me
55   From giving reins and spurs to my free speech,
Which else would post° until it had returned   *ride fast*
These terms of treason doubled down his throat.
Setting aside his high blood's royalty,[6]
And let him be° no kinsman to my liege,   *And as if he were*
60   I do defy him, and I spit at him,
Call him a slanderous coward and a villain;
Which to maintain I would allow him odds,
And meet him, were I tied° to run afoot   *obliged*
Even to the frozen ridges of the Alps,
65   Or any other ground inhabitable,
Wherever Englishman durst set his foot.
Meantime let this defend my loyalty:
By all my hopes, most falsely doth he lie.
    BOLINGBROKE [*throwing down his gage*][7] Pale trembling coward,
        there I throw my gage,
70   Disclaiming here the kindred of[8] the King,
And lay aside my high blood's royalty,
Which fear, not reverence, makes thee to except.°   *set aside*
If guilty dread have left thee so much strength
As to take up mine honour's pawn,° then stoop.   *(the gage)*
75   By that, and all the rites of knighthood else,
Will I make good against thee, arm to arm,
What I have spoke or thou canst worse devise.
    MOWBRAY [*taking up the gage*] I take it up,[9] and by that sword I swear
    Which gently laid my knighthood on my shoulder,
80   I'll answer thee in any fair degree°
Or chivalrous design of knightly trial;   *honorable manner*
And when I mount, alive may I not light°
If I be traitor or unjustly fight!   *dismount*
    KING RICHARD [*to* BOLINGBROKE] What doth our cousin lay to
      Mowbray's charge?
85   It must be great that can inherit us°   *make us have*
So much as of a thought of ill in him.
    BOLINGBROKE Look what I speak, my life shall prove it true:
That Mowbray hath received eight thousand nobles°   *gold coins*
In name of lendings° for your highness' soldiers,   *As advances on pay*
90   The which he hath detained for lewd employments,°   *improper uses*
Like a false traitor and injurious villain.
Besides I say, and will in battle prove,
Or° here or elsewhere, to the furthest verge°   *Either / horizon*
That ever was surveyed by English eye,
95   That all the treasons for these eighteen years[1]
Complotted° and contrivèd in this land   *Plotted*
Fetch° from false Mowbray their first head° and spring.   *Derive / source*
Further I say, and further will maintain
Upon his bad life, to make all this good,

6. Bolingbroke as well as Richard was a grandson of Edward III.
7. Pledge to combat—probably a glove.
8. The privilege of kinship with.
9. Thereby accepting the challenge.
1. Since the Peasants' Revolt of 1381.

100   That he did plot the Duke of Gloucester's death,[2]
    Suggest° his soon-believing° adversaries,   *Incite / credulous*
    And consequently,° like a traitor-coward,   *subsequently*
    Sluiced° out his innocent soul through streams of blood;   *Let flow*
    Which blood, like sacrificing Abel's,[3] cries
105   Even from the tongueless caverns of the earth
    To me for justice and rough chastisement.
    And, by the glorious worth of my descent,
    This arm shall do it or this life be spent.
    KING RICHARD   How high a pitch[4] his resolution soars!
110   Thomas of Norfolk, what sayst thou to this?
    MOWBRAY   O, let my sovereign turn away his face,
    And bid his ears a little while be deaf,
    Till I have told this slander of his blood°   *disgrace to his ancestry*
    How God and good men hate so foul a liar!
115   KING RICHARD   Mowbray, impartial are our eyes and ears.
    Were he my brother, nay, my kingdom's heir,
    As he is but my father's brother's son,
    Now by my sceptre's awe I make a vow
    Such neighbour-nearness to our sacred blood
120   Should nothing privilege him, nor partialize°   *bias*
    The unstooping firmness of my upright soul.
    He is our subject, Mowbray; so art thou.
    Free speech and fearless I to thee allow.
    MOWBRAY   Then, Bolingbroke, as low as to thy heart
125   Through the false passage of thy throat thou liest!
    Three parts of that receipt° I had for Calais   *money received*
    Disbursed I duly to his highness' soldiers.
    The other part reserved I by consent,
    For that my sovereign liege was in my debt
130   Upon remainder of a dear account[5]
    Since last I went to France to fetch his queen.
    Now swallow down that lie. For Gloucester's death,
    I slew him not, but to my own disgrace
    Neglected my sworn duty in that case.[6]
135   For you, my noble lord of Lancaster,
    The honourable father to my foe,
    Once did I lay an ambush for your life,
    A trespass that doth vex my grievèd soul;
    But ere I last received the Sacrament
140   I did confess it, and exactly° begged   *expressly*
    Your grace's pardon, and I hope I had it.
    This is my fault. As for the rest appealed,°   *accused*
    It issues from the rancour of a villain,
    A recreant° and most degenerate° traitor,   *faithless / cowardly*
145   Which in myself° I boldly will defend,   *my own person*
        [*He throws down his gage*]
    And interchangeably° hurl down my gage   *reciprocally*

2. Thomas of Woodstock, Duke of Gloucester, was mysteriously murdered while in the custody of Mowbray. Richard had reason to hate him; earlier Woodstock had attempted to curtail the young King's power by placing authority in the hands of a royal council, of which Woodstock was the head.
3. In Genesis 4, Cain murders his brother Abel because God prefers Abel's offering of sheep to Cain's fruits of the ground.
4. Highest point of a falcon's flight.
5. For the balance of a large sum.
6. Mowbray is circumspect here; in the next scene, Gaunt and the Duchess assert less ambiguously that Richard ordered him to kill Woodstock.

Upon this overweening traitor's foot,
To prove myself a loyal gentleman
Even in the best blood chambered° in his bosom;   *enclosed*
150   In haste whereof° most heartily I pray   *To hasten which*
Your highness to assign our trial day.
       [BOLINGBROKE *takes up the gage*]
KING RICHARD   Wrath-kindled gentlemen, be ruled by me.
Let's purge this choler without letting blood.[7]
This we prescribe, though no physician:
155   Deep malice[8] makes too deep incision;
Forget, forgive, conclude,° and be agreed;   *come to terms*
Our doctors say this is no time to bleed.
Good uncle, let this end where it begun.
We'll calm the Duke of Norfolk, you your son.
160   JOHN OF GAUNT   To be a make-peace shall become my age.
Throw down, my son, the Duke of Norfolk's gage.[9]
KING RICHARD   And, Norfolk, throw down his.
JOHN OF GAUNT   When, Harry, when?
Obedience bids I should not bid again.
KING RICHARD   Norfolk, throw down! We bid; there is no boot.°   *help for it*
165   MOWBRAY [*kneeling*]   Myself I throw, dread sovereign, at thy foot.
My life thou shalt command, but not my shame.
The one my duty owes, but my fair name,
Despite of death that lives upon my grave,
To dark dishonour's use thou shalt not have.
170   I am disgraced, impeached, and baffled[1] here,
Pierced to the soul with slander's venomed spear,
The which no balm can cure but his heart blood
Which breathed° this poison.   *uttered*
KING RICHARD   Rage must be withstood.
Give me his gage. Lions make leopards tame.[2]
175   MOWBRAY [*standing*]   Yea, but not change his spots.[3] Take but my shame,
And I resign my gage. My dear dear lord,
The purest treasure mortal times° afford   *earthly lives*
Is spotless reputation; that away,
Men are but gilded loam, or painted clay.
180   A jewel in a ten-times barred-up chest
Is a bold spirit in a loyal breast.
Mine honour is my life. Both grow in one.°   *united*
Take honour from me, and my life is done.
Then, dear my liege, mine honour let me try.°   *put to the test*
185   In that I live, and for that will I die.
KING RICHARD   Cousin, throw down your gage. Do you begin.
BOLINGBROKE   O God defend my soul from such deep sin!
Shall I seem crest-fallen in my father's sight?
Or with pale beggar-fear impeach my height°   *disgrace my rank*
190   Before this out-dared dastard?° Ere my tongue   *coward*
Shall wound my honour with such feeble wrong,
Or sound so base a parle,° my teeth shall tear   *trumpet call for a truce*
The slavish motive° of recanting fear,   *instrument (the tongue)*

7. Let's expel the bile (thought to be the physiological cause of anger) without bloodletting (in combat; as a medical remedy).
8. Enmity; virulence (of a disease).
9. As a gesture of reconciliation.

1. Publicly stripped of knighthood (a chivalric term).
2. Lions were the King's emblem; leopards were Mowbray's. Heraldic banners are likely to be displayed onstage in this scene.
3. Leopard spots; stains of reproach.

And spit it bleeding in his° high disgrace   *its*
195 Where shame doth harbour, even in Mowbray's face.

                              Exit [JOHN OF] GAUNT

KING RICHARD   We were not born to sue, but to command;
Which since we cannot do to make you friends,
Be ready, as your lives shall answer it,
At Coventry upon Saint Lambert's day.°   *September 17*
200 There shall your swords and lances arbitrate
The swelling difference of your settled hate.
Since we cannot atone° you, we shall see   *reconcile*
Justice design the victor's chivalry.[4]
Lord Marshal, command our officers-at-arms
205 Be ready to direct these home alarms.°   *Exeunt*   *domestic disturbances*

1.2

    Enter JOHN OF GAUNT [*Duke of Lancaster*], *with* DUCH-
    ESS OF GLOUCESTER

JOHN OF GAUNT   Alas, the part I had in Gloucester's blood[1]
Doth more solicit me than your exclaims°   *exclamations*
To stir against the butchers of his life.
But since correction lieth in[2] those hands
5 Which made the fault that we cannot correct,
Put we our quarrel to the will of heaven,
Who, when they see the hours ripe on earth,
Will rain hot vengeance on offenders' heads.
DUCHESS OF GLOUCESTER   Finds brotherhood in thee no sharper spur?
10 Hath love in thy old blood no living fire?
Edward's° seven sons, whereof thyself art one,   *Edward III's*
Were as seven vials of his sacred blood,
Or seven fair branches springing from one root.
Some of those seven are dried by nature's course,
15 Some of those branches by the destinies cut;
But Thomas, my dear lord, my life, my Gloucester,
One vial full of Edward's sacred blood,
One flourishing branch of his most royal root,
Is cracked, and all the precious liquor spilt;
20 Is hacked down, and his summer leaves all faded
By envy's° hand and murder's bloody axe.   *hatred's*
Ah, Gaunt, his blood was thine! That bed, that womb,
That mettle,° that self° mould that fashioned thee,   *substance / same*
Made him a man; and though thou liv'st and breathest,
25 Yet art thou slain in him. Thou dost consent
In some large measure to thy father's death
In that thou seest thy wretched brother die,
Who was the model of thy father's life.
Call it not patience, Gaunt, it is despair.
30 In suff'ring thus thy brother to be slaughtered
Thou show'st the naked° pathway to thy life,   *defenseless; obvious*
Teaching stern murder how to butcher thee.
That which in mean° men we entitle patience   *common*
Is pale cold cowardice in noble breasts.

---

4. Indicate the victor in knightly combat.
1.2 Location: John of Gaunt's house.
1. Thomas of Woodstock, Duke of Gloucester, was

Gaunt's younger brother.
2. Since punishment depends on (Gaunt blames Richard for Woodstock's death).

35   What shall I say? To safeguard thine own life
        The best way is to venge° my Gloucester's death.   *avenge*
  JOHN OF GAUNT   God's is the quarrel; for God's substitute,
        His deputy anointed in his sight,
        Hath caused his death; the which if wrongfully,
40   Let heaven revenge, for I may never lift
        An angry arm against his minister.°   *agent*
  DUCHESS OF GLOUCESTER   Where then, alas, may I complain myself?
  JOHN OF GAUNT   To God, the widow's champion and defence.
  DUCHESS OF GLOUCESTER   Why then, I will. Farewell, old Gaunt.
45   Thou goest to Coventry, there to behold
        Our cousin° Hereford and fell° Mowbray fight.   *kinsman / ruthless*
        O, set my husband's wrongs on Hereford's spear,
        That it may enter butcher Mowbray's breast!
        Or if misfortune miss the first career,[3]
50   Be Mowbray's sins so heavy in his bosom
        That they may break his foaming courser's back
        And throw the rider headlong in the lists,
        A caitiff,° recreant° to my cousin Hereford!   *A wretch / yielding*
        Farewell, old Gaunt. Thy sometimes° brother's wife   *former*
55   With her companion, grief, must end her life.
  JOHN OF GAUNT   Sister, farewell. I must to Coventry.
        As much good stay with thee as go with me.
  DUCHESS OF GLOUCESTER   Yet one word more. Grief boundeth[4]
           where it falls,
        Not with the empty hollowness, but weight.[5]
60   I take my leave before I have begun,
        For sorrow ends not when it seemeth done.
        Commend me to thy brother, Edmund York.
        Lo, this is all.—Nay, yet depart not so!
        Though this be all, do not so quickly go.
65   I shall remember more. Bid him—ah, what?—
        With all good speed at Pleshey[6] visit me.
        Alack, and what shall good old York there see
        But empty lodgings° and unfurnished walls,   *rooms*
        Unpeopled offices,° untrodden stones,   *servants' quarters*
70   And what hear there for welcome but my groans?
        Therefore commend me; let him not come there
        To seek out sorrow that dwells everywhere.
        Desolate, desolate will I hence and die.
        The last leave of thee takes my weeping eye. *Exeunt [severally]°*   *separately*

1.3

Enter LORD MARSHAL *[with officers setting out
chairs], and Duke [of]* AUMERLE
  LORD MARSHAL   My lord Aumerle, is Harry Hereford armed?
  AUMERLE   Yea, at all points,° and longs to enter in.   *completely*
  LORD MARSHAL   The Duke of Norfolk, sprightfully° and bold,   *spiritedly*
        Stays° but the summons of the appellant's° trumpet.   *Awaits / accuser's*
5   AUMERLE   Why then, the champions are prepared, and stay
        For nothing but his majesty's approach.

---

3. If (Mowbray's) downfall fail to occur at the first encounter.
4. Rebounds (causing further sound; the Duchess apologizes for continuing to speak).
5. Not because it is hollow, like a bouncing ball, but because it is heavy.
6. Gloucester's house in Essex.
1.3 Location: The lists (tournament arena) at Coventry.

The trumpets sound, and KING [RICHARD] *enters with*
[JOHN OF] GAUNT, BUSHY, BAGOT, GREEN, *and other*
nobles. When they are set, enter MOWBRAY *Duke of Nor-*
folk, defendant, in arms, and a HERALD [*to Mowbray*]

KING RICHARD   Marshal, demand of yonder champion
The cause of his arrival here in arms.
Ask him his name, and orderly° proceed   *according to the rules*
10 To swear him in the justice of his cause.
LORD MARSHAL [*to* MOWBRAY]   In God's name and the King's,
    say who thou art,
And why thou com'st thus knightly clad in arms,
Against what man thou com'st, and what thy quarrel.
Speak truly on thy knighthood and thy oath,
15 As so defend thee heaven and thy valour!
MOWBRAY   My name is Thomas Mowbray, Duke of Norfolk,
Who hither come engagèd by my oath—
Which God defend° a knight should violate—   *forbid*
Both to defend my loyalty and truth
20 To God, my king, and my succeeding issue,
Against the Duke of Hereford that appeals me;
And by the grace of God and this mine arm
To prove him, in defending of myself,
A traitor to my God, my king, and me.
25 And as I truly fight, defend me heaven!
     [*He sits.*]
      The trumpets sound. Enter [BOLINGBROKE] *Duke of*
      Hereford, appellant, in armour, and HERALD
KING RICHARD   Marshal, ask yonder knight in arms
Both who he is and why he cometh hither
Thus plated in habiliments of war;[1]
And formally, according to our law,
30 Depose° him in the justice of his cause.   *Take testimony from*
LORD MARSHAL [*to* BOLINGBROKE]   What is thy name? And
    wherefore com'st thou hither
Before King Richard in his royal lists?
Against whom comest thou? And what's thy quarrel?
Speak like a true knight, so defend thee heaven!
35 BOLINGBROKE   Harry of Hereford, Lancaster, and Derby
Am I, who ready here do stand in arms
To prove by God's grace and my body's valour
In lists on Thomas Mowbray, Duke of Norfolk,
That he is a traitor foul and dangerous
40 To God of heaven, King Richard, and to me.
And as I truly fight, defend me heaven!
     [*He sits*]
LORD MARSHAL   On pain of death, no person be so bold
Or daring-hardy as to touch the lists
Except the Marshal and such officers
45 Appointed to direct these fair designs.°   *procedures*
BOLINGBROKE [*standing*]   Lord Marshal, let me kiss my sovereign's hand
And bow my knee before his majesty,
For Mowbray and myself are like two men
That vow a long and weary pilgrimage;

---

1. Wearing plated battle armor.

50   Then let us take a ceremonious leave
        And loving farewell of our several° friends.   *respective*
LORD MARSHAL [*to* KING RICHARD]   The appellant in all duty
        greets your highness,
        And craves to kiss your hand and take his leave.
KING RICHARD   We will descend and fold him in our arms.
        [*He descends from his seat and embraces* BOLINGBROKE]
55   Cousin of Hereford, as° thy cause is just,   *insofar as*
        So be thy fortune in this royal fight.
        Farewell, my blood, which if today thou shed,
        Lament we may, but not revenge thee dead.
BOLINGBROKE   O, let no noble eye profane° a tear   *misuse*
60   For me if I be gored with Mowbray's spear.
        As confident as is the falcon's flight
        Against a bird do I with Mowbray fight.
        [*To the* LORD MARSHAL] My loving lord, I take my leave of you;
        [*To* AUMERLE] Of you, my noble cousin, Lord Aumerle;
65   Not sick, although I have to do with death,
        But lusty,° young, and cheerly drawing breath.   *vigorous*
        Lo, as at English feasts, so I regreet°   *greet*
        The daintiest[2] last, to make the end most sweet.
        [*To* GAUNT, *kneeling*] O thou, the earthly author of my blood,
70   Whose youthful spirit in me regenerate°   *reborn*
        Doth with a two-fold vigour lift me up
        To reach at victory above my head,
        Add proof° unto mine armour with thy prayers,   *invulnerability*
        And with thy blessings steel° my lance's point,   *harden*
75   That it may enter Mowbray's waxen° coat   *(that is, soft)*
        And furbish new the name of John a Gaunt
        Even in the lusty haviour° of his son.   *conduct*
JOHN OF GAUNT   God in thy good cause make thee prosperous!
        Be swift like lightning in the execution,
80   And let thy blows, doubly redoublèd,
        Fall like amazing° thunder on the casque°   *stupefying / helmet*
        Of thy adverse pernicious enemy.
        Rouse up thy youthful blood, be valiant, and live.
BOLINGBROKE [*standing*]   Mine innocence and Saint George to
        thrive!
85 MOWBRAY [*standing*]   However God or fortune cast my lot,
        There lives or dies, true to King Richard's throne,
        A loyal, just, and upright gentleman.
        Never did captive with a freer heart
        Cast off his chains of bondage and embrace
90   His golden uncontrolled enfranchisement°   *unrestrained liberation*
        More than my dancing soul doth celebrate
        This feast of battle with mine adversary.
        Most mighty liege, and my companion peers,
        Take from my mouth the wish of happy years.
95   As gentle and as jocund as to jest°   *take part in revels*
        Go I to fight. Truth hath a quiet breast.
KING RICHARD   Farewell, my lord. Securely° I espy   *Confidently*
        Virtue with valour couchèd[3] in thine eye. —
        Order the trial, Marshal, and begin.

---

2. Finest thing, like a dessert.   3. Lodged; aimed in readiness (like a lance).

100   LORD MARSHAL   Harry of Hereford, Lancaster, and Derby,
      Receive thy lance; and God defend the right!
        [*An officer bears a lance to* BOLINGBROKE]
      BOLINGBROKE   Strong as a tower in hope, I cry 'Amen!'°   *from Psalms 61:3*
      LORD MARSHAL [*to an officer*]   Go bear this lance to Thomas,
      Duke of Norfolk.
        [*An officer bears a lance to* MOWBRAY]
      FIRST HERALD   Harry of Hereford, Lancaster, and Derby
105   Stands here for God, his sovereign, and himself,
      On pain to be found false and recreant,
      To prove the Duke of Norfolk, Thomas Mowbray,
      A traitor to his God, his king, and him,
      And dares him to set forward to the fight.
110   SECOND HERALD   Here standeth Thomas Mowbray, Duke of Norfolk,
      On pain to be found false and recreant,
      Both to defend himself and to approve°   *prove*
      Henry of Hereford, Lancaster, and Derby
      To God his sovereign and to him disloyal,
115   Courageously and with a free desire
      Attending but the signal to begin.
      LORD MARSHAL   Sound trumpets, and set forward combatants!
        [*A charge is sounded.*]
        [KING RICHARD *throws down his warder*]°   *staff*
      Stay, the King hath thrown his warder down.
      KING RICHARD   Let them lay by their helmets and their spears,
120   And both return back to their chairs again.
        [BOLINGBROKE *and* MOWBRAY *disarm and sit*]
      [*To the nobles*] Withdraw with us, and let the trumpets sound
      While we return° these dukes what we decree.   *Until we deliver to*
        A long flourish° [*during which* KING RICHARD *and his*   *extended trumpet call*
        nobles withdraw and hold council, then come forward.
        KING RICHARD *addresses* BOLINGBROKE *and* MOWBRAY]
      Draw near, and list what with our council we have done.
      For that° our kingdom's earth should not be soiled   *Because*
125   With that dear blood which it hath fosterèd,
      And for° our eyes do hate the dire aspect°   *because / spectacle*
      Of civil wounds ploughed up with neighbours' swords,[4]
127.1   *And for we think the eagle-wingèd pride*
         Of sky-aspiring and ambitious thoughts
         With rival-hating envy set on you°   *malice set you on*
         To wake our peace, which in our country's cradle
127.5   *Draws the sweet infant breath of gentle sleep,*
      Which, so roused up with boist'rous untuned drums,
      With harsh-resounding trumpets' dreadful bray,
130   And grating shock of wrathful iron arms,
      Might from our quiet confines fright fair peace
      And make us wade even in our kindred's blood,
      Therefore we banish you our territories.
      You, cousin Hereford, upon pain° of life,   *loss*
135   Till twice five summers have enriched our fields
      Shall not regreet° our fair dominions,   *greet again*
      But tread the stranger° paths of banishment.   *foreign*

---

4. The following indented passage (lines 127.1–127.5)   it as part of his limited revisions to the text.
appears in Q1 but not in F. Shakespeare probably deleted

BOLINGBROKE   Your will be done. This must my comfort be:
That sun that warms you here shall shine on me,
140   And those his golden beams to you here lent
Shall point on me and gild my banishment.
KING RICHARD   Norfolk, for thee remains a heavier doom,°   *sentence*
Which I with some unwillingness pronounce.
The sly° slow hours shall not determinate°   *stealthy / bring to an end*
145   The dateless limit° of thy dear° exile.   *limitless period / grievous*
The hopeless word of 'never to return'
Breathe I against thee, upon pain of life.
MOWBRAY   A heavy sentence, my most sovereign liege,
And all unlooked-for from your highness' mouth.
150   A dearer merit,° not so deep a maim°   *better reward / an injury*
As to be cast forth in the common air,
Have I deservèd at your highness' hands.
The language I have learnt these forty years,
My native English, now I must forgo,
155   And now my tongue's use is to me no more
Than an unstringèd viol° or a harp,   *six-stringed instrument*
Or like a cunning° instrument cased up,   *skillfully made*
Or, being open, put into his hands
That knows no touch to tune the harmony.
160   Within my mouth you have enjailed my tongue,
Doubly portcullised° with my teeth and lips,   *Shut in by an iron gate*
And dull unfeeling barren ignorance
Is made my jailer to attend on me.
I am too old to fawn upon a nurse,
165   Too far in years to be a pupil now.
What is thy sentence then but speechless death,
Which robs my tongue from breathing native breath?
KING RICHARD   It boots° thee not to be compassionate.°   *helps / sorrowful*
After our sentence, plaining° comes too late.   *lamenting*
170   MOWBRAY   Then thus I turn me from my country's light,
To dwell in solemn shades of endless night.
KING RICHARD   Return again, and take an oath with thee.
[*To both*] Lay on our royal sword your banished hands.
Swear by the duty that you owe to God—
175   Our part therein⁵ we banish with yourselves—
To keep the oath that we administer.
You never shall, so help you truth and God,
Embrace each other's love in banishment,
Nor never look upon each other's face,
180   Nor never write, regreet, nor reconcile
This low'ring tempest of your home-bred hate,
Nor never by advisèd° purpose meet   *deliberated*
To plot, contrive, or complot any ill
'Gainst us, our state, our subjects, or our land.
BOLINGBROKE   I swear.
185   MOWBRAY   And I, to keep all this.
BOLINGBROKE   Norfolk, so far as to mine enemy:
By this time, had the King permitted us,
One of our souls had wandered in the air,

5. Your allegiance to me as God's deputy.

Banished this frail sepulchre of our flesh,
190 As now our flesh is banished from this land.
Confess thy treasons ere thou fly the realm.
Since thou hast far to go, bear not along
The clogging° burden of a guilty soul.   *encumbering*
MOWBRAY   No, Bolingbroke, if ever I were traitor,
195 My name be blotted from the book of life,°   *eternal life*
And I from heaven banished as from hence.
But what thou art, God, thou, and I do know,
And all too soon I fear the King shall rue.
Farewell, my liege. Now no way can I stray:°   *lose my way*
200 Save back to England, all the world's my way.   *Exit*
KING RICHARD   Uncle, even in the glasses° of thine eyes   *windows*
I see thy grievèd heart. Thy sad aspect°   *appearance*
Hath from the number of his banished years
Plucked four away. [*To* BOLINGBROKE] Six frozen winters spent,
205 Return with welcome home from banishment.
BOLINGBROKE   How long a time lies in one little word!
Four lagging winters and four wanton° springs   *luxuriant*
End in a word: such is the breath of kings.
JOHN OF GAUNT   I thank my liege that in regard of me
210 He shortens four years of my son's exile.
But little vantage° shall I reap thereby,   *profit*
For ere the six years that he hath to spend
Can change their moons and bring their times about,
My oil-dried lamp and time-bewasted° light   *extinguished by time*
215 Shall be extinct with age and endless night.
My inch of taper will be burnt and done,
And blindfold⁶ death not let me see my son.
KING RICHARD   Why, uncle, thou hast many years to live.
JOHN OF GAUNT   But not a minute, King, that thou canst give.
220 Shorten my days thou canst with sudden sorrow,
And pluck nights from me, but not lend a morrow.
Thou canst help time to furrow me with age,
But stop no wrinkle in his pilgrimage.
Thy word is current° with him for my death,   *valid*
225 But dead, thy kingdom cannot buy my breath.
KING RICHARD   Thy son is banished upon good advice,
Whereto thy tongue a party verdict⁷ gave.
Why at our justice seem'st thou then to lour?°   *frown*
JOHN OF GAUNT   Things sweet to taste prove in digestion sour.
230 You urged me as a judge, but I had rather
You would have bid me argue like a father.
Alas, I looked when° some of you should say   *I expected that*
I was too strict to make mine own away,
But you gave leave to my unwilling tongue
235 Against my will to do myself this wrong.⁸
235.1 *O, had't been a stranger, not my child,*
To smooth° his fault I should have been more mild.   *To gloss over*
A partial slander° sought I to avoid,   *A suspicion of partiality*
And in the sentence my own life destroyed.

---

6. Because death's emblem is a hooded figure or an eyeless skull, and because the dead cannot see.
7. A share in the joint verdict.

8. The following indented passage (lines 235.1–235.4)
appears only in Q1.

KING RICHARD   Cousin, farewell; and uncle, bid him so.
Six years we banish him, and he shall go.
Flourish. Exeunt [all but AUMERLE, *the* LORD MARSHAL,
JOHN OF GAUNT, *and* BOLINGBROKE]
AUMERLE [*to* BOLINGBROKE]   Cousin, farewell. What presence
must not know,[9]
From where you do remain° let paper show.   [*Exit*]   stay
LORD MARSHAL [*to* BOLINGBROKE]   My lord, no leave take I, for I
240   will ride
As far as land will let me by your side.
JOHN OF GAUNT [*to* BOLINGBROKE]   O, to what purpose dost
thou hoard thy words,
That thou return'st no greeting to thy friends?
BOLINGBROKE   I have too few to take my leave of you,
245   When the tongue's office° should be prodigal   function
To breathe the abundant dolour of the heart.
JOHN OF GAUNT   Thy grief is but thy absence for a time.
BOLINGBROKE   Joy absent, grief is present for that time.
JOHN OF GAUNT   What is six winters? They are quickly gone.
250   BOLINGBROKE   To men in joy, but grief makes one hour ten.
JOHN OF GAUNT   Call it a travel that thou tak'st for pleasure.
BOLINGBROKE   My heart will sigh when I miscall it so,
Which finds it an enforcèd pilgrimage.
JOHN OF GAUNT   The sullen passage of thy weary steps
255   Esteem as foil[1] wherein thou art to set
The precious jewel of thy home return.[2]
256.1   BOLINGBROKE   *Nay, rather every tedious stride I make*
Will but remember° what a deal° of world   remind me / an extent
I wander from the jewels that I love.
Must I not serve a long apprenticehood
256.5   *To foreign passages, and in the end,*
Having my freedom, boast of nothing else
But that I was a journeyman[3] to grief?
JOHN OF GAUNT   *All places that the eye of heaven° visits*   sun; God's presence
Are to a wise man ports and happy havens.
256.10   *Teach thy necessity to reason thus;*
There is no virtue like necessity.
Think not the King did banish thee,
But thou the King. Woe doth the heavier sit
Where it perceives it is but faintly° borne.   faintheartedly
256.15   *Go, say I sent thee forth to purchase° honour,*   acquire
And not the King exiled thee; or suppose
Devouring pestilence hangs in our air
And thou art flying to a fresher clime.
Look what° thy soul holds dear, imagine it   Whatever
256.20   *To lie that way thou goest, not whence thou com'st.*
Suppose the singing birds musicians,
The grass whereon thou tread'st the presence strewed,[4]
The flowers fair ladies, and thy steps no more
Than a delightful measure° or a dance;   a stately dance

---

9. What you cannot tell me personally because of your
absence.
1. Thin metal against which jewels were set to enhance
their luster.

2. The following indented passage (lines 256.1–256.26)
appears only in Q1.
3. Person who has finished an apprenticeship.
4. The royal presence chamber strewn with rushes.

256.25 *For gnarling° sorrow hath less power to bite*   snarling
        The man that mocks at it and sets it light.°   values it lightly
        BOLINGBROKE   O, who can hold a fire in his hand
        By thinking on the frosty Caucasus,[5]
        Or cloy the hungry edge of appetite
260   By bare imagination of a feast,
        Or wallow naked in December snow
        By thinking on fantastic° summer's heat?   imagined
        O no, the apprehension of the good
        Gives but the greater feeling to the worse.
265   Fell sorrow's tooth doth never rankle° more   irritate
        Than when he bites, but lanceth[6] not the sore.
        JOHN OF GAUNT   Come, come, my son, I'll bring thee on thy way.
        Had I thy youth and cause, I would not stay.°   linger
        BOLINGBROKE   Then England's ground, farewell. Sweet soil, adieu,
270   My mother and my nurse that bears me yet!
        Where'er I wander, boast of this I can:
        Though banished, yet a trueborn Englishman.   *Exeunt*

1.4

        Enter KING [RICHARD] *with* GREEN *and* BAGOT *at one*
        door, and the Lord AUMERLE *at another*
        KING RICHARD   We did observe.[1]—Cousin Aumerle,
        How far brought you high Hereford on his way?
        AUMERLE   I brought high Hereford, if you call him so,
        But to the next highway, and there I left him.
5   KING RICHARD   And say, what store of parting tears were shed?
        AUMERLE   Faith, none for me,° except the north-east wind,   my part
        Which then grew bitterly against our faces,
        Awaked the sleeping rheum,° and so by chance   tears
        Did grace our hollow parting with a tear.
10   KING RICHARD   What said our cousin when you parted with him?
        AUMERLE   'Farewell.' And for° my heart disdainèd that my tongue   because
        Should so profane the word, that[2] taught me craft
        To counterfeit oppression of such grief
        That words seemed buried in my sorrow's grave.
15   Marry,° would the word 'farewell' have lengthened hours   Indeed
        And added years to his short banishment,
        He should have had a volume of farewells;
        But since it would not, he had none of me.
        KING RICHARD   He is our cousin, cousin;[3] but 'tis doubt,
20   When time shall call him home from banishment,
        Whether our kinsman come to see his friends.°   relatives
        Ourself and Bushy, Bagot here, and Green
        Observed his courtship to the common people,
        How he did seem to dive into their hearts
25   With humble and familiar courtesy,
        What reverence he did throw away on slaves,
        Wooing poor craftsmen with the craft of smiles
        And patient underbearing° of his fortune,   enduring

---

5. Mountain range between the Black and Caspian Seas.
6. Probes (to release the pus from an abscess).
1.4 Location: The court.
1. The scene begins in mid-conversation; the King is
replying to a remark by Bagot or Green.

2. His heart. Unwilling to give Hereford good wishes
insincerely, Aumerle pretends to be overwhelmed with
grief.
3. Richard, Bolingbroke, and Aumerle were sons of three
brothers.

As 'twere to banish their affects with him.[4]

30   Off goes his bonnet° to an oysterwench.   *cap*

A brace of draymen° bid God speed him well,   *A couple of cart drivers*

And had the tribute of his supple knee

With 'Thanks, my countrymen, my loving friends',

As were our England in reversion[5] his,

35   And he our subjects' next degree in hope.

GREEN   Well, he is gone, and with him go these thoughts.

Now for the rebels which stand out in Ireland.

Expedient manage° must be made, my liege,   *Hasty arrangements*

Ere further leisure yield them further means

40   For their advantage and your highness' loss.

KING RICHARD   We will ourself in person to this war,

And for° our coffers with too great a court   *because*

And liberal largess are grown somewhat light,

We are enforced to farm our royal realm,[6]

45   The revenue whereof shall furnish us

For our affairs in hand. If that come short,

Our substitutes° at home shall have blank charters,[7]   *deputies*

Whereto, when they shall know what men are rich,

They shall subscribe them° for large sums of gold,   *write down their names*

50   And send them after to supply our wants;

For we will make for Ireland presently.°   *at once*

        Enter BUSHY

Bushy, what news?

BUSHY   Old John of Gaunt is grievous sick, my lord,

Suddenly taken, and hath sent post-haste

55   To entreat your majesty to visit him.

KING RICHARD   Where lies he?

BUSHY   At Ely House.

KING RICHARD   Now put it, God, in his physician's mind

To help him to his grave immediately.

60   The lining[8] of his coffers shall make coats

To deck our soldiers for these Irish wars.

Come, gentlemen, let's all go visit him.

Pray God we may make haste and come too late!   *Exeunt*

2.1

Enter JOHN OF GAUNT [*Duke of Lancaster*], *sick,* [*carried*
in a chair,] *with Duke of* YORK

JOHN OF GAUNT   Will the King come, that I may breathe my last

In wholesome counsel to his unstaid° youth?   *unruly*

YORK   Vex not yourself, nor strive not with your breath,

For all in vain comes counsel to his ear.

5   JOHN OF GAUNT   O, but they say the tongues of dying men

Enforce attention, like deep harmony.

Where words are scarce they are seldom spent in vain,

For they breathe truth that breathe their words in pain.

He that no more must say is listened more

10   Than they whom youth and ease have taught to glose.°   *talk speciously*

---

4. As if taking their affections with him into exile.
5. A legal term for property that reverts to the original owner on the expiring of a contract.
6. To lease the King's right to tax.
7. Documents enabling the King to raise money by

forced loans; the deputies can fill in the blanks with any amount they see fit.
8. Contents (playing on "lining cloth").
2.1 Location: Ely House.

More are men's ends marked than their lives before.
 The setting sun, and music at the close,
As the last taste of sweets, is sweetest last,
Writ in remembrance more than things long past.
15 Though Richard my life's counsel would not hear,
My death's sad tale may yet undeaf his ear.
YORK No, it is stopped with other, flattering sounds,
As praises of whose taste the wise are feared,°   *wary*
Lascivious metres to whose venom sound
20 The open ear of youth doth always listen,
Report of fashions in proud Italy,
Whose manners still° our tardy-apish[1] nation   *always*
Limps after in base imitation.
Where doth the world thrust forth a vanity —
25 So° it be new there's no respect° how vile —   *Provided / regard for*
That is not quickly buzzed into his ears?
Then all too late comes counsel, to be heard
Where will doth mutiny with wit's regard.[2]
Direct not him whose way himself will choose:
30 'Tis breath thou lack'st, and that breath wilt thou lose.
JOHN OF GAUNT Methinks I am a prophet new-inspired,
And thus, expiring, do foretell of him.
His rash, fierce blaze of riot° cannot last,   *wastefulness*
For violent fires soon burn out themselves.
35 Small showers last long, but sudden storms are short.
He tires betimes° that spurs too fast betimes.   *soon*
With eager feeding food doth choke the feeder.
Light vanity, insatiate cormorant,[3]
Consuming means, soon preys upon itself.
40 This royal throne of kings, this sceptred isle,
This earth of majesty, this seat of Mars,°   *war god's dwelling*
This other Eden, demi-paradise,
This fortress built by nature for herself
Against infection° and the hand of war,   *disease; depravity*
45 This happy breed of men, this little world,
This precious stone set in the silver sea,
Which serves it in the office° of a wall,   *function*
Or as a moat defensive to a house
Against the envy° of less happier lands;   *malice*
50 This blessèd plot, this earth, this realm, this England,
This nurse, this teeming womb of royal kings,
Feared by their breed[4] and famous by their birth,
Renownèd for their deeds as far from home
For Christian service and true chivalry[5]
55 As is the sepulchre, in stubborn Jewry,[6]
Of the world's ransom, blessèd Mary's son;
This land of such dear souls, this dear dear land,
Dear for her reputation through the world,
Is now leased out — I die pronouncing it —
60 Like to a tenement° or pelting° farm. *rental property / worthless*
England, bound in with the triumphant sea,

1. Imitative but outmoded.
2. Where willfulness overthrows sound judgment.
3. Glutton (literally, a bird that swallows fish whole).
4. For their inherited valor.
5. Alluding to the English kings' accomplishments in the Crusades.
6. Judea, stubborn in its resistance to Christianity.

Whose rocky shore beats back the envious siege
Of wat'ry Neptune, is now bound in with shame,
With inky blots and rotten parchment bonds.[7]
65   That England that was wont to conquer others
Hath made a shameful conquest of itself.
Ah, would the scandal vanish with my life,
How happy then were my ensuing death!

> *Enter* KING [RICHARD], QUEEN, [*Duke of*] AUMERLE,
> BUSHY, GREEN, BAGOT, [*Lord*] ROSS, *and* [*Lord*] WIL-
> LOUGHBY

YORK   The King is come. Deal mildly with his youth,
70   For young hot colts, being reined, do rage the more.
QUEEN   How fares our noble uncle Lancaster?
KING RICHARD   What comfort, man? How is't with agèd Gaunt?
JOHN OF GAUNT   O, how that name befits my composition!°   *constitution*
  Old Gaunt indeed, and gaunt in being old.
75   Within me grief hath kept a tedious fast,
  And who abstains from meat° that is not gaunt?   *food*
  For sleeping England long time have I watched.°   *stayed awake*
  Watching breeds leanness, leanness is all gaunt.
  The pleasure that some fathers feed upon
80   Is my strict fast: I mean my children's looks.[8]
  And therein fasting, hast thou made me gaunt.
  Gaunt am I for the grave, gaunt as a grave,
  Whose hollow womb inherits naught but bones.
KING RICHARD   Can sick men play so nicely° with their names?   *subtly*
85 JOHN OF GAUNT   No, misery makes sport to mock itself.
  Since thou dost seek to kill my name in me,[9]
  I mock my name, great King, to flatter thee.
KING RICHARD   Should dying men flatter with those that live?
JOHN OF GAUNT   No, no, men living flatter those that die.
90 KING RICHARD   Thou now a-dying sayst thou flatt'rest me.
JOHN OF GAUNT   O no: thou diest, though I the sicker be.
KING RICHARD   I am in health; I breathe, and see thee ill.
JOHN OF GAUNT   Now He that made me knows I see thee ill:
  Ill in myself to see, and in thee seeing ill.[1]
95   Thy deathbed is no lesser than thy land,
  Wherein thou liest in reputation sick;
  And thou, too careless patient as thou art,
  Committ'st thy anointed body to the cure
  Of those physicians[2] that first wounded thee.
100   A thousand flatterers sit within thy crown,
  Whose compass° is no bigger than thy head,   *circumference*
  And yet, encagèd in so small a verge,[3]
  The waste[4] is no whit lesser than thy land.
  O, had thy grandsire with a prophet's eye
105   Seen how his son's son should destroy his sons,
  From forth° thy reach he would have laid thy shame,   *out of*
  Deposing thee before thou wert possessed,[5]
  Which art possessed° now to depose thyself.   *in a diabolical frenzy*

7. Richard's "blank charters."
8. Since Bolingbroke is exiled.
9. Destroy my family (by exiling Bolingbroke).
1. Too ill to see well, and seeing evil in you.
2. Richard's favorites, or his own bad impulses.

3. Area; distance of twelve miles around the court, to which special rules applied.
4. Destruction (specifically, injury done to a property by a tenant); waist, narrowest part.
5. In possession of the crown.

Why, cousin,° wert thou regent° of the world   *kinsman / ruler*
110   It were a shame to let this land by lease.
But, for thy world, enjoying but this land,[6]
Is it not more than shame to shame it so?
Landlord of England art thou now, not king.
Thy state of law[7] is bondslave to the law,
115   And—
KING RICHARD   And thou, a lunatic lean-witted fool,
Presuming on an ague's privilege,°   *the privilege of the sick*
Dar'st with thy frozen° admonition   *rigid; caused by a chill*
Make pale our cheek, chasing the royal blood
120   With fury from his native residence.°   *its natural place*
Now by my seat's° right royal majesty,   *throne's*
Wert thou not brother to great Edward's son,[8]
This tongue that runs so roundly° in thy head   *freely*
Should run thy head from thy unreverent shoulders.
125   JOHN OF GAUNT   O, spare me not, my brother Edward's son,
For that I was his father Edward's son.
That blood already, like the pelican,[9]
Hast thou tapped out[1] and drunkenly caroused.
My brother Gloucester, plain well-meaning soul—
130   Whom fair befall in heaven 'mongst happy souls—
May be a precedent and witness good
That thou respect'st not spilling° Edward's blood.   *don't hesitate to spill*
Join with the present sickness that I have,
And thy unkindness be like crookèd age,
135   To crop° at once a too-long withered flower.   *cut*
Live in thy shame, but die not shame with thee.[2]
These words hereafter thy tormentors be.
[*To attendants*] Convey me to my bed, then to my grave.
Love they to live that love and honour have.
Exit [*carried in a chair*]
140   KING RICHARD   And let them die that age and sullens° have,   *sulks*
For both hast thou, and both become the grave.
YORK   I do beseech your majesty impute his words
To wayward sickliness and age in him.
He loves you, on my life, and holds you dear
145   As Harry Duke of Hereford, were he here.
KING RICHARD   Right, you say true: as Hereford's love, so his.[3]
As theirs, so mine; and all be as it is.
Enter [*Earl of*] NORTHUMBERLAND
NORTHUMBERLAND   My liege, old Gaunt commends him to your majesty.
KING RICHARD   What says he?
NORTHUMBERLAND   Nay, nothing: all is said.
150   His tongue is now a stringless instrument.
Words, life, and all, old Lancaster hath spent.
YORK   Be York the next that must be bankrupt so!
Though death be poor, it ends a mortal woe.
KING RICHARD   The ripest fruit first falls, and so doth he.

6. Since this realm alone constitutes your world.
7. Legal status (as landlord, not King).
8. Edward the Black Prince, Edward III's son and Richard's father.
9. A mother pelican was thought to wound her breast so her ungrateful young could feed on her blood.

1. Let run as from a barrel tap.
2. May your shame outlive you.
3. York claims that Gaunt loves Richard as much as he loves his own son; Richard deliberately misconstrues York to mean Gaunt loves Richard as much as Hereford does.

155 His time is spent; our pilgrimage must be.°   *continue*
So much for that. Now for our Irish wars.
We must supplant those rough rug-headed kerns,[4]
Which live like venom where no venom else
But only they have privilege to live.[5]
160 And for° these great affairs do ask some charge,[6]   *because*
Towards our assistance we do seize to us
The plate, coin, revenues, and movables°   *personal property*
Whereof our uncle Gaunt did stand possessed.

YORK   How long shall I be patient? Ah, how long
165 Shall tender° duty make me suffer wrong?   *scrupulous*
Not Gloucester's death, nor Hereford's banishment,
Nor Gaunt's rebukes, nor England's private wrongs,[7]
Nor the prevention of poor Bolingbroke
About his marriage,[8] nor my own disgrace,
170 Have ever made me sour my patient cheek,
Or bend one wrinkle° on my sovereign's face.   *one frown*
I am the last of noble Edward's sons,
Of whom thy father, Prince of Wales, was first.
In war was never lion raged more fierce,
175 In peace was never gentle lamb more mild,
Than was that young and princely gentleman.
His face thou hast, for even so looked he,
Accomplished with the number of thy hours.°   *When he was your age*
But when he frowned it was against the French,
180 And not against his friends. His noble hand
Did win what he did spend, and spent not that
Which his triumphant father's hand had won.
His hands were guilty of no kindred blood,
But bloody with the enemies of his kin.
185 O, Richard, York is too far gone with grief,
Or else he never would compare between.

KING RICHARD   Why uncle, what's the matter?
YORK   O my liege,
Pardon me if you please; if not, I, pleased
Not to be pardoned, am content withal.°   *nevertheless*
190 Seek you to seize and grip into your hands
The royalties[9] and rights of banished Hereford?
Is not Gaunt dead? And doth not Hereford live?
Was not Gaunt just? And is not Harry true?
Did not the one deserve to have an heir?
195 Is not his heir a well-deserving son?
Take Hereford's rights away, and take from Time
His° charters and his customary rights: *Its*
Let not tomorrow then ensue° today;   *follow*
Be not thyself, for how art thou a king
200 But by fair sequence and succession?
Now afore God—God forbid I say true!—
If you do wrongfully seize Hereford's rights,
Call in° the letters patents that he hath   *Revoke*

4. Shaggy Irish foot soldiers.
5. Alluding to the legend that St. Patrick drove snakes out of Ireland.
6. Do demand some expenditure.
7. Wrongs committed against private individuals.
8. Richard intervened against Bolingbroke's proposed marriage to the King of France's cousin.
9. Privileges granted by a king through "letters patents" (line 203).

By his attorneys general to sue
205 His livery, and deny his offered homage,[1]
You pluck° a thousand dangers on your head,   *pull*
You lose a thousand well-disposèd hearts,
And prick my tender patience to those thoughts
Which honour and allegiance cannot think.
210 KING RICHARD   Think what you will, we seize into our hands
His plate, his goods, his money, and his lands.
YORK   I'll not be by the while.[2] My liege, farewell.
What will ensue hereof there's none can tell.
But by bad courses may be understood
215 That their events° can never fall out good.   *Exit*   *outcomes*
KING RICHARD   Go, Bushy, to the Earl of Wiltshire straight.
Bid him repair° to us to Ely House   *go*
To see° this business. Tomorrow next   *attend to*
We will for Ireland, and 'tis time, I trow.°   *think*
220 And we create, in absence of ourself,
Our uncle York Lord Governor of England;
For he is just and always loved us well. —
Come on, our Queen; tomorrow must we part.
Be merry, for our time of stay is short.
       Flourish. Exeunt KING [RICHARD], QUEEN[, AUMERLE,
       GREEN, *and* BAGOT *at one door,* BUSHY *at another door*].
       Manent° NORTHUMBERLAND, WILLOUGHBY, *and* ROSS   *Remain*
225 NORTHUMBERLAND   Well, lords, the Duke of Lancaster is dead.
ROSS   And living too, for now his son is Duke.
WILLOUGHBY   Barely in title, not in revenues.
NORTHUMBERLAND   Richly in both, if justice had her right.
ROSS   My heart is great,° but it must break with silence   *full of emotion*
230 Ere't be disburdened with a liberal° tongue.   *unrestrained*
NORTHUMBERLAND   Nay, speak thy mind, and let him ne'er
       speak more
That speaks thy words again to do thee harm.
WILLOUGHBY   Tends that that thou wouldst speak to[3] the Duke
       of Hereford?
If it be so, out with it boldly, man.
235 Quick is mine ear to hear of good towards him.
ROSS   No good at all that I can do for him,
Unless you call it good to pity him,
Bereft and gelded of his patrimony.
NORTHUMBERLAND   Now afore God, 'tis shame such wrongs are borne
240 In him, a royal prince, and many more
Of noble blood in this declining land.
The King is not himself, but basely led
By flatterers; and what they will inform
Merely in° hate 'gainst any of us all,   *Purely out of*
245 That will the King severely prosecute
'Gainst us, our lives, our children, and our heirs.
ROSS   The commons° hath he pilled° with grievous taxes,   *common people / stripped*
And quite lost their hearts. The nobles hath he fined
For ancient quarrels, and quite lost their hearts.

---

1. The letters patent allow Hereford, through his legal representatives ("attorneys general"), to make a legal claim for the inheritance of his land ("sue" for delivery), pro-vided he swears allegiance to the King ("offers homage").
2. Present during the seizure.
3. Does what you would say concern.

250 WILLOUGHBY   And daily new exactions are devised,
As blanks, benevolences,° and I wot° not what.   *forced loans / know*
But what, a' God's name, doth become of this?°   *this money*
NORTHUMBERLAND   Wars hath not wasted it; for warred he hath not,
But basely yielded upon compromise
255 That which his ancestors achieved with blows.[4]
More hath he spent in peace than they in wars.
ROSS   The Earl of Wiltshire hath the realm in farm.[5]
WILLOUGHBY   The King's grown bankrupt like a broken man.
NORTHUMBERLAND   Reproach and dissolution hangeth over him.
260 ROSS   He hath not money for these Irish wars,
His burdenous taxations notwithstanding,
But by the robbing of the banished Duke.
NORTHUMBERLAND   His noble kinsman. Most degenerate King!
But, lords, we hear this fearful tempest sing,
265 Yet seek no shelter to avoid the storm.
We see the wind sit sore° upon our sails,   *blow hard*
And yet we strike[6] not, but securely° perish.   *heedlessly*
ROSS   We see the very wreck that we must suffer,
And unavoided° is the danger now   *unavoidable*
270 For suffering° so the causes of our wreck.   *enduring*
NORTHUMBERLAND   Not so: even through the hollow eyes° of death   *eye sockets*
I spy life peering; but I dare not say
How near the tidings of our comfort is.
WILLOUGHBY   Nay, let us share thy thoughts, as thou dost ours.
275 ROSS   Be confident to speak, Northumberland.
We three are but thyself, and, speaking so,
Thy words are but as thoughts. Therefore be bold.
NORTHUMBERLAND   Then thus. I have from Port le Blanc,
A bay in Brittaine,[7] received intelligence
280 That Harry Duke of Hereford, Reinold Lord Cobham,
Thomas son and heir to the Earl of Arundel[8]
That late broke from the Duke of Exeter,
His[9] brother, Archbishop late° of Canterbury,   *until recently*
Sir Thomas Erpingham, Sir Thomas Ramston,
285 Sir John Norbery,
Sir Robert Waterton, and Francis Coint,
All these well furnished by the Duke of Brittaine
With eight tall ships, three thousand men of war,°   *soldiers*
Are making hither with all due expedience,
290 And shortly mean to touch our northern shore.
Perhaps they had ere this, but that they stay
The first departing of the King[1] for Ireland.
If then we shall shake off our slavish yoke,
Imp out[2] our drooping country's broken wing,
295 Redeem from broking pawn° the blemished crown,   *pawnbrokers*
Wipe off the dust that hides our sceptre's gilt,
And make high majesty look like itself,
Away with me in post° to Ravenspurgh.[3]   *speedily*

4. Referring to the ceding of Brest, a city in western
France, to the Duke of Brittany.
5. *in farm*: on lease (as in 1.4.44–46).
6. Lower sails; deliver blows.
7. Brittany, in northwest France.
8. An editorial approximation of a line missing from early

texts. Shakespeare's source states that Arundel's son
escaped from Exeter's custody.
9. The Earl of Arundel's.
1. *they stay . . . King*: they wait for the King to depart first.
2. Engraft new feathers on (from falconry).
3. Then a port on the river Humber, in Yorkshire.

But if you faint,° as fearing to do so,   *are fainthearted*
300 Stay, and be secret, and myself will go.
ROSS To horse, to horse! Urge doubts to them that fear.
WILLOUGHBY Hold out my horse,° and I will first be there.   *If my horse holds up*
                                          Exeunt

2.2
Enter the QUEEN, BUSHY, [*and*] BAGOT
BUSHY Madam, your majesty is too much sad.[1]
You promised when you parted with the King
To lay aside life-harming heaviness°   *melancholy*
And entertain° a cheerful disposition.   *assume*
5 QUEEN To please the King I did; to please myself
I cannot do it. Yet I know no cause
Why I should welcome such a guest as grief,
Save bidding farewell to so sweet a guest
As my sweet Richard. Yet again, methinks
10 Some unborn sorrow, ripe in fortune's womb,
Is coming towards me; and my inward soul
At nothing trembles. With something it grieves
More than with parting from my lord the King.
BUSHY Each substance of a grief hath twenty shadows
15 Which shows like grief itself but is not so.
For sorrow's eye, glazèd with blinding tears,
Divides one thing entire to many objects—
Like perspectives, which, rightly gazed upon,
Show nothing but confusion; eyed awry,
20 Distinguish form.[2] So your sweet majesty,
Looking awry upon your lord's departure,
Find shapes° of grief more than himself to wail,°   *images / bewail*
Which, looked on as it is, is naught but shadows
Of what it is not. Then, thrice-gracious Queen,
25 More than your lord's departure weep not: more is not seen,
Or if it be, 'tis with false sorrow's eye,
Which for things true weeps things imaginary.
QUEEN It may be so, but yet my inward soul
Persuades me it is otherwise. Howe'er it be,
30 I cannot but be sad: so heavy-sad
As thought—on thinking on no thought I think[3]—
Makes me with heavy nothing faint and shrink.
BUSHY 'Tis nothing but conceit,° my gracious lady.   *imagination*
QUEEN 'Tis nothing less:[4] conceit is still° derived   *always*
35 From some forefather grief; mine is not so;
For nothing hath begot my something° grief—   *substantial*
Or something hath the nothing that I grieve[5]—
'Tis in reversion that I do possess[6]—

2.2 Location: Windsor Castle.
1. Shakespeare makes Richard's Queen a mature young woman; the historical Isabella was married to Richard at seven years and was ten at the time of Bolingbroke's invasion.
2. *For . . . form*: Bushy compares the Queen's eye first to a perspective glass that multiplies one image into many, then to a perspective picture that looks distorted unless viewed at an angle ("awry").
3. *As thought . . . think*: a difficult line. The Oxford editors adopt the Q1 version, "thought"; other editors adopt the F version, "though," which is hardly less obscure. The Queen is playing with the paradox that her premonition, a thought of nothing, or "no thought," is nonetheless almost physically oppressive.
4. Anything but conceit.
5. Or the grief that I feel apparently over nothing actually has some cause.
6. It will come at a later date (that is, her grief anticipates its occasion).

But what it is that is not yet known what,
40   I cannot name; 'tis nameless woe, I wot.
       Enter GREEN
GREEN   God save your majesty, and well met, gentlemen.
  I hope the King is not yet shipped for Ireland.
QUEEN   Why hop'st thou so? 'Tis better hope he is,
  For his designs crave° haste, his haste good hope.   *need*
45   Then wherefore dost thou hope he is not shipped?
GREEN   That he, our hope, might have retired his power,°   *brought back his forces*
  And driven into despair an enemy's hope,
  Who strongly hath set footing in this land.
  The banished Bolingbroke repeals° himself,   *recalls from exile*
50   And with uplifted arms° is safe arrived   *weapons*
  At Ravenspurgh.
QUEEN   Now God in heaven forbid!
GREEN   Ah madam, 'tis too true! And, that is worse,
  The Lord Northumberland, his son young Harry Percy,
  The Lords of Ross, Beaumont, and Willoughby,
55   With all their powerful friends, are fled to him.
BUSHY   Why have you not proclaimed Northumberland,
  And all the rest, revolted faction-traitors?°   *treasonous conspirators*
GREEN   We have; whereupon the Earl of Worcester
  Hath broke his staff,[7] resigned his stewardship,
60   And all the household servants fled with him
  To Bolingbroke.
QUEEN   So, Green, thou art the midwife to my woe,
  And Bolingbroke my sorrow's dismal heir.
  Now hath my soul brought forth her prodigy,°   *monstrous birth; portent*
65   And I, a gasping new-delivered mother,
  Have woe to woe, sorrow to sorrow joined.
BUSHY   Despair not, madam.
QUEEN   Who shall hinder me?
  I will despair, and be at enmity
  With cozening° hope. He° is a flatterer,   *cheating / (Hope)*
70   A parasite, a keeper-back of death,
  Who° gently would dissolve° the bonds of life, *(Death) / loosen*
  Which false hope lingers in extremity.
       Enter [Duke of] YORK [*wearing a gorget*][8]
GREEN   Here comes the Duke of York.
QUEEN   With signs of war about his agèd neck.
75   O, full of careful business° are his looks!   *anxious preoccupation*
  Uncle, for God's sake speak comfortable° words.   *comforting*
YORK   Should I do so, I should belie my thoughts.
  Comfort's in heaven, and we are on the earth,
  Where nothing lives but crosses,° cares, and grief.   *misfortunes*
80   Your husband, he is gone to save far off,
  Whilst others come to make him lose at home.
  Here am I, left to underprop his land,
  Who, weak with age, cannot support myself.
  Now comes the sick hour that his surfeit made.
85   Now shall he try° his friends that flattered him.   *test*
       Enter a [SERVINGMAN]

7. Symbolically resigning his office as lord steward of the King's household. Worcester is Northumberland's brother.
8. Piece of armor protecting the throat.

SERVINGMAN My lord, your son was gone before I came.

YORK He was? Why so, go all which way it will.
The nobles they are fled. The commons° they are cold,   *common people*
And will, I fear, revolt on Hereford's side.

90   Sirrah, get thee to Pleshey, to my sister° Gloucester.   *sister-in-law*
Bid her send me presently° a thousand pound—   *immediately*
Hold; take my ring.⁹

SERVINGMAN My lord, I had forgot to tell your lordship,
Today as I came by I callèd there—

95   But I shall grieve you to report the rest.

YORK What is't, knave?°   *fellow*

SERVINGMAN An hour before I came, the Duchess died.

YORK God for his mercy, what a tide of woes
Comes rushing on this woeful land at once!

100   I know not what to do. I would to God,
So my untruth° had not provoked him to it,   *disloyalty*
The King had cut off my head with my brother's.
What, are there no posts° dispatched for Ireland?   *fast messengers*
How shall we do for money for these wars?

105   [*To the* QUEEN] Come, sister—cousin, I would say; pray pardon me.¹
[*To the* SERVINGMAN] Go, fellow, get thee home. Provide some carts,
And bring away the armour that is there.   [*Exit* SERVINGMAN]
Gentlemen, will you go muster men?
If I know how or which way to order these affairs

110   Thus disorderly thrust into my hands,
Never believe me. Both are my kinsmen.
T'one is my sovereign, whom both my oath
And duty bids defend; t'other again
Is my kinsman, whom the King hath wronged,

115   Whom conscience and my kindred bids to right.
Well, somewhat we must do. [*To the* QUEEN] Come, cousin,
I'll dispose of° you.—   *make arrangements for*
Gentlemen, go muster up your men,
And meet me presently at Berkeley Castle.²

120   I should to Pleshey too, but time will not permit.
All is uneven,
And everything is left at six and seven.°   *in confusion*

                 Exeunt Duke [*of* YORK *and*] QUEEN.
                 Manent BUSHY, GREEN [*and* BAGOT]

BUSHY The wind sits fair³ for news to go for Ireland,
But none returns. For us to levy power

125   Proportionable to the enemy
Is all unpossible.

GREEN Besides, our nearness to the King in love
Is near° the hate of those love not the King.   *Implies*

BAGOT And that is the wavering commons; for their love

130   Lies in their purses, and whoso empties them
By so much fills their hearts with deadly hate.

BUSHY Wherein the King stands generally condemned.

BAGOT If judgement lie in them,° then so do we,   *is in the people's hands*
Because we ever have been near the King.

---

9. As proof that he comes with York's authorization.
1. The Duchess's death is uppermost in York's mind.

2. In Gloucestershire, in western England.
3. The wind blows from a favorable direction.

135 GREEN   Well, I will for refuge straight to Bristol Castle.
    The Earl of Wiltshire is already there.
  BUSHY   Thither will I with you; for little office°   *service*
    Will the hateful commoners perform for us,
    Except like curs to tear us all to pieces.
140   [*To* BAGOT] Will you go along with us?
  BAGOT   No, I will to Ireland, to his majesty.
    Farewell: if heart's presages be not vain
    We three here part that ne'er shall meet again.
  BUSHY   That's as York thrives[4] to beat back Bolingbroke.
145 GREEN   Alas, poor Duke, the task he undertakes
    Is numb'ring sands and drinking oceans dry.
    Where one on his side fights, thousands will fly.
  BAGOT   Farewell at once, for once, for all and ever.
  BUSHY   Well, we may meet again.
  BAGOT   I fear me never.
            Exeunt [BUSHY *and* GREEN *at one door,*
            and BAGOT *at another door*]

2.3

Enter [BOLINGBROKE *Duke of Lancaster and*] *Hereford,*
and [*the Earl of*] NORTHUMBERLAND

  BOLINGBROKE   How far is it, my lord, to Berkeley now?
  NORTHUMBERLAND   Believe me, noble lord,
    I am a stranger here in Gloucestershire.
    These high wild hills and rough uneven ways
5   Draws out our miles and makes them wearisome;
    And yet your fair discourse hath been as sugar,
    Making the hard way sweet and delectable.
    But I bethink me what a weary way
    From Ravenspurgh to Cotswold[1] will be found
10   In° Ross and Willoughby, wanting° your company,   *By / lacking*
    Which I protest hath very much beguiled
    The tediousness and process° of my travel.   *tedious course*
    But theirs is sweetened with the hope to have
    The present benefit which I possess;
15   And hope to joy is little less in joy
    Than hope enjoyed. By this° the weary lords   *this expectation*
    Shall make their way seem short as mine hath done
    By sight of what I have: your noble company.
  BOLINGBROKE   Of much less value is my company
20   Than your good words.
        Enter HARRY PERCY
               But who comes here?
  NORTHUMBERLAND   It is my son, young Harry Percy,[2]
    Sent from my brother Worcester, whencesoever.°   *wherever he may be*
    Harry, how fares your uncle?°   *Worcester*
  HARRY PERCY   I had thought, my lord, to have learned his
    health of you.
25 NORTHUMBERLAND   Why, is he not with the Queen?
  HARRY PERCY   No, my good lord; he hath forsook the court,

---

4. That depends on York's success.
2.3 Location: Gloucestershire.
1. Hilly part of Gloucestershire.

2. Shakespeare makes Harry Percy, the Hotspur of *1
Henry IV*, a boy here; the historical Percy was two years
older than Bolingbroke.

Broken his staff of office, and dispersed
The household of the King.
NORTHUMBERLAND   What was his reason?
He was not so resolved when last we spake together.
30   HARRY PERCY   Because your lordship was proclaimèd traitor.
But he, my lord, is gone to Ravenspurgh
To offer service to the Duke of Hereford,
And sent me over by Berkeley to discover
What power the Duke of York had levied there,
35   Then with directions to repair to Ravenspurgh.
NORTHUMBERLAND   Have you forgot the Duke of Hereford, boy?[3]
HARRY PERCY   No, my good lord, for that is not forgot
Which ne'er I did remember. To my knowledge,
I never in my life did look on him.
40   NORTHUMBERLAND   Then learn to know him now. This is the Duke.
HARRY PERCY   My gracious lord, I tender you my service,
Such as it is, being tender, raw, and young,
Which elder days shall ripen and confirm
To more approvèd° service and desert.   *more fully demonstrated*
45   BOLINGBROKE   I thank thee, gentle Percy, and be sure
I count myself in nothing else so happy
As in a° soul rememb'ring my good friends;   *my*
And as my fortune ripens with thy love,
It shall be still thy true love's recompense.
50   My heart this covenant makes; my hand thus seals it.
        [*He gives* PERCY *his hand*]
NORTHUMBERLAND   How far is it to Berkeley, and what stir°   *activity*
Keeps good old York there with his men of war?
HARRY PERCY   There stands the castle, by yon tuft of trees,
Manned with three hundred men, as I have heard,
55   And in it are the Lords of York, Berkeley, and Seymour,
None else of name° and noble estimate.°   *title / reputation*
       Enter [*Lord*] ROSS *and* [*Lord*] WILLOUGHBY
NORTHUMBERLAND   Here come the Lords of Ross and Willoughby,
Bloody with spurring, fiery red with haste.
BOLINGBROKE   Welcome, my lords. I wot° your love pursues   *know*
60   A banished traitor. All my treasury
Is yet but unfelt° thanks, which, more enriched,   *immaterial*
Shall be your love and labour's recompense.
ROSS   Your presence makes us rich, most noble lord.
WILLOUGHBY   And far surmounts our labour to attain it.
65   BOLINGBROKE   Evermore thank's the exchequer[4] of the poor,
Which till my infant fortune comes to years°   *of age*
Stands for° my bounty.   *in place of*
       Enter BERKELEY
          But who comes here?
NORTHUMBERLAND   It is my lord of Berkeley, as I guess.
BERKELEY   My lord of Hereford, my message is to you.
70   BOLINGBROKE   My lord, my answer is to 'Lancaster',[5]
And I am come to seek that name in England,

---

3. Northumberland scolds his son for not greeting Bolingbroke respectfully.
4. Gratitude is always the treasury.

5. I only reply to the title of Lancaster (which Richard
took away).

And I must find that title in your tongue
Before I make reply to aught you say.
BERKELEY   Mistake me not, my lord, 'tis not my meaning
75   To raze one title of your honour out.
To you, my lord, I come—what lord you will—
From the most gracious regent of this land,
The Duke of York, to know what pricks you on°   *incites you*
To take advantage of the absent time°   *time of absence*
80   And fright our native peace with self-borne⁶ arms.
        Enter [Duke of] YORK
BOLINGBROKE   I shall not need transport my words by you.
Here comes his grace in person.—My noble uncle!
        [He kneels]
YORK   Show me thy humble heart, and not thy knee,
Whose duty is deceivable° and false.   *deceptive*
85 BOLINGBROKE   My gracious uncle—
YORK   Tut, tut, grace me no grace, nor uncle me no uncle.
I am no traitor's uncle, and that word 'grace'
In an ungracious mouth is but profane.
Why have those banished and forbidden legs
90   Dared once to touch a dust° of England's ground?   *speck*
But then more 'why': why have they dared to march
So many miles upon her peaceful bosom,
Frighting her pale-faced villages with war
And ostentation° of despisèd arms?   *display*
95   Com'st thou because the anointed King is hence?
Why, foolish boy, the King is left behind,
And in my loyal bosom lies his power.
Were I but now the lord of such hot youth
As when brave Gaunt, thy father, and myself
100   Rescued the Black Prince, that young Mars of men,
From forth the ranks of many thousand French,
O then how quickly should this arm of mine,
Now prisoner to the palsy, chastise thee
And minister correction° to thy fault!   *administer punishment*
105 BOLINGBROKE   My gracious uncle, let me know my fault.
On what condition stands it and wherein?⁷
YORK   Even in condition of the worst degree:
In gross rebellion and detested treason.
Thou art a banished man, and here art come
110   Before the expiration of thy time
In braving° arms against thy sovereign.   *defiant*
BOLINGBROKE *[standing]*   As I was banished, I was banished Hereford;
But as I come, I come for Lancaster.
And, noble uncle, I beseech your grace,
115   Look on my wrongs with an indifferent° eye.   *impartial*
You are my father, for methinks in you
I see old Gaunt alive. O then, my father,
Will you permit that I shall stand condemned
A wandering vagabond, my rights and royalties
120   Plucked from my arms perforce and given away
To upstart unthrifts?° Wherefore was I born?   *spendthrifts*

---

6. Borne for oneself, not for the King; borne against fel-   7. What is its nature, and in what does it consist?
low countrymen.

If that my cousin King be King in England,
It must be granted I am Duke of Lancaster.
You have a son, Aumerle my noble kinsman.
125 Had you first died and he been thus trod down,
He should have found his uncle Gaunt a father
To rouse his wrongs and chase them to the bay.[8]
I am denied to sue my livery[9] here,
And yet my letters patents give me leave.
130 My father's goods are all distrained° and sold,   *confiscated*
And these and all are all amiss employed.
What would you have me do? I am a subject,
And I challenge law;° attorneys are denied me;   *demand my rights*
And therefore personally I lay my claim
135 To my inheritance of free descent.°   *legal succession*
NORTHUMBERLAND   The noble Duke hath been too much abused.
ROSS   It stands your grace upon[1] to do him right.
WILLOUGHBY   Base men by his endowments° are made great.   *property*
YORK   My lords of England, let me tell you this.
140 I have had feeling of my cousin's wrongs,
And laboured all I could to do him right.
But in this kind° to come, in braving arms,   *manner*
Be his own carver,[2] and cut out his way
To find out right with wrong[3]—it may not be.
145 And you that do abet him in this kind
Cherish rebellion, and are rebels all.
NORTHUMBERLAND   The noble Duke hath sworn his coming is
But for his own, and for the right of that
We all have strongly sworn to give him aid;
150 And let him never see joy that breaks that oath.
YORK   Well, well, I see the issue° of these arms.   *consequence*
I cannot mend it, I must needs confess,
Because my power° is weak and all ill-left.   *army*
But if I could, by Him that gave me life,
155 I would attach° you all, and make you stoop   *arrest*
Unto the sovereign mercy of the King.
But since I cannot, be it known to you
I do remain as neuter.° So fare you well—   *neutral*
Unless you please to enter in the castle
160 And there repose you for this night.
BOLINGBROKE   An offer, uncle, that we will accept.
But we must win° your grace to go with us   *persuade*
To Bristol Castle, which they say is held
By Bushy, Bagot, and their complices,°   *accomplices*
165 The caterpillars° of the commonwealth,   *devourers*
Which I have sworn to weed and pluck away.
YORK   It may be I will go with you—but yet I'll pause,
For I am loath to break our country's laws.
Nor° friends nor foes, to me welcome you are.   *Neither*
170 Things past redress are now with me past care.   *Exeunt*

---

8. *rouse*: startle an animal from its cover. *bay*: point
where the animal turns on its pursuers.
9. See note to 2.1.205.

1. It is incumbent on your grace.
2. Help himself to meat (instead of waiting to be served).
3. To illegally obtain what he deserves.

2.4

Enter Earl of SALISBURY *and a* WELSH CAPTAIN

WELSH CAPTAIN   My lord of Salisbury, we have stayed° ten days,   *waited*
   And hardly° kept our countrymen together,   *with difficulty*
   And yet we hear no tidings from the King.
   Therefore we will disperse ourselves. Farewell.
5 SALISBURY   Stay yet another day, thou trusty Welshman.
   The King reposeth all his confidence in thee.
WELSH CAPTAIN   'Tis thought the King is dead. We will not stay.
   The bay trees in our country are all withered,
   And meteors fright the fixèd stars of heaven.
10 The pale-faced moon looks bloody on the earth,[1]
   And lean-looked prophets whisper fearful change.
   Rich men look sad, and ruffians dance and leap;
   The one in fear to lose what they enjoy,
   The other to enjoy° by rage and war.   *hoping to profit*
15 These signs forerun the death or fall of kings.
   Farewell. Our countrymen are gone and fled,
   As well assured Richard their king is dead.   *Exit*
SALISBURY   Ah, Richard! With the eyes of heavy mind
   I see thy glory, like a shooting star,
20 Fall to the base earth from the firmament.
   Thy sun sets weeping in the lowly west,
   Witnessing° storms to come, woe, and unrest.   *Testifying to*
   Thy friends are fled to wait upon thy foes,
   And crossly° to thy good all fortune goes.   *Exit*   *adversely*

3.1

Enter BOLINGBROKE [*Duke of Lancaster and Hereford,*
Duke of] YORK, [*Earl of*] NORTHUMBERLAND, [*Lord*]
ROSS, [HARRY] PERCY, [*and Lord*] WILLOUGHBY

BOLINGBROKE   Bring forth these men.
   [*Enter*] BUSHY *and* GREEN, [*guarded as*] *prisoners*
   Bushy and Green, I will not vex° your souls,   *afflict*
   Since presently° your souls must part your bodies,   *immediately*
   With too much urging° your pernicious lives,   *emphasizing*
5 For 'twere no charity. Yet to wash your blood
   From off my hands, here in the view of men
   I will unfold some causes of your deaths.
   You have misled a prince, a royal king,
   A happy° gentleman in blood and lineaments,[1]   *fortunate*
10 By you unhappied and disfigured clean.°   *utterly*
   You have, in manner,° with your sinful hours   *so to speak*
   Made a divorce betwixt his queen and him,
   Broke the possession of a royal bed,
   And stained the beauty of a fair queen's cheeks
15 With tears drawn from her eyes by your foul wrongs.[2]
   Myself—a prince by fortune of my birth,
   Near to the King in blood, and near in love
   Till you did make him misinterpret me—
   Have stooped my neck under your injuries,

2.4 Location: A camp in Wales.
1. Holinshed records the first of these omens (line 8); the others are poetic commonplaces.
3.1 Location: Before Bristol Castle.

1. In descent and qualities.
2. Bolingbroke implies that Bushy and Green had homosexual relations with Richard; Holinshed claims that they procured female paramours for him.

20 And sighed my English breath in foreign clouds,°   *air*
    Eating the bitter bread of banishment,
    Whilst you have fed upon my signories,°   *estates*
    Disparked my parks[3] and felled my forest woods,
    From my own windows torn my household coat,[4]
25 Razed° out my imprese,° leaving me no sign,   *Scraped / heraldic emblem*
    Save men's opinions and my living blood,
    To show the world I am a gentleman.
    This and much more, much more than twice all this,
    Condemns you to the death.—See them delivered over
30 To execution and the hand of death.
    BUSHY   More welcome is the stroke of death to me
      Than Bolingbroke to England.
    GREEN   My comfort is that heaven will take our souls,
      And plague injustice with the pains of hell.
35 BOLINGBROKE   My lord Northumberland, see them dispatched.
      [*Exit* NORTHUMBERLAND, *with* BUSHY *and* GREEN, *guarded*]
    Uncle, you say the Queen is at your house.
    For God's sake, fairly° let her be intreated.°   *courteously / treated*
    Tell her I send to her my kind commends.°   *greetings*
    Take special care my greetings be delivered.
40 YORK   A gentleman of mine I have dispatched
    With letters of your love to her at large.°   *fully described*
    BOLINGBROKE   Thanks, gentle uncle.—Come, lords, away,
    To fight with Glyndŵr[5] and his complices.
    A while to work, and after, holiday.   *Exeunt*

3.2

Drums. Flourish. Enter [KING] RICHARD, [*Duke of*]
AUMERLE, [BISHOP OF] CARLISLE, *and soldiers* [*with*]
colours°   *flags*
    KING RICHARD   Harlechly Castle call they this at hand?
    AUMERLE   Yea, my lord. How brooks° your grace the air   *enjoys*
      After your late° tossing on the breaking seas?   *recent*
    KING RICHARD   Needs must° I like it well. I weep for joy   *Necessarily*
5   To stand upon my kingdom once again.
      [*He touches the ground*]
    Dear earth, I do salute thee with my hand,
    Though rebels wound thee with their horses' hoofs.
    As a long-parted mother with her child
    Plays fondly with her tears, and smiles in meeting,
10 So, weeping, smiling, greet I thee my earth,
    And do thee favours with my royal hands.
    Feed not thy sovereign's foe, my gentle earth,
    Nor with thy sweets° comfort his ravenous sense;[1]   *bounty*
    But let thy spiders that suck up thy venom[2]
15 And heavy-gaited toads[3] lie in their way,
    Doing annoyance to the treacherous feet
    Which with usurping steps do trample thee.
    Yield stinging nettles to mine enemies,

---

3. Put my hunting lands to other uses.
4. Removed the stained glass bearing my coat of arms.
5. This character appears in *1 Henry IV* and is perhaps to
be identified with the Welsh captain of 2.4.
3.2 Location: Near Harlech Castle, on the coast of

Gwynedd, Wales.
1. Appetite; intention.
2. It was thought that spiders drew their venom from the
earth.
3. Also thought to be poisonous.

And when they from thy bosom pluck a flower

20   Guard it, I pray thee, with a lurking adder,

Whose double° tongue may with a mortal touch   *forked*

Throw death upon thy sovereign's enemies. —

Mock not my senseless conjuration,[4] lords.

This earth shall have a feeling, and these stones

25   Prove armèd soldiers, ere her native king°   *King entitled by birth*

Shall falter under foul rebellion's arms.

BISHOP OF CARLISLE   Fear not, my lord. That power that made you king

Hath power to keep you king in spite of all.[5]

28.1   *The means that heavens yield must be embraced*

     And not neglected; else° heaven would,   *otherwise*

     And we will not: heaven's offer we refuse,

     The proffered means of succour and redress.

AUMERLE   He means, my lord, that we are too remiss,

30   Whilst Bolingbroke, through our security,°   *overconfidence*

Grows strong and great in substance and in friends.

KING RICHARD   Discomfortable° cousin, know'st thou not   *Disheartening*

That when the searching eye of heaven is hid

Behind the globe, that lights the lower world,

35   Then thieves and robbers range abroad unseen

In murders and in outrage bloody here;

But when from under this terrestrial ball

He fires° the proud tops of the eastern pines,   *lights up*

And darts his light through every guilty hole,

40   Then murders, treasons, and detested sins,

The cloak of night being plucked from off their backs,

Stand bare and naked, trembling at themselves?

So when this thief, this traitor, Bolingbroke,

Who all this while hath revelled in the night

45   Whilst we were wand'ring with the Antipodes,[6]

Shall see us rising in our throne, the east,

His treasons will sit blushing in his face,

Not able to endure the sight of day,

But, self-affrighted, tremble at his sin.

50   Not all the water in the rough rude sea

Can wash the balm° from an anointed king.   *oil of consecration*

The breath of worldly men cannot depose

The deputy elected by the Lord.

For every man that Bolingbroke hath pressed°   *drafted*

55   To lift shrewd° steel against our golden crown,   *wicked; sharp*

God for his Richard hath in heavenly pay

A glorious angel. Then if angels fight,

Weak men must fall; for heaven still° guards the right.   *always*

     Enter [Earl of] SALISBURY

Welcome, my lord. How far off lies your power?

60 SALISBURY   Nor nea'er° nor farther off, my gracious lord,   *Neither nearer*

Than this weak arm. Discomfort guides my tongue,

And bids me speak of nothing but despair.

One day too late, I fear me, noble lord,

Hath clouded all thy happy days on earth.

---

4. Injunction addressed to an insentient being (the earth).
5. The following indented passage (lines 28.1–28.4) appears only in Q1.
6. *That when . . . east:* Richard compares the sun ("the

searching eye of heaven," line 33), the antipodes, or "lower world" on the other side of the globe, to himself leaving England to visit Ireland. Unlike the sun, however, Richard arrives from the west.

65   O, call back yesterday, bid time return,
        And thou shalt have twelve thousand fighting men.
        Today, today, unhappy day too late,
        Overthrows thy joys, friends, fortune, and thy state;°   *prosperity; nation*
        For all the Welshmen, hearing thou wert dead,
70   Are gone to Bolingbroke, dispersed, and fled.
        AUMERLE   Comfort, my liege. Why looks your grace so pale?
        KING RICHARD   But now° the blood of twenty thousand men   *A moment ago*
        Did triumph° in my face, and they are fled;   *shine*
        And till so much blood thither come again
75   Have I not reason to look pale and dead?
        All souls that will be safe fly from my side,
        For time hath set a blot upon my pride.
        AUMERLE   Comfort, my liege. Remember who you are.
        KING RICHARD   I had forgot myself. Am I not King?
80   Awake, thou sluggard majesty, thou sleep'st!
        Is not the King's name forty thousand names?
        Arm, arm, my name! A puny subject strikes
        At thy great glory. Look not to the ground,
        Ye favourites of a king: are we not high?
85   High be our thoughts. I know my uncle York
        Hath power enough to serve our turn.
                Enter SCROPE
                                                But who comes here?
        SCROPE   More health and happiness betide my liege
        Than can my care-tuned[7] tongue deliver° him.   *offer*
        KING RICHARD   Mine ear is open and my heart prepared.
90   The worst is worldly loss thou canst unfold.
        Say, is my kingdom lost? Why 'twas my care,°   *trouble*
        And what loss is it to be rid of care?
        Strives Bolingbroke to be as great as we?
        Greater he shall not be. If he serve God
95   We'll serve Him too, and be his fellow so.[8]
        Revolt our subjects? That we cannot mend.
        They break their faith to God as well as us.
        Cry° woe, destruction, ruin, loss, decay: *Though you may cry*
        The worst is death, and death will have his° day.   *its*
100   SCROPE   Glad am I that your highness is so armed
        To bear the tidings of calamity.
        Like an unseasonable stormy day,
        Which makes the silver rivers drown their shores
        As if the world were all dissolved to tears,
105   So high above his limits° swells the rage   *bounds; banks*
        Of Bolingbroke, covering your fearful° land   *alarmed*
        With hard bright steel, and hearts harder than steel.
        Whitebeards have armed their thin and hairless scalps
        Against thy majesty. Boys with women's voices
110   Strive to speak big, and clap their female° joints   *weak*
        In stiff unwieldy arms° against thy crown.   *armor*
        Thy very beadsmen[9] learn to bend their bows
        Of double-fatal[1] yew against thy state.

---

7. Tuned to the key of sorrow.
8. Be Bolingbroke's equal in that regard.
9. Poor elderly men who received charity in return for

praying for their benefactors' souls.
1. Because yew is poisonous, and its wood was used to make bows.

Yea, distaff-women° manage rusty bills[2]   *spinners*
115 Against thy seat.° Both young and old rebel,   *throne*
And all goes worse than I have power to tell.
KING RICHARD   Too well, too well thou tell'st a tale so ill.
Where is the Earl of Wiltshire? Where is Bagot?[3]
What is become of Bushy, where is Green,
120 That they have let the dangerous enemy
Measure our confines[4] with such peaceful° steps?   *unopposed*
If we prevail, their heads shall pay for it.
I warrant they have made peace with Bolingbroke.
SCROPE   Peace have they made with him indeed, my lord.
125 KING RICHARD   O villains, vipers damned without redemption!
Dogs easily won to fawn on any man!
Snakes in my heart-blood warmed, that sting my heart!
Three Judases, each one thrice-worse than Judas![5]
Would they make peace? Terrible hell make war
130 Upon their spotted° souls for this offence!   *blemished*
SCROPE   Sweet love, I see, changing his property,°   *its quality*
Turns to the sourest and most deadly hate.
Again uncurse their souls. Their peace is made
With heads, and not with hands. Those whom you curse
135 Have felt the worst of death's destroying wound,
And lie full low, graved in the hollow ground.
AUMERLE   Is Bushy, Green, and the Earl of Wiltshire dead?
SCROPE   Ay, all of them at Bristol lost their heads.
AUMERLE   Where is the Duke my father, with his power?
140 KING RICHARD   No matter where. Of comfort no man speak.
Let's talk of graves, of worms and epitaphs,
Make dust our paper, and with rainy eyes
Write sorrow on the bosom of the earth.
Let's choose executors and talk of wills—
145 And yet not so, for what can we bequeath
Save our deposèd° bodies to the ground?   *dethroned; prostrate*
Our lands, our lives, and all are Bolingbroke's;
And nothing can we call our own but death,
And that small model[6] of the barren earth
150 Which serves as paste[7] and cover to our bones.
[*Sitting*] For God's sake, let us sit upon the ground,
And tell sad stories of the death of kings—
How some have been deposed, some slain in war,
Some haunted by the ghosts they have deposed,
155 Some poisoned by their wives, some sleeping killed,
All murdered. For within the hollow crown
That rounds° the mortal temples of a king   *encircles*
Keeps Death his court; and there the antic° sits,   *jester*
Scoffing his state[8] and grinning at his pomp,
160 Allowing him a breath, a little scene,
To monarchize,° be feared, and kill with looks,[9]   *play the monarch*
Infusing him with self and vain conceit,[1]
As if this flesh which walls about our life

2. Spiked axes on long shafts.
3. Bagot is not one of the "three Judases" (line 128) actually executed by Bolingbroke; he reappears in 4.1.
4. Travel over our territories.
5. Disciple who betrayed Jesus.
6. Microcosm (the body); enveloping shape (the grave).
7. Pastry shell (also known as "coffin").
8. Mocking the King's regality.
9. Order executions with a glance.
1. Instilling in him vain ideas about himself.

Were brass impregnable; and humoured thus,[2]
165 Comes at the last, and with a little pin
Bores through his castle wall; and farewell, king.
Cover your heads,[3] and mock not flesh and blood
With solemn reverence. Throw away respect,
Tradition, form, and ceremonious duty,
170 For you have but mistook me all this while.
I live with bread, like you; feel want,
Taste grief, need friends. Subjected thus,[4]
How can you say to me I am a king?
BISHOP OF CARLISLE   My lord, wise men ne'er wail their present woes,
175 But presently prevent the ways to wail.[5]
To fear the foe, since fear oppresseth° strength,   *suppresses*
Gives in your weakness strength unto your foe;
And so your follies fight against yourself.
Fear, and be slain. No worse can come to fight;°   *in fighting*
180 And fight and die is death destroying death,[6]
Where fearing dying pays death servile breath.
AUMERLE   My father hath a power.° Enquire of him,   *an army*
And learn to make a body of a limb.
KING RICHARD [*standing*]   Thou chid'st me well. Proud Boling-
broke, I come
185 To change blows with thee for our day of doom.[7]
This ague-fit° of fear is overblown.°   *chill / blown over*
An easy task it is to win our own.
Say, Scrope, where lies our uncle with his power?
Speak sweetly, man, although thy looks be sour.
190 SCROPE   Men judge by the complexion° of the sky   *appearance*
The state and inclination of the day.
So may you by my dull and heavy eye
My tongue hath but a heavier tale to say.
I play the torturer by small and small°   *little by little*
195 To lengthen out the worst that must be spoken.
Your uncle York is joined with Bolingbroke,
And all your northern castles yielded up,
And all your southern gentlemen° in arms   *men of rank*
Upon his faction.
KING RICHARD   Thou hast said enough.
200 [*To* AUMERLE] Beshrew° thee, cousin, which didst lead me forth   *Woe to*
Of that sweet way I was in to despair.
What say you now? What comfort have we now?
By heaven, I'll hate him everlastingly
That bids me be of comfort any more.
205 Go to Flint Castle;° there I'll pine away.   *Welsh castle near Chester*
A king, woe's slave, shall kingly woe obey.
That power I have, discharge, and let them go
To ear° the land that hath some hope to grow;   *till*
For I have none. Let no man speak again
210 To alter this, for counsel is but vain.
AUMERLE   My liege, one word.
KING RICHARD   He does me double wrong

---

2. And Death having thus amused himself.
3. Replace your hats (do not respectfully remain bare-headed).
4. Made a subject to such needs (with pun).

5. But immediately vanquish the causes of grief.
6. To die fighting is to destroy death's power by dying.
7. To exchange blows with you in order to determine our fates.

That wounds me with the flatteries of his tongue.
Discharge my followers. Let them hence away
From Richard's night to Bolingbroke's fair day.   *Exeunt*

3.3

Enter BOLINGBROKE [*Duke of Lancaster and Hereford,*
Duke of] YORK, [*Earl of*] NORTHUMBERLAND, [*and sol-*
diers] *with drum and colours*

BOLINGBROKE   So that by this intelligence° we learn   *information*
    The Welshmen are dispersed, and Salisbury
    Is gone to meet the King, who lately landed
    With some few private friends upon this coast.
5 NORTHUMBERLAND   The news is very fair and good, my lord.
    Richard not far from hence hath hid his head.
  YORK   It would beseem the Lord Northumberland
    To say 'King Richard'. Alack the heavy day
    When such a sacred king should hide his head!
10 NORTHUMBERLAND   Your grace mistakes. Only to be brief
    Left I his title out.
  YORK   The time hath been,
    Would you have been so brief with him, he would
    Have been so brief with you to shorten you,
    For taking so the head,[1] your whole head's length.
15 BOLINGBROKE   Mistake not, uncle, further than you should.
  YORK   Take not, good cousin, further than you should,
    Lest you mistake° the heavens are over our heads.   *forget*
  BOLINGBROKE   I know it, uncle, and oppose not myself
    Against their will.
        Enter [HARRY] PERCY [*and a trumpeter*]
               But who comes here?
20 Welcome, Harry. What, will not this castle yield?
  HARRY PERCY   The castle royally is manned, my lord,
    Against thy entrance.
  BOLINGBROKE   Royally?
    Why, it contains no king.
  HARRY PERCY   Yes, my good lord,
    It doth contain a king. King Richard lies
25   Within the limits of yon lime and stone,
    And with him are the Lord Aumerle, Lord Salisbury,
    Sir Stephen Scrope, besides a clergyman
    Of holy reverence; who, I cannot learn.
  NORTHUMBERLAND   O, belike° it is the Bishop of Carlisle.   *probably*
30 BOLINGBROKE [*to* NORTHUMBERLAND]   Noble lord,
    Go to the rude ribs° of that ancient castle;   *rough walls*
    Through brazen trumpet send the breath of parley
    Into his ruined ears,° and thus deliver.   *its battered loopholes*
    Henry Bolingbroke
35   Upon his knees doth kiss King Richard's hand,
    And sends allegiance and true faith of heart
    To his most royal person, hither come
    Even at his feet to lay my arms and power,
    Provided that my banishment repealed°   *revoked*
40 And lands restored again be freely granted.

3.3 Location: Before Flint Castle.   1. For omitting the title thus; for acting without restraint.

If not, I'll use the advantage of my power,
And lay° the summer's dust with showers of blood   *make settle*
Rained from the wounds of slaughtered Englishmen;
The which how far off from the mind of Bolingbroke
45   It is such crimson tempest should bedrench
The fresh green lap of fair King Richard's land,
My stooping duty° tenderly shall show.   *submissive kneeling*
Go, signify as much, while here we march
Upon the grassy carpet of this plain.
50   Let's march without the noise of threat'ning drum,
That from this castle's tottered° battlements   *dilapidated*
Our fair appointments° may be well perused.   *equipment*
Methinks King Richard and myself should meet
With no less terror than the elements
55   Of fire and water° when their thund'ring shock   *lightning and rain*
At meeting tears the cloudy cheeks of heaven.
Be he the fire, I'll be the yielding water.
The rage be his, whilst on the earth I rain°   *(punning on "reign"?)*
My waters: on the earth, and not on him.—
60   March on, and mark King Richard, how he looks.

> [*They march about the stage; then* BOLINGBROKE, YORK,
> PERCY, *and soldiers stand at a distance from the walls;*
> NORTHUMBERLAND *and a trumpeter advance to the
> walls.*] *The trumpets sound* [a] *parley without, and* [an]
> *answer within; then a flourish* [*within.* KING] RICHARD
> *appeareth on the walls,*[2] [*with* BISHOP OF] CARLISLE,
> [*Duke of*] AUMERLE, SCROPE, [*and Earl of*] SALISBURY

See, see, King Richard doth himself appear,
As doth the blushing[3] discontented sun
From out the fiery portal of the east
When he perceives the envious° clouds are bent   *malicious*
65   To dim his glory and to stain the track
Of his bright passage to the occident.
YORK   Yet looks he like a king. Behold, his eye,
As bright as is the eagle's, lightens forth[4]
Controlling majesty. Alack, alack for woe
70   That any harm should stain so fair a show!
KING RICHARD [*to* NORTHUMBERLAND]   We are amazed; and
        thus long have we stood
To watch° the fearful bending of thy knee,   *wait for*
Because we thought ourself thy lawful king.
An if° we be, how dare thy joints forget   *An if = If*
75   To pay their aweful° duty to our presence?   *reverential*
If we be not, show us the hand of God
That hath dismissed us from our stewardship.
For well we know no hand of blood and bone
Can grip° the sacred handle of our sceptre,   *seize*
80   Unless he do profane, steal, or usurp.
And though you think that all—as you have done—
Have torn° their souls by turning them from us,   *ruined (by disloyalty)*
And we are barren and bereft of friends,

---

2. That is, on the balcony of the tiring-house at the back   weather).
of the stage.   4. Flashes out (the eagle is a traditional royal symbol).
3. Red (proverbially, a red morning sky anticipates bad

Yet know my master, God omnipotent,
85 Is mustering in his clouds on our behalf
Armies of pestilence; and they shall strike
Your children yet unborn and unbegot,
That lift your vassal hands against my head
And threat° the glory of my precious crown.   *threaten*
90 Tell Bolingbroke, for yon methinks he is,
That every stride he makes upon my land
Is dangerous treason. He is come to open
The purple testament° of bleeding war;   *blood-red document*
But ere the crown he looks for live in peace
95 Ten thousand bloody crowns° of mothers' sons   *heads*
Shall ill become the flower of England's face,[5]
Change the complexion of her maid-pale° peace   *innocent white*
To scarlet indignation, and bedew
Her pastures' grass with faithful English blood.
NORTHUMBERLAND [*kneeling*]   The King of heaven forbid our
100   lord the King
Should so with civil and uncivil[6] arms
Be rushed upon. Thy thrice-noble cousin
Harry Bolingbroke doth humbly kiss thy hand,
And by the honourable tomb he swears,
105 That stands upon your royal grandsire's° bones,   *(Edward III's)*
And by the royalties of both your bloods,
Currents that spring from one most gracious head,°   *source*
And by the buried hand of warlike Gaunt,
And by the worth and honour of himself,
110 Comprising all that may be sworn or said,
His coming hither hath no further scope°   *aim*
Than for his lineal royalties,° and to beg   *hereditary rights*
Enfranchisement° immediate on his knees;   *Recall from exile*
Which on thy royal party° granted once,   *part*
115 His glittering arms he will commend° to rust,   *commit*
His barbèd° steeds to stables, and his heart   *armed*
To faithful service of your majesty.
This swears he as he is a prince and just,
And as I am a gentleman I credit° him.   *believe*
120 KING RICHARD   Northumberland, say thus the King returns:°   *replies*
His noble cousin is right welcome hither,
And all the number of his fair demands
Shall be accomplished without contradiction.
With all the gracious utterance thou hast,
125 Speak to his gentle hearing kind commends.°   *regards*
          [NORTHUMBERLAND *and the trumpeter return to*
          BOLINGBROKE]
          [*To* AUMERLE] We do debase ourself, cousin, do we not,
To look so poorly° and to speak so fair?   *abjectly*
Shall we call back Northumberland, and send
Defiance to the traitor, and so die?
130 AUMERLE   No, good my lord, let's fight with gentle words
Till time lend friends, and friends their helpful swords.
KING RICHARD   O God, O God, that e'er this tongue of mine,
That laid the sentence of dread banishment

5. Blooming surface of England; faces of England's choicest youth.   6. Of the same country and violent; playing on "civil" as "peaceful" and "uncivil" as "alien."

On yon proud man, should take it off again
135 With words of sooth!° O, that I were as great   *soothing words*
As is my grief, or lesser than my name,
Or that I could forget what I have been,
Or not remember what I must be now!
Swell'st thou, proud heart? I'll give thee scope to beat,
140 Since foes have scope to beat both thee and me.
             [NORTHUMBERLAND *advances to the walls*]
AUMERLE Northumberland comes back from Bolingbroke.
KING RICHARD What must the King do now? Must he submit?
The King shall do it. Must he be deposed?
The King shall be contented. Must he lose
145 The name of King? A° God's name, let it go.   *In*
I'll give my jewels for a set of beads,°   *rosary*
My gorgeous palace for a hermitage,
My gay apparel for an almsman's° gown,   *a beggar's*
My figured° goblets for a dish of wood,   *engraved*
150 My sceptre for a palmer's° walking staff,   *pilgrim's*
My subjects for a pair of carvèd saints,
And my large kingdom for a little grave,
A little, little grave, an obscure grave;
Or I'll be buried in the King's highway,°   *(as suicides were)*
155 Some way of common trade° where subjects' feet   *passage*
May hourly trample on their sovereign's head,
For on my heart they tread now, whilst I live,
And buried once, why not upon my head?
Aumerle, thou weep'st, my tender-hearted cousin.
160 We'll make foul weather with despisèd tears.
Our sighs and they shall lodge° the summer corn,   *beat down*
And make a dearth° in this revolting° land.   *famine / rebellious*
Or shall we play the wantons° with our woes,   *we frolic*
And make some pretty match° with shedding tears;   *clever game*
165 As thus to drop them still° upon one place   *continually*
Till they have fretted° us a pair of graves   *eroded for*
Within the earth, and therein laid? 'There lies
Two kinsmen digged their graves with weeping eyes.'
Would not this ill do well? Well, well, I see
170 I talk but idly° and you mock at me.   *foolishly*
Most mighty prince, my lord Northumberland,
What says King Bolingbroke? Will his majesty
Give Richard leave to live till Richard die?
You make a leg,° and Bolingbroke says 'Ay'.   *an obeisance*
175 NORTHUMBERLAND My lord, in the base court° he doth attend   *outer courtyard*
To speak with you. May it please you to come down?
KING RICHARD Down, down I come like glist'ring Phaethon,[7]
Wanting the manage° of unruly jades.[8]   *Lacking control*
In the base court: base court where kings grow base
180 To come at traitors' calls, and do them grace.°   *favor them*
In the base court, come down: down court, down King,
For night-owls shriek where mounting larks should sing.
             [*Exeunt* KING RICHARD *and his party*]

---

7. In Greek myth, the son of the sun god. He attempted to drive his father's sun chariot but was too weak to control the horses; Zeus, king of the gods, struck him down with a thunderbolt to prevent him from destroying the earth.
8. Horses (contemptuous).

[NORTHUMBERLAND *returns to* BOLINGBROKE]

BOLINGBROKE   What says his majesty?

NORTHUMBERLAND   Sorrow and grief of heart

Makes him speak fondly,° like a frantic° man.   *foolishly / an insane*

[*Enter* KING RICHARD *and his party below*]

Yet he is come.

185   BOLINGBROKE   Stand all apart,

And show fair duty to his majesty.

He kneels down

My gracious lord.

KING RICHARD   Fair cousin, you debase your princely knee

To make the base earth proud with kissing it.

190   Me rather had° my heart might feel your love   *I had rather*

Than my unpleased eye see your courtesy.

Up, cousin, up. Your heart is up, I know,

Thus high at least,⁹ although your knee be low.

BOLINGBROKE   My gracious lord, I come but for mine own.

195   KING RICHARD   Your own is yours, and I am yours, and all.

BOLINGBROKE   So far be mine, my most redoubted° lord,   *dreaded*

As my true service shall deserve your love.

KING RICHARD   Well you deserve. They well deserve to have

That know the strong'st and surest way to get.

[BOLINGBROKE *rises*]

200   [*To* YORK] Uncle, give me your hands. Nay, dry your eyes.

Tears show their love, but want their remedies.°   *do no good*

[*To* BOLINGBROKE] Cousin, I am too young to be your father,

Though you are old enough to be my heir.

What you will have I'll give, and willing too;

205   For do we must what force will have us do.

Set on towards London, cousin: is it so?

BOLINGBROKE   Yea, my good lord.

KING RICHARD   Then I must not say no.

Flourish. Exeunt.

3.4

Enter the QUEEN *with her two* LADIES

QUEEN   What sport shall we devise here in this garden,

To drive away the heavy thought of care?

FIRST LADY   Madam, we'll play at bowls.°   *lawn bowling*

QUEEN   'Twill make me think the world is full of rubs,¹

5   And that my fortune runs against the bias.²

SECOND LADY   Madam, we'll dance.

QUEEN   My legs can keep no measure° in delight   *dance step*

When my poor heart no measure° keeps in grief;   *moderation*

Therefore no dancing, girl. Some other sport.

10   FIRST LADY   Madam, we'll tell tales.

QUEEN   Of sorrow or of joy?

FIRST LADY   Of either, madam.

QUEEN   Of neither, girl.

For if of joy, being altogether wanting,

15   It doth remember° me the more of sorrow.   *remind*

---

9. Richard touches his crown.
3.4 Location: The Duke of York's garden.
1. Impediments (a term from the game of bowls).

2. Runs askew. *bias:* literally, a lead weight in the bowl
that makes it run smoothly.

Or if of grief, being altogether had,°   *possessed*
It adds more sorrow to my want of joy.
For what I have I need not to repeat,
And what I want it boots° not to complain.   *helps*
    SECOND LADY   Madam, I'll sing.
20   QUEEN   'Tis well that thou hast cause;
    But thou shouldst please me better wouldst thou weep.
    SECOND LADY   I could weep, madam, would it do you good.
    QUEEN   And I could sing, would weeping do me good,
    And never borrow any tear of thee.
                Enter a GARDENER *and two* [MEN]
25   But stay; here come the gardeners.
    Let's step into the shadow of these trees.
    My wretchedness unto a row of pins³
    They will talk of state, for everyone doth so
    Against° a change. Woe is forerun with woe.   *In anticipation of*
             [*The* QUEEN *and her* LADIES *stand apart*]
30 GARDENER [*to* FIRST MAN]   Go, bind thou up young dangling apricots
    Which, like unruly children, make their sire
    Stoop with oppression of their prodigal° weight.   *excessive*
    Give some supportance to the bending twigs.
    [*To* SECOND MAN] Go thou, and, like an executioner,
35   Cut off the heads of too fast-growing sprays
    That look too lofty in our commonwealth.
    All must be even° in our government.   *equal*
    You thus employed, I will go root away
    The noisome° weeds which without profit suck   *harmful*
40   The soil's fertility from wholesome flowers.
    FIRST MAN   Why should we, in the compass of a pale,⁴
    Keep law and form and due proportion,
    Showing as in a model our firm estate,°   *stable government*
    When our sea-wallèd garden, the whole land,
45   Is full of weeds, her fairest flowers choked up,
    Her fruit trees all unpruned, her hedges ruined,
    Her knots⁵ disordered, and her wholesome herbs
    Swarming with caterpillars?
    GARDENER   Hold thy peace.
    He that hath suffered° this disordered spring   *permitted*
50   Hath now himself met with the fall of leaf.
    The weeds which his broad spreading leaves did shelter,
    That seemed in eating him to hold him up,
    Are plucked up, root and all, by Bolingbroke—
    I mean the Earl of Wiltshire, Bushy, Green.
    SECOND MAN   What, are they dead?
55 GARDENER   They are; and Bolingbroke
    Hath seized the wasteful King. O, what pity is it
    That he had not so trimmed and dressed° his land   *cultivated*
    As we this garden! We at time of year°   *in season*
    Do wound the bark, the skin of our fruit trees,⁶
60   Lest, being over-proud in° sap and blood,   *excessively swollen with*
    With too much riches it confound° itself.   *ruin*

---

3. I'll bet my great wretchedness against a trivial row of pins.
4. In the limits of a fenced enclosure.

5. Intricate flowerbeds; social bonds.
6. *Do . . . trees*: this restricts the tree's food supply, encouraging fruit buds to form.

Had he done so to great and growing men,
They might have lived to bear, and he to taste,
Their fruits of duty. Superfluous branches
65 We lop away, that bearing boughs may live.
Had he done so, himself had borne° the crown,[7]   *retained*
Which waste of idle hours hath quite thrown down.
FIRST MAN   What, think you then the King shall be deposed?
GARDENER   Depressed° he is already, and deposed   *Brought low*
70 'Tis doubt° he will be. Letters came last night   *feared*
To a dear friend of the good Duke of York's
That tell black tidings.
QUEEN   O, I am pressed to death through want of speaking![8]
        [*She comes forward*]
Thou, old Adam's[9] likeness, set to dress° this garden,   *cultivate*
75 How dares thy harsh rude° tongue sound this unpleasing news?   *ignorant*
What Eve, what serpent hath suggested° thee   *tempted*
To make a second fall of cursèd man?
Why dost thou say King Richard is deposed?
Dar'st thou, thou little better thing than earth,
80 Divine° his downfall? Say where, when, and how   *Prophesy*
Cam'st thou by this ill tidings? Speak, thou wretch!
GARDENER   Pardon me, madam. Little joy have I
To breathe this news, yet what I say is true.
King Richard he is in the mighty hold
85 Of Bolingbroke. Their fortunes both are weighed.
In your lord's scale is nothing but himself
And some few vanities that make him light.
But in the balance of great Bolingbroke,
Besides himself, are all the English peers,
90 And with that odds he weighs King Richard down.
Post° you to London and you will find it so.   *Hasten*
I speak no more than everyone doth know.
QUEEN   Nimble mischance that art so light of foot,
Doth not thy embassage° belong to me,   *message*
95 And am I last that knows it? O, thou think'st
To serve me last, that I may longest keep
Thy sorrow in my breast. Come, ladies, go
To meet at London London's king in woe.
What, was I born to this, that my sad look
100 Should grace the triumph° of great Bolingbroke?   *triumphal procession*
Gard'ner, for telling me these news of woe,
Pray God the plants thou graft'st may never grow.
                                Exit [*with her* LADIES]
GARDENER   Poor Queen, so that° thy state might be no worse   *if as a result*
I would my skill were subject to thy curse.
105 Here did she fall° a tear. Here in this place   *drop*
I'll set a bank of rue,[1] sour herb-of-grace.
Rue even for ruth° here shortly shall be seen   *pity*
In the remembrance of a weeping queen.   *Exeunt*

---

7. Playing on the "crown" of a tree.
8. In medieval and Renaissance England, indicted persons who refused to plead guilty or not guilty were killed
with weights laid on the stomach.
9. Adam was the first gardener.
1. Herb associated with compassion and repentance.

4.1

Enter, as to Parliament, BOLINGBROKE *[Duke of Lancaster and Hereford, Duke of]* AUMERLE, *[Earl of]*
NORTHUMBERLAND, *[*HARRY*]* PERCY, *[Lord]* FITZWALTER,
[Duke of] SURREY, *[*BISHOP OF*]* CARLISLE, *[and the]*
ABBOT OF WESTMINSTER

BOLINGBROKE   Call forth Bagot.

Enter BAGOT, *[with] officers*

                         Now, Bagot, freely speak thy mind:
What thou dost know of noble Gloucester's death,
Who wrought it with[1] the King, and who performed
The bloody office° of his timeless° end.   *deed / untimely*

5   BAGOT   Then set before my face the Lord Aumerle.

BOLINGBROKE *[to* AUMERLE*]*   Cousin, stand forth, and look
      upon that man.

      *[*AUMERLE *stands forth]*

BAGOT   My lord Aumerle, I know your daring tongue
Scorns to unsay° what once it hath delivered.   *deny*
In that dead° time when Gloucester's death was plotted   *fatal; dark*

10 I heard you say 'Is not my arm of length,°   *long enough*
That reacheth from the restful English court
As far as Calais, to mine uncle's head?'
Amongst much other talk that very time[2]
I heard you say that you had rather refuse

15 The offer of an hundred thousand crowns
Than° Bolingbroke's return to England,   *Than accept*
Adding withal° how blest this land would be   *besides*
In this your cousin's death.

AUMERLE   Princes and noble lords,
What answer shall I make to this base man?

20 Shall I so much dishonour my fair stars°   *honorable birth*
On equal terms to give him chastisement?[3]
Either I must, or have mine honour soiled
With the attainder° of his slanderous lips.   *accusation*

      [He throws down his gage]

There is my gage, the manual seal of death

25 That marks thee out for hell. I say thou liest,
And will maintain° what thou hast said is false   *will uphold in combat*
In thy heart blood, though being all too base
To stain the temper[4] of my knightly sword.

BOLINGBROKE   Bagot, forbear. Thou shalt not take it up.

30 AUMERLE   Excepting one,° I would he° were the best *(Bolingbroke) / (Bagot)*
In all this presence that hath moved° me so.   *angered*

FITZWALTER   If that thy valour stand on sympathy,[5]
There is my gage, Aumerle, in gage to thine.

      [He throws down his gage]

By that fair sun which shows me where thou stand'st,

35 I heard thee say, and vauntingly° thou spak'st it,   *boastfully*
That thou wert cause of noble Gloucester's death.
If° thou deny'st it twenty times, thou liest,   *Even if*

4.1 Location: Westminster Hall.
1. Who persuaded; who collaborated with.
2. *that very time*: inconsistent, since Gloucester was killed long before Bolingbroke's exile.

3. Punishment (a lord could refuse to fight a lowborn man in the trial by combat).
4. Quality (literally, "hardness").
5. Insists on equality of rank.

And I will turn thy falsehood to thy heart,
Where it was forgèd, with my rapier's point.
40 AUMERLE   Thou dar'st not, coward, live to see that day.
FITZWALTER   Now by my soul, I would it were this hour.
AUMERLE   Fitzwalter, thou art damned to hell for this.
HARRY PERCY   Aumerle, thou liest. His honour is as true
In this appeal° as thou art all unjust;   accusation
45 And that thou art so, there I throw my gage
   [*He throws down his gage*]
To prove it on thee to the extremest point
Of mortal breathing. Seize it if thou dar'st.
AUMERLE   An if I do not, may my hands rot off,
And never brandish more° revengeful steel   again
50 Over the glittering helmet of my foe.[6]
50.1   ANOTHER LORD   *I task the earth to the like, forsworn Aumerle,*
             And spur thee on with full as many lies°   accusations of lying
             As may be hollowed° in thy treacherous ear   shouted
             From sun to sun.° There is my honour's pawn.   sunrise to sunset
50.5   *Engage it to[7] the trial if thou darest.*
             [*He throws down his gage*]
        AUMERLE   *Who sets° me else? By heaven, I'll throw[8] at all.*   challenges (in gambling)
             I have a thousand spirits in one breast
             To answer twenty thousand such as you.
SURREY   My lord Fitzwalter, I do remember well
The very time Aumerle and you did talk.
FITZWALTER   'Tis very true. You were in presence° then,   were present
And you can witness with me this is true.
55 SURREY   As false, by heaven, as heaven itself is true.
FITZWALTER   Surrey, thou liest.
SURREY   Dishonourable boy,
That lie shall lie so heavy on my sword
That it shall render vengeance and revenge,
Till thou, the lie-giver, and that lie do lie
60 In earth as quiet as thy father's skull;
In proof whereof, there is my honour's pawn.
   [*He throws down his gage*]
Engage it to the trial if thou dar'st.
FITZWALTER   How fondly dost thou spur a forward horse!
If I dare eat, or drink, or breathe, or live,
65 I dare meet Surrey in a wilderness
And spit upon him whilst I say he lies,
And lies, and lies.[9] There is my bond of faith
To tie thee to my strong correction.
As I intend to thrive in this new world,
70 Aumerle is guilty of my true appeal.°   accusation
Besides, I heard the banished Norfolk° say   (Mowbray)
That thou, Aumerle, didst send two of thy men
To execute the noble Duke at Calais.
AUMERLE   Some honest Christian trust me with° a gage.   lend me
   [*He takes another's gage and throws it down*]

6. The following indented passage (lines 50.1–50.8)   8. Defeat (as by throwing dice).
appears only in Q1.   9. Fitzwalter may throw down another gage here.
7. Accept it as a pledge ("gage") for.

75　　That Norfolk lies, here do I throw down this,
　　　If he may be repealed,° to try his honour.　　　　　　　　　　*recalled from exile*
　　BOLINGBROKE　These differences shall all rest under gage[1]
　　　Till Norfolk be repealed. Repealed he shall be,
　　　And, though mine enemy, restored again
80　　To all his lands and signories.° When he is returned,　　　　　*estates*
　　　Against Aumerle we will enforce his trial.
　　BISHOP OF CARLISLE　That honourable day shall never be seen.
　　　Many a time hath banished Norfolk fought
　　　For Jesu Christ in glorious Christian field,[2]
85　　Streaming the ensign of the Christian cross
　　　Against black pagans, Turks, and Saracens;
　　　And, toiled° with works of war, retired himself　　　　　　　*exhausted*
　　　To Italy, and there at Venice gave
　　　His body to that pleasant country's earth,
90　　And his pure soul unto his captain, Christ,
　　　Under whose colours he had fought so long.
　　BOLINGBROKE　Why, Bishop of Carlisle, is Norfolk dead?
　　BISHOP OF CARLISLE　As surely as I live, my lord.
　　BOLINGBROKE　Sweet peace conduct his sweet soul to the bosom
95　　Of good old Abraham![3] Lords appellants,
　　　Your differences° shall all rest under gage　　　　　　　　　*disputes*
　　　Till we assign you to your days of trial.
　　　　　　Enter [Duke of] YORK
　　YORK　Great Duke of Lancaster, I come to thee
　　　From plume-plucked° Richard, who with willing soul　　　　*humbled*
100　　Adopts thee heir, and his high sceptre yields
　　　To the possession of thy royal hand.
　　　Ascend his throne, descending now from him,
　　　And long live Henry, of that name the fourth!
　　BOLINGBROKE　In God's name I'll ascend the regal throne.
105　BISHOP OF CARLISLE　Marry, God forbid!
　　　Worst° in this royal presence may I speak,　　　　　　　　*Least worthy*
　　　Yet best beseeming° me to speak the truth.　　　　　*fitting (as a clergyman)*
　　　Would God that any in this noble presence
　　　Were enough noble to be upright judge
110　　Of noble Richard. Then true noblesse° would　　　　　　　*nobility*
　　　Learn° him forbearance from so foul a wrong.　　　　　　　*Teach*
　　　What subject can give sentence on his king?
　　　And who sits here that is not Richard's subject?
　　　Thieves are not judged but° they are by° to hear,　　*except when / present*
115　　Although apparent° guilt be seen in them;　　　　　　　　*obvious*
　　　And shall the figure° of God's majesty,　　　　　　　　　　*image*
　　　His captain, steward, deputy elect,°　　　　　　　　　　　*chosen*
　　　Anointed, crownèd, planted many years,
　　　Be judged by subject and inferior breath,
120　　And he himself not present? O, forfend° it, God,　　　　　*prohibit*
　　　That in a Christian climate souls refined[4]
　　　Should show so heinous, black, obscene° a deed!　　　　　*odious*
　　　I speak to subjects, and a subject speaks
　　　Stirred up by God thus boldly for his king.

1. Shall remain as standing challenges.　　　　16:22.
2. In battle for the Christian cause.　　　　　　4. Spiritually improved; aristocratic.
3. *the bosom . . . Abraham:* that is, heavenly rest; see Luke

125 My lord of Hereford here, whom you call king,
Is a foul traitor to proud Hereford's king;
And, if you crown him, let me prophesy
The blood of English shall manure the ground,
And future ages groan for this foul act.

130 Peace shall go sleep with Turks and infidels,
And in this seat° of peace tumultuous wars   *region; throne*
Shall kin with kin and kind with kind confound.[5]
Disorder, horror, fear, and mutiny
Shall here inhabit, and this land be called

135 The field of Golgotha[6] and dead men's skulls.
O, if you rear this house against this house°   *(Lancaster against York)*
It will the woefullest division prove
That ever fell upon this cursèd earth!
Prevent, resist it; let it not be so,

140 Lest child, child's children, cry against you woe.
NORTHUMBERLAND   Well have you argued, sir, and for your pains
Of capital treason we arrest you here.
My lord of Westminster, be it your charge
To keep him safely till his day of trial.[7]

145 May it please you, lords, to grant the Commons' suit?[8]
BOLINGBROKE   Fetch hither Richard, that in common° view   *public*
He may surrender.[9] So we shall proceed
Without suspicion.
YORK   I will be his conduct.°   *Exit*   *escort*
BOLINGBROKE   Lords, you that here are under our arrest,

150 Procure your sureties for your days of answer.[1]
Little are we beholden to your love,
And little looked for° at your helping hands.   *expected*
      Enter RICHARD *and [Duke of]* YORK *[with attendants*
      bearing the crown and sceptre]
RICHARD   Alack, why am I sent for to a king
Before I have shook off the regal thoughts

155 Wherewith I reigned? I hardly yet have learned
To insinuate, flatter, bow, and bend my knee.
Give sorrow leave awhile to tutor me
To this submission. Yet I well remember
The favours° of these men. Were they not mine?   *faces; benefits*

160 Did they not sometime cry 'All hail!' to me?
So Judas did to Christ. But He in twelve
Found truth in all but one; I, in twelve thousand, none.
God save the King! Will no man say 'Amen'?
Am I both priest and clerk?[2] Well then, Amen.

165 God save the King, although I be not he.
And yet Amen, if heaven do think him me.
To do what service am I sent for hither?
YORK   To do that office° of thine own good will   *task; ceremony*
Which tired majesty did make thee offer:

5. Shall destroy kinsman by fellow kinsman and country-man by fellow countryman.
6. Place of Christ's crucifixion, the name of which means "place of dead men's skulls."
7. The passage that follows, to line 308, is not included in the earliest texts. See Textual Variants.
8. The House of Commons' request that Richard should have judgment passed on him.
9. Abdicate (the legitimacy of the Commons' suit depended on Richard's having given up the crown and thus his royal immunity from prosecution).
1. Procure persons guaranteeing your appearance on the day of trial.
2. Priest's assistant who utters the responses to prayers.

170   The resignation of thy state and crown
       To Henry Bolingbroke.
      RICHARD [*to an attendant*]   Give me the crown. [*To* BOLING-
        BROKE] Here, cousin, seize the crown.
      Here, cousin. On this side my hand, on that side thine.
      Now is this golden crown like a deep well
175   That owes° two buckets filling one another,[3]   *has*
      The emptier ever dancing in the air,
      The other down, unseen, and full of water.
      That bucket down and full of tears am I,
      Drinking my griefs, whilst you mount up on high.
180   BOLINGBROKE   I thought you had been willing to resign.
      RICHARD   My crown I am, but still my griefs are mine.
      You may my glories and my state° depose,   *royal status*
      But not my griefs; still° am I king of those.   *permanently*
      BOLINGBROKE   Part of your cares you give me with your crown.
185   RICHARD   Your cares set up do not pluck my cares down.
      My care is loss of care by old care done;
      Your care is gain of care by new care won.[4]
      The cares I give I have, though given away;
      They 'tend° the crown, yet still with me they stay.   *attend, accompany*
190   BOLINGBROKE   Are you contented to resign the crown?
      RICHARD   Ay, no; no, ay; for I must nothing be;[5]
      Therefore no, no, for I resign to thee.
      Now mark me how I will undo° myself.   *ruin; strip*
      I give this heavy weight from off my head,
        [BOLINGBROKE *accepts the crown*]
195   And this unwieldy sceptre from my hand,
        [BOLINGBROKE *accepts the sceptre*]
      The pride of kingly sway from out my heart.
      With mine own tears I wash away my balm,
      With mine own hands I give away my crown,
      With mine own tongue deny my sacred state,°   *divine right to be King*
200   With mine own breath release all duteous oaths.°   *oaths of allegiance*
      All pomp and majesty I do forswear.
      My manors, rents, revenues I forgo.
      My acts, decrees, and statutes I deny.°   *repudiate*
      God pardon all oaths that are broke to me.
205   God keep all vows unbroke are made to thee.
      Make me, that nothing have, with nothing grieved,[6]
      And thou with all pleased, that hast all achieved.
      Long mayst thou live in Richard's seat to sit,
      And soon lie Richard in an earthy pit.
210   'God save King Henry,' unkinged Richard says,
      'And send him many years of sunshine° days.'   *sunny*
      What more remains?
      NORTHUMBERLAND [*giving* RICHARD *papers*]
                  No more but that you read°   *read aloud*
      These accusations and these grievous crimes
      Committed by your person and your followers

3. That is, the raising of one causing the other to descend and fill.
4. *Your cares . . . won:* an extended wordplay on "care": Your assuming cares of state does not relieve me of grief. I mourn the loss of responsibility, by lack of diligence in the past; you concern yourself with gaining responsibility, won by effort.
5. Playing on "ay" (yes) and "I": since I am no thing, then "I," that is, "ay," is "no."
6. Grieved at nothing; grieved at having nothing.

215 Against the state and profit° of this land,   *established prosperity*
    That by confessing them, the souls of men
    May deem that you are worthily deposed.
    RICHARD   Must I do so? And must I ravel out
    My weaved-up follies? Gentle Northumberland,
220 If thy offences were upon record,
    Would it not shame thee in so fair a troop°   *company*
    To read a lecture° of them? If thou wouldst,   *give a public reading*
    There shouldst thou find one heinous article
    Containing the deposing of a king
225 And cracking the strong warrant of an oath,
    Marked with a blot, damned in the book of heaven.
    Nay, all of you that stand and look upon
    Whilst that my wretchedness doth bait⁷ myself,
    Though some of you, with Pilate, wash your hands,⁸
230 Showing an outward pity, yet you Pilates
    Have here delivered me to my sour° cross,   *bitter*
    And water cannot wash away your sin.
    NORTHUMBERLAND   My lord, dispatch.° Read o'er these articles.   *hurry up*
    RICHARD   Mine eyes are full of tears; I cannot see.
235 And yet salt water blinds them not so much
    But they can see a sort° of traitors here.   *pack*
    Nay, if I turn mine eyes upon myself
    I find myself a traitor with the rest,
    For I have given here my soul's consent
240 T'undeck the pompous° body of a king,   *splendidly dressed*
    Made glory base and sovereignty a slave,
    Proud majesty a subject, state° a peasant.   *royalty*
    NORTHUMBERLAND   My lord—
    RICHARD   No lord of thine, thou haught°-insulting man,   *haughty*
245 Nor no man's lord. I have no name, no title,
    No, not that name was given me at the font,
    But 'tis usurped. Alack the heavy day,
    That I have worn so many winters out
    And know not now what name to call myself!
250 O, that I were a mockery king of snow,
    Standing before the sun of Bolingbroke
    To melt myself away in water-drops!
    Good king, great king—and yet not greatly good—
    An if my word be sterling° yet in England,   *valid (like currency)*
255 Let it command a mirror hither straight,°   *immediately*
    That it may show me what a face I have,
    Since it is bankrupt of his° majesty.   *its*
    BOLINGBROKE   Go some of you and fetch a looking-glass.
                                                   [*Exit one or more*]
    NORTHUMBERLAND   Read o'er this paper while the glass° doth   *until the mirror*
         come.
260 RICHARD   Fiend, thou torment'st me ere I come to hell.
    BOLINGBROKE   Urge it no more, my lord Northumberland.
    NORTHUMBERLAND   The Commons will not then be satisfied.
    RICHARD   They shall be satisfied. I'll read enough
         When I do see the very book indeed

---

7. Torment (as in bearbaiting).
8. Pilate, Jesus' judge, washed his hands to signify his dis-   claiming of responsibility for the death sentence he
                                                                  imposed at the request of the Jews.

265   Where all my sins are writ, and that's myself.
            Enter one with a glass
    Give me that glass, and therein will I read.
          [RICHARD *takes the glass and looks in it*]
    No deeper wrinkles yet? Hath sorrow struck
    So many blows upon this face of mine
    And made no deeper wounds? O flatt'ring glass,
270   Like to my followers in prosperity,
    Thou dost beguile me! Was this face the face
    That every day under his household roof
    Did keep ten thousand men? Was this the face
    That like the sun did make beholders wink?°   *shut their eyes*
275   Is this the face which faced[9] so many follies,
    That was at last outfaced° by Bolingbroke?   *stared down*
    A brittle glory shineth in this face.
    As brittle as the glory is the face,
          [*He shatters the glass*]
    For there it is, cracked in an hundred shivers.
280   Mark, silent King, the moral of this sport:
    How soon my sorrow hath destroyed my face.
   BOLINGBROKE   The shadow[1] of your sorrow hath destroyed
    The shadow° of your face.   *image*
   RICHARD   Say that again:
    'The shadow of my sorrow'—ha, let's see.
285   'Tis very true: my grief lies all within,
    And these external manner of laments
    Are merely shadows to the unseen grief
    That swells with silence in the tortured soul.
    There lies the substance, and I thank thee, King,
290   For thy great bounty that not only giv'st
    Me cause to wail, but teachest me the way
    How to lament the cause. I'll beg one boon,°   *favor*
    And then be gone and trouble you no more.
    Shall I obtain it?
   BOLINGBROKE   Name it, fair cousin.
295   RICHARD   Fair cousin? I am greater than a king;
    For when I was a king my flatterers
    Were then but subjects; being now a subject,
    I have a king here to my flatterer.
    Being so great, I have no need to beg.
300   BOLINGBROKE   Yet ask.
   RICHARD   And shall I have?
   BOLINGBROKE   You shall.
   RICHARD   Then give me leave to go.
   BOLINGBROKE   Whither?
305   RICHARD   Whither you will, so° I were from your sights.   *provided that*
   BOLINGBROKE   Go some of you, convey° him to the Tower.   *conduct*
   RICHARD   O good, 'convey'!° Conveyors are you all,   *steal*
    That rise thus nimbly by a true king's fall.
                      [*Exit, guarded*]
   BOLINGBROKE   On Wednesday next we solemnly set down

---

9. Countenanced; adorned (as a garment trimmed with "facings").
1. Darkness; outward display; image, reflection; unhappi-ness (Richard plays on the word's various meanings in the following passage).

310   Our coronation. Lords, prepare yourselves.
                  Exeunt. Manent [ABBOT OF] WESTMINSTER,
                  [BISHOP OF] CARLISLE, [*and*] AUMERLE
ABBOT OF WESTMINSTER   A woeful pageant have we here beheld.
BISHOP OF CARLISLE   The woe's to come, the children yet unborn
    Shall feel this day as sharp to them as thorn.
AUMERLE   You holy clergymen, is there no plot
315   To rid the realm of this pernicious blot?
ABBOT OF WESTMINSTER   My lord, before I freely speak my
        mind herein,
    You shall not only take the sacrament[2]
    To bury mine intents,[3] but also to effect
    Whatever I shall happen to devise.
320   I see your brows are full of discontent,
    Your hearts of sorrow, and your eyes of tears.
    Come home with me to supper. I will lay
    A plot shall show us all a merry day.   *Exeunt*

5.1

Enter the QUEEN *with her* LADIES
QUEEN   This way the King will come. This is the way
    To Julius Caesar's ill-erected Tower,[1]
    To whose flint bosom my condemnèd lord
    Is doomed a prisoner by proud Bolingbroke.
5   Here let us rest, if this rebellious earth
    Have any resting for her true king's queen.
            Enter RICHARD, *and guard*
    But soft,° but see—or rather do not see—   *wait*
    My fair rose wither. Yet look up, behold,
    That you in pity may dissolve to dew,
10   And wash him fresh again with true-love tears.—
    Ah, thou the model where old Troy did stand![2]
    Thou map° of honour, thou King Richard's tomb,   *epitome*
    And not King Richard! Thou most beauteous inn:
    Why should hard-favoured° grief be lodged in thee,   *ugly; unfortunate*
15   When triumph is become an alehouse[3] guest?
RICHARD   Join not with grief, fair woman, do not so,
    To make my end too sudden. Learn, good soul,
    To think our former state a happy dream,
    From which awaked, the truth of what we are
20   Shows us but this. I am sworn brother, sweet,
    To grim necessity, and he and I
    Will keep a league till death. Hie° thee to France,   *Hasten*
    And cloister thee in some religious house.°   *convent*
    Our holy lives must win a new world's° crown,   *(heaven's)*
25   Which our profane hours here have stricken down.
QUEEN   What, is my Richard both in shape and mind
    Transformed and weakenèd? Hath Bolingbroke
    Deposed thine intellect? Hath he been in thy heart?
    The lion dying thrusteth forth his paw

---

2. A solemn oath, accompanied by the rite of communion.
3. To keep my intentions secret.
5.1 Location: A street near the Tower of London.
1. The Tower of London (popularly thought to have been built by Caesar). *ill-erected:* poorly built; erected for evil ends.
2. The pattern of fallen greatness, like Troy.
3. Poorer class of lodging (referring to Bolingbroke) than an "inn."

30 And wounds the earth, if nothing else, with rage
To be° o'erpowered; and wilt thou, pupil-like,   *At being*
Take the correction, mildly kiss the rod,
And fawn on rage with base humility,
Which art a lion and the king of beasts?
35 RICHARD   A king of beasts[4] indeed! If aught but beasts,
I had been still a happy king of men.
Good sometimes° Queen, prepare thee hence for France.   *former*
Think I am dead, and that even here thou tak'st,
As from my death-bed, thy last living leave.
40 In winter's tedious nights, sit by the fire
With good old folks, and let them tell thee tales
Of woeful ages long ago betid;[5]
And ere thou bid goodnight, to quit their griefs°   *repay their sad tales*
Tell thou the lamentable fall of me,
45 And send the hearers weeping to their beds;
Forwhy the senseless brands will sympathize[6]
The heavy accent of thy moving[7] tongue,
And in compassion weep the fire out;
And some° will mourn in ashes, some coal black,   *(firebrands)*
50 For the deposing of a rightful king.
    Enter [Earl of] NORTHUMBERLAND
NORTHUMBERLAND   My lord, the mind of Bolingbroke is changed.
You must to Pomfret,° not unto the Tower.   *castle in Yorkshire*
And, madam, there is order ta'en[8] for you.
With all swift speed you must away to France.
55 RICHARD   Northumberland, thou ladder wherewithal
The mounting Bolingbroke ascends my throne,
The time shall not be many hours of age
More than it is ere foul sin, gathering head,
Shall break into corruption.[9] Thou shalt think,
60 Though he divide the realm and give thee half,
It is too little helping[1] him to all.
He shall think that thou, which know'st the way
To plant unrightful kings, wilt know again,
Being ne'er so little urged another way,
65 To pluck him headlong from the usurpèd throne.
The love of wicked friends converts to fear,
That fear to hate, and hate turns one or both
To worthy° danger and deservèd death.   *severe*
NORTHUMBERLAND   My guilt be on my head, and there an end.[2]
70 Take leave and part,° for you must part° forthwith.   *separate / depart*
RICHARD   Doubly divorced! Bad men, you violate
A twofold marriage: 'twixt my crown and me,
And then betwixt me and my married wife.
[*To the* QUEEN] Let me unkiss the oath 'twixt thee and me—
75 And yet not so, for with a kiss 'twas made.
Part us, Northumberland: I towards the north,
Where shivering cold and sickness pines the clime;°   *afflicts the region*
My queen to France, from whence set forth in pomp

---

4. Lion (Richard's emblem); ruler of beastly men.
5. Woe that happened long ago.
6. Because even the insentient firewood will respond empathetically.
7. Physically and emotionally.
8. Arrangements have been made.
9. Pus (the image is of a swelling abscess).
1. *helping:* since you helped.
2. Recalling the cry of the Jews at Jesus' trial: "His death be upon our heads, and the heads of our children."

She came adornèd hither like sweet May,
80 Sent back like Hallowmas° or short'st of day.[3]   *November 1*
QUEEN And must we be divided? Must we part?
RICHARD Ay, hand from hand, my love, and heart from heart.
QUEEN Banish us both, and send the King with me.
NORTHUMBERLAND That were some love, but little policy.°   *but politically naive*
85 QUEEN Then whither he goes, thither let me go.
RICHARD So two together weeping make one woe.
   Weep thou for me in France, I for thee here.
   Better far off than, near, be ne'er the nea'er.[4]
   Go count thy way with sighs, I mine with groans.
90 QUEEN So longest way shall have the longest moans.
RICHARD Twice for one step I'll groan, the way being short,
   And piece the way out° with a heavy heart.   *lengthen the way*
   Come, come, in wooing sorrow let's be brief,
   Since, wedding it, there is such length in grief.
95 One kiss shall stop our mouths, and dumbly° part.   *silently*
   Thus give I mine, and thus take I thy heart.
      [*They kiss*]
QUEEN Give me mine own again. 'Twere no good part[5]
   To take on me to keep and kill thy heart.
      [*They kiss*]
   So now I have mine own again, be gone,
100 That I may strive to kill it with a groan.
RICHARD We make woe wanton[6] with this fond delay.
   Once more, adieu. The rest let sorrow say.
      Exeunt [RICHARD, *guarded, and* NORTHUMBERLAND *at one
         door, the* QUEEN *and her* LADIES *at another door*]

5.2

Enter DUKE *and* DUCHESS OF YORK
DUCHESS OF YORK My lord, you told me you would tell the rest,
   When weeping made you break the story off,
   Of our two cousins'° coming into London.   *kinsmen's*
YORK Where did I leave?
DUCHESS OF YORK   At that sad stop, my lord,
5 Where rude misgoverned° hands from windows' tops°   *unruly / upper windows*
   Threw dust and rubbish on King Richard's head.
YORK Then, as I said, the Duke, great Bolingbroke,
   Mounted upon a hot and fiery steed,
   Which his aspiring rider[1] seemed to know,
10 With slow but stately pace kept on his course,
   Whilst all tongues cried 'God save thee, Bolingbroke!'
   You would have thought the very windows spake,
   So many greedy looks of young and old
   Through casements darted their desiring eyes
15 Upon his visage, and that all the walls
   With painted imagery[2] had said at once,
   'Jesu preserve thee! Welcome, Bolingbroke!'

---

3. Winter solstice.
4. Better to be far away than to be near but never nearer
to our happiness.
5. It would not be good of me.
6. We make our woe unrestrained; we make a sport of

our grief.
5.2 Location: The Duke of York's house.
1. Object of "seemed to know."
2. Painted cloths, hung on walls in pageants; figures in
these sometimes had "speech bubbles."

Whilst he, from the one side to the other turning,
Bare-headed, lower than his proud steed's neck,
20 Bespake° them thus: 'I thank you, countrymen',   *Addressed*
And thus still doing, thus he passed along.
DUCHESS OF YORK Alack, poor Richard! Where rode he the whilst?
YORK As in a theatre the eyes of men,
After a well-graced actor leaves the stage,
25 Are idly bent on him that enters next,
Thinking his prattle to be tedious,
Even so, or with much more contempt, men's eyes
Did scowl on gentle Richard. No man cried 'God save him!'
No joyful tongue gave him his welcome home;
30 But dust was thrown upon his sacred head,
Which with such gentle sorrow he shook off,
His face still combating° with tears and smiles,   *continually struggling*
The badges° of his grief and patience,   *emblems*
That had not God for some strong purpose steeled
35 The hearts of men, they must perforce have melted,
And barbarism itself have pitied him.
But heaven hath a hand in these events,
To whose high will we bound our calm contents.[3]
To Bolingbroke are we sworn subjects now,
40 Whose state and honour I for aye allow.°   *forever acknowledge*
    Enter [Duke of] AUMERLE
DUCHESS OF YORK Here comes my son Aumerle.
YORK   Aumerle that was;[4]
But that is lost for being Richard's friend,
And, madam, you must call him 'Rutland' now.
I am in Parliament pledge for his truth°   *guarantor of his loyalty*
45 And lasting fealty° to the new-made King.   *fidelity*
DUCHESS OF YORK Welcome, my son. Who are the violets now
That strew the green lap of the new-come spring?
AUMERLE Madam, I know not, nor I greatly care not.
God knows I had as lief° be none as one.   *had rather*
50 YORK Well, bear you well in this new spring of time,
Lest you be cropped° before you come to prime.   *cut*
What news from Oxford? Hold these jousts and triumphs?°   *processions*
AUMERLE For aught I know, my lord, they do.
YORK You will be there, I know.
55 AUMERLE If God prevent it not, I purpose so.
YORK What seal is that that hangs without thy bosom?[5]
Yea, look'st thou pale? Let me see the writing.
AUMERLE My lord, 'tis nothing.
YORK   No matter, then, who see it.
I will be satisfied. Let me see the writing.
60 AUMERLE I do beseech your grace to pardon me.
It is a matter of small consequence,
Which for some reasons I would not have seen.
YORK Which for some reasons, sir, I mean to see.
I fear, I fear!
DUCHESS OF YORK What should you fear?

---

3. Bound ourselves to be calmly contented.
4. Aumerle has been deprived of his dukedom; he remains Earl of Rutland.

5. The document is in Aumerle's doublet, with the seal on a visibly dangling slip of attached paper.

65	'Tis nothing but some bond that he is entered into	
	For gay apparel 'gainst° the triumph day.	*in time for*
	YORK Bound to himself?[6] What doth he with a bond	
	That he is bound to? Wife, thou art a fool.	
	Boy, let me see the writing.	
70	AUMERLE I do beseech you, pardon me. I may not show it.	
	YORK I will be satisfied. Let me see it, I say.	
	He plucks it out of [Aumerle's] bosom, and reads it	
	Treason, foul treason! Villain, traitor, slave!	
	DUCHESS OF YORK What is the matter, my lord?	
	YORK Ho, who is within there? Saddle my horse. —	
75	God for his mercy, what treachery is here!	
	DUCHESS OF YORK Why, what is it, my lord?	
	YORK Give me my boots, I say. Saddle my horse. —	
	Now by mine honour, by my life, my troth,	
	I will appeach° the villain.	*accuse*
80	DUCHESS OF YORK What is the matter?	
	YORK Peace, foolish woman.	
	DUCHESS OF YORK I will not peace. What is the matter, son?	
	AUMERLE Good mother, be content. It is no more	
	Than my poor life must answer.	
	DUCHESS OF YORK Thy life answer?	
85	YORK Bring me my boots. I will unto the King.	
	His man enters with his boots	
	DUCHESS OF YORK Strike him,° Aumerle! Poor boy, thou art	*(the servant)*
	amazed.°	*distraught*
	[*To York's man*] Hence, villain! Never more come in my sight.	
	YORK Give me my boots, I say.	
	DUCHESS OF YORK Why, York, what wilt thou do?	
	Wilt thou not hide the trespass of thine own?	
90	Have we more sons?[7] Or are we like to have?	
	Is not my teeming date° drunk up with time?	*my period of childbearing*
	And wilt thou pluck my fair son from mine age,	
	And rob me of a happy mother's name?	
	Is he not like thee? Is he not thine own?	
95	YORK Thou fond,° mad woman,	*foolish*
	Wilt thou conceal this dark conspiracy?	
	A dozen of them here have ta'en the sacrament,	
	And interchangeably set down their hands[8]	
	To kill the King at Oxford.	
	DUCHESS OF YORK He shall be none.°	*not be one of them*
100	We'll keep him here, then what is that to him?	
	YORK Away, fond woman! Were he twenty times my son	
	I would appeach him.	
	DUCHESS OF YORK Hadst thou groaned° for him	*suffered labor pains*
	As I have done thou wouldst be more pitiful.	
	But now I know thy mind: thou dost suspect	
105	That I have been disloyal to thy bed,	
	And that he is a bastard, not thy son.	
	Sweet York, sweet husband, be not of that mind.	
	He is as like thee as a man may be,	

6. If Aumerle had signed a bond to borrow money, the creditor would have the bond.
7. Actually, Aumerle had a brother and a sister, and the

Duchess of York, the Duke's second wife, was Aumerle's stepmother.
8. And mutually committed themselves in writing.

Not like to me or any of my kin,
And yet I love him.
110 YORK   Make way, unruly woman.

Exit [with his man]

DUCHESS OF YORK   After, Aumerle! Mount thee upon his horse.
Spur, post,° and get before him to the King,   *Ride fast*
And beg thy pardon ere he do accuse thee.
I'll not be long behind—though I be old,
115 I doubt not but to ride as fast as York—
And never will I rise up from the ground
Till Bolingbroke have pardoned thee. Away, be gone!

Exeunt [severally]

5.3

Enter BOLINGBROKE, [*crowned* KING HENRY,] *with*
[HARRY] PERCY, *and other nobles*

KING HENRY   Can no man tell of my unthrifty son?[1]
'Tis full three months since I did see him last.
If any plague hang over us, 'tis he.
I would to God, my lords, he might be found.
5 Enquire at London 'mongst the taverns there,
For there, they say, he daily doth frequent
With unrestrainèd loose companions—
Even such, they say, as stand in narrow lanes
And beat our watch° and rob our passengers°—   *watchmen / wayfarers*
10 Which he, young wanton and effeminate° boy,   *pleasure-seeking*
Takes on° the point of honour to support   *Makes it*
So dissolute a crew.
HARRY PERCY   My lord, some two days since,° I saw the Prince,   *ago*
And told him of these triumphs held at Oxford.
15 KING HENRY   And what said the gallant?
HARRY PERCY   His answer was he would unto the stews,°   *brothels*
And from the common'st creature pluck a glove,
And wear it as a favour,[2] and with that
He would unhorse the lustiest° challenger.   *most vigorous*
20 KING HENRY   As dissolute as desperate.° Yet through both   *reckless*
I see some sparks of better hope, which elder days
May happily[3] bring forth.

Enter [Duke of] AUMERLE, *amazed*

                   But who comes here?
AUMERLE   Where is the King?
KING HENRY   What means our cousin that he stares and looks so wildly?
25 AUMERLE [*kneeling*]   God save your grace! I do beseech your majesty
To have some conference with your grace alone.
KING HENRY [*to lords*]   Withdraw yourselves, and leave us here alone.

[*Exeunt all but* KING HENRY *and* AUMERLE]

What is the matter with our cousin now?
AUMERLE   For ever may my knees grow° to the earth,   *be fixed*
30 My tongue cleave to the roof within my mouth,
Unless a pardon ere I rise or speak.
KING HENRY   Intended or committed was this fault?

5.3 Location: Windsor Castle.
1. Henry's oldest son is Prince Hal of *1* and *2 Henry IV*,
later King Henry V. *unthrifty*: dissolute.

2. Lady's gift to a knight worn in combat.
3. Perhaps; with good fortune.

If on the first,° how heinous e'er it be,   *If only intended*
To win thy after-love I pardon thee.
35   AUMERLE [*rising*]   Then give me leave that I may turn the key,
That no man enter till my tale be done.
KING HENRY   Have thy desire.
        [AUMERLE *locks the door.*]
        The Duke of YORK *knocks at the door and crieth*
YORK [*within*]   My liege, beware! Look to thyself!
Thou hast a traitor in thy presence there.
        [KING HENRY *draws his sword*]
KING HENRY [*to* AUMERLE]   Villain, I'll make thee safe.°   *harmless*
40   AUMERLE   Stay° thy revengeful hand! Thou hast no cause to fear.   *Restrain*
YORK [*knocking within*]   Open the door, secure° foolhardy King!   *overconfident*
Shall I for° love speak treason⁴ to thy face?   *out of*
Open the door, or I will break it open.
        [KING HENRY *opens the door.*] *Enter* [*Duke of*] YORK
KING HENRY   What is the matter, uncle? Speak,
45   Recover breath, tell us how near is danger,
That we may arm us to encounter it.
YORK   Peruse this writing here, and thou shalt know
The treason that my haste⁵ forbids me show.°   *explain*
        [*He gives* KING HENRY *the paper*]
AUMERLE   Remember, as thou read'st, thy promise past.
50   I do repent me. Read not my name there.
My heart is not confederate with my hand.°   *signature*
YORK   It was, villain, ere thy hand did set it down.
I tore it° from the traitor's bosom, King.   *(the bond)*
Fear, and not love, begets his penitence.
55   Forget to pity him, lest pity prove
A serpent that will sting thee to the heart.
KING HENRY   O, heinous, strong, and bold conspiracy!
O loyal father of a treacherous son!
Thou sheer,° immaculate, and silver fountain,   *clear*
60   From whence this stream through muddy passages
Hath held his current and defiled himself,
Thy overflow of good converts to bad,
And thy abundant goodness shall excuse
This deadly° blot in thy digressing⁶ son.   *damnable; death-dealing*
65   YORK   So shall my virtue be his vice's bawd,
And he shall spend mine honour with his shame,
As thriftless sons their scraping fathers' gold.
Mine honour lives when his dishonour dies,
Or my shamed life in his dishonour lies.
70   Thou kill'st me in his life: giving him breath
The traitor lives, the true man's put to death.
DUCHESS OF YORK [*within*]   What ho, my liege, for God's sake let me in!
KING HENRY   What shrill-voiced suppliant makes this eager cry?
DUCHESS OF YORK [*within*]   A woman, and thy aunt, great King; 'tis I.
75   Speak with me, pity me! Open the door!
A beggar begs that never begged before.
KING HENRY   Our scene is altered from a serious thing,
And now changed to 'The Beggar and the King'.°   *(the name of a ballad)*

---

4. Disrespectfully criticize (as "secure" and "foolhardy").   6. Diverging from course (as of a stream); transgressing.
5. York is out of breath.

My dangerous cousin, let your mother in.
80   I know she is come to pray for your foul sin.
        [AUMERLE *opens the door.*] *Enter* DUCHESS [OF YORK]
  YORK   If thou do pardon, whosoever pray,
    More sins for this forgiveness prosper may.
    This festered joint° cut off, the rest rest sound.   *infected limb*
    This let alone will all the rest confound.°   *destroy*
  DUCHESS OF YORK [*kneeling*]   O King, believe not this hard-
85   hearted man.
    Love loving not itself, none other can.[7]
  YORK   Thou frantic woman, what dost thou make° here?   *do*
    Shall thy old dugs° once more a traitor rear?   *breasts*
  DUCHESS OF YORK   Sweet York, be patient.—Hear me, gentle liege.
  KING HENRY   Rise up, good aunt.
90   DUCHESS OF YORK   Not yet, I thee beseech.
    Forever will I kneel upon my knees,
    And never see day that the happy sees,
    Till thou give joy, until thou bid me joy
    By pardoning Rutland, my transgressing boy.
95   AUMERLE [*kneeling*]   Unto° my mother's prayers I bend my knee.   *In support of*
  YORK [*kneeling*]   Against them both my true joints bended be.
    Ill mayst thou thrive if thou grant any grace.
  DUCHESS OF YORK   Pleads he in earnest? Look upon his face.
    His eyes do drop no tears, his prayers are in jest.
100   His words come from his mouth; ours from our breast.
    He prays but faintly, and would be denied;
    We pray with heart and soul, and all beside.
    His weary joints would gladly rise, I know;
    Our knees shall kneel till to the ground they grow.
105   His prayers are full of false hypocrisy;
    Ours of true zeal and deep integrity.
    Our prayers do outpray his; then let them have
    That mercy which true prayer ought to have.
  KING HENRY   Good aunt, stand up.
  DUCHESS OF YORK   Nay, do not say 'Stand up'.
110   Say 'Pardon' first, and afterwards 'Stand up'.
    An if° I were thy nurse, thy tongue to teach,   *An if = If*
    'Pardon' should be the first word of thy speech.
    I never longed to hear a word till now.
    Say 'Pardon', King. Let pity teach thee how.
115   The word is short, but not so short as sweet;
    No word like 'Pardon' for kings' mouths so meet.°   *fit*
  YORK   Speak it in French, King: say 'Pardonnez-moi'.[8]
  DUCHESS OF YORK   Dost thou teach pardon pardon to destroy?[9]
    Ah, my sour° husband, my hard-hearted lord   *harsh*
120   That sets the word itself against the word!
    Speak 'Pardon' as 'tis current in our land;
    The chopping[1] French we do not understand.
    Thine eye begins to speak; set thy tongue there;
    Or in thy piteous heart plant thou thine ear,
125   That hearing how our plaints and prayers do pierce,

---

7. If one does not love one's own flesh and blood, one can love no one else (not even the King).
8. "Excuse me," a polite refusal.
9. Rhymes with "moi" in anglicized pronunciation.
1. Logic-chopping, changing the meaning.

Pity may move thee 'Pardon' to rehearse.°   *recite*
KING HENRY   Good aunt, stand up.
DUCHESS OF YORK   I do not sue to stand.
  Pardon is all the suit I have in hand.
KING HENRY   I pardon him as God shall pardon me.
    [YORK *and* AUMERLE *rise*]
130   DUCHESS OF YORK   O, happy vantage° of a kneeling knee!   *gain; position*
  Yet am I sick for fear. Speak it again.
  Twice saying pardon doth not pardon twain,°   *divide*
  But makes one pardon strong.
KING HENRY   I pardon him
  With all my heart.
DUCHESS OF YORK [*rising*]   A god on earth thou art.
135   KING HENRY   But for our trusty brother-in-law[2] and the Abbot,
  With all the rest of that consorted° crew,   *confederated*
  Destruction straight shall dog them at the heels.
  Good uncle, help to order several powers°   *forces*
  To Oxford, or where'er these traitors are.
140   They shall not live within this world, I swear,
  But I will have them if I once know where.
  Uncle, farewell; and cousin, so adieu.
  Your mother well hath prayed; and prove you true.°   *loyal*
DUCHESS OF YORK   Come, my old[3] son. I pray God make thee new.
     Exeunt [KING HENRY *at one door;* YORK,
             DUCHESS OF YORK, *and* AUMERLE
                    at another door]

5.4

Enter Sir Piers EXTON, *and* [MEN]
EXTON   Didst thou not mark the King, what words he spake?
  'Have I no friend will rid me of this living fear?'
  Was it not so?
FIRST MAN   Those were his very words.
EXTON   'Have I no friend?' quoth he. He spake it twice,
5   And urged it twice together, did he not?
SECOND MAN   He did.
EXTON   And speaking it, he wishtly° looked on me,   *intently*
  As who° should say 'I would thou wert the man   *As if he*
  That would divorce this terror from my heart',
10   Meaning the King at Pomfret. Come, let's go.
  I am the King's friend, and will rid° his foe.   *Exeunt*   *will get rid of*

5.5

Enter RICHARD, *alone*
RICHARD   I have been studying how I may compare
  This prison where I live unto the world;
  And for because the world is populous,
  And here is not a creature but myself,
5   I cannot do it. Yet I'll hammer° it out.   *work*
  My brain I'll prove the female° to my soul,   *(that is, receptive)*
  My soul the father, and these two beget

2. The Duke of Exeter and Earl of Huntington, husband of Bolingbroke's sister; like Aumerle, he had been deprived of his dukedom.
3. Unregenerate (recalling the baptism service: "O mer-ciful God, grant that the old Adam in this child may be so buried that the new man may be raised up in him").
5.4 Location: Windsor Castle.
5.5 Location: Pomfret Castle.

A generation of still-breeding° thoughts; *ever-breeding*
And these same thoughts people this little world
10 In humours[1] like the people of this world.° *(the real world)*
For no thought is contented. The better sort,
As thoughts of things divine, are intermixed
With scruples,° and do set the faith itself *doubts*
Against the faith,[2] as thus: 'Come, little ones',[3]
15 And then again,
'It is as hard to come as for a camel
To thread the postern of a small needle's eye.'[4]
Thoughts° tending to ambition, they do plot *Other thoughts*
Unlikely wonders:° how these vain weak nails *miracles*
20 May tear a passage through the flinty ribs
Of this hard world, my ragged° prison walls; *rugged*
And for they cannot, die in their own pride.° *prime of life; arrogance*
Thoughts tending to content° flatter themselves *contentment*
That they are not the first of fortune's slaves,
25 Nor shall not be the last—like seely° beggars, *simpleminded*
Who, sitting in the stocks, refuge[5] their shame
That many have, and others must, set there;
And in this thought they find a kind of ease,
Bearing their own misfortunes on the back
30 Of such as have before endured the like.
Thus play I in one person many people,
And none contented. Sometimes am I king;
Then treason makes me wish myself a beggar,
And so I am. Then crushing penury
35 Persuades me I was better when a king.
Then am I kinged again, and by and by
Think that I am unkinged by Bolingbroke,
And straight° am nothing. But whate'er I be, *at once*
Nor I, nor any man that but° man is, *merely*
40 With nothing shall be pleased till he be eased
With being nothing.
    The music plays
                Music do I hear.
Ha, ha; keep time! How sour sweet music is
When time is broke and no proportion kept.
So is it in the music of men's lives.
45 And here have I the daintiness of ear
To check° time broke in a disordered string;° *rebuke / string instrument*
But for the concord° of my state and time *harmony*
Had not an ear to hear my true time broke.
I wasted time, and now doth time waste me,
50 For now hath time made me his numb'ring clock.[6]
My thoughts are minutes, and with sighs they jar
Their watches° on unto mine eyes, the outward watch[7] *periods of vigil*
Whereto my finger, like a dial's point,° *clock's hand*

---

1. Temperaments; caprices.
2. *the faith . . . faith*: scriptural passage against scriptural passage.
3. From Matthew 19:14, Mark 10:14, and Luke 18:25, implying the ease of obtaining salvation.
4. Adapting Matthew 19:24, Mark 10:25, or Luke 18:25, which describe the unlikeliness of the rich reaching heaven.
5. Find refuge for; rationalize.
6. Clock that counts hours and minutes, not an hourglass.
7. Clock face; mind's external watcher.

Is pointing still° in cleansing them from tears.[8]   *always*
55 Now, sir, the sounds that tell what hour it is
Are clamorous groans that strike upon my heart,
Which is the bell. So sighs, and tears, and groans
Show minutes, hours, and times. But my time
Runs posting° on in Bolingbroke's proud joy,   *speeding*
60 While I stand fooling here, his jack of the clock.[9]
This music mads° me. Let it sound no more,   *maddens*
For though it have holp° madmen to their wits,   *helped*
In me it seems it will make wise men mad.
     [*The music ceases*]
Yet blessing on his heart that gives it me,
65 For 'tis a sign of love, and love to Richard
Is a strange brooch° in this all-hating world.   *rare ornament*
     Enter a GROOM *of the stable*
GROOM   Hail, royal Prince!
RICHARD   Thanks, noble peer.
The cheapest of us is ten groats too dear.[1]
What art thou, and how com'st thou hither,
70 Where no man never comes but that sad dog
That brings me food to make misfortune live?
GROOM   I was a poor groom of thy stable, King,
When thou wert king; who, travelling towards York,
With much ado at length have gotten leave
75 To look upon my sometimes° royal master's face.   *former*
O, how it erned° my heart when I beheld   *grieved*
In London streets, that coronation day,
When Bolingbroke rode on roan Barbary,
That horse that thou so often hast bestrid,
80 That horse that I so carefully have dressed!°   *groomed*
RICHARD   Rode he on Barbary? Tell me, gentle friend,
How went he under him?
GROOM   So proudly as if he disdained the ground.
RICHARD   So proud that Bolingbroke was on his back.
85 That jade° hath eat bread from my royal hand;   *nag*
This hand hath made him proud with clapping° him.   *patting*
Would he not stumble, would he not fall down—
Since pride must have a fall—and break the neck
Of that proud man that did usurp his back?
90 Forgiveness, horse! Why do I rail on thee,
Since thou, created to be awed by man,
Wast born to bear? I was not made a horse,
And yet I bear a burden like an ass,
Spur-galled[2] and tired by jauncing° Bolingbroke.   *rough-riding*
     Enter KEEPER *to* RICHARD, *with meat*
95 KEEPER [*to* GROOM]   Fellow, give place.° Here is no longer stay.   *leave*
RICHARD [*to* GROOM]   If thou love me, 'tis time thou wert away.
GROOM   What my tongue dares not, that my heart shall say.
                              Exit

KEEPER   My lord, will't please you to fall to?

---

8. Wiping tears from my eyes.
9. Manikin that strikes the clock's bell.
1. You have overpriced the cheaper of us (me, a prisoner) in calling me "royal." The difference between the coins

"royal" (ten shillings) and "noble" (six shillings eight pence) is "ten groats" (forty pence). In other words, we are equal in worth.
2. Made sore by spurring.

RICHARD   Taste of it first,³ as thou art wont to do.
100   KEEPER   My lord, I dare not. Sir Piers of Exton,
      Who lately came from the King, commands the contrary.
     RICHARD [*striking the* KEEPER]   The devil take Henry of Lancaster and thee!
      Patience is stale, and I am weary of it.
     KEEPER   Help, help, help!
          EXTON *and his* [*men*] *rush in*
105   RICHARD   How now! What means death in this rude assault?
      [*He seizes a weapon from a man, and kills him*]
      Villain, thy own hand yields thy death's instrument.
      [*He kills another*]
      Go thou, and fill another room in hell.
          Here EXTON *strikes him down*
     RICHARD   That hand shall burn in never-quenching fire
      That staggers thus my person.° Exton, thy fierce hand   *thus makes me stagger*
110   Hath with the King's blood stained the King's own land.
      Mount, mount, my soul; thy seat° is up on high,   *residence*
      Whilst my gross flesh sinks downward, here to die.   [*He dies*]
     EXTON   As full of valour as of royal blood.
      Both have I spilt. O, would the deed were good!
115   For now the devil that told me I did well
      Says that this deed is chronicled in hell.
      This dead King to the living King I'll bear.
      Take hence the rest, and give them burial here.
          Exeunt [EXTON *with Richard's body at one door, and*
          his men with the other bodies at another door]

5.6

     Flourish. Enter [KING HENRY] *with* [*Duke of*] YORK, *with*
     other lords and attendants
     KING HENRY   Kind uncle York, the latest news we hear
      Is that the rebels have consumed with fire
      Our town of Ci'cester° in Gloucestershire;   *Cirencester*
      But whether they be ta'en or slain we hear not.
          Enter [*Earl of*] NORTHUMBERLAND
5   Welcome, my lord. What is the news?
     NORTHUMBERLAND   First, to thy sacred state wish I all happiness.
      The next news is, I have to London sent
      The heads of Salisbury, Spencer, Blunt, and Kent.
      The manner of their taking may appear
10   At large discoursèd° in this paper here.   *Narrated in full*
          [*He gives the paper to* KING HENRY]
     KING HENRY   We thank thee, gentle Percy, for thy pains,
      And to thy worth will add right worthy° gains.   *valuable; well-deserved*
          Enter Lord FITZWALTER
     FITZWALTER   My lord, I have from Oxford sent to London
      The heads of Brocas and Sir Bennet Seely,
15   Two of the dangerous consorted° traitors   *confederated*
      That sought at Oxford thy dire overthrow.
     KING HENRY   Thy pains, Fitzwalter, shall not be forgot.
      Right noble is thy merit, well I wot.°   *know*
          Enter HARRY PERCY [*with the* BISHOP OF] CARLISLE
          [*guarded*]

---

3. To make sure it is not poisoned.   5.6 Location: Windsor Castle.

HARRY PERCY   The grand conspirator Abbot of Westminster,
20   With clog° of conscience and sour melancholy,   *burden*
        Hath yielded up his body to the grave.
        But here is Carlisle living, to abide
        Thy kingly doom° and sentence of his pride.   *judgment*
KING HENRY   Carlisle, this is your doom.
25   Choose out some secret place, some reverent room
        More than thou hast,¹ and with it joy° thy life.   *enjoy*
        So as thou liv'st in peace, die free from strife.
        For though mine enemy thou hast ever been,
        High sparks of honour in thee have I seen.
            Enter EXTON *with [his men bearing] a coffin*
30 EXTON   Great King, within this coffin I present
        Thy buried fear. Herein all breathless lies
        The mightiest of thy greatest enemies,
        Richard of Bordeaux, by me hither brought.
KING HENRY   Exton, I thank thee not, for thou hast wrought
35   A deed of slander° with thy fatal hand   *disgrace*
        Upon my head and all this famous land.
EXTON   From your own mouth, my lord, did I this deed.
KING HENRY   They love not poison that do poison need;
        Nor do I thee. Though I did wish him dead,
40   I hate the murderer, love him murderèd.
        The guilt of conscience take thou for thy labour,
        But neither my good word nor princely favour.
        With Cain² go wander through the shades of night,
        And never show thy head by day nor light.
            [Exeunt EXTON *and his men]*
45   Lords, I protest my soul is full of woe
        That blood should sprinkle me to make me grow.
        Come mourn with me for what I do lament,
        And put on sullen black incontinent.°   *immediately*
        I'll make a voyage to the Holy Land
50   To wash this blood off from my guilty hand.
        March sadly after. Grace my mournings here
        In weeping after this untimely bier.   *Exeunt [with the coffin]*

---

1. More reverent than the prison cell you inhabit now.   demned to be a vagabond (Genesis 4:14).
2. After Cain murdered his brother Abel, he was con-

TEXTUAL VARIANTS

Control text: Q1; additional matter from F

F: The Folio of 1623
Q1: The Quarto of 1597
Q2, Q3: Quartos of 1598
Q4: The Quarto of 1608
Q5: The Quarto of 1615
Q6: The Quarto of 1634

Title: The Tragedie of Richard II [Q] The life and death of King Richard the Second [F]

s.p. KING RICHARD *King* [to 5.1]

1.1.118 by my [F] by **152 gentlemen** [F] gentleman **157 time** [F] month **162–63 Harry, when? / Obedience bids** *Harrie,* when? Obedience bids, / Obedience bids [F] Harry? when obedience bids, / Obedience bids **186 down** [F] vp
1.2.1 Gloucester's [F]; Woodstockes **58 it** [Q2, F] is
1.3.33 comest [Q5] comes [Q1] com'st [F] **55 just** [F] right **127 swords** [F] sword **127–28 swords, / Which** [F; Q1 has a five-line passage after line 127 omitted in F, indented in this edition. See Textual Note.] **166 then** [F; not in Q] **174 you owe** [F] y'owe **215 night** [Q4, F] nightes **220 sudden** [F] sullen **231–32 father. / Alas** [F; Q has a four-line passage omitted in F, indented in this edition after line 235.] **251 travel** trauaile **256–57 return. / s.p. BOLINGBROKE** [F; Q has twenty-six lines omitted from F, indented in this edition after line 256.] **256.2 remember** remember me
1.4.7 grew [F] blew **19 cousin, cousin** [F] Coosens Coosin **22 Bushy, Bagot here, and Green** [Q6] Bushie, [Q1] Bushy: heere *Bagot* and *Greene* [F] **51–52 *Enter Bushy / Bushy, what news?* [F] *Enter Bushie with newes.* [Q1] **58 in his** [F] in the [Q1] into the [Q2] **63 late!** [F] late, / Amen [indented]
2.1.18 whose taste the wise are feared whose taste the wise are found [Q1] Whose state the wise are found [Q2] his state: then there are sound [F] **48 as a** [Q4, F] as **70 reined** ragde **102 encagèd** [F] inraged **113 now,** now not, **115–16 And— / s.p. KING RICHARD And thou, a** [F] And thou / *King.* A **125 brother** [Q2] brothers **178 the** [F] a **233 that thou wouldst** thou wouldst [Q1] thou'dst [F] **255 his** [F] his noble **258 King's grown** [Q3, F] King growen **278 Port le** [F] le Port **281 Thomas . . . Arundel** [not in Q1, F; a line is missing, probably a result of censorship.] **284 Thomas Ramston** John Ramston **286 Coint** [F] Coines
2.2.12 At . . . With With . . . at **16 eye** [F] eyes **31 As thought—** As thought [Q1] As though [Q2, F] **59 broke** [Q2, F] broken **119 Castle** [F; not in Q1] **138 commoners** commons **148–49 s.p. BAGOT Farewell . . . / BUSHY Well** [continued to Green] Farewell . . . / *Bush⟨ie⟩* Well [Q1] *Bush⟨y⟩*. Farewell . . . Well [F]
2.3.36 Hereford, [Q3] Herefords **98 the** [F; not in Q1] **124 kinsman** [F] cousin **157 to** [Q2, F] vnto
3.1.32 England. [F] England, Lords farewell.
3.2.1 Harlechly Barkloughly **28–29 all. / s.p. AUMERLE** [F; Q1 has four lines omitted in F, indented in this edition after line 28.] **31 friends** [F] power **36 bloody** [Q2, F] bouldy **51 from** [F] off from **80 sluggard** [F] coward **81 forty** [F] twenty **98 loss,** [F] and **130 offence** [F; not in Q1] **174 wail their present woes** [F] sit and wail theyr woes **199 faction** [F] partie
3.3.13 with you [F; not in Q1] **35 Upon** [F] on both **58–59 rain / My waters** [F] raigne. / My water's **90 is** [F] standes **118 a prince and** princesse [Q1] a Prince [Q3] a Prince, is [F] **126 We** [Q4, F] *King.* We **126 ourself** [F] our selues **170 mock** [F] laugh
3.4.11 joy grief **35 too** [F] two **58 garden! We at** garden at [Q1] garden, at [Q3, F] **68 then** [not in Q1, F] **81 Cam'st** [Q2, F] them
4.1.21 him [Q3, F] them **50–51 foe. / s.p. SURREY** [F; Q1 has an eight-line passage omit-

ted from F, indented in this edition after line 50.] **50.3 may** it may **50.4 sun to sun** sinne to sinne **67 my** [Q3, F; not in Q1] the [Q2] **92 Bishop of Carlisle** Bishop [Q3, F] B. [Q1] **103 of that name the fourth** [F] fourth of that name **136 you** [Q2, F] yon **136 rear** [F] raise **139 Prevent** Preuent it **145–308 May . . . fall** [F (and similarly Q4); not in Q1. Only departures from F are noted for these lines.] **227 upon** [Q4] vpon me **241 and** [Q4] a **245 Nor** [Q4] No, nor **309–10 On . . . yourselves** [Q4, F] Let it be so, and loe on wednesday next, / We solemnly proclaime our Coronation, / Lords be ready all [Q1] **322 I will** Ile

5.1.25 stricken [F] throwne **44 fall** [F] tale **66 friends** [F] men **78 queen** [F] wife **84 s.p. NORTHUMBERLAND** [F] *King.*

5.2.52 Hold these jousts and triumphs Hold those Iusts & Triumphs [F] do these iusts & triumphs hold **55 prevent it** preuent **78 by my life, my** by my life, by my [Q1] my life, my [Q2, F] **82 son** [F] Aumerle

5.3.1 tell [F] tell me **14 these** [F] those **21 days** [F] yeares **30 the** my **35 I may** [Q2, F] May **55 lest** lest thy **73 voiced** [Q3, F] voice **91 kneel** [F] walke **100 mouth** [Q2, F] month **109 s.p. KING HENRY** [Q2, F] *yorke* **142 so** [not in Q1, F] too [Q6]

5.4.3, 6 s.p. FIRST, SECOND [not in Q1, F] **3 Those** [F] These

5.5.13–14 faith . . . faith [F] word . . . word **33 treason makes** [F] treasons make **55 sounds that tell** sound that tells **56 that** [F] which **58 hours, and times** [F] times, and houres **65 a sign** [Q2, F] asigne **94 spur-galled** [F] Spurrde, galld

5.6.8 Salisbury, Spencer, Blunt [F] Oxford, Salisbury, Blunt [Q1] Oxford, Salisbury [Q2] **17 not** [Q2, F1] nor **43 through the** [F] through

The Life and Death of King John

Historical narrative normally attributes a fundamental meaning to history. *The Life and Death of King John* (1596) is an exception. Though focusing on historical process, on how events fit together over time, it suggests the larger significance of John's reign (1199–1216) only in a way that is deeply disorienting. The problem is less history's meaninglessness than its excessive meaningfulness: the plot promises more coherence than it delivers. The apparent trajectory of events repeatedly proves illusory; seemingly decisive moments turn out to be mere episodes in the open-ended, ironic, unpredictable movement of history. The play thus breaks with the providential conclusion to Shakespeare's first tetralogy (four related plays) provided by *Richard III* (1592–93) and, more generally, with the moralizing strategy of Renaissance humanist historians. It moves Shakespeare closer to the pragmatic, secular political thinking of Niccolò Machiavelli.

The logic of the plot is to undermine logic, to frustrate expectation, to reveal the uncertain relation between intention and outcome in a world that offers only fragments of an overarching religious consolation for the frequent futility of human endeavor. The basic conflict turns on John's efforts to retain the crown. The opening struggle over inheritance between the Bastard and his younger half-brother Robert Falconbridge leads to the surprising conclusion that bastardy is no barrier to inheritance. Even more surprisingly, the Bastard then renounces that inheritance. Similarly, when the English and French battle to a stalemate in seeking the loyalty of Angers, they first decide to level the town to punish its autonomy and then instead resolve to end their quarrel—and thus spare the town—through a cynical political marriage. This resolution proves as transitory as the previous ones when Pandolf, the papal legate, excommunicates John, and France as a result repudiates the deal. Though John now appears in trouble, his ensuing military triumph seems to shift his fortunes again. Yet by then ordering the murder of Arthur, his young nephew and chief rival for the throne, he undermines his own position. At first, it seems that John will be rescued from the consequences of his crime when Hubert, the executioner, spares Arthur. But Arthur dies attempting to escape, an accident the English lords interpret as murder. Their defection to the invading French army seems to seal John's fate. Though John tries to remove the rationale for the invasion by belatedly submitting to the pope, this characteristically has no effect. When the lords learn that the Dauphin, son of the King of France, plans to kill them after securing the English throne, however, they scurry back to John.

The war itself is marked less by climactic battles than by both sides' careless habit of losing their armies at sea: nature too intervenes to subvert probability. But even this is not enough to save John. Hated by the English clergy for his earlier extortions from the monasteries, he is poisoned by a vengeful monk. This is an outcome that lacks dramatic logic: the pillaging of the monasteries is undramatized in the play and given very little weight, John's resistance to Catholic domination is viewed positively if peripherally, he has been reconciled with Rome, and he is apparently dying of a fever even before he is poisoned. Finally, Prince Henry, the King's son and a child like Arthur, is pulled from a hat and recognized as the legitimate heir just as peace breaks out between England and France. Accordingly, the orthodox ending, in which the dead King is succeeded by his son and rightful heir, feels highly contingent.

This view of history, in which the meaning of events proves unstable and problematic, is of a piece with Shakespeare's treatment of contemporary politics, his sources, his central themes, and his major characters, as well as with the play's later fortunes in the theater. For its early audiences, *King John* may have provided a compelling projection back into the thirteenth century of the highly charged issue of the legitimacy of Queen Elizabeth and the competing claims of Mary, Queen of Scots. The parallels are numerous and striking. First, John's claim to the crown depends on the legally questionable will of his oldest brother, Richard I (the Lionheart); the will of Elizabeth's father, Henry VIII, made Elizabeth the heir, but the legitimacy of appointing one's successors by will had been challenged even in Henry's lifetime. Second, Shakespeare's John is accused of being a bastard and is excommunicated by the pope; Elizabeth was declared a bastard by her father and excommunicated by the pope. Third, John's rival, Arthur, is the son of Geoffrey, John's other older brother (along with Richard), and succession routinely passed to the offspring of the older child. In like manner, Mary, Queen of Scots, was the daughter of Henry's older sister, but Henry's will violated custom by excluding this sister's descendants from the succession. Elizabeth's legal claim to the crown was thus arguably weaker than Mary's. Fourth, Arthur's cause is championed by King Philip of France; Mary too enjoyed the support of foreign Catholic monarchs, including King Philip II of Spain. Fifth, after ordering Arthur's death, John unsuccessfully tries to absolve himself of the crime he commissioned but did not commit; in 1587, Mary was executed for comparable reasons by command of Elizabeth, who distanced herself from the judicial murder she had in fact ordered. Sixth, Arthur's death provokes an invasion from France to impose foreign and Catholic rule. The invaders are led by the Dauphin, Philip of France's son and heir, whose claim to the English crown is based on his marriage to John's niece. Analogous motives led Philip II of Spain, the widowed husband of Elizabeth's older sister, who was her predecessor as queen, to launch the Spanish Armada the year after Mary's death. Finally, in *King John*, England is saved by a providential storm that destroys much of the French navy. So too a storm wrecked much of the armada, a catastrophe interpreted in England as God's deliverance of Protestant England from its enemies intent on conquest and Catholic rule.

The coronation of King John. From Matthew of Westminster, *Flores Historiarum* (late thirteenth or early fourteenth century).

Though these summaries oversimplify theater and history alike, they suggest the explosive issues Shakespeare dramatized—the struggle with the papacy, the threat of invasion, and especially the problem of legitimate rule. To be sure, there were risks in questioning Elizabeth's royal legitimacy or in accusing her of murdering the rightful queen. But *King John* raises these matters not to resolve them but to meditate on their complexity. John both is and is not Arthur's murderer; he both is and is not the legitimate King.

Shakespeare's use of his sources reveals the same pattern—an attraction to politically powerful material combined with an impulse toward undermining ideological certainty. *King John*'s closest analogue is the anonymous play *The Troublesome Reign of John, King of England* (published 1591), which most critics believe is Shakespeare's primary source (on the two plays' relative chronology, see the Textual Note). If *The Troublesome Reign* is the earlier work, as is assumed here, it relies in part on Raphael Holinshed's *Chronicles of England, Scotland, and Ireland* (second edition, 1587), the nonfictional narrative of English history on which Shakespeare himself drew extensively during the 1590s for his other English history plays. *The Troublesome Reign*'s author reshapes chronology and invents episodes, changes that *King John* generally adopts, and promotes conventional Protestant and English chauvinism, which *King John* mutes. From early in the English Reformation, John was seen as a proto-Protestant royal martyr who temporarily stood up to the Roman Catholic Church, both in rejecting the papal choice for archbishop of Canterbury and in heavily taxing the church. More closely following Holinshed, who combines this Protestant view with a centuries-old Catholic hostility to John that endured into the Renaissance, Shakespeare tones down the rhetoric of *The Troublesome Reign*. While that play justifies John's taxes on the monasteries by portraying monks engaged in outrageous sexual conduct, Shakespeare omits the scene and calls John's policy pillaging. Similarly, although John's submission to Rome is lamented in *King John*, Shakespeare hardly makes the decision catastrophic. But he does retain some of *The Troublesome Reign*'s anti-Catholicism—for instance, in John's defense of an English church. Overall, however, the play's Protestantism is unmilitant: *King John* offers scant comfort to Catholics but little more to Protestants.

Shakespeare also tones down *The Troublesome Reign*'s commitment to English national chauvinism. *King John* concludes with the Bastard's patriotic credo:

> This England never did, nor never shall,
> Lie at the proud foot of a conqueror
> But when it first did help to wound itself.
> Now these her princes are come home again,
> Come the three corners of the world in arms
> And we shall shock them. Naught shall make us rue
> If England to itself do rest but true.
>
> (5.7.112–18)

Yet these lines are more ambiguous than they first appear. Though they firmly oppose foreign conquest of England, the play has seriously entertained the possibility that such domination is a lesser evil than continued rule by a murderous English monarch. Moreover, the "if" in the final sentence tempers optimism, especially given the conduct of the aristocracy.

A more vexed question is the nature of "England" itself. Temporally, *King John* differs from Shakespeare's other history plays of the 1590s: it treats the early thirteenth rather than the late fourteenth and fifteenth centuries. In addition, it is not part of a tetralogy, and hence it does not develop the resonance of "England" by depicting the sequence of reigns. Sociologically, the play also stands alone. Today, John's reign is remembered for the Magna Carta and the adventures of Robin Hood. Both concern resistance to royal tyranny, by the aristocracy and the lower class, respectively. Though both stories were available in the 1590s, neither appears in the play. The lords rebel late in the action, but the issue of the balance of power between King and nobility remains secondary. And despite a brief reference to popular unrest, *King John* accords the English people an even more marginal role in constituting the nation. This treatment of aristocracy and populace contrasts with Shakespeare's approach in his history plays of the next three years, *1* and *2 Henry IV* and *Henry V.*

The relative underdevelopment of "England" encourages a different focus—on the tension between royal legitimacy and fitness to rule. Although *King John* shares this concern with *Richard II* (1595), the most interesting gloss comes from a later play:

> Why 'bastard'? Wherefore 'base',
> . . . .
> . . . Why brand they us
> With 'base', with 'baseness, bastardy—base, base'—
> . . . .
> Legitimate Edgar, I must have your land.
> . . . .
> . . . Fine word, 'legitimate'.
> Well, my legitimate, if this letter speed
> And my invention thrive, Edmond the base
> Shall to th' legitimate. I grow, I prosper.
> Now gods, stand up for bastards!
> (*The Tragedy of King Lear* 1.2.6–22)

Despite Edmond's plea, the gods in *King Lear* do not stand up for bastards. That work asks instead whether hereditary legitimacy can coincide with fitness to rule. By contrast, *King John's* "fine word" is "illegitimate": it asks whether hereditary illegitimacy can coincide with fitness to rule. In *King John*, the gods stand up for bastards.

The play's treatment of this issue, which often seems like a formal debate, turns on the relationship between John, the protagonist, and Arthur, the central victim. John's legitimacy is already disputed in *The Troublesome Reign*, and Shakespeare further weakens the King's legal position. When John explains why he will prevail against the French and Arthur—"Our strong possession and our right for us" (1.1.39)—his mother cautions, "Your strong possession much more than your right" (line 40). Her denial of legality has particular authority because—not surprisingly—she supports John. John unwittingly concedes her point when faced with the parallel case of Robert Falconbridge, who wants to inherit his father's lands, as his father's will provides. But John correctly interprets the law, which stipulates that the offspring of a wife's extramarital affair is the legitimate child of her husband. John thus finds in favor of the Bastard, Robert's older half-brother, who is the result of their mother's adulterous liaison with Richard the Lionheart. In matters of inheritance, the law takes precedence over a will. Yet when Arthur's mother, Constance, asserts his right to the throne, Eleanor replies, "I can produce / A will that bars the title of thy son" (2.1.191–92). The will is King Richard's, in which John is named successor. But since the law calls for inheritance through the line of Geoffrey, John's older brother and Arthur's father, Arthur's claim is legitimate and John's is not. "Legitimate" and "fit" are not synonymous, however. After undermining John's hereditary right, Shakespeare complicates the question. He departs from his sources by making Arthur a helpless child heavily dependent on his mother, on the King of France, and on King Richard's slayer (the Duke of Austria). Arthur also has no interest in being King: his unfitness to rule means that John's "strong possession" carries real weight.

The dispute between John and Arthur is carried out by proxy. Eleanor and especially Constance, whose part Shakespeare expanded from his sources, initially have more active roles than do their sons and (with the Bastard) rhetorically dominate the stage—most strikingly in their confrontation in 2.1 and in Constance's subsequent lamentations. Going beyond the common female role—victim of history—these women attempt to direct the action. Moreover, Constance and Eleanor question each other's sexual honor—an issue that is broached earlier when the Bastard's mother acknowledges her adulterous affair with King Richard. This recurrent concern underscores the uncertainty of biologically legitimate patriarchal succession. Hereditary descent from father to son tacitly accords a central role to women, whose sexual fidelity is felt to be necessary but unreliable. *King John* emphasizes the dubious fidelity of women but denies its necessity: the mothers too weaken traditional notions of legitimacy. Yet Constance's powerful rhetoric changes no one's mind, and midway through the play both she and Eleanor disappear from the plot. With them go the challenges they pose.

Perhaps as a result of the mothers' deaths, the sons become increasingly inept. They are most memorable not in themselves but for the way that physical imagery running through *King John*, often as personification, is ultimately reliteralized in the accounts of their own bodily suffering. Arthur leaps to his accidental, meaningless death when the "Good ground" of England, which he hopes does "not break my limbs," proves to be inhospitable "stones" (4.3.2, 6, 9). Earlier, the motif of fire and heat is picked up in the threat to burn out Arthur's eyes, a threat echoed in, to use John's words, the "tyrant fever [that] burns me up" and the poison that produces "so hot a summer in my bosom" (5.3.14, 5.7.30). More generally, John's stunned response to his mother's death helps explain the radical transformation in his behavior—from confident leadership to helpless passivity. By the last part of the play, he is neither tragic nor villainous but simply beside the point, his fall having coincided with the Bastard's rise.

That rise makes possible a defense of illegitimacy. An almost entirely unhistorical personage in the least historical of Shakespeare's history plays, the Bastard is the most prominent character in the work but arguably less a coherent fictional figure than a series of discontinuous theatrical functions. His changes seem to be dictated more by the twists of the plot than by shifts in his personality. At first, the Bastard primarily embodies a mischievous popular culture. Theatrically, he descends from the devilish Vice figure, a character in the earlier English morality plays. The Vice combined a commitment to evil, an intimacy with the audience, and an attractive penchant for fun. Similarly, the Bastard speaks to and for the audience in asides and soliloquies, denouncing the moral failings of the rich and powerful while cheerfully conceding that he too is out for himself. He takes pleasure in promoting discord and destruction, and he appears immune to bodily harm, an immunity that wins him repeated description as the devil.

Another side of the Bastard also appears early on but becomes dominant only in the second half of the play. After John deems him legitimate, the Bastard rejects his previous patrimony in order to be knighted and recognized as the dead King Richard's illegitimate son, an act that allows the identification of royalty with illegitimacy. His unswerving loyalty contrasts with the cynical deal between John and the King of France—a deal that the Bastard memorably denounces as "commodity," or self-interest (2.1.562–99). Later, that loyalty casts a harsh light on the treasonous alliance with the French formed by the English aristocrats, who are motivated by a mixture of principle and "commodity"—the very considerations that soon prompt them to change sides again and renew their allegiance to

King John's tomb in Worcester Cathedral. From Francis Sanford, *A Genealogical History of the Kings and Queens of England* (1707).

John. In response to Arthur's death and John's decline, the Bastard at this point becomes a more responsible if less entertaining figure—a shift Shakespeare manages by keeping the character offstage for five hundred lines. Horrified by Arthur's death but persuaded that it was an accident, he undertakes the defense of the crown as well as the realm. In this endeavor, he proves the ethical, in addition to the merely rhetorical, center of a world otherwise almost devoid of positive value. He owes this unique authority to his unparalleled range of social and theatrical roles. As the spirit of his biological father in the play, he reflects both badly and well on the King. Compared with the Bastard, whose heroic, comic, and at times misguided swashbuckling style includes the easy exaction of family vengeance through the killing of Austria, John looks mediocre at best. Yet the Bastard's presence suggests that Richard guards the throne, that John is the right person for the job. Fitness to rule may be found in the ostensibly illegitimate.

But by ordering Arthur's murder, John squanders his authority, thereby also weakening the play's concern with the possible conflict between hereditary legitimacy and rightful rule. In the end, *King John*'s skepticism about the meaningfulness of historical process weakens even what is apparently its central theme. A similar fate is reserved for its central character: despite his crucial role in recognizing John's legitimate heir and in articulating a vision of national unity, the Bastard too is partly undermined. In Holinshed, John "lost a great part of his army" to drowning; in *The Troublesome Reign*, the Bastard reports to John that the sea has "swallowed up the most of all our men." *King John* forces the Bastard to narrate this event twice, both times in language that seems to make him more directly responsible for the debacle—"half my power," "the best part of my power" (5.6.40, 5.7.61). Ineptitude is soon replaced by irrelevance: the Bastard opts for war after others have already negotiated peace. Though he is not simply shunted aside by the unpredictable concatenation of historical events, the meaningful resolution he ultimately seeks to impose has less to do with human intention and achievement than with the fortuitous collapse of both contending parties.

Finally, the distinctive, enigmatic logic of *King John*'s plot has affected its theatrical fortunes. Since the eighteenth century, the play has been cut to make its uncertain nationalism less ambiguous. In the nineteenth century, its discontinuities and many dramatically effective confrontations between characters encouraged productions in which narrative sweep was sacrificed to pageantry and individual scenes (especially involving Constance). In related fashion, *King John* has proven useful for political allegory in times of crisis. It was prominent in the unsuccessful battle against the censorship legislation of the 1737 Licensing Act, and it was marshaled to support loyalist opposition to the Catholic Jacobite invasion of England in 1745. It served similar ends in the French and Indian War fifteen years later, during the Napoleonic Wars at the beginning of the nineteenth century, as a justification for British imperialism at the time of the Boer War in South Africa in 1899, and as a rallying cry before and during World War II. A 1961 production took the contested city of Angers as an image of Berlin, recently divided between East and West, and subsequent decades saw performances in several Eastern European Communist countries. Though *King John* was the first of Shakespeare's plays to be filmed (in 1899, an extremely brief version consisting of three scenes—John's temptation of Hubert, Constance's lamentation, and John's death scene), the work's theatrical standing has declined, at least throughout this century. There may be promise, however, in the rebellion during the last generation against politically orthodox interpretations in criticism and performance alike. Perhaps a revival of interest depends less on the play's pageantry or jingoism than on its disabused view of power and its refusal to find reassurance in the interconnected, yet uncertain, sequence of historical events.

WALTER COHEN

TEXTUAL NOTE

The initial printing of *The Life and Death of King John* was in the First Folio of 1623 (F). The text published there probably goes back to an authorial manuscript, or "foul papers," from 1596 that was subsequently copied between 1609 and 1623 by two scribes. Their transcript, though not a promptbook, seems to have been designed with future theatrical performance in mind. The second scribe moved further from Shakespeare's manuscript toward stage-ready copy than did the first. In response to a law of 1606 prohibiting oaths, the scribes probably cleaned up Shakespeare's language, replacing, for instance, "God" with "heaven."

The *Norton Shakespeare* reverses that process so as to restore what Shakespeare wrote but retains other scribal innovations, such as the introduction of act and scene divisions. In F, these are messy and illogical, perhaps in part because two compositors set the type for the play. This edition follows earlier editors in treating F's "Scaena Secunda" as 2.1, and its "Actus Secundus" as 2.2, though this is not the only reasonable solution. Still another judgment call is necessary. Beginning at the present edition's 2.1.325, F starts calling the Citizen of Angers "Hubert." The shift may indicate a desire to double the parts (that is, to have the same actor play both roles) or to conflate the two characters. If the latter, the extant text does not complete the job: the two men do not seem like the same person. Accordingly, this edition emends F to keep the two characters separate.

King John's initial publication date of 1623 helps determine when it was written. Partly on the basis of the work's recourse to rhetoric reminiscent of the period of the Spanish Armada (1588), a few scholars place its composition in 1590 or earlier and see it as a source for the anonymous play *The Troublesome Reign of John, King of England* (published in 1591). Yet a direct link between the wording of two stage directions in *The Troublesome Reign* and their analogues in *King John* is easily explained only on the assumption that the anonymous play came first and that Shakespeare was familiar with it. Shakespeare could have read the relevant stage directions of *The Troublesome Reign* in the 1591 edition of that play, but it is not clear how the author of *The Troublesome Reign* could have known of Shakespeare's unpublished stage directions. Stylistic and metrical tests, which date *King John* to roughly 1596, strongly support this hypothesis.

SELECTED BIBLIOGRAPHY

Braunmuller, A. R. "*King John* and Historiography." *ELH* 55 (1988): 309–32.

Burckhardt, Sigurd. *Shakespearean Meanings.* Princeton: Princeton University Press, 1968. 116–43.

Curren-Aquino, Deborah T., ed. "*King John*": *New Perspectives.* Newark: University of Delaware Press, 1989.

Danby, John F. *Shakespeare's Doctrine of Nature: A Study of "King Lear."* London: Faber and Faber, 1949. 67–79.

Dusinberre, Juliet. "*King John* and Embarrassing Women." *Shakespeare Survey* 42 (1989): 37–52.

Elliot, John R. "Shakespeare and the Double Image of King John." *Shakespeare Studies* 1 (1965): 64–84.

Grennan, Eamon. "Shakespeare's Satirical History: A Reading of *King John*." *Shakespeare Studies* 11 (1978): 21–38.

Hodgdon, Barbara. *The End Crowns All: Closure and Contradiction in Shakespeare's History.* Princeton: Princeton University Press, 1991. 22–43.

Shirley, Frances A., ed. "*King John*" *and* "*Henry VIII*": *Critical Essays.* New York: Garland, 1988.

Womersly, David. "The Politics of Shakespeare's *King John*." *Review of English Studies*, n.s., 40 (1989): 497–515.

King John

KING JOHN of England
QUEEN ELEANOR, his mother
LADY FALCONBRIDGE
Philip the BASTARD, later knighted as Sir Richard Plantagenet,
    her illegitmate son by King Richard I (Coeur-de-lion)
Robert FALCONBRIDGE, her legitimate son
James GURNEY, her attendant
Lady BLANCHE of Spain, niece of King John
PRINCE HENRY, son of King John
HUBERT, a follower of King John
Earl of SALISBURY
Earl of PEMBROKE
Earl of ESSEX
Lord BIGOT
KING PHILIP of France
LOUIS THE DAUPHIN, his son
ARTHUR, Duke of Brittaine, nephew of King John
Lady CONSTANCE, his mother
Duke of AUSTRIA (Limoges)
CHÂTILLON, ambassador from France to England
Count MELUN
A CITIZEN of Angers
Cardinal PANDOLF, a legate from the Pope
PETER OF POMFRET, a prophet
HERALDS
EXECUTIONERS
MESSENGERS
SHERIFF
Lords, soldiers, attendants

1.1

[*Flourish.*] *Enter* KING JOHN, QUEEN ELEANOR,[1] [*and the
Earls of*] PEMBROKE, ESSEX, *and* SALISBURY; *with the*[m]
        CHÂTILLON *of France*

KING JOHN   Now say, Châtillon, what would France with us?[2]
CHÂTILLON   Thus, after greeting, speaks the King of France,
    In my behaviour,° to the majesty—   *person*
    The borrowed° majesty—of England here.   *usurped*
5 QUEEN ELEANOR   A strange beginning: 'borrowed majesty'?
KING JOHN   Silence, good mother, hear the embassy.°   *message*
CHÂTILLON   Philip of France, in right and true behalf

1.1 Location: John's court in London.
1. This scene, which occupies the first act, is unhistorical. The youngest son of Henry II and "Queen Eleanor" (Eleanor of Aquitaine), John (1167–1216) succeeded his brother, the famed crusader Richard I (the Lionheart), in

1199 and ruled until his death. Eleanor of Aquitaine (c. 1122–1204) was Queen first of France and then of England.
2. What does (the King of) France wish with us?

Of thy deceasèd brother Geoffrey's[3] son,
Arthur Plantagenet,[4] lays most lawful claim
10 To this fair island and the territories,
To Ireland, Poitou, Anjou, Touraine, Maine;[5]
Desiring thee to lay aside the sword
Which sways° usurpingly these several titles,°   *rules / separate lands*
And put the same into young Arthur's hand,
15 Thy nephew and right royal sovereign.
KING JOHN   What follows if we disallow of this?
CHÂTILLON   The proud control° of fierce and bloody war,   *compulsion*
To enforce these rights so forcibly withheld—
KING JOHN   Here have we war for war, and blood for blood,
20 Controlment for controlment: so answer France.
CHÂTILLON   Then take my king's defiance from my mouth,
The farthest limit of my embassy.
KING JOHN   Bear mine° to him, and so depart in peace.   *my defiance*
Be thou as lightning in the eyes of France,
25 For ere thou canst report,[6] I will be there;
The thunder of my cannon° shall be heard.   *(anachronism)*
So hence. Be thou the trumpet of our wrath,
And sullen presage° of your own decay.°—   *gloomy omen / downfall*
An honourable conduct° let him have;   *escort*
30 Pembroke, look to't.—Farewell, Châtillon.
                    Exeunt CHÂTILLON *and* PEMBROKE
QUEEN ELEANOR   What now, my son? Have I not ever° said   *always*
How that ambitious Constance[7] would not cease
Till she had kindled France and all the world
Upon° the right and party of her son?   *On behalf of*
35 This might have been prevented and made whole°   *settled*
With very easy arguments of love,°   *friendly discussions*
Which now the manage° of two kingdoms must   *government*
With fearful-bloody issue° arbitrate.   *outcome*
KING JOHN   Our strong possession and our right for us.°   *on our side*
QUEEN ELEANOR [*aside to* KING JOHN]   Your strong possession
40   much more than your right,
Or else it must go wrong with you and me:
So much my conscience whispers in your ear,
Which none but heaven and you and I shall hear.
                    Enter a SHERIFF [*who whispers to* ESSEX]
ESSEX   My liege,° here is the strangest controversy,   *lord*
45 Come from the country to be judged by you,
That e'er I heard. Shall I produce the men?
KING JOHN   Let them approach.—   [*Exit* SHERIFF]

---

3. Geoffrey was older than John and younger than Richard I; he died before Henry II. Because of changes in the laws of inheritance, John's claims to the throne would have been weaker in Shakespeare's lifetime—and are so represented—than they were in his own day, the early thirteenth century.
4. "Plantagenet" was the family name of most English monarchs from the accession of Henry II in 1154 to the deposition of Richard III in 1485. The historical Arthur was in his late teens; Shakespeare makes him much younger.

5. Except for Ireland, English territories in western and central France. Historically, it was these French territories, rather than the English crown itself, that Arthur claimed.
6. Before you can deliver your message (pun on noise of thunder or cannon).
7. Arthur's mother, Geoffrey's widow in Shakespeare and in his main source, *The Troublesome Reign of King John*. Historically, Constance remarried twice after Geoffrey's death.

Our abbeys and our priories shall pay[8]
This expeditious charge.°   *sudden cost (of war)*

Enter Robert FALCONBRIDGE *and Philip [the* BASTARD,[9]
with the Sheriff]
                                            What men are you?
50 BASTARD   Your faithful subject I, a gentleman
Born in Northamptonshire, and eldest son,
As I suppose, to Robert Falconbridge,
A soldier, by the honour-giving hand
Of Cœur-de-lion° knighted in the field.   *Richard the Lionheart*
55 KING JOHN   What art thou?
FALCONBRIDGE   The son and heir to that same Falconbridge.
KING JOHN   Is that the elder, and art thou the heir?
You came not of one mother then, it seems.
BASTARD   Most certain of one mother, mighty King—
60 That is well known—and, as I think, one father.
But for the certain knowledge of that truth
I put you o'er to° heaven, and to my mother.   *refer you to*
Of that° I doubt as all men's children may.   *(truth)*
QUEEN ELEANOR   Out on thee,° rude man! Thou dost shame   *Away with you*
thy mother
65 And wound her honour with this diffidence.°   *distrust*
BASTARD   I, Madam? No, I have no reason for it.
That is my brother's plea and none of mine,
The which if he can prove, a pops me out°   *he deprives me of*
At least from fair five hundred pound a year.
70 Heaven guard my mother's honour, and my land!
KING JOHN   A good blunt fellow.—Why, being younger born,
Doth he lay claim to thine inheritance?
BASTARD   I know not why, except to get the land;
But once he slandered me with bastardy.
75 But whe'er° I be as true° begot or no,   *whether / legitimately*
That still I lay upon my mother's head;°   *I let my mother answer*
But that I am as well begot, my liege—
Fair fall the bones that took the pains for me[1]—
Compare our faces and be judge yourself.
80 If old Sir Robert did beget us both
And were our father, and this son like him,
O old Sir Robert, father, on my knee
I give heaven thanks I was not like to thee.
KING JOHN   Why, what a madcap hath heaven lent us here!
85 QUEEN ELEANOR[2]   He hath a trick° of Cœur-de-lion's face;   *distinguishing trait*
The accent of his tongue affecteth° him.   *resembles*
Do you not read some tokens of my son
In the large composition° of this man?   *openness; build*
KING JOHN   Mine eye hath well examinèd his parts,°   *attributes*
And finds them perfect Richard.
90 [*To Robert* FALCONBRIDGE]   Sirrah,° speak: *(used to inferiors)*
What doth move you to claim your brother's land?

---

8. Alluding to John's much-resented taxation of the monastic orders.
9. Drawing upon a passing reference in Holinshed's *Chronicles, The Troublesome Reign* invents a major role for this character, a role that Shakespeare further expands.

1. May good fortune befall the bones (of the dead man) who went to the trouble of begetting me.
2. The Queen may speak the following lines privately to John.

BASTARD   Because he hath a half-face° like my father!   *profile; thin face*
    With half that face³ would he have all my land,
    A half-faced groat⁴ five hundred pound a year.
95   FALCONBRIDGE   My gracious liege, when that my father lived,
    Your brother° did employ my father much—   *(Richard)*
    BASTARD   Well, sir, by this you cannot get my land.
    Your tale must be how he employed my mother.
    FALCONBRIDGE   And once dispatched him in an embassy
100   To Germany, there with the Emperor
    To treat of high affairs touching that time.
    Th'advantage of his absence took the King,
    And in the meantime sojourned at my father's,
    Where how he did prevail I shame to speak.
105   But truth is truth: large lengths of seas and shores
    Between my father and my mother lay,
    As I have heard my father speak himself,
    When this same lusty° gentleman was got.°   *vigorous / conceived*
    Upon his deathbed he by will bequeathed
110   His lands to me, and took it on his death°   *solemnly swore*
    That this my mother's son was none of his;
    And if he were, he came into the world
    Full fourteen weeks before the course of time.
    Then, good my liege, let me have what is mine,
115   My father's land, as was my father's will.
    KING JOHN   Sirrah, your brother is legitimate.°   *(legally correct)*
    Your father's wife did after wedlock bear him,
    And if she did play false, the fault was hers,
    Which fault lies on the hazards of° all husbands   *is a risk for*
120   That marry wives. Tell me, how if my brother,
    Who, as you say, took pains to get this son,
    Had of your father claimed this son for his?
    In sooth, good friend, your father might have kept
    This calf, bred from his cow, from all the world;
125   In sooth he might. Then if he were my brother's,
    My brother might not claim him, nor your father,
    Being none of his, refuse him.⁵ This concludes:
    My mother's son did get your father's heir;
    Your father's heir must have your father's land.
130   FALCONBRIDGE   Shall then my father's will be of no force
    To dispossess that child which is not his?
    BASTARD   Of no more force to dispossess me, sir,
    Than was his will° to get me, as I think.   *legal instrument; lust*
    QUEEN ELEANOR   Whether hadst° thou rather be: a Falconbridge,   *Which would*
135   And like thy brother to enjoy thy land,
    Or the reputed son of Cœur-de-lion,
    Lord of thy presence,° and no land beside?   *yourself*
    BASTARD   Madam, an if° my brother had my shape,   *an if = if*
    And I had his, Sir Robert's his° like him,   *Sir Robert's*
140   And if my legs were two such riding-rods,°   *their riding switches*
    My arms such eel-skins stuffed, my face so thin
    That in mine ear I durst not stick a rose

---

3. Half of his father's face, since Falconbridge inherits maternal features as well; "face" is also "impudence."
4. A coin showing the monarch's head in profile; also Falconbridge, who as a person is worth only as much as a groat (four pence), despite his inheritance.
5. *nor . . . him:* nor could your father, though not the biological father to the Bastard, disown him.

Lest men should say 'Look where three-farthings goes!',[6]
And, to° his shape, were heir to all this land,   *in addition to*
145   Would I might never stir from off this place.[7]
I would give it every foot° to have this face;   *every foot of it*
It would not be Sir Nob in any case.[8]
QUEEN ELEANOR   I like thee well. Wilt thou forsake thy fortune,
Bequeath thy land to him, and follow me?
150   I am a soldier and now bound to France.
BASTARD   Brother, take you my land; I'll take my chance.
Your face hath got five hundred pound a year,
Yet sell your face for fivepence and 'tis dear.°—   *expensive*
Madam, I'll follow you unto the death.
155   QUEEN ELEANOR   Nay, I would have you go before me thither.
BASTARD   Our country manners give our betters way.[9]
KING JOHN   What is thy name?
BASTARD   Philip, my liege, so is my name begun:
Philip, good old Sir Robert's wife's eldest son.
160   KING JOHN   From henceforth bear his name whose form thou bear'st.
Kneel thou down Philip, but arise more great:
[*He knights the* BASTARD]
Arise Sir Richard and Plantagenet.
BASTARD   Brother by th' mother's side, give me your hand.
My father gave me honour, yours gave land.
165   Now blessèd be the hour, by night or day,
When I was got, Sir Robert was away.
QUEEN ELEANOR   The very spirit of Plantagenet!
I am thy grandam, Richard; call me so.
BASTARD   Madam, by chance, but not by truth;° what though?°   *chastely / but so what?*
170   Something about,° a little from the right,°   *a bit off / unlawful*
In at the window, or else o'er the hatch;[1]
Who dares not stir by day must walk° by night,   *go; rob (sexually)*
And have is have, however men do catch.[2]
Near or far off, well won is still well shot,[3]
175   And I am I, howe'er I was begot.
KING JOHN   Go, Falconbridge, now hast thou thy desire:
A landless knight° makes thee a landed squire.—   *(the Bastard)*
Come, madam, and come, Richard; we must speed
For France; for France, for it is more than need.
180   BASTARD   Brother, adieu. Good fortune come to thee,
For thou wast got i'th' way of honesty.
Exeunt all but [*the*] BASTARD
A foot of honour[4] better than I was,
But many a many foot of land the worse.
Well, now can I make any Joan° a lady.   *lower-class woman*

6. A rose appeared behind the Queen's head on a three-
farthing coin, which was thin and of small value (less than
a penny).
7. May I be struck dead here and now.
8. My appearance would not be that of Sir Robert under
any circumstances. The speech is full of sexual innuendo.
"Riding-rods" (line 140) and "eel-skins" (line 141) hint at
sexual inadequacy associated with a thin penis. "Nob"
(line 147) is also slang for "penis." "Rose" (line 142),
"shape" (line 144), and "case" (line 147) may refer to the
vagina; "riding" (line 140), "stuffed" (line 141), "stick a
rose" (line 142), and "foot" (line 146) suggest copulation;

and "stir" (line 145) can mean "sexually arouse."
9. The Bastard jokes that it's proper to let social superiors
go first.
1. Both phrases are proverbial for birth out of wedlock.
hatch: the lower half of a divided door.
2. That is, possession is nine-tenths of the law.
3. Archery metaphor, with sexual innuendo, as with "stir"
(line 172). The entire passage is also marked by mock-
proverbial expressions.
4. A degree of status. The Bastard contrasts his aristocratic "honour" with Falconbridge's middle-class "honesty" (line 181).

185 'Good e'en, Sir Richard'—'God-a-mercy[5] fellow';
And if his name be George I'll call him Peter,
For new-made honour doth forget men's names;
'Tis too respective and too sociable
For your conversion.[6] Now your traveller,
190 He and his toothpick at my worship's mess;
And when my knightly stomach is sufficed,
Why then I suck my teeth[7] and catechize
My pickèd° man of countries. 'My dear sir,'   affected; tooth-picked
Thus leaning on mine elbow I begin,
195 'I shall beseech you—'. That is Question now;
And then comes Answer like an Absey book.°   a school (ABC) primer
'O sir,' says Answer, 'at your best command,
At your employment, at your service, sir.'
'No sir,' says Question, 'I, sweet sir, at yours.'
200 And so, ere Answer knows what Question would,°   wishes
Saving in dialogue of compliment,°   Except empty flattery
And talking of the Alps and Apennines,
The Pyrenean and the River Po,
It draws toward supper° in conclusion so.   (another meal)
205 But this is worshipful society,
And fits the mounting spirit° like myself;   ambitious character
For he is but a bastard to° the time   no true child of
That doth not smack of observation;°   courtly obsequiousness
And so am I°—whether I smack or no,   so I intend
210 And not alone in habit° and device,°   clothes / heraldic emblem
Exterior form, outward accoutrement,
But from the inward motion°—to deliver   impulse
Sweet, sweet, sweet poison° for the age's tooth;°   flattery / appetite
Which,° though I will not practise° to deceive,   (flattery) / make a habit
215 Yet to avoid deceit° I mean to learn;   being deceived
For it shall strew the footsteps of my rising.[8]
        Enter LADY FALCONBRIDGE *and James* GURNEY
But who comes in such haste in riding-robes?
What woman-post° is this? Hath she no husband   female dispatch rider
That will take pains to blow a horn[9] before her?
220 O me, 'tis my mother! How now, good lady?
What brings you here to court so hastily?
LADY FALCONBRIDGE   Where is that slave thy brother? Where is he
That holds in chase° mine honour up and down?   Who hunts
BASTARD   My brother Robert, old Sir Robert's son?
225 Colbrand the Giant,[1] that same mighty man?
Is it Sir Robert's son that you seek so?
LADY FALCONBRIDGE   Sir Robert's son, ay, thou unreverent boy,

---

5. God reward you: the patronizing reply of a social superior. The Bastard imagines himself, newly promoted,
encountering a social inferior who says "Good evening."
His soliloquy continues in this vein, parodying the affectation of courtiers and foreign travelers, in part through the
ironic use of religious rhetoric—"conversion" (line 189,
referring to his new rank), "my worship's mess" (line 190;
"my worship" means both "a lord" and "the Lord"; "mess"
means both "a dinner table" and "the Mass," the commemoration of Christ's Last Supper), and "catechize"
(line 192; orally question, usually about religious principles).

6. 'Tis . . . conversion: Remembering names is beneath
the dignity of a newly created knight.
7. The Bastard defiantly cleans his teeth in the vulgar
English fashion, rather than resorting to the traveler's and
courtier's affectation of a toothpick.
8. For flattery will ease my ascent; awareness of deceptive
flattery will do so.
9. Post horn announcing the rider's approach; also, the
symbol of a cuckold.
1. Danish giant killed by Guy in the popular romance
Guy of Warwick.

Sir Robert's son. Why scorn'st thou at Sir Robert?
He is Sir Robert's son, and so art thou.

230 BASTARD   James Gurney, wilt thou give us leave° awhile?   *leave us*
GURNEY   Good leave, good Philip.
BASTARD   Philip Sparrow,[2] James!
There's toys abroad;[3] anon I'll tell thee more.

Exit James [GURNEY]

Madam, I was not old Sir Robert's son.
Sir Robert might have eat his part in me
235 Upon Good Friday, and ne'er broke his fast.
Sir Robert could do° well, marry° to confess,   *(sexual) / indeed*
Could a get° me! Sir Robert could not do it: *Could he have begotten*
We know his handiwork.° Therefore, good mother,   *(Falconbridge)*
To whom am I beholden for these limbs?
240 Sir Robert never holp° to make this leg.   *helped*
LADY FALCONBRIDGE   Hast thou conspirèd with thy brother too,
That for thine own gain shouldst defend mine honour?
What means this scorn, thou most untoward° knave?   *unmannerly*
BASTARD   Knight, knight, good mother, Basilisco-like![4]
245 What! I am dubbed; I have it° on my shoulder.   *(a sword tap)*
But, mother, I am not Sir Robert's son.
I have disclaimed Sir Robert; and my land,
Legitimation, name, and all is gone.
Then, good my mother, let me know my father;
250 Some proper man, I hope; who was it, mother?
LADY FALCONBRIDGE   Hast thou denied thyself a Falconbridge?
BASTARD   As faithfully as I deny the devil.
LADY FALCONBRIDGE   King Richard Cœur-de-lion was thy father.
By long and vehement suit I was seduced
255 To make room for him in my husband's bed.
Heaven lay not my transgression to my charge!
Thou art the issue° of my dear° offence,   *result / costly; loving*
Which was so strongly urged past my defence.
BASTARD   Now by this light, were I to get° again,   *be conceived*
260 Madam, I would not wish a better father.
Some sins do bear their privilege° on earth,   *are pardonable*
And so doth yours; your fault was not your folly.°   *your sin wasn't foolish*
Needs must you lay your heart at his dispose,°   *disposal*
Subjected tribute to commanding love,
265 Against whose fury and unmatchèd force
The aweless° lion could not wage the fight,   *fearless*
Nor keep his princely heart from Richard's hand.
He that perforce° robs lions of their hearts[5]   *by his strength*
May easily win a woman's. Ay, my mother,
270 With all my heart I thank thee for my father.
Who lives and dares but say thou didst not well
When I was got, I'll send his soul to hell.
Come, lady, I will show thee to my kin,
    And they shall say, when Richard me begot,

2. Recalling the popularity of Philip as a name for a mere bird, the Bastard considers the name beneath him.
3. There's trivial news (ironic).
4. The cowardly braggart Basilisco in an anonymous play *Solyman and Perseda*, probably from the early 1590s, calls himself a knight while his servant calls him a knave.
5. Alluding to Richard I's legendary feat of killing a lion by putting his hand down its throat and pulling out its heart (hence the epithet Coeur-de-lion, Lionheart).

275 If thou hadst said him nay, it had been sin.
    Who says it was, he lies: I say 'twas not.[6]

                                 Exeunt

2.1

      [*Flourish.*] *Enter before Angers* [*at one door*] PHILIP
      King of France, LOUIS [THE] DAUPHIN, [*Lady*] CON-
      STANCE, *and* ARTHUR [*Duke of Brittaine, with soldiers;*
      at another door the Duke of] AUSTRIA [*wearing a lion's*
      hide, with soldiers][1]
KING PHILIP   Before Angers well met, brave Austria. —
    Arthur, that great forerunner of thy blood,
    Richard° that robbed the lion of his heart   *(Arthur's uncle)*
    And fought the holy wars in Palestine,°   *third crusade (1191–92)*
5   By this brave duke came early to his grave;[2]
    And, for amends to his posterity,
    At our importance° hither is he come   *urgent request*
    To spread his colours,° boy, in thy behalf,   *battle flags*
    And to rebuke the usurpation
10   Of thy unnatural uncle, English John.
    Embrace him, love him, give him welcome hither.
ARTHUR [*to* AUSTRIA]   God shall forgive you Cœur-de-lion's death,
    The rather that° you give his offspring life,   *All the more because*
    Shadowing° their right under your wings of war.   *Protecting*
15   I give you welcome with a powerless hand,
    But with a heart full of unstainèd love.
    Welcome before the gates of Angers, Duke.
KING PHILIP   A noble boy. Who would not do thee right?
AUSTRIA [*kissing* ARTHUR]   Upon thy cheek lay I this zealous kiss
20   As seal to this indenture° of my love: *contract*
    That to my home I will no more return
    Till Angers and the right thou hast in France,
    Together with that pale, that white-faced shore,°   *chalk cliffs of Dover*
    Whose foot° spurns back the ocean's roaring tides   *(of the cliffs)*
25   And coops° from other lands her islanders,   *protects*
    Even till that England, hedged in with the main,°   *ocean*
    That water-wallèd bulwark, still° secure   *always*
    And confident from foreign purposes,
    Even till that utmost corner of the west
30   Salute thee for her king. Till then, fair boy,
    Will I not think of home, but follow arms.
CONSTANCE   O, take his mother's thanks, a widow's thanks,
    Till your strong hand shall help to give him strength
    To make a more° requital to your love.   *greater*
35 AUSTRIA   The peace of heaven is theirs that lift their swords
    In such a just and charitable war.
KING PHILIP   Well then, to work! Our cannon shall be bent°   *aimed*

---

6. Not a sin; nought (nothing); naughty, and hence
something, a sin.
2.1 Location: Before the town wall of Angers.
1. This is "Scaena Secunda" in F (see the Textual Note).
The back of the stage represents the town wall, with the
town notionally behind it. Hubert's entry "upon the
walls" (line 200) is onto the upper stage. Below the upper
stage, central tiring-house doors would probably represent

the gates of Angers, the capital of John's French holdings.
These remain closed; the French and English armies
appear from side entrances.
2. Austria, the "brave duke," imprisoned Richard, but
Richard was actually killed while besieging the castle of
the Viscount of Limoges in France. Shakespeare follows
his main source in combining the two historical figures
in the character of Austria.

Against the brows° of this resisting town.   *walls*
Call for our chiefest men of discipline°   *military skill*
40   To cull the plots of best advantages.³
We'll lay before this town our royal bones,
Wade to the market-place in Frenchmen's blood,
But we will° make it subject to this boy.   *In order to; unless we*
CONSTANCE   Stay for an answer to your embassy,
45   Lest unadvised° you stain your swords with blood.   *rashly*
My lord Châtillon may from England bring
That right in peace which here we urge° in war,   *seek*
And then we shall repent each drop of blood
That hot rash haste so indirectly° shed.   *wrongfully*
          Enter CHÂTILLON
50   KING PHILIP   A wonder, lady: lo upon thy wish
Our messenger Châtillon is arrived.—
What England° says, say briefly, gentle lord;   *the King of England*
We coldly° pause for thee. Châtillon, speak.   *calmly*
CHÂTILLON   Then turn your forces from this paltry siege,
55   And stir them up against a mightier task.
England, impatient of your just demands,
Hath put himself in arms. The adverse winds,
Whose leisure I have stayed,° have given him time   *Which I had to wait out*
To land his legions all as soon as I.
60   His marches are expedient° to this town,   *coming quickly*
His forces strong, his soldiers confident.
With him along is come the Mother-Queen,
An Ate° stirring him to blood and strife;   *goddess of discord*
With her her niece,⁴ the Lady Blanche of Spain;
65   With them a bastard of the King's deceased;°   *of Richard's*
And all th'unsettled humours⁵ of the land—
Rash, inconsiderate,° fiery voluntaries,°   *imprudent / volunteers*
With ladies'° faces and fierce dragons' spleens°—   *beardless / tempers*
Have sold their fortunes at their native homes,
70   Bearing their birthrights proudly on their backs,⁶
To make a hazard of° new fortunes here.   *To take a chance on*
In brief, a braver choice of dauntless spirits
Than now the English bottoms° have waft o'er   *ships*
Did never float upon the swelling tide
75   To do offence and scathe° in Christendom.   *damage*
          Drum beats
The interruption of their churlish drums
Cuts off more circumstance.° They are at hand;   *detail*
To parley or to fight therefore prepare.
KING PHILIP   How much unlooked-for is this expedition!°   *military force; speed*
80   AUSTRIA   By how much unexpected, by so much
We must awake endeavour for defence,
For courage mounteth with occasion.°   *necessity*
Let them be welcome then: we are prepared.

---

3. To pick the positions of greatest advantage (for the cannons).
4. Actually, Eleanor's granddaughter: "niece" is used in a broad sense.
5. Men of discontented spirits; masterless men of no fixed abode. The soldiers are seen as "humors" (physical

elements of the body, which affect temperament) discharged from the body of England.
6. In the form of armor bought by selling their land ("birthrights" and "fortunes," line 69). "All his clothes are on his back" is proverbial.

Enter [marching] KING [JOHN] *of England, [the]* BAS-
TARD, QUEEN [ELEANOR], *[Lady]* BLANCHE, *[the Earl of]*
PEMBROKE, *and [soldiers]*

KING JOHN   Peace be to France, if France in peace permit
85   Our just and lineal° entrance to our own.°   *hereditary / Angers*
       If not, bleed France,° and peace ascend to heaven,   *let France bleed*
       Whiles we, God's wrathful agent, do correct°   *punish*
       Their proud contempt that beats his peace to heaven.
KING PHILIP   Peace be to England, if that war return
90   From France to England, there to live in peace.
       England we love, and for that England's sake
       With burden of our armour here we sweat.
       This toil of ours should be a work of thine;
       But thou from loving England art so far
95   That thou hast underwrought° his lawful king,   *undermined*
       Cut off the sequence of posterity,°   *the succession*
       Outfacèd infant state,° and done a rape   *Defied Arthur's right*
       Upon the maiden virtue of the crown.
       [*Pointing to* ARTHUR]
       Look here upon thy brother Geoffrey's face.
100   These eyes, these brows, were moulded out of his;
       This little abstract° doth contain that large°   *précis / full version*
       Which died in Geoffrey; and the hand of time
       Shall draw this brief° into as huge a volume.   *summary*
       That Geoffrey was thy elder brother born,
105   And this his son; England was Geoffrey's right,
       And this is Geoffrey's.° In the name of God,   *(son and heir)*
       How comes it then that thou art called a king,
       When living blood doth in these temples beat,
       Which owe° the crown that thou o'ermasterest?   *own*
110 KING JOHN   From whom hast thou this great commission, France,
       To draw my answer from thy articles?°   *charges*
KING PHILIP   From that supernal° judge that stirs good thoughts   *heavenly*
       In any breast of strong authority°   *In any powerful ruler*
       To look into the blots and stains of right.
115   That judge hath made me guardian to this boy,
       Under whose warrant I impeach° thy wrong,   *challenge*
       And by whose help I mean to chastise it.
KING JOHN   Alack, thou dost usurp authority.
KING PHILIP   Excuse it is to beat usurping down.[7]
120 QUEEN ELEANOR   Who is it thou dost call usurper, France?
CONSTANCE   Let me make answer: thy usurping son.
QUEEN ELEANOR   Out,° insolent! Thy bastard shall be king   *Begone*
       That thou mayst be a queen and check° the world.   *master*
CONSTANCE   My bed was ever° to thy son as true   *always*
125   As thine was to thy husband; and this boy
       Liker in feature to his father Geoffrey
       Than thou and John in manners, being as like
       As rain to water, or devil to his dam.°   *mother*
       My boy a bastard? By my soul I think
130   His father never was so true begot.
       It cannot be, an if° thou wert his mother.   *an if = if*

---

7. My (so-called) usurpation is excusable because I am using it to put down (real) usurpation.

QUEEN ELEANOR [*to* ARTHUR]   There's a good mother, boy, that
    blots° thy father.   *slanders*

CONSTANCE [*to* ARTHUR]   There's a good grandam, boy, that
    would blot thee.

AUSTRIA   Peace!

BASTARD   Hear the crier![8]

AUSTRIA   What the devil art thou?

135 BASTARD   One that will play the devil, sir, with you,
    An a° may catch your hide[9] and you alone.   *If he (I)*
    You are the hare° of whom the proverb goes,   *coward*
    Whose valour plucks dead lions by the beard.°   *(an insult)*
    I'll smoke your skin-coat° an I catch you right—   *thrash your hide*
140   Sirrah,° look to't—i'faith I will, i'faith!   *Boy (an insult)*

BLANCHE   O, well did he° become that lion's robe!   *(Richard)*
    That did disrobe the lion of that robe!

BASTARD   It lies as sightly° on the back of him   *fitly*
    As great Alcides' shows[1] upon an ass.
145   But, ass, I'll take that burden from your back,
    Or lay on that° shall make your shoulders crack.   *that burden which*

AUSTRIA   What cracker° is this same that deafs our ears   *boaster*
    With this abundance of superfluous breath?—
    King Philip, determine what we shall do straight.°   *immediately*

150 KING PHILIP   Women and fools,° break off your conference.—   *children*
    King John, this is the very sum of all:
    England and Ireland, Anjou,[2] Touraine, Maine,
    In right of Arthur do I claim of thee.
    Wilt thou resign them and lay down thy arms?

155 KING JOHN   My life as soon. I do defy thee, France.—
    Arthur of Brittaine, yield thee to my hand,
    And out of my dear love I'll give thee more
    Than e'er the coward hand of France can win.
    Submit thee, boy.

QUEEN ELEANOR [*to* ARTHUR]   Come to thy grandam, child.

160 CONSTANCE [*to* ARTHUR]   Do, child, go to it° grandam, child.   *its*
    Give grandam kingdom, and it grandam will
    Give it a plum, a cherry, and a fig.°   *(obscene)*
    There's a good grandam.°   *(sarcastic baby talk)*

ARTHUR   Good my mother, peace.
    I would that I were low laid in my grave.
165   I am not worth this coil° that's made for me.   *commotion*
    [*He weeps*]

QUEEN ELEANOR   His mother shames him so, poor boy, he weeps.

CONSTANCE   Now shame upon you, whe'er° she does or no!   *whether*
    His grandam's wrongs, and not his mother's shames,
    Draw those heaven-moving pearls from his poor eyes,
170   Which heaven shall take in nature° of a fee;   *as a kind*
    Ay, with these crystal beads° heaven shall be bribed   *tears*
    To do him justice and revenge on you.

QUEEN ELEANOR   Thou monstrous slanderer of heaven and earth!

---

8. The Bastard mockingly compares Austria to an officer
in a law court who calls for order.
9. The lion skin Austria wears, which, as a memento of
his father's death, antagonizes the Bastard.
1. As the lion skin of Hercules would appear (alluding to
his legendary size and strength, and to the proverbial "ass

in a lion's skin").
2. Here and at line 488, Shakespeare appears to confuse
the province (Anjou) with the besieged town (Angers; F:
Angiers). Elsewhere, he maintains a distinction, as do his
sources.

CONSTANCE   Thou monstrous injurer of heaven and earth!
175 Call not me slanderer. Thou and thine usurp
The dominations, royalties° and rights   *royal powers*
Of this oppressèd boy. This is thy eld'st son's son,[3]
Infortunate in nothing but in thee.
Thy sins are visited° in this poor child;   *punished*
180 The canon of the law° is laid on him,   *biblical decree*
Being but the second generation
Removèd from thy sin-conceiving womb.[4]
KING JOHN   Bedlam,° have done.   *Lunatic*
CONSTANCE   I have but this to say:
That he° is not only plaguèd for her sin,°   *(Arthur) / (adultery)*
185 But God hath made her sin° and her the plague   *(John)*
On this removèd issue,° plagued for her   *(Arthur)*
And with her plague;[5] her sin his injury,
Her injury the beadle to her sin;
All punished in the person of this child,
190 And all for her.[6] A plague upon her!
QUEEN ELEANOR   Thou unadvisèd° scold, I can produce   *rash*
A will that bars the title of thy son.
CONSTANCE   Ay, who doubts that? A will, a wicked will,
A woman's will,[7] a cankered grandam's will!
195 KING PHILIP   Peace, lady; pause or be more temperate.
It ill beseems this presence° to cry aim   *royal assembly*
To[8] these ill-tunèd repetitions. —
Some trumpet summon hither to the walls
These men of Angers. Let us hear them speak
200 Whose title they admit, Arthur's or John's.
        Trumpet sounds. Enter a CITIZEN[9] *upon the walls*
CITIZEN   Who is it that hath warned° us to the walls?   *summoned*
KING PHILIP   'Tis France for England.
KING JOHN   England for itself.
You men of Angers and my loving subjects—
KING PHILIP   You loving men of Angers, Arthur's subjects,
205 Our trumpet called you to this gentle parle°—   *parley*
KING JOHN   For our° advantage; therefore hear us first.   *(England's; John's)*
These flags of France that are advancèd here
Before the eye and prospect of your town,
Have hither marched to your endamagement.
210 The cannons have their bowels full of wrath,
And ready mounted are they to spit forth
Their iron indignation 'gainst your walls.
All preparation for a bloody siege
And merciless proceeding by these French
215 Confront your city's eyes, your winking° gates;   *closed (in sleep)*

---

3. Oldest grandson; but perhaps deliberately meant to produce the false inference that Arthur is really the "eld'st son's [Richard's] son."
4. Implying sexual infidelity in the conception of John. These lines (especially 179) echo the Second Commandment (Exodus 20:5, "the law" of line 180): "visiting the iniquities of the fathers upon the children, upon the third generation and upon the fourth."
5. *plagued . . . plague:* punished because of and by her.
6. *her sin his injury . . . her:* her wrongful action is like a parish constable (a "beadle," who whipped petty criminals) urging on her son to afflict Arthur; all (Eleanor's sin,

John as its embodiment) are punished in Arthur, and all because of Eleanor.
7. Testament influenced by a woman (Eleanor; ironically, it was illegal for women to make wills themselves, for fear their husbands would influence them); a woman's desire (as in the proverbial "A woman will have her will").
8. *to cry aim / To:* to encourage.
9. Shakespeare may have taken some steps toward conflating this character with Hubert, who figures prominently later in the play (see note to line 325 and Textual Note), but no early text survives in which such an identification of characters has been fully effected.

And but for our approach, those sleeping stones
That as a waist° doth girdle you about,   *girdle*
By the compulsion of their ordinance,°   *artillery*
By this time from their fixèd beds of lime°   *their foundations*
220 Had been dishabited,° and wide havoc made   *dislodged*
For bloody power to rush upon your peace.
But on the sight of us your lawful king,
Who painfully,° with much expedient° march,   *laboriously / hurried*
Have brought a countercheck before your gates
225 To save unscratched your city's threatened cheeks,
Behold the French, amazed,° vouchsafe° a parle;   *terrified / grant*
And now instead of bullets wrapped in fire
To make a shaking fever in your walls,
They shoot but calm words folded up in smoke°   *deceit*
230 To make a faithless error° in your ears;   *lie*
Which trust accordingly, kind citizens,
And let us in, your king, whose laboured° spirits,   *worn out*
Forwearied in this action of swift speed,
Craves harbourage within your city walls.
235 KING PHILIP   When I have said, make answer to us both.
[*He takes Arthur's hand*]
Lo, in this° right hand, whose protection   *(Philip's)*
Is most divinely vowed upon the right
Of him° it holds, stands young Plantagenet,   *(Arthur)*
Son to the elder brother of this man°   *(John)*
240 And king o'er him and all that he enjoys.
For this downtrodden equity° we tread   *right*
In warlike march these greens before your town,
Being no further enemy to you
Than the constraint° of hospitable zeal   *necessity*
245 In the relief of this oppressèd child
Religiously° provokes. Be pleasèd then   *Solemnly*
To pay that duty which you truly owe
To him that owes° it, namely this young prince;   *has a right to*
And then our arms, like to a muzzled bear,
250 Save in aspect,° hath all offence° sealed up: *appearance / aggression*
Our cannons' malice vainly shall be spent
Against th'invulnerable clouds of heaven,
And with a blessèd and unvexed retire,°   *unmolested retreat*
With unhacked swords and helmets all unbruised,
255 We will bear home that lusty blood again
Which here we came to spout against your town,
And leave your children, wives, and you in peace.
But if you fondly° pass our proffered offer,   *foolishly*
'Tis not the roundure° of your old-faced walls   *roundness; circumference*
260 Can hide you from our messengers of war,°   *cannon balls*
Though all these English and their discipline°   *military skill*
Were harboured in their rude° circumference.   *rugged*
Then tell us, shall your city call us lord
In that behalf which° we have challenged it,   *in which; for whom*
265 Or shall we give the signal to our rage,
And stalk in blood to our possession?
CITIZEN   In brief, we are the King of England's subjects.
For him and in his right we hold this town.
KING JOHN   Acknowledge then the King, and let me in.

270	CITIZEN That can we not; but he that proves° the king,	*proves to be*
	To him will we prove loyal; till that time	
	Have we rammed up our gates against the world.	
	KING JOHN Doth not the crown of England prove the king?	
	And if not that, I bring you witnesses:	
275	Twice fifteen thousand hearts of England's breed—	
	BASTARD [*aside*] Bastards and else.°	*others*
	KING JOHN To verify our title with their lives.	
	KING PHILIP As many and as well-born bloods as those—	
	BASTARD [*aside*] Some bastards too.	
280	KING PHILIP Stand in his face° to contradict his claim.	*against him*
	CITIZEN Till you compound° whose right is worthiest,	*settle*
	We for the worthiest hold° the right from both.	*withhold*
	KING JOHN Then God forgive the sin of all those souls	
	That to their everlasting residence,	
285	Before the dew of evening fall, shall fleet°	*leave their bodies*
	In dreadful trial of° our kingdom's king.	*contest to determine*
	KING PHILIP Amen, Amen! Mount, chevaliers!° To arms!	*horsemen*
	BASTARD Saint George that swinged° the dragon, and e'er since	*thrashed*
	Sits on's horseback at mine hostess' door,[1]	
290	Teach us some fence!° [*To* AUSTRIA] Sirrah, were I at home	*swordsmanship*
	At your den, sirrah, with your lioness,°	*whore; wife*
	I would set an ox-head° to your lion's hide	*add cuckold's horns*
	And make a monster of you.	
	AUSTRIA Peace, no more.	
	BASTARD O tremble, for you hear the lion roar!	
295	KING JOHN Up higher to the plain, where we'll set forth	
	In best appointment° all our regiments.	*readiness*
	BASTARD Speed then, to take advantage of the field.°	*best battle positions*
	KING PHILIP It shall be so, and at the other hill	
	Command the rest to stand.[2] God and our right!°	*(English royal motto)*
	Exeunt [*severally*° KING JOHN *and* KING PHILIP *with their*	*separately*
	powers. The CITIZEN *remains on the walls*]	
	[*Alarum.*] *Here, after excursions,*° *enter* [*at one door*] *the*	*onstage skirmishes*
	HERALD *of France, with* [*a*] *trumpet*[*er*], *to the gates*	
300	FRENCH HERALD You men of Angers, open wide your gates	
	And let young Arthur Duke of Brittaine in,	
	Who by the hand of France this day hath made	
	Much work for tears in many an English mother,	
	Whose sons lie scattered on the bleeding ground;	
305	Many a widow's husband grovelling lies,	
	Coldly embracing the discoloured earth;	
	And victory with little loss doth play	
	Upon the dancing banners of the French,	
	Who are at hand, triumphantly displayed,°	*drawn up*
310	To enter conquerors, and to proclaim	
	Arthur of Brittaine England's king and yours.	
	Enter [*at another door the*] *English* HERALD, *with* [*a*]	
	trumpet[*er*]	
	ENGLISH HERALD Rejoice, you men of Angers, ring your bells!	
	King John, your king and England's, doth approach,	

1. The idea that Saint George, England's patron saint, is ever on horseback yet never rides was proverbial. *at mine hostess' door*: on an inn sign.

2. Command the reserves to be in readiness. (This concludes an unheard conversation in parallel with John's.)

Commander of this hot malicious day.
315 Their armours that marched hence so silver-bright
Hither return all gilt° with Frenchmen's blood.   *smeared; golden*
There stuck no plume in any English crest°   *(on a helmet)*
That is removèd by a staff° of France;   *spear*
Our colours° do return in those same hands   *banners*
320 That did display them when we first marched forth;
And like a jolly troop of huntsmen come
Our lusty English, all with purpled hands
Dyed in the dying slaughter of their foes.
Open your gates and give the victors way.
325 CITIZEN[3] Heralds, from off our towers we might° behold   *could*
From first to last the onset and retire
Of both your armies, whose equality
By our best eyes cannot be censurèd.°   *differentiated*
Blood hath bought blood and blows have answered blows,
330 Strength matched with strength and power confronted power.
Both are alike, and both alike we like.
One must prove greatest. While they weigh so even,
We hold our town for neither, yet for both.
      Enter the two kings with their powers,° at several doors   *armies*
      [at one door KING JOHN, *the* BASTARD, QUEEN ELEANOR
      and Lady BLANCHE, *with soldiers; at another door* KING
      PHILIP, LOUIS THE DAUPHIN, *and the Duke of* AUSTRIA
      with soldiers][4]
KING JOHN France, hast thou yet more blood to cast away?
335 Say, shall the current of our right run on,
Whose passage, vexed with thy impediment,
Shall leave his native channel° and o'erswell°   *normal course / flood*
With course disturbed even thy confining shores,
Unless thou let his silver water keep
340 A peaceful progress to the ocean?
KING PHILIP England, thou hast not saved one drop of blood
In this hot trial more than we of France;
Rather, lost more. And by this hand I swear,
That sways the earth this climate° overlooks,   *part of the sky*
345 Before we will lay down our just-borne arms,
We'll put thee down 'gainst whom these arms we bear,
Or add a royal number° to the dead,   *(Philip)*
Gracing the scroll that tells of this war's loss
With slaughter coupled to the name of kings.
350 BASTARD Ha, majesty! How high thy glory towers
When the rich blood of kings is set on fire!
O, now doth Death line his dead chaps° with steel;   *deadly jaws*
The swords of soldiers are his teeth, his fangs;
And now he feasts, mousing° the flesh of men   *tearing; biting*
355 In undetermined differences° of kings.   *unresolved disputes*
Why stand these royal fronts° amazèd thus?   *faces*
Cry havoc,[5] Kings! Back to the stainèd field,
You equal potents,° fiery-kindled spirits!   *equally strong rulers*

---

3. This and subsequent speeches of the Citizen are attributed to Hubert in the earliest Folio text. See note to line 200.
4. F calls for "the two Kings with their powers"; this seems to exclude Constance and Arthur.
5. Order given to troops for pillaging and merciless slaughter.

<table>
<tr><td></td><td>Then let confusion° of one part° confirm</td><td>let overthrow / side</td></tr>
<tr><td>360</td><td>The other's peace; till then, blows, blood, and death!</td><td></td></tr>
</table>

Then let confusion° of one part° confirm *let overthrow / side*
360 The other's peace; till then, blows, blood, and death!
KING JOHN Whose party do the townsmen yet admit?
KING PHILIP Speak, citizens, for England: who's your king?
CITIZEN The King of England, when we know the King.
KING PHILIP Know him in us,° that here hold up his right. *me*
365 KING JOHN In us, that are our own great deputy° *representative*
And bear possession of our person° here, *represent my own claim*
Lord of our presence,° Angers, and of you. *myself*
CITIZEN A greater power than we denies all this,
And, till it be undoubted, we do lock
370 Our former scruple in our strong-barred gates,
Kinged of° our fear, until our fears resolved *Commanded by*
Be by some certain king, purged and deposed.
BASTARD By heaven, these scroyles° of Angers flout you, Kings, *scoundrels*
And stand securely on their battlements
375 As in a theatre, whence they gape and point
At your industrious scenes and acts of death.
Your royal presences° be ruled by me. *persons*
Do like the mutines of Jerusalem:[6]
Be friends awhile, and both conjointly° bend *together*
380 Your sharpest deeds of malice on this town.
By east and west let France and England mount
Their battering cannon, chargèd to° the mouths, *loaded to*
Till their soul-fearing° clamours have brawled° down *terrifying / broken*
The flinty ribs° of this contemptuous city. *walls*
385 I'd play incessantly upon these jades,[7]
Even till unfencèd° desolation *unwalled*
Leave them as naked as the vulgar° air. *common*
That done, dissever your united strengths,
And part your mingled colours once again;
390 Turn face to face, and bloody point to point.
Then in a moment Fortune shall cull° forth *choose*
Out of one side her happy minion,° *darling*
To whom in favour she shall give the day,° *victory*
And kiss him with a glorious victory.
395 How like you this wild counsel, mighty states?° *rulers*
Smacks it not something of the policy?° *political cunning*
KING JOHN Now, by the sky that hangs above our heads,
I like it well.—France, shall we knit° our powers, *join*
And lay this Angers even with the ground,
400 Then after fight who shall be king of it?
BASTARD [*to* KING PHILIP] An if thou hast the mettle of a king,
Being wronged as we are by this peevish° town, *obstinate*
Turn thou the mouth of thy artillery,
As we will ours, against these saucy° walls; *presumptuous*
405 And when that we have dashed them to the ground,
Why, then defy each other, and pell-mell° *quickly*
Make work upon ourselves, for[8] heaven or hell.
KING PHILIP Let it be so.—Say, where will you assault?

---

6. Warring factions of Jerusalem who temporarily united against besieging Roman forces in A.D. 70.
7. I'd unceasingly fire at (or torment) these wretches. (A "jade" was a decrepit horse or an insulting term for a woman—and hence a double insult when applied to a man.)
8. On behalf of; for the destination of.

KING JOHN   We from the west will send destruction
410 Into this city's bosom.
  AUSTRIA   I from the north.
  KING PHILIP   Our thunder° from the south   *cannon*
 Shall rain their drift of bullets° on this town. *shower of cannonballs*
  BASTARD [*to* KING JOHN]   O prudent discipline!° From north to south *tactics*
415 Austria and France shoot in each other's mouth.
 I'll stir them to it. Come, away, away!
  CITIZEN   Hear us, great Kings, vouchsafe a while to stay,
 And I shall show you peace and fair-faced league.
 Win you this city without stroke or wound;
420 Rescue those breathing lives to die in beds,
 That here come sacrifices for the field.
 Persever not, but hear me, mighty Kings.
  KING JOHN   Speak on with favour;° we are bent° to hear. *permission / willing*
  CITIZEN   That daughter there of Spain, the Lady Blanche,
425 Is niece to England. Look upon the years°   *ages*
 Of Louis the Dauphin and that lovely maid.
 If lusty love should go in quest of beauty,
 Where should he find it fairer than in Blanche?
 If zealous° love should go in search of virtue,   *pious*
430 Where should he find it purer than in Blanche?
 If love ambitious sought a match of birth,
 Whose veins bound° richer blood than Lady Blanche? *contain*
 Such as she is in beauty, virtue, birth,
 Is the young Dauphin every way complete;°   *perfect*
435 If not complete, O, say he is not she;
 And she again wants nothing—to name want—
 If want it be not that she is not he.[9]
 He is the half part of a blessèd man,
 Left to be finishèd by such as she;
440 And she a fair divided excellence,
 Whose fullness of perfection lies in him.
 O, two such silver currents when they join
 Do glorify the banks that bound them in,
 And two such shores to two such streams made one,
445 Two such controlling bounds, shall you be, Kings,
 To these two princes if you marry them.
 This union shall do more than battery can
 To our fast-closèd gates, for at this match,[1]
 With swifter spleen° than powder can enforce,   *passion*
450 The mouth of passage shall we fling wide ope,
 And give you entrance. But without this match
 The sea enragèd is not half so deaf,
 Lions more confident, mountains and rocks
 More free from motion, no, not Death himself
455 In mortal fury half so peremptory,°   *resolved*
 As we to keep this city.
  BASTARD [*aside*]   Here's a stay°   *an obstacle; cease-fire*
 That shakes the rotten carcass of old Death
 Out of his rags.[2] Here's a large mouth,° indeed, *(of a cannon or human)*

9. *If not . . . he:* The Dauphin is perfect insofar 1. Marriage; device for lighting gun "powder" (line 449).
as he lacks Blanche, and vice versa. *wants:* lacks. *to:* if I 2. *That . . . rags:* That steals what belongs to death.
must.

	That spits forth Death and mountains, rocks and seas,	
460	Talks as familiarly of roaring lions	
	As maids of thirteen do of puppy-dogs.	
	What cannoneer begot this lusty blood?	
	He speaks plain cannon: fire, and smoke, and bounce;°	*bang*
	He gives the bastinado° with his tongue;	*a cudgeling*
465	Our ears are cudgelled; not a word of his	
	But buffets better than a fist of France.	
	Zounds!° I was never so bethumped with words	*God's wounds*
	Since I first called my brother's father Dad.	
	QUEEN ELEANOR [*aside to* KING JOHN] Son, list° to this conjunc-	*listen*
	tion,° make this match,	*proposition*
470	Give with our niece a dowry large enough;	
	For, by this knot, thou shalt so surely tie	
	Thy now unsured assurance to the crown	
	That yon green° boy shall have no sun to ripe	*unripe; young*
	The bloom that promiseth a mighty fruit.	
475	I see a yielding in the looks of France;	
	Mark how they whisper. Urge them while their souls	
	Are capable of° this ambition,	*susceptible to*
	Lest zeal,° now melted by the windy breath	*(on Arthur's behalf)*
	Of soft petitions, pity, and remorse,	
480	Cool and congeal° again to what it was.	*freeze*
	CITIZEN Why answer not the double majesties	
	This friendly treaty° of our threatened town?	*entreaty; proposal*
	KING PHILIP Speak England first, that hath been forward first	
	To speak unto this city: what say you?	
485	KING JOHN If that the Dauphin there, thy princely son,	
	Can in this book of beauty° read 'I love',	*(Blanche)*
	Her dowry shall weigh equal with a queen;	
	For Anjou and fair Touraine, Maine, Poitou,³	
	And all that we upon this side the sea—	
490	Except this city now by us besieged—	
	Find liable° to our crown and dignity,	*subject*
	Shall gild her bridal bed, and make her rich	
	In titles, honours, and promotions,°	*elevations in rank*
	As she in beauty, education, blood,	
495	Holds hand with° any princess of the world.	*Is equal to*
	KING PHILIP What sayst thou, boy? Look in the lady's face.	
	LOUIS THE DAUPHIN I do, my lord, and in her eye I find	
	A wonder, or a wondrous miracle,	
	The shadow of myself formed in her eye;	
500	Which, being but the shadow of your son,	
	Becomes a sun and makes your son a shadow.⁴	
	I do protest I never loved myself	
	Till now enfixèd° I beheld myself	*imprinted*
	Drawn in the flattering table° of her eye.	*surface*
	[*He*] *whispers with* BLANCHE	
505	BASTARD [*aside*] Drawn in the flattering table of her eye,	
	Hanged in the frowning wrinkle of her brow,	

3. The French territories claimed by both John and Arthur will go to the Dauphin.
4. *The shadow of myself . . . a shadow*: The Dauphin speaks in elaborate clichés of courtly love poetry: the conceit is common, as is the "sun/son" wordplay. He claims that his "shadow," from being a mere reflection or pale imitation of the King's son (or a shadow of the sun) in Blanche's eyes, becomes a "sun" because her eyes are so bright, with the result that the actual "son" becomes a mere "shadow" of his own reflection.

And quartered in her heart:[5] he doth espy
Himself love's traitor. This is pity now,
That hanged and drawn and quartered there should be
510 In such a love so vile a lout as he.
BLANCHE [*to* LOUIS THE DAUPHIN] My uncle's will in this respect is mine.
If he see aught° in you that makes him like,   *anything*
That anything he sees which moves his liking
I can with ease translate it to my will;
515 Or if you will, to speak more properly,°   *precisely*
I will enforce it easily to my love.
Further I will not flatter you, my lord,
That all I see in you is worthy° love,   *deserving of*
Than this:[6] that nothing do I see in you,
520 Though churlish° thoughts themselves should be your judge,   *grudging*
That I can find should merit any hate.
KING JOHN What say these young ones? What say you, my niece?
BLANCHE That she is bound in honour still° to do   *always*
What you in wisdom shall vouchsafe° to say.   *deign*
525 KING JOHN Speak then, Prince Dauphin, can you love this lady?
LOUIS THE DAUPHIN Nay, ask me if I can refrain from love,
For I do love her most unfeignedly.
KING JOHN Then do I give Volquessen,[7] Maine,
Poitou, and Anjou, these five provinces,
530 With her to thee, and this addition more:
Full thirty thousand marks° of English coin.   *£ 20,000*
Philip of France, if thou be pleased withal,°   *with this*
Command thy son and daughter to join hands.
KING PHILIP It likes° us well.—Young princes, close your hands.   *pleases*
535 AUSTRIA And your lips too, for I am well assured
That I did so when I was first assured.°   *betrothed*
[LOUIS THE DAUPHIN *and Lady* BLANCHE *join hands and kiss*]
KING PHILIP Now citizens of Angers, ope your gates.
Let in that amity which you have made,
For at Saint Mary's chapel presently°   *immediately*
540 The rites of marriage shall be solemnized.—
Is not the Lady Constance in this troop?
[*Aside*] I know she is not, for this match made up
Her presence would have interrupted much.
[*Aloud*] Where is she and her son? Tell me who knows.
545 LOUIS THE DAUPHIN She is sad and passionate° at your highness' tent.   *sorrowful*
KING PHILIP And by my faith this league that we have made
Will give her sadness very little cure.—
Brother of England, how may we content
This widow lady? In her right we came,
550 Which we, God knows, have turned another way
To our own vantage.°   *advantage*
KING JOHN   We will heal up all,
For we'll create young Arthur Duke of Brittaine[8]
And Earl of Richmond, and this rich fair town
We make him lord of. Call the Lady Constance.

---

5. *Drawn . . . heart:* the Bastard alludes to the punishment of being hanged, drawn (disemboweled; but also, painted, line 504), and quartered (cut in pieces; but also, lodged) for treason. The rhyme scheme of lines 505–10 mimics the last six lines of a Shakespearean sonnet.

6. Taking up "Further," line 517.
7. Modern Vexin, northwest of Paris.
8. An inconsistency: Arthur already holds this title, as John himself acknowledges (line 156).

555	Some speedy messenger bid her repair°	*come*
	To our solemnity.° I trust we shall,	*(marriage) ceremony*
	If not fill up the measure of her will,	
	Yet in some measure satisfy her so	
	That we shall stop her exclamation.°	*loud reproaches*
560	Go we as well as haste will suffer° us	*allow*
	To this unlooked-for, unprepared pomp.°	*ceremony*

[*Flourish.*] *Exeunt* [*all but the* BASTARD]

	BASTARD Mad world, mad kings, mad composition!°	*treaty*
	John, to stop Arthur's title in the whole,	
	Hath willingly departed° with a part;	*parted*
565	And France, whose armour conscience buckled on,	
	Whom zeal and charity brought to the field	
	As God's own soldier, rounded° in the ear	*whispered to*
	With° that same purpose-changer,⁹ that sly devil,	*By*
	That broker that still breaks the pate¹ of faith,	
570	That daily break-vow, he that wins of° all,	*gets the best of*
	Of kings, of beggars, old men, young men, maids,—	
	Who° having no external° thing to lose	*(maids) / material*
	But the word 'maid',° cheats° the poor maid of that—	*virginity / he cheats*
	That smooth-faced° gentleman, tickling° commodity;	*plausible / cajoling*
575	Commodity, the bias² of the world,	
	The world who of itself is peisèd° well,	*balanced*
	Made to run even upon even ground,	
	Till this advantage, this vile-drawing° bias,	*drawing to evil*
	This sway° of motion, this commodity,	*swayer; swerver*
580	Makes it take head° from all indifferency,°	*flee / impartiality*
	From all direction, purpose, course, intent;	
	And this same bias, this commodity,	
	This bawd,° this broker, this all-changing word,	*procurer*
	Clapped on the outward eye³ of fickle France,	
585	Hath drawn him from his own determined aid,	
	From a resolved and honourable war,	
	To a most base and vile-concluded peace.	
	And why rail I on this commodity?	
	But for° because he hath not wooed me yet—	*Only*
590	Not that I have the power to clutch° my hand	*clench (in refusal)*
	When his fair angels would salute⁴ my palm,	
	But for° my hand, as unattempted° yet,	*Because / untempted*
	Like a poor beggar raileth on the rich.	
	Well, whiles I am a beggar I will rail,	
595	And say there is no sin but to be rich,	
	And being rich, my virtue then shall be	
	To say there is no vice but beggary.	
	Since kings break faith upon° commodity,	*on account of*
	Gain, be my lord, for I will worship thee.	*Exit*

9. "Purpose-changer," as well as the subsequent noun phrases in lines 568–70, is in apposition to those in line 574, in particular "commodity" (self-interest, profit seeking: that which translates everything into its market value to the exclusion of noneconomic considerations).
1. Cracks the skull (giving colloquial vigor to "breaks faith"). *broker:* go-between, procurer (leading to wordplay in "breaks" and "break-vow," lines 569–70).
2. Literally, in the game of bowls, the off-center weight of a bowl that causes it to veer from a straight course.

3. Fixed its hold on the outer edge of a bowl so as to make it swerve from a true course; suddenly caught the "outward eye" of self-interest as opposed to the inward eye of conscience. Both meanings are applicable to King Philip.
4. *angels would salute:* ten-shilling coins (with the archangel Michael on them) would kiss (greet); alluding to the Annunciation and Michael's "salute" to the Virgin Mary.

2.2

Enter [Lady] CONSTANCE, ARTHUR *[Duke of Brittaine],*
and [the Earl of] SALISBURY[1]

CONSTANCE *[to* SALISBURY*]* Gone to be married? Gone to swear a peace?
False blood to false blood joined! Gone to be friends?
Shall Louis have Blanche, and Blanche those provinces?
It is not so, thou hast misspoke, misheard.

5   Be well advised,° tell o'er thy tale again.   *Consider carefully*
It cannot be, thou dost but say 'tis so.
I trust I may not trust thee, for thy word
Is but the vain breath of a common° man.   *(as opposed to royal)*
Believe me, I do not believe thee, man;

10   I have a king's oath to the contrary.
Thou shalt be punished for thus frighting me;
For I am sick and capable of° fears;   *susceptible to*
Oppressed with wrongs, and therefore full of fears;
A widow husbandless, subject to fears;

15   A woman naturally born to fears;
And though° thou now confess thou didst but jest,   *even if*
With my vexed spirits I cannot take a truce,°   *make peace*
But they will quake and tremble all this day.
What dost thou mean by shaking of thy head?

20   Why dost thou look so sadly on my son?
What means that hand upon that breast of thine?
Why holds thine eye that lamentable rheum,°   *tears*
Like a proud° river peering o'er his bounds?°   *swollen / banks*
Be these sad signs confirmers of thy words?

25   Then speak again—not all thy former tale,
But this one word: whether thy tale be true.
SALISBURY   As true as I believe you think them° false   *(the French and English)*
That give you cause to prove my saying true.
CONSTANCE   O, if thou teach me to believe this sorrow,

30   Teach thou this sorrow how to make me die;
And let belief and life encounter so
As doth the fury of two desperate men
Which in the very meeting fall and die.[2]
Louis marry Blanche! *[To* ARTHUR*]* O boy, then where art thou?

35   France friend with England!—What becomes of me?
[To SALISBURY*]* Fellow,° be gone, I cannot brook° thy sight;   *(an insult) / endure*
This news hath made thee a most ugly man.
SALISBURY   What other harm have I, good lady, done,
But spoke the harm that is by others done?

40   CONSTANCE   Which harm within itself so heinous is
As it makes harmful all that speak of it.
ARTHUR   I do beseech you, madam, be content.°   *calm*
CONSTANCE   If thou that bidd'st me be content wert grim,
Ugly and sland'rous to thy mother's womb,[3]

45   Full of unpleasing blots and sightless° stains,   *unsightly*
Lame, foolish, crooked, swart,° prodigious,[4]   *dark*
Patched° with foul moles and eye-offending marks,   *Blotched*
I would not care, I then would be content,

2.2 Location: The French camp by Angers.
1. This is "Actus Secundus" in F (see Textual Note).
2. *O . . . die:* in this image, drawn from emblem-book
representations of Fury, sorrow (or belief) dies as Constance does.
3. Malformed babies were seen as a divine punishment
for wickedness.
4. Monstrous (and thereby foretelling evil).

For then I should not love thee, no, nor thou
50 Become thy great birth, nor deserve a crown.
But thou art fair, and at thy birth, dear boy,
Nature and Fortune joined to make thee great.
Of Nature's gifts thou mayst with lilies boast,
And with the half-blown° rose. But Fortune, O,   *half-blossomed; young*
55 She is corrupted, changed, and won from thee;
Sh'adulterates° hourly with thine uncle John,   *prostitutes herself*
And with her golden hand hath plucked on° France   *enticed*
To tread down fair respect of sovereignty,°   *(Arthur's rights)*
And made his majesty the bawd to theirs.[5]
60 France is a bawd to Fortune and King John,
That strumpet Fortune, that usurping John.
[*To* SALISBURY] Tell me, thou fellow, is not France forsworn?°   *an oath breaker*
Envenom° him with words, or get thee gone   *Poison*
And leave those woes alone, which I alone
Am bound to underbear.°   *suffer under*
65 SALISBURY   Pardon me, madam,
I may not go without you to the Kings.
CONSTANCE   Thou mayst, thou shalt; I will not go with thee.
I will instruct my sorrows to be proud,
For grief is proud and makes his owner stoop.
[*She sits upon the ground*]
70 To me and to the state° of my great grief   *throne (ironic)*
Let kings assemble, for my grief's so great
That no supporter but the huge firm earth
Can hold it up. Here I and sorrows sit;
Here is my throne; bid kings come bow to it.
[*Exeunt* SALISBURY *and* ARTHUR]

3.1

[*Flourish.*] *Enter* KING JOHN [*and* KING PHILIP *of*]
France [*hand in hand*; LOUIS THE] DAUPHIN [*and Lady*]
BLANCHE, [*married*; QUEEN] ELEANOR, *Philip* [*the* BAS-
TARD, *and the Duke of*] AUSTRIA[1]
KING PHILIP [*to* BLANCHE]   'Tis true,[2] fair daughter, and this blessèd day
Ever in France shall be kept festival.
To solemnize this day, the glorious sun
Stays in his course° and plays the alchemist,[3]   *Stands still*
5 Turning with splendour of his precious eye
The meagre cloddy earth to glittering gold.
The yearly course that brings this day about
Shall never see it but a holy day.
CONSTANCE [*rising*]   A wicked day, and not a holy day!
10 What hath this day deserved? What hath it done,
That it in golden letters should be set
Among the high tides° in the calendar?   *great festivals*

---

5. And made Philip the go-between for John and Fortune.
3.1 Location: The French camp by Angers.
1. Shakespeare originally intended no act break, though
that division, which appears in F, probably indicates a
pause in the performance when the play was revived with
act divisions. Salisbury and Arthur might stay onstage, but
they have no further part in the scene's action. Their exit,
if it occurs, may be followed by a brief pause with Constance alone onstage. She remains unobserved until line
9. F's stage directions have her enter with the others at
the start of the act, perhaps because they merely list all
the characters who need to be onstage after a break in the
action. But her words of 2.2.67–74 are incompatible with
her entry here, which is therefore omitted.
2. King Philip enters in midconversation.
3. Alchemists sought to turn base metals such as lead into
gold.

Nay, rather turn this day out of the week,
This day of shame, oppression, perjury.
Or if it must stand still,° let wives with child   *remain*
Pray that their burdens may not fall° this day,   *they not give birth*
Lest that their hopes prodigiously[4] be crossed;
But° on this day let seamen fear no wreck;   *Except*
No bargains break that are not this day made;
This day all things begun come to ill end,
Yea, faith itself to hollow falsehood change.
KING PHILIP   By heaven, lady, you shall have no cause
To curse the fair proceedings of this day.
Have I not pawned° to you my majesty?°   *pledged / royal word*
CONSTANCE   You have beguiled me with a counterfeit°   *false coin or portrait*
Resembling majesty, which being touched and tried°   *tested for gold*
Proves valueless. You are forsworn, forsworn.
You came in arms to spill mine enemies' blood,
But now in arms you strengthen it with yours.[5]
The grappling vigour and rough frown of war
Is cold in amity and painted° peace,   *counterfeit*
And our oppression° hath made up° this league.   *affliction / possible*
Arm, arm, you heavens, against these perjured Kings!
A widow cries, be husband to me, God!
Let not the hours of this ungodly day
Wear out° the day in peace, but ere sun set   *Finish*
Set armèd discord 'twixt these perjured Kings.
Hear me, O hear me!
AUSTRIA   Lady Constance, peace.
CONSTANCE   War, war, no peace! Peace is to me a war.
O Limoges, O Austria,[6] thou dost shame
That bloody spoil.° Thou slave, thou wretch, thou coward!   *(the lion skin)*
Thou little valiant, great in villainy;
Thou ever strong upon the stronger side;
Thou Fortune's champion, that dost never fight
But when her humorous ladyship° is by   *changeable Fortune*
To teach thee safety. Thou art perjured too,
And sooth'st up greatness.° What a fool art thou,   *flatter the powerful*
A ramping° fool, to brag and stamp, and swear   *showily threatening*
Upon my party!° Thou cold-blooded slave,   *cause*
Hast thou not spoke like thunder on my side,°   *behalf*
Been sworn my soldier, bidding me depend
Upon thy stars, thy fortune, and thy strength?
And dost thou now fall over° to my foes?   *defect*
Thou wear a lion's hide! Doff it, for shame,
And hang a calf's-skin[7] on those recreant° limbs.   *cowardly; traitorous*
AUSTRIA   O, that a man should speak those words to me!
BASTARD   And hang a calf's-skin on those recreant limbs.
AUSTRIA   Thou dar'st not say so, villain, for thy life.
BASTARD   And hang a calf's-skin on those recreant limbs.
KING JOHN [*to the* BASTARD]   We like not this. Thou dost forget
thyself.°   *your rank; protocol*

4. By an ominously monstrous child.
5. "In arms" (arm in arm, but also militarily), France strengthens John's "blood" (legitimacy, line 28) through
"yours" (your blood in marriage).
6. See note to 2.1.5.
7. Symbolizing cowardice or folly.

Enter [Cardinal] PANDOLF

KING PHILIP   Here comes the holy legate of the Pope.[8]

PANDOLF   Hail, you anointed deputies of God.° —   *kings*
   To thee, King John, my holy errand is.
   I Pandolf, of fair Milan Cardinal,
65 And from Pope Innocent the legate here,
   Do in his name religiously demand
   Why thou against the Church, our Holy Mother,
   So wilfully dost spurn, and force perforce[9]
   Keep Stephen Langton, chosen° Archbishop   *(by the pope)*
70 Of Canterbury, from that holy see.
   This, in our foresaid Holy Father's name,
   Pope Innocent, I do demand of thee.

KING JOHN   What earthy name to interrogatories
   Can task the free breath of a sacred king?[1]
75 Thou canst not, Cardinal, devise a name
   So slight, unworthy, and ridiculous
   To charge me to an° answer, as the Pope.   *to make an*
   Tell him this tale, and from the mouth of England
   Add thus much more: that no Italian priest°   *the pope*
80 Shall tithe or toll° in our dominions;   *collect church revenue*
   But as we, under God, are supreme head,[2]
   So, under him, that great supremacy°   *sovereignty*
   Where we do reign we will alone uphold
   Without th'assistance of a mortal hand.
85 So tell the Pope, all reverence set apart°   *rejected*
   To him and his usurped authority.

KING PHILIP   Brother of England, you blaspheme in this.

KING JOHN   Though you and all the kings of Christendom
   Are led so grossly by this meddling priest,
90 Dreading the curse that money may buy out,[3]
   And by the merit of vile gold, dross, dust,
   Purchase corrupted pardon of a man,[4]
   Who in that sale sells pardon from himself;[5]
   Though you and all the rest so grossly led
95 This juggling° witchcraft with revenue cherish;   *deceiving*
   Yet I alone, alone do me oppose
   Against the Pope, and count his friends my foes.

PANDOLF   Then by the lawful power that I have
   Thou shalt stand cursed and excommunicate;°   *excommunicated*
100 And blessèd shall he be that doth revolt
   From his allegiance to an heretic;
   And meritorious shall that hand be called,
   Canonizèd and worshipped as a saint,
   That takes away by any secret course
   Thy hateful life.

8. As he does in the use of Austria to represent two of Richard I's adversaries, Shakespeare follows his main source in combining two papal legates in one.
9. *dost . . . perforce*: set yourself, and forcibly.
1. *What . . . king?*: What person holding an earthly title (the pope or his deputy) can demand answers from a King who governs by divine right? John attributes to himself the divine authority he has just denied the pope.
2. "Supreme head" of the English church is the title adopted in 1534 by Henry VIII, Elizabeth's father, in defiance of the papacy. This passage is perhaps the most openly and anachronistically Protestant, anti-Catholic moment in the play.
3. Excommunication is the "curse" that a bribe can buy off, or reverse.
4. An allusion to the sale of indulgences, or papal dispensations for sin, by a member of the Catholic clergy ("a man").
5. The clergyman "sells" (gives up) hope of God's forgiveness for himself and is hence damned by his selling. The pardon he sells lacks efficacy because it comes "from himself," rather than from God.

105	CONSTANCE O lawful let it be	
	That I have room° with Rome to curse awhile.	*opportunity*
	Good Father Cardinal, cry thou 'Amen'	
	To my keen curses, for without my wrong°	*the wrongs done to me*
	There is no tongue hath power to curse him right.°	*properly*
110	PANDOLF There's law and warrant, lady, for my curse.	
	CONSTANCE And for mine too. When law can do no right,	
	Let it be lawful that law bar no wrong.°	*cursing*
	Law cannot give my child his kingdom here,	
	For he that holds his kingdom holds the law.	
115	Therefore, since law° itself is perfect wrong,	*(secular)*
	How can the law° forbid my tongue to curse?	*(ecclesiastical)*
	PANDOLF Philip of France, on peril of a curse,°	*excommunication*
	Let go the hand of that arch-heretic,	
	And raise the power of France upon his head,	
120	Unless he do submit himself to Rome.	
	QUEEN ELEANOR Look'st thou pale, France? Do not let go thy hand.	
	CONSTANCE [*to* KING JOHN] Look to it, devil, lest that France repent,	
	And by disjoining hands hell lose a soul.	
	AUSTRIA King Philip, listen to the Cardinal.	
125	BASTARD And hang a calf's-skin on his recreant limbs.	
	AUSTRIA Well, ruffian, I must pocket up° these wrongs,	*put up with*
	Because—	
	BASTARD Your breeches best may carry them.[6]	
	KING JOHN Philip, what sayst thou to the Cardinal?	
	CONSTANCE What should he say, but as° the Cardinal?	*the same as*
130	LOUIS THE DAUPHIN Bethink you, Father, for the difference	
	Is purchase of a heavy curse from Rome,	
	Or the light loss of England for a friend.	
	Forgo the easier.	
	BLANCHE That's the curse of Rome.	
	CONSTANCE O Louis, stand fast; the devil tempts thee here	
135	In likeness of a new untrimmèd° bride.	*virginal*
	BLANCHE The Lady Constance speaks not from her faith,	
	But from her need.	
	CONSTANCE [*to* KING PHILIP] O if thou grant my need,	
	Which only lives but by the death of faith,[7]	
	That need must needs infer this principle:[8]	
140	That faith would live again by death of need.°	*by the end of my woes*
	O, then tread down my need, and faith mounts up;	
	Keep my need up, and faith is trodden down.	
	KING JOHN The King is moved, and answers not to this.	
	CONSTANCE [*to* KING PHILIP] O, be removed from him, and answer well.	
145	AUSTRIA Do so, King Philip, hang no more in doubt.	
	BASTARD Hang nothing but a calf's-skin, most sweet lout.	
	KING PHILIP I am perplexed, and know not what to say.	
	PANDOLF What canst thou say but will perplex° thee more,	*trouble*
	If thou stand excommunicate and cursed?	
150	KING PHILIP Good Reverend Father, make my person yours,°	*put yourself in my place*
	And tell me how you would bestow yourself.°	*what you would do*
	This royal hand and mine are newly knit,°	*joined*

---

6. Probably, you may best carry them (the "wrongs" of line 126, or kicks) in the pocket of your breeches; possibly implying that Austria will be kicked in the breeches.
7. Which (my need) exists only because of your broken

faith (the pledge to support Arthur) or my loss of faith in you; perhaps, which will live only if you break your faith (to the church).
8. That need necessarily implies this truth.

And the conjunction of our inward souls
Married in league, coupled and linked together
155   With all religious strength of sacred vows;
The latest breath that gave the sound of words
Was deep-sworn faith, peace, amity, true love,
Between our kingdoms and our royal selves;
And even° before this truce, but new° before,   *just / only just*
160   No longer than we well could wash our hands°   *(of blood)*
To clap this royal bargain up of peace,[9]
God knows, they were besmeared and over-stained
With slaughter's pencil,° where Revenge did paint   *paintbrush*
The fearful difference° of incensèd kings;   *dispute*
165   And shall these hands, so lately purged of blood,
So newly joined in love, so strong in both,°   *(blood and love)*
Unyoke this seizure[1] and this kind regreet,°   *return of salutation*
Play fast and loose with faith, so jest with heaven,
Make such unconstant children of ourselves,
170   As now again to snatch our palm from palm,
Unswear faith sworn, and on the marriage-bed
Of smiling peace to march a bloody host,
And make a riot on the gentle brow
Of true sincerity? O holy sir,
175   My Reverend Father, let it not be so.
Out of your grace, devise, ordain, impose
Some gentle order, and then we shall be blessed
To do your pleasure and continue friends.
PANDOLF   All form is formless, order orderless,
180   Save what is opposite to England's love.
Therefore to arms, be champion of our Church,
Or let the Church, our mother, breathe her curse,
A mother's curse, on her revolting son.
France, thou mayst hold° a serpent by the tongue,   *may more easily hold*
185   A crazèd lion by the mortal° paw,   *deadly*
A fasting tiger safer by the tooth,
Than keep in peace that hand which thou dost hold.
KING PHILIP   I may disjoin my hand, but not my faith.
PANDOLF   So mak'st thou faith an enemy to faith,[2]
190   And like a civil war, sett'st oath to oath,
Thy tongue against thy tongue. O, let thy vow,
First made to heaven, first be to heaven performed;
That is, to be the champion of our Church.
What since thou swor'st[3] is sworn against thyself,
195   And may not be performèd by thyself;
For that which thou hast sworn to do amiss
Is not amiss when it is truly done;[4]
And being not done where doing tends to ill,
The truth is then most done not doing it.
200   The better act of purposes mistook[5]
Is to mistake again; though indirect,°   *circuitous; wrong*

9. To seal this royal peace treaty by shaking hands.
1. Of hands joined together.
2. You set your faith to John against your faith to the
church. The confusing rhetoric of this speech exemplifies
the elaborate and sometimes equivocal reasoning known
as casuistry that was practiced by sixteenth-century Catholics and hated by English Protestants.
3. What you've subsequently sworn (amity with John).
4. *For . . . done:* For it's not immoral to break an immoral
vow. *truly done:* not done at all because it is immoral.
5. The better act when you've done wrong.

Yet indirection thereby grows direct,
And falsehood falsehood cures, as fire cools fire
Within the scorchèd veins of one new burned.[6]

205 It is religion that doth make vows kept;°   *make us honor our vows*
But thou hast sworn against religion;
By what thou swear'st, against the thing thou swear'st;[7]
And mak'st an oath the surety for thy troth:[8]
Against an oath, the truth. Thou art unsure

210 To swear: swear'st only not to be forsworn—
Else what a mockery should it be to swear!—
But thou dost swear only to be forsworn,
And most forsworn to keep what thou dost swear;
Therefore thy later vows against thy first

215 Is in thyself rebellion to° thyself,   *against*
And better conquest never canst thou make
Than arm thy constant and thy nobler parts
Against these giddy loose suggestions;°   *dissolute temptations*
Upon° which better part° our prayers come in   *On behalf of / side*

220 If thou vouchsafe° them. But if not, then know   *accept*
The peril of our curses light on thee
So heavy as thou shalt not shake them off,
But in despair° die under their black weight.   *(because damned)*

AUSTRIA   Rebellion, flat rebellion!
BASTARD   Wilt not be?[9]
225 Will not a calf's-skin stop that mouth of thine?

LOUIS THE DAUPHIN   Father, to arms!
BLANCHE   Upon thy wedding day?
Against the blood that thou hast married?
What, shall our feast be kept with° slaughtered men?   *attended by*
Shall braying trumpets and loud churlish drums,

230 Clamours of hell, be measures° to our pomp?°   *music / celebration*
    [*She kneels*]
O husband, hear me! Ay, alack, how new
Is 'husband' in my mouth! Even for that name
Which till this time my tongue did ne'er pronounce,
Upon my knee I beg, go not to arms
Against mine uncle.

235 CONSTANCE [*kneeling*]   O, upon my knee
Made hard with kneeling, I do pray to thee,
Thou virtuous Dauphin, alter not the doom°   *fate*
Forethought by heaven.[1]

BLANCHE [*to* LOUIS THE DAUPHIN]   Now shall I see thy love:
    what motive may
240 Be stronger with thee than the name of wife?

CONSTANCE   That which upholdeth him that thee upholds:°   *who supports you*
His honour.—O thine honour, Louis, thine honour!

LOUIS THE DAUPHIN [*to* KING PHILIP]   I muse your majesty doth
    seem so cold

---

6. *as fire . . . burned:* the theory that one fire cools
another was proverbial but false.
7. By your oath to John, you break your oath to your religion, the basis for all other vows.
8. You make an oath the guarantee of your "troth"
(agreement with John); but with a pun on its opposite—
the "truth" (or religious faith) of the next line.

9. Is it all in vain; won't you be quiet?
1. Constance self-interestedly treats as a single issue
John's two separate matters—Arthur's right to the throne
and Pandolf's insistence on papal right. The belief that
people are preordained for either salvation or damnation
("doom / Forethought by heaven") is more Protestant
than Catholic.

When such profound respects° do pull you on.   *weighty considerations*
245 PANDOLF   I will denounce a curse upon his head.
KING PHILIP   Thou shalt not need.—England, I will fall from° thee.   *desert*
    [*He takes his hand from King John's hand.* BLANCHE
    and CONSTANCE *rise*]
CONSTANCE   O, fair return of banished majesty!
QUEEN ELEANOR   O, foul revolt of French inconstancy!
KING JOHN   France, thou shalt rue this hour within this hour.
250 BASTARD   Old Time the clock-setter, that bald sexton Time,
    Is it as he will?—Well then, France shall rue.²
BLANCHE   The sun's o'ercast with blood; fair day, adieu!
    Which is the side that I must go withal?°   *with*
    I am with both, each army hath a hand,
255   And in their rage, I having hold of both,
    They whirl asunder° and dismember me.   *dash apart*
    Husband, I cannot pray that thou mayst win.—
    Uncle, I needs must pray that thou mayst lose.—
    Father,° I may not wish the fortune thine.—   *Father-in-law (Philip)*
260   Grandam, I will not wish thy wishes thrive.
    Whoever wins, on that side shall I lose,
    Assurèd loss before the match be played.
LOUIS THE DAUPHIN   Lady, with me, with me thy fortune° lies.   *prosperity*
BLANCHE   There where my fortune° lives, there° my life dies.   *fate / (with Louis)*
KING JOHN [*to the* BASTARD]   Cousin, go draw our puissance°   *army*
265   together.—   [*Exit the* BASTARD]
    France, I am burned up with inflaming wrath,
    A rage whose heat hath this condition:
    That nothing can allay,° nothing but blood,   *cure*
    The blood, and dearest-valued blood, of France.
270 KING PHILIP   Thy rage shall burn thee up, and thou shalt turn
    To ashes ere our blood shall quench that fire.
    Look to thyself, thou art in jeopardy.
KING JOHN   No more than he that threats.—To arms let's hie!°   *hasten*
    Exeunt [*severally*]

3.2

    Alarum;° excursions.° Enter [*the*] BASTARD, *with* [*the*   *Call to arms / battles*
    Duke of*] Austria's head*
BASTARD   Now, by my life, this day grows wondrous hot;
    Some airy devil¹ hovers in the sky
    And pours down mischief. Austria's head lie there,
    While Philip breathes.
    Enter [KING] JOHN, ARTHUR [*Duke of Brittaine, and*]
    HUBERT
5 KING JOHN   Hubert, keep this boy.—Philip,° make up!°   *(the Bastard) / press on*
    My mother is assailèd in our tent,
    And ta'en° I fear.   *captured*
BASTARD   My lord, I rescued her;

---

2. *Old . . . rue*: The sexton set the church clock and dug graves. Hence, the "hour" (line 249), or time, which was usually portrayed as bald, will indeed be fatal. "Time" and "rue" recall the punning proverb about herbs, "Thyme and rue grow both in one garden," in which the pleasant taste of thyme is contrasted with the bitterness of rue: the passage of time is accompanied by regret. Together the two lines mean something like "If things proceed according to the fatal effects of time, France will indeed be sorry, because time (thyme) and rue go together."
3.2 Location: Plains near Angers.
1. Aerial devils or spirits held to cause thunderstorms and subsequent death.

Her highness is in safety; fear you not.
But on, my liege, for very little pains
10   Will bring this labour to an happy end.
            Exeunt [KING JOHN *and the* BASTARD *at one door,*
                    HUBERT *and* ARTHUR *at another door*]

3.3

Alarum; excursions; retreat.° *Enter* [KING] JOHN,   *signal for retreat*
[QUEEN] ELEANOR, ARTHUR [*Duke of Brittaine, the*] BAS-
TARD, HUBERT, *lords* [*with soldiers*]¹
KING JOHN [*to* QUEEN ELEANOR] So shall it be; your grace shall
      stay behind²
So° strongly guarded. [*To* ARTHUR] Cousin,° look not sad;   *Thus / Kinsman*
Thy grandam loves thee, and thy uncle will
As dear be to thee as thy father was.
5   ARTHUR O, this will make my mother die with grief.
KING JOHN [*to the* BASTARD] Cousin, away for England! Haste before,°   *Go ahead*
And ere our coming, see thou shake the bags
Of hoarding abbots.³ The fat ribs of peace
Must by the hungry now be fed upon.
10   Imprisoned angels° set at liberty.⁴   *gold coins; spirits*
Use our commission° in his° utmost force.   *(to tax) / its*
BASTARD Bell, book, and candle⁵ shall not drive me back
When gold and silver becks° me to come on.   *beckons*
I leave your highness.—Grandam, I will pray,
15   If ever I remember to be holy,
For your fair safety. So I kiss your hand.
QUEEN ELEANOR Farewell, gentle cousin.
KING JOHN   Coz, farewell.
                                    [*Exit the* BASTARD]
QUEEN ELEANOR Come hither, little kinsman. Hark, a word.
      [*She takes* ARTHUR *aside*]
KING JOHN Come hither, Hubert.
      [*He takes* HUBERT *aside*]
                      O my gentle Hubert,
20   We owe thee much. Within this wall of flesh°   *(John's body)*
There is a soul counts thee her creditor,
And with advantage° means to pay thy love;   *interest*
And, my good friend, thy voluntary oath°   *oath of allegiance*
Lives in this bosom, dearly cherishèd.
Give me thy hand.
      [*He takes Hubert's hand*]
25   I had a thing to say,
But I will fit it with some better tune.°   *words; reward*
By heaven, Hubert, I am almost ashamed
To say what good respect° I have of thee.   *opinion*
HUBERT I am much bounden° to your majesty.   *indebted*

3.3 Location: Scene continues.
1. F does not begin a new scene here, but it does empty the stage—hence the scene division adopted here and in most modern editions.
2. In France, to control the French possessions while John returns to England.
3. *shake . . . abbots:* pillage the monasteries, which have

hoarded up wealth. When Henry VIII made himself head of the English church, he confiscated monastic treasure.
4. F places this line right after "abbots" (line 8), perhaps because a marginal addition in the foul papers was misplaced in the scribal transcript.
5. Articles used in the rite of excommunication.

30 KING JOHN   Good friend, thou hast no cause to say so yet,
 But thou shalt have; and creep time ne'er so slow,
 Yet it shall come for me to do thee good.
 I had a thing to say—but let it go.
 The sun is in the heaven, and the proud day,
35 Attended with the pleasures of the world,
 Is all too wanton° and too full of gauds°   *merry / playthings*
 To give me audience.° If the midnight bell   *For you to listen*
 Did with his iron tongue and brazen mouth
 Sound on into the drowsy race° of night;   *course*
40 If this same were a churchyard° where we stand,   *graveyard*
 And thou possessèd° with a thousand wrongs;   *obsessed*
 Or if that surly spirit, melancholy,
 Had baked° thy blood and made it heavy, thick,   *congealed*
 Which else° runs tickling up and down the veins,   *otherwise*
45 Making that idiot,° laughter, keep° men's eyes   *jester / stay in*
 And strain their cheeks to idle merriment—
 A passion° hateful to my purposes—   *mood*
 Or if that thou couldst see me without eyes,
 Hear me without thine ears, and make reply
50 Without a tongue, using conceit° alone,   *understanding*
 Without eyes, ears, and harmful sound of words;
 Then in despite° of broad-eyed watchful day   *defiance*
 I would into thy bosom pour my thoughts.
 But, ah, I will not. Yet I love thee well,
55 And by my troth,° I think thou lov'st me well.   *faith*
 HUBERT   So well that what you bid me undertake,
 Though that° my death were adjunct to my act,   *Even if*
 By heaven, I would do it.
 KING JOHN   Do not I know thou wouldst?
 Good Hubert, Hubert, Hubert, throw thine eye
60 On yon young boy. I'll tell thee what, my friend,
 He is a very serpent in my way,
 And wheresoe'er this foot of mine doth tread,
 He lies before me. Dost thou understand me?
 Thou art his keeper.
 HUBERT   And I'll keep him so
65 That he shall not offend your majesty.
 KING JOHN   Death.
 HUBERT   My lord.
 KING JOHN   A grave.
 HUBERT   He shall not live.
 KING JOHN   Enough.
 I could be merry now. Hubert, I love thee.
 Well, I'll not say what I intend for thee.
 Remember. [*To* QUEEN ELEANOR] Madam, fare you well.
70 I'll send those powers° o'er to your majesty.   *troops*
 QUEEN ELEANOR   My blessing go with thee.
 KING JOHN [*to* ARTHUR]   For England, cousin, go.
 Hubert shall be your man, attend on you
 With all true duty.—On toward Calais, ho!
                    Exeunt [QUEEN ELEANOR, *attended, at one door,*
                              the rest at another door]

3.4

Enter [KING PHILIP *of*] *France,* [LOUIS THE] DAUPHIN,
[*Cardinal*] PANDOLF, [*and*] *attendants*

KING PHILIP   So, by a roaring tempest on the flood,
A whole armada of convicted sail
Is scattered and disjoined from fellowship.[1]

PANDOLF   Courage and comfort; all shall yet go well.

5   KING PHILIP   What can go well when we have run° so ill?   *performed; run away*
Are we not beaten? Is not Angers lost,
Arthur ta'en prisoner, divers° dear friends slain,   *various*
And bloody England° into England gone,   *John*
O'erbearing interruption, spite[2] of France?

10 LOUIS THE DAUPHIN   What he hath won, that hath he fortified.
So hot a speed, with such advice disposed,°   *judgment regulated*
Such temperate° order in so fierce a cause,   *calm*
Doth want example.° Who hath read or heard   *lack precedent*
Of any kindred action like to this?

15 KING PHILIP   Well could I bear that England had this praise,
So° we could find some pattern° of our shame.   *If / precedent*

Enter CONSTANCE [*distracted,° with her hair about her*   *wild, mad*
ears]

Look who comes here! A grave° unto a soul,   *(Constance's body)*
Holding th'eternal spirit against her will[3]
In the vile prison of afflicted breath.°—   *life*

20 I prithee, lady, go away with me.

CONSTANCE   Lo, now, now see the issue° of your peace!   *outcome*

KING PHILIP   Patience, good lady; comfort, gentle Constance.

CONSTANCE   No, I defy all counsel, all redress,°   *comfort*
But that which ends all counsel, true redress:

25 Death, Death, O amiable, lovely Death!
Thou odoriferous° stench, sound rottenness!   *fragrant*
Arise forth from the couch of lasting° night,   *bed of everlasting*
Thou hate and terror to prosperity,
And I will kiss thy detestable bones,

30 And put my eyeballs in thy vaulty brows,[4]
And ring these fingers with thy household worms,[5]
And stop this gap of breath with fulsome dust,[6]
And be a carrion° monster like thyself.   *corpse-eating*
Come grin on me, and I will think thou smil'st,

35 And buss° thee as thy wife. Misery's love,   *kiss*
O, come to me!

KING PHILIP   O fair affliction,° peace!   *afflicted one*

CONSTANCE   No, no, I will not, having breath to cry.
O, that my tongue were in the thunder's mouth!
Then with a passion° would I shake the world,   *an emotional outcry*

40 And rouse from sleep that fell anatomy,°   *fierce skeleton*
Which cannot hear a lady's feeble voice,
Which scorns a modern invocation.°   *an ordinary plea*

PANDOLF   Lady, you utter madness, and not sorrow.

3.4 Location: The French camp by Angers.
1. *So . . . fellowship:* this French naval defeat is not in
Shakespeare's sources. It is probably a reference to the
Spanish Armada of 1588 (see the Introduction). *convicted
sail:* doomed ships.
2. Overcoming hindrances, in spite.

3. *Holding . . . will:* that is, she wants to die.
4. Hollow forehead; the eye sockets of the imagined skull
of death's corpse.
5. And wear the worms that serve you and live inside you
as rings around my fingers.
6. And kiss this mouth with nauseous dust.

CONSTANCE   Thou art not holy to belie me so.
45   I am not mad: this hair I tear is mine;
      My name is Constance; I was Geoffrey's wife;
      Young Arthur is my son; and he is lost.
      I am not mad; I would to God I were,
      For then 'tis like° I should forget myself.   *likely*
50   O, if I could, what grief should I forget!
      Preach some philosophy to make me mad,
      And thou shalt be canonized, Cardinal.
      For, being not mad, but sensible° of grief,   *subject to feelings*
      My reasonable part produces reason
55   How I may be delivered of° these woes,   *freed from*
      And teaches me to kill or hang myself.
      If I were mad I should forget my son,
      Or madly think a babe of clouts° were he.   *cloth doll*
      I am not mad; too well, too well I feel
60   The different plague° of each calamity.   *distinct affliction*
KING PHILIP   Bind up those tresses. O, what love I note
      In the fair multitude of those her hairs!
      Where but by chance a silver drop° hath fallen,   *tear*
      Even to that drop ten thousand wiry friends°   *hairs*
65   Do glue themselves° in sociable grief,   *mat together*
      Like true, inseparable, faithful loves,
      Sticking together in calamity.
CONSTANCE   To England, if you will.[7]
KING PHILIP   Bind up your hairs.
CONSTANCE   Yes, that I will. And wherefore will I do it?
70   I tore them from their bonds, and cried aloud,
      'O that these hands could so redeem my son,
      As they have given these hairs their liberty!'
      But now I envy at their liberty,
      And will again commit them to their bonds,
75   Because my poor child is a prisoner.
      [*She binds up her hair*]
      And Father Cardinal, I have heard you say
      That we shall see and know our friends in heaven.
      If that be true, I shall see my boy again;
      For since the birth of Cain, the first male child,
80   To him that did but yesterday suspire,°   *take his first breath*
      There was not such a gracious creature born.
      But now will canker-sorrow eat my bud,[8]
      And chase the native beauty from his cheek;
      And he will look as hollow as a ghost,
85   As dim and meagre° as an ague's° fit,   *pale and thin / fever's*
      And so he'll die; and rising so again,
      When I shall meet him in the court of heaven,
      I shall not know him; therefore never, never
      Must I behold my pretty Arthur more.
90 PANDOLF   You hold too heinous a respect° of grief.   *view*
CONSTANCE   He talks to me that never had a son.
KING PHILIP   You are as fond of grief as of your child.

7. Apparently a reply to line 20, delayed because of Constance's distraction. Possibly the intervening passage is a
revision interpolated after the original composition.

8. But now sorrow, like a cankerworm, will eat my flower
(Arthur); this is proverbial.

CONSTANCE   Grief fills the room up of my absent child,
Lies in his bed, walks up and down with me,
95   Puts on his pretty looks, repeats his words,
Remembers° me of all his gracious parts,   *Reminds*
Stuffs out his vacant garments with his form;
Then have I reason to be fond of grief.
Fare you well. Had you such a loss as I,
100   I could give better comfort than you do.
[*She unbinds her hair*]
I will not keep this form upon my head
When there is such disorder in my wit.
O Lord, my boy, my Arthur, my fair son,
My life, my joy, my food, my all the world,
105   My widow-comfort, and my sorrow's cure!   *Exit*
KING PHILIP   I fear some outrage,° and I'll follow her.   *(perhaps suicide)*
Exit [attended]
LOUIS THE DAUPHIN   There's nothing in this world can make me joy.
Life is as tedious as a twice-told tale,
Vexing the dull ear of a drowsy man;
110   And bitter shame hath spoiled the sweet world's taste,
That° it yields naught but shame and bitterness.   *So that*
PANDOLF   Before the curing of a strong disease,
Even in the instant of repair and health,
The fit° is strongest. Evils that take leave,   *symptom*
115   On their departure most of all show evil.
What have you lost by losing of this day?
LOUIS THE DAUPHIN   All days of glory, joy, and happiness.
PANDOLF   If you had won it, certainly you had.
No, no; when Fortune means° to men most good,   *intends*
120   She looks upon them with a threat'ning eye.
'Tis strange to think how much King John hath lost
In this which he accounts so clearly won.
Are not you grieved that Arthur is his prisoner?
LOUIS THE DAUPHIN   As heartily as he is glad he hath him.
125   PANDOLF   Your mind is all as youthful as your blood.
Now hear me speak with a prophetic spirit,
For even the breath of what I mean to speak
Shall blow each dust,° each straw, each little rub,°   *speck / obstacle*
Out of the path which shall directly lead
130   Thy foot to England's throne. And therefore mark.
John hath seized Arthur, and it cannot be
That whiles warm life plays in that infant's veins
The misplaced° John should entertain an hour,   *usurping*
One minute, nay, one quiet breath of rest.
135   A sceptre snatched with an unruly hand
Must be as boisterously° maintained as gained;   *violently*
And he that stands upon a slipp'ry place
Makes nice of no vile hold to stay[9] him up.
That John may stand, then Arthur needs must fall;
140   So be it, for it cannot be but so.
LOUIS THE DAUPHIN   But what shall I gain by young Arthur's fall?
PANDOLF   You, in the right of Lady Blanche your wife,
May then make all the claim that Arthur did.[1]

---

9. Is not fussy about the vileness of any hold to keep.   1. In Shakespeare's sources but not historical.

LOUIS THE DAUPHIN   And lose it, life and all, as Arthur did.
145 PANDOLF   How green you are, and fresh in this old world!
John lays you plots;° the times conspire with you;   *plots to your benefit*
For he that steeps his safety in true° blood   *legitimate*
Shall find but bloody safety and untrue.[2]
This act, so vilely born, shall cool the hearts
150 Of all his people, and freeze up their zeal,°   *enthusiastic loyalty*
That none so small advantage shall step forth
To check his reign but they will cherish it;[3]
No natural exhalation° in the sky,   *meteor*
No scope° of nature, no distempered° day,   *effect / stormy*
155 No common wind, no customèd event,
But they will pluck away his° natural cause,   *its*
And call them meteors,° prodigies, and signs,   *portents*
Abortives,[4] presages, and tongues of° heaven   *signs from*
Plainly denouncing vengeance upon John.
160 LOUIS THE DAUPHIN   Maybe he will not touch young Arthur's life,
But hold° himself safe in his prisonment.   *consider*
PANDOLF   O sir, when he shall hear of your approach,
If that young Arthur be not gone already,
Even at that news he dies; and then the hearts
165 Of all his people shall revolt from him,
And kiss the lips of unacquainted° change,   *unfamiliar*
And pick strong matter of° revolt and wrath   *reasons for*
Out of the bloody fingers' ends° of John.   *deeds*
Methinks I see this hurly all on foot,°   *commotion all under way*
170 And O, what better matter breeds for you
Than I have named! The Bastard Falconbridge
Is now in England, ransacking the Church,
Offending charity. If but a dozen French
Were there in arms, they would be as a call°   *decoy; call to arms*
175 To train° ten thousand English to their side,   *draw*
Or as a little snow tumbled about
Anon becomes a mountain. O noble Dauphin,
Go with me to the King. 'Tis wonderful
What may be wrought out of their discontent
180 Now that their souls are top-full of offence.°   *grievances*
For England, go! I will whet on° the King.   *provoke*
LOUIS THE DAUPHIN   Strong reasons make strange actions. Let us go.
If you say ay, the King will not say no.   *Exeunt*

4.1

Enter HUBERT, *and* EXECUTIONERS [*with a rope and irons*]
HUBERT   Heat me these irons hot, and look thou stand
Within the arras.[1] When I strike my foot
Upon the bosom of the ground, rush forth
And bind the boy which you shall find with me
5 Fast to the chair. Be heedful. Hence, and watch!
EXECUTIONER   I hope your warrant will bear out° the deed.   *authorize*
HUBERT   Uncleanly° scruples: fear not you. Look to't!°   *Improper / Do it*
[*The* EXECUTIONERS *withdraw behind the arras*]

2. Compare Genesis 9:6: "Whoso sheddeth man's blood, by man shall his blood be shed." *untrue:* untrustworthy.
3. *none . . . it:* they will seize the smallest opportunity to dethrone him.
4. Untimely or monstrous births (seen as portents).
4.1 Location: A castle prison in England.
1. Behind the tapestry hangings.

Young lad, come forth, I have to say° with you.   *something to discuss*
    Enter ARTHUR [*Duke of Brittaine*]
ARTHUR Good morrow, Hubert.
HUBERT   Good morrow, little Prince.
10   ARTHUR As little prince, having so great a title
    To be more prince, as may be.² You are sad.
HUBERT Indeed I have been merrier.
ARTHUR   Mercy on me!
    Methinks nobody should be sad but I.
    Yet I remember, when I was in France,
15   Young gentlemen would be as sad as night
    Only for wantonness.° By my christendom,°   *affectation / faith*
    So° I were out of prison and kept sheep,   *If*
    I should be as merry as the day is long;
    And so I would be here, but that I doubt°   *fear*
20   My uncle practises° more harm to me.   *plots*
    He is afraid of me, and I of him.
    Is it my fault that I was Geoffrey's son?
    No, indeed is't not, and I would to God
    I were your son, so you would love me, Hubert.
25   HUBERT [*aside*] If I talk to him, with his innocent prate°   *prattle*
    He will awake my mercy, which lies dead;
    Therefore I will be sudden, and dispatch.
ARTHUR Are you sick, Hubert? You look pale today.
    In sooth, I would° you were a little sick,   *Truly, I wish*
30   That I might sit all night and watch with you.
    I warrant I love you more than you do me.
HUBERT [*aside*] His words do take possession of my bosom.
    [*He shows* ARTHUR *a paper*]
    Read here, young Arthur. [*Aside*] How now: foolish rheum,°   *tears*
    Turning dispiteous° torture out of door?   *pitiless*
35   I must be brief, lest resolution drop
    Out at mine eyes in tender womanish tears.
    [*To* ARTHUR] Can you not read it? Is it not fair writ?°   *legible; legal ?*
ARTHUR Too fairly, Hubert, for so foul effect.
    Must you with hot irons burn out both mine eyes?³
HUBERT Young boy, I must.
ARTHUR   And will you?
40   HUBERT   And I will.
ARTHUR Have you the heart? When your head did but ache
    I knit my handkerchief about your brows,
    The best I had—a princess wrought it° me,   *made it for*
    And I did never ask it you° again—   *back from you*
45   And with my hand at midnight held your head,
    And like the watchful minutes to the hour
    Still and anon° cheered up the heavy time,⁴   *Continually*
    Saying 'What lack you?' and 'Where lies your grief?'°   *pain*
    Or 'What good love° may I perform for you?'   *loving deed*
50   Many a poor man's son would have lain still
    And ne'er have spoke a loving word to you,

---

2. *As . . . be:* Although I have title to be a great prince (king), I am as little a prince as is possible.
3. The order to blind Arthur here is at odds with the death sentence of 3.3.66, as well as with Hubert's decision later in this scene (line 127) falsely to report Arthur's death, a decision he makes good on in 4.2.
4. The minutes are seen as breaking up the time to make it pass easily.

But you at your sick service had a prince.
Nay, you may think my love was crafty love,
And call it cunning. Do, an if you will.
55 If heaven be pleased that you must use me ill,
Why then you must. Will you put out mine eyes,
These eyes that never did, nor never shall,
So much as frown on you?
HUBERT   I have sworn to do it,
And with hot irons must I burn them out.
60 ARTHUR   Ah, none but in this iron age⁵ would do it.
The iron of itself, though heat° red hot,   *heated*
Approaching near these eyes would drink my tears,
And quench his° fiery indignation   *its*
Even in the matter° of mine innocence;   *substance; tears*
65 Nay, after that, consume° away in rust,   *dissolve*
But° for containing fire to harm mine eye.   *Merely*
Are you more stubborn-hard than hammered iron?
An if an angel should have come to me
And told me Hubert should put out mine eyes,
70 I would not have believed him; no tongue but Hubert's.
          [HUBERT *stamps his foot*]
HUBERT   Come forth!
          [*The* EXECUTIONERS *come forth*]
                    Do as I bid you do.
ARTHUR   O, save me, Hubert, save me! My eyes are out
Even with the fierce looks of these bloody men.
HUBERT [*to the* EXECUTIONERS]   Give me the iron, I say, and bind him here.
          [*He takes the iron*]
75 ARTHUR   Alas, what need you be so boisterous-rough?
I will not struggle; I will stand stone-still.
For God's sake, Hubert, let me not be bound.
Nay, hear me, Hubert! Drive these men away,
And I will sit as quiet as a lamb;
80 I will not stir, nor wince, nor speak a word,
Nor look upon the iron angerly.°   *angrily*
Thrust but these men away, and I'll forgive you,
Whatever torment you do put me to.
HUBERT [*to the* EXECUTIONERS]   Go stand within. Let me alone with him.
85 EXECUTIONER   I am best pleased to be from° such a deed.   *away from*
          [*Exeunt* EXECUTIONERS]
ARTHUR   Alas, I then have chid° away my friend!   *scolded*
He hath a stern look, but a gentle heart.
Let him come back, that his compassion may
Give life to yours.
HUBERT   Come, boy, prepare yourself.
ARTHUR   Is there no remedy?
90 HUBERT   None but to lose your eyes.
ARTHUR   O God, that there were but a mote° in yours,   *speck of dust*
A grain, a dust, a gnat, a wandering hair,
Any annoyance in that precious sense,°   *sight*
Then, feeling what small things are boisterous° there,   *painful*
95 Your vile intent must needs seem horrible.
HUBERT   Is this your promise? Go to,° hold your tongue!   *Stop it (rebuke)*

---

5. Cruel degenerate world, in contrast to the legendary "golden" and "silver" ages; with a play on the hot irons.

ARTHUR   Hubert, the utterance of a brace of tongues
      Must needs want pleading for a pair of eyes.[6]
      Let° me not hold my tongue, let me not, Hubert;   *Make*
100   Or, Hubert, if you will, cut out my tongue,
      So° I may keep mine eyes. O, spare mine eyes,   *If*
      Though to no use but still to look on you.
      Lo, by my troth,° the instrument is cold   *faith*
      And would not harm me.
HUBERT   I can heat it, boy.
105 ARTHUR   No, in good sooth:° the fire is dead with grief,   *truly*
      Being create° for comfort, to be° used   *created / at being*
      In undeserved extremes.° See else yourself.[7]   *extreme suffering*
      There is no malice in this burning coal;
      The breath of heaven hath blown his spirit° out,   *(dead person's) soul*
110   And strewed repentant ashes° on his head.   *(of a penitent sinner)*
HUBERT   But with my breath I can revive it, boy.
ARTHUR   An if you do, you will but make it blush
      And glow with shame of your proceedings, Hubert.
      Nay, it perchance will sparkle° in your eyes,   *cast sparks*
115   And like a dog that is compelled to fight,
      Snatch at his master that doth tarre° him on.   *set*
      All things that you should° use to do me wrong   *would*
      Deny their office;° only you do lack   *Disobey*
      That mercy which fierce fire and iron extends,
120   Creatures of note° for mercy-lacking uses.   *Things noteworthy*
HUBERT   Well, see to live.[8] I will not touch thine eye
      For all the treasure that thine uncle owes.°   *owns*
      Yet am I sworn, and I did purpose, boy,
      With this same very iron to burn them out.
125 ARTHUR   O, now you look like Hubert. All this while
      You were disguisèd.
HUBERT   Peace, no more. Adieu.
      Your uncle must not know but° you are dead.   *otherwise than that*
      I'll fill these doggèd° spies with false reports;   *unfeeling*
      And, pretty child, sleep doubtless° and secure   *without fear*
130   That Hubert, for the wealth of all the world,
      Will not offend° thee.   *harm*
ARTHUR   O God! I thank you, Hubert.
HUBERT   Silence, no more. Go closely° in with me.   *secretly*
      Much danger do I undergo for thee.   *Exeunt*

4.2

[*Flourish.*] *Enter* [KING] JOHN, [*the Earls of*] PEMBROKE
and SALISBURY, *and other lords.* [KING JOHN *ascends the
throne*]

KING JOHN   Here once again we sit, once again crowned,[1]
      And looked upon, I hope, with cheerful eyes.
PEMBROKE   This 'once again', but that your highness pleased,
      Was once superfluous.[2] You were crowned before,

---

6. *the utterance . . . eyes:* not even a pair of tongues would
be enough to plead for a pair of eyes.
7. If you don't believe me, see for yourself.
8. Live, and retain your sight.
4.2 Location: John's court in England.

1. John has had a second coronation. Its purpose,
according to Shakespeare's main source, was to get the
English lords again to swear allegiance to him.
2. *but . . . superfluous:* but for the fact that you wanted
this second coronation, it would have been one too many.

5   And that high royalty was ne'er plucked off,
The faiths of men ne'er stainèd with revolt;
Fresh expectation° troubled not the land   *Hope of a new king*
With any longed-for change or better state.[3]

SALISBURY   Therefore to be possessed with double pomp,
10   To guard° a title that was rich before,   *adorn*
To gild refinèd gold, to paint the lily,
To throw a perfume on the violet,
To smooth the ice, or add another hue
Unto the rainbow, or with taper-light°   *candlelight*
15   To seek the beauteous eye of heaven to garnish,°   *the sun to adorn*
Is wasteful and ridiculous excess.

PEMBROKE   But that your royal pleasure must be done,
This act is as an ancient tale new-told,
And in the last repeating troublesome,
20   Being urgèd at a time unseasonable.°   *inappropriate*

SALISBURY   In this the antique and well-noted° face   *familiar*
Of plain old form° is much disfigurèd,   *custom*
And like a shifted wind unto a sail,
It makes the course of thoughts to fetch about,°   *change directions*
25   Startles and frights consideration,[4]
Makes sound opinion sick, and truth suspected
For putting on so new a fashioned robe.[5]

PEMBROKE   When workmen strive to do better than well,
They do confound° their skill in covetousness;[6]   *destroy*
30   And oftentimes excusing of a fault
Doth make the fault the worser by th'excuse;
As patches set upon a little breach°   *tear*
Discredit more in hiding of the fault
Than did the fault before it was so patched.

35   SALISBURY   To this effect: before you were new-crowned
We breathed our counsel,° but it pleased your highness   *spoke our advice*
To overbear° it; and we are all well pleased,   *overrule*
Since all and every part of what we would°   *wish*
Doth make a stand° at what your highness will.°   *stop; resist / desires*

40   KING JOHN   Some reasons of this double coronation
I have possessed you with,° and think them strong.   *instructed you in*
And more, more strong, when lesser is my fear
I shall endue° you with. Meantime but ask   *supply*
What you would have reformed that is not well,
45   And well shall you perceive how willingly
I will both hear and grant you your requests.[7]

PEMBROKE   Then I, as one that am the tongue° of these   *spokesman*
To sound° the purposes of all their hearts,   *express*
Both for myself and them, but chief of all
50   Your safety, for the which myself and them
Bend° their best studies,° heartily request   *Direct / efforts*
Th'enfranchisement° of Arthur, whose restraint   *release*

---

3. Better government; better living conditions.
4. Encourages questions about John's claim to the throne.
5. For behaving so uncustomarily; for donning a coronation robe.

6. By greedily trying to do even better.
7. Lines 43–46 may allude to the historical King John's submission to the baronial demands spelled out in the Magna Carta. See also line 168 and 5.2.20–23.

Doth move the murmuring lips of discontent
To break into this dangerous argument:
55   If what in rest° you have, in right you hold,   *in peace*
Why then your fears—which, as they say, attend
The steps of wrong—should move you to mew up°   *confine*
Your tender kinsman, and to choke his days
With barbarous ignorance, and deny his youth
60   The rich advantage of good exercise?°   *education*
That the time's enemies may not have this
To grace occasions,° let it be our suit   *To justify opposition*
That you have bid us ask, his liberty;
Which for our goods we do no further ask
65   Than whereupon our weal, on you depending,
Counts it your weal he have his liberty.[8]
      Enter HUBERT
KING JOHN   Let it be so. I do commit his youth
To your direction.—Hubert, what news with you?
      [*He takes* HUBERT *aside*]
PEMBROKE   This is the man should do the bloody deed:
70   He showed his warrant to a friend of mine.
The image of a wicked heinous fault°   *crime*
Lives in his eye; that close aspect° of his   *furtive appearance*
Does show the mood of a much troubled breast;
And I do fearfully believe 'tis done
75   What we so feared he had a charge to do.
SALISBURY   The colour of the King doth come and go
Between his purpose and his conscience,
Like heralds 'twixt two dreadful battles set.°   *armies set for battle*
His passion is so ripe it needs must break.°   *burst (like a boil)*
80   PEMBROKE   And when it breaks, I fear will issue thence
The foul corruption° of a sweet child's death.   *pus*
KING JOHN [*coming forward*]   We cannot hold° mortality's strong hand. *hold back*
Good lords, although my will to give is living,
The suit which you demand is gone and dead.
85   He tells us Arthur is deceased tonight.°   *last night*
SALISBURY   Indeed we feared his sickness was past cure.
PEMBROKE   Indeed we heard how near his death he was,
Before the child himself felt he was sick.
This must be answered,° either here or hence.°   *answered for / in heaven*
90   KING JOHN   Why do you bend such solemn brows on me?
Think you I bear the shears of destiny?[9]
Have I commandment on the pulse of life?
SALISBURY   It is apparent° foul play, and 'tis shame   *blatant*
That greatness should so grossly offer° it.   *brazenly flaunt*
95   So thrive it in your game;[1] and so, farewell.
PEMBROKE   Stay yet, Lord Salisbury; I'll go with thee,
And find th'inheritance of this poor child,
His little kingdom of a forcèd° grave.   *violently imposed*
That blood which owed° the breadth of all this isle   *owned (by right)*
100   Three foot of it doth hold. Bad world the while.°   *while such deeds occur*

8. *Which . . . liberty:* Which we ask for ourselves only
insofar as concern for our benefit, which depends on you,
leads to the conclusion that it is to your benefit to free
him.

9. The shears with which, in Greek myth, the Fates cut
the thread of life.
1. May you suffer a similar fate.

This must not be thus borne. This will break out° *break out in conflict*
To all our sorrows; and ere long, I doubt.° *fear*
 Exeunt [PEMBROKE, SALISBURY, *and other lords*]
KING JOHN They burn in indignation. I repent.
There is no sure foundation set on blood,
105 No certain life achieved by others' death.
 Enter [*a*] MESSENGER
A fearful eye thou hast. Where is that blood
That I have seen inhabit in those cheeks?
So foul a sky° clears not without a storm; *(his face)*
Pour down thy weather: how goes all° in France? *everything; everyone*
110 MESSENGER From France to England. Never such a power
For any foreign preparation° *military expedition*
Was levied in the body of a land.
The copy° of your speed is learned by them, *example*
For when you should be told they do prepare,
115 The tidings comes that they are all arrived.
KING JOHN O, where hath our intelligence° been drunk? *spy network*
Where hath it slept? Where is my mother's ear,
That such an army could be drawn in France,
And she not hear of it?
MESSENGER My liege, her ear
120 Is stopped with dust. The first of April died
Your noble mother. And as I hear, my lord,
The Lady Constance in a frenzy died
Three days before; but this from rumour's tongue
I idly heard; if true or false I know not.
125 KING JOHN Withhold thy speed,° dreadful Occasion;° *Slow down / events*
O, make a league with me till I have pleased
My discontented peers. What, Mother dead?
How wildly then walks my estate° in France!— *fare my possessions*
Under whose conduct came those powers of France
130 That thou for truth giv'st out° are landed here? *claim*
MESSENGER Under the Dauphin.
 Enter [*the*] BASTARD *and* PETER OF POMFRET[2]
KING JOHN Thou hast made me giddy
With these ill tidings. [*To the* BASTARD] Now, what says the world
To your proceedings?° Do not seek to stuff *(monastic pillaging)*
My head with more ill news, for it is full.
135 BASTARD But if you be afeard to hear the worst,
Then let the worst, unheard, fall on your head.
KING JOHN Bear with me, cousin, for I was amazed° *confused; stunned*
Under the tide;° but now I breathe again *sea (of bad tidings)*
Aloft the flood, and can give audience
140 To any tongue, speak it of what it will.
BASTARD How I have sped° among the clergymen *fared*
The sums I have collected shall express.
But as I travelled hither through the land,
I find the people strangely fantasied,° *full of peculiar ideas*
145 Possessed with rumours, full of idle° dreams, *foolish*
Not knowing what they fear, but full of fear.
And here's a prophet that I brought with me
From forth the streets of Pomfret, whom I found

2. Modern Pontefract, west Yorkshire.

With many hundreds treading on his heels;
150 To whom he sung, in rude,° harsh-sounding rhymes,   *unpolished*
That ere the next Ascension Day³ at noon
Your highness should deliver up° your crown.   *give up*
KING JOHN   Thou idle dreamer, wherefore didst thou so?
PETER OF POMFRET   Foreknowing that the truth will fall out so.
155 KING JOHN   Hubert, away with him! Imprison him,
And on that day, at noon, whereon he says
I shall yield up my crown, let him be hanged.
Deliver him to safety,° and return,   *custody*
For I must use thee. [*Exeunt* HUBERT *and* PETER OF POMFRET]
O my gentle cousin,
160 Hear'st thou the news abroad, who are arrived?
BASTARD   The French, my lord: men's mouths are full of it.
Besides, I met Lord Bigot and Lord Salisbury
With eyes as red° as new-enkindled fire,   *(in rage)*
And others more, going to seek the grave
165 Of Arthur, whom they say is killed tonight°   *last night*
On your suggestion.
KING JOHN   Gentle kinsman, go
And thrust thyself into their companies.
I have a way to win their loves again.
Bring them before me.
BASTARD   I will seek them out.
170 KING JOHN   Nay, but make haste, the better foot before.°   *go quickly*
O, let me have no subject° enemies   *subjects who are my*
When adverse foreigners affright my towns
With dreadful pomp of stout invasion!
Be Mercury, set feathers to thy heels,⁴
175 And fly like thought° from them to me again.   *(proverbially swift)*
BASTARD   The spirit of the time° shall teach me speed.   *Exit*   *present occasion*
KING JOHN   Spoke like a sprightful° noble gentleman!—   *spirited*
Go after him, for he perhaps shall need
Some messenger betwixt me and the peers,
180 And be thou he.
MESSENGER   With all my heart, my liege.   [*Exit*]
KING JOHN   My mother dead!
Enter HUBERT
HUBERT   My lord, they say five moons° were seen tonight,   *(an ominous portent)*
Four fixèd, and the fifth did whirl about
185 The other four in wondrous motion.
KING JOHN   Five moons?
HUBERT   Old men and beldams° in the streets   *crones*
Do prophesy upon it dangerously.
Young Arthur's death is common in their mouths,
And when they talk of him they shake their heads,
190 And whisper one another in the ear;
And he that speaks doth grip the hearer's wrist,
Whilst he that hears makes fearful action,°   *shows fear*
With wrinkled brows, with nods, with rolling eyes.
I saw a smith stand with his hammer, thus,
195 The whilst his iron did on the anvil cool,

3. The Thursday, forty days after Easter, on which Christ   4. Mercury, swift messenger of the Greek gods, wore
is supposed to have ascended to heaven.   winged sandals.

With open mouth swallowing a tailor's news,
Who, with his shears and measure in his hand,
Standing on slippers which his nimble haste
Had falsely thrust upon contrary° feet,   *the wrong*
200 Told of a many thousand warlike French
That were embattailèd° and ranked in Kent.   *in battle order*
Another lean unwashed artificer°   *artisan*
Cuts off his° tale, and talks of Arthur's death.   *(the tailor's)*
KING JOHN   Why seek'st thou to possess me with these fears?
205 Why urgest thou so oft young Arthur's death?
Thy hand hath murdered him. I had a mighty cause
To wish him dead, but thou hadst none to kill him.
HUBERT   No had,° my lord? Why, did you not provoke me?   *Hadn't I*
KING JOHN   It is the curse of kings to be attended
210 By slaves that take their humours° for a warrant   *whims*
To break within the bloody house of life,[5]
And on the winking° of authority   *hint; lapse*
To understand a law,° to know the meaning   *To infer a command*
Of dangerous majesty, when perchance it frowns
215 More upon humour than advised respect.°   *considered opinion*
HUBERT   Here is your hand° and seal for what I did.   *signature*
        [*He shows a paper*]
KING JOHN   O, when the last account 'twixt heaven and earth
Is to be made,[6] then shall this hand and seal
Witness against us to damnation!
220 How oft the sight of means to do ill deeds
Make deeds ill done! Hadst not thou been by,°   *on hand*
A fellow by the hand of nature marked,°   *(by ugliness)*
Quoted,° and signed° to do a deed of shame,   *Noted / marked*
This murder had not come into my mind.
225 But taking note of thy abhorred aspect,°   *appearance*
Finding thee fit for bloody villainy,
Apt, liable° to be employed in danger,°   *suitable / doing harm*
I faintly broke° with thee of Arthur's death;   *vaguely spoke*
And thou, to be endearèd to a king,
230 Made it no conscience° to destroy a prince.   *no matter of conscience*
HUBERT   My lord—
KING JOHN   Hadst thou but shook thy head or made a pause
When I spake darkly° what I purposèd,   *insinuated*
Or turned an eye of doubt upon my face,
235 As° bid me tell my tale in express° words,   *As if to / plain*
Deep shame had struck me dumb, made me break off,
And those thy fears might have wrought fears in me.
But thou didst understand me by my signs,
And didst in signs again parley° with sin;   *negotiate*
240 Yea, without stop, didst let thy heart consent,
And consequently thy rude° hand to act   *rough*
The deed which both our tongues held vile° to name.   *refused*
Out of my sight, and never see me more!
My nobles leave me, and my state is braved,°   *challenged*
245 Even at my gates, with ranks of foreign powers;
Nay, in the body of this fleshly land,°   *(John's body)*

5. The human body, which contains blood and which   6. *when . . . made*: when Judgment Day arrives.
murder makes bloody.

This kingdom, this confine° of blood and breath,   *territory*
Hostility and civil tumult reigns
Between my conscience and my cousin's death.
250 HUBERT   Arm you against your other enemies;
I'll make a peace between your soul and you.
Young Arthur is alive. This hand of mine
Is yet a maiden° and an innocent hand,   *virgin*
Not painted with the crimson spots of blood.
255 Within this bosom never entered yet
The dreadful motion° of a murderous thought;   *impulse*
And you have slandered nature° in my form,°   *my nature / appearance*
Which, howsoever rude exteriorly,
Is yet the cover of a fairer mind
260 Than to be butcher of an innocent child.
KING JOHN   Doth Arthur live? O, haste thee to the peers;
Throw this report° on their incensèd° rage,   *(like water) / burning*
And make them tame to their obedience.°   *(to John)*
Forgive the comment that my passion made
265 Upon thy feature,° for my rage was blind,   *features*
And foul imaginary eyes of blood[7]
Presented thee more hideous than thou art.
O, answer not, but to my closet° bring   *private room*
The angry lords with all expedient° haste.   *quick*
270 I conjure° thee but slowly; run more fast.   *Exeunt [severally]*   *urge*

4.3

Enter ARTHUR [Duke of Brittaine] on the walls [dis-
guised as a ship-boy]
ARTHUR   The wall is high, and yet will I leap down.
Good ground, be pitiful, and hurt me not.
There's few or none do know me; if they did,
This ship-boy's semblance° hath disguised me quite.°   *disguise / completely*
5 I am afraid, and yet I'll venture it.
If I get down and do not break my limbs,
I'll find a thousand shifts° to get away.   *stratagems*
As good to die and go, as die and stay.
    [He leaps down]
O me! My uncle's spirit is in these stones.
10 Heaven take my soul, and England keep my bones!
                                                    [He] dies
Enter [the Earls of] PEMBROKE [and] SALISBURY, and
[Lord] BIGOT
SALISBURY   Lords, I will meet him° at Saint Edmundsbury.[1]   *(the Dauphin)*
It is our safety,° and we must embrace   *means of safety*
This gentle offer of the perilous time.
PEMBROKE   Who brought that letter from the Cardinal?°   *Pandolf*
15 SALISBURY   The Count Melun, a noble lord of France,
Who's private with° me of the Dauphin's love;   *Who has confided in*
'Tis much more general° than these lines import.   *much greater*
BIGOT   Tomorrow morning let us meet him then.
SALISBURY   Or rather, then set forward, for 'twill be
20 Two long days' journey, lords, or ere° we meet.   *before*

---

7. John's, bloody from rage; Hubert's, bloody from guilt;   **4.3** Location: Outside the castle.
Arthur's, bloody from murder.   1. Bury St. Edmunds, Suffolk (a place of pilgrimage).

Enter [the] BASTARD

BASTARD   Once more today well met, distempered° lords.   *ill-humored*
    The King by me requests your presence straight.°   *immediately*
SALISBURY   The King hath dispossessed himself of us.
    We will not line his thin bestainèd cloak
25   With our pure honours, nor attend the foot
    That leaves the print of blood where'er it walks.
    Return and tell him so; we know the worst.
BASTARD   Whate'er you think, good words I think were best.
SALISBURY   Our griefs and not our manners reason now.
30 BASTARD   But there is little reason in your grief.
    Therefore 'twere reason° you had manners now.   *reasonable*
PEMBROKE   Sir, sir, impatience hath his privilege.°   *its particular right*
BASTARD   'Tis true—to hurt his master, no man else.[2]
SALISBURY   This is the prison.
    [*He sees Arthur's body*]
                What is he lies here?
35 PEMBROKE   O death, made proud with pure and princely beauty!
    The earth had not a hole° to hide this deed.   *grave*
SALISBURY   Murder, as° hating what himself hath done,   *as though*
    Doth lay it open° to urge on revenge.   *on public display*
BIGOT   Or when he° doomed this beauty to a grave,   *(murder)*
40   Found it too precious-princely for a grave.
SALISBURY [*to the* BASTARD]   Sir Richard, what think you? You have beheld.
    Or have you° read or heard; or could you think,   *Have you either*
    Or do you almost think, although you see,
    That you do see? Could thought, without this object,
45   Form such another?[3] This is the very top,
    The height, the crest,° or crest unto the crest,   *(atop a coat of arms)*
    Of murder's arms; this is the bloodiest shame,
    The wildest savagery, the vilest stroke
    That ever wall-eyed° wrath or staring rage   *glaring*
50   Presented to the tears of soft remorse.°   *pity*
PEMBROKE   All murders past do stand excused in° this,   *in comparison with*
    And this, so sole° and so unmatchable,   *unique*
    Shall give a holiness, a purity,
    To the yet-unbegotten sin of times,°   *the future*
55   And prove a deadly bloodshed but a jest,
    Exampled by° this heinous spectacle.   *Given the precedent of*
BASTARD   It is a damnèd and a bloody work,
    The graceless° action of a heavy° hand—   *impious / an oppressive*
    If that it be the work of any hand.
60 SALISBURY   If that it be the work of any hand?
    We had a kind of light° what would ensue: *premonition*
    It is the shameful work of Hubert's hand,
    The practice° and the purpose of the King;   *plot*
    From whose obedience I forbid my soul,
65   Kneeling before this ruin of sweet life,
    And breathing to his breathless excellence
    The incense of a vow, a holy vow,
    Never to taste the pleasures of the world,

2. Angry words hurt no one but the speaker (proverbial).
3. *Or do . . . another:* Could you even approach the thought of what you actually see here? Without seeing Arthur's body, would it be possible to imagine such a sight?

Never to be infected with delight,
70 Nor conversant with ease and idleness,
Till I have set a glory to this hand°   (his own; Arthur's)
By giving it the worship° of revenge.   honor
PEMBROKE *and* BIGOT   Our souls religiously confirm thy words.
          Enter HUBERT
HUBERT   Lords, I am hot with haste in seeking you.
75   Arthur doth live; the King hath sent for you.
SALISBURY   O, he is bold, and blushes not at death!—
      Avaunt,° thou hateful villain, get thee gone!   Begone
HUBERT   I am no villain.
SALISBURY   Must I rob the law?[4]
          [*He draws his sword*]
BASTARD   Your sword is bright,° sir; put it up° again.   unused / sheathe it
80 SALISBURY   Not till I sheathe it in a murderer's skin.
HUBERT [*drawing his sword*]   Stand back, Lord Salisbury, stand back, I say!
      By heaven, I think my sword's as sharp as yours.
      I would not have you, lord, forget yourself,[5]
      Nor tempt° the danger of my true° defence,   test / honest; able
85   Lest I, by marking of° your rage, forget   responding to
      Your worth, your greatness and nobility.
BIGOT   Out, dunghill! Dar'st thou brave° a nobleman?   defy
HUBERT   Not for my life; but yet I dare defend
      My innocent life against an emperor.
SALISBURY   Thou art a murderer.
90 HUBERT   Do not prove me so;°   (by making me kill)
      Yet° I am none. Whose tongue soe'er speaks false,   Up to now
      Not truly speaks; who speaks not truly, lies.
PEMBROKE   Cut him to pieces!
BASTARD [*drawing his sword*]   Keep the peace, I say!
SALISBURY   Stand by,° or I shall gall° you, Falconbridge.   aside / wound
95 BASTARD   Thou wert better gall the devil, Salisbury.
      If thou but frown on me, or stir thy foot,
      Or teach thy hasty spleen° to do me shame,   temper
      I'll strike thee dead. Put up thy sword betime,°   immediately
      Or I'll so maul you and your toasting-iron°   sword (belittling)
100   That you shall think the devil is come from hell.
BIGOT   What wilt thou do, renownèd Falconbridge,
      Second° a villain and a murderer?   Back up
HUBERT   Lord Bigot, I am none.
BIGOT   Who killed this prince?
HUBERT   'Tis not an hour since I left him well.
105   I honoured him, I loved him, and will weep
      My date° of life out for his sweet life's loss.   term
SALISBURY   Trust not those cunning waters of his eyes,
      For villainy is not without such rheum,
      And he, long traded° in it, makes it seem   experienced
110   Like rivers of remorse and innocency.
      Away with me, all you whose souls abhor
      Th'uncleanly savours° of a slaughter-house,   odors
      For I am stifled with this smell of sin.
BIGOT   Away toward Bury,° to the Dauphin there.   Bury St. Edmunds

4. Deprive the law of its due by killing Hubert.   able for a lord to challenge a commoner, or vice versa, as
5. Lose self-control; forget your rank (it not being honor-   lines 85–86 suggest).

115 PEMBROKE   There, tell the King, he may enquire° us out.   *seek*
        Exeunt Lords [PEMBROKE, SALISBURY, *and* BIGOT]
  BASTARD   Here's a good world! Knew you of this fair work?
    Beyond the infinite and boundless reach
    Of mercy, if thou didst this deed of death
    Art thou damned, Hubert.
120 HUBERT   Do but hear me, sir.
  BASTARD   Ha! I'll tell thee what:
    Thou'rt damned as black—nay nothing is so black—
    Thou art more deep damned than Prince Lucifer;
    There is not yet so ugly a fiend of hell
125   As thou shalt be if thou didst kill this child.
  HUBERT   Upon my soul—
  BASTARD   If thou didst but consent
    To this most cruel act, do but despair;[6]
    And if thou want'st° a cord, the smallest thread   *lack*
    That ever spider twisted from her womb
130   Will serve to strangle thee; a rush° will be a beam   *reed*
    To hang thee on; or wouldst thou° drown thyself,   *if you wish to*
    Put but a little water in a spoon
    And it shall be, as all the ocean,
    Enough to stifle such a villain up.
135   I do suspect thee very grievously.
  HUBERT   If I in act, consent, or sin of thought
    Be guilty of the stealing that sweet breath
    Which was embounded° in this beauteous clay,°   *enclosed / (Arthur's body)*
    Let hell want pains enough to torture me.
    I left him well.
140 BASTARD   Go bear him in thine arms.
    I am amazed,° methinks, and lose my way   *bewildered*
    Among the thorns and dangers of this world.
      [HUBERT *takes up* ARTHUR *in his arms*]
    How easy dost thou take all England up!
    From forth° this morsel of dead royalty,   *Out of*
145   The life, the right, and truth of all this realm
    Is fled to heaven, and England now is left
    To tug and scramble, and to part by th' teeth
    The unowed interest[7] of proud swelling state.
    Now for the bare-picked bone of majesty
150   Doth doggèd° war bristle his angry crest,[8]   *cruel*
    And snarleth in the gentle eyes of peace;
    Now powers from home° and discontents at home   *foreign armies*
    Meet in one line,° and vast confusion waits,°   *rank / chaos awaits*
    As doth a raven on a sick-fall'n beast,
155   The imminent decay of wrested pomp.°   *usurped power*
    Now happy he whose cloak and cincture° can   *belt*
    Hold out this tempest. Bear away that child,
    And follow me with speed. I'll to the King.
    A thousand businesses are brief in hand,°   *need urgent action*
160   And heaven itself doth frown upon the land. *Exeunt* [*severally*]

---

6. Lose all hope of salvation and hence commit suicide.
7. Contested or unowned possession; obedience ("interest") that is not due ("unowed"), because John lacks legitimacy.
8. Dog's hackles (hairs on neck and back); crest on a coat
of arms.

5.1

[Flourish.] Enter KING JOHN *and [Cardinal]* PANDOLF,
[with] attendants

KING JOHN *[giving* PANDOLF *the crown]*   Thus have I yielded up
    into your hand
  The circle of my glory.
PANDOLF *[giving back the crown]*   Take again
  From this my hand, as holding of° the Pope,   *as land rented from*
  Your sovereign greatness and authority.
5 KING JOHN   Now keep your holy word: go meet the French,
  And from his Holiness° use all your power   *the pope*
  To stop their marches 'fore we are enflamed.
  Our discontented counties° do revolt,   *shires; nobles*
  Our people quarrel with obedience,
10 Swearing allegiance and the love of soul
  To stranger° blood, to foreign royalty.   *foreign*
  This inundation of mistempered humour
  Rests by you only to be qualified.[1]
  Then pause not, for the present time's so sick
15 That present° med'cine must be ministered,   *immediate*
  Or overthrow incurable ensues.
PANDOLF   It was my breath° that blew this tempest up,   *words*
  Upon your stubborn usage of the Pope,
  But since you are a gentle convertite,°   *convert*
20 My tongue shall hush again this storm of war
  And make fair weather in your blust'ring land.
  On this Ascension Day, remember well,
  Upon your oath of service to the Pope,
  Go I to make the French lay down their arms.
                    Exeunt [all but KING JOHN*]*[2]
25 KING JOHN   Is this Ascension Day? Did not the prophet
  Say that before Ascension Day at noon
  My crown I should give off?[3] Even so I have.
  I did suppose it should be on constraint,
  But, heaven be thanked, it is but voluntary.
           Enter BASTARD
30 BASTARD   All Kent hath yielded; nothing there holds out
  But Dover Castle. London hath received,
  Like a kind host, the Dauphin and his powers.°   *army*
  Your nobles will not hear you, but are gone
  To offer service to your enemy;
35 And wild amazement hurries° up and down   *confusion drives*
  The little number of your doubtful° friends.   *untrustworthy; fearful*
KING JOHN   Would not my lords return to me again
  After they heard young Arthur was alive?
BASTARD   They found him dead and cast into the streets,
40 An empty casket, where the jewel of life
  By some damned hand was robbed and ta'en away.
KING JOHN   That villain Hubert told me he did live.
BASTARD   So on my soul he did, for aught he knew.
  But wherefore do you droop? Why look you sad?

5.1 Location: John's court.
1. *This . . . qualified:* Only you can cure this surge of diseased behavior.

2. F leaves the attendants onstage with John. But even in
that case, this speech could easily be a soliloquy.
3. See 4.2.147–52.

45   Be great in act as you have been in thought.
    Let not the world see fear and sad distrust
    Govern the motion of a kingly eye.
    Be stirring as the time,[4] be fire with° fire;   *against*
    Threaten the threat'ner, and outface the brow
50   Of bragging horror. So shall inferior eyes,
    That borrow their behaviours from the great,
    Grow great by your example, and put on
    The dauntless spirit of resolution.
    Away, and glisten like the god of war
55   When he intendeth to become the field.°   *adorn the battlefield*
    Show boldness and aspiring confidence.
    What, shall they seek the lion in his den
    And fright him there, and make him tremble there?
    O, let it not be said! Forage,° and run   *Range (for prey)*
60   To meet displeasure farther from the doors,
    And grapple with him ere he come so nigh.
  KING JOHN   The legate of the Pope hath been with me,
    And I have made a happy peace with him,
    And he hath promised to dismiss the powers
    Led by the Dauphin.
65   BASTARD   O inglorious league!
    Shall we, upon the footing of our land,°   *standing on our own soil*
    Send fair-play orders,° and make compromise,   *equitable conditions*
    Insinuation,° parley, and base truce   *Ingratiating proposals*
    To arms invasive?° Shall a beardless boy,   *invading*
70   A cockered silken wanton,° brave our fields   *spoiled dandyish child*
    And flesh his spirit[5] in a warlike soil,
    Mocking the air with colours idly° spread,   *carelessly*
    And find no check? Let us, my liege, to arms!
    Perchance the Cardinal cannot make your peace,
75   Or if he do, let it at least be said
    They saw we had a purpose of defence.
  KING JOHN   Have thou the ordering of this present time.
  BASTARD   Away, then, with good courage! [*Aside*] Yet I know
    Our party may well meet a prouder foe.[6]   *Exeunt*

5.2

    *Enter [marching] (in arms) [*LOUIS THE*] DAUPHIN, [the*
    Earl of] SALISBURY, [Count] MELUN, [the Earl of] PEM-
    BROKE, [and Lord] BIGOT, [with] soldiers
  LOUIS THE DAUPHIN   My Lord Melun, let this[1] be copied out,
    And keep it safe for our remembrance.
    Return the precedent° to these lords again,   *original copy*
    That having our fair order° written down,   *arrangements*
5   Both they and we, perusing o'er these notes,
    May know wherefore we took the sacrament[2]
    And keep our faiths firm and inviolable.
  SALISBURY   Upon our sides it never shall be broken.
    And, noble Dauphin, albeit we swear

---

4. Be as vigorous as the times demand.
5. Initiate himself in bloodshed (in the "soil," as a sword is "fleshed" in a body).
6. Is well able to handle an even stronger enemy than the French; may be up against an enemy more powerful than we are.
5.2 Location: St. Edmundsbury (Bury St. Edmunds) in Suffolk.
1. This agreement with the English lords.
2. The Mass, taken as a solemn dedication to the task.

10   A voluntary zeal° and an unurgèd° faith   *commitment / unforced*
    To your proceedings, yet believe me, Prince,
    I am not glad that such a sore of time
    Should seek a plaster° by contemnèd° revolt,   *bandage / despised*
    And heal the inveterate canker° of one wound   *infection*
15   By making many. O, it grieves my soul
    That I must draw this metal° from my side   *(his sword)*
    To be a widow-maker! O, and there
    Where honourable rescue and defence
    Cries out upon[3] the name of Salisbury!
20   But such is the infection of the time,
    That for the health and physic° of our right,   *cure*
    We cannot deal but with the very hand
    Of stern injustice and confusèd wrong.[4]
    And is't not pity, O my grievèd friends,
25   That we the sons and children of this isle
    Was born to see so sad an hour as this,
    Wherein we step after a stranger,° march   *foreigner*
    Upon her gentle bosom, and fill up
    Her enemies' ranks? I must withdraw and weep
30   Upon the spot° of this enforcèd cause—   *place; stain*
    To grace the gentry of a land remote,
    And follow unacquainted colours° here.   *unfamiliar banners*
    What, here? O nation, that thou couldst remove;°   *move elsewhere*
    That Neptune's arms° who clippeth thee about°   *the sea / embraces you*
35   Would bear thee from the knowledge of thyself
    And gripple° thee unto a pagan shore,   *join*
    Where these two Christian armies might combine
    The blood of malice in a vein of league,°   *(against a pagan foe)*
    And not to spend° it so unneighbourly.   *shed*
40 LOUIS THE DAUPHIN   A noble temper° dost thou show in this,   *disposition*
    And great affections,° wrestling in thy bosom,   *emotions; loyalties*
    Doth make an earthquake of nobility.°   *out of a noble nature*
    O, what a noble combat hast thou fought
    Between compulsion° and a brave respect!°   *necessity / patriotism*
45   Let me wipe off this honourable dew
    That silverly doth progress on thy cheeks.
    My heart hath melted at a lady's tears,
    Being an ordinary inundation;
    But this effusion of such manly drops,
50   This shower blown up by tempest of the soul,
    Startles mine eyes, and makes me more amazed
    Than had I seen the vaulty° top of heaven   *arched*
    Figured quite o'er° with burning meteors.[5]   *Adorned thoroughly*
    Lift up thy brow, renownèd Salisbury,
55   And with a great heart heave away this storm;
    Commend° these waters to those baby eyes   *Leave*
    That never saw the giant° world enraged,   *grown-up*
    Nor met with Fortune other than at feasts,
    Full warm of° blood, of mirth, of gossiping.   *with*
60   Come, come, for thou shalt thrust thy hand as deep

---

3. Exclaim against; appeal to.
4. *We ... wrong:* We cannot act except with unjust means; or, possibly, we cannot act except against the unjust hand of John.
5. Meteors were seen as portents of disaster.

Into the purse of rich prosperity
As Louis himself. So, nobles, shall you all
That knit your sinews° to the strength of mine.   *join your powers*
        [*A trumpet sounds*]
And even there methinks an angel[6] spake!
        Enter [*Cardinal*] PANDOLF
65   Look where the holy legate comes apace,
     To give us warrant from the hand of heaven,°   *the pope; God*
     And on our actions set the name of right
     With holy breath.
PANDOLF   Hail, noble prince of France!
     The next° is this. King John hath reconciled   *next thing I have to say*
70   Himself to Rome; his spirit is come in°   *has submitted*
     That so stood out against the Holy Church,
     The great metropolis and See of Rome;
     Therefore thy threat'ning colours° now wind up,°   *banners / put away*
     And tame the savage spirit of wild war,
75   That like a lion fostered up at hand°   *by human hand*
     It may lie gently at the foot of peace,
     And be no further harmful than in show.
LOUIS THE DAUPHIN   Your grace shall pardon me: I will not back.° *go back*
     I am too high-born to be propertied,°   *manipulated*
80   To be a secondary° at control,   *subordinate*
     Or useful serving-man and instrument
     To any sovereign state° throughout the world.   *(the papacy)*
     Your breath first kindled the dead coal of wars
     Between this chastised kingdom and myself,
85   And brought in matter° that should feed this fire;   *fuel*
     And now 'tis far too huge to be blown out
     With that same weak wind which enkindled it.
     You taught me how to know the face of right,°   *my rightful claim*
     Acquainted me with interest° to this land,   *my claim*
90   Yea, thrust this enterprise into my heart;
     And come ye now to tell me John hath made
     His peace with Rome? What is that peace to me?
     I, by the honour of my marriage bed,
     After young Arthur, claim this land for mine;
95   And now it is half conquered, must I back
     Because that John hath made his peace with Rome?
     Am I Rome's slave? What penny hath Rome borne,°   *contributed*
     What men provided, what munition sent
     To underprop° this action? Is't not I   *support*
100 That undergo this charge? Who else but I,
     And such as to my claim are liable,°   *are liable to me*
     Sweat in this business and maintain° this war?   *pay for*
     Have I not heard these islanders shout out
     'Vive le Roi!' as I have banked their towns?
105 Have I not here the best cards for the game,
     To win this easy match played for a crown?

---

6. The trumpet, an editorial addition, is seen as an
angel's affirmation of the Dauphin's speech. The stage
direction may not be necessary, however. "Angel" might
also mean "gold coin," developing the money imagery of
lines 61–63—"purse of rich prosperity," "nobles" (also a
coin), and perhaps "sinews" (where "sinews of war" con-
notes money). The Dauphin's point, perhaps made in an
aside, would be that money talks in persuading the
English peers to join his cause.

And shall I now give o'er the yielded set?[7]
No, no, on my soul, it never shall be said.
PANDOLF You look but on the outside of this work.

110 LOUIS THE DAUPHIN Outside or inside, I will not return
Till my attempt° so much be glorified   *warlike enterprise*
As to my ample hope was promisèd
Before I drew° this gallant head of war,°   *gathered / army*
And culled° these fiery spirits from the world   *picked out*

115 To outlook conquest° and to win renown   *To defy defeat*
Even in the jaws of danger and of death.
[*A trumpet sounds*]
What lusty° trumpet thus doth summon us?   *vigorous*
Enter [the] BASTARD

BASTARD According to the fair play° of the world,   *code of chivalry*
Let me have audience; I am sent to speak.

120 My holy lord of Milan, from the King
I come to learn how you have dealt for him,
And as° you answer I do know the scope   *according to how*
And warrant limited unto my tongue.
PANDOLF The Dauphin is too wilful-opposite,°   *stubbornly hostile*

125 And will not temporize with° my entreaties.   *will not heed*
He flatly says he'll not lay down his arms.
BASTARD By all the blood that ever fury breathed,
The youth says well. Now hear our English king,
For thus his royalty doth speak in me.

130 He is prepared, and reason too he should.°   *as he should be*
This apish and unmannerly approach,
This harnessed masque and unadvisèd revel,[8]
This unhaired° sauciness and boyish troops,   *youthful*
The King doth smile at, and is well prepared

135 To whip this dwarfish war, these pigmy arms,
From out the circle° of his territories.   *confines*
That hand which had the strength even at your door
To cudgel you and make you take the hatch,°   *beat a hasty retreat*
To dive like buckets in concealèd wells,

140 To crouch in litter° of your stable planks,   *animal's bedding*
To lie like pawns° locked up in chests and trunks,   *pawned goods*
To hug° with swine, to seek sweet safety out   *bed down*
In vaults and prisons, and to thrill° and shake   *shiver*
Even at the crying of your nation's crow,°   *the cock*

145 Thinking his voice an armèd Englishman;
Shall that victorious hand be feebled here
That in your chambers° gave you chastisement?   *your own home*
No! Know the gallant monarch is in arms,
And like an eagle o'er his eyrie towers°   *soars over his nest*

150 To souse° annoyance that comes near his nest.   *swoop down on*
[*To the English lords*]
And you degenerate, you ingrate revolts,°   *ungrateful rebels*
You bloody Neros, ripping up the womb
Of your dear mother England,[9] blush for shame;

---

7. 'Vive . . . set: the Dauphin uses an extended card-playing metaphor, including "Vive le Roi" ("Long live the King"), "banked" (put in the bank, won; but also, sailed by the banks of), "cards," "game," "match played," "crown" (the coin as a stake in a card game; John's crown), and "yielded set" (the hand already won).
8. This courtly entertainment in armor and rashly undertaken revelry.
9. The Roman emperor Nero was supposed to have murdered his mother by ripping open her womb.

For your own ladies and pale-visaged maids
155 Like Amazons[1] come tripping after drums;
Their thimbles into armèd gauntlets° change,   *steel-plated gloves*
Their needles to lances, and their gentle hearts
To fierce and bloody inclination.°   *disposition*
LOUIS THE DAUPHIN   There end thy brave,° and turn thy face°   *defiance / return*
in peace.
160 We grant thou canst outscold us. Fare thee well:
We hold our time too precious to be spent
With such a brabbler.°   *quarreler*
PANDOLF   Give me leave to speak.
BASTARD   No, I will speak.
LOUIS THE DAUPHIN   We will attend° to neither.—   *listen*
Strike up the drums, and let the tongue of war
165 Plead for our interest and our being here.
BASTARD   Indeed your drums, being beaten, will cry out;
And so shall you, being beaten. Do but start
An echo with the clamour of thy drum,
And even at hand a drum is ready braced°   *ready to be struck*
170 That shall reverberate all as loud as thine.
Sound but another, and another shall
As loud as thine rattle the welkin's° ear,   *sky's*
And mock° the deep-mouthed thunder; for at hand, *outrival*
Not trusting to this halting° legate here,   *wavering*
175 Whom he hath used rather for sport than need,
Is warlike John; and in his forehead sits
A bare-ribbed Death, whose office° is this day   *task*
To feast upon whole thousands of the French.
LOUIS THE DAUPHIN   Strike up our drums to find this danger out.
180 BASTARD   And thou shalt find it, Dauphin, do not doubt.
                    [*Drums beat.*] *Exeunt* [*the* BASTARD *at one door,*
                    all the rest, marching, at another door]

5.3

Alarum. Enter [KING] JOHN [*at one door*] *and* HUBERT
[*at another door*]
KING JOHN   How goes the day with us? O, tell me, Hubert.
HUBERT   Badly, I fear. How fares your majesty?
KING JOHN   This fever that hath troubled me so long
Lies heavy on me. O, my heart is sick!
        Enter a MESSENGER
5 MESSENGER   My lord, your valiant kinsman Falconbridge
Desires your majesty to leave the field,
And send him word by me which way you go.
KING JOHN   Tell him toward Swineshead,° to the abbey there.   *(in Lincolnshire)*
MESSENGER   Be of good comfort, for the great supply°   *reinforcements*
10 That was expected by the Dauphin here
Are wrecked three nights ago on Goodwin Sands.°   *shoals off Kent*
This news was brought to Richard,° but even now   *(the Bastard)*
The French fight coldly and retire themselves.°   *retreat*
KING JOHN   Ay me, this tyrant fever burns me up,

---

1. Female warriors of classical legend.   5.3 Location: The battlefield.

15   And will not let me welcome this good news.
      Set on toward Swineshead. To my litter straight;°   *portable bed at once*
      Weakness possesseth me, and I am faint.   *Exeunt*

                              5.4

      [*Alarum.*] *Enter* [*the Earls of*] SALISBURY [*and*] PEM-
      BROKE, *and* [*Lord*] BIGOT
      SALISBURY   I did not think the King so stored° with friends.   *well provided*
      PEMBROKE   Up once again; put spirit in the French.
           If they miscarry,° we miscarry too.   *fail*
      SALISBURY   That misbegotten devil Falconbridge,
5   In spite of spite,° alone upholds the day.°   *everything / battle*
      PEMBROKE   They say King John, sore° sick, hath left the field.   *grievously*
           Enter [*Count*] MELUN, *wounded* [*led by a soldier*]
      MELUN   Lead me to the revolts° of England here.   *rebels*
      SALISBURY   When we were happy, we had other names.
      PEMBROKE   It is the Count Melun.
      SALISBURY   Wounded to death.
10   MELUN   Fly, noble English, you are bought and sold.°   *betrayed*
           Unthread the rude eye of rebellion,[1]
           And welcome home again discarded faith;
           Seek out King John and fall before his feet,
           For if the French be lords of° this loud° day   *win / hectic*
15   He° means to recompense the pains you take   *(Louis)*
           By cutting off your heads. Thus hath he sworn,
           And I with him, and many more with me,
           Upon the altar at Saint Edmundsbury,
           Even on that altar where we swore to you
20   Dear amity and everlasting love.
      SALISBURY   May this be possible? May this be true?
      MELUN   Have I not hideous death within my view,
           Retaining but a quantity of life,
           Which bleeds away, even as a form of wax
25   Resolveth from his figure° 'gainst the fire?   *Melts out of shape*
           What in the world should make me now deceive,
           Since I must lose the use of all deceit?
           Why should I then be false, since it is true
           That I must die here, and live hence° by truth?   *in the next world*
30   I say again, if Louis do win the day,
           He is forsworn° if e'er those eyes of yours   *perjured*
           Behold another daybreak in the east;
           But even this night, whose black contagious breath
           Already smokes about the burning cresset°   *suspended torch*
35   Of the old, feeble, and day-wearied sun,
           Even this ill night your breathing shall expire,
           Paying the fine of rated° treachery   *assessed (as penalty)*
           Even with a treacherous fine° of all your lives,   *payment; end*
           If Louis by your assistance win the day.
40   Commend me to one Hubert with your king.
           The love of him, and this respect° besides,   *consideration*
           For that° my grandsire was an Englishman,   *Because*

5.4 Location: Scene continues.   which you've been led (like a thread that has been
1. Turn back from the barbarous path of rebellion down   inserted into the needle's eye and must be pulled out).

Awakes my conscience to confess all this;
In lieu° whereof, I pray you bear me hence   *recompense*
45   From forth the noise and rumour° of the field,   *tumult*
Where I may think the remnant of my thoughts
In peace, and part this body and my soul
With contemplation and devout desires.
SALISBURY   We do believe thee; and beshrew° my soul   *woe to*
50   But° I do love the favour° and the form   *Unless / look*
Of this most fair occasion; by the which
We will untread° the steps of damnèd flight,°   *retrace / desertion*
And like a bated° and retirèd flood,   *an abated*
Leaving our rankness° and irregular course,   *flooding*
55   Stoop low within those bounds we have o'erlooked,°   *overflowed; ignored*
And calmly run on in obedience
Even to our ocean, to our great King John.
My arm shall give thee help to bear thee hence,
For I do see the cruel pangs of death
60   Right in thine eye.—Away, my friends! New flight,°   *change of allegiance*
And happy newness that intends old right.²   *Exeunt*

5.5

[*Alarum; retreat.*] *Enter* [LOUIS THE] DAUPHIN, *and his*
train
LOUIS THE DAUPHIN   The sun of heaven, methought, was loath to set,
But stayed and made the western welkin blush,
When English measured° backward their own ground   *crossed*
In faint retire.° O, bravely came we off,¹   *weak retreat*
5   When with a volley of our needless° shot,   *unnecessary*
After such bloody toil, we bid good night,
And wound our tatt'ring colours clearly up,²
Last in the field and almost lords of it.
Enter a MESSENGER
MESSENGER   Where is my prince the Dauphin?
LOUIS THE DAUPHIN   Here. What news?
10   MESSENGER   The Count Melun is slain; the English lords
By his persuasion are again fall'n off;°   *changed in allegiance*
And your supply° which you have wished so long   *supplies*
Are cast away and sunk on Goodwin Sands.
LOUIS THE DAUPHIN   Ah, foul shrewd° news! Beshrew° thy very   *harmful / Curse*
heart!
15   I did not think to be so sad tonight
As this hath made me. Who was he that said
King John did fly an hour or two before
The stumbling night³ did part our weary powers?
MESSENGER   Whoever spoke it, it is true, my lord.
20   LOUIS THE DAUPHIN   Well, keep good quarter° and good care tonight.   *guard*
The day shall not be up so soon as I,
To try the fair adventure° of tomorrow.   *Exeunt*   *chance*

---

2. That intends to restore the ancient right—John's claim   2. We rolled our tattered (waving) banners up without
to rule and our just conduct.   obstruction from the English.
5.5 Location: Scene continues.   3. That is, night that causes stumbling.
1. We acquitted ourselves valiantly.

5.6

Enter [the] BASTARD *[with a light] and* HUBERT *[with a pistol], severally*

HUBERT Who's there? Speak, ho! Speak quickly, or I shoot.

BASTARD A friend. What art thou?

HUBERT   Of the part° of England.   side

BASTARD Whither dost thou go?

HUBERT   What's that to thee?

Why may not I demand of thine affairs

5   As well as thou of mine?

BASTARD Hubert, I think.

HUBERT Thou hast a perfect° thought.   correct

I will upon all hazards° well believe   against all odds

Thou art my friend that know'st my tongue so well.

Who art thou?

10 BASTARD   Who thou wilt. An if thou please,

Thou mayst befriend me so much as to think

I come one way° of the Plantagenets.   by one parent

HUBERT Unkind remembrance!¹ Thou and eyeless° night   blind

Have done me shame. Brave soldier, pardon me

15 That any accent° breaking from thy tongue   sound

Should 'scape the true acquaintance of mine ear.

BASTARD Come, come, sans compliment.° What news abroad?   no formalities

HUBERT Why, here walk I in the black brow of night

To find you out.

BASTARD   Brief, then, and what's the news?

20 HUBERT O my sweet sir, news fitting to the night:

Black, fearful, comfortless, and horrible.

BASTARD Show me the very wound of this ill news;

I am no woman, I'll not swoon at it.

HUBERT The King, I fear, is poisoned by a monk.

25 I left him almost speechless, and broke out°   hurried away

To acquaint you with this evil, that you might

The better arm you to the sudden time°   for this emergency

Than if you had at leisure° known of this.   later

BASTARD How did he take it?° Who did taste to° him?   (poison) / (the food) for

30 HUBERT A monk, I tell you, a resolvèd villain,²

Whose bowels suddenly burst out. The King

Yet° speaks, and peradventure may recover.   Still

BASTARD Who didst thou leave to tend his majesty?

HUBERT Why, know you not? The lords are all come back,

35 And brought Prince Henry³ in their company,

At whose request the King hath pardoned them,

And they are all about his majesty.

BASTARD Withhold thine indignation, mighty heaven,

And tempt us not to bear above our power.⁴

40 I'll tell thee, Hubert, half my power this night,

Passing these flats, are taken° by the tide.   drowned

These Lincoln Washes⁵ have devourèd them;

5.6 Location: Near Swineshead Abbey.
1. Bad memory (criticizing himself for not recognizing the Bastard).
2. A "resolvèd villain" since, as the person whose job it was to protect the King by tasting his food, he knowingly took poison himself just so that he could succeed in poisoning the King.

3. John's son; later, King Henry III.
4. And don't push us (or me) past our power to endure. "Bear above our power" may hint at the Bastard's previous thoughts, here put aside, of assuming the throne himself.
5. The tides of the Wash (tidal flatlands south of Lincolnshire).

Myself, well mounted, hardly° have escaped.   *barely; with trouble*
Away before!° Conduct me to the King.   *Go on ahead*
45 I doubt° he will be dead or ere° I come.   *Exeunt*   *fear / before*

5.7

Enter PRINCE HENRY, *[the Earl of]* SALISBURY, *and*
[Lord] BIGOT

PRINCE HENRY   It is too late. The life of all his blood
Is touched° corruptibly, and his pure° brain,   *infected / (once) lucid*
Which some suppose the soul's frail dwelling-house,
Doth by the idle° comments that it makes   *foolish*
5   Foretell the ending of mortality.°   *mortal life*

Enter [the Earl of] PEMBROKE

PEMBROKE   His highness yet doth speak, and holds belief
That being brought into the open air,
It would allay the burning quality
Of that fell° poison which assaileth him.   *savage*
10 PRINCE HENRY   Let him be brought into the orchard here.—
                            [Exit Lord BIGOT*]*[1]
Doth he still rage?
PEMBROKE   He is more patient
Than when you left him. Even° now, he sung.   *Just*
PRINCE HENRY   O, vanity° of sickness! Fierce extremes°   *delusion / (of pain)*
In their continuance will not feel themselves.[2]
15 Death, having preyed upon the outward parts,°   *the body*
Leaves them invincible,° and his siege is now   *(because overcome)*
Against the mind; the which he pricks and wounds
With many legions of strange fantasies,
Which in their throng and press to that last hold°   *stronghold (the mind)*
20 Confound° themselves. 'Tis strange that death should sing. *Destroy*
I am the cygnet° to this pale faint swan,   *young swan*
Who chants a doleful hymn to his own death,[3]
And from the organ-pipe° of frailty sings   *voice box*
His soul and body to their lasting rest.
25 SALISBURY   Be of good comfort, Prince, for you are born
To set a form upon that indigest°   *chaos*
Which he hath left so shapeless and so rude.°   *formless*
        [KING] JOHN *[is] brought in [with Lord* BIGOT *attending]*
KING JOHN   Ay marry, now° my soul hath elbow-room;   *now being outdoors*
It would not out at° windows nor at doors.   *go out through*
30 There is so hot a summer in my bosom
That all my bowels crumble up to dust;
I am a scribbled form, drawn with a pen
Upon a parchment, and against° this fire°   *before / (of poison)*
Do I shrink up.
PRINCE HENRY   How fares your majesty?
35 KING JOHN   Poisoned, ill fare!° Dead, forsook, cast off; *food; state of things*
And none of you will bid the winter come
To thrust his icy fingers in my maw,°   *stomach; mouth; throat*
Nor let my kingdom's rivers take their course
Through my burned bosom, nor entreat the north

5.7 Location: The orchard of Swineshead Abbey.
1. F has no stage direction. Someone must fetch John:
either Bigot here or Pembroke after line 12.

2. By continuing for a long time will cease to be felt.
3. John's swan song; swans were thought to sing only as
they died.

40 To make his bleak winds kiss my parchèd lips
And comfort me with cold. I do not ask you much;
I beg cold° comfort, and you are so strait°   *slight; cooling / mean*
And so ingrateful you deny me that.
PRINCE HENRY   O, that there were some virtue° in my tears   *remedial power*
That might relieve you!
45 KING JOHN   The salt in them is hot.
Within me is a hell, and there the poison
Is, as a fiend, confined to tyrannize
On unreprievable condemnèd blood.

       Enter [the] BASTARD

BASTARD   O, I am scalded with my violent motion°   *haste*
50 And spleen° of speed to see your majesty!   *impetuosity*
KING JOHN   O cousin, thou art come to set° mine eye.   *close*
The tackle° of my heart is cracked and burnt,   *rigging (heartstrings)*
And all the shrouds° wherewith my life should sail   *sail ropes*
Are turnèd to one thread, one little hair;
55 My heart hath one poor string to stay° it by,   *support*
Which holds but till thy news be utterèd,
And then all this thou seest is but a clod
And module° of confounded° royalty.   *counterfeit / destroyed*
BASTARD   The Dauphin is preparing° hitherward,   *coming*
60 Where God He knows how we shall answer him;
For in a° night the best part of my power,   *a single*
As I upon° advantage did remove,   *to gain*
Were in the Washes all unwarily
Devourèd by the unexpected flood.

       [KING JOHN *dies*]

65 SALISBURY   You breathe these dead° news in as dead an ear.   *fatal*
[*To* KING JOHN] My liege, my lord!—But° now a king, now thus.   *Just*
PRINCE HENRY   Even so must I run on, and even so stop.
What surety of the world, what hope, what stay,°   *support; continuation*
When this was now a king and now is clay?
70 BASTARD [*to* KING JOHN]   Art thou gone so? I do but stay behind
To do the office° for thee of revenge,   *duty*
And then my soul shall wait on° thee to heaven,   *follow*
As it on earth hath been thy servant still.°   *always*
[*To the lords*] Now, now, you stars° that move in your right spheres,[4] *(the nobles)*
75 Where be your powers?° Show now your mended faiths,° *armies / loyalties*
And instantly return with me again,
To push destruction and perpetual shame
Out of the weak door of our fainting° land.   *dispirited*
Straight° let us seek, or straight we shall be sought.   *Immediately*
80 The Dauphin rages at our very heels.
SALISBURY   It seems you know not, then, so much as we.
The Cardinal Pandolf is within at rest,
Who half an hour since came from the Dauphin,
And brings from him such offers of our peace
85 As we with honour and respect may take,
With purpose presently° to leave this war.   *immediately*
BASTARD   He will the rather do it when he sees
Ourselves well-sinewed° to our own defence.   *strongly armed*
SALISBURY   Nay, 'tis in a manner done already,

---

4. Proper orbits, around the King, as the stars were thought to orbit the earth.

90   For many carriages° he hath dispatched   *vehicles*
      To the sea-side, and put his cause and quarrel
      To the disposing of the Cardinal,
      With° whom yourself, myself, and other lords,   *To*
      If you think meet,° this afternoon will post°   *fit / hurry*
95   To consummate° this business happily.   *conclude*
    BASTARD   Let it be so.—And you, my noble prince,
      With other princes° that may best be spared,   *nobles*
      Shall wait upon° your father's funeral.   *attend*
    PRINCE HENRY   At Worcester must his body be interred,
      For so he willed it.
100   BASTARD   Thither shall it then,
      And happily° may your sweet self put on   *with good fortune*
      The lineal state° and glory of the land,   *inherited kingship*
      To whom with all submission, on my knee,
      I do bequeath° my faithful services   *give*
105   And true subjection everlastingly.
        [*He kneels*]
    SALISBURY   And the like tender° of our love we make,   *offer*
      To rest° without a spot° for evermore.   *remain / blemish*
        [SALISBURY, PEMBROKE *and* BIGOT *kneel*]
    PRINCE HENRY   I have a kind of soul that would give thanks,
      And knows not how to do it but with tears.
        [*He weeps*]
110   BASTARD [*rising*]   O, let us pay the time but needful° woe,   *only the necessary*
      Since it hath been beforehand with our griefs.[5]
      This England never did, nor never shall,
      Lie at the proud foot of a conqueror
      But° when it first did help to wound itself.   *Except*
115   Now these her princes are come home again,
      Come the three corners of the world[6] in arms
      And we shall shock° them. Naught shall make us rue   *resist; repel*
      If England to itself do rest but true.
          [*Flourish.*] *Exeunt* [*with the body*]

TEXTUAL VARIANTS

Control text: F

F: The Folio of 1623

s.p. KING JOHN [F's use of *King John*, *John*, and *England* has been standardized throughout.]

s.p. QUEEN ELEANOR [F most often uses *Eleanor*, but also *Queen*, *Queen Mother*, and *Old Queen*. The choice of speech prefix often corresponds to the immediate context; they have been standardized throughout.]

s.p. BASTARD [F uses *Philip* until line 138 and *Bastard* almost exclusively thereafter: standardized throughout.]

s.p. FALCONBRIDGE [F's use of *Robert* has been altered throughout.]

s.p. KING PHILIP [In many places, noted individually below, F confuses the King with the

5. Since we have already suffered and grieved—perhaps with the additional implication that the suffering is now over.

6. England itself is seen as the fourth corner.

Dauphin *(Lewis)*. Otherwise, F's use of *King*, *Philip*, and *France* has been standardized throughout.]

s.p. LOUIS THE DAUPHIN [F uses *Dauphin (Dolphin)* alone: expanded throughout.]

1.1.11 Poitou *Poyctiers* **161 arise** rise **188 'Tis too** 'Tis two **208 smack** smoake **237 Could a** Could **257 Thou** That

2.1.1, 18 s.p. KING PHILIP *Lewis* **63 Ate** Ace **113 breast** beast **144 shows** shooes **149 King Philip** King *Lewis* **150 s.p. KING PHILIP** *Lew⟨is⟩* **152 Anjou** *Angiers* **169 Draw** Drawes **215 Confront your** Comfort yours **325 s.p. CITIZEN** *Hubert.* **327 your** yonr **335 run** rome **362 who's** whose **368 s.p. CITIZEN** *Fra⟨nce⟩* **371 Kinged** Kings **425 niece** neere **435 complete, O** compleat of **488 Anjou** *Angiers* **489 side** fide **501 sun** sonne **524 shall** still **540 rites** rights **572 lose** loose

3.1.34 God heauens **36 day** daies **62 God** heauen **74 task** tast **81 God** heauen **122 it** that **162 God** Heauen **185 crazèd** cased **208 troth** truth **210 swear'st** sweares **224 Wilt** Wil't

3.3.8–10 Of . . . liberty. Of hoording Abbots: imprisoned angells / Set at libertie: the fat ribs of peace / Must by the hungry now be fed vpon: **52 broad-eyed** brooded

3.4.44 art not art **48 God** heauen **64 Friends** fiends **110 world's** words **149 vilely born** euilly borne **182 make** makes

4.1.23 God heauen **63 his** this **77 God's** heauen **91 God** heauen **114 eyes** eye **131 God** heauen

4.2.1 again against **31 worser** worse **42 when** then **73 Does** Do **117 ear** care

4.3.16 Who's Whose **17 'Tis** Is **33 man** mans **147 scramble** scamble **156 cincture** center

5.1.54 glisten glister

5.2.36 gripple cripple **43 thou** [not in F] **133 unhaired** vn-heard **135 these** this **145 his** this

5.3.8 Swineshead *Swinsted*

5.4.34 cresset Crest

5.5.3 measured measure **7 tatt'ring** tott'ring

5.6.13 eyeless endles

5.7.16 invincible inuisible **17 mind** winde **21 cygnet** Symet **42 strait** straight **60 God** heauen **88 our own** our **108 kind of** kinde

I Henry IV

A roadside inn that fails to provide chamber pots for its customers, a castle in Wales where a magician summons spirits to be his musicians, a battlefield where the King of England has many nobles dress like himself—these are but a few of the memorable venues where the action of 1 Henry IV occurs. With this drama, the Shakespearean history play reaches out to encompass a rich diversity of languages, characters, and locales. Nothing in Shakespeare's earlier English histories quite anticipates this one. The great prose chronicles of the sixteenth century, such as Raphael Holinshed's *Chronicles of England, Scotland, and Ireland* (second edition, 1587), which Shakespeare consulted and whose materials he freely adapted and supplemented, stand behind all his history plays. The earlier plays, however, like the chronicles, focus primarily on the world of court and battlefield in which the monarch and his nobles appear as history's significant players, their rivalries and their achievements the focal point of the action. Common people such as Jack Cade make appearances, in both chronicle and stage play, but their stories are typically subordinated to the monarchical plot. In 1 Henry IV, something different happens. Several lines of action unfold at once, each connected to particular geographical locales, and each commenting upon, without simply displacing, the others. Henry IV, who had seized the throne from Richard II, is the play's title character, but from the start he is a beleaguered figure. He is kept from his dream of making a crusade to the Holy Land by discontent and rebellion among his nobles, especially the Percy family, and burdened with an oldest son, Prince Hal, who acts more like a prodigal child than the heir to the throne. The King appears in some key scenes, but for long stretches the action focuses on other characters and on places the King never visits.

Some events take place in the north of England, in the Northumberland stronghold of the Percy family. The play is set in the early fifteenth century, but even in the late sixteenth century the north of England was popularly regarded as lawless and wild, its nobility not fully incorporated into the increasingly centralized state being constructed by the Tudor monarchs. In 1569, members of the Percy family had been prominent in the Northern Rebellion, an attempt to overthrow Queen Elizabeth and put Mary Queen of Scots on the throne. In drawing his portrait of the Percys, Shakespeare makes their champion, Hotspur, an impassioned embodiment of medieval chivalry, eager above all for honor and for the glory to be won in battle. While the historical Hotspur was actually much older than the King's son, Prince Hal, Shakespeare follows Samuel Daniel's poem *The Civil Wars between Lancaster and York* (1595) in making him Hal's coequal in years and his rival for preeminence in the kingdom. He is joined in rebellion by other figures from the threatening territories on the perimeter of England: by the Earl of Douglas, a formidable Scottish warrior, and by the Welshman Owen Glyndŵr, a self-proclaimed magician with a fiery temper, a lyrical temperament, and a daughter who marries Edmund Mortimer, the man presented in this play as Richard II's designated heir to the throne. Wales thus harbors both rebellion and the man who was arguably the legitimate King of England.

A tavern in Eastcheap, a commercial district in the east of London, is another important locale. This tavern is Prince Hal's second home, where he comes to drink and amuse himself and particularly to carouse with Falstaff, the dissipated knight who is the young Prince's tutor in folly, his intimate friend, and surrogate father. In the tavern, Hal rubs elbows with commoners—with Mistress Quickly, the Hostess; with Francis, the inarticulate apprentice tapster; and with other common people. Shakespeare took his cue about Hal's presence amid this crew from the many popular accounts of the Prince's dissolute youth, especially from a play printed in 1598 called *The Famous Victories of Henry V*,

The historical Owain Glyndŵr claimed the title of Prince of Wales. His great seal, both sides of which are shown here, bears the inscription "Owain, by the grace of God, prince of Wales" and depicts four upreared (rampant) lions, the coat of arms of the Gwynedd dynasty to which Glyndŵr belonged.

some version of which seems to have been staged in the late 1580s. It depicts not only episodes from Hal's madcap youth but also his eventual reformation and assumption of the throne. Shakespeare elaborated extensively on this story of youthful prodigality. Mistress Quickly, for example, is entirely his invention, and the character of Falstaff, while loosely modeled on a figure in *The Famous Victories*, is utterly transformed by Shakespeare into what has remained one of the great comic creations of the English theater. In depicting Falstaff and the Eastcheap milieu, Shakespeare employed a racy, colloquial prose quite unlike the elevated poetry that noble characters usually speak in Shakespearean drama and in which the entirety of his previous history, *Richard II*, had been written.

One of the objections to English popular theater voiced by a contemporary poet, Sir Philip Sidney, was that it mingled clowns with kings in a way that violated codes of aesthetic and social decorum; these codes insisted on the strict separation of high and low subject matter, language, and people. *1 Henry IV*, however, is thoroughly hybrid in its mingling of the high matter of rebellion and affairs of state with the low matter of drinking, jokes, and highway robbery. The play is also a temporal hybrid, in that the tavern scenes seem to take place not in the early fifteenth century, when Henry IV was struggling to secure his rule, but more nearly in the late sixteenth century, when Shakespeare was actually writing his play. In the tavern scenes, for example, characters make fun of plays and modes of writing popular in the 1570s and 1580s, such as Thomas Preston's ranting tyrant play *Cambyses* (1569) and the baroquely ornate rhetoric popularized by John Lyly in his *Euphues* (1578). The tavern world is also filled with references to the commodities that passed through London's markets in the late sixteenth century. The characters there drink sack, Madeira, and bastard—popular alcoholic beverages, some (such as Madeira) imported from as far away as an island off the coast of west Africa; and they refer to articles of clothing, such as the Spanish-leather wallets and leather jerkins with crystal buttons, worn by London's aspiring mercantile classes. Eastcheap itself, where the tavern is located, was a major market street in Shakespeare's London, and the tavern scenes are steeped in references to the commercial culture, including the theatrical culture, of early modern England.

There is every indication, however, that if a Sidney would have found the hybridity of the play a problem, ordinary consumers did not. Judging by its publication history, in its own time *1 Henry IV* was one of Shakespeare's most popular plays. It appeared in two quarto versions in 1598 and then in five more before the First Folio was printed in 1623. Even after that, individual quarto editions of the play continued to appear. Part of its popularity may have derived from the diversity it encompasses. Recent critics have argued that with *1 Henry IV*, the Shakespearean history play moves to supplement chronicle history, which focuses on monarchs, nobles, and affairs of state, with chorography: that is, with a mode of writing popular in the late sixteenth century that described and surveyed the land of England focusing on the products, the terrain, and the customs of England's various regions. *1 Henry IV* is a chorography in the sense that while the play's distinct lines of action comment on one another, each is defined in relation to specific places, customs, and social groups. The commercial, bawdy world of the tavern, with its cast of lowlife characters and its rituals of drinking and play, is very different from the more formal milieu of Westminster, where the King and his nobles, speaking mainly in poetry, are immersed in the tasks of statecraft, and different again from the world of passion and magic centered in Glyndŵr's Welsh castle. Through the multiple plots, the spectator watching the play experiences the illusion of complex temporal simultaneity and social and geographical heterogeneity. Thus in successive scenes, the rebels, in Wales, plot the dismemberment of England and listen to a song sung in Welsh (3.1); King Henry, in Westminster, berates his wayward son (3.2); Falstaff, in Eastcheap, tries to cheat Mistress Quickly by claiming that his ring was stolen in her tavern (3.3). All these actions go on cotemporally but in widely disparate locales, creating a theatrical illusion of the rich diversity encompassed by the ongoing life of the nation and its bordering regions.

But the play's rich elaboration of difference also makes evident its monarch's central problem: how to maintain control over and enforce unity upon the territories over which he claims dominion, but which threaten to break away or assert a worrisome autonomy. The problem is especially pressing for Henry IV because he did not lineally inherit the throne; he seized it from Richard II. He is on shaky ground, then, should he try to unify England under the banner of his own legitimacy. In fact, for much of the play, Henry is a king in search of a strategy of rule. He had hoped to unify his people, and quiet his conscience for his part in Richard's deposition and death, by undertaking a crusade to recover Jerusalem for European Christianity. Trouble at home, however, bubbling up on the Scottish border, on the Welsh border, in the northern counties, and even in the church, in the person of the Archbishop of York, keeps him from enacting this plan. The land seethes with the murmurings of rebels.

In the England of the 1590s, the monarch's most pressing problem of control was posed by Ireland; there, after 1595, the Earl of Tyrone was an important figure in challenging English rule. Like Glyndŵr, Tyrone was educated in England and in some accounts was even Glyndŵr's descendant. While Ireland is not directly depicted in *1 Henry IV*, Hotspur verbally links Wales and Ireland. Urged to listen to a song sung in Welsh, he says that he would rather hear his hunting dog howl in Irish (3.1.232), thereby confirming the common English view that Welsh and Irish were equally barbarous languages. More important, Wales stands in the play as a displaced image of the contemporary Irish situation. Wales had officially been incorporated into England in the 1530s, though in the popular imagination it could still seem a foreign place of mystery and danger. In *1 Henry IV*, Wales represents the threat not only of rebellion but also of effeminization and seduction. Mortimer, the supposed heir to the English throne, falls in love with Glyndŵr's daughter, promises to learn her language, and never appears on the battlefield against Henry's forces. In essence, he "goes native," a persistent fear voiced by the English concerning their soldiers and settlers in Ireland. The English had long worried that through prolonged contact with the Irish, English men and women might adopt their barbarous ways and forfeit their English identity. They even feared that their children, in drinking the milk of Irish wet nurses, could be transformed into people more Irish than English.

In *1 Henry IV*, the threat posed by the dangerous Celtic borderlands and the Percy faction is a direct challenge to the King's authority, menacing his control over the territories to which he lays claim. Hampered by the questionable means by which he came to the throne, Henry ultimately finds force and guile the most effective instruments for maintaining his power. He can win battles, and he is willing to use deception to improve his position. At Shrewsbury, his major battle against the rebels, a number of Henry's nobles dress like the King, frustrating the enemy's ability to identify the true King and encouraging

Henry's own forces by the seeming ubiquity of their monarch. Perpetual battle, however, is a costly way to rule, and having many nobles dress like him runs counter to Henry's stated belief that the King should be seldom seen in order to be the more wondered at when he does appear. To have many men marching in the King's clothing and answering to the King's name might, in fact, subversively suggest that "King" is a part any man could play, given the right accoutrements.

Prince Hal faces the pressing task of finding better strategies for ruling the changed world his father brought into being by his deposition of King Richard. Hal cannot assume that his kingship will be uncontested simply because he is Henry's son. A usurper's off-spring has more legitimacy than a usurper, but not much. Rather, Hal must *make* himself King by a convincing performance of the part, and he must beat out those who would be his rivals, such as Harry Hotspur. Viewed one way, *1 Henry IV* is a study in the political and theatrical skills necessary for rule in a world where the inevitability and assumed legitimacy of inherited kingship has been called into question. In 1532, Niccolò Machiavelli's *The Prince*, a manual of practical statecraft, was published and quickly became notorious throughout Europe. Machiavelli taught rulers how to maintain their power through a mixture of guile, alliance, warfare, and personal force of character. Popularly viewed as irreligious and amoral, Machiavelli nonetheless was a byword for political pragmatism.

In his sophisticated manipulation of power, Hal shows himself a good student of Machiavelli, and the Machiavellian strand of his characterization has caused a split in critical assessments of him. To many, Hal personifies the ideal English king, the perfect mean between the self-indulgence of Falstaff and the impassioned inflexibility of a Hotspur. He is thus an object of desire and emulation. Other critics focus on what they perceive as a lack of humanity at the heart of this consummate politician and recoil from his calculated use of other people to serve his own ends. For example, at the end of the first scene in which he appears, Hal in soliloquy speaks about his tavern mates:

> I know you all, and will a while uphold
> The unyoked humour of your idleness.
> Yet herein will I imitate the sun,
> Who doth permit the base contagious clouds
> To smother up his beauty from the world,
> That when he please again to be himself,
> Being wanted he may be more wondered at
> By breaking through the foul and ugly mists
> Of vapours that did seem to strangle him.
>   (1.2.173–81)

The soliloquy continues, but these lines reveal the calculation that is one part of this character's representation. Comparing himself to the royal symbol, the sun, Hal casts his companions as the contaminating clouds and ugly mists that temporarily obscure his own radiance. Hal is chillingly disdainful of those he elsewhere treats as boon companions, but he also finds their baseness *useful*, since it will set in high relief his own glory, once he has cast them off.

Hal is an interesting dramatic character and not merely a personification of political expediency, however, precisely because his calculated use of his companions does not necessarily preclude his being attracted to them and to the world of play and good fellowship they represent. In *1 Henry IV*, Hal is not yet King, and the moment of repudiation is not yet upon him. In this play, Hal can both enjoy his time in Eastcheap and, ironically, acquire skills there he will need when he ascends his father's troubled throne. In the tavern, for example, he and Falstaff take turns playing King and Prince in a theatrical staging of the prodigal Hal's encounter with his reproving father. Hal rehearses the cadences and the sentiments of royal speech, trying out a part, learning to inhabit it convincingly. But it is not just his own part he masters. Unlike his father, Hal does not hold himself aloof from his would-be subjects. His ventures into Eastcheap are in part a mapping of one corner of England, a survey of the customs and strange languages of this locale. To Ned Poins he boasts that having been instructed by three tapsters in the terminology of drinking, "I can drink with any tinker in his own language during my life" (2.5.16–17).

In the tavern, Hal also meditates on the strange tongue of his great rival, Hotspur, whose impatient but impassioned speech Hal parodies:

> I am not yet of Percy's mind, the Hotspur of the North—he that kills me some six or seven dozen of Scots at a breakfast, washes his hands, and says to his wife, 'Fie upon this quiet life! I want work.' 'O my sweet Harry,' says she, 'how many hast thou killed today?' 'Give my roan horse a drench,' says he, and answers, 'Some fourteen,' an hour after; 'a trifle, a trifle.' I prithee call in Falstaff. I'll play Percy, and that damned brawn shall play Dame Mortimer his wife. (2.5.94–101)

Learning the language of others and rehearsing their tongues is, for Hal, one of the arts of power. He can—and later he will—repudiate some of those whose language and customs he has imbibed, making the repudiation a justification for his own rule. Knowing disorderliness, the King will use his office to punish it. He can also appropriate the language of others, as at Shrewsbury he appropriates the chivalric accents of Hotspur; or he can co-opt others to serve his own purposes by speaking to them in a tongue they can comprehend. By his own account, Hal is beloved of the tapsters who have taught him their language, and they have promised that when he is King, he "shall command all the good lads in Eastcheap" (2.5.12–13). Many of them he will eventually quite literally command in his wars in France. It can be argued, therefore, that there is a profound instrumentality to Hal's sojourn outside the court milieu that should be his "natural" home. He is acquiring theatrical skills, linguistic skills, and above all a knowledge of the diverse corners of an England he must rule by a mixture of charm, guile, and strategic severity—demonizing some objects to win the loyalty of others, outstripping rivals by outdoing them at their own particular strengths.

Yet Hal is only part of this play, and *1 Henry IV*'s uniqueness consists in good part in the way it plays off one dramatic perspective, one line of action, against another. The young Prince is certainly the focus of the play's narrative of reform, and he is the only character who can move with seeming ease among the worlds of tavern, court, and battlefield. Yet even as he surveys and judges those around him, the play's structure of geographical juxtapositions and its vivid depiction of other characters and other modes of being invite the audience to submit the Prince himself to critical scrutiny. Consider, for example, 3.1 and 3.2, the scenes at the center of the play that take the audience first to Glyndŵr's castle in Wales, where he, Hotspur, Mortimer, and Worcester are plotting their rebellion, and then to the King's palace at Westminster to which Henry has summoned his son. The first scene graphically establishes the kingdom-cleaving threat posed by the rebels. They have a map and are planning how they will divide the territory of England into three parts. But the scene also establishes the danger, mystery, and beauty of this borderland. Glyndŵr is a man trained in occult arts who boasts that the earth shook at his birth and that he can summon spirits to do his bidding. Hotspur scoffs, but when Glyndŵr's daughter promises to sing in Welsh, Glyndŵr says.

> Do so, and those musicians that shall play to you
> Hang in the air a thousand leagues from hence,
> And straight they shall be here. Sit and attend.
> (3.1.220–22)

Three lines later, music plays, its origins a mystery. When Glyndŵr speaks, Wales seems a land of enchantment, haunted by spirits.

It is also a place of strong and undisguised emotions: Hotspur's irascible impatience, Glyndŵr's pride, Mortimer and the Welsh woman's passion for one another. Women, in fact, are important in the rebel scenes as they are not anywhere else in the play. Except for Mistress Quickly, Kate Percy and Glyndŵr's daughter are the play's only two female characters; and 3.1, the play's only scene in which two women are onstage at the same time, is largely Shakespeare's invention. In the chronicles, Glyndŵr, Mortimer, and Hotspur's proposed division of conquered territory is negotiated by representatives in the Archbishop of Bangor's house. In short, Shakespeare went to some trouble to link the rebels with women—more specifically, with wives and daughters. The question is why. In part, the choice portrays the rebels, unlike the Lancastrians, as having private as well as public lives. Glyndŵr is fond of his daughter and worries about her happiness. Mortimer dotes on this same daughter and seems to have married her for love as much as for political alliance. Hotspur's affection for his wife is displayed through the teasing banter with which he persistently addresses her. Scornful of mooning lovers, he nonetheless is careful to take his wife with him when he journeys to Wales.

The passions so nakedly on display in this scene clearly signal the rebels' vulnerabilities. In the patriarchal thought of the period, men were presented as superior to women because they were supposedly more rational and less subject to their passions. If men loved women too much, they risked becoming effeminate, that is, *like* a woman in placing desire above reason, especially if that desire kept a man from performing his public duties, such as going to war. Hotspur prizes his masculinity and the public honor to be won in battle. He is contemptuous of the affected courtier who appeared at Holmedon after the fighting, demanding Hotspur's prisoners (1.3.28–68). In his dealings with his wife, Hotspur seems to use banter and jokes to maintain control of his affection for her. He would not, for a woman, forgo the man-to-man erotics of battle when, "hot horse to horse" (4.1.123), he clashes against the bosom of Prince Hal. Mortimer, by contrast, simply succumbs to the charms of the Welsh woman. He never appears in battle: Wales and a wife swallow him up.

This Welsh world of danger, mystery, and passion sits strangely against the world of calculation that unfolds immediately thereafter, when in 3.2 King Henry castigates Prince Hal for his dissolute life and together they discuss strategies of monarchical self-presentation. The throne room is a place not of enchantment but of business. No women are shown at court, and passion manifests itself most strongly as the desire to rule. Father and son are both preoccupied with the tactics and strategies by which they can most effectively command the loyalty of subjects. While Henry fears his son misunderstands the task before him, Hal shows that he is every bit as astute as his father. But after the high emotions and alluring lyricism of the Welsh scene, the throne room at Westminster can seem a pragmatic and claustrophobic space. In concentrating their energies on rule, Henry and Hal here are divorced from many things that give the rebel world its charm.

Falstaff and the tavern pose a different challenge to the values of Westminster. As recent criticism has shown, the fat man's tutoring of Hal in riotous living mimics the pedagogical relationship of master to student that was sometimes eroticized in the early modern period. Much of the poignancy of the play's depiction of the friendship between the two comes from the tension between their apparent intimacy and the Prince's stated intention to repudiate his companion. Falstaff's threat to monarchical values is obvious. Against the future-oriented calculations of Hal and his father, he insists on living in the present. As his huge body testifies, he demands the immediate gratification of physical desires. To eat, drink, and jest—these are pleasures that for Falstaff brook no delay. Hal can discipline himself. He is thin, as Falstaff remarks, and he can plot a personal reformation sometime far in the future and work toward that end. Falstaff cannot; and yet, while a figure of disorder, he has for many readers been the play's most interesting and memorable character. Aside from Hamlet, no other Shakespearean figure has attracted as much critical attention as the fat knight.

When Shakespeare first wrote the play, he called this character Sir John Oldcastle. The choice was unfortunate, for the Cobham family, descendants of the historical Oldcastle, protested. William Brook, the seventh Lord Cobham, had been lord chamberlain from August 1596 to March 1597, the very months when most scholars believe Shakespeare completed 1 Henry IV. Since the lord chamberlain oversaw the licensing of plays through the office of the Master of the Revels, Cobham was in an especially favorable position to object to this comic rendition of his ancestor. Shakespeare apparently changed the character's name in response to this act of censorship, though traces of his original intentions can be discerned, including the fact that in 1.2.37 Falstaff is still referred to as "my old lad of the castle." In addition, in the first complete quarto of *1 Henry IV*, there are a few traces of the fact that Peto once bore the name "Harvey," and Bardolph the name "Russell." Again, the objections of powerful figures may have forced changes. "Russell" was the family name of the prominent earls of Bedford, and "Harvey" the name of the stepfather of the Earl of Southampton.

Falstaff and Mistress Quickly; part of the frontispiece to *The Wits, or Sport upon Sport* (1662), a collection of short dramatic pieces, one of which featured Falstaff and his exploits.

Recently, some critics (including the editors of the Oxford text) have argued that the names "Peto," "Bardolph," and "Falstaff" should be replaced by the names Shakespeare originally intended: namely, "Harvey," "Russell," and "Oldcastle." They suggest that such a replacement would undo an act of censorship that thwarted Shakespeare's original intentions. This edition retains the substituted names primarily because these are the names Shakespeare consistently used after the initial act of censorship, and they have become part of the textual and dramatic history of this and other plays. Only in a few instances do traces of the original names survive in stage directions or speech prefixes or text. In subsequent plays in which Falstaff appears or is mentioned—*2 Henry IV*, *Henry V*, and *The Merry Wives of Windsor*—the new names are also used. While it is important to point out that an act of censorship occurred, to "undo" it creates new erasures in the textual and cultural history of the play. For Shakespeare, "Falstaff," not "Oldcastle," became the word linking the various textual manifestations of his fat knight; and that name, in turn, is the bridge to a rich critical literature on Shakespeare's comic figure.

It is of interest, however, to ask why Shakespeare first used the name "Oldcastle" in his play. The historical Oldcastle was a knight who served Henry IV in battle in both France and Wales, but who was also a Lollard; that is, he was connected with the religious group often seen as a forerunner of English Protestantism for its critiques of the Catholic Church and its advocacy of a vernacular Bible to be made available to lay people. At first, Henry IV treated Oldcastle's religious views leniently, but eventually he was sent to the Tower of London and condemned as a heretic by the Archbishop of Canterbury. He escaped, and Henry was warned that Oldcastle was leading an armed force against him. Oldcastle was captured in 1417 and eventually hung in chains and then burned on the gallows.

The esteem in which Oldcastle was held depended, in the sixteenth century, very much on one's religious perspective. To many zealous Protestants, such as John Foxe, Oldcastle was a Protestant hero, a victim of Catholic oppression rather than a traitor; Foxe included Oldcastle in his *Book of Martyrs*. But by the 1590s, Lollards were also sometimes linked with "extremist" Protestant groups pushing for radical reforms in the Church of England. Making a well-known Lollard martyr a fat figure of disorder therefore did not necessarily signal Catholic sympathies. It might simply be a way of suggesting the hypocrisy of zealous reformers. In other plays, especially in his portrait of Malvolio in *Twelfth Night*,

This knight suggests Shakespeare's portrait of the chivalric heroes, Prince Hal and Hotspur, at the battle of Shrewsbury. From Henry Peacham's *Minerva Britanna* (1612).

Shakespeare makes fun of "Puritans" who claimed a greater righteousness and strictness of life than their more moderate contemporaries. In *1 Henry IV*, Falstaff's language is liberally studded with biblical quotations, most of which he misapplies or contradicts by his behavior. Thus he tells Hal that one must labor in one's vocation (1.2.92–93), an injunction found in 1 Corinthians 7:20 and in Ephesians 4:1. But the vocation in which *he* would labor is that of thief—not exactly what Protestant divines meant when discussing the virtues of a vocation. Moreover, by making Falstaff so obviously a glutton and lover of sack, Shakespeare could be making fun of the hypocrisy of Puritans, as Ben Jonson was to do in *Bartholemew Fair* and Thomas Middleton in *The Chaste Maid in Cheapside*.

The name Shakespeare fastened upon to replace Oldcastle had its own history. The historical Fastolf (1378?–1459) was a courageous officer in Henry VI's war in France, though in some chronicles he appears erroneously to have been called a coward, a detail that Shakespeare repeats in *1 Henry VI*. Having once used the name without repercussion in the former play, Shakespeare may have felt it was safe to employ it as a replacement for "Oldcastle" and to play upon the figure's reputation for cowardice.

Yet it may be a mistake to connect Shakespeare's character too strictly to any historical counterpart. As scholarship has shown, Falstaff is a rich amalgam of popular and literary traditions. Viewed morally, he looks like the irreverent Vice figure from the medieval morality plays, trying to lure Hal from the path of virtue; but he also recalls the topsy-turvy world of Carnival in which rulers are temporarily displaced and the body's pleasures (eating, drinking, breaking wind, having sex) are celebrated before the arrival of abstemious Lent. Falstaff has touches, as well, of the braggart warrior (who is actually a coward) from the classical tradition, but above all he embodies traditions of popular critique associated with the stage clown. In early productions, Will Kemp, the famous clown in Shakespeare's company, probably played the part. As the clown, Falstaff had precedent for his irreverent ways. Sometimes speaking from a downstage position near the audience, the clown traditionally poked fun at upstage authority figures. Falstaff does so in spades, whether mocking the elevated speech of King Henry or twitting Hal for being so skinny. But Falstaff is more than a gadfly or a parasite swollen fat on others' folly. He also embodies a mode of being in the world that serves as a powerful alternative both to the calculations of Hal and to Hotspur's headlong, death-courting pursuit of honor. At Shrewsbury, where the play's final battle occurs, Falstaff carries a bottle of sack in his pistol case and feigns death when attacked by Douglas. Though Hotspur and others are slain, Falstaff rises up. He embraces neither honor nor death, but life.

The play's disparate strands of action and character come together at the Battle of Shrewsbury, where Hotspur, the King, Prince Hal, and even Falstaff all appear. It is perhaps Hal's happiest hour. At Shrewsbury, he finds a way to redeem his reputation and distinguish himself from Falstaff without being forced to repudiate his friend, just as he can kill Hotspur while paying homage to his courage. But the equipoise of this battle's conclusion is precarious. Hal is not yet King and must still delay his assumption of the throne. Falstaff has not reformed and probably never will. And the rebels have not been destroyed. Hotspur is dead, but the Archbishop of York, Glyndŵr, and Mortimer are still in arms. In other words, it is an illusion that Hal has carried all before him. In the corners and crevices of the realm, dissension and difference remain. In such conditions, the work of rule is a performance with no end.

JEAN E. HOWARD

TEXTUAL NOTE

The first quarto edition of *1 Henry IV* was printed in 1598. Only a fragment, comprising 1.3.199 through 2.3.19 of a single copy, now remains. This quarto, usually designated as Qo but in the Oxford edition called Q1, was the basis for a second quarto edition printed later in 1598. This text, Q2, serves as the control text for most modern editions. The manuscript behind Q1 does not seem to have been marked up for the theater, so it was probably not the promptbook. The manuscript was either a corrected copy of Shakespeare's "foul papers" or, more probably, a transcription of them made by a professional scribe. This manuscript was prepared with unusual care, perhaps to show that changes required by the Master of the Revels had been made in the text. Originally, the characters Falstaff, Peto, and Bardolph had been assigned the names "Oldcastle," "Harvey," and "Russell." Objections from the Cobham family, descendants of Oldcastle, and perhaps from other powerful people seem to have forced Shakespeare to change these names (see the Introduction for a fuller discussion of this act of censorship).

Five other quarto editions were published, in 1599, 1604, 1608, 1613, and 1622, before the publication of the First Folio (F) in 1623. These all derive from Q2 and have no independent authority. The Folio text derives from the 1613 Quarto, but act and scene divisions were added, speech prefixes and stage directions altered, and oaths were softened or removed and biblical allusions altered in compliance with the 1606 edict forbidding profanity on the stage. The party responsible for these changes is uncertain. Some changes may have been made by the compositors who set the text or by someone acting as editor (perhaps John Heminges or Henry Condell, Shakespeare's fellow shareholders in the King's Men who oversaw the production of the First Folio). The Oxford editors plausibly argue that these changes may in part derive from a manuscript prepared by the same scribe who prepared a similarly "literary" manuscript for *2 Henry IV*: that is, a manuscript less attuned to playhouse requirements than to the rationalization of the text as a written document. This scribal manuscript may itself have derived from a promptbook whose theatrical features were largely obscured by the transcription. The Oxford editors also believe that a few of the changes made in F may reflect Shakespeare's own revisions of Q.

The act and scene divisions of F are followed except for the marking of new scenes at 2.3 and 5.3. The latter scene break, regularly inserted in most modern editions, indicates a clearing of the stage in the middle of the Battle of Shrewsbury; 2.3 is added to mark the moment at Gad's Hill when, Falstaff and his friends having led off the travelers they have captured, Hal and Poins come onstage disguised in their buckram suits.

As explained in the Introduction, for this play Norton is using the names "Falstaff," "Peto," and "Bardolph" (rather than Oxford's "Oldcastle," "Harvey," and "Russell"). Consequently, Oxford speech prefixes and stage directions, and in a few places the Oxford text, have been silently altered where these three characters are concerned in order to return to the names and language appearing in the printed quarto texts of 1598. Textual deviations from Q are marked in the variants, and Norton's standardization of Q speech prefixes is delineated immediately before those variants. In particular, "Falstaff," rather than Oxford's "Sir John," has been used in speech prefixes in this play as well as in *2 Henry IV*.

SELECTED BIBLIOGRAPHY

Barber, C. L. "Rule and Misrule in *Henry IV.*" *Shakespeare's Festive Comedy: A Study of Dramatic Form and Its Relation to Social Custom.* Princeton: Princeton University Press, 1959. 192–221.

Bristol, Michael D. "The Festive Agon: The Politics of Carnival." *Carnival and Theater: Plebeian Culture and the Structure of Authority in Renaissance England.* New York: Routledge, 1989. 197–213.

Goldberg, Jonathan. "Desiring Hal." *Sodometries: Renaissance Texts, Modern Sexualities.* Stanford: Stanford University Press, 1992. 145–75.

Greenblatt, Stephen. "Invisible Bullets." *Shakespearean Negotiations: The Circulation of Social Energy in Renaissance England.* Berkeley: University of California Press, 1988. 21–65.

Highley, Christopher. "Wales, Ireland, and *1 Henry IV.*" *Renaissance Drama*, n.s., 21 (1990): 91–114.

Howard, Jean E., and Phyllis Rackin. "Gender and Nation: Anticipations of Modernity in the Second Tetralogy." *Engendering a Nation: A Feminist Account of Shakespeare's English Histories.* London: Routledge, 1997. 137–215.

Kastan, David Scott. " 'The King Hath Many Marching in His Coats'; or, What Did You Do During the War, Daddy?" *Shakespeare Right and Left.* Ed. Ivo Kamps. New York: Routledge, 1991. 241–58.

McMillan, Scott. *Henry IV, Part One: Shakespeare in Performance.* Manchester: Manchester University Press, 1991.

Mullaney, Steven. "The Rehearsal of Cultures." *The Place of the Stage: License, Play, and Power in Renaissance England.* Chicago: University of Chicago Press, 1988. 60–87.

Taylor, Gary. "The Fortunes of Oldcastle." *Shakespeare Survey* 38 (1985): 85–100.

The History of Henry the Fourth

The Persons of the Play

KING HENRY IV
PRINCE HARRY, Prince of Wales,
    familiarly known as Hal   } King Henry's sons
Lord JOHN OF LANCASTER
Earl of WESTMORLAND
Sir Walter BLUNT
Earl of WORCESTER
Percy, Earl of NORTHUMBERLAND, his brother
Henry Percy, known as HOTSPUR,
    Northumberland's son
Kate, LADY PERCY, Hotspur's wife
Lord Edmund MORTIMER, called Earl of March,   rebels
    Lady Percy's brother   against
LADY MORTIMER, his wife   King Henry
Owain GLYNDŴR, Lady Mortimer's father
Earl of DOUGLAS
Sir Richard VERNON
Scrope, ARCHBISHOP of York
SIR MICHAEL, a member of the Archbishop's
    household
Sir John FALSTAFF
Edward (Ned) POINS
BARDOLPH
PETO
Mistress Quickly, HOSTESS of   associates of Prince Harry
a tavern in Eastcheap
FRANCIS, a drawer
VINTNER
GADSHILL
CARRIERS
CHAMBERLAIN
OSTLER
TRAVELLERS
SHERIFF
MESSENGERS
SERVANT
Lords, soldiers

1.1

Enter KING [HENRY], *Lord* JOHN OF LANCASTER, [*and
the*] *Earl of* WESTMORLAND, *with other* [*lords*]

KING HENRY So shaken as we are, so wan with care,
  Find we° a time for frighted peace to pant   *Let us find*
  And breathe short-winded accents° of new broils   *words*
  To be commenced in strands afar remote.[1]

[handwritten: personification of peace. representing the third soldier.]

1.1 Location: The palace, London.
1. On distant shores. King Henry is alluding to the Holy   Land, to which he vowed to lead a crusade at the close of *Richard II.*

5	No more the thirsty entrance° of this soil	*parched mouth*
	Shall daub her lips with her own children's blood.	
	No more shall trenching° war channel° her fields,	*cutting / furrow*
	Nor bruise her flow'rets with the armèd hoofs	
	Of hostile paces.° Those opposèd eyes,	*horses' footsteps*
10	Which, like the meteors of a troubled heaven,[2]	
	All of one nature, of one substance bred,	
	Did lately meet in the intestine° shock	*internal*
	And furious close° of civil butchery,	*hand-to-hand combat*
	Shall now in mutual well-beseeming° ranks	*orderly*
15	March all one way, and be no more opposed	
	Against acquaintance, kindred, and allies.	
	The edge of war, like an ill-sheathèd knife,	
	No more shall cut his° master. Therefore, friends,	*its*
	As far as to the sepulchre of Christ—	
20	Whose soldier now, under whose blessèd cross	
	We are impressèd° and engaged to fight—	*conscripted*
	Forthwith a power of English shall we levy,	
	Whose arms were moulded in their mothers' womb	
	To chase these pagans in those holy fields	
25	Over whose acres walked those blessèd feet	
	Which fourteen hundred years ago were nailed,	
	For our advantage, on the bitter cross.	
	But this our purpose now is twelve month old,	
	And bootless° 'tis to tell you we will go.	*useless*
30	Therefor° we meet not now. Then let me hear	*On that account*
	Of you, my gentle cousin° Westmorland,	*my noble kinsman*
	What yesternight our Council did decree	
	In forwarding this dear expedience.°	*urgent undertaking*
	WESTMORLAND My liege, this haste was hot in question,°	*under urgent debate*
35	And many limits of the charge[3] set down	
	But yesternight, when all athwart° there came	*at cross-purposes*
	A post° from Wales, loaden with heavy news,	*messenger*
	Whose worst was that the noble Mortimer,	
	Leading the men of Herefordshire to fight	
40	Against the irregular and wild Glyndŵr,[4]	
	Was by the rude hands of that Welshman taken,	
	A thousand of his people butcherèd,	
	Upon whose dead corpse'° there was such misuse,	*corpses*
	Such beastly shameless transformation,[5]	
45	By those Welshwomen done as may not be	
	Without much shame retold or spoken of.	
	KING HENRY It seems then that the tidings of this broil	
	Brake° off our business for the Holy Land.	*Broke*
	WESTMORLAND This matched with other did, my gracious lord,	
50	For more uneven° and unwelcome news	*disturbing*
	Came from the north, and thus it did import:	

2. Unusual events in the sky, such as comets or shooting stars, were thought to portend strife and disaster.
3. Many particulars concerning responsibilities and expenses.
4. In most editions, Glyndŵr's name is given as "Glendower," an anglicized version of the Welsh word used in this text. Glyndŵr is probably "irregular" in the sense of using guerrilla tactics in his warfare; possibly, the word alludes to his alleged sorcery.

5. Mutilation. Holinshed's 1587 *Chronicles*, one of Shakespeare's sources, says the Welsh women's acts on this occasion were too shameful to relate, but Abraham Fleming in the same edition of the *Chronicles* includes an account of another battle in which Welsh women cut off the sexual organs and the noses of conquered enemies and put them, respectively, in the mouths and anuses of these enemies.

On Holy-rood day[6] the gallant Hotspur there—
Young Harry Percy—and brave Archibald,
That ever valiant and approvèd° Scot,   *worthy*
55 At Holmedon[7] met,
Where they did spend a sad and bloody hour,
As by° discharge of their artillery   *As judging by*
And shape of likelihood° the news was told;   *And probable outcome*
For he that brought them° in the very heat   *(the news)*
60 And pride° of their contention did take horse,   *height*
Uncertain of the issue° any way.   *outcome*
KING HENRY   Here is a dear, a true industrious friend,
Sir Walter Blunt,[8] new lighted from his horse,
Stained with the variation of each soil
65 Betwixt that Holmedon and this seat° of ours;   *dwelling*
And he hath brought us smooth° and welcome news.   *agreeable*
The Earl of Douglas is discomfited.
Ten thousand bold Scots, two-and-twenty knights,
Balked° in their own blood did Sir Walter see   *Heaped up; thwarted*
70 On Holmedon's plains. Of prisoners Hotspur took
Mordake the Earl of Fife and eldest son
To beaten Douglas,[9] and the Earl of Athol,
Of Moray, Angus, and Menteith;
And is not this an honourable spoil,
75 A gallant prize? Ha, cousin, is it not?
WESTMORLAND   In faith, it is a conquest for a prince to boast of.
KING HENRY   Yea, there thou mak'st me sad, and mak'st me sin
In envy that my lord Northumberland
Should be the father to so blest a son—
80 A son who is the theme of honour's tongue,
Amongst a grove the very straightest plant,
Who is sweet Fortune's minion° and her pride—   *favorite*
Whilst I by looking on the praise of him
See riot and dishonour stain the brow
85 Of my young Harry. O, that it could be proved
That some night-tripping fairy[1] had exchanged
In cradle clothes our children where they lay,
And called mine Percy, his Plantagenet![2]
Then would I have his Harry, and he mine.
90 But let him° from my thoughts. What think you, coz,°   *let him go / kinsman*
Of this young Percy's pride? The prisoners
Which he in this adventure hath surprised°   *captured*
To his own use[3] he keeps, and sends me word
I shall have none but Mordake Earl of Fife.
95 WESTMORLAND   This is his uncle's teaching. This is Worcester,
Malevolent to you in all aspects,[4]

6. Holy Cross Day, September 14.
7. Holmedon (also spelled "Humbleton") in Northumberland was the site in 1402 of a Scottish invasion of
England.
8. It is not clear whether Blunt comes onstage now. He
could have entered at the beginning of the scene; alternatively, as in this edition, he may not come onstage at all.
Blunt has no lines in the scene, and Henry could at this
point receive a letter containing Blunt's news or could be
reporting news he has already learned. "Here" would thus
refer in a general way to Blunt's being at court.
9. Mordrake was not actually Douglas's son, but an

understandable misreading of Holinshed led Shakespeare
to believe he was.
1. It was popularly believed that fairies stole beautiful
children and left bad or malformed ones in their places.
2. Henry was descended from the Plantagenet dynasty;
and the Percys were a distinguished family from the north
of England to which Hotspur belonged.
3. Prisoners were routinely used as a source of revenue.
4. Habitually hostile to you. The line suggests that Worcester is a planet whose influence is always harmful, whatever his position, or "aspect," in the sky.

Which makes him prune[5] himself, and bristle up
The crest of youth against your dignity.

KING HENRY   But I have sent for him to answer this;
100 And for this cause awhile we must neglect
Our holy purpose to Jerusalem.
Cousin, on Wednesday next our Council we
Will hold at Windsor. So inform the lords.
But come yourself with speed to us again,
105 For more is to be said and to be done
Than out of anger can be uttered.

WESTMORLAND   I will, my liege.

Exeunt [KING HENRY, LANCASTER, *and other lords*
at one door; WESTMORLAND *at another door*]

1.2

Enter [HARRY][1] *Prince of Wales and Sir John* FALSTAFF[2]

FALSTAFF   Now, Hal, what time of day is it, lad?

PRINCE HARRY   Thou art so fat-witted° with drinking of old sack,[3]   *thick-witted*
and unbuttoning thee after supper, and sleeping upon benches
after noon, that thou hast forgotten to demand that truly which
5 thou wouldst truly know. What a devil hast thou to do with the
time of the day? Unless hours were cups of sack, and minutes
capons,[4] and clocks the tongues of bawds, and dials° the signs   *clock faces; sundials*
of leaping-houses,° and the blessed sun himself a fair hot   *brothels*
wench in flame-coloured taffeta,[5] I see no reason why thou
10 shouldst be so superfluous° to demand the time of the day.   *needlessly curious*

FALSTAFF   Indeed you come near me° now, Hal, for we that take   *are near the mark*
purses go by the moon and the seven stars,[6] and not 'By Phoe-
bus, he, that wand'ring knight so fair'.[7] And I prithee, sweet
wag,° when thou art a king, as God save thy grace—'majesty' I   *mischievous boy*
15 should say, for grace[8] thou wilt have none—

PRINCE HARRY   What, none?

FALSTAFF   No, by my troth, not so much as will serve to be prologue to an egg and butter.

PRINCE HARRY   Well, how then? Come, roundly,° roundly.   *to the point*

20 FALSTAFF   Marry° then, sweet wag, when thou art king let not us   *By Mary (a mild oath)*
that are squires of the night's body[9] be called thieves of the
day's beauty. Let us be 'Diana's foresters',[1] 'gentlemen of the
shade', 'minions of the moon', and let men say we be men of
good government,° being governed, as the sea is, by our noble   *conduct*
25 and chaste mistress the moon, under whose countenance° we   *face; protection*
steal.

PRINCE HARRY   Thou sayst well, and it holds well° too, for the   *the comparison is apt*
fortune of us that are the moon's men doth ebb and flow like

5. A term from falconry suggesting the hawk's trimming
of its feathers as preparation for action.
1.2 Location: A room in the Prince's apartments, London.
1. F's stage direction reads, "Henry Prince of Wales"; Q
reads, "prince of Wales." Norton speech prefixes refer to
this character as "Prince Harry," and the same designa-
tion is used, as here, in stage directions.
2. See Introduction and Textual Note for a discussion of
Falstaff's name.
3. Spanish white wine.
4. Castrated male chickens (an Elizabethan delicacy).
5. Silk cloth, which in some contexts was associated with
prostitutes.
6. The constellation known as the Pleiades. *go by the*

moon: go about at moonlight; tell time by the light of the
moon.
7. Evidently a line from a contemporary ballad or
romance about Phoebus, the sun god of classical myth.
8. Virtue; with a pun also on "grace" as meaning "God's
favor" and "a prayer before meals." Falstaff asserts that
Hal has none of these and so must be called "your majesty," rather than "your grace," which was also a title of
honor.
9. Let not we who steal by night. Falstaff alludes to the
attendants of knights known as "squires of the body."
1. Hunters by moonlight; thieves. In classical myth,
Diana was goddess of the moon.

the sea, being governed as the sea is by the moon. As for proof
now: a purse of gold most resolutely snatched on Monday
night, and most dissolutely spent on Tuesday morning; got with
swearing 'lay by!',[2] and spent with crying 'bring in!';[3] now in as
low an ebb as the foot of the ladder, and by and by in as high a
flow as the ridge° of the gallows.[4]   *crossbar*

FALSTAFF By the Lord, thou sayst true, lad; and is not my Hostess of the tavern a most sweet wench?

PRINCE HARRY As the honey of Hybla,[5] my old lad of the castle;[6]
and is not a buff jerkin[7] a most sweet robe of durance?°   *durability; imprisonment*

FALSTAFF How now, how now, mad wag? What, in thy quips
and thy quiddities?° What a plague have I to do with a buff   *quibbles (wordplay)*
jerkin?

PRINCE HARRY Why, what a pox[8] have I to do with my Hostess
of the tavern?

FALSTAFF Well, thou hast called her to a reckoning[9] many a
time and oft.

PRINCE HARRY Did I ever call for thee to pay thy part?[1]

FALSTAFF No, I'll give thee thy due, thou hast paid all there.

PRINCE HARRY Yea, and elsewhere so far as my coin would
stretch;[2] and where it would not, I have used my credit.

FALSTAFF Yea, and so used it that were it not here <u>apparent that
thou art heir apparent</u>—but I prithee, sweet wag, shall there be
gallows standing in England when thou art king, and resolution
thus fubbed[3] as it is with the rusty curb of old father Antic° the   *buffoon*
law? Do not thou when thou art king hang a thief.

PRINCE HARRY No, thou shalt.

FALSTAFF Shall I? O, rare! By the Lord, I'll be a brave° judge!   *fine; well-dressed*

PRINCE HARRY Thou judgest false already. I mean thou shalt
have the hanging of the thieves, and so become a rare
hangman.

FALSTAFF Well, Hal, well; and in some sort it jumps° with my   *agrees*
humour° as well as waiting in the court,[4] I can tell you.   *temperament*

PRINCE HARRY For obtaining of suits?[5]

FALSTAFF Yea, for obtaining of suits, whereof the hangman hath
no lean wardrobe. 'Sblood,[6] I am as melancholy as a gib cat,°   *tomcat*
or a lugged bear.[7]

PRINCE HARRY Or an old lion, or a lover's lute.

FALSTAFF Yea, or the drone of a Lincolnshire bagpipe.

PRINCE HARRY What sayst thou to a hare,[8] or the melancholy of
Moor-ditch?[9]

FALSTAFF Thou hast the most unsavoury similes, and art indeed

[handwritten marginal note: A game. Challenge to play in words.]

2. A thief's cry similar to "Hands up!"
3. A tavern customer's call for more food or wine.
4. The Prince's speech is riddled with sexual slang, including "purse" (line 30) as meaning "vagina" or "scrotum"; "snatched" (line 30) as "forcibly had sexual relations with"; "spent" (line 31) as "exhausted by sexual activity"; "lay by" (line 32) as "lie back"; "spent with" (line 32) as "reached orgasm with"; and "low" (line 33) and "high" (line 33) as referring to a penis, first limp and then erect.
5. Region of Sicily renowned for its honey.
6. Slang for "roisterer"; also a play on the name "Oldcastle" (see Introduction).
7. Leather jacket often worn by jailers.
8. The equivalent of "what the devil." The pox literally was plague or syphilis.

9. You have asked that she present the bill; asked that she show her value sexually.
1. To pay your bill; to use your penis.
2. So far as my money would go; so far as my ability to engender, or "coin," a child would take me.
3. And valor (of thieves) thus thwarted.
4. Being in attendance at the royal court or at the court of justices.
5. Petitions; clothing. The hangman was entitled to claim the victims' clothing.
6. By His blood (an oath alluding to Christ's crucifixion).
7. A baited bear. In a popular form of entertainment, bears were led in chains and set upon by dogs.
8. The hare's sadness was proverbial. Its flesh, when eaten, was supposed to generate melancholy.
9. An open sewer outside the walls of London.

the most comparative,° rascalliest sweet young Prince. But Hal, *quick at comparisons*
I prithee trouble me no more with vanity.° I would to God thou *worthless things*
and I knew where a commodity° of good names° were to be *supply / reputations*
bought. An old lord of the Council rated me the other day in
75 the street about you, sir, but I marked him not; and yet he
talked very wisely, but I regarded him not; and yet he talked
wisely, and in the street too.

PRINCE HARRY Thou didst well, for wisdom cries out in the
streets, and no man regards it.[1]

80 FALSTAFF O, thou hast damnable iteration,[2] and art indeed able
to corrupt a saint. Thou hast done much harm upon me, Hal,
God forgive thee for it. Before I knew thee, Hal, I knew nothing; and now am I, if a man should speak truly, little better
than one of the wicked. I must give over this life, and I will
85 give it over. By the Lord, an° I do not, I am a villain. I'll be *if*
damned for never a° king's son in Christendom. *for no*

PRINCE HARRY Where shall we take a purse tomorrow, Jack?

FALSTAFF Zounds,[3] where thou wilt, lad! I'll make one;° an I do *I'll take part*
not, call me villain and baffle me.[4]

90 PRINCE HARRY I see a good amendment of life in thee, from
praying to purse-taking.

FALSTAFF Why, Hal, 'tis my vocation,° Hal. 'Tis no sin for a man *calling*
to labour in his vocation.[5]

Enter POINS

Poins! Now shall we know if Gadshill[6] have set a match.° O, if *planned a theft*
95 men were to be saved by merit,[7] what hole in hell were hot
enough for him? This is the most omnipotent villain that ever
cried 'Stand!' to a true° man. *an honest*

PRINCE HARRY Good morrow, Ned.

POINS Good morrow, sweet Hal. [*To* FALSTAFF] What says
100 Monsieur Remorse? What says Sir John, sack-and-sugar Jack?[8]
How agrees the devil and thee about thy soul, that thou soldest
him on Good Friday[9] last, for a cup of Madeira[1] and a cold
capon's leg?

PRINCE HARRY Sir John stands to° his word, the devil shall have *keeps*
105 his bargain, for he was never yet a breaker of proverbs: he will
give the devil his due.

POINS [*to* FALSTAFF] Then art thou damned for keeping thy
word with the devil.

PRINCE HARRY Else he had been damned for cozening° the *cheating*
110 devil.

POINS But my lads, my lads, tomorrow morning by four o'clock
early, at Gads Hill, there are pilgrims going to Canterbury with
rich offerings, and traders riding to London with fat purses. I
have visors° for you all; you have horses for yourselves. Gadshill *masks*

1. A biblical allusion to Proverbs 1:20–24.
2. You have a soul-endangering way of reading Scripture.
This is one of several speeches in which Falstaff uses a
language associated with Puritans.
3. By Christ's wounds (a strong oath).
4. And subject me to public disgrace. Falstaff alludes to
the practice of "baffling," in which perjured knights or
effigies of them were hung upside down in public places.
5. Allusion to 1 Corinthians 7:20 and Ephesians 4:1. Falstaff is misusing the biblical injunction to work at one's
vocation to justify robbery.
6. A thief named after Gad's Hill, the place where he

practices his robberies. This hill, near Rochester on the
road from Canterbury to London, was notorious for highway robberies.
7. By good works (as opposed to salvation by God's
grace).
8. "Jack" is a nickname for "John," but the word also
means "a drinking vessel" or "a knave." Falstaff likes sugar
in his sack, or sweet white wine.
9. The strictest of fast days in the Christian calendar.
1. A white wine exported from Madeira, an island off the
coast of west Africa.

115 lies° tonight in Rochester. I have bespoke° supper tomorrow *lodges / ordered*
night in Eastcheap.[2] We may do it as secure° as sleep. If you *safely*
will go, I will stuff your purses full of crowns; if you will not,
tarry at home and be hanged.

FALSTAFF   Hear ye, Edward, if I tarry at home and go not, I'll
120 hang you for going.

POINS   You will, chops?°   *fat cheeks*

FALSTAFF   Hal, wilt thou make one?

PRINCE HARRY   Who, I rob? I a thief? Not I, by my faith.

FALSTAFF   There's neither honesty,° manhood, nor good fellow-   *honor*
125 ship in thee, nor thou camest not of the blood royal, if thou
darest not stand for° ten shillings.[3]   *fight for; be worth*

PRINCE HARRY   Well then, once in my days I'll be a madcap.

FALSTAFF   Why, that's well said.

PRINCE HARRY   Well, come what will, I'll tarry at home.

130 FALSTAFF   By the Lord, I'll be a traitor then, when thou art king.

PRINCE HARRY   I care not.

POINS   Sir John, I prithee leave the Prince and me alone. I will
lay him down such reasons for this adventure that he shall go.

FALSTAFF   Well, God give thee the spirit of persuasion and him
135 the ears of profiting, that what thou speakest may move and
what he hears may be believed, that the true prince may, for
recreation' sake, prove a false thief; for the poor abuses of the
time want countenance.[4] Farewell. You shall find me in Eastcheap.

140 PRINCE HARRY   Farewell, the latter spring; farewell, All-hallown
summer.[5]   [*Exit* FALSTAFF]

POINS   Now, my good sweet honey lord, ride with us tomorrow.
I have a jest to execute that I cannot manage alone. Falstaff,
Peto, Bardolph, and Gadshill shall rob those men that we have
145 already waylaid—yourself and I will not be there— and when
they have the booty, if you and I do not rob them, cut this head
off from my shoulders.

PRINCE HARRY   But how shall we part with them in setting forth?

POINS   Why, we will set forth before or after them and appoint
150 them a place of meeting, wherein it is at our pleasure to fail.
And then will they adventure upon the exploit themselves,
which they shall have no sooner achieved but we'll set upon
them.

PRINCE HARRY   Ay, but 'tis like that they will know us by our
155 horses, by our habits,° and by every other appointment,° to be   *clothing / item*
ourselves.

POINS   Tut, our horses they shall not see—I'll tie them in the
wood; our visors we will change after we leave them; and, sirrah,[6] I have cases of buckram for the nonce,[7] to immask° our   *hide*
160 noted° outward garments.   *known*

PRINCE HARRY   But I doubt they will be too hard for us.[8]

POINS   Well, for two of them, I know them to be as true-bred
cowards as ever turned back; and for the third, if he fight longer

---

2. A street and market district in London, evidently the
location of the play's tavern.
3. A ten-shilling coin was called a "royal," thus punning
on the Prince's "blood royal."
4. Lack encouragement (from those of high rank).
5. Addressing Falstaff as youth in age (a second spring)
and likening him to a period of unusually mild weather

(a second summer) occurring around All Hallow's Day,
November 1.
6. A familiar form of address, conventionally used with
social inferiors.
7. I have suits of coarse cloth for the purpose.
8. But I fear they will be more than we can manage.

than he sees reason, I'll forswear arms. The virtue of this jest
165   will be the incomprehensible° lies that this same fat rogue will   *boundless*
tell us when we meet at supper: how thirty at least he fought
with, what wards,° what blows, what extremities he endured;   *parries*
and in the reproof° of this lives the jest.   *disproof*

PRINCE HARRY   Well, I'll go with thee. Provide us all things nec-
170   essary, and meet me tomorrow night in Eastcheap; there I'll
sup. Farewell.

POINS   Farewell, my lord.   *Exit*

PRINCE HARRY   I know you all, and will a while uphold
The unyoked humour° of your idleness.   *unbridled whims*
175   Yet herein will I imitate the sun,
Who doth permit the base contagious° clouds   *disease-carrying*
To smother up his beauty from the world,
That° when he please again to be himself,   *So that*
Being wanted° he may be more wondered at   *Having been missed*
180   By breaking through the foul and ugly mists
Of vapours that did seem to strangle him.
If all the year were playing holidays,
To sport would be as tedious as to work;
But when they seldom come, they wished-for come,
185   And nothing pleaseth but rare accidents.°   *exceptional events*
So when this loose behaviour I throw off
And pay the debt I never promisèd,
By how much better than my word I am,
By so much shall I falsify men's hopes;°   *expectations*
190   And like bright metal on a sullen ground,°   *dull background*
My reformation, glitt'ring o'er my fault,
Shall show more goodly and attract more eyes
Than that which hath no foil to set it off.
I'll so offend to° make offence a skill,°   *as to / an art*
195   Redeeming time[9] when men think least I will.   *Exit*

1.3

Enter the KING, [*the Earls of*] NORTHUMBERLAND [*and*]
WORCESTER, HOTSPUR, *Sir Walter* BLUNT, *with other*
[*lords*]

KING HENRY [*to* HOTSPUR, NORTHUMBERLAND, *and* WORCESTER]
My blood hath been too cold and temperate,
Unapt° to stir at these indignities,   *Slow*
And you have found me,° for accordingly   *discovered this fact*
You tread upon my patience; but be sure
5   I will from henceforth rather be myself,°   *(i.e., my royal self)*
Mighty and to be feared, than my condition,[1]
Which hath been smooth as oil, soft as young down,
And therefore lost that title of° respect   *claim to*
Which the proud soul ne'er pays but to the proud.
10   WORCESTER   Our house,[2] my sovereign liege, little deserves
The scourge of greatness to be used on it,
And that same greatness too, which our own hands
Have holp° to make so portly.°   *helped / majestic*

9. Making amends for misspent time. Injunctions to redeem time were both proverbial and biblical: see Ephesians 5:16 or Colossians 4:5.
1.3 Location: A royal residence, probably Windsor Castle.

1. My natural (mild) temperament.
2. The Percy family, which had supported Henry against Richard II.

NORTHUMBERLAND [*to the* KING]   My lord—
KING HENRY   Worcester, get thee gone, for I do see
15   Danger and disobedience in thine eye.
        O sir, your presence is too bold and peremptory,°   *proud*
        And majesty might never yet endure
        The moody frontier[3] of a servant brow.
        You have good leave° to leave us. When we need   *full permission*
20   Your use and counsel we shall send for you.   *Exit* WORCESTER
        You were about to speak.
        NORTHUMBERLAND   Yea, my good lord.
        Those prisoners in your highness' name demanded,
        Which Harry Percy here at Holmedon took,
        Were, as he says, not with such strength denied
25   As was delivered° to your majesty,   *reported*
        Who either through envy° or misprision°   *malice / error*
        Was guilty of this fault, and not my son.
        HOTSPUR [*to the* KING]   My liege, I did deny no prisoners;
        But I remember, when the fight was done,
30   When I was dry° with rage and extreme toil,   *thirsty*
        Breathless and faint, leaning upon my sword,
        Came there a certain lord, neat and trimly dressed,
        Fresh as a bridegroom, and his chin, new-reaped,[4]
        Showed° like a stubble-land at harvest-home.[5]   *Looked*
35   He was perfumèd like a milliner,[6]
        And 'twixt his finger and his thumb he held
        A pouncet-box,[7] which ever and anon
        He gave his nose and took't away again—
        Who° therewith angry, when it next came there   *(the nose)*
40   Took it in snuff[8]—and still he smiled and talked;
        And as the soldiers bore dead bodies by,
        He called them untaught knaves, unmannerly
        To bring a slovenly° unhandsome corpse   *base; nasty*
        Betwixt the wind and his nobility.
45   With many holiday and lady° terms   *dainty and effeminate*
        He questioned me; amongst the rest demanded
        My prisoners in your majesty's behalf.
        I then, all smarting with my wounds being cold—
        To be so pestered with a popinjay!°—   *parrot; vain dandy*
50   Out of my grief° and my impatience   *pain*
        Answered neglectingly,° I know not what—   *negligently*
        He should, or should not—for he made me mad
        To see him shine so brisk, and smell so sweet,
        And talk so like a waiting gentlewoman
55   Of guns, and drums, and wounds, God save the mark![9]
        And telling me the sovereign'st° thing on earth   *best*
        Was parmacity[1] for an inward bruise,
        And that it was great pity, so it was,

---

3. The angry expression (punning on "frontier" as meaning both "forehead" and "military fortifications").
4. Newly trimmed. London in the 1590s witnessed a
fashion for close-shaved beards.
5. At the end of harvest (when the fields are cut back to
stubble).
6. Seller of finely scented apparel such as bonnets, rib-
bons, and gloves. The name derives from the fact that

these goods were often imports from Milan.
7. Perfume box with a perforated lid.
8. Took offense at it; inhaled it.
9. God keep evil away (an expression of indignation).
1. Spermaceti, an oily substance from the sperm whale
that was used in various medicines and potions. The spelling "parmacity" probably derives from the ointment's
association with the Italian city of Parma.

This villainous saltpetre² should be digged
60   Out of the bowels of the harmless earth,
Which many a good tall° fellow had destroyed   *brave*
So cowardly, and but for these vile guns
He would himself have been a soldier.
This bald unjointed° chat of his, my lord,   *This trivial incoherent*
65   Made me to answer indirectly, as I said,
And I beseech you, let not his report
Come current° for an accusation   *Be taken as valid*
Betwixt my love and your high majesty.
BLUNT [*to the* KING]   The circumstance considered, good my lord,
70   Whate'er Lord Harry Percy then had said
To such a person, and in such a place,
At such a time, with all the rest retold,
May reasonably die, and never rise
To do him wrong or any way impeach
75   What then he said, so° he unsay it now.   *if*
KING HENRY   Why, yet he doth deny° his prisoners,   *refuse to hand over*
But with proviso and exception
That we at our own charge shall ransom straight°   *immediately*
His brother-in-law the foolish Mortimer,³
80   Who, on my soul, hath wilfully betrayed
The lives of those that he did lead to fight
Against that great magician, damned Glyndŵr—
Whose daughter, as we hear, the Earl of March
Hath lately married. Shall our coffers, then,
85   Be emptied to redeem a traitor home?
Shall we buy treason, and indent with fears⁴
When they have lost and forfeited themselves?
No, on the barren mountains let him starve;
For I shall never hold that man my friend
90   Whose tongue shall ask me for one penny cost
To ransom home revolted° Mortimer—   *rebellious*
HOTSPUR   Revolted Mortimer?
He never did fall off,° my sovereign liege,   *change allegiance*
But by the chance of war. To prove that true
95   Needs no more but one tongue for all those wounds,
Those mouthèd° wounds, which valiantly he took   *gaping; eloquent*
When on the gentle Severn's⁵ sedgy° bank,   *marshy*
In single opposition, hand to hand,
He did confound° the best part of an hour   *consume*
100   In changing hardiment° with great Glyndŵr.   *matching valor*
Three times they breathed,° and three times did they drink,   *rested*
Upon agreement, of swift Severn's flood,
Who, then affrighted with their bloody looks,
Ran fearfully among the trembling reeds,
105   And hid his crisp° head in the hollow bank,   *rippled*
Bloodstainèd with these valiant combatants.

---

2. The main ingredient of gunpowder.
3. Shakespeare follows Holinshed's *Chronicles* in confusing or conflating two Mortimers. One was captured by
Glyndŵr and later became Glyndŵr's son-in-law and Hotspur's brother-in-law. The other, the fifth Earl of March,
was his nephew and claimed the English throne as a
descendant of Lionel, Duke of Clarence, third son of
Edward III. This Mortimer was the one named by Richard II as his presumptive heir.
4. And bargain with those whom we have reason to fear.
5. The Severn River flows from Wales into Bristol Channel in England.

      Never did bare and rotten policy°   *cunning*
      Colour° her working with such deadly wounds,   *Disguise*
      Nor never could the noble Mortimer
110   Receive so many, and all willingly.
      Then let not him be slandered with revolt.[6]
      KING HENRY   Thou dost belie° him, Percy, thou dost belie him.   *misrepresent*
      He never did encounter with Glyndŵr. I tell thee,
      He durst as well have met the devil alone
115   As Owain Glyndŵr for an enemy.
      Art thou not ashamed? But, sirrah, henceforth
      Let me not hear you speak of Mortimer.
      Send me your prisoners with the speediest means,
      Or you shall hear in such a kind from me
120   As will displease you. — My lord Northumberland,
      We license your departure with your son.
      [*To* HOTSPUR] Send us your prisoners, or you'll hear of it.
                Exeunt [*all but* HOTSPUR *and* NORTHUMBERLAND]
      HOTSPUR   An if° the devil come and roar for them   *An if = If*
      I will not send them. I will after straight°   *go after him at once*
125   And tell him so, for I will ease my heart,
      Although it be with hazard of my head.
      NORTHUMBERLAND   What, drunk with choler?° Stay and pause awhile.   *anger*
                Enter [*the Earl of*] WORCESTER
      Here comes your uncle.
      HOTSPUR   Speak of Mortimer?
      Zounds, I will speak of him, and let my soul
130   Want mercy° if I do not join with him.   *Be damned*
      In his behalf I'll empty all these veins,
      And shed my dear blood drop by drop in the dust,
      But I will lift the downfall° Mortimer   *downfallen*
      As high in the air as this unthankful King,
135   As this ingrate and cankered° Bolingbroke.[7]   *corrupted*
      NORTHUMBERLAND [*to* WORCESTER]   Brother, the King hath
          made your nephew mad.
      WORCESTER   Who struck this heat up after I was gone?
      HOTSPUR   He will forsooth have all my prisoners;
      And when I urged the ransom once again
140   Of my wife's brother, then his cheek looked pale,
      And on my face he turned an eye of death,°   *a menacing look*
      Trembling even at the name of Mortimer.
      WORCESTER   I cannot blame him: was not he proclaimed
      By Richard, that dead is, the next of blood?°   *heir to the throne*
145   NORTHUMBERLAND   He was; I heard the proclamation.
      And then it was when the unhappy° King,   *unfortunate*
      Whose wrongs in us° God pardon, did set forth   *done by us*
      Upon his Irish expedition,[8]
      From whence he, intercepted,° did return   *interrupted*
150   To be deposed, and shortly murderèd.
      WORCESTER   And for whose death we in the world's wide mouth
      Live scandalized° and foully spoken of.   *disgraced*

---

6. With the accusation of having revolted.
7. Henry's family name. Hotspur's use of it suggests his
unwillingness to acknowledge Henry as King.

8. As Shakespeare dramatizes in *Richard II*, Bolingbroke
returned to England from exile in France while Richard
was at war in Ireland.

HOTSPUR But soft,° I pray you; did King Richard then   *wait*
    Proclaim my brother° Edmund Mortimer   *brother-in-law*
    Heir to the crown?
155 NORTHUMBERLAND   He did; myself did hear it.
HOTSPUR Nay, then I cannot blame his cousin[9] King
    That wished him on the barren mountains starve.
    But shall it be that you that set the crown
    Upon the head of this forgetful man,
160   And for his sake wear the detested blot
    Of murderous subornation,[1] shall it be
    That you a world of curses undergo,
    Being the agents or base second means,
    The cords, the ladder, or the hangman, rather?
165   O, pardon me that I descend so low
    To show the line and the predicament
    Wherein you range[2] under this subtle° King!   *cunning*
    Shall it for shame be spoken in these days,
    Or fill up chronicles in time to come,
170   That men of your nobility and power
    Did gage° them both in an unjust behalf,°   *pledge / cause*
    As both of you, God pardon it, have done:
    To put down Richard, that sweet lovely rose,
    And plant this thorn, this canker,[3] Bolingbroke?
175   And shall it in more shame be further spoken
    That you are fooled, discarded, and shook off
    By him for whom these shames ye underwent?
    No; yet time serves° wherein you may redeem   *is available*
    Your banished honours, and restore yourselves
180   Into the good thoughts of the world again,
    Revenge the jeering and disdained° contempt   *disdainful*
    Of this proud King, who studies day and night
    To answer° all the debt he owes to you   *satisfy*
    Even with the bloody payment of your deaths.
    Therefore, I say—
185 WORCESTER   Peace, cousin, say no more.
    And now I will unclasp a secret book,
    And to your quick-conceiving discontents
    I'll read you matter deep and dangerous,
    As full of peril and adventurous spirit
190   As to o'erwalk° a current roaring loud   *walk across*
    On the unsteadfast footing of a spear.
HOTSPUR If he fall in, good night, or sink or swim.[4]
    Send danger from the east unto the west,
    So° honour cross it from the north to south;   *Provided*
195   And let them grapple. O, the blood more stirs
    To rouse a lion than to start a hare!
NORTHUMBERLAND [*to* WORCESTER]   Imagination of some great exploit
    Drives him beyond the bounds of patience.
HOTSPUR By heaven, methinks it were an easy leap
200   To pluck bright honour from the pale-faced moon,

9. Punning on "cozen" (cheat).
1. Of assisting with a murder.
2. *To . . . range:* To show the degree and category into which you might be classified (with a pun on "line" as meaning "hangman's rope" and on "predicament" as meaning "an unpleasant situation").
3. Wild and inferior kind of rose; also, cankerworm (which destroys plants), or ulcerated sore.
4. Farewell to him, whether he sinks or manages to swim for a short time.

Or dive into the bottom of the deep,
Where fathom-line[5] could never touch the ground,
And pluck up drownèd honour by the locks,
So he that doth redeem her thence might wear,
205 Without corrival,° all her dignities.   *competitor*
But out upon this half-faced fellowship!°   *paltry sharing of honors*
WORCESTER [*to* NORTHUMBERLAND]   He apprehends a world of
     figures[6] here,
But not the form of what he should attend.°   *pay attention to*
[*To* HOTSPUR] Good cousin, give me audience for a while,
210 And list° to me.   *listen*
HOTSPUR   I cry you mercy.°   *I beg your pardon*
WORCESTER   Those same noble Scots[7]
   That are your prisoners—
HOTSPUR   I'll keep them all.
By God, he shall not have a Scot of them;
No, if a scot would save his soul he shall not.
I'll keep them, by this hand.
215 WORCESTER   You start away,
And lend no ear unto my purposes.
Those prisoners you shall keep.
HOTSPUR   Nay, I will; that's flat.
He said he would not ransom Mortimer,
Forbade my tongue to speak of Mortimer;
220 But I will find him when he lies asleep,
And in his ear I'll hollo 'Mortimer!'
Nay, I'll have a starling shall be taught to speak
Nothing but 'Mortimer', and give it him
To keep his anger still° in motion.   *constantly*
225 WORCESTER   Hear you, cousin, a word.
HOTSPUR   All studies here I solemnly defy,°   *renounce*
Save how to gall and pinch° this Bolingbroke.   *torture*
And that same sword-and-buckler[8] Prince of Wales—
But that I think his father loves him not
230 And would be glad he met with some mischance—
I would have him poisoned with a pot of ale.[9]
WORCESTER   Farewell, kinsman. I'll talk to you
When you are better tempered to attend.
NORTHUMBERLAND [*to* HOTSPUR]   Why, what a wasp-stung and
     impatient fool
235 Art thou to break into this woman's mood,[1]
Tying thine ear to no tongue but thine own!
HOTSPUR   Why, look you, I am whipped and scourged with rods,
Nettled and stung with pismires,° when I hear   *ants*
Of this vile politician° Bolingbroke.   *schemer*
240 In Richard's time—what d'ye call the place?
A plague upon't, it is in Gloucestershire.
'Twas where the madcap Duke his uncle kept—
His uncle York—where I first bowed my knee

---

5. A weighted line used in testing the depth of the sea.
6. Figures of speech; fantasies.
7. Inhabitants of Scotland (with a pun in the following lines on "scot" as meaning "a small sum").
8. In Elizabethan England, the sword and buckler, or small shield, were associated with ordinary fighting men. A prince should use rapier and dagger.
9. A drink associated with the common people.
1. Alluding to the commonplace that women were, by nature, unable to hold their tongues.

Unto this king of smiles, this Bolingbroke.
245 'Sblood, when you and he came back from Ravenspurgh.[2]
NORTHUMBERLAND At Berkeley castle.
HOTSPUR   You say true.
Why, what a candy deal of° courtesy   *quantity of sweet*
This fawning greyhound then did proffer me!
'Look when° his infant fortune came to age',   *Whenever; as soon as*
250 And 'gentle Harry Percy', and 'kind cousin'.
O, the devil take such cozeners!°—God forgive me.   *cheaters*
Good uncle, tell your tale; I have done.
WORCESTER Nay, if you have not, to't again.
We'll stay° your leisure.   *await*
HOTSPUR   I have done, i'faith.
255 WORCESTER Then once more to your Scottish prisoners.
Deliver them up° without their ransom straight;   *Release them*
And make the Douglas'[3] son your only mean°   *agent; means*
For powers° in Scotland, which, for divers reasons   *raising an army*
Which I shall send you written, be assured
260 Will easily be granted. [To NORTHUMBERLAND] You, my lord,
Your son in Scotland being thus employed,
Shall secretly into the bosom creep
Of that same noble prelate well-beloved,
The Archbishop.
HOTSPUR   Of York, is't not?
WORCESTER   True, who bears hard°   *resents*
265 His brother's death at Bristol, the Lord Scrope.[4]
I speak not this in estimation,°   *as a guess*
As what I think might be, but what I know
Is ruminated, plotted, and set down,
And only stays° but to behold the face   *waits*
270 Of that occasion that shall bring it on.
HOTSPUR I smell it; upon my life, it will do well!
NORTHUMBERLAND Before the game is afoot thou still lett'st slip.[5]
HOTSPUR Why, it cannot choose but be a noble plot—
And then the power° of Scotland and of York   *army*
To join with Mortimer, ha?
275 WORCESTER   And so they shall.
HOTSPUR In faith, it is exceedingly well aimed.
WORCESTER And 'tis no little reason bids us speed
To save our heads by raising of a head;°   *an army*
For, bear ourselves as even° as we can,   *carefully*
280 The King will always think him in our debt,
And think we think ourselves unsatisfied
Till he hath found a time to pay us home.°   *repay us fully*
And see already how he doth begin
To make us strangers to his looks of love.
285 HOTSPUR He does, he does. We'll be revenged on him.
WORCESTER Cousin, farewell. No further go in this
Than I by letters shall direct your course.

2. Bolingbroke's landing place at the mouth of the Humber River in Yorkshire upon his return from exile.
3. The "the" before Douglas's name indicates that he is head of a Scottish clan or noble family.
4. Richard Scroop, the Archbishop of York and an ally of the rebels in this play, was actually a distant cousin of William Scroop, Earl of Wiltshire, who was a favorite of Richard II and was executed by Henry IV in 1399. His death is mentioned in *Richard II* 3.2.
5. Before the quarry is even in the field, you always let loose the dogs. This image from hunting implies that Hotspur habitually jumps the gun.

When time is ripe, which will be suddenly,°   *soon*
I'll steal to Glyndŵr and Lord Mortimer,
290 Where you and Douglas and our powers at once,
As I will fashion it, shall happily meet,
To bear our fortunes in our own strong arms,
Which now we hold at° much uncertainty.   *with*
NORTHUMBERLAND Farewell, good brother. We shall thrive, I
    trust.
295 HOTSPUR [*to* WORCESTER] Uncle, adieu. O, let the hours be short
  Till fields° and blows and groans applaud our sport!   *battlefields*
                     Exeunt [WORCESTER *at one door,*
      NORTHUMBERLAND *and* HOTSPUR *at another door*]

2.1

Enter a CARRIER,[1] *with a lantern in his hand*
FIRST CARRIER Heigh-ho! An't° be not four by the day,° I'll be   *If it / in the morning*
  hanged. Charles's Wain[2] is over the new chimney, and yet our
  horse° not packed. What, ostler![3]   *horses*
OSTLER [*within*] Anon,° anon!   *Right away*
5 FIRST CARRIER I prithee, Tom, beat cut's saddle,[4] put a few
  flocks in the point.[5] Poor jade is wrung in the withers,[6] out of
  all cess.°   *measure*
      Enter another CARRIER
SECOND CARRIER Peas and beans° are as dank here as a dog, and   *(horse feed)*
  that is the next way to give poor jades the bots.° This house is   *intestinal worms*
10 turned upside down since Robin Ostler died.
FIRST CARRIER Poor fellow never joyed since the price of oats
  rose; it was the death of him.
SECOND CARRIER I think this be the most villainous house in all
  London road for fleas. I am stung like a tench.[7]
15 FIRST CARRIER Like a tench? By the mass, there is ne'er a king
  christen° could be better bit than I have been since the first   *Christian king*
  cock.°   *midnight*
SECOND CARRIER Why, they will allow us ne'er a jordan,° and   *chamber pot*
  then we leak° in your chimney, and your chamber-lye° breeds   *urinate / urine*
20 fleas like a loach.[8]
FIRST CARRIER What, ostler! Come away, and be hanged, come
  away!
SECOND CARRIER I have a gammon of bacon° and two races° of   *a ham / roots*
  ginger to be delivered as far as Charing Cross.[9]
25 FIRST CARRIER God's body, the turkeys in my pannier° are quite   *basket*
  starved! What, ostler! A plague on thee, hast thou never an eye
  in thy head? Canst not hear? An° 'twere not as good deed as   *If*
  drink to break the pate° on thee, I am a very villain. Come, and   *skull*
  be hanged! Hast no faith° in thee?   *responsibility*
      Enter GADSHILL

2.1 Location: An innyard in Rochester, Kent.
1. One who transports goods for hire.
2. The constellation now known as the Plough or the Great Bear.
3. One who attends to horses at an inn.
4. Soften the horse's saddle. "Cut" was a term for a horse with a docked tail or a gelding; here, it may be the horse's name.
5. Put a few tufts of wood in the saddle's pommel (to soften it).

6. The poor old horse is extremely sore in the ridge between its shoulder blades.
7. A spotted fish whose markings may have looked like flea bites.
8. A fish. The comparison means that urine breeds fleas either as a loach breeds loaches or as a loach breeds fleas. There was a popular belief that some fish spawned flies or fleas.
9. A village between London and Winchester.

30 GADSHILL   Good morrow, carriers. What's o'clock?

FIRST CARRIER   I think it be two o'clock.

GADSHILL   I prithee lend me thy lantern to see my gelding in the
stable.

FIRST CARRIER   Nay, by God, soft.° I know a trick worth two of   *wait*
35 that, i'faith.

GADSHILL [*to* SECOND CARRIER]   I pray thee, lend me thine.

SECOND CARRIER   Ay, when? Canst tell?[1] 'Lend me thy lantern,'
quoth a.° Marry, I'll see thee hanged first.   *says he*

GADSHILL   Sirrah carrier, what time do you mean to come to
40 London?

SECOND CARRIER   Time enough to go to bed with a candle, I
warrant° thee. — Come, neighbour Mugs, we'll call up the gen-   *assure*
tlemen. They will along° with company, for they have great   *travel*
charge.°   *Exeunt* [CARRIERS]   *have valuable cargo*

45 GADSHILL   What ho, chamberlain![2]

Enter CHAMBERLAIN

CHAMBERLAIN   'At hand' quoth Pickpurse.[3]

GADSHILL   That's even as fair° as '"At hand" quoth the chamber-   *good*
lain', for thou variest no more from picking of purses than giv-
ing direction doth from labouring:[4] thou layest the plot° how.   *plan*

50 CHAMBERLAIN   Good morrow, Master Gadshill. It holds current
that° I told you yesternight. There's a franklin in the Weald[5] of   *holds true what*
Kent hath brought three hundred marks[6] with him in gold. I
heard him tell it to one of his company last night at supper — a
kind of auditor, one that hath abundance of charge too, God
55 knows what. They are up already, and call for eggs and butter;
they will away presently.

GADSHILL   Sirrah, if they meet not with Saint Nicholas's clerks,[7]
I'll give thee this neck.

CHAMBERLAIN   No, I'll none of it; I pray thee keep that for the
60 hangman, for I know thou worshippest Saint Nicholas as truly
as a man of falsehood may.

GADSHILL   What talkest thou to me of the hangman? If I hang,
I'll make a fat pair of gallows, for if I hang, old Sir John hangs
with me, and thou knowest he's no starveling. Tut, there are
65 other Trojans[8] that thou dreamest not of, the which° for sport'   *who*
sake are content to do the profession° some grace, that would,   *(of robbery)*
if matters should be looked into, for their own credit' sake make
all whole.° I am joined with no foot-landrakers,[9] no long-staff   *set things right*
sixpenny strikers,[1] none of these mad mustachio purple-hued
70 maltworms,[2] but with nobility and tranquillity, burgomasters
and great 'oyez'-ers;[3] such as can hold in,° such as will strike   *can keep a secret*
sooner than speak, and speak sooner than drink, and drink
sooner than pray. And yet, zounds, I lie, for they pray continu-

1. A retort similar to "Never."
2. Bedroom attendant. In popular discourse, chamber-lains were notorious for their complicity with thieves.
3. "I am at your disposal," as the thief said (evidently a popular tag).
4. For you are not more different from a pickpocket than an overseer is from a laborer.
5. There's a small landowner in the wooded region.
6. Coins worth two-thirds of a pound each.
7. Slang for "highway robbers." St. Nicholas was variously regarded as the patron saint of travelers and of thieves.
8. Slang for "roisterers."
9. Highwaymen who travel on foot (rather than on horse).
1. Thieves who carried crude weapons and robbed for small sums.
2. These drunkards with wild mustaches and purple faces.
3. Court officials who cried "Oyez," or "Hear ye."

ally to their saint the commonwealth; or rather, not pray to her,
but prey on her; for they ride up and down[4] on her and make
her their boots.°   *booty; footwear*

CHAMBERLAIN What, the commonwealth their boots? Will she
hold out water in foul way?[5]

GADSHILL She will, she will, justice hath liquored her.[6] We steal
as in a castle,° cocksure; we have the recipe of fern-seed,[7] we   *in complete safety*
walk invisible.

CHAMBERLAIN Nay, by my faith, I think you are more beholden
to the night than to fern-seed for your walking invisible.

GADSHILL Give me thy hand; thou shalt have a share in our
purchase,° as I am a true man.   *plunder*

CHAMBERLAIN Nay, rather let me have it as you are a false thief.

GADSHILL Go to, 'homo'° is a common name to all men. Bid the   *man*
ostler bring my gelding out of the stable. Farewell, you muddy°   *stupid*
knave.   *Exeunt [severally]°*   *separately*

2.2

Enter PRINCE [HARRY], POINS, PETO [*and* BARDOLPH][1]

POINS Come, shelter, shelter!

          [*Exeunt* PETO *and* BARDOLPH *at another door*]
I have removed Falstaff's horse, and he frets° like a gummed   *worries; frays*
velvet.[2]

PRINCE HARRY Stand close!°   [*Exit* POINS]   *concealed*
          Enter FALSTAFF

FALSTAFF Poins! Poins, and be hanged! Poins!

PRINCE HARRY Peace, ye fat-kidneyed rascal! What a brawling
dost thou keep!

FALSTAFF Where's Poins, Hal?

PRINCE HARRY He is walked up to the top of the hill. I'll go seek
him.   [*Exit*]

FALSTAFF I am accursed to rob in that thief's company. The
rascal hath removed my horse and tied him I know not where.
If I travel but four foot by the square° further afoot, I shall break   *(a measuring tool)*
my wind.° Well, I doubt not but to die a fair death, for[3] all   *be breathless; fart*
this—if I scape hanging for killing that rogue. I have forsworn
his company hourly any time this two-and-twenty years, and yet
I am bewitched with the rogue's company. If the rascal have
not given me medicines° to make me love him, I'll be hanged.   *love potions*
It could not be else: I have drunk medicines. Poins! Hal! A
plague upon you both! Bardolph! Peto! I'll starve ere I'll rob a
foot further. An 'twere not as good a deed as drink to turn true
man° and to leave these rogues, I am the veriest varlet that ever   *repent; turn informer*
chewed with a tooth. Eight yards of uneven ground is three-
score and ten miles afoot with me, and the stony-hearted villains know it well enough. A plague upon't when thieves cannot be true one to another!

---

4. They travel (with a pun on "ride" as meaning "to
mount sexually").
5. Will she keep water out (off your feet) on a muddy
road; will she protect you in difficulty?
6. Greased her (as one waterproofs leather); bribed her.
7. Popularly supposed to make those who wore it invisible.

2.2 Location: The highway, Gad's Hill.
1. For a discussion of the names of "Bardolph" and
"Peto," see the Textual Note and Introduction.
2. Like cheap velvet treated with gum. Gummed velvet
was shiny but wore out quickly.
3. Die a natural death, despite.

They whistle. [Enter PRINCE HARRY, POINS, PETO, *and*
BARDOLPH]⁴

Whew! A plague upon you all! Give me my horse, you rogues,
give me my horse, and be hanged!

PRINCE HARRY   Peace, ye fat-guts. Lie down, lay thine ear close
30   to the ground, and list if thou canst hear the tread of travellers.

FALSTAFF   Have you any levers to lift me up again, being down?
'Sblood, I'll not bear my own flesh so far afoot again for all the
coin in thy father's exchequer. What a plague mean ye to colt°   trick
me thus?

35   PRINCE HARRY   Thou liest: thou art not colted, thou art uncolted.°   unhorsed

FALSTAFF   I prithee, good Prince Hal, help me to my horse, good
king's son.

PRINCE HARRY   Out, ye rogue, shall I be your ostler?

FALSTAFF   Hang thyself in thine own heir-apparent garters!⁵ If I
40   be ta'en, I'll peach° for this. An I have not ballads made on you   inform against you
all and sung to filthy tunes,⁶ let a cup of sack be my poison.
When a jest is so forward, and afoot too!⁷ I hate it.

Enter GADSHILL *[visored]*°   wearing a mask

GADSHILL   Stand!

FALSTAFF   So I do, against my will.

45   POINS   O, 'tis our setter,° I know his voice. Gadshill, what news?   one who sets up a crime

GADSHILL⁸   Case ye,° case ye, on with your visors! There's money   Disguise yourselves
of the King's coming down the hill; 'tis going to the King's
exchequer.

FALSTAFF   You lie, ye rogue, 'tis going to the King's tavern.

50   GADSHILL   There's enough to make° us all.   make fortunes for

FALSTAFF   To be hanged.

[They put on visors]

PRINCE HARRY   Sirs, you four shall front° them in the narrow   confront
lane. Ned Poins and I will walk lower. If they scape from your
encounter, then they light on us.

55   PETO   How many be there of them?

GADSHILL   Some eight or ten.

FALSTAFF   Zounds, will they not rob us?

PRINCE HARRY   What, a coward, Sir John Paunch?

FALSTAFF   Indeed I am not John of Gaunt⁹ your grandfather, but
60   yet no coward, Hal.

PRINCE HARRY   Well, we leave that to the proof.°   test

POINS   Sirrah Jack, thy horse stands behind the hedge. When
thou needest him, there thou shalt find him. Farewell, and
stand fast.

65   FALSTAFF   Now cannot I strike him if I should be hanged.

PRINCE HARRY *[aside to* POINS*]*   Ned, where are our disguises?

POINS *[aside to the* PRINCE*]*   Here, hard by. Stand close.

---

4. It is not clear exactly when the Prince and his companions show themselves to the frustrated Falstaff. They can
all enter here, or the Prince and Poins could enter at line
28 and Bardolph and Peto at the same time as Gadshill at
line 42.
5. Falstaff's version of the proverb "He may hang himself
in his own garters." As the heir to the throne, the Prince
was a member of the Order of the Garter, the highest
order of English knighthood.
6. Ballads on topical themes were sung by ballad singers
and sold cheaply as broadsides in streets, theaters, and
other public places.

7. When a plot (to rob) is so advanced and goes so well;
when a joke (on me) goes so far and makes me go on foot.
8. In Q, this speech is assigned to Bardolph; but Poins
has just asked Gadshill a question, so one expects an
answer to come from him. It has been conjectured that
the confusion here may reflect confusion in Shakespeare's foul papers about whether Bardolph and Gadshill
were to be two characters or one. See note to 2.5.159.
9. Henry IV's father. Falstaff puns on "Gaunt" as meaning "lean"; in fact, his name is derived from "Ghent," his
birthplace.

[Exeunt the PRINCE *and* POINS]

FALSTAFF   Now, my masters, happy man be his dole,[1] say I; every
man to his business.

[They stand aside.]
Enter the TRAVELLERS *[amongst them the* CARRIERS]

70   FIRST TRAVELLER   Come, neighbour, the boy shall lead our
horses down the hill. We'll walk afoot a while, and ease their
legs.

THIEVES *[coming forward]*   Stand!

SECOND TRAVELLER   Jesus bless us!

75   FALSTAFF   Strike, down with them, cut the villains' throats! Ah,
whoreson caterpillars,[2] bacon-fed knaves! They hate us youth.
Down with them, fleece them!

FIRST TRAVELLER   O, we are undone, both we and ours for ever!

FALSTAFF   Hang ye, gorbellied° knaves, are ye undone? No, ye   *pot-bellied*
80   fat chuffs;[3] I would your store° were here. On, bacons,° on!   *all you own / fat men*
What, ye knaves! Young men must live. You are grand-jurors,[4]
are ye? We'll jure ye, faith.

Here they rob them and bind them. Exeunt [the THIEVES
with the TRAVELLERS]

2.3

Enter PRINCE *[*HARRY*] and* POINS *[disguised in buckram
suits]*

PRINCE HARRY   The thieves have bound the true° men; now   *honest*
could thou and I rob the thieves, and go merrily to London. It
would be argument° for a week, laughter for a month, and a   *topic for discussion*
good jest for ever.

5   POINS   Stand close; I hear them coming.

[They stand aside]
*Enter [*FALSTAFF, BARDOLPH, PETO, *and* GADSHILL, *with
the travellers' money]*

FALSTAFF   Come, my masters, let us share, and then to horse
before day. An° the Prince and Poins be not two arrant cowards,   *If*
there's no equity stirring.° There's no more valour in that Poins   *justice to be found*
than in a wild duck.

As they are sharing, the PRINCE *and* POINS *set upon
them*

10   PRINCE HARRY   Your money!

POINS   Villains!

*They all [*GADSHILL, BARDOLPH, *and* PETO] *run away
[severally] and* FALSTAFF, *after a blow or two, [roars and]
runs away too, leaving the booty behind them*

PRINCE HARRY   Got with much ease. Now merrily to horse.
The thieves are all scattered, and possessed with fear
So strongly that they dare not meet each other.

15   Each takes his fellow for an officer.
Away, good Ned. Falstaff sweats to death,
And lards° the lean earth as he walks along.   *drips fat on*
Were't not for laughing, I should pity him.

POINS   How the fat rogue roared!   *Exeunt [with the booty]*

---

1. Proverbial expression meaning "Good luck to
everyone."
2. Parasites. *whoreson:* an insult derived from "whore's
son."
3. Country bumpkins; misers.
4. Referring to the fact that only prosperous citizens
served on grand juries.
2.3 Location: Scene continues.

2.4

Enter HOTSPUR, *reading a letter*

HOTSPUR 'But for mine own part, my lord, I could be well contented to be there, in respect of the love I bear your house.'°—   *family*
He could be contented; why is he not then? In respect of the
love he bears our house! He shows in this he loves his own
5   barn better than he loves our house. Let me see some more.—
'The purpose you undertake is dangerous'— Why, that's certain: 'tis dangerous to take a cold, to sleep, to drink; but I tell
you, my lord fool, out of this nettle danger we pluck this flower
safety.— 'The purpose you undertake is dangerous, the friends
10   you have named uncertain, the time itself unsorted,° and your   *unsuitable*
whole plot too light for the counterpoise of° so great an opposi-   *to counterbalance*
tion.'— Say you so, say you so? I say unto you again, you are a
shallow, cowardly hind,° and you lie. What a lack-brain is this!   *peasant*
By the Lord, our plot is a good plot as ever was laid, our friends
15   true and constant; a good plot, good friends, and full of expectation; an excellent plot, very good friends. What a frosty-spirited
rogue is this! Why, my lord of York° commends the plot and   *(Archbishop Scrope)*
the general course of the action. Zounds, an I were now by this
rascal, I could brain him with his lady's fan! Is there not my
20   father, my uncle, and myself? Lord Edmund Mortimer, my
lord of York, and Owain Glyndŵr? Is there not besides the
Douglas? Have I not all their letters, to meet me in arms by the
ninth of the next month? And are they not some of them set
forward already? What a pagan rascal is this, an infidel! Ha,
25   you shall see now, in very sincerity of fear and cold heart will
he to the King, and lay open all our proceedings! O, I could
divide myself and go to buffets[1] for moving° such a dish of   *urging*
skim-milk with so honourable an action! Hang him! Let him
tell the King we are prepared; I will set forward tonight.

Enter his Lady [LADY PERCY]

30   How now, Kate? I must leave you within these two hours.
LADY PERCY O my good lord, why are you thus alone?
For what offence have I this fortnight been
A banished woman from my Harry's bed?
Tell me, sweet lord, what is't that takes from thee
35   Thy stomach,° pleasure, and thy golden sleep?   *appetite*
Why dost thou bend thine eyes upon the earth,
And start so often when thou sitt'st alone?
Why hast thou lost the fresh blood in thy cheeks,
And given my treasures and my rights[2] of thee
40   To thick-eyed° musing and curst melancholy?   *vacantly staring*
In thy faint° slumbers I by thee have watched,   *restless*
And heard thee murmur tales of iron wars,
Speak terms of manège° to thy bounding steed,   *horsemanship*
Cry 'Courage! To the field!' And thou hast talked
45   Of sallies and retires,° of trenches, tents,   *advances and retreats*
Of palisadoes,[3] frontiers,° parapets,   *ramparts*

2.4 Location: The Percys' home, Warkworth Castle, in
Northumberland.
1. I could split myself into two and fall to blows with
myself.
2. Marriage rights. Alluding to the belief that husbands

and wives owe a mutual marriage debt that obliges them
regularly to engage in sexual relations with one another.
3. Pointed stakes driven into the ground as defensive barriers.

Of basilisks, of cannon, culverin,[4]
Of prisoners ransomed, and of soldiers slain,
And all the currents of a heady° fight.   *headlong*
50   Thy spirit within thee hath been so at war,
And thus hath so bestirred thee in thy sleep,
That beads of sweat have stood upon thy brow
Like bubbles in a late-disturbèd° stream;   *recently disturbed*
And in thy face strange motions have appeared,
55   Such as we see when men restrain their breath
On some great sudden hest.° O, what portents are these?   *command*
Some heavy° business hath my lord in hand,   *serious; sad*
And I must know it, else he loves me not.
HOTSPUR   What ho!
                    [*Enter* SERVANT]
                        Is Gilliams with the packet gone?
60   SERVANT   He is, my lord, an hour ago.
HOTSPUR   Hath Butler brought those horses from the sheriff?
SERVANT   One horse, my lord, he brought even now.
HOTSPUR   What horse? A roan, a crop-ear, is it not?
SERVANT   It is, my lord.
HOTSPUR   That roan shall be my throne.
65   Well, I will back him straight.—O, *Esperance!*[5]—
Bid Butler lead him forth into the park.
LADY PERCY   But hear you, my lord.
HOTSPUR   What sayst thou, my lady?
LADY PERCY   What is it carries you away?
HOTSPUR   Why, my horse,
My love, my horse.
LADY PERCY   Out, you mad-headed ape!
70   A weasel hath not such a deal of spleen°   *impulsiveness; anger*
As you are tossed with.
In faith, I'll know your business, Harry, that I will.
I fear my brother Mortimer doth stir
About his title, and hath sent for you
75   To line° his enterprise; but if you go—   *strengthen*
HOTSPUR   So far afoot? I shall be weary, love.
LADY PERCY   Come, come, you paraquito,° answer me   *little parrot*
Directly to this question that I ask.
In faith, I'll break thy little finger,° Harry,   *(euphemism for "penis")*
80   An if thou wilt not tell me all things true.
HOTSPUR   Away, away, you trifler! Love? I love thee not,
I care not for thee, Kate. This is no world
To play with maumets[6] and to tilt° with lips.   *duel*
We must have bloody noses and cracked crowns,[7]
85   And pass them current,[8] too. God's me,° my horse!—   *God save me*
What sayst thou, Kate? What wouldst thou have with me?
LADY PERCY   Do you not love me? Do you not indeed?
Well, do not, then, for since you love me not

---

4. *basilisks*: large cannons, named after a deadly mythological reptile. *culverin*: a name for both a kind of long
cannon and a firearm noted for its ability to fire over a
long range.
5. Referring to the Percy motto, *Esperance ma comforte,*
or "Hope is my reliance."
6. Breasts; dolls; false gods. The term derived from
"mahomet," whom English Protestants viewed as a false

god worshipped by heathen peoples.
7. Punning on "cracked crowns" as meaning "broken
heads" and "counterfeit currency." Hotspur may be alluding to the acts of rape associated with warfare: "nose" is
slang for "penis," and a "cracked crown" can mean a
"whore" or "deflowered woman."
8. Establish them as the norm; let them circulate.

I will not love myself. Do you not love me?
90 Nay, tell me if you speak in jest or no.
HOTSPUR   Come, wilt thou see me ride?
And when I am a-horseback,[9] I will swear
I love thee infinitely. But hark you, Kate.
I must not have you henceforth question me
95 Whither I go, nor reason whereabout.°   *discuss about what*
Whither I must, I must; and, to conclude,
This evening must I leave you, gentle Kate.
I know you wise, but yet no farther wise
Than Harry Percy's wife; constant you are,
100 But yet a woman;[1] and for secrecy
No lady closer,° for I well believe   *more secretive*
Thou wilt not utter what thou dost not know.
And so far will I trust thee, gentle Kate.
LADY PERCY   How, so far?
105 HOTSPUR   Not an inch further. But hark you, Kate,
Whither I go, thither shall you go too.
Today will I set forth, tomorrow you.
Will this content you, Kate?
LADY PERCY   It must, of force.°   *Exeunt*   *of necessity*

2.5

Enter PRINCE [HARRY]

PRINCE HARRY   Ned, prithee come out of that fat° room, and lend   *stuffy*
me thy hand to laugh a little.
    Enter POINS [*at another door*]
POINS   Where hast been, Hal?
PRINCE HARRY   With three or four loggerheads,° amongst three   *blockheads*
5 or fourscore hogsheads.° I have sounded the very bass-string of   *casks for liquor*
humility. Sirrah, I am sworn brother to a leash of drawers,° and   *set of three tapsters*
can call them all by their christen names, as 'Tom', 'Dick', and
'Francis'. They take it already, upon their salvation, that though
I be but Prince of Wales yet I am the king of courtesy, and tell
10 me flatly I am no proud jack° like Falstaff, but a Corinthian,[1] a   *fellow*
lad of mettle, a good boy—by the Lord, so they call me; and
when I am King of England I shall command all the good lads
in Eastcheap. They call drinking deep 'dyeing scarlet',[2] and
when you breathe in your watering[3] they cry 'Hem!' and bid
15 you 'Play it off!'° To conclude, I am so good a proficient in one   *Drink up*
quarter of an hour that I can drink with any tinker in his own
language during my life. I tell thee, Ned, thou hast lost much
honour that thou wert not with me in this action. But, sweet
Ned—to sweeten which name of Ned I give thee this penny-
20 worth of sugar,[4] clapped even now into my hand by an under-
skinker,° one that never spake other English in his life than   *assistant tapster*
'Eight shillings and sixpence', and 'You are welcome', with this
shrill addition, 'Anon,° anon, sir! Score° a pint of bastard[5] in   *At once / Chalk up*

---

9. On my horse; having sexual intercourse.
1. Women were assumed to be great talkers who could keep no secrets.
2.5 Location: An inn in Eastcheap, London.
1. A rich, licentious man. In contemporary texts, ancient Corinth was famous for wealth and sensuality.
2. Referring to the ruddy complexion associated with

drunkards or to the fact that urine, a product of drink, was used to dye wool.
3. When you pause to breathe in your drink.
4. Tapsters sold sugar to sweeten wine.
5. A Spanish wine, so named because it was mixed or adulterated with honey.

the Half-moon!'[6] or so. But, Ned, to drive away the time till
Falstaff come, I prithee do thou stand in some by-room, while
I question my puny° drawer to what end he gave me the sugar, *inexperienced*
and do thou never leave calling 'Francis!', that his tale to me
may be nothing but 'Anon!' Step aside, and I'll show thee a
precedent.°   [*Exit* POINS] *give you a foretaste*

POINS [*within*] Francis!
PRINCE HARRY Thou art perfect.
POINS [*within*] Francis!
          Enter [FRANCIS, *a*] *drawer*
FRANCIS Anon, anon, sir!—Look down into the Pomegranate,[7]
Ralph!
PRINCE HARRY Come hither, Francis.
FRANCIS My lord.
PRINCE HARRY How long hast thou to serve,[8] Francis?
FRANCIS Forsooth, five years, and as much as to—
POINS [*within*] Francis!
FRANCIS Anon, anon, sir!
PRINCE HARRY Five year! By'r Lady,[9] a long lease for the clinking
of pewter. But Francis, darest thou be so valiant as to play the
coward with thy indenture,° and show it a fair pair of heels, and *contract*
run from it?
FRANCIS O Lord, sir, I'll be sworn upon all the books° in *(Bibles)*
England, I could find in my heart— →never answers the question. leaves his interpretation open.
POINS [*within*] Francis!
FRANCIS Anon, sir!
PRINCE HARRY How old art thou, Francis?
FRANCIS Let me see, about Michaelmas[1] next I shall be—
POINS [*within*] Francis!
FRANCIS Anon, sir! [*To the* PRINCE] Pray, stay a little, my lord.
PRINCE HARRY Nay, but hark you, Francis. For the sugar thou
gavest me, 'twas a pennyworth, was't not?
FRANCIS O Lord, I would it had been two!
PRINCE HARRY I will give thee for it a thousand pound. Ask me
when thou wilt, and thou shalt have it—
POINS [*within*] Francis!
FRANCIS Anon, anon!
PRINCE HARRY Anon, Francis? No, Francis, but tomorrow, Fran-
cis; or, Francis, o' Thursday; or, indeed, Francis, when thou
wilt. But Francis.
FRANCIS My lord.
PRINCE HARRY Wilt thou rob this leathern-jerkin, crystal-button,
knot-pated, agate-ring, puke-stocking, caddis-garter, smooth-
tongue, Spanish-pouch?[2]
FRANCIS O Lord, sir, who do you mean?
PRINCE HARRY Why, then, your brown bastard is your only

---

6. Name of the inn room to which the wine is to be
charged.
7. Name of another room in the inn.
8. Serve as apprentice. Apprenticeship typically began at
age twelve or fourteen and lasted seven years.
9. By our Lady (an oath invoking the Virgin Mary).
1. September 29, a holy day honoring the archangel
Michael and signifying to tradespeople the close of an
accounting period.
2. Referring (satirically) to Francis's employer, who would

be robbed of Francis's labor if the apprentice were to run
away. This employer is imagined as dressing in the manner of an upwardly mobile Londoner, wearing a leather
jacket ("jerkin") with crystal buttons and keeping his hair
close-cropped ("knot-pated"). He also wears a signet ring
with a carved agate, dark ("puke") stockings, and garters
made from caddis ribbon (a cheaper alternative to silk).
He has a simpering style of speech and carries a vintner's
pouch made of Spanish leather.

drink!³ For look you, Francis, your white canvas doublet will
70 sully.° In Barbary,⁴ sir, it cannot come to° so much.   *get dirty / be worth*
FRANCIS What, sir?
POINS [*within*] Francis!
PRINCE HARRY Away, you rogue! Dost thou not hear them call?
     [*As he departs* POINS *and the* PRINCE] *both call him.*
     The Drawer stands amazed, not knowing which way to go.
     Enter VINTNER°   *Innkeeper*
VINTNER What, standest thou still, and hearest such a calling?
75 Look to the guests within.   [*Exit* FRANCIS]
     My lord, old Sir John with half a dozen more are at the door.
     Shall I let them in?
PRINCE HARRY Let them alone a while, and then open the door.
                                                    [*Exit* VINTNER]
     Poins!
80 POINS [*within*] Anon, anon, sir!
     Enter POINS
PRINCE HARRY Sirrah, Falstaff and the rest of the thieves are at
     the door. Shall we be merry?
POINS As merry as crickets, my lad. But hark ye, what cunning
     match° have you made with this jest of the drawer? Come,   *game*
85 what's the issue?°   *outcome*
PRINCE HARRY I am now of all humours that have showed them-
     selves humours⁵ since the old days of goodman° Adam to the   *(title for a farmer)*
     pupil° age of this present twelve o'clock at midnight.   *youthful*
     [*Enter* FRANCIS]
     What's o'clock, Francis?
90 FRANCIS Anon, anon, sir!   [*Exit at another door*]
PRINCE HARRY That ever this fellow should have fewer words
     than a parrot, and yet the son of a woman! His industry is
     upstairs and downstairs, his eloquence the parcel of a reckon-
     ing.° I am not yet of Percy's mind, the Hotspur of the North—   *items of a bill*
95 he that kills me° some six or seven dozen of Scots at a breakfast, *he that slays*
     washes his hands, and says to his wife, 'Fie upon this quiet life!
     I want work.' 'O my sweet Harry,' says she, 'how many hast
     thou killed today?' 'Give my roan horse a drench,'° says he, and *dose of medicine*
     answers, 'Some fourteen,' an hour after; 'a trifle, a trifle.' I
100 prithee call in Falstaff. I'll play Percy, and that damned brawn°   *fat boar*
     shall play Dame Mortimer his wife. 'Rivo!'⁶ says the drunkard.
     Call in Ribs, call in Tallow.°   *fat drippings*
     Enter FALSTAFF [*with sword and buckler,* BARDOLPH,
     PETO, *and* GADSHILL, *followed by* FRANCIS, *with wine*]
POINS Welcome, Jack. Where hast thou been?
FALSTAFF A plague of all cowards, I say, and a vengeance too,
105 marry and amen!—Give me a cup of sack, boy.—Ere I lead
     this life long, I'll sew netherstocks,° and mend them and foot° *stockings / make a new foot f*
     them too. A plague of all cowards!—Give me a cup of sack,
     rogue. Is there no virtue extant?
     He drinketh

---

3. The best of all drinks; the only drink you'll get (if you
stay in the tavern). This entire speech seems meant to
mystify Francis while obliquely warning him that he will
get dirty and be poor if he fulfills his apprenticeship.
4. North African region from which England acquired
sugar.

5. That is, I am in the mood for anything. Renaissance
medical theory held that four body fluids, or humors,
determined by their relative proportions the health, temperament, and moods of an individual.
6. An exclamation associated with boisterous drinking.

PRINCE HARRY   Didst thou never see Titan° kiss a dish of butter *the sun*
110 pitiful hearted Titan—that melted at the sweet tale of the sun's?
If thou didst, then behold that compound.[7]
FALSTAFF [*to* FRANCIS]   You rogue, here's lime[8] in this sack too.
There is nothing but roguery to be found in villainous man,
yet a coward is worse than a cup of sack with lime in it.
[*Exit* FRANCIS][9]
115 A villainous coward! Go thy ways, old Jack, die when thou wilt.
If manhood, good manhood, be not forgot upon the face of the
earth, then am I a shotten herring.[1] There lives not three good
men unhanged in England, and one of them is fat and grows
old, God help the while.° A bad world, I say. I would I were a *these times*
120 weaver[2]—I could sing psalms, or anything. A plague of all cowards, I say still.
PRINCE HARRY   How now, woolsack, what mutter you?
FALSTAFF   A king's son! If I do not beat thee out of thy kingdom
with a dagger of lath,[3] and drive all thy subjects afore thee like
125 a flock of wild geese, I'll never wear hair on my face more. You,
Prince of Wales!
PRINCE HARRY   Why, you whoreson round man, what's the
matter?
FALSTAFF   Are not you a coward? Answer me to that. And Poins
130 there?
POINS   Zounds, ye fat paunch, an ye call me coward, by the Lord
I'll stab thee.
FALSTAFF   I call thee coward? I'll see thee damned ere I call thee
coward, but I would give a thousand pound I could run as fast
135 as thou canst. You are straight enough in the shoulders; you
care not who sees your back. Call you that backing of your
friends? A plague upon such backing! Give me them that will
face me. Give me a cup of sack. I am a rogue if I drunk today.
PRINCE HARRY   O villain, thy lips are scarce wiped since thou
140 drunkest last.
FALSTAFF   All is one for that.° *It doesn't matter*
He drinketh
A plague of all cowards, still say I.
PRINCE HARRY   What's the matter?
FALSTAFF   What's the matter? There be four of us here have ta'en
145 a thousand pound this day morning.° *this morning*
PRINCE HARRY   Where is it, Jack, where is it?
FALSTAFF   Where is it? Taken from us it is. A hundred upon poor
four of us.
PRINCE HARRY   What, a hundred, man?
150 FALSTAFF   I am a rogue if I were not at half-sword° with a dozen *dueling closely*
of them, two hours together. I have scaped by miracle. I am
eight times thrust through the doublet,° four through the hose,° *short jacket / breeches*
my buckler° cut through and through, my sword hacked like a *shield*
handsaw. *Ecce signum*.[4]

7. Combination; that is, the melted butter (referring to Falstaff).
8. Often added to bad wine to make it dry and sparkling.
9. Neither Q nor F indicates when Francis leaves the stage. He plays no further part in the action after this, so an exit here avoids the problem of having a character onstage with no obvious function.
1. A herring that has spawned its roe and is thus very thin.

2. Weavers were reputed to sing the Psalms of the Bible at work. Many were Puritans, and some had emigrated from the zealously Protestant Low Countries.
3. A wooden dagger, which was the weapon associated with the Vice figure in medieval morality plays (see note to line 413).
4. Behold the evidence (Latin).

[*He shows his sword*]

155 I never dealt better since I was a man. All would not do.⁵ A
plague of all cowards! [*Pointing to* GADSHILL, PETO, *and* BAR-
DOLPH] Let them speak. If they speak more or less than truth,
they are villains and the sons of darkness.

PRINCE HARRY⁶   Speak, sirs, how was it?

160 GADSHILL   We four set upon some dozen—

FALSTAFF [*to the* PRINCE]   Sixteen at least, my lord.

GADSHILL   And bound them.

PETO   No, no, they were not bound.

FALSTAFF   You rogue, they were bound every man of them, or I
165   am a Jew else, an Hebrew Jew.

GADSHILL   As we were sharing, some six or seven fresh men set
upon us.

FALSTAFF   And unbound the rest; and then come in the other.

PRINCE HARRY   What, fought you with them all?

170 FALSTAFF   All? I know not what you call all, but if I fought not
with fifty of them, I am a bunch of radish. If there were not
two- or three-and-fifty upon poor old Jack, then am I no two-
legged creature.

PRINCE HARRY   Pray God you have not murdered some of them.

175 FALSTAFF   Nay, that's past praying for. I have peppered° two of   *made it hot for*
them. Two I am sure I have paid°—two rogues in buckram   *killed*
suits. I tell thee what, Hal, if I tell thee a lie, spit in my face,
call me horse. Thou knowest my old ward°—   *posture of defense*
[*He stands as to fight*]
here I lay,° and thus I bore my point.° Four rogues in buckram   *stood / sword point*
180   let drive at me.

PRINCE HARRY   What, four? Thou saidst but two even now.

FALSTAFF   Four, Hal, I told thee four.

POINS   Ay, ay, he said four.

FALSTAFF   These four came all afront,° and mainly° thrust at me.   *abreast / mightily*
185   I made me no more ado, but took all their seven points in my
target,° thus.   *shield*
[*He wards himself with his buckler*]

PRINCE HARRY   Seven? Why, there were but four even now.

FALSTAFF   In buckram?

POINS   Ay, four in buckram suits.

190 FALSTAFF   Seven, by these hilts,° or I am a villain else.   *sword handle*

PRINCE HARRY [*aside to* POINS]   Prithee, let him alone. We shall
have more anon.

FALSTAFF   Dost thou hear me, Hal?

PRINCE HARRY   Ay, and mark° thee too, Jack.   *pay attention to; count*

195 FALSTAFF   Do so, for it is worth the listening to. These nine in
buckram that I told thee of—

PRINCE HARRY [*aside to* POINS]   So, two more already.

FALSTAFF   Their points⁷ being broken—

POINS [*aside to the* PRINCE]   Down fell their hose.

200 FALSTAFF   Began to give me ground. But I followed me° close,   *I followed*

---

5. All I did was not enough; the whole group was insuffi-
cient opposition.
6. This is a second place (see 2.2.46) where textual confusion surrounds the character of Gadshill. In Q, this line
is assigned to Gadshill and the following line to Russell
(whose name was changed to "Bardolph" as a result of
censorship; see Introduction). In F, this line is assigned to

the Prince and the following line to Gadshill. The next
two speeches here assigned to Gadshill were also given to
Russell in Q. The F assignment of these lines to Gadshill
may indicate that at some point Shakespeare divided
between two characters a role originally designed for one.
7. Sword points, but Poins takes it as meaning "fastenings
for hose."

came in foot and hand, and, with a thought,° seven of the eleven
I paid.

swift as thought

PRINCE HARRY [*aside to* POINS] O monstrous! Eleven buckram
men grown out of two!

205 FALSTAFF But, as the devil would have it, three misbegotten
knaves in Kendal green[8] came at my back and let drive at me;
for it was so dark, Hal, that thou couldst not see thy hand.

PRINCE HARRY These lies are like their father that begets them—
gross as a mountain, open, palpable. Why, thou clay-brained
210 guts, thou knotty-pated° fool, thou whoreson obscene greasy
tallow-catch[9]—

blockheaded

FALSTAFF What, art thou mad? Art thou mad? Is not the truth
the truth?

PRINCE HARRY Why, how couldst thou know these men in Ken-
215 dal green when it was so dark thou couldst not see thy hand?
Come, tell us your reason. What sayst thou to this?

POINS Come, your reason, Jack, your reason.

FALSTAFF What, upon compulsion? Zounds, an I were at the
strappado,[1] or all the racks[2] in the world, I would not tell you
220 on compulsion. Give you a reason on compulsion? If reasons
were as plentiful as blackberries, I would give no man a reason
upon compulsion, I.

PRINCE HARRY I'll be no longer guilty of this sin. This sanguine°
coward, this bed-presser,° this horse-back-breaker, this huge hill
225 of flesh—

red-faced
licentious man

FALSTAFF 'Sblood, you starveling, you elf-skin, you dried neat's°
tongue, you bull's pizzle, you stock-fish[3]—O, for breath to utter
what is like thee!— you tailor's yard,[4] you sheath, you bow-
case, you vile standing tuck[5]—

ox's

230 PRINCE HARRY Well, breathe awhile, and then to't again, and
when thou hast tired thyself in base comparisons, hear me
speak but this.

POINS Mark, Jack.

PRINCE HARRY We two saw you four set on four, and bound
235 them, and were masters of their wealth.—Mark now how a
plain tale shall put you down.—Then did we two set on you
four, and, with a word, outfaced you from your prize, and have
it; yea, and can show it you here in the house. And Falstaff,
you carried your guts away as nimbly, with as quick dexterity,
240 and roared for mercy, and still run and roared, as ever I heard
bull-calf. What a slave art thou, to hack thy sword as thou hast
done, and then say it was in fight! What trick, what device,
what starting-hole° canst thou now find out to hide thee from
this open and apparent shame?

refuge

245 POINS Come, let's hear, Jack; what trick hast thou now?

FALSTAFF By the Lord, I knew ye as well as he that made ye.

8. A coarse green cloth made in Kendal, Cumbria. It was associated with poor country people, especially forest dwellers, as well as outlaws.
9. Greasy lump of fat (gathered by butchers for candle making),.
1. A torture device in which victims were lifted off the ground by ropes attached to their hands, which were tied behind their backs, and then let fall.
2. A torture device in which victims' limbs were pulled apart.

3. *bull's pizzle*: a bull's penis that when dried and stretched was used as a whip. *stock-fish*: dried cod.
4. Tailors were popularly imagined to lack virility. Falstaff puns on "yard" as referring both to a tailor's measuring stick and to his penis.
5. *sheath*: empty case (punning on "sheath" as meaning "foreskin"). *bow-case*: a long, thin case for unstrung bows. *standing tuck*: a stiff rapier (with a pun on "standing" as meaning "sexually erect").

Why, hear you, my masters. Was it for me to kill the heir-
apparent? Should I turn upon the true prince? Why, thou
knowest I am as valiant as Hercules;[6] but beware instinct. The
250   lion will not touch the true prince[7] — instinct is a great matter.
I was now a coward on instinct. I shall think the better of myself
and thee during my life — I for a valiant lion, and thou for a true
prince. But by the Lord, lads, I am glad you have the money. —
[Calling] Hostess, clap to the doors. — Watch tonight, pray
255   tomorrow.[8] Gallants, lads, boys, hearts of gold, all the titles of
good fellowship come to you! What, shall we be merry, shall
we have a play extempore?

PRINCE HARRY   Content, and the argument° shall be thy running   subject
away.

260 FALSTAFF   Ah, no more of that, Hal, an thou lovest me.

          Enter HOSTESS

HOSTESS   O Jesu, my lord the Prince!

PRINCE HARRY   How now, my lady the Hostess, what sayst thou
to me?

HOSTESS   Marry, my lord, there is a nobleman of the court at
265   door would speak with you. He says he comes from your father.

PRINCE HARRY   Give him as much as will make him a royal
man,[9] and send him back again to my mother.

FALSTAFF   What manner of man is he?

HOSTESS   An old man.

270 FALSTAFF   What doth gravity out of his bed at midnight? Shall I
give him his answer?

PRINCE HARRY   Prithee do, Jack.

FALSTAFF   Faith, and I'll send him packing.   Exit

PRINCE HARRY   Now, sirs; [to GADSHILL] by'r Lady, you fought
275   fair — so did you, Peto, so did you, Bardolph. You are lions
too — you ran away upon instinct, you will not touch the true
prince; no, fie!

BARDOLPH   Faith, I ran when I saw others run.

PRINCE HARRY   Faith, tell me now in earnest, how came Fal-
280   staff's sword so hacked?

PETO   Why, he hacked it with his dagger, and said he would
swear truth out of England[1] but he would make you believe it
was done in fight, and persuaded us to do the like.

BARDOLPH   Yea, and to tickle our noses with speargrass,[2] to make
285   them bleed; and then to beslubber our garments with it, and
swear it was the blood of true men. I did that° I did not this   what
seven year before — I blushed to hear his monstrous devices.

PRINCE HARRY   O villain, thou stolest a cup of sack eighteen years
ago, and wert taken with the manner,° and ever since thou hast   caught in the act
290   blushed extempore.° Thou hadst fire[3] and sword on thy side,   spontaneously
and yet thou rannest away. What instinct hadst thou for it?

BARDOLPH   [indicating his face]   My lord, do you see these meteors? Do you behold these exhalations?[4]

---

6. In classical mythology, a hero who performed prodigious acts of strength and courage.
7. A popular belief derived from classical texts.
8. Falstaff alludes here to Matthew 26:41: "Watch, and
pray, that ye enter not into temptation." He puns on
"watch" as meaning "keep vigil" and "carouse" and on
"pray" as meaning "prey."
9. Punning on "nobles" and "royals" as names of coins,
the latter being more valuable.

1. Swear so excessively that Truth, imagined as an allegorical figure, would run out of England to escape him.
2. A plant with sharply pointed leaves.
3. A reference to Bardolph's red face, the focus of the
jests that follow.
4. "Meteors" and "exhalations" refer to the red blotches
on Bardolph's face, here compared to disturbances in the
heavens.

anger ↗ *Noose.*

PRINCE HARRY   I do.
295 BARDOLPH   What think you they portend?°   *signify*
PRINCE HARRY   Hot livers,[5] and cold° purses.   *empty*
BARDOLPH   Choler,[6] my lord, if rightly taken.°   [*Exit*][7]   *understood*
PRINCE HARRY   No, if rightly taken, halter.[8]

Enter FALSTAFF   ⤷ *justifiably arrested.*

Here comes lean Jack; here comes bare-bone. How now, my
300 sweet creature of bombast?[9] How long is't ago, Jack, since thou
sawest thine own knee?
FALSTAFF   My own knee? When I was about thy years, Hal, I was
not an eagle's talon in the waist; I could have crept into any
alderman's thumb-ring. A plague of sighing and grief—it blows
305 a man up like a bladder. There's villainous news abroad. Here
was Sir John Bracy from your father; you must to the court in
the morning. That same mad fellow of the North, Percy, and
he of Wales that gave Amamon° the bastinado,° and made Luc-   *(a devil) / a beating*
ifer cuckold,[1] and swore the devil his true liegeman° upon the   *subject*
310 cross of a Welsh hook[2] —what a plague call you him?
POINS   Owain Glyndŵr.
FALSTAFF   Owain, Owain, the same; and his son-in-law Mortimer, and old Northumberland, and that sprightly Scot of Scots
Douglas, that runs a-horseback up a hill perpendicular—
315 PRINCE HARRY   He that rides at high speed and with his pistol
kills a sparrow flying.
FALSTAFF   You have hit it.
PRINCE HARRY   So did he never the sparrow.
FALSTAFF   Well, that rascal hath good mettle in him; he will not
320 run.
PRINCE HARRY   Why, what a rascal art thou, then, to praise him
so for running!
FALSTAFF   A-horseback, ye cuckoo, but afoot he will not budge a
foot.
325 PRINCE HARRY   Yes, Jack, upon instinct.
FALSTAFF   I grant ye, upon instinct. Well, he is there too, and
one Mordake, and a thousand blue-caps° more. Worcester is   *Scottish soldiers*
stolen away tonight. Thy father's beard is turned white with the
news. You may buy land now as cheap as stinking mackerel.
330 PRINCE HARRY   Why then, it is like, if there come a hot June and
this civil buffeting hold,° we shall buy maidenheads as they buy   *continue*
hobnails: by the hundreds.[3]
FALSTAFF   By the mass, lad, thou sayst true; it is like we shall
have good trading that way. But tell me, Hal, art not thou horri-
335 ble afeard? Thou being heir-apparent, could the world pick
thee out three such enemies again as that fiend Douglas, that
spirit Percy, and that devil Glyndŵr? Art thou not horribly
afraid? Doth not thy blood thrill° at it?°   *shudder*
PRINCE HARRY   Not a whit, i'faith. I lack some of thy instinct.

5. Short tempers; livers inflamed by drink.
6. The humor associated with an angry disposition.
7. Neither Q nor F marks an exit for Bardolph here, but both indicate that he reenters at line 439. The necessary exit might well follow this discussion of his inflamed face.
8. No, if rightly arrested, a noose. The Prince forces a legal reading on the previous line, playing on "choler" as "collar," or "noose," and taking "taken" to mean "arrested."
9. Cotton padding; pompous speech.
1. Slept with the devil's own wife; gave the devil his horns (the proverbial sign of a cuckold).
2. A heavy weapon with a crooked end, lacking the cross shape on which oaths were usually made.
3. Alluding to rape as a practice of war or to the notion that women would be likely to relinquish their virginity cheaply during wartime.

340 FALSTAFF Well, thou wilt be horribly chid tomorrow when thou
comest to thy father. If thou love me, practise an answer.

PRINCE HARRY Do thou stand for° my father, and examine me *impersonate*
upon the particulars of my life.

FALSTAFF Shall I? Content. This chair shall be my state,° this *throne*
345 dagger my sceptre, and this cushion my crown.

[*He sits*]

PRINCE HARRY Thy state is taken for a joint-stool,[4] thy golden
sceptre for a leaden dagger, and thy precious rich crown for a
pitiful bald crown.

FALSTAFF Well, an° the fire of grace be not quite out of thee, *if*
350 now shalt thou be moved. Give me a cup of sack to make my
eyes look red, that it may be thought I have wept; for I must
speak in passion, and I will do it in King Cambyses' vein.[5]

PRINCE HARRY [*bowing*] Well, here is my leg.° *bow*

FALSTAFF And here is my speech. [To PETO, POINS, and GADS-
355 HILL] Stand aside, nobility.

HOSTESS O Jesu, this is excellent sport, i'faith.

FALSTAFF Weep not, sweet Queen,[6] for trickling tears are vain.

HOSTESS O the Father, how he holds his countenance!° *keeps a straight face*

FALSTAFF For God's sake, lords, convey° my tristful° Queen, *lead away / sad*
360 For tears do stop° the floodgates of her eyes. *fill*

HOSTESS O Jesu, he doth it as like one of these harlotry° players *vagabond; scurvy*
as ever I see!

FALSTAFF Peace, good pint-pot; peace, good tickle-brain.[7] —
Harry, I do not only marvel where thou spendest thy time, but
365 also how thou art accompanied. For though the camomile,° *an herb*
the more it is trodden on, the faster it grows, yet youth, the
more it is wasted, the sooner it wears.[8] That thou art my son I
have partly thy mother's word, partly my own opinion, but
chiefly a villainous trick° of thine eye, and a foolish hanging of *trait*
370 thy nether° lip, that doth warrant° me. If then thou be son to *lower / assure*
me, here lies the point. Why, being son to me, art thou so
pointed at?° Shall the blessed sun of heaven prove a micher,° *criticized / truant*
and eat blackberries?—A question not to be asked. Shall the
son of England prove a thief, and take purses?—A question to
375 be asked. There is a thing, Harry, which thou hast often heard
of, and it is known to many in our land by the name of pitch.° *sticky, black tar*
This pitch, as ancient writers do report, doth defile.[9] So doth
the company thou keepest. For Harry, now I do not speak to
thee in drink, but in tears; not in pleasure, but in passion; not
380 in words only, but in woes also. And yet there is a virtuous man
whom I have often noted in thy company, but I know not his
name.

PRINCE HARRY What manner of man, an it like your majesty?

FALSTAFF A goodly, portly man, i'faith, and a corpulent; of a
385 cheerful look, a pleasing eye, and a most noble carriage;° and, *bearing*
as I think, his age some fifty, or, by'r Lady, inclining to threescore. And now I remember me, his name is Falstaff. If that

---

4. A stool made of wooden pieces fitted or joined together.
5. In the exaggerated rhetorical style associated with such
early Elizabethan plays as *Cambyses*, a tragedy about a
despotic Persian king.
6. Possibly addressed to the Hostess, with a pun on
"quean" as slang for "whore."

7. Slang term for a strong alcoholic drink, and hence for
the drinker.
8. Falstaff's entire speech is a parody of the previously
fashionable ornate rhetoric exemplified by John Lyly's
Euphues (1578).
9. See Ecclesiasticus 13:1 (also cited in Lyly's *Euphues*).

man should be lewdly given,° he deceiveth me; for, Harry, I   *be lustful*
see virtue in his looks. If, then, the tree may be known by the
390 fruit, as the fruit by the tree,[1] then peremptorily I speak it—
there is virtue in that Falstaff. Him keep with; the rest banish.
And tell me now, thou naughty varlet, tell me, where hast thou
been this month?
PRINCE HARRY   Dost thou speak like a king? Do thou stand for
395 me, and I'll play my father.
FALSTAFF [*standing*]   Depose me. If thou dost it half so gravely,
so majestically both in word and matter, hang me up by the
heels for a rabbit sucker,° or a poulter's hare.[2]   *an unweaned rabbit*
PRINCE HARRY [*sitting*]   Well, here I am set.°   *seated*
400 FALSTAFF   And here I stand. [*To the others*] Judge, my masters.
PRINCE HARRY   Now, Harry, whence come you?
FALSTAFF   My noble lord, from Eastcheap.
PRINCE HARRY   The complaints I hear of thee are grievous.
FALSTAFF   'Sblood, my lord, they are false. [*To the others*] Nay,
405 I'll tickle ye for° a young prince, i'faith.   *amuse you as*
PRINCE HARRY   Swearest thou, ungracious boy? Henceforth ne'er
look on me. Thou art violently carried away from grace. There
is a devil haunts thee in the likeness of an old fat man; a tun°   *large barrel*
of man is thy companion. Why dost thou converse° with that   *associate*
410 trunk of humours,[3] that bolting-hutch° of beastliness, that swol-   *sifting bin*
len parcel of dropsies, that huge bombard° of sack, that stuffed   *leather wine vessel*
cloak-bag° of guts, that roasted Manningtree[4] ox with the pud-   *suitcase*
ding° in his belly, that reverend Vice,[5] that grey Iniquity, that   *stuffing*
father Ruffian, that Vanity in Years? Wherein is he good,° but   *virtuous; proficient*
415 to taste sack and drink it? Wherein neat and cleanly,° but to   *deft*
carve a capon and eat it? Wherein cunning, but in craft?
Wherein crafty, but in villainy? Wherein villainous, but in all
things? Wherein worthy, but in nothing?
FALSTAFF   I would your grace would take me with you.° Whom   *explain what you mean*
420 means your grace?
PRINCE HARRY   That villainous, abominable misleader of youth,
Falstaff; that old white-bearded Satan.
FALSTAFF   My lord, the man I know.
PRINCE HARRY   I know thou dost.
425 FALSTAFF   But to say I know more harm in him than in myself
were to say more than I know. That he is old, the more the
pity, his white hairs do witness it. But that he is, saving your
reverence,[6] a whoremaster, that I utterly deny. If sack and sugar
be a fault, God help the wicked. If to be old and merry be a
430 sin, then many an old host° that I know is damned. If to be fat   *innkeeper*
be to be hated, then Pharaoh's lean kine[7] are to be loved. No,
my good lord, banish Peto, banish Bardolph, banish Poins, but
for sweet Jack Falstaff, kind Jack Falstaff, true Jack Falstaff, valiant Jack Falstaff, and therefore more valiant being, as he is,
435 old Jack Falstaff,
Banish not him thy Harry's company,

1. An allusion to Matthew 12:33 (which also appears in Lyly's *Euphues*).
2. A hare sold in a poultry shop.
3. A chest full of body fluids, whose excess, according to Renaissance medical theory, was extremely unhealthy.
4. Market town in Essex, noted for the Manningtree Fair, where a roasted ox may have been part of the festivities.
5. An irreverent, comic, and (usually) youthful character representing evil and sin in the medieval morality plays.
6. If you will excuse the expression.
7. In a biblical story in Genesis, Pharaoh dreams of seven lean cows ("kine") that portend seven years of famine.

Banish not him thy Harry's company.
Banish plump Jack, and banish all the world.
PRINCE HARRY   I do; I will.
                [*Knocking within. Exit* HOSTESS.]⁸
            Enter BARDOLPH, *running*

440 BARDOLPH   O my lord, my lord, the sheriff with a most mon-
        strous watch° is at the door.   *group of constables*
    FALSTAFF   Out, ye rogue! Play out the play! I have much to say
        in the behalf of that Falstaff.
            Enter the HOSTESS
    HOSTESS   O Jesu! My lord, my lord!
445 PRINCE HARRY   Heigh, heigh, the devil rides upon a fiddlestick!⁹
        What's the matter?
    HOSTESS   The sheriff and all the watch are at the door. They are
        come to search the house. Shall I let them in?
    FALSTAFF   Dost thou hear, Hal? Never call a true piece of gold a
450   counterfeit—thou art essentially made, without seeming so.¹
    PRINCE HARRY   And thou a natural coward without instinct.
    FALSTAFF   I deny your major.° If you will deny² the sheriff, so. If   *main premise*
        not, let him enter. If I become° not a cart° as well as another   *adorn / hangman's cart*
        man, a plague on my bringing up. I hope I shall as soon be
455   strangled with a halter as another.
    PRINCE HARRY   Go, hide thee behind the arras.° The rest walk up   *tapestry wall hanging*
        above. Now, my masters, for a true face and good conscience.
                    [*Exeunt* POINS, BARDOLPH, *and* GADSHILL]
    FALSTAFF   Both which I have had, but their date is out;° and   *has expired*
        therefore I'll hide me.
            [*He withdraws behind the arras*]
460 PRINCE HARRY [*to* HOSTESS]   Call in the sheriff.   [*Exit* HOSTESS]
            Enter SHERIFF *and* [*a*] CARRIER
        Now, master sheriff, what is your will with me?
    SHERIFF   First, pardon me, my lord. A hue and cry³
        Hath followed certain men unto this house.
    PRINCE HARRY   What men?
465 SHERIFF   One of them is well known, my gracious lord,
        A gross, fat man.
    CARRIER   As fat as butter.
    PRINCE HARRY   The man, I do assure you, is not here,
        For I myself at this time have employed him.
        And, sheriff, I will engage° my word to thee   *pledge*
470   That I will by tomorrow dinner-time
        Send him to answer thee, or any man,
        For anything he shall be charged withal.
        And so let me entreat you leave the house.
    SHERIFF   I will, my lord. There are two gentlemen
475   Have in this robbery lost three hundred marks.
    PRINCE HARRY   It may be so. If he have robbed these men,
        He shall be answerable. And so, farewell.
    SHERIFF   Good night, my noble lord.
    PRINCE HARRY   I think it is good morrow, is it not?

---

8. Neither F nor Q marks an exit for the Hostess, but
both indicate her reentry at line 443. It makes sense for
her to exit here to see about the commotion at her door.
9. That is, what a row about nothing.
1. A famously difficult passage. Falstaff may be insisting

he is true gold, not a counterfeit (and so should not be
turned over to the watch) just as Hal is a true Prince
("essentially made") despite appearances.
2. If you will refuse to let in.
3. A group of citizens who pursue a criminal.

480 SHERIFF   Indeed, my lord, I think it be two o'clock.

Exeunt [SHERIFF *and* CARRIER]

PRINCE HARRY   This oily rascal is known as well as Paul's.°   *St. Paul's Cathedral*
Go call him forth.

PETO   Falstaff!

[*He draws back the arras, revealing* FALSTAFF *asleep*]

Fast asleep
Behind the arras, and snorting like a horse.

PRINCE HARRY   Hark how hard he fetches breath. Search his pockets.

[PETO] *searcheth his pocket and findeth certain papers.*
[*He closeth the arras and cometh forward*]

What hast thou found?

485 PETO   Nothing but papers, my lord.

PRINCE HARRY   Let's see what they be. Read them.

PETO [*reads*]   Item: a capon.   2s. 2d.
Item: sauce.   4d.
Item: sack, two gallons.   5s. 8d.
490 Item: anchovies and sack after supper.   2s. 6d.
Item: bread.   ob.°   *obolus (halfpenny)*

PRINCE HARRY   O monstrous! But one halfpennyworth of bread
to this intolerable deal° of sack! What there is else, keep close;   *quantity*
we'll read it at more advantage.° There let him sleep till day.   *a better opportunity*
495 I'll to the court in the morning. We must all to the wars, and
thy place shall be honourable. I'll procure this fat rogue a
charge of foot,[4] and I know his death will be a march of twelve
score.[5] The money shall be paid back again, with advantage.°   *interest*
Be with me betimes° in the morning; and so good morrow,   *early*
500 Peto.

PETO   Good morrow, good my lord.   *Exeunt* [*severally*]

3.1

Enter HOTSPUR, [*the Earl of*] WORCESTER, *Lord* MORTI-
MER, [*and*] *Owain* GLYNDŴR [*with a map*]

MORTIMER   These promises are fair, the parties sure,
And our induction° full of prosperous hope.[1]   *beginning*

HOTSPUR   Lord Mortimer and cousin Glyndŵr,
Will you sit down? And uncle Worcester?

[MORTIMER, GLYNDŴR, *and* WORCESTER *sit*]

5 A plague upon it, I have forgot the map!

GLYNDŴR   No, here it is. Sit, cousin Percy, sit,
Good cousin Hotspur;

[HOTSPUR *sits*]

For by that name
As oft as Lancaster[2] doth speak of you,
His cheek looks pale, and with a rising sigh
He wisheth you in heaven.

10 HOTSPUR   And you in hell,
As oft as he hears Owain Glyndŵr spoke of.

GLYNDŴR   I cannot blame him. At my nativity

---

4. Command of an infantry company.
5. I know it will kill him to march twelve times twenty
yards or paces.
3.1 Location: Glyndŵr's castle, Wales. According to Holinshed's *Chronicles*, the events of this scene take place in
the house of the Archdeacon of Bangor; but he is not
present in Shakespeare's scene, and Glyndŵr acts as host
throughout.
1. Full of the hope of prospering.
2. Referring to Henry's title as Duke and hence implying
a denial of the legitimacy of his kingship.

The front° of heaven was full of fiery shapes,   *forehead*
Of burning cressets;[3] and at my birth
15 The frame and huge foundation of the earth
Shaked like a coward.
HOTSPUR   Why, so it would have done
At the same season if your mother's cat
Had but kittened, though yourself had never been born.
GLYNDŴR   I say the earth did shake when I was born.
20 HOTSPUR   And I say the earth was not of my mind
If you suppose as fearing you it shook.
GLYNDŴR   The heavens were all on fire, the earth did tremble—
HOTSPUR   O, then the earth shook to see the heavens on fire,
And not in fear of your nativity.
25 Diseasèd nature oftentimes breaks forth
In strange eruptions; oft the teeming° earth   *fertile*
Is with a kind of colic pinched and vexed
By the imprisoning of unruly wind
Within her womb, which for enlargement° striving   *release*
30 Shakes the old beldam° earth, and topples down   *grandmother*
Steeples and moss-grown towers. At your birth
Our grandam earth, having this distemp'rature,°   *disorder*
In passion shook.
GLYNDŴR   Cousin, of many men
I do not bear these crossings.° Give me leave   *contradictions*
35 To tell you once again that at my birth
The front of heaven was full of fiery shapes,
The goats ran from the mountains, and the herds
Were strangely clamorous to the frighted fields.
These signs have marked me extraordinary,
40 And all the courses of my life do show
I am not in the roll of common men.
Where is he living, clipped in with° the sea   *encircled by*
That chides the banks° of England, Scotland, Wales,   *shores*
Which° calls me pupil or hath read to° me?   *Who / tutored*
45 And bring him out° that is but woman's son   *show me any man*
Can trace° me in the tedious ways of art,[4]   *follow*
And hold me pace° in deep experiments.   *keep up with me*
HOTSPUR [*standing*]   I think there's no man speaketh better Welsh.[5]
I'll to dinner.
50 MORTIMER   Peace, cousin Percy, you will make him mad.
GLYNDŴR   I can call spirits from the vasty deep.°   *lower world*
HOTSPUR   Why, so can I, or so can any man;
But will they come when you do call for them?
GLYNDŴR   Why, I can teach you, cousin, to command the devil.
55 HOTSPUR   And I can teach thee, coz, to shame the devil,
By telling truth: 'Tell truth, and shame the devil'.
If thou have power to raise him, bring him hither,
And I'll be sworn I have power to shame him hence.
O, while you live, tell truth and shame the devil.
60 MORTIMER   Come, come, no more of this unprofitable chat.
GLYNDŴR   Three times hath Henry Bolingbroke made head°   *raised an army*

---

3. Metal baskets of fire suspended from long poles; meteors.
4. The long, laborious ways of magic.
5. The Welsh language was often described by English

writers as a barbaric one, and "to speak Welsh" commonly meant to use a strange, unintelligible language. Hotspur implies that Glyndŵr speaks nonsense.

Against my power;° thrice from the banks of Wye   *army*
And sandy-bottomed Severn have I sent him
Bootless° home, and weather-beaten back.[6]   *Unsuccessful*
65 HOTSPUR   Home without boots, and in foul weather too!
How scapes he agues,° in the devil's name?   *fevers*
GLYNDŴR   Come, here's the map. Shall we divide our right,°   *what we are entitled to*
According to our threefold order ta'en?[7]
MORTIMER   The Archdeacon hath divided it
70 Into three limits° very equally.   *regions*
England from Trent and Severn hitherto°   *to here*
By south and east is to my part assigned;
All westward—Wales beyond the Severn shore
And all the fertile land within that bound—
75 To Owain Glyndŵr; [*to* HOTSPUR] and, dear coz, to you
The remnant northward lying off from Trent.
And our indentures tripartite° are drawn,   *in triplicate*
Which, being sealèd interchangeably[8]—
A business that this night may execute°—   *may be done tonight*
80 Tomorrow, cousin Percy, you and I
And my good lord of Worcester will set forth
To meet your father and the Scottish power,
As is appointed us, at Shrewsbury.
My father,° Glyndŵr, is not ready yet,   *father-in-law*
85 Nor shall we need his help these fourteen days.
Within that space you may have drawn together
Your tenants, friends, and neighbouring gentlemen.
GLYNDŴR   A shorter time shall send me to you, lords;
And in my conduct° shall your ladies come,   *escort*
90 From whom you now must steal and take no leave;
For there will be a world of water shed
Upon the parting of your wives and you.
HOTSPUR   Methinks my moiety° north from Burton here   *portion*
In quantity equals not one° of yours.   *either*
95 See how this river comes me cranking in,[9]
And cuts me from the best of all my land
A huge half-moon, a monstrous cantle,° out.   *piece*
I'll have the current in this place dammed up,
And here the smug° and silver Trent shall run   *smooth*
100 In a new channel fair and evenly.
It shall not wind with such a deep indent,
To rob me of so rich a bottom° here.   *lowland plain*
GLYNDŴR   Not wind? It shall, it must; you see it doth.
MORTIMER   Yea, but mark how he bears his course, and runs me up°   *turns upward*
105 With like advantage on the other side,
Gelding the opposèd continent[1] as much
As on the other side it takes from you.
WORCESTER   Yea, but a little charge° will trench° him here,   *expense / rechannel*
And on this north side win this cape of land,
110 And then he runs straight and even.
HOTSPUR   I'll have it so; a little charge will do it.

6. According to Holinshed, Glyndŵr used magic to raise   68–76). *order ta'en:* agreement made.
storms that frustrated Henry's attacks.   8. Bearing the seals of all three nobles.
7. *threefold:* either an agreement made in triplicate (see   9. Comes bending in on my shores.
line 77) or an agreement having three parts (see the   1. Cutting a vital piece from ("gelding") the opposite
rebels' plan to divide the island into three pieces at lines   bank.

GLYNDŴR   I'll not have it altered.

HOTSPUR   Will not you?

GLYNDŴR   No, nor you shall not.

115   HOTSPUR   Who shall say me nay?

GLYNDŴR   Why, that will I.

HOTSPUR   Let me not understand you, then: speak it in Welsh.

GLYNDŴR   I can speak English, lord, as well as you;

   For I was trained up in the English court,

120   Where, being but young, I framèd to the harp

   Many an English ditty lovely well,

   And gave the tongue a helpful ornament[2] —

   A virtue that was never seen in you.

HOTSPUR   Marry, and I am glad of it, with all my heart.

125   I had rather be a kitten and cry 'mew'

   Than one of these same metre ballad-mongers.

   I had rather hear a brazen canstick turned,[3]

   Or a dry wheel grate on the axle-tree,°   *axle*

   And that would set my teeth nothing on edge,

130   Nothing so much as mincing° poetry.   *affected*

   'Tis like the forced gait of a shuffling° nag.   *hobbled*

GLYNDŴR   Come, you shall have Trent turned.

HOTSPUR   I do not care. I'll give thrice so much land

   To any well-deserving friend;

135   But in the way of bargain—mark ye me—

   I'll cavil on° the ninth part of a hair.   *quibble about*

   Are the indentures drawn? Shall we be gone?

GLYNDŴR   The moon shines fair. You may away by night.

   I'll haste the writer, and withal°   *simultaneously*

140   Break with° your wives of your departure hence.   *Inform*

   I am afraid my daughter will run mad,

   So much she doteth on her Mortimer.   *Exit*

MORTIMER   Fie, cousin Percy, how you cross my father!

HOTSPUR   I cannot choose. Sometime he angers me

145   With telling me of the moldwarp[4] and the ant,

   Of the dreamer Merlin[5] and his prophecies,

   And of a dragon and a finless fish,

   A clip-winged griffin[6] and a moulten° raven,   *moulted*

   A couching lion and a ramping cat,[7]

150   And such a deal of skimble-skamble° stuff   *stupid*

   As puts me from my faith.[8] I tell you what,

   He held me last night at the least nine hours

   In reckoning up the several devils' names

   That were his lackeys. I cried, 'Hum!' and, 'Well, go to!',

155   But marked him not a word. O, he is as tedious

   As a tired horse, a railing wife,

   Worse than a smoky house. I had rather live

---

2. And gave the English language the ornament of a musical setting; and supplemented the English lyrics with pleasing music.

3. A brazen candlestick scraped and polished on a lathe after casting. John Stow's *Survey of London* records contemporary complaints about the noise of candlestick making.

4. Mole. Holinshed records a prophecy whereby Henry, figured as a mole, would be overthrown by a dragon, a lion, and a wolf, representing Glyndŵr, Percy, and Mortimer, respectively.

5. Legendary Welsh prophet, wizard, and bard at King Arthur's court.

6. A fabulous beast, part lion and part eagle.

7. Alluding to the heraldic terms "couchant" and "rampant," which mean "crouching" and "rearing fiercely." Hotspur is making fun of Glyndŵr's heraldic preoccupations.

8. As makes me a skeptic, even of religion.

	With cheese and garlic, in a windmill, far,	
	Than feed on cates° and have him talk to me	*delicacies*
160	In any summer house° in Christendom.	*luxurious residence*
	MORTIMER In faith, he is a worthy gentleman,	
	Exceedingly well read, and profited°	*proficient*
	In strange concealments,° valiant as a lion,	*In occult arts*
	And wondrous affable, and as bountiful	
165	As mines of India. Shall I tell you, cousin?	
	He holds your temper in a high respect,	
	And curbs himself even of his natural scope°	*freedom of speech*
	When you come 'cross° his humour; faith, he does.	*contradict*
	I warrant you, that man is not alive	
170	Might so have tempted° him as you have done	*provoked*
	Without the taste of danger and reproof.	
	But do not use it oft, let me entreat you.	
	WORCESTER [*to* HOTSPUR] In faith, my lord, you are too wilful-blame,°	*stubborn*
	And since your coming hither have done enough	
175	To put him quite besides° his patience.	*out of*
	You must needs learn, lord, to amend this fault.	
	Though sometimes it show greatness, courage, blood°—	*spirit; noble birth*
	And that's the dearest grace° it renders you—	*best distinction*
	Yet oftentimes it doth present° harsh rage,	*show*
180	Defect of manners, want of government,	
	Pride, haughtiness, opinion,° and disdain,	*self-conceit*
	The least of which haunting a nobleman	
	Loseth men's hearts, and leaves behind a stain	
	Upon the beauty of all parts besides,°	*all other qualities*
185	Beguiling° them of commendation.	*Depriving*
	HOTSPUR Well, I am schooled. Good manners be your speed!°	*give you success*
	Enter GLYNDŴR *with the Ladies* [LADY PERCY *and Morti-*	
	mer's wife]	
	Here come our wives, and let us take our leave.	
	[*Mortimer's wife weeps, and speaks to him in Welsh*]	
	MORTIMER This is the deadly spite° that angers me:	*vexation*
	My wife can speak no English, I no Welsh.	
190	GLYNDŴR My daughter weeps she'll not part with you.	
	She'll be a soldier, too; she'll to the wars.	
	MORTIMER Good father, tell her that she and my aunt Percy[9]	
	Shall follow in your conduct speedily.	
	GLYNDŴR *speaks to her in Welsh, and she answers*	
	him in the same	
	GLYNDŴR She is desperate here,° a peevish self-willed harlotry,°	*on this point / hussy*
195	One that no persuasion can do good upon.	
	The lady speaks in Welsh	
	MORTIMER I understand thy looks. That pretty Welsh°	*(i.e., her tears)*
	Which thou down pourest from these swelling heavens°	*overflowing eyes*
	I am too perfect° in, and but for shame	*proficient*
	In such a parley° should I answer thee.	*In a similar language*
	The lady [*kisses him, and speaks*] *again in Welsh*	
200	MORTIMER I understand thy kisses, and thou mine,	
	And that's a feeling disputation;[1]	
	But I will never be a truant, love,	

---

9. Kate, Lady Percy. Her historical counterpart was the   1. A conversation rooted in emotions or in touch.
sister, not the aunt, of Glyndŵr's son-in-law.

Till I have learnt thy language, for thy tongue
Makes Welsh as sweet as ditties highly° penned,   *eloquently*
205 Sung by a fair queen in a summer's bower
With ravishing division,° to her lute.   *embellishments*
GLYNDŴR   Nay, if you melt,° then will she run mad.   *weep*
        The lady [sits on the rushes² and] speaks again in Welsh
MORTIMER   O, I am ignorance itself in this!
GLYNDŴR   She bids you on the wanton° rushes lay you down   *luxurious*
210 And rest your gentle head upon her lap,³
And she will sing the song that pleaseth you,
And on your eyelids crown the god of sleep,
Charming your blood with pleasing heaviness,°   *sleepiness*
Making such difference 'twixt wake and sleep
215 As is the difference betwixt day and night
The hour before the heavenly-harnessed team⁴
Begins his golden progress in the east.
MORTIMER   With all my heart, I'll sit and hear her sing.
By that time will our book,° I think, be drawn.   *document*
        [He sits, resting his head on the Welsh lady's lap]
220 GLYNDŴR   Do so, and those musicians that shall play to you
Hang in the air a thousand leagues from hence,
And straight they shall be here. Sit and attend.
HOTSPUR   Come, Kate, thou art perfect in lying down.°   *expert at lovemaking*
Come, quick, quick, that I may lay my head in thy lap.⁵
225 LADY PERCY   [*sitting*]   Go, ye giddy goose!
        [HOTSPUR sits, resting his head on Lady Percy's lap.] The
        music plays⁶
HOTSPUR   Now I perceive the devil understands Welsh;
And 'tis no marvel, he is so humorous.°   *eccentric; whimsical*
By'r Lady, he's a good musician.
LADY PERCY   Then should you be nothing but musical,
230 For you are altogether governed by humours.°   *whims*
Lie still, ye thief, and hear the lady sing in Welsh.
HOTSPUR   I had rather hear Lady my brach° howl in Irish.   *female hunting dog*
LADY PERCY   Wouldst thou have thy head broken?
HOTSPUR   No.
235 LADY PERCY   Then be still.
HOTSPUR   Neither—'tis a woman's fault.⁷
LADY PERCY   Now God help thee!
HOTSPUR   To the Welsh lady's bed.
LADY PERCY   What's that?
240 HOTSPUR   Peace; she sings.
        Here the lady sings a Welsh song
HOTSPUR   Come, Kate, I'll have your song too.
LADY PERCY   Not mine, in good sooth.°   *truth*
HOTSPUR   Not yours, in good sooth! Heart,° you swear like a   *By God's heart*
comfit-maker's° wife: 'Not you, in good sooth!' and 'As true as   *confectioner's*
245 I live!' and
'As God shall mend me!' and 'As sure as day!';

---

2. Used as a floor covering, both in houses and on the
theater stage.
3. Often a euphemism for the genitals.
4. The sun was supposedly carried in a chariot drawn by
horses.
5. "Head" was slang for "penis" and "lap" for "vagina."

6. Instrumental music would probably be played in a so-
called music house behind the upper stage in the Elizabethan theater, and so might well seem to "hang in the
air" (see lines 220–21).
7. No, I won't be still—it is a woman's trait (and I am a
man).

And giv'st such sarcenet[8] surety for thy oaths
As if thou never walk'st further than Finsbury.[9]
Swear me, Kate, like a lady as thou art,
250 A good mouth-filling oath, and leave 'in sooth'
And such protest of pepper gingerbread[1]
To velvet-guards and Sunday citizens.[2]
Come, sing.

LADY PERCY   I will not sing.

255 HOTSPUR   'Tis the next° way to turn tailor,[3] or be redbreast   *quickest*
teacher.° [*Rising*] An the indentures be drawn, I'll away within   *or teach birds to sing*
these two hours; and so come in when ye will.   *Exit*

GLYNDŴR   Come, come, Lord Mortimer. You are as slow
As hot Lord Percy is on fire to go.
260 By this° our book is drawn. We'll but seal,   *now*
And then to horse immediately.

MORTIMER [*rising*]   With all my heart.
                    [*The ladies rise, and all*] *exeunt*

3.2

Enter KING [HENRY], PRINCE [HARRY], *and* [*lords*]

KING HENRY   Lords, give us leave—the Prince of Wales and I
Must have some private conference—but be near at hand,
For we shall presently have need of you.   *Exeunt lords*
I know not whether God will have it so
5 For some displeasing service I have done,
That in his secret doom° out of my blood°   *judgment / lineage*
He'll breed revengement and a scourge for me,
But thou dost in thy passages° of life   *course*
Make me believe that thou art only marked
10 For° the hot vengeance and the rod of heaven   *To be*
To punish my mistreadings. Tell me else,
Could such inordinate° and low desires,   *unsuitable*
Such poor, such bare, such lewd, such mean attempts,°   *base undertakings*
Such barren pleasures,[1] rude society,
15 As thou art matched withal° and grafted to,   *with*
Accompany the greatness of thy blood,
And hold their level° with thy princely heart?   *And claim equality*

PRINCE HARRY   So please your majesty, I would I could
Quit° all offences with as clear excuse   *Clear myself of*
20 As well as I am doubtless° I can purge   *certain*
Myself of many I am charged withal;
Yet such extenuation let me beg
As, in reproof° of many tales devised—   *upon disproof*
Which oft the ear of greatness needs must hear
25 By smiling pickthanks° and base newsmongers°—   *flatterers / gossips*
I may, for some things true wherein my youth
Hath faulty wandered and irregular,
Find pardon on my true submission.°   *admission of guilt*

KING HENRY   God pardon thee! Yet let me wonder, Harry,

---

8. Flimsy (from the name of a fine silk).
9. Finsbury Fields, north of London, was a popular resort for London's middling classes. Hotspur implies that
Kate's mild oaths make her sound like a burgher's wife.
1. Watered-down oaths. Gingerbread was cheaply available at fairs and markets, and sometimes pepper was used
as an inexpensive substitute for ginger.

2. Citizens who doff their work clothes and dress up only
on Sundays. To *velvet-guards*: To those, like citizens'
wives, whose clothes are trimmed ("guarded") with velvet.
3. Tailors were noted for singing.
3.2 Location: The palace, London.
1. Unprofitable habits; nonreproductive erotic pursuits.

30   At thy affections,° which do hold a wing   *inclinations*
     Quite from[2] the flight of all thy ancestors.
     Thy place in Council thou hast rudely[3] lost—
     Which by thy younger brother is supplied—
     And art almost an alien to the hearts
35   Of all the court and princes of my blood.
     The hope and expectation of thy time°   *time of life; youth*
     Is ruined, and the soul of every man
     Prophetically do forethink thy fall.
     Had I so lavish of my presence been,
40   So common-hackneyed[4] in the eyes of men,
     So stale and cheap to vulgar company,
     Opinion,° that did help me to the crown,   *Public opinion*
     Had still kept loyal to possession,[5]
     And left me in reputeless° banishment,   *inglorious*
45   A fellow of no mark nor likelihood.°   *promise of success*
     By being seldom seen, I could not stir
     But, like a comet, I was wondered at,
     That men would tell their children 'This is he.'
     Others would say 'Where, which is Bolingbroke?'
50   And then I stole all courtesy from heaven,[6]
     And dressed myself in such humility
     That I did pluck allegiance from men's hearts,
     Loud shouts and salutations from their mouths,
     Even in the presence of the crownèd King.
55   Thus did I keep my person fresh and new,
     My presence like a robe pontifical°—   *churchman's rich dress*
     Ne'er seen but wondered at—and so my state,°   *magnificence; royalty*
     Seldom but sumptuous, showed like a feast,
     And won by rareness such solemnity.
60   The skipping King, he ambled up and down
     With shallow jesters and rash bavin° wits,   *brushwood*
     Soon kindled and soon burnt, carded his state,[7]
     Mingled his royalty with cap'ring fools,
     Had his great name profanèd with their scorns,°   *by their scornful manners*
65   And gave his countenance,° against his name,[8]   *approval*
     To laugh at gibing boys, and stand the push°   *tolerate the impudence*
     Of every beardless vain comparative;°   *wit*
     Grew a companion to the common streets,
     Enfeoffed° himself to popularity,   *Surrendered*
70   That, being daily swallowed by men's eyes,
     They surfeited with honey, and began
     To loathe the taste of sweetness, whereof a little
     More than a little is by much too much.
     So when he had occasion to be seen,
75   He was but as the cuckoo is in June,[9]
     Heard, not regarded, seen but with such eyes
     As, sick and blunted with community,°   *familiarity*

2. *which . . . from:* which do fly a course contrary to.
3. By violence. Perhaps alluding to the story, dramatized in *The Famous Victories of Henry V,* that Prince Hal boxed the Lord Chief Justice on the ear and was subsequently punished.
4. Cheapened. A hackney was a horse available for common hire.
5. The possessor of the throne (Richard II).

6. That is, surpassed heaven itself for graciousness.
7. Adulterated his royal dignity. The term refers to a process ("carding") whereby wool or liquids were mixed with inferior substances.
8. To the detriment of his reputation.
9. Referring to a proverbial saying, "No one regards the June cuckoo's song."

Afford no extraordinary gaze
Such as is bent on sun-like majesty
80 When it shines seldom in admiring eyes,
But rather drowsed and hung their eyelids down,
Slept in his face,° and rendered such aspect°   *before his eyes / looks*
As cloudy° men use to their adversaries,   *sullen*
Being with his presence glutted, gorged, and full.
85 And in that very line,° Harry, standest thou;   *category*
For thou hast lost thy princely privilege
With vile participation.° Not an eye   *base companionship*
But is a-weary of thy common sight,
Save mine, which hath desired to see thee more,
90 Which now doth that° I would not have it do—   *what*
Make blind itself with foolish tenderness.
    [*He weeps*]
PRINCE HARRY   I shall hereafter, my thrice-gracious lord,
Be more myself.
KING HENRY   For all the world,
As thou art to this hour was Richard then,
95 When I from France set foot at Ravenspurgh,
And even as I was then is Percy now.
Now by my sceptre, and my soul to boot,
He hath more worthy interest° to the state   *more claim by worth*
Than thou, the shadow° of succession;   *mere image*
100 For, of° no right, nor colour° like to right,   *having / pretext*
He doth fill fields with harness° in the realm,   *armor*
Turns head° against the lion's° armèd jaws,   *Leads a revolt / king's*
And, being no more in debt to years than thou,
Leads ancient lords and reverend bishops on
105 To bloody battles, and to bruising arms.
What never-dying honour hath he got
Against renownèd Douglas!—whose high deeds,
Whose hot incursions and great name in arms,
Holds from all soldiers chief majority°   *preeminence*
110 And military title capital[1]
Through all the kingdoms that acknowledge Christ.
Thrice hath this Hotspur, Mars° in swaddling-clothes,   *god of war*
This infant warrior, in his enterprises
Discomfited° great Douglas; ta'en him once;   *Defeated*
115 Enlargèd° him; and made a friend of him   *Released*
To fill the mouth of deep defiance up,[2]
And shake the peace and safety of our throne.
And what say you to this? Percy, Northumberland,
The Archbishop's grace of York, Douglas, Mortimer,
120 Capitulate° against us, and are up.°   *Combine / up in arms*
But wherefore do I tell these news to thee?
Why, Harry, do I tell thee of my foes,
Which° art my near'st and dearest enemy?—   *Who*
Thou that art like enough, through vassal° fear,   *servile*
125 Base inclination, and the start of spleen,°   *fit of temper*
To fight against me under Percy's pay,
To dog his heels, and curtsy at his frowns,

1. And claim to the title of principal (capital) warrior.   the appetite of deep defiance.
2. To add volume to the voice of deep defiance; to fill up

To show how much thou art degenerate.

PRINCE HARRY Do not think so; you shall not find it so.
130 And God forgive them that so much have swayed
Your majesty's good thoughts away from me.
I will redeem all this on Percy's head,
And in the closing of some glorious day
Be bold to tell you that I am your son;
135 When I will wear a garment all of blood,
And stain my favours° in a bloody mask,   *features*
Which, washed away, shall scour my shame with it.
And that shall be the day, whene'er it lights,°   *comes*
That this same child of honour and renown,
140 This gallant Hotspur, this all-praisèd knight,
And your unthought-of Harry chance to meet.
For every honour sitting on his helm,
Would they were multitudes, and on my head
My shames redoubled; for the time will come
145 That I shall make this northern youth exchange
His glorious deeds for my indignities.
Percy is but my factor,° good my lord,   *agent*
To engross up° glorious deeds on my behalf;   *amass*
And I will call him to so strict account
150 That he shall render every glory up,
Yea, even the slightest worship of his time,°   *honor of his life*
Or I will tear the reckoning from his heart.
This, in the name of God, I promise here,
The which if he be pleased I shall perform,
155 I do beseech your majesty may salve°   *heal*
The long-grown wounds of my intemperature;°   *disorder; intemperance*
If not, the end of life cancels all bonds,
And I will die a hundred thousand deaths
Ere break the smallest parcel of this vow.
160 **KING HENRY** A hundred thousand rebels die in this.
Thou shalt have charge° and sovereign trust herein.   *military command*
              Enter [Sir Walter] BLUNT
How now, good Blunt? Thy looks are full of speed.
BLUNT So hath the business that I come to speak of.
Lord Mortimer of Scotland[3] hath sent word
165 That Douglas and the English rebels met
The eleventh of this month at Shrewsbury.
A mighty and a fearful head° they are,   *army*
If promises be kept on every hand,
As ever offered foul play in a state.
170 **KING HENRY** The Earl of Westmorland set forth today,
With him my son Lord John of Lancaster,
For this advertisement° is five days old.   *news*
On Wednesday next, Harry, you shall set forward.
On Thursday we ourselves will march.
175 Our meeting is Bridgnorth,[4] and, Harry, you
Shall march through Gloucestershire, by which account,°   *calculation*
Our business valuèd,° some twelve days hence   *taken into account*
Our general forces at Bridgnorth shall meet.

---

3. A Scottish lord who is unrelated to Glyndŵr's son-in-   4. A town about twenty miles south of Shrewsbury.
law.

Our hands are full of business; let's away.
180 Advantage feeds him fat[5] while men delay.   *Exeunt*

3.3

Enter FALSTAFF [*with a truncheon° at his waist*], *and*   officer's club
BARDOLPH

FALSTAFF Bardolph, am I not fallen away° vilely since this last   shrunk
action?[1] Do I not bate?° Do I not dwindle? Why, my skin hangs   grow thin
about me like an old lady's loose gown. I am withered like an
old apple-john.[2] Well, I'll repent, and that suddenly, while I
5 am in some liking.° I shall be out of heart[3] shortly, and then I   in the mood
shall have no strength to repent. An I have not forgotten what
the inside of a church is made of, I am a peppercorn, a brewer's
horse°—the inside of a church! Company, villainous company,   an old workhorse
hath been the spoil of me.
10 BARDOLPH Sir John, you are so fretful you cannot live long.
FALSTAFF Why, there is it. Come, sing me a bawdy song, make
me merry. I was as virtuously given° as a gentleman need to be: inclined
virtuous enough; swore little; diced not—above seven times a
week; went to a bawdy-house not—above once in a quarter—
15 of an hour; paid money that I borrowed—three or four times;
lived well, and in good compass.° And now I live out of all   limits
order, out of all compass.
BARDOLPH Why, you are so fat, Sir John, that you must needs
be out of all compass,° out of all reasonable compass, Sir John.   circumference; girth
20 FALSTAFF Do thou amend thy face, and I'll amend my life.
Thou art our admiral,° thou bearest the lantern in the poop[4]—   flagship
but 'tis in the nose of thee. Thou art the Knight of the Burning
Lamp.[5]
BARDOLPH Why, Sir John, my face does you no harm.
25 FALSTAFF No, I'll be sworn; I make as good use of it as many a
man doth of a death's head,[6] or a *memento mori*.[7] I never see
thy face but I think upon hell-fire and Dives that lived in purple—for there he is in his robes, burning, burning.[8] If thou
wert any way given to virtue, I would swear by thy face; my oath
30 should be 'By this fire that's God's angel!' But thou art altogether given over,° and wert indeed, but for the light in thy   dedicated to vice
face, the son of utter darkness. When thou rannest up Gads
Hill in the night to catch my horse, if I did not think thou hadst
been an *ignis fatuus* or a ball of wildfire,[9] there's no purchase
35 in money. O, thou art a perpetual triumph,° an everlasting bon-   torchlight procession
fire-light! Thou hast saved me a thousand marks[1] in links° and   small torches
torches, walking with thee in the night betwixt tavern and tav-

---

5. Opportunities (for rebellion) flourish; the superior position (of the rebels) improves.
3.3 Location: The inn in Eastcheap, London.
1. This last military engagement (referring to the Gad's Hill episode).
2. A kind of apple often eaten long after picking, when its skin was shriveled.
3. Disinclined; weary.
4. The ship's main deck.
5. Parodying figures from popular romance such as Amadis, the Knight of the Burning Sword.
6. A skull, or representation of a skull, such as was engraved as an emblem of mortality on seal rings.
7. An object serving as a reminder of mortality (Latin for "remember you must die").

8. Referring to a biblical parable about a rich man "clothed in purple and fine linen" who regularly refused to feed the beggar Lazarus and was ultimately forced to suffer in hell for his sin (Luke 16:19–23); also referring to Bardolph's body as bearing the signs of venereal disease. "Burning" implies "on fire with lust" as well as "infected with syphilitic sores."
9. A flaming explosive used in warfare or in fireworks; skin marked by erysipelas, an inflammatory disease. *ignis fatuus*: will-of-the wisp (Latin for "foolish fire"); a phenomenon in which phosphorescent light appears on marshy ground.
1. Considerable money (each mark was worth two-thirds of a pound).

ern — but the sack that thou hast drunk me° would have bought   *drunk (at my cost)*
me lights as good cheap° at the dearest chandler's² in Europe.   *as cheaply*

40   I have maintained that salamander³ of yours with fire any time
this two-and-thirty years, God reward me for it.

BARDOLPH   'Sblood, I would my face were in your belly!⁴

FALSTAFF   God-a-mercy! So should I be sure to be heartburnt.

    Enter HOSTESS

How now, Dame Partlet⁵ the hen, have you enquired yet who

45   picked my pocket?

HOSTESS   Why, Sir John, what do you think, Sir John? Do you
think I keep thieves in my house? I have searched, I have
enquired; so has my husband, man by man, boy by boy, servant
by servant. The tithe° of a hair was never lost in my house   *tenth part*

50   before.

FALSTAFF   Ye lie, Hostess: Bardolph was shaved and lost many a
hair,⁶ and I'll be sworn my pocket was picked. Go to, you are a
woman, go.

HOSTESS   Who, I? No, I defy thee! God's light, I was never called

55   so in mine own house before.

FALSTAFF   Go to, I know you well enough.

HOSTESS   No, Sir John, you do not know me,⁷ Sir John; I know
you, Sir John. You owe me money, Sir John, and now you pick
a quarrel to beguile me of it. I bought you a dozen of shirts to

60   your back.

FALSTAFF   Dowlas,° filthy dowlas. I have given them away to   *Coarse linen*
bakers' wives; they have made bolters° of them.   *sieves*

HOSTESS   Now as I am a true woman, holland° of eight shillings   *fine linen*
an ell.° You owe money here besides, Sir John: for your diet,   *a measure of 45 inches*

65   and by-drinkings,° and money lent you, four-and-twenty pound.   *drinks between meals*

FALSTAFF   [*pointing at* BARDOLPH]   He had his part of it. Let him
pay.

HOSTESS   He? Alas, he is poor; he hath nothing.

FALSTAFF   How, poor? Look upon his face. What call you rich?

70   Let them coin his nose, let them coin his cheeks, I'll not pay a
denier.⁸ What, will you make a younker° of me? Shall I not   *novice; gull*
take mine ease in mine inn, but I shall have my pocket picked?
I have lost a seal-ring of my grandfather's worth forty mark.

HOSTESS   O Jesu, [*to* BARDOLPH] I have heard the Prince tell

75   him, I know not how oft, that that ring was copper.

FALSTAFF   How? The Prince is a jack,° a sneak-up.° [*Raising his*   *rascal / sly villain*
truncheon] 'Sblood, an he were here I would cudgel him like a
dog if he would say so.

    Enter PRINCE [HARRY *and* PETO], *marching; and* FAL-
    STAFF *meets* [*them*], *playing upon his truncheon like a*
    fife

How now, lad, is the wind in that door,° i'faith? Must we all   *quarter*

80   march?

BARDOLPH   Yea, two and two, Newgate fashion.⁹

---

2. The most expensive candle maker's.
3. A fabled lizard capable of living in fire. The implication is that Falstaff has maintained the salamander Bardolph with the "fires" of sack or lust.
4. Equivalent to "Stick it down your throat" (a proverbial
retort to an insult).
5. A traditional name for hens and for women supposed
to talk too much.

6. Had his beard cut; was cheated or robbed of his
money; lost his hair because of syphilis.
7. That is, you don't know how honest I am; you don't
have sexual knowledge of me.
8. French copper coin of little value.
9. Bound like convicts taken to and from London's Newgate prison.

HOSTESS   My lord, I pray you hear me.

PRINCE HARRY   What sayst thou, Mistress Quickly? How doth
    thy husband?
    I love him well; he is an honest man.

85 HOSTESS   Good my lord, hear me!

FALSTAFF   Prithee, let her alone, and list to me.

PRINCE HARRY   What sayst thou, Jack?

FALSTAFF   The other night I fell asleep here behind the arras,
    and had my pocket picked. This house is turned bawdy-house:
90 they pick pockets.

PRINCE HARRY   What didst thou lose, Jack?

FALSTAFF   Wilt thou believe me, Hal, three or four bonds of forty
    pound apiece, and a seal-ring of my grandfather's.

PRINCE HARRY   A trifle, some eightpenny matter.

95 HOSTESS   So I told him, my lord; and I said I heard your grace
    say so; and, my lord, he speaks most vilely of you, like a foul-
    mouthed man as he is, and said he would cudgel you.

PRINCE HARRY   What? He did not!

HOSTESS   There's neither faith, truth, nor womanhood in me
100   else.

FALSTAFF   There's no more faith in thee than in a stewed prune,[1]
    nor no more truth in thee than in a drawn fox;[2] and, for wom-
    anhood, Maid Marian[3] may be the deputy's wife of the ward
    to° thee. Go, you thing,[4] go!   compared to

105 HOSTESS   Say, what thing, what thing?

FALSTAFF   What thing? Why, a thing to thank God on.

HOSTESS   I am no thing to thank God on. I would thou shouldst
    know it, I am an honest man's wife; and setting thy knighthood
    aside, thou art a knave to call me so.

110 FALSTAFF   Setting thy womanhood aside, thou art a beast to say
    otherwise.

HOSTESS   Say, what beast, thou knave, thou?

FALSTAFF   'What beast? Why, an otter.

PRINCE HARRY   An otter, Sir John? Why an otter?

115 FALSTAFF   Why? She's neither fish nor flesh;[5] a man knows not
    where to have her.[6]

HOSTESS   Thou art an unjust man in saying so. Thou or any man
    knows where to have me, thou knave, thou.

PRINCE HARRY   Thou sayst true, Hostess, and he slanders thee
120   most grossly.

HOSTESS   So he doth you, my lord, and said this other day you
    owed him a thousand pound.

PRINCE HARRY   [to FALSTAFF]   Sirrah, do I owe you a thousand
    pound?

125 FALSTAFF   A thousand pound, Hal? A million! Thy love is worth
    a million; thou owest me thy love.

HOSTESS   Nay, my lord, he called you 'jack' and said he would
    cudgel you.

FALSTAFF   Did I, Bardolph?

---

1. Symbol of a bawd. Brothels often displayed a dish of
stewed prunes in the window.
2. A hunted fox drawn out from its hiding spot; a dead
fox dragged to lay a false trail.
3. A disreputable character, usually played by a cross-
dressed man, in the boisterous May games and morris
dances denounced by Puritan preachers. The figure is
here juxtaposed to the respectable wife of the deputy of
the ward.
4. A euphemism for "female genitalia."
5. The otter's unusual appearance led to debates about
whether it was a fish or an animal.
6. How to understand her; how to have sexual relations
with her.

130 BARDOLPH   Indeed, Sir John, you said so.

FALSTAFF   Yea, if he said my ring was copper.

PRINCE HARRY   I say 'tis copper; darest thou be as good as thy
word now?

FALSTAFF   Why, Hal, thou knowest as thou art but man I dare,
135   but as thou art prince, I fear thee as I fear the roaring of the
lion's whelp.°   cub

PRINCE HARRY   And why not as the lion?

FALSTAFF   The King himself is to be feared as the lion. Dost thou
think I'll fear thee as I fear thy father? Nay, an I do, I pray God
140   my girdle break.

PRINCE HARRY   O, if it should, how would thy guts fall about thy
knees! But sirrah, there's no room for faith, truth, nor honesty
in this bosom of thine; it is all filled up with guts and midriff.
Charge an honest woman with picking thy pocket? Why, thou
145   whoreson impudent embossed rascal,⁷ if there were anything
in thy pocket but tavern reckonings, memorandums of bawdy-
houses, and one poor pennyworth of sugar-candy to make thee
long-winded°—if thy pocket were enriched with any other   to give you energy
injuries⁸ but these, I am a villain. And yet you will stand to it,°   persist
150   you will not pocket up° wrong. Art thou not ashamed?   keep quiet about

FALSTAFF   Dost thou hear, Hal? Thou knowest in the state of
innocency Adam fell, and what should poor Jack Falstaff do in
the days of villainy? Thou seest I have more flesh than another
man, and therefore more frailty. You confess, then, you picked
155   my pocket.

PRINCE HARRY   It appears so by the story.

FALSTAFF   Hostess, I forgive thee. Go make ready breakfast. Love
thy husband, look to thy servants, cherish thy guests. Thou shalt
find me tractable to any honest reason; thou seest I am pacified
160   still.° Nay, prithee, be gone.   Exit HOSTESS   always
Now, Hal, to the news at court. For the robbery, lad, how is
that answered?°   settled

PRINCE HARRY   O, my sweet beef, I must still be good angel to
thee. The money is paid back again.

165 FALSTAFF   O, I do not like that paying back; 'tis a double labour.

PRINCE HARRY   I am good friends with my father, and may do
anything.

FALSTAFF   Rob me the exchequer the first thing thou dost, and
do it with unwashed hands° too.   do it at once

170 BARDOLPH   Do, my lord.

PRINCE HARRY   I have procured thee, Jack, a charge of foot.°   an infantry command

FALSTAFF   I would it had been of horse! Where shall I find one°   someone
that can steal well? O, for a fine thief of the age of two-and-
twenty or thereabouts! I am heinously unprovided.° Well, God   ill-equipped
175   be thanked for these rebels—they offend none but the virtuous.
I laud them, I praise them.

PRINCE HARRY   Bardolph.

BARDOLPH   My lord?

PRINCE HARRY [giving letters]   Go bear this letter to Lord John
of Lancaster,
180   To my brother John; this to my lord of Westmorland.

---

7. *embossed rascal:* bloated rogue; hunted deer, ex-   8. Any other things whose loss causes you injury.
hausted and foaming at the mouth.

[*Exit* BARDOLPH]

Go, Peto, to horse, to horse, for thou and I
Have thirty miles to ride yet ere dinner time. [*Exit* PETO]
Jack, meet me tomorrow in the Temple Hall⁹
At two o'clock in the afternoon.
185   There shalt thou know thy charge, and there receive
Money and order for their furniture.°   *equipment*
The land is burning, Percy stands on high,
And either we or they must lower lie.   [*Exit*]
FALSTAFF   Rare words! Brave world! [*Calling*] Hostess, my
    breakfast, come!—
190   O, I could wish this tavern were my drum!¹   *Exit*

4.1

Enter HOTSPUR *and* [*the Earls of*] WORCESTER *and*
DOUGLAS

HOTSPUR   Well said, my noble Scot! If speaking truth
In this fine age were not thought flattery,
Such attribution° should the Douglas have   *praise*
As not a soldier of this season's stamp°   *coinage*
5   Should go so general current° through the world.   *be so widely accepted*
By God, I cannot flatter, I do defy
The tongues of soothers,° but a braver place   *flatterers*
In my heart's love hath no man than yourself.
Nay, task° me to my word, approve° me, lord.   *hold / test*
10 DOUGLAS   Thou art the king of honour.
No man so potent breathes upon the ground
But I will beard° him.   *defy*
HOTSPUR   Do so, and 'tis well.
      Enter a MESSENGER *with letters*
What letters hast thou there? I can but thank you.
MESSENGER   These letters come from your father.
15 HOTSPUR   Letters from him? Why comes he not himself?
MESSENGER   He cannot come, my lord, he is grievous sick.
HOTSPUR   Zounds, how has he the leisure to be sick
In such a jostling° time? Who leads his power?   *turbulent*
Under whose government° come they along?   *command*
20 MESSENGER   His letters bears his mind, not I, my lord.
    [HOTSPUR *reads the letter*]
WORCESTER   I prithee tell me, doth he keep his bed?
MESSENGER   He did, my lord, four days ere I set forth;
And at the time of my departure thence
He was much feared° by his physicians.   *feared for*
25 WORCESTER   I would the state of time° had first been whole°   *of the times / healthy*
Ere he by sickness had been visited.
His health was never better worth° than now.   *of more value*
HOTSPUR   Sick now? Droop now? This sickness doth infect
The very life-blood of our enterprise.
30   'Tis catching° hither, even to our camp.   *infectious*
He writes me here that inward sickness stays him,
And that his friends by deputation°   *through deputies*

---

9. One of the Inns of Court, London's law schools.
1. A disputed passage. Perhaps Falstaff means he wishes
that he could stay at the tavern rather than go to war or
that he could make the tavern ring with the noise of his

departure. He puns on "taborn," a kind of drum used to
call soldiers to battle.
4.1 Location: The rebel camp near Shrewsbury.

Could not so soon be drawn;° nor did he think it meet°   *assembled / suitable*
To lay so dangerous and dear a trust
35 On any soul removed° but on his own.   *not directly involved*
Yet doth he give us bold advertisement°   *counsel*
That with our small conjunction° we should on,   *joint force*
To see how fortune is disposed to us;
For, as he writes, there is no quailing now,
40 Because the King is certainly possessed°   *informed*
Of all our purposes. What say you to it?
WORCESTER   Your father's sickness is a maim to us.
HOTSPUR   A perilous gash, a very limb lopped off.
And yet, in faith, it is not. His present want°   *absence*
45 Seems more than we shall find it. Were it good
To set° the exact wealth of all our states°   *stake / resources*
All at one cast,° to set so rich a main¹   *throw of the dice*
On the nice hazard° of one doubtful hour?   *precarious chance*
It were not good, for therein should we read
50 The very bottom and the sole² of hope,
The very list,° the very utmost bound,   *limit*
Of all our fortunes.
DOUGLAS   Faith, and so we should, where now remains
A sweet reversion°—we may boldly spend   *future inheritance*
55 Upon the hope of what is to come in.
A comfort of retirement³ lives in this.
HOTSPUR   A rendezvous, a home to fly unto,
If that the devil and mischance look big°   *threateningly*
Upon the maidenhead° of our affairs.   *virgin state; start*
60 WORCESTER   But yet I would your father had been here.
The quality and hair° of our attempt   *character*
Brooks° no division. It will be thought   *Tolerates*
By some that know not why he is away
That wisdom, loyalty, and mere° dislike   *absolute*
65 Of our proceedings kept the Earl from hence;
And think how such an apprehension
May turn the tide of fearful faction,°   *timid support*
And breed a kind of question in our cause.
For, well you know, we of the off'ring° side   *challenging*
70 Must keep aloof from strict arbitrement,°   *rigorous judgment*
And stop all sight-holes, every loop° from whence   *loophole*
The eye of reason may pry in upon us.
This absence of your father's draws° a curtain   *opens*
That shows the ignorant a kind of fear
Before not dreamt of.
75 HOTSPUR   You strain too far.
I rather of his absence make this use:
It lends a lustre, and more great opinion,°   *prestige*
A larger dare° to our great enterprise,   *daring*
Than if the Earl were here; for men must think
80 If we without his help can make a head°   *raise an army*
To push against a kingdom, with his help
We shall o'erturn it topsy-turvy down.
Yet° all goes well, yet all our joints° are whole.   *So far / limbs*

1. A stake in gambling; an army.   3. Refuge to which one can retreat.
2. Undersurface (as of a shoe), with a pun on "soul."

DOUGLAS   As heart can think, there is not such a word
85 Spoke of in Scotland as this term of fear.
        Enter Sir Richard VERNON
HOTSPUR   My cousin Vernon! Welcome, by my soul!
VERNON   Pray God my news be worth a welcome, lord.
    The Earl of Westmorland, seven thousand strong,
    Is marching hitherwards; with him Prince John.
HOTSPUR   No harm. What more?
90 VERNON   And further I have learned
    The King himself in person is set forth,
    Or hitherwards intended speedily,
    With strong and mighty preparation.
HOTSPUR   He shall be welcome too. Where is his son,
95 The nimble-footed madcap Prince of Wales,
    And his comrades that daffed° the world aside   tossed
    And bid it pass?
VERNON   All furnished,° all in arms,   equipped
    All plumed like ostriches,[4] that with the wind
    [   ]
100 Baiting° like eagles having lately bathed,   Beating their wings
    Glittering in golden coats like images,°   gilded statues
    As full of spirit as the month of May,
    And gorgeous as the sun at midsummer;
    Wanton° as youthful goats, wild as young bulls.   Frisky
105 I saw young Harry with his beaver° on,   visor; helmet
    His cuishes° on his thighs, gallantly armed,   armor for the thighs
    Rise from the ground like feathered Mercury,[5]
    And vaulted with such ease into his seat
    As if an angel dropped down from the clouds
110 To turn and wind° a fiery Pegasus,[6]   wheel about
    And witch° the world with noble horsemanship.   bewitch
HOTSPUR   No more, no more! Worse than the sun in March,
    This praise doth nourish agues.[7] Let them come!
    They come like sacrifices in their trim,°   fine trappings
115 And to the fire-eyed maid of smoky war°   Bellona, goddess of war
    All hot and bleeding will we offer them.
    The mailèd° Mars shall on his altar sit   dressed in armor
    Up to the ears in blood. I am on fire
    To hear this rich reprisal° is so nigh,   prize
120 And yet not ours! Come, let me taste° my horse,   test, try
    Who is to bear me like a thunderbolt
    Against the bosom of the Prince of Wales.
    Harry to Harry shall, hot horse to horse,
    Meet and ne'er part till one drop down a corpse.
    O, that Glyndŵr were come!
125 VERNON   There is more news.
    I learned in Worcester, as I rode along,
    He cannot draw° his power this fourteen days.   assemble
DOUGLAS   That's the worst tidings that I hear of yet.

4. Some editors follow Q in printing "estridges" (goshawks, a kind of hawk) here. Various emendations have been proposed for this and the following lines. The Oxford editors assume a line has been lost, as the brackets indicate.
5. The messenger of the gods, often represented as a
young man with winged sandals or a winged hat.
6. A winged horse of classical myth.
7. The March sun was popularly imagined as warm enough to kindle feverish diseases ("agues") without being strong enough to dispel them.

WORCESTER   Ay, by my faith, that bears a frosty sound.
130 HOTSPUR   What may the King's whole battle° reach unto?   *army*
VERNON   To thirty thousand.
HOTSPUR   Forty let it be.
My father and Glyndŵr being both away,
The powers° of us may serve so great a day.   *armies*
Come, let us take a muster speedily.
135 Doomsday is near: die all, die merrily.
DOUGLAS   Talk not of dying; I am out of° fear   *free from*
Of death or death's hand for this one half year.   *Exeunt*

4.2

Enter FALSTAFF *and* BARDOLPH

FALSTAFF   Bardolph, get thee before to Coventry; fill me a bottle
of sack. Our soldiers shall march through. We'll to Sutton
Coldfield[1] tonight.
BARDOLPH   Will you give me money, captain?
5 FALSTAFF   Lay out,° lay out.   *Use your own*
BARDOLPH   This bottle makes an angel.[2]
FALSTAFF [*giving* BARDOLPH *money*]   An if° it do, take it for thy   *An if = If*
labour; an if it make twenty, take them all; I'll answer the coin-
age.[3] Bid my lieutenant Peto meet me at town's end.
10 BARDOLPH   I will, captain. Farewell.   *Exit*
FALSTAFF   If I be not ashamed of my soldiers, I am a soused
gurnet.° I have misused the King's press[4] damnably. I have got   *a pickled fish*
in exchange of one hundred and fifty soldiers three hundred
and odd pounds. I press me° none but good householders, yeo-   *I draft*
15 men's sons, enquire me out contracted° bachelors, such as had   *engaged to be wed*
been asked twice on the banns,[5] such a commodity of warm
slaves[6] as had as lief° hear the devil as a drum, such as fear the   *willingly*
report of a caliver° worse than a struck° fowl or a hurt wild   *musket / wounded*
duck. I pressed me none but such toasts and butter,° with hearts   *such weaklings*
20 in their bellies no bigger than pins' heads, and they have
bought out their services;[7] and now my whole charge consists
of ensigns, corporals, lieutenants, gentlemen of companies[8]—
slaves as ragged as Lazarus[9] in the painted cloth,° where the   *cheap wall hangings*
glutton's dogs licked his sores—and such as indeed were never
25 soldiers, but discarded unjust° servingmen, younger sons to   *dishonest*
younger brothers, revolted° tapsters, and ostlers trade-fallen,°   *runaway / out of work*
the cankers° of a calm world and a long peace, ten times more   *cankerworms; parasites*
dishonourable-ragged than an old feazed ensign;° and such   *tattered flag*
have I to fill up the rooms of them as° have bought out their   *places of those who*
30 services, that you would think that I had a hundred and fifty
tattered prodigals lately come from swine-keeping, from eating
draff and husks.[1] A mad fellow met me on the way and told me
I had unloaded all the gibbets° and pressed the dead bodies.   *gallows*

4.2 Location: The road approaching Coventry.
1. Town about twenty miles northwest of Coventry in
Warwickshire.
2. Brings my outlay to several shillings (an "angel"). Falstaff retorts by punning on "makes" as meaning "earns a
profit of."
3. I'll be responsible for the money coined.
4. Commission for conscripting soldiers.
5. Proclamations made on three consecutive Sundays
affirming one's intent to marry.

6. Such a quantity of well-off or comfort-loving cowards.
7. They have paid me to excuse them from military service.
8. Gentlemen volunteers who were not officers.
9. For the story of Lazarus and the rich man, see note to
3.3.28.
1. Alluding to the biblical parable of the prodigal son,
who longs to eat swill ("draff") and corn husks meant for
pigs after he has squandered his inheritance in debauchery (see Luke 15:11–16).

No eye hath seen such scarecrows. I'll not march through Coventry with them, that's flat. Nay, and the villains march wide
betwixt the legs, as if they had gyves° on, for indeed I had the   *fetters*
most of them out of prison. There's not a shirt and a half in all
my company; and the half-shirt is two napkins tacked together
and thrown over the shoulders like a herald's coat without
sleeves; and the shirt, to say the truth, stolen from my host° at   *innkeeper*
Saint Albans, or the red-nose innkeeper of Daventry.² But that's
all one; they'll find linen enough on every hedge.³
    Enter PRINCE [HARRY] *and the Lord [Earl] of* WESTMOR-
    LAND
PRINCE HARRY   How now, blown Jack?⁴ How now, quilt?
FALSTAFF   What, Hal! How now, mad wag? What a devil dost
thou in Warwickshire? My good lord of Westmorland, I cry you
mercy!° I thought your honour had already been at Shrews-   *I beg your pardon*
bury.
WESTMORLAND   Faith, Sir John, 'tis more than time that I were
there, and you too; but my powers are there already. The King,
I can tell you, looks for us all. We must away° all night.   *must march*
FALSTAFF   Tut, never fear° me. I am as vigilant as a cat to steal   *worry about*
cream.
PRINCE HARRY   I think to steal cream indeed, for thy theft hath
already made thee butter.⁵ But tell me, Jack, whose fellows are
these that come after?
FALSTAFF   Mine, Hal, mine.
PRINCE HARRY   I did never see such pitiful rascals.
FALSTAFF   Tut, tut, good enough to toss,⁶ food for powder,° food   *cannon fodder*
for powder. They'll fill a pit as well as better. Tush, man, mortal
men, mortal men.
WESTMORLAND   Ay, but Sir John, methinks they are exceeding
poor and bare,° too beggarly.   *threadbare*
FALSTAFF   Faith, for their poverty, I know not where they had
that, and for their bareness, I am sure they never learned that
of me.
PRINCE HARRY   No, I'll be sworn, unless you call three fingers in
the ribs⁷ bare. But sirrah, make haste. Percy is already in the
field.   *Exit*
FALSTAFF   What, is the King encamped?
WESTMORLAND   He is, Sir John. I fear we shall stay too long.
    [Exit]
FALSTAFF   Well, to the latter end of a fray
And the beginning of a feast
Fits a dull fighter and a keen guest.   *Exit*

4.3

    Enter HOTSPUR, *[the Earls of]* WORCESTER *[and]* DOUG-
    LAS, *and [Sir Richard]* VERNON
HOTSPUR   We'll fight with him tonight.
WORCESTER   It may not be.

2. Saint Albans is a town north of London, Daventry a town southeast of Coventry.
3. Where laundresses set it out to dry.
4. Punning on "jack" as referring to what many Elizabethan soldiers wore: a quilted jacket covered with leather or cloth and worn over iron plates. *blown:* swollen; short-winded.
5. The riches ("cream") you have stolen have made you rich, or turned you into fat.
6. Good enough to be tossed on pikes.
7. Three fingers of fat over the ribs. A finger was a measure of three-quarters of an inch.
4.3 Location: The rebels' camp, Shrewsbury.

DOUGLAS   You give him then advantage.
VERNON   Not a whit.
HOTSPUR   Why say you so? Looks he not for supply?°   *reinforcements*
VERNON   So do we.
HOTSPUR   His is certain; ours is doubtful.
5   WORCESTER   Good cousin, be advised. Stir not tonight.
VERNON [*to* HOTSPUR]   Do not, my lord.
DOUGLAS   You do not counsel well.
   You speak it out of fear and cold heart.
VERNON   Do me no slander, Douglas. By my life—
   And I dare well maintain it with my life—
10   If well-respected° honour bid me on,   *well-considered*
   I hold as little counsel with weak fear
   As you, my lord, or any Scot that this day lives.
   Let it be seen tomorrow in the battle
   Which of us fears.
15   DOUGLAS   Yea, or tonight.
VERNON   Content.
HOTSPUR   Tonight, say I.
VERNON   Come, come, it may not be. I wonder much,
   Being men of such great leading° as you are,   *leadership*
20   That you foresee not what impediments
   Drag back our expedition.° Certain horse°   *rapid progress / cavalry*
   Of my cousin Vernon's are not yet come up.
   Your uncle Worcester's horse came but today,
   And now their pride° and mettle is asleep,   *spirit*
25   Their courage with hard labour tame and dull,
   That not a horse is half the half himself.
HOTSPUR   So are the horses of the enemy
   In general journey-bated° and brought low.   *weary from travel*
   The better part of ours are full of rest.
30   WORCESTER   The number of the King exceedeth our.
   For God's sake, cousin, stay° till all come in.   *wait*
         The trumpet sounds a parley[1] [*within*]. *Enter*
         Sir Walter BLUNT
BLUNT   I come with gracious offers from the King,
   If you vouchsafe me hearing and respect.
HOTSPUR   Welcome, Sir Walter Blunt; and would to God
35   You were of our determination.°   *on our side*
   Some of us love you well, and even those some°   *those same persons*
   Envy your great deservings and good name,
   Because you are not of our quality,°   *party*
   But stand against us like an enemy.
40   BLUNT   And God defend° but still I should stand so,   *forbid*
   So long as out of limit° and true rule   *bounds of allegiance*
   You stand against anointed majesty.
   But to my charge. The King hath sent to know
   The nature of your griefs,° and whereupon   *grievances*
45   You conjure from the breast of civil peace
   Such bold hostility, teaching his duteous land
   Audacious cruelty. If that the King
   Have any way your good deserts forgot,
   Which he confesseth to be manifold,

1. Summons to a conference with the enemy.

50 He bids you name your griefs, and with all speed
 You shall have your desires, with interest,
 And pardon absolute for yourself and these
 Herein misled by your suggestion.°   *instigation*
HOTSPUR The King is kind, and well we know the King
55 Knows at what time to promise, when to pay.
 My father and my uncle and myself
 Did give him that same royalty he wears;
 And when he was not six-and-twenty strong,
 Sick in the world's regard, wretched and low,
60 A poor unminded° outlaw sneaking home,   *insignificant*
 My father gave him welcome to the shore;
 And when he heard him swear and vow to God
 He came but to be Duke of Lancaster,
 To sue his livery,[2] and beg his peace
65 With tears of innocency and terms of zeal,
 My father, in kind heart and pity moved,
 Swore him assistance, and performed it too.
 Now when the lords and barons of the realm
 Perceived Northumberland did lean to him,
70 The more and less came in with cap and knee,[3]
 Met him in boroughs, cities, villages,
 Attended him on bridges, stood in lanes,[4]
 Laid gifts before him, proffered him their oaths,
 Gave him their heirs as pages, followed him,
75 Even at the heels, in golden° multitudes.   *resplendent*
 He presently, as greatness knows itself,°   *recognizes its power*
 Steps me° a little higher than his vow   *Steps*
 Made to my father while his blood° was poor   *spirit*
 Upon the naked shore at Ravenspurgh,
80 And now forsooth takes on him to reform
 Some certain edicts and some strait° decrees   *strict*
 That lie too heavy on the commonwealth,
 Cries out upon abuses, seems to weep
 Over his country's wrongs; and by this face,°   *outward show*
85 This seeming brow of justice, did he win
 The hearts of all that he did angle for;
 Proceeded further, cut me off° the heads   *cut off*
 Of all the favourites that the absent King
 In deputation° left behind him here   *As deputies*
90 When he was personal° in the Irish war.   *engaged in person*
BLUNT Tut, I came not to hear this.
HOTSPUR   Then to the point.
 In short time after, he deposed the King,
 Soon after that deprived him of his life,
 And in the neck of that tasked° the whole state; *And immediately taxed*
95 To make that worse, suffered his kinsman March[5] —
 Who is, if every owner were well placed,[6]
 Indeed his king—to be engaged° in Wales,   *held hostage*
 There without ransom to lie forfeited;°   *unredeemed*

2. To plead for the restitution of his lands (which Richard
II had seized when John of Gaunt, Bolingbroke's father,
died).
3. Those of both high and low social status deferentially
presented themselves (with cap in hand and bended knee).

4. Stood in rows along the roadways.
5. The Earl of March. For his claim to the throne, see
note to 1.3.79.
6. If everyone had possessions according to his entitle-
ment.

Disgraced me in my happy victories,
100 Sought to entrap me by intelligence,°   *spying*
Rated° mine uncle from the Council-board,   *Drove away*
In rage dismissed my father from the court,
Broke oath on oath, committed wrong on wrong,
And in conclusion drove us to seek out
105 This head of safety,[7] and withal° to pry   *also*
Into his title, the which we find
Too indirect° for long continuance.   *irregular*
BLUNT   Shall I return this answer to the King?
HOTSPUR   Not so, Sir Walter. We'll withdraw awhile.
110 Go to the King, and let there be impawned°   *pledged*
Some surety for a safe return again;
And in the morning early shall mine uncle
Bring him our purposes. And so, farewell.
BLUNT   I would you would accept of grace and love.
HOTSPUR   And maybe so we shall.
115 BLUNT   Pray God you do.
          Exeunt [HOTSPUR, WORCESTER, DOUGLAS, *and*
          VERNON *at one door,* BLUNT *at another door*]

4.4

Enter the ARCHBISHOP *of York, and* SIR MICHAEL

ARCHBISHOP [*giving letters*]   Hie, good Sir Michael, bear this sealèd brief°   *dispatch*
With wingèd haste to the Lord Marshal,
This to my cousin Scrope, and all the rest
To whom they are directed. If you knew
5 How much they do import, you would make haste.
SIR MICHAEL   My good lord,
I guess their tenor.
ARCHBISHOP   Like enough you do.
Tomorrow, good Sir Michael, is a day
Wherein the fortune of ten thousand men
10 Must bide the touch;° for, sir, at Shrewsbury,   *stand the test*
As I am truly given to understand,
The King with mighty and quick-raisèd power
Meets with Lord Harry. And I fear, Sir Michael,
What with the sickness of Northumberland,
15 Whose power was in the first proportion,°   *magnitude*
And what with Owain Glyndŵr's absence thence,
Who with them was a rated sinew[1] too,
And comes not in, overruled by prophecies,
I fear the power of Percy is too weak
20 To wage an instant° trial with the King.   *immediate*
SIR MICHAEL   Why, my good lord, you need not fear; there is Douglas
And Lord Mortimer.
ARCHBISHOP   No, Mortimer is not there.
SIR MICHAEL   But there is Mordake, Vernon, Lord Harry Percy;
And there is my lord of Worcester, and a head°   *troop*
25 Of gallant warriors, noble gentlemen.
ARCHBISHOP   And so there is; but yet the King hath drawn
The special head of all the land together—

---

7. That is, safety in these gathered forces.   1. A much-valued source of strength.
4.4 Location: The archbishop's palace, York.

The Prince of Wales, Lord John of Lancaster,
The noble Westmorland, and warlike Blunt,
30 And many more corrivals,° and dear° men   *associates / noble*
Of estimation° and command in arms.   *reputation*
SIR MICHAEL   Doubt not, my lord, they shall be well opposed.
ARCHBISHOP   I hope no less, yet needful 'tis to fear;
And to prevent the worst, Sir Michael, speed.
35 For if Lord Percy thrive not, ere the King
Dismiss his power he means to visit us,
For he hath heard of our confederacy,
And 'tis but wisdom to make strong against him;
Therefore make haste. I must go write again
40 To other friends; and so farewell, Sir Michael.   *Exeunt [severally]*

5.1

Enter KING [HENRY], PRINCE [HARRY], *Lord* JOHN OF LAN-
CASTER, [*the*] *Earl of* WESTMORLAND, *Sir Walter* BLUNT,
and FALSTAFF

KING HENRY   How bloodily the sun begins to peer
Above yon bulky hill! The day looks pale
At his distemp'rature.°   *sick appearance*
PRINCE HARRY   The southern wind
Doth play the trumpet to his° purposes,   *(the sun's)*
5 And by his hollow whistling in the leaves
Foretells a tempest and a blust'ring day.
KING HENRY   Then with the losers let it sympathize,°   *accord*
For nothing can seem foul to those that win.
*The trumpet sounds [a parley within]. Enter [the Earl
of]* WORCESTER [*and Sir Richard* VERNON][1]
How now, my lord of Worcester? 'Tis not well
10 That you and I should meet upon such terms
As now we meet. You have deceived our trust,
And made us doff our easy robes of peace
To crush our old limbs in ungentle steel.
This is not well, my lord, this is not well.
15 What say you to it? Will you again unknit
This churlish knot of all-abhorrèd war,
And move in that obedient orb[2] again
Where you did give a fair and natural light,
And be no more an exhaled meteor,[3]
20 A prodigy of fear,° and a portent   *A fearful omen*
Of broachèd mischief° to the unborn times?   *Of evil set flowing*
WORCESTER   Hear me, my liege.
For mine own part, I could be well content
To entertain the lag-end° of my life   *latter end*
25 With quiet hours; for I protest,
I have not sought the day of this dislike.°   *discord*
KING HENRY   You have not sought it? How comes it, then?
FALSTAFF   Rebellion lay in his way, and he found it.

5.1 Location: King Henry's camp at Shrewsbury.
1. Neither Q nor F indicates that Vernon accompanies
Worcester in this scene, but it seems lacking in ceremony
for Worcester to go to King Henry's camp alone. Also, in
the next scene, Worcester discusses with Vernon what the
King has said and whether to inform Hotspur, making it
appear that Vernon was present at this meeting.

2. Orbit. Henry, drawing on a conventional analogy between social and cosmological order, compares Worcester
to a star or a planet that, in Ptolemaic cosmology, should
move properly in its sphere (orbit) around the earth.
3. Meteors were thought to be made of gas exhaled by
the sun and were considered bad omens.

PRINCE HARRY Peace, chewet,° peace!   *jackdaw; chatterer*
30 WORCESTER [*to the* KING] It pleased your majesty to turn your looks
Of favour from myself and all our house;
And yet I must remember° you, my lord,   *remind*
We were the first and dearest of your friends.
For you my staff of office did I break
35 In Richard's time, and posted° day and night   *rode swiftly*
To meet you on the way and kiss your hand
When yet you were in place° and in account°   *social status / esteem*
Nothing so strong and fortunate as I.
It was myself, my brother, and his son
40 That brought you home, and boldly did outdare
The dangers of the time. You swore to us,
And you did swear that oath at Doncaster,
That you did nothing purpose° 'gainst the state,   *intend*
Nor claim no further than your new-fall'n right,[4]
45 The seat° of Gaunt, dukedom of Lancaster.   *estate*
To this we swore our aid, but in short space
It rained down fortune show'ring on your head,
And such a flood of greatness fell on you,
What with our help, what with the absent King,
50 What with the injuries° of a wanton° time,   *evils / lawless*
The seeming sufferances° that you had borne,   *wrongs*
And the contrarious° winds that held the King   *adverse*
So long in his unlucky Irish wars
That all in England did repute him dead;
55 And from this swarm of fair advantages
You took occasion to be quickly wooed
To gripe° the general sway into your hand,   *seize*
Forgot your oath to us at Doncaster,
And being fed by us, you used us so
60 As that ungentle gull,° the cuckoo's bird,   *rude young bird*
Useth the sparrow[5]—did oppress our nest,
Grew by our feeding to so great a bulk
That even our love° durst not come near your sight   *we who loved you*
For fear of swallowing.° But with nimble wing   *being swallowed*
65 We were enforced for safety' sake to fly
Out of your sight, and raise this present head,
Whereby we stand opposèd° by such means   *in opposition to you*
As you yourself have forged against yourself,
By unkind usage, dangerous° countenance,   *threatening*
70 And violation of all faith and troth
Sworn to us in your younger enterprise.
KING HENRY These things indeed you have articulate,°   *expressed*
Proclaimed at market crosses, read in churches,
To face° the garment of rebellion   *adorn*
75 With some fine colour° that may please the eye   *hue; pretext*
Of fickle changelings° and poor discontents,   *turncoats*
Which gape and rub the elbow[6] at the news
Of hurly-burly innovation;°   *rebellion*
And never yet did insurrection want°   *lack*

---

4. The right newly descended to you (upon the death of your father).
5. The female cuckoo lays its eggs in the nests of smaller birds such as the sparrow, who raises the cockoo's young
until they grow so large they threaten the sparrow and her nest.
6. And hug themselves with crossed arms (conventional expression of delight).

80 Such water-colours to impaint his cause,
    Nor moody beggars starving for a time
    Of pell-mell° havoc and confusion.   *chaotic*
PRINCE HARRY In both our armies there is many a soul
    Shall pay full dearly for this encounter
85 If once they join in trial.° Tell your nephew   *combat*
    The Prince of Wales doth join with all the world
    In praise of Henry Percy. By my hopes,
    This present enterprise set off his head,°   *not counted against him*
    I do not think a braver gentleman,
90 More active-valiant or more valiant-young,
    More daring, or more bold, is now alive
    To grace this latter age with noble deeds.
    For my part, I may speak it to my shame,
    I have a truant been to chivalry;
95 And so I hear he doth account me too.
    Yet this, before my father's majesty:
    I am content that he shall take the odds°   *have the advantage*
    Of his great name and estimation,°   *reputation*
    And will, to save the blood on either side,
100 Try fortune with him in a single fight.
KING HENRY And, Prince of Wales, so dare we venture thee,
    Albeit° considerations infinite   *Were it not that*
    Do make against it. No, good Worcester, no.
    We love our people well; even those we love
105 That are misled upon your cousin's° part;   *kinsman's*
    And will they take the offer of our grace,°   *mercy*
    Both he and they and you, yea, every man
    Shall be my friend again, and I'll be his.
    So tell your cousin, and bring me word
110 What he will do. But if he will not yield,
    Rebuke and dread correction wait on° us,   *serve*
    And they shall do their office. So be gone.
    We will not now be troubled with reply.
    We offer fair; take it advisedly.
                    Exeunt WORCESTER [*and* VERNON]
115 PRINCE HARRY It will not be accepted, on my life.
    The Douglas and the Hotspur both together
    Are confident against the world in arms.
KING HENRY Hence, therefore, every leader to his charge,
    For on their answer will we set on them,
120 And God befriend us as our cause is just!
                    Exeunt. Manent° *Prince* [HARRY] *and* FALSTAFF   *Remain*
FALSTAFF Hal, if thou see me down in the battle, and bestride
    me,° so.° 'Tis a point of friendship.   *stand over me / good*
PRINCE HARRY Nothing but a colossus[7] can do thee that friend-
    ship. Say thy prayers, and farewell.
125 FALSTAFF I would 'twere bed-time, Hal, and all well.
PRINCE HARRY Why, thou owest God a death.   [*Exit*]
FALSTAFF 'Tis not due yet. I would be loath to pay him before
    his day. What need I be so forward with him that calls not on
    me? Well, 'tis no matter; honour pricks° me on. Yea, but how   *spurs*

---

7. Referring to a massive statue of Apollo that purportedly stood over the entrance to the harbor in ancient Rhodes and was referred to as the Colossus of Rhodes.

130 if honour prick me off[8] when I come on? How then? Can
honour set-to° a leg? No. Or an arm? No. Or take away the   *mend*
grief of a wound? No. Honour hath no skill in surgery, then?
No. What is honour? A word. What is in that word 'honour'?
What is that 'honour'? Air. A trim reckoning!° Who hath it? He   *A nice summing up*
135 that died o'Wednesday. Doth he feel it? No. Doth he hear it?
No. 'Tis insensible[9] then? Yea, to the dead. But will it not live
with the living? No. Why? Detraction° will not suffer° it. There-   *Slander / allow*
fore I'll none of it. Honour is a mere scutcheon.[1] And so ends
my catechism.   *Exit*

5.2

Enter [the Earl of] WORCESTER *and Sir Richard*
VERNON

WORCESTER   O no, my nephew must not know, Sir Richard,
The liberal and kind offer of the King.
VERNON   'Twere best he did.
WORCESTER   Then are we all undone.
It is not possible, it cannot be,
5 The King should keep his word in loving us.
He will suspect us still,° and find a time   *always*
To punish this offence in other faults.
Supposition all our lives shall be stuck full of eyes,[1]
For treason is but trusted like the fox,
10 Who, ne'er so° tame, so cherished, and locked up,   *no matter how*
Will have a wild trick of his ancestors.
Look how we can, or° sad or merrily,   *whether*
Interpretation will misquote our looks,
And we shall feed like oxen at a stall,
15 The better cherished still the nearer death.
My nephew's trespass may be well forgot;
It hath the excuse of youth and heat of blood,
And an adopted name of privilege[2] —
A hare-brained Hotspur, governed by a spleen.°   *hot temper*
20 All his offences live upon my head,
And on his father's. We did train° him on,   *lead*
And, his corruption being ta'en from us,
We as the spring° of all shall pay for all.   *source*
Therefore, good cousin, let not Harry know
25 In any case the offer of the King.
VERNON   Deliver what you will; I'll say 'tis so.
        Enter HOTSPUR *[and the Earl of* DOUGLAS*]*
Here comes your cousin.
HOTSPUR   My uncle is returned.
Deliver up[3] my lord of Westmorland.
Uncle, what news?
30 WORCESTER   The King will bid you battle presently.
DOUGLAS   Defy him by the Lord of Westmorland.
HOTSPUR   Lord Douglas, go you and tell him so.

8. Selects me to die; marks me off the list.
9. Imperceptible to the senses.
1. Heraldic shield exhibited at funerals displaying the deceased person's coat of arms.
5.2 Location: The rebels' camp.
1. The King's suspicion will cause him constantly to spy on us. Worcester is referring to an allegorical representa-

tion of Suspicion dressed in a coat of eyes or to secret agents similar to those whom Elizabeth's government maintained.
2. A nickname, "Hotspur," which may excuse his rashness.
3. Release (as the hostage for the safe return of Worcester and Vernon).

DOUGLAS Marry, and shall, and very willingly.   *Exit*

WORCESTER There is no seeming° mercy in the King.   semblance of

35 HOTSPUR Did you beg any? God forbid!

WORCESTER I told him gently of our grievances,
    Of his oath-breaking, which he mended thus:
    By now forswearing that he is forsworn.
    He calls us 'rebels', 'traitors', and will scourge
40   With haughty arms this hateful name in us.

    Enter [the Earl of] DOUGLAS

DOUGLAS Arm, gentlemen, to arms, for I have thrown
    A brave° defiance in King Henry's teeth—   proud
    And Westmorland that was engaged° did bear it—   held as hostage
    Which cannot choose but bring him quickly on.

WORCESTER [*to* HOTSPUR] The Prince of Wales stepped forth
45   before the King
    And, nephew, challenged you to single fight.

HOTSPUR O, would the quarrel lay upon our heads,
    And that no man might draw short breath today
    But I and Harry Monmouth![4] Tell me, tell me,
50   How showed his tasking?° Seemed it in contempt?   challenge

VERNON No, by my soul, I never in my life
    Did hear a challenge urged more modestly,
    Unless a brother should a brother dare
    To gentle° exercise and proof of arms.[5]   noble
55   He gave you all the duties of° a man,   respect due to
    Trimmed up your praises[6] with a princely tongue,
    Spoke your deservings like a chronicle,
    Making you ever better than his praise
    By still° dispraising praise valued with you;[7]   constantly
60   And, which became him like a prince indeed,
    He made a blushing cital° of himself,   mention
    And chid his truant youth with such a grace
    As if he mastered there a double spirit
    Of teaching and of learning instantly.°   simultaneously
65   There did he pause; but let me tell the world,
    If he outlive the envy° of this day,   malice
    England did never owe° so sweet a hope,   own
    So much misconstrued in his wantonness.°   self-indulgence

HOTSPUR Cousin, I think thou art enamourèd
70   On° his follies. Never did I hear   Of
    Of any prince so wild a liberty.°   such unrestrained license
    But be he as he will, yet once ere night
    I will embrace him with a soldier's arm,
    That he shall shrink under my courtesy.
75   Arm, arm, with speed! And fellows, soldiers, friends,
    Better consider what you have to do
    Than I, that have not well the gift of tongue,
    Can lift your blood[8] up with persuasion.

    Enter a MESSENGER

MESSENGER My lord, here are letters for you.

80 HOTSPUR I cannot read them now.   [*Exit* MESSENGER]

4. Harry of Monmouth, the town in Wales where the Prince was born.
5. Trial of skill at weapons.
6. Embellished his praises of you.

7. As measured against you (because your merit exceeds all praise).
8. Rebelliousness; self-indulgence.

O gentlemen, the time of life is short.
To spend that shortness basely were too long
If life did ride upon a dial's point,
Still ending at the arrival of an hour.⁹
85   An if we live, we live to tread on kings;
If die, brave death when princes die with us!
Now for our consciences: the arms are fair
When the intent of bearing them is just.
            Enter another MESSENGER
MESSENGER   My lord, prepare; the King comes on apace. [*Exit*]
90   HOTSPUR   I thank him that he cuts me from my tale,
For I profess not° talking, only this: *am not skilled at*
Let each man do his best. And here draw I
A sword whose temper° I intend to stain   *tempered steel*
With the best blood that I can meet withal
95   In the adventure of this perilous day.
Now *Esperance!*¹ Percy! And set on!
Sound all the lofty instruments of war,
And by that music let us all embrace,
For, heaven to earth,² some of us never shall
100   A second time do such a courtesy.
            The trumpets sound. Here they embrace. [*Exeunt*]

5.3

KING [HENRY] *enters with his power. Alarum*¹ [*and exe-
unt*] *to the battle. Then enter* [*the Earl of*] DOUGLAS,
and Sir Walter BLUNT [*disguised as the* KING]
BLUNT   What is thy name, that in the battle thus
Thou crossest me? What honour dost thou seek
Upon my head?
DOUGLAS   Know then my name is Douglas,
And I do haunt thee in the battle thus
5   Because some tell me that thou art a king.
BLUNT   They tell thee true.
DOUGLAS   The Lord of Stafford dear today hath bought
Thy likeness,² for instead of thee, King Harry,
This sword hath ended him. So shall it thee,
10   Unless thou yield thee as my prisoner.
BLUNT   I was not born a yielder, thou proud Scot,
And thou shalt find a king that will revenge
Lord Stafford's death.
            They fight. DOUGLAS *kills* BLUNT. *Then enter* HOTSPUR
HOTSPUR   O Douglas, hadst thou fought at Holmedon thus,
15   I never had triumphed upon a Scot.
DOUGLAS   All's done, all's won: here breathless lies the King.
HOTSPUR   Where?
DOUGLAS   Here.
HOTSPUR   This, Douglas? No, I know this face full well.
20   A gallant knight he was; his name was Blunt—

---

9. *To spend . . . hour*: that is, If life only lasted an hour
(*dial's point*: hand of a clock), it would still be too long if
it were basely spent.
1. Hope (the Percy motto; see note to 2.4.65).
2. The odds are as great as the distance from heaven to
earth.

5.3 Location: The remaining scenes take place on the
battlefield at Shrewsbury.
1. A call to arms, usually sounded on drum or trumpets.
2. *hath . . . likeness*: has paid for impersonating you; has
paid for his resemblance to you.

Semblably furnished° like the King himself.   *Similarly equipped*
DOUGLAS [*to Blunt's body*]   A fool go with thy soul,³ whither it goes!
A borrowed title hast thou bought too dear.
Why didst thou tell me that thou wert a king?
25 HOTSPUR   The king hath many marching in his coats.⁴
DOUGLAS   Now by my sword, I will kill all his coats.
I'll murder all his wardrobe, piece by piece,
Until I meet the King.
HOTSPUR   Up and away!
Our soldiers stand full fairly for the day.⁵
                              Exeunt [leaving Blunt's body]
              Alarum. Enter FALSTAFF
30 FALSTAFF   Though I could scape shot-free⁶ at London, I fear the
shot here. Here's no scoring⁷ but upon the pate. — Soft, who
are you? — Sir Walter Blunt. There's honour for you. Here's no
vanity. I am as hot as molten lead, and as heavy too. God keep
lead out of me; I need no more weight than mine own bowels.
35 I have led my ragamuffins where they are peppered; there's not
three of my hundred and fifty left alive, and they are for the
town's end,⁸ to beg during life.
              Enter PRINCE [HARRY]
But who comes here?
PRINCE HARRY   What, stand'st thou idle here? Lend me thy sword.
40 Many a noble man lies stark and stiff
Under the hoofs of vaunting enemies,
Whose deaths as yet are unrevenged. I prithee
Lend me thy sword.
45 FALSTAFF   O Hal, I prithee give me leave to breathe awhile.
Turk Gregory⁹ never did such deeds in arms
As I have done this day. I have paid° Percy,   *settled with (killed)*
I have made him sure.¹
PRINCE HARRY   He is indeed,
And living to kill thee. I prithee
Lend me thy sword.
FALSTAFF   Nay, before God, Hal,
50 If Percy be alive thou gett'st not my sword;
But take my pistol if thou wilt.
PRINCE HARRY   Give it me. What, is it in the case?
FALSTAFF   Ay, Hal;
'Tis hot, 'tis hot. There's that will sack a city.
              The PRINCE *draws it out, and finds it to be a bottle of
              sack*
PRINCE HARRY   What, is it a time to jest and dally now?
                              He throws the bottle at him. Exit
55 FALSTAFF   Well, if Percy be alive, I'll pierce him. If he do come
in my way, so; if he do not, if I come in his willingly, let him
make a carbonado° of me. I like not such grinning honour as   *meat slashed to grill*

---

3. May the title of "fool" go with your soul (for impersonating the King).
4. In his surcoat, or loose robes of rich material, embroidered with the royal coat of arms and worn over armor.
5. Our soldiers look as though they will win the day.
6. Escape without paying the tavern bill ("shot"), with a
pun in the following line on "shot" as ammunition (pro-
jectiles, cannon shot, etc.).
7. Recording of debts by means of "scores," or notches

on a board (customary in taverns); wounding or cutting.
8. By the town gates, where people often begged.
9. A conflation of the idea of the Turk, taken to be a
cruel and fierce fighter and an enemy of Protestant
England, and either Pope Gregory VII or Pope Gregory
XIII, both regarded as violent and cruel by Protestant
writers.
1. I have killed him; but the Prince takes "sure" to mean
"secure."

Sir Walter hath. Give me life, which if I can save, so; if not,
honour comes unlooked for, and there's an end.

Exit [with Blunt's body]

5.4

Alarum. Excursions. Enter KING [HENRY], PRINCE
[HARRY, *wounded*], *Lord* JOHN OF LANCASTER, *and [the]*
Earl of WESTMORLAND

KING HENRY   I prithee, Harry, withdraw thyself, thou bleed'st too much.
    Lord John of Lancaster, go you with him.

JOHN OF LANCASTER   Not I, my lord, unless I did bleed too.

PRINCE HARRY [*to the* KING]   I beseech your majesty, make up,°   *go forward*
5   Lest your retirement do amaze° your friends.   *alarm*

KING HENRY   I will do so. My lord of Westmorland,
    Lead him to his tent.

WESTMORLAND [*to the* PRINCE]   Come, my lord, I'll lead you to your tent.

PRINCE HARRY   Lead me, my lord? I do not need your help,
10   And God forbid a shallow scratch should drive
    The Prince of Wales from such a field as this,
    Where stained[1] nobility lies trodden on,
    And rebels' arms triumph in massacres.

JOHN OF LANCASTER   We breathe° too long. Come, cousin Westmorland,   *rest*
15   Our duty this way lies. For God's sake, come.

                     [*Exeunt* LANCASTER *and* WESTMORLAND]

PRINCE HARRY   By God, thou hast deceived me, Lancaster;
    I did not think thee lord of such a spirit.
    Before I loved thee as a brother, John,
    But now I do respect thee as my soul.
20 KING HENRY   I saw him hold Lord Percy at the point°   *sword point*
    With lustier maintenance° than I did look for   *more valiant bearing*
    Of such an ungrown warrior.

PRINCE HARRY   O, this boy lends mettle to us all!   *Exit*

             Enter [the Earl of] DOUGLAS

DOUGLAS   Another king! They grow like Hydra's heads.[2]
25   I am the Douglas, fatal to all those
    That wear those colours on them. What art thou
    That counterfeit'st the person of a king?

KING HENRY   The King himself, who, Douglas, grieves at heart
    So many of his shadows° thou hast met   *likenesses*
30   And not the very King. I have two boys
    Seek° Percy and thyself about the field;   *Who seek*
    But seeing thou fall'st on me so luckily,
    I will assay° thee; and defend thyself.   *challenge*

DOUGLAS   I fear thou art another counterfeit;
35   And yet, in faith, thou bear'st thee like a king.
    But mine° I am sure thou art, whoe'er thou be,   *(my prize of war)*
    And thus I win thee.

         They fight. The KING *being in danger, enter* PRINCE
         [HARRY]

PRINCE HARRY   Hold up thy head, vile Scot, or thou art like
    Never to hold it up again. The spirits

5.4
1. Bloodstained; disgraced by defeat.
2. A monster of classical myth that grew two heads whenever one was cut off. The hydra was a common image of
political disorder.

40 Of valiant Shirley, Stafford, Blunt, are in my arms.
It is the Prince of Wales that threatens thee,
Who never promiseth but he means to pay.
        They fight. DOUGLAS *flieth*
Cheerly, my lord! How fares your grace?
Sir Nicholas Gawsey hath for succour sent,
45 And so hath Clifton. I'll to Clifton straight.
KING HENRY   Stay and breathe awhile.
Thou hast redeemed thy lost opinion,°   *reputation*
And showed thou mak'st some tender of° my life,   *have some regard for*
In this fair rescue thou hast brought to me.
50 PRINCE HARRY   O God, they did me too much injury
That ever said I hearkened for° your death.   *desired*
If it were so, I might have let alone
The insulting° hand of Douglas over you,   *scornful*
Which would have been as speedy in your end
55 As all the poisonous potions in the world,
And saved the treacherous labour of your son.
KING HENRY   Make up° to Clifton; I'll to Sir Nicholas Gawsey.   *Go forward*
                                                        Exit
        Enter HOTSPUR
HOTSPUR   If I mistake not, thou art Harry Monmouth.
PRINCE HARRY   Thou speak'st as if I would deny my name.
HOTSPUR   My name is Harry Percy.
60 PRINCE HARRY   Why then, I see
A very valiant rebel of the name.
I am the Prince of Wales; and think not, Percy,
To share with me in glory any more.
Two stars keep not their motion in one sphere,³
65 Nor can one England brook° a double reign   *endure*
Of Harry Percy and the Prince of Wales.
HOTSPUR   Nor shall it, Harry, for the hour is come
To end the one of us, and would to God
Thy name in arms were now as great as mine.
70 PRINCE HARRY   I'll make it greater ere I part from thee,
And all the budding honours on thy crest°   *helmet; coat of arms*
I'll crop° to make a garland for my head.   *cut*
HOTSPUR   I can no longer brook thy vanities.°   *empty boasts*
        They fight.
        Enter FALSTAFF
FALSTAFF   Well said, Hal! To it, Hal! Nay, you shall find no boy's
75 play here, I can tell you.
        Enter DOUGLAS. *He fighteth with* FALSTAFF, *who falls*
        down as if he were dead. [*Exit* DOUGLAS.] *The* PRINCE
        killeth [HOTSPUR]
HOTSPUR   O Harry, thou hast robbed me of my youth.
I better brook the loss of brittle life
Than those proud titles thou hast won of me.
They wound my thoughts worse than thy sword my flesh.
80 But thoughts, the slaves of life, and life, time's fool,
And time, that takes survey of all the world,
Must have a stop.° O, I could prophesy,   *an end*

---

3. Alluding to the theory that stars moved in concentric spheres around a center. Only one star could occupy a single sphere.

But that the earthy and cold hand of death
Lies on my tongue. No, Percy, thou art dust,
85 And food for—   [*He dies*]
PRINCE HARRY   For worms, brave Percy. Fare thee well, great heart.
Ill-weaved ambition, how much art thou shrunk!
When that this body did contain a spirit,
A kingdom for it was too small a bound,
90 But now two paces of the vilest earth
Is room enough. This earth that bears thee dead
Bears not alive so stout° a gentleman.   *valiant*
If thou wert sensible° of courtesy,   *conscious*
I should not make so dear° a show of zeal;°   *heartfelt / emotion*
95 But let my favours⁴ hide thy mangled face,
    [*He covers Hotspur's face*]
And even in thy behalf I'll thank myself
For doing these fair rites of tenderness.
Adieu, and take thy praise with thee to heaven.
Thy ignominy sleep with thee in the grave,
100 But not remembered in thy epitaph.
        He spieth FALSTAFF *on the ground*
What, old acquaintance! Could not all this flesh
Keep in a little life? Poor Jack, farewell.
I could have better spared a better man.
O, I should have a heavy° miss of thee,   *sad; weighty*
105 If I were much in love with vanity.
Death hath not struck so fat a deer today,
Though many dearer in this bloody fray.
Embowelled⁵ will I see thee by and by.
Till then, in blood by noble Percy lie.   *Exit*
        FALSTAFF *riseth up*
110 FALSTAFF   Embowelled? If thou embowel me today, I'll give you
leave to powder° me, and eat me too, tomorrow. 'Sblood, 'twas   *pickle in salt*
time to counterfeit, or that hot termagant⁶ Scot had paid me,
scot and lot° too. Counterfeit? I lie, I am no counterfeit. To die   *in full*
is to be a counterfeit, for he is but the counterfeit of a man who
115 hath not the life of a man. But to counterfeit dying when a
man thereby liveth is to be no counterfeit, but the true and
perfect image of life indeed. The better part of valour is discretion, in the which better part° I have saved my life. Zounds, I   *role*
am afraid of this gunpowder Percy, though he be dead. How if
120 he should counterfeit too, and rise? By my faith, I am afraid he
would prove the better counterfeit. Therefore I'll make him
sure; yea, and I'll swear I killed him. Why may not he rise as
well as I? Nothing confutes me but eyes,⁷ and nobody sees me.
Therefore, sirrah, [*stabbing* HOTSPUR] with a new wound in
125 your thigh, come you along with me.
        He takes up HOTSPUR *on his back.*
    Enter PRINCE [HARRY] *and* [*Lord*] JOHN OF LANCASTER
PRINCE HARRY   Come, brother John. Full bravely hast thou fleshed
Thy maiden sword.⁸

4. Ornaments such as plumes or gloves worn into battle.
5. Prepared for embalming and burial as noblemen were;
disemboweled in the manner of a hunted deer.
6. A quarrelsome or shrewish person; the name of an
imaginary deity who, according to medieval morality

plays, was worshipped by followers of Mohammed.
7. No one could confute my story but an eyewitness.
8. *Full . . . sword:* How courageously or splendidly have
you initiated in bloodshed your untried weapon (fought
your first battle). The phrase alludes to hunting practices

JOHN OF LANCASTER   But soft; whom have we here?
Did you not tell me this fat man was dead?
PRINCE HARRY   I did; I saw him dead,
Breathless and bleeding on the ground.
130   [*To* FALSTAFF]   Art thou alive?
Or is it fantasy that plays upon our eyesight?
I prithee speak; we will not trust our eyes
Without our ears. Thou art not what thou seem'st.
FALSTAFF   No, that's certain: I am not a double man.° But if I be   *ghost; two men*
135   not Jack Falstaff, then am I a jack.° There is Percy. If your   *knave*
father will do me any honour, so; if not, let him kill the next
Percy himself. I look to be either earl or duke, I can assure you.
PRINCE HARRY   Why, Percy I killed myself, and saw thee dead.
FALSTAFF   Didst thou? Lord, Lord, how this world is given to
140   lying! I grant you I was down and out of breath, and so was he;
but we rose both at an instant,° and fought a long hour by   *simultaneously*
Shrewsbury clock. If I may be believed, so; if not, let them that
should reward valour bear the sin upon their own heads. I'll
take't on my death° I gave him this wound in the thigh. If the   *swear on my deathbed*
145   man were alive and would deny it, zounds, I would make him
eat a piece of my sword.
JOHN OF LANCASTER   This is the strangest tale that e'er I heard.
PRINCE HARRY   This is the strangest fellow, brother John.
[*To* FALSTAFF] Come, bring your luggage nobly on your back.
150   For my part, if a lie may do thee grace,°   *get you favor*
I'll gild it with the happiest° terms I have.   *most favorable*
        A retreat is sounded
The trumpet sounds retreat; the day is our.
Come, brother, let us to the highest° of the field   *highest ground*
To see what friends are living, who are dead.
        Exeunt [the PRINCE *and* LANCASTER]
155   FALSTAFF   I'll follow, as they say, for reward. He that rewards me,
God reward him. If I do grow great, I'll grow less; for I'll purge,⁹
and leave sack, and live cleanly, as a nobleman should do.
        Exit [bearing Hotspur's body]

5.5

The trumpets sound. Enter KING [HENRY], PRINCE
[HARRY], *Lord* JOHN OF LANCASTER, [*the*] *Earl of* WEST-
MORLAND, *with* [*the Earl of*] WORCESTER *and* [*Sir Rich-
ard*] VERNON, *prisoners* [*and soldiers*]
KING HENRY   Thus ever did rebellion find rebuke.
Ill-spirited Worcester, did not we send grace,
Pardon, and terms of love to all of you?
And wouldst thou turn our offers contrary,
5   Misuse the tenor° of thy kinsman's trust?   *Abuse the substance*
Three knights upon our party slain today,
A noble earl, and many a creature else,
Had been alive this hour
If like a Christian thou hadst truly borne
10   Betwixt our armies true intelligence.°   *information*

---

in which hawks or hounds were "fleshed," or made eager
for prey by the taste of blood. Also alluding, by way of the
slang meaning of "sword" as "penis," to a man's first sex-

ual encounters with the flesh of others.
9. I'll take laxatives (to reduce my weight); I'll repent.

WORCESTER   What I have done my safety urged me to,
    And I embrace this fortune patiently,
    Since not to be avoided it falls on me.
KING HENRY   Bear Worcester to the death, and Vernon too.
15   Other offenders we will pause upon.°   reflect upon
                Exeunt WORCESTER *and* VERNON [*guarded*]
    How goes the field?
PRINCE HARRY   The noble Scot Lord Douglas, when he saw
    The fortune of the day quite turned from him,
    The noble Percy slain, and all his men
20   Upon the foot of fear,° fled with the rest;   Fleeing in fear
    And falling from a hill he was so bruised
    That the pursuers took him. At my tent
    The Douglas is, and I beseech your grace
    I may dispose of him.
25   KING HENRY   With all my heart.
PRINCE HARRY   Then, brother John of Lancaster,
    To you this honourable bounty° shall belong.   act of generosity
    Go to the Douglas, and deliver him
    Up to his pleasure ransomless and free.
30   His valours shown upon our crests° today   helmets
    Have taught us how to cherish such high deeds
    Even in the bosom of our adversaries.
JOHN OF LANCASTER   I thank your grace for this high courtesy,
    Which I shall give away immediately.
35   KING HENRY   Then this remains, that we divide our power.
    You, son John, and my cousin Westmorland,
    Towards York shall bend you° with your dearest speed   direct your course
    To meet Northumberland and the prelate Scrope,
    Who, as we hear, are busily in arms.
40   Myself and you, son Harry, will towards Wales,
    To fight with Glyndŵr and the Earl of March.
    Rebellion in this land shall lose his sway,
    Meeting the check of such another day;
    And since this business so fair is done,
45   Let us not leave° till all our own be won.   leave off
                Exeunt [*the* KING, *the* PRINCE, *and their power*
                at one door, LANCASTER, WESTMORLAND, *and their*
                                power at another door]

TEXTUAL VARIANTS

Control text: Q1 for 1.3.199–2.3.19, Q2 elsewhere

F: The Folio of 1623
Q1: Remaining fragment of the Quarto of 1598
Q2: The complete Quarto of 1598
Q3: The Quarto of 1599
Q4: The Quarto of 1604
Q5: The Quarto of 1608
Q6: The Quarto of 1613

Q5b, Q6b: Successive states of Q5 and Q6 incorporating various print-shop corrections and changes
Q7: The Quarto of 1622

Title: THE / HISTORY OF / HENRIE THE / FOURTH; / With the battell at Shrewsburie, / *betweene the King and Lord* / Henry Percy, surnamed / Henrie Hotspur of / the North. / *With the humorous conceits of Sir* / John Falstalffe [Q2 title page] The First Part of Henry the Fourth, / with the Life and Death of HENRY / Sirnamed HOT-SPURRE. [F head title]

s.p. KING HENRY [Q's use of *King* has been changed throughout.]
s.p. PRINCE HARRY [Q's use of *Prince* has been changed throughout.]
s.p. POINS [Q's use of *Poines / Poynes* has been standardized throughout.]
s.p. HOTSPUR [Q's use of *Hotspur / Percy* has been standardized throughout.]
s.p. FIRST TRAVELLER and **SECOND TRAVELLER** [Q's *Traveler* of 2.2 has been differentiated into two persons.]
s.p. LADY PERCY [Q's use of *Lady* has been changed throughout.]
s.p. BARDOLPH [Q's use of *Russell / Bardoll* has been standardized throughout.]
s.p. GLYNDŴR [Q's use of *Glendower* has been changed throughout.]
s.p. SIR MICHAEL [Q's use of *Sir M⟨ighell⟩* in 4.4 has been modernized.]
s.p. JOHN OF LANCASTER [Q's use of *Prince John / John / John of Lancaster* has been standardized throughout.]

1.1.39 Herefordshire [Q7, F] Herdforshire **40 Glyndŵr** Glendower [similarly throughout] **62 a dear** [Q5b, F] deere **71 the Earl** Earle **73 Moray** Murrey **75–76 not? /** **s.p. WESTMORLAND In faith, it is a** not? In faith it is. / *West⟨merland⟩*. A
1.2.70 similes [Q6]; smiles **71 sweet** [Q3, F]; sweer **100 John, sack-and-sugar Jack?** John Sacke, and Sugar Jacke? **114 visors** vizards **144 Peto, Bardolph** Harvey, Rossill **148 But how** [F] How **154 Ay** [F] Yea **158 visors** vizards **161 But** [F] Yea, but
1.3.12 too [F] to **25 was** [F] is **26 Who either through envy** [F] Either envie therefore **27 Was** [F] Is **52 or** [F] or he **65 Made me to answer** [F] I answered **83 the** [Q3, F] that **115 Owain** Owen [similarly throughout] **122 you'll** [F] you wil **126 Although it be with** [F] Albeit I make a **131 In his behalf** [F] Yea on his part **133 downfall** [F] down-trod **199 s.p. HOTSPUR** [Q6, F; no s.p. in Q1] **209–10 a while . . . me.** [F] a while. **237 whipped** [Q2, F] whip **240 d'ye** [F] do you **241 upon't** [F] upon it **253 to't** [F] to it **254 We'll** [F] We wil **264 is't** [F] is it **265 Bristol** Bristow **Scrope** Scroop **289 Lord** Lo: **292 our** [Q2, F] out
2.1.1 An't [F] An it **23 races** razes **38 quoth a** [F] quoth he **51 Weald** wild **64 he's** [F] he is **68 foot-landrakers** [Q4, F] footland rakers **71 'oyez'-ers** Oneyres **80 recipe** receyte
2.2.16 two-and-twenty [F] xxii: **25 upon't** [F] upon it **45–46 Gadshill, what news? /** **s.p.** **GADSHILL** Bardoll, what newes. / *Bar⟨doll⟩*. **46 visors** vizards **70, 78 s.p. FIRST TRAVEL-LER** [unnumbered in Q] **71 their** our **74 s.p. SECOND TRAVELLER** [unnumbered in Q]
2.4.2 respect [Q7, F] the respect **42 thee** the **48 ransomed** ransome **63 A roan** [Q4, F] Roane **78 to** unto **83 maumets** mammets
2.5.29 precedent [F] present **32 s.p. POINS** [Q5, F] *Prin⟨ce⟩*. **61 o' a** **110 sun's** sonnes **159 s.p. PRINCE HARRY** [F] *Gad⟨shill⟩*. **160, 162, 166 s.p. GADSHILL** [F] *Ross⟨ill⟩*. **230 to't** [F] to it **303 talon** talent **311 Owain** O **346 joint-stool** joynd stoole **358 Father** [F] father **359 tristful** trustfull **366 yet** [Q4, F] so **431 lean** [Q3, F] lane **478, 479 Good . . . good** God . . . god **487 s.p. PETO** [F; not in Q] **492 s.p. PRINCE HARRY** [F; not in Q]
3.1.48 speaketh speakes **67 here's** [F] here is **97 cantle** [F] scantle **126 metre** miter **129 on an** **152 the least** least **182 nobleman** [F] noble man **197 thou down pourest** thou powrest downe **228 he's** [F] he is
3.2.59 won wan **84 gorged** [Q3, F] gordge **96 then** [F] than **112 swaddling-clothes**

swathling cloaths 156 **intemperature** [F] intemperance 157 **bonds** bands

3.3.30 **that's** [Q4] that 49 **tithe** tight 65 **four-and-twenty** [F] xxiiii. 107 **no thing** [F] nothing 122 **owed** ought 158 **guests** [F] ghesse 173–4 **two-and-twenty** [F] xxii. 184 **o'clock** of clocke

4.1.18 **jostling** justling 20 **my lord** my mind 31 **sickness stays him** sicknesse 50 **sole** soule 55 **is** [F] tis 98 **ostriches** Estridges 98–100 **that with the wind /** [. . .] **/ Baiting that with the wind /** Baited 106 **cuishes** cushes 109 **dropped** [Q3, F] drop 117 **altar** [Q5, F] altars 124 **corpse** coarse 127 **cannot** [Q6b, F] can 128 **yet** [Q6, F] it 135 **merrily** [F] merely

4.2.3 **Coldfield** cop- / hill 14–15 **yeomen's** Yeomans 22 **ensigns** Ancients 28 **feazed ensign** fazd ancient 31 **tattered** tottered

4.3.23 **horse** [Q5, F] horses 26 **the half** the halfe of 84 **country's** [Q6b, F] Countrey

4.4.30 **more** mo

5.1.42, 58 **Doncaster** [F] Dancaster 83 **our** [F] your 135 **o'** a 136 **will it** [Q3, F] wil

5.2.3 **undone** [Q6, F] under one 10 **ne'er** [F] never

5.3.1 **in the** in 22 **A fool** Ah foole 35 **ragamuffins** rag of Muffins 39 **stand'st** [F] stands 42 **as yet** are yet 50 **gett'st** [F] gets

5.4.57 **Sir S.** 67 **Nor** [F] Now 91 **thee** the 97 **rites** [F] rights 108 **Embowelled** Inboweld 110 **Embowelled** Inboweld 110 **embowel** inbowel 144 **take't on** [F] take it upon 147 **e'er** [F] ever

The Second Part of Henry IV

The title page of the 1600 Quarto of 2 Henry IV describes the play as *The Second Part of Henry the Fourth, Continuing to His Death, and Coronation of Henry the Fifth. With the Humours of Sir John Falstaff, and Swaggering Pistol.* Its first focus is the "high" historical matter of the reign of kings. For this part of the play, Shakespeare drew primarily on the second edition of Raphael Holinshed's *Chronicles of England, Scotland, and Ireland* (1587), though he probably consulted other sources, including Samuel Daniel's *First Four Books of the Civil Wars* (1595). In regard to this historical material, the title page particularly highlights the delicate moment of succession when one king dies and another is crowned. Shakespeare's audience was facing such a moment at the end of the 1590s. Elizabeth I was old, having been on the English throne since 1558; and because she had never married, she had no heirs. The uncertainties of the coming succession may have, by contrast, heightened the pleasure of watching Henry IV followed upon the throne by his male heir, Henry V—the king who, whatever his father's sins in seizing the crown from Richard II, had become in the popular imagination a symbol of kingly perfection and English masculinity. The numerous stories of Hal's wild youth merely served as the perfect foil to set off the glory of his eventual reformation and triumphant reign.

The play also deals, however, in some decidedly "low" and mostly unhistorical matter, suggested on the title page by mention of the "humours" of Falstaff and the presence of swaggering Pistol. These characters hold pride of place alongside Henry IV and Henry V, indicating the popularity of the antic parts of the play—Falstaff's jokes and his flouting of authority or Pistol's madly bombastic language. Some of the matter for the play's comic scenes probably derives from *The Famous Victories of Henry V*, a popular play about the life of Henry V first published in 1598 but believed to have been performed well before that date. In 2 Henry IV, Prince Hal does not mingle with the comic figures as freely as he is shown to do in 1 Henry IV; in fact, he appears only once, in 2.4, in the Eastcheap tavern where Falstaff holds court. Nonetheless, the total number of low, unhistorical characters expands considerably in this play. Pistol is a new character, and Mistress Quickly is joined in her Eastcheap tavern by Doll Tearsheet, a prostitute whose name graphically suggests one consequence of unrestrained fornication. Further, a number of country characters are introduced: the Gloustershire justices of the peace, Shallow and Silence; Shallow's servant, Davy; and the five rural recruits (Mouldy, Bullcalf, Wart, Feeble, and Shadow) whom Falstaff considers for conscription into the army. 2 Henry IV is the only history play of which more than half is written in prose, and much of that richly varied prose occurs in the numerous scenes involving these humble figures Shakespeare added to the historical narrative of one king's death and another's coronation.

It appears that 2 Henry IV was written soon after the very popular 1 Henry IV, which was published in 1598 but probably written and staged in 1596–97. While the quarto was published in 1600, there is a reference to the character of Justice Silence in Ben Jonson's *Every Man out of His Humour*, published in 1599. 2 Henry IV was therefore probably performed sometime between February 1598, when 1 Henry IV was entered in the Stationers' Register with no indication it was the first part of a two-part play, and early in 1599. It is likely that censorship of Shakespeare's original naming of Falstaff as "Oldcastle," Bardolph as "Russell," and Peto as "Harvey" (see Introduction to 1 Henry IV) had occurred before Shakespeare completed 2 Henry IV, though a few traces of the original names appear in the speech prefixes and stage directions in the first two acts of the quarto version.

THE
Second part of Henrie
the fourth, continuing to his death,
and coronation of Henrie
the fift.

With the humours of sir Iohn Fal-
staffe, and swaggering
Pistoll.

As it hath been sundrie times publikely
acted by the right honourable, the Lord
Chamberlaine his seruants.

Written by William Shakespeare.

LONDON
Printed by V.S. for Andrew Wise, and
William Aspley.
1600.

Title page of the 1600 Quarto of *2 Henry IV*, promising to combine royal history and the comic
events involving Falstaff and his tavern companions.

Shakespeare may have interrupted his composition of 2 *Henry IV* to write *The Merry Wives of Windsor*, a play that could have been performed as early as 1597. If so, he would have written the last acts of 2 *Henry IV* well after the censorship of the offending names in *1 Henry IV* had occurred, and he would consequently have altered the names in the final acts of the play.

Narrowing down the play's date of composition, however, does not answer the question of why Shakespeare wrote two plays dealing with the reign of Henry IV. Some critics believe that the playwright once intended to encompass all the material of both plays in one, but in writing what we now call *1 Henry IV* he found he had room to depict only the events up to the Battle of Shrewsbury and Hal's emergence as a chivalric hero through his defeat of Hotspur. Therefore, what was "left over" was, in effect, put into 2 *Henry IV* with the patchwork addition of enough comic material to scrape together a play. It is also possible that Shakespeare intended to dramatize only the events now in *1 Henry IV*, but that having done so, he was encouraged by his success to add another chapter to the story of Hal's reformation and gradual progression toward the throne. Alternatively, Shakespeare may have planned two plays from the beginning, intending to undertake two quite different explorations of the prodigal narrative by which the wild Prince becomes first a chivalric hero and eventually the King of England.

Whatever the original impetus for writing it, the finished play we call 2 *Henry IV* has an integrity of its own and a set of preoccupations that clearly distinguishes it from *1 Henry IV*. The rebels, for example, are a less flamboyant crew than in the earlier play, and they are not vanquished in combat as at Shrewsbury; rather, at Gaultres, Prince John tricks them into laying down their weapons. Policy, not chivalry, wins the day. Hal's challenge, moreover, is no longer to prove himself the prince of chivalry, with the rebel Henry Percy (Hotspur) as his main antagonist. Rather, he must show himself fit for civil rule. Hence the importance in 2 *Henry IV* of the Lord Chief Justice, a figure who in popular accounts of Hal's life had had the Prince imprisoned for impudently giving him a box on the ear. This event is not dramatized in either of Shakespeare's Henry IV plays, as it had been in *The Famous Victories*, but it is several times alluded to. In 2 *Henry IV*, the Chief Justice emerges as the main foil to the disorderly Falstaff. Upon hearing that Henry IV is dead and Hal is King, the fat knight exclaims, "The laws of England are at my commandment" (5.3.125–26). It seems quite possible that under Henry V, law will give way before the appetites and desires of individual subjects. Hal and the Chief Justice do not share the stage until 5.2, but their encounter is a pivotal moment in the text, revealing whether Hal will appropriate the mantle of civil justice from the Chief Justice, as he had appropriated Hotspur's reputation for chivalrous deeds, or will follow Falstaff in flouting the law.

Also unique to this play is its pervasive concern with the passing of time. As Hastings says at the end of Act 1, "We are time's subjects" (1.3.110); arguably, he sounds the play's central theme. Even the King, to whom so many are subject, is himself subject to time. Shakespeare portrays him as old and sick, though the historical Henry successfully ruled England for ten years after the Battle of Shrewsbury. His sickness and the urgency of the rebel threat pressure the Prince, forcing him to realize that his idle days in the tavern are numbered and that if he lingers longer, he will "profane the precious time" (2.4.331), time he should spend coming to terms with his father and defending a kingdom still threatened by rebels. Even the irrepressible Falstaff now feels time's hand. He enters the play in 1.2 asking what the doctor has said about the urine he has sent for examination, and to Quickly and Tearsheet he confesses, "I am old, I am old" (2.4.244). If *1 Henry IV* is an expansive work, infused with a feeling of infinite play and infinite possibility, 2 *Henry IV* has a melancholy, autumnal aura. It is a play of limits and constrictions. Shallow intones: "Death, as the Psalmist saith, is certain to all; all shall die" (3.2.33–34). 2 *Henry IV*, with its many images of sickness, disease, and old age, drives home this point.

The play's portrayal of Prince Hal shares in the somber mood that permeates all of 2 *Henry IV*. When the audience first sees him, he is with Poins (2.2), brooding on the impasse to which his own actions have brought him. Rather than keeping a controlling distance from his tavern companion, Hal ruefully acknowledges what he shares with common men. Tired, he desires nothing more exalted than small beer, the common drink of every London apprentice. He admits that he should not, because of his rank, be intimate with Poins; and yet he confesses that he is, revealing how thoroughly he knows his companion's wardrobe and using Poins as a sounding board for his misgivings about his own behavior and its consequences. While the scene's mood changes when Bardolph enters with an absurdly pompous letter from Falstaff, its fretful beginning indicates a new strain in Shakespeare's depiction of Hal's progress toward the throne. In *1 Henry IV*, everything seemed easy for the Prince. He announced a course of reform and enacted it with little apparent cost to himself. In *2 Henry IV*, Shakespeare constructs a more sober Prince who articulates anxiety about the gap between his plebeian taste for small beer and the grandeur of the office he will assume, a Prince who knows that to have acted the wastrel in order to make a dazzling reform may have cost him his father's affection and made it impossible for him to express his own love for the King without appearing a hypocrite. In the opening acts of *2 Henry IV*, Hal's capacity for self-critique and for uncertainty makes him more vulnerable, and perhaps more likable, than the shiny and assured paragon of *1 Henry IV*.

As with Hal, Shakespeare creates in this play a Henry who shows a new capacity for introspection. In 3.1, speaking about the burdens of office, he acknowledges the costs of his success and admits that at the beginning of his reign he could little foresee the changes time would bring to his door. Yet like his son, at the end of the day Henry finds his office worth the cost. Power may bring burdens, but for both characters it is irresistible. Each sentimentally envies common men (whose poverty and powerlessness they do not share), but neither, tellingly, renounces the office of king. And neither ever gives up the attempt to control his destiny. Having contemplated the many unforeseen changes of his reign, Henry IV finally breaks off his revery to plan a campaign against the rebels.

> Are these things then necessities?
> Then let us meet them like necessities;
> And that same word even now cries out on us.
> They say the Bishop and Northumberland
> Are fifty thousand strong.
>
> (3.1.87–91)

This is the pragmatic voice of rule, the blunt determination that Shakespeare attributes both to Prince Hal and to his father.

Yet despite (and perhaps because of) their similarities, Shakespeare makes the relationship of Henry and Hal a troubled one. Part of the complexity of *2 Henry IV* is that while it tellingly anatomizes how these kings, father and then son, acquire and maintain power, it simultaneously creates the impression of a psychodrama between the two of them that, though inseparable from their political roles, is never fully understood by either of them. Hal, despite telling Poins he loves his father, does not appear in the King's presence until the end of Act 4, when Henry is on his deathbed. Then, with what has seemed to many to be unseemly haste, Hal takes the crown from the pillow by his sleeping father and sets it on his own head, believing his father dead. Is this, as the King fears, Hal's acting out of a fantasy of parricide? Or, as Hal protests, is it his attempt to come to terms with the burdens of office that have hastened his father's death and that will now fall to him?

In part, the relationship between Hal and Henry is complicated by the guilt each feels about the politically useful and carefully managed "wildness" that each has employed. Hal, of course, has cultivated wildness as a prelude to reform. It is the foil by which he aims to set off his achievement of perfect chivalry and justice. But it is important to remember that to come by his throne, Henry himself had to enact the wildness of usurpation, seizing the crown from a lawfully anointed king, an act Shakespeare depicted in *Richard II*. To be sure, once in the seat of rule, Henry repudiated such wildness and embraced the law, justifying his own reign in part by presenting himself as the bulwark against disorder — that of the rebels and even that of his son. There is no doubt that Hal displays prodigal behavior, spending time in the tavern rather than at court, but his father dwells on and exaggerates his son's lawlessness, picturing England's distress when ruled by a man who "from curbed licence plucks / The muzzle of restraint" (4.3.258–59). This preoccupation with Hal's lawlessness may signal Henry's guilt about his own act of usurpation, for which he has long planned a penitential crusade to the Holy Land (a crusade that we eventually learn would *also* have the effect of distracting his nobles from thoughts of rebellion at home). But what Henry does not seem able to see is those ways in which his son's tactics resemble his own. Truly his father's child, Hal angles for power with an unerring sense of when to embrace wildness and when to repudiate it. Ironically, as Henry's act of seizing the crown raises the specter of parricide, Henry's obsession with curbing Hal's wildness hints of castration. Without seeming fully to realize the consequences of his own actions, he would cut off one source of Hal's power, even though he himself once embraced disorder and still needs it to justify his rule.

In Henry's last conversation with Hal and at his death, father and son switch positions in the discourse of "wildness" that runs through the play. The King has been the principle of order, the Prince the ungovernable prodigal. On his deathbed, however, the King acknowledges to Hal:

> God knows, my son,
> By what bypaths and indirect crook'd ways
> I met this crown; and I myself know well
> How troublesome it sat upon my head.
> To thee it shall descend with better quiet,
> Better opinion, better confirmation;
> For all the soil of the achievement goes
> With me into the earth.
> (4.3.311–18)

He represents himself as a man stained by his own errancy, but one whose sins can be buried with his death. Hal picks up the theme when he announces after his father's death, "My father is gone wild into his grave" (5.2.122), as if Henry himself embodied the principle of disorder, now buried. Yet Hal continues, suddenly making problematic whose wildness the grave holds:

> For in his tomb lie my affections;
> And with his spirits sadly I survive
> To mock the expectation of the world.
> (5.2.123–25)

Now it is *Hal's* wildness that the grave holds, his father's sober spirits that live on in the son. Shedding his prodigality is now not an act of disempowerment but its opposite. The wild Prince has become the order-loving King. It will now be his turn to repudiate disorder, beginning with Falstaff.

Critics have argued that 2 *Henry IV* looks forward to the tragedies in its somber tone and its focus upon the tortured self-divisions of the King and his son. There is truth in this claim, but one must also recognize that while the play allows the audience to read doubt and self-division in Henry and the Prince, at the end it moves to install Hal unambiguously in the position of the reformed Prince and law-abiding King. Hal's apparent self-division holds the attention of the audience just as his carefully managed reform wins the admiration of his subjects. But when the time is right, whatever the "personal" cost, he embraces the law in the person of the Chief Justice while burying wildness in the person of his father and publicly repudiating it in the person of Falstaff. In so doing, he follows perfectly the laws of power.

But though Hal publicly repudiates wildness, the play does not. Wildness surges up unpredictably, not only in the actions of the rebels but also in the actions and particularly in the unruly language of those many "minor" characters who are Shakespeare's additions to his historical sources and whose existence is signaled on the title page by reference to the humors of Falstaff and swaggering Pistol. In the late sixteenth century, the English language was undergoing both expansion and regularization. Many writers were interested in making English a fit language in which to write verse that would rival the achievements of classical literature. Writers experimented with imitating the verse forms used by Latin writers in particular; they also coined new words, and they attempted to purge English of uncouth or infelicitous elements. But it was not just poets who affected the language. Trade brought new products to England, and those products had to have names. Foreign visitors, merchants, and workers were a common sight in the London landscape, and they, of course, brought their languages with them. Meanwhile, the theater daily offered its auditors the linguistic pleasures of the high-sounding rhetoric of kings and tyrants, while London preachers made their reputations by dazzling displays of oratorical power.

This atmosphere generated an infectious excitement about language, and not all of this excitement was easy to control. Rhetorical handbooks proliferated, each sketching out the styles and figures of speech appropriate to different occasions, and each also listing rhetorical "vices," examples of indecorous or ungrammatical or infelicitous speech. 2 *Henry IV* could be considered a casebook of linguistic vices. The minor characters speak a wild farrago of tongues that defy the desire for linguistic order. Swaggering Pistol is a case in point. Much of his speech is composed of scraps of rhetoric he has picked up from going to the London theater. He imitates Tamburlaine, for example, the hero of Marlowe's two-part play about a Scythian shepherd who became one of the great military conquerors of all time—a character to whom Marlowe gave an expansive, hyperbolic rhetoric often imitated and parodied by later dramatists. But Pistol mangles his references to Marlowe's hero, intermingling what he can remember of Tamburlaine's speeches with a mishmash of fine-sounding names and lines from drinking songs, as when he proclaims:

> Shall pack-horses
> And hollow pampered jades of Asia,
> Which cannot go but thirty mile a day,
> Compare with Caesars and with cannibals,
> And Trojan Greeks?
> Nay, rather damn them with King Cerberus,
> And let the welkin roar. Shall we fall foul for toys?
> (2.4.140–46)

Pistol's "mistakes" are pervasive. First he imitates what he can remember of the moment when Tamburlaine taunts the conquered kings whom he has put in harness to draw his chariot. But then he veers into nonsense, mistaking "cannibal" for "Hannibal," the heroic leader of Carthage; describing Greeks as Trojans, while in *The Iliad* the Greeks and Trojans were separate, and warring, peoples; then attributing a crown to Cerberus, the three-headed dog who guarded the gates of hell; and ending with a tag from a drinking song: "And let the welkin roar." The sheer exuberance of the speech is partly what makes it pleasurable—Pistol's delight in the sound of big words, whatever those words may mean—along with the lawless incongruity with which one bit of remembered rhetoric is stitched onto the next. Self-mockingly, but also self-importantly, the passage points to the power of the theater to fill the spectators' heads with fine language, even if all that language is not completely understood. Choleric, explosive, overflowing with the excesses of stage rhetoric, Pistol is a wild card in the play's quest for order and the rule of law.

He is not alone. The play opens with a prologue spoken by Rumour, whose business is telling lies, substituting the untrue for the true. That Shakespeare prefaced the play with this figure indicates his concern with the vagaries and waywardness of language. Sometimes language is maliciously used to deceive, as with Rumour or Prince John's double-edged speech at Gaultres. Sometimes, as with Pistol's bombast, his language seems simply to reveal a delight in how words sound, regardless of what they mean. By contrast, Falstaff's puns, which play on the similar sound of dissimilar words, reveal the double and triple meanings that can be activated from a simple utterance. To take a small example from the many that could be cited, consider Falstaff's anger in 1.2 at the prosperous merchant who refuses to give him twenty-two yards of satin without his providing adequate security, that is, adequate goods or money to cover the debt. To his Page Falstaff sputters, "Well, he may sleep in security, for he hath the horn of abundance, and the lightness of his wife shines through it; and yet cannot he see, though he have his own lanthorn to light him" (1.2.39–42). The subversive wittiness of this passage depends on Falstaff's punning on the fact that "horn" can mean the horn lanterns sold by merchants, the cornucopia that is a symbol of abundance, or the horns of a man who has been sexually betrayed by his wife, while "lightness" can mean both illumination and sexual promiscuity. On the surface, Falstaff is grudgingly admitting that the merchant is rich and graced with a wife. But the puns tell another story: that of a blind cuckold whose wife's sexual infidelity is visible to everyone but himself. In Falstaff's mouth, language is a slippery thing and often a devastating tool for confounding an enemy.

The Rumour of Shakespeare's Induction is derived from the classical figure of Fame, here depicted as covered with ears (to gather reports from all quarters) and blowing a horn (to broadcast news abroad). From Vicenzo Cartari, *Imagines deorum* (1581).

One of the play's most remarkable rhetoricians, Mistress Quickly, did not make it to the title page of the quarto, but her verbal blunders are another example of language's unpredictable qualities. Quickly is quite a different person here than in *1 Henry IV*. For one thing, she seems to have lost the husband who was mentioned often, though never glimpsed, in the previous play; and she has acquired a new companion in the person of the prostitute Doll Tearsheet. Unmarried, economically independent, and associated with the criminality of prostitution and perhaps of murder (in 5.4, the women are accused with Pistol of having beaten a man to death), Quickly emerges as one of the figures of disorder that must be purged from a reformed commonwealth. Yet she embodies a principle of linguistic anarchy that defies control. Her signature utterance is the malapropism, the verbal blunder by which one word is mistaken for another. For example, telling the Chief Justice of Falstaff's whereabouts, she says he was "indicted," meaning "invited," to dinner (2.1.24). The malapropism is interesting because it is a kind of lawless speech in which the speaker is guided by the sound of words, or by a private logic, rather than by the usual rules of sense. Quickly, for example, in mistaking "indicted" for "invited" has blundered into her own kind of sense, since she would indeed like to see Falstaff indicted, or brought to legal judgment, for the debts he owes her. Malapropisms, to those who know better, make the speaker appear foolish. Yet they also can disrupt the institutions that depend on clear and predictable communication. Not even the Chief Justice knows quite what to make of Quickly, so persistently does her speech elude the net of common sense, enveloping her in a tangle of meanings—some obscene, some suggestively significant—that she may or may not intend. Sir Francis Bacon called revenge "wild justice"; the malapropism might be called "wild speech," so thoroughly does it defy semantic predictability.

The distinctiveness of the prose assigned to the comic figures in *2 Henry IV* is one of the play's most striking features. Clearly this shows Shakespeare's ability to delineate character by means of linguistic differences. Shallow's mindless repetition of simple words, Falstaff's puns, Quickly's malapropisms, and Pistol's bombast are all ways of individuating these figures. They also suggest the fecundity of speech in Henry's England and register, at the linguistic level, a wild disorder no principle of decorum or law can entirely contain. By means of the double entendre, much of the prose spoken in the tavern alludes to the body and its pleasures, even as it seems to speak of something else. For example, Quickly, complaining of Falstaff to the Chief Justice, says, "he stabbed me in mine own house, most beastly, in good faith. A cares not what mischief he does; if his weapon be out, he will foin like any devil, he will spare neither man, woman, nor child" (2.1.12–15). "Foin" means "thrust" or "strike." Overtly, Quickly describes a Falstaff who takes out his sword or dagger and indiscriminately stabs whoever happens to be handy. Indirectly, and perhaps inadvertently, she describes a Falstaff who, when his sexual "weapon," or penis, is out, will indiscriminately engage in sex with whoever happens to be near. The tavern scenes teem with similar instances of sexualized speech or, more accurately, speech that tells two stories at the same time, with one of them a story of sex: its pleasures and diseases and persistence. The bawdy doubleness of tavern prose contrasts sharply with the elevated poetry in which the King most often speaks. Worrying, planning, commanding, the King constructs himself as a bulwark against disorder. But the disorderly, bombastic, vibrant, and lewd speech of the tavern suggests at the level of language the difficulties of controlling the manifold energies of his subjects.

Thinking about the play's control of or its failure to control unsanctioned energies provides a context for considering what traditionally has been the most discussed aspect of *2 Henry IV*: the Prince's final public repudiation of Falstaff. In this play, Falstaff is kept separate from the Prince except for the one scene (2.4) in which the Prince disguises himself as a tavern barman and overhears Falstaff talking with Doll and Quickly. Moreover, the exploitative side of Falstaff is more fully displayed here than in the earlier play. He leeches off Quickly; he takes bribes to release able-bodied men from service in the army; he worms a thousand pounds from Shallow. Yet he is still able, as in the stunning speech in which he indicts Prince John for cold-bloodedness (4.2.78–111), to offer a telling critique of his betters and to embody a frank physicality they eschew. The new King's

A seventeenth-century tavern scene recalling Mistress Quickly's Eastcheap tavern. From Peter Rollos, *Le centre de l'amour* (1680).

repudiation of Falstaff—"I know thee not, old man. Fall to thy prayers" (5.5.45)—continues to trouble critics and audiences. Certainly, how the moment is staged can mitigate or harshen its implications. In Terry Hands's 1975 Royal Shakespeare Company production, for example, the newly crowned King came onstage in glittering gold and masked, the epitome of detached and heartless power. In other productions, he rejects his former friend with a sob, emphasizing his own sense of loss and his continuing affection for Falstaff. But however it is staged, there is little doubt that the new King, whatever his "personal" feelings, has turned Falstaff away to consolidate his power in his new position.

But the final scene is not the play's last word: it is followed by an epilogue. It is likely that this Epilogue was spoken by the company's clown, in this case Will Kemp, a famed comic actor who in this play is believed to have played Falstaff. It is especially likely that Kemp spoke the Epilogue because of the several references in it to the actor's willingness to use his legs, or to dance, should his words not prove agreeable. Kemp was a skilled dancer, and when he left Shakespeare's company in 1599, he undertook a famous morris dance from London to Norwich. The Epilogue gives the common actor who had played Falstaff the play's last word and its final display of physical skill. At Shrewsbury, Hal had thought Falstaff dead, but, faking death, the fat man had arisen. In 2 *Henry IV*, the old knight is banished from the King's presence in the play's final scene, but in the Epilogue, the actor who had played him reappears—soliciting the audience's applause, denying that Falstaff is a representation of the Lollard martyr, Sir John Oldcastle (see the Introduction to 1 *Henry IV*), and kicking up his heels in a virtuoso display of dancing skill. The Epilogue partly undoes what the dramatic fiction has done, namely, demonize and repudiate the energies associated with popular culture and the low life of the tavern. The body of the common actor holds center stage as Kemp, throwing aside the character Falstaff's mantle of age, delights the audience with a jig.

The Epilogue has another effect. It pluralizes the "authorities" to which the theater is beholden. With its references to the Oldcastle controversy and its final allusion to praying for Queen Elizabeth, the Epilogue acknowledges the power embodied in the person of the monarch and in the state's censorship apparatus. But it also refers to pleasing both the gentlewomen and the gentlemen of the audience—in other words, the paying customers who came to the theater for all sorts of pleasures. If the title page of the quarto is to be believed, readers, and probably audiences, were as much delighted by the irrepressible and irresponsible antics of Falstaff and swaggering Pistol as by the sober reformation of Hal and the suffering of his father, just as they were undoubtedly as delighted by the mangling of the King's English as by its decorous deployment. In short, while in this play the rule of law unmistakably and officially triumphs over the forces of disorder, the comic actor has the last dance, and theater finds a way to offer pleasures in excess of what the sober historical narrative allows.

JEAN E. HOWARD

TEXTUAL NOTE

2 *Henry IV* was entered in the Stationers' Register on August 23, 1600, and first printed in a quarto version dated that same year. This quarto had two issues, the first of which, QA, lacks the present 3.1, in which the sleepless King Henry meditates on the passage of time and the ironies of history. In QB, this scene is included. The text was not printed again until it appeared in a significantly different version in the First Folio of 1623 (F). The Folio text contains eight fairly substantial passages, totaling about 160 lines, not found in Q (A or B). It also differs from the quarto text in a number of other ways: oaths have been excised; punctuation, syntax, and certain aspects of style have been regularized; stage directions have been altered, and in several scenes the names of characters have been "massed" together in an initial stage direction even if some of these characters only enter

at a later point in the scene; some quarto lines are missing and new part lines appear, as does a table of "The Actors Names" listing all the speaking parts.

The important debate about the play's textual history concerns the relation of Q to F. Q shows signs—such as the use of a number of different speech prefixes for the same character—of having been printed directly from the author's "foul papers," which do not appear to have been marked up for use in a theatrical performance. One explanation for the absence of 3.1 in QA is that the scene was marked for excision in the foul papers, either because it was politically sensitive or to reduce the length of the play. Others have argued that the scene was written on a separate manuscript leaf that became detached from its proper place in the foul papers and so was overlooked by the compositor. The Oxford editors believe that this scene was added by Shakespeare *after* the rest of the manuscript had been written as the first step in his ongoing reworking of the play. They postulate that the compositor who set this part of QA missed the marks indicating where the scene was to be added to the foul papers.

F, by contrast, shows signs of having been prepared by a professional scribe in its regularization of a number of aspects of the text, though these changes also introduce errors and obscure the exact nature of the manuscript underlying the transcription. The excision of oaths is undoubtedly a result of the 1606 statute against profanity on the stage. Some further changes found in F may be due to the special problems facing the compositors setting the text. It appears that too little space had been allocated in F for setting this play in type. Consequently, a group of four additional sheets was added, but the compositor still had to omit words, compressing one part of the text, and to add words and phrases, expanding other parts of the text, in order to fit the play into its allotted space. It is possible that the list of "The Actors Names" was added to fill up a blank page.

Some editors argue that the eight substantial passages found in F but missing from Q were originally present in the manuscript used for setting Q but were marked for excision, either because they were politically sensitive or for theatrical reasons such as the need to reduce the length of the speeches assigned to actors doubling in two roles. These editors grant priority to the quarto text (which appears to be printed from Shakespeare's foul papers and which does not contain the errors and changes made by the scribe who prepared the Folio manuscript), but they usually add the eight additional passages on the grounds that they were originally part of the manuscript behind the quarto.

The Oxford editors work from different assumptions; specifically, they argue that beginning with 3.1, Shakespeare himself made a series of revisions to the play, perhaps recording these in the fair copy that was to serve as the promptbook. They argue that he did so as part of a consistent strategy to augment the historical portions of the play and to connect it more fully to *Richard II* and *1 Henry IV*. They agree that two of the eight additional Folio passages represent cuts in the quarto text because they deal with the politically sensitive matter of rebellion, but they also hold that the remaining six are Shakespeare's later *additions* to the play. They further argue that some of the other changes in F, such as the deletion of specific lines, show authorial intervention in the interest of making the play more stageworthy. The Oxford editors therefore postulate that the scribe who produced the copy used for setting F, while having a copy of Q to consult, was working primarily from a theatrical promptbook that registered some authorial revisions to the quarto version of the play, though the theatrical nature of that promptbook has been obscured by the "literary" habits of the scribe. As a consequence, this edition of the play, while using Q as its control text, accepts a higher number of Folio readings than is true for many other editions in an attempt to reproduce the stage version of the play the Oxford editors believe underlies F.

The eight substantial new passages found in F deserve further discussion. Interestingly, all of them involve figures who are of the rebels' party. The Oxford editors agree that two of them were censored because they too compellingly justified rebellion. These are 1.1.188–208, Morton's speech announcing that the Archbishop of York has joined the rebellion, using the murder of Richard II as partial justification, and 4.1.55–79, the Archbishop's speech justifying the rebels' position and exclaiming against the King's indifference to their grievances. Other passages are in greater dispute. For example, 2.3.23–45, part of Lady Percy's magnificent speech in praise of Hotspur, does not appear in Q. Is this because Shakespeare had not yet written it? Or had it been cut from the original manuscript because the praise of Hotspur could be read as indirect praise of the Earl of Essex, the dashing, headstrong noble whose triumphal return from a 1599 campaign against the Irish Shakespeare was to anticipate with excitement in *Henry V*—but who in actuality returned home in disgrace and shortly thereafter led an abortive rebellion against Elizabeth? Or was it cut because the boy actor playing Lady Percy also was to play Doll Tearsheet in the next scene and had to have the number of lines he spoke reduced? Each of the eight additional Folio passages, which include 1.1.165–78, 1.3.21–24, 1.3.36–55, 1.3.85–108, and 4.1.101–37 (as well as the three passages already mentioned), is flagged in the notes so that readers can consider each case for themselves. The principal passages deleted from this text but present in Q and in most modern editions of the text are indented and printed as inset passages at the points where they appeared in Q.

Apart from Act 4, this text follows Folio act and scene divisions, although in F the Induction is marked as a separate scene. As for Act 4, F divides it into two scenes, and in many modern editions, it is divided into five scenes; this edition divides it into three, ignoring the interpolated scene breaks often added by modern editors after 4.1.226, when Prince John marches onstage to speak with the rebels at Gaultres and after 4.3.132, when the King is carried to the Jerusalem Chamber. It retains, however, the interpolated break after 4.1.349 in which Falstaff enters with Coleville after Prince John has departed the stage, on the grounds that unlike the other two instances, this is a place where the stage is cleared and the action is therefore not continuous. It also retains the Folio scene break (now 4.3) when King Henry first comes onstage sick and in his bed.

SELECTED BIBLIOGRAPHY

Barkan, Leonard. "The Human Body and the Commonwealth." *Nature's Work of Art: The Human Body as Image of the World.* New Haven: Yale University Press. 61–115.

Calderwood, James L. *Metadrama in Shakespeare's Henriad: "Richard II" to "Henry V."* Berkeley: University of California Press, 1979. See especially 88–133.

Crewe, Jonathan. "Reforming Prince Hal: The Sovereign Inheritor in *2 Henry IV.*" *Renaissance Drama*, n.s., 21 (1990): 225–42.

Hodgdon, Barbara. " 'Let the End Try the Man': *1* and *2 Henry IV.*" *The End Crowns All: Closure and Contradiction in Shakespeare's History.* Princeton: Princeton University Press, 1991. 151–84.

Knights, L. C. "Time's Subjects: The Sonnets and *King Henry IV, Part II.*" *Some Shakespearean Themes.* London: Chatto and Windus, 1959. 45–64.

Macdonald, Ronald R. "Uses of Diversity: Bakhtin's Theory of Utterance and Shakespeare's Second Tetralogy." *"Henry IV Parts One and Two": Theory in Practice.* Ed. Nigel Wood. Buckingham, England: Open University Press, 1995. 65–91.

Mullaney, Steven. "The Rehearsal of Cultures." *The Place of the Stage: License, Play, and Power in Renaissance England.* Chicago: University of Chicago Press, 1988. 60–87.

Rackin, Phyllis. "Historical Kings / Theatrical Clowns." *Stages of History: Shakespeare's English Chronicles.* Ithaca: Cornell University Press, 1990. 201–47.

Wiles, David. *Shakespeare's Clowns: Actor and Text in the Elizabethan Playhouse.* Cambridge: Cambridge University Press, 1987. See especially "Kemp's Jigs" (43–60), and "Falstaff" (116–35).

Young, David P., ed. *Twentieth Century Interpretations of "Henry IV, Part II."* Englewood Cliffs, N.J.: Prentice-Hall, 1968.

The Second Part of Henry the Fourth

THE PERSONS OF THE PLAY

RUMOUR, the Presenter
EPILOGUE
KING HENRY IV
PRINCE HARRY, later crowned King Henry V ⎫
PRINCE JOHN of Lancaster   ⎬ sons of King
Humphrey, Duke of GLOUCESTER   ⎪ Henry IV
Thomas, Duke of CLARENCE   ⎭
Percy, Earl of NORTHUMBERLAND, of the rebels' party
LADY NORTHUMBERLAND
LADY PERCY, their son Hotspur's widow
TRAVERS, Northumberland's servant
MORTON, a bearer of news from Shrewsbury
Scrope, ARCHBISHOP of York
LORD BARDOLPH   ⎫
Thomas, Lord MOWBRAY, the Earl Marshal   ⎬ rebels against
Lord HASTINGS   ⎪ King Henry IV
Sir John COLEVILLE   ⎭
LORD CHIEF JUSTICE
His SERVANT
GOWER, a Messenger
Sir John FALSTAFF ⎫
His PAGE   ⎪
BARDOLPH   ⎬ 'irregular humorists'
POINS   ⎪
Ensign PISTOL   ⎪
PETO   ⎭
MISTRESS QUICKLY, hostess of a tavern
DOLL TEARSHEET, a whore
SNARE ⎫
       ⎬ sergeants
FANG   ⎭
Neville, Earl of WARWICK   ⎫
Earl of SURREY   ⎪
Earl of WESTMORLAND   ⎬ supporters of King Henry
HARCOURT   ⎪
Sir John Blunt   ⎭
Robert SHALLOW ⎫
                ⎬ country justices
SILENCE   ⎭
DAVY, Shallow's servant
Ralph MOULDY   ⎫
Simon SHADOW   ⎪
Thomas WART   ⎬ men levied to fight for King Henry
Francis FEEBLE ⎪
Peter BULLCALF ⎭
PORTER of Northumberland's household
DRAWERS

BEADLES
GROOMS
MESSENGER
Sneak and other musicians
Lord Chief Justice's men, soldiers and attendants

Induction

Enter RUMOUR[1] *[in a robe] painted full of tongues*

RUMOUR Open your ears; for which of you will stop°		*plug up*
The vent of hearing° when loud Rumour speaks?		*The ear*
I from the orient° to the drooping west,		*east*
Making the wind my post-horse,° still° unfold		*hired horse / continually*
5 The acts commencèd on this ball of earth.		
Upon my tongues continual slanders ride,		
The which in every language I pronounce,		
Stuffing the ears of men with false reports.		
I speak of peace, while covert enmity		
10 Under the smile of safety wounds the world;		
And who but Rumour, who but only I,		
Make fearful musters and prepared defence[2]		
Whiles the big° year, swoll'n with some other griefs,		*pregnant*
Is thought with child by the stern tyrant war,		
15 And no such matter? Rumour is a pipe		
Blown by surmises, Jealousy's conjectures,		
And of so easy and so plain a stop[3]		
That the blunt° monster with uncounted° heads,		*stupid / innumerable*
The still-discòrdant wav'ring multitude,		
20 Can play upon it. But what° need I thus		*why*
My well-known body to anatomize°		*dissect; lay open*
Among my household?° Why is Rumour here?		*(the theater audience)*
I run before King Harry's victory,		
Who in a bloody field by Shrewsbury[4]		
25 Hath beaten down young Hotspur and his troops,		
Quenching the flame of bold rebellion		
Even with the rebels' blood. But what mean I		
To speak so true at first? My office is		
To noise abroad that Harry Monmouth[5] fell		
30 Under the wrath of noble Hotspur's sword,		
And that the King before the Douglas' rage		
Stooped his anointed head as low as death.		
This have I rumoured through the peasant° towns		*rural*
Between that royal field of Shrewsbury		
35 And this worm-eaten hold° of raggèd stone,		*stronghold*

Induction Location: Outside Northumberland's castle at Warkworth.

1. A personification possibly based on Virgil's "Fama," a female monster with many eyes, ears, and tongues who circulated both true and false accounts of events. See *Aeneid* 4.179–90.

2. Cause soldiers, prompted by fear, to assemble and defenses to be made ready. These lines may be topical: fear of imminent Spanish invasion led the Privy Council to mobilize militia forces frequently throughout the latter years of Elizabeth's reign.

3. And whose "stops," or openings, are so easy to play upon. The ease with which Rumour's pipe can be played means that even the common people can do it. In the next lines, Rumour refers to these commoners as a many-headed monster, a common derogatory image of the people, especially when they aspire to participation in governance. By contrast, the proper head of the realm was held to be the single sovereign.

4. In Shakespeare's rendition of the Battle of Shrewsbury, staged in *1 Henry IV*, Prince Hal kills Henry Percy (Hotspur) and his forces capture the Scottish Earl of Douglas, two of the principal leaders of rebellion. In 1.1 of this play, the announcement of Henry Percy's death invokes considerable wordplay on his nickname, his "hot" spur being transformed into a "cold" spur by death.

5. Prince Hal was called Harry Monmouth in honor of his birthplace, Monmouth, in Wales.

Where Hotspur's father, old Northumberland,
Lies crafty-sick.° The posts come tiring on,[6]   *pretending to be ill*
And not a man of them brings other news
Than they have learnt of me. From Rumour's tongues
40   They bring smooth comforts false, worse than true wrongs.

                                                              Exit

1.1

Enter LORD BARDOLPH[1] *at one door. [He crosses the*
stage to another door]

LORD BARDOLPH
Who keeps the gate here, ho?
       Enter PORTER [*above*][2]
                                    Where is the Earl?
PORTER   What shall I say you are?
LORD BARDOLPH   Tell thou the Earl
That the Lord Bardolph doth attend° him here.   *await*
PORTER   His lordship is walked forth into the orchard.
5   Please it your honour knock but at the gate,
And he himself will answer.
       Enter the Earl NORTHUMBERLAND [*at the other door, as*
       sick, with a crutch and coif]°   *nightcap*
LORD BARDOLPH   Here comes the Earl.
                                    [*Exit* PORTER]
NORTHUMBERLAND   What news, Lord Bardolph? Every minute now
Should be the father of some stratagem.
The times are wild; contention, like a horse
10   Full of high feeding,° madly hath broke loose,   *overly rich food*
And bears down all before him.
LORD BARDOLPH   Noble Earl,
I bring you certain news from Shrewsbury.
NORTHUMBERLAND   Good, an° God will.   *if*
LORD BARDOLPH   As good as heart can wish.
The King is almost wounded to the death;
15   And, in the fortune° of my lord your son,   *good luck*
Prince Harry slain outright; and both the Blunts[3]
Killed by the hand of Douglas; young Prince John
And Westmorland and Stafford fled the field;
And Harry Monmouth's brawn,° the hulk Sir John,   *fattened pig*
20   Is prisoner to your son. O, such a day,
So fought, so followed,° and so fairly won,   *carried through*
Came not till now to dignify the times
Since Caesar's fortunes!°   *successes*
NORTHUMBERLAND   How is this derived?
Saw you the field? Came you from Shrewsbury?
25   LORD BARDOLPH   I spake with one, my lord, that came from thence,
A gentleman well bred and of good name,
That freely rendered me these news for true.

---

6. The messengers, exhausting themselves, gallop on.
1.1. Location: Scene continues.
1. A nobleman associated with the rebel Percy faction;
Falstaff's companion with the same name is unrelated.
2. Having the Porter enter on the upper playing space is
conjectural, but it effectively suggests that Northumber-

land is in a stronghold where his retainers are wary of
intruders. The upper stage, however, does not appear to
have been used elsewhere in the play.
3. In *1 Henry IV*, only one Blunt, Sir Walter, dies at
Shrewsbury.

Enter TRAVERS

NORTHUMBERLAND   Here comes my servant Travers, who I sent
  On Tuesday last to listen after news.

30 LORD BARDOLPH   My lord, I overrode° him on the way,   *overtook*
  And he is furnished with no certainties
  More than he haply° may retail from me.   *perhaps*

NORTHUMBERLAND   Now, Travers, what good tidings comes with you?

TRAVERS   My lord, Lord Bardolph turned me back[4]

35 With joyful tidings, and being better horsed
  Outrode me. After him came spurring hard
  A gentleman almost forspent° with speed,   *worn out*
  That stopped by me to breathe° his bloodied horse.   *rest*
  He asked the way to Chester,[5] and of him

40 I did demand what news from Shrewsbury.
  He told me that rebellion had ill luck,
  And that young Harry Percy's spur was cold.
  With that he gave his able horse the head,
  And, bending forward, struck his armèd heels

45 Against the panting sides of his poor jade°   *worn-out horse*
  Up to the rowel-head;[6] and starting so,
  He seemed in running to devour the way,
  Staying° no longer question.   *Awaiting*

NORTHUMBERLAND   Ha? Again:
  Said he young Harry Percy's spur was cold?

50 Of Hotspur, 'Coldspur'? that rebellion
  Had met ill luck?

LORD BARDOLPH   My lord, I'll tell you what:
  If my young lord your son have not the day,
  Upon mine honour, for a silken point°   *lace for tying a garment*
  I'll give my barony. Never talk of it.

55 NORTHUMBERLAND   Why should the gentleman that rode by Travers
  Give then such instances of loss?

LORD BARDOLPH   Who, he?
  He was some hilding° fellow that had stol'n   *worthless*
  The horse he rode on, and, upon my life,
  Spoke at a venture.°   *at random*

Enter MORTON

                    Look, here comes more news.

60 NORTHUMBERLAND   Yea, this man's brow, like to a title leaf,
  Foretells the nature of a tragic volume.[7]
  So looks the strand° whereon the imperious flood   *shore*
  Hath left a witnessed usurpation.[8]
  Say, Morton, didst thou come from Shrewsbury?

65 MORTON   I ran from Shrewsbury, my noble lord,
  Where hateful death put on his ugliest mask
  To fright our party.

---

4. In Q, Travers says that Sir John Umfreuile, not Lord
Bardolph, turned him back. Since Lord Bardolph reports
having met Travers on the road, most critics agree that
Umfreuile and Lord Bardolph are the same character
whose name got changed at some point. At 1.1.161, Q
assigns one line to "Umfr.," another indication that a
character with this name was once to figure in the play.
This line does not appear in F or in the present text.
5. A town north of Shrewsbury.

6. The spiked wheel at the end of the spur.
7. Alluding to the descriptive title pages of early modern
printed books, which often indicated the principal actions
of the work and sometimes characterized them as tragic
or comic. For an example, see the descriptive title page
of the quarto version of this play, reprinted in the Introduction.
8. *whereon . . . usurpation*: where the sea has left evidence of its conquest (of the land).

NORTHUMBERLAND   How doth my son and brother?[9]
  Thou tremblest, and the whiteness in thy cheek
  Is apter than thy tongue to tell thy errand.
70 Even such a man, so faint, so spiritless,
  So dull, so dead in look, so woebegone,
  Drew Priam's curtain[1] in the dead of night,
  And would have told him half his Troy was burnt;
  But Priam found the fire ere he his tongue,
75 And I my Percy's death ere thou report'st it.
  This thou wouldst say: 'Your son did thus and thus,
  Your brother thus; so fought the noble Douglas',
  Stopping° my greedy ear with their bold deeds;   *Filling*
  But in the end, to stop° my ear indeed,   *plug up, obstruct*
80 Thou hast a sigh to blow away this praise,
  Ending with 'Brother, son, and all are dead.'
MORTON   Douglas is living, and your brother yet;
  But for my lord your son—
NORTHUMBERLAND   Why, he is dead.
  See what a ready tongue suspicion hath!
85 He that but fears the thing he would not know
  Hath by instinct knowledge from others' eyes
  That what he feared is chanced.° Yet speak, Morton.   *has happened*
  Tell thou an earl his divination lies,[2]
  And I will take it as a sweet disgrace,
90 And make thee rich for doing me such wrong.
MORTON   You are too great to be by me gainsaid,
  Your spirit is too true, your fears too certain.
NORTHUMBERLAND   Yet for all this, say not that Percy's dead.
  I see a strange confession in thine eye—
95 Thou shak'st thy head, and hold'st it fear or sin
  To speak a truth. If he be slain, say so.
  The tongue offends not that reports his death;
  And he doth sin that doth belie the dead,
  Not he which says the dead is not alive.
100 Yet the first bringer of unwelcome news
  Hath but a losing office,° and his tongue   *thankless duty*
  Sounds ever after as a sullen° bell   *mournful*
  Remembered knolling a departing friend.
LORD BARDOLPH   I cannot think, my lord, your son is dead.
105 MORTON [*to* NORTHUMBERLAND]   I am sorry I should force you to believe
  That which I would to God I had not seen;
  But these mine eyes saw him in bloody state,
  Rend'ring faint quittance,[3] wearied and out-breathed,°   *out of breath*
  To Harry Monmouth, whose swift wrath beat down
110 The never-daunted Percy to the earth,
  From whence with life he never more sprung up.
  In few,° his death, whose spirit lent a fire   *In short*
  Even to the dullest peasant in his camp,

9. The Earl of Worcester, who helped lead the rebellion staged in *1 Henry IV*.
1. Opened Priam's bed curtain. Priam was King of Troy during the Trojan War. This may allude to a scene from Virgil's *Aeneid* in which Hector appears to Aeneas, not Priam, in a dream, warning him of danger. Aeneas wakes to find Troy in flames.
2. Tell me, who am an earl, that in my prophecy I lie. To say a social superior lies would normally be a grave offense, but Northumberland would be happy to be proven wrong.
3. Repayment (return of blows).

	Being bruited° once, took fire and heat away	*reported*
115	From the best-tempered courage[4] in his troops;	
	For from his metal° was his party steeled,	*steel; courage*
	Which once in him abated,° all the rest	*blunted*
	Turned on themselves,[5] like dull and heavy lead;	
	And, as the thing that's heavy in itself	
120	Upon enforcement° flies with greatest speed,	*When forced into motion*
	So did our men, heavy in Hotspur's loss,	
	Lend to this weight such lightness with their fear	
	That arrows fled not swifter toward their aim	
	Than did our soldiers, aiming at their safety,	
125	Fly from the field. Then was that noble Worcester	
	Too soon ta'en prisoner; and that furious Scot	
	The bloody Douglas, whose well-labouring sword	
	Had three times slain th'appearance of the King,[6]	
	Gan vail his stomach,[7] and did grace° the shame	*sanction*
130	Of those that turned their backs, and in his flight,	
	Stumbling in fear, was took. The sum of all	
	Is that the King hath won, and hath sent out	
	A speedy power° to encounter you, my lord,	*quick-moving army*
	Under the conduct° of young Lancaster	*command*
135	And Westmorland. This is the news at full.	

NORTHUMBERLAND   For this I shall have time enough to mourn.

	In poison there is physic;° and these news,	*medicine*
	Having been° well, that would have made me sick,	*If I had been*
	Being sick, have in some measure made me well;	
140	And, as the wretch whose fever-weakened joints,	
	Like strengthless hinges, buckle under life,[8]	
	Impatient of his fit, breaks like a fire	
	Out of his keeper's° arms, even so my limbs,	*nurse's*
	Weakened with grief, being now enraged with grief,	
	Are thrice themselves.	

[He casts away his crutch]

	Hence therefore, thou nice° crutch!	*unmanly*
145	A scaly° gauntlet now with joints of steel	*mailed*
	Must glove this hand.	

[He snatches off his coif]

	And hence, thou sickly coif!	
	Thou art a guard too wanton° for the head	*effeminate; luxurious*
	Which princes fleshed with conquest[9] aim to hit.	
150	Now bind my brows with iron, and approach	
	The ragged'st° hour that time and spite dare bring	*roughest*
	To frown upon th'enraged Northumberland!	
	Let heaven kiss earth! Now let not nature's hand	
	Keep the wild flood confined! Let order die!	
155	And let this world no longer be a stage	
	To feed contention in a ling'ring act;[1]	

4. Courage of the finest quality. The implicit comparison is to steel that had been tempered, or made strong, by extreme heat.
5. Bent backward (like soft metal); fled.
6. In *1 Henry IV*, at the Battle of Shrewsbury, members of the rebel faction slew several noblemen dressed in the King's coats whom they mistook for Henry himself.
7. Began to lose courage (stomach).

8. Collapse from the burden of living.
9. Which princes made eager for bloody victories by having tasted raw flesh (been victorious). Hounds were "fleshed," given a taste of raw meat, to prepare them for the hunt.
1. *And let . . . act:* And let the world stop being a stage where strife is encouraged in a prolonged action.

But let one spirit of the first-born Cain[2]
Reign in all bosoms, that each heart being set
On bloody courses, the rude scene may end,
160 And darkness be the burier of the dead!
LORD BARDOLPH   Sweet Earl, divorce not wisdom from your honour.
MORTON   The lives of all your loving complices°   associates
Lean on your health, the which, if you give o'er
To stormy passion, must perforce decay.[3]
165 You cast th'event° of war, my noble lord,   calculated the outcome
And summed° the account of chance, before you said   added up
'Let us make head'.° It was your presurmise   raise an army
That in the dole° of blows your son might drop.   dealing out
You knew he walked o'er perils on an edge,°   a narrow blade
170 More likely to fall in than to get o'er.
You were advised° his flesh was capable   aware
Of wounds and scars, and that his forward spirit
Would lift him where most trade of° danger ranged.°   dealing in / was displayed
Yet did you say, 'Go forth'; and none of this,
175 Though strongly apprehended, could restrain
The stiff-borne° action. What hath then befall'n?   stubbornly pursued
Or what doth this bold enterprise bring forth,
More than that being° which was like to be?   event
LORD BARDOLPH   We all that are engagèd° to this loss   involved in
180 Knew that we ventured on such dangerous seas
That if we wrought out life was ten to one;[4]
And yet we ventured for the gain proposed,
Choked the respect of° likely peril feared;   Refused to consider
And since we are o'erset,° venture again.   overthrown
185 Come, we will all put forth body and goods.
MORTON   'Tis more than time; and, my most noble lord,
I hear for certain, and dare speak the truth,[5]
The gentle Archbishop of York is up°   up in arms
With well-appointed powers.° He is a man   well-equipped forces
190 Who with a double surety binds his followers.[6]
My lord, your son had only but the corpse,°   mere bodies
But shadows and the shows of men, to fight;
For that same word 'rebellion' did divide
The action of their bodies from their souls,
195 And they did fight with queasiness, constrained,
As men drink potions, that their weapons only
Seemed on our side; but, for their spirits and souls,
This word 'rebellion', it had froze them up,
As fish are in a pond. But now the Bishop
200 Turns insurrection to religion.
Supposed sincere and holy in his thoughts,
He's followed both with body and with mind,
And doth enlarge his rising[7] with the blood
Of fair King Richard, scraped from Pomfret stones;[8]

---

2. In the Bible, the first human being to be born and the murderer of his brother.
3. Lines 165–78 are not included in Q. (See Textual Note.)
4. The odds were ten to one against our preserving life.
5. Lines 188–208 are missing from Q. It is generally agreed that these lines were cut for political reasons.
6. Referring to the fact that the Archbishop, unlike Hot-

spur, might use his religious as well as his temporal authority to secure his soldiers' fidelity.
7. And increases the size or enhances the reputation of his rebellion.
8. Alluding to Henry IV's responsibility for the murder of Richard at Pontefract Castle (Pomfret), as staged in Act 5 of *Richard II*. Richard's blood is treated as a holy saint's relic.

205 Derives from heaven his quarrel and his cause;
Tells them he doth bestride° a bleeding land   *protect by standing over*
Gasping for life under great Bolingbroke;°   *(Henry IV)*
And more and less° do flock to follow him.   *people of all ranks*
NORTHUMBERLAND   I knew of this before, but, to speak truth,
210 This present grief had wiped it from my mind.
Go in with me, and counsel every man
The aptest way for safety and revenge.
Get posts° and letters, and make° friends with speed.   *messengers / gather*
Never so few, and never yet more need.   *Exeunt*

1.2

Enter Sir John FALSTAFF, *[followed by] his* PAGE *bearing*
his sword and buckler°   *shield*
FALSTAFF   Sirrah,[1] you giant, what says the doctor to my water?°   *urine*
PAGE   He said, sir, the water itself was a good healthy water, but,
for the party that owed° it, he might have more diseases than   *owned*
he knew for.°   *was aware of*
5 FALSTAFF   Men of all sorts take a pride to gird° at me. The brain   *mock*
of this foolish-compounded clay,[2] man, is not able to invent
anything that tends to laughter more than I invent, or is
invented on me. I am not only witty in myself, but the cause
that wit is in other men. I do here walk before thee like a sow
10 that hath o'erwhelmed° all her litter but one. If the Prince put   *crushed*
thee into my service for any other reason than to set me off,[3]
why then, I have no judgement. Thou whoreson mandrake,[4]
thou art fitter to be worn in my cap than to wait at my heels. I
was never manned with° an agate[5] till now; but I will set you   *attended by*
15 neither in gold nor silver, but in vile apparel, and send you
back again to your master for a jewel—the juvenal° the Prince   *youth*
your master, whose chin is not yet fledge.° I will sooner have a   *covered with down*
beard grow in the palm of my hand than he shall get one off
his cheek; and yet he will not stick° to say his face is a face-   *hesitate*
20 royal.[6] God may finish it when he will; 'tis not a hair amiss yet.
He may keep it still at° a face-royal, for a barber shall never   *at the value of*
earn sixpence out of it. And yet he'll be crowing as if he had
writ man° ever since his father was a bachelor. He may keep   *called himself a man*
his own grace,° but he's almost out of mine, I can assure him.   *title (Prince); favor*
25 What said Master Dumbleton about the satin for my short
cloak and slops?[7]
PAGE   He said, sir, you should procure him better assurance
than Bardolph. He would not take his bond and yours; he liked
not the security.
30 FALSTAFF   Let him be damned like the glutton![8] Pray God his

---

1.2 Location: A street in London.
1. Form of address to a social inferior.
2. Clay compounded with foolishness (an image derived from the biblical account of the first human being as formed out of clay).
3. To make me stand out by contrast. The page is tiny, and Falstaff is huge.
4. An herb with a forked root that was popularly supposed to resemble a miniature man. It was believed to shriek when pulled from the ground and to have aphrodisiac powers. *whoreson*: an insult, derived from the phrase

"whore's son."
5. A small jewel often carved with images of people and worn in caps.
6. The face of royalty (with a pun on "royal," a coin worth ten shillings and stamped with the monarch's face).
7. Baggy knee breeches, fashionable in Elizabethan London.
8. Referring to the biblical parable of a rich glutton who ignored the pleas of the beggar Lazarus, and at death was condemned to hell (see Luke 16:19–31).

tongue be hotter! A whoreson Achitophel,[9] a rascally yea-
forsooth knave,[1] to bear a gentleman in hand° and then stand   *lead a gentleman on*
upon security! The whoreson smooth-pates[2] do now wear noth-
ing but high shoes and bunches of keys at their girdles;[3] and if
35   a man is through with them in honest taking-up,[4] then they
must stand upon security. I had as lief° they would put rats-   *gladly*
bane° in my mouth as offer to stop it with security. I looked a°   *rat poison / that he*
should have sent me two and twenty yards of satin, as I am a
true knight,[5] and he sends me 'security'! Well, he may sleep in
40   security, for he hath the horn of abundance, and the lightness
of his wife shines through it;[6] and yet cannot he see, though he
have his own lanthorn to light him. Where's Bardolph?
PAGE   He's gone in Smithfield[7] to buy your worship a horse.
FALSTAFF   I bought him in Paul's,[8] and he'll buy me a horse in
45   Smithfield. An° I could get me but a wife in the stews,° I were   *If / brothels*
manned, horsed, and wived.
Enter [the] LORD CHIEF JUSTICE *and [his]* SERVANT
PAGE   Sir, here comes the nobleman that committed° the Prince   *imprisoned*
for striking him about Bardolph.[9]
FALSTAFF [*moving away*]   Wait close;° I will not see him.[1]   *concealed*
50 LORD CHIEF JUSTICE [*to his* SERVANT]   What's he that goes there?
SERVANT   Falstaff, an't please your lordship.
LORD CHIEF JUSTICE   He that was in question° for the robbery?[2]   *under investigation*
SERVANT   He, my lord; but he hath since done good service at
Shrewsbury, and, as I hear, is now going with some charge° to   *command of soldiers*
55   the Lord John of Lancaster.
LORD CHIEF JUSTICE   What, to York? Call him back again.
SERVANT   Sir John Falstaff!
FALSTAFF   Boy, tell him I am deaf.
PAGE [*to the* SERVANT]   You must speak louder; my master is
60   deaf.
LORD CHIEF JUSTICE   I am sure he is to the hearing of anything
good. [*To the* SERVANT] Go pluck him by the elbow; I must
speak with him.
SERVANT   Sir John!
65 FALSTAFF   What, a young knave and begging! Is there not wars?[3]
Is there not employment? Doth not the King lack subjects? Do
not the rebels want soldiers? Though it be a shame to be on
any side but one, it is worse shame to beg than to be on the

9. A biblical figure, King David's trusted counselor, who
betrayed him by supporting the treason of the king's son
(2 Samuel 15).
1. A villainous knave who appears to be agreeable. A
"yea-forsooth" knave makes promises with mild oaths (but
then breaks them).
2. Alluding disparagingly to the fashion among tradesmen for short hair.
3. Wear the most fashionable shoes and display a mass of
keys (habits suggesting pride and conspicuous consumption).
4. If a man makes a deal with them for a purchase on
credit.
5. Referring to Tudor sumptuary codes, which prescribed
the fabrics that could be worn by people of different social
ranks. As a knight, Falstaff can wear satin.
6. For he is rich and his wife's promiscuity is visible to
all, with puns on "horn" as referring to the horn lanterns
sold by merchants; to a symbol of overflowing plenty (a

cornucopia); and to cuckoldry (deceived husbands were
said to wear horns). "Lightness" can mean both illumination and sexual promiscuity.
7. A district northwest of London's city walls, used as a
market for animals.
8. St. Paul's Cathedral in London, where masterless men
presented themselves for employment.
9. Alluding to the apocryphal account of the youthful
Prince's assault on the Lord Chief Justice, staged in *The
Famous Victories of Henry V*, the anonymous play from
which Shakespeare's is partly derived.
1. Falstaff's determination not to acknowledge the Lord
Chief Justice presumably causes him to turn his back on
the magistrate or walk off in another direction.
2. The Gadshill robbery, in which Falstaff took part. See
1 Henry IV, 2.2.
3. Alluding to the Elizabethan practice of mass conscription of impoverished men.

worst side, were it worse than the name of rebellion can tell
70   how to make° it.   *regard*

SERVANT   You mistake me, sir.

FALSTAFF   Why, sir, did I say you were an honest man? Setting
my knighthood and my soldiership aside, I had lied in my
throat° if I had said so.   *deliberately lied*

75 SERVANT   I pray you, sir, then set your knighthood and your soldiership aside, and give me leave to tell you you lie in your
throat if you say I am any other than an honest man.

FALSTAFF   I give thee leave to tell me so? I lay aside that which
grows to me?° If thou gettest any leave of me, hang me. If thou   *is part of me*
80   takest leave, thou wert better be hanged. You hunt counter.[4]
Hence, avaunt!°   *be gone*

SERVANT   Sir, my lord would speak with you.

LORD CHIEF JUSTICE   Sir John Falstaff, a word with you.

FALSTAFF   My good lord! God give your lordship good time of
85   day. I am glad to see your lordship abroad. I heard say your
lordship was sick. I hope your lordship goes abroad by advice.°   *by medical advice*
Your lordship, though not clean past your youth, have yet some
smack of age in you, some relish of the saltness of time in you;
and I most humbly beseech your lordship to have a reverent
90   care of your health.

LORD CHIEF JUSTICE   Sir John, I sent for you before your expedition to Shrewsbury.

FALSTAFF   An't please your lordship, I hear his majesty is
returned with some discomfort from Wales.[5]

95 LORD CHIEF JUSTICE   I talk not of his majesty. You would not
come when I sent for you.

FALSTAFF   And I hear, moreover, his highness is fallen into this
same whoreson apoplexy.°   *paralysis*

LORD CHIEF JUSTICE   Well, God mend him! I pray you, let me
100   speak with you.

FALSTAFF   This apoplexy is, as I take it, a kind of lethargy, an't
please your lordship, a kind of sleeping in the blood, a
whoreson tingling.

LORD CHIEF JUSTICE   What° tell you me of it? Be it as it is.   *Why*

105 FALSTAFF   It hath it original° from much grief, from study, and   *its origin*
perturbation of the brain. I have read the cause of his effects in
Galen.[6] It is a kind of deafness.

LORD CHIEF JUSTICE   I think you are fallen into the disease, for
you hear not what I say to you.

110 FALSTAFF   Very well, my lord, very well. Rather, an't please you,
it is the disease of not listening, the malady of not marking, that
I am troubled withal.°   *with*

LORD CHIEF JUSTICE   To punish you by the heels[7] would amend
the attention of your ears, and I care not if I do become your
115   physician.

FALSTAFF   I am as poor as Job,[8] my lord, but not so patient. Your
lordship may minister the potion of imprisonment to me in

---

4. You pursue the scent of the game in the wrong direction.
5. Some discouragement from Wales (where the King
promised to fight Glyndŵr and Mortimer at the end of *1
Henry IV*).
6. Ancient Greek physician whose anatomical texts were
widely translated and printed in early modern Europe.

Galen was commonly regarded as the chief authority in
human physiology.
7. By putting your feet in the stocks or in shackles.
8. A biblical figure who, in the Book of Job, patiently
endured the many adversities with which God afflicted
him, including poverty.

respect of° poverty; but how I should be your patient to follow | *on account of*
your prescriptions, the wise may make some dram of a scruple,
120   or indeed a scruple itself.[9]

LORD CHIEF JUSTICE   I sent for you, when there were matters
against you for your life,[1] to come speak with me.

FALSTAFF   As I was then advised by my learned counsel in the
laws of this land-service,° I did not come. | *military duty*

125   LORD CHIEF JUSTICE   Well, the truth is, Sir John, you live in
great infamy.

FALSTAFF   He that buckles himself in my belt cannot live in less.

LORD CHIEF JUSTICE   Your means are very slender, and your waste
is great.

130   FALSTAFF   I would it were otherwise; I would my means were
greater and my waist slenderer.

LORD CHIEF JUSTICE   You have misled the youthful Prince.

FALSTAFF   The young Prince hath misled me. I am the fellow
with the great belly, and he my dog.[2]

135   LORD CHIEF JUSTICE   Well, I am loath to gall° a new-healed | *to injure by rubbing*
wound. Your day's service at Shrewsbury hath a little gilded
over your night's exploit on Gads Hill. You may thank th'un-
quiet time for your quiet o'erposting° that action. | *passing swiftly over*

FALSTAFF   My lord—

140   LORD CHIEF JUSTICE   But since all is well, keep it so. Wake not a
sleeping wolf.

FALSTAFF   To wake a wolf is as bad as smell a fox.° | *as being suspicious*

LORD CHIEF JUSTICE   What! You are as a candle, the better part
burnt out.

145   FALSTAFF   A wassail candle,[3] my lord, all tallow—if I did say of
wax,[4] my growth would approve° the truth. | *attest to*

LORD CHIEF JUSTICE   There is not a white hair in your face but
should have his effect° of gravity. | *manifestation*

FALSTAFF   His effect of gravy, gravy, gravy.[5]

150   LORD CHIEF JUSTICE   You follow the young Prince up and down
like his ill angel.° | *evil spirit*

FALSTAFF   Not so, my lord; your ill angel is light,[6] but I hope he
that looks upon me will take me without weighing. And yet in
some respects, I grant, I cannot go.° I cannot tell, virtue is of so | *walk; be circulated*
155   little regard in these costermongers' times[7] that true valour is
turned bearherd;[8] pregnancy° is made a tapster, and his quick | *mental agility*
wit wasted in giving reckonings;° all the other gifts appertinent° | *tavern bills / belonging*
to man, as the malice of this age shapes them, are not worth a
gooseberry. You that are old consider not the capacities of us
160   that are young. You do measure the heat of our livers with the
bitterness of your galls.[9] And we that are in the vanguard° of | *most advanced stage*
our youth, I must confess, are wags too.

---

9. The wise may feel a particle of doubt. Drams and scruples were small weights used to measure medicines in apothecary shops.
1. For which your life was at stake.
2. An obscure allusion. It may refer to the man in the moon, a mythical figure who supposedly carried a bush and was accompanied by a dog.
3. A large fat candle used at holiday festivities.
4. Beeswax, with pun on "wax" as meaning "grow."
5. Grease; sweat. Falstaff implies that sweat should drop from his face as fat (gravy) drops from hot meat.

6. Your bad coin weighs less. Falstaff puns on "angel" as the name of a gold coin that could illegally be clipped so that it weighed less than it should.
7. In these commercial times. A costermonger sold trifling commodities such as fruits and vegetables.
8. Keeper of bears, such as those used for the popular entertainment of bearbaiting.
9. You measure the strength of our passions by the bitterness of your melancholy. The liver was believed to be the seat of youthful passions, and bile or gall produced the melancholy and anger characteristic of old age.

LORD CHIEF JUSTICE   Do you set down your name in the scroll
of youth, that are written down old with all the characters° of   *letters; signs*
165   age? Have you not a moist eye, a dry hand, a yellow cheek, a
white beard, a decreasing leg, an increasing belly? Is not your
voice broken, your wind short, your chin double, your wit single, and every part about you blasted with antiquity? And will
you yet call yourself young? Fie, fie, fie, Sir John!

170   FALSTAFF   My lord, I was born about three of the clock in the
afternoon with a white head, and something a° round belly.   *a somewhat*
For my voice, I have lost it with hallowing° and singing of   *shouting to hounds*
anthems. To approve° my youth further, I will not. The truth   *prove*
is, I am only old in judgement and understanding; and he that
175   will caper° with me for a thousand marks,[1] let him lend me the   *dance (in competition)*
money, and have at him! For the box of th'ear that the Prince
gave you, he gave it like a rude° prince, and you took it like a   *violent; an uncivilized*
sensible[2] lord. I have checked him for it, and the young lion
repents—[*aside*] marry,° not in ashes and sackcloth, but in new   *by the Virgin Mary (oath)*
180   silk and old sack.[3]

LORD CHIEF JUSTICE   Well, God send the Prince a better companion!

FALSTAFF   God send the companion a better prince! I cannot rid
my hands of him.

185   LORD CHIEF JUSTICE   Well, the King hath severed you and Prince
Harry. I hear you are going with Lord John of Lancaster against
the Archbishop and the Earl of Northumberland.

FALSTAFF   Yea, I thank your pretty sweet wit for it. But look° you   *see that*
pray, all you that kiss my lady Peace at home, that our armies
190   join not in a hot day; for, by the Lord, I take but two shirts out
with me, and I mean not to sweat extraordinarily. If it be a hot
day and I brandish anything but my bottle, would I might never
spit white again.[4] There is not a dangerous action° can peep   *military action*
out his head but I am thrust upon it. Well, I cannot last ever.
195   But it was alway yet the trick° of our English nation, if they   *habit*
have a good thing, to make it too common. If ye will needs say
I am an old man, you should give me rest. I would to God my
name were not so terrible to the enemy as it is. I were better to
be eaten to death with a rust than to be scoured to nothing with
200   perpetual motion.

LORD CHIEF JUSTICE   Well, be honest, be honest, and God bless
your expedition.

FALSTAFF   Will your lordship lend me a thousand pound to furnish me forth?

205   LORD CHIEF JUSTICE   Not a penny, not a penny. You are too
impatient to bear crosses.[5] Fare you well. Commend me to my
cousin Westmorland.
            [*Exeunt* LORD CHIEF JUSTICE *and his* SERVANT]

FALSTAFF   If I do, fillip° me with a three-man beetle.[6] A man can   *strike*

---

1. A unit of money; one mark was equal to two-thirds of
a pound.
2. Like a reasonable lord; like a lord capable of feeling
pain. For the story of Hal's striking the Chief Justice, see
note to 1.2.48.
3. A Spanish white wine that improved with age.

4. A disputed passage. Perhaps, may I never drink again
(white spit was thought to be the result of heavy drinking).
5. To endure afflictions like a good Christian; to carry
silver coins, which bear the sign of a cross.
6. A huge sledgehammer designed to be lifted by three
laborers at once.

no more separate age and covetousness than a°° can part young   *he*
210 limbs and lechery; but the gout[7] galls the one and the pox
pinches° the other, and so both the degrees prevent my curses.[8]   *syphilis torments*
Boy!

PAGE   Sir.

FALSTAFF   What money is in my purse?

215 PAGE   Seven groats° and two pence.   *coins worth fourpence*

FALSTAFF   I can get no remedy against this consumption of the
purse. Borrowing only lingers and lingers it out, but the disease
is incurable. [*Giving letters*] Go bear this letter to my lord of
Lancaster; this to the Prince; this to the Earl of Westmorland;
220 and this to old Mistress Ursula,[9] whom I have weekly sworn to
marry since I perceived the first white hair of my chin. About
it. You know where to find me.   [*Exit* PAGE][1]
A pox of this gout!—or a gout of this pox!—for the one or the
other plays the rogue with my great toe. 'Tis no matter if I do
225 halt;° I have the wars for my colour,° and my pension shall   *limp / pretext*
seem the more reasonable. A good wit will make use of any-
thing. I will turn diseases to commodity.°   *Exit*   *profit*

1.3

Enter the ARCHBISHOP [*of York*], *Thomas* MOWBRAY [*the*]
Earl Marshal,[1] *Lord* HASTINGS, *and* LORD BARDOLPH

ARCHBISHOP OF YORK   Thus have you heard our cause and
      known our means,
And, my most noble friends, I pray you all
Speak plainly your opinions of our hopes.
And first, Lord Marshal, what say you to it?
5 MOWBRAY   I well allow the occasion of our arms,[2]
But gladly would be better satisfied
How in our means° we should advance ourselves   *with our resources*
To look with forehead bold and big enough
Upon the power and puissance° of the King.   *strength*
10 HASTINGS   Our present musters grow upon the file°   *according to our list*
To five-and-twenty thousand men of choice,°   *choice men*
And our supplies° live largely in the hope   *reinforcements*
Of great Northumberland, whose bosom burns
With an incensèd fire of injuries.
15 LORD BARDOLPH   The question then, Lord Hastings, standeth thus:
Whether our present five-and-twenty thousand
May hold up head° without Northumberland.   *May succeed*
HASTINGS   With him we may.

---

7. A disease characterized by painful inflammation of the joints, often of the toe joints in particular, and associated with the excessive consumption of rich food and alcohol. Falstaff is bothered by gout, and it may have been the reason he sent his urine to be examined by the doctor at the beginning of this scene.
8. So both conditions (age and youth) anticipate my curses. Venereal disease torments young lecherous men; gout afflicts old men.
9. A name nowhere else mentioned in this play. It could be the first name of Mistress Quickly. It may also be an

inadvertent reference to the Ursula of *Much Ado About Nothing,* a play also printed in 1600.
1. Neither Q nor F marks a separate exit for the Page. F indicates a plural "Exeunt" at the end of the scene, suggesting that Falstaff and the Page exit together. But clearly the fat knight's concluding lines are a private meditation on his diseases best spoken after he has sent the Page off to deliver his letter.
1.3 Location: The Archbishop's palace in York.
1. The officer in charge of arranging royal ceremonies.
2. I grant the justice of our taking arms.

LORD BARDOLPH   Yea, marry, there's the point;
But if without him we be thought too feeble,
20   My judgement is, we should not step too far[3]
Till we had his assistance by the hand;
For in a theme° so bloody-faced as this,   *matter*
Conjecture, expectation, and surmise
Of aids uncertain should not be admitted.
25   ARCHBISHOP OF YORK   'Tis very true, Lord Bardolph, for indeed
It was young Hotspur's case at Shrewsbury.
LORD BARDOLPH   It was, my lord; who lined° himself with hope,   *strengthened*
Eating the air on promise of supply,[4]
Flatt'ring himself with project of a power°   *expectation of an army*
30   Much smaller° than the smallest of his thoughts;   *smaller in actuality*
And so, with great imagination
Proper to madmen, led his powers to death,
And winking° leapt into destruction.   *shutting his eyes*
HASTINGS   But by your leave, it never yet did hurt
35   To lay down likelihoods and forms of hope.[5]
LORD BARDOLPH   Yes, if this present quality° of war—   *condition*
Indeed the instant° action, a cause on foot°—   *present / in motion*
Lives so in hope; as in an early spring
We see th'appearing buds, which to prove° fruit   *mature into*
40   Hope gives not so much warrant as despair
That frosts will bite them.[6] When we mean to build
We first survey the plot,[7] then draw the model;°   *design*
And when we see the figure° of the house,   *design*
Then must we rate the cost of the erection,
45   Which if we find outweighs ability,
What do we then but draw anew the model
In fewer offices,° or, at least,° desist   *rooms / worst*
To build at all? Much more in this great work—
Which is almost to pluck a kingdom down
50   And set another up—should we survey
The plot of situation and the model,
Consent° upon a sure foundation,   *Agree*
Question surveyors,° know our own estate,°   *architects / resources*
How able such a work to undergo,
55   To weigh against his opposite;[8] or else
We fortify in paper and in figures,
Using the names of men instead of men,
Like one that draws the model of an house
Beyond his power to build it, who, half-through,
60   Gives o'er, and leaves his part-created cost[9]
A naked subject° to the weeping clouds,   *An exposed object*
And waste for churlish winter's tyranny.
HASTINGS   Grant that our hopes, yet° likely of fair birth,   *still*
Should be stillborn, and that we now possessed
65   The utmost man of expectation,[1]

3. Lines 21–24 are not present in Q.
4. Sustaining himself on nothing but the promise of aid;
believing the empty words he had heard concerning
promised aid.
5. And hopeful plans. Lines 36–55 are not present in Q.
6. *as in . . . them:* an obscure passage. Bardolph may
mean that optimism in this instance is ill-advised, just as
it is ill-advised to hope that early spring buds will mature

into fruit rather than be killed by frost.
7. Plan. What follows is an elaboration on a biblical parable in Luke 14:28–30 about a wise builder.
8. *To weigh . . . opposite:* To put in the balance against
contrary arguments. Bardolph is urging the rebels to evaluate their strengths against their weaknesses.
9. And leaves his costly building half completed.
1. The last man whom we can expect.

I think we are a body strong enough,
Even as we are, to equal with the King.

LORD BARDOLPH   What, is the King but five-and-twenty thousand?

HASTINGS   To us no more, nay, not so much, Lord Bardolph;
70   For his divisions, as the times do brawl,°   *are full of conflict*
Are in three heads: one power against the French,
And one against Glyndŵr, perforce a third
Must take up us.° So is the unfirm King   *oppose us*
In three divided, and his coffers sound
75   With hollow poverty and emptiness.

ARCHBISHOP OF YORK   That he should draw his several° strengths together   *separate*
And come against us in full puissance
Need not be dreaded.

HASTINGS   If he should do so,
He leaves his back unarmed, the French and Welsh
80   Baying him at the heels.[2] Never fear that.

LORD BARDOLPH   Who is it like° should lead his forces hither?   *likely*

HASTINGS   The Duke of Lancaster and Westmorland;
Against the Welsh, himself and Harry Monmouth;
But who is substituted° 'gainst the French   *delegated*
I have no certain notice.[3]

85   ARCHBISHOP OF YORK   Let us on,
And publish° the occasion of our arms.   *make public*
The commonwealth is sick of their own choice;
Their over-greedy love hath surfeited.[4]
An habitation giddy and unsure
90   Hath he that buildeth on the vulgar° heart.   *common*
O thou fond° many, with what loud applause   *foolish*
Didst thou beat° heaven with blessing Bolingbroke,   *assail*
Before he was what thou wouldst have him be!
And being now trimmed° in thine own desires,   *decked out*
95   Thou, beastly feeder, art so full of him
That thou provok'st thyself to cast him up.
So, so, thou common dog, didst thou disgorge
Thy glutton bosom of the royal Richard,
And now thou wouldst eat thy dead vomit up,
100   And howl'st to find it. What trust is in these times?
They that when Richard lived would have him die
Are now become enamoured on his grave.
Thou that threw'st dust upon his goodly head,
When through proud London he came sighing on
105   After th'admirèd heels of Bolingbroke,
Cri'st now, 'O earth, yield us that king again,
And take thou this!' O thoughts of men accursed!
Past and to come seems best; things present, worst.

MOWBRAY   Shall we go draw our numbers° and set on?   *gather our forces*
110   HASTINGS   We are time's subjects, and time bids be gone.   *Exeunt*

---

2. That is, following him like hunting dogs.   4. Became sick through overindulgence.
3. Lines 85–108 are not present in Q.

2.1

*Enter [*MISTRESS QUICKLY *the] hostess of [a] tavern, and
an officer,* FANG *[followed at a distance by another offi-
cer],* SNARE[1]

MISTRESS QUICKLY   Master Fang, have you entered the action?°   *begun the lawsuit*
FANG   It is entered.
MISTRESS QUICKLY   Where's your yeoman?° Is't a lusty[2] yeoman?   *assistant*
Will a stand to't?[3]
FANG   Sirrah!—Where's Snare?
MISTRESS QUICKLY   O Lord, ay, good Master Snare.
SNARE [*coming forward*]   Here, here.
FANG   Snare, we must arrest Sir John Falstaff.
MISTRESS QUICKLY   Yea, good Master Snare, I have entered him[4]
and all.
SNARE   It may chance° cost some of us our lives, for he will stab.   *perhaps*
MISTRESS QUICKLY   Alas the day, take heed of him; he stabbed[5]
me in mine own house, most beastly, in good faith. A cares not
what mischief he does; if his weapon° be out, he will foin° like   *dagger; penis / thrust*
any devil, he will spare neither man, woman, nor child.
FANG   If I can close[6] with him, I care not for his thrust.
MISTRESS QUICKLY   No, nor I neither. I'll be at your elbow.
FANG   An I but fist° him once, an a come but within my   *seize; masturbate*
vice°—   *grasp*
MISTRESS QUICKLY   I am undone by his going, I warrant you; he's
an infinitive thing upon my score.[7] Good Master Fang, hold
him sure. Good Master Snare, let him not scape. A comes continuantly to Pie Corner[8]—saving your manhoods—to buy a
saddle,[9] and he is indited° to dinner to the Lubber's Head[1] in   *(for "invited")*
Lombard Street, to Master Smooth's the silkman. I pray you,
since my exion is entered,[2] and my case° so openly known to   *lawsuit; vagina*
the world, let him be brought in to his answer. A hundred mark
is a long one° for a poor lone woman to bear; and I have borne,[3]   *huge account*
and borne, and borne, and have been fobbed off, and fobbed
off, and fobbed off, from this day to that day, that it is a shame
to be thought on. There is no honesty in such dealing, unless
a woman should be made an ass and a beast, to bear every
knave's wrong.

2.1 Location: Eastcheap, a street and market in London.
1. That Snare should linger behind Fang is suggested by the subsequent lines in which Fang cannot locate his fellow officer. Perhaps Snare is slow and lazy; or perhaps he deliberately lags behind to sniff out trouble and "ensnare" villains.
2. Sturdy; lustful. The following lines are full of sexual puns.
3. Will he fight vigorously? Will he maintain an erect penis?
4. I have brought suit against him, with a pun on "entered him" as meaning "had sexual relations with him." The phrase usually denotes a man's sexual entry into a woman.
5. With a pun on "stabbed" as meaning "sexually penetrated."
6. Fight hand to hand; clinch.
7. "Infinitive" is Quickly's malapropism, or verbal blun-

der, for "infinite." She implies that the board ("score") on which her accounts are tallied has innumerable markings corresponding to Falstaff's debts to her.
8. Piecorner was an area of Smithfield named for its cooks' shops and known for its commerce in horses and sex. *continuantly*: blunder for "continually" or "incontinently."
9. With a pun on "saddle" as also meaning "female genitalia."
1. Blunder for "Libbard's," an Elizabethan form of "Leopard's." The silk merchant's shop sign evidently contained the image of a leopard's head.
2. Since my legal action has begun, with a pun on "entered" suggesting sexual penetration.
3. Endured, with a pun on "have borne" as meaning "have supported the weight of a partner in sexual relations."

Enter Sir John FALSTAFF, BARDOLPH, *and the* [PAGE][4]

Yonder he comes, and that arrant° malmsey-nose[5] knave Bar-   *notorious*
35   dolph with him. Do your offices,° do your offices, Master Fang   *duties*
and Master Snare; do me,[6] do me, do me your offices.

FALSTAFF   How now, whose mare's dead? What's the matter?

FANG   Sir John, I arrest you at the suit of Mistress Quickly.

FALSTAFF [*drawing*]   Away, varlets! Draw, Bardolph! Cut me off
40   the villain's head! Throw the quean° in the channel!°   *whore / street gutter*

[BARDOLPH *draws*]

MISTRESS QUICKLY   Throw me in the channel? I'll throw thee in
the channel!

[*A brawl*]

Wilt thou, wilt thou, thou bastardly rogue? Murder, murder!
Ah, thou honeysuckle[7] villain, wilt thou kill God's officers, and
45   the King's? Ah, thou honeyseed° rogue! Thou art a honeyseed,   *(for "homicidal")*
a man-queller, and a woman-queller.

FALSTAFF   Keep them off, Bardolph!

FANG   A rescue,[8] a rescue!

MISTRESS QUICKLY   Good people, bring a rescue or two. Thou
50   wot,° wot thou? Thou wot, wot'a? Do, do, thou rogue, do, thou   *You will*
hempseed![9]

PAGE   Away, you scullion,° you rampallian,° you fustilarian![1] I'll   *kitchen wench / ruffian*
tickle your catastrophe![2]

Enter [*the*] LORD CHIEF JUSTICE *and his men*

LORD CHIEF JUSTICE   What is the matter? Keep the peace here,
55   ho!

[*Brawl ends.* FANG *seizes* FALSTAFF][3]

MISTRESS QUICKLY   Good my lord, be good to me; I beseech you,
stand to me.[4]

LORD CHIEF JUSTICE   How now, Sir John? What, are you brawling here?

Doth this become your place,° your time° and business?   *social place / age*
60   You should have been well on your way to York.
[*To* FANG] Stand from him, fellow. Wherefore hang'st thou
upon him?

MISTRESS QUICKLY   O my most worshipful lord, an't° please your   *if it*
grace, I am a poor widow of Eastcheap, and he is arrested at
my suit.

65 LORD CHIEF JUSTICE   For what sum?

MISTRESS QUICKLY   It is more than for some, my lord, it is for all,
all I have. He hath eaten me out of house and home. He hath
put all my substance into that fat belly of his; [*to* FALSTAFF] but
I will have some of it out again, or I will ride thee a-nights like
70   the mare.[5]

---

4. As here, Q's stage directions sometimes refer to "the
boy" rather than "the page." These have been standardized to "Page" throughout.
5. Red-nosed from drinking alcohol. Malmsey was a
strong red wine named after its place of origin in Greece
and available from Spain, Portugal, and their colonies as
well as Greece.
6. Do your jobs for me, with a pun on "do me" as slang
for "have sexual relations with me."
7. For "homicidal," with a pun on "honey" as slang for
"sexual pleasure."
8. A cry for help in resisting arrest. Fang fears Falstaff is
being rescued, but Quickly in the next line takes "rescue"
to mean "reinforcements" and seems to call for the rescue

Fang is trying to stop.
9. Another version of "homicide," with an allusion to the
hangman's hempen rope.
1. Fat, unkempt woman.
2. Expression meaning "I'll whip your rear end."
3. There are considerable opportunities for comic stage
business here. Someone has to be hanging on Falstaff at
this point, because at line 61, the Lord Chief Justice tells
a "fellow" to let go. Perhaps Fang has twined himself
around Falstaff's legs or has even (living up to his name)
lodged his teeth in Falstaff's clothing or anatomy.
4. Support me; be sexually erect for me.
5. Referring to a kind of goblin supposed to produce
nightmares by sitting on the chest of a sleeper, with puns

FALSTAFF   I think I am as like to ride the mare, if I have any
vantage of ground to get up.°   *mount*
LORD CHIEF JUSTICE   How comes this, Sir John? Fie, what man
of good temper would endure this tempest of exclamation? Are
75   you not ashamed, to enforce a poor widow to so rough a course
to come by her own?
FALSTAFF [*to the Hostess*]   What is the gross sum that I owe thee?
MISTRESS QUICKLY   Marry, if thou wert an honest man, thyself,
and the money too. Thou didst swear to me upon a parcel-gilt°   *partly gilded*
80   goblet, sitting in my Dolphin chamber,° at the round table, by   *(an inn room)*
a sea-coal fire,[6] upon Wednesday in Wheeson° week, when the   *Whitsun (Pentecost)*
Prince broke thy head for liking° his father to a singing-man of   *likening*
Windsor[7]—thou didst swear to me then, as I was washing thy
wound, to marry me, and make me my lady thy wife. Canst
85   thou deny it? Did not goodwife Keech[8] the butcher's wife
come in then, and call me 'Gossip[9] Quickly'—coming in to
borrow a mess of° vinegar, telling us she had a good dish of   *some*
prawns, whereby thou didst desire to eat some, whereby I told
thee they were ill for a green° wound? And didst thou not,   *fresh*
90   when she was gone downstairs, desire me to be no more so
familiarity° with such poor people, saying that ere long they   *(for "familiar")*
should call me 'madam'?[1] And didst thou not kiss me, and bid
me fetch thee thirty shillings? I put thee now to thy book-oath;°   *oath on the Bible*
deny it if thou canst.
[*She weeps*]
95   FALSTAFF   My lord, this is a poor mad soul, and she says up and
down the town that her eldest son is like you. She hath been in
good case,° and the truth is, poverty hath distracted her.[2] But   *prosperous*
for these foolish officers, I beseech you I may have redress
against them.
100   LORD CHIEF JUSTICE   Sir John, Sir John, I am well acquainted
with your manner of wrenching the true cause the false way. It
is not a confident brow,° nor the throng of words that come   *countenance*
with such more than impudent sauciness from you, can thrust
me from a level° consideration. You have, as it appears to me,   *just*
105   practised upon the easy-yielding spirit of this woman, and made
her serve your uses both in purse and in person.
MISTRESS QUICKLY   Yea, in truth, my lord.
LORD CHIEF JUSTICE   Pray thee, peace. [*To* FALSTAFF] Pay her
the debt you owe her, and unpay the villainy you have done
110   with her. The one you may do with sterling money, and the
other with current° repentance.   *genuine*
FALSTAFF   My lord, I will not undergo this sneap° without reply.   *reproof*
You call honourable boldness 'impudent sauciness'; if a man
will make curtsy and say nothing, he is virtuous. No, my lord,
115   my humble duty° remembered, I will not be your suitor. I say   *due respect to you*
to you I do desire deliverance from these officers, being upon
hasty employment in the King's affairs.
LORD CHIEF JUSTICE   You speak as having power to do wrong;

---

on "ride" as meaning "mount sexually" and on "mare" as
a disparaging term for "woman."
6. Fire generated from charcoal shipped by sea rather
than by the inferior, locally produced charcoal.
7. One of the professional singers in the chapel at Windsor, a royal residence west of London.
8. "Goodwife" was the title of a married woman. "Keech"

meant "a lump of animal fat."
9. Familiar form of address for a female friend, derived
from "godmother," the name for the female guardian of a
newly christened child.
1. A form of address for a knight's wife; a whore.
2. Driven her mad.

but answer in th'effect of your reputation,° and satisfy the poor   *as befits your status*
120   woman.
FALSTAFF [*drawing apart*]   Come hither, hostess.
    [*She goes to him*]
    Enter M[aster] GOWER, *a messenger*
LORD CHIEF JUSTICE   Now, Master Gower, what news?
GOWER   The King, my lord, and Harry Prince of Wales
    Are near at hand; the rest the paper tells.
    [LORD CHIEF JUSTICE *reads the paper, and converses*
    apart with GOWER]
125 FALSTAFF   As I am a gentleman!
MISTRESS QUICKLY   Faith, you said so before.
FALSTAFF   As I am a gentleman! Come, no more words of it.
MISTRESS QUICKLY   By this heavenly ground I tread on, I must be
    fain° to pawn both my plate and the tapestry of my dining-   *content*
130   chambers.
FALSTAFF   Glasses, glasses, is the only drinking;[3] and for thy
    walls, a pretty slight drollery,° or the story of the Prodigal,[4] or   *comic painting*
    the German hunting in waterwork,[5] is worth a thousand of
    these bed-hangers° and these fly-bitten tapestries. Let it be ten   *bed curtains*
135   pound if thou canst. Come, an 'twere not for thy humours,°   *moods*
    there's not a better wench in England. Go, wash thy face, and
    draw° the action. Come, thou must not be in this humour with   *withdraw*
    me. Dost not know me? Come, I know thou wast set on to this.
MISTRESS QUICKLY   Pray thee, Sir John, let it be but twenty
140   nobles.[6] I'faith, I am loath to pawn my plate, so God save me,
    la!
FALSTAFF   Let it alone; I'll make other shift.° You'll be a fool   *I'll manage otherwise*
    still.°   *always*
MISTRESS QUICKLY   Well, you shall have it, though I pawn my
145   gown. I hope you'll come to supper. You'll pay me altogether?
FALSTAFF   Will I live? [*To* BARDOLPH *and the* PAGE] Go with her,
    with her. Hook on,° hook on!   *Stick to her*
MISTRESS QUICKLY   Will you have Doll[7] Tearsheet meet you at
    supper?
150 FALSTAFF   No more words; let's have her.
    Exeunt [MISTRESS QUICKLY, BARDOLPH,
    the PAGE, FANG *and* SNARE]
LORD CHIEF JUSTICE [*to* GOWER]   I have heard better news.
FALSTAFF   What's the news, my good lord?
LORD CHIEF JUSTICE [*to* GOWER]   Where lay the King tonight?°   *last night*
GOWER   At Basingstoke,[8] my lord.
155 FALSTAFF [*to* LORD CHIEF JUSTICE]   I hope, my lord, all's well.
    What is the news, my lord?
LORD CHIEF JUSTICE [*to* GOWER]   Come all his forces back?
GOWER   No; fifteen hundred foot, five hundred horse,
    Are marched up to my lord of Lancaster
160   Against Northumberland and the Archbishop.
FALSTAFF [*to* LORD CHIEF JUSTICE]   Comes the King back from
    Wales, my noble lord?

---

3. Glass drinking vessels began to replace metal tankards in the late sixteenth century.
4. Alluding to a biblical parable about a profligate son who repents, which was a frequent subject for cheap painted cloths.
5. A hunting scene of German or Dutch origin painted on a wall in imitation of tapestry.
6. Gold coins. Twenty were worth about six pounds.
7. A common name for a prostitute.
8. A town forty-six miles west of London.

LORD CHIEF JUSTICE [*to* GOWER] You shall have letters of me
    presently.°   *at once*
Come, go along with me, good Master Gower.
    [*They are going*]
FALSTAFF My lord!
165 LORD CHIEF JUSTICE What's the matter?
FALSTAFF Master Gower, shall I entreat you with me to dinner?
GOWER I must wait upon my good lord here, I thank you, good
    Sir John.
LORD CHIEF JUSTICE Sir John, you loiter here too long, being
170 you are to take soldiers up° in counties as you go.   *levy soldiers*
FALSTAFF Will you sup with me, Master Gower?
LORD CHIEF JUSTICE What foolish master taught you these man-
    ners, Sir John?
FALSTAFF Master Gower, if they become me not, he was a fool
175 that taught them me.[9] [*To* LORD CHIEF JUSTICE] This is the
    right fencing grace,° my lord—tap for tap, and so part fair.°   *style / on good terms*
LORD CHIEF JUSTICE Now the Lord lighten° thee; thou art a   *enlighten; make thin*
    great fool.   *Exeunt* [LORD CHIEF JUSTICE *and* GOWER *at one*
                             door, FALSTAFF *at another*]

2.2

Enter PRINCE HARRY *and* POINS[1]
PRINCE HARRY Before God, I am exceeding weary.
POINS Is't come to that? I had thought weariness durst not have
    attached° one of so high blood.   *laid hold of*
PRINCE HARRY Faith, it does me, though it discolours the com-
5 plexion of my greatness[2] to acknowledge it. Doth it not show
    vilely in me to desire small° beer?   *weak*
POINS Why, a prince should not be so loosely studied° as to   *disposed*
    remember so weak a composition.
PRINCE HARRY Belike then my appetite was not princely got; for,
10 by my troth, I do now remember the poor creature small beer.
    But indeed, these humble considerations make me out of love
    with my greatness. What a disgrace is it to me to remember thy
    name![3] Or to know thy face tomorrow! Or to take note how
    many pair of silk stockings thou hast—videlicet° these, and   *namely*
15 those that were thy peach-coloured ones! Or to bear° the inven-   *remember*
    tory of thy shirts—as one for superfluity,° and another for use.   *as a spare*
    But that the tennis-court keeper knows better than I, for it is a
    low ebb of linen with thee when thou keepest not racket° there;   *do not play*
    as thou hast not done a great while, because the rest of thy low
20 countries have made a shift to eat up thy holland.[4]
20.1   *And God knows whether those that bawl out the ruins of*

9. Falstaff suggests that the habit of ignoring others is
something he learned from a fool, namely the Chief Justice, who a few lines earlier would not answer Falstaff's
questions.
2.2 Location: Prince Hal's dwelling.
1. Q's stage direction reads: "Enter the Prince, Poynes,
Sir John Russel, with other." This is the only place in Q
where the name "Russel" is employed instead of "Bardolph," but it indicates that Shakespeare had been working on some portion of this play before he was forced to
change "Oldcastle" to "Falstaff," "Russell" to "Bardolph,"
and "Harvey" to "Peto" (see Introduction to *1 Henry IV*).
2. It mars my noble countenance (by turning it pale from
weakness or red from shame).

3. Men of high rank should not be on familiar terms
with, or remember the names of, those below them in
status.
4. Because the brothels ("low countries") have contrived
to eat up all the money you would have spent on linen
("holland"). With puns on "low countries" as also meaning "sexual organs" and "the Netherlands" as well as
"brothels"; and with a pun on "holland" as referring to
the country of Holland as well as to the fine linen made
there. Poins has either spent his money on whores or on
providing linen for the babies he has prodigally fathered.
His lack of shirts makes it impossible for him to play at
the tennis courts, where players sweat so much that shirts
were frequently changed.

thy linen⁵ shall inherit his kingdom°—*but the midwives*   *go to heaven*
say the children are not in the fault, whereupon the
world increases, and kindreds are mightily strengthened.

POINS   How ill it follows, after you have laboured so hard, you
should talk so idly! Tell me, how many good young princes
would do so, their fathers lying so sick as yours is?

PRINCE HARRY   Shall I tell thee one thing, Poins?

25   POINS   Yes, faith, and let it be an excellent good thing.

PRINCE HARRY   It shall serve among wits of no higher breeding
than thine.

POINS   Go to, I stand the push of° your one thing that you'll tell.   *I can tolerate*

PRINCE HARRY   Marry, I tell thee, it is not meet° that I should be   *appropriate*
30   sad now my father is sick; albeit I could tell to thee, as to one
it pleases me, for fault° of a better, to call my friend, I could be   *lack*
sad; and sad indeed too.

POINS   Very hardly,° upon such a subject.   *With great difficulty*

PRINCE HARRY   By this hand, thou thinkest me as far in the devil's
35   book as thou and Falstaff, for obduracy° and persistency. Let   *stubbornness*
the end try the man. But I tell thee, my heart bleeds inwardly
that my father is so sick; and keeping such vile company as
thou art hath, in reason, taken from me all ostentation° of   *signs*
sorrow.

40   POINS   The reason?

PRINCE HARRY   What wouldst thou think of me if I should weep?

POINS   I would think thee a most princely hypocrite.

PRINCE HARRY   It would be every man's thought, and thou art a
blessed fellow to think as every man thinks. Never a man's
45   thought in the world keeps the roadway⁶ better than thine.
Every man would think me an hypocrite indeed. And what
accites° your most worshipful thought to think so?   *induces*

POINS   Why, because you have been so lewd,° and so much   *base*
engrafted° to Falstaff.   *attached*

50   PRINCE HARRY   And to thee.

POINS   By this light, I am well spoke on;° I can hear it with mine   *of*
own ears. The worst that they can say of me is that I am a
second brother,⁷ and that I am a proper fellow of my hands;°   *a good fighter*
and those two things I confess I cannot help.

       Enter BARDOLPH [*followed by the* PAGE]
55   By the mass, here comes Bardolph.

PRINCE HARRY   And the boy that I gave Falstaff. A° had him from   *He*
me Christian, and look if the fat villain have not transformed
him ape.⁸

BARDOLPH   God save your grace!

60   PRINCE HARRY   And yours, most noble Bardolph!

POINS [*to* BARDOLPH]   Come, you virtuous ass, you bashful fool,
must you be blushing?⁹ Wherefore blush you now? What a

The lines 20.1–20.4 do not appear in F but are in Q.
The Oxford editors assume they were cut by Shakespeare
during revision of the play.
5. The bastard children who are wrapped in your old
shirts.
6. Adheres to the popular viewpoint.
7. That is, a younger brother (and therefore without pros-

pect of inheritance).
8. Made him look ridicuous, like an ape or a monkey
rather than a human being. Falstaff has perhaps dressed
the Page in an outlandish livery or uniform.
9. The jokes in this portion of the scene often refer to
Bardolph's notoriously red face. The color may be due to
drink, venereal disease, or some form of acne or rosacea.

maidenly man at arms are you become! Is't such a matter° to   *so difficult*
get a pottle-pot's maidenhead?[1]

65 PAGE A calls me e'en now, my lord, through a red lattice,[2] and
I could discern no part of his face from the window. At last I
spied his eyes, and methought he had made two holes in the
ale-wife's red petticoat, and so peeped through.

PRINCE HARRY [*to* POINS] Has not the boy profited?°   *(from Falstaff)*

70 BARDOLPH [*to the* PAGE] Away, you whoreson upright rabbit,
away!

PAGE Away, you rascally Althea's[3] dream, away!

PRINCE HARRY Instruct us, boy; what dream, boy?

PAGE Marry, my lord, Althea dreamt she was delivered of a
75 firebrand, and therefore I call him her dream.

PRINCE HARRY [*giving him money*] A crown's-worth of good
interpretation! There 'tis, boy.

POINS O, that this good blossom could be kept from cankers!°   *cankerworms*
[*Giving the* PAGE *money*] Well, there is sixpence to preserve
80 thee.

BARDOLPH An° you do not make him hanged among you, the   *If*
gallows shall be wronged.

PRINCE HARRY And how doth thy master, Bardolph?

BARDOLPH Well, my good lord. He heard of your grace's coming
85 to town. There's a letter for you.

POINS Delivered with good respect.° And how doth the Mar-   *(said ironically)*
tlemas[4] your master?

BARDOLPH In bodily health, sir.
        [PRINCE HARRY *reads the letter*]

POINS Marry, the immortal part° needs a physician, but that   *the soul*
90 moves not him. Though that be sick, it dies not.

PRINCE HARRY I do allow this wen° to be as familiar with me as   *wart*
my dog; and he holds his place,° for look you how he writes.   *maintains his position*
        [*He gives* POINS *the letter*][5]

POINS 'John Falstaff, knight'.—Every man must know that,° as   *(Falstaff's rank)*
oft as he has occasion to name himself; even like those that are
95 kin to the King, for they never prick their finger but they say
'There's some of the King's blood spilt.' 'How comes that?' says
he that takes upon him not to conceive.° The answer is as ready   *understand*
as a borrower's cap:[6] 'I am the King's poor cousin,° sir.'   *relative*

PRINCE HARRY Nay, they will be kin to us, or they will fetch it°   *derive kinship*
100 from Japhet.[7] [*Taking the letter*] But the letter. 'Sir John Falstaff, knight, to the son of the King nearest his father, Harry
Prince of Wales, greeting.'

POINS Why, this is a certificate!°   *legal document*

PRINCE HARRY Peace!— 'I will imitate the honourable Romans
105 in brevity.'

POINS [*taking the letter*] Sure he means brevity in breath, short

---

1. To open and drain a two-quart tankard of ale (with
implicit comparison to penetrating a virgin).
2. Sign of an alehouse window.
3. A conflation of two dreams from classical myth. It was
Hecuba, the Queen of Troy, who, when pregnant with
Paris, dreamed she gave birth to a firebrand that set fire
to her city. Althaea was told that her newborn son, Meleager, would live only as long as a brand in the fire was
not consumed, so she snatched it from the hearth.
4. Fatted cattle or pigs that were slaughtered on Novem-

ber 11, the feast day of St. Martin (Martlemas).
5. The reading of the letter is another occasion for comic
horseplay. The Prince and Poins may pass it back and
forth, or Poins may read it over Prince Harry's shoulder,
or snatch it away.
6. As readily produced as the cap of one looking for
money.
7. One of Noah's sons (Genesis 10:2–5), imagined to be
the common ancestor of all Europeans.

winded. [*Reads*] 'I commend me to thee, I commend thee, and
I leave thee. Be not too familiar with Poins, for he misuses thy
favours so much that he swears thou art to marry his sister Nell.
110 Repent at idle times as thou mayst. And so, farewell.
      Thine by yea and no[8]—which is as much as to say, as
thou usest him—Jack Falstaff with my familiars,° John   *friends*
with my brothers and sisters, and Sir John with all
Europe.'
115 My lord, I'll steep this letter in sack and make him eat it.
PRINCE HARRY   That's to make him eat twenty of his words. But
do you use me thus, Ned? Must I marry your sister?
POINS   God send the wench no worse fortune, but I never said
so.
120 PRINCE HARRY   Well, thus we play the fools with the time, and
the spirits of the wise sit in the clouds and mock us. [*To* BAR-
DOLPH] Is your master here in London?
BARDOLPH   Yea, my lord.
PRINCE HARRY   Where sups he? Doth the old boar feed in the
125 old frank?[9]
BARDOLPH   At the old place, my lord, in Eastcheap.
PRINCE HARRY   What company?
PAGE   Ephesians, my lord, of the old church.[1]
PRINCE HARRY   Sup any women with him?
130 PAGE   None, lord, but old Mistress Quickly and Mistress Doll
Tearsheet.
PRINCE HARRY   What pagan° may that be?   *heathen*
PAGE   A proper gentlewoman, sir, and a kinswoman of my mas-
ter's.
135 PRINCE HARRY   Even such kin as the parish heifers are to the
town bull. Shall we steal upon them, Ned, at supper?
POINS   I am your shadow, my lord; I'll follow you.
PRINCE HARRY   Sirrah, you, boy, and Bardolph, no word to your
master that I am yet come to town. [*Giving money*] There's for
140 your silence.
BARDOLPH   I have no tongue, sir.
PAGE   And for mine, sir, I will govern it.
PRINCE HARRY   Fare you well; go.
                    [*Exeunt* BARDOLPH *and the* PAGE]
This Doll Tearsheet should be some road.[2]
145 POINS   I warrant you, as common as the way between Saint
Albans[3] and London.
PRINCE HARRY   How might we see Falstaff bestow° himself   *behave*
tonight in his true colours, and not ourselves be seen?
POINS   Put on two leathern jerkins° and aprons, and wait upon   *jackets*
150 him at his table like drawers.°   *tavern servants*
PRINCE HARRY   From a god to a bull—a heavy declension°—it   *a sad degradation*
was Jove's case.[4] From a prince to a prentice—a low transfor-

---

8. Parodying the mild oaths associated with Puritans.
9. Pigsty. Possibly a reference to Eastcheap's famous tavern the Boar's Head.
1. Carousers of the usual kind. The Page alludes to the
biblical account of the Ephesians, whom St. Paul admon-
ished against lust and drunkenness before their conversion, with a possible reference to Catholics (members of
"the old church"), whom English Protestants accused of
moral laxity.
2. Some common prostitute. "Road" is slang for "vagina."
3. Town on the heavily traveled road north from London.
4. Referring to Jove's transformation into a bull before his
rape of Europa.

mation—that shall be mine; for in everything the purpose must
weigh with° the folly. Follow me, Ned.   *Exeunt*   *match*

2.3

Enter [the Earl of] NORTHUMBERLAND, LADY [NORTHUM-
BERLAND] *and* LADY PERCY[1]

NORTHUMBERLAND   I pray thee, loving wife and gentle
    daughter,°   *daughter-in-law*
  Give even way° unto my rough affairs.   *Allow free scope*
  Put not you on the visage of the times
  And be like them to Percy troublesome.
5 LADY NORTHUMBERLAND   I have given over; I will speak no more.
  Do what you will; your wisdom be your guide.
NORTHUMBERLAND   Alas, sweet wife, my honour is at pawn,
  And, but° my going, nothing can redeem it.   *except by*
LADY PERCY   O yet, for God's sake, go not to these wars!
10 The time was, father, that you broke your word[2]
  When you were more endeared° to it than now—   *bound*
  When your own Percy, when my heart's dear Harry,
  Threw many a northward look to see his father
  Bring up his powers; but he did long in vain.
15 Who then persuaded you to stay at home?
  There were two honours lost, yours and your son's.
  For yours, the God of heaven brighten it!
  For his, it stuck upon him as the sun
  In the grey° vault of heaven, and by his light   *pale blue*
20 Did all the chivalry° of England move   *chivalrous warriors*
  To do brave acts. He was indeed the glass°   *mirror*
  Wherein the noble youth did dress themselves.[3]
  He had no legs that practised not his gait;[4]
  And speaking thick,[5] which nature made his blemish,
25 Became the accents of the valiant;
  For those that could speak low and tardily°   *slowly*
  Would turn their own perfection to abuse
  To seem like him. So that in speech, in gait,
  In diet, in affections° of delight,   *choice*
30 In military rules, humours of blood,°   *disposition*
  He was the mark° and glass, copy° and book,   *target / example*
  That fashioned others. And him—O wondrous him!
  O miracle of men!—him did you leave,
  Second to none, unseconded° by you,   *unsupported*
35 To look upon the hideous god of war
  In disadvantage, to abide a field°   *confront a battle*
  Where nothing but the sound of Hotspur's name
  Did seem defensible;° so you left him.   *to provide a defense*
  Never, O never do his ghost the wrong
40 To hold your honour more precise and nice°   *exacting*
  With others than with him. Let them alone.

2.3 Location: Outside Northumberland's castle at Warkworth.
1. Q's stage direction designates the women only as wives:
"Enter Northumberland, his wife, and the wife to Harry
Percie."
2. Alluding to Northumberland's absence from the Battle
of Shrewsbury. See *1 Henry IV.*
3. Lines 23–45 do not appear in Q.
4. There was no man able to walk who did not try to
move as Hotspur did.
5. Speaking rapidly. The phrase has often been taken to
mean that Hotspur had a speech defect. A long stage tradition made him a stutterer.

The Marshal and the Archbishop are strong.
Had my sweet Harry had but half their numbers,
Today might I, hanging on Hotspur's neck,
Have talked of Monmouth's° grave.   *Prince Hal's*

45 NORTHUMBERLAND   Beshrew your heart,
Fair daughter, you do draw my spirits from me
With new lamenting ancient oversights.
But I must go and meet with danger there,
Or it will seek me in another place,
And find me worse provided.

50 LADY NORTHUMBERLAND   O fly to Scotland,
Till that the nobles and the armèd commons
Have of their puissance° made a little taste.   *strength*

LADY PERCY   If they get ground and vantage of the King,
Then join you with them like a rib of steel,
55 To make strength stronger; but, for all our loves,
First let them try themselves. So did your son.
He was so suffered.° So came I a widow,   *allowed to proceed*
And never shall have length of life enough
To rain upon remembrance with mine eyes,[6]
60 That it may grow and sprout as high as heaven
For recordation° to my noble husband.   *As a memorial*

NORTHUMBERLAND   Come, come, go in with me. 'Tis with my mind
As with the tide swelled up unto his height,
That makes a still stand,° running neither way.   *standstill*
65 Fain would I go to meet the Archbishop,
But many thousand reasons hold me back.
I will resolve for Scotland. There am I
Till time and vantage° crave my company.   *Exeunt*   *opportunity*

2.4

[*A table and chairs set forth.*][1] Enter a DRAWER° [*with*   *servant in a tavern*
wine and another DRAWER *with a dish of apple-johns*][2]

FIRST DRAWER   What the devil hast thou brought there—apple-
johns? Thou knowest Sir John cannot endure an apple-john.

SECOND DRAWER   Mass,[3] thou sayst true. The Prince once set a
dish of apple-johns before him; and told him, there were five
5 more Sir Johns; and, putting off his hat, said 'I will now take
my leave of these six dry, round, old, withered knights.' It
angered him to the heart. But he hath forgot that.

FIRST DRAWER   Why then, cover,° and set them down; and see if   *spread the cloth*
thou canst find out Sneak's noise.° Mistress Tearsheet would   *band of musicians*
10 fain hear some music.   [*Exit the* SECOND DRAWER]

[*The* FIRST DRAWER *covers the table.*]

[*Enter the* SECOND DRAWER]

---

6. To rain tears upon his memory, here imagined as a
plant—perhaps rosemary, the conventional symbol of
remembrance.
2.4 Location: A tavern, perhaps the Boar's Head, in Eastcheap.
1. Changes were made to this scene at some point. In Q,
dialogue occurs between Francis and "a Drawer or two."
At 2.4.13, Q's stage direction reads: "Enter Will." This
character has no lines, and probably his part was later
deleted. In F, the dialogue is somewhat rearranged and

occurs between two drawers, as here. However many servants are onstage, though, the point of their scurrying
about is to create excitement about Falstaff's arrival and
the trick to be played on him.
2. A kind of apple that could be kept for two years and
was meant to be eaten when the skin was wrinkled and
shriveled up.
3. An oath derived from the name of the Catholic church
service.

SECOND DRAWER   Sirrah, here will be the Prince and Master
Poins anon,° and they will put on two of our jerkins and aprons,   *soon*
and Sir John must not know of it. Bardolph hath brought word.

FIRST DRAWER   By the mass, here will be old utis!° It will be an   *merrymaking; a din*
15 excellent stratagem.

SECOND DRAWER   I'll see if I can find out Sneak.   *Exeunt*
Enter MISTRESS QUICKLY *and* DOLL TEARSHEET [*drunk*]

MISTRESS QUICKLY   I'faith, sweetheart, methinks now you are in
an excellent good temperality.° Your pulsidge[4] beats as extraor-   *(for "temper")*
dinarily as heart would desire, and your colour, I warrant you,
20 is as red as any rose, in good truth, la; but i'faith, you have
drunk too much canaries,[5] and that's a marvellous searching°   *strong*
wine, and it perfumes the blood ere we can say 'What's this?'
How do you now?

DOLL TEARSHEET   Better than I was.—Hem!

25 MISTRESS QUICKLY   Why, that's well said! A good heart's worth
gold.
Enter Sir John FALSTAFF
Lo, here comes Sir John.

FALSTAFF [*sings*]   'When Arthur first in court'[6]—[*Calls*] Empty
the jordan!°—[*Sings*] 'And was a worthy king'—How now, Mis-   *chamber pot*
30 tress Doll?

MISTRESS QUICKLY   Sick of a qualm,° yea, good faith.   *fainting fit*

FALSTAFF   So is all her sect;° an they be once in a calm,[7] they   *kind; sex*
are sick.

DOLL TEARSHEET   A pox damn you, you muddy rascal![8] Is that
35 all the comfort you give me?

FALSTAFF   You make fat rascals, Mistress Doll.

DOLL TEARSHEET   I make them? Gluttony and diseases make
them; I make them not.

FALSTAFF   If the cook help to make the gluttony, you help to
40 make the diseases, Doll. We catch of you,° Doll, we catch of   *are infected by you*
you; grant that, my poor virtue, grant that.

DOLL TEARSHEET   Yea, Jesu, our chains and our jewels.[9]

FALSTAFF   'Your brooches, pearls, and ouches'[1]—for to serve
bravely is to come halting off,[2] you know; to come off the
45 breach with his pike bent bravely,[3] and to surgery bravely; to
venture upon the charged chambers[4] bravely.

MISTRESS QUICKLY   By my troth, this is the old fashion. You two
never meet but you fall to some discord. You are both, i' good
truth, as rheumatic° as two dry toasts; you cannot one bear with   *(for "choleric")*
50 another's confirmities.° What the goodyear, one must bear,[5] [*to*   *(for "infirmities")*
DOLL] and that must be you. You are the weaker vessel, as they
say, the emptier vessel.

---

4. For "pulse."
5. Sweet wine from the Canary Islands.
6. Lines from the ballad "Sir Lancelot du Lake."
7. Quiet; not sexually active (punning on "qualm" in the prior line).
8. You dull knave. A "rascal" was a young, lean deer. They were called "muddy" when sluggish and out of season. In his next speech, Falstaff will accuse Doll of making even lean deer fat, probably by tempting them to gluttony and vice.
9. Yes, you steal ("catch") our valuables.
1. Perhaps a line from a ballad, with puns on the three items of jewelry as slang for the carbuncles and sores that

result from venereal disease.
2. To fight bravely is to return limping; to engage in vigorous sex is to be wounded in the process.
3. To come away from the gap in the fortifications (the breech) with one's weapon finely bent (with puns on "breech" as slang for "female genitalia" and "pike" as slang for "penis").
4. Interior of a mine loaded with munitions; the sexually aroused interior of a woman.
5. Endure; carry goods; support the weight of a sexual partner; give birth. *What the goodyear*: a phrase probably meaning "What the devil."

DOLL TEARSHEET   Can a weak empty vessel bear such a huge full
hogshead?° There's a whole merchant's venture° of Bordeaux   cask / cargo
55   stuff° in him; you have not seen a hulk better stuffed in the   wine
hold.— Come, I'll be friends with thee, Jack. Thou art going
to the wars, and whether I shall ever see thee again or no there
is nobody cares.

Enter [a] DRAWER

DRAWER   Sir, Ensign⁶ Pistol's below, and would speak with you.
60   DOLL TEARSHEET   Hang him, swaggering° rascal, let him not   blustering; quarreling
come hither. It is the foul-mouthedest rogue in England.
MISTRESS QUICKLY   If he swagger, let him not come here. No, by
my faith! I must live among my neighbours; I'll no swaggerers.
I am in good name and fame with the very best. Shut the door;
65   there comes no swaggerers here. I have not lived all this while
to have swaggering now. Shut the door, I pray you.
FALSTAFF   Dost thou hear, hostess?
MISTRESS QUICKLY   Pray ye pacify yourself, Sir John. There
comes no swaggerers here.
70   FALSTAFF   Dost thou hear? It is mine ensign.
MISTRESS QUICKLY   Tilly-fally,° Sir John, ne'er tell me. Your   Nonsense
ensign-swaggerer comes not in my doors. I was before Master
Tisick⁷ the debuty° t'other day, and, as he said to me—'twas no   (for "deputy")
longer ago than Wed'sday last, i' good faith—'Neighbour
75   Quickly,' says he—Master Dumb our minister was by then—
'Neighbour Quickly,' says he, 'receive those that are civil, for,'
said he, 'you are in an ill name.' Now a said so, I can tell
whereupon.⁸ 'For,' says he, 'you are an honest woman, and well
thought on; therefore take heed what guests you receive.
80   Receive,' says he, 'no swaggering companions.' There comes
none here. You would bless you° to hear what he said. No, I'll   feel fortunate
no swaggerers.
FALSTAFF   He's no swaggerer, hostess—a tame cheater,⁹ i'faith.
You may stroke him as gently as a puppy greyhound. He'll not
85   swagger with a Barbary hen,° if her feathers turn back in any   guinea hen; prostitute
show of resistance.—Call him up, drawer.   [*Exit DRAWER*]
MISTRESS QUICKLY   Cheater¹ call you him? I will bar no honest
man my house, nor no cheater, but I do not love swaggering,
by my troth, I am the worse when one says 'swagger'. Feel,
90   masters, how I shake, look you, I warrant you.
DOLL TEARSHEET   So you do, hostess.
MISTRESS QUICKLY   Do I? Yea, in very truth do I, an 'twere° an   as if I were
aspen leaf. I cannot abide swaggerers.

Enter PISTOL, BARDOLPH, and [the PAGE]

PISTOL   God save you, Sir John.
95   FALSTAFF   Welcome, Ensign Pistol. Here, Pistol, I charge you²
with a cup of sack. Do you discharge³ upon mine hostess.
PISTOL   I will discharge upon her, Sir John, with two bullets.°   (slang for "testicles")
FALSTAFF   She is pistol-proof, sir, you shall not hardly offend°   injure
her.

---

6. A military title for the army's standard-bearer.
7. The name signifies a hacking cough.
8. Now I can tell why he ("a") said so.
9. A decoy in a scheme to defraud people.
1. Quickly apparently understands the word as "es-

cheator," an officer responsible for returning to the crown
property whose title had lapsed.
2. Toast to you; load you with ammunition (punning on
Pistol's name); arouse you sexually.
3. Return the toast; empty the cup; shoot; ejaculate.

100 MISTRESS QUICKLY   Come, I'll drink no proofs, nor no bullets. I'll
drink no more than will do me good, for no man's pleasure, I.

PISTOL   Then to you, Mistress Dorothy! I will charge° you.   *toast; arouse; order*

DOLL TEARSHEET   Charge me? I scorn you, scurvy companion.
What, you poor, base, rascally, cheating, lack-linen mate!°   *fellow who has no linen*

105 Away, you mouldy rogue, away! I am meat for your master.[4]

PISTOL   I know you, Mistress Dorothy.

DOLL TEARSHEET   Away, you cutpurse° rascal, you filthy bung,[5]   *thieving; castrated*
away! By this wine, I'll thrust my knife in your mouldy chaps°   *cheeks, buttocks*
an you play the saucy cuttle with me![6]
[*She brandishes a knife*]

110 Away, you bottle-ale rascal, you basket-hilt stale juggler,[7] you!
[PISTOL *draws his sword*]
Since when, I pray you, sir? God's light, with two points[8] on
your shoulder! Much!

PISTOL   God let me not live, but I will murder your ruff° for this.   *starched collar*

MISTRESS QUICKLY   No, good Captain Pistol; not here, sweet cap-
115 tain.

DOLL TEARSHEET   Captain? Thou abominable damned cheater,
art thou not ashamed to be called 'captain'? An captains were
of my mind, they would truncheon° you out, for taking their   *cudgel*
names upon you before you have earned them. You a captain?

120 You slave! For what? For tearing a poor whore's ruff in a bawdy-
house! He a captain? Hang him, rogue, he lives upon mouldy
stewed prunes[9] and dried cakes. A captain? God's light, these
villains will make the word 'captain' odious; therefore captains
had need look to't.

125 BARDOLPH   Pray thee, go down, good ensign.

FALSTAFF   Hark thee hither, Mistress Doll.
[*He takes her aside*]

PISTOL   Not I! I tell thee what, Corporal Bardolph, I could tear
her! I'll be revenged of her.

PAGE   Pray thee, go down.

130 PISTOL   I'll see her damned first
To Pluto's damned lake,° by this hand,[1]   *(the lake of hell)*
To th'infernal deep,
Where Erebus,° and tortures vile also.   *the underworld*
'Hold hook and line!' say I.

135 Down, down, dogs; down, Fates.
Have we not Hiren here?[2]

MISTRESS QUICKLY   Good Captain Pizzle,° be quiet. 'Tis very   *Penis*
late, i'faith. I beseek you now, aggravate° your choler.   *(for "moderate")*

PISTOL   These be good humours indeed!

140 Shall pack-horses

---

4. That is, I am superior to you; with a pun on "meat" as
meaning "a body available for sexual pleasure."
5. Thief; anus.
6. If you continue to abuse me (with a pun on "cuttle" as
signifying both "knife" and "cuttlefish," which was supposed to vomit a black liquid to conceal itself from enemies).
7. You imposter with a cheap, outdated sword. Basket-
work hilts were used on inexpensive weapons or those
used only for practice.
8. Tags for fastening armor.
9. Available in brothels as a supposed preventative of

venereal disease, with a pun on "stew" as meaning
"brothel."
1. In this and subsequent speeches, Pistol rants in an
affected style that recalls and parodies the language of
sensational plays from the 1590s and earlier, which were
often set in non-European locales and involved military
and erotic adventures.
2. Apparently a line from *The Turkish Mohamet and
Hiren [Irene] the Fair Greek*, a lost play by George Peele.
Pistol may be referring to his sword as "Hiren" with a pun
on "iron."

And hollow pampered jades of Asia,[3]
Which cannot go but thirty mile a day,
Compare with Caesars and with cannibals,[4]
And Trojan Greeks?

145 Nay, rather damn them with King Cerberus,[5]
And let the welkin° roar. Shall we fall foul for toys?[6]   *heavens*

MISTRESS QUICKLY   By my troth, captain, these are very bitter
words.

BARDOLPH   Be gone, good ensign; this will grow to a brawl anon.

150 PISTOL   Die men like dogs! Give crowns like pins![7]
Have we not Hiren here?

MISTRESS QUICKLY   O' my word, captain, there's none such here.
What the goodyear, do you think I would deny her? For God's
sake, be quiet.

155 PISTOL   Then feed and be fat, my fair Calipolis.[8]
Come, give's some sack.
Si fortune me tormente, sperato me contento.[9]
Fear we broadsides? No; let the fiend give fire!°   *shoot*
Give me some sack; and, sweetheart, lie thou there.
       [*He lays down his sword*]

160 Come we to full points here? And are etceteras nothings?[1]
       [*He drinks*]

FALSTAFF   Pistol, I would be quiet.

PISTOL   Sweet knight, I kiss thy neaf.° What, we have seen the   *fist*
seven stars![2]

DOLL TEARSHEET   For God's sake, thrust him downstairs. I can

165 not endure such a fustian° rascal.   *worthless*

PISTOL   Thrust him downstairs? Know we not Galloway nags?[3]

FALSTAFF   Quoit° him down, Bardolph, like a shove-groat shil-   *Throw*
ling.[4] Nay, an a do° nothing but speak nothing, a shall be noth-   *if he does*
ing here.

170 BARDOLPH [*to* PISTOL]   Come, get you downstairs.

PISTOL [*taking up his sword*]   What, shall we have incision?
       Shall we imbrue?°   *steep in blood*
Then death rock me asleep, abridge my doleful days.
Why then, let grievous, ghastly, gaping wounds
Untwine the Sisters Three.[5] Come, Atropos, I say!

175 MISTRESS QUICKLY   Here's goodly stuff toward!°   *about to happen*

FALSTAFF   Give me my rapier, boy.

DOLL TEARSHEET   I pray thee, Jack, I pray thee, do not draw.

FALSTAFF [*taking his rapier and speaking to* PISTOL]   Get you
downstairs.
       [FALSTAFF, BARDOLPH, *and* PISTOL *brawl*]

---

3. A garbled allusion to Marlowe's 2 *Tamburlaine* 4.3.1–
2, in which Tamburlaine taunts the kings whom he has
captured and whom he uses in lieu of horses to draw his
chariot.
4. Pistol may mean "Hannibals." Hannibal was a famous
general of Carthage.
5. In classical mythology, the three-headed dog guarding
the underworld.
6. Quarrel over trifles.
7. Alluding to Tamburlaine's extravagance in distributing
the crowns of conquered kings among his followers.
8. Echoing Peele's *Battle of Alcazar*, in which the Moor-
ish King Muly Mahomet offers his starving wife the raw
flesh of a lion he has just killed.

9. If fortune torments me, hope contents me (a motto
that Pistol renders in a mixture of Italian, French, and
Spanish).
1. That is, have we come to a stop? Is there no further
satisfaction to be had in the rest (the "etceteras")? Pistol
puns on "etceteras" and "nothings" as slang for "female
genitalia."
2. We have caroused all night (with an allusion to the
Ursa Major constellation).
3. Small Scottish horses; prostitutes.
4. Shilling coin used in a game like shuffleboard.
5. The three Fates: Clotho, Lachesis, and Atropos. Atropos cut the thread of life.

180 MISTRESS QUICKLY   Here's a goodly tumult! I'll forswear keeping
house afore I'll be in these tirrits° and frights!   *(for "terrors" or "fits")*
> [FALSTAFF *thrusts at* PISTOL]

So!
> [PISTOL *thrusts at* FALSTAFF]

Murder, I warrant now! Alas, alas, put up your naked weapons,
put up your naked weapons!
> [*Exit* PISTOL, *pursued by* BARDOLPH]

185 DOLL TEARSHEET   I pray thee, Jack, be quiet; the rascal's gone.
Ah, you whoreson little valiant villain, you!

MISTRESS QUICKLY [*to* FALSTAFF] Are you not hurt i'th' groin?
Methought a made a shrewd° thrust at your belly.   *vicious*
> [*Enter* BARDOLPH]

FALSTAFF   Have you turned him out o'doors?

190 BARDOLPH   Yea, sir. The rascal's drunk. You have hurt him, sir,
i'th' shoulder.

FALSTAFF   A rascal, to brave° me!   *defy*

DOLL TEARSHEET   Ah, you sweet little rogue, you! Alas, poor ape,
how thou sweatest! Come, let me wipe thy face; come on, you
195 whoreson chops.° Ah rogue, i'faith, I love thee. Thou art as   *fat cheeks*
valorous as Hector of Troy,⁶ worth five of Agamemnon,⁷ and
ten times better than the Nine Worthies.⁸ Ah, villain!

FALSTAFF   A rascally slave! I will toss the rogue in a blanket.⁹

DOLL TEARSHEET   Do, an thou darest for thy heart. An thou dost,
200 I'll canvas° thee between a pair of sheets.   *toss*
> *Enter* music[*ians*]

PAGE   The music is come, sir.

FALSTAFF   Let them play. — Play, sirs!
> [*Music plays*]

Sit on my knee, Doll. A rascal bragging slave! The rogue fled
from me like quicksilver.°   *mercury*
205 DOLL TEARSHEET   I'faith, and thou followed'st him like a church.° *(i.e., sedately)*
Thou whoreson little tidy° Bartholomew boar-pig,¹ when wilt   *plump*
thou leave fighting o'days, and foining° o'nights, and begin to   *thrusting*
patch up thine old body for heaven?
> *Enter* PRINCE [HARRY] *and* POINS, *disguised* [*as drawers*]

FALSTAFF   Peace, good Doll, do not speak like a death's-head,²
210 do not bid me remember mine end.

DOLL TEARSHEET   Sirrah, what humour's° the Prince of?   *disposition is*

FALSTAFF   A good shallow young fellow. A would have made a
good pantler;° a would ha' chipped° bread well.   *pantry worker / cut*

DOLL TEARSHEET   They say Poins has a good wit.

215 FALSTAFF   He a good wit? Hang him, baboon! His wit's as thick
as Tewkesbury³ mustard; there's no more conceit° in him than   *intellect*
is in a mallet.

DOLL TEARSHEET   Why does the Prince love him so, then?

FALSTAFF   Because their legs are both of a bigness, and a° plays   *he*
220 at quoits⁴ well, and eats conger and fennel,⁵ and drinks off can-

---

6. The greatest Trojan warrior in Homer's *Iliad*.
7. Leader of the Greeks in the battle for Troy.
8. Nine legendary brave men: three Christians — Arthur, Charlemagne, Godfrey of Boulogne; three pagans — Hector, Alexander, Julius Caesar; and three Jews — Joshua, David, Judas Maccabeus.
9. A punishment for cowardice.
1. A roasted pig associated with an annual London carni-

val held on August 24, St. Bartholomew's Day.
2. Skull or representation of a skull used as a reminder of mortality.
3. Market town in Gloucestershire famed for its mustard.
4. A game involving the throwing of a heavy iron ring toward a target on the ground.
5. Conger eel, a heavy, hard-to-digest food, was served with fennel.

dles' ends for flap-dragons,[6] and rides the wild mare[7] with the boys, and jumps upon joint-stools, and swears with a good grace, and wears his boot very smooth like unto the sign of the leg,[8] and breeds no bate° with telling of discreet stories, and *discord*
225 such other gambol° faculties a has that show a weak mind and *sportive* an able body; for the which the Prince admits him; for the Prince himself is such another—the weight of a hair will turn the scales between their avoirdupois.° *weight*

PRINCE HARRY [*aside to* POINS]   Would not this nave° of a wheel *hub*
230 have his ears cut off?

POINS   Let's beat him before his whore.

PRINCE HARRY   Look whe'er the withered elder[9] hath not his poll° *head* clawed like a parrot.[1]

POINS   Is it not strange that desire should so many years outlive
235 performance?

FALSTAFF   Kiss me, Doll.
              [*They kiss*]

PRINCE HARRY [*aside to* POINS]   Saturn and Venus[2] this year in conjunction! What says th'almanac to that?

POINS   And look whether the fiery Trigon[3] his man be not lisping
240 to his master's old tables,° his note-book, his counsel-keeper![4] *writing tablets*

FALSTAFF [*to* DOLL]   Thou dost give me flattering busses.° *kisses*

DOLL TEARSHEET   By my troth, I kiss thee with a most constant heart.

FALSTAFF   I am old, I am old.

245 DOLL TEARSHEET   I love thee better than I love e'er a scurvy young boy of them all.

FALSTAFF   What stuff° wilt have a kirtle° of? I shall receive money *material / skirt* o'Thursday; shalt° have a cap tomorrow.—A merry song! *you shall*
              [*The music plays again*]
Come, it grows late; we'll to bed. Thou'lt forget me when I am
250 gone.

DOLL TEARSHEET   By my troth, thou'lt set me a-weeping an thou sayst so. Prove° that ever I dress myself handsome till thy *If you ever prove* return—well, hearken° a'th' end. *judge*

FALSTAFF   Some sack, Francis.

255 PRINCE *and* POINS [*coming forward*]   Anon, anon, sir.

FALSTAFF   Ha, a bastard son of the King's!—And art not thou Poins his brother?° *the brother of Poins*

PRINCE HARRY   Why, thou globe of sinful continents,[5] what a life dost thou lead!

260 FALSTAFF   A better than thou: I am a gentleman, thou art a drawer.

PRINCE HARRY   Very true, sir, and I come to draw you out by the ears.

MISTRESS QUICKLY   O, the Lord preserve thy grace! By my troth,

6. Referring to a tavern game in which one drank liquor on which burning objects (flapdragons) had been set afloat.
7. Plays at a form of leapfrog; has sexual relations with a woman.
8. As in the sign over the bootmaker's shop (depicting a well-booted leg).
9. Sapless elder tree; impotent old man.
1. Doll may here be running her hands through Falstaff's hair.

2. The planets governing old age and love.
3. The signs of the zodiac were divided into four sets of three (trigons). Aries, Leo, and Sagittarius are the "fiery trigon," being hot and dry. Poins alludes to Bardolph's red face.
4. Apparently Bardolph is wooing Quickly, here referred to as Falstaff's confidante and the keeper of his secrets.
5. World composed of sinful lands; a vast receptacle of sin.

265 welcome to London! Now the Lord bless that sweet face of
thine! O Jesu, are you come from Wales?

FALSTAFF [*to* PRINCE HARRY]   Thou whoreson mad compound of
majesty! By this light°—flesh and corrupt blood, thou art wel-   *(a conventional oath)*
come.

270 DOLL TEARSHEET   How, you fat fool? I scorn you.

POINS [*to* PRINCE HARRY]   My lord, he will drive you out of your
revenge and turn all to a merriment, if you take not the heat.°   *don't act at once*

PRINCE HARRY [*to* FALSTAFF]   You whoreson candlemine° you,   *storehouse of tallow*
how vilely did you speak of me now, before this honest,° virtu-   *chaste*

275 ous, civil gentlewoman!

MISTRESS QUICKLY   God's blessing of your good heart, and so she
is, by my troth!

FALSTAFF [*to* PRINCE HARRY]   Didst thou hear me?

PRINCE HARRY   Yea, and you knew me as you did when you ran

280 away by Gads Hill;[6] you knew I was at your back, and spoke it
on purpose to try my patience.

FALSTAFF   No, no, no, not so, I did not think thou wast within
hearing.

PRINCE HARRY   I shall drive you, then, to confess the wilful

285 abuse, and then I know how to handle you.

FALSTAFF   No abuse, Hal; o'mine honour, no abuse.

PRINCE HARRY   Not? To dispraise me, and call me 'pantler' and
'bread-chipper' and I know not what?

FALSTAFF   No abuse, Hal.

290 POINS   No abuse?

FALSTAFF   No abuse, Ned, i'th' world, honest Ned, none. I dis-
praised him before the wicked, that the wicked might not fall
in love with him; [*to* PRINCE HARRY] in which doing I have
done the part of a careful° friend and a true subject, and thy   *caring*

295 father is to give me thanks for it. No abuse, Hal; none, Ned,
none; no, faith, boys, none.

PRINCE HARRY   See now whether pure fear and entire cowardice
doth not make thee wrong this virtuous gentlewoman to close
with° us. Is she of the wicked? Is thine hostess here of the   *in order to pacify*

300 wicked? Or is thy boy of the wicked? Or honest Bardolph,
whose zeal burns in his nose, of the wicked?

POINS [*to* FALSTAFF]   Answer, thou dead elm, answer.

FALSTAFF   The fiend hath pricked down Bardolph irrecover-
able,[7] and his face is Lucifer's privy° kitchen, where he doth   *private*

305 nothing but roast malt-worms.° For the boy, there is a good   *weevils; drunkards*
angel about him, but the devil outbids him,° too.   *(the good angel)*

PRINCE HARRY   For the women?

FALSTAFF   For one of them, she's in hell already, and burns°   *infects with syphilis*
poor souls. For th'other, I owe her money, and whether she be

310 damned for that I know not.[8]

MISTRESS QUICKLY   No, I warrant you.

FALSTAFF   No, I think thou art not; I think thou art quit for° that.   *acquitted of*
Marry, there is another indictment upon thee, for suffering
flesh to be eaten in thy house, contrary to the law,[9] for the

315 which I think thou wilt howl.

---

6. Referring to events staged in Act 2 of *1 Henry IV*.
7. Marked Bardolph as beyond redemption.
8. Referring to the view that usury (lending money at
interest) was a sin.

9. Alluding to laws enacted against eating meat during
the Christian penitential days known as Lent as well as
to laws against the sex trade, with a pun on "house" as
"brothel."

MISTRESS QUICKLY   All victuallers° do so. What's a joint of mut-   innkeepers; bawds
ton° or two in a whole Lent?   piece of lamb; whore
PRINCE HARRY   You, gentlewoman—
DOLL TEARSHEET   What says your grace?
320   FALSTAFF   His grace says that which his flesh rebels against.[1]
                   PETO knocks at door [within]
MISTRESS QUICKLY   Who knocks so loud at door? [Calls] Look to
th' door there, Francis.
                   Enter PETO
PRINCE HARRY   Peto, how now, what news?
PETO   The King your father is at Westminster;
325   And there are twenty weak and wearied posts°   messengers
Come from the north; and as I came along
I met and overtook a dozen captains,
Bareheaded, sweating, knocking at the taverns,
And asking every one for Sir John Falstaff.
330   PRINCE HARRY   By heaven, Poins, I feel me much to blame
So idly to profane the precious time,
When tempest of commotion, like the south°   the south wind
Borne° with black vapour, doth begin to melt   Laden
And drop upon our bare unarmèd heads.—
335   Give me my sword and cloak.—Falstaff, good night.
                   Exeunt PRINCE [HARRY] and POINS
FALSTAFF   Now comes in the sweetest morsel of the night, and
we must hence and leave it unpicked.
                   [Knocking within. Exit BARDOLPH]
More knocking at the door!
                   [Enter BARDOLPH]
How now, what's the matter?
340   BARDOLPH   You must away to court, sir, presently.°   at once
A dozen captains stay° at door for you.   wait
FALSTAFF [to the PAGE]   Pay the musicians, sirrah. Farewell, hostess; farewell, Doll. You see, my good wenches, how men of
merit are sought after. The undeserver° may sleep, when the   unimportant officer
345   man of action is called on. Farewell, good wenches. If I be not
sent away post,° I will see you again ere I go.   hastily
                   [Exeunt musicians]
DOLL TEARSHEET [weeping]   I cannot speak. If my heart be not
ready to burst—well, sweet Jack, have a care of thyself.
FALSTAFF   Farewell, farewell!
                   Exit [with BARDOLPH, PETO, and the PAGE]
350   MISTRESS QUICKLY   Well, fare thee well. I have known thee these
twenty-nine years come peascod-time,[2] but an honester and
truer-hearted man—well, fare thee well.
                   [Enter BARDOLPH]
BARDOLPH   Mistress Tearsheet!
MISTRESS QUICKLY   What's the matter?
355   BARDOLPH   Bid Mistress Tearsheet come to my master.   [Exit]
MISTRESS QUICKLY   O run, Doll; run, run, good Doll!
                   Exeunt [DOLL at one door, MISTRESS QUICKLY at another door]

---

1. Implying that the Prince's virtuous speech can't hide a
body filled with lust for Tearsheet.

2. The time of year when peas form in the pod (early
spring).

3.1

Enter KING [HENRY] *in his nightgown,°* with a page   dressing gown

KING HENRY [*giving letters*]   Go call the Earls of Surrey and of Warwick.
But ere they come, bid them o'er-read these letters
And well consider of them. Make good speed.   *Exit* [*page*]
How many thousand of my poorest subjects

5   Are at this hour asleep? O sleep, O gentle sleep,
Nature's soft nurse, how have I frighted° thee,   frightened
That thou no more wilt weigh my eyelids down
And steep my senses in forgetfulness?
Why rather, sleep, liest thou in smoky cribs,°   hovels

10   Upon uneasy pallets° stretching thee,   hard straw beds
And hushed with buzzing night-flies to thy slumber,
Than in the perfumed chambers of the great,
Under the canopies of costly state,°   splendor
And lulled with sound of sweetest melody?

15   O thou dull° god, why li'st thou with the vile°   drowsy / lowly
In loathsome beds, and leav'st the kingly couch
A watch-case,° or a common 'larum-bell?   sentry box
Wilt thou upon the high and giddy mast
Seal up the ship-boy's eyes, and rock his brains

20   In cradle of the rude° imperious surge,   rough
And in the visitation of the winds,
Who take the ruffian billows by the top,
Curling their monstrous heads, and hanging them
With deafing° clamour in the slippery clouds,   deafening

25   That, with the hurly,° death itself awakes?   tumult
Canst thou, O partial sleep, give thy repose
To the wet sea-boy in an hour so rude,°   wild
And in the calmest and most stillest night,
With all appliances° and means to boot,°   devices / as well

30   Deny it to a king? Then happy low,° lie down.   happy humble people
Uneasy lies the head that wears a crown.
    Enter [*the Earls of*] WARWICK *and* SURREY
WARWICK   Many good morrows to your majesty!
KING HENRY   Is it good morrow, lords?
WARWICK   'Tis one o'clock, and past.
KING HENRY   Why then, good morrow to you all, my lords.

35   Have you read o'er the letter that I sent you?
WARWICK   We have, my liege.°   sovereign
KING HENRY   Then you perceive the body of our kingdom,
How foul it is, what rank° diseases grow,   loathsome
And with what danger near the heart of it.

40 WARWICK   It is but as a body yet distempered,°   sick
Which to his former strength may be restored
With good advice and little medicine.
My lord Northumberland will soon be cooled.
KING HENRY   O God, that one might read the book of fate,

45   And see the revolution of the times[1]
Make mountains level, and the continent,°   dry land
Weary of solid firmness, melt itself
Into the sea; and other times to see

3.1 Location: The palace at Westminster.   1. The changes that time will bring.

The beachy girdle of° the ocean   *girdle of beaches around*
50   Too wide for Neptune's² hips; how chance's mocks
And changes fill the cup of alteration
With divers° liquors!³   *various*
52.1   *O, if this were seen,*
The happiest youth, viewing his progress through,°   *through life*
What perils past, what crosses° to ensue,   *afflictions*
Would shut the book and sit him down and die.
'Tis not ten years gone
Since Richard and Northumberland, great friends,
Did feast together; and in two year after
55   Were they at wars. It is but eight years since
This Percy° was the man nearest my soul,   *(Northumberland)*
Who like a brother toiled in my affairs,
And laid his love and life under my foot,°   *at my disposal*
Yea, for my sake, even to° the eyes of Richard   *before*
60   Gave him defiance. But which of you was by—
[*To* WARWICK] You, cousin Neville,⁴ as I may remember—
When Richard, with his eye brimful of tears,
Then checked and rated° by Northumberland,   *chided*
Did speak these words,⁵ now proved a prophecy?—
65   'Northumberland, thou ladder by the which
My cousin Bolingbroke ascends my throne'—
Though then, God knows, I had no such intent,
But that necessity so bowed the state
That I and greatness were compelled to kiss—
70   'The time shall come'—thus did he follow it—
'The time will come that foul sin, gathering head,⁶
Shall break into corruption'; so went on,
Foretelling this same time's condition,
And the division of our amity.
75   WARWICK   There is a history in all men's lives
Figuring° the natures of the times deceased;°   *Showing / past*
The which observed, a man may prophesy,
With a near aim, of the main chance° of things   *general probability*
As yet not come to life, who° in their seeds   *which*
80   And weak beginnings lie intreasurèd.°   *stored*
Such things become the hatch and brood° of time;   *progeny and offspring*
And by the necessary form of this⁷
King Richard might create a perfect guess
That great Northumberland, then false to him,
85   Would of that seed grow to a greater falseness,
Which should not find a ground to root upon
Unless on you.
KING HENRY   Are these things then necessities?
Then let us meet them like necessities;

---

2. In classical myth, the god of the sea. Here the seashore is depicted as a girdle worn by Neptune. That the girdle is too wide or too large indicates that the sea is retreating from the land, in contrast to the prior image of land being absorbed into the ocean.
3. The following three and a half lines (52.1–52.4) do not appear in F, though they are in the 1600 Quarto version of the play.
4. An apparent error. The King is addressing the Earl of Warwick, whose surname was Beauchamp, not Neville. Shakespeare may be confusing him with Richard Neville, an important character in his plays on the life of Henry VI.
5. See *Richard II* 5.1, in which similar lines are spoken, though neither Bolingbroke nor Warwick was present.
6. Coming to maturity; coming to a head, like pus on a sore.
7. And by this requisite pattern (of cause and effect).

And that same word even now cries out on° us.   *denounces*
90   They say the Bishop and Northumberland
      Are fifty thousand strong.
WARWICK   It cannot be, my lord.
      Rumour doth double, like the voice and echo,
      The numbers of the feared. Please it your grace
      To go to bed? Upon my soul, my lord,
95   The powers that you already have sent forth
      Shall bring this prize in very easily.
      To comfort you the more, I have received
      A certain instance° that Glyndŵr is dead.   *proof*
      Your majesty hath been this fortnight ill,
100   And these unseasoned° hours perforce must add   *irregular*
      Unto your sickness.
KING HENRY   I will take your counsel.
      And were these inward° wars once out of hand,   *civil*
      We would, dear lords, unto the Holy Land.   *Exeunt*

3.2

Enter Justice SHALLOW *and Justice* SILENCE

SHALLOW   Come on, come on, come on! Give me your hand,
      sir, give me your hand, sir. An early stirrer, by the rood!° And   *cross*
      how doth my good cousin° Silence?   *kinsman*
SILENCE   Good morrow, good cousin Shallow.
5   SHALLOW   And how doth my cousin your bedfellow? And your
      fairest daughter and mine, my god-daughter Ellen?
SILENCE   Alas, a black ouzel,[1] cousin Shallow.
SHALLOW   By yea and no, sir, I dare say my cousin William is
      become a good scholar. He is at Oxford still, is he not?
10   SILENCE   Indeed, sir, to my cost.
SHALLOW   A° must then to the Inns o' Court[2] shortly. I was once   *He*
      of Clement's Inn,[3] where I think they will talk of mad Shallow
      yet.
SILENCE   You were called 'lusty Shallow' then, cousin.
15   SHALLOW   By the mass, I was called anything; and I would have
      done anything indeed, too, and roundly,° too. There was I, and   *thoroughly*
      little John Doit of Staffordshire, and black George Barnes, and
      Francis Pickbone, and Will Squeal, a Cotswold man; you had
      not four such swinge-bucklers° in all the Inns o' Court again.   *swashbucklers*
20   And I may say to you, we knew where the bona-robas° were,   *well-dressed prostitutes*
      and had the best of them all at commandment. Then was Jack
      Falstaff, now Sir John, a boy, and page to Thomas Mowbray,
      Duke of Norfolk.
SILENCE   This Sir John, cousin, that comes hither anon° about   *soon*
25   soldiers?
SHALLOW   The same Sir John, the very same. I see him break
      Scoggin's[4] head at the court gate when a was a crack,° not thus   *young fellow*
      high. And the very same day did I fight with one Samson Stock-

---

3.2 Location: Outside Justice Shallow's house in Gloucestershire.
1. Blackbird. Women with black hair and/or complex-
ions were often viewed as "foul" rather than "fair."
2. Prestigious legal schools in London that admitted men

to the bar.
3. One of the Inns of Chancery, less prestigious legal colleges.
4. A buffoon (possibly referring to Edward IV's court jester
of that name).

fish, a fruiterer, behind Gray's Inn.[5] Jesu, Jesu, the mad days
30 that I have spent! And to see how many of my old acquaintance
are dead.
SILENCE   We shall all follow, cousin.
SHALLOW   Certain, 'tis certain; very sure, very sure. Death, as the
Psalmist saith, is certain to all; all shall die. How° a good yoke   What's the price of
35 of bullocks at Stamford fair?
SILENCE   By my troth, I was not there.
SHALLOW   Death is certain. Is old Double of your town living
yet?
SILENCE   Dead, sir.
40 SHALLOW   Jesu, Jesu, dead! A° drew a good bow; and dead! A   He
shot a fine shoot. John o' Gaunt° loved him well, and betted   (Henry IV's father)
much money on his head. Dead! A would have clapped i'th'
clout at twelve score,[6] and carried you a forehand shaft a fourteen and fourteen and a half,[7] that it would have done a man's
45 heart good to see. How a score of ewes now?
SILENCE   Thereafter as they be.[8] A score of good ewes may be
worth ten pounds.
SHALLOW   And is old Double dead?
         Enter BARDOLPH *and [the* PAGE*]*[9]
SILENCE   Here come two of Sir John Falstaff's men, as I think.
50 SHALLOW   Good morrow, honest gentlemen.
BARDOLPH   I beseech you, which is Justice Shallow?
SHALLOW   I am Robert Shallow, sir, a poor esquire of this county,
and one of the King's Justices of the Peace. What is your good
pleasure with me?
55 BARDOLPH   My captain, sir, commends him° to you—my captain   sends his respects
Sir John Falstaff, a tall° gentleman, by heaven, and a most gal-   valiant
lant leader.
SHALLOW   He greets me well, sir. I knew him a good backsword
man.° How doth the good knight? May I ask how my lady his   fencer
60 wife doth?
BARDOLPH   Sir, pardon, a soldier is better accommodated than
with a wife.
SHALLOW   It is well said, in faith, sir, and it is well said indeed,
too. 'Better accommodated'—it is good; yea, indeed is it. Good
65 phrases are surely, and ever were, very commendable. 'Accommodated'—it comes of 'accommodo'. Very good, a good phrase.
BARDOLPH   Pardon, sir, I have heard the word—'phrase' call you
it?—By this day, I know not the phrase; but I will maintain the
word with my sword to be a soldier-like word, and a word of
70 exceeding good command,° by heaven. 'Accommodated'; that   fit for many uses
is, when a man is, as they say, accommodated; or when a man
is being whereby a may be thought to be accommodated;
which is an excellent thing.
         Enter Sir John FALSTAFF
SHALLOW   It is very just.° Look, here comes good Sir John. [*To*   true
75 FALSTAFF] Give me your hand, give me your worship's good

---

5. One of the Inns of Court.
6. Hit the target from 240 yards.
7. He could shoot an arrow straight, to 280 or 290 yards.
A "forehand shaft" is an arrow shot in a straight line rather
than with the curved trajectory common for long shots.
8. The price depends on their quality.

9. In F, Bardolph enters with "his Boy." In Q, he enters
"and one with him." It is reasonable to assume, but not
certain, that Falstaff's page is Bardolph's companion. The
use of a boy actor for this part would allow the number of
adult actors required for the rest of the scene to be
reduced by one.

hand. By my troth, you like well,° and bear your years very well.   *you are thriving*
Welcome, good Sir John.

FALSTAFF   I am glad to see you well, good Master Robert Shallow. [*To* SILENCE] Master Surecard, as I think.

80 SHALLOW   No, Sir John, it is my cousin Silence, in commission[1]
with me.

FALSTAFF   Good Master Silence, it well befits you should be of
the peace.

SILENCE   Your good worship is welcome.

85 FALSTAFF   Fie, this is hot weather, gentlemen. Have you provided me here half a dozen sufficient° men?   *able*

SHALLOW   Marry, have we, sir. Will you sit?

FALSTAFF   Let me see them, I beseech you.
[*He sits*]

SHALLOW   Where's the roll,° where's the roll, where's the roll?   *list*
90 Let me see, let me see, let me see; so, so, so, so, so. Yea, marry,
sir: 'Ralph Mouldy'. [*To* SILENCE] Let them appear as I call,
let them do so, let them do so. Let me see, [*calls*] where is
Mouldy?
[*Enter* MOULDY][2]

MOULDY   Here, an't please you.

95 SHALLOW   What think you, Sir John? A good-limbed fellow,
young, strong, and of good friends.°   *well-connected*

FALSTAFF   Is thy name Mouldy?

MOULDY   Yea, an't please you.

FALSTAFF   'Tis the more time° thou wert used.   *well past time*

100 SHALLOW   Ha, ha, ha, most excellent, i'faith! Things that are
mouldy lack use. Very singular good, in faith, well said, Sir
John, very well said.

FALSTAFF   Prick him.°   *Mark his name*

MOULDY   I was pricked[3] well enough before, an you could have
105 let me alone. My old dame° will be undone now for one to do   *wife*
her husbandry[4] and her drudgery. You need not to have
pricked me; there are other men fitter to go out than I.

FALSTAFF   Go to, peace, Mouldy. You shall go, Mouldy; it is
time you were spent.°   *used up*

110 MOULDY   Spent?

SHALLOW   Peace, fellow, peace. Stand aside; know you where
you are?
[MOULDY *stands aside*]
For th'other, Sir John, let me see: 'Simon Shadow' —

FALSTAFF   Yea, marry, let me have him to sit under. He's like to
115 be a cold° soldier.   *dead; cowardly*

SHALLOW [*calls*]   Where's Shadow?
[*Enter* SHADOW]

SHADOW   Here, sir.

FALSTAFF   Shadow, whose son art thou?

SHADOW   My mother's son, sir.

120 FALSTAFF   Thy mother's son! Like enough, and thy father's
shadow.° So the son of the female is the shadow° of the male —   *likeness / faint copy*

---

1. Having a position (as justice of the peace).
2. In F, the recruits enter at the beginning of the scene with Silence and Shallow. But they have nothing to do until this point in the scene. It is better to have them all enter with Mouldy and be called forward one by one; or,
as here, to enter separately as each name is called.
3. Vexed; provided with a penis.
4. Will be lacking someone to perform the sexual duties of a husband; will be lacking someone to do the work of the farm.

it is often so indeed—but not of the father's substance.[5]
SHALLOW   Do you like him, Sir John?
FALSTAFF   Shadow will serve for summer. Prick him, for we have
125   a number of shadows[6] fill up the muster book.
        [SHADOW *stands aside*]
SHALLOW [*calls*]   'Thomas Wart.'
FALSTAFF   Where's he?
        [*Enter* WART]
WART   Here, sir.
FALSTAFF   Is thy name Wart?
130   WART   Yea, sir.
FALSTAFF   Thou art a very ragged wart.
SHALLOW   Shall I prick him, Sir John?
FALSTAFF   It were superfluous, for his apparel is built° upon his   *pieced together*
        back, and the whole frame stands upon pins.[7] Prick him no
135   more.
SHALLOW   Ha, ha, ha, you can do it, sir, you can do it! I com-
        mend you well.
        [WART *stands aside*]
      [*Calls*] 'Francis Feeble.'
        [*Enter* FEEBLE]
FEEBLE   Here, sir.
140   SHALLOW   What trade art thou, Feeble?
FEEBLE   A woman's tailor,[8] sir.
SHALLOW   Shall I prick him, sir?
FALSTAFF   You may, but if he had been a man's tailor, he'd ha'
        pricked[9] you. [*To* FEEBLE] Wilt thou make as many holes in
145   an enemy's battle° as thou hast done in a woman's petticoat?   *army*
FEEBLE   I will do my good will,° sir; you can have no more.   *do my best*
FALSTAFF   Well said, good woman's tailor; well said, courageous
        Feeble! Thou wilt be as valiant as the wrathful dove or most
        magnanimous° mouse. Prick the woman's tailor. Well, Master   *brave*
150   Shallow; deep, Master Shallow.
FEEBLE   I would Wart might have gone, sir.
FALSTAFF   I would thou wert a man's tailor, that thou mightst
        mend him and make him fit to go.° I cannot put him to a   *to serve; to have sex*
        private soldier[1] that is the leader of so many thousands.° Let   *(of lice)*
155   that suffice, most forcible Feeble.
FEEBLE   It shall suffice, sir.
FALSTAFF   I am bound to thee, reverend Feeble.
        [FEEBLE *stands aside*]
      Who is next?
SHALLOW [*calls*]   'Peter Bullcalf o'th' green.'
160   FALSTAFF   Yea, marry, let's see Bullcalf.
        [*Enter* BULLCALF]
BULLCALF   Here, sir.
FALSTAFF   Fore God, a likely° fellow! Come, prick Bullcalf till   *promising*
        he roar again.

---

5. Not born from the father's body (because born from
the mother's); not the father's true son.
6. Fictitious names that officers recorded in order to collect additional pay from the crown.
7. The whole structure depends upon pegs ("pins");
stands upon legs ("pins").

8. Women's tailors were bywords for effeminacy and
cowardice.
9. Dressed; stabbed; penetrated.
1. Make him a private soldier; offer him sexually to a private soldier.

BULLCALF   O Lord, good my lord captain!
165   FALSTAFF   What, dost thou roar before thou'rt pricked?
BULLCALF   O Lord, sir, I am a diseased man.
FALSTAFF   What disease hast thou?
BULLCALF   A whoreson cold, sir; a cough, sir, which I caught
with ringing in the King's affairs[2] upon his coronation day, sir.
170   FALSTAFF   Come, thou shalt go to the wars in a gown.° We will   *dressing gown*
have away° thy cold, and I will take such order° that thy friends   *get rid / measures*
shall ring for thee.[3]
[BULLCALF *stands aside*]
Is here all?
SHALLOW   There is two more called than your number. You
175   must have but four here,[4] sir, and so I pray you go in with me
to dinner.
FALSTAFF   Come, I will go drink with you, but I cannot tarry°   *stay for*
dinner. I am glad to see you, by my troth, Master Shallow.
SHALLOW   O, Sir John, do you remember since we lay all night
180   in the Windmill in Saint George's Field?[5]
FALSTAFF   No more of that, good Master Shallow, no more of
that.
SHALLOW   Ha, 'twas a merry night! And is Jane Nightwork alive?
FALSTAFF   She lives, Master Shallow.
185   SHALLOW   She never could away with° me.   *tolerate*
FALSTAFF   Never, never. She would always say she could not
abide Master Shallow.
SHALLOW   By the mass, I could anger her to th' heart. She was
then a bona-roba. Doth she hold her own well?
190   FALSTAFF   Old, old, Master Shallow.
SHALLOW   Nay, she must be old; she cannot choose but be old;
certain she's old; and had Robin Nightwork by old Nightwork
before I came to Clement's Inn.
SILENCE   That's fifty-five year ago.
195   SHALLOW   Ha, cousin Silence, that thou hadst seen that that this
knight and I have seen! Ha, Sir John, said I well?
FALSTAFF   We have heard the chimes at midnight, Master
Shallow.
SHALLOW   That we have, that we have; in faith, Sir John, we
200   have. Our watchword was 'Hem° boys!' Come, let's to dinner;   *Drink up*
come, let's to dinner. Jesus, the days that we have seen! Come,
come.   *Exeunt* [SHALLOW, SILENCE, *and* FALSTAFF]
BULLCALF [*coming forward*]   Good Master Corporate° Bardolph,   *(for "Corporal")*
stand° my friend, and here's four Harry ten shillings in French   *act as*
205   crowns for you.[6] In very truth, sir, I had as lief° be hanged, sir,   *willingly*
as go. And yet for mine own part, sir, I do not care; but rather
because I am unwilling, and, for mine own part, have a desire
to stay with my friends. Else, sir, I did not care, for mine own
part, so much.
210   BARDOLPH [*taking the money*]   Go to; stand aside.
[BULLCALF *stands aside*]

2. Ringing the church bells in the King's honor.
3. In your place; at your death.
4. An inconsistency: there have been five, not six, recruits called.
5. A region of London south of the Thames near Southwark, known as a market for sex. "The Windmill" was the name of a brothel or inn.

6. An elaborate way of offering a bribe. The reference to "Harry ten shillings" is anachronistic; shillings originated during Henry VII's reign and by the 1590s had been devalued to half their original worth. Therefore, Bullcalf is offering about one pound to be paid in French crowns (coins worth four shillings each).

MOULDY [*coming forward*]   And, good Master Corporal Captain,
for my old dame's sake stand my friend. She has nobody to do
anything about her when I am gone, and she is old and cannot
help herself. You shall have forty,° sir.   *(shillings)*

215 BARDOLPH   Go to; stand aside.
                    [MOULDY *stands aside*]

FEEBLE   By my troth, I care not. A man can die but once. We
owe God a death. I'll ne'er bear a base mind. An't be my des-
tiny, so; an't be not, so. No man's too good to serve's° prince.   *serve his*
And let it go which way it will, he that dies this year is quit for°   *released from (dying)*
220 the next.

BARDOLPH   Well said; thou'rt a good fellow.

FEEBLE   Faith, I'll bear no base mind.
                    Enter [Sir John] FALSTAFF[, SHALLOW, *and* SILENCE]

FALSTAFF   Come, sir, which men shall I have?

SHALLOW   Four of which you please.

225 BARDOLPH [*to* FALSTAFF]   Sir, a word with you. [*Aside to him*] I
have three pound to free Mouldy and Bullcalf.

FALSTAFF   Go to, well.

SHALLOW   Come, Sir John, which four will you have?

FALSTAFF   Do you choose for me.

230 SHALLOW   Marry, then: Mouldy, Bullcalf, Feeble, and Shadow.

FALSTAFF   Mouldy and Bullcalf. For you, Mouldy, stay at home
till you are past service;[7] and for your part, Bullcalf, grow till
you come unto it.[8] I will none of you.
                    [*Exeunt* BULLCALF *and* MOULDY]

SHALLOW   Sir John, Sir John, do not yourself wrong. They are
235 your likeliest men, and I would have you served with the best.

FALSTAFF   Will you tell me, Master Shallow, how to choose a
man? Care I for the limb, the thews,° the stature, bulk, and big   *strength*
assemblance° of a man? Give me the spirit, Master Shallow.   *composition*
Here's Wart; you see what a ragged appearance it is? A shall
240 charge you and discharge you° with the motion of a pewterer's   *load and fire*
hammer,° come off and on swifter than he that gibbets on the   *with a steady motion*
brewer's bucket.[9] And this same half-faced° fellow Shadow;   *thin-faced*
give me this man. He presents no mark° to the enemy; the   *target*
foeman may with as great aim level at° the edge of a penknife.   *fire against*
245 And for a retreat, how swiftly will this Feeble the woman's tailor
run off! O, give me the spare men, and spare me the great
ones.—Put me a caliver° into Wart's hand, Bardolph.   *musket*

BARDOLPH [*giving* WART *a caliver*]   Hold, Wart. Traverse°—thas,   *March*
thas, thas!
                    [WART *marches*]

250 FALSTAFF [*to* WART]   Come, manage me your caliver. So; very
well. Go to, very good, exceeding good. O, give me always a
little, lean, old, chapped, bald shot!° Well said, i'faith, Wart;   *marksman*
thou'rt a good scab. Hold; [*giving a coin*] there's a tester° for   *sixpence*
thee.

255 SHALLOW   He is not his craft's master; he doth not do it right. I
remember at Mile-End Green,[1] when I lay° at Clement's   *lodged*

---

7. Past the time of military duty; past the time of sexual
potency.
8. That is, grow until you come into the time of military
service; the time of sexual potency. Falstaff plays on the
fact that Bullcalf is a *calf*, not a *bull*.

9. Retreat and advance, or raise and lower your gun,
faster than he who hangs pails on each end of the wooden
bar (gibbet) that a brewer carries on his shoulders.
1. Open land east of London used as a training ground
for citizen militias and for fairs and shows.

Inn—I was then Sir Dagonet in Arthur's show[2]—there was a
little quiver° fellow, and a would manage you his piece thus,   *nimble*
and a would about and about, and come you in° and come you   *thrust at you*
260   in. 'Ra-ta-ta!' would a say; 'Bounce!'° would a say; and away   *Bang*
again would a go; and again would a come. I shall ne'er see
such a fellow.

FALSTAFF   These fellows will do well, Master Shallow. God keep
you, Master Silence; I will not use many words with you. Fare
265   you well, gentlemen both; I thank you. I must° a dozen mile   *must go*
tonight.—Bardolph, give the soldiers coats.

SHALLOW   Sir John, the Lord bless you; God prosper your affairs!
God send us peace! As you return, visit my house; let our old
acquaintance be renewed. Peradventure I will with ye to the
270   court.

FALSTAFF   Fore God, would you would!

SHALLOW   Go to, I have spoke at a word.° God keep you!   *spoken sincerely*

FALSTAFF   Fare you well, gentle gentlemen.

                   Exeunt [SHALLOW *and* SILENCE]

On, Bardolph, lead the men away.

          [*Exeunt* BARDOLPH, WART, SHADOW, *and* FEEBLE]

275   As I return, I will fetch off° these justices. I do see the bottom   *defraud*
of Justice Shallow. Lord, Lord, how subject we old men are to
this vice of lying! This same starved justice hath done nothing
but prate to me of the wildness of his youth and the feats he
hath done about Turnbull Street;[3] and every third word a lie,
280   duer paid° to the hearer than the Turk's tribute.[4] I do remem-   *sooner paid*
ber him at Clement's Inn, like a man made after supper of a
cheese paring. When a was naked, he was for all the world like
a forked radish,[5] with a head fantastically carved upon it with a
knife. A was so forlorn° that his dimensions, to any thick° sight,   *thin / imperfect*
285   were invisible. A was the very genius° of famine.[6]   *spirit*
285.1   *yet lecherous as a monkey; and the whores called him*
'mandrake'. A came ever in the rearward of the fashion,
and sung those tunes to the overscutched hussies° that   *worn-out whores*
he heard the carmen° whistle, and sware they were his   *wagoners*
285.5   *fancies or his good-nights.°*   *his own love songs*
And now is this Vice's dagger[7] become a squire, and talks as familiarly of John o' Gaunt as if he had been sworn brother to him,
and I'll be sworn a ne'er saw him but once, in the Tilt-yard,°   *tournament arena*
and then he° burst his° head for crowding among the marshal's   *(Gaunt) / (Shallow's)*
290   men. I saw it, and told John o' Gaunt he beat his own
name;[8] for you might have trussed° him and all his apparel into   *packed*
an eel-skin. The case of a treble hautboy° was a mansion for   *oboe*
him, a court. And now has he land and beeves.° Well, I'll be   *oxen*
acquainted with him if I return; and't shall go hard but I'll
295   make him a philosopher's two stones to me.[9] If the young dace°   *small fish*

---

2. Referring to his role as King Arthur's fool in an archery
pageant in which each participant took the name of one
of the knights of the Round Table.
3. An area of Smithfield associated with criminal activities.
4. Money extracted from those the Turkish sultan conquered or who engaged in trade with him. The penalty
for failure to pay was death, so presumably money was
paid punctually. Shallow is even quicker to tell lies.
5. A mandrake root, said to resemble a man's body. See

note to 1.2.12.
6. The following inset lines (285.1–285.5) appear in Q
but not in F.
7. The wooden dagger used by the Vice, or comic character, in medieval morality plays.
8. Attacked someone very gaunt or thin.
9. I'll make him twice as valuable to me as the philosopher's stone that was supposed to transmute base metals
into gold, with a pun on "stones" as meaning "testicles."

be a bait for the old pike, I see no reason in the law of nature
but I may snap at him. Let time shape, and there an end.

Exit

4.1

Enter [in arms] the ARCHBISHOP [*of York*], [*Thomas*]
MOWBRAY, [*Lord*] HASTINGS, [*and*] COLEVILLE,[1] *within*
the Forest of Gaultres[2]

ARCHBISHOP OF YORK What is this forest called?
HASTINGS 'Tis Gaultres Forest, an't° shall please your grace.   *if it*
ARCHBISHOP OF YORK Here stand, my lords, and send discoverers° forth   *scouts*
  To know the numbers of our enemies.
HASTINGS We have sent forth already.
5 ARCHBISHOP OF YORK   'Tis well done.
  My friends and brethren in these great affairs,
  I must acquaint you that I have received
  New-dated° letters from Northumberland,   *Recent*
  Their cold intent, tenor, and substance, thus:
10 Here doth he wish his person, with such powers
  As might hold sortance° with his quality,°   *accord / rank*
  The which he could not levy; whereupon
  He is retired to ripe° his growing fortunes   *ripen*
  To Scotland, and concludes in hearty prayers
15 That your attempts may overlive the hazard
  And fearful meeting of their opposite.°   *enemy*
MOWBRAY Thus do the hopes we have in him touch ground
  And dash themselves to pieces.
      Enter a MESSENGER
HASTINGS   Now, what news?
MESSENGER West of this forest, scarcely off a mile,
20 In goodly form° comes on the enemy;   *battle array*
  And, by the ground they hide,° I judge their number   *cover*
  Upon or near the rate of thirty thousand.
MOWBRAY The just proportion° that we gave them out.°   *exact size / estimated*
  Let us sway on, and face them in the field.
      Enter [the Earl] of WESTMORLAND
25 ARCHBISHOP OF YORK What well-appointed leader fronts° us here?   *confronts*
MOWBRAY I think it is my lord of Westmorland.
WESTMORLAND Health and fair greeting from our general,
  The Prince, Lord John and Duke of Lancaster.
ARCHBISHOP OF YORK Say on, my lord of Westmorland, in peace,
  What doth concern your coming.
30 WESTMORLAND   Then, my lord,
  Unto your grace do I in chief address
  The substance of my speech. If that rebellion
  Came like itself, in base and abject routs,°   *lowborn disorderly bands*
  Led on by bloody youth, guarded° with rags,   *adorned*
35 And countenanced° by boys and beggary;   *approved*
  I say, if damned commotion so appeared

4.1 Location: Gaultres Forest in Yorkshire.
1. In F, this initial stage direction includes Westmorland, who actually enters later in the scene, and Coleville, a rebel captured by Falstaff in 4.2. Most editors delete both figures from the initial stage direction. The Oxford editors speculate that Coleville is the captain who at 4.1.295–97 is sent to tell the rebel army to disperse after peace is made, so they include him in the scene from the beginning.
2. Gaultres was a royal forest north and west of York. In Holinshed's *Chronicles* and in Q and F, it is spelled "Gaultree," a spelling adopted in most editions.

In his true native and most proper shape,
You, reverend father, and these noble lords
Had not been here to dress the ugly form
40 Of base and bloody insurrection
With your fair honours. You, Lord Archbishop,
Whose see° is by a civil peace maintained,   *diocese*
Whose beard the silver hand of peace hath touched,
Whose learning and good letters° peace hath tutored,   *scholarship*
45 Whose white investments figure° innocence,   *robes represent*
The dove and very blessèd spirit of peace,
Wherefore do you so ill translate° yourself   *transform*
Out of the speech of peace that bears such grace
Into the harsh and boist'rous tongue of war,
50 Turning your books to graves, your ink to blood,
Your pens to lances, and your tongue divine
To a loud trumpet and a point° of war?   *signal*
ARCHBISHOP OF YORK   Wherefore do I this? So the question stands.
Briefly, to this end: we are all diseased,[3]
55 And with our surfeiting° and wanton hours   *overfeeding*
Have brought ourselves into a burning fever,
And we must bleed° for it—of which disease   *be bled as a cure*
Our late King Richard, being infected, died.
But, my most noble lord of Westmorland,
60 I take not on me here as a physician,
Nor do I as an enemy to peace
Troop in the throngs of military men;
But rather show° a while like fearful war   *appear*
To diet rank° minds, sick of happiness,   *swollen; overindulged*
65 And purge th'obstructions which begin to stop
Our very veins of life. Hear me more plainly.
I have in equal balance justly weighed
What wrongs our arms may do, what wrongs we suffer,
And find our griefs heavier than our offences.
70 We see which way the stream of time doth run,
And are enforced from our most quiet shore
By the rough torrent of occasion;°   *events*
And have the summary of all our griefs,
When time shall serve, to show in articles,°   *an itemized list*
75 Which long ere this we offered to the King,
And might by no suit gain our audience.
When we are wronged, and would unfold our griefs,
We are denied access unto his person
Even by those men that most have done us wrong.
80 The dangers of the days but newly gone,
Whose memory is written on the earth
With yet° appearing blood, and the examples   *still*
Of every minute's instance,° present now, *Occurring every minute*
Hath put us in these ill-beseeming° arms,   *unsuitable*
85 Not to break peace, or any branch of it,
But to establish here a peace indeed,
Concurring both in name and quality.
WESTMORLAND   Whenever yet was your appeal denied?

---

3. Lines 55–79 are missing from Q, perhaps because they state the case for rebellion too forcefully.

Wherein have you been gallèd° by the King?   *vexed; grieved*
90   What peer hath been suborned to grate on° you,   *induced to annoy*
That you should seal° this lawless bloody book   *license*
Of forged rebellion with a seal divine?[4]
ARCHBISHOP OF YORK   My brother general, the commonwealth
I make my quarrel in particular.[5]
95   WESTMORLAND   There is no need of any such redress;
Or if there were, it not belongs to you.
MOWBRAY   Why not to him in part, and to us all
That feel the bruises of the days before,
And suffer the condition of these times
100   To lay a heavy and unequal° hand   *unjust*
Upon our honours?[6]
WESTMORLAND   O my good Lord Mowbray,
Construe the times to° their necessities,   *according to*
And you shall say indeed it is the time,
And not the King, that doth you injuries.
105   Yet for your part, it not appears° to me,   *it does not appear*
Either from the King or in the present time,
That you should have an inch of any ground
To build a grief on. Were you not restored
To all the Duke of Norfolk's signories,°   *properties*
110   Your noble and right well-remembered father's?
MOWBRAY   What thing in honour had my father lost
That need to be revived and breathed° in me?   *brought to life*
The King that loved him, as the state stood then,
Was force perforce° compelled to banish him;   *against his will*
115   And then that Henry Bolingbroke and he,
Being mounted and both rousèd° in their seats,   *raised*
Their neighing coursers daring of the spur,[7]
Their armèd staves in charge,[8] their beavers° down,   *helmet visors*
Their eyes of fire sparkling through sights° of steel,   *visor slits*
120   And the loud trumpet blowing them together,
Then, then, when there was nothing could have stayed°   *kept*
My father from the breast of Bolingbroke—
O, when the King did throw his warder° down,   *staff of command*
His own life hung upon the staff he threw;
125   Then threw he down himself and all their lives
That by indictment° and by dint of sword   *legal accusations*
Have since miscarried under Bolingbroke.
WESTMORLAND   You speak, Lord Mowbray, now you know not what.
The Earl of Hereford° was reputed then   *(Bolingbroke)*
130   In England the most valiant gentleman.
Who knows on whom fortune would then have smiled?
But if your father had been victor there,
He ne'er had borne it out of Coventry;[9]
For all the country in a general voice
135   Cried hate upon him, and all their prayers and love

---

4. Alluding to bishops as official licensers of books with the ability to exercise censorship. Westmorland accuses the Archbishop of *not* censoring the book of rebellion.
5. *My . . . particular*: these two lines are obscure. York seems to be saying he is making the cause of the commonwealth his own because all men are his brothers.
6. The second half of line 101 and lines 102–37 do not appear in Q. They recount a version of events depicted

in Shakespeare's *Richard II* in which Richard stopped a formal combat between Thomas Mowbray, father of the Mowbray of this play, and Bolingbroke, now Henry IV.
7. Daring the spur to prick them forward.
8. Their steel-tipped lances ready for the charge.
9. He never would have carried away the prize from Coventry (where the duel was to take place).

Were set on Hereford, whom they doted on
And blessed and graced, indeed, more than the King.
But this is mere digression from my purpose.
Here come I from our princely general
140 To know your griefs, to tell you from his grace
That he will give you audience; and wherein
It shall appear that your demands are just,
You shall enjoy them, everything set off°   *forgotten*
That might so much as think you enemies.
145 MOWBRAY   But he hath forced us to compel this offer,
And it proceeds from policy,° not love.   *political cunning*
WESTMORLAND   Mowbray, you overween° to take it so.   *presume too much*
This offer comes from mercy, not from fear;
For lo, within a ken° our army lies,   *the field of vision*
150 Upon mine honour, all too confident
To give admittance to a thought of fear.
Our battle° is more full of names° than yours,   *army / titled men*
Our men more perfect in the use of arms,
Our armour all as strong, our cause the best.
155 Then reason will° our hearts should be as good.   *it follows that*
Say you not then our offer is compelled.
MOWBRAY   Well, by my will we shall admit no parley.°   *discussion of terms*
WESTMORLAND   That argues but the shame of your offence.
A rotten case° abides no handling.   *cause*
160 HASTINGS   Hath the Prince John a full commission,
In very ample virtue° of his father,   *With full authority*
To hear and absolutely to determine
Of what° conditions we shall stand upon?   *whatever*
WESTMORLAND   That is intended° in the general's name.   *indicated*
165 I muse° you make so slight a question.   *wonder*
ARCHBISHOP OF YORK   Then take, my lord of Westmorland, this schedule;°   *document*
For this contains our general grievances.
Each several° article herein redressed,   *individual*
All members of our cause, both here and hence,
170 That are ensinewed° to this action   *tightly bound (by sinews)*
Acquitted° by a true substantial form,°   *Pardoned / binding act*
And present execution of our wills
To us and to our purposes consigned,[1]
We come within our awe-full banks again,[2]
175 And knit our powers to the arm of peace.
WESTMORLAND *[taking the schedule]*   This will I show the general.
Please you, lords,
In sight of both our battles we may meet,
And either end in peace—which God so frame°—   *bring to pass*
Or to the place of diff'rence° call the swords   *conflict*
Which must decide it.
180 ARCHBISHOP OF YORK   My lord, we will do so.   *Exit* WESTMORLAND
MOWBRAY   There is a thing within my bosom tells me
That no conditions of our peace can stand.
HASTINGS   Fear you not that. If we can make our peace

---

1. *And . . . consigned:* And immediate ("present") fulfillment of our demands allowed us. The emendation to "consigned" of Q's and F's "confinde" allows three parallel clauses to follow one another, each dealing with one

of the rebels' conditions for putting down their arms.
2. We come again within the bounds of respect (with the suggestion of a flooded river returning to its banks).

Upon such large° terms and so absolute   *liberal*
185   As our conditions shall consist° upon,   *insist*
Our peace shall stand as firm as rocky mountains.
MOWBRAY   Yea, but our valuation° shall be such   *the value we are held in*
That every slight and false-derivèd° cause,   *wrongly attributed*
Yea, every idle, nice,° and wanton° reason,   *petty / frivolous*
190   Shall to the King taste of this action,°   *(of rebellion)*
That, were our royal faiths martyrs in love,[3]
We shall be winnowed with so rough a wind
That even our corn shall seem as light as chaff,
And good from bad find no partition.°   *distinction*
195 ARCHBISHOP OF YORK   No, no, my lord; note this. The King is weary
Of dainty and such picking° grievances,   *trivial*
For he hath found to end one doubt° by death   *fear*
Revives two greater in the heirs of life;
And therefore will he wipe his tables° clean,   *tablets*
200   And keep no tell-tale to his memory
That may repeat and history° his loss   *retell*
To new remembrance; for full well he knows
He cannot so precisely weed this land
As his misdoubts° present occasion.   *suspicions*
205 His foes are so enrooted with his friends
That, plucking to unfix an enemy,
He doth unfasten so and shake a friend;
So that this land, like an offensive wife
That hath enraged him on to offer strokes,°   *attempt beatings*
210 As he is striking, holds his infant up,
And hangs resolved correction in the arm
That was upreared to execution.[4]
HASTINGS   Besides, the King hath wasted all his rods°   *means of punishment*
On late° offenders, that he now doth lack   *recent*
215 The very instruments of chastisement;
So that his power, like to a fangless lion,
May offer,° but not hold.   *threaten*
ARCHBISHOP OF YORK   'Tis very true.
And therefore be assured, my good Lord Marshal,
If we do now make our atonement° well,   *reconciliation*
220 Our peace will, like a broken limb united,
Grow stronger for the breaking.
MOWBRAY   Be it so.
      Enter WESTMORLAND
Here is returned my lord of Westmorland.
WESTMORLAND   The Prince is here at hand. Pleaseth your lordship
To meet his grace just° distance 'tween our armies?   *equal*
225 MOWBRAY   Your grace of York, in God's name then set forward.
ARCHBISHOP OF YORK   Before, and greet his grace! — My lord, we come.
      [*They march over the stage.*]
      Enter PRINCE JOHN [*with one or more soldiers carrying*
      wine]
PRINCE JOHN   You are well encountered here, my cousin Mowbray.
Good day to you, gentle lord Archbishop;

---

3. So that even if our loyalty to the King made us loving martyrs.

4. *And . . . execution:* And so punishment that was about to be executed is held in suspended action.

And so to you, Lord Hastings, and to all.
230 My lord of York, it better showed with you
When that your flock, assembled by the bell,
Encircled you to hear with reverence
Your exposition on the holy text,
Than now to see you here an iron° man,   *armored; a fierce*
235 Cheering a rout° of rebels with your drum,   *disorderly band*
Turning the word° to sword, and life to death.   *(Scripture)*
That man that sits within a monarch's heart
And ripens in the sunshine of his favour,
Would he° abuse the countenance° of the King,   *Should he / favor*
240 Alack, what mischiefs might he set abroach°   *afoot*
In shadow° of such greatness! With you, Lord Bishop,   *Under cover*
It is even so. Who hath not heard it spoken
How deep you were within the books of God—
To us, the speaker in his° parliament,   *(God's)*
245 To us, th'imagined voice of God himself,
The very opener° and intelligencer°   *interpreter / informer*
Between the grace, the sanctities of heaven
And our dull workings?° O, who shall believe   *ignorant thoughts*
But you misuse the reverence of your place,
250 Employ the countenance and grace of heav'n
As a false favourite doth his prince's name
In deeds dishonourable? You have ta'en up,°   *enlisted*
Under the counterfeited zeal of[5] God,
The subjects of his substitute, my father;
255 And, both against the peace of heaven and him,
Have here upswarmèd them.[6]

ARCHBISHOP OF YORK   Good my lord of Lancaster,
I am not here against your father's peace;
But, as I told my lord of Westmorland,
The time misordered doth, in common sense,
260 Crowd us and crush us to this monstrous form,
To hold our safety up. I sent your grace
The parcels° and particulars of our grief,   *items; details*
The which hath been with scorn shoved from the court,
Whereon this Hydra son[7] of war is born;
265 Whose dangerous eyes may well be charmed asleep[8]
With grant° of our most just and right desires,   *the granting*
And true obedience, of this madness cured,
Stoop tamely to the foot of majesty.

MOWBRAY   If not, we ready are to try our fortunes
To the last man.

270 HASTINGS   And though we here fall down,
We have supplies° to second our attempt.   *reinforcements*
If they miscarry, theirs shall second them;
And so success of° mischief shall be born,   *from*
And heir from heir shall hold this quarrel up,
275 Whiles° England shall have generation.°   *As long as / offspring*

---

5. Under the pretense of zeal toward God; under the pretense of God's approval.
6. Have raised them up in angry swarms (like bees).
7. Hydra-like offspring. The Archbishop alludes to the many-headed monster of classical myth, which was al-most impossible to kill because its heads grew again as fast as they were cut off.
8. Alluding to another monster of classical myth, the hundred-eyed Argus, which Mercury overcame by charming it to sleep.

PRINCE JOHN You are too shallow, Hastings, much too shallow,
  To sound the bottom of the after-times.°   *future*
WESTMORLAND Pleaseth your grace to answer them directly
  How far forth you do like their articles?
280 PRINCE JOHN I like them all, and do allow° them well,   *grant*
  And swear here, by the honour of my blood,
  My father's purposes have been mistook,
  And some about him have too lavishly°   *freely*
  Wrested his meaning and authority.
285 [*To the* ARCHBISHOP] My lord, these griefs shall be with speed redressed;
  Upon my soul they shall. If this may please you,
  Discharge your powers unto their several counties,
  As we will ours; and here between the armies
  Let's drink together friendly and embrace,
290 That all their eyes may bear those tokens home
  Of our restorèd love and amity.
ARCHBISHOP OF YORK I take your princely word for these redresses.
PRINCE JOHN I give it you, and will maintain my word;
  And thereupon I drink unto your grace.
            [*He drinks*]
295 HASTINGS [*to* COLEVILLE] Go, captain, and deliver to the army
  This news of peace. Let them have pay, and part.
  I know it will well please them. Hie thee,° captain.   *Get thee gone*
                        Exit [COLEVILLE]
ARCHBISHOP OF YORK To you, my noble lord of Westmorland!
  [*He drinks*]
WESTMORLAND [*drinking*] I pledge your grace. An if you knew what pains
300 I have bestowed to breed this present peace,
  You would drink freely; but my love to ye
  Shall show itself more openly hereafter.
ARCHBISHOP OF YORK I do not doubt you.
WESTMORLAND   I am glad of it.
  [*Drinking*] Health to my lord and gentle cousin Mowbray!
305 MOWBRAY You wish me health in very happy season,°   *at an apt moment*
  For I am on the sudden something ill.
ARCHBISHOP OF YORK Against° ill chances men are ever merry;   *Before*
  But heaviness° foreruns the good event.   *sorrow*
WESTMORLAND Therefore be merry, coz,° since sudden sorrow   *kinsman*
310 Serves to say thus: some good thing comes tomorrow.
ARCHBISHOP OF YORK Believe me, I am passing° light in spirit.   *exceptionally*
MOWBRAY So much the worse, if your own rule be true.
                        Shout [*within*]
PRINCE JOHN The word of peace is rendered. Hark how they
  shout.
MOWBRAY This had° been cheerful after victory.   *would have*
315 ARCHBISHOP OF YORK A peace is of the nature of a conquest,
  For then both parties nobly are subdued,
  And neither party loser.
PRINCE JOHN [*to* WESTMORLAND] Go, my lord,
  And let our army be dischargèd too.   *Exit* [WESTMORLAND]
  [*To the* ARCHBISHOP] And, good my lord, so please you, let our trains°   *troops*
320 March by us, that we may peruse the men
  We should have coped withal.°   *fought against*
ARCHBISHOP OF YORK   Go, good Lord Hastings,
  And ere they be dismissed, let them march by.   *Exit* [HASTINGS]

PRINCE JOHN   I trust, lords, we shall lie° tonight together.   *lodge*
    Enter [the Earl of] WESTMORLAND *[with captains]*
  Now, cousin, wherefore stands our army still?
325   WESTMORLAND   The leaders, having charge from you to stand,
  Will not go off until they hear you speak.
PRINCE JOHN   They know their duties.
    Enter [Lord] HASTINGS
HASTINGS *[to the* ARCHBISHOP*]*   Our army is dispersed.
  Like youthful steers unyoked, they take their courses,
  East, west, north, south; or, like a school broke up,
330   Each hurries toward his home and sporting place.
WESTMORLAND   Good tidings, my lord Hastings, for the which
  I do arrest thee, traitor, of high treason;
  And you, Lord Archbishop, and you, Lord Mowbray,
  Of capital treason I attach° you both.   *arrest*
    [The captains guard HASTINGS, *the* ARCHBISHOP, *and*
    MOWBRAY*]*
335   MOWBRAY   Is this proceeding just and honourable?
WESTMORLAND   Is your assembly so?
ARCHBISHOP OF YORK   Will you thus break your faith?
PRINCE JOHN   I pawned° thee none.   *pledged*
  I promised you redress of these same grievances
340   Whereof you did complain; which, by mine honour,
  I will perform with a most Christian care.
  But for you rebels, look to taste the due
  Meet° for rebellion and such acts as yours.   *Appropriate*
  Most shallowly did you these arms° commence,   *military exploits*
345   Fondly° brought here, and foolishly sent hence. —   *Foolishly*
  Strike up our drums, pursue the scattered stray.°   *stragglers*
  God, and not we, hath safely fought today.
  Some guard these traitors to the block of death,
  Treason's true bed and yielder up of breath.   *Exeunt*

4.2

Alarum. Excursions. Enter [Sir John] FALSTAFF *and*
COLEVILLE
FALSTAFF   What's your name, sir, of what condition° are you,   *social status*
  and of what place, I pray?
COLEVILLE   I am a knight, sir, and my name is Coleville of the
  Dale.
5   FALSTAFF   Well then, Coleville is your name, a knight is your
  degree,° and your place the Dale. Coleville shall be still your   *rank*
  name, a traitor your degree, and the dungeon your place — a
  place deep enough, so shall you be still Coleville of the Dale.
COLEVILLE   Are not you Sir John Falstaff?
10   FALSTAFF   As good a man as he, sir, whoe'er I am. Do ye yield,
  sir, or shall I sweat for you? If I do sweat, they are the drops°   *tears*
  of thy lovers,° and they weep for thy death; therefore rouse up fear   *friends*
  and trembling, and do observance° to my mercy.   *pay homage (kneel)*
COLEVILLE *[kneeling]*   I think you are Sir John Falstaff, and in
15   that thought yield me.
FALSTAFF *[aside]*   I have a whole school of tongues in this belly
  of mine, and not a tongue of them all speaks any other word

---

4.2 Location: Scene continues.

but my name. An I had but a belly of any indifferency,° I were   *of moderate size*
simply the most active fellow in Europe. My womb,° my   *belly*
20   womb, my womb undoes me.
　　　　　 Enter PRINCE JOHN, [*the Earl of*] WESTMORLAND, [*Sir*
　　　　　 John Blunt,] *and* [*other lords and soldiers*]
　　 Here comes our general.
　　 PRINCE JOHN　The heat° is past; follow no further now.   *chase*
　　　　 [*A*] *retreat* [*is sounded*]
　　 Call in the powers, good cousin Westmorland.
　　　　　　　　　　　　　 [*Exit* WESTMORLAND]
　　 Now, Falstaff, where have you been all this while?
25   When everything is ended, then you come.
　　 These tardy tricks of yours will, on my life,
　　 One time or other break some gallows' back.[1]
　　 FALSTAFF　I would be sorry, my lord, but it should be thus. I
　　 never knew yet but rebuke and check° was the reward of valour.   *censure*
30   Do you think me a swallow, an arrow, or a bullet? Have I in
　　 my poor and old motion the expedition° of thought? I have   *speed*
　　 speeded hither with the very extremest° inch of possibility; I   *utmost*
　　 have foundered° nine-score and odd posts;° and here, travel-   *made lame / horses*
　　 tainted as I am, have in my pure and immaculate valour taken
35   Sir John Coleville of the Dale, a most furious knight and valor-
　　 ous enemy. But what of that? He saw me, and yielded, that I
　　 may justly say, with the hook-nosed fellow of Rome, 'I came,
　　 saw, and overcame.'[2]
　　 PRINCE JOHN　It was more of his courtesy than your deserving.
40   FALSTAFF　I know not. Here he is, and here I yield him; and I
　　 beseech your grace, let it be booked with the rest of this day's
　　 deeds; or, by the Lord, I will have it in a particular ballad[3] else,
　　 with mine own picture on the top on't, Coleville kissing my
　　 foot; to the which course if I be enforced, if you do not all show
45   like gilt twopences to me,[4] and I in the clear sky of fame o'er-
　　 shine you as much as the full moon doth the cinders of the
　　 element,° which show like pins' heads to her, believe not the   *the stars*
　　 word of the noble. Therefore let me have right, and let desert
　　 mount.°   *merit be rewarded*
50   PRINCE JOHN　Thine's too heavy to mount.
　　 FALSTAFF　Let it shine then.
　　 PRINCE JOHN　Thine's too thick° to shine.   *opaque; dim*
　　 FALSTAFF　Let it do something, my good lord, that may do me
　　 good, and call it what you will.
　　 PRINCE JOHN　Is thy name Coleville?
55   COLEVILLE　　　　　　　　　　　 It is, my lord.
　　 PRINCE JOHN　A famous rebel art thou, Coleville.
　　 FALSTAFF　And a famous true subject took him.
　　 COLEVILLE　I am, my lord, but as my betters are
　　 That led me hither. Had they been ruled by me,
60   You should have won them dearer° than you have.   *at greater cost*
　　 FALSTAFF　I know not how—they sold themselves, but thou
　　 Like a kind fellow gav'st thyself away,
　　 And I thank thee for thee.

1. Cause you to be hanged, which will break the gallows.
2. Referring to Julius Caesar, whose portrait and imperial exploits would be familiar to Elizabethans through
Thomas North's translation of Plutarch.

3. Ballad specifically about me. Ballads often reported
contemporary scandals and events.
4. If you do not all look like counterfeits when compared
with me.

Enter [the Earl of] WESTMORLAND

PRINCE JOHN   Have you left pursuit?

WESTMORLAND   Retreat is made, and execution stayed.°   *stopped*

65 PRINCE JOHN   Send Coleville with his confederates

To York, to present° execution.   *immediate*

Blunt, lead him hence, and see you guard him sure.

Exit [Blunt,] with COLEVILLE

And now dispatch we toward the court, my lords.

I hear the King my father is sore° sick.   *severely*

70 [*To* WESTMORLAND] Our news shall go before us to his majesty,

Which, cousin, you shall bear to comfort him;

And we with sober speed will follow you.

FALSTAFF   My lord, I beseech you give me leave to go

Through Gloucestershire, and when you come to court

75 Stand,° my good lord, pray, in your good report.   *Let me stand*
                                                                           position

PRINCE JOHN   Fare you well, Falstaff. I in my condition°

Shall better speak of you than you deserve.

Exeunt [all but FALSTAFF]

FALSTAFF   I would you had but the wit; 'twere better than your

dukedom. Good faith, this same young sober-blooded boy doth

80 not love me, nor a man cannot make him laugh. But that's no

marvel; he drinks no wine. There's never none of these demure

boys come to any proof;° for thin drink doth so overcool their   *turn out well*

blood, and making many fish meals, that they fall into a kind

of male green-sickness;[5] and then when they marry, they get

85 wenches.° They are generally fools and cowards—which some   *beget females*

of us should be too, but for inflammation.[6] A good sherry-sack°   *Spanish sherry*

hath a two-fold operation in it. It ascends me into the brain,

dries me there[7] all the foolish and dull and crudy° vapours   *coagulated*

which environ° it, makes it apprehensive,° quick, forgetive,[8]   *surround / witty*

90 full of nimble, fiery, and delectable shapes, which, delivered

o'er to the voice, the tongue, which is the birth, becomes excel-

lent wit. The second property of your excellent sherry is the

warming of the blood, which, before cold and settled,° left the   *stagnant*

liver[9] white and pale, which is the badge of pusillanimity and

95 cowardice. But the sherry warms it, and makes it course from

the inwards to the parts' extremes;° it illuminateth the face,   *extremities*

which, as a beacon, gives warning to all the rest of this little

kingdom, man, to arm; and then the vital commoners and

inland° petty spirits[1] muster me° all to their captain, the heart;   *internal / assemble*

100 who, great and puffed up with his retinue, doth any deed of

courage. And this valour comes of sherry. So that skill in the

weapon is nothing without sack, for that sets it a-work; and

learning a mere hoard of gold kept by a devil,[2] till sack com-

mences it and sets it in act and use.[3] Hereof comes it that

---

5. An anemic condition that affected young women in
puberty and that was supposed to be cured through sexual
activity. Throughout this speech, Falstaff indicts John for
lacking the heat necessary for masculine valor and the
begetting of male children. Diet was believed to affect the
balance of the four humors, or fluids, that determined
temperament and the relative "heat" of the body.
6. The passions that alcohol inflames.
7. It ascends into the brain and to my benefit dries up.
8. Inventive.

9. The supposed seat of the passions.
1. Alluding to the medical doctrine of "vital spirits," or
highly refined fluids, that were supposed to suffuse the
blood.
2. Referring to the popular belief that hidden treasures
were guarded by evil spirits.
3. Until sack sets learning free; confers a degree upon
learning (punning on "commencement" and "act," two
terms used for the granting of a university degree).

105	Prince Harry is valiant; for the cold blood he did naturally
inherit of his father he hath, like lean,° sterile, and bare land,	barren
manured, husbanded,° and tilled, with excellent endeavour of	cultivated
drinking good, and good store of fertile sherry, that he is
become very hot and valiant. If I had a thousand sons, the first
110	human principle I would teach them should be to forswear
thin potations, and to addict themselves to sack.

Enter BARDOLPH

How now, Bardolph?

BARDOLPH   The army is dischargèd all and gone.

FALSTAFF   Let them go. I'll through Gloucestershire, and there
115   will I visit Master Robert Shallow, Esquire. I have him already
tempering[4] between my finger and my thumb, and shortly will
I seal with him.[5] Come, away!   *Exeunt*

4.3

Enter KING [HENRY *in his bed,*[1] *attended by the Earl of*]
WARWICK, *Thomas Duke of* CLARENCE, *Humphrey*
[*Duke*] *of* GLOUCESTER [*and others*]

KING HENRY   Now, lords, if God doth give successful end
To this debate° that bleedeth at our doors,	conflict
We will our youth lead on to higher fields,[2]
And draw no swords but what are sanctified.
5	Our navy is addressed,° our power collected,	prepared
Our substitutes in absence well invested,°	installed in office
And everything lies level to° our wish;	in accordance with
Only we want a little personal strength,
And pause us till these rebels now afoot
10 | Come underneath the yoke of government.

WARWICK   Both which we doubt not but your majesty
Shall soon enjoy.

KING HENRY   Humphrey, my son of Gloucester,
Where is the Prince your brother?

GLOUCESTER   I think he's gone to hunt, my lord, at Windsor.

KING HENRY   And how accompanied?

15   GLOUCESTER   I do not know, my lord.

KING HENRY   Is not his brother Thomas of Clarence with him?

GLOUCESTER   No, my good lord, he is in presence here.

CLARENCE   What would my lord and father?

KING HENRY   Nothing but well to thee, Thomas of Clarence.
20   How chance thou art not with the Prince thy brother?
He loves thee, and thou dost neglect him, Thomas.
Thou hast a better place in his affection

Than all thy brothers. Cherish it, my boy,
And noble offices° thou mayst effect	duties
25	Of mediation, after I am dead,
Between his greatness and thy other brethren.
Therefore omit° him not, blunt not his love,	neglect
Nor lose the good advantage of his grace

---

4. Softening like warm sealing wax.
5. Mold him to my use; conclude with him.
4.3 Location: The Jerusalem Chamber, the palace at Westminster. (This room is actually in Westminster Abbey.)

1. Henry may enter walking or carried in a chair or, as here, in a bed thrust out from behind the stage. The use of a bed emphasizes the severity of his illness.
2. That is, those of Palestine, where the King proposes to lead a crusade.

By seeming cold or careless of his will;
30 For he is gracious, if he be observed;°   *shown respect*
He hath a tear for pity, and a hand
Open as day for melting° charity.   *compassionate*
Yet notwithstanding, being incensed, he is flint,
As humorous° as winter, and as sudden   *changeable*
35 As flaws congealèd° in the spring° of day.   *As snowflakes / dawn*
His temper therefore must be well observed.
Chide him for faults, and do it reverently,
When you perceive his blood inclined to mirth;
But being moody, give him line and scope°   *free range*
40 Till that his passions, like a whale on ground,
Confound° themselves with working. Learn this, Thomas,   *Exhaust*
And thou shalt prove a shelter to thy friends,
A hoop of gold³ to bind thy brothers in,
That the united vessel of their blood,⁴
45 Mingled with venom of suggestion°—   *malicious gossip*
As force perforce the age will pour it in—
Shall never leak, though it do work as strong
As aconitum⁵ or rash gunpowder.
CLARENCE   I shall observe him with all care and love.
50 KING HENRY   Why art thou not at Windsor with him, Thomas?
CLARENCE   He is not there today; he dines in London.
KING HENRY   And how accompanied? Canst thou tell that?
CLARENCE   With Poins and other his continual° followers.   *constant*
KING HENRY   Most subject is the fattest° soil to weeds,   *richest*
55 And he, the noble image of my youth,
Is overspread with them; therefore my grief
Stretches itself beyond the hour of death.
The blood weeps from my heart when I do shape
In forms imaginary th'unguided days°   *days lacking a ruler*
60 And rotten times that you shall look upon
When I am sleeping with my ancestors;
For when his headstrong riot hath no curb,
When rage° and hot blood are his counsellors,   *passion*
When means° and lavish manners meet together,   *opportunity*
65 O, with what wings shall his affections° fly   *desires; inclinations*
Towards fronting peril and opposed decay?⁶
WARWICK   My gracious lord, you look beyond° him quite.   *misjudge*
The Prince but studies his companions,
Like a strange tongue,° wherein, to gain the language,   *foreign language*
70 'Tis needful that the most immodest word
Be looked upon and learnt, which once attained,
Your highness knows, comes to no further use
But to be known and hated; so, like gross° terms,   *vulgar; common*
The Prince will in the perfectness of time
75 Cast off his followers, and their memory
Shall as a pattern or a measure live
By which his grace must mete° the lives of other,°   *appraise / others*
Turning past evils to advantages.

---

3. A barrel with a golden hoop; a golden ring.
4. The vessel—a vial or chalice—that holds their blood.
5. Wolfsbane, an especially virulent poison.
6. Toward the peril and destruction that confront him.

KING HENRY   'Tis seldom when the bee doth leave her comb
    In the dead carrion.⁷
         Enter [the Earl of] WESTMORLAND
80   Who's here? Westmorland?
WESTMORLAND   Health to my sovereign, and new happiness
    Added to that that I am to deliver!
    Prince John your son doth kiss your grace's hand.
    Mowbray, the Bishop Scrope, Hastings, and all
85   Are brought to the correction of your law.
    There is not now a rebel's sword unsheathed,
    But peace puts forth her olive everywhere.
    The manner how this action hath been borne
    Here at more leisure may your highness read,
90   With every course° in his° particular.   *stage in the action / its*
         [He gives the KING *papers]*
KING HENRY   O Westmorland, thou art a summer bird
    Which ever in the haunch° of winter sings   *hind part*
    The lifting up of day.°   *dawn*
         Enter HARCOURT
             Look, here's more news.
HARCOURT   From enemies heaven keep your majesty;
95   And when they stand against you, may they fall
    As those that I am come to tell you of!
    The Earl Northumberland and the Lord Bardolph,
    With a great power of English and of Scots,
    Are by the sheriff of Yorkshire overthrown.
100   The manner and true order of the fight
    This packet, please it you, contains at large.
         [He gives the KING *papers]*
KING HENRY   And wherefore should these good news make me sick?
    Will fortune never come with both hands full,
    But write her fair words still in foulest letters?
105   She either gives a stomach° and no food—   *an appetite*
    Such are the poor in health—or else a feast,
    And takes away the stomach—such are the rich,
    That have abundance and enjoy it not.
    I should rejoice now at this happy news,
110   And now my sight fails, and my brain is giddy.
    O me! Come near me now; I am much ill.
         [He swoons]
GLOUCESTER   Comfort, your majesty!
CLARENCE   O my royal father!
WESTMORLAND   My sovereign lord, cheer up yourself, look up.°   *take courage*
WARWICK   Be patient, princes; you do know these fits
115   Are with his highness very ordinary.
    Stand from him, give him air; he'll straight be well.
CLARENCE   No, no, he cannot long hold out° these pangs.   *endure*
    Th'incessant care and labour of his mind
    Hath wrought the mure° that should confine it in   *made the wall*
120   So thin that life looks through and will break out.
GLOUCESTER   The people fear° me, for they do observe   *frighten*

---

7. *'Tis . . . carrion:* It is rare that the bee who has placed her honeycomb in a carcass abandons it. (So the new King will be unlikely to abandon his old pleasures.)

Unfathered heirs and loathly births of nature.[8]
The seasons change their manners, as° the year   *as if*
Had found some months asleep and leaped them over.
125 CLARENCE   The river° hath thrice flowed, no ebb between,   *(the Thames)*
And the old folk, time's doting chronicles,
Say it did so a little time before
That our great grandsire Edward sicked and died.
WARWICK   Speak lower, princes, for the King recovers.
130 GLOUCESTER   This apoplexy will certain be his end.
KING HENRY   I pray you take me up and bear me hence
Into some other chamber; softly, pray.
      [The KING is carried over the stage in his bed]
Let there be no noise made, my gentle friends,
Unless some dull° and favourable hand   *restful*
135 Will whisper music to my weary spirit.
WARWICK   Call for the music in the other room.
                  [Exit one or more. Still° music within]   *Soft*
KING HENRY   Set me the crown upon my pillow here.
      [CLARENCE takes the crown from the King's head, and
      sets it on his pillow][9]
CLARENCE   His eye is hollow, and he changes° much.   *(in complexion)*
      [A noise within]
WARWICK   Less noise, less noise!
      Enter PRINCE HARRY
PRINCE HARRY   Who saw the Duke of Clarence?
140 CLARENCE   I am here, brother, full of heaviness.°   *sadness*
PRINCE HARRY   How now, rain within doors, and none abroad?
  How doth the King?
GLOUCESTER   Exceeding ill.
PRINCE HARRY   Heard he the good news yet? Tell it him.
GLOUCESTER   He altered much upon the hearing it.
145 PRINCE HARRY   If he be sick with joy, he'll recover without physic.
WARWICK   Not so much noise, my lords! Sweet prince, speak low.
  The King your father is disposed to sleep.
CLARENCE   Let us withdraw into the other room.
WARWICK   Will't please your grace to go along with us?
150 PRINCE HARRY   No, I will sit and watch here by the King.
      [Exeunt all but the KING and PRINCE HARRY]
Why doth the crown lie there upon his pillow,
Being so troublesome a bedfellow?
O polished perturbation,° golden care,   *source of unease*
That keep'st the ports° of slumber open wide   *gates (the eyes)*
155 To many a watchful° night!—Sleep with it° now;   *wakeful / (the crown)*
Yet not so sound, and half so deeply sweet,
As he whose brow with homely biggen° bound   *nightcap*
Snores out the watch of night.[1] O majesty,
When thou dost pinch thy bearer, thou dost sit
160 Like a rich armour worn in heat of day,
That scald'st with safety.—By his gates of breath°   *his lips*
There lies a downy feather which stirs not.
Did he suspire,° that light and weightless down   *If he breathed*

---

8. Children supernaturally begotten and malformed offspring resulting from normal conception.
9. It is unclear who removes the crown: the weakened

King or his son Clarence, who is the next to speak.
1. Nighttime. "Watch" alludes to the periods of sentry
duty into which the night was divided.

Perforce must move.—My gracious lord, my father!—
165   This sleep is sound indeed. This is a sleep
That from this golden rigol° hath divorced   *ring*
So many English kings.—Thy due from me
Is tears and heavy sorrows of the blood,
Which nature, love, and filial tenderness
170   Shall, O dear father, pay thee plenteously.
My due from thee is this imperial crown,
Which, as immediate from° thy place and blood,   *as next in line to*
Derives itself° to me.   *Descends*
          [*He puts the crown on his head*]
                        Lo where it sits,
Which God shall guard; and put the world's whole strength
175   Into one giant arm, it shall not force
This lineal° honour from me. This from thee   *hereditary*
Will I to mine leave, as 'tis left to me.   *Exit*
          [*Music ceases. The* KING *awakes*]
KING HENRY   Warwick, Gloucester, Clarence!
          Enter [*the Earl of*] WARWICK, [*and the Dukes of*]
              GLOUCESTER [*and*] CLARENCE
CLARENCE   Doth the King call?
WARWICK   What would your majesty? How fares your grace?
180   KING HENRY   Why did you leave me here alone, my lords?
CLARENCE   We left the Prince my brother here, my liege,
    Who undertook to sit and watch by you.
KING HENRY   The Prince of Wales? Where is he? Let me see him.
WARWICK   This door is open; he is gone this way.
185   GLOUCESTER   He came not through the chamber where we stayed.
KING HENRY   Where is the crown? Who took it from my pillow?
WARWICK   When we withdrew, my liege, we left it here.
KING HENRY   The Prince hath ta'en it hence. Go seek him out.
    Is he so hasty that he doth suppose
190   My sleep my death?
    Find him, my lord of Warwick; chide him hither.   [*Exit* WARWICK]
    This part° of his conjoins° with my disease,   *act / unites*
    And helps to end me. See, sons, what things you are,
    How quickly nature falls into revolt
195   When gold becomes her object!
    For this the foolish over-careful fathers
    Have broke their sleep with thoughts, their brains with care,
    Their bones with industry; for this they have
    Engrossèd° and piled up the cankered° heaps   *Gathered / diseased*
200   Of strange-achievèd gold;[2] for this they have
    Been thoughtful° to invest their sons with arts   *careful*
    And martial exercises; when, like the bee
    Culling from every flower the virtuous sweets,
    Our thighs packed with wax, our mouths with honey,
205   We bring it to the hive; and, like the bees,
    Are murdered for our pains. This bitter taste
    Yields his engrossments to the ending father.[3]
              Enter [*the Earl of*] WARWICK

---

2. Gold gained in foreign lands or by unnatural or unusual means.

3. *This . . . father:* This bitter taste is all the dying father's
amassing of wealth amounts to.

Now where is he that will not stay so long
Till his friend sickness have determined° me?   *put an end to*
210 WARWICK My lord, I found the Prince in the next room,
Washing with kindly° tears his gentle° cheeks   *filial / noble*
With such a deep demeanour,° in great sorrow,   *sad countenance*
That tyranny, which never quaffed° but blood,   *drank*
Would, by beholding him, have washed his knife
215 With gentle eye-drops.° He is coming hither.   *tears*
KING HENRY But wherefore did he take away the crown?
     Enter PRINCE HARRY [*with the crown*]
Lo where he comes.—Come hither to me, Harry.
[*To the others*] Depart the chamber; leave us here alone.
     Exeunt [*all but the* KING *and* PRINCE HARRY]
PRINCE HARRY I never thought to hear you speak again.
220 KING HENRY Thy wish was father, Harry, to that thought.
I stay too long by thee, I weary thee.
Dost thou so hunger for mine empty chair
That thou wilt needs invest thee with my honours
Before thy hour be ripe? O foolish youth,
225 Thou seek'st the greatness that will overwhelm thee!
Stay but a little, for my cloud of dignity°   *fragile greatness*
Is held from falling with so weak a wind°   *(his breath)*
That it will quickly drop. My day is dim.
Thou hast stol'n that which after some few hours
230 Were thine without offence, and at my death
Thou hast sealed up° my expectation.   *confirmed*
Thy life did manifest thou loved'st me not,
And thou wilt have me die assured of it.
Thou hid'st a thousand daggers in thy thoughts,
235 Whom° thou hast whetted on thy stony heart   *Which*
To stab at half an hour of my life.
What, canst thou not forbear me° half an hour?   *grant me but*
Then get thee gone and dig my grave thyself,
And bid the merry bells ring to thine ear
240 That thou art crownèd, not that I am dead.
Let all the tears that should bedew my hearse°   *coffin*
Be drops of balm⁴ to sanctify thy head.
Only compound° me with forgotten dust.   *mix*
Give that which gave thee life unto the worms.
245 Pluck down my officers, break my decrees;
For now a time is come to mock at form°—   *decorum*
Harry the Fifth is crowned. Up, vanity!
Down, royal state!° All you sage counsellors, hence!   *ceremony*
And to the English court assemble now
250 From every region, apes° of idleness!   *fools*
Now, neighbour confines,° purge you of your scum!   *bordering regions*
Have you a ruffian that will swear, drink, dance,
Revel the night, rob, murder, and commit
The oldest sins the newest kind of ways?
255 Be happy; he will trouble you no more.
England shall double gild° his treble guilt,   *paint over*
England shall give him office, honour, might;

4. The consecrated oils with which new monarchs were anointed during their coronation.

For the fifth Harry from curbed licence⁵ plucks
The muzzle of restraint, and the wild dog
260 Shall flesh his tooth on° every innocent.   *taste the flesh of*
O my poor kingdom, sick with civil blows!°   *domestic conflicts*
When that my care could not withhold° thy riots,°   *control / strife*
What wilt thou do when riot is thy care?⁶
O, thou wilt be a wilderness again,
265 Peopled with wolves, thy old inhabitants.
PRINCE HARRY   O pardon me, my liege! But for my tears,
The moist impediments unto my speech,
I had forestalled this dear° and deep rebuke   *grievous*
Ere you with grief had spoke and I had heard
270 The course of it so far. There is your crown;
    [*He returns the crown and kneels*]
And He° that wears the crown immortally   *(God)*
Long guard it yours! If I affect° it more   *desire*
Than as your honour and as your renown,
Let me no more from this obedience rise,
275 Which my most true and inward duteous spirit
Teacheth this prostrate and exterior° bending.   *outward*
God witness with me, when I here came in
And found no course of breath within your majesty,
How cold it struck my heart. If I do feign,
280 O, let me in my present wildness° die,   *sinfulness*
And never live to show th'incredulous world
The noble change that I have purposèd.°   *intended*
Coming to look on you, thinking you dead,
And dead almost, my liege, to think you were,
285 I spake unto this crown as having sense,°   *as if it had senses*
And thus upbraided it: 'The care on thee depending⁷
Hath fed upon the body of my father;
Therefore thou best of gold art worst of gold.
Other, less fine in carat, is more precious,
290 Preserving life in medicine potable;⁸
But thou, most fine, most honoured, most renowned,
Hast eat thy bearer up.' Thus, my royal liege,
Accusing it, I put it on my head,
To try° with it, as with an enemy   *struggle*
295 That had before my face murdered my father,
The quarrel of a true inheritor.°   *legitimate heir*
But if it did infect my blood with joy
Or swell my thoughts to any strain of pride,
If any rebel or vain spirit of mine
300 Did with the least affection of° a welcome   *inclination toward*
Give entertainment to the might of it,
Let God for ever keep it from my head,
And make me as the poorest vassal is,
That doth with awe and terror kneel to it.
305 KING HENRY   O my son,
God put it in thy mind to take it hence,

---

5. *Licence:* excessive freedom. The image is of a wild dog that has been curbed, kept under restraint, until his muzzle is removed and chaos ensues.
6. When debauchery (in the person of Hal) is your caretaker; when strife becomes your concern (rather than mine after my death).
7. The trouble that comes along with the crown.
8. Gold in a drinkable solution ("potable") was widely considered healthful.

That thou mightst win the more thy father's love,
Pleading so wisely in excuse of it!
Come hither, Harry; sit thou by my bed,
310 And hear, I think, the very latest° counsel   *last*
That ever I shall breathe.
        [PRINCE HARRY *rises from kneeling and sits by the bed*]
                        God knows, my son,
By what bypaths and indirect crook'd ways
I met this crown; and I myself know well
How troublesome it sat upon my head.
315 To thee it shall descend with better quiet,
Better opinion,° better confirmation;   *public support*
For all the soil° of the achievement goes   *stain*
With me into the earth. It seemed in me
But as an honour snatched with boist'rous hand;
320 And I had many living to upbraid
My gain of it by their assistances,⁹
Which daily grew to quarrel and to bloodshed,
Wounding supposèd peace. All these bold fears°   *fearful acts*
Thou seest with peril I have answerèd;
325 For all my reign hath been but as a scene
Acting that argument.° And now my death   *theme*
Changes the mood, for what in me was purchased¹
Falls upon thee in a more fairer sort,
So thou the garland wear'st successively.²
330 Yet though thou stand'st more sure than I could do,
Thou art not firm enough, since griefs are green,°   *grievances are fresh*
And all thy friends—which thou must make thy friends—
Have but their stings and teeth newly ta'en out,
By whose fell° working I was first advanced,   *cruel*
335 And by whose power I well might lodge a fear
To be again displaced; which to avoid
I cut them off, and had a purpose now
To lead out many to the Holy Land,
Lest rest and lying still might make them look°   *examine*
340 Too near° unto my state. Therefore, my Harry,   *Too closely*
Be it thy course to busy giddy° minds   *restless*
With foreign quarrels, that action° hence borne out   *military exploits*
May waste° the memory of the former days.   *obliterate*
More would I, but my lungs are wasted so
345 That strength of speech is utterly denied me.
How I came by the crown, O God forgive,
And grant it may with thee in true peace live!
PRINCE HARRY   My gracious liege,
You won it, wore it, kept it, gave it me;
350 Then plain and right must my possession be,
Which I with more than with a common pain°   *effort*
'Gainst all the world will rightfully maintain.
        Enter [PRINCE] JOHN of Lancaster [*followed by the Earl
        of*] WARWICK [*and others*]
KING HENRY   Look, look, here comes my John of Lancaster.

---

9. *And . . . assistances:* And many were living who made
demands on me and reproved me on the strength of the
fact that they had helped me to seize the throne.

1. Was acquired by acts, not by inheritance.
2. So that you wear the sign of victory (the crown) by
right of succession.

PRINCE JOHN Health, peace, and happiness to my royal father!
355 KING HENRY Thou bring'st me happiness and peace, son John;
But health, alack, with youthful wings is flown
From this bare withered trunk. Upon thy sight
My worldly business makes a period.°   *an end*
Where is my lord of Warwick?
PRINCE HARRY   My lord of Warwick!
[WARWICK *comes forward to the* KING]
360 KING HENRY Doth any name particular belong
Unto the lodging° where I first did swoon?   *room*
WARWICK 'Tis called Jerusalem, my noble lord.
KING HENRY Laud be to God! Even there my life must end.
It hath been prophesied to me many years
365 I should not die but in Jerusalem,
Which vainly I supposed the Holy Land;
But bear me to that chamber; there I'll lie;
In that Jerusalem shall Harry die.
Exeunt [bearing the KING *in his bed]*

5.1

Enter SHALLOW, SILENCE,[1] *[Sir John]* FALSTAFF, BAR-
DOLPH, *and [the]* PAGE
SHALLOW *[to* FALSTAFF] By cock and pie,[2] you shall not away
tonight.—What, Davy, I say!
FALSTAFF You must excuse me, Master Robert Shallow.
SHALLOW I will not excuse you; you shall not be excused;
5   excuses shall not be admitted; there is no excuse shall serve;
you shall not be excused.—Why, Davy!
[*Enter* DAVY]
DAVY Here, sir.
SHALLOW Davy, Davy, Davy; let me see, Davy; let me see. Wil-
liam Cook—bid him come hither.—Sir John, you shall not be
10   excused.
DAVY Marry, sir, thus: those precepts° cannot be served. And   *warrants*
again,° sir: shall we sow the headland[3] with wheat?   *Moreover*
SHALLOW With red wheat, Davy. But for William Cook; are there
no young pigeons?
15   DAVY Yes, sir. Here is now the smith's note° for shoeing and   *bill*
plough-irons.
SHALLOW Let it be cast° and paid. Sir John, you shall not be   *calculated*
excused.
DAVY Sir, a new link° to the bucket must needs be had; and, sir,   *chain*
20   do you mean to stop any of William's wages, about the sack he
lost at Hinkley[4] Fair?
SHALLOW A° shall answer° it. Some pigeons, Davy, a couple of   *He / pay for*
short-legged hens, a joint of mutton, and any pretty little tiny
kickshaws,° tell William Cook.   *fancy dishes*
25   DAVY Doth the man of war stay all night, sir?
SHALLOW Yea, Davy. I will use him well; a friend i'th' court is

---

5.1 Location: Shallow's house in Gloucestershire.
1. F includes Silence in this scene; Q does not. If present, he lives up to his name, getting no lines.
2. A mild oath. "Cock" was a euphemism for "God," and
"pie" was a colloquial word for the collection of rules by

which the pre-Reformation church ordered the church
calendar.
3. Unplowed strip of land between two fields.
4. A market town near Coventry.

better than a penny in purse. Use his men well, Davy, for they
are arrant knaves, and will backbite.° *slander*

DAVY   No worse than they are back-bitten,° sir, for they have mar- *(by fleas)*
30 vellous° foul linen. *amazingly*

SHALLOW   Well conceited,° Davy. About thy business, Davy. *quipped*

DAVY   I beseech you, sir, to countenance° William Visor of *favor*
Wo'ncot against Clement Perks o'th' Hill.[5]

SHALLOW   There is many complaints, Davy, against that Visor.
35 That Visor is an arrant knave, on my knowledge.

DAVY   I grant your worship that he is a knave, sir; but yet God
forbid, sir, but a knave should have some countenance at his
friend's request. An honest man, sir, is able to speak for himself,
when a knave is not. I have served your worship truly, sir, this
40 eight years. An I cannot once or twice in a quarter bear out° a *support*
knave against an honest man, I have little credit with your worship. The knave is mine honest friend, sir; therefore I beseech
you let him be countenanced.

SHALLOW   Go to; I say he shall have no wrong. Look about,
45 Davy.   [*Exit* DAVY]
Where are you, Sir John? Come, off with your boots.— Give
me your hand, Master Bardolph.

BARDOLPH   I am glad to see your worship.

SHALLOW   I thank thee with all my heart, kind Master Bardolph.
50 [*To the* PAGE] And welcome, my tall° fellow.—Come, Sir John. *valiant*

FALSTAFF   I'll follow you, good Master Robert Shallow.
                              [*Exit* SHALLOW *with* SILENCE]
Bardolph, look to our horses.   [*Exit* BARDOLPH *with the* PAGE]
If I were sawed into quantities,° I should make four dozen of *pieces*
such bearded hermits' staves as Master Shallow. It is a wonder-
55 ful thing to see the semblable coherence° of his men's spirits *close correspondence*
and his. They, by observing him, do bear themselves like
foolish justices; he, by conversing° with them, is turned into a *associating*
justice-like servingman. Their spirits are so married in conjunction, with the participation of society,° that they flock *by close association*
60 together in consent like so many wild geese. If I had a suit to
Master Shallow, I would humour his men with the imputation
of being near their master; if to his men, I would curry° with *employ flattery*
Master Shallow that no man could better command his ser-
vants. It is certain that either wise bearing or ignorant carriage° *demeanor*
65 is caught as men take° diseases, one of another; therefore let *catch*
men take heed of their company. I will devise matter enough
out of this Shallow to keep Prince Harry in continual laughter
the wearing out of six fashions—which is four terms,[6] or two
actions°—and a shall laugh without intervallums.[7] O, it is *lawsuits*
70 much that a lie with a slight oath, and a jest with a sad° brow, *serious*
will do with a fellow that never had the ache in his shoulders![8]
O, you shall see him laugh till his face be like a wet cloak ill
laid up![9]

SHALLOW [*within*]   Sir John!

75 FALSTAFF   I come, Master Shallow; I come, Master Shallow.
                                                                    Exit

---

5. Possibly Stinchcombe Hill, not far from "Wo'ncot"
(the local pronunciation of Woodmancot in Gloucestershire).
6. Alluding to the four divisions of the judicial year.

7. Time between terms.
8. With someone who has not experienced old age or
troubles.
9. *ill laid up:* carelessly put away (so that it is wrinkled).

5.2

Enter the Earl of WARWICK [*at one door*], *and the* LORD
CHIEF JUSTICE [*at another door*]

WARWICK   How now, my Lord Chief Justice, whither away?
LORD CHIEF JUSTICE   How doth the King?
WARWICK   Exceeding well: his cares are now all ended.
LORD CHIEF JUSTICE   I hope not dead.
WARWICK   He's walked the way of nature,
5   And to our purposes he lives no more.
LORD CHIEF JUSTICE   I would his majesty had called me with him.
    The service that I truly did his life
    Hath left me open to all injuries.
WARWICK   Indeed I think the young King loves you not.
10   LORD CHIEF JUSTICE   I know he doth not, and do arm myself
    To welcome the condition° of the time,   *(new) circumstances*
    Which cannot look more hideously upon me
    Than I have drawn it in my fantasy.
        Enter [PRINCE] JOHN *of Lancaster,* [*and the Dukes of*]
        CLARENCE *and* GLOUCESTER
WARWICK   Here come the heavy issue° of dead Harry.   *sad offspring*
15   O, that the living Harry had the temper
    Of he the worst of these three gentlemen!
    How many nobles then should hold their places,
    That must strike sail° to spirits of vile sort!°   *submit / low rank*
LORD CHIEF JUSTICE   O God, I fear all will be overturned.
20   PRINCE JOHN   Good morrow, cousin Warwick, good morrow.
GLOUCESTER *and* CLARENCE   Good morrow, cousin.
PRINCE JOHN   We meet like men that had forgot to speak.
WARWICK   We do remember, but our argument°   *subject matter*
    Is all too heavy to admit much talk.
25   PRINCE JOHN   Well, peace be with him that hath made us heavy!
LORD CHIEF JUSTICE   Peace be with us, lest we be heavier!
GLOUCESTER   O good my lord, you have lost a friend indeed;
    And I dare swear you borrow not that face
    Of seeming sorrow—it is sure your own.
PRINCE JOHN [*to* LORD CHIEF JUSTICE]   Though no man be
30   assured what grace to find,°   *favor he will find*
    You stand in coldest expectation.
    I am the sorrier; would 'twere otherwise.
CLARENCE [*to* LORD CHIEF JUSTICE]   Well, you must now speak
        Sir John Falstaff fair,
    Which swims against your stream of quality.°   *character; rank*
35   LORD CHIEF JUSTICE   Sweet princes, what I did I did in honour,
    Led by th'impartial conduct of my soul;
    And never shall you see that I will beg
    A raggèd° and forestalled remission.[1]   *base*
    If truth and upright innocency fail me,
40   I'll to the King my master, that is dead,
    And tell him who hath sent me after him.
        Enter PRINCE HARRY [*as King*]
WARWICK   Here comes the Prince.
LORD CHIEF JUSTICE   Good morrow, and God save your majesty!

5.2 Location: The palace at Westminster.
1. Either a pardon sure to be denied or a pardon secured in advance (by an act of submission).

PRINCE HARRY   This new and gorgeous garment, majesty,
45 Sits not so easy on me as you think.
Brothers, you mix your sadness with some fear.
This is the English not the Turkish court;
Not Amurath an Amurath succeeds,[2]
But Harry Harry. Yet be sad, good brothers,
50 For, by my faith, it very well becomes you.
Sorrow so royally in you appears
That I will deeply° put the fashion on,   *solemnly*
And wear it in my heart. Why then, be sad;
But entertain no more of it, good brothers,
55 Than a joint burden laid upon us all.
For me, by heaven, I bid you be assured
I'll be your father and your brother too.
Let me but bear° your love, I'll bear your cares.   *have; carry*
Yet weep that Harry's dead, and so will I;
60 But Harry lives that shall convert those tears
By number° into hours of happiness.   *One by one*
PRINCE JOHN, GLOUCESTER, *and* CLARENCE   We hope no other
    from your majesty.
PRINCE HARRY   You all look strangely on me, [*to* LORD CHIEF
    JUSTICE] and you most.
You are, I think, assured I love you not.
65 LORD CHIEF JUSTICE   I am assured, if I be measured rightly,
Your majesty hath no just cause to hate me.
PRINCE HARRY   No? How might a prince of my great hopes forget
So great indignities you laid upon me?
What—rate,° rebuke, and roughly send to prison   *chide*
70 Th'immediate heir of England? Was this easy?
May this be washed in Lethe[3] and forgotten?
LORD CHIEF JUSTICE   I then did use the person° of your father.   *act as a deputy*
The image of his power lay then in me;
And in th'administration of his law,
75 Whiles I was busy for the commonwealth,
Your highness pleasèd to forget my place,°   *rank, position*
The majesty and power of law and justice,
The image of the King whom I presented,
And struck me in my very seat of judgement;
80 Whereon, as° an offender to your father,   *as you were*
I gave bold way to my authority
And did commit° you. If the deed were ill,   *imprison*
Be you contented, wearing now the garland,°   *crown*
To have a son set your decrees at naught—
85 To pluck down justice from your awe-full° bench,   *awe-inspiring*
To trip the course of law, and blunt the sword
That guards the peace and safety of your person,
Nay, more, to spurn at your most royal image,
And mock your workings in a second body?°   *representative*
90 Question your royal thoughts, make the case yours,
Be now the father, and propose° a son;   *imagine*
Hear your own dignity so much profaned,

2. An English name for the Turkish Sultan Murad III, who had his brothers executed upon his succession in 1574. Turks were bywords for cruelty and tyranny in early modern England.
3. The river in Hades that induced forgetfulness.

See your most dreadful laws so loosely slighted,
Behold yourself so by a son disdained;
95 And then imagine me taking your part,
And in your power soft° silencing your son.   *gently*
After this cold considerance, sentence me;
And, as you are a king, speak in your state°   *role as monarch*
What I have done that misbecame my place,
100 My person, or my liege's sovereignty.
PRINCE HARRY   You are right Justice,° and you weigh this well.   *perfect justice*
Therefore still bear the balance and the sword;[4]
And I do wish your honours may increase
Till you do live to see a son of mine
105 Offend you and obey you as I did.
So shall I live to speak my father's words:
'Happy am I that have a man so bold
That dares do justice on my proper° son,   *own*
And not less happy having such a son
110 That would deliver up his greatness so
Into the hands of justice.' You did commit° me,   *imprison*
For which I do commit° into your hand   *place*
Th'unstainèd sword that you have used° to bear,   *were accustomed*
With this remembrance:° that you use the same   *reminder*
115 With the like bold, just, and impartial spirit
As you have done 'gainst me. There is my hand.
You shall be as a father to my youth;
My voice shall sound° as you do prompt mine ear,   *speak*
And I will stoop and humble my intents
120 To your well-practised wise directions. —
And princes all, believe me, I beseech you,
My father is gone wild into his grave,
For in his tomb lie my affections;°   *wild passions*
And with his spirits sadly I survive
125 To mock° the expectation of the world,   *defy*
To frustrate prophecies, and to raze out
Rotten opinion, who hath writ me down
After my seeming.[5] The tide of blood° in me   *of passion*
Hath proudly flowed in vanity till now.
130 Now doth it turn, and ebb back to the sea,
Where it shall mingle with the state of floods,°   *the majesty of the sea*
And flow henceforth in formal majesty.
Now call we our high court of Parliament,
And let us choose such limbs° of noble counsel   *members*
135 That the great body of our state may go
In equal rank with the best-governed nation;
That war, or peace, or both at once, may be
As things acquainted and familiar to us;
[*to* LORD CHIEF JUSTICE] In which you, father, shall have foremost hand.
140 [*To all*]   Our coronation done, we will accite,°   *summon*
As I before remembered, all our state;°   *nobility*
And, God consigning to° my good intents,   *endorsing*
No prince nor peer shall have just cause to say,
'God shorten Harry's happy life one day.'   *Exeunt*

---

4. The traditional emblems of justice.
5. According to my (false) appearance.

5.3

[*A table and chairs set forth.*] *Enter Sir John* FALSTAFF,
SHALLOW, SILENCE, DAVY [*with vessels for the table*],
BARDOLPH, *and* [*the*] PAGE

SHALLOW [*to* FALSTAFF] Nay, you shall see my orchard, where,
in an arbour, we will eat a last year's pippin¹ of mine own
grafting, with a dish of caraways,² and so forth—come, cousin
Silence—and then to bed.

5   FALSTAFF Fore God, you have here a goodly dwelling and a rich.
SHALLOW Barren, barren, barren; beggars all, beggars all, Sir
John. Marry, good air.—Spread, Davy; spread, Davy.
[DAVY *begins to spread the table*]
Well said,° Davy.   *done*

FALSTAFF This Davy serves you for good uses; he is your serving-
10   man and your husband.°   *steward*
SHALLOW A good varlet,° a good varlet, a very good varlet, Sir   *servant*
John.—By the mass, I have drunk too much sack at supper.—A
good varlet. Now sit down, now sit down. [*To* SILENCE] Come,
cousin.

15   SILENCE Ah, sirrah, quoth-a,° we shall   *said he*
[*sings*] Do nothing but eat and make good cheer,
And praise God for the merry year,
When flesh is cheap and females dear,
And lusty lads roam here and there
20   So merrily,
And ever among so merrily.

FALSTAFF There's a merry heart, good Master Silence! I'll give
you a health° for that anon.   *drink a toast to you*

SHALLOW Good Master Bardolph!—Some wine, Davy.

25   DAVY [*to* FALSTAFF] Sweet sir, sit. [*To* BARDOLPH] I'll be with you
anon. [*To* FALSTAFF] Most sweet sir, sit. Master page, good master page, sit.
[*All but* DAVY *sit.* DAVY *pours wine*]
Proface!³ What you want° in meat, we'll have in drink; but you   *lack*
must bear;° the heart's all.   *be forbearing*

30   SHALLOW Be merry, Master Bardolph and my little soldier there,
be merry.

SILENCE [*sings*] Be merry, be merry, my wife has all,
For women are shrews, both short and tall,
'Tis merry in hall when beards wags all,
35   And welcome merry shrovetide.⁴
Be merry, be merry.

FALSTAFF I did not think Master Silence had been a man of this
mettle.°   *boldness*

SILENCE Who, I? I have been merry twice and once ere now.
Enter DAVY [*with a dish of apples*]

40   DAVY There's a dish of leather-coats° for you.   *russet apples*
SHALLOW Davy!
DAVY Your worship! I'll be with you straight. [*To* FALSTAFF] A
cup of wine, sir?

5.3 Location: Shallow's garden in Gloucestershire.
1. A kind of apple traditionally kept for a year before eating.
2. Caraway seeds or sweet biscuits containing these seeds,
often eaten with apples.

3. A greeting used as a welcome to a meal, from an Italian phrase meaning "May it do you good."
4. The season of festivities preceding the Christian penitential season, Lent.

SILENCE [*sings*]   A cup of wine
45   That's brisk and fine,
                         And drink unto thee, leman° mine,   sweetheart
                         And a merry heart lives long-a.
FALSTAFF   Well said, Master Silence.
SILENCE   And we shall be merry; now comes in the sweet o'th'
50   night.
FALSTAFF   Health and long life to you, Master Silence!
        [*He drinks*]
SILENCE   Fill the cup and let it come. I'll pledge you a mile to
     th' bottom.[5]
SHALLOW   Honest Bardolph, welcome! If thou want'st anything
55   and wilt not call, beshrew thy heart! [*To the* PAGE] Welcome,
     my little tiny thief, and welcome indeed, too!—I'll drink to
     Master Bardolph, and to all the cavalieros° about London.   fine fellows
        [*He drinks*]
DAVY   I hope to see London once ere I die.
BARDOLPH   An I might see you there, Davy!
60   SHALLOW   By the mass, you'll crack° a quart together, ha, will   drink
     you not, Master Bardolph?
BARDOLPH   Yea, sir, in a pottle-pot.°   two-quart glass
SHALLOW   By God's liggens,[6] I thank thee. The knave will stick
     by thee, I can assure thee that; a will not out;° 'tis true-bred.   drop out
65   BARDOLPH   And I'll stick by him, sir.
SHALLOW   Why, there spoke a king! Lack nothing, be merry!
        One knocks at [*the*] *door* [*within*]
     Look who's at door there, ho! Who knocks?   [*Exit* DAVY]
        [SILENCE *drinks*]
FALSTAFF [*to* SILENCE]   Why, now you have done me right![7]
SILENCE [*sings*]   Do me right,
70   And dub me knight—
                         Samingo.[8]
     Is't not so?
FALSTAFF   'Tis so.
SILENCE   Is't so?—Why then, say an old man can do somewhat.
        [*Enter* DAVY]
75   DAVY   An't please your worship, there's one Pistol come from the
     court with news.
FALSTAFF   From the court? Let him come in.
        Enter PISTOL
     How now, Pistol?
PISTOL   Sir John, God save you.
80   FALSTAFF   What wind blew you hither, Pistol?
PISTOL   Not the ill wind which blows no man to good.
     Sweet knight, thou art now one of the greatest men in this
     realm.
SILENCE   By'r Lady, I think a be—but goodman° Puff of Bar'son.[9]   except for yeoman
85   PISTOL   Puff?
     Puff in thy teeth, most recreant coward base!—

---

5. I'll drink to the bottom of the cup, even if it were a
mile.
6. An obscure oath, possibly derived from "by God's
(eye)lid."
7. Done me justice (by drinking well).
8. Translated lines from a French drinking song, "Mon-

sieur Mingo." "Sa" may be a mispronunciation of "Sir."
"Mingo" means "I urinate."
9. Referring either to Barcheston, a town ten miles south
of Stratford, or Barston, a town between Coventry and
Solihull.

Sir John, I am thy Pistol and thy friend,
And helter-skelter have I rode to thee,
And tidings do I bring, and lucky joys,
90 And golden times, and happy news of price.
FALSTAFF   I pray thee now, deliver them like a man of this world.
PISTOL   A foutre° for the world and worldlings base!   *fig*
I speak of Africa and golden joys.
FALSTAFF   O base Assyrian knight,[1] what is thy news?
95 Let King Cophetua[2] know the truth thereof.
SILENCE [*singing*]   'And Robin Hood, Scarlet, and John.'[3]
PISTOL   Shall dunghill curs confront the Helicons?[4]
And shall good news be baffled?°   *disgraced*
Then Pistol lay thy head in Furies'[5] lap.
100 SHALLOW   Honest gentleman, I know not your breeding.
PISTOL   Why then, lament therefor.
SHALLOW   Give me pardon, sir. If, sir, you come with news from
the court, I take it there's but two ways: either to utter them, or
conceal them. I am, sir, under the King in some authority.
105 PISTOL   Under which king, besonian?° Speak, or die.   *beggarly fellow*
SHALLOW   Under King Harry.
PISTOL   Harry the Fourth, or Fifth?
SHALLOW   Harry the Fourth.
PISTOL   A foutre for thine office!
Sir John, thy tender lambkin now is king.
Harry the Fifth's the man. I speak the truth.
110 When Pistol lies, do this, [*making the fig*][6] and fig me,
Like the bragging Spaniard.
FALSTAFF   What, is the old King dead?
PISTOL   As nail in door. The things I speak are just.°   *true*
FALSTAFF   Away, Bardolph, saddle my horse! Master Robert
Shallow, choose what office thou wilt in the land; 'tis thine.
115 Pistol, I will double-charge thee[7] with dignities.
BARDOLPH   O joyful day!
I would not take a knighthood for my fortune.
PISTOL   What, I do bring good news?
FALSTAFF [*to* DAVY]   Carry Master Silence to bed.
                                    [*Exit* DAVY *with* SILENCE]
120 Master Shallow—my lord Shallow—be what thou wilt, I am
fortune's steward—get on thy boots; we'll ride all night.—O
sweet Pistol!—Away, Bardolph!   [*Exit* BARDOLPH]
Come, Pistol, utter more to me, and withal° devise something   *at the same time*
to do thyself good. Boot, boot, Master Shallow! I know the
125 young King is sick for me. Let us take any man's horses—the
laws of England are at my commandment. Blessed are they
that have been my friends, and woe to my Lord Chief Justice.
PISTOL   Let vultures vile seize on his lungs also!

---

1. Adopting Pistol's elevated rhetorical style, Falstaff calls
him a knight of Assyria, an Asian empire that the Elizabethans associated with pillage and robbery.
2. Alluding to the African king who marries a beggar in
the popular ballad "A Beggar and a King."
3. A line from the ballad "Robin Hood and the Jolly
Pinder of Wakesfield."
4. That is, "the true Muses." Pistol conflates the Muses
of classical mythology with Mt. Helicon, part of the Parnassus mountain range on which they dwelt.
5. Then let Pistol appeal to the goddesses of revenge.
6. An obscene gesture, known as "the Spanish fig," in
which the thumb is put between the fore and middle fingers in a way meant to be suggestive of genitalia and sex
acts. In the next line, Pistol refers to a "bragging" (lying)
Spaniard who was "figged."
7. Load you (with honors) twice over; load you like a gun
twice over, with a pun on Pistol's name.

'Where is the life that late I led?'[8] say they.
130 Why, here it is. Welcome these pleasant days.   *Exeunt*

5.4
Enter Beadles, [dragging in MISTRESS] QUICKLY *and*
DOLL TEARSHEET[1]

MISTRESS QUICKLY   No, thou arrant knave! I would to God that I
might die, that I might have thee hanged. Thou hast drawn my
shoulder out of joint.
FIRST BEADLE   The constables have delivered her over to me;
5   and she shall have whipping-cheer,[2] I warrant her. There hath
been a man or two killed about her.[3]
DOLL TEARSHEET   Nut-hook,[4] nut-hook, you lie! Come on, I'll
tell thee what, thou damned tripe-visaged° rascal, an° the child   *flabby-faced / if*
I go with do miscarry,[5] thou wert better thou hadst struck thy
10   mother, thou paper-faced° villain.   *white-faced*
MISTRESS QUICKLY   O the Lord, that Sir John were come! He
would make this a bloody day to somebody. But I pray God the
fruit of her womb miscarry!
FIRST BEADLE   If it do, you shall have a dozen of cushions again;
15   you have but eleven now.[6] Come, I charge you both go with
me, for the man is dead that you and Pistol beat amongst you.
DOLL TEARSHEET   I'll tell you what, you thin man in a censer,[7] I
will have you as soundly swinged° for this, you bluebottle[8]   *beaten*
rogue, you filthy famished correctioner! If you be not swinged,
20   I'll forswear half-kirtles.°   *give up wearing skirts*
FIRST BEADLE   Come, come, you she knight-errant, come!
MISTRESS QUICKLY   O God, that right should thus o'ercome might!
Well, of sufferance° comes ease.   *from suffering*
DOLL TEARSHEET   Come, you rogue, come; bring me to a justice.
25   MISTRESS QUICKLY   Ay, come, you starved bloodhound.
DOLL TEARSHEET   Goodman death, goodman bones!
MISTRESS QUICKLY   Thou atomy,° thou!   *(for "anatomy"; skeleton)*
DOLL TEARSHEET   Come, you thin thing; come, you rascal.
FIRST BEADLE   Very well.   *Exeunt*

5.5
Enter two GROOMS[, *strewing rushes*[1]]

FIRST GROOM   More rushes, more rushes!
SECOND GROOM   The trumpets have sounded twice.
FIRST GROOM   'Twill be two o'clock ere they come from the cor-
onation.   *Exeunt*

---

8. A line from a lost poem or ballad.
5.4 Location: A street in London.
1. Q says, "Enter Sinklo and three or foure officers." Sinklo was probably an actor's name. He was evidently very
thin, for this scene contains a number of unflattering references to one of the officer's skinniness.
2. That is, a whipping for her entertainment or supper
("cheer"). Beadle (the parish officers responsible for
enforcing laws) commonly meted out this punishment for
prostitution.
3. Because of her; in her company.
4. A hook for pulling nuts from trees; the arresting con-

stable.
5. Women who were pregnant might escape the full
force of the law until after they gave birth.
6. Implying that Tearsheet feigns pregnancy by carrying
one of Quickly's pillows under her gown.
7. You figure of a man embossed on the lid of a pot for
burning incense.
8. Alluding to the blue tunics worn by beadles.
5.5 Location: A public place near Westminster Abbey.
1. Floor coverings, here strewn on the ground before the
King's entrance.

Enter [Sir John] FALSTAFF, SHALLOW, PISTOL, BAR-
DOLPH, *and [the]* PAGE[2]

5 FALSTAFF   Stand here by me, Master Robert Shallow. I will make
the King do you grace.° I will leer upon him as a comes by,   *honor*
and do but mark the countenance that he will give me.
PISTOL   God bless thy lungs, good knight.
FALSTAFF   Come here, Pistol; stand behind me. [*To* SHALLOW]
10 O, if I had had time to have made new liveries,[3] I would have
bestowed° the thousand pound I borrowed of you! But 'tis no   *spent*
matter; this poor show doth better; this doth infer° the zeal I   *imply*
had to see him.
SHALLOW   It doth so.
15 FALSTAFF   It shows my earnestness of affection —
PISTOL   It doth so.
FALSTAFF   My devotion —
PISTOL   It doth, it doth, it doth.
FALSTAFF   As it were, to ride day and night, and not to deliberate,
20 not to remember, not to have patience to shift me° —   *change my clothes*
SHALLOW   It is most certain.
FALSTAFF   But to stand stained with travel and sweating with
desire to see him, thinking of nothing else, putting all affairs in
oblivion, as if there were nothing else to be done but to see
25 him.
PISTOL   'Tis *semper idem*, for *absque hoc nihil est:*[4] 'tis all in every
part.
SHALLOW   'Tis so indeed.
PISTOL   My knight, I will inflame thy noble liver,
30 And make thee rage.
Thy Doll, and Helen[5] of thy noble thoughts,
Is in base durance° and contagious° prison,   *imprisonment / noxious*
Haled° thither   *Dragged*
By most mechanical° and dirty hand.   *menial*
35 Rouse up Revenge from ebon den° with fell Alecto's snake,[6]   *dark cave (hell)*
For Doll is in. Pistol speaks naught but truth.
FALSTAFF   I will deliver her.
      [*Shouts within.*] *Trumpets sound*
PISTOL   There roared the sea, and trumpet-clangour sounds!
      Enter KING HARRY *the Fifth,* [PRINCE JOHN *of Lancaster,*
      the Dukes of CLARENCE *and* GLOUCESTER, *the*] LORD
      CHIEF JUSTICE [*and others*]
FALSTAFF   God save thy grace, King Hal, my royal Hal!
40 PISTOL   The heavens thee guard and keep, most royal imp° of fame!   *offspring*
FALSTAFF   God save thee, my sweet boy!
KING HARRY   My Lord Chief Justice, speak to that vain° man.   *foolish*
LORD CHIEF JUSTICE [*to* FALSTAFF]   Have you your wits? Know
      you what 'tis you speak?
FALSTAFF   My king, my Jove,[7] I speak to thee, my heart!

---

2. In Q, Falstaff and his friends enter after "Trumpets
sound, and the King, and his train passe over the stage."
There are thus two royal processions, one before Falstaff
enters and one later in the scene. F contains only the
latter procession, which immediately precedes the climactic moment when Hal rejects Falstaff.
3. Uniforms such as those worn by the retainers in a
noble household.

4. The first Latin motto, "ever the same," was associated
with Queen Elizabeth; the second means "apart from
this, there is nothing."
5. The famously beautiful woman whose abduction by
Paris is said to have started the Trojan War.
6. Alecto was one of the Furies in classical myth; her
head was covered with snakes.
7. In classical myth, the ruler of the gods.

45 KING HARRY I know thee not, old man. Fall to thy prayers.
How ill white hairs becomes a fool and jester!
I have long dreamt of such a kind of man,
So surfeit-swelled,° so old, and so profane;   *bloated from excess*
But being awake, I do despise my dream.
50 Make less thy body hence,° and more thy grace.   *henceforth*
Leave gormandizing;° know the grave doth gape   *gluttony*
For thee thrice wider than for other men.
Reply not to me with a fool-born jest.
Presume not that I am the thing I was,
55 For God doth know, so shall the world perceive,
That I have turned away my former self;
So will I those that kept me company.
When thou dost hear I am as I have been,
Approach me, and thou shalt be as thou wast,
60 The tutor and the feeder of my riots.
Till then I banish thee, on pain of death,
As I have done the rest of my misleaders,
Not to come near our person by ten mile.
For competence of life[8] I will allow you,
65 That lack of means enforce you not to evils;
And as we hear you do reform yourselves,
We will, according to your strengths and qualities,°   *attainments*
Give you advancement. [*To* LORD CHIEF JUSTICE] Be it your
  charge, my lord,
To see performed the tenor of our word. [*To his train*] Set on!
Exeunt KING [HARRY *and his train*]
70 FALSTAFF Master Shallow, I owe you a thousand pound.
SHALLOW Yea, marry, Sir John; which I beseech you to let me
have home with me.
FALSTAFF That can hardly be, Master Shallow. Do not you
grieve at this. I shall be sent for in private to him. Look you, he
75 must seem thus to the world. Fear not your advancements. I
will be the man yet that shall make you great.
SHALLOW I cannot perceive how, unless you give me your doublet and stuff me out with straw. I beseech you, good Sir John,
let me have five hundred of my thousand.
80 FALSTAFF Sir, I will be as good as my word. This that you heard
was but a colour.°   *pretense*
SHALLOW A colour[9] I fear that you will die in, Sir John.
FALSTAFF Fear no colours. Go with me to dinner. Come, Lieu-
tenant Pistol; come, Bardolph. I shall be sent for soon at night.
Enter [*the* LORD CHIEF] JUSTICE *and* PRINCE JOHN [*with
officers*]
LORD CHIEF JUSTICE [*to officers*] Go carry Sir John Falstaff to
85   the Fleet.°   *(a London prison)*
Take all his company along with him.
FALSTAFF My lord, my lord!
LORD CHIEF JUSTICE I cannot now speak. I will hear you soon.—
Take them away.

---

8. An allowance sufficient to supply life's necessities.   9. Punning on "collar" as meaning "hangman's noose."

90 PISTOL *Si fortuna me tormenta, spero me contenta.*[1]

Exeunt. Manent° Lancaster [PRINCE JOHN]   *Remain*
and [LORD] CHIEF JUSTICE

PRINCE JOHN   I like this fair proceeding of the King's.
He hath intent his wonted° followers   *customary*
Shall all be very well provided for,
But all are banished till their conversations°   *conduct*
95 Appear more wise and modest to the world.
LORD CHIEF JUSTICE   And so they are.
PRINCE JOHN   The King hath called his parliament, my lord.
LORD CHIEF JUSTICE   He hath.
PRINCE JOHN   I will lay odds that, ere this year expire,
100 We bear our civil swords and native fire[2]
As far as France. I heard a bird so sing,
Whose music, to my thinking, pleased the King.
Come, will you hence?   *Exeunt*

Epilogue

[*Enter* EPILOGUE]

EPILOGUE   First my fear, then my curtsy,° last my speech.   *bow*
My fear is your displeasure; my curtsy, my duty; and my
speech to beg your pardons. If you look for a good speech now,
you undo° me; for what I have to say is of mine own making,   *ruin*
5 and what indeed I should say will, I doubt,° prove mine own   *fear*
marring. But to the purpose, and so to the venture.° Be it   *hazard*
known to you, as it is very well, I was lately here in the end of
a displeasing play, to pray your patience for it, and to promise
you a better. I did mean indeed to pay you with this; which, if
10 like an ill venture[1] it come unluckily home, I break,° and you,   *go bankrupt*
my gentle creditors, lose. Here I promised you I would be, and
here I commit my body to your mercies. Bate° me some, and I   *Excuse*
will pay you some, and, as most debtors do, promise you infinitely.[2]
15 If my tongue cannot entreat you to acquit me, will you command me to use my legs? And yet that were but light payment,
to dance out of your debt. But a good conscience will make
any possible satisfaction, and so would I. All the gentlewomen
here have forgiven me; if the gentlemen will not, then the gen-
20 tlemen do not agree with the gentlewomen, which was never
seen before in such an assembly.
One word more, I beseech you. If you be not too much
cloyed with fat meat, our humble author will continue the story
with Sir John in it,[3] and make you merry with fair Catherine of
25 France; where, for anything I know, Falstaff shall die of a
sweat[4]—unless already a° be killed with your hard opinions.   *he*

---

1. See note to 2.4.157.
2. Our swords used up to now in civil war and our native zeal.
Epilogue
1. An unlucky commercial speculation, especially in a cargo at sea.
2. Q here inserts the lines "and so I kneele downe before you; but indeed, to pray for the Queene," which con-

clude the Epilogue in F. This is one of several indications that the Epilogue was rewritten and expanded at some point, but that in Q these lines, with their reference to the queen, were not moved to their proper place at the end of the speech.
3. In fact, Sir John Falstaff does not appear in *Henry V*, the play here anticipated.
4. A sweating sickness; the plague; a venereal disease.

For Oldcastle[5] died a martyr, and this is not the man. My tongue is weary; when my legs are too, I will bid you good night, and so kneel down before you—but, indeed, to pray for
30   the Queen.

[*He dances, then kneels for applause. Exit*]

TEXTUAL VARIANTS

Control text: Q; additional passages from F

F: The Folio of 1623
Q: The Quarto of 1600
QA: First issue of 1600 Q, lacking 3.1
QB: Second issue of 1600, containing 3.1

Title: THE / Second part of Henrie / the fourth, continuing to his death, / *and coronation of Henrie* / the fift. / With the humours of Sir John Fal- / *staffe, and swaggering* / Pistoll. [Q title page] The Second Part of Henry the Fourth, / Containing his Death: and the Coronation / of King Henry the Fift. [F head title]

s.p. LORD BARDOLPH [Q's use of *Bardolph* (for the nobleman) has been changed throughout.]
s.p. NORTHUMBERLAND [Q's use of *Earl* / *Northumberland* has been standardized throughout.]
s.p. FALSTAFF [Q's use of *Oldcastle* / *John* / *Sir John* / *Falstaff* has been standardized throughout.]
s.p. PAGE [Q's use of *Boy* / *Page* has been standardized throughout.]
s.p. LORD CHIEF JUSTICE [Q's use of *Lord* / *Justice* has been standardized throughout.]
s.p. ARCHBISHOP OF YORK [Q's use of *Bishop* has been changed throughout.]
s.p. MOWBRAY [Q's use of *Marshall* / *Mowbray* has been standardized throughout.]
s.p. MISTRESS QUICKLY [Q's use of *Hostess* / *Quickly* has been standardized throughout.]
s.p. GOWER [Q's use of *Gower* / *Messenger* has been standardized throughout.]
s.p. PRINCE HARRY [Q's use of *Prince* / *Harry* has been standardized throughout.]
s.p. LADY NORTHUMBERLAND [Q's use of *Wife* has been changed throughout.]
s.p. LADY PERCY [Q's use of *Kate* has been changed throughout.]
s.p. FIRST DRAWER and **SECOND DRAWER** [Q's use of *Francis* and *Drawer* has been changed throughout (with some speeches redistributed).]
s.p. DOLL TEARSHEET [Q's use of *Tere-sheet* / *Doll* / *Dorothy* / *Whoore* has been standardized throughout.]
s.p. PRINCE JOHN [Q's use of *John* / *Prince* / *Lancaster* has been standardized throughout.]
s.p. KING HENRY [Q's use of *King* has been changed throughout.]
s.p. GLOUCESTER [Q's use of *Humphrey* / *Gloucester* has been standardized throughout.]
s.p. FIRST and **SECOND GROOM** [Q's use of *Strewers of Rushes 1, 2*, and *3* has been changed throughout (with some speeches redistributed).]
s.p. FIRST BEADLE [Q's use of *Sinklo* has been changed throughout.]

The following variants record only where the Norton text departs from Q, the control text. 3.1, missing in QA, is based on QB, but where material in QA was reset in QB, QA remains the authoritative text. F, however, contains eight lengthy passages (and some shorter ones) that do not appear in Q (1.1.165–78, 1.1.188–208, 1.3.21–24, 1.3.36–55, 1.3.85–108, 2.3.23–45, 4.1.55–79, 4.1.101–37). These are marked in the variants and are based on F

---

5. Alluding to the fact that Sir John was originally called "Oldcastle" in *1 Henry IV*. See the Introduction to that play.

Material originally in Q but absent in F (and in the Oxford text) is printed in the variants or in inset passages within this text. For a much fuller collation of Q and F, see Oxford's *William Shakespeare: A Textual Companion*.

Induction [F; heading not in Q] **s.p. RUMOUR** [not in Q] **13 griefs** [F] griefe **21 anatomize** anothomize **35 hold** hole **36 Where** [F] When

1.1.34 Lord Bardolph Sir John Umfreuile **41 ill** [F] bad **55 should the** [F] should that **59 a venture** a venter **96 say so** [F; not in Q] **103 knolling** [F] tolling **126 Too** [F] So **161 s.p. LORD BARDOLPH** [F] *Umfr⟨euile⟩*. This strained passion doth you wrong my lord. / *Bard⟨olfe⟩*. **163 Lean on your** [F] Leave on you **165–78 You . . . be?** [F; not in Q] **177 doth** hath **181 was** [F] twas **188–208 The . . . him.** [F; not in Q]

1.2.3 more moe **6 clay, man** clay-man **7 tends** [F] intends **10 o'erwhelmed** [F] overwhelmd **14 set** [F] in-set **25 Dumbleton** Dommelton [Q] *Dombledon* [F] **26 slops** [F] my sloppes **31 rascally** [F] rascall **33 smooth-pates** [F] smoothy-pates **41 it;** [F] it: wheres Bardolf, **42 him. Where's Bardolph?** [F] him. **45 An** and **67 want** [F] need **88 age** [F] an ague **93 An't** andt **101 is, as I take it, a** [F] as I take it? is a **110 s.p. FALSTAFF** [F] Old⟨castle⟩. **131 waist** waste **slenderer** [F] slender **156 bearherd** Berod **158 this** [F] his **them, are** [F] the one **161 vanguard** vaward **176 th'ear** [F] the yeere **185–86 and Prince Harry** [not in Q] **192 my bottle, would** [F] a bottle. I would

1.3.21–24 Till . . . admitted. [F; not in Q] **26 case** [F] cause **28 on** [F] and **29 with** [F] in **36–55 Yes . . . else** [F; not in Q] **58 one on** 66 a [F] so **71 Are** [F] And **78 not** [F] not to **79 He . . . Welsh** [F] French and Welch he leaves his back unarmde, they **84 'gainst** [F] against **85–108 s.p. ARCHBISHOP OF YORK . . . worst.** [F; not in Q] **109 s.p. MOWBRAY** [F] *Bish⟨op⟩*.

2.1.18 An I and I **an a** and a **19 vice** [F] view **22–23 continuantly** [F] continually **25 Lombard** [F] Lumbert **29 fobbed** fubd **38 Sir John** [F; not in Q] **44 Ah a** 45 **Ah a** **48 s.p. FANG** [F] *Offic⟨er⟩*. **52 s.p. PAGE** [F] *Boy* **66–67 all, all** [F] al **73 Fie, what** [F] what **95 mad** made **134 tapestries** [F] tapestrie **134–35 ten pound** [F] X £. **138 Come** [F] come, come **152 good** [F; not in Q] **154 Basingstoke** [F] Billingsgate

2.2.14 hast—videlicet these [F] hast with these **15 ones** [F] once **19 thy** [F] the **20 made a shift to** [F; not in Q] **holland.** [F; Q here prints additional lines, and these are included as an inset passage after 2.2.20 of the text.] **23 lying** [F] being **yours** [F] yours at this time **28 you'll** [F] you will **49 engrafted** engraffed **65 A calls me e'en now** A calls me enow **68 red petticoat** peticote **70 rabbit** [F] rabble **72 Althea** [F] Althear **78 good** [F; not in Q] **81 An** And **82 be wronged** [F] have wrong **84 my good** [F] my **98 borrower's** borowed **106 Sure he** [F] He sure **112 familiars** [F] family **115 My lord . . .** [F; no speech prefix before this line] *Poynes* My lord . . . **144 road** rode **150 like** [F] as **151 declension** [F] descension **152 prince** [F] pince **153 everything** [F] enery thing

2.3.11 endeared [F] endeere **23–45 He . . . grave** [F; not in Q]

2.4.1 s.p. FIRST DRAWER [F] *Fran⟨cis⟩*. **3 s.p. SECOND DRAWER** [F] *Draw⟨er⟩*. **8 s.p. FIRST DRAWER** [F] *Fran⟨cis⟩*. **11 s.p. SECOND DRAWER** [F] *Francis*. **14 s.p. FIRST DRAWER** [F] *Dra⟨wer⟩*. **16 s.p. SECOND DRAWER** [F] *Francis*. **20 in good truth, la** in good truth, law **22 we** [F] one **32 an** and **38 them; I** [F] I **42 Yea, Jesu** Yea, joy **46 bravely.** [F] bravely. / *Doll* Hang your selfe, you muddie Cunger, hang your selfe. **48–49 i'good truth** ygood truth **59 Ensign** Antient [similarly elsewhere] **71 your** [F] & your **113 this.** [F] this. / *Sir John* No more Pistoll, I would not have you go off here, discharge your selfe of our company, Pistoll. **117 An** and **123 'captain' odious** [F] as odious as the word occupy, which was an excellent good worde before it was il sorted **133 Where** [F] with **135 Fates** [F] faters **144 Trojan** troiant **150 Die men** [F] Men **152 O' A** **168 an a** and a **189 o' a** **198 A** [F] Ah **207 o' . . . o' a . . . a** **213 ha' chipped** a chipt **223 boot** [F] bootes **228 the scales** [F] scales **240 master's** [F] master **248 o'Thursday** a thursday **251 By my troth, thou'lt** By my troth thou't **an** and **286 o' a** **293 him** [F]

thee **306 outbids** [F] blinds **356 good Doll.** [F] good Doll, come, shee comes blub-
berd, yea? wil you come Doll?

3.1.1–103 [QB; not in QA] **18 mast** [F] masse **22 billows** [F] pillowes **26 thy** [F]
them **27 sea-boy** [F] season **52 liquors!** [F; Q here contains additional lines printed
in this text as an inset passage after this word.] **80 beginnings** [F] beginning

3.2.11 o' a **19 o'** a **20 bona-robas** [F] bona robes **35 Stamford** [F] Samforth **41 o'**
Gaunt a Gaunt **42 i'th'** ith **50** s.p. SHALLOW [F] *Bardolfe* [QA] **61 accommodated**
[F] accommodate **75 your** [F] your good **79 Surecard** [F] Soccard **90 so. Yea** so (so,
so) yea **94 an't** and't **98 an't** and't **103** s.p. FALSTAFF **Prick him.** [F] *John prickes him.*
[Q s.d. is indented from right-hand margin on same type line as "well said."] **104 an**
and **122 not** [F] much **133 for his** [F] for **143 he'd ha'** hee'd a **165 thou'rt** [F] thou
art **168 caught** [F] cought **174 There** [F] Here **181–82 good Master Shallow, no**
more of that [F] master Shallow. **199 in** [F] that we have, in **200 Hem boys** [F]
Hemboies **205 lief** [F] live **217 I'll ne'er** ile nere **217–18 An't . . . an't** and't . . .
and't **252 chapped** chopt **263 will** wooll **268 As you** [F] at your **my house** [F] our
house **274 On** [F] *Shal⟨low⟩.* On **285 invisible** invincible **famine.** [Q here contains
additional lines printed in this text as an inset passage after this word.] **285.2 ever** [F]
over **291 trussed** [F] thrust

4.1.34 rags rage **36 appeared** appeare **55–79 And . . . wrong.** [F; not in Q] **71 shore**
there **80 days** [F] daie's **101–37 O . . . King.** [F; not in Q. The s.p. "*West.*" is set before
4.1.138 in Q.] **114 force** forc'd **137 indeed** and did **173 to our** [F] our **consigned**
confinde **178 And At 234 Than** [F] That **man** [F] man talking **245 th'imagined**
th'imagine **250 Employ** Imply **274 this** [F] his **292–93 redresses.** s.p. / PRINCE JOHN
I [F] redresses, / I **295** s.p. HASTINGS [F] *Prince* **327 Our . . . dispersed** [F] My lord,
our army is disperst already **343 rebellion . . . yours.** [F] rebellion: **348 these** this **trai-**
tors [F] traitour

4.2.2 I pray [F; not in Q] **37 Rome** [F] Rome, there cosin **62 gav'st away** [F] gavest
away gratis **63 Have** [F] Now, have **75 pray** [F; not in Q] **78 but** [F; not in Q] **96**
illuminateth [F] illumineth **100 his** [F] this

4.3.32 melting [F] meeting **39 line** [F] time **52 accompanied? Canst thou tell that?**
[F] accompanied **94 heaven** [F] heavens **104 write . . . letters** [F] wet . . . termes **120**
and will break out [F; not in Q] **132 chamber; softly, pray** [F] chamber **179 How**
fares your grace? [F; not in Q] **183 him.** [F] him: he is not here. **203 Culling** [F]
toling **203–4 the virtuous sweets, / Our thighs** [F] Our thigh **209 have** hands **275**
true and inward [F] inward true and **288 worst of** [F] worse then **289 fine in carat,**
is [F] fine, in karrat **292 my** [F] my most **305 O my son** [F; not in Q] **306 put it** [F]
put **348 My gracious leige** [F; not in Q]

5.1.1 pie [F] pie sir **8 Davy, Davy, Davy** [F] Davy, Davy, Davy, Davy **8–9 see. William**
[F] see Davy, let me see, yea mary William **12 headland** [F] hade land **19 Sir** [F]
Now sir **21 Hinkley** [F] Hunkly **29–30 marvellous** [F] marvailes **33 o'th'** a'th' **40**
An and **46 Come,** [F] come, come, come **49 all** [F; not in Q]

5.2.21 s.p. GLOUCESTER *and* CLARENCE [F] *Princ. ambo* **46 mix** [F] mixt **62** s.p. PRINCE
. . . CLARENCE *Bro.* other [F] otherwise

5.3.3 grafting graffing **5 here a . . . and a** [F] here . . . and **24 Good Master Bardolph!**
[F] Give master Bardolfe **46 thee** the **52–53 to th' too'th 57 cavalieros** [F] cabi-
leros **59 An** And **64 'tis** a tis **75 An't** And't **84 By'r Lady** Birlady **86 in thy** [F] ith
thy **95 Cophetua** Covetua **117 knighthood** [F] Knight

5.4.8 an and **11 He** [F] I **22 o'ercome** overcom

5.5.1–3 s.p. FIRST GROOM, SECOND GROOM, FIRST GROOM [Q opens with s.d. *Enter strew-*
ers of rushes. The first three speeches are assigned to *1, 2,* and *3,* each presumably a
strewer.] **3 o'** a **3–4 coronation.** *Exeunt / Enter* coronation, dispatch, dispatch. / *Trum-*
pets sound, and the King, and his traine passe over the Stage; after them enter **5 Robert**
[F; not in Q] **14** s.p. SHALLOW [F] *Pist⟨ol⟩.* **21–22 most certain. /** s.p. FALSTAFF **But**
[F] best certaine: but **23 affairs** [F] affaires else **26 *absque* obsque** all [F; not in

Q] **49 awake** [F] awakt **53 fool-born** fool-borne **69 our** [F] my **82 I fear that** [F] that I feare

Epilogue 9 did mean [F; in F, the Epilogue is set in italics] meant **13–14 infinitely.** [F] infinitely: and so I kneele downe before you; but indeed, to pray for the Queene. **21 before** [F; not in Q] **27 died a** [F] died **29–30 and . . . Queen** [F; in Q, these lines follow Epilogue 15] **29 kneel** [F] I kneele

Henry V

From a military point of view, Henry V was perhaps the most capable king England ever had. In 1414, reviving an English royal claim on the French throne, Henry invaded France. The following year, he won the Battle of Agincourt against impossible odds, forcing the King of France to declare him his heir and marry him to his daughter. Not surprisingly, Henry's story was a favorite with his English compatriots. It was lovingly chronicled by the historians Raphael Holinshed (died c. 1580) and Edward Hall (d. 1547), and probably dramatized once or more by other playwrights before Shakespeare brought his own version to the stage in 1599.

Shakespeare's *Henry V* is the last written of a set of eight plays on medieval English history. His first four history plays had dealt with the tumultuous years of the Wars of the Roses, 1422–1485. Shakespeare wrote another four plays several years later, presenting the events of 1398 to 1420 that led up to these long wars over the royal succession. *Richard II* depicts Henry Bolingbroke's successful rebellion against Richard II and his coronation as Henry IV. The next two plays describe the troubled reign of the usurper, whose former allies turn against him and whose son keeps company with thieves. At the end of *2 Henry IV*, the King dies and young Prince Hal ascends the throne as Henry V, quickly belying his wastrel reputation and proving himself an astute leader in the play that bears his name. In the final lines of *Henry V*, however, the Chorus foresees Henry's imminent death, after which civil strife will break out once again.

Henry V is, therefore, one of a group of plays rather than a freestanding work. It refers constantly to events before and after its own temporal limits, events familiar to Shakespeare's audience from plays they had already seen performed. These references complicate the play's tone considerably. The Chorus's final predictions, for instance, darken the otherwise straightforwardly triumphal conclusion. Surely our awareness of the internecine strife that precedes and follows Henry's reign reinforces our admiration for him—he prospers where others have failed, and will again fail, miserably. At the same time, *Henry V* is haunted by problems merely deferred, not resolved; in the long view, its hero's success looks transitory, even futile.

In 1599, such complexities may have seemed especially pertinent. England was mobilizing for a major campaign against Ireland to be led by Elizabeth's dashing young favorite, the Earl of Essex. *Henry V* registers both the patriotic excitement generated by the prospect of a military venture in foreign parts and the dread of war in a notoriously difficult environment (in the event, Essex's expedition was a disaster). These acutely mixed feelings were symptomatic of more general disputes about England's foreign policy. For much of the sixteenth century, England had attempted merely to defend its borders, but as it became wealthier and more powerful, expansion seemed feasible again. Ireland and the Netherlands beckoned; so did the New World, where France and Spain had already established colonies. Henry V's foray into France typified the kind of aggressive enterprise some of Shakespeare's contemporaries wished their nation to underwrite and others denounced as wasteful and dangerous.

Given the circumstances in which *Henry V* was originally written, it is not surprising that it has generated striking interpretive disagreements, or that the play continues to be viewed through the lens of contemporary events. In Laurence Olivier's film version, made during World War II, *Henry V* is a vindication of England's excellence, and the victory at Agincourt a hopeful precedent for success in a justified European war. Kenneth Branagh's 1989 film, on the other hand, reflects the murkier experience of more recent conflicts: the American intervention in Vietnam, the British in the Falkland Islands. Did Shakespeare

Henricus v. From John Rastell, *The Pastyme of People* (1529).

intend the play as a paean to militarism or as an exposé of war's pointless brutality? Is Henry supposed to be a heroic or a repellent character? Is the war in France justified or purely expedient?

Henry's grandeur is repeatedly emphasized by the Chorus, by his followers, and even occasionally by his enemies. He not merely copes with but triumphs over the difficult circumstances bequeathed him: uniting his disputatious people against an external enemy, spending their aggressions abroad instead of at home, and gaining himself a kingdom to boot. His combination of personal bravery and splendid eloquence proves inspiring to his men throughout the campaign in France, in the smaller skirmishes as well as in the desperate moments before Agincourt; his "Once more unto the breach" speech (3.1.1–34) and his prophetic vision of aged veterans boasting to their compatriots on St. Crispin's Day (4.3.41ff.) have often been held up as models of their kind.

On the other hand, *Henry V* clearsightedly acknowledges, as had *Richard II* and *1* and *2 Henry IV*, that the factors that render someone an effective king are not necessarily morally admirable ones. Even while Shakespeare displays Henry's charisma to the full, he refuses to be entirely dazzled by his allure. In the early sixteenth century, Machiavelli had introduced Renaissance political thinkers to the notion that success as a ruler might be separable from, or even inimical to, what was conventionally considered virtuous behavior. Shakespeare's Henry is certainly no monster of iniquity, but his career poses some of the same questions that Machiavelli had in *The Prince* about the relationship of political success to personal goodness: about what the relationship is and whether it should matter.

A closer look at *Henry V* reveals a play not only deeply equivocal but self-consciously so. The capstone of Shakespeare's years of experimentation in the history play form, *Henry V* seems profoundly aware of the way generic constraints bear in upon its hero. Comedy and tragedy form themselves upon the rhythms of an individual life, ending in marriage or in death. History plays, by contrast, even when they seem to concentrate on the fortunes of a single character, dramatize the life of a nation, or at least its governing class. Characters in history plays are conceived as an endless generational succession, inheriting a political and historical situation from their ancestors and passing it down to their descendants. When one person dies, another steps into his place. The king's marriage represents not merely a natural culmination of his personal story, but one episode in a family's attempt to perpetuate a dynasty.

The young King Henry V is, therefore, both more and less than a talented and intelligent individual. One of a series, like the play that bears his name, he must come to terms with what it means to be part of a family line, what it means for one's "career" to begin before birth, end long after death. And Henry's family line is, of course, a tangled matter. His dubious title to the English throne reflects some of the instabilities in the concept of inheritance: what can it mean to acquire name and title "legitimately" from a man who stole the throne? The passing of property and title from one generation to the next might seem to reflect facts of nature, but it is also, as the Archbishop of Canterbury's discussion of "Salic law" reveals in 1.2, a matter of custom, a cultural construction. Inheritance can be altered as well by force or by negotiation: Henry IV compelled Richard to abdicate, and Henry V's victory at Agincourt requires the French King to recognize an English conqueror rather than his own son as heir to the French throne.

Troubles over the way proper generational sequence ought to be defined resonate throughout the play. War, in particular, seems intimately tied up with questions of lineage. Battlefield heroics can reinforce and clarify the relationship between fathers and sons. King Charles of France, for instance, describes Henry's belligerence as his birthright:

> The kindred of him hath been fleshed upon us,
> And he is bred out of that bloody strain
> That haunted us in our familiar paths.
> Witness our too-much-memorable shame
> When Crécy battle fatally was struck,
> And all our princes captived by the hand
> Of that black name, Edward, Black Prince of Wales,
> Whiles that his mountant sire, on mountain standing,
> Up in the air, crowned with the golden sun,
> Saw his heroical seed and smiled to see him
> Mangle the work of nature and deface
> The patterns that by God and by French fathers
> Had twenty years been made.
>
> (2.4.50–62)

Henry's great-uncle, Edward the Black Prince, butchers the French while the Prince's father, King Edward III, gladly looks on. There seem to be no mothers in this entirely male domain, merely God and fathers in alliance, so that Edward III himself seems rather improbably deified, "up in the air, crowned with the golden sun." Henry, in his stirring speech to his troops at Harfleur, evidences a similar pattern of assumptions:

> On, on, you noblest English,
> Whose blood is fet from fathers of war-proof,
> Fathers that like so many Alexanders
> Have in these parts from morn till even fought,
> And sheathed their swords for lack of argument.
> Dishonor not your mothers; now attest
> That those whom you called fathers did beget you.
>
> (3.1.17–23)

Once again, fathers set demanding precedents for sons eager to duplicate their exploits but inevitably threatened by the possibility of falling short. The French King and Henry imagine inheritance, which might seem a rather passive process, as a strenuous, anxious endeavor.

For if battle clarifies the pedigrees of winners, it simultaneously obscures those of the losers. In practical terms, of course, Henry's victory debars the Dauphin, the French heir apparent, from assuming his father's title. More generally, however, as both Henry and the French King insist, defeat in battle disrupts familial affinity, defacing paternal patterns, dishonoring mothers. Negotiating with Harfleur's governor, Henry predicts the consequences of the town's refusal to surrender quietly.

> why, in a moment look to see
> The blind and bloody soldier with foul hand
> Defile the locks of your shrill-shrieking daughters;
> Your fathers taken by the silver beards,
> And their most reverend heads dashed to the walls;
> Your naked infants spitted upon pikes,

> Whiles the mad mothers with their howls confused
> Do break the clouds, as did the wives of Jewry
> At Herod's bloody-hunting slaughtermen.
>
> (3.3.110–18)

On the face of it, it might seem surprising for a general to characterize his own troops as rapists and murderers. Yet Henry's rhetorical tactics are entirely deliberate: by describing his soldiers' potential victims as members of families—as daughters, fathers, infants, mothers—he heightens the impact of their violence. The rampaging army, he implies, will shatter not merely individuals but whole networks of affiliation. The speech effectively intimidates his auditors, who give up without a fight.

Unfortunately, even soldiers in the "winning" camp, insofar as they are vulnerable to the enemy, are liable to similar familial disasters. Exeter's description of war's misfortunes exempts neither side from calamity, from

> the widows' tears, the orphans' cries,
> The dead men's blood, the pining maidens' groans,
> For husbands, fathers, and betrothèd lovers. . . .
>
> (2.4.106–8)

Although Henry's invasion leaves the French more bloodied and tearful than the English, the English too suffer emotional and practical losses. Henry's soldiers are wasted by disease, hanged, occasionally even killed in battle. In 4.1, the common soldier worries, in an age without veteran's benefits, of dying with "wives left poor behind them" and "children rawly left" (lines 132–34). The process of proving Henry's family tree, in other words, may disrupt not only his enemies' but his subordinates'. If infants are slaughtered, daughters raped, fathers torn from dependents, how can families be reconstituted? How can legitimate inheritance possibly be determined?

The difficulties of succession and inheritance are issues for Shakespeare the playwright, as well as for his protagonist. Just as the character Henry V must strive to match and excel the patterns set by his ancestors, so the play *Henry V* must concern itself with what it means to be a sequel in two different senses: the way in which it re-presents actual historical events in a necessarily diminished theatrical form, and the way in which it must struggle to gratify

Soldiers using a battering ram. From Flauius Vegetus Renatus, *The Foure Bookes of Flauius Vegetus Renatus Briefly Containing a Plain Form and Perfect Knowledge of Martiall Policye* (1572).

an audience whose expectations had been formed by three exceedingly popular plays in the same series. At the beginning of every act, a Chorus pointedly emphasizes the play's self-conscious lack of realism: for example,

> Can this cock-pit hold
> The vasty fields of France? Or may we cram
> Within this wooden O the very casques
> That did affright the air at Agincourt?
> (Prologue, lines 11–14)

Of course, *Henry V* is no more implausible than most other Renaissance plays. But in a sense, the theatrical anxieties of *Henry V* are cognate with the personal anxieties of its hero; the play is afraid of degenerating from its precursors, proving an inadequate replica of a distinguished original. And just as Henry V seems to overcompensate, not merely living up to his illustrious predecessors but going beyond them, so too *Henry V*, like many sequels, copes with its belatedness by a strategy of overstatement. It exaggerates some of the themes and issues of the earlier plays. In *1 Henry IV*, Hotspur, Prince Hal's valiant antagonist, epitomized many of the traditional ideals of chivalry—a word derived from the French *cheval*, "horse." In *Henry V*, Bourbon, one of Henry's new opponents, writes a sonnet to his horse that begins "Wonder of nature"—for, he says, "my horse is my mistress" (3.7.36–37,40). Hotspur's chivalry, caricatured to the point of ridiculousness, degenerates in *Henry V* into bestiality jokes made at the expense of a blustering fop.

Shakespeare dramatizes Henry's success, in other words, not merely by magnifying his exploits but by minimizing the threat from possible competitors. Although the enemies of Henry's adulthood are technically more formidable than the enemies of his adolescence, they are characterized as bumbling and laughable, so that Henry's victory over them seems virtually preordained. Henry's allies seem similarly diminished. Falstaff, who dominated much of *1* and *2 Henry IV*, dies without reappearing in *Henry V*, leaving his cronies Bardolph, Nym, and Pistol to accompany Henry to France. They are joined by Fluellen, a Welsh soldier; MacMorris, an Irish one; Jamy, a Scots one; and Williams, a rural English one. This miscellany is proof of Henry's charisma; while in the previous plays the Irish, Scots, and Welsh were up in arms, Henry V successfully enlists them in his cause—not by homogenizing their differences, but by inspiring their allegiance to him even as they quarrel furiously with one another. Henry's triumph at Agincourt, Shakespeare claims, involves the whole British nation. At the same time, these loyal adherents are given little of Falstaff's subversive wit, presumably because Falstaff's wholesale critique of military valor would undercut too thoroughly the premises of Henry's royal magnetism. Even the bluff yeoman Williams, who complains of the disproportionate suffering common people undergo to satisfy the ambitions of their betters, does not dissent from the fundamental principle of social and military hierarchy: to disobey one's superiors, he claims, "were against all proportion of subjection" (4.1.138). For better or worse, everyone seems to agree, the subject's life is at the ruler's disposal.

Shakespeare's excision of Falstaff's skeptical intelligence from *Henry V* means that there is no one within the play to point out the ironies of many of the turns of the plot. Presumably, though no one comments explicitly upon it, the venality of the clerics who finance Henry's expedition to France is sufficiently clear to the audience. Likewise, when Gower loyally remarks that Henry, unlike Alexander, never killed any of his friends, we are likely to think back to Falstaff's death, reported earlier in the play, and also to reflect that of Henry's other Eastcheap chums only Pistol has survived the "great victory" at Agincourt. Elsewhere it is unclear how or even whether the audience is expected to grasp an irony. In 1.1, Henry decides to press his claim on the French throne through the female line of descent. Shortly thereafter, he executes three erstwhile friends for conspiring against his life. In fact their plot was inspired by the conviction that Henry's title to the English throne was obstructed by the Earl of Mortimer's daughter, the Earl of Cambridge's wife. In other words, Henry employs against the French a principle that, if it were enforced against him, would strip him of both English and French kingdoms. Yet the point is made so obliquely that only a spectator cognizant of the tangled Plantagenet genealogy is likely to catch it.

As the stature of Henry's foes and associates diminishes, the ethical problems posed by his exploits are correspondingly aggravated. As we have already seen, Henry's self-assertion necessarily occurs at the expense of others, thereby raising the question of the extent to which his interests ought to take precedence over competing claims. Neither we nor Henry can be certain whether his exceptional situation and abilities exempt him from the criteria by which common persons are judged. In fact, Henry's unusual gifts as a leader render the uncertainty more pointed. Richard II disregarded common folk, and Henry IV deliberately avoided them; but Henry V inspires them by his capacity to immerse himself sympathetically in their lives. His insistence upon his ordinariness becomes a strategy of rule — part of what he is loved for during his lifetime and what becomes legendary after his death. But then, when he insists on seeing himself as a unique case nonetheless, he seems not merely to be asserting a king's usual prerogatives, but to be inconsistently or hypocritically making special allowances for himself. "Nice customs curtsy to great kings," he tells Catherine (5.2.250), and so, perhaps, do more important precepts.

This unresolved ambivalence becomes obvious in 4.1, when Henry disguises himself as a commoner and ventures among his rank and file. Initially, he argues for the essential similarity between himself and his followers.

> I think the King is but a man, as I am. The violet smells to him as it doth to me; the element shows to him as it doth to me. All his senses have but human conditions. His ceremonies laid by, in his nakedness he appears but a man, and though his affections are higher mounted than ours, yet when they stoop, they stoop with the like wing. (lines 99–104)

The ordinary soldiers, Williams and Bates, are unconvinced, pointing out that if they lose the battle, the King will be ransomed while they will be killed. On the other hand, they note, because they are required to obey the King under any circumstances, they need not concern themselves with the justice of the King's cause: their blood will be on Henry's head if he is waging an unjust war. The common soldiers see the King as unlike themselves, with special responsibilities that compensate for his special privileges. Henry responds indignantly:

> The King is not bound to answer the particular endings of his soldiers, the father of his son, nor the master of his servant, for they purpose not their deaths when they propose their services. Besides, there is no king, be his cause never so spotless, if it come to the arbitrament of swords, can try it out with all unspotted soldiers. Some, peradventure, have on them the guilt of premeditated and contrived murder; some, of beguiling virgins with the broken seals of perjury; some, making the wars their bulwark, that have before gored the gentle bosom of peace with pillage and robbery. (lines 146–55)

Henry resists accepting the extraordinary moral burden his followers would confer upon him. Yet his refusal is based not on his earlier assertion of the shared humanity of King and subject, but on a conviction of the King's special position. He distinguishes sharply and problematically between the King's "superior" violence — the violence of war — and the violence of individual subjects, which is merely criminal. After the soldiers leave, Henry exclaims bitterly:

> Upon the King.
> 'Let us our lives, our souls, our debts, our care-full wives,
> Our children, and our sins, lay on the King.'
> We must bear all. O hard condition,
> Twin-born with greatness: subject to the breath
> Of every fool, whose sense no more can feel
> But his own wringing. What infinite heartsease
> Must kings neglect that private men enjoy?
> (lines 212–19)

It is hard to take this self-pity seriously, given that Henry attempts to deflect all blame for his actions onto enemies and inferiors, even while accepting as his due the rewards that accrue to him by virtue of his exceptional status.

On the other hand, Shakespeare also shows effectively the King's genuine isolation from ordinary pleasures of work and play that normal people can take for granted. Though he repudiates Falstaff, the King retains a distinctly sportive quality; but the moral and practical gap that yawns between the ascendant Henry and his correspondingly diminished associates complicates the effect of his playfulness. In 2.2, with a typical flourish, he pretends to hand the traitors Scrope, Grey, and Cambridge their military commissions, after feigning to inquire about mercy for traitors. Actually, he gives them letters showing that he knows of their plot. This is splendid theater, but it is also quite chilling: Henry plays with his guilty victims as a cat plays with a mouse. His joke signifies not true contest, but absolute control.

Elsewhere too Henry's power tips the balance of hostility and affection that usually characterizes practical jokes in a markedly aggressive direction. In disguise on the eve of the Battle of Agincourt, he argues with the commoner Williams, as we have already seen, over the question of the King's responsibility for his subjects. He and Williams exchange gloves so they will be able to resume the quarrel after the battle. In 4.7, with victory assured, Henry gives Williams's glove to Fluellen to see what Williams will do when he sees it again. When Williams attacks Fluellen, Henry stops the fight, pretending to be angry at the insult to himself. Williams—technically guilty of the capital crime of mutiny—defends himself boldly enough, and Henry, thinking to be generous, returns Williams's glove to him filled with coins. Yet Williams fails to thank Henry, and when Fluellen attempts to add to the gift, he spurns it angrily. It is unclear from the script whether Williams eventually accepts the gold; either way, Henry's power contaminates what he wants to see as a game. While in the earlier plays Prince Hal always had the advantage of rank, it was still possible for Falstaff to give him almost as good as he got. Now that Henry is King and Falstaff is dead, Henry is always the winner, and so the game is no game at all. Arguably, in fact, Henry goes to war with France because he misses a sense of *competition*—because the fate of the effective King is that he cannot find real opposition at home.

Henry's wooing of Catherine in 5.2 is typified by the same dubious sense of fun. This scene, often quite endearing onstage, is also entirely beside the point. We hear from the Chorus in 3.0 that the French King offered Catherine to Henry before his forces arrived

Game of tennis. From Comenius, *Orbis Sensualism Pictus* (1659).

in France, but he rejected the offer because the suggested dowry—some "petty and unprofitable dukedoms"—did not suffice. Nonetheless, in 5.2, Henry calls Catherine his "capital demand" and presents himself to her as a wooer. He pretends that Catherine is free to reject him, even though the marriage is already arranged as part of the peace treaty. Rather like Williams, Catherine refuses to play along: when he asks, "Canst thou love me?" she replies, "I cannot tell." "Wilt thou have me?" "Dat is as it shall please de *roi mon père*" (lines 183ff.). Is Catherine being coy, or is she simply speaking the literal truth? In the game as Henry constructs it, Catherine's refusals can as easily be interpreted as coquettishness as real denial. In other words, even if she refuses to play Henry's game, she necessarily plays it anyhow. In *Henry V*, Shakespeare must cope with a knotty dramatic problem: how to interest an audience in a man who has, or wins, everything—whose life seems an unbroken series of successes. In the final scene as in the rest of the play, Shakespeare fascinates us by exhibiting the inevitably equivocal nature of kingly glory.

KATHARINE EISAMAN MAUS

TEXTUAL NOTE

Henry V exists in the 1623 First Folio (F) version and in a quarto version first issued in 1600 and reprinted in 1602 and 1619. The F version is generally accepted as the most authoritative text and was probably derived from Shakespeare's "foul papers," or manuscript, but there are also signs that the compositor consulted the 1619 Quarto (Q3) when setting up the F text. F is not, however, a wholly reliable source; it contains a fairly large number of readings rejected by modern editors, probably the result of a compositor misreading a handwritten text. The Oxford editors argue that Q, although printed much earlier than F and obviously corrupt in some respects, actually represents a later stage of the text and may therefore incorporate some of Shakespeare's second thoughts and modifications. They believe that Q is based on memorial reconstruction by actors who played the parts of Exeter and Gower, for the text is far more reliable when these characters are onstage than for other scenes.

The Q text also has a slightly different cast of characters than F: F's Bedford is Q's Clarence, F's Westmoreland is Q's Warwick, and speeches assigned in F to Britain and to the Dauphin in the Agincourt scenes are given to Bourbon in Q. The most important substitution is the last, Bourbon's replacement of the Dauphin in 3.7, 4.2, and 4.5. In F, the Dauphin's substantial role sets him up as Henry's personal adversary, much as Hotspur was in *1 Henry IV*. Also in F, the Dauphin's amply demonstrated folly seems to warrant his eventual displacement by Henry. The Q speech assignments, on the other hand, are consistent with King Charles's order in 3.5 that the Dauphin remain with him at Rouen. In Q, the Dauphin's absence from the battlefield, rather than his extravagantly frivolous presence, implies his unfitness for rule.

Although most editors accept the F speech assignments, Gary Taylor, editor of the Oxford text, argues that Shakespeare in fact vacillated about whether to include the Dauphin in the Agincourt scenes and that Q represents his final decision not to do so. In consequence, although F remains the Oxford control text, Taylor adopts many more readings from Q than do most editors. In this respect, the Oxford *Henry V* seems to depart from the editors' usual policy of not conflating distinctly different texts of the same play (the policy that produces the two *King Lears* later in this volume). Taylor provides information on the tangled textual history of the play and a full explanation of his editorial choices in his single-volume edition of *Henry V* (Oxford: Clarendon Press, 1982).

SELECTED BIBLIOGRAPHY

Altman, Joel. " 'Vile Participation': The Amplification of Violence in the Theatre of *Henry V*." *Shakespeare Quarterly* 42 (1991): 1–32.

Barton, Anne. "The King Disguised: Shakespeare's *Henry V* and the Comical History." *The Triple Bond: Plays, Mainly Shakespearean, in Performance*. Ed. Joseph Price. University Park: Pennsylvania State University Press, 1975. 92–117.

Calderwood, James. "*Henry V*: English, Rhetoric, Theater." *Metadrama in Shakespeare's Henriad: Richard II to Henry V*. Berkeley: University of California Press, 1979. 162–81.

Danson, Lawrence. "*Henry V*: King, Chorus, and Critics." *Shakespeare Quarterly* 34 (1983): 27–43.

Dollimore, Jonathan, and Alan Sinfield. "History and Ideology, Masculinity and Miscegenation." *Faultlines: Cultural Materialism and the Politics of Dissident Reading*. By Alan Sinfield. Berkeley: University of California Press, 1992. 109–42.

Greenblatt, Stephen. "Invisible Bullets: Renaissance Authority and Its Subversion, *Henry IV* and *Henry V*." *Political Shakespeare: New Essays in Cultural Materialism*. Ed. Jonathan Dollimore and Alan Sinfield. Manchester: Manchester University Press, 1985. 18–47.

Ornstein, Robert. "*Henry V*." *A Kingdom for a Stage: The Achievement of Shakespeare's History Plays*. Cambridge: Harvard University Press, 1972. 175–202.

Quint, David. "Alexander the Pig: Shakespeare on History and Poetry." *Boundary 2* 10 (1982): 49–63.

Rabkin, Norman. "Rabbits, Ducks, and *Henry V*." *Shakespeare Quarterly* 28 (1977): 279–96.

Taylor, Gary. *Three Studies in the Text of "Henry V."* Oxford: Clarendon Press, 1979.

The Life of Henry the Fifth

THE PERSONS OF THE PLAY

CHORUS
KING HARRY V of England, claimant to the French throne
Duke of GLOUCESTER ⎱
Duke of CLARENCE ⎰ his brothers
Duke of EXETER, his uncle
Duke of YORK
SALISBURY
WESTMORLAND
WARWICK
Archbishop of CANTERBURY
Bishop of ELY
Richard, Earl of CAMBRIDGE ⎫
Henry, Lord SCROPE of Masham ⎬ traitors
Sir Thomas GREY ⎭
PISTOL ⎫
NIM ⎬ formerly Falstaff's companions
BARDOLPH ⎭
BOY, formerly Falstaff's page
HOSTESS, formerly Mistress Quickly, now Pistol's wife
Captain GOWER, an Englishman
Captain FLUELLEN, a Welshman
Captain MACMORRIS, an Irishman
Captain JAMY, a Scot
Sir Thomas ERPINGHAM
John BATES ⎫
Alexander COURT ⎬ English soldiers
Michael WILLIAMS ⎭
HERALD
KING CHARLES VI of France
ISABEL, his wife and queen
The DAUPHIN, their son and heir
CATHERINE, their daughter
ALICE, an old gentlewoman
The CONSTABLE of France ⎫
Duke of BOURBON ⎪
Duke of ORLÉANS ⎪
Duke of BERRI ⎬ French noblemen at Agincourt
Lord RAMBURES ⎪
Lord GRANDPRÉ ⎭
Duke of BURGUNDY
MONTJOY, the French Herald
GOVERNOR of Harfleur
French AMBASSADORS to England

Prologue

*Enter [*CHORUS *as*] *Prologue*

CHORUS   O for a muse of fire, that would ascend
    The brightest heaven of invention:°   *imagination*
    A kingdom for a stage, princes to act,
    And monarchs to behold the swelling° scene.   *expansive; splendid*
5   Then should the warlike Harry, like himself,
    Assume the port° of Mars,° and at his heels,   *bearing / god of war*
    Leashed in like hounds, should famine, sword, and fire
    Crouch for employment. But pardon, gentles° all,   *gentle folk*
    The flat unraisèd° spirits that hath dared   *uninspired*
10   On this unworthy scaffold° to bring forth   *platform*
    So great an object. Can this cock-pit° hold   *small cockfighting arena*
    The vasty fields of France? Or may we cram
    Within this wooden O° the very casques°   *round theater / helmets*
    That did affright the air at Agincourt?[1]
15   O pardon: since a crookèd figure[2] may
    Attest° in little place a million,   *Represent*
    And let us, ciphers° to this great account,°   *zeroes / sum; story*
    On your imaginary forces° work.   *powers of imagination*
    Suppose within the girdle of these walls
20   Are now confined two mighty monarchies,
    Whose high uprearèd and abutting fronts°   *frontiers*
    The perilous narrow ocean° parts asunder.   *(English Channel)*
    Piece out our imperfections with your thoughts:
    Into a thousand parts divide one man,
25   And make imaginary puissance.
    Think, when we talk of horses, that you see them,
    Printing their proud hoofs i'th' receiving earth;
    <u>For 'tis your thoughts that now must deck° our kings,</u>   *equip*
    Carry them here and there, jumping o'er times,
30   Turning th'accomplishment of many years
    Into an hourglass—for the which supply,°   *to supplement which*
    Admit me Chorus to this history,
    Who Prologue-like your humble patience pray
    Gently to hear, kindly to judge, our play.   *Exit*

1.1

Enter the [Archbishop] of CANTERBURY *and [the Bishop of]* ELY

CANTERBURY   My lord, I'll tell you. That self° bill is urged   *same*
    Which in th'eleventh year of the last king's reign
    Was like,° and had indeed against us passed,   *likely*
    But that the scrambling and unquiet time
5   Did push it out of farther question.°   *consideration*
ELY   But how, my lord, shall we resist it now?
CANTERBURY   It must be thought on. If it pass against us,
    We lose the better half of our possession,
    For all the temporal lands[1] which men devout
10   By testament have given to the Church
    Would they strip from us—being valued thus:

---

1. Site of Henry's famous victory over the French in 1415.
2. A zero, which multiplies a digit's value by ten. *crookèd:* curved.
1.1 Location: In Henry's court.
1. Land devoted to secular uses.

As much as would maintain, to the King's honour,
Full fifteen earls and fifteen hundred knights,
Six thousand and two hundred good esquires;[2]
15 And, to relief of lazars° and weak age,   *lepers*
Of indigent faint souls past corporal° toil,   *bodily*
A hundred almshouses right well supplied;
And to the coffers of the King beside
A thousand pounds by th' year. Thus runs the bill.
20 ELY   This would drink deep.
CANTERBURY   'Twould drink the cup and all.
ELY   But what prevention?
CANTERBURY   The King is full of grace and fair regard.°   *kindly inclination*
ELY   And a true lover of the holy Church.
25 CANTERBURY   The courses of his youth promised it not.
The breath no sooner left his father's body
But that his wildness, mortified° in him,   *struck dead*
Seemed to die too. Yea, at that very moment
Consideration° like an angel came   *Spiritual reflection*
30 And whipped th'offending Adam° out of him,   *innate depravity*
Leaving his body as a paradise
T'envelop and contain celestial spirits.
Never was such a sudden scholar made;
Never came reformation in a flood
35 With such a heady currance° scouring faults;   *headlong current*
Nor never Hydra-headed[3] wilfulness
So soon did lose his seat°—and all at once—   *throne*
As in this king.
ELY   We are blessèd in the change.
CANTERBURY   Hear him but reason in divinity°   *theology*
40 And, all-admiring, with an inward wish
You would desire the King were made a prelate;°   *an important clergyman*
Hear him debate of commonwealth affairs,
You would say it hath been all-in-all his study;
List° his discourse of war, and you shall hear   *Listen to*
45 A fearful battle rendered you in music;
Turn him to any cause of policy,°   *political issue*
The Gordian knot[4] of it he will unloose,
Familiar° as his garter—that when he speaks,   *Offhandedly*
The air, a chartered libertine,° is still,   *licensed freedman*
50 And the mute wonder lurketh in men's ears
To steal his sweet and honeyed sentences:
So that the art and practic part of life
Must be the mistress to this theoric.[5]
Which is a wonder how his grace should glean it,
55 Since his addiction° was to courses vain,   *inclination*
His companies° unlettered, rude, and shallow,   *companions*
His hours filled up with riots,° banquets, sports,   *reveling*
And never noted in him any study,
Any retirement, any sequestration°   *removal*
60 From open haunts and popularity.[6]

2. Gentlemen below knightly rank.
3. Many-headed (the Hydra was a monstrous snake, killed by Hercules).
4. It was foretold that whoever untied the intricate Gordian knot would rule Asia; Alexander the Great cut it with
his sword.
5. *the art . . . theoric:* practical experience must have taught him the theory.
6. From public places and unrefined companions.

ELY   The strawberry grows underneath the nettle,
　　　And wholesome berries thrive and ripen best
　　　Neighboured by fruit of baser quality;
　　　And so the Prince obscured his contemplation
65　　Under the veil of wildness—which, no doubt,
　　　Grew like the summer grass, fastest by night,
　　　Unseen, yet crescive in his faculty.[7]
CANTERBURY   It must be so, for miracles are ceased,[8]
　　　And therefore we must needs admit the means°　　　　　　　　　　*natural causes*
　　　How things are perfected.
70　ELY　　　　　　　　　　　But, my good lord,
　　　How now for mitigation of this bill
　　　Urged by the Commons? Doth his majesty
　　　Incline to it, or no?
CANTERBURY　　　　　　He seems indifferent,
　　　Or rather swaying more upon our part
75　　Than cherishing th'exhibitors[9] against us;
　　　For I have made an offer to his majesty,
　　　Upon our spiritual convocation[1]
　　　And in regard of causes now in hand,
　　　Which I have opened° to his grace at large:　　　　　　　　　　　　　*expounded*
80　　As touching France, to give a greater sum
　　　Than ever at one time the clergy yet
　　　Did to his predecessors part withal.°　　　　　　　　　　　　　　　*with*
ELY   How did this offer seem received, my lord?
CANTERBURY   With good acceptance of his majesty,
85　　Save that there was not time enough to hear,
　　　As I perceived his grace would fain° have done,　　　　　　　　　　　*gladly*
　　　The severals[2] and unhidden passages°　　　　　　　　　*channels of descent*
　　　Of his true titles to some certain dukedoms,
　　　And generally to the crown and seat of France,
90　　Derived from Edward,° his great-grandfather.　　　　　　　　　*King Edward III*
ELY   What was th'impediment that broke this off?
CANTERBURY   The French ambassador upon that instant
　　　Craved audience—and the hour I think is come
　　　To give him hearing. Is it four o'clock?
95　ELY   It is.
CANTERBURY   Then go we in, to know his embassy°—　　　　　　　　　　*message*
　　　Which I could with a ready guess declare
　　　Before the Frenchman speak a word of it.
ELY   I'll wait upon you, and I long to hear it.　　　　　　　*Exeunt*

1.2

Enter KING [HARRY, *the Dukes of* GLOUCESTER], CLARENCE, *and*
EXETER, [*and the Earls of*] WARWICK [*and*] WESTMORLAND
KING HARRY   Where is my gracious lord of Canterbury?
EXETER   Not here in presence.
KING HARRY　　　　　　　　Send for him, good uncle.
WESTMORLAND   Shall we call in th'ambassador, my liege?

---

7. Yet growing according to its natural ability.
8. Protestants believed that no miracles occurred after scriptural times (anachronistic in the mouth of a medieval archbishop).
9. Parliamentary sponsors of the bill.

1. On behalf of the assembled clergy.
2. Legal means by which land is conveyed in separate parts to different heirs.
1.2 Location: The royal court.

KING HARRY   Not yet, my cousin.[1] We would be resolved,
5   Before we hear him, of some things of weight
     That task° our thoughts, concerning us and France.   *exercise*
             Enter [Archbishop of CANTERBURY *and Bishop of* ELY]
CANTERBURY   God and his angels guard your sacred throne,
     And make you long become° it.   *adorn*
KING HARRY   Sure we thank you.
     My learnèd lord, we pray you to proceed,
10   And justly and religiously unfold
     Why the law Salic[2] that they have in France
     Or° should or should not bar us in our claim.   *Either*
     And God forbid, my dear and faithful lord,
     That you should fashion, wrest, or bow your reading,[3]
15   Or nicely charge° your understanding soul   *foolishly burden*
     With opening titles miscreate,[4] whose right
     Suits not in native colours° with the truth;   *Does not accord*
     For God doth know how many now in health
     Shall drop their blood in approbation°   *confirmation*
20   Of what your reverence shall incite us to.
     Therefore take heed how you impawn° our person,   *pledge*
     How you awake our sleeping sword of war;
     We charge you in the name of God take heed.
     For never two such kingdoms did contend
25   Without much fall of blood, whose guiltless drops
     Are every one a woe, a sore complaint
     'Gainst him whose wrongs gives edge unto the swords
     That makes such waste in brief mortality.°   *short-lived humankind*
     Under this conjuration° speak, my lord,   *injunction*
30   For we will hear, note, and believe in heart
     That what you speak is in your conscience washed
     As pure as sin with baptism.
CANTERBURY   Then hear me, gracious sovereign, and you peers
     That owe your selves, your lives, and services
35   To this imperial throne. There is no bar
     To make against your highness' claim to France
     But this, which they produce from Pharamond:°   *legendary French king*
     'In terram Salicam mulieres ne succedant' —
     'No woman shall succeed in Salic[5] land' —
40   Which 'Salic land' the French unjustly gloss°   *interpret*
     To be the realm of France, and Pharamond
     The founder of this law and female bar.[6]
     Yet their own authors faithfully affirm
     That the land Salic is in Germany,
45   Between the floods° of Saale and of Elbe,   *rivers*
     Where, Charles the Great having subdued the Saxons,
     There left behind and settled certain French
     Who, holding in disdain the German women
     For some dishonest° manners of their life,   *unchaste*
50   Established there this law: to wit, no female
     Should be inheritrix in Salic land —
     Which Salic, as I said, 'twixt Elbe and Saale,

---

1. Kinsman; complimentary form of address from king to
nobles.
2. Explained below, lines 35ff.
3. Should shape, pervert, or bend your interpretation.

4. With explicating false property rights.
5. Referring to an ancient Frankish tribe that lived beside
the Rhine River.
6. And prohibition of female inheritance.

Is at this day in Germany called Meissen.
Then doth it well appear the Salic Law
55 Was not devisèd for the realm of France.
Nor did the French possess the Salic land
Until four hundred one-and-twenty years
After defunction° of King Pharamond,   *death*
Idly° supposed the founder of this law,   *Foolishly*
60 Who died within the year of our redemption°   *A.D.*
Four hundred twenty-six; and Charles the Great°   *Charlemagne*
Subdued the Saxons, and did seat° the French   *establish*
Beyond the river Saale, in the year
Eight hundred five. Besides, their writers say,
65 King Pépin, which deposèd Childéric,
Did, as heir general[7] — being descended
Of Blithild, which was daughter to King Clotaire —
Make claim and title to the crown of France.
Hugh Capet also — who usurped the crown
70 Of Charles the Duke of Lorraine, sole heir male
Of the true line and stock of Charles the Great —
To fine° his title with some shows of truth,   *complete; purify*
Though in pure truth it was corrupt and naught,
Conveyed himself as heir to th' Lady Lingard,
75 Daughter to Charlemain, who was the son
To Louis the Emperor, and Louis the son
Of Charles the Great. Also, King Louis the Ninth,
Who was sole heir to the usurper Capet,
Could not keep quiet in his conscience,
80 Wearing the crown of France, till satisfied
That fair Queen Isabel, his grandmother,
Was lineal of° the Lady Ermengarde,   *descended from*
Daughter to Charles, the foresaid Duke of Lorraine;
By the which marriage, the line of Charles the Great
85 Was reunited to the crown of France.
So that, as clear as is the summer's sun,
King Pépin's title and Hugh Capet's claim,
King Louis his° satisfaction, all appear   *(Louis's)*
To hold in right and title of the female;
90 So do the kings of France unto this day,
Howbeit they would hold up this Salic Law
To bar your highness claiming from the female,
And rather choose to hide them in a net°   *complexities*
Than amply to embar° their crookèd titles,   *frankly to rule out*
95 Usurped from you and your progenitors.
KING HARRY   May I with right and conscience make this claim?
CANTERBURY   The sin upon my head, dread sovereign.
For in the Book of Numbers° is it writ,   *Numbers 27:8*
'When the son dies, let the inheritance
100 Descend unto the daughter.' Gracious lord,
Stand for your own; unwind your bloody flag;
Look back into your mighty ancestors.
Go, my dread lord, to your great-grandsire's tomb,
From whom you claim;[8] invoke his warlike spirit,

---

7. One who inherits through either the male or female line.

8. Edward III claimed the French throne through his mother, Isabella.

105 And your great-uncle's, Edward the Black Prince,
Who on the French ground played a tragedy,
Making defeat° on the full power of France,   *(at Crécy, in 1346)*
Whiles his most mighty father° on a hill   *(Edward III)*
Stood smiling to behold his lion's whelp
110 Forage in blood of French nobility.
O noble English, that could entertain°   *encounter*
With half their forces the full pride of France,
And let another half stand laughing by,
All out of work, and cold for° action.   *for want of*
115 ELY   Awake remembrance of those valiant dead,
And with your puissant° arm renew their feats.   *powerful*
You are their heir, you sit upon their throne,
The blood and courage that renownèd them°   *made them famous*
Runs in your veins—and my thrice-puissant liege
120 Is in the very May-morn of his youth,
Ripe for exploits and mighty enterprises.
EXETER   Your brother kings and monarchs of the earth
Do all expect that you should rouse yourself
As did the former lions of your blood.
125 WESTMORLAND   They know your grace hath cause; and means and might,
So hath your highness. Never king of England
Had nobles richer and more loyal subjects,
Whose hearts have left their bodies here in England
And lie pavilioned° in the fields of France.   *encamped*
130 CANTERBURY   O let their bodies follow, my dear liege,
With blood and sword and fire, to win your right.
In aid whereof, we of the spiritualty°   *clergy*
Will raise your highness such a mighty sum
As never did the clergy at one time
135 Bring in to any of your ancestors.
KING HARRY   We must not only arm t'invade the French,
But lay down our proportions[9] to defend
Against the Scot, who will make raid upon us
With all advantages.°   *Given any opportunity*
140 CANTERBURY   They of those marches,° gracious sovereign,   *borderlands*
Shall be a wall sufficient to defend
Our inland from the pilfering borderers.
KING HARRY   We do not mean the coursing snatchers° only,   *mounted raiders*
But fear the main intendment° of the Scot,   *hostile intention*
145 Who hath been still a giddy° neighbour to us.   *always an unreliable*
For you shall read that my great-grandfather
Never unmasked his power unto France
But that the Scot on his unfurnished° kingdom   *unprotected*
Came pouring like the tide into a breach°   *gap in a dike*
150 With ample and brim fullness of his force
Galling° the gleanèd° land with hot assays,°   *Hurting / depleted / attacks*
Girding with grievous siege castles and towns,
That England, being empty of defence,
Hath shook and trembled at the bruit° thereof.   *noise*
155 CANTERBURY   She hath been then more feared than harmed, my liege.
For hear her but exampled° by herself: *given an example*
When all her chivalry hath been in France

---

9. Decide the distribution of our forces.

And she a mourning widow of her nobles,
She hath herself not only well defended
160 But taken and impounded as a stray
The King of Scots,[1] whom she did send to France
To fill King Edward's fame with prisoner kings
And make your chronicle as rich with praise
As is the ooze and bottom of the sea
165 With sunken wrack° and sumless treasuries.[2]   *shipwrecks*
A LORD   But there's a saying very old and true:
          'If that you will France win,
          Then with Scotland first begin.'
For once the eagle England being in prey,°   *out hunting*
170 To her unguarded nest the weasel Scot
Comes sneaking, and so sucks her princely eggs,
Playing the mouse in absence of the cat,
To 'tame[3] and havoc° more than she can eat.   *spoil*
EXETER   It follows then the cat must stay at home.
175 Yet that is but a crushed° necessity,   *forced*
Since we have locks to safeguard necessaries
And pretty° traps to catch the petty thieves.   *clever*
While that the armèd hand doth fight abroad,
Th'advisèd° head defends itself at home.   *well-advised*
180 For government, though high and low and lower,[4]
Put into parts,[5] doth keep in one consent,°   *harmony*
Congreeing° in a full and natural close,°   *Coming together / cadence*
Like music.
CANTERBURY   True. Therefore doth heaven divide
The state of man in divers functions,
185 Setting endeavour in continual motion;
To which is fixèd, as an aim or butt,°   *target*
Obedience. For so work the honey-bees,
Creatures that by a rule in nature teach
The act of order to a peopled kingdom.
190 They have a king,[6] and officers of sorts,
Where some like magistrates correct at home;
Others like merchants venture trade abroad;
Others like soldiers, armèd in their stings,
Make boot upon° the summer's velvet buds,   *Plunder*
195 Which pillage they with merry march bring home
To the tent royal of their emperor,
Who busied in his majesty surveys
The singing masons building roofs of gold,
The civil citizens lading° up the honey,   *weighing*
200 The poor mechanic° porters crowding in   *menial*
Their heavy burdens at his narrow gate,
The sad-eyed justice with his surly hum
Delivering o'er to executors° pale   *executioners*
The lazy yawning drone. I this infer:
205 That many things, having full reference
To one consent,[7] may work contrariously.°   *disparately*

---

1. David II of Scotland, taken prisoner in 1346, when Edward III was in France; actually, he was imprisoned in London.
2. Incalculable riches.
3. Attame, or meddle with.
4. That is, composed of three social classes.
5. Divided into different functions.
6. The queen bee was thought to be male.
7. *having . . . consent:* united by a common purpose.

As many arrows, loosèd several ways,°   *from different places*
Fly to one mark, as many ways meet in one town,
As many fresh streams meet in one salt sea,
210   As many lines close in the dial's° centre,   *sundial's*
So may a thousand actions once afoot
End in one purpose, and be all well borne
Without defect. Therefore to France, my liege.
Divide your happy England into four,
215   Whereof take you one quarter into France,
And you withal shall make all Gallia° shake.   *France*
If we with thrice such powers left at home
Cannot defend our own doors from the dog,
Let us be worried,° and our nation lose   *savaged*
220   The name° of hardiness and policy.[8]   *reputation*
KING HARRY   Call in the messengers sent from the Dauphin.[9]
                                        [*Exit one or more*]
Now are we well resolved, and by God's help
And yours, the noble sinews of our power,
France being ours we'll bend it to our awe,°   *make it submit to us*
225   Or break it all to pieces. Or° there we'll sit,   *Either*
Ruling in large and ample empery°   *sovereignty*
O'er France and all her almost kingly dukedoms,
Or lay these bones in an unworthy urn,
Tombless, with no remembrance over them.
230   Either our history shall with full mouth
Speak freely of our acts, or else our grave,
Like Turkish mute,[1] shall have a tongueless mouth,
Not worshipped with a waxen epitaph.[2]
                Enter AMBASSADORS *of France* [*with a tun*]°   *chest; barrel*
Now are we well prepared to know the pleasure
235   Of our fair cousin Dauphin, for we hear
Your greeting is from him, not from the King.
AMBASSADOR   May't please your majesty to give us leave
Freely to render what we have in charge,
Or shall we sparingly show you far off[3]
240   The Dauphin's meaning and our embassy?
KING HARRY   We are no tyrant, but a Christian king,
Unto whose grace our passion is as subject
As is our wretches fettered in our prisons.
Therefore with frank and with uncurbèd plainness
Tell us the Dauphin's mind.
245   AMBASSADOR   Thus then in few:°   *short*
Your highness lately sending into France
Did claim some certain dukedoms, in the right
Of your great predecessor, King Edward the Third.
In answer of which claim, the Prince our master
250   Says that you savour° too much of your youth,   *show traces*
And bids you be advised, there's naught in France
That can be with a nimble galliard° won: *lively dance*
You cannot revel into dukedoms there.
He therefore sends you, meeter° for your spirit,   *more appropriate*

8. Political discernment.   and deprived of speech.
9. Title of the French heir apparent.   2. Not dignified with (even) a perishable memorial.
1. Turkish harem attendants were reportedly castrated   3. Show you in an abridged and roundabout way.

255   This tun of treasure, and in lieu of this
       Desires you let the dukedoms that you claim
       Hear no more of you. This the Dauphin speaks.
     KING HARRY What treasure, uncle?
     EXETER [*opening the tun*]   Tennis balls, my liege.
     KING HARRY We are glad the Dauphin is so pleasant° with us.   *jocular*
260   His present and your pains we thank you for.
       When we have matched our rackets to these balls,
       We will in France, by God's grace, play a set
       Shall strike his father's crown° into the hazard.[4]   *royal crown; coin*
       Tell him he hath made a match with such a wrangler
265   That all the courts of France will be disturbed
       With chases.[5] And we understand him well,
       How he comes o'er° us with our wilder days,   *taunts*
       Not measuring what use we made of them.
       We never valued this poor seat° of England,   *throne*
270   And therefore, living hence,° did give ourself   *away from court*
       To barbarous licence—as 'tis ever common
       That men are merriest when they are from home.
       But tell the Dauphin I will keep my state,°   *dignity; territory*
       Be like a king, and show my sail of greatness
275   When I do rouse me in° my throne of France.   *about*
       For that have I laid by my majesty
       And plodded like a man for working days,
       But I will rise there with so full a glory
       That I will dazzle all the eyes of France,
280   Yea strike the Dauphin blind to look on us.
       And tell the pleasant Prince this mock of his
       Hath turned his balls to gunstones,° and his soul   *cannonballs*
       Shall stand sore chargèd° for the wasteful vengeance   *heavily burdened*
       That shall fly from them—for many a thousand widows
285   Shall this his mock mock out of their dear husbands,
       Mock mothers from their sons, mock castles down;
       Ay, some are yet ungotten and unborn
       That shall have cause to curse the Dauphin's scorn.
       But this lies all within the will of God,
290   To whom I do appeal, and in whose name
       Tell you the Dauphin I am coming on
       To venge me° as I may, and to put forth   *avenge myself*
       My rightful hand in a well-hallowed cause.
       So get you hence in peace. And tell the Dauphin
295   His jest will savour but of shallow wit
       When thousands weep more than did laugh at it.—
       Convey them with safe conduct.—Fare you well.
                           Exeunt AMBASSADORS
     EXETER This was a merry message.
     KING HARRY We hope to make the sender blush at it.
300   Therefore, my lords, omit no happy hour
       That may give furth'rance to our expedition;
       For we have now no thought in us but France,
       Save those to God, that run before our business.

4. Jeopardy; aperture in the back wall of an Elizabethan tennis court.
5. Military pursuit; in tennis, second impact of a missed return, rated by its proximity to the back wall (a disputable point, hence "wrangler" in line 264).

Therefore let our proportions for these wars
305 Be soon collected, and all things thought upon
That may with reasonable swiftness add
More feathers to our wings; for, God before,[6]
We'll chide this Dauphin at his father's door.
Therefore let every man now task his thought,
310 That this fair action may on foot be brought.

Exeunt. Flourish

2.0

Enter CHORUS

CHORUS Now all the youth of England are on fire,
And silken° dalliance in the wardrobe lies;   *luxurious*
Now thrive the armourers, and honour's thought
Reigns solely in the breast of every man.
5 They sell the pasture now to buy the horse,
Following the mirror° of all Christian kings   *exemplar*
With wingèd heels, as English Mercuries.[1]
For now sits expectation in the air
And hides a sword from hilts unto the point
10 With crowns imperial, crowns° and coronets,   *titles; coins*
Promised to Harry and his followers.
The French, advised by good intelligence°   *espionage*
Of this most dreadful preparation,
Shake in their fear, and with pale policy°   *feeble intrigue*
15 Seek to divert the English purposes.
O England!—model° to thy inward greatness,   *small replica*
Like little body with a mighty heart,
What mightst thou do, that honour would thee do,
Were all thy children kind and natural?
20 But see, thy fault France hath in thee found out:
A nest of hollow[2] bosoms, which he fills
With treacherous crowns; and three corrupted men—
One, Richard, Earl of Cambridge; and the second
Henry, Lord Scrope of Masham; and the third
25 Sir Thomas Grey, knight, of Northumberland—
Have, for the gilt[3] of France—O guilt indeed!—
Confirmed conspiracy with fearful° France;   *frightened*
And by their hands this grace of kings must die,
If hell and treason hold° their promises,   *keep*
30 Ere he take ship for France, and in Southampton.
Linger your patience on, and we'll digest
Th'abuse of distance, force—perforce—a play.[4]
The sum is paid, the traitors are agreed,
The King is set from London, and the scene
35 Is now transported, gentles, to Southampton.
There is the playhouse now, there must you sit,
And thence to France shall we convey you safe,
And bring you back, charming the narrow seas
To give you gentle pass—for if we may
40 We'll not offend one stomach[5] with our play.

---

6. With God leading us; if God leads us.
2.0
1. Messenger of the gods; patron of thieves.
2. Hypocritical; empty (as receptacles for money).

3. Gold; gold leaf (suggesting superficiality).
4. *digest . . . play*: incorporate (and make acceptable) a violation of the unity of place, and stuff a play with events.
5. Offend anyone; make anyone seasick.

But till the King come forth, and not till then,
Unto Southampton do we shift our scene.   *Exit*

2.1

Enter Corporal NIM *and Lieutenant* BARDOLPH

BARDOLPH   Well met, Corporal Nim.

NIM   Good morrow, Lieutenant Bardolph.

BARDOLPH   What, are Ensign° Pistol and you friends yet?   *flag bearer*

NIM   For my part, I care not. I say little, but when time shall
5   serve, there shall be smiles—but that shall be as it may. I dare
    not fight, but I will wink° and hold out mine iron.° It is a simple   *close my eyes / sword*
    one, but what though?° It will toast cheese, and it will endure   *of that*
    cold, as another man's sword will—and there's an end.

BARDOLPH   I will bestow a breakfast to make you friends, and
10   we'll be all three sworn brothers to France. Let't be so, good
    Corporal Nim.

NIM   Faith, I will live so long as I may, that's the certain of it,
    and when I cannot live any longer, I will do as I may. That is
    my rest, that is the rendezvous° of it.   *last word?*

15 BARDOLPH   It is certain, corporal, that he is married to Nell
    Quickly, and certainly she did you wrong, for you were troth-
    plight° to her.   *betrothed*

NIM   I cannot tell. Things must be as they may. Men may sleep,
    and they may have their throats about them at that time, and
20   some say knives have edges. It must be as it may. Though
    Patience be a tired mare, yet she will plod. There must be
    conclusions. Well, I cannot tell.

Enter [Ensign] PISTOL *and* HOSTESS *Quickly*

BARDOLPH   Good morrow, Ensign Pistol.[1] *[To* NIM*]* Here comes
    Ensign Pistol and his wife. Good Corporal, be patient here.

25 NIM   How now, mine host° Pistol?   *tavern keeper; pimp*

PISTOL   Base tick, call'st thou me host? Now by Gad's lugs°   *God's ears*
    I swear I scorn the term. Nor shall my Nell keep lodgers.

HOSTESS   No, by my troth, not long, for we cannot lodge and
    board a dozen or fourteen gentlewomen that live honestly by
30   the prick° of their needles, but it will be thought we keep a   *(unwittingly obscene)*
    bawdy-house straight.

*[*NIM *draws his sword]*

    O well-a-day,° Lady![2] If he be not hewn now, we shall see wilful   *alas*
    adultery° and murder committed.   *(for "assault")*

*[*PISTOL *draws his sword]*

BARDOLPH   Good lieutenant, good corporal, offer nothing° here.   *don't fight*

35 NIM   Pish.

PISTOL   Pish for thee, Iceland dog.° Thou prick-eared cur of   *small, hairy breed*
    Iceland.

HOSTESS   Good Corporal Nim, show thy valour, and put up°   *away*
    your sword.

[They sheathe their swords]

NIM   Will you shog off?° I would have you *solus.*[3]   *move along*

40 PISTOL   '*Solus*', egregious dog? O viper vile!
    The *solus* in thy most marvellous face,

2.1 Location: Eastcheap, a slum section of London, site
of the tavern scenes in *1* and *2 Henry IV*. Bardolph, Pistol,
and Hostess Quickly were featured in the *Henry IV* plays;
Nim (slang for "thief") is a new character.

1. Sixteenth-century pistols were notoriously noisy and
inaccurate.
2. By our Lady, a mild oath.
3. Alone; unmarried.

The *solus* in thy teeth, and in thy throat,
And in thy hateful lungs, yea in thy maw pardie[4]—
And which is worse, within thy nasty mouth.
45 I do retort° the *solus* in thy bowels,   send back
For I can take,° and Pistol's cock is up,[5]   take fire; strike
And flashing fire will follow.
NIM   I am not Barbason,° you cannot conjure me.[6] I have an   (the name of a devil)
humour° to knock you indifferently well. If you grow foul with   inclination
50 me, Pistol, I will scour you with my rapier, as I may, in fair
terms.° If you would walk off, I would prick your guts a little,   pretty thoroughly
in good terms, as I may, and that's the humour of it.
PISTOL   O braggart vile, and damnèd furious wight!°   creature
The grave doth gape and doting death is near.
55 Therefore ex-hale.°   draw (your sword)
          [PISTOL *and* NIM] *draw* [*their swords*]
BARDOLPH   Hear me, hear me what I say.
          [*He draws his sword*]
He that strikes the first stroke, I'll run him up to the hilts, as I
am a soldier.
PISTOL   An oath of mickle° might, and fury shall abate.   great
          [*They sheathe their swords*]
60 [*To* NIM] Give me thy fist,° thy forefoot to me give.   (i.e., hand)
Thy spirits are most tall.°   valiant
NIM   I will cut thy throat one time or other, in fair terms, that is
the humour of it.
PISTOL   *Couple a gorge,*[7]
65 That is the word. I thee defy again.
O hound of Crete, think'st thou my spouse to get?
No, to the spital[8] go,
And from the powd'ring tub[9] of infamy
Fetch forth the lazar kite of Cressid's kind,[1]
70 Doll Tearsheet[2] she by name, and her espouse.
I have, and I will hold, the quondam° Quickly   former
For the only she, and—*pauca,*° there's enough. Go to.   few (words)
          Enter the BOY [*running*]
BOY   Mine host Pistol, you must come to my master,° and you,   (Sir John Falstaff)
hostess. He is very sick, and would to bed.— Good Bardolph,
75 put thy face between his sheets, and do the office of a warming-
pan.[3]—Faith, he's very ill.
BARDOLPH   Away, you rogue!
HOSTESS   By my troth, he'll yield the crow a pudding[4] one of
these days. The King has killed his heart.[5] Good husband,
80 come home presently.°   *Exit* [*with* BOY]   right away
BARDOLPH   Come, shall I make you two friends? We must to
France together. Why the devil should we keep knives to cut
one another's throats?
PISTOL   Let floods o'erswell,[6] and fiends for food howl on!
85 NIM   You'll pay me the eight shillings I won of you at betting?

---

4. *in thy maw pardie*: in your stomach, indeed (old-fashioned).
5. Pistol's trigger is cocked (unwittingly obscene).
6. Frighten me with big words.
7. Corrupt French for "Cut the throat."
8. Hospital; in Elizabethan times, a filthy, disease-ridden place occupied by indigents near death.
9. Sweat bath, used in treating syphilis.

1. The diseased, scavenging whore (Cressida, a faithless Trojan woman, was a pattern of female wickedness).
2. A prostitute who appears in 2 *Henry IV*.
3. Referring to Bardolph's "fiery" complexion.
4. He'll feed the crows (after his death).
5. By rejecting him, in the last scene of 2 *Henry IV*.
6. Let destruction reign (perhaps an unidentified quotation).

PISTOL   Base is the slave that pays.

NIM   That now I will have. That's the humour of it.

PISTOL   As manhood shall compound.° Push home.   *valor will determine*

[PISTOL *and* NIM] *draw* [*their swords*]

BARDOLPH [*drawing his sword*]   By this sword, he that makes the
90   first thrust, I'll kill him. By this sword, I will.

PISTOL   Sword is an oath,[7] and oaths must have their course.

[*He sheathes his sword*]

BARDOLPH   Corporal Nim, an° thou wilt be friends, be friends.   *if*
An thou wilt not, why then be enemies with me too. Prithee,
put up.

95   NIM   I shall have my eight shillings?

PISTOL   A noble° shalt thou have, and present pay,[8]   *6 shillings 8 pence*
And liquor likewise will I give to thee,
And friendship shall combine, and brotherhood.
I'll live by Nim, and Nim shall live by me.
100   Is not this just? For I shall sutler[9] be
Unto the camp, and profits will accrue.
Give me thy hand.

NIM   I shall have my noble?

PISTOL   In cash, most justly paid.

105   NIM   Well then, that's the humour of't.

[NIM *and* BARDOLPH *sheathe their swords*]
Enter HOSTESS [*Quickly*]

HOSTESS   As ever you come of women, come in quickly to Sir
John. Ah, poor heart, he is so shaked of a burning quotidian-
tertian,[1] that it is most lamentable to behold. Sweet men, come
to him.   [*Exit*]

110   NIM   The King hath run bad humours on° the knight, that's the   *shows ill will toward*
even° of it.   *truth*

PISTOL   Nim, thou hast spoke the right.
His heart is fracted° and corroborate.[2]   *broken*

NIM   The King is a good king, but it must be as it may. He passes
115   some humours and careers.°   *behaves strangely*

PISTOL   Let us condole° the knight—for, lambkins, we will live.   *console*
                    Exeunt

2.2

Enter [*Duke of*] EXETER, [*Duke of* GLOUCESTER,] *and*
[*Earl of*] WESTMORLAND

GLOUCESTER   Fore God, his grace is bold to trust these traitors.

EXETER   They shall be apprehended by and by.

WESTMORLAND   How smooth and even they do bear themselves,
As if allegiance in their bosoms sat,
5   Crownèd with faith and constant loyalty.

GLOUCESTER   The King hath note of all that they intend,
By interception which they dream not of.

EXETER   Nay, but the man that was his bedfellow,[1]
Whom he hath dulled and cloyed° with gracious favours—   *tired and sated*
10   That he should for a foreign purse so sell
His sovereign's life to death and treachery.

---

7. Punning on "'s word," by God's word.
8. And immediate payment.
9. Seller of provisions (notoriously dishonest).
1. Dangerous fever (the Hostess conflates quotidian fever,
which recurs daily, with tertian fever, which recurs every

third day).
2. Confirmed (error for "corrupted").
2.2 Location: Southampton, a port in the south of
England.
1. It was common for men to share a bed.

Sound trumpets. Enter KING [HARRY, *Lord*] SCROPE,
[*Earl of*] CAMBRIDGE, *and* [*Sir Thomas*] GREY

KING HARRY   Now sits the wind fair, and we will aboard.
My lord of Cambridge, and my kind lord of Masham,
And you, my gentle knight, give me your thoughts.

15 Think you not that the powers we bear with us
Will cut their passage through the force of France,
Doing the execution° and the act   destruction
For which we have in head° assembled them?   an army

SCROPE   No doubt, my liege, if each man do his best.

20 KING HARRY   I doubt not that, since we are well persuaded
We carry not a heart with us from hence
That grows not in a fair consent with ours,
Nor leave not one behind that doth not wish
Success and conquest to attend on us.

25 CAMBRIDGE   Never was monarch better feared and loved
Than is your majesty. There's not, I think, a subject
That sits in heart-grief and uneasiness
Under the sweet shade of your government.

GREY   True. Those that were your father's enemies

30 Have steeped their galls° in honey, and do serve you   bitterness
With hearts create of duty and of zeal.

KING HARRY   We therefore have great cause of thankfulness,
And shall forget the office° of our hand   use
Sooner than quittance° of desert and merit,   payment

35 According to their weight and worthiness.

SCROPE   So service shall with steelèd sinews toil,
And labour shall refresh itself with hope,
To do your grace incessant services.

KING HARRY   We judge no less.—Uncle of Exeter,

40 Enlarge° the man committed° yesterday   Release / imprisoned
That railed against our person. We consider
It was excess of wine that set him on,
And on his more advice° we pardon him.   sober reconsideration

SCROPE   That's mercy, but too much security.°   complacency

45 Let him be punished, sovereign, lest example
Breed, by his sufferance,° more of such a kind.   by pardoning him

KING HARRY   O let us yet be merciful.

CAMBRIDGE   So may your highness, and yet punish too.

GREY   Sir, you show great mercy if you give him life,

50 After the taste of much correction.

KING HARRY   Alas, your too much love and care of me
Are heavy orisons° 'gainst this poor wretch.   weighty pleas
If little faults proceeding on distemper°   from drunkenness
Shall not be winked at,° how shall we stretch our eye   overlooked

55 When capital crimes, chewed, swallowed, and digested,[2]
Appear before us? We'll yet° enlarge that man,   nonetheless
Though Cambridge, Scrope, and Grey, in their dear° care   loving
And tender preservation of our person,
Would have him punished. And now to our French causes.
Who are the late[3] commissioners?

60 CAMBRIDGE   I one, my lord.
Your highness bade me ask for it° today.   (the commission)

---

2. That is, crimes thoroughly premeditated.   3. Newly appointed (to govern during Henry's absence).

SCROPE   So did you me, my liege.

GREY   And I, my royal sovereign.

KING HARRY   Then Richard, Earl of Cambridge, there is yours;
    There yours, Lord Scrope of Masham, and sir knight,
65 Grey of Northumberland, this same is yours.
    Read them, and know I know your worthiness.—
    My lord of Westmorland, and Uncle Exeter,
    We will aboard tonight.—Why, how now, gentlemen?
    What see you in those papers, that you lose
70 So much complexion?—Look ye how they change:
    Their cheeks are paper.—Why, what read you there
    That have so cowarded and chased your blood
    Out of appearance?°   *sight*

CAMBRIDGE   I do confess my fault,
    And do submit me to your highness' mercy.

75 GREY *and* SCROPE   To which we all appeal.

KING HARRY   The mercy that was quick° in us but late   *alive*
    By your own counsel is suppressed and killed.
    You must not dare, for shame, to talk of mercy,
    For your own reasons turn into your bosoms,
80 As dogs upon their masters, worrying° you.—   *tearing*
    See you, my princes and my noble peers,
    These English monsters?[4] My lord of Cambridge here,
    You know how apt our love was to accord°   *agree*
    To furnish him with all appurtenants°   *privileges*
85 Belonging to his honour; and this vile man
    Hath for a few light crowns lightly conspired
    And sworn unto the practices° of France   *plots*
    To kill us here in Hampton. To the which
    This knight,° no less for bounty bound to us   *(Grey)*
90 Than Cambridge is, hath likewise sworn. But O
    What shall I say to thee, Lord Scrope, thou cruel,
    Ingrateful, savage, and inhuman creature?
    Thou that didst bear the key of all my counsels,
    That knew'st the very bottom of my soul,
95 That almost mightst ha' coined me into gold
    Wouldst thou ha' practised on° me for thy use: *conspired against*
    May it be possible that foreign hire
    Could out of thee extract one spark of evil
    That might annoy my finger? 'Tis so strange
100 That though the truth of it stands off as gross°   *clearly*
    As black on white, my eye will scarcely see it.
    Treason and murder ever kept together,
    As two yoke-devils sworn to either's purpose,
    Working so grossly in a natural° cause   *(for devils)*
105 That admiration° did not whoop° at them;   *astonishment / cry out*
    But thou, 'gainst all proportion,° didst bring in   *natural order*
    Wonder to wait on° treason and on murder.   *consort with*
    And whatsoever cunning fiend it was
    That wrought upon thee so preposterously°   *unnaturally*
110 Hath got the voice° in hell for excellence.   *vote*
    And other devils that suggest° by treasons   *seduce*
    Do botch and bungle up° damnation   *clumsily conceal*

---

4. "Monsters" were usually imported freaks.

With patches, colours,° and with forms, being fetched°   *pretexts / derived*
From glist'ring semblances of piety;
115   But he that tempered° thee, bade thee stand up,°   *molded / rebel*
Gave thee no instance° why thou shouldst do treason,   *motive*
Unless to dub thee with the name⁵ of traitor.
If that same demon that hath gulled° thee thus   *duped*
Should with his lion gait walk the whole world,
120   He might return to vasty Tartar° back   *to huge hell*
And tell the legions,° 'I can never win   *armies of devils*
A soul so easy as that Englishman's.'
O how hast thou with jealousy° infected   *suspicion*
The sweetness of affiance.° Show men dutiful?   *trust*
125   Why so didst thou. Seem they grave and learned?
Why so didst thou. Come they of noble family?
Why so didst thou. Seem they religious?
Why so didst thou. Or are they spare in diet,
Free from gross passion, or° of mirth or anger,   *either*
130   Constant in spirit, not swerving with the blood,°   *passion*
Garnished and decked in modest complement,°   *appearance*
Not working with the eye without the ear,
And but in purgèd° judgement trusting neither?   *purified*
Such, and so finely boulted,° didst thou seem.   *sifted*
135   And thus thy fall hath left a kind of blot
To mark the full-fraught° man, and best endowed,   *packed (with excellences)*
With some suspicion. I will weep for thee,
For this revolt of thine methinks is like
Another fall of man.—Their faults are open.°   *obvious*
140   Arrest them to the answer of the law,
And God acquit them of their practices.
EXETER   I arrest thee of high treason, by the name of Richard,
Earl of Cambridge.— I arrest thee of high treason, by the name
of Henry, Lord Scrope of Masham.— I arrest thee of high trea-
145   son, by the name of Thomas Grey, knight, of Northumberland.
SCROPE   Our purposes God justly hath discovered,°   *revealed*
And I repent my fault more than my death,
Which I beseech your highness to forgive
Although my body pay the price of it.
150   CAMBRIDGE   For me, the gold of France did not seduce,
Although I did admit it as a motive
The sooner to effect what I intended.⁶
But God be thankèd for prevention,
Which heartily in sufferance° will rejoice,   *suffering punishment*
155   Beseeching God and you to pardon me.
GREY   Never did faithful subject more rejoice
At the discovery of most dangerous treason
Than I do at this hour joy o'er myself,
Prevented from a damnèd enterprise.
160   My fault, but not my body, pardon, sovereign.
KING HARRY   God 'quit° you in his mercy. Hear your sentence.   *acquit*
You have conspired against our royal person,
Joined with an enemy proclaimed and fixed,

---

5. To knight you with the title.
6. The Earl of Cambridge was heir of Edmund Mortimer
through his wife, Edmund's sister, and Mortimer arguably

had a better claim to the English throne than did Henry
himself. Henry's adherence to a principle of inheritance
"through the female line" is hardly absolute.

And from his coffers
165 Received the golden earnest of° our death,   *advance payment for*
Wherein you would have sold your king to slaughter,
His princes and his peers to servitude,
His subjects to oppression and contempt,
And his whole kingdom into desolation.
170 Touching our person seek we no revenge,
But we our kingdom's safety must so tender,°   *regard*
Whose ruin you have sought, that to her laws
We do deliver you. Get ye therefore hence,
Poor miserable wretches, to your death;
175 The taste whereof, God of his mercy give
You patience to endure, and true repentance
Of all your dear° offences. — Bear them hence.   *grievous*
                    Exeunt [the traitors, guarded]
Now lords for France, the enterprise whereof
Shall be to you, as us, like° glorious.   *equally*
180 We doubt not of a fair and lucky war,
Since God so graciously hath brought to light
This dangerous treason lurking in our way
To hinder our beginnings. We doubt not now
But every rub° is smoothèd on our way.   *obstacle*
185 Then forth, dear countrymen. Let us deliver
Our puissance° into the hand of God,   *power*
Putting it straight in expedition.°   *at once in action*
Cheerly to sea, the signs° of war advance: *flags*
No king of England, if not king of France.   *Flourish. Exeunt*

2.3

Enter [Ensign] PISTOL, *[Corporal]* NIM, *[Lieutenant]*
BARDOLPH, BOY, *and* HOSTESS *[Quickly]*
HOSTESS   Prithee, honey, sweet husband, let me bring° thee to   *accompany*
    Staines.[1]
PISTOL   No, for my manly heart doth erne.° Bardolph,   *grieve*
    Be blithe; Nim, rouse thy vaunting veins; boy, bristle
5   Thy courage up. For Falstaff he is dead,
    And we must erne therefore.
BARDOLPH   Would I were with him, wheresome'er he is, either
    in heaven or in hell.
HOSTESS   Nay, sure he's not in hell. He's in Arthur's bosom,[2] if
10 ever man went to Arthur's bosom. A° made a finer end, and   *He*
    went away an° it had been any christom[3] child. A parted ev'n *as if*
    just between twelve and one, ev'n at the turning o'th' tide—for
    after I saw him fumble with the sheets, and play with flowers,° *(on the bedclothes)*
    and smile upon his finger's end, I knew there was but one way.
15 For his nose was as sharp as a pen, and a babbled of green
    fields.[4] 'How now, Sir John?' quoth I. 'What, man! Be o' good
    cheer.' So a cried out, 'God, God, God', three or four times.
    Now I, to comfort him, bid him a should not think of God; I
    hoped there was no need to trouble himself with any such

2.3 Location: Eastcheap.
1. Town on the road to Southampton.
2. Mistake for "Abraham's bosom," heaven.
3. Error for "chrisom," just christened.
4. Falstaff was reciting the Twenty-third Psalm ("The

Lord is my shepherd"), but Hostess Quickly does not recognize it. The text is corrupt at this point, reading "a
Table of green fields," and was corrected by the eighteenth-century editor Louis Theobald in a famous emendation.

20   thoughts yet. So a bade me lay more clothes on his feet. I put
      my hand into the bed and felt them, and they were as cold as
      any stone. Then I felt to his knees, and so up'ard and up'ard,
      and all was as cold as any stone.
      NIM   They say he cried out of sack.[5]
25   HOSTESS   Ay, that a did.
      BARDOLPH   And of women.
      HOSTESS   Nay, that a did not.
      BOY   Yes, that a did, and said they were devils incarnate.
      HOSTESS   A could never abide carnation, 'twas a colour he never
30   liked.
      BOY   A said once the devil would have him about women.
      HOSTESS   A did in some sort, indeed, handle° women — but then   *discuss*
      he was rheumatic,[6] and talked of the Whore of Babylon.[7]
      BOY   Do you not remember, a saw a flea stick upon Bardolph's
35   nose, and a said it was a black soul burning in hell-fire.
      BARDOLPH   Well, the fuel[8] is gone that maintained that fire.
      That's all the riches I got in his service.
      NIM   Shall we shog? The King will be gone from Southampton.
      PISTOL   Come, let's away. — My love, give me thy lips.
            [*He kisses her*]
40   Look to my chattels and my movables.°   *personal property*
      Let senses rule. The word is 'Pitch and pay'.°   *Cash down, no credit*
      Trust none, for oaths are straws, men's faiths are wafer-cakes,°   *fragile*
      And Holdfast is the only dog,[9] my duck.°   *darling*
      Therefore *caveto*° be thy counsellor.   *beware*
45   Go, clear thy crystals.° — Yokefellows in arms,   *wipe your eyes*
      Let us to France, like horseleeches, my boys,
      To suck, to suck, the very blood to suck!
      BOY [*aside*]   And that's but unwholesome food, they say.
      PISTOL   Touch her soft mouth, and march.
50   BARDOLPH   Farewell, hostess.
            [*He kisses her*]
      NIM   I cannot kiss, that is the humour of it, but adieu.
      PISTOL [*to* HOSTESS]   Let housewifery appear. Keep close,° I   *Stay indoors; be thrifty*
      thee command.
      HOSTESS   Farewell! Adieu!   *Exeunt* [*severally*]°   *separately*

2.4

Flourish. Enter KING [CHARLES *the Sixth of France*], *the*
DAUPHIN, [*the* CONSTABLE,] *and the Dukes of* BERRI *and*
[BOURBON]
KING CHARLES   Thus comes the English with full power upon us,
      And more than carefully it us concerns
      To answer royally in our defences.
      Therefore the Dukes of Berri and of Bourbon,
5   Of Brabant and of Orléans shall make forth,
      And you Prince Dauphin, with all swift dispatch
      To line° and new-repair our towns of war   *garrison*

---

5. *of sack*: against wine, formerly one of Falstaff's great
indulgences.
6. Error for "lunatic," delirious.
7. The scarlet woman of Revelation, identified by Protestants with the Catholic Church.

8. That is, Falstaff's liquor.
9. Alluding to the proverb "Brag is a good dog, but Hold-
fast is better."
2.4 Location: France, where the remainder of the play
takes place. The King's court at Rouen.

With men of courage and with means defendant.°   *of defense*
For England° his approaches makes as fierce   *the King of England*
10 As waters to the sucking of a gulf.°   *whirlpool*
It fits us then to be as provident
As fear may teach us, out of late° examples   *recent*
Left by the fatal and neglected[1] English
Upon our fields.
DAUPHIN   My most redoubted° father,   *formidable*
15 It is most meet° we arm us 'gainst the foe,   *proper*
For peace itself should not so dull a kingdom—
Though war, nor no known quarrel, were in question—
But that defences, musters, preparations
Should be maintained, assembled, and collected
20 As° were a war in expectation.   *As if*
Therefore, I say, 'tis meet we all go forth
To view the sick and feeble parts of France.
And let us do it with no show of fear,
No, with no more than if we heard that England
25 Were busied with a Whitsun morris dance[2]
For, my good liege, she is so idly° kinged,   *frivolously*
Her sceptre so fantastically° borne   *irrationally*
By a vain, giddy, shallow, humorous° youth,   *capricious*
That fear attends her not.
CONSTABLE   O peace, Prince Dauphin.
30 You are too much mistaken in this king.
Question your grace the late° ambassadors   *recent*
With what great state he heard their embassy,
How well supplied with agèd counsellors,
How modest in exception,° and withal   *objecting*
35 How terrible° in constant resolution,   *fearsome*
And you shall find his vanities forespent°   *his former follies*
Were but the outside of the Roman Brutus,[3]
Covering discretion with a coat of folly,
As gardeners do with ordure° hide those roots   *manure*
40 That shall first spring and be most delicate.
DAUPHIN Well, 'tis not so, my Lord High Constable.
But though° we think it so, it is no matter.   *if*
In cases of defence 'tis best to weigh°   *consider*
The enemy more mighty than he seems.
45 So the proportions of defence are filled[4]—
Which, of a weak and niggardly projection,°   *scale*
Doth like a miser spoil his coat with scanting°   *skimping*
A little cloth.
KING CHARLES Think we King Harry strong.
And princes, look you strongly arm to meet him.
50 The kindred of him hath been fleshed[5] upon us,
And he is bred out of that bloody strain
That haunted us in our familiar paths.
Witness our too-much-memorable shame

1. The fatally underestimated, at the Battles of Crécy (1346) and Poitiers (1356).
2. Folk dance celebrating Whitsuntide, a summer holiday.
3. Lucius Junius Brutus pretended idiocy to disarm the tyrant Tarquinius Superbus, against whom he led a successful revolt.
4. A proper defense is mounted.
5. Have been given their first taste of blood.

When Crécy battle fatally was struck,°   *fought*

55 And all our princes captived by the hand
Of that black name, Edward, Black Prince of Wales,
Whiles that his mountant° sire, on mountain standing,   *ascendant*
Up in the air, crowned with the golden sun,
Saw his heroical seed and smiled to see him

60 Mangle the work of nature and deface
The patterns that by God and by French fathers
Had twenty years been made. This is a stem
Of that victorious stock, and let us fear
The native° mightiness and fate° of him.   *hereditary / fortune*

    Enter a MESSENGER

65 MESSENGER   Ambassadors from Harry, King of England,
Do crave admittance to your majesty.
KING CHARLES   We'll give them present audience. Go and bring them.
                           [*Exit* MESSENGER]
You see this chase is hotly followed, friends.
DAUPHIN   Turn head[6] and stop pursuit. For coward dogs

70 Most spend their mouths° when what they seem to threaten   *bark the loudest*
Runs far before them. Good my sovereign,
Take up the English short, and let them know
Of what a monarchy you are the head.
Self-love, my liege, is not so vile a sin
As self-neglecting.

    Enter [*Duke of*] EXETER [*attended*]

75 KING CHARLES   From our brother England?
EXETER   From him, and thus he greets your majesty:
He wills you, in the name of God Almighty,
That you divest yourself and lay apart°   *aside*
The borrowed glories that by gift of heaven,

80 By law of nature and of nations, 'longs°   *belongs*
To him and to his heirs, namely the crown,
And all wide-stretchèd honours that pertain
By custom and the ordinance of times°   *laws of ages*
Unto the crown of France. That you may know

85 'Tis no sinister° nor no awkward° claim,   *illegitimate / oblique*
Picked from the worm-holes of long-vanished days,
Nor from the dust of old oblivion raked,
He sends you this most memorable line,°   *pedigree*
In every branch truly demonstrative,°   *conclusive*

90 Willing you over-look° this pedigree,   *Wishing you to look over*
And when you find him evenly derived°   *directly descended*
From his most famed of famous ancestors,
Edward the Third, he bids you then resign
Your crown and kingdom, indirectly° held   *unjustly*

95 From him, the native and true challenger.°   *claimant*
KING CHARLES   Or else what follows?
EXETER   Bloody constraint. For if you hide the crown
Even in your hearts, there will he rake for it.
Therefore in fierce tempest is he coming,

100 In thunder and in earthquake, like a Jove,
That if requiring° fail, he will compel;   *requesting*

---

6. Make a stand (a hunting term).

And bids you, in the bowels° of the Lord,   *compassion*
Deliver up the crown, and to take mercy
On the poor souls for whom this hungry war
105 Opens his vasty jaws; and on your head
Turns he the widows' tears, the orphans' cries,
The dead men's blood, the pining maidens' groans,
For husbands, fathers, and betrothèd lovers
That shall be swallowed in this controversy.
110 This is his claim, his threat'ning, and my message —
Unless the Dauphin be in presence here,
To whom expressly I bring greeting too.
KING CHARLES For us, we will consider of this further.
Tomorrow shall you bear our full intent
Back to our brother England.
115 DAUPHIN   For the Dauphin,
I stand here for him. What to him from England?
EXETER Scorn and defiance, slight regard, contempt;
And anything that may not misbecome
The mighty sender, doth he prize° you at.   *assess*
120 Thus says my king: an if° your father's highness *an if = if*
Do not, in grant° of all demands at large,° *concession / in full*
Sweeten the bitter mock you sent his majesty,
He'll call you to so hot an answer for it
That caves and womby vaultages° of France   *hollow caverns*
125 Shall chide your trespass and return your mock
In second accent° of his ordinance.°   *echo / artillery*
DAUPHIN Say if my father render fair return
It is against my will, for I desire
Nothing but odds° with England. To that end,   *strife*
130 As matching to his youth and vanity,°   *frivolity*
I did present him with the Paris° balls.   *tennis*
EXETER He'll make your Paris Louvre° shake for it, *French royal palace*
Were it the mistress° court of mighty Europe. *principal (in tennis)*
And be assured, you'll find a diff'rence,
135 As we his subjects have in wonder found,
Between the promise of his greener° days   *younger*
And these he masters now: now he weighs time
Even to the utmost grain.° That you shall read *smallest unit*
In your own losses, if he stay in France.
140 KING CHARLES [*rising*] Tomorrow shall you know our mind at full.
    Flourish[7]
EXETER Dispatch us with all speed, lest that our king
Come here himself to question our delay —
For he is footed° in this land already.   *come ashore*
KING CHARLES You shall be soon dispatched with fair conditions.
145 A night is but small breath° and little pause   *small time*
To answer matters of this consequence. *Exeunt. Flourish*

7. Fanfare (to signal the end of the interview; Exeter unceremoniously continues).

3.0

Enter CHORUS

CHORUS   Thus with imagined wing° our swift scene flies   *wings of imagination*
In motion of no less celerity
Than that of thought. Suppose that you have seen
The well-appointed° king at Dover pier   *well-equipped*
5   Embark his royalty, and his brave fleet
With silken streamers the young Phoebus fanning.¹
Play with your fancies,° and in them behold   *imagination*
Upon the hempen tackle ship-boys climbing;
Hear the shrill whistle,° which doth order give   *(of the ship's captain)*
10   To sounds confused; behold the threaden° sails,   *woven of thread*
Borne with th'invisible and creeping wind,
Draw the huge bottoms° through the furrowed sea,   *hulls*
Breasting the lofty surge. O do but think
You stand upon the rivage° and behold   *shore*
15   A city on th'inconstant billows dancing—
For so appears this fleet majestical,
Holding due course to Harfleur.² Follow, follow!
Grapple° your minds to sternage° of this navy,   *Fasten / the sterns*
And leave your England, as dead midnight still,
20   Guarded with grandsires, babies, and old women,
Either past or not arrived to pith° and puissance.   *strength*
For who is he, whose chin is but enriched
With one appearing hair, that will not follow
These culled° and choice-drawn cavaliers to France?   *select*
25   Work, work your thoughts, and therein see a siege.
Behold the ordnance° on their carriages,   *cannons*
With fatal mouths gaping on girded° Harfleur.   *encircled*
Suppose th'ambassador from the French comes back,
Tells Harry that the King doth offer him
30   Catherine his daughter, and with her, to° dowry,   *as*
Some petty and unprofitable dukedoms.
The offer likes° not, and the nimble gunner   *pleases*
With linstock° now the devilish cannon touches,   *lighting stick*
       Alarum, and chambers° go off   *small cannon*
And down goes all before them. Still be kind,
35   And eke out our performance with your mind.   *Exit*

3.1

Alarum. Enter KING [HARRY *and the English army, with*]
scaling ladders

KING HARRY   Once more unto the breach,¹ dear friends, once more,
Or close the wall up with our English dead.
In peace there's nothing so becomes a man
As modest stillness and humility,
5   But when the blast of war blows in our ears,
Then imitate the action of the tiger.
Stiffen the sinews, conjure up the blood,
Disguise fair nature with hard-favoured rage.
Then lend the eye a terrible aspect,

3.0
1. *the . . . fanning*: fluttering toward the rising sun.
2. French port on the mouth of the Seine.

3.1 Location: Before Harfleur.
1. Gap in the fortifications, created by artillery bombard-ment.

10	Let it pry° through the portage² of the head	*peer*
	Like the brass cannon, let the brow o'erwhelm° it	*overhang*
	As fearfully as doth a gallèd° rock	*worn*
	O'erhang and jutty° his confounded° base,	*jut out over / ruined*
	Swilled° with the wild and wasteful° ocean.	*Washed / destructive*
15	Now set the teeth and stretch the nostril wide,	
	Hold hard the breath, and bend up every spirit	
	To his full height. On, on, you noblest English,	
	Whose blood is fet° from fathers of war-proof,°	*fetched / proven in war*
	Fathers that like so many Alexanders³	
20	Have in these parts from morn till even fought,	
	And sheathed their swords for lack of argument.°	*opposition*
	Dishonour not your mothers; now attest	
	That those whom you called fathers did beget you.	
	Be copy° now to men of grosser° blood,	*example / less noble*
25	And teach them how to war. And you, good yeomen,°	*men below noble rank*
	Whose limbs were made in England, show us here	
	The mettle° of your pasture; let us swear	*quality*
	That you are worth your breeding—which I doubt not,	
	For there is none of you so mean and base	
30	That hath not noble lustre in your eyes.	
	I see you stand like greyhounds in the slips,°	*leashes*
	Straining upon the start. The game's afoot.	
	Follow your spirit, and upon this charge	
	Cry, 'God for Harry! England and Saint George!'°	*patron saint of England*

Alarum, and chambers go off. [Exeunt]

3.2

Enter NIM, BARDOLPH, *[Ensign]* PISTOL, *and* BOY

(margin note, handwritten: undercuts the overblown rhetoric)

BARDOLPH   On, on, on, on, on! To the breach, to the breach!

NIM   Pray thee corporal, stay. The knocks are too hot, and for

mine own part I have not a case° of lives. The humour of it is   *set*

too hot, that is the very plainsong° of it.   *plain truth*

5   PISTOL   'The plainsong' is most just,° for humours do abound.   *apt*

Knocks go and come, God's vassals drop and die,

[*sings*]   And sword and shield

In bloody field

Doth win immortal fame.

10   BOY   Would I were in an alehouse in London. I would give all

my fame for a pot of ale, and safety.

PISTOL [*sings*]   And I.

If wishes would prevail with me°   *in my case*

My purpose should not fail with me

15   But thither would I hie.°   *go*

BOY [*sings*]   As duly

But not as truly

As bird doth sing on bough.

Enter [Captain] FLUELLEN *and beats them in*

FLUELLEN   God's plud!¹ Up to the breaches, you dogs! Avaunt,

20   you cullions!²

PISTOL   Be merciful, great duke, to men of mould.³

---

2. Portholes (that is, eye sockets).
3. Alexander the Great complained because no worlds remained for him to conquer.
3.2 Scene continues.

1. Blood (Fluellen's Welsh accent substitutes "p" for "b," and also "f" for "v" and "ch" for "j").
2. Be off, you wretches. *cullions:* testicles.
3. Earth (that is, mortal men).

Abate thy rage, abate thy manly rage,
Abate thy rage, great duke. Good bawcock,[4] bate
Thy rage. Use lenity,° sweet chuck.   *leniency*
25 NIM   These be good humours![5]
     [FLUELLEN *begins to beat* NIM]
Your honour runs bad humours.°   *Exeunt [all but the* BOY]   *is ill-tempered*
BOY   As young as I am, I have observed these three swashers.° I   *swashbucklers*
am boy to them all three, but all they three, though they should
serve me, could not be man[6] to me, for indeed three such
30 antics° do not amount to a man. For Bardolph, he is white-   *buffoons*
livered° and red-faced—by the means whereof a° faces it out,   *cowardly / he*
but fights not. For Pistol, he hath a killing tongue and a quiet
sword—by the means whereof a breaks words, and keeps whole
weapons. For Nim, he hath heard that men of few words are
35 the best men, and therefore he scorns to say his prayers, lest a
should be thought a coward. But his few bad words are
matched with as few good deeds—for a never broke any man's
head but his own, and that was against a post, when he was
drunk. They will steal anything, and call it 'purchase'.[7] Bar-
40 dolph stole a lute case, bore it twelve leagues,° and sold it for   *about 36 miles*
three halfpence. Nim and Bardolph are sworn brothers in
filching,° and in Calais[8] they stole a fire shovel. I knew by that   *stealing*
piece of service the men would carry coals.[9] They would have
me as familiar with men's pockets as their gloves or their hand-
45 kerchiefs—which makes° much against my manhood, if I   *offends*
should take from another's pocket to put into mine, for it is
plain pocketing up of wrongs.[1] I must leave them, and seek
some better service. Their villainy goes against my weak stomach, and therefore I must cast it up.°   *Exit*   *vomit it; leave it*

3.3

Enter [Captain] GOWER *[and Captain* FLUELLEN,
meeting]

GOWER   Captain Fluellen, you must come presently° to the   *immediately*
mines.[1] The Duke of Gloucester would speak with you.
FLUELLEN   To the mines? Tell you the Duke it is not so good to
come to the mines. For look you, the mines is not according to
5 the disciplines° of the war. The concavities° of it is not suffi-   *tactics, art / depth*
cient. For look you, th'athversary, you may discuss unto the
Duke, look you, is digt° himself, four yard under, the count-   *digged (dug)*
ermines.[2] By Cheshu,° I think a will plow° up all, if there is not   *Jesu / blow*
better directions.
10 GOWER   The Duke of Gloucester, to whom the order° of the   *supervision*
siege is given, is altogether directed by an Irishman, a very valiant gentleman, i'faith.
FLUELLEN   It is Captain MacMorris, is it not?
GOWER   I think it be.
15 FLUELLEN   By Cheshu, he is an ass, as[3] in the world. I will verify

---

4. Fine chap (French *beau coq*).
5. This is fine behavior (sarcastic).
6. Punning on the sense "personal servant."
7. Booty (seized in combat).
8. French port town.
9. Do dirty work; tolerate insults.

1. Pocketing stolen goods; putting up with insults (unmanly behavior).
3.3 Location: Outside Harfleur.
1. Tunnels dug to undermine a besieged fortress.
2. Tunnels dug to undermine enemy "mines."
3. *he is an ass, as:* he is as big an ass as there is.

as much in his beard.° He has no more directions in the true   *to his face*
disciplines of the wars, look you—of the *Roman* disciplines—
than is a puppy dog.

    Enter [Captain] MACMORRIS *and Captain* JAMY

GOWER   Here a comes, and the Scots captain, Captain Jamy,
20   with him.

FLUELLEN   Captain Jamy is a marvellous falorous° gentleman,   *valorous*
   that is certain, and of great expedition° and knowledge in th'an-   *quick-wittedness*
   cient wars, upon my particular knowledge of his directions. By
   Cheshu, he will maintain his argument as well as any military
25   man in the world, in the disciplines of the pristine wars of the
   Romans.

JAMY   I say gud day, Captain Fluellen.

FLUELLEN   Good e'en to your worship, good Captain James.

GOWER   How now, Captain MacMorris, have you quit the
30   mines? Have the pioneers given o'er?°   *diggers stopped work*

MACMORRIS   By Chrish law,[4] 'tish ill done. The work ish give
   over, the trumpet sound the retreat. By my hand I swear, and
   my father's soul, the work ish ill done, it ish give over. I would
   have blowed up the town, so Chrish save me law, in an hour.
35   O 'tish ill done, 'tish ill done, by my hand 'tish ill done.

FLUELLEN   Captain MacMorris, I beseech you now, will you
   vouchsafe° me, look you, a few disputations with you, as partly   *allow*
   touching or concerning the disciplines of the war, the Roman
   wars, in the way of argument, look you, and friendly communi-
40   cation? Partly to satisfy my opinion and partly for the satisfaction, look you, of my mind. As touching the direction of the
   military discipline, that is the point.

JAMY   It sall be vary gud, gud feith, gud captains bath,° and I sall   *both*
   quite° you with gud leve, as I may pick occasion. That sall I,   *requite, answer*
45   marry.

MACMORRIS   It is no time to discourse, so Chrish save me. The
   day is hot, and the weather and the wars and the King and the
   dukes. It is no time to discourse. The town is besieched. An the
   trumpet call us to the breach, and we talk and, be Chrish, do
50   nothing, 'tis shame for us all. So God sa'° me, 'tis shame to   *save*
   stand still, it is shame by my hand. And there is throats to be
   cut, and works to be done, and there ish nothing done, so
   Christ sa' me law.

JAMY   By the mess,° ere these eyes of mine take themselves to   *By the mass (an oath)*
55   slumber, ay'll de gud service, or I'll lig° i'th' grund for it. Ay   *lie*
   owe Got a death, and I'll pay't as valorously as I may, that sall I
   suirely do, that is the brief and the long. Marry, I wad full fain
   heard° some question 'tween you twae.°   *eagerly have heard / two*

FLUELLEN   Captain MacMorris, I think, look you, under your
60   correction, there is not many of your nation—

MACMORRIS   Of my nation? What ish my nation? Ish a villain
   and a bastard and a knave and a rascal? What ish my nation?
   Who talks of my nation?

FLUELLEN   Look you, if you take the matter otherwise than is
65   meant, Captain MacMorris, peradventure I shall think you do
   not use me with that affability as in discretion you ought to use

---

4. La (adds force to an utterance).

me, look you, being as good a man as yourself, both in the
disciplines of war and in the derivation of my birth, and in
other particularities.

70 MACMORRIS   I do not know you so good a man as myself. So
Chrish save me, I will cut off your head.

GOWER   Gentlemen both, you will mistake each other.

JAMY   Ah, that's a foul fault.

A parley⁵ [is sounded]

GOWER   The town sounds a parley.

75 FLUELLEN   Captain MacMorris, when there is more better
opportunity to be required, look you, I will be so bold as to tell
you I know the disciplines of war. And there is an end.   *Exit*

[Flourish.] Enter KING [HARRY] *and all his train before*
the gates

KING HARRY   How yet resolves the Governor of the town?
This is the latest parle° we will admit.   *last parley*
80 Therefore to our best mercy give yourselves,
Or like to men proud of° destruction   *glorying in*
Defy us to our worst. For as I am a soldier,
A name that in my thoughts becomes me best,
If I begin the batt'ry° once again   *bombardment*
85 I will not leave the half-achievèd Harfleur
Till in her ashes she lie buried.
The gates of mercy shall be all shut up,
And the fleshed° soldier, rough and hard of heart,   *inflamed*
In liberty of bloody hand shall range
90 With conscience wide° as hell, mowing like grass   *permissive*
Your fresh fair virgins and your flow'ring infants.
What is it then to me if impious war
Arrayed in flames like to the prince of fiends
Do with his smirched complexion all fell° feats   *cruel*
95 Enlinked to waste° and desolation?   *destruction*
What is't to me, when you yourselves are cause,
If your pure maidens fall into the hand
Of hot and forcing violation?
What rein can hold licentious wickedness
100 When down the hill he holds° his fierce career?°   *maintains / gallop*
We may as bootless° spend our vain command   *unprofitably*
Upon th'enragèd soldiers in their spoil
As send precepts° to the leviathan°   *summons / sea monster*
To come ashore. Therefore, you men of Harfleur,
105 Take pity of your town and of your people
Whiles yet my soldiers are in my command,
Whiles yet the cool and temperate wind of grace
O'erblows° the filthy and contagious clouds⁶   *Disperses*
Of heady° murder, spoil, and villainy.   *headstrong*
110 ⎧ If not—why, in a moment look to see 4 ← blood thirsty.
   ⎪ The blind and bloody soldier with foul hand
   ⎩ Defile the locks of your shrill-shrieking daughters;
     Your fathers taken by the silver beards,
     And their most reverend heads dashed to the walls;
115 Your naked infants spitted° upon pikes,   *impaled*
     Whiles the mad mothers with their howls confused

---

5. Trumpet call requesting negotiation.   6. Pestilence was believed to drop from the sky.

Do break the clouds, as did the wives of Jewry[7]
At Herod's bloody-hunting slaughtermen.
What say you? Will you yield, and this avoid?
120 Or, guilty in defence, be thus destroyed?
  — *Enter* GOVERNOR [*on the wall*]
GOVERNOR   Our expectation hath this day an end.
The Dauphin, whom of succours we entreated,
Returns° us that his powers are yet not ready   *Replies to*
To raise so great a siege. Therefore, dread King,
125 We yield our town and lives to thy soft mercy.
Enter our gates, dispose of us and ours,
For we no longer are defensible.
KING HARRY   Open your gates.   [*Exit* GOVERNOR]
                    Come, Uncle Exeter,
Go you and enter Harfleur. There remain,
130 And fortify it strongly 'gainst the French.
Use mercy to them all. For us, dear uncle,
The winter coming on, and sickness growing
Upon our soldiers, we will retire to Calais.
Tonight in Harfleur will we be your guest;
135 Tomorrow for the march are we addressed.°   *ready*
  [*The gates are opened.*] *Flourish, and* [*they*] *enter the town*

3.4

Enter [*Princess*] CATHERINE *and* ALICE, *an old gentle-*
woman

CATHERINE   Alice, tu as été en Angleterre, et tu bien parles
le langage.[1]
ALICE   Un peu, madame.
CATHERINE   Je te prie, m'enseignez. Il faut que j'apprenne à
5 parler. Comment appelez-vous la main en anglais?
ALICE   La main? Elle est appelée *de hand*.
CATHERINE   *De hand*. Et les doigts?
ALICE   Les doigts? Ma foi, j'oublie les doigts, mais je me souvien-
drai. Les doigts—je pense qu'ils sont appelés *de fingres*. Oui, *de*
10 *fingres*.
CATHERINE   La main, *de hand*; les doigts, *de fingres*. Je pense que
je suis la bonne écolière; j'ai gagné deux mots d'anglais vite-
ment. Comment appelez-vous les ongles?
ALICE   Les ongles? Nous les appelons *de nails*.
15 CATHERINE   *De nails*. Écoutez—dites-moi si je parle bien: *de*
hand, de fingres, et *de nails*.
ALICE   C'est bien dit, madame. Il est fort bon anglais.
CATHERINE   Dites-moi l'anglais pour le bras.

7. Judaea; see Matthew 2:16–18.
3.4 Location: The French King's palace.
1. A translation of this French scene follows, with editorial comments in brackets.

CATHERINE   Alice, you've been in England, and you speak the language well.
ALICE   A little, madam.
CATHERINE   Please teach me. I must learn to speak it. What do you call *la main* in English?
ALICE   *La main?* It is called "de hand."
CATHERINE   De hand. And *les doigts?*
ALICE   *Les doigts?* Faith, I forget *les doigts*, but I'll remember. *Les doigts*—I think they're called "de fingres." Yes,
de fingres.
CATHERINE   *Le main*, de hand; *les doigts*, de fingres. I think I'm a good scholar; I've learned two words of English
quickly. What do you call *les ongles?*
ALICE   *Les ongles?* We call them "de nails."
CATHERINE   De nails. Listen—tell me if I speak well: de hand, de fingres, and de nails.

ALICE *De arma,* madame.

20 CATHERINE Et le coude?

ALICE *D'elbow.*

CATHERINE *D'elbow.* Je m'en fais la répétition de tous les mots que vous m'avez appris dès à présent.

ALICE Il est trop difficile, madame, comme je pense.

25 CATHERINE Excusez-moi, Alice. Écoutez: *d'hand, de fingre, de nails, d'arma, de bilbow.*

ALICE *D'elbow,* madame.

CATHERINE O Seigneur Dieu, je m'en oublie! *D'elbow.* Comment appelez-vous le col?

30 ALICE *De nick,* madame.

CATHERINE *De nick.* Et le menton?

ALICE *De chin.*

CATHERINE *De sin.* Le col, *de nick;* le menton, *de sin.*

ALICE Oui. Sauf votre honneur, en vérité vous prononcez les
35 mots aussi droit que les natifs d'Angleterre.

CATHERINE Je ne doute point d'apprendre, par la grâce de Dieu, et en peu de temps.

ALICE N'avez-vous y déjà oublié ce que je vous ai enseigné?

CATHERINE Non, et je réciterai à vous promptement: *d'hand, de*
40 *fingre, de mailès—*

ALICE *De nails,* madame.

CATHERINE *De nails, de arma, de ilbow—*

ALICE Sauf votre honneur, *d'elbow.*

CATHERINE Ainsi dis-je. *D'elbow, de nick,* et *de sin.* Comment
45 appelez-vous les pieds et la robe?

ALICE *De foot,* madame, et *de cown?*

CATHERINE *De foot* et *de cown?* O Seigneur Dieu! Ils sont les mots de son mauvais, corruptible, gros, et impudique, et non pour les dames d'honneur d'user. Je ne voudrais prononcer ces
50 mots devant les seigneurs de France pour tout le monde. Foh! *De foot* et *de cown!* Néanmoins, je réciterai une autre fois ma

ALICE That's well said, madam. It is very good English.
CATHERINE Tell me the English for *le bras.*
ALICE "De arma," madam.
CATHERINE And *le coude?*
ALICE "D'elbow."
CATHERINE D'elbow. I'll repeat all the words you have taught me so far.
ALICE It is too difficult, madam, in my opinion.
CATHERINE Excuse me, Alice. Listen: d'hand, de fingre, de nails, d'arma, de bilbow.
ALICE D'elbow, madam.
CATHERINE O Lord God, I forgot. D'elbow. What do you call *le col?*
ALICE "De nick," madam.
CATHERINE De nick. And *le menton?*
ALICE "De chin."
CATHERINE De sin. *Le col,* de nick; *le menton,* de sin.
ALICE Yes. Saving your honor, to tell the truth you pronounce the words just as properly as the native English.
CATHERINE I don't doubt that I'll learn, with God's help, and in a short time.
ALICE Haven't you already forgotten what I have taught you?
CATHERINE No, I shall recite to you right now: d'hand, de fingre, de mailès—
ALICE De nails, madam.
CATHERINE De nails, de arma, de ilbow—
ALICE Saving your honor, d'elbow.
CATHERINE That's what I said. D'elbow, de nick, and de sin. What do you call *les pieds* and *la robe?*
ALICE "De foot," madam, and "de cown" [gown].
CATHERINE De foot and de cown? O Lord God, those are evil-sounding words, easily misconstrued, vulgar, and immodest, and not for respectable ladies to use. [They sound like the French *foutre,* "fuck," and *con,* "cunt."] I wouldn't speak those words in front of French gentlemen for all the world. Ugh! de foot and de cown! Still, I shall recite my entire lesson once more. D'hand, de fingre, de nails, d'arma, d'elbow, de nick, de sin, de foot, de cown.
ALICE Excellent, madam!
CATHERINE That's enough for one time. Let's go to dinner.

leçon ensemble. *D'hand, de fingre, de nails, d'arma, d'elbow,*
de nick, de sin, de foot, de cown.
ALICE Excellent, madame!
55 CATHERINE *C'est assez pour une fois. Allons-nous à dîner.*

Exeunt

3.5

Enter KING [CHARLES *the Sixth*] *of France*, DAUPHIN,
CONSTABLE, [DUKE *of*] BOURBON, *and others*

KING CHARLES 'Tis certain he hath passed the River Somme.
CONSTABLE And if he be not fought withal,° my lord,   *with*
   Let us not live in France; let us quit all
   And give our vineyards to a barbarous people.
5 DAUPHIN *O Dieu vivant!*° Shall a few sprays[1] of us,   *O living God*
   The emptying of our fathers' luxury,[2]
   Our scions,° put in wild and savage stock,   *grafts*
   Spirt° up so suddenly into the clouds   *Sprout*
   And over-look their grafters?
10 BOURBON Normans, but bastard Normans, Norman bastards!
   Mort de ma vie,° if they march along   *Death of my life*
   Unfought withal, but I will sell my dukedom
   To buy a slobb'ry° and a dirty farm   *muddy*
   In that nook-shotten[3] isle of Albion.°   *England*
15 CONSTABLE *Dieu de batailles!*° Where° have they this mettle? *God of battles / Whence*
   Is not their climate foggy, raw, and dull,
   On whom as in despite° the sun looks pale,   *contempt*
   Killing their fruit with frowns? Can sodden° water, *boiled, to make ale*
   A drench for sur-reined jades[4]—their barley-broth—
20 Decoct° their cold blood to such valiant heat?   *Boil, to purify*
   And shall our quick blood, spirited with wine,
   Seem frosty? O for honour of our land
   Let us not hang like roping° icicles   *rope-like*
   Upon our houses' thatch, whiles a more frosty people
25 Sweat drops of gallant youth in our rich fields—
   'Poor' may we call them,° in their native lords.   *(the fields)*
DAUPHIN By faith and honour,
   Our madams mock at us and plainly say
   Our mettle is bred out,° and they will give   *is exhausted*
30 Their bodies to the lust of English youth,
   To new-store France with bastard warriors.
BOURBON They bid us, 'To the English dancing-schools,
   And teach lavoltas° high and swift corantos'[5]—   *leaping dance*
   Saying our grace is only in our heels,
35 And that we are most lofty runaways.
KING CHARLES Where is Montjoy the herald? Speed° him hence. *Quickly send*
   Let him greet England with our sharp defiance.
   Up, princes, and with spirit of honour edged
   More sharper than your swords, hie° to the field.   *go*
40 Charles Delabret, High Constable of France,
   You Dukes of Orléans, Bourbon, and of Berri,
   Alençon, Brabant, Bar, and Burgundy,

3.5 Location: The French King's court.   3. With an indented shore.
1. Offshoots (bastards).   4. A tonic for overworked horses.
2. The discharge ("emptying") of our forefathers' lust.   5. Running dance.

Jaques Châtillion, Rambures, Vaudemont,
Beaumont, Grandpré, Roussi, and Fauconbridge,
45 Foix, Lestrelles, Boucicault, and Charolais,
High dukes, great princes, barons, lords, and knights,
For your great seats now quit you⁶ of great shames.
Bar Harry England, that sweeps through our land
With pennons° painted in the blood of Harfleur;   *banners*
50 Rush on his host, as doth the melted snow
Upon the valleys, whose low vassal seat
The Alps doth spit and void his rheum° upon.   *empty its moisture*
Go down upon him, you have power enough,
And in a captive chariot into Rouen
Bring him our prisoner.
55 CONSTABLE   This becomes the great.°   *befits noblemen*
Sorry am I his numbers are so few,
His soldiers sick and famished in their march,
For I am sure when he shall see our army
He'll drop his heart into the sink° of fear   *pit*
60 And, fore achievement,° offer us his ransom.   *instead of battle*
KING CHARLES   Therefore, Lord Constable, haste on Montjoy,
And let him say to England that we send
To know what willing ransom he will give.—
Prince Dauphin, you shall stay with us in Rouen.
65 DAUPHIN   Not so, I do beseech your majesty.
KING CHARLES   Be patient, for you shall remain with us.—
Now forth, Lord Constable, and princes all,
And quickly bring us word of England's fall. *Exeunt [severally]*

3.6

Enter Captains GOWER *and* FLUELLEN [*meeting*]
GOWER   How now, Captain Fluellen, come you from the bridge?
FLUELLEN   I assure you there is very excellent services committed at the bridge.
GOWER   Is the Duke of Exeter safe?
5 FLUELLEN   The Duke of Exeter is as magnanimous as Agamemnon,¹ and a man that I love and honour with my soul and my
heart and my duty and my live and my living and my uttermost
power. He is not, God be praised and blessed, any hurt in the
world, but keeps the bridge most valiantly, with excellent disci-
10 pline. There is an ensign lieutenant there at the pridge, I think
in my very conscience he is as valiant a man as Mark Antony,
and he is a man of no estimation° in the world, but I did see   *fame*
him do as gallant service.
GOWER   What do you call him?
15 FLUELLEN   He is called Ensign Pistol.
GOWER   I know him not.
            Enter Ensign PISTOL
FLUELLEN   Here is the man.
PISTOL   Captain, I thee beseech to do me favours.
The Duke of Exeter doth love thee well.
20 FLUELLEN   Ay, I praise God, and I have merited some love at his
hands.

---

6. *For . . . you:* In defense of your high ranks, now revenge   3.6 Location: The English camp.
yourselves.   1. Greek general in the Trojan War.

PISTOL   Bardolph, a soldier firm and sound of heart,
  Of buxom° valour, hath by cruel fate   *lively*
  And giddy Fortune's furious fickle wheel,
25 That goddess blind that stands upon the rolling restless stone—
FLUELLEN   By your patience, Ensign Pistol: Fortune is painted
  blind, with a muffler° afore her eyes, to signify to you that For- *blindfold*
  tune is blind. And she is painted also with a wheel, to signify to
  you—which is the moral of it—that she is turning and incon-
30 stant and mutability and variation. And her foot, look you, is
  fixed upon a spherical stone, which rolls and rolls and rolls. In
  good truth, the poet makes a most excellent description of it;
  Fortune is an excellent moral.°   *symbolic emblem*
PISTOL   Fortune is Bardolph's foe and frowns on him,
35 For he hath stol'n a pax,[2] and hangèd must a° be.   *he*
  A damnèd death—
  Let gallows gape for dog, let man go free,
  And let not hemp[3] his windpipe suffocate.
  But Exeter hath given the doom° of death   *sentence*
40 For pax of little price.
  Therefore go speak, the Duke will hear thy voice,
  And let not Bardolph's vital thread be cut
  With edge of penny cord and vile reproach.
  Speak, captain, for his life, and I will thee requite.
45 FLUELLEN   Ensign Pistol, I do partly understand your meaning.
PISTOL   Why then rejoice therefor.
FLUELLEN   Certainly, ensign, it is not a thing to rejoice at. For
  if, look you, he were my brother, I would desire the Duke to
  use his good pleasure, and put him to executions. For disci-
50 pline ought to be used.
PISTOL   Die and be damned! and *fico*[4] for thy friendship.
FLUELLEN   It is well.
PISTOL   The fig of Spain.
FLUELLEN   Very good.
55 PISTOL   I say the fig within thy bowels and thy dirty maw. *Exit*
FLUELLEN   Captain Gower, cannot you hear it lighten and
  thunder?
GOWER   Why, is this the ensign you told me of? I remember him
  now. A bawd, a cutpurse.°   *thief*
60 FLUELLEN   I'll assure you, a uttered as prave words at the pridge
  as you shall see in a summer's day. But it is very well. What he
  has spoke to me, that is well, I warrant you, when time is serve.
GOWER   Why 'tis a gull,° a fool, a rogue, that now and then goes *simpleton*
  to the wars, to grace himself at his return into London under
65 the form of a soldier. And such fellows are perfect in the great
  commanders' names, and they will learn° you by rote where *teach*
  services were done— at such and such a sconce,° at such a *fortification*
  breach, at such a convoy, who came off bravely, who was shot,
  who disgraced, what terms the enemy stood on—and this they
70 con° perfectly in the phrase of war, which they trick up° with *memorize / adorn*
  new-tuned° oaths. And what a beard of the General's cut and a *newly coined*
  horrid suit of the camp[5] will do among foaming bottles and ale-

---

2. Small tablet with a crucifix stamped on it.
3. Of which ropes were made.
4. Spanish for "fig"; obscene gesture made by thrusting

the thumb between two fingers.
5. *horrid . . . camp*: frightening soldier's attire.

washed wits is wonderful to be thought on. But you must learn
to know such slanders° of the age, or else you may be marvel-
75 lously mistook.

FLUELLEN   I tell you what, Captain Gower, I do perceive he is
not the man that he would gladly make show to the world he
is. If I find a hole in his coat,° I will tell him my mind.

[A drum is heard]

Hark you, the King is coming, and I must speak with him from
80 the pridge.

Enter KING [HARRY] *and his poor soldiers, [with] drum
and colours°*

God pless your majesty.

KING HARRY   How now, Fluellen, com'st thou from the bridge?

FLUELLEN   Ay, so please your majesty. The Duke of Exeter has
very gallantly maintained the pridge. The French is gone off,
85 look you, and there is gallant and most prave passages.° Marry,
th'athversary was have possession of the pridge, but he is
enforced to retire, and the Duke of Exeter is master of the
pridge. I can tell your majesty, the Duke is a prave man.

KING HARRY   What men have you lost, Fluellen?

90 FLUELLEN   The perdition° of th'athversary hath been very great,
reasonable great. Marry, for my part I think the Duke hath lost
never a man, but one that is like to be executed for robbing a
church, one Bardolph, if your majesty know the man. His face
is all bubuncles and whelks° and knobs and flames o' fire, and
95 his lips blows at his nose, and it is like a coal of fire, sometimes
plue and sometimes red. But his nose is executed,[6] and his
fire's out.

KING HARRY   We would have all such offenders so cut off, and
we here give express charge that in our marches through the
100 country there be nothing compelled from the villages, nothing
taken but° paid for, none of the French upbraided or abused in
disdainful language. For when lenity° and cruelty play for a
kingdom, the gentler gamester is the soonest winner.

Tucket.° Enter MONTJOY

MONTJOY   You know me by my habit.°

105 KING HARRY   Well then, I know thee. What shall I know of thee?

MONTJOY   My master's mind.

KING HARRY   Unfold it.

MONTJOY   Thus says my King:
'Say thou to Harry of England, though we seemed dead, we did
but sleep. Advantage° is a better soldier than rashness. Tell
him, we could have rebuked him at Harfleur, but that we
110 thought not good to bruise an injury° till it were full ripe. Now
we speak upon our cue,° and our voice is imperial. England
shall repent his folly, see his weakness, and admire our sufferance.° Bid him therefore consider of his ransom, which must
proportion the losses we have borne, the subjects we have lost,
115 the disgrace we have digested°—which in weight to re-answer,°
his pettiness would bow under. For our losses, his exchequer°
is too poor; for th'effusion of our blood, the muster[7] of his kingdom too faint a number; and for our disgrace, his own person
kneeling at our feet but a weak and worthless satisfaction. To
120 this add defiance, and tell him for conclusion he hath betrayed

---

*Glosses (right margin):*
disgraces
means of exposing him
drummer and flag bearer
altercations
loss
abscesses and pimples
unless
leniency
Trumpet call
herald's coat
Circumspection
squeeze a pimple
at the proper time
wonder at our patience
endured / compensate
King's treasury

---

6. Slit (in the pillory before he is hanged).   7. Entire population, assembled for military service.

his followers, whose condemnation is pronounced.'
So far my King and master; so much my office.
KING HARRY   What is thy name? I know thy quality.°   rank
MONTJOY   Montjoy.
125   KING HARRY   Thou dost thy office fairly. Turn thee back
And tell thy king I do not seek him now,
But could be willing to march on to Calais
Without impeachment,° for to say the sooth°—   hindrance / truth
Though 'tis no wisdom to confess so much
130   Unto an enemy of craft and vantage°—   cunning and superiority
My people are with sickness much enfeebled,
My numbers lessened, and those few I have
Almost no better than so many French;
Who when they were in health—I tell thee herald,
135   I thought upon one pair of English legs
Did march three Frenchmen. Yet forgive me, God,
That I do brag thus. This your air of France
Hath blown that vice in me. I must repent.
Go, therefore, tell thy master here I am;
140   My ransom is this frail and worthless trunk,°   body
My army but a weak and sickly guard.
Yet, God before, tell him we will come on,
Though France himself and such another neighbour
Stand in our way. There's for thy labour, Montjoy.[8]
145   Go bid thy master well advise himself.
If we may pass, we will; if we be hindered,
We shall your tawny ground with your red blood
Discolour. And so, Montjoy, fare you well.
The sum of all our answer is but this:
150   We would not seek a battle as we are,
Nor as we are we say we will not shun it.
So tell your master.
MONTJOY   I shall deliver so. Thanks to your highness.   *Exit*
GLOUCESTER   I hope they will not come upon us now.
155   KING HARRY   We are in God's hand, brother, not in theirs.
March to the bridge. It now draws toward night.
Beyond the river we'll encamp ourselves,
And on tomorrow bid them march away.   *Exeunt*

3.7

Enter the CONSTABLE, *Lord* RAMBURES, [*Dukes of*]
ORLÉANS [*and*] BOURBON,[1] *with others*

CONSTABLE   Tut, I have the best armour of the world. Would it
were day.
ORLÉANS   You have an excellent armour. But let my horse have
his due.
5   CONSTABLE   It is the best horse of Europe.
ORLÉANS   Will it never be morning?
BOURBON   My lord of Orléans and my Lord High Constable, you
talk of horse and armour?
ORLÉANS   You are as well provided of both as any prince in the
10   world.
BOURBON   What a long night is this! I will not change my horse

---

8. Henry generously "tips" the enemy herald.
3.7 Location: The French camp near Agincourt.

1. As in Q; F has "Dauphin" in this scene and in 4.2 and
4.5. See Textual Note.

with any that treads but on four pasterns.° Ah ha! He bounds   *hooves*
from the earth as if his entrails were hares—*le cheval volant,*
the Pegasus, *qui a les narines de feu!*[2] When I bestride him, I
15   soar, I am a hawk; he trots the air, the earth sings when he
touches it,[3] the basest horn° of his hoof is more musical than   *lowest part (with pun)*
the pipe of Hermes.[4]

ORLÉANS   He's of the colour of the nutmeg.

BOURBON   And of the heat of the ginger.[5] It is a beast for Per-
20   seus. He is pure air and fire, and the dull elements of earth and
water never appear in him, but only in patient stillness while
his rider mounts him. He is indeed a horse, and all other jades°   *nags*
you may call beasts.

CONSTABLE   Indeed, my lord, it is a most absolute° and excellent   *perfect*
25   horse.

BOURBON   It is the prince of palfreys.° His neigh is the bidding   *warhorses*
of a monarch, and his countenance enforces homage.

ORLÉANS   No more, cousin.

BOURBON   Nay, the man hath no wit, that cannot from the ris-
30   ing of the lark to the lodging of the lamb vary deserved praise
on my palfrey. It is a theme as fluent° as the sea. Turn the sands   *flowing; abundant*
into eloquent tongues, and my horse is argument° for them all.   *subject*
'Tis a subject for a sovereign to reason on, and for a sovereign's
sovereign to ride on, and for the world, familiar to us and
35   unknown, to lay apart their particular functions, and wonder at
him. I once writ a sonnet in his praise, and began thus: 'Wonder of nature!—'

ORLÉANS   I have heard a sonnet begin so to one's mistress.

BOURBON   Then did they imitate that which I composed to my
40   courser, for my horse is my mistress.

ORLÉANS   Your mistress bears well.[6]

BOURBON   *Me* well, which is the prescribed praise and perfection
of a good and particular° mistress.   *private*

CONSTABLE   Nay, for methought yesterday your mistress shrewdly°   *severely*
45   shook your back.

BOURBON   So perhaps did yours.

CONSTABLE   Mine was not bridled.

BOURBON   O then belike she was old and gentle, and you rode
like a kern° of Ireland, your French hose° off, and in your strait   *soldier / wide breeches*
50   strossers.°   *tights*

CONSTABLE   You have good judgement in horsemanship.

BOURBON   Be warned by me then: they that ride so, and ride not
warily, fall into foul bogs. I had rather have my horse to my
mistress.

55 CONSTABLE   I had as lief have my mistress a jade.°   *horse; whore*

BOURBON   I tell thee, Constable, my mistress wears his own
hair.[7]

CONSTABLE   I could make as true a boast as that, if I had a sow
to my mistress.

60 BOURBON   *'Le chien est retourné à son propre vomissement, et la*

---

2. The flying horse . . . with nostrils of fire. Pegasus was a
mythological flying horse, ridden by the hero Perseus.
3. When Pegasus struck Mount Helicon with his hoof,
the fountain of the Muses sprang forth.
4. Greek messenger god, whose sweet playing on the
pipe charmed the many-eyed guard Argus, allowing the
imprisoned Io to escape.

5. Horses' colors supposedly suggested their dispositions:
"nutmeg" meant "pleasant and nimble"; "ginger" meant
"hot and skittish."
6. Carries weight (with obscene innuendo).
7. Implying that the constable's mistress does not, having
lost it to syphilis.

truie lavée au bourbier.'[8] Thou makest use of anything.

CONSTABLE   Yet do I not use my horse for my mistress, or any
such proverb so little kin to the purpose.

RAMBURES   My Lord Constable, the armour that I saw in your
tent tonight, are those stars or suns upon it?

CONSTABLE   Stars, my lord.

BOURBON   Some of them will fall tomorrow, I hope.

CONSTABLE   And yet my sky shall not want.

BOURBON   That may be, for you bear a many superfluously,
and 'twere more honour some were away.

CONSTABLE   Even as your horse bears your praises, who would
trot as well were some of your brags dismounted.

BOURBON   Would I were able to load him with his desert! Will it
never be day? I will trot tomorrow a mile, and my way shall
be paved with English faces.

CONSTABLE   I will not say so, for fear I should be faced out of my
way.° But I would it were morning, for I would fain° be about   *turned aside / gladly*
the ears of the English.

RAMBURES   Who will go to hazard° with me for twenty prisoners?   *wager*

CONSTABLE   You must first go yourself to hazard, ere you have
them.

BOURBON   'Tis midnight. I'll go arm myself.   *Exit*

ORLÉANS   The Duke of Bourbon longs for morning.

RAMBURES   He longs to eat the English.

CONSTABLE   I think he will eat all he kills.

ORLÉANS   By the white hand of my lady, he's a gallant prince.

CONSTABLE   Swear by her foot, that she may tread out° the oath.   *erase with her foot*

ORLÉANS   He is simply the most active gentleman of France.

CONSTABLE   Doing is activity, and he will still be doing.

ORLÉANS   He never did harm that I heard of.

CONSTABLE   Nor will do none tomorrow. He will keep that good
name still.

ORLÉANS   I know him to be valiant.

CONSTABLE   I was told that by one that knows him better than
you.

ORLÉANS   What's he?

CONSTABLE   Marry, he told me so himself, and he said he cared
not who knew it.

ORLÉANS   He needs not; it is no hidden virtue in him.

CONSTABLE   By my faith, sir, but it is. Never anybody saw it but
his lackey.[9] 'Tis a hooded valour, and when it appears it will
bate.[1]

ORLÉANS   'Ill will never said well.'

CONSTABLE   I will cap that proverb with 'There is flattery in
friendship.'

ORLÉANS   And I will take up that with 'Give the devil his due.'

CONSTABLE   Well placed! There stands your friend for the devil.
Have at the very eye° of that proverb with 'A pox of the devil!'   *bull's-eye*

ORLÉANS   You are the better at proverbs by how much 'a fool's
bolt° is soon shot'.   *short, blunt arrow*

---

8. "The dog is returned to his vomit, and the sow that
was washed, to the wallowing in the mire" (quoting 2
Peter 2:22).
9. That is, the only person he is brave enough to beat is
his servant.
1. Beat its wings (like a hawk, which was kept "hooded"
until prey was sighted); also, abate.

CONSTABLE You have shot over.°   *overshot the target*

ORLÉANS 'Tis not the first time you were overshot.°   *defeated*

Enter a MESSENGER

MESSENGER My Lord High Constable, the English lie within
fifteen hundred paces of your tents.

115   CONSTABLE Who hath measured the ground?

MESSENGER The Lord Grandpré.

CONSTABLE A valiant and most expert gentleman.

                                         [*Exit* MESSENGER]

Would it were day! Alas, poor Harry of England. He longs not
for the dawning as we do.

120   ORLÉANS What a wretched and peevish fellow is this King of
England, to mope° with his fat-brained followers so far out of   *wander*
his knowledge.

CONSTABLE If the English had any apprehension,° they would   *sense*
run away.

125   ORLÉANS That they lack—for if their heads had any intellectual
armour, they could never wear such heavy headpieces.

RAMBURES That island of England breeds very valiant creatures.
Their mastiffs are of unmatchable courage.

ORLÉANS Foolish curs, that run winking° into the mouth of a   *with closed eyes*

130   Russian bear[2], and have their heads crushed like rotten apples.
You may as well say, 'That's a valiant flea that dare eat his
breakfast on the lip of a lion.'

CONSTABLE Just,° just. And the men do sympathize with the   *True*
mastiffs in robustious and rough coming on, leaving their wits

135   with their wives. And then, give them great meals of beef,[3] and
iron and steel, they will eat like wolves and fight like devils.

ORLÉANS Ay, but these English are shrewdly° out of beef.   *badly*

CONSTABLE Then shall we find tomorrow they have only stom-
achs° to eat, and none to fight. Now is it time to arm. Come,   *appetite*

140   shall we about it?

ORLÉANS It is now two o'clock. But let me see—by ten
We shall have each a hundred Englishmen.   *Exeunt*

4.0

[*Enter*] CHORUS

CHORUS Now entertain conjecture of° a time   *imagine*
When creeping murmur and the poring° dark   *pouring; eye-straining*
Fills the wide vessel of the universe.
From camp to camp through the foul womb of night

5   The hum of either army stilly sounds,
That° the fixed sentinels almost receive   *So that*
The secret whispers of each other's watch.
Fire answers fire, and through their paly° flames   *pale*
Each battle sees the other's umbered° face.   *shadowed*

10   Steed threatens steed, in high and boastful neighs
Piercing the night's dull ear, and from the tents
The armourers, accomplishing° the knights,   *equipping*
With busy hammers closing rivets up,
Give dreadful note of preparation.

15   The country cocks do crow, the clocks do toll

---

2. Referring to the sport of bearbaiting, in which dogs   3. A traditional English food.
were set upon bears chained to a post.

And the third hour of drowsy morning name.
Proud of their numbers and secure in soul,
The confident and overlusty French
Do the low-rated° English play at dice,[1]   *underrated*
20   And chide the cripple tardy-gaited night,
Who like a foul and ugly witch doth limp
So tediously away. The poor condemnèd English,
Like sacrifices, by their watchful fires
Sit patiently and inly° ruminate   *inwardly*
25   The morning's danger; and their gesture sad,
Investing° lank lean cheeks and war-worn coats,   *Accompanying*
Presented them unto the gazing moon
So many horrid ghosts. O now, who will behold
The royal captain of this ruined band
30   Walking from watch to watch, from tent to tent,
Let him cry, 'Praise and glory on his head!'
For forth he goes and visits all his host,°   *army*
Bids them good morrow with a modest smile
And calls them brothers, friends, and countrymen.
35   Upon his royal face there is no note°   *sign*
How dread an army hath enrounded° him;   *encircled*
Nor doth he dedicate° one jot of colour   *lose*
Unto the weary and all-watchèd night,
But freshly looks and overbears attaint[2]
40   With cheerful semblance and sweet majesty,
That every wretch, pining and pale before,
Beholding him, plucks comfort from his looks.
A largess universal,° like the sun,   *wealth available to all*
His liberal eye doth give to everyone,
45   Thawing cold fear, that mean and gentle° all   *lowborn and noble*
Behold, as may unworthiness define,[3]
A little touch of Harry in the night.
And so our scene must to the battle fly,
Where O for pity, we shall much disgrace,
50   With four or five most vile and ragged foils,°   *swords*
Right ill-disposed in brawl ridiculous,
The name of Agincourt. Yet sit and see,
Minding° true things by what their mock'ries be.   *Exit*   *Imagining*

4.1

Enter KING [HARRY] *and* [*Duke of*] GLOUCESTER [*then
the Duke of* CLARENCE]
KING HARRY   Gloucester, 'tis true that we are in great danger;
The greater therefore should our courage be.
Good morrow, brother Clarence. God Almighty!
There is some soul of goodness in things evil,
5   Would men observingly distil it out—
For our bad neighbour makes us early stirrers,
Which is both healthful and good husbandry.°   *economy*
Besides, they are our outward consciences,
And preachers to us all, admonishing
10   That we should dress us fairly° for our end.   *prepare adequately*

4.0
1. See 3.7.79.
2. And suppresses signs of exhaustion.

3. As far as their limited capacities permit.
4.1 Location: The English camp at Agincourt.

Thus may we gather honey from the weed
And make a moral of the devil himself.
        Enter [Sir Thomas] ERPINGHAM
Good morrow, old Sir Thomas Erpingham.
A good soft pillow for that good white head
15 Were better than a churlish turf of France.
ERPINGHAM Not so, my liege. This lodging likes° me better,   *pleases*
        Since I may say, 'Now lie I like a king.'
KING HARRY 'Tis good for men to love their present pains
        Upon example.[1] So the spirit is eased,
20 And when the mind is quickened, out of doubt
        The organs, though defunct and dead before,
        Break up their drowsy grave and newly move
        With casted slough[2] and fresh legerity.°   *nimbleness*
        Lend me thy cloak, Sir Thomas.
        [He puts on Erpingham's cloak]
                        Brothers both,
25 Commend me to the princes in our camp.
        Do my good morrow° to them, and anon   *Say good morning*
        Desire them all to my pavilion.
GLOUCESTER We shall, my liege.
ERPINGHAM Shall I attend your grace?
30 KING HARRY No, my good knight.
        Go with my brothers to my lords of England.
        I and my bosom must debate awhile,
        And then I would no other company.
ERPINGHAM The Lord in heaven bless thee, noble Harry.
35 KING HARRY God-a-mercy,° old heart, thou speak'st cheerfully.   *Thank you*
                        Exeunt [all but KING HARRY]
        Enter PISTOL *[to him]*
PISTOL *Qui vous là?*°   *Who goes there*
KING HARRY A friend.
PISTOL Discuss unto me: art thou officer,
        Or art thou base, common, and popular?°   *plebeian*
40 KING HARRY I am a gentleman of a company.
PISTOL Trail'st thou the puissant pike?°   *Are you an infantryman*
KING HARRY Even so. What are you?
PISTOL As good a gentleman as the Emperor.
KING HARRY Then you are a better than the King.
45 PISTOL The King's a bawcock and a heart-of-gold,
        A lad of life, an imp of fame,°   *a scion of noble stock*
        Of parents good, of fist most valiant.
        I kiss his dirty shoe, and from heartstring
        I love the lovely bully.° What is thy name?   *lovable swashbuckler*
50 KING HARRY Harry *le roi.*°   *the King*
PISTOL Leroi? A Cornish name. Art thou of Cornish crew?
KING HARRY No, I am a Welshman.
PISTOL Know'st thou Fluellen?
KING HARRY Yes.
55 PISTOL Tell him I'll knock his leek about his pate
        Upon Saint Davy's day.[3]
KING HARRY Do not you wear your dagger in your cap that day,
        lest he knock that about yours.

---

1. By the pattern provided by others.
2. Old skin having been cast off (like a snake).

3. October 1, Welsh national holiday celebrating St. David's victory over the Saxons.

PISTOL Art thou his friend?

60 KING HARRY And his kinsman too.

PISTOL The *fico*[4] for thee then.

KING HARRY I thank you. God be with you.

PISTOL My name is Pistol called.

KING HARRY It sorts° well with your fierceness.   *Exit* [PISTOL]   *agrees*
          Enter [*Captains*] FLUELLEN *and* GOWER [*severally.* KING
          HARRY *stands apart*]

65 GOWER Captain Fluellen!

FLUELLEN So! In the name of Jesu Christ, speak fewer. It is the
          greatest admiration° in the universal° world, when the true and   *wonder / whole*
          ancient prerogatifs and laws of the wars is not kept. If you
          would take the pains but to examine the wars of Pompey the

70   Great,[5] you shall find, I warrant you, that there is no tiddle-
          taddle nor pibble-babble° in Pompey's camp. I warrant you,   *chattering*
          you shall find the ceremonies of the wars, and the cares of it,
          and the forms of it, and the sobriety of it, and the modesty of
          it, to be otherwise.

75 GOWER Why, the enemy is loud. You hear him all night.

FLUELLEN If the enemy is an ass and a fool and a prating cox-
          comb,° is it meet,° think you, that we should also, look you, be   *yammering fool / proper*
          an ass and a fool and a prating coxcomb? In your own con-
          science now?

80 GOWER I will speak lower.

FLUELLEN I pray you and beseech you that you will.
                                        Exeunt [FLUELLEN *and* GOWER]

KING HARRY Though it appear a little out of fashion,°   *unconventional*
          There is much care and valour in this Welshman.
              Enter three soldiers: John BATES, *Alexander* COURT, *and*
              Michael WILLIAMS

COURT Brother John Bates, is not that the morning which breaks

85   yonder?

BATES I think it be. But we have no great cause to desire the
       approach of day.

WILLIAMS We see yonder the beginning of the day, but I think
          we shall never see the end of it.—Who goes there?

90 KING HARRY A friend.

WILLIAMS Under what captain serve you?

KING HARRY Under Sir Thomas Erpingham.

WILLIAMS A good old commander and a most kind gentleman.
          I pray you, what thinks he of our estate?°   *situation*

95 KING HARRY Even as men wrecked upon a sand, that look to be
          washed off the next tide.

BATES He hath not told his thought to the King?

KING HARRY No, nor it is not meet he should. For though I speak
          it to you, I think the King is but a man, as I am. The violet

100   smells to him as it doth to me; the element shows° to him as it   *the sky appears*
          doth to me. All his senses have but human conditions.° His   *limitations*
          ceremonies laid by, in his nakedness he appears but a man,
          and though his affections° are higher mounted than ours, yet   *desires*
          when they stoop,[6] they stoop with the like wing. Therefore,

105   when he sees reason of fears,° as we do, his fears, out of doubt,   *to fear*

---

4. See 3.6.51.   6. Plummet down (term from falconry).
5. Roman general, defeated by Julius Caesar.

be of the same relish° as ours are. Yet, in reason, no man should   *taste; kind*
possess him with⁷ any appearance of fear, lest he, by showing
it, should dishearten his army.

BATES   He may show what outward courage he will, but I
110   believe, as cold a night as 'tis, he could wish himself in Thames
up to the neck. And so I would he were, and I by him, at all
adventures,⁸ so we were quit° here.   *away from*

KING HARRY   By my troth,° I will speak my conscience of the   *oath*
King. I think he would not wish himself anywhere but where
115   he is.

BATES   Then I would he were here alone. So should he be sure
to be ransomed, and a many poor men's lives saved.

KING HARRY   I dare say you love him not so ill to wish him here
alone, howsoever you speak this to feel° other men's minds.   *test*
120   Methinks I could not die anywhere so contented as in the
King's company, his cause being just and his quarrel honourable.

WILLIAMS   That's more than we know.

BATES   Ay, or more than we should seek after. For we know
125   enough if we know we are the King's subjects. If his cause be
wrong, our obedience to the King wipes the crime of it out of
us.

WILLIAMS   But if the cause be not good, the King himself hath a
130   heavy reckoning to make, when all those legs and arms and
heads chopped off in a battle shall join together at the latter
day,⁹ and cry all, 'We died at such a place'—some swearing,
some crying for a surgeon, some upon their wives left poor
behind them, some upon the debts they owe, some upon their
children rawly° left. I am afeard there are few die well that die   *abruptly; poorly*
135   in a battle, for how can they charitably dispose of anything,
when blood is their argument?° Now, if these men do not die   *business*
well, it will be a black matter for the King that led them to it—
who° to disobey were against all proportion of subjection.¹   *whom*

KING HARRY   So, if a son that is by his father sent about merchan-
140   dise do sinfully miscarry upon the sea, the imputation of° his   *blame for*
wickedness, by your rule, should be imposed upon his father,
that sent him. Or if a servant, under his master's command
transporting a sum of money, be assailed by robbers, and die in
many irreconciled iniquities,° you may call the business of the   *unatoned sins*
145   master the author of the servant's damnation. But this is not so.
The King is not bound to answer the particular endings of his
soldiers, the father of his son, nor the master of his servant, for
they purpose not their deaths when they propose their services.
Besides, there is no king, be his cause never so spotless, if it
150   come to the arbitrament° of swords, can try it out with all   *settlement*
unspotted° soldiers. Some, peradventure,° have on them the   *unblemished / perhaps*
guilt of premeditated and contrived murder; some, of beguiling
virgins with the broken seals of perjury; some, making the wars
their bulwark,° that have before gored the gentle bosom of   *defense (against the law)*
155   peace with pillage and robbery. Now, if these men have

---

7. Induce him to experience.
8. Whatever might happen.
9. Last Judgment, when human beings are to be resur-

rected in the body.
1. *against . . . subjection:* to defy all proper relationships
of authority and subordination.

defeated the law and outrun native° punishment, though they
can outstrip men, they have no wings to fly from God. War is
his beadle.° War is his vengeance. So that here men are punished for before-breach° of the King's laws, in now the King's
160 quarrel. Where they feared the death, they have borne life
away; and where they would be safe, they perish. Then if they
die unprovided,° no more is the King guilty of their damnation
than he was before guilty of those impieties for the which they
are now visited.° Every subject's duty is the King's, but every
165 subject's soul is his own. Therefore should every soldier in the
wars do as every sick man in his bed: wash every mote° out of
his conscience. And dying so, death is to him advantage;° or
not dying, the time was blessedly lost wherein such preparation
was gained. And in him that escapes, it were not sin to think
170 that, making God so free an offer, he° let him outlive that day
to see his greatness and to teach others how they should prepare.
BATES 'Tis certain, every man that dies ill,° the ill upon his own
head. The King is not to answer it. I do not desire he
175 should answer for me, and yet I determine to fight lustily for
him.
KING HARRY I myself heard the King say he would not be ransomed.
WILLIAMS Ay, he said so, to make us fight cheerfully, but when
180 our throats are cut he may be ransomed, and we ne'er the
wiser.
KING HARRY If I live to see it, I will never trust his word after.
WILLIAMS You pay him then! That's a perilous shot out of an
elder-gun,° that a poor and a private displeasure can do against
185 a monarch. You may as well go about to turn the sun to ice
with fanning in his face with a peacock's feather. You'll never
trust his word after! Come, 'tis a foolish saying.
KING HARRY Your reproof is something too round.° I should be
angry with you, if the time were convenient.
190 WILLIAMS Let it be a quarrel between us, if you live.
KING HARRY I embrace it.
WILLIAMS How shall I know thee again?
KING HARRY Give me any gage° of thine, and I will wear it in my
bonnet. Then if ever thou darest acknowledge it, I will make it
195 my quarrel.
WILLIAMS Here's my glove. Give me another of thine.
KING HARRY There.
    [They exchange gloves]
WILLIAMS This will I also wear in my cap. If ever thou come to
me and say, after tomorrow, 'This is my glove', by this hand I
200 will take thee a box on the ear.
KING HARRY If ever I live to see it, I will challenge it.
WILLIAMS Thou darest as well be hanged.
KING HARRY Well, I will do it, though I take thee in the King's
company.
205 WILLIAMS Keep thy word. Fare thee well.
BATES Be friends, you English fools, be friends. We have French
quarrels enough, if you could tell how to reckon.°
KING HARRY Indeed, the French may lay twenty French crowns°
to one they will beat us, for they bear them on their shoulders.

Glosses (right margin):
at home
police officer
earlier breaking
unprepared
punished
speck
profit
(God)
in sin
a popgun
blunt
token
count
coins; heads

210 But it is no English treason to cut French crowns,[2] and tomor-
     row the King himself will be a clipper.   *Exeunt soldiers*
     Upon the King.
     'Let us our lives, our souls, our debts, our care-full wives,
     Our children, and our sins, lay on the King.'
215 We must bear all. O hard condition,
     Twin-born with greatness: subject to the breath
     Of every fool, whose sense no more can feel
     But his own wringing.° What infinite heartsease   *pain*
     Must kings neglect that private men enjoy?
220 And what have kings that privates have not too,
     Save ceremony, save general ceremony?
     And what art thou, thou idol ceremony?
     What kind of god art thou, that suffer'st more
     Of mortal griefs than do thy worshippers?
225 What are thy rents?° What are thy comings-in?°   *revenues / income*
     O ceremony, show me but thy worth.
     What is thy soul of adoration?[3]
     Art thou aught° else but place, degree, and form,   *anything*
     Creating awe and fear in other men?
230 Wherein thou art less happy, being feared,
     Than they in fearing.
     What drink'st thou oft, instead of homage sweet,
     But poisoned flattery? O be sick, great greatness,
     And bid thy ceremony give thee cure.
235 Think'st thou the fiery fever will go out
     With titles blown from adulation?
     Will it give place to flexure° and low bending?   *bowing*
     Canst thou, when thou command'st the beggar's knee,
     Command the health of it? No, thou proud dream
240 That play'st so subtly with a king's repose;
     I am a king that find° thee, and I know   *expose*
     'Tis not the balm, the sceptre, and the ball,°   *orb (royal accessory)*
     The sword, the mace, the crown imperial,
     The intertissued robe of gold and pearl,
245 The farcèd° title running fore the king,   *stuffed*
     The throne he sits on, nor the tide of pomp
     That beats upon the high shore of this world—
     No, not all these, thrice-gorgeous ceremony,
     Not all these, laid in bed majestical,
250 Can sleep so soundly as the wretched slave
     Who with a body filled and vacant mind
     Gets him to rest, crammed with distressful bread;
     Never sees horrid night, the child of hell,
     But like a lackey° from the rise to set   *servant*
255 Sweats in the eye of Phoebus,° and all night   *the sun*
     Sleeps in Elysium;° next day, after dawn   *classical paradise*
     Doth rise and help Hyperion° to his horse,   *the sun's charioteer*
     And follows so the ever-running year
     With profitable labour to his grave.
260 And but for ceremony such a wretch,
     Winding up days with toil and nights with sleep,

Vulnerbility (handwritten in margin)

---

2. "Clipping" (line 211), or shaving, precious metal off   3. What is the secret of the adoration you inspire?
coins was punishable as treason.

Had the forehand° and vantage of a king.   advantage
The slave, a member of the country's peace,
Enjoys it, but in gross brain little wots°   thinks
265 What watch the King keeps to maintain the peace,
Whose hours the peasant best advantages.°   profits most from
     Enter [Sir Thomas] ERPINGHAM
ERPINGHAM My lord, your nobles, jealous of° your absence,   concerned about
Seek through your camp to find you.
KING HARRY   Good old knight,
Collect them all together at my tent.
I'll be before thee.
270 ERPINGHAM   I shall do't, my lord.   *Exit*
KING HARRY O God of battles, steel my soldiers' hearts.
Possess them not with fear. Take from them now
The sense of reck'ning,° ere th'opposèd numbers   ability to count
Pluck their hearts from them. Not today, O Lord,
275 O not today, think not upon the fault
My father made in compassing the crown.[4]
I Richard's body have interrèd new,°   buried anew
And on it have bestowed more contrite tears
Than from it issued forcèd drops of blood.
280 Five hundred poor have I in yearly pay
Who twice a day their withered hands hold up°   (in prayer)
Toward heaven to pardon blood. And I have built
Two chantries,[5] where the sad and solemn priests
Sing still for Richard's soul. More will I do,
285 Though all that I can do is nothing worth,
Since that my penitence comes after ill,°   sin
Imploring pardon.
     Enter the [Duke of] GLOUCESTER
GLOUCESTER My liege.
KING HARRY My brother Gloucester's voice? Ay.
290 I know thy errand, I will go with thee.
The day, my friends, and all things stay° for me.   *Exeunt*   wait

4.2

     Enter [Dukes of BOURBON *and]* ORLÉANS, *and [Lord]*
     RAMBURES
ORLÉANS The sun doth gild our armour. Up, my lords!
BOURBON *Monte cheval!°* My horse! *Varlet, lacquais!°* Ha!   To horse / valet
ORLÉANS O brave spirit!
BOURBON *Via les eaux et terre!*
5 ORLÉANS *Rien plus? L'air et feu!*[1]
BOURBON *Cieux,°* cousin Orléans!   To the heavens
     Enter CONSTABLE
Now, my Lord Constable!
CONSTABLE Hark how our steeds for present° service neigh.   immediate
BOURBON Mount them and make incision in their hides,
10 That their hot blood may spin in English eyes
And dout° them with superfluous courage. Ha!   extinguish
RAMBURES What, will you have them weep our horses' blood?

---

4. Henry's father usurped the throne from its rightful possessor, Richard II.
5. Chapels where masses for the dead were sung.
4.2 Location: The French camp.

1. Away over water and earth!
No more? Air and fire! (Playing on the four elements, of which fire was the highest.)

How shall we then behold their natural tears?
Enter MESSENGER
MESSENGER   The English are embattled,[2] you French peers.
15   CONSTABLE   To horse, you gallant princes, straight to horse!
Do but behold yon poor and starvèd band,
And your fair show° shall suck away their souls,   *appearance*
Leaving them but the shells and husks of men.
There is not work enough for all our hands,
20   Scarce blood enough in all their sickly veins
To give each naked curtal-axe° a stain   *cutlass*
That our French gallants shall today draw out
And sheathe for lack of sport. Let us but blow on them,
The vapour of our valour will o'erturn them.
25   'Tis positive 'gainst all exceptions,° lords,   *'Tis definitely true*
That our superfluous lackeys and our peasants,
Who in unnecessary action swarm
About our squares of battle, were enough
To purge this field of such a hilding° foe,   *worthless*
30   Though we upon this mountain's basis by°   *foot nearby*
Took stand° for idle speculation,   *Stood still*
But that our honours must not. What's to say?
A very little little let us do
And all is done. Then let the trumpets sound
35   The tucket sonance° and the note to mount,   *trumpet signal*
For our approach shall so much dare the field
That England shall couch down in fear and yield.
Enter [Lord] GRANDPRÉ
GRANDPRÉ   Why do you stay so long, my lords of France?
Yon island carrions,° desperate of their bones,   *cadavers*
40   Ill-favouredly become the morning field.
Their ragged curtains° poorly are let loose   *banners*
And our air shakes them passing scornfully.
Big Mars° seems bankrupt in their beggared host   *god of war*
And faintly through a rusty beaver° peeps.   *visor*
45   The horsemen sit like fixèd candlesticks
With torchstaves° in their hands, and their poor jades   *tapers*
Lob° down their heads, drooping the hides and hips,   *Hang*
The gum down-roping° from their pale dead eyes,   *mucus dripping*
And in their palled° dull mouths the gimmaled° bit   *pale / jointed*
50   Lies foul with chewed grass, still and motionless.
And their executors,[3] the knavish crows,
Fly o'er them all impatient for their hour.
Description cannot suit itself in words
To demonstrate the life of° such a battle   *depict realistically*
55   In life so lifeless as it shows itself.
CONSTABLE   They have said their prayers, and they stay° for death.   *wait*
BOURBON   Shall we go send them dinners and fresh suits
And give their fasting horses provender,°   *food*
And after° fight with them?   *afterward*
60   CONSTABLE   I stay but for my guidon.° To the field!   *pennant*
I will the banner from a trumpet° take   *trumpeter*
And use it for my haste. Come, come away!
The sun is high, and we outwear° the day.   *Exeunt*   *waste*

2. Drawn into lines of battle.   3. Administrators of wills (who dispose of the remains of the dead)

4.3

*Enter [Dukes of] GLOUCESTER, [CLARENCE, and] EXE-
TER, [Earls of] SALISBURY and [WARWICK, and Sir
Thomas] ERPINGHAM, with all [the] host*

GLOUCESTER Where is the King?

CLARENCE The King himself is rode to view their battle.°   *army*

WARWICK Of fighting men they have full threescore thousand.°   *60,000*

EXETER There's five to one. Besides, they all are fresh.

5 SALISBURY God's arm strike with us! 'Tis a fearful odds.

   God b'wi' you, princes all. I'll to my charge.°   *command post*

   If we no more meet till we meet in heaven,

   Then joyfully, my noble Lord of Clarence,

   My dear Lord Gloucester, and my good Lord Exeter,

10   And [*to* WARWICK] my kind kinsman, warriors all, adieu.

CLARENCE Farewell, good Salisbury, and good luck go with thee.

EXETER Farewell, kind lord. Fight valiantly today —

   And yet I do thee wrong to mind° thee of it,   *remind*

   For thou art framed of the firm truth of valour.

                                       [*Exit* SALISBURY]

15 CLARENCE He is as full of valour as of kindness,

   Princely in both.

               Enter KING [HARRY, *behind*]

WARWICK   O that we now had here

   But one ten thousand of those men in England

   That do no work today.

KING HARRY   What's he that wishes so?

   My cousin Warwick? No, my fair cousin.

20   If we are marked to die, we are enough

   To do our country loss;° and if to live,   *For our country to lose*

   The fewer men, the greater share of honour.

   God's will, I pray thee wish not one man more.

   By Jove, I am not covetous for gold,

25   Nor care I who doth feed upon my cost;

   It ernes° me not if men my garments wear;   *grieves*

   Such outward things dwell not in my desires.

   But if it be a sin to covet honour

   I am the most offending soul alive.

30   No, faith, my coz,° wish not a man from England.   *kinsman*

   God's peace, I would not lose so great an honour

   As one man more methinks would share° from me   *deprive*

   For the best hope I have. O do not wish one more.

   Rather proclaim it presently° through my host°   *immediately / army*

35   That he which hath no stomach° to this fight,   *appetite; courage*

   Let him depart. His passport shall be made

   And crowns for convoy° put into his purse.   *money for transport*

   We would not die in that man's company

   That fears his fellowship° to die with us.   *duty as our companion*

40   This day is called the Feast of Crispian.[1]

   He that outlives this day and comes safe home

   Will stand a-tiptoe when this day is named

   And rouse him at the name of Crispian.

   He that shall see this day and live t'old age

4.3 Location: The English camp.

1. October 25, dedicated to the martyred brothers Crispin and Crispianus.

45	Will yearly on the vigil° feast his neighbours	*eve of the saint's day*
	And say, 'Tomorrow is Saint Crispian.'	
	Then will he strip his sleeve and show his scars	
	And say, 'These wounds I had on Crispin's day.'	
	Old men forget; yet all shall be forgot,	
50	But he'll remember, with advantages,°	*embellishments*
	What feats he did that day. Then shall our names,	
	Familiar in his mouth as household words—	
	Harry the King, Bedford and Exeter,	
	Warwick and Talbot, Salisbury and Gloucester—	
55	Be in their flowing cups freshly remembered.	
	This story shall the good man teach his son,	
	And Crispin Crispian shall ne'er go by	
	From this day to the ending of the world	
	But we in it shall be rememberèd,	
60	We few, we happy few, we band of brothers.	
	For he today that sheds his blood with me	
	Shall be my brother; be he ne'er so vile,°	*lowborn*
	This day shall gentle his condition.[2]	
	And gentlemen in England now abed	
65	Shall think themselves accursed they were not here,	
	And hold their manhoods cheap whiles any speaks	
	That fought with us upon Saint Crispin's day.	

Enter [Earl of] SALISBURY

	SALISBURY My sovereign lord, bestow yourself° with speed.	*take your positions*
	The French are bravely in their battles° set	*battle lines*
70	And will with all expedience° charge on us.	*speed*
	KING HARRY All things are ready if our minds be so.	
	WARWICK Perish the man whose mind is backward now.	
	KING HARRY Thou dost not wish more help from England, coz?	
	WARWICK God's will, my liege, would you and I alone,	
75	Without more help, could fight this royal battle.	
	KING HARRY Why now thou hast unwished five thousand men,	
	Which likes° me better than to wish us one.—	*pleases*
	You know your places. God be with you all.	

Tucket. Enter MONTJOY

	MONTJOY Once more I come to know of thee, King Harry,	
80	If for thy ransom thou wilt now compound°	*make terms*
	Before thy most assurèd overthrow.	
	For certainly thou art so near the gulf	
	Thou needs must be englutted.° Besides, in mercy	*swallowed*
	The Constable desires thee thou wilt mind°	*remind*
85	Thy followers of repentance, that their souls	
	May make a peaceful and a sweet retire	
	From off these fields where, wretches, their poor bodies	
	Must lie and fester.	
	KING HARRY Who hath sent thee now?	
90	MONTJOY The Constable of France.	
	KING HARRY I pray thee bear my former answer back.	
	Bid them achieve° me, and then sell my bones.	*get*
	Good God, why should they mock poor fellows thus?	
	The man that once did sell the lion's skin	
95	While the beast lived, was killed with hunting him.[3]	

2. Shall raise him to gentlemanly rank.   3. *The man . . . him:* alluding to one of Aesop's fables.

A many of our bodies shall no doubt
Find native° graves, upon the which, I trust,   (English)
Shall witness live in brass of this day's work.
And those that leave their valiant bones in France,
100 Dying like men, though buried in your dunghills
They shall be famed. For there the sun shall greet them
And draw their honours reeking° up to heaven,   steaming; stinking
Leaving their earthly parts to choke your clime,
The smell whereof shall breed a plague in France.
105 Mark then abounding valour in our English,
That, being dead, like to the bullets grazing°   ricocheting
Break out into a second course of mischief,
Killing in relapse of mortality.°   another fatal outbreak
Let me speak proudly. Tell the Constable
110 We are but warriors for the working day.°   workaday warriors
Our gayness and our gilt are all besmirched
With rainy marching in the painful field.
There's not a piece of feather° in our host—   decorative plume
Good argument, I hope, we will not fly—
115 And time hath worn us into slovenry.°   filth
But by the mass, our hearts are in the trim.°   fine shape
And my poor soldiers tell me, yet ere night
They'll be in fresher robes, as they will pluck
The gay new coats o'er your French soldiers' heads,
120 And turn them out of service.[4] If they do this—
As if God please, they shall—my ransom then
Will soon be levied.[5] Herald, save thou thy labour.
Come thou no more for ransom, gentle herald.
They shall have none, I swear, but these my joints—
125 Which if they have as I will leave 'em them,
Shall yield them little. Tell the Constable.
MONTJOY   I shall, King Harry. And so fare thee well.
Thou never shalt hear herald any more.
KING HARRY   I fear thou wilt once more come for a ransom.
                                        Exit [MONTJOY]
     Enter [*Duke of* YORK]
130 YORK   My lord, most humbly on my knee I beg
The leading of the vanguard.
KING HARRY   Take it, brave York.—Now soldiers, march away,
And how thou pleasest, God, dispose the day.   *Exeunt*

4.4

     Alarum. Excursions.° Enter PISTOL, [*a*] FRENCH SOL-   Skirmishes
          DIER, [*and the*] BOY
PISTOL   Yield, cur.
FRENCH SOLDIER   *Je pense que vous êtes le gentilhomme de bon*
     qualité.[1]
PISTOL   *Qualité? 'Calin o custure me!*[2]
5   Art thou a gentleman? What is thy name? Discuss.
FRENCH SOLDIER   *O Seigneur Dieu!*°   O Lord God
PISTOL [*aside*]   O Seigneur Dew should be a gentleman.—

---

4. Dismiss them, stripped of their servant's uniforms.
5. Collected (from the French themselves).
4.4 Location: The battlefield.

1. I think you are a gentleman of high rank.
2. The Irish refrain of a popular ballad, meaning "I am a girl from beside the Suir."

	Perpend° my words, O Seigneur Dew, and mark:	*Weigh*
	O Seigneur Dew, thou diest, on point of fox,°	*sword*
10	Except, O Seigneur, thou do give to me	
	Egregious° ransom.	*Extraordinary*

FRENCH SOLDIER   *O prenez miséricorde! Ayez pitié de moi!*[3]

PISTOL   'Moy' shall not serve, I will have forty 'moys',[4]
Or I will fetch thy rim° out at thy throat   *stomach lining*

15   In drops of crimson blood.

FRENCH SOLDIER   *Est-il impossible d'échapper la force de ton bras?*[5]

PISTOL   Brass, cur? Thou damnèd and luxurious° mountain goat,   *lecherous*
Offer'st me brass?

FRENCH SOLDIER   *O pardonne-moi!*

20   PISTOL   Sayst thou me so? Is that a ton of moys? —
Come hither boy. Ask me this slave in French
What is his name.

BOY   *Écoutez: comment êtes-vous appelé?*[6]

FRENCH SOLDIER   *Monsieur le Fer.*

25   BOY   He says his name is Master Fer.

PISTOL   Master Fer? I'll fer him, and firk° him, and ferret° him.   *beat / savage*
Discuss the same in French unto him.

BOY   I do not know the French for fer and ferret and firk.

PISTOL   Bid him prepare, for I will cut his throat.

30   FRENCH SOLDIER   *Que dit-il, monsieur?*°   *What does he say, sir*

BOY   *Il me commande à vous dire que vous faites vous prêt, car ce
soldat ici est disposé tout à cette heure de couper votre gorge.*°   *(translates Pistol)*

PISTOL   *Oui, couper la gorge, par ma foi,*[7]
Peasant, unless thou give me crowns, brave crowns;

35   Or mangled shalt thou be by this my sword.

FRENCH SOLDIER   *O je vous supplie, pour l'amour de Dieu, me
pardonner. Je suis le gentilhomme de bonne maison. Gardez ma
vie, et je vous donnerai deux cents écus.*°   *(translated by the boy)*

PISTOL   What are his words?

40   BOY   He prays you to save his life. He is a gentleman of a good
house, and for his ransom he will give you two hundred
crowns.

PISTOL   Tell him, my fury shall abate, and I the crowns will take.

FRENCH SOLDIER   *Petit monsieur, que dit-il?*[8]

45   BOY   *Encore qu'il est contre son jurement de pardonner aucun
prisonnier; néanmoins, pour les écus que vous lui ci promettez, il
est content à vous donner la liberté, le franchisement.*

FRENCH SOLDIER   [*kneeling to* PISTOL]   *Sur mes genoux je vous
donne mille remerciements, et je m'estime heureux que j'ai*

50   *tombé entre les mains d'un chevalier, comme je pense, le plus
brave, vaillant, et treis-distingué seigneur d'Angleterre.*°   *(translated by the boy)*

PISTOL   Expound unto me, boy.

BOY   He gives you upon his knees a thousand thanks, and he
esteems himself happy that he hath fallen into the hands of

55   one, as he thinks, the most brave, valorous, and thrice-worthy
seigneur of England.

PISTOL   As I suck blood, I will some mercy show.
Follow me.

---

3. O take pity! Have pity on me!
4. Pistol mistakes *moi* for the name of a coin.
5. Is it impossible to escape the strength of your arm?

6. Listen: what's your name?
7. Yes, cut your throat, by my faith.
8. Little sir, what says he?

BOY   *Suivez-vous le grand capitaine.*[9]

                              [*Exeunt* PISTOL *and* FRENCH SOLDIER]

60   I did never know so full a voice issue from so empty a heart.
    But the saying is true: 'The empty vessel makes the greatest
    sound.' Bardolph and Nim had ten times more valour than this
    roaring devil i'th' old play, that everyone may pare his nails
    with a wooden dagger,[1] and they are both hanged, and so
65   would this be, if he durst steal anything adventurously.° I must   *recklessly*
    stay with the lackeys with the luggage of our camp. The French
    might have a good prey of us, if he knew of it, for there is none
    to guard it but boys.   *Exit*

4.5

Enter CONSTABLE, [*Dukes of*] ORLÉANS [*and*] BOURBON,
    and [*Lord*] RAMBURES

CONSTABLE   *O diable!*

ORLÉANS   *O Seigneur! Le jour est perdu, tout est perdu!*

BOURBON   *Mort de ma vie!*[1] All is confounded,° all.   *lost*
    Reproach and everlasting shame
5   Sits mocking in our plumes.
        A short alarum
    O méchante fortune!° — [*To* RAMBURES] Do not run away.   *evil fate*

ORLÉANS   We are enough yet living in the field
    To smother up the English in our throngs,
    If any order might be thought upon.

10 BOURBON   The devil take order. Once more back again!
    And he that will not follow Bourbon now,
    Let him go home, and with his cap in hand
    Like a base leno° hold the chamber door   *pimp*
    Whilst by a slave no gentler° than my dog   *better born*
15   His fairest daughter is contaminated.

CONSTABLE   Disorder that hath spoiled° us friend° us now.   *ruined / befriend*
    Let us on heaps go offer up our lives.

BOURBON   I'll to the throng.
    Let life be short, else shame will be too long.[2]   *Exeunt*

4.6

Alarum. Enter KING [HARRY] *and his train,*° *with pris-*   *followers*
    oners

KING HARRY   Well have we done, thrice-valiant countrymen.
    But all's not done; yet keep the French the field.
              [*Enter the Duke of* EXETER]

EXETER   The Duke of York commends him to your majesty.

KING HARRY   Lives he, good uncle? Thrice within this hour
5   I saw him down, thrice up again and fighting.
    From helmet to the spur, all blood he was.

EXETER   In which array, brave soldier, doth he lie,
    Larding° the plain. And by his bloody side,   *Moistening*
    Yokefellow to his honour-owing° wounds,   *honorable*
10   The noble Earl of Suffolk also lies.

---

9. Follow the great captain.
1. Allegorical "Vice" characters in old-fashioned morality
plays were typically armed with wooden daggers.
4.5 Location: The battlefield.
1. O the devil!

O God! The day is lost, all is lost!
  Death of my life!
2. See Additional Passages at end of play for the Folio
and quarto versions of this scene.
4.6 Location: The battlefield.

Suffolk first died, and York, all haggled over,°   *hacked up*
Comes to him, where in gore he lay insteeped,°   *soaked*
And takes him by the beard, kisses the gashes
That bloodily did yawn upon his face,
15   And cries aloud, 'Tarry, dear cousin Suffolk.
My soul shall thine keep company to heaven.
Tarry, sweet soul, for mine, then fly abreast,
As in this glorious and well-foughten field
We kept together in our chivalry.'
20   Upon these words I came and cheered him up.
He smiled me in the face, raught° me his hand,   *reached*
And with a feeble grip says, 'Dear my lord,
Commend my service to my sovereign.'
So did he turn, and over Suffolk's neck
25   He threw his wounded arm, and kissed his lips,
And so espoused to death, with blood he sealed
A testament of noble-ending love.
The pretty and sweet manner of it forced
Those waters from me which I would have stopped.
30   But I had not so much of man in me,
And all my mother° came into mine eyes   *(feminine) tenderness*
And gave me up to tears.
KING HARRY   I blame you not,
For hearing this I must perforce compound°   *come to terms*
With mistful eyes, or they will issue° too.   *weep*
       Alarum
35   But hark, what new alarum is this same?
The French have reinforced their scattered men.
Then every soldier kill his prisoners.
       [The soldiers kill their prisoners][1]
Give the word through.
PISTOL   *Coup' la gorge.*°   *Exeunt*   *Cut the throat*

4.7

    Enter [Captains] FLUELLEN *and* GOWER

FLUELLEN   Kill the poys and the luggage! 'Tis expressly against
    the law of arms. 'Tis as arrant a piece of knavery, mark you
    now, as can be offert. In your conscience now, is it not?
GOWER   'Tis certain there's not a boy left alive. And the cowardly
5   rascals that ran from the battle ha' done this slaughter. Besides,
    they have burned and carried away all that was in the King's
    tent; wherefore the King most worthily hath caused every sol-
    dier to cut his prisoner's throat. O 'tis a gallant king.
FLUELLEN   Ay, he was porn at Monmouth.° Captain Gower,   *(in Wales)*
10   what call you the town's name where Alexander the Pig was
    born?
GOWER   Alexander the Great.
FLUELLEN   Why I pray you, is not 'pig' great? The pig or the
    great or the mighty or the huge or the magnanimous are all
15   one reckonings, save the phrase is a little variations.°   *(for "varied")*
GOWER   I think Alexander the Great was born in Macedon. His
    father was called Philip of Macedon, as I take it.
FLUELLEN   I think it is e'en Macedon where Alexander is porn.

---

1. This may or may not be done onstage.   4.7 Location: Before Henry's pavilion.

I tell you, captain, if you look in the maps of the world I warrant
20   you sall find, in the comparisons between Macedon and Monmouth, that the situations, look you, is both alike. There is a
river in Macedon, and there is also moreover a river at Monmouth. It is called Wye at Monmouth, but it is out of my prains
what is the name of the other river—but 'tis all one, 'tis alike as
25   my fingers is to my fingers, and there is salmons in both. If you
mark Alexander's life well, Harry of Monmouth's life is come
after it indifferent well.¹ For there is figures° in all things. Alex-   *comparisons*
ander, God knows, and you know, in his rages and his furies
and his wraths and his cholers° and his moods and his displea-   *angers*
30   sures and his indignations, and also being a little intoxicates in
his prains, did in his ales and his angers, look you, kill his best
friend Cleitus—

GOWER   Our King is not like him in that. He never killed any of
his friends.

35 FLUELLEN   It is not well done, mark you now, to take the tales
out of my mouth ere it is made an end and finished. I speak
but in the figures and comparisons of it. As Alexander killed his
friend Cleitus, being in his ales and his cups, so also Harry
Monmouth, being in his right wits and his good judgements,
40   turned away the fat knight with the great-belly doublet—he was
full of jests and gipes° and kneveries and mocks—I have forgot   *gibes*
his name.

GOWER   Sir John Falstaff.

FLUELLEN   That is he. I'll tell you, there is good men porn at
45   Monmouth.

GOWER   Here comes his majesty.

    Alarum. Enter KING HARRY *and* [*the English army*], *with*
    [*Duke of*] BOURBON, [*Duke of* ORLÉANS, *and other*] *pris-*
    *oners.*² *Flourish*

KING HARRY   I was not angry since I came to France
Until this instant. Take a trumpet, herald;
Ride thou unto the horsemen on yon hill.
50   If they will fight with us, bid them come down,
Or void° the field: they do offend our sight.   *leave*
If they'll do neither, we will come to them,
And make them skirr° away as swift as stones   *scurry*
Enforcèd° from the old Assyrian slings.   *Driven*
55   Besides, we'll cut the throats of those we have,
And not a man of them that we shall take
Shall taste our mercy. Go and tell them so.

    Enter MONTJOY

EXETER   Here comes the herald of the French, my liege.

GLOUCESTER   His eyes are humbler than they used to be.

60 KING HARRY   How now, what means this, herald? Know'st thou not
That I have fined° these bones of mine for ransom?   *pledged*
Com'st thou again for ransom?

MONTJOY   No, great King.
I come to thee for charitable licence,°   *permission*
That we may wander o'er this bloody field
65   To book° our dead and then to bury them,   *register*

1. *is . . . well*: resembles it fairly well.
2. This is a second batch of prisoners, captured after the French counterattack.

To sort our nobles from our common men—
For many of our princes, woe the while,
Lie drowned and soaked in mercenary blood.[3]
So do our vulgar° drench their peasant limbs   *common people*
70   In blood of princes, and our wounded steeds
Fret fetlock°-deep in gore, and with wild rage   *ankle*
Jerk out their armèd heels at their dead masters,
Killing them twice. O give us leave, great King,
To view the field in safety, and dispose
Of their dead bodies.
75   KING HARRY   I tell thee truly, herald,
I know not if the day be ours or no,
For yet a many of your horsemen peer°   *appear*
And gallop o'er the field.
MONTJOY   The day is yours.
KING HARRY   Praisèd be God, and not our strength, for it.
80   What is this castle called that stands hard by?
MONTJOY   They call it Agincourt.
KING HARRY   Then call we this the field of Agincourt,
Fought on the day of Crispin Crispian.
FLUELLEN   Your grandfather of famous memory, an't° please   *if it*
85   your majesty, and your great-uncle Edward the Plack Prince of
Wales, as I have read in the chronicles, fought a most prave
pattle here in France.
KING HARRY   They did, Fluellen.
FLUELLEN   Your majesty says very true. If your majesties is
90   remembered of it, the Welshmen did good service in a garden
where leeks did grow, wearing leeks in their Monmouth caps,[4]
which your majesty know to this hour is an honourable badge
of the service. And I do believe your majesty takes no scorn to
wear the leek upon Saint Tavy's day.
95   KING HARRY   I wear it for a memorable honour,
For I am Welsh, you know, good countryman.
FLUELLEN   All the water in Wye° cannot wash your majesty's   *Welsh river*
Welsh plood out of your pody, I can tell you that. God pless it
and preserve it, as long as it pleases his grace, and his majesty
100   too.
KING HARRY   Thanks, good my countryman.
FLUELLEN   By Jeshu, I am your majesty's countryman. I care not
who know it, I will confess it to all the world. I need not to be
ashamed of your majesty, praised be God, so long as your maj-
105   esty is an honest man.
KING HARRY   God keep me so.
        Enter WILLIAMS [*with a glove in his cap*]
                        Our heralds go with him.
Bring me just notice° of the numbers dead   *accurate record*
On both our parts.
        Exeunt [MONTJOY, GOWER, *and English*] *heralds*
                Call yonder fellow hither.
EXETER [*to* WILLIAMS]   Soldier, you must come to the King.
110   KING HARRY   Soldier, why wearest thou that glove in thy cap?
WILLIAMS   An't please your majesty, 'tis the gage° of one that I   *token*
should fight withal, if he be alive.

---

3. Common soldiers, unlike noblemen, fought for pay.   4. Tall, tapering caps without brims.

KING HARRY   An Englishman?

WILLIAMS   An't please your majesty, a rascal, that swaggered with
115   me last night—who, if a live, and ever dare to challenge this
glove, I have sworn to take him a box o'th' ear; or if I can see
my glove in his cap—which he swore, as he was a soldier, he
would wear if a lived—I will strike it out soundly.

KING HARRY   What think you, Captain Fluellen? Is it fit this sol-
120   dier keep his oath?

FLUELLEN   He is a craven° and a villain else, an't please your   *coward*
majesty, in my conscience.

KING HARRY   It may be his enemy is a gentleman of great sort,
quite from the answer of his degree.[5]

125 FLUELLEN   Though he be as good a gentleman as the devil is, as
Lucifer and Beelzebub° himself, it is necessary, look your   *Satan*
grace, that he keep his vow and his oath. If he be perjured, see
you now, his reputation is as arrant a villain and a Jack-sauce°   *saucy knave*
as ever his black shoe trod upon God's ground and his earth,
130   in my conscience, law.

KING HARRY   Then keep thy vow, sirrah, when thou meetest the
fellow.

WILLIAMS   So I will, my liege, as I live.

KING HARRY   Who serv'st thou under?

135 WILLIAMS   Under Captain Gower, my liege.

FLUELLEN   Gower is a good captain, and is good knowledge and
literatured° in the wars.   *well-read*

KING HARRY   Call him hither to me, soldier.

WILLIAMS   I will, my liege.   *Exit*

140 KING HARRY [*giving him Williams's other glove*]   Here, Fluellen,
wear thou this favour for me and stick it in thy cap. When
Alençon and myself were down together, I plucked this glove
from his helm. If any man challenge this, he is a friend to
Alençon and an enemy to our person. If thou encounter any
145   such, apprehend° him, an° thou dost me love.   *arrest / if*

FLUELLEN   Your grace does me as great honours as can be
desired in the hearts of his subjects. I would fain° see the man   *gladly*
that has but two legs that shall find himself aggriefed at this
glove, that is all; but I would fain see it once. An't please God
150   of his grace, that I would see.

KING HARRY   Know'st thou Gower?

FLUELLEN   He is my dear friend, an't please you.

KING HARRY   Pray thee, go seek him and bring him to my tent.

FLUELLEN   I will fetch him.   *Exit*

155 KING HARRY   My lord of Warwick and my brother Gloucester,
Follow Fluellen closely at the heels.
The glove which I have given him for a favour
May haply purchase him a box o'th' ear.
It is the soldier's. I by bargain should
160   Wear it myself. Follow, good cousin Warwick.
If that the soldier strike him, as I judge
By his blunt bearing he will keep his word,
Some sudden mischief may arise of it,
For I do know Fluellen valiant
165   And touched with choler,° hot as gunpowder,   *made angry*

---

5. Quite above responding to a challenge from one of Williams's rank.

And quickly will return an injury.°   insult
Follow, and see there be no harm between them.
Go you with me, uncle of Exeter.   *Exeunt [severally]*

4.8

Enter [Captain] GOWER *and* WILLIAMS
WILLIAMS   I warrant° it is to knight you, captain.   *I'm sure*
          Enter [Captain] FLUELLEN
FLUELLEN   God's will and his pleasure, captain, I beseech you
          now, come apace° to the King. There is more good toward you,   *quickly*
          peradventure,° than is in your knowledge to dream of.   *perhaps*
5   WILLIAMS   Sir, know you this glove?
    FLUELLEN   Know the glove? I know the glove is a glove.
    WILLIAMS   [*plucking the glove from Fluellen's cap*]   I know this,
          and thus I challenge it.
          [*He*] strikes [FLUELLEN]
    FLUELLEN   God's plood, and his! An arrant traitor as any's in the
10   universal world, or in France, or in England.
    GOWER   [*to* WILLIAMS]   How now, sir? You villain!
    WILLIAMS   Do you think I'll be forsworn?
    FLUELLEN   Stand away, Captain Gower. I will give treason his
          payment into plows, I warrant you.
15 WILLIAMS   I am no traitor.
    FLUELLEN   That's a lie in thy throat. I charge you in his majesty's
          name, apprehend him. He's a friend of the Duke Alençon's.
          Enter [Earl of] WARWICK *and [Duke of]* GLOUCESTER
    WARWICK   How now, how now, what's the matter?
    FLUELLEN   My lord of Warwick, here is—praised be God for it—
20   a most contagious° treason come to light, look you, as you shall   *noxious*
          desire in a summer's day.
          Enter KING [HARRY] *and [Duke of]* EXETER
          Here is his majesty.
    KING HARRY   How now, what is the matter?
    FLUELLEN   My liege, here is a villain and a traitor that, look your
25   grace, has struck the glove which your majesty is take out of
          the helmet of Alençon.
    WILLIAMS   My liege, this was my glove—here is the fellow° of   *mate*
          it—and he that I gave it to in change promised to wear it in his
          cap. I promised to strike him, if he did. I met this man with my
30   glove in his cap, and I have been as good as my word.
    FLUELLEN   Your majesty hear now, saving your majesty's man-
          hood, what an arrant rascally beggarly lousy knave it is. I hope
          your majesty is pear° me testimony and witness, and will   *(for "will bear")*
          avouchment° that this is the glove of Alençon that your maj-   *(for "vouch")*
35   esty is give me, in your conscience now.
    KING HARRY   Give me thy glove, soldier.
          Look, here is the fellow of it.
          'Twas I indeed thou promisèd'st to strike,
          And thou hast given me most bitter terms.°   *words*
40 FLUELLEN   An't please your majesty, let his neck answer for it, if
          there is any martial law in the world.
    KING HARRY   How canst thou make me satisfaction?
    WILLIAMS   All offences, my lord, come from the heart. Never

4.8 Location: Before Henry's pavilion.

came any from mine that might offend your majesty.
45 KING HARRY It was ourself thou didst abuse.
WILLIAMS Your majesty came not like yourself. You appeared to
me but as a common man. Witness the night, your garments,
your lowliness. And what your highness suffered under that
shape, I beseech you take it for your own fault, and not mine,
50 for had you been as I took you for, I made no offence. Therefore I beseech your highness pardon me.
KING HARRY Here, Uncle Exeter, fill this glove with crowns
And give it to this fellow. — Keep it, fellow,
And wear it for an honour in thy cap
55 Till I do challenge it. — Give him the crowns.
— And captain, you must needs be friends with him.
FLUELLEN By this day and this light, the fellow has mettle
enough in his belly. — Hold, there is twelve pence for you, and
I pray you to serve God, and keep you out of prawls and prab-
60 bles and quarrels and dissensions, and I warrant you it is the
better for you.
WILLIAMS I will none of your money.
FLUELLEN It is with a good will. I can tell you, it will serve you
to mend your shoes. Come, wherefore should you be so pash-
65 ful? Your shoes is not so good. 'Tis a good shilling, I warrant
you, or I will change it.¹
        Enter [an English] HERALD
KING HARRY Now, herald, are the dead numbered?
HERALD Here is the number of the slaughtered French.
KING HARRY What prisoners of good sort° are taken, uncle?   *high rank*
70 EXETER Charles, Duke of Orléans, nephew to the King;
Jean, Duke of Bourbon, and Lord Boucicault;
Of other lords and barons, knights and squires,
Full fifteen hundred, besides common men.
KING HARRY This note doth tell me of ten thousand French
75 That in the field lie slain. Of princes in this number
And nobles bearing banners,° there lie dead   *coats of arms*
One hundred twenty-six; added to these,
Of knights, esquires, and gallant gentlemen,
Eight thousand and four hundred, of the which
80 Five hundred were but yesterday dubbed knights.
So that in these ten thousand they have lost
There are but sixteen hundred mercenaries;
The rest are princes, barons, lords, knights, squires,
And gentlemen of blood and quality.
85 The names of those their nobles that lie dead:
Charles Delabret, High Constable of France;
Jaques of Châtillion, Admiral of France;
The Master of the Crossbows, Lord Rambures;
Great-Master of France, the brave Sir Guiscard Dauphin;
90 Jean, Duke of Alençon; Antony, Duke of Brabant,
The brother to the Duke of Burgundy;
And Édouard, Duke of Bar; of lusty earls,
Grandpré and Roussi, Fauconbridge and Foix,
Beaumont and Marle, Vaudemont and Lestrelles.
95 Here was a royal fellowship of death.

1. Williams may or may not take the money.

Where is the number of our English dead?
    [*He is given another paper*]
Edward the Duke of York, the Earl of Suffolk,
Sir Richard Keighley, Davy Gam Esquire;
None else of name,° and of all other men   *high rank*
100 But five-and-twenty. O God, thy arm was here,
And not to us, but to thy arm alone
Ascribe we all. When, without stratagem,
But in plain shock° and even play of battle,   *confrontation*
Was ever known so great and little loss
105 On one part and on th'other? Take it God,
For it is none but thine.
EXETER   'Tis wonderful.
KING HARRY Come, go we in procession to the village,
And be it death proclaimèd through our host
To boast of this, or take that praise from God
110 Which is his only.
FLUELLEN Is it not lawful, an't please your majesty, to tell how
   many is killed?
KING HARRY Yes, captain, but with this acknowledgement,
That God fought for us.
115 FLUELLEN Yes, in my conscience, he did us great good.
KING HARRY Do we all holy rites:
Let there be sung *Non nobis* and *Te Deum*,[2]
The dead with charity enclosed in clay;°   *buried with pious love*
And then to Calais, and to England then,
120 Where ne'er from France arrived more-happy° men. *Exeunt* *more fortunate*

5.0

Enter CHORUS
CHORUS Vouchsafe° to those that have not read the story   *Allow*
That I may prompt them—and of such as have,
I humbly pray them to admit th'excuse
Of time, of numbers, and due course of things,
5 Which cannot in their huge and proper life
Be here presented. Now we bear the King
Toward Calais. Grant him there; there seen,
Heave him away upon your wingèd thoughts
Athwart the sea. Behold, the English beach
10 Pales-in° the flood, with men, maids, wives, and boys,   *Fences in*
Whose shouts and claps out-voice the deep-mouthed sea,
Which like a mighty whiffler[1] fore the King
Seems to prepare his way. So let him land,
And solemnly see him set on to London.
15 So swift a pace hath thought, that even now
You may imagine him upon Blackheath,[2]
Where that his lords desire him to have borne
His bruisèd helmet and his bended sword
Before him through the city; he forbids it,
20 Being free from vainness and self-glorious pride,
Giving full trophy, signal, and ostent°   *honor for the victory*

---

2. *Non nobis* is Psalm 115, beginning "Not unto us, O
Lord, not unto us, but unto thy name give the glory." *Te
Deum* is a canticle of thanks beginning "We praise thee,
O God."

5.0
1. Official who cleared the way for a procession.
2. Open space outside London.

Quite from himself, to God. But now behold,
In the quick forge and working-house of thought,
How London doth pour out her citizens.
25 The Mayor and all his brethren, in best sort,°   *clothing*
Like to the senators of th'antique Rome
With the plebeians° swarming at their heels,   *commoners*
Go forth and fetch their conqu'ring Caesar in —
As, by a lower but high-loving likelihood,[3]
30 Were now the General of our gracious Empress[4] —
As in good time he may — from Ireland coming,
Bringing rebellion broachèd° on his sword,   *impaled*
How many would the peaceful city quit
To welcome him! Much more, and much more cause,
35 Did they this Harry. Now in London place him;
As yet the lamentation of the French
Invites the King of England's stay at home.
The Emperor's coming[5] in behalf of France,
To order peace between them [
40   ] [6] and omit
All the occurrences, whatever chanced,
Till Harry's back-return again to France.[7]
There must we bring him, and myself have played
The interim by rememb'ring° you 'tis past.   *reminding*
45 Then brook° abridgement, and your eyes advance,   *tolerate*
After your thoughts, straight back again to France.   *Exit*

5.1

Enter [Captain] GOWER *and [Captain]* FLUELLEN *[with
a leek in his cap and a cudgel]*

GOWER Nay, that's right. But why wear you your leek today?
Saint Davy's day is past.
FLUELLEN There is occasions and causes why and wherefore in
all things. I will tell you, ass my friend, Captain Gower. The
5 rascally scald° beggarly lousy pragging knave Pistol — which you   *scabby*
and yourself and all the world know to be no petter than a
fellow, look you now, of no merits — he is come to me, and
prings me pread and salt yesterday,° look you, and bid me eat   *(on St. Davy's Day)*
my leek. It was in a place where I could not breed no con-
10 tention with him, but I will be so bold as to wear it in my cap
till I see him once again, and then I will tell him a little piece
of my desires.

Enter [Ensign] PISTOL

GOWER Why, here a° comes, swelling like a turkey-cock.   *he*
FLUELLEN 'Tis no matter for his swellings nor his turkey-
15 cocks. — God pless you Ensign Pistol, you scurvy lousy knave,
God pless you.
PISTOL Ha, art thou bedlam?° Dost thou thirst, base Trojan,°   *crazy / villain*
To have me fold up Parca's[1] fatal web?
Hence! I am qualmish° at the smell of leek.   *nauseated*

---

3. Lovingly anticipated probability.
4. *General . . . Empress:* Earl of Essex (see Introduction).
5. Sigismund, the Holy Roman Emperor, attempted, and
failed, to negotiate a peace between France and England.
6. A line is evidently missing here.

7. Henry invaded France a second and third time, in
1417 and 1420; Act 5 begins in the latter year.
5.1 Location: The English camp.
1. The Parcae were the mythological Fates who spun and
cut the thread of life.

20 FLUELLEN I peseech you heartily, scurvy lousy knave, at my
desires and my requests and my petitions, to eat, look you, this
leek. Because, look you, you do not love it, nor your affections
and your appetites and your digestions does not agree with it, I
would desire you to eat it.

25 PISTOL Not for Cadwallader° and all his goats.   *last Welsh king*

FLUELLEN There is one goat for you. [*He*] *strikes* [PISTOL] Will
you be so good, scald° knave, as eat it?   *worthless*

PISTOL Base Trojan, thou shalt die.

FLUELLEN You say very true, scald knave, when God's will is. I

30 will desire you to live in the mean time, and eat your victuals.°   *food*
Come, there is sauce for it. [*He strikes him*] You called me
yesterday 'mountain-squire',° but I will make you today a   *(Wales is moutainous)*
'squire of low degree'. I pray you, fall to. If you can mock a leek
you can eat a leek.
[*He strikes him*]

35 GOWER Enough, captain, you have astonished° him.   *stunned*

FLUELLEN By Jesu, I will make him eat some part of my leek, or
I will peat his pate° four days and four nights.—Bite, I pray you.   *head*
It is good for your green° wound and your ploody coxcomb.°   *fresh / head*

PISTOL Must I bite?

40 FLUELLEN Yes, certainly, and out of doubt and out of question
too, and ambiguities.

PISTOL By this leek, I will most horribly revenge—
[FLUELLEN *threatens him*]
I eat and eat—I swear—

FLUELLEN Eat, I pray you. Will you have some more sauce to

45 your leek? There is not enough leek to swear by.

PISTOL Quiet thy cudgel,° thou dost see I eat.   *wooden club*

FLUELLEN Much good do you, scald knave, heartily. Nay, pray
you throw none away. The skin is good for your broken coxcomb. When you take occasions to see leeks hereafter, I pray

50 you mock at 'em, that is all.

PISTOL Good.

FLUELLEN Ay, leeks is good. Hold you, there is a groat° to heal   *fourpence*
your pate.

PISTOL Me, a groat?

55 FLUELLEN Yes, verily,° and in truth you shall take it, or I have   *truly*
another leek in my pocket which you shall eat.

PISTOL I take thy groat in earnest° of revenge.   *advance payment*

FLUELLEN If I owe you anything, I will pay you in cudgels. You
shall be a woodmonger, and buy nothing of me but cudgels.

60 God b'wi' you, and keep you, and heal your pate.   *Exit*

PISTOL All hell shall stir for this.

GOWER Go, go, you are a counterfeit cowardly knave. Will you
mock at an ancient tradition, begun upon an honourable
respect and worn as a memorable trophy of predeceased

65 valour, and dare not avouch° in your deeds any of your words?   *prove*
I have seen you gleeking and galling° at this gentleman twice   *jesting and annoying*
or thrice. You thought, because he could not speak English in
the native garb, he could not therefore handle an English cudgel. You find it otherwise. And henceforth let a Welsh correc-

70 tion teach you a good English condition. Fare ye well.   *Exit*

PISTOL Doth Fortune play the hussy° with me now?   *whore*
News have I that my Nell is dead

I'th' spital of a malady of France,°   *venereal disease*
And there my rendezvous° is quite cut off.   *refuge*
75   Old I do wax, and from my weary limbs
Honour is cudgelled. Well, bawd° I'll turn,   *pimp*
And something lean to cutpurse of quick hand.
To England will I steal, and there I'll steal,
And patches will I get unto these cudgelled scars,
80   And swear I got them in the Gallia° wars.   *Exit*   *French*

5.2

Enter at one door KING [HARRY, *Dukes of*] EXETER [*and*
CLARENCE, *Earl of*] WARWICK, *and other lords; at
another,* KING [CHARLES *the Sixth*] *of France,* QUEEN ISA-
BEL, *the Duke of* BURGUNDY, *and other French,* [*among
them Princess*] CATHERINE [*and* ALICE]

KING HARRY   Peace to this meeting, wherefor° we are met.   *for which*
Unto our brother France and to our sister,
Health and fair time of day. Joy and good wishes
To our most fair and princely cousin Catherine;
5   And as a branch and member of this royalty,
By whom this great assembly is contrived,
We do salute you, Duke of Burgundy.
And princes French, and peers, health to you all.
KING CHARLES   Right joyous are we to behold your face.
10   Most worthy brother England, fairly met.
So are you, princes English, every one.
QUEEN ISABEL   So happy be the issue,° brother England,   *outcome*
Of this good day and of this gracious meeting,
As we are now glad to behold your eyes—
15   Your eyes which hitherto have borne in them,
Against the French that met them in their bent,°   *glance*
The fatal balls° of murdering basilisks.[1]   *eyeballs; cannonballs*
The venom of such looks we fairly hope
Have lost their quality,° and that this day   *nature*
20   Shall change all griefs and quarrels into love.
KING HARRY   To cry amen to that, thus we appear.
QUEEN ISABEL   You English princes all, I do salute you.
BURGUNDY   My duty to you both, on equal love,
Great Kings of France and England. That I have laboured
25   With all my wits, my pains, and strong endeavours,
To bring your most imperial majesties
Unto this bar° and royal interview,   *court*
Your mightiness on both parts best can witness.
Since, then, my office hath so far prevailed
30   That face to face and royal eye to eye
You have congreeted,° let it not disgrace me   *met*
If I demand, before this royal view,
What rub° or what impediment there is   *hindrance*
Why that the naked, poor, and mangled peace,
35   Dear nurse of arts, plenties, and joyful births,
Should not in this best garden of the world,
Our fertile France, put up her lovely visage?
Alas, she hath from France too long been chased,

5.2 Location: The French court.   1. Fabulous animals able to kill with a glance.

40	And all her husbandry° doth lie on heaps,	*agriculture*
	Corrupting in it° own fertility.	*its*
	Her vine, the merry cheerer of the heart,	
	Unprunèd dies; her hedges even-plashed°	*interwoven*
	Like prisoners wildly overgrown with hair	
	Put forth disordered twigs; her fallow leas°	*unplanted fields*
45	The darnel, hemlock, and rank fumitory°	*kinds of weeds*
	Doth root upon, while that the coulter° rusts	*plow*
	That should deracinate° such savagery.	*root out*
	The even mead°—that erst brought sweetly forth	*meadow*
	The freckled cowslip, burnet, and green clover—	
50	Wanting the scythe, all uncorrected, rank,	
	Conceives by idleness,° and nothing teems	*Breeds worthless things*
	But hateful docks, rough thistles, kecksies, burs,°	*(all are weeds)*
	Losing both beauty and utility.	
	An° all our vineyards, fallows, meads, and hedges,	*And if*
55	Defective in their natures, grow to wildness,	
	Even so our houses and ourselves and children	
	Have lost, or do not learn for want of time,	
	The sciences° that should become° our country,	*knowledge / adorn*
	But grow like savages—as soldiers will	
60	That nothing do but meditate on blood—	
	To swearing and stern looks, diffused° attire,	*disordered*
	And everything that seems unnatural.	
	Which to reduce into our former favour²	
	You are assembled, and my speech entreats	
65	That I may know the let° why gentle peace	*impediment*
	Should not expel these inconveniences	
	And bless us with her former qualities.	
	KING HARRY If, Duke of Burgundy, you would the peace	
	Whose want gives growth to th'imperfections	
70	Which you have cited, you must buy that peace	
	With full accord to all our just demands,	
	Whose tenors° and particular effects	*general principles*
	You have enscheduled briefly in your hands.	
	BURGUNDY The King hath heard them, to the which as yet	
	There is no answer made.	
75	KING HARRY Well then, the peace,	
	Which you before so urged, lies in his answer.	
	KING CHARLES I have but with a cursitory° eye	*cursory*
	O'erglanced the articles. Pleaseth your grace	
	To appoint some of your council presently	
80	To sit with us once more, with better heed	
	To re-survey them, we will suddenly	
	Pass our accept and peremptory° answer.	*approved and definite*
	KING HARRY Brother, we shall.—Go, Uncle Exeter	
	And brother Clarence, and you, brother Gloucester;	
85	Warwick and Huntingdon, go with the King,	
	And take with you free power to ratify,	
	Augment, or alter, as your wisdoms best	
	Shall see advantageable for our dignity,	
	Anything in or out of our demands,	
90	And we'll consign° thereto.—Will you, fair sister,	*agree*

2. To revert to our old appearance.

Go with the princes, or stay here with us?

QUEEN   Our gracious brother, I will go with them.
Haply° a woman's voice may do some good   *Perhaps*
When articles too nicely° urged be stood on.   *punctiliously*

95   KING HARRY   Yet leave our cousin Catherine here with us.
She is our capital° demand, comprised   *chief*
Within the fore-rank of our articles.

QUEEN   She hath good leave.

Exeunt [all but] KING HARRY, CATHERINE, *and* [ALICE]
the gentlewoman

KING HARRY   Fair Catherine, and most fair,
Will you vouchsafe to teach a soldier terms

100   Such as will enter at a lady's ear
And plead his love-suit to her gentle heart?

CATHERINE   Your majesty shall mock at me. I cannot speak your
England.

KING HARRY   O fair Catherine, if you will love me soundly with

105   your French heart, I will be glad to hear you confess it brokenly
with your English tongue. Do you like me, Kate?

CATHERINE   *Pardonnez-moi,*° I cannot tell vat is 'like me'.   *Excuse me*

KING HARRY   An angel is like you, Kate, and you are like an
angel.

110   CATHERINE   *[to* ALICE*]   Que dit-il?—que je suis semblable à les
anges?*

ALICE   *Oui, vraiment—sauf votre grâce—ainsi dit-il.*[3]

KING HARRY   I said so, dear Catherine, and I must not blush to
affirm it.

115   CATHERINE   *O bon Dieu!*° *Les langues des hommes sont pleines*   *O good God*
de tromperies.°   *(translated below)*

KING HARRY   What says she, fair one? That the tongues of men
are full of deceits?

ALICE   *Oui,* dat de tongeus of de mans is be full of deceits—dat

120   is de Princess.

KING HARRY   The Princess is the better Englishwoman. I'faith,
Kate, my wooing is fit for thy understanding. I am glad thou
canst speak no better English, for if thou couldst, thou wouldst
find me such a plain king that thou wouldst think I had sold

125   my farm to buy my crown. I know no ways to mince it in love,
but directly to say, 'I love you'; then if you urge me farther than
to say, 'Do you in faith?', I wear out my suit. Give me your
answer, i'faith do, and so clap° hands and a bargain. How say   *shake*
you, lady?

130   CATHERINE   *Sauf votre honneur,*° me understand well.   *Save your honor*

KING HARRY   Marry, if you would put me to verses, or to dance
for your sake, Kate, why, you undid me. For the one I have
neither words nor measure,° and for the other I have no   *meter*
strength in measure°—yet a reasonable measure in strength. If   *talent for dancing*

135   I could win a lady at leap-frog, or by vaulting into my saddle
with my armour on my back, under the correction of bragging
be it spoken, I should quickly leap into a wife. Or if I might
buffet° for my love, or bound my horse for her favours, I could   *box*
lay on like a butcher, and sit like a jackanapes,° never off. But   *monkey*

140   before God, Kate, I cannot look greenly,° nor gasp out my elo-   *abashed*

3. What does he say? That I am like an angel? Yes, truly, save your grace, he says that.

quence, nor I have no cunning in protestation—only downright oaths, which I never use till urged, nor never break for
urging. If thou canst love a fellow of this temper,° Kate, whose   makeup
face is not worth sunburning, that never looks in his glass° for   mirror
145   love of anything he sees there, let thine eye be thy cook. I speak
to thee plain soldier: if thou canst love me for this, take me. If
not, to say to thee that I shall die, is true—but for thy love, by
the Lord, no. Yet I love thee, too. And while thou livest, dear
Kate, take a fellow of plain and uncoined° constancy, for he   not in common use
150   perforce must do thee right, because he hath not the gift to
woo in other places. For these fellows of infinite tongue, that
can rhyme themselves into ladies' favours, they do always reason themselves out again. What! A speaker is but a prater,° a   chatterer
rhyme is but a ballad; a good leg will fall, a straight back will
155   stoop, a black beard will turn white, a curled pate will grow
bald, a fair face will wither, a full eye will wax° hollow, but a   become
good heart, Kate, is the sun and the moon—or rather the sun
and not the moon, for it shines bright and never changes, but
keeps his course truly. If thou would have such a one, take me;
160   and take me, take a soldier; take a soldier, take a king. And
what sayst thou then to my love? Speak, my fair—and fairly, I
pray thee.
CATHERINE   Is it possible dat I sould love de *ennemi* of France?
KING HARRY   No, it is not possible you should love the enemy of
165   France, Kate. But in loving me, you should love the friend of
France, for I love France so well that I will not part with a
village of it, I will have it all mine; and Kate, when France is
mine, and I am yours, then yours is France, and you are mine.
CATHERINE   I cannot tell vat is dat.
170   KING HARRY   No, Kate? I will tell thee in French—which I am
sure will hang upon my tongue like a new-married wife about
her husband's neck, hardly to be shook off. *Je quand suis le
possesseur de France, et quand vous avez le possession de moi—*
let me see, what then? Saint Denis be my speed!—*donc vôtre
175   est France, et vous êtes mienne.*[4] It is as easy for me, Kate, to
conquer the kingdom as to speak so much more French. I shall
never move° thee in French, unless it be to laugh at me.   persuade
CATHERINE   *Sauf votre honneur, le français que vous parlez, il est
meilleur que l'anglais lequel je parle.*[5]
180   KING HARRY   No, faith, is't not, Kate. But thy speaking of my
tongue, and I thine, most truly-falsely, must needs be granted
to be much at one.° But Kate, dost thou understand thus much   alike; united
English? Canst thou love me?
CATHERINE   I cannot tell.
185   KING HARRY   Can any of your neighbours tell, Kate? I'll ask them.
Come, I know thou lovest me, and at night when you come
into your closet° you'll question this gentlewoman about me,   bedchamber
and I know, Kate, you will to her dispraise those parts° in me   qualities
that you love with your heart. But good Kate, mock me merci-
190   fully—the rather, gentle princess, because I love thee cruelly.
If ever thou be'st mine, Kate—as I have a saving faith within
me tells me thou shalt—I get thee with scrambling,° and thou   fighting

---

4. Translation of the last part of his previous speech.
5. Saving your honor, the French you speak is better than the English I speak.

must therefore needs prove a good soldier-breeder. Shall not
thou and I, between Saint Denis and Saint George,[6] com-
195   pound a boy, half-French half-English, that shall go to Constantinople and take the Turk by the beard? Shall we not? What
sayst thou, my fair flower-de-luce?[7]

CATHERINE   I do not know dat.

KING HARRY   No, 'tis hereafter to know, but now to promise. Do
200   but now promise, Kate, you will endeavour for your French
part of such a boy, and for my English moiety° take the word   *half*
of a king and a bachelor. How answer you, *la plus belle Cather-*
ine du monde, mon très chère et divine déesse?[8]

CATHERINE   Your *majesté 'ave faux*° French enough to deceive   *false*
205   de most sage *demoiselle*° dat is *en France.*   *maiden*

KING HARRY   Now fie upon my false French! By mine honour,
in true English, I love thee, Kate. By which honour I dare not
swear thou lovest me, yet my blood° begins to flatter me that   *instinct*
thou dost, notwithstanding the poor and untempering° effect of   *uningratiating*
210   my visage. Now beshrew° my father's ambition! He was think-   *curse*
ing of civil wars when he got me; therefore was I created with
a stubborn outside, with an aspect° of iron, that when I come   *a face*
to woo ladies I fright them. But in faith, Kate, the elder I wax
the better I shall appear. My comfort is that old age, that ill
215   layer-up° of beauty, can do no more spoil upon my face. Thou   *preserver*
hast me, if thou hast me, at the worst, and thou shalt wear me,
if thou wear me, better and better; and therefore tell me, most
fair Catherine, will you have me? Put off your maiden blushes,
avouch the thoughts of your heart with the looks of an empress,
220   take me by the hand and say, 'Harry of England, I am thine'—
which word thou shalt no sooner bless mine ear withal, but I
will tell thee aloud, 'England is thine, Ireland is thine, France
is thine, and Henry Plantagenet is thine'—who, though I speak
it before his face, if he be not fellow° with the best king, thou   *equal*
225   shalt find the best king of good fellows. Come, your answer in
broken music°—for thy voice is music and thy English broken.   *music in parts*
Therefore, queen of all, Catherine, break thy mind to me in
broken English: wilt thou have me?

CATHERINE   Dat is as it shall please de *roi mon père.*°   *King my father*

230 KING HARRY   Nay, it will please him well, Kate. It shall please
him, Kate.

CATHERINE   Den it sall also content me.

KING HARRY   Upon that I kiss your hand, and I call you my
queen.

235 CATHERINE   *Laissez, mon seigneur, laissez, laissez! Ma foi, je ne*
veux point que vous abbaissez votre grandeur en baisant la main
d'une de votre seigneurie indigne serviteur. Excusez-moi, je vous
supplie, mon treis-puissant seigneur.[9]

KING HARRY   Then I will kiss your lips, Kate.

240 CATHERINE   *Les dames et demoiselles pour être baisées devant*
leurs noces, il n'est pas la coutume de France.°   *(translated below)*

KING HARRY [*to* ALICE]   Madam my interpreter, what says she?

ALICE   Dat it is not be de *façon pour les*° ladies of France—I   *fashion for the*

---

6. Patron saints of France and England.
7. Fleur-de-lis, French national emblem.
8. The most beautiful Catherine in the world, my very
dear and divine goddess.

9. Stop, my lord, stop, stop! My faith, I do not want you
to lower your grandeur by kissing the hand of one of your
humble servants. Excuse me, I beseech you, my very powerful lord.

cannot tell vat is *baiser en*° Anglish.   *"kiss" in*

245 KING HARRY   To kiss.

ALICE   Your *majesté entend* bettre *que moi.*[1]

KING HARRY   It is not a fashion for the maids in France to kiss
before they are married, would she say?

ALICE   *Oui, vraiment.*°   *Yes, truly*

250 KING HARRY   O Kate, nice° customs curtsy to great kings. Dear   *fastidious*
Kate, you and I cannot be confined within the weak list° of a   *barrier*
country's fashion. We are the makers of manners, Kate, and the
liberty that follows our places stops the mouth of all find-faults,
as I will do yours, for upholding the nice fashion of your coun-

255 try in denying me a kiss. Therefore, patiently and yielding. [*He
kisses her*] You have witchcraft in your lips, Kate. There is more
eloquence in a sugar touch of them than in the tongues of the
French Council, and they should sooner persuade Harry of
England than a general petition of monarchs. Here comes

260 your father.

> *Enter* KING [CHARLES, QUEEN ISABEL, *the Duke of* BUR-
> GUNDY,] *and the French* [*and*] *English lords*

BURGUNDY   God save your majesty. My royal cousin, teach you
our princess English?

KING HARRY   I would have her learn, my fair cousin, how perfectly I love her, and that is good English.

265 BURGUNDY   Is she not apt?

KING HARRY   Our tongue is rough, coz,° and my condition is not   *kinsman*
smooth, so that having neither the voice nor the heart of flattery
about me I cannot so conjure up the spirit of love in her that
he will appear in his true likeness.

270 BURGUNDY   Pardon the frankness of my mirth, if I answer you for
that. If you would conjure in her, you must make a circle;[2] if
conjure up love in her in his true likeness, he must appear
naked and blind.° Can you blame her then, being a maid yet   *(like Cupid, god of love)*
rosed over with the virgin crimson of modesty, if she deny the

275 appearance of a naked blind boy in her naked seeing self? It
were, my lord, a hard condition for a maid to consign to.

KING HARRY   Yet they do wink° and yield, as love is blind and   *close their eyes*
enforces.

BURGUNDY   They are then excused, my lord, when they see not

280 what they do.

KING HARRY   Then, good my lord, teach your cousin to consent
winking.

BURGUNDY   I will wink on her to consent, my lord, if you will
teach her to know my meaning. For maids, well summered

285 and warm kept, are like flies at Bartholomew-tide:° blind,   *August 24*
though they have their eyes. And then they will endure handling, which before would not abide looking on.

KING HARRY   This moral ties me over to time and a hot summer,
and so I shall catch the fly, your cousin, in the latter end,[3] and

290 she must be blind too.

BURGUNDY   As love is, my lord, before that it loves.

KING HARRY   It is so. And you may, some of you, thank love for
my blindness, who cannot see many a fair French city for one

---

1. Your majesty understands better than I.   devils).
2. By embracing her (sorcerers drew circles to call up   3. At last; in the backside.

fair French maid that stands in my way.

295 KING CHARLES Yes, my lord, you see them perspectively,[4] the
cities turned into a maid—for they are all girdled with maiden
walls that war hath never entered.

KING HARRY Shall Kate be my wife?

KING CHARLES So please you.

300 KING HARRY I am content, so the maiden° cities you talk of may   *unconquered*
wait on her: so the maid that stood in the way for my wish shall
show me the way to my will.

KING CHARLES We have consented to all terms of reason.

KING HARRY Is't so, my lords of England?

305 WARWICK The King hath granted every article:
His daughter first, and so in sequel all,
According to their firm proposèd natures.

EXETER Only he hath not yet subscribèd° this: *signed to*
where your majesty demands that the King of France, having
310 any occasion to write for matter of grant,° shall name your high-   *in formal documents*
ness in this form and with this addition: [*reads*] in French,
Notre très cher fils Henri, Roi d'Angleterre, Héritier de France,
and thus in Latin, *Praeclarissimus filius noster Henricus, Rex
Angliae et Haeres Franciae.*[5]

315 KING CHARLES Nor this I have not, brother, so denied,
But your request shall make me let it pass.

KING HARRY I pray you then, in love and dear alliance,
Let that one article rank with the rest,
And thereupon give me your daughter.

320 KING CHARLES Take her, fair son, and from her blood raise up
Issue° to me, that the contending kingdoms   *Offspring*
Of France and England, whose very shores look pale
With envy of each other's happiness,
May cease their hatred, and this dear conjunction°   *loving union*
325 Plant neighbourhood° and Christian-like accord   *neighborliness*
In their sweet bosoms, that never war advance
His bleeding sword 'twixt England and fair France.

ALL Amen.

KING HARRY Now welcome, Kate, and bear me witness all
330 That here I kiss her as my sovereign Queen.
Flourish

QUEEN ISABEL God, the best maker of all marriages,
Combine your hearts in one, your realms in one.
As man and wife, being two, are one in love,
So be there 'twixt your kingdoms such a spousal
335 That never may ill office° or fell° jealousy,   *bad action / cruel*
Which troubles oft the bed of blessèd marriage,
Thrust in between the paction° of these kingdoms   *agreement*
To make divorce of their incorporate league;
That English may as French, French Englishmen,
340 Receive each other, God speak this 'Amen'.

ALL Amen.

KING HARRY Prepare we for our marriage. On which day,
My lord of Burgundy, we'll take your oath,
And all the peers', for surety of our leagues.

---

4. In a lens that produces optical illusions.
5. Our very dear son Henry, King of England, heir of France.

345 Then shall I swear to Kate, and you to me,
     And may our oaths well kept and prosp'rous be.

     Sennet.° Exeunt   *Ceremonial trumpet call*

Epilogue

     Enter CHORUS[1]
CHORUS Thus far with rough and all-unable pen
     Our bending° author hath pursued the story,   *(over a desk)*
     In little room confining mighty men,
     Mangling by starts the full course of their glory.
5   Small time, but in that small most greatly lived
     This star of England. Fortune made his sword,
     By which the world's best garden he achieved,
     And of it left his son imperial lord.
     Henry the Sixth, in infant bands° crowned king   *swaddling clothes*
10   Of France and England, did this king succeed,
     Whose state so many had the managing
     That they lost France and made his England bleed,
     Which oft our stage hath shown[2] — and, for their sake,
     In your fair minds let this acceptance take.°   [*Exit*]   *this play find favor*

Additional Passages

The Dauphin / Bourbon variant, which usually involves only the speech prefixes, has several consequences for the dialogue and structure of 4.5. Following are the edited Folio and quarto versions of this scene.

A: Folio

     Enter CONSTABLE, ORLÉANS, BOURBON, DAUPHIN, *and*
          RAMBURES
CONSTABLE   O diable!
ORLÉANS   O Seigneur! Le jour est perdu, tout est perdu.
DAUPHIN   Mort de ma vie! All is confounded, all.
     Reproach and everlasting shame
5   Sits mocking in our plumes.
          A short alarum
     O méchante fortune! Do not run away.   [*Exit* RAMBURES]
CONSTABLE   Why, all our ranks are broke.
DAUPHIN   O perdurable shame! Let's stab ourselves:
     Be these the wretches that we played at dice for?
10   ORLÉANS   Is this the king we sent to for his ransom?
BOURBON   Shame, an eternall shame, nothing but shame!
     Let us die in pride. In once more, back again!
     And he that will not follow Bourbon now,
     Let him go home, and with his cap in hand
15   Like a base leno hold the chamber door,
     Whilst by a slave no gentler than my dog
     His fairest daughter is contaminated.
CONSTABLE   Disorder that hath spoiled us, friend us now,
     Let us on heaps go offer up our lives.
20   ORLÉANS   We are enough yet living in the field
     To smother up the English in our throngs,

1. The following lines form a sonnet.
2. In *1 Henry VI*, *The First Part of the Contention* (2   *Henry VI*), *Richard Duke of York* (*3 Henry VI*), *and Richard III*.

If any order might be thought upon.
BOURBON   The devil take order now. I'll to the throng.
Let life be short, else shame will be too long.   *Exeunt*

B. Quarto
        Enter the four French lords: [*the* CONSTABLE, ORLÉANS,
            BOURBON, *and* GEBON]
GEBON   *O diabello!*°   devil
CONSTABLE   *Mort de ma vie!*
ORLÉANS   O what a day is this!
BOURBON   *O jour de honte,*° all is gone, all is lost.   day of shame
5 CONSTABLE   We are enough yet living in the field
To smother up the English,
If any order might be thought upon.
BOURBON   A plague of order! Once more to the field!
And he that will not follow Bourbon now,
10 Let him go home, and with his cap in hand,
Like a base leno hold the chamber door,
Whilst by a slave no gentler than my dog
His fairest daughter is contaminated.
CONSTABLE   Disorder that hath spoiled us, right us now.
15 Come we in heaps, we'll offer up our lives
Unto these English, or else die with fame.
BOURBON   Come, come along.
Let's die with honour, our shame doth last too long.   *Exeunt*

TEXTUAL VARIANTS

Control text: F; additional matter from Q1

F: The Folio of 1623
Q1: The Quarto of 1600
Q3: The Quarto of 1619

s.p. KING HARRY [F's use of *King* has been standardized throughout.]
s.p. KING CHARLES [F's use of *King* has been standardized throughout.]

1.2.38 succedant succedual **50 there** [Q] then **72 fine** [Q] find **74 heir** [Q]
th'Heire **77 Ninth** Tenth **99 son** man **115 those** these **131 blood** Bloods **147
unmasked his power** [Q] went with his forces **unto** into **154 the bruit thereof** the
brute hereof [Q] th'ill neighborhood **163 your** [Q] their **166 A LORD** [Q] *Bish⟨op of⟩
Ely.* **183 True.** [Q; not in F] **197 majesty** [Q] Maiesties **208 Fly** [Q] Come **212 end**
[Q] And **213 defect** [Q] defeat **276 have I** I haue [F] haue we [Q1] we haue
[Q3] **284 from** [Q] with **287 Ay,** [Q] And
2.0.32 — perforce — [not in F]
2.1.21 mare [Q] name **23 Good morrow, Ensign Pistol** [Q; not in F] **25 NIM** [Q; not
in F] **26 Gad's lugs** [Q] this hand **65 thee defy** [Q] defie thee **72 enough.** [Q]
enough to **73 you** your **95 s.p. NIM** I shall have my eight shillings? *Nim.* I shal haue
my eight shillings I woon of you at beating? [Q; not in F] **105 that's** that
2.2.1 s.p. GLOUCESTER [Q; throughout scene] *Bed⟨ford⟩.* [F; throughout scene] **35 their**
[Q] the **84 him** [Q; not in F] **85 vile** [Q; not in F] **95 ha'** [Q1] haue **104 a** an **136
mark** make **the** thee **144 Henry** [Q] *Thomas* **154 heartily in sufferance** in sufferance

heartily **163 and fixed** [Q; not in F] **172 have** [Q; not in F] **173 ye** [Q1] you

2.3.15 babbled Table **22 up'ard and up'ard** vpward and vpward [Q] up-peer'd and upward

29 s.p. HOSTESS *Woman.* **35 hell-fire** [Q1] Hell **41 word** [Q1] world

2.4.4 Bourbon [Q] Britaine **33 agèd** [Q] Noble **57 mountant** Mountaine **75 England** [Q1] of England **106 Turns he** [Q] Turning **107 pining** [Q] priuy **123 for** [Q] of

3.0.6 fanning fayning

3.1.7 conjure commune **17 noblest** Noblish **24 men** me **32 Straining** Straying

3.2.19 God's plud [Q; not in F] **19 breaches** [Q] breach **26 runs** wins

3.3 s.p. FLUELLEN [Q; throughout scene] *Welch.* [F; throughout scene] **s.p. JAMY** [Q; throughout scene] *Scot.* [F; throughout scene] **s.p. MACMORRIS** [Q; throughout scene] *Irish.* [F; throughout scene] **55–56 Aye owe Got a** aye, or goe to **109 heady** headly **112 Defile** Desire **124 dread** [Q] great

3.4.3 Un *En* **4 j'apprenne** *ie apprend* **5 parler** *parlen* **Comment** *Comient* **6 La main?** **Elle est appelée** *Le main il & appelle* **7 Et les doigts** [continued to Catherine] *Alice.* *E le doyts.* **8 s.p. ALICE** *Kat⟨herine⟩* **8–9 souviendrai** *souemeray* **9 sont** *ont* **fingers.** Oui *fingres, ou* **11 s.p. CATHERINE** *Alice.* **12 la bonne écolière; j'ai** *le bon escholier. / Kat⟨herine⟩. I'ay* **13 les** *le* **14 Les** *Le* **15 De nails.** Ecoutez— De Nayles escoute: **19** *arma* Arme **20 le** *de* **22 la répétition** *le repeticio* **39 Non, et** *Nome* **43 Sauf** *Sans* **honneur** *honeus* **44 dis** *de* **45 pieds** *pied* **la robe** [Q] *de roba* **46 De foot** *Le foot* **46, 47, 51, 53** *cown* con [Q] *Count* **47 De foot et de** Le Foot, *& le* Ils Il **51 De foot et de** Le Foot *& le* **Néanmoins** *neant moys* **53 foot, de** foote, e de [Q] Foot, le

3.5.10, 32 s.p. BOURBON [Q] *Brit⟨ain⟩.* **11 de** du **26 'Poor' may we** Poore we **45 Foix** Loys **46 knights** Kings

3.6.23 Of and of **27 her** [Q] his **49 executions** [Q] execution **58 is this the ensign you told me of** [Q] this is an arrant counterfeit Rascall **82 com'st** cam'st **99 here** [Q; not in F] **102 lenity** [Q] Leuitie

3.7.7 s.p. BOURBON [Q; throughout scene] *Dolph⟨in⟩.* [F; throughout scene] **12 Ah ha** Ch'ha **14 qui a** ches **60 vomissement** vemissement *et est* **61 truie** leuye **83 Duke of Bourbon** [Q] Dolphin

4.0.16 name nam'd

4.1.92 Thomas Iohn **148 deaths** [Q] death **propose** purpose **173 s.p. BATES** 3. *Lord.* [Q] *Will⟨iams⟩.* **227 adoration** odoration **267 or** of **280 have I** [Q] I haue **286 ill** all

4.2 s.p. BOURBON [Q; throughout scene] *Dolph⟨in⟩.* [F; throughout scene] **5 plus?** puis **6 Cieux** Cein **11 dout** doubt **25 'gainst** against **35 sonance** Sonuance **46 hands** hand **47 drooping** dropping **49 palled** pale **60 guidon** Guard: on

4.3.2 s.p. CLARENCE *Bed⟨ford⟩.* **3 s.p. WARWICK** [Q; throughout scene] *West⟨merland⟩.* [F; throughout scene] **8 Clarence** [Q] Bedford **11, 15 s.p. CLARENCE** *Bed⟨ford⟩.* [F; speeches not in Q] **44 t'old** old **48 And . . . day.'** [Q; not in F] **106 grazing** crasing **118 as** or **119 your** [Q] the **129 come** come againe

4.4.4 Qualité 'Calin *o* Qualitie calmie **12 miséricorde** miserecordie **pitié** pité **14 Or** for **46 prisonnier** prisonner **néanmoins** neant-mons **47 lui ci** layt a **promettez** promets **48 je** se **49 remerciements** remercious **49–50 j'ai tombé** Ie intombe **50 mains** main. **comme** [not in F] **pense** peuse **51 treis-distingué** tres distinie **59 Suivez** Saaue

4.5 [Both Bourbon and the Dauphin appear in this scene in F. Whereas in most instances the textual differences between Q and F merely involve speech prefixes, here they are more substantial. See Additional Passages, pp. 1520–21, for F and Q versions of this scene.] **2 Seigneur** sigueur **perdu . . . perdu** perdia . . . perdie **3 s.p. BOURBON** [Q] *Dol⟨phin⟩.* **Mort de** Mor Dieu **7–9 We are . . . upon** [Q; F places after 4.5.17] **10 order** [Q] Order now **12 home** [Q] hence **13 leno** [Q] Pander **14 by a slave** [Q] a base slaue

4.6.14–15 face, / And [Q] face. / He **15 dear** [Q] my **39 s.p. PISTOL** Coup' la gorge. [Q; not in F]

4.7.18 e'en in **19 world** Orld **36 made an end** [Q] made **83 Crispian** *Crispianus* **102 countryman** [Q] Countrymen **115 a live** aliue **118 a lived** aliue **150 that I would see** that I might see
4.8.9 God's plood, and his Gode plut, and his [Q1] 'Sblud **23 what is** [Q1] what's **94 Vaudemont** *Vandemont* **98 Keighley** Ketly **107 we** me **118 in** [Q; no in F]
5.0.10 maids [not in F] **29 high-loving** by loving
5.1.13 a [Q1] hee **36 By Jesu** [Q1] I say **37 and four nights** [Q; not in F] **80 swear** [Q] swore
5.2.50 scythe, all Sythe, withall **169 vat** wat **172–73** *suis le possesseur* sur le possession **236 grandeur** grandeus **237 de votre seigneurie** nostre Seigneur **indigne** indignie **244 vat** wat **246 entend** entendre **291 before that it** before it **297 never** [not in F] **305 s.p. WARWICK** West⟨merland⟩. **306 so** [not in F] **328 ALL** Lords. **337 paction** Pation

Sir Thomas More: Passages Attributed to Shakespeare

Early in the seventeenth century (probably 1603–4), Shakespeare seems to have participated in the revision of *Sir Thomas More*, a play originally composed between late 1592
and mid-1595, probably in 1592–93, by Anthony Munday, Henry Chettle, and perhaps a
third writer (Thomas Dekker?). This original version was designed for Lord Strange's Men,
who presumably intended to stage it at their regular theater, the Rose. Drawing on Raphael
Holinshed's *Chronicles of England, Scotland, and Ireland* (1587), Nicholas Harpsfield's
Life and Death of Sir Thomas More, and Thomas Stapleton's Latin biography, *Vita Tho-
mae Mori*, the play conforms to the popular tragic model known in Latin as *de casibus
virorum illustrium* (on the fall of illustrious men). It follows the career of More—leading
English Renaissance humanist and author of *Utopia*, Lord Chancellor of England and
persecutor of Protestants, and, finally, Catholic martyr when the religious tide turned. The
work focuses on his success as sheriff in peacefully quelling the anti-alien London riots of
May Day 1517; his elevation to the post of Lord Chancellor; and his eventual execution
for refusing to subscribe to certain of the king's articles. Throughout and especially at the
end, the witty and wise protagonist is treated with almost uncritical admiration.

Strange's Men specialized in plays on English subjects with a loosely nationalist appeal;
they also liked to live dangerously. *Sir Thomas More* was doubly dangerous. First, though
it carefully converts the issue that led to More's death (papal versus royal supremacy of the
church) into a less concrete conflict between worldly authority and individual conscience
that would appeal to a Puritan-leaning audience, it sympathetically dramatizes the life of
a Catholic martyr killed by Henry VIII, the father of the ruling Protestant monarch, Queen
Elizabeth. Second, though it shows More successfully preventing popular protest that historically he was unable to control, the play exploits contemporary antiforeign resentment,
which was noticeable by late 1592 and led to rioting and harsh government reprisals
between 1593 and 1595. On neither issue does the absolute monarch end up looking
particularly good. Before the first performance, however, the censor, Sir Edmund Tilney,
Master of the Revels, demanded substantial rewriting, in particular a toning down of the
attack on foreigners and the elimination of the scene dramatizing the 1517 rebellion
against them. Apparently before the manuscript could be revised, an outbreak of plague
closed the theaters for most of the period from mid-1592 to mid-1594, and the actors
abandoned the play.

Early in the seventeenth century, the text was revised for performance—possibly at the
Fortune, the regular theater of Lord Admiral's Men/Prince Henry's Men, conceivably at
the Globe by Shakespeare's company, the Lord Chamberlain's Men/King's Men. (On
James I's accession in 1603, Prince Henry and his father the king assumed the patronage
of the Lord Admiral's and Lord Chamberlain's companies.) The play fit the strategy of the
Lord Admiral's Men in the years immediately after 1600, when they specialized in revivals
from the Strange's repertory of the early 1590s and the Admiral's own of 1594–97. Also,
during the same period, both the Lord Admiral's and the Lord Chamberlain's Men
mounted a number of plays set during the reign of Henry VIII. A new monarch and the
absence of the dangerous political context of the 1590s allowed the revisers to imagine
how they might take account of the censor's earlier concerns. But they could not disregard
the fact that the play as originally written required more actors than were in either company, and they adapted the text accordingly. No record of performance exists.

For the original version, Anthony Munday (manuscript Hand S) had copied out the entire text, modifying the work of his collaborator(s). The revision, which also significantly improved the quality of the play, was undertaken by Henry Chettle (Hand A), Thomas Dekker (Hand E), probably Thomas Heywood (Hand B), a playhouse scribe (Hand C), and very probably Shakespeare (Hand D). The result, *The Book of Sir Thomas More* (British Library MS Harleian 7368)—where "Book" means theatrical promptbook—was not printed until the nineteenth century. It is worth emphasizing the existence of other possible explanations, and three in particular, of the text besides the one offered here. The revisions may have occurred immediately following the initial composition of the play, either before or after Tilney's censorship. Second, a small minority deny that Shakespeare

From Anthony Munday and others, "The Booke of Sir Thomas Moore" (British Library, MS Harley 7368), fol. 9a. This is the most legible of the pages believed to be in Shakespeare's hand.

is Hand D. Third and most striking, it has been argued that Hand D, whatever his identity, was one of the original playwrights rather than a reviser.

Hand D is present in the first of the two passages printed here, Add.II.D (Addition II, Hand D; 8^r, 8^v, 9^r), which was subsequently edited by Hand C, partly to make it conform to the other revisions. If Add.II.D is Shakespearean, it is by far the longest extant specimen of Shakespeare's handwriting and as such is of considerable scholarly, as well as theatrical and literary, value. It shows what a Shakespearean first draft looks like and hence some of the challenges a scribe or printer had to contend with. The attribution to Shakespeare is based on resemblances to his other extant handwriting (almost exclusively signatures), spelling similarities to printed texts that probably are directly based on manuscripts in Shakespeare's hand, and stylistic affinities. The text printed here excludes the emendations Hand C made to Add.II.D. Normally, this edition opts for the theatrical, rather than the authorial, version of a play on the grounds that Shakespeare was aware of and accepted the revisions introduced by his acting company when preparing his manuscript for the stage. In this instance, however, his involvement in rehearsal and performance is less likely than usual. The second passage included here, Add.III (folio 11^{*b}), is in Hand C and is attributed to Shakespeare, with somewhat less confidence, on stylistic grounds. Normally, as well, this edition prints an entire play rather than a fragment. Here, however, Shakespeare's contribution is small and his involvement probably late—long after the play had been conceptualized and indeed written.

Add.II.D constitutes almost the first two-thirds of what one modern edition calls Scene 6 and another Act 2, Scene 3. Earlier in the play, the citizens of London, angered by the high-handed, legally protected behavior of foreigners, prepare to take bloody revenge. Here, More, acting on behalf of a state otherwise prepared to meet force with force, talks the assembled crowd out of violence and into submission to the king. Shakespeare's revision belittles the protesters, depriving them of an individuality they possessed earlier in the play and reducing them to the idiotic fear of disease-causing foreign vegetables (the parsnip and the pumpkin, lines 10–19). Though the rhetoric of More's arguments for obedience is clever and even arresting in its evocation of "the wretched strangers" leaving England (line 81), the claims are orthodox and traditional. They may represent changes from the original manuscript and, like the imagery, certainly have parallels in Shakespeare's other plays, most tellingly in Ulysses' speech on degree in 1.3 of *Troilus and Cressida* (probably from 1602). Though the lines seem at least partly designed to reassure the censor, their political implications also point in a different direction. Once the crowd has listened to More, whom they already trust and respect, they willingly submit to royal authority. The text demonstrates the fundamental decency of the common folk. And More's brilliant success provides a plausible if historically inaccurate explanation of his appointment as Lord Chancellor.

Like Ulysses' speech, however, More's is undermined by the rest of the play. The passage also engages in powerfully ironic foreshadowing at the expense of the monarchy. More promises,

> Submit you to these noble gentlemen,
> Entreat their mediation to the King,
> Give up yourself to form, obey the magistrate,
> And there's no doubt but mercy may be found,
> If you so seek it.

(lines 157–61)

There is, however, a "doubt": Lincoln goes to the scaffold, his noble death anticipating More's own fate. More also insists that

> to the King God hath his office lent
> . . . .
> What do you then,

> Rising 'gainst him that God himself installs,
> But rise 'gainst God?
>
> (lines 107, 113–15)

The equation of God and King, the divine sanction for royal authority—these are the principles that More repudiates, at the cost of his life. A similar effect is achieved in Add.III, which opens Scene 8 of one modern edition and Act 3, Scene 1, of another. Newly named Lord Chancellor, More soliloquizes on the suddenness of his ascent, in which he sees evidence of a providential force at odds with explanations based on "our fortunes" (line 2; Fortune is usually represented in *de casibus* tragedy by the image of the turning wheel). This view leads him to predict, accurately, that "to be great / Is" to be "greatly undone" (lines 19–21)—where the greatness of the undoing can refer both to the height from which he falls and to the stature of the cause for which he goes to his death.

WALTER COHEN

SELECTED BIBLIOGRAPHY

Fox, Alistair. "The Paradoxical Design of *The Book of Sir Thomas More.*" *Renaissance and Reformation / Renaissance et Réforme,* n.s. 5 (1981): 162–73.

Gabrieli, Vittorio. "*Sir Thomas More:* Sources, Characters, Ideas." *Moreana* 23 (June 1986): 17–43.

Honigmann, E. A. J. "The Play of *Sir Thomas More* and Some Contemporary Events." *Shakespeare Survey* 42 (1990): 77–84.

Howard-Hill, T. H., ed. *Shakespeare and "Sir Thomas More": Essays on the Play and Its Shakespearian Interest.* Cambridge: Cambridge University Press, 1989.

McMillin, Scott. *The Elizabethan Theatre and "The Book of Sir Thomas More."* Ithaca, N.Y.: Cornell University Press, 1987.

Munday, Anthony, and others. Revised by Henry Chettle, Thomas Dekker, Thomas Heywood, and William Shakespeare. *Sir Thomas More.* Ed. Vittorio Gabrieli and Giorgio Melchiori. The Revels Plays. Manchester: Manchester University Press, 1990.

Pollard, Alfred W., et al. *Shakespeare's Hand in "The Play of Sir Thomas More."* Cambridge: Cambridge University Press, 1923.

Sir Thomas More: Passages Attributed to Shakespeare

Add.II.D

[*John*] LINCOLN [*a broker*],° DOLL, BETTS, [SHERWIN (*a*   *buying and selling agent*
goldsmith), *and prentices*° *armed; Thomas* MORE (*sheriff*   *apprentices*
of the City of London), *the other sheriff, Sir Thomas*
PALMER, *Sir Roger* CHOLMELEY,] *and a* SERJEANT-*at-*
arms [*stand aloof*]

LINCOLN [*to the prentices*]   Peace, hear me! He that will not see°   *tolerate*
a red herring at a Harry groat,° butter at eleven pence a pound,   *cost fourpence*
meal at nine shillings a bushel, and beef at four nobles a stone,
list¹ to me.

5   OTHER   It will come to that pass if strangers be suffered.² Mark
him.

LINCOLN   Our country is a great eating country; argo,³ they eat
more in our country than they do in their own.

OTHER   By a halfpenny loaf a day, troy weight.°   *standard measure*

10   LINCOLN   They bring in strange roots,⁴ which is merely° to the   *entirely*
undoing of poor prentices, for what's a sorry parsnip⁵ to a good
heart?

OTHER   Trash, trash. They breed sore eyes, and 'tis enough to
infect the city with the palsy.

15   LINCOLN   Nay, it has infected it with the palsy, for these bastards
of dung⁶—as you know, they grow in dung—have infected us,
and it is our infection will make the city shake, which partly
comes through the eating of parsnips.

OTHER   True, and pumpions° together.   *pumpkins*

SERJEANT [*coming forward*]   What say you to the mercy of the
20   King?
Do you refuse it?

LINCOLN   You would have us upon th'hip,° would you? No,   *at a disadvantage*
marry, do we not. We accept of the King's mercy; but we will
show no mercy upon the strangers.

25   SERJEANT   You are the simplest things
That ever stood in such a question.⁷

LINCOLN   How say you now? Prentices 'simple'? [*To the pren-*
tices] Down with him!

ALL   Prentices simple! Prentices simple!

Add.II.D Location: St. Martin's Lane, London; May Day
1517.
1. *noble*: gold coin worth six shillings eight pence. *stone*:
fourteen pounds. *list*: listen. These prices would have
seemed high to a contemporary audience.
2. If foreigners ("strangers" means "foreigners" throughout the scene) are allowed (to remain in London).
3. As Lincoln says, England had a reputation for gluttony. *argo*: for Latin *ergo* (therefore).

4. Foreign vegetables.
5. Lincoln confuses parsnips with potatoes, which were
introduced to England from the Americas in the 1580s
and were rumored to cause disease.
6. Illegitimate growths made still more repugnant by
their association with excrement; perhaps merely abusive.
7. Stood their ground in such circumstances (against the
King's wishes).

Enter the Lord MAYOR, [*the Earl of*] SURREY, [*and the Earl of*] SHREWSBURY

30 SHERIFF [*to the prentices*]   Hold in the King's name! Hold!

SURREY [*to the prentices*]   Friends, masters, countrymen—

MAYOR [*to the prentices*]   Peace ho, peace! I charge you, keep the peace!

SHREWSBURY [*to the prentices*]   My masters, countrymen—

SHERWIN   The noble Earl of Shrewsbury, let's hear him.

35 BETTS   We'll hear the Earl of Surrey.

LINCOLN   The Earl of Shrewsbury.

BETTS   We'll hear both.

ALL   Both, both, both, both!

LINCOLN   Peace, I say peace! Are you men of wisdom, or what

40   are you?

SURREY   What you will have them,° but not men of wisdom.   *Whatever you call them*

SOME   We'll not hear my Lord of Surrey.

OTHERS   No, no, no, no, no! Shrewsbury, Shrewsbury!

MORE [*to the nobles and officers*]   Whiles they are o'er the bank of their obedience,

45   Thus will they bear down all things.[8]

LINCOLN [*to the prentices*]   Sheriff More speaks. Shall we hear Sheriff More speak?

DOLL   Let's hear him. A keeps a plentiful shrievaltry,[9] and a made my brother Arthur Watchins Sergeant Safe's yeoman.°   *assistant*

50   Let's hear Sheriff More.

ALL   Sheriff More, More, More, Sheriff More!

MORE   Even by the rule you have among yourselves,
Command still audience.°   *quiet hearing*

SOME   Surrey, Surrey!

55 OTHERS   More, More!

LINCOLN *and* BETTS   Peace, peace, silence, peace!

MORE   You that have voice and credit with the number,°   *the crowd*
Command them to a stillness.

LINCOLN   A plague on them! They will not hold their peace.

60   The devil cannot rule them.

MORE   Then what a rough and riotous charge° have you,   *duty*
To lead those that the devil cannot rule.
[*To the prentices*] Good masters, hear me speak.

DOLL   Ay, by th' mass, will we. More, thou'rt a good house-

65   keeper,[1] and I thank thy good worship for my brother Arthur
Watchins.

ALL   Peace, peace!

MORE   Look, what you do offend you cry upon,[2]
That is the peace. Not one of you here present,

70   Had there such fellows lived when you were babes
That could have topped the peace as now you would,
The peace wherein you have till now grown up
Had been ta'en from you, and the bloody times
Could not have brought you to the state of men.[3]

---

8. The image is of water flooding over the banks (of obedience), destroying everything in its path.
9. He ("A") is a generous sheriff.
1. Patron; head of a well-to-do household.
2. By yelling "peace" (though you call for peace), you break the peace. More's speeches to the crowd, especially lines 79–94, echo Ulysses' speech on degree in *Troilus*

and Cressida 1.3.74–137, in particular lines 110–24. Both of these sincere expositions of orthodoxy are ironized by the ensuing events.
3. *Not one . . . men:* If such peace breakers as you had been around when you were children, you wouldn't have had peaceful times to grow up in, and you wouldn't have lived to become men.

75   Alas, poor things, what is it you have got,
     Although we grant you get the thing you seek?
   BETTS   Marry, the removing of the strangers, which cannot
     choose but much advantage the poor handicrafts° of the city.   *craftspeople*
   MORE   Grant them removed, and grant that this your noise
80   Hath chid down all the majesty of England.[4]
     Imagine that you see the wretched strangers,
     Their babies at their backs, with their poor luggage
     Plodding to th' ports and coasts for transportation,
     And that you sit as kings in your desires,
85   Authority quite silenced by your brawl
     And you in ruff of your opinions clothed:[5]
     What had you got? I'll tell you. You had taught
     How insolence and strong hand° should prevail,   *force*
     How order should be quelled—and by this pattern
90   Not one of you should live an agèd man,
     For other ruffians as their fancies wrought
     With selfsame hand, self reasons, and self right
     Would shark° on you, and men like ravenous fishes   *prey*
     Would feed on one another.
95   DOLL   Before God, that's as true as the gospel.
   BETTS   Nay, this'° a sound fellow, I tell you. Let's mark° him.   *this is / listen to*
   MORE   Let me set up before your thoughts, good friends,
     One supposition,° which if you will mark   *proposition*
     You shall perceive how horrible a shape
100 Your innovation° bears. First, 'tis a sin   *rebellion*
     Which oft th'apostle° did forewarn us of,   *Paul (Romans 13:1–5)*
     Urging obedience to authority;
     And 'twere no error if I told you all
     You were in arms 'gainst God.
105 ALL   Marry, God forbid that!
   MORE   Nay, certainly you are.
     For to the King God hath his office lent
     Of dread,° of justice, power and command,   *fearful respect*
     Hath bid him rule and willed you to obey;
110 And to add ampler majesty to this,
     He hath not only lent the King his figure,
     His throne and sword, but given him his own name,
     Calls him a god on earth. What do you then,
     Rising 'gainst him that God himself installs,
115 But rise 'gainst God?[6] What do you to your souls
     In doing this? O desperate as you are,
     Wash your foul minds with tears, and those same hands
     That you like rebels lift against the peace
     Lift up for peace; and your unreverent knees,
120 Make them your feet. To kneel to be forgiven
     Is safer wars than ever you can make,
     Whose discipline is riot.[7]
     In, in, to your obedience![8] Why, even your hurly°   *riot*

4. *grant that . . . England:* suppose your action overthrew the state.
5. And you wearing the clothes ("ruff" was a fancy starched collar; also, the highest pride; alluding to Elizabethan sumptuary laws, which determined, according to rank and income, the clothes one was permitted to wear).
6. More argues in this speech that the monarch's authority has divine sanction—ironically, a position that, as the end of the play reveals, he later repudiated at the cost of his life.
7. *Is . . . riot:* Is a safer means of fighting (for your goals) than your rebellion.
8. Get back within the boundaries of your obedience.

Cannot proceed but by obedience.
125 What rebel captain,
As mut'nies are incident,° by his name   *about to happen*
Can still the rout?° Who will obey a traitor?   *quiet the rabble*
Or how can well that proclamation sound,
When there is no addition° but 'a rebel'   *title of rank*
130 To qualify° a rebel? You'll put down strangers,   *signify*
Kill them, cut their throats, possess their houses,
And lead the majesty of law in lyam°   *on a leash*
To slip° him like a hound—alas, alas!   *release*
Say now the King,
135 As he is clement° if th'offender mourn,°   *merciful / repent*
Should so much come too short of your great trespass[9]
As but to banish you: whither would you go?
What country, by° the nature of your error,   *in light of*
Should give you harbour? Go you to France or Flanders,
140 To any German province, Spain or Portugal,
Nay, anywhere that not adheres[1] to England—
Why, you must needs° be strangers. Would you be pleased   *necessarily*
To find a nation of such barbarous temper
That breaking out in hideous violence
145 Would not afford you an abode on earth,
Whet° their detested knives against your throats,   *But would whet*
Spurn you like dogs, and like as if that God
Owed° not nor made not you, nor that the elements   *Owned*
Were not all appropriate° to your comforts   *available*
150 But chartered unto° them, what would you think   *reserved only for*
To be thus used? This is the strangers' case,
And this your mountainish° inhumanity.   *gross, coarse*
ONE [*to the others*]   Faith, a° says true. Let's do as we may be   *he*
done by.
155 ANOTHER [*to* MORE]   We'll be ruled by you, Master More, if
you'll stand our friend to procure our pardon.
MORE   Submit you to these noble gentlemen,
Entreat their mediation to the King,
Give up yourself to form,° obey the magistrate,   *correct behavior*
160 And there's no doubt but mercy may be found,
If you so seek it.[2]

Add.III

Enter [Sir Thomas] MORE

MORE   It is in heaven that I am thus and thus,[1]
And that which we profanely term our fortunes
Is the provision of the power above,
Fitted and shaped just to that strength of nature
5 Which we are born withal.° Good God, good God,   *with*
That I from such an humble bench[2] of birth
Should step as 'twere up to my country's head
And give the law out there; ay, in my father's life

---

9. Should reduce by so much the punishment for your great offense.
1. Anywhere whose customs don't conform.
2. In the event, More's intercession is unable to save Lincoln, whose noble death on the scaffold foreshadows More's own and, like his, reflects badly on the King—the

dying men's loyal words notwithstanding.
Add.III Location: The chancery staterooms in Westminster.
1. It is up to heaven that I am one thing and then another.
2. Legal position; foot of the table: hence, origin.

To take prerogative and tithe of knees[3]
10 From elder kinsmen, and him bind by my place
To give the smooth and dexter way to me[4]
That owe it him by nature!° Sure these things,   *by birth*
Not physicked° by respect, might turn our blood   *regulated*
To much corruption. But More, the more thou hast
15 Either of honour, office, wealth and calling,
Which might accite° thee to embrace and hug them,   *entice*
The more do thou e'en° serpents' natures think them: *even*
Fear their gay skins, with thought of their sharp stings,
And let this be thy maxim: to be great
20 Is, when the thread of hazard is once spun,
A bottom great wound up, greatly undone.[5]

TEXTUAL VARIANTS

Control text: British Library MS Harley 7368: Add.II.D. (fols. 8ʳ–9ʳ); Add.III (fol. 11*ᵛ)

Add.II.D s.d. [*John . . . aloof*] *Enter Lincoln. Doll. Clown. Georg betts williamson others And a sergaunt at armes* **27 now? Prentices 'simple'?** now prenty prentisses symple **34 s.p. SHERWIN** Sher [Hand D, crossed out] williamson [Hand C] **42 s.p. SOME** all **43 s.p. OTHERS** all [Hand D, crossed out] **54 s.p. SOME** all **55 s.p. OTHERS** all **89 order** orderd (?) **153 s.p. ONE** all
Add.III 18 stings state

3. *To . . . knees:* To have preeminence and the deference of having others curtsy.
4. *and him . . . me:* and for my rank to force ("bind") someone ("him") to yield the right-hand side and the smooth part of the road.
5. *to be great . . . undone:* worldly power, when the thread that Fortune ("hazard") allots has been all wound up onto a big spool ("bottom"; or, when the hazards of reaching a high position have been surmounted), simply means a greater fall (or, falling only for something important). In Greek mythology, the end of a life occurred when the Fates cut a person's thread. Regardless of the exact interpretation of the passage, it accurately predicts More's fate.

All Is True (Henry VIII)

All Is True (Henry VIII; 1613) is the Shakespearean play that brought down the house. During a performance on June 29, 1613, when it "had beene acted not passinge 2 or 3 times before," "certain Chambers" (small cannons) were shot off. The thatch of the Globe Theatre ignited, and the building burned down. Contemporary accounts disagree about whether the accident occurred early in the play, when King Henry participates in "a Masque at the Cardinal Wolsey's house" and the stage direction reads "Chambers discharged" (1.4.50), or, more improbably, when it "was almost ended." Apparently there was only one injury, to a man who "had his breeches set on fire, that would perhaps have broyled him, if he had not by the benefit of a provident wit put it out with bottle Ale." Another version, perhaps of the same incident, claims that the injured man "was scalded with the fire by adventuring in to save a child which otherwise had been burnt."

The play itself does indeed show "a provident wit" and "save a child" (though perhaps not in the fashion the two commentators had in mind), through the mixing of dramatic genres: in All Is True, the national history play meets the tragicomic romance. Known as Henry VIII at least since 1623, the text is a collaborative effort of Shakespeare and John Fletcher—with Shakespeare apparently the senior partner. In drawing on narratives of relatively recent English history—primarily Raphael Holinshed's Chronicles of England, Scotland, and Ireland (1587), Shakespeare's main source for his earlier English history plays, and, for much of Act 5, John Foxe's epic of Protestant propaganda, Book of Martyrs— the playwrights returned to a genre that Shakespeare had dominated during its heyday in the 1590s. By contrast, tragicomic romance, influenced by late Renaissance elite Italian theater, was very much in vogue in 1613 thanks largely to the recent works of Shakespeare, Francis Beaumont, and Fletcher. The Shakespearean history play focuses on dynastic instabilities and civil conflicts of the late fourteenth and fifteenth centuries, and especially on the national implications of struggles between aristocratic factions. Shakespearean romance characteristically deploys a fictional plot in which long suffering and separation (often across the sea) are transcended through the virtuous daughter who redeems her father and through magical interventions that produce providential outcomes. The synthesis of romance and history in All Is True thus emphasizes a providential interpretation of English history. Here, as in the other romances, the royal family is identified with the family of James I. The resulting implication—that the antagonisms of earlier history are justified by the felicity of the present reign—risks chauvinistic sycophancy. Yet All Is True also challenges this celebratory interpretation: it is in the tension between these two tendencies that the play's interest lies.

The historical narrative, which combines close reliance on the sources with chronological compression and rearrangement, spans almost twenty-five years. Its principal structural unit is de casibus tragedy, which recounts the fall of illustrious figures and resembles the morality play's abstractly allegorical focus on virtue and vice. The wheel of fortune is the form's dominant, cyclical image: what goes up must come down. Providential romance, however, is teleological: it has an end in view. So much of All Is True concerns not the ups and downs of monarchs and their rivals, as in Shakespeare's earlier histories, but the successive falls of Buckingham, Katherine, and Cardinal Wolsey, and the near fall of Cranmer, Archbishop of Canterbury. Each gets a day in court—his or her fifteen minutes of fame—before passing from the scene. These downfalls, like other events in the play, are rendered through stirring speeches and pageantry that for centuries made the work a success on the stage and that recall the spectacle of the contemporary court theatrical form known as the "masque."

Now, to let matters of State ſleep, I will entertain you at the preſent with what hath happened this week at the banks ſide. The Kings Players had a new Play, called *All ú true*, repreſenting ſome principall pieces of the raign of *Henry* 8. which was ſet forth with many extraordinary circumſtances of Pomp and Majeſty, even to the matting of the ſtage; the Knights of the Order, with their Georges and Garter, the Guards with their embroidered Coats, and the like: ſufficient in truth within a while to make greatneſs very familiar, if not ridiculous. Now, King *Henry* making a Maſque at the Cardinal *Wolſey*'s houſe, and certain Chambers being ſhot off at his entry, ſome of the paper, or other ſtuff wherewith one of them was ſtopped, did light on the thatch, where being thought at firſt but an idle ſmoak, and their eyes more attentive to the ſhow, it kindled inwardly, and ran round like a train, conſuming within leſs then an hour the whole houſe to the very grounds.

This was the fatal period of that vertuous fabrique, wherein yet nothing did periſh, but wood and ſtraw, and a few forſaken cloaks; only one man had his breeches ſet on fire, that would perhaps have broyled him, if he had not by the benefit of a provident wit put it out with bottle Ale. The reſt when we meet: till when, I proteſt every minute is the ſiege of Troy. Gods dear bleſſings till then and ever be with you.

Your poor Uncle and faithful ſervant.

HENRY WOTTON.

The burning of the Globe Theater. From a letter of July 2, 1613, in *Letters of Sir Henry Wotton to Sir Edmund Bacon* (1661).

Initially, the repetitive *de casibus* structure doesn't seem to be heading anywhere. Yet the linguistic patterning suggests a larger purpose. Beginning with the Prologue's invocation of tears and pity (lines 5–6), the play emphasizes suffering, the burden of life, acquiescence in defeat, forgiveness of one's foes, patience, religious serenity, and an understanding of the fall from power as part of a natural pattern like life itself. Cardinal Wolsey's undoing offers a striking instance of the transformation of conflict into reconciliation. When Surrey, who correctly blames Wolsey for the execution of Buckingham (Surrey's father-in-law), taunts the Cardinal at the moment of his ruin, he is finally rebuked:

LORD CHAMBERLAIN   O, my lord,
Press not a falling man too far. 'Tis virtue.
His faults lie open to the laws. Let them,
Not you, correct him. My heart weeps to see him
So little of his great self.
SURREY   I forgive him.
(3.2.333–37)

Once the lords have departed, the hitherto villainous Wolsey experiences a shift in outlook that aligns him with his victims, Buckingham and Katherine. Characterization counts for little as the Cardinal discovers his religious vocation only following the collapse of his secular career. Asked how he feels, Wolsey replies:

Why, well—
Never so truly happy, my good Cromwell.
I know myself now, and I feel within me
A peace above all earthly dignities,
A still and quiet conscience.
(3.2.377–81)

Cardinal Wolsey is forced "to render up the great seal" to Norfolk and Suffolk (3.2.230). From George Cavendish, *The Life and Death of Cardinal Wolsey* (1557).

Thus, like Buckingham's and Katherine's falls, but also like Adam and Eve's, Wolsey's fall is a fortunate one.

The Cardinal considers his former responsibilities "a burden / Too heavy for a man that hopes for heaven" (3.2.385–86). But not too heavy for a woman: the burden is delivered at the end of the play when Queen Anne gives birth to the future Queen Elizabeth—the moment toward which all previous events have been tending. The critic Northrop Frye noted in the play "an invisible but omnipotent and ruthless providence who is ready to tear the whole social and religious structure of England to pieces in order to get Queen Elizabeth born." Buckingham has a serious claim to the crown, so he must be removed. Katherine's defect is that she is not the queen who will bear Elizabeth. Wolsey, who favors a diplomatically useful French alliance for Henry and hence opposes the king's marriage to Anne, unwittingly brings them together at a party he hosts (1.4). The individual tragedies are thus both personally and politically fortunate. Elizabeth's birth promises not only her own reign but also that of her successor, James, and praise of these two monarchs is accompanied by compliments to James's daughter Elizabeth, who was married in February 1613. Archbishop Cranmer's concluding prophecy makes the link explicit:

> when
> The bird of wonder dies—the maiden phoenix—
> Her ashes new create another heir
> As great in admiration as herself.
>
> (5.4.39–42)

Though Queen Elizabeth is the "maiden phoenix" and James the heir, James's daughter was also compared to the phoenix at the time of her marriage.

This connection also lays to rest Henry's persistent desire for a male heir. That absent royal son earlier justifies Henry's divorce of Katherine:

> methought
> I stood not in the smile of heaven. . . .
> . . . .
> I weighed the danger which my realms stood in
> By this my issue's fail, and that gave to me
> Many a groaning throe.
>
> (2.4.183–96)

Henry assumes the burden himself, experiencing "many a groaning throe" as if he could deliver the son that Katherine cannot. When Anne takes on the burden, Henry reveals his ongoing anxiety:

> KING HENRY   Is the Queen delivered?
> Say, 'Ay, and of a boy.'
> OLD LADY   Ay, ay, my liege,
> And of a lovely boy. The God of heaven
> Both now and ever bless her! 'Tis a girl
> Promises boys hereafter.
>
>   (5.1.163–67)

The Old Lady's flattery reveals the truth: Elizabeth *is* "a girl / Promises boys hereafter." In having James succeed her, she fulfills the properly self-effacing function of women in this patriarchal fantasy and delivers to Henry what Anne could not—a male heir.

Providence also enters the play through the standard sea journeys of Shakespearean romance, journeys that typically bring separation, suffering, and a transformation whose association with water links it to baptism. Set entirely in England, *All Is True* seems remote from such concerns. Yet the aquatic and nautical imagery of destruction pervades the play. Buckingham, for instance, warns against false friends, who,

>   when they once perceive
> The least rub in your fortunes, fall away
> Like water from ye, never found again
> But where they mean to sink ye.
>
>   (2.1.129–32)

Henry finds himself "hulling in / The wild sea of my conscience" over his marriage to Katherine (2.4.196–97), who worries about her "shipwrecked" ladies-in-waiting. Wolsey's foes are "rav'nous fishes" who ineffectually attack his "new trimmed . . . vessel" (1.2.80–81). Wolsey himself is a "rock" that threatens Buckingham and will protect Henry "against the chiding flood" of danger and rebellion (1.1.113; 3.2.198). He is a boat that "coasts / And hedges" but will "founder" (3.2.38–40). He has swum "far beyond my depth" and is at "the mercy / Of a rude stream that must for ever hide me" (3.2.362–65). He has borne "a load would sink a navy" (3.2.384), but he tells Cromwell that he, who "sounded all the depths and shoals of honour, / Found thee a way, out of his wreck, to rise in" (3.2.437–38). Approaching death, Wolsey is "broken with the storms of state" (4.2.21).

Positive associations with water and the sea are often connected with colonialism. The English nobility in France were so opulently attired they "made Britain India" (1.1.21)—an image of fabulous wealth. Similarly, "Our King has all the Indies in his arms" (4.1.45) when he embraces Anne, a "very fresh fish" at court (2.3.87). At her public appearance, "such a noise arose / As the shrouds make at sea in a stiff tempest" (4.1.73–74). The perilous journeys and shipwrecks are redeemed by Elizabeth's watery baptism, which has the crowd appeal of "some strange Indian with the great tool" (5.3.32). Speaking of James, Cranmer predicts,

> Wherever the bright sun of heaven shall shine,
> His honour and the greatness of his name
> Shall be, and make new nations.
>
>   (5.4.50–52)

The capital of the "new nation" is Jamestown and the nation itself Virginia, named for "the maiden phoenix" who died "yet a virgin" (5.4.60)—James's predecessor, the infant Elizabeth.

Although the providential logic that leads first Elizabeth and then James to the throne often works against human intentions, Henry takes an increasingly active role in securing the destined end. The crucial moment is Cranmer's trial. Just before it begins, the stage direction reads "*Enter* KING [HENRY] . . . *at a window, above*" (5.2.18). There, seeing but unseen, he is quasi-divine, as he himself suggests in angrily observing the council's humiliation of Cranmer: "Is this the honour they do one another? / 'Tis well there's one above 'em yet" (5.2.25–26). The "one above 'em" can be either God or the King, a distinction the scene blurs. This elevated perspective presumably pleased James, who held an absolutist, divine-right view of monarchy. Henry's intervention later in the scene to protect Cranmer preserves the man who later established the doctrinal basis of the English Reformation. As suggested by Cranmer's prophetic promise about Elizabeth's reign — "God shall be truly known" (5.4.36) — this religious outcome is also part of the providential pattern. Yet except in Cranmer's conflict with the Catholic Gardiner, who accuses him of being "a sectary" and Cromwell of being "a favourer / Of this new sect" (5.2.104, 114–15), and in Wolsey's dismissive description of Anne as "a spleeny Lutheran" (3.2.100), little is made of the central event of Henry's reign: the break with Rome. The characters are judged not by their religious sympathies but by their integrity. Accordingly, the outstanding figures are an English Protestant, Cranmer, and a Spanish Catholic, Katherine. The notion of conscience, which is far more prominent here than in Holinshed's *Chronicles* and which Protestants used against the papacy to repudiate blind adherence to any human doctrinal authority, is deployed by the playwrights to judge Catholics and Protestants alike. Though this impartiality may be more the work of Shakespeare than of Fletcher (see the Textual Note), the overall result is the characteristic national reconciliation of Shakespeare's history plays.

National reconciliation also transcends class antagonism, an issue largely absent from the sources. Like the other lords, the Duke of Buckingham resents the usurpation of the nobility's traditional power by the proud "beggar" Wolsey, a "butcher's cur" (1.1.122, 120): the Cardinal's father was supposedly a butcher. On similar grounds, Wolsey opposes Henry's marriage to Anne, who came from the gentry rather than the nobility and who had been one of Katherine's ladies-in-waiting: "A knight's daughter / To be her mistress' mistress? The Queen's queen?" (3.2.95–96). But the play also posits a harmony between upper class and lower that can be disturbed only by self-serving intermediaries who mistreat humble folk. Buckingham is betrayed to Wolsey by his surveyor, whom he fired for oppressing his tenants. Katherine gets Henry to repeal a tax levied by Wolsey that is so onerous it drives the poor to rebellion. Interclass unity is affirmed in the popular excitement about the baby Elizabeth, which the play refracts through the lower-class prose of the exasperated Porter (5.3) — a prose noteworthy in a play composed overwhelmingly in blank verse. Similarly, at Anne's earlier coronation, one of the gentlemen, who play the role of a chorus absent from the sources, remarks,

> The citizens,
> I am sure, have shown at full their royal minds —
> As, let 'em have their rights, they are ever forward.
> (4.1.7–9)

And in slightly different fashion, Cranmer renders hereditary class hierarchy a thing of the past. "Those about" Elizabeth "from her shall read the perfect ways of honour, / And by those claim their greatness, not by blood" (5.4.36–38).

Yet as recent productions have emphasized, *All Is True* offers a critical account of Henry's reign. All is true: the historical figures who fall from the heights are not simply guilty; they carry a certain truth to their graves. Buckingham has been betrayed, as his father was, "by those men we loved most" (2.1.123). The innocent and virtuous Katherine is given a strength of character, consequent impressiveness, and spiritual coronation absent both from Holinshed's portrayal and from her successor, Anne. And in a departure from Holinshed, even Wolsey gets a moving repentance.

The play also implicitly suggests the costs of the Elizabethan Protestant succession. Though only Buckingham is executed, *All Is True* makes that execution resonate. Henry's "princely commendations" to the dying Katherine are "like a pardon after execution" (4.2.119, 122). As Katherine is succeeded by Anne, so Wolsey is replaced by Sir Thomas More, Cromwell, and Cranmer (3.2.392–460), all four of whom were also later executed.

Wolsey hopes More will "do justice / For truth's sake and his conscience" (lines 397–98)—principles that were to cost the Catholic More his life. Anne actually predicts her own fate in lamenting Katherine's mistreatment:

> Much better
> She ne'er had known pomp; though't be temporal,
> Yet if that quarrel, fortune, do divorce
> It from the bearer, 'tis a sufferance panging
> As soul and bodies severing.
>
> (2.3.12–16)

Wolsey advises Cromwell:

> Be just, and fear not.
> Let all the ends thou aim'st at be thy country's,
> Thy God's, and truth's. Then if thou fall'st, O Cromwell,
> Thou fall'st a blessèd martyr.
>
> (3.2.447–50)

Gardiner's anti-Protestant attacks on Cranmer and Cromwell foreshadow his later success in sending both men to their death. Even Elizabeth's christening evokes execution: "Belong to th' gallows, and be hanged" (5.3.5).

Ambivalence extends as well to the centrally providential characters. No man utters anything but praise for the "beauty and honour" of that "angel" Anne Boleyn (2.3.76, 4.1.44). But a woman does. When Anne denies any desire for political advancement, the Old Lady calls this position "hypocrisy," ridicules Anne's pliant "conscience," and finds her claim "strange" (2.3.26, 32, 36). Yet Anne does become queen, without an explanation of her supposed change of heart but with a suggestive pun on "quean" (whore) characteristic of the entire sexualized exchange and of Anne's earlier banter (1.4.46–49). The scene with the Old Lady, apparently invented by Shakespeare, thus sullies Anne before she becomes a purely ceremonial figure reduced to bearing royal children. Moreover, Elizabeth's conception before Henry and Anne's marriage may be alluded to in the "great-bellied women" at Anne's coronation and the "fry of fornication" at Elizabeth's christening (4.1.78, 5.3.33–34).

As for Henry himself, though he is repeatedly praised by his victims (2.1.87–95, 3.2.381–93, 4.2.161–65), his increasing attention to government raises retrospective questions about his earlier behavior. It is tempting to wonder: how much did the King know, and when did he know it? The Henry of the play, more troubling than Holinshed's, seems oddly abstracted, either culpably unaware or disingenuously disavowing knowledge of foreign affairs, taxation, and treason. He often seems the Teflon king, to whom no blame sticks. The self-destructive zigzags in foreign policy—alliance with France, alliance with Spain, attempted alliance with France—are Wolsey's doings, not his: the buck stops elsewhere. Moreover,

Henry VIII, aged 53 in 1544, in the portrait engraving by Cornelius Matsuys. Gardiner's unsuccessful attack on Cranmer probably occurred around this time.

his interventions are not fully reassuring. His charges against Wolsey ignore major issues to focus on personal, peripheral concerns. Even his protection of Cranmer is necessary only because Henry allows his biased council to proceed in the first place. Indeed, the play suggests that the law serves the man with power, whether Wolsey or the King.

Explicit skepticism about Henry is produced by his divorce proceedings. *All Is True* shows a man "afflicted" by a "wounded conscience," by "conscience, conscience," by "my conscience" (2.2.62, 74, 142; 2.4.167, 179, 200). But earlier, at Wolsey's banquet, it shows a man attracted to Anne Boleyn: "The fairest hand I ever touched. O beauty, / Till now I never knew thee" (1.4.76–77). This meeting is the play's invention. A disabused view is openly voiced later:

> LORD CHAMBERLAIN It seems the marriage with his brother's wife
>   Has crept too near his conscience.
> SUFFOLK   No, his conscience
>   Has crept too near another lady.
>
>   (2.2.15–17)

Even apologists for Henry's behavior suspect his motives. Overwhelmed by the sight of Anne, the Second Gentleman remarks, "I cannot blame his conscience" (4.1.47). It is hard to determine whether such criticism undermines the providential pattern or renders the pattern's transcendence of such formidable obstacles all the more miraculous. Like many Shakespearean plays, *All Is True* opposes means and ends, showing and telling, dramatized plot and asserted conclusion, pity and jubilation.

The critique of Henry may have been targeted at James as well, despite the play's closing compliment to him. The satire on French fashion (1.3) ridicules behavior at James's court in which the King participated. Like Henry, James neglected affairs of state, to the dismay of his subjects. His court was riven by factionalism; his absolutist view of monarchy at times resulted in a subordination of law to royal desire. Yet the crucial contemporary parallels lie elsewhere. In urging punishment of Cranmer's Protestantism, Gardiner warns that laxity leads to falling dominoes:

> Commotions, uproars—with a general taint
> Of the whole state, as of late days our neighbours,
> The upper Germany, can dearly witness.
>
>   (5.2.62–64)

The reference is to the Peasants' War in Germany (1524–26), in which the German aristocracy massacred perhaps 100,000 peasants. The danger of popular unrest in England is suggested by the court's fear of "loud rebellion" and the unruly "rabble" (1.2.30, 5.3.65). The rowdies at Elizabeth's christening are "your faithful friends o'th' suburbs" (5.3.66)— the location of the outdoor public theaters, such as the Globe, where *All Is True* was performed. The Porter's Man equates the crowd at the christening with the crowd at the Globe: "You great fellow, / Stand close up, or I'll make your head ache" (5.3.81–82). The Porter remarks, "These are the youths that thunder at a playhouse, and fight for bitten apples, that no audience but the tribulation of Tower Hill or the limbs of Limestone, their dear brothers, are able to endure" (5.3.55–58). The comparison is between the unruly apprentices who come to the theater and the rough crowds who attend public executions or frequent the dockyards. A christening recalls an execution; an ostensibly orthodox play in a suburban theater emphasizes the criminal character of suburb and audience alike.

It is thus the interaction between *All Is True* and its audience that undermines orthodoxy. According to Sir Henry Wotton, a spectator at the fateful performance when the Globe burned down, the work represented "some principall pieces of the reign of Henry VIII, which was set forth with many extraordinary circumstances of pomp and majesty . . . sufficient in truth within a while to make greatness very familiar, if not ridiculous." Rather than dazzling into awestruck submission, the play's pageantry reduces the mystique of monarchy, turning the politically disenfranchised popular audience into moral arbiters of royal power. James's favorite, the Duke of Buckingham, may have felt as much when, in 1628, he commissioned a performance of *All Is True*, only to walk out after his namesake's beheading. In 1649, a Parliament driven by popular pressure emulated the play by staging an execution of its own. This time, however, the victim was James I's own son: the man on the scaffold was the king.

Walter Cohen

TEXTUAL NOTE

Although the play was initially printed in the First Folio of 1623 (F) under the title *The Famous History of the Life of Henry the Eight* and today is generally known as *Henry VIII*, comments on early performances suggest that it was originally called *All Is True*. Perhaps the compilers of the Folio changed its title to make it conform to the pattern of using monarchs' names for the English history plays: it is placed at the end of this group of plays. Or perhaps John Fletcher, Shakespeare's collaborator on the play, is responsible for the switch (see below). The text is based not on an authorial manuscript but on a scribal copy; either the authorial or the scribal version may have been slightly revised for theatrical performance. F's division into acts and scenes is followed in the present edition; some editors, however, introduce a scene division after 5.2.34.

All Is True probably has links to the marriage on February 14, 1613, of Princess Elizabeth, King James's daughter, to the German Prince Frederick, the Elector Palatine. If so, it might have been written in late 1612. Unlike other plays by Shakespeare, it was not performed at court as part of the wedding festivities, but it just conceivably could have been staged around that time at Blackfriars, the King's Men's indoor, "private," winter commercial theater. But the accidental burning of the Globe Theatre at one of the first performances of the play on June 29, 1613, makes composition following the marriage, with the initial performance at the Globe in June 1613, far more likely. (See the Introduction.)

F attributes the play to Shakespeare. But beginning in the eighteenth century and especially since 1850, many critics have concluded that John Fletcher, who succeeded Shakespeare as the principal dramatist of the King's Men, collaborated on *All Is True*. External evidence for this position is inferential and inconclusive. Toward the end of his career, as perhaps at the beginning, Shakespeare seems to have turned to collaboration— in *Pericles*, the lost *Cardenio*, and *The Two Noble Kinsmen*. In the last two plays, dating from 1612–14, he apparently worked with Fletcher. On the other hand, these plays were all excluded from F by the editors, who were Shakespeare's fellow actors in the King's Men. Though a minority of scholars continue to believe that Shakespeare was the sole author of *All Is True*, the internal stylistic and linguistic evidence strongly suggests that Fletcher wrote at least one-quarter of the piece—primarily 1.3–4, 3.1, and 5.2–4. (He seems to have written a little more than half of *The Two Noble Kinsmen*.) Yet the problem of attribution is not that simple. Shakespeare may have had some role in 3.1 and especially 5.2–4. Fletcher is likely to have played a part in 2.1–2 and 4.1–2. The unusually full stage directions may also be his work. Fletcher's sections of the play arguably have a more pro-Protestant outlook than Shakespeare's relatively balanced and uncommitted treatment of religious controversy. And this distinction may even extend to the title, with *All Is True* representing Shakespeare's evenhanded view and *The Famous History of the Life of Henry the Eight* Fletcher's celebration of the king who broke with Rome. Finally, scholarly skepticism about the attribution of certain scenes (notably 2.1 and 4.1) to either Shakespeare or Fletcher has led to speculation about a third author. Francis Beaumont, who regularly collaborated with Fletcher, has been proposed, but the suggestion remains conjectural.

In short, both the broad conception of the play and most of the "big" scenes appear to be Shakespeare's.

SELECTED BIBLIOGRAPHY

Bergeron, David M. *Shakespeare's Romances and the Royal Family*. Lawrence: University Press of Kansas, 1985. 203–22.

Cespedes, Frank V. " 'We are one in fortunes': The Sense of History in *Henry VIII*." *English Literary Renaissance* 10 (1980): 413–38.

Felperin, Howard. *Shakespearean Romance*. Princeton: Princeton University Press, 1972. 196–210.

Kermode, Frank. "What Is Shakespeare's *Henry VIII* About?" *Shakespeare: The Histories*. Ed. Eugene M. Waith. Englewood Cliffs, N.J.: Prentice Hall, 1965. 168–79.

Knight, G. Wilson. *The Crown of Life*. London: Oxford University Press, 1947. 256–336.

Kurland, Stuart M. "*Henry VIII* and James I: Shakespeare and Jacobean Politics." *Shakespeare Studies* 19 (1987): 203–17.

Noling, Kim H. "Grubbing Up the Stock: Dramatizing Queens in *Henry VIII*." *Shakespeare Quarterly* 39 (1988): 291–306.

Rudnytsky, Peter L. "*Henry VIII* and the Deconstruction of History." *Shakespeare Survey* 43 (1991): 43–57.

Shirley, Frances A., ed. *"King John" and "Henry VIII": Critical Essays*. New York: Garland, 1988.

Slights, Camille Wells. "The Politics of Conscience in *All Is True* (or *Henry VIII*)." *Shakespeare Survey* 43 (1991): 59–68.

All Is True

THE PERSONS OF THE PLAY

PROLOGUE
KING HENRY the Eighth
Duke of BUCKINGHAM
Lord ABERGAVENNY } his sons-in-law
Earl of SURREY
Duke of NORFOLK
Duke of SUFFOLK
LORD CHAMBERLAIN
LORD CHANCELLOR
Lord SANDS (also called Sir William SANDS)
Sir Thomas LOVELL
Sir Anthony DENNY
Sir Henry GUILDFORD
CARDINAL WOLSEY
Two SECRETARIES
BUCKINGHAM'S SURVEYOR
CARDINAL CAMPEIUS
GARDINER, the King's new secretary, later Bishop of Winchester
His PAGE
Thomas CROMWELL
CRANMER, Archbishop of Canterbury
QUEEN KATHERINE, later KATHERINE, Princess Dowager
GRIFFITH, her gentleman usher
PATIENCE, her waiting-woman
Other WOMEN
Six spirits, who dance before Katherine in a vision
A MESSENGER
Lord CAPUTIUS
ANNE Boleyn
An OLD LADY
BRANDON } who arrest Buckingham and Abergavenny
SERJEANT-at-arms
Sir Nicholas VAUX ⎫
Tipstaves ⎬ after Buckingham's arraignment
Halberdiers ⎪
Common people ⎭
Two vergers ⎫
Two SCRIBES ⎪
Archbishop of Canterbury ⎪
Bishop of LINCOLN ⎪
Bishop of Ely ⎬ appearing at the Legatine Court
Bishop of Rochester ⎪
Bishop of Saint Asaph ⎪
Two priests ⎪
Serjeant-at-arms ⎪
Two noblemen ⎪
A CRIER ⎭

Three GENTLEMEN ⎫
Two judges ⎪
Choristers ⎪
Lord Mayor of London ⎪
Garter King-of-Arms ⎪
Marquis Dorset ⎬ appearing in the Coronation
Four Barons of the Cinque Ports ⎪
Stokesley, Bishop of London ⎪
Old Duchess of Norfolk ⎪
Countesses ⎭

A DOORKEEPER ⎫
Doctor BUTTS, the King's physician ⎬ At Cranmer's trial
Pursuivants, pages, footboys, grooms ⎭

A PORTER ⎫
His MAN ⎪
Two aldermen ⎪
Lord Mayor of London ⎪
GARTER King-of-Arms ⎬ at the Christening
Six noblemen ⎪
Old Duchess of Norfolk, godmother ⎪
The child, Princess Elizabeth ⎪
Marchioness Dorset, godmother ⎭

EPILOGUE
Ladies, gentlemen, a SERVANT, guards, attendants, trumpeters

Prologue

[*Enter* PROLOGUE]

PROLOGUE I come no more to make you laugh. Things now
    That bear a weighty and a serious brow,
    Sad, high, and working,° full of state° and woe—   *full of pathos / grandeur*
    Such noble scenes as draw the eye to flow
5   We now present. Those that can pity[1] here
    May, if they think it well, let fall a tear.
    The subject will deserve it. Such as give
    Their money out of hope they may believe,
    May here find truth,[2] too. Those that come to see
10   Only a show or two, and so agree
    The play may pass, if they be still, and willing,
    I'll undertake may see away their shilling
    Richly in two short hours.[3] Only they
    That come to hear a merry bawdy play,
15   A noise of targets,° or to see a fellow   *shields*
    In a long motley coat guarded[4] with yellow,
    Will be deceived. For, gentle hearers, know
    To rank our chosen truth with such a show
    As fool and fight is, beside forfeiting
20   Our own brains, and the opinion that we bring
    To make that only true we now intend,[5]

---

1. A major theme of the play.
2. Another major theme of the play.
3. *Those . . . hours:* If those who come only for a spectacle ("show") and approve the play on those terms are quiet and willing, I promise they'll get their shilling's worth (the price of more expensive, genteel seating) in two hours (plays ran two to three hours).
4. Ornamented on its border. The fool's "motley," or

patchwork, coat may refer to other plays about Henry's life, including Samuel Rowley's *When You See Me You Know Me* (1605), which featured Henry's fool, Will Summers, and was reprinted and perhaps revived in 1613.
5. *beside . . . intend:* in addition to wasting our mental labor, and our intention of presenting an entirely truthful representation.

Will leave us never an understanding[6] friend.
Therefore, for goodness' sake, and as you are known
The first and happiest hearers° of the town,   *finest audience*
25 Be sad° as we would make ye. Think ye see   *grave*
The very persons of our noble story
As they were living; think you see them great,°   *of high rank*
And followed with the general throng and sweat
Of thousand friends; then, in a moment, see
30 How soon this mightiness meets misery.[7]
And if you can be merry then, I'll say
A man may weep upon his wedding day.   [*Exit*]

1.1

[*A cloth of state throughout the play.*][1] *Enter the Duke*
of NORFOLK *at one door; at the other* [*door enter*] *the*
Duke of BUCKINGHAM *and the Lord* ABERGAVENNY

BUCKINGHAM [*to* NORFOLK] Good morrow, and well met. How have ye done
Since last we saw° in France?   *met*
NORFOLK   I thank your grace,
Healthful, and ever since a fresh° admirer   *an eager*
Of what I saw there.[2]
BUCKINGHAM   An untimely ague
5 Stayed me a prisoner in my chamber[3] when
Those suns of glory, those two lights of men,
Met in the vale of Ardres.
NORFOLK   'Twixt Guisnes and Ardres.[4]
I was then present, saw them salute on horseback,
Beheld them when they lighted,° how they clung   *got off*
10 In their embracement as° they grew together,   *as if*
Which had they,° what four throned ones could have weighed[5]   *if they had*
Such a compounded one?
BUCKINGHAM   All the whole time
I was my chamber's prisoner.
NORFOLK   Then you lost
The view of earthly glory. Men might say
15 Till this time pomp was single, but now married
To one above itself.[6] Each following day
Became the next day's master, till the last
Made former wonders its.[7] Today the French,
All clinquant° all in gold, like heathen gods   *glittering*
20 Shone down the English; and tomorrow they
Made Britain India.[8] Every man that stood
Showed like a mine. Their dwarfish pages were

6. Punning reference to the lower-class groundlings, who are literally "understanding" in the sense of "standing under" the raised stage.
7. The rise and fall of public figures is still another central theme.
1.1. Location: The court at London.
1. A seat under a canopy for the King or Cardinal Wolsey, perhaps onstage throughout the play. The original Globe performances also had "matting" (a woven straw floor-covering) on the stage.
2. The reference is to the rendezvous of Henry VIII and Francis I of France near Calais in June 1520, at the Field of the Cloth of Gold, named for the sumptuous displays by the two kings.
3. Actually, Buckingham was present, if reluctantly

(because of the expense), at the Field of the Cloth of Gold. The fictional "ague," or fever, allows the dramatist to show Buckingham responding to Norfolk's detailed description.
4. Guisnes belonged to England, Ardres to France.
5. Been as heavy as.
6. *Till . . . itself:* The pomp of each King now joins ("marries") that of the other, making a greater pomp than either alone could display.
7. *Each . . . its:* Each day learned wonders from the previous one, making the last day the most wonderful of all. *master:* standard.
8. *they . . . India:* the English made Britain look as (fabulously) rich as India or the West Indies.

As cherubim, all gilt;[9] the *mesdames*,° too,		*ladies*
Not used to toil, did almost sweat to bear		
25 The pride° upon them, that° their very labour		*fancy adornment / so that*
Was to them as a painting.[1] Now this masque		
Was cried° incomparable, and th'ensuing night		*said to be*
Made it a fool and beggar. The two kings		
Equal in lustre, were now best, now worst,		
30 As presence did present them.[2] Him in eye		
Still him in praise,[3] and being present both,		
'Twas said they saw but one, and no discerner		
Durst wag his tongue in censure.[4] When these suns—		
For so they phrase 'em—by their heralds challenged		
35 The noble spirits to arms, they did perform		
Beyond thought's compass, that former fabulous story		
Being now seen possible enough, got credit		
That *Bevis* was believed.[5]		

BUCKINGHAM   O, you go far!

NORFOLK   As I belong to worship,° and affect   *the aristocracy*
40 In honour honesty,[6] the tract of ev'rything
Would by a good discourser lose some life
Which action's self was tongue to.[7] All was royal.
To the disposing° of it naught rebelled.   *arrangement*
Order gave each thing view. The office did
Distinctly[8] his full function.

45 BUCKINGHAM   Who did guide—
I mean, who set the body and the limbs
Of this great sport° together, as you guess?   *show*

NORFOLK   One, certes, that promises no element[9]
In such a business.

BUCKINGHAM   I pray you who, my lord?

50 NORFOLK   All this was ordered by the good discretion
Of the right reverend Cardinal of York.°   *(Wolsey)*

BUCKINGHAM   The devil speed° him! No man's pie is freed   *ruin*
From his ambitious finger. What had he
To do in these fierce° vanities? I wonder   *excessive*
55 That such a keech[1] can, with his very bulk,
Take up the rays o'th' beneficial sun,°   *(Henry)*
And keep it from the earth.

NORFOLK   Surely, sir,
There's in him stuff that puts° him to these ends.   *spurs*
For being not propped by ancestry, whose grace
60 Chalks successors their way,[2] nor called upon
For high feats done to th' crown, neither allied
To eminent assistants,° but spider-like,   *ministers of state*
Out of his self-drawing° web, a° gives us note   *spun from himself / he*

---

9. Gold-plated statues of cherubim, often found in
churches.
1. Made them rosy, as if with makeup.
2. According to who was present.
3. *Him . . . praise:* To the King on display at the time
went all the acclaim.
4. *no . . . censure:* no one watching dared say one out-
shone the other.
5. *they did . . . believed:* their performance was such that
stories formerly deemed mere fables, now looking possible, gained plausibility. Even *Sir Bevis of Hampton*
(Southampton), a popular medieval romance, was be-

lieved.
6. *and . . . honesty:* and honorably love truth.
7. *the tract . . . to:* the events surpass their telling.
8. *Order . . . Distinctly:* Careful organization made everything appropriately visible. Each responsible person properly fulfilled.
9. One, without doubt, who seems out of place.
1. Hunk of fat from a slaughtered animal. Wolsey was
said to be a butcher's son.
2. *ancestry . . . way:* noble ancestors, whose honorable
qualities pave the way for future generations.

The force of his own merit makes his way—
65 A gift that heaven gives for him which buys
A place next to the King.

ABERGAVENNY   I cannot tell
What heaven hath given him—let some graver eye
Pierce into that; but I can see his pride
Peep through each part of him. Whence has he that?°   (such pride)
70 If not from hell, the devil is a niggard°   selfish
Or has given all before,° and he° begins   already / (Wolsey)
A new hell in himself.

BUCKINGHAM   Why the devil,
Upon this French going out,° took he upon him   journey
Without the privity° o'th' King t'appoint   private sanction
75 Who should attend on him? He makes up the file°   roll
Of all the gentry, for the most part such
To whom as great a charge as little honour
He meant to lay upon;³ and his own letter,
The honourable board of council out,
Must fetch him in, he papers.⁴

80 ABERGAVENNY   I do know
Kinsmen of mine—three at the least—that have
By this so sickened° their estates that never   wasted
They shall abound as formerly.

BUCKINGHAM   O, many
Have broke their backs with laying manors on 'em⁵
85 For this great journey. What did this vanity
But minister communication of
A most poor issue?⁶

NORFOLK   Grievingly I think
The peace between the French and us not values°   does not merit
The cost that did conclude it.

BUCKINGHAM   Every man,
90 After the hideous storm that followed, was
A thing inspired, and, not consulting,° broke   without conferring
Into a general° prophecy—that this tempest,   collective
Dashing the garment of this peace, aboded°   prophesied
The sudden breach on't.°   of it

NORFOLK   Which is budded out°—   has occurred
95 For France hath flawed° the league, and hath attached°   betrayed / seized
Our merchants' goods at Bordeaux.

ABERGAVENNY   Is it therefore°   on this account
Th'ambassador is silenced?

NORFOLK   Marry is't.°   Of course it is

ABERGAVENNY A proper title of a° peace, and purchased   A fine thing to call
At a superfluous rate.°   too high a cost

BUCKINGHAM   Why, all this business
Our reverend Cardinal carried.°   oversaw
100 NORFOLK   Like it° your grace,   May it please
The state takes notice of the private difference

---

3. *To whom . . . upon:* (Wolsey gave) places of little honor
to the noblemen on whom he laid the greatest expense
for the display.
4. *and . . . papers:* and with the council ignored ("out"),
his own summons ("letter") forces every person he lists
("papers") to comply.

5. *many . . . 'em:* many have sold off their estates—and
thus bankrupted themselves—to pay for a costly wardrobe.
6. *What . . . issue:* What did such wasteful expense do but
bankrupt their own children ("poor issue"); or encourage
talk for a trivial outcome ("poor issue")?

Betwixt you and the Cardinal. I advise you—
And take it from a heart that wishes towards you
Honour and plenteous safety—that you read°   assess
105   The Cardinal's malice and his potency
Together; to consider further that
What his high hatred would effect wants° not   lacks
A minister° in his power. You know his nature,   An agent
That he's revengeful; and I know his sword
110   Hath a sharp edge—it's long, and't may be said
It reaches far; and where 'twill not extend
Thither he darts it. Bosom up° my counsel,   Keep secret; take to heart
You'll find it wholesome. Lo, where comes that rock
That I advise your shunning.

> *Enter* CARDINAL WOLSEY, *the purse*[7] *[containing the*
> *great seal] borne before him. [Enter with him] certain of*
> *the guard, and two* SECRETARIES *with papers. The* CARDI-
> NAL *in his passage fixeth his eye on* BUCKINGHAM *and*
> BUCKINGHAM *on him, both full of disdain*

CARDINAL WOLSEY [*To a* SECRETARY]   The Duke of Buckingham's
115   surveyor,° ha?   overseer of an estate
Where's his examination?°   testimony
SECRETARY   Here, so please you.
CARDINAL WOLSEY   Is he in person ready?
SECRETARY   Ay, please your grace.
CARDINAL WOLSEY   Well, we shall then know more, and Buckingham
Shall lessen this big° look.   pompous

> *Exeunt* CARDINAL [WOLSEY] *and his train*

120   BUCKINGHAM   This butcher's cur is venom-mouthed, and I
Have not the power to muzzle him; therefore best
Not wake him in his slumber. A beggar's book°   learning
Outworths a noble's blood.°   inherited privilege
NORFOLK   What, are you chafed?°   annoyed
Ask God for temp'rance; that's th'appliance only°   the only medicine
Which your disease requires.
125   BUCKINGHAM   I read in's looks
Matter against me, and his eye reviled
Me as his abject° object. At this instant   discarded
He bores° me with some trick. He's gone to th' King—   defrauds
I'll follow, and outstare him.
NORFOLK   Stay, my lord,
130   And let your reason with your choler question°   dispute
What 'tis you go about. To climb steep hills
Requires slow pace at first. Anger is like
A full hot° horse who, being allowed his way,   feisty
Self-mettle° tires him. Not a man in England   His own disposition
135   Can advise me like you. Be to yourself
As you would to your friend.[8]
BUCKINGHAM   I'll to the King,
And from a mouth of honour° quite cry down   a gentleman's mouth
This Ipswich° fellow's insolence, or proclaim   (Wolsey's birthplace)
There's difference in no persons.°   Rank no longer matters

---

7. A special bag that held the "great seal," part of the
Lord Chancellor's insignia of office.

8. *Be . . . friend:* Don't do anything you wouldn't advise a
friend to do.

NORFOLK   Be advised.°   *Be careful*
140 Heat not a furnace for your foe so hot
That it do singe yourself. We may outrun
By violent swiftness that which we run at,°   *toward*
And lose by over-running. Know you not
The fire that mounts° the liquor till't run o'er   *swells (by boiling)*
145 In seeming to augment it wastes it? Be advised.
I say again there is no English soul
More stronger to direct you than yourself,
If with the sap of reason you would quench
Or but allay° the fire of passion.   *abate*
BUCKINGHAM   Sir,
150 I am thankful to you, and I'll go along
By your prescription; but this top-proud° fellow—   *proudest of all*
Whom from the flow of gall I name not, but
From sincere motions[9]—by intelligence,°   *covert information*
And proofs as clear as founts° in July when   *springs*
155 We see each grain of gravel, I do know
To be corrupt and treasonous.
NORFOLK   Say not 'treasonous'.
BUCKINGHAM   To th' King I'll say't, and make my vouch° as strong   *case*
As shore of rock. Attend: this holy fox,
Or wolf, or both—for he is equal° rav'nous   *as*
160 As he is subtle, and as prone to mischief
As able to perform't, his mind and place°   *high position*
Infecting one another, yea, reciprocally—
Only to show his pomp as well in France
As here at home, suggests° the King our master   *tempts*
165 To this last° costly treaty, th'interview°   *latest / the meeting*
That swallowed so much treasure and, like a glass,
Did break i'th' rinsing.
NORFOLK   Faith, and so it did.
BUCKINGHAM   Pray give me favour,° sir. This cunning Cardinal,   *let me continue*
The articles o'th' combination° drew   *terms of the treaty*
170 As himself pleased, and they were ratified
As he cried 'Thus let be', to as much end°   *effect*
As give a crutch to th' dead. But our count-Cardinal[1]
Has done this, and 'tis well for worthy Wolsey,
Who cannot err, he did it. Now this follows—
175 Which, as I take it, is a kind of puppy
To th'old dam,° treason—Charles the Emperor,[2]   *bitch; mother*
Under pretence to see the Queen his aunt°—   *(Katherine)*
For 'twas indeed his colour,° but he came   *alibi*
To whisper° Wolsey—here makes visitation.   *meet covertly with*
180 His fears were that the interview betwixt
England and France might through their amity
Breed him some prejudice, for from this league
Peeped harms that menaced him. Privily° he   *Clandestinely*
Deals with our Cardinal and, as I trow°—   *believe*
185 Which I do well, for I am sure the Emperor
Paid ere he promised, whereby his suit was granted

---

9. *Whom . . . motions:* Whom I name not from a rancorous impulse but from pure motives.
1. Church leader assuming secular, aristocratic rank

(compare "King-Cardinal," 2.2.18).
2. Charles V, Holy Roman Emperor and King of Spain.

Ere it was asked—but when the way was made,
And paved with gold, the Emperor thus desired
That he° would please to alter the King's course   *(Wolsey)*
190 And break the foresaid peace. Let the King know,
As soon he shall by me, that thus the Cardinal
Does buy and sell his° honour as he° pleases,   *(Henry's) / (Wolsey)*
And for his own advantage.
NORFOLK   I am sorry
To hear this of him, and could wish he were
Something mistaken° in't.   *Partly misrepresented*
195 BUCKINGHAM   No, not a syllable.
I do pronounce him in that very shape
He shall appear in proof.°   *in practice*
       Enter BRANDON, *a* SERJEANT-*at-arms before him, and two*
       or three of the guard
BRANDON   Your office, serjeant, execute it.
SERJEANT   Sir.
    [*To* BUCKINGHAM] My lord the Duke of Buckingham and Earl
200 Of Hereford, Stafford, and Northampton, I
Arrest thee of high treason in the name
Of our most sovereign King.
BUCKINGHAM [*to* NORFOLK]   Lo° you, my lord,   *Look*
The net has fall'n upon me. I shall perish
Under device and practice.°   *trickery and schemes*
BRANDON   I am sorry
205 To see you ta'en from liberty to look on³
The business present. 'Tis his highness' pleasure
You shall to th' Tower.
BUCKINGHAM   It will help me nothing
To plead mine innocence, for that dye is on me
Which makes my whit'st part black. The will of heav'n
210 Be done in this and all things. I obey.
O, my lord Abergavenny, fare you well.
BRANDON   Nay, he must bear you company.
    [*To* ABERGAVENNY]   The King
Is pleased you shall to th' Tower till you know
How he determines further.
ABERGAVENNY   As the Duke said,
215 The will of heaven be done and the King's pleasure
By me obeyed.
BRANDON   Here is a warrant from
The King t'attach° Lord Montague and the bodies   *to seize*
Of the duke's confessor, John de la Car,
One Gilbert Perk, his chancellor—
BUCKINGHAM   So, so;
220 These are the limbs o'th' plot. No more, I hope.
BRANDON   A monk o'th' Chartreux.°   *Carthusian*
BUCKINGHAM   O, Nicholas Hopkins?
BRANDON   He.
BUCKINGHAM   My surveyor is false. The o'er-great Cardinal
Hath showed him gold. My life is spanned° already.   *marked out*
225 I am the shadow of poor Buckingham,

---

3. *to look on:* and (sorry) to behold.

Whose figure even this instant cloud puts on
By dark'ning my clear sun.[4] *[To* NORFOLK*]* My lord, farewell.

                *Exeunt [*NORFOLK *at one door,* BUCKINGHAM *and*
                ABERGAVENNY *under guard at another]*

1.2

Cornetts. Enter KING HENRY *leaning on Cardinal [Wol-*
sey]'s shoulder. [Enter with them Wolsey's two SECRETAR-
IES,*] the nobles, and Sir Thomas* LOVELL*. [The* KING
ascends to his seat under the cloth of state;] CARDINAL
*[*WOLSEY*] places himself under the King's feet° on his*   *below the throne*
right side

KING HENRY *[to* WOLSEY*]*   My life itself and the best heart° of it   *essential core*
Thanks you for this great care. I stood i'th' level°   *line of fire*
Of a full-charged confederacy,° and give thanks   *loaded conspiracy*
To you that choked it. Let be called before us
5 That gentleman of Buckingham's.° In person   *(the surveyor)*
I'll hear him his confessions justify,°   *verify*
And point by point the treasons of his master
He shall again relate.
    CRIER *(within)*   Room for the Queen, ushered by the Duke of Norfolk.

        Enter QUEEN *[*KATHERINE, *the Duke of]* NORFOLK, *and*
        [the Duke of] SUFFOLK*. She kneels.* KING *[*HENRY*] riseth*
        from his state,° takes her up, and kisses her   *throne*
10 QUEEN KATHERINE   Nay, we must longer kneel. I am a suitor.
KING HENRY   Arise, and take place by us.

        [He] placeth [her] by him
                        Half your suit
Never name to us. You have half our power,
The other moiety° ere you ask is given.   *half*
Repeat your will° and take it.   *State your wish*
QUEEN KATHERINE   Thank your majesty.
15 That you would love yourself, and in that love
Not unconsidered leave your honour nor
The dignity of your office, is the point
Of my petition.
KING HENRY   Lady mine, proceed.
QUEEN KATHERINE   I am solicited,° not by a few,   *apprised*
20 And those of true condition,° that your subjects   *loyal character*
Are in great grievance. There have been commissions
Sent down among 'em[1] which hath flawed° the heart   *broken*
Of all their loyalties; wherein, although,
My good lord Cardinal, they vent reproaches
25 Most bitterly on you, as putter-on°   *inciter*
Of these exactions, yet the King our master—
Whose honour heaven shield from soil°—even he escapes not   *blemish*
Language unmannerly, yea, such which breaks
The sides[2] of loyalty, and almost appears
In loud rebellion.
30 NORFOLK   Not 'almost appears'—
It doth appear; for upon these taxations

---

4. A cloud having overshadowed my former glory and
come between me and my king ("sun" may refer to either
Buckingham or Henry).
1.2 Location: A council chamber at court.

1. *There . . . 'em:* They have received writs authorizing
the collection of taxes.
2. *which . . . sides:* which oversteps the limits.

The clothiers all, not able to maintain
The many to them 'longing,° have put off°   *they employ / let go*
The spinsters, carders, fullers,[3] weavers, who,
35 Unfit for other life, compelled by hunger
And lack of other means, in desperate manner
Daring th'event to th' teeth,[4] are all in uproar,
And danger° serves among them.   *roguery*
KING HENRY   Taxation?
Wherein, and what taxation? My lord Cardinal,
40 You that are blamed for it alike with us,
Know you of this taxation?
CARDINAL WOLSEY   Please you, sir,
I know but of a single° part in aught°   *(his own) / anything*
Pertains to th' state, and front but in that file
Where others tell steps with me.[5]
QUEEN KATHERINE   No, my lord?
45 You know no more than others? But you frame
Things that are known alike, which are not wholesome
To those which would not know them, and yet must
Perforce be their acquaintance.[6] These exactions
Whereof my sovereign would have note,° they are   *knowledge*
50 Most pestilent to th' hearing, and to bear 'em
The back is sacrifice to° th' load. They say   *broken by*
They are devised by you, or else you suffer
Too hard an exclamation.°   *a complaint*
KING HENRY   Still exaction!
The nature of it? In what kind, let's know,
Is this exaction?
55 QUEEN KATHERINE   I am much too venturous
In tempting of your patience, but am boldened
Under your promised pardon. The subjects' grief°   *grievance*
Comes through commissions which compels from each
The sixth part of his substance° to be levied   *wealth*
60 Without delay, and the pretence for this
Is named your wars in France. This makes bold mouths.
Tongues spit their duties out, and cold hearts freeze
Allegiance in them. Their curses now
Live where their prayers did, and it's come to pass
65 This tractable obedience is a slave
To each incensèd will.[7] I would your highness
Would give it quick consideration, for
There is no primer° business.   *more pressing*
KING HENRY   By my life,
This is against our pleasure.
CARDINAL WOLSEY   And for me,
70 I have no further gone in this than by
A single voice,[8] and that not passed me but
By learnèd approbation° of the judges. If I am   *approval*
Traduced° by ignorant tongues, which neither know   *Slandered*

3. All involved in wool production: "spinsters" spun the wool; "carders" combed through, extracting impurities; and "fullers" beat the wool to thicken and cleanse it.
4. Refusing adamantly to comply with the result.
5. *front . . . me:* I walk at the front of a line of those who have power equal to my own (literally, who march in step behind me).

6. *But . . . acquaintance:* But you originate measures that all know, that harm even those who would rather not accept them, yet must.
7. *This . . . will:* Each subject's anger dominates his former compliant obedience.
8. *I . . . voice:* I have only cast my single vote; I have concurred with a unanimous vote.

My faculties° nor person yet will be		*abilities*

My faculties° nor person yet will be   *abilities*
75 The chronicles of my doing, let me say
'Tis but the fate of place,° and the rough brake°   *rank / thicket*
That virtue must go through. We must not stint°   *halt*
Our necessary actions in the fear
To cope° malicious censurers, which ever,   *Of facing*
80 As rav'nous fishes, do a vessel follow
That is new trimmed,° but benefit no further   *newly rigged*
Than vainly longing. What we oft do best,
By sick interpreters, once weak ones, is
Not ours or not allowed;⁹ what° worst, as oft,   *what we do*
85 Hitting a grosser quality,° is cried up   *Appealing to the base*
For our best act. If we shall stand still,
In fear our motion° will be mocked or carped at,   *For fear our proposal*
We should take root here where we sit,
Or sit state-statues only.¹
KING HENRY   Things done well,
90 And with a care, exempt themselves from fear;
Things done without example,° in their issue°   *precedent / effects*
Are to be feared. Have you a precedent
Of this commission? I believe not any.
We must not rend our subjects from our laws
95 And stick them in our will.° Sixth part of each?   *use them at our whim*
A trembling contribution! Why, we take
From every tree lop,° bark, and part o'th' timber,   *branches*
And though we leave it with a root, thus hacked
The air will drink the sap. To every county
100 Where this is questioned° send our letters with   *challenged*
Free pardon to each man that has denied°   *refused*
The force of this commission. Pray look to't—
I put it to your care.
CARDINAL WOLSEY [*to a* SECRETARY]   A word with you.
Let there be letters writ to every shire
Of the King's grace° and pardon.   *mercy*
105 [*Aside to the* SECRETARY]   The grievèd commons
Hardly° conceive of me. Let it be noised°   *Severely / rumored*
That through our intercession this revokement
And pardon comes. I shall anon advise you
Further in the proceeding.   *Exit* SECRETARY
Enter [BUCKINGHAM'S] SURVEYOR
110 QUEEN KATHERINE [*to the* KING]   I am sorry that the Duke of Buckingham
Is run in° your displeasure.   *Has provoked*
KING HENRY   It grieves many.
The gentleman is learnèd, and a most rare speaker,
To nature none more bound;² his training such
That he may furnish and instruct great teachers
115 And never seek for aid out of° himself. Yet see,   *outside of*
When these so noble benefits shall prove
Not well disposed,° the mind growing once corrupt,   *employed*
They turn to vicious forms ten times more ugly
Than ever they were fair. This man so complete,°   *accomplished*

9. *What . . . allowed:* Formerly foolish, now corrupt ("sick") observers never attribute to us or approve in us what we do best.
1. Or become nothing but decorative statues of leaders.
2. No man has been given greater gifts by nature.

120 Who was enrolled 'mongst wonders—and when we
Almost with ravished° list'ning could not find   *spellbound*
His hour of speech a minute—he, my lady,
Hath into monstrous habits° put the graces   *shapes; behavior*
That once were his, and is become as black
125 As if besmeared in hell. Sit by us. You shall hear—
This was his gentleman in trust of him—
Things to strike honour sad.
[*To* WOLSEY]   Bid him recount
The fore-recited practices° whereof   *schemes*
We cannot feel too little, hear too much.
CARDINAL WOLSEY [*to the* SURVEYOR]   Stand forth, and with bold
130   spirit relate what you
Most like a careful subject have collected°   *gathered as evidence*
Out of° the Duke of Buckingham.   *(by observing)*
KING HENRY [*to the* SURVEYOR]   Speak freely.
BUCKINGHAM'S SURVEYOR   First, it was usual with him, every day
It would infect his speech, that if the King
135 Should without issue die, he'll carry it so°   *arrange so as*
To make the sceptre his. These very words
I've heard him utter to his son-in-law,
Lord Abergavenny, to whom by oath he menaced
Revenge upon the Cardinal.
CARDINAL WOLSEY [*to the* KING]   Please your highness note
140 His dangerous conception in this point,
Not friended by his wish to your high person.³
His will is most malignant, and it stretches
Beyond you to your friends.
QUEEN KATHERINE   My learned Lord Cardinal,
Deliver° all with charity.   *Recount*
KING HENRY [*to the* SURVEYOR]   Speak on.
145 How grounded he his title to the crown
Upon our fail?° To this point hast thou heard him   *childlessness; death*
At any time speak aught?
BUCKINGHAM'S SURVEYOR   He was brought to this
By a vain prophecy of Nicholas Hopkins.
KING HENRY   What was that Hopkins?
BUCKINGHAM'S SURVEYOR   Sir, a Chartreux friar,
150 His confessor, who fed him every minute
With words of sovereignty.
KING HENRY   How know'st thou this?
BUCKINGHAM'S SURVEYOR   Not long before your highness sped to France,
The Duke being at the Rose⁴, within the parish
Saint Lawrence Poutney, did of me demand
155 What was the speech° among the Londoners   *gossip*
Concerning the French journey. I replied
Men feared the French would prove perfidious,
To the King's danger; presently° the Duke   *at once*
Said 'twas the fear indeed, and that he doubted°   *suspected*
160 'Twould prove the verity of certain words
Spoke by a holy monk that oft, says he,
'Hath sent to me, wishing me to permit

3. Since he has not been granted ("friended by") his wish   4. Manor owned by Buckingham just outside London.
that the King die without an heir.

John de la Car, my chaplain, a choice hour°   *a suitable time*
To hear from him a matter of some moment;
165 Whom after under the confession's seal
He solemnly had sworn, that what he spoke
My chaplain to no creature living but
To me should utter, with demure° confidence   *grave*
This pausingly ensued: "neither the King nor's heirs",
170 Tell you the Duke, "shall prosper. Bid him strive
To win the love o'th' commonalty.° The Duke   *common people*
Shall govern England."'
QUEEN KATHERINE   If I know you well,
You were the Duke's surveyor, and lost your office
On the complaint o'th' tenants. Take good heed
175 You charge not in your spleen° a noble person   *spite*
And spoil° your nobler soul. I say, take heed;   *ruin*
Yes, heartily beseech you.
KING HENRY   Let him on.°   *continue*
[*To the* SURVEYOR] Go forward.
BUCKINGHAM'S SURVEYOR   On my soul I'll speak but truth.
I told my lord the Duke, by th' devil's illusions
180 The monk might be deceived, and that 'twas dangerous
To ruminate on this so far until
It forged him some design which, being believed,
It was much like to do.⁵ He answered, 'Tush,
It can do me no damage', adding further
185 That had the King in his last sickness failed,°   *died*
The Cardinal's and Sir Thomas Lovell's heads
Should have gone off.
KING HENRY   Ha? What, so rank?° Ah, ha!   *rotten*
There's mischief in this man. Canst thou say further?
BUCKINGHAM'S SURVEYOR   I can, my liege.
KING HENRY   Proceed.
BUCKINGHAM'S SURVEYOR   Being at Greenwich,
190 After your highness had reproved the Duke
About Sir William Bulmer—
KING HENRY   I remember
Such a time, being my sworn servant,
The Duke retained him his.° But on—what hence?   *for his own*
BUCKINGHAM'S SURVEYOR   'If', quoth he, 'I for this had been committed'—
195 As to the Tower, I thought—'I would have played
The part my father⁶ meant to act upon
Th'usurper Richard who, being at Salisbury,
Made suit to come in's presence; which if granted,
As he made semblance of his duty,° would   *seemed to kneel*
Have put his knife into him.'
200 KING HENRY   A giant traitor!
CARDINAL WOLSEY [*to the* QUEEN]   Now, madam, may° his highness   *can*
          live in freedom,
And this man out of prison?
QUEEN KATHERINE   God mend all.

---

5. *until . . . do:* until the Duke's ruminations made him
imagine ("forged him") some scheme that, if he believed
in it (and hence in the Monk's prophecy), he would probably undertake.
6. The Duke of Buckingham during Richard III's reign.

KING HENRY [*to the* SURVEYOR]   There's something more would
    out of thee—what sayst?
BUCKINGHAM'S SURVEYOR   After 'the Duke his father', with 'the knife',
205 He stretched him,° and with one hand on his dagger,   *stood up straight*
    Another spread on's breast, mounting° his eyes,   *raising up*
    He did discharge a horrible oath whose tenor
    Was, were he evil used,° he would outgo   *poorly treated*
    His father by as much as a performance°   *true performance*
    Does an irresolute purpose.
210 KING HENRY   There's his period°—   *ultimate goal*
    To sheathe his knife in us. He is attached.°   *arrested*
    Call him to present° trial. If he may   *immediate*
    Find mercy in the law, 'tis his; if none,
    Let him not seek't of us. By day and night,
215 He's traitor to th' height.°   [*Flourish.*] *Exeunt*   *to the greatest degree*

1.3

Enter [the] LORD CHAMBERLAIN *and Lord* SANDS
LORD CHAMBERLAIN   Is't possible the spells of France should juggle°   *enchant*
    Men into such strange mysteries?°   *outlandish conduct*
SANDS   New customs,
    Though they be never so ridiculous—
    Nay, let 'em be unmanly°—yet are followed.   *effeminate*
5 LORD CHAMBERLAIN   As far as I see, all the good our English
    Have got by the late voyage° is but merely   *(to France)*
    A fit or two o'th' face.° But they are shrewd ones,   *Odd new expressions*
    For when they hold 'em° you would swear directly   *maintain these looks*
    Their very noses had been counsellors
10 To Pépin or Clotharius, they keep state so.[1]
SANDS   They have all new legs,° and lame ones; one would take it,   *new walks and bows*
    That never see 'em pace° before, the spavin   *saw them walk*
    Or spring-halt reigned among 'em.[2]
LORD CHAMBERLAIN   Death,° my lord,   *By God's death*
    Their clothes are after such a pagan cut to't
    That sure they've worn out Christendom.[3]
Enter Sir Thomas LOVELL
15   How now—
    What news, Sir Thomas Lovell?
LOVELL   Faith, my lord,
    I hear of none but the new proclamation
    That's clapped upon the court gate.
LORD CHAMBERLAIN   What is't for?
LOVELL   The reformation of our travelled gallants
20 That fill the court with quarrels, talk, and tailors.
LORD CHAMBERLAIN   I'm glad 'tis there. Now I would pray our '*messieurs*'
    To think an English courtier may be wise
    And never see the Louvre.°   *French king's palace*
LOVELL   They must either,
    For so run the conditions, leave those remnants

1.3 Location: The court.
1. *To . . . so:* To sixth- and seventh-century kings of
France, their noses ("they") have such dignified (but con-
voluted) postures.
2. *the spavin . . . 'em:* they seem to be lame. *spavin:* swelling in horses' legs. *spring-halt:* spasms in horses' legs.

3. *Their . . . Christendom:* They have run out of the fashions of Christendom and have moved on to pagan habits.
This mockery reflects contemporary anxieties about the
"effeminacy" of imported continental fashions. *are after:*
have.

25 Of fool and feather° that they got in France,   *folly and adornment*
    With all their honourable points of ignorance[4]
    Pertaining thereunto—as fights and fireworks,°   *whoring*
    Abusing better men than they can be
    Out of a foreign wisdom, renouncing clean
30 The faith they have in tennis and tall stockings,
    Short blistered breeches, and those types of travel[5]—
    And understand again like honest men,
    Or pack° to their old playfellows. There, I take it,   *return*
    They may, *cum privilegio, 'oui'* away
35 The lag end of their lewdness[6] and be laughed at.
SANDS   'Tis time to give 'em physic,° their diseases   *medicine*
    Are grown so catching.
LORD CHAMBERLAIN   What a loss our ladies
    Will have of these trim vanities!°   *well-dressed fops*
LOVELL   Ay, marry,°   *indeed*
    There will be woe indeed, lords. The sly whoresons
40 Have got a speeding° trick to lay down° ladies.   *an expeditious / seduce*
    A French song and a fiddle has no fellow.°   *equal*
SANDS   The devil fiddle 'em! I am glad they are going,
    For sure there's no converting of 'em.° Now   *changing their ways*
    An honest country lord, as I am, beaten
45 A long time out of play,° may bring his plainsong°   *love / unadorned tune*
    And have an hour of hearing, and, by'r Lady,
    Held current° music, too.   *modern; stylish*
LORD CHAMBERLAIN   Well said, Lord Sands.
    Your colt's tooth is not cast yet?[7]
SANDS   No, my lord,
    Nor shall not while I have a stump.°   *(of a tooth—sexual)*
LORD CHAMBERLAIN [*to* LOVELL]   Sir Thomas,
    Whither were you a-going?
50 LOVELL   To the Cardinal's.
    Your lordship is a guest too.
LORD CHAMBERLAIN   O, 'tis true.
    This night he makes° a supper, and a great one,   *holds*
    To many lords and ladies. There will be
    The beauty of this kingdom, I'll assure you.
55 LOVELL   That churchman bears a bounteous mind indeed,
    A hand as fruitful° as the land that feeds us.   *benevolent*
    His dews fall everywhere.
LORD CHAMBERLAIN   No doubt he's noble.
    He had a black mouth that said other of him.[8]
SANDS   He may, my lord; he's wherewithal.° In him   *he can afford to*
60 Sparing° would show a worse sin than ill doctrine.°   *Stinginess / heresy*
    Men of his way° should be most liberal.   *profession*
    They are set here for examples.
LORD CHAMBERLAIN   True, they are so,
    But few now give so great ones.° My barge stays.°   *examples / waits*
    Your lordship shall along.° [*To* LOVELL] Come, good Sir Thomas,   *join me*

---

4. Which, in their ignorance, they consider honorable.
5. *Abusing . . . travel*: They must stop "abusing" their betters out of a misplaced faith in French wisdom, and start "renouncing" French habits like tennis, tall stockings, puffed breeches, and such marks of travel (which were affected by Henry VIII and James I, as well as James's courtiers).

6. *They . . . lewdness*: They may, with immunity ("*cum privilegio*"), indulge their remaining decadence by copying the French. *oui*: yes.
7. You haven't abandoned your youthful lasciviousness ("colt's tooth") yet?
8. Anyone who denies this generosity must have an evil mouth.

65 We shall be late else, which I would not be,
    For I was spoke to,° with Sir Henry Guildford,   *invited*
    This night to be comptrollers.°   *stewards*
SANDS   I am your lordship's.   *Exeunt*

1.4

Hautboys.[1] *[Enter servants with] a small table for* CARDI-
NAL *[*WOLSEY *which they place] under the [cloth of]*
state, [and] a longer table for the guests. Then enter at
one door ANNE *Boleyn and divers other ladies and gentle-*
men as guests, [and] at another door enter Sir Henry
GUILDFORD

GUILDFORD   Ladies, a general welcome from his grace
Salutes ye all. This night he dedicates
To fair content and you. None here, he hopes,
In all this noble bevy,° has brought with her   *company*
5 One care abroad. He would have all as merry
As feast, good company, good wine, good welcome
Can make good people.
        Enter [the] LORD CHAMBERLAIN, *Lord* SANDS, *and [Sir*
        Thomas] LOVELL
[*To the* LORD CHAMBERLAIN] O, my lord, you're tardy.
The very thought of this fair company
Clapped wings to me.
LORD CHAMBERLAIN   You are young, Sir Harry Guildford.
10 SANDS   Sir Thomas Lovell, had the Cardinal
But half my lay° thoughts in him, some of these   *secular*
Should find a running banquet,[2] ere they rested,
I think would better please 'em. By my life,
They are a sweet society of fair ones.
15 LOVELL   O, that your lordship were but now confessor
To one or two of these.
SANDS   I would I were.
They should find easy penance.
LOVELL   Faith, how easy?
SANDS   As easy as a down bed would afford it.
LORD CHAMBERLAIN   Sweet ladies, will it please you sit?
[*To* GUILDFORD]   Sir Harry,
20 Place you° that side, I'll take the charge of this.   *Arrange seating on*
        [*They sit about the longer table. A noise within*]
His grace is ent'ring. Nay, you must not freeze—
Two women placed together makes cold weather.
My lord Sands, you are one will keep 'em waking.°   *spirited*
Pray sit between these ladies.
SANDS   By my faith,
And thank your lordship.
        [*He sits between* ANNE *and another*]
25   By your leave, sweet ladies.
If I chance to talk a little wild, forgive me.
I had it from my father.
ANNE   Was he mad, sir?

1.4 Location: Westminster, a hall in York Place.   2. Light refreshments; furtive, stolen pleasures.
1. Early reeded wind instrument, ancestor of the oboe.

SANDS   O, very mad; exceeding mad—in love, too.
But he would bite° none. Just as I do now,   *(sign of madness)*
He would kiss you twenty with a breath.[3]
          [*He kisses her*]

30   LORD CHAMBERLAIN   Well said,° my lord.   *done*
So now you're fairly seated. Gentlemen,
The penance lies on you if these fair ladies
Pass away frowning.
SANDS   For my little cure,°   *duty; (of souls)*

35   Let me alone.
          Hautboys. Enter CARDINAL WOLSEY [*who*] *takes his* [*seat*
          at the small table under the] *state°*   *chair of state*
CARDINAL WOLSEY   You're welcome, my fair guests. That noble lady
Or gentleman that is not freely merry
Is not my friend. This, to confirm my welcome,
And to you all, good health!
          [*He drinks*]
SANDS   Your grace is noble.

40   Let me have such a bowl may° hold my thanks,   *as may*
And save me so much talking.
CARDINAL WOLSEY   My lord Sands,
I am beholden to you. Cheer° your neighbours.   *Amuse*
Ladies, you are not merry! Gentlemen,
Whose fault is this?
SANDS   The red wine first must rise

45   In their fair cheeks, my lord, then we shall have 'em
Talk us to silence.
ANNE   You are a merry gamester,°   *fellow; gambler*
My lord Sands.
SANDS   Yes, if I make my play.[4]
Here's to your ladyship; and pledge it,° madam,   *drink to it*
For 'tis to such a thing—
ANNE   You cannot show me.°   *(sexual)*
SANDS [*to* WOLSEY]   I told your grace they would talk anon.
          Drum and trumpet. Chambers discharged[5]

50   CARDINAL WOLSEY   What's that?
LORD CHAMBERLAIN [*to the* SERVANTS]
Look out there, some of ye.   [*Exit a* SERVANT]
CARDINAL WOLSEY   What warlike voice,
And to what end is this? Nay, ladies, fear not.
By all the laws of war you're privileged.°   *safe from harm*
          Enter [*the*] SERVANT
LORD CHAMBERLAIN   How now—what is't?
SERVANT   A noble troop of strangers,

55   For so they seem. They've left their barge and landed,
And hither make as° great ambassadors   *come like*
From foreign princes.
CARDINAL WOLSEY   Good Lord Chamberlain,
Go give 'em welcome—you can speak the French tongue.
And pray receive 'em nobly, and conduct 'em

---

3. He would kiss you twenty times with a single breath.
4. If I win my hand (at cards or love).
5. Small cannon fired. The firing of this cannon in a June

29, 1613, performance of the play probably caused the fire
that destroyed the Globe Theatre. See the Introduction.

60   Into our presence where this heaven of beauty
Shall shine at full upon them. Some attend him.
       [*Exit* CHAMBERLAIN, *attended*]
     All rise, and [some servants] remove [the] tables
You have now a broken banquet, but we'll mend it.
A good digestion to you all, and once more
I shower a welcome on ye—welcome all.
     Hautboys. Enter, ushered by the LORD CHAMBERLAIN,
     KING [HENRY] *and others as masquers habited like shep-*
     herds. They pass directly before CARDINAL [WOLSEY] *and*
     gracefully salute him
65   A noble company. What are their pleasures?
LORD CHAMBERLAIN   Because they speak no English, thus they prayed
To tell your grace, that, having heard by fame°   *rumor*
Of this so noble and so fair assembly
This night to meet here, they could do no less,
70   Out of the great respect they bear to beauty,
But leave their flocks, and, under your fair conduct,°   *if you'll permit me*
Crave leave to view these ladies, and entreat
An hour of revels° with 'em.   *entertainment*
CARDINAL WOLSEY   Say, Lord Chamberlain,
They have done my poor house grace, for which I pay 'em
75   A thousand thanks, and pray 'em take their pleasures.
     [*The masquers*] *choose ladies.* [*The*] KING [*chooses*]
     ANNE *Boleyn*
KING HENRY [*to* ANNE]   The fairest hand I ever touched. O beauty,
Till now I never knew thee.
     Music. [*They*] *dance*
CARDINAL WOLSEY [*to the* LORD CHAMBERLAIN]   My lord.
LORD CHAMBERLAIN   Your grace.
80   CARDINAL WOLSEY   Pray tell 'em thus much from me.
There should be one amongst 'em by his person
More worthy this place° than myself, to whom,   *chair of state*
If I but knew him, with my love and duty
I would surrender it.
LORD CHAMBERLAIN   I will, my lord.
     [*He*] *whisper[s with the masquers]*
CARDINAL WOLSEY   What say they?
85   LORD CHAMBERLAIN   Such a one they all confess
There is indeed, which they would have your grace
Find out, and he will take it.°   *(the place of honor)*
CARDINAL WOLSEY [*standing*]   Let me see then.
By all your good leaves, gentlemen, here I'll make
My royal choice.
     [*He bows before the* KING]
KING HENRY [*unmasking*]   Ye have found him, Cardinal.
90   You hold a fair assembly. You do well, lord.
You are a churchman, or I'll tell you, Cardinal,
I should judge now unhappily.[6]
CARDINAL WOLSEY   I am glad
Your grace is grown so pleasant.°   *merry*
KING HENRY   My Lord Chamberlain,
Prithee come hither.

6. I would judge such ostentatiousness unfavorably.

[*Gesturing towards* ANNE]   What fair lady's that?

LORD CHAMBERLAIN   An't° please your grace, Sir Thomas   *If it*
95   Boleyn's daughter—
The Viscount Rochford—one of her highness' women.

KING HENRY   By heaven, she is a dainty one. [*To* ANNE] Sweetheart,
I were unmannerly to take you out°   *(to dance)*
And not to kiss you [*kisses her*]. A health,° gentlemen;   *toast*
[*He drinks*]
100   Let it go round.

CARDINAL WOLSEY   Sir Thomas Lovell, is the banquet ready
I'th' privy chamber?

LOVELL   Yes, my lord.

CARDINAL WOLSEY [*to the* KING]   Your grace
I fear with dancing is a little heated.

KING HENRY   I fear too much.

105   CARDINAL WOLSEY   There's fresher air, my lord,
In the next chamber.

KING HENRY   Lead in your ladies, every one. [*To* ANNE] Sweet partner,
I must not yet forsake you. [*To* WOLSEY] Let's be merry,
Good my lord Cardinal. I have half a dozen healths
110   To drink to these fair ladies, and a measure°   *majestic dance*
To lead 'em once again, and then let's dream
Who's best in favour.[7] Let the music knock it.°   *strike it up*

Exeunt with trumpets

2.1

Enter two GENTLEMEN, *at several*° *doors*   *separate*

FIRST GENTLEMAN   Whither away so fast?

SECOND GENTLEMAN   O, God save ye.
Ev'n to the hall° to hear what shall become   *Westminster Hall*
Of the great Duke of Buckingham.

FIRST GENTLEMAN   I'll save you
That labour, sir. All's now done but the ceremony
Of bringing back the prisoner.

5   SECOND GENTLEMAN   Were you there?

FIRST GENTLEMAN   Yes, indeed was I.

SECOND GENTLEMAN   Pray speak what has happened.

FIRST GENTLEMAN   You may guess quickly what.

SECOND GENTLEMAN   Is he found guilty?

FIRST GENTLEMAN   Yes, truly is he, and condemned upon't.

SECOND GENTLEMAN   I am sorry for't.

10   FIRST GENTLEMAN   So are a number more.

SECOND GENTLEMAN   But pray, how passed it?°   *how did the trial go*

FIRST GENTLEMAN   I'll tell you in a little.° The great Duke   *concisely*
Came to the bar, where to his accusations
He pleaded still not guilty, and alleged°   *offered up*
15   Many sharp reasons to defeat the law.°   *the Crown's case*
The King's attorney, on the contrary,
Urged on the examinations,° proofs,° confessions,   *depositions / statements*
Of divers witnesses, which the Duke desired
To him brought *viva voce*° to his face—   *in person*
20   At which appeared against him his surveyor,
Sir Gilbert Perk his chancellor, and John Car,

---

7. Who's most popular with the ladies; who's best looking.   **2.1** Location: A street in Westminster.

Confessor to him, with that devil-monk,
Hopkins, that made this mischief.
SECOND GENTLEMAN   That was he
That fed him with his prophecies.
FIRST GENTLEMAN   The same.
25 All these accused him strongly, which he fain[1]
Would have flung from him, but indeed he could not.
And so his peers, upon this evidence,
Have found him guilty of high treason. Much
He spoke, and learnèdly, for life, but all
30 Was either pitied in him or forgotten.[2]
SECOND GENTLEMAN   After all this, how did he bear himself?
FIRST GENTLEMAN   When he was brought again to th' bar to hear
His knell rung out, his judgement,° he was stirred   *sentence*
With such an agony he sweat extremely,
35 And something spoke in choler,° ill and hasty;   *anger*
But he fell to° himself again, and sweetly   *got control of*
In all the rest showed a most noble patience.
SECOND GENTLEMAN   I do not think he fears death.
FIRST GENTLEMAN   Sure he does not.
He never was so womanish. The cause
He may a little grieve at.
40 SECOND GENTLEMAN   Certainly
The Cardinal is the end° of this.   *source*
FIRST GENTLEMAN   'Tis likely
By all conjectures: first, Kildare's attainder,
Then deputy of Ireland,[3] who, removed,
Earl Surrey was sent thither—and in haste, too,
Lest he should help his father.°   *father-in-law*
45 SECOND GENTLEMAN   That trick of state
Was a deep envious° one.   *deeply spiteful*
FIRST GENTLEMAN   At his return
No doubt he will requite it. This is noted,
And generally:° whoever the King favours,   *by all*
The Card'nal instantly will find employment—
And far enough from court, too.
50 SECOND GENTLEMAN   All the commons
Hate him perniciously° and, o' my conscience,   *want him dead*
Wish him ten fathom deep. This Duke as much
They love and dote on, call him 'bounteous Buckingham,
The mirror° of all courtesy'—   *exemplar*

> *Enter [the Duke of] BUCKINGHAM from his arraignment,*
> *tipstaves before him, the axe with the edge towards him,*
> *halberd[ier]s on each side, accompanied with Sir*
> *Thomas LOVELL, Sir Nicholas VAUX, Sir [William]*
> *SANDS,[4] and common people*

FIRST GENTLEMAN   Stay there, sir,
55 And see the noble ruined man you speak of.

1. Which accusations he gladly.
2. *all . . . forgotten:* (Buckingham's defense) either was
fruitless or brought only pity.
3. Thomas Kildare, Lord Lieutenant of Ireland, lost his
estates and position ("attainder") and was sentenced to
death by Wolsey.
4. *tipstaves:* court-appointed officers who carried tipstaves, staffs tipped with metal. *halberdiers:* guards who
carried halberds, long-handled weapons with both spear
tips and battle-axe blades. "Sir William Sands" is called
"Lord Sands" in the stage directions at the beginning of
1.3 and at 1.4.7. The discrepancy occurs because the play
violates chronology here: Henry and Anne actually met
years after Buckingham's trial, and Sands became a baron
in the interim.

SECOND GENTLEMAN   Let's stand close° and behold him.   *aside; silent*
     [*They stand apart*]
BUCKINGHAM [*to the common people*]   All good people,
     You that thus far have come to pity me,
     Hear what I say, and then go home and lose° me.   *forget*
     I have this day received a traitor's judgement,°   *sentence*
60   And by that name must die. Yet, heaven bear witness,
     And if I have a conscience let it sink° me,   *destroy*
     Even as the axe falls, if I be not faithful.
     The law I bear no malice for my death.
     'T has done, upon the premises,° but justice.   *evidence*
65   But those that sought it I could wish more° Christians.   *truer*
     Be what they will, I heartily forgive 'em.
     Yet let 'em look° they glory not in mischief,   *beware*
     Nor build their evils on the graves of great men,⁵
     For then my guiltless blood must cry against 'em.
70   For further life in this world I ne'er hope,
     Nor will I sue, although the King have mercies
     More than I dare make faults.° You few that loved me,   *commit misdeeds*
     And dare be bold to weep for Buckingham,
     His noble friends and fellows, whom to leave
75   Is only bitter to him, only dying,⁶
     Go with me like good angels to my end,
     And, as the long divorce° of steel falls on me,   *(of body and soul)*
     Make of your prayers one sweet sacrifice,°   *offering*
     And lift my soul to heaven. [*To the guard*] Lead on, i' God's name.
80   LOVELL   I do beseech your grace, for charity,
     If ever any malice in your heart
     Were hid against me, now to forgive me frankly.
     BUCKINGHAM   Sir Thomas Lovell, I as free forgive you
     As I would be forgiven. I forgive all.
85   There cannot be those numberless offences
     'Gainst me that I cannot take° peace with. No black envy°   *make / spite*
     Shall mark my grave. Commend me to his grace,
     And if he speak of Buckingham, pray tell him
     You met him half in heaven. My vows and prayers
90   Yet are the King's, and, till my soul forsake,°   *depart (my body)*
     Shall cry for blessings on him. May he live
     Longer than I have time to tell° his years;   *count*
     Ever beloved and loving may his rule be;
     And, when old time° shall lead him to his end,   *old age*
95   Goodness and he fill up one monument.°   *share one tomb*
     LOVELL   To th' waterside I must conduct your grace,
     Then give my charge up to Sir Nicholas Vaux,
     Who undertakes° you to your end.   *leads*
     VAUX [*to an attendant*]   Prepare there—
     The Duke is coming. See the barge be ready,
100 And fit it with such furniture° as suits   *trappings*
     The greatness of his person.
     BUCKINGHAM   Nay, Sir Nicholas,
     Let it alone. My state° now will but mock me.   *position*
     When I came hither I was Lord High Constable

---

5. Nor advance their evil designs through plotting the   6. *His . . . dying*: Leaving his friends is the only bitter part
downfall of noblemen.   of Buckingham's sentence, the only death.

And Duke of Buckingham; now, poor Edward Bohun.[7]
105 Yet I am richer than my base accusers,
That never knew what truth meant. I now seal it,°   *attest to truth*
And with that blood will make 'em one day groan for't.
My noble father, Henry of Buckingham,
Who first raised head° against usurping Richard,   *an army*
110 Flying for succour to his servant Banister,
Being distressed, was by that wretch betrayed,
And without trial fell. God's peace be with him.
Henry the Seventh succeeding, truly pitying
My father's loss, like a most royal prince,
115 Restored me to my honours, and out of ruins
Made my name once more noble. Now his son,
Henry the Eighth, life, honour, name, and all
That made me happy, at one stroke has taken
For ever from the world. I had my trial,
120 And must needs say a noble one; which makes me
A little happier than my wretched father.
Yet thus far we are one in fortunes: both
Fell by our servants, by those men we loved most—
A most unnatural and faithless service.
125 Heaven has an end° in all. Yet, you that hear me,   *a purpose*
This from a dying man receive as certain—
Where you are liberal of your loves and counsels,
Be sure you be not loose;° for those you make friends   *unrestrained*
And give your hearts to, when they once perceive
130 The least rub° in your fortunes, fall away   *obstacle*
Like water from ye, never found again
But where they mean to sink° ye. All good people   *destroy*
Pray for me. I must now forsake ye. The last hour
Of my long weary life is come upon me.
135 Farewell, and when you would say something that is sad,
Speak how I fell. I have done, and God forgive me.
              Exeunt [the] Duke [of BUCKINGHAM] *and train*
              [*The two* GENTLEMEN *come forward*]
FIRST GENTLEMAN   O, this is full of pity, sir; it calls,
I fear, too many curses on their heads
That were the authors.
SECOND GENTLEMAN   If the Duke be guiltless,
140 'Tis full of woe. Yet I can give you inkling°   *forewarning*
Of an ensuing evil, if it fall,°   *should occur*
Greater than this.
FIRST GENTLEMAN   Good angels keep it from us.
What may it be? You do not doubt my faith, sir?
SECOND GENTLEMAN   This secret is so weighty, 'twill require
A strong faith° to conceal it.   *discretion*
145 FIRST GENTLEMAN   Let me have it—
I do not talk much.
SECOND GENTLEMAN   I am confident;°   *I trust you*
You shall, sir. Did you not of late days hear
A buzzing° of a separation   *gossip*
Between the King and Katherine?
FIRST GENTLEMAN   Yes, but it held not.°   *did not persist*

---

7. Actually Edward Stafford; Shakespeare copies Holinshed's mistake.

150   For when the King once heard it, out of anger
         He sent command to the Lord Mayor straight
         To stop the rumour and allay° those tongues   *suppress*
         That durst disperse it.
         SECOND GENTLEMAN   But that slander, sir,
         Is found a truth now, for it grows again
155   Fresher than e'er it was, and held° for certain   *believed*
         The King will venture at it. Either the Cardinal
         Or some about him near° have, out of malice   *his confidants*
         To the good Queen, possessed him with a scruple
         That will undo her. To confirm this, too,
160   Cardinal Campeius[8] is arrived, and lately,
         As all think, for this business.
         FIRST GENTLEMAN   'Tis the Cardinal;
         And merely to revenge him on the Emperor[9]
         For not bestowing on him at his asking
         The Archbishopric of Toledo this is purposed.
         SECOND GENTLEMAN   I think you have hit the mark.° But is't not   *guessed correctly*
165   cruel
         That she should feel the smart of this? The Cardinal
         Will have his will, and she must fall.
         FIRST GENTLEMAN   'Tis woeful.
         We are too open° here to argue this.   *exposed*
         Let's think in private more.   *Exeunt*

                                    2.2
                    Enter [the] LORD CHAMBERLAIN *[with a] letter*
         LORD CHAMBERLAIN *[reads]* 'My lord, the horses your lordship
         sent for, with all the care I had, I saw well chosen, ridden, and
         furnished.° They were young and handsome, and of the best   *trained and equipped*
         breed in the north. When they were ready to set out for Lon-
5   don, a man of my lord Cardinal's, by commission and main
         power,[1] took 'em from me with this reason—his master would
         be served before a subject, if not before the King; which
         stopped our mouths, sir.'
         I fear he will indeed. Well, let him have them.
10   He will have all, I think.
                    Enter to the LORD CHAMBERLAIN *the Dukes of* NORFOLK
                    and SUFFOLK
         NORFOLK   Well met, my Lord Chamberlain.
         LORD CHAMBERLAIN   Good day to both your graces.
         SUFFOLK   How is the King employed?
         LORD CHAMBERLAIN   I left him private,°   *alone*
         Full of sad° thoughts and troubles.   *grave*
         NORFOLK   What's the cause?
15   LORD CHAMBERLAIN   It seems the marriage with his brother's wife
         Has crept too near his conscience.
         SUFFOLK   No, his conscience
         Has crept too near another lady.

---

8. Henry had to get a special dispensation from the Pope
before marrying Katherine, because her previous husband
was Prince Arthur, Henry's brother, who died a year after
the marriage took place. Wolsey had Cardinal Laurence
Campeius (Lorenzo Campeggio) come to London as a
papal legate in 1528 to reopen debate about the marriage
and to aid his plot to have it annulled.
9. Charles V, Holy Roman Emperor and King of Spain,
was Katherine's nephew.
2.2 Location: The court at London.
1. By warrant and superior strength.

NORFOLK   'Tis so.
This is the Cardinal's doing. The King-Cardinal,
That blind priest, like the eldest son of fortune,
20   Turns what he list.² The King will know him° one day.   *(for what he is)*
SUFFOLK   Pray God he do. He'll never know himself else.
NORFOLK   How holily he° works in all his business,   *(Wolsey)*
And with what zeal! For now he has cracked the league
Between us and the Emperor, the Queen's great-nephew,³
25   He dives into the King's soul and there scatters
Dangers, doubts, wringing° of the conscience,   *affliction*
Fears, and despairs—and all these for his marriage.
And out of all these, to restore the King,
He counsels a divorce—a loss of her
30   That like a jewel has hung twenty years
About his neck, yet never lost her lustre;
Of her that loves him with that excellence°   *great virtue*
That angels love good men with; even of her
That, when the greatest stroke° of fortune falls,   *severest blow*
35   Will bless the King⁴—and is not this course° pious?   *(of action)*
LORD CHAMBERLAIN   Heaven keep me from such counsel! 'Tis most true—
These news are everywhere, every tongue speaks 'em,
And every true heart weeps for't. All that dare
Look into these affairs see this main end°—   *ultimate aim*
40   The French king's sister.⁵ Heaven will one day open
The King's eyes, that so long have slept, upon
This bold bad man.
SUFFOLK   And free us from his slavery.
NORFOLK   We had need pray,
45   And heartily, for our deliverance,
Or this imperious man will work us all
From princes into pages. All men's honours
Lie like one lump° before him, to be fashioned   *(of clay)*
Into what pitch° he please.   *stature*
SUFFOLK   For me, my lords,
50   I love him not, nor fear him—there's my creed.
As I am made without him, so I'll stand,⁶
If the King please. His curses and his blessings
Touch me alike; they're breath I° not believe in.   *I do*
I knew him, and I know him; so I leave him
To him that made him proud—the Pope.
55   NORFOLK   Let's in,
And with some other business put the King
From these sad thoughts that work too much upon him.
[*To the* LORD CHAMBERLAIN] My lord, you'll bear us company?
LORD CHAMBERLAIN   Excuse me,
The King has sent me otherwhere. Besides,
60   You'll find a most unfit time to disturb him.
Health to your lordships.

2. *The King-Cardinal . . . list:* Like Fortune, his mother, Wolsey blindly turns the wheel of fortune as he likes ("list").
3. Wolsey has now broken the alliance between Henry and Charles V to get additional revenge on Charles: see 2.1.161–64. Previously (1.1.176–93), to gain favor with Charles, he engineered the breaking of the treaty with France sealed at the Field of the Cloth of Gold.
4. Prophetic: Katherine does later "bless the King" who has repudiated her (4.2.164).
5. Henry's marriage to the Duchess of Alençon will reunite the English and French kings, thus still further injuring Charles V. See 3.2.86–87.
6. Since not Wolsey but the King granted my nobility of rank, I'll remain firm in my position.

NORFOLK   Thanks, my good Lord Chamberlain.

Exit [the] LORD CHAMBERLAIN

KING [HENRY] *draws the curtain,[7] and sits reading pen-
sively*

SUFFOLK   How sad° he looks! Sure he is much afflicted.°   *grave / distressed*

KING HENRY   Who's there? Ha?

NORFOLK   Pray God he be not angry.

KING HENRY   Who's there, I say? How dare you thrust yourselves
65   Into my private meditations!
Who am I? Ha?

NORFOLK   A gracious king that pardons all offences
Malice ne'er meant. Our breach of duty this way°   *in this respect*
Is business of estate,° in which we come   *state*
To know your royal pleasure.

70   KING HENRY   Ye are too bold.
Go to, I'll make ye know your times of business.
Is this an hour for temporal affairs? Ha?

*Enter [CARDINAL] WOLSEY and [CARDINAL] CAMPEIUS,
[the latter] with a commission*

Who's there? My good lord Cardinal? O, my Wolsey,
The quiet° of my wounded conscience,   *ease*
Thou art a cure° fit for a king.   *balm; curate (priest)*
75   [*To* CAMPEIUS]   You're welcome,
Most learnèd reverend sir, into our kingdom.
Use us, and it. [*To* WOLSEY] My good lord, have great care
I be not found a talker.[8]

CARDINAL WOLSEY   Sir, you cannot.
I would your grace would give us but an hour
Of private conference.

80   KING HENRY [*to* NORFOLK *and* SUFFOLK]   We are busy; go.

[NORFOLK *and* SUFFOLK *speak privately to one another
as they depart*]

NORFOLK   This priest has no pride in him!

SUFFOLK   Not to speak of.
I would not be so sick, though, for his place[9]—
But this cannot continue.

NORFOLK   If it do
I'll venture one have-at-him.°   *thrust (in fencing)*

SUFFOLK   I another.

Exeunt NORFOLK *and* SUFFOLK

CARDINAL WOLSEY [*to the* KING]   Your grace has given a precedent°   *model*
85   of wisdom
Above all princes in committing freely
Your scruple to the voice of Christendom.[1]
Who can be angry now? What envy reach you?
The Spaniard,° tied by blood and favour to her,   *Charles V*
90   Must now confess, if they have any goodness,
The trial just and noble. All the clerks°—   *clerics*
I mean the learnèd ones in Christian kingdoms—
Have their free voices.° Rome, the nurse of judgement,   *may vote freely*

Invited by your noble self, hath sent
95 One general tongue° unto us: this good man,   *representative voice*
This just and learnèd priest, Card'nal Campeius,
Whom once more I present unto your highness.
KING HENRY [*embracing* CAMPEIUS] And once more in mine
    arms I bid him welcome,
And thank the holy conclave° for their loves.   *College of Cardinals*
100 They have sent me such a man I would have wished for.
CARDINAL CAMPEIUS Your grace must needs deserve all strangers'° loves,   *foreigners'*
You are so noble. To your highness' hand
I tender my commission,
    [*He gives the commission to the* KING]
[*to* WOLSEY]   by whose virtue,
The Court of Rome commanding, you, my lord
105 Cardinal of York, are joined with me their servant
In the unpartial° judging of this business.   *impartial*
KING HENRY Two equal° men. The Queen shall be acquainted°   *fair / apprised*
Forthwith for what you come. Where's Gardiner?
CARDINAL WOLSEY I know your majesty has always loved her
110 So dear in heart not to deny her that°   *that which*
A woman of less place° might ask by law—   *rank*
Scholars allowed freely to argue for her.
KING HENRY Ay, and the best she shall have, and my favour
To him that does best, God forbid else. Cardinal,
115 Prithee call Gardiner to me, my new secretary.[2]
    [CARDINAL WOLSEY *goes to the door and calls* GARDINER]
I find him a fit fellow.
    Enter GARDINER
CARDINAL WOLSEY [*aside to* GARDINER] Give me your hand. Much joy
    and favour to you.
You are the King's now.
GARDINER [*aside to* WOLSEY] But to be commanded
For ever by your grace, whose hand has raised me.
120 KING HENRY Come hither, Gardiner.
    [*The* KING] *walks* [*with* GARDINER] *and whispers* [*with
    him*]
CARDINAL CAMPEIUS [*to* WOLSEY] My lord of York, was not one
    Doctor Pace[3]
In this man's place before him?
CARDINAL WOLSEY   Yes, he was.
CARDINAL CAMPEIUS Was he not held a learnèd man?
CARDINAL WOLSEY   Yes, surely.
CARDINAL CAMPEIUS Believe me, there's an ill opinion spread then,
    Even of yourself, lord Cardinal.
125 CARDINAL WOLSEY   How? Of me?
CARDINAL CAMPEIUS They will not stick° to say you envied him,   *scruple*
And fearing he would rise, he was so virtuous,
Kept him a foreign man still,° which so grieved him   *always abroad*
That he ran mad and died.
CARDINAL WOLSEY   Heav'n's peace be with him—
130 That's Christian care enough. For living murmurers°   *malcontents*

2. Stephen Gardiner, former secretary to Wolsey, became Henry's secretary in July 1529 through Wolsey's preferment, and Bishop of Winchester in 1531.
3. Richard Pace, the King's former secretary, was now sent frequently abroad by Wolsey on diplomatic business, apparently as punishment for becoming too close to the King.

There's places of rebuke. He was a fool,
For he would needs be virtuous.
[*Gesturing towards* GARDINER]   That good fellow,
If I command him, follows my appointment.°   orders
I will have none so near[4] else. Learn this, brother:
135   We live not to be griped° by meaner persons.   grasped familiarly
KING HENRY [*to* GARDINER]   Deliver this with modesty° to th'   Announce this mildly
        Queen.   *Exit* GARDINER
The most convenient place that I can think of
For such receipt of° learning is Blackfriars;   accommodating such
There ye shall meet about this weighty business.
140   My Wolsey, see it furnished.° O, my lord,   fitted out properly
Would it not grieve an able° man to leave   a (sexually) vigorous
So sweet a bedfellow? But conscience, conscience—
O, 'tis a tender place,° and I must leave her.   *Exeunt*   (conscience); (sexual)

2.3

Enter ANNE *Boleyn and an* OLD LADY

ANNE   Not for that neither. Here's the pang that pinches°—   torments
His highness having lived so long with her, and she
So good a lady that no tongue could ever
Pronounce dishonour of her—by my life,
5   She never knew harm-doing—O now, after
So many courses of the sun° enthronèd,   years
Still° growing in a majesty and pomp the which   Ever
To leave a thousandfold more bitter than
'Tis sweet at first t'acquire—after this process,
10   To give her the avaunt,° it is a pity   boot
Would move a monster.
OLD LADY   Hearts of most hard temper°   constitution
Melt and lament for her.
ANNE   O, God's will! Much better
She ne'er had known pomp; though't be temporal,°   only of this world
Yet if that quarrel,° fortune, do divorce   quarreler
15   It from the bearer, 'tis a sufferance panging°   as painful
As soul and bodies severing.
OLD LADY   Alas, poor lady!
She's a stranger° now again.   foreigner
ANNE   So much the more
Must pity drop upon her. Verily,
I swear, 'tis better to be lowly born
20   And range with humble livers in content
Than to be perked up in a glist'ring grief[1]
And wear a golden sorrow.
OLD LADY   Our content
Is our best having.°   possession
ANNE   By my troth° and maidenhead,   faith
I would not be a queen.
OLD LADY   Beshrew me,° I would—   Devil take me
25   And venture maidenhead for't; and so would you,
For all this spice° of your hypocrisy.   sample
You, that have so fair parts° of woman on you,   qualities; beauty

4. I want no one else on such intimate terms with the   1. *'tis . . . grief*: it's better to be born poor and to occupy
King.   a lowly rank happily than to be unhappy despite one's
2.3 Location: The Queen's apartments at court.   riches (literally, to be dressed up in a glittering sadness).

Have, too, a woman's heart which ever yet
Affected° eminence, wealth, sovereignty;   *Craved*
30   Which, to say sooth,° are blessings; and which gifts,   *truth*
Saving your mincing,° the capacity   *Despite your affectation*
Of your soft cheveril° conscience would receive   *kid leather (pliant)*
If you might please to stretch it.
ANNE   Nay, good troth.[2]
OLD LADY   Yes, troth and troth. You would not be a queen?
35   ANNE   No, not for all the riches under heaven.
OLD LADY   'Tis strange. A threepence bowed would hire me,
Old as I am, to queen it.[3] But I pray you,
What think you of a duchess? Have you limbs
To bear that load of title?
ANNE   No, in truth.
40   OLD LADY   Then you are weakly made. Pluck off[4] a little;
I would not be a young count in your way
For more than blushing comes to.[5] If your back
Cannot vouchsafe this burden,[6] 'tis too weak
Ever to get a boy.
ANNE   How you do talk!
45   I swear again, I would not be a queen
For all the world.
OLD LADY   In faith, for little England
You'd venture an emballing;[7] I myself
Would for Caernarfonshire,[8] although there 'longed°   *belonged*
No more to th' crown but that. Lo, who comes here?
            Enter [the] LORD CHAMBERLAIN
50   LORD CHAMBERLAIN   Good morrow, ladies. What were't worth to know
The secret of your conference?°   *conversation*
ANNE   My good lord,
Not your demand; it values not° your asking.   *does not merit*
Our mistress' sorrows we were pitying.
LORD CHAMBERLAIN   It was a gentle business, and becoming
55   The action of good women. There is hope
All will be well.
ANNE   Now I pray God, amen.
LORD CHAMBERLAIN   You bear a gentle mind, and heav'nly blessings
Follow such creatures. That you may, fair lady,
Perceive I speak sincerely, and high note's
60   Ta'en of your many virtues, the King's majesty
Commends his good opinion of you,° and   *Sends his compliments*
Does purpose° honour to you no less flowing°   *intend / copious*
Than Marchioness of Pembroke; to which title
A thousand pound a year annual support
Out of his grace he adds.
65   ANNE   I do not know
What kind° of my obedience I should tender.   *manner*

---

2. Faith (exclamatory); perhaps a pun on "trot," a demeaning term for an old woman.
3. *A threepence . . . it:* A bent ("bowed") and hence worthless coin would convince me to be a Queen. Sexual puns ("queen"—"quean," or whore; "bowed"—bawd) continue through the scene.
4. Come lower in rank; undress.
5. *I . . . to:* If you persist in this "way" (path; being unable to bear the load of being duchess), a "count" (an earl, the

rank below duke) will get no more from you than blushes. Also: I wouldn't give up being a young virginal cunt ("count") like you with more than a blush.
6. Cannot bear these honors. "Burden," like "bear" (line 39), suggests both intercourse and childbearing.
7. *for . . . emballing:* for England you'd accept investiture with the royal emblem of ball and scepter (you'd get laid).
8. Particularly poor Welsh county.

More than my all is nothing; nor my prayers
Are not° words duly hallowed, nor my wishes   *no more than*
More worth than empty vanities; yet prayers and wishes
70 Are all I can return. Beseech your lordship,
Vouchsafe° to speak my thanks and my obedience,   *Condescend*
As from a blushing handmaid to his highness,
Whose health and royalty I pray for.

LORD CHAMBERLAIN   Lady,
I shall not fail t'approve° the fair conceit°   *endorse / opinion*
75 The King hath of you. [*Aside*] I have perused her well.
Beauty and honour in her are so mingled
That they have caught the King, and who knows yet
But from this lady may proceed a gem
To lighten[9] all this isle. [*To* ANNE] I'll to the King
80 And say I spoke with you.

ANNE   My honoured lord.

Exit [the] LORD CHAMBERLAIN

OLD LADY   Why, this it is—see, see!
I have been begging sixteen years in court,
Am yet a courtier beggarly,° nor could   *still begging*
85 Come pat betwixt too early and too late
For any suit of pounds;[1] and you—O, fate!—
A very fresh fish here—fie, fie upon
This compelled° fortune!—have your mouth filled up   *forced upon you*
Before you open it.

ANNE   This is strange to me.
90 OLD LADY   How tastes it? Is it bitter? Forty pence, no.[2]
There was a lady once—'tis an old story—
That would not be a queen, that would she not,
For all the mud in Egypt.[3] Have you heard it?

ANNE   Come, you are pleasant.°   *merry; joking*

OLD LADY   With your theme I could
95 O'ermount the lark. The Marchioness of Pembroke?
A thousand pounds a year, for pure° respect?   *mere*
No other obligation? By my life,
That promises more thousands. Honour's train
Is longer than his foreskirt.[4] By this time
100 I know your back will bear a duchess. Say,
Are you not stronger than you were?

ANNE   Good lady,
Make yourself mirth with your particular fancy,°   *private fantasies*
And leave me out on't. Would I had no being,
If this salute° my blood a jot. It faints me°   *agitates / I faint*
105 To think what follows.[5]
The Queen is comfortless, and we forgetful
In our long absence. Pray do not deliver
What here you've heard to her.

OLD LADY   What do you think me—

Exeunt

9. To bring light to (alluding to Elizabeth).
1. *nor . . . pounds:* nor could I arrive at just the right moment to succeed in any petition for money.
2. I'll bet a small sum (conventionally, forty pence) that
it isn't.
3. For all the wealth (in this case, the fertile land, or

"mud") of Egypt.
4. *That . . . foreskirt:* Future rewards will exceed present
ones, just as a noblewoman's dress is longer in back than
in front.
5. "What follows," ultimately, is Anne's execution at Henry's order in 1536, on the charge of adultery.

2.4

Trumpets: sennet.° [Then] cornetts. Enter two vergers¹   fanfare
with short silver wands; next them two SCRIBES *in the*
habit of doctors;² after them the [Arch]bishop of Canter-
bury alone; after him the Bishops of LINCOLN, *Ely, Roch-*
ester, and Saint Asaph; next them, with some small
distance, follows a gentleman bearing [both] the purse
[containing] the great seal and a cardinal's hat; then
two priests bearing each a silver cross; then a gentleman
usher, bare-headed, accompanied with a serjeant-at-arms
bearing a silver mace;° then two gentlemen bearing two   ceremonial staff
great silver pillars; after them, side by side, the two cardi-
*nals, [*WOLSEY *and* CAMPEIUS; *then] two noblemen with*
the sword and mace. The KING *[ascends to his seat]*
under the cloth of state; the two cardinals sit under him
as judges; the QUEEN *[attended by* GRIFFITH *her gentle-*
man usher] takes place some distance from the KING; *the*
Bishops place themselves on each side the court in [the]
manner of a consistory,° below them, the SCRIBES. *The*   church court
lords sit next the Bishops. The rest of the attendants
stand in convenient order about the stage

CARDINAL WOLSEY Whilst our commission from Rome is read
  Let silence be commanded.
KING HENRY   What's the need?
  It hath already publicly been read,
  And on all sides th'authority allowed.°   accepted
  You may then spare that time.
5 CARDINAL WOLSEY   Be't so. Proceed.
SCRIBE [*to the* CRIER] Say, 'Henry, King of England, come into the court'.
CRIER Henry, King of England, come into the court.
KING HENRY Here.
SCRIBE [*to the* CRIER] Say, 'Katherine, Queen of England, come
  into the court'.
10 CRIER Katherine, Queen of England, come into the court.
    The QUEEN *makes no answer, [but] rises out of her chair,*
    goes about the court, comes to the KING, *and kneels at*
    his feet. Then [she] speaks
QUEEN KATHERINE Sir, I desire you do me right and justice,
  And to bestow your pity on me; for
  I am a most poor woman, and a stranger,°   foreigner
  Born out of your dominions, having here
15 No judge indifferent,° nor no more assurance   impartial
  Of equal° friendship and proceeding.° Alas, sir,   just / legal order
  In what have I offended you? What cause
  Hath my behaviour given to your displeasure
  That thus you should proceed to put me off,°   abandon me
20 And take your good grace° from me? Heaven witness   good will; yourself
  I have been to you a true and humble wife,
  At all times to your will conformable,

2.4 Location: A hall in Blackfriars.   authority of office) before a bishop or other dignitary.
1. Officials who carry the verge (a staff symbolizing the 2. Furred black gown and flat caps of doctors of law.

Ever in fear to kindle your dislike,
Yea, subject to your countenance, glad or sorry
25 As I saw it inclined. When was the hour
I ever contradicted your desire,
Or made it not mine too? Or which of your friends
Have I not strove to love, although I knew
He were mine enemy? What friend of mine
30 That had to him derived° your anger did I   incurred
Continue in my liking? Nay, gave notice
He was from thence discharged? Sir, call to mind
That I have been your wife in this obedience
Upward of twenty years, and have been blessed
35 With many children by you.[3] If, in the course
And process of this time, you can report—
And prove it, too—against mine honour aught,°   anything
My bond to wedlock, or my love and duty
Against° your sacred person, in God's name   Toward
40 Turn me away, and let the foul'st contempt
Shut door upon me, and so give me up
To the sharp'st kind of justice. Please you, sir,
The King your father was reputed for
A prince most prudent, of an excellent
45 And unmatched wit° and judgement. Ferdinand   wisdom
My father, King of Spain, was reckoned one
The wisest[4] prince that there had reigned by many
A year before. It is not to be questioned
That they had gathered a wise council to them
50 Of every realm, that did debate this business,
Who deemed our marriage lawful. Wherefore I humbly
Beseech you, sir, to spare me till I may
Be by my friends in Spain advised, whose counsel
I will implore. If not, i'th' name of God,
Your pleasure be fulfilled.
55 CARDINAL WOLSEY   You have here, lady,
And of your choice, these reverend fathers, men
Of singular integrity and learning,
Yea, the elect o'th' land, who are assembled
To plead your cause. It shall be therefore bootless°   pointless
60 That longer you desire° the court, as well   beg (for a delay)
For your own quiet,° as to rectify   composure
What is unsettled in the King.
CARDINAL CAMPEIUS   His grace
Hath spoken well and justly. Therefore, madam,
It's fit this royal session do proceed,
65 And that without delay their arguments
Be now produced and heard.
QUEEN KATHERINE [to WOLSEY] Lord Cardinal,
To you I speak.
CARDINAL WOLSEY Your pleasure, madam.
QUEEN KATHERINE   Sir,
I am about to weep, but thinking that
We are a queen, or long have dreamed so, certain°   without doubt

---

3. Queen Katherine bore five of Henry's children. All but   4. was . . . wisest: was judged the very wisest.
one, later Queen Mary, died at birth or in infancy.

70　　The daughter of a king, my drops of tears
　　　I'll turn to sparks of fire.
　　CARDINAL WOLSEY　　　　Be patient yet.
　　QUEEN KATHERINE　　I will when you are humble! Nay, before,
　　　Or God will punish me. I do believe,
　　　Induced° by potent circumstances, that　　　　　　　　　　　*Convinced*
75　　You are mine enemy, and make my challenge°　　　　　　*legal objection that*
　　　You shall not be my judge. For it is you
　　　Have blown this coal betwixt my lord and me,
　　　Which God's dew quench. Therefore I say again,
　　　I utterly abhor,° yea, from my soul,　　　　　　　　　　　*loathe; reject*
80　　Refuse you for my judge, whom yet once more
　　　I hold my most malicious foe, and think not
　　　At all a friend to truth.
　　CARDINAL WOLSEY　　　　I do profess°　　　　　　　　*declare*
　　　You speak not like yourself, who ever yet°　　　　　　　*always*
　　　Have stood to° charity, and displayed th'effects　　　　*upheld*
85　　Of disposition gentle and of wisdom
　　　O'er-topping woman's power. Madam, you do me wrong.
　　　I have no spleen° against you, nor injustice　　　　　　*malevolence*
　　　For you or any. How far I have proceeded,
　　　Or how far further shall, is warranted
90　　By a commission from the consistory,°　　　　　*College of Cardinals*
　　　Yea, the whole consistory of Rome. You charge me
　　　That I 'have blown this coal'. I do deny it.
　　　The King is present. If it be known to him
　　　That I gainsay my deed,° how may he wound,　　　*deny what took place*
95　　And worthily,° my falsehood—yea, as much　　　　　　　*justly*
　　　As you have done my truth. If he know
　　　That I am free of your report, he knows
　　　I am not of your wrong.[5] Therefore in him
　　　It lies to cure° me, and the cure is to　　　　　　　　　*absolve*
100　　Remove these thoughts from you. The which before
　　　His highness shall speak in,° I do beseech　　　　　　　*about*
　　　You, gracious madam, to unthink your speaking,
　　　And to say so no more.
　　QUEEN KATHERINE　　　　My lord, my lord—
　　　I am a simple woman, much too weak
105　　T'oppose your cunning. You're meek and humble-mouthed;
　　　You sign your place and calling, in full seeming,
　　　With meekness and humility[6]—but your heart
　　　Is crammed with arrogancy, spleen,° and pride.　　　　　*malice*
　　　You have by fortune and his highness' favours
110　　Gone slightly° o'er low steps, and now are mounted　　　*effortlessly*
　　　Where powers are your retainers, and your words,
　　　Domestics to you, serve your will as't please
　　　Yourself pronounce their office.[7] I must tell you,
　　　You tender more° your person's honour than　　　*have more regard for*
115　　Your high profession spiritual, that again
　　　I do refuse you for my judge, and here,

5. *If . . . wrong:* If he agrees that I am innocent ("free") of
your accusation, then he knows that I have done you no
wrong; and that I have no part in the wrong you do me by
thus accusing me.
6. *You . . . humility:* You mark your office and role with

great outward display of meekness and humility.
7. *and now . . . office:* and now have attained a place
where men of authority ("powers") serve you, and your
words are like attendants ("domestics"), which transform
into deeds anything you pronounce as your will.

Before you all, appeal unto the Pope,
To bring my whole cause 'fore his holiness,
And to be judged by him.
She curtsies to the KING *and [begins] to depart*
CARDINAL CAMPEIUS   The Queen is obstinate,
120 Stubborn° to justice, apt to accuse it, and   *Impervious*
Disdainful to be tried by't. 'Tis not well.
She's going away.
KING HENRY [*to the* CRIER]   Call her again.
CRIER   Katherine, Queen of England, come into the court.
GRIFFITH [*to the* QUEEN]   Madam, you are called back.
QUEEN KATHERINE   What° need you note it? Pray you keep your   *Why*
125 way.°   *keep going*
When *you* are called, return. Now the Lord help.
They vex me past my patience. Pray you, pass on.
I will not tarry; no, nor ever more
Upon this business my appearance make
In any of their courts.
Exeunt QUEEN [KATHERINE] *and her attendants*
130 KING HENRY   Go thy ways, Kate.
That man i'th' world who shall report he has
A better wife, let him in naught be trusted
For speaking false in that. Thou art alone—
If thy rare qualities, sweet gentleness,
135 Thy meekness saint-like, wife-like government,°   *restraint*
Obeying in commanding,[8] and thy parts°   *qualities*
Sovereign and pious else° could speak thee out°—   *besides / describe you*
The queen of earthly queens. She's noble born,
And like her true nobility she has
Carried° herself towards me.   *Conducted*
140 CARDINAL WOLSEY   Most gracious sir,
In humblest manner I require° your highness   *entreat*
That it shall please you to declare in hearing
Of all these ears—for where I am robbed and bound,
There must I be unloosed, although not there
145 At once and fully satisfied°—whether ever I   *given recompense*
Did broach this business to your highness, or
Laid any scruple in your way which might
Induce you to the question on't,° or ever   *of it*
Have to you, but with thanks to God for such
150 A royal lady, spake one the least° word that might   *the very least*
Be to the prejudice of her present state,
Or touch° of her good person?   *censure*
KING HENRY   My lord Cardinal,
I do excuse you;° yea, upon mine honour,   *forgive you fully*
I free you from't. You are not° to be taught   *do not require*
155 That you have many enemies that know not
Why they are so, but, like to village curs,
Bark when their fellows do. By some of these
The Queen is put in anger. You're excused.
But will you be more justified?° You ever   *vindicated*
160 Have wished the sleeping of this business, never desired
It to be stirred, but oft have hindered, oft,

8. Acting like an obedient wife even as you rule like a Queen.

	The passages° made toward it. On my honour	*proceedings*
	I speak my good lord Card'nal to this point,	
	And thus far clear him.[9] Now, what moved me to't,°	*convinced me of it*
165	I will be bold with time and your attention.	
	Then mark th'inducement.° Thus it came—give heed to't.	*what influenced me*
	My conscience first received a tenderness,°	*sensitivity*
	Scruple, and prick, on° certain speeches uttered	*from*
	By th' Bishop of Bayonne, then French Ambassador,	
170	Who had been hither sent on the debating	
	A marriage 'twixt the Duke of Orléans[1] and	
	Our daughter Mary. I'th' progress of this business,	
	Ere a determinate resolution,° he—	*decisive settlement*
	I mean the Bishop—did require a respite	
175	Wherein he might the King his lord advertise°	*make aware*
	Whether our daughter were legitimate,	
	Respecting this our marriage with the dowager,	
	Sometimes° our brother's wife. This respite shook	*Formerly*
	The bosom of my conscience, entered me,	
180	Yea, with a spitting° power, and made to tremble	*piercing*
	The region of my breast; which forced such way	
	That many mazed considerings did throng	
	And prest in with this caution.[2] First, methought	
	I stood not in the smile of heaven, who had	
185	Commanded nature that my lady's womb,	
	If it conceived a male child by me, should	
	Do no more offices of life to't than	
	The grave does yield to th' dead. For her male issue	
	Or° died where they were made, or shortly after	*Either*
190	This world had aired them.° Hence I took a thought	*given them life*
	This was a judgement on me that my kingdom,	
	Well worthy the best heir o'th' world, should not	
	Be gladded° in't by me. Then follows that	*made joyful*
	I weighed the danger which my realms stood in	
195	By this my issue's fail,° and that gave to me	*lack; death*
	Many a groaning throe.° Thus hulling in[3]	*pang*
	The wild sea of my conscience, I did steer	
	Toward this remedy, whereupon we are	
	Now present here together—that's to say	
200	I meant to rectify my conscience, which	
	I then did feel full sick, and yet° not well,	*still*
	By all the reverend fathers of the land	
	And doctors learned. First I began in private	
	With you, my lord of Lincoln.[4] You remember	
205	How under my oppression I did reek°	*sweat*
	When I first moved° you.	*appealed to*
	LINCOLN Very well, my liege.	
	KING HENRY I have spoke long. Be pleased yourself to say	
	How far you satisfied me.	

---

9. *I speak . . . Him:* Here the King speaks to the court as a whole, announcing that up to this point he exonerates the Cardinal of any wrongdoing.
1. Second son of King Francis I of France, he later became Henry II of France.
2. *many . . . caution:* many confused thoughts crowded in at this warning.
3. Floating aimlessly, like a ship adrift in the current that is not making use of its sails.
4. The Bishop of Lincoln, according to Holinshed, was the King's confessor.

LINCOLN   So please your highness,
    The question did at first so stagger me,
210   Bearing a state of mighty moment° in't   *matter of such weight*
    And consequence of dread,° that I committed   *dire consequences*
    The daring'st counsel which I had to doubt,[5]
    And did entreat your highness to this course
    Which you are running here.
KING HENRY [*to Canterbury*]   I then moved you,
215   My lord of Canterbury, and got your leave
    To make this present summons. Unsolicited
    I left no reverend person in this court,
    But by particular consent proceeded
    Under your hands and seals.[6] Therefore, go on,
220   For no dislike i'th' world against the person
    Of the good Queen, but the sharp thorny points
    Of my allegèd° reasons, drives this forward.   *advanced by me*
    Prove but our marriage lawful, by my life
    And kingly dignity, we are contented
225   To wear our mortal state to come with her,
    Katherine, our queen, before the primest° creature   *most perfect*
    That's paragoned o'°th' world.   *considered a model by*
CARDINAL CAMPEIUS   So please your highness,
    The Queen being absent, 'tis a needful fitness°   *only appropriate*
    That we adjourn this court till further° day.   *a later*
230   Meanwhile must be an earnest motion°   *plea*
    Made to the Queen to call back her appeal
    She intends unto his holiness.
KING HENRY [*aside*]   I may perceive
    These cardinals trifle with me. I abhor
    This dilatory sloth and tricks of Rome.
235   My learned and well-belovèd servant, Cranmer,
    Prithee return.[7] With thy approach I know
    My comfort comes along. [*Aloud*] Break up the court.
    I say, set on.°   *Exeunt in manner as they entered*   *proceed*

3.1

Enter QUEEN [KATHERINE] *and her women, as at work*
QUEEN KATHERINE   Take thy lute, wench. My soul grows sad with troubles.
    Sing, and disperse 'em if thou canst. Leave° working.   *Cease*
GENTLEWOMAN [*sings*]   Orpheus[1] with his lute made trees,
        And the mountain tops that freeze,
5   Bow themselves when he did sing.
        To his music plants and flowers
        Ever sprung, as° sun and showers   *as if*
          There had made a lasting spring.
        Everything that heard him play,
10   Even the billows of the sea,
          Hung their heads, and then lay by.°   *were still*

---

5. *I committed . . . doubt*: I distrusted even the boldest advice I myself could offer.
6. With your written agreement.
7. The King here apostrophizes Thomas Cranmer, who is not present but is traveling on the continent collecting opinions on the status of Henry and Katherine's marriage.

See 3.2.401–2 for mention of his return and his elevation to the position of Archbishop of Canterbury.
3.1 Location: The Queen's apartments at court.
1. In Greek mythology, he was famous for the power of his music.

In sweet music is such art,
Killing care and grief of heart
Fall asleep, or hearing, die.
Enter [GRIFFITH,] *a gentleman*

15 QUEEN KATHERINE How now?
GRIFFITH An't please your grace, the two great cardinals
Wait in the presence.°   *reception chamber*
QUEEN KATHERINE   Would they speak with me?
GRIFFITH They willed me say so, madam.
QUEEN KATHERINE   Pray their graces
To come near.   [*Exit* GRIFFITH]
       What can be their business
20 With me, a poor weak woman, fall'n from favour?
I do not like their coming, now I think on't;
They should be good men, their affairs as righteous —
But all hoods make not monks.[2]
       Enter the two cardinals, WOLSEY *and* CAMPEIUS [*ushered*
       by GRIFFITH]
CARDINAL WOLSEY   Peace to your highness.
QUEEN KATHERINE Your graces find me here part of a housewife —
25 I would be all,[3] against° the worst may happen.   *in case*
What are your pleasures with me, reverend lords?
CARDINAL WOLSEY May it please you, noble madam, to withdraw
Into your private chamber, we shall give you
The full cause of our coming.
QUEEN KATHERINE   Speak it here.
30 There's nothing I have done yet, o' my conscience,
Deserves a corner.° Would all other women   *subterfuge*
Could speak this with as free° a soul as I do.   *innocent*
My lords, I care not — so much I am happy°   *favored*
Above a number° — if my actions   *many*
35 Were tried by ev'ry tongue, ev'ry eye saw 'em,
Envy and base opinion° set against 'em,   *Spite and base gossip*
I know my life so even.° If your business   *uniformly virtuous*
Seek me out and that way I am wife in,[4]
Out with it boldly. Truth loves open dealing.
40 CARDINAL WOLSEY *Tanta est erga te mentis integritas, Regina serenissima*[5] —
QUEEN KATHERINE O, good my lord, no Latin.
I am not such a truant° since my coming°   *so idle / (to England)*
As not to know the language I have lived in.
A strange° tongue makes my cause more strange suspicious° —   *foreign / unusually*
45 Pray, speak in English. Here are some will thank you,
If you speak truth, for their poor mistress' sake.
Believe me, she has had much wrong. Lord Cardinal,
The willing'st° sin I ever yet committed   *most premeditated*
May be absolved in English.
CARDINAL WOLSEY   Noble lady,
50 I am sorry my integrity should breed —
And service to his majesty and you —
So deep suspicion, where all faith° was meant.   *loyalty*
We come not by the way° of accusation,   *for the sake*

2. Proverbial: religious trappings do not ensure piety.
3. I would like to be not just partly but completely a housewife.
4. *If . . . in:* If your business concerns me and my behav-ior as wife.
5. So great, most royal Queen, is the integrity of (my) mind toward you (Latin).

55	To taint that honour every good tongue blesses,	
	Nor to betray you any way° to sorrow—	*by any means*
	You have too much, good lady—but to know	
	How you stand minded° in the weighty difference	*Your deliberation*
	Between the King and you, and to deliver,°	*recount*
	Like free° and honest men, our just opinions	*candid*
60	And comforts to your cause.	

CARDINAL CAMPEIUS   Most honoured madam,

	My lord of York, out of his noble nature,	
	Zeal, and obedience he still bore° your grace,	*has always borne*
	Forgetting, like a good man, your late censure	
	Both of his truth and him—which was° too far—	*went*
65	Offers, as I do, in a sign of peace,	
	His service and his counsel.	

QUEEN KATHERINE [*aside*]   To betray me.

[*Aloud*] My lords, I thank you both for your good wills.

	Ye speak like honest men—pray God ye prove so.	
	But how to make ye suddenly° an answer	*without deliberation*
70	In such a point of weight, so near° mine honour—	*bound up with*
	More near my life, I fear—with my weak wit,°	*comprehension*
	And to such men of gravity and learning,	
	In truth I know not. I was set° at work	*sitting*
	Among my maids, full little—God knows—looking	
75	Either for such men or such business.	
	For her sake that I have been[6]—for I feel	
	The last fit° of my greatness—good your graces,	*spell*
	Let me have time and counsel for my cause.	
	Alas, I am a woman friendless, hopeless.	

CARDINAL WOLSEY   Madam, you wrong the King's love with these fears.

Your hopes and friends are infinite.

QUEEN KATHERINE   In England

	But little for my profit.° Can you think, lords,	*of little use to me*
	That any Englishman dare give me counsel,	
	Or be a known friend 'gainst his highness' pleasure—	
85	Though he be grown so desperate° to be honest—	*rash enough*
	And live a subject?° Nay, forsooth, my friends,	*survive in this land*
	They that must weigh out° my afflictions,	*offset*
	They that my trust must grow to, live not here.	
	They are, as all my other comforts, far hence,	
	In mine own country, lords.	

CARDINAL CAMPEIUS   I would your grace

Would leave your griefs and take my counsel.

QUEEN KATHERINE   How, sir?

CARDINAL CAMPEIUS   Put your main cause into the King's protection.

	He's loving and most gracious. 'Twill be much	
	Both for your honour better and your cause,	
95	For if the trial of the law o'ertake ye	
	You'll part away° disgraced.	*leave*

CARDINAL WOLSEY [*to the* QUEEN]   He tells you rightly.

QUEEN KATHERINE   Ye tell me what ye wish for both—my ruin.

Is this your Christian counsel? Out upon ye!

Heaven is above all yet—there sits a judge

That no king can corrupt.

6. For the sake of the woman—the Queen—I once was.

100	CARDINAL CAMPEIUS Your rage mistakes° us.	*misrepresents*

QUEEN KATHERINE   The more shame for ye! Holy men I thought ye,
Upon my soul, two reverend cardinal virtues[7] —
But cardinal sins and hollow hearts I fear ye.

	Mend° 'em, for shame, my lords! Is this your comfort?	*Reform*
105	The cordial° that ye bring a wretched lady,	*balm*
	A woman lost° among ye, laughed at, scorned?	*ruined*

I will not wish ye half my miseries —
I have more charity. But say I warned ye.

	Take heed, for heaven's sake take heed, lest at once°	*all at once*
110	The burden of my sorrows fall upon ye.	
	CARDINAL WOLSEY Madam, this is a mere distraction.°	*sheer madness*
	You turn the good we offer into envy.°	*malevolence*

QUEEN KATHERINE   Ye turn me into nothing. Woe upon ye,

	And all such false professors.° Would you have me —	*(of religion)*
115	If you have any justice, any pity,	
	If ye be anything but churchmen's habits° —	*vestments*

Put my sick cause into his hands that hates me?
Alas, he's banished me his bed already —
His love, too, long ago. I am old, my lords,
120 And all the fellowship I hold now with him
Is only my obedience. What can happen

	To me above° this wretchedness? All your studies	*beyond*
	Make me accursed like this.[8]	*immediate*
	CARDINAL CAMPEIUS Your fears are worse.°	*(than reality)*
	QUEEN KATHERINE Have I lived thus long — let me speak° myself,	*represent*
125	Since virtue finds no friends — a wife, a true one?	
	A woman, I dare say, without vainglory,°	*conceit*

Never yet branded with suspicion?
Have I with all my full affections

	Still° met the King, loved him next° heav'n, obeyed him,	*Always / next to*
130	Been out of fondness superstitious° to him,	*overly devoted*

Almost forgot my prayers to content him?
And am I thus rewarded? 'Tis not well, lords.
Bring me a constant woman to her husband,
One that ne'er dreamed a joy beyond his pleasure,
135 And to that woman when she has done most,

	Yet will I add an° honour, a great patience.	*another*
	CARDINAL WOLSEY Madam, you wander from° the good we aim at.	*misinterpret*

QUEEN KATHERINE   My lord, I dare not make myself so guilty
To give up willingly that noble title
140 Your master wed me to. Nothing but death
Shall e'er divorce my dignities.
CARDINAL WOLSEY   Pray, hear me.
QUEEN KATHERINE   Would I had never trod this English earth,
Or felt the flatteries that grow upon it.
Ye have angels' faces, but heaven knows your hearts.
145 What will become of me now, wretched lady?
I am the most unhappy woman living.
[*To her women*] Alas, poor wenches, where are now your forturnes?

---

7. The cardinal virtues (justice, temperance, prudence, and fortitude, with a play on their rank), which, along with the three theological virtues (faith, hope, and charity), constitute the seven virtues. These oppose the seven deadly ("cardinal," punning on "carnal") sins referred to in the next line.

8. *All . . . this:* All your endeavors (and inquiries) bring me only these miseries; I defy you, with all your clerical learning, to imagine a more terrible fate than this.

Shipwrecked upon a kingdom where no pity,
No friends, no hope, no kindred weep for me?
150 Almost no grave allowed me? Like the lily,
That once was mistress of the field and flourished,
I'll hang my head and perish.

CARDINAL WOLSEY   If your grace
Could but be brought to know our ends° are honest,   *intentions*
You'd feel more comfort. Why should we, good lady,
155 Upon what cause, wrong you? Alas, our places,°   *official duties*
The way of our profession, is against it.
We are to cure such sorrows, not to sow 'em.
For goodness' sake, consider what you do,
How you may hurt yourself, ay, utterly
160 Grow from the King's acquaintance by this carriage.°   *behavior*
The hearts of princes kiss obedience,
So much they love it, but to stubborn spirits
They swell and grow as terrible as storms.
I know you have a gentle noble temper,°   *temperament*
165 A soul as even° as a calm. Pray, think us   *unwavering*
Those we profess—peacemakers, friends, and servants.

CARDINAL CAMPEIUS   Madam, you'll find it so. You wrong your virtues
With these weak women's fears. A noble spirit,
As yours was put° into you, ever casts   *given*
170 Such doubts as false coin from it. The King loves you.
Beware you lose it not. For° us, if you please   *As for*
To trust us in your business, we are ready
To use our utmost studies in your service.

QUEEN KATHERINE   Do what ye will, my lords, and pray forgive me.
175 If I have used° myself unmannerly,   *handled*
You know I am a woman, lacking wit°   *understanding*
To make a seemly answer to such persons.
Pray do my service° to his majesty.   *give my respects*
He has my heart yet, and shall have my prayers
180 While I shall have my life. Come, reverend fathers,
Bestow your counsels on me. She now begs
That° little thought, when she set footing here,°   *Who / (in England)*
She should have bought her dignities so dear.   *Exeunt*

3.2

Enter the Duke of NORFOLK, [*the*] *Duke of* SUFFOLK,
Lord SURREY, *and* [*the*] LORD CHAMBERLAIN

NORFOLK   If you will now unite in your complaints,
And force them with a constancy,° the Cardinal   *persevere in them*
Cannot stand under them. If you omit°   *forgo*
The offer of this time,° I cannot promise   *This opportunity*
5 But that you shall sustain more new disgraces
With these you bear already.

SURREY   I am joyful
To meet the least occasion that may give me
Remembrance of my father-in-law the Duke,°   *(of Buckingham)*
To be revenged on him.°   *(Wolsey)*

SUFFOLK   Which of the peers
10 Have uncontemned gone° by him, or at least   *not been disdained*
Strangely neglected?° When did he regard   *snubbed*

3.2 Location: The court.

The stamp of nobleness in any person
Out of° himself? *Aside from*
LORD CHAMBERLAIN   My lords, you speak your pleasures.
What he deserves of you and me I know;
15 What we can do to him—though now the time
Gives way to° us—I much fear. If you cannot *Favors*
Bar his access to th' King, never attempt
Anything on° him, for he hath a witchcraft *against*
Over the King in's tongue.
NORFOLK   O, fear him not.
20 His spell in that is out.° The King hath found *past*
Matter against him that for ever mars
The honey of his language. No, he's settled,
Not to come off,° in his° displeasure. *evade / (the king's)*
SURREY   Sir,
I should be glad to hear such news as this
Once every hour.
25 NORFOLK   Believe it, this is true.
In the divorce his contrary proceedings° *double-dealing*
Are all unfolded,° wherein he appears *exposed*
As I would wish mine enemy.
SURREY   How came
His practices° to light? *schemes*
SUFFOLK   Most strangely.
SURREY   O, how, how?
30 SUFFOLK   The Cardinal's letters to the Pope miscarried,° *were diverted*
And came to th'eye o'th' King, wherein was read
How that the Cardinal did entreat his holiness
To stay° the judgement o'th' divorce, for if *delay*
It did take place, 'I do', quoth he, 'perceive
35 My king is tangled in affection to
A creature° of the Queen's, Lady Anne Boleyn'. *servant*
SURREY   Has the King this?
SUFFOLK   Believe it.
SURREY   Will this work?
LORD CHAMBERLAIN   The King in this perceives him how he coasts° *sails indirectly*
And hedges° his own way. But in this point *moves secretly*
40 All his tricks founder, and he brings his physic° *medicine*
After his patient's death. The King already
Hath married the fair lady.
SURREY   Would he had.
SUFFOLK   May you be happy in your wish, my lord,
For I profess you have it.
SURREY   Now all my joy
Trace the conjunction.° *Follow the union*
SUFFOLK   My amen to't.
45 NORFOLK   All men's.
SUFFOLK   There's order given for her coronation.
Marry, this is yet but young,° and may be left *recent*
To some ears unrecounted. But, my lords,
She is a gallant° creature, and complete° *an excellent / perfect*
50 In mind and feature. I persuade me,° from her *am sure*
Will fall some blessing to this land which shall
In it be memorized.[1]

1. Be made memorable (alluding to Elizabeth).

SURREY　　　　　　　But will the King
Digest° this letter of the Cardinal's?　　　　　　　　　　　　　*Tolerate*
The Lord forbid!
NORFOLK　　　　　Marry, amen.
SUFFOLK　　　　　　　　　No, no—
55　There be more wasps that buzz about his nose
Will make this sting the sooner. Cardinal Campeius
Is stol'n away to Rome; hath ta'en no leave;
Has left the cause o'th' King unhandled,° and　　　　　　*unsettled*
Is posted° as the agent of our Cardinal　　　　　　　　　*Has rushed*
60　To second all his plot. I do assure you
The King cried 'Ha!'[2] at this.
LORD CHAMBERLAIN　　　　Now God incense him,
And let him cry 'Ha!' louder.
NORFOLK　　　　　　　　But, my lord,
When returns Cranmer?
SUFFOLK　　He is returned in his opinions, which
65　Have satisfied the King for his divorce,
Together with all famous colleges,
Almost, in Christendom.[3] Shortly, I believe,
His second marriage shall be published,° and　　　　*announced publicly*
Her coronation. Katherine no more
70　Shall be called 'Queen', but 'Princess Dowager',
And 'widow to Prince Arthur'.
NORFOLK　　　　　　　This same Cranmer's
A worthy fellow, and hath ta'en much pain°　　　　　　*great pains*
In the King's business.
SUFFOLK　　　　　　He has, and we shall see him
For it an archbishop.
NORFOLK　　　　　So I hear.
SUFFOLK　　　　　　　　'Tis so.
　　　　　　Enter [CARDINAL] WOLSEY *and* CROMWELL
The Cardinal.
75　NORFOLK　　　　Observe, observe—he's moody.
　　　[*They stand apart and observe* WOLSEY *and* CROMWELL]
CARDINAL WOLSEY [*to* CROMWELL]　　The packet,° Cromwell—　　*parcel of letters*
　　gave't you the King?
CROMWELL　　To his own hand, in's bedchamber.
CARDINAL WOLSEY　　　　　　　　Looked he
O'th' inside of the paper?°　　　　　　　　　　　　　　　*wrapper*
CROMWELL　　　　　Presently°　　　　　　　　　　*Immediately*
He did unseal them, and the first he viewed
80　He did it with a serious mind; a heed°　　　　　*concerned look*
Was in his countenance. You he bade
Attend him here this morning.
CARDINAL WOLSEY　　　　　Is he ready
To come abroad?
CROMWELL　　I think by this° he is.　　　　　　　　*by this time*
85　CARDINAL WOLSEY　　Leave me a while.　　　*Exit* CROMWELL
[*Aside*] It shall be to the Duchess of Alençon,
The French King's sister—he shall marry her.

---

2. Henry's characteristic expression of impatience and part of his legend in the Renaissance. See, for instance, 1.2.187 and 2.2.64, 66.
3. *He . . . Christendom*: Cranmer has sent ahead the opin-ions concerning the King's marriage that he collected on the continent, and the results have satisfied both the King and most learned clerics.

Anne Boleyn? No, I'll no Anne Boleyns for him.
There's more in't than fair visage. Boleyn?
90 No, we'll no Boleyns. Speedily I wish
To hear from Rome. The Marchioness of Pembroke?
[*The nobles speak among themselves*]

NORFOLK   He's discontented.

SUFFOLK   Maybe he hears the King
Does whet his anger to° him.   *against*

SURREY   Sharp enough,
Lord, for thy justice.

CARDINAL WOLSEY [*aside*]   The late° Queen's gentlewoman? A   *former*
95   knight's daughter
To be her mistress' mistress? The Queen's queen?
This candle burns not clear;° 'tis I must snuff it,   *bright*
Then out it goes. What though I know her virtuous
And well deserving? Yet I know her for
100 A spleeny Lutheran,[4] and not wholesome° to   *beneficial*
Our cause, that she should lie i'th' bosom of
Our hard-ruled° King. Again, there is sprung up   *hard-to-advise*
An heretic, an arch-one, Cranmer, one°   *one who*
Hath crawled into the favour of the King
And is his oracle.°   *most trusted counsel*
[*The nobles speak among themselves*]

105 NORFOLK   He is vexed at something.
Enter KING [HENRY] *reading a schedule*° [*and* LOVELL   *scroll*
    with him]

SURREY   I would 'twere something that would fret the string,
The master-cord on's heart![5]

SUFFOLK   The King, the King!

KING HENRY [*aside*]   What piles of wealth hath he accumulated
To his own portion?° And what expense by th' hour   *share*
110 Seems to flow from him? How i'th' name of thrift
Does he rake this together? [*To the nobles*] Now, my lords,
Saw you the Cardinal?

NORFOLK   My lord, we have
Stood here observing him. Some strange commotion°   *rebellion*
Is in his brain. He bites his lip, and starts,
115 Stops on a sudden, looks upon the ground,
Then lays his finger on his temple, straight°   *immediately*
Springs out into fast gait, then stops again,
Strikes his breast hard, and anon he casts
His eye against the moon. In most strange postures
We have seen him set himself.

120 KING HENRY   It may well be
There is a mutiny in's mind. This morning
Papers of state he sent me to peruse
As I required, and wot° you what I found   *know*
There, on my conscience put unwittingly?
125 Forsooth, an inventory thus importing°   *delineating*
The several parcels of his plate,[6] his treasure,

---

4. Passionate Lutheran. It is possible that Wolsey objected
to Henry's marriage to Anne on religious grounds, as well
as on the class grounds he outlines in this speech.
5. *would . . . heart:* would eat through ("fret") the heart-

strings (tying Henry to Wolsey), with a musical allusion:
"fret" (fingering bar), "string," and "cord" (chord).
6. *plate:* gold and silver functional household equipment
that also stored and displayed wealth.

Rich stuffs, and ornaments of household which
I find at such proud rate° that it outspeaks   *high value*
Possession of a subject.[7]
NORFOLK   It's heaven's will.
130   Some spirit put this paper in the packet
To bless your eye withal.°   *with*
KING HENRY   If we did think
His contemplation were above the earth
And fixed on spiritual object, he should still
Dwell in his musings. But I am afraid
135   His thinkings are below the moon,° not worth   *mundane*
His serious considering.
       [*The*] KING *takes his seat* [*and*] *whispers* [*with*] LOVELL,
           who [*then*] *goes to the* CARDINAL
CARDINAL WOLSEY   Heaven forgive me!
[*To the* KING] Ever God bless your highness!
KING HENRY   Good my lord,
You are full of heavenly stuff,[8] and bear the inventory
Of your best graces in your mind, the which
140   You were now running o'er. You have scarce time
To steal from spiritual leisure a brief span
To keep your earthly audit. Sure, in that,
I deem you an ill husband, and am glad
To have you therein my companion.[9]
CARDINAL WOLSEY   Sir,
145   For holy offices I have a time; a time
To think upon the part of business which
I bear i'th' state; and nature does require
Her times of preservation which, perforce,
I, her frail son, amongst my brethren mortal,
Must give my tendance to.°   *take care of*
150 KING HENRY   You have said well.
CARDINAL WOLSEY   And ever may your highness yoke together,
As I will lend you cause, my doing well
With my well-saying.
KING HENRY   'Tis well said again,
And 'tis a kind of good deed to say well—
155   And yet words are no deeds. My father loved you.
He said he did, and with his deed did crown°   *make good*
His word upon you. Since I had my office,
I have kept you next° my heart, have not alone   *nearest to*
Employed you where high profits might come home,
160   But pared my present havings° to bestow   *given up possessions*
My bounties upon you.
CARDINAL WOLSEY [*aside*] What should this mean?
SURREY [*aside*]   The Lord increase this business!
KING HENRY   Have I not made you
The prime° man of the state? I pray you tell me   *principal*
If what I now pronounce you have found true,

---

7. *a . . . subject*: it inventories more wealth than is fit for
a subject.
8. Godly qualities, but Henry's ironic language ("stuff,"
"steal," "audit") refers to both worldly and spiritual matters.
9. Henry jokes that both he and Wolsey are "ill hus-

bands," Wolsey because he cannot manage ("husband")
his household resources (ostensibly, he is otherworldly,
but really he is a greedy spendthrift) and because he now
opposes Henry's remarriage, and Henry because he has
literally been a poor husband to Katherine.

165   And, if you may confess it, say withal
      If you are bound to us or no. What say you?
      CARDINAL WOLSEY   My sovereign, I confess your royal graces°   favors
      Showered on me daily have been more than could
      My studied purposes° requite, which went   deliberate efforts
170   Beyond all man's endeavours. My endeavours
      Have ever come too short of my desires,°   aspirations
      Yet filed° with my abilities. Mine own ends°   matched / aims
      Have been mine so that° evermore they pointed   only insofar as
      To th' good of your most sacred person and
175   The profit of the state. For your great graces
      Heaped upon me, poor undeserver, I
      Can nothing render but allegiant° thanks,   loyal
      My prayers to heaven for you, my loyalty,
      Which ever has and ever shall be growing,
      Till death, that winter, kill it.
180   KING HENRY   Fairly answered.
      A loyal and obedient subject is
      Therein illustrated. The honour of it
      Does pay the act of it, as, i'th' contrary,
      The foulness is the punishment.¹ I presume
185   That as my hand has opened° bounty to you,   freely offered
      My heart dropped love, my power rained honour, more
      On you than any, so your hand and heart,
      Your brain, and every function of your power,
      Should, notwithstanding that° your bond of duty,°   despite / (to Rome)
190   As 'twere in love's particular,° be more   peculiar intimacy
      To me, your friend, than any.
      CARDINAL WOLSEY   I do profess
      That for your highness' good I ever laboured
      More than mine own; that am, have,° and will be—   have been
      Though all the world should crack° their duty to you,   forswear
195   And throw it from their soul, though perils did
      Abound, as thick as thought could make 'em, and
      Appear in forms more horrid—yet, my duty,
      As doth a rock against the chiding° flood,   roaring
      Should the approach of this wild river break,°   check
      And stand unshaken yours.
200   KING HENRY   'Tis nobly spoken.
      Take notice, lords, he has a loyal breast,
      For you have seen him open't. [To WOLSEY] Read o'er this,
            [He gives him a paper]
      And after this [giving him another paper], and then to breakfast with
      What appetite you have.
                        Exit KING [HENRY], frowning upon the
                        CARDINAL. The nobles throng after
                        [the KING], smiling and whispering
      CARDINAL WOLSEY   What should this mean?
205   What sudden anger's this? How have I reaped° it?   acquired
      He parted frowning from me, as if ruin
      Leaped from his eyes. So looks the chafèd° lion   angry
      Upon the daring huntsman that has galled° him,   wounded

1. *The honour . . . punishment:* The reward for loyalty and obedience is the honor they bring. Similarly, disloyalty and corruption are their own punishment, causing the subject dishonor.

Then makes him nothing.° I must read this paper—   *slaughters the hunter*
I fear, the story of his anger.
      [*He reads one of the papers*]
210   'Tis so.
This paper has undone° me. 'Tis th'account   *ruined*
Of all that world° of wealth I have drawn together   *vast quantity*
For mine own ends—indeed, to gain the popedom,
And fee° my friends in Rome. O negligence,   *pay off*
215 Fit for a fool to fall by! What cross° devil   *perverse*
Made me put this main° secret in the packet   *most important*
I sent the King? Is there no way to cure this?
No new device to beat this from his brains?
I know 'twill stir him strongly. Yet I know
220 A way, if it take right,° in spite of fortune   *if it succeed*
Will bring me off° again. What's this?   *save me*
      [*He reads the other paper*]
               'To th' Pope'?
The letter, as I live, with all the business
I writ to's holiness. Nay then, farewell.
I have touched the highest point of all my greatness,
225 And from that full meridian° of my glory   *a star's highest point*
I haste now to my setting. I shall fall
Like a bright exhalation° in the evening,   *shooting star*
And no man see me more.
      Enter to [CARDINAL] WOLSEY *the Dukes of* NORFOLK *and*
      SUFFOLK, *the Earl of* SURREY, *and the* LORD CHAMBER-
      LAIN
NORFOLK   Hear the King's pleasure, Cardinal, who commands you
230 To render up the great seal presently°   *immediately*
Into our hands, and to confine yourself
To Asher House, my lord of Winchester's,
Till you hear further from his highness.
CARDINAL WOLSEY   Stay—
Where's your commission,° lords? Words cannot carry   *written warrant*
Authority so weighty.
235 SUFFOLK   Who dare cross° 'em   *challenge*
Bearing the King's will from his mouth expressly?
CARDINAL WOLSEY   Till I find more than will or words to do it—
I mean your malice—know, officious lords,
I dare and must deny it. Now I feel
240 Of what coarse metal° ye are moulded—envy.°   *(also) mettle / malice*
How eagerly ye follow my disgraces
As if it fed ye, and how sleek° and wanton°   *obsequious / impetuous*
Ye appear in everything may bring my ruin!
Follow your envious courses, men of malice.
245 You have Christian warrant for 'em, and no doubt
In time will find their fit rewards.[2] That seal
You ask with such a violence,° the King,   *vehemence*
Mine and your master, with his own hand gave me,
Bade me enjoy it, with the place° and honours,   *position*
250 During my life; and, to confirm his goodness,
Tied it by letters patents.° Now, who'll take it?   *open letters*
SURREY   The King that gave it.

---

2. *You . . . rewards:* You emulate other, equally unjust Christians and will reap their "rewards" (punishments).

CARDINAL WOLSEY   It must be himself then.
SURREY   Thou art a proud traitor, priest.
CARDINAL WOLSEY   Proud lord, thou liest.
Within these forty hours Surrey durst better
Have burnt that tongue than said so.
255 SURREY   Thy ambition,
Thou scarlet sin,³ robbed this bewailing land
Of noble Buckingham, my father-in-law.
The heads of all thy brother cardinals
With thee and all thy best parts° bound together   *attributes*
260 Weighed° not a hair of his. Plague of° your policy,   *Equaled / on*
You sent me deputy for Ireland,
Far from his succour, from the King, from all
That might have mercy on the fault thou gav'st him;°   *charged him wtih*
Whilst your great goodness, out of holy pity,
Absolved him with an axe.
265 CARDINAL WOLSEY   This, and all else
This talking lord can lay upon my credit,°   *good reputation*
I answer is most false. The Duke by law
Found his deserts. How innocent I was
From° any private malice in his end,   *Of*
270 His noble jury and foul cause can witness.
If I loved many words, lord, I should tell you
You have as little honesty as honour,
That° in the way of loyalty and truth   *I who*
Toward the King, my ever royal master,
275 Dare mate° a sounder man than Surrey can be,   *rival*
And all that love his follies.
SURREY   By my soul,
Your long coat, priest, protects you; thou shouldst feel
My sword i'th' life-blood of thee else. My lords,
Can ye endure to hear this arrogance,
280 And from this fellow?° If we live thus tamely,   *(contemptuous)*
To be thus jaded° by a piece of scarlet,   *cowed*
Farewell nobility. Let his grace go forward
And dare us with his cap, like larks.⁴
CARDINAL WOLSEY   All goodness
Is poison to thy stomach.
SURREY   Yes, that goodness
285 Of gleaning all the land's wealth into one,
Into your own hands, Card'nal, by extortion;
The goodness of your intercepted packets
You writ to th' Pope against the King; your goodness—
Since you provoke me—shall be most notorious.
290 My lord of Norfolk, as you are truly noble,
As you respect the common good, the state
Of our despised nobility, our issues°—   *sons*
Whom if he° live will scarce be gentlemen—   *(Wolsey)*
Produce the grand sum of his sins, the articles°   *charges against him*
295 Collected from his life. [*To* WOLSEY] I'll startle you

3. *scarlet*: referring to the cardinal's robes; see line 281 and 3.1.103. *scarlet sin*: egregious sin in the Bible; see Isaiah 1:18.

4. And befuddle us with his scarlet cap, as larks are caught by dazzling them with scarlet cloth.

Worse than the sacring-bell when the brown wench
Lay kissing in your arms,[5] lord Cardinal.

CARDINAL WOLSEY [*aside*]   How much, methinks, I could despise this man,
But that I am bound in charity against it.

300 NORFOLK [*to* SURREY]   Those articles, my lord, are in the King's hand;°   *possession*
But thus° much—they are foul ones.   *I'll tell you this*

CARDINAL WOLSEY   So much fairer
And spotless shall mine innocence arise
When the King knows my truth.°   *loyalty*

SURREY   This cannot save you.
305 I thank my memory I yet remember
Some of these articles, and out they shall.
Now, if you can blush and cry 'Guilty', Cardinal,
You'll show a little honesty.

CARDINAL WOLSEY   Speak on, sir;
I dare your worst objections.° If I blush,   *accusations*
It is to see a nobleman want° manners.   *lack*

310 SURREY   I had rather want those than my head. Have at you!°   *(a challenge)*
First, that without the King's assent or knowledge
You wrought to be a legate,[6] by which power
You maimed the jurisdiction of all bishops.

NORFOLK [*to* WOLSEY]   Then, that in all you writ to Rome, or else
315 To foreign princes, '*Ego et Rex meus*'[7]
Was still° inscribed—in which you brought the King   *always*
To be your servant.

SUFFOLK [*to* WOLSEY]   Then, that without the knowledge
Either of King or Council, when you went
Ambassador to the Emperor,° you made bold   *Charles V*
320 To carry into Flanders the great seal.

SURREY [*to* WOLSEY]   Item,° you sent a large commission°   *Next / delegation*
To Gregory de Cassado, to conclude,
Without the King's will or the state's allowance,°   *consent*
A league between his highness and Ferrara.

325 SUFFOLK [*to* WOLSEY]   That out of mere° ambition you have caused   *pure*
Your holy hat to be stamped on the King's coin.[8]

SURREY [*to* WOLSEY]   Then, that you have sent innumerable substance°—   *untold riches*
By what means got, I leave to your own conscience—
To furnish° Rome, and to prepare the ways   *supply; bribe*
330 You have for dignities to the mere undoing°   *complete destruction*
Of all the kingdom. Many more there are,
Which since they are of you, and odious,
I will not taint my mouth with.

LORD CHAMBERLAIN   O, my lord,
Press° not a falling man too far. 'Tis virtue.°   *Oppress / (not to)*
335 His faults lie open to° the laws. Let them,   *exposed before*
Not you, correct him. My heart weeps to see him
So little of his great self.

SURREY   I forgive him.

---

5. *I'll . . . arms:* The small "sacring bell" was rung at mass
when the priest elevated the consecrated Host. Surrey
imagines Wolsey surprised with a country girl ("brown"
because tanned or dirty from working, or perhaps ugly or
promiscuous) when he should have been at mass.
6. You schemed to be a papal representative.
7. I and my King. Norfolk accuses Wolsey of putting himself before the King and of making the King his depen-

dent. Technically, however, the Latin word order is correct and means "my King and I," thus making it less
offensive.
8. Allowed to produce half groats and half pennies with
his insignia in his home diocese of York, Wolsey had his
cardinal's hat stamped on a groat, thereby usurping the
King's monopoly on coins of larger denominations.

SUFFOLK   Lord Cardinal, the King's further pleasure is—
Because all those things you have done of late,
340   By your power legantine within this kingdom,
Fall into th' compass of a praemunire[9]—
That therefore such a writ be sued° against you,   *served*
To forfeit all your goods, lands, tenements,
Chattels,° and whatsoever, and to be   *Personal property*
345   Out of the King's protection. This is my charge.
NORFOLK [*to* WOLSEY]   And so we'll leave you to your meditations
How to live better. For your stubborn answer
About the giving back the great seal to us,
The King shall know it and, no doubt, shall thank you.
350   So fare you well, my little good lord Cardinal.   *Exeunt all but* WOLSEY
CARDINAL WOLSEY   So farewell—to the little good you bear me.
Farewell, a long farewell, to all my greatness!
This is the state of man. Today he puts forth
The tender leaves of hopes; tomorrow blossoms,
355   And bears his blushing° honours thick upon him;   *resplendent*
The third day comes a frost, a killing frost,
And when he thinks, good easy° man, full surely   *trusting*
His greatness is a-ripening, nips his root,
And then he falls, as I do. I have ventured,
360   Like little wanton boys that swim on bladders,[1]
This many summers in a sea of glory,
But far beyond my depth; my high-blown pride
At length broke under me, and now has left me
Weary, and old with service, to the mercy
365   Of a rude stream° that must for ever hide me.   *turbulent current*
Vain pomp and glory of this world, I hate ye!
I feel my heart new opened. O, how wretched
Is that poor man that hangs on princes' favours!
There is betwixt that smile we would aspire to,
370   That sweet aspect of princes, and their ruin,[2]
More pangs and fears than wars or women have,
And when he falls, he falls like Lucifer,°   *(from heaven to hell)*
Never to hope again.
            Enter CROMWELL, [*who then*] *stand*[*s*] *amazed*
                        Why, how now, Cromwell?
CROMWELL   I have no power to speak, sir.
CARDINAL WOLSEY   What, amazed
375   At my misfortunes? Can thy spirit wonder
A great man should decline?°   *fall from power*
            [CROMWELL *begins to weep*]
                        Nay, an° you weep   *if*
I am fall'n indeed.
CROMWELL   How does your grace?
CARDINAL WOLSEY   Why, well—
Never so truly happy, my good Cromwell.
I know myself now, and I feel within me

9. Having made himself a papal legate, Wolsey is subject
to punishment because he has broken the law of *praemunire* by appealing to an outside (here, papal) court when
the offense fell under the jurisdiction of English courts.
Wolsey is charged with elevating the Pope's authority over

his sovereign's.
1. Like frolicsome little boys who stay afloat (only by)
using inflated membranes from an animal's body.
2. *their ruin:* the destruction they cause.

380 A peace above all earthly dignities,
A still and quiet conscience. The King has cured me.
I humbly thank his grace, and from these shoulders,
These ruined pillars,³ out of pity, taken
A load would sink a navy—too much honour.
385 O, 'tis a burden, Cromwell, 'tis a burden
Too heavy for a man that hopes for heaven.
CROMWELL   I am glad your grace has made that right use of it.
CARDINAL WOLSEY   I hope I have. I am able now, methinks,
Out of a fortitude of soul I feel,
390 To endure more miseries and greater far
Than my weak-hearted enemies dare offer.
What news abroad?
CROMWELL   The heaviest and the worst
Is your displeasure° with the King.   *disgrace*
CARDINAL WOLSEY   God bless him.
CROMWELL   The next is that Sir Thomas More is chosen
Lord Chancellor in your place.
395 CARDINAL WOLSEY   That's somewhat sudden.
But he's a learnèd man. May he continue
Long in his highness' favour, and do justice
For truth's sake and his conscience, that his bones,
When he has run his course and sleeps in blessings,
400 May have a tomb of orphans' tears wept on him.⁴
What more?
CROMWELL   That Cranmer is returned° with welcome,   *(from the continent)*
Installed lord Archbishop of Canterbury.⁵
CARDINAL WOLSEY   That's news indeed.
CROMWELL   Last, that the Lady Anne,
Whom the King hath in secrecy long married,
405 This day was viewed in open as his queen,
Going to chapel, and the voice° is now   *gossip*
Only about her coronation.
CARDINAL WOLSEY   There was the weight that pulled me down.
O, Cromwell,
The King has gone beyond° me. All my glories   *overreached*
410 In° that one woman I have lost for ever.   *Due to*
No sun shall ever usher forth mine honours,
Or gild again the noble troops° that waited   *retainers*
Upon my smiles. Go, get thee from me, Cromwell,
I am a poor fall'n man, unworthy now
415 To be thy lord and master. Seek the King—
That sun I pray may never set—I have told him
What and how true thou art. He will advance thee.
Some little memory of me will stir him.
I know his noble nature not to let
420 Thy hopeful service perish too. Good Cromwell,
Neglect him not. Make use° now, and provide   *Seize your chance*
For thine own future safety.
CROMWELL [*weeping*]   O, my lord,
Must I then leave you? Must I needs forgo°   *renounce*

---

3. Perhaps the pillars carried during Wolsey's triumphal entrance in 2.4.
4. The Lord Chancellor's duties included guardianship of all children under twenty-one, particularly orphans.

Henry had More beheaded in 1535 for his Catholicism.
5. In 1533; Cranmer was beheaded by Henry's oldest daughter, Queen Mary, in 1556 for his Protestantism.

So good, so noble, and so true a master?
425 Bear witness, all that have not hearts of iron,
With what a sorrow Cromwell leaves his lord.
The King shall have my service, but my prayers
For ever and for ever shall be yours.
CARDINAL WOLSEY [*weeping*]   Cromwell, I did not think to shed a tear
430 In all my miseries, but thou hast forced me,
Out of thy honest truth, to play the woman.°   *to weep*
Let's dry our eyes, and thus far hear me, Cromwell,
And when I am forgotten, as I shall be,
And sleep in dull cold marble, where no mention
435 Of me more must be heard of, say I taught thee—
Say Wolsey, that once trod the ways of glory,
And sounded° all the depths and shoals of honour,   *fathomed*
Found thee a way, out of his wreck,° to rise in,   *shipwreck*
A sure and safe one, though thy master missed it.
440 Mark but my fall, and that that ruined me.
Cromwell, I charge thee, fling away ambition.[6]
By that sin fell the angels. How can man, then,
The image of his maker, hope to win° by it?   *profit*
Love thyself last. Cherish those hearts that hate thee.
445 Corruption wins not more than honesty.
Still° in thy right hand carry gentle peace   *Ever*
To silence envious tongues. Be just, and fear not.
Let all the ends thou aim'st at be thy country's,
Thy God's, and truth's. Then if thou fall'st, O Cromwell,
450 Thou fall'st a blessèd martyr.[7]
Serve the King. And prithee, lead me in—
There take an inventory of all I have:
To the last penny 'tis the King's. My robe,
And my integrity to heaven, is all
455 I dare now call mine own. O Cromwell, Cromwell,
Had I but served my God with half the zeal
I served my King, He would not in mine age
Have left me naked° to mine enemies.   *utterly exposed*
CROMWELL   Good sir, have patience.
CARDINAL WOLSEY   So I have. Farewell
460 The hopes of court; my hopes in heaven do dwell.   *Exeunt*

4.1
Enter [the] two GENTLEMEN *meeting one another. [The
first holds a paper]*
FIRST GENTLEMAN   You're well met once again.[1]
SECOND GENTLEMAN   So are you.
FIRST GENTLEMAN   You come to take your stand here and behold
The Lady Anne pass from her coronation?
SECOND GENTLEMAN   'Tis all my business. At our last encounter
5 The Duke of Buckingham came from his trial.
FIRST GENTLEMAN   'Tis very true. But that time offered sorrow,
This, general joy.
SECOND GENTLEMAN   'Tis well. The citizens,

6. Cromwell did not take Wolsey's advice; Henry had him beheaded in 1540 for treason and heresy after an even more rapid rise and fall than Wolsey's.
7. As Cromwell was sometimes thought to be in Shake-
speare's time.
4.1 Location: A street in Westminster.
1. See 2.1.

I am sure, have shown at full their royal minds°—   *royalist allegiance*
As, let 'em have their rights, they are ever forward²—
10   In celebration of this day with shows,
Pageants, and sights of honour.
FIRST GENTLEMAN   Never greater,
Nor, I'll assure you, better taken,° sir.   *received*
SECOND GENTLEMAN   May I be bold to ask what that contains,
That paper in your hand?
FIRST GENTLEMAN   Yes, 'tis the list
15   Of those that claim their offices this day
By custom of the coronation.
The Duke of Suffolk is the first, and claims
To be High Steward; next, the Duke of Norfolk,
He to be Earl Marshal. You may read the rest.
           [*He gives him the paper*]
20 SECOND GENTLEMAN   I thank you, sir. Had I not known those customs,
I should have been beholden to your paper.
But I beseech you, what's become of Katherine,
The Princess Dowager? How goes her business?
FIRST GENTLEMAN   That I can tell you too. The Archbishop
25   Of Canterbury, accompanied with other
Learnèd and reverend fathers of his order,
Held a late° court at Dunstable, six miles off   *Recently held a*
From Ampthill, where the Princess lay;° to which   *resided*
She was often cited° by them, but appeared not.   *summoned*
30   And, to be short, for not appearance, and
The King's late scruple, by the main assent°   *consensus*
Of all these learnèd men, she was divorced,
And the late marriage made of none effect,°   *null*
Since which she was removed to Kimbolton,
Where she remains now sick.
35 SECOND GENTLEMAN   Alas, good lady!
         [*Flourish of trumpets within*]
The trumpets sound. Stand close.° The Queen is coming.   *aside*
         [*Enter the coronation procession, which*] *pass*[*es*] *over*
         the stage in order and state. Hautboys [*within,*
         play during the procession]

         THE ORDER OF THE CORONATION

    1. [*First, enter*] *trumpet*[*ers, who play*] *a lively flourish.*
    2. Then, [*enter*] *two judges.*
    3. [*Then, enter the*] LORD CHANCELLOR, *with* [*both the*]
    purse [*containing the great seal*] *and* [*the*] *mace* [*borne*]
    before him.
    4. [*Then, enter*] *choristers singing;* [*with them,*]
    music[*ians playing.*]
    5. [*Then, enter the Lord*] *Mayor of London bearing the*
    mace, [*followed by*] *Garter* [*King-of-Arms° wearing*] *his*   *chief herald*
    coat of arms and a gilt copper crown.
    6. [*Then, enter*] *Marquis Dorset bearing a sceptre of*
    gold, [*and wearing,*] *on his head, a demi-coronal of gold*
    [*and, about his neck, a collar of esses*].³ *With him*

---

2. As, to give them their due, they are always eager to demonstrate.

3. Heavy gold chain made of S-shaped links worn around the neck by men of high office.

[*enter*] *the Earl of* SURREY *bearing the rod of silver with
the dove, crowned with an earl's coronet,* [*and also wearing a*] *collar of esses.*
7. [*Next, enter the*] *Duke of* SUFFOLK *as High Steward,
in his robe of estate,* [*with*] *his coronet on his head,*
[*and*] *bearing a long white wand. With him,* [*enter*] *the
Duke of* NORFOLK *with the rod of marshalship* [*and*] *a
coronet on his head.* [*Each wears a*] *collar of esses.*
8. [*Then,*] *under a canopy borne by four* [*barons*] *of the
Cinque Ports,*[4] [*enter*] ANNE, *the* [*new*] *Queen, in her
robe. Her hair,* [*which hangs loose,*°] *richly adorned*   *(a bridal custom)*
with pearl. [*She wears a*] *crown.* [*Accompanying*] *her on*
[*either*] *side* [*are*] *the Bishops of London and Winchester.*
9. [*Next, enter*] *the old Duchess of Norfolk, in a coronal
of gold wrought with flowers, bearing the Queen's train.*
10. [*Finally, enter*] *certain ladies or countesses, with
plain circlets of gold without flowers.*
[*The two* GENTLEMEN *comment on the procession as it
passes over the stage*]

SECOND GENTLEMAN A royal train,° believe me. These I know.   *procession*
  Who's that that bears the sceptre?
FIRST GENTLEMAN   Marquis Dorset.
  And that, the Earl of Surrey with the rod.
40 SECOND GENTLEMAN A bold brave gentleman. That should be
  The Duke of Suffolk?
FIRST GENTLEMAN   'Tis the same: High Steward.
SECOND GENTLEMAN And that, my lord of Norfolk?
FIRST GENTLEMAN   Yes.
SECOND GENTLEMAN [*seeing* ANNE]   Heaven bless thee!
  Thou hast the sweetest face I ever looked on.
  Sir, as I have a soul, she is an angel.
45 Our King has all the Indies[5] in his arms,
  And more, and richer, when he strains° that lady.   *embraces*
  I cannot blame his conscience.
FIRST GENTLEMAN   They that bear
  The cloth of honour° over her are four barons   *canopy*
  Of the Cinque Ports.
50 SECOND GENTLEMAN Those men are happy,
  And so are all° are near her.   *all who*
  I take it she that carries up the train
  Is that old noble lady, Duchess of Norfolk.
FIRST GENTLEMAN It is. And all the rest are countesses.
55 SECOND GENTLEMAN Their coronets say so. These are stars indeed—
FIRST GENTLEMAN And sometimes falling ones.°   *meteors; (sexual)*
SECOND GENTLEMAN   No more of that.
     Exit [*the last of the procession,*] *and then
      a great flourish of trumpets* [*within*]
    Enter a third GENTLEMAN [*in a sweat*]
FIRST GENTLEMAN God save you, sir. Where have you been broiling?°   *overheating*
THIRD GENTLEMAN Among the crowd i'th' Abbey, where a finger

---

4. By traditional prerogative, the barons of the Cinque
Ports (Hastings, Sandwich, Dover, Romney, and Hythe
on the southeast coast of England) carried a canopy over
the sovereign at state occasions.
5. The East and West Indies were considered sources of
great wealth. See 1.1.21.

60	Could not be wedged in more. I am stifled With the mere rankness° of their joy.	*exuberance; odor*
	SECOND GENTLEMAN You saw the ceremony?	
	THIRD GENTLEMAN That I did.	
	FIRST GENTLEMAN How was it?	
	THIRD GENTLEMAN Well worth the seeing.	
	SECOND GENTLEMAN Good sir, speak° it to us.	*describe*
	THIRD GENTLEMAN As well as I am able. The rich stream	
65	Of lords and ladies, having brought the Queen	
	To a prepared place in the choir, fell off°	*drew back*
	A distance from her, while her grace sat down	
	To rest a while—some half an hour or so—	
	In a rich chair of state, opposing° freely	*displaying*
70	The beauty of her person to the people.	
	Believe me, sir, she is the goodliest° woman	*fairest*
	That ever lay by man; which when the people	
	Had the full view of, such a noise arose	
	As the shrouds° make at sea in a stiff tempest,	*ship's rigging*
75	As loud and to as many tunes. Hats, cloaks—	
	Doublets,° I think—flew up, and had their faces	*Short jackets*
	Been loose, this day they had been lost. Such joy	
	I never saw before. Great-bellied women,	
	That had not half a week to go, like rams°	*battering rams*
80	In the old time of war, would shake the press,°	*crowd*
	And make 'em reel before 'em. No man living	
	Could say 'This is my wife' there, all were woven	
	So strangely in one piece.	
	SECOND GENTLEMAN But what followed?	
	THIRD GENTLEMAN At length her grace rose, and with modest paces	
85	Came to the altar, where she kneeled, and saint-like	
	Cast her fair eyes to heaven, and prayed devoutly,	
	Then rose again, and bowed her to the people,	
	When by the Archbishop of Canterbury	
	She had all the royal makings° of a queen,	*essential trappings*
90	As holy oil, Edward Confessor's crown,	
	The rod and bird of peace, and all such emblems	
	Laid nobly on her. Which performed, the choir,	
	With the choicest music° of the kingdom,	*musicians*
	Together sung *Te Deum.*⁶ So she parted,°	*departed*
95	And with the same full state° paced back again	*ceremony*
	To York Place, where the feast is held.	
	FIRST GENTLEMAN Sir,	
	You must no more call it York Place—that's past,	
	For since the Cardinal fell, that title's lost.	
	'Tis now the King's, and called Whitehall.	
	THIRD GENTLEMAN I know it,	
100	But 'tis so lately altered that the old name	
	Is fresh about me.	
	SECOND GENTLEMAN What two reverend bishops	
	Were those that went on each side of the Queen?	
	THIRD GENTLEMAN Stokesley and Gardiner, the one of Winchester—	

---

6. Hymn of praise and thanksgiving beginning "*Te Deum laudamus,*" "We praise thee, O Lord."

Newly preferred° from the King's secretary—   *promoted*
The other London.[7]
105 SECOND GENTLEMAN   He of Winchester
Is held no great good lover of the Archbishop's,
The virtuous Cranmer.
THIRD GENTLEMAN   All the land knows that.
However, yet there is no great breach. When it comes,
Cranmer will find a friend will not° shrink from him.   *who will not*
SECOND GENTLEMAN   Who may that be, I pray you?
110 THIRD GENTLEMAN   Thomas Cromwell,
A man in much esteem with th' King, and truly
A worthy friend. The King has made him
Master o'th' Jewel House,
And one already of the Privy Council.
SECOND GENTLEMAN   He will deserve more.
115 THIRD GENTLEMAN   Yes, without all doubt.
Come, gentlemen, ye shall go my way,
Which is to th' court, and there ye shall be my guests.
Something° I can command. As I walk thither   *Some influence*
I'll tell ye more.
FIRST *and* SECOND GENTLEMEN   You may command us, sir.
                                                                    Exeunt

4.2

[*Three chairs.*] *Enter* KATHERINE *Dowager, sick, led*
between GRIFFITH *her gentleman usher, and* PATIENCE
her woman
GRIFFITH   How does your grace?
KATHERINE   O Griffith, sick to death.
My legs, like loaden° branches, bow to th' earth,   *heavily laden*
Willing to leave their burden. Reach a chair.
[*A chair is brought to her. She sits*]
So now, methinks, I feel a little ease.
5   Didst thou not tell me, Griffith, as thou led'st me,
That the great child of honour,° Cardinal Wolsey,   *(ironic)*
Was dead?
GRIFFITH   Yes, madam, but I think your grace,
Out of the pain you suffered, gave no ear to't.
KATHERINE   Prithee, good Griffith, tell me how he died.
10   If well, he stepped before me happily°   *aptly*
For my example.
GRIFFITH   Well, the voice° goes, madam.   *talk*
For after the stout Earl Northumberland
Arrested him at York, and brought him forward,
As a man sorely tainted,° to his answer,°   *disgraced / hearing*
15   He fell sick, suddenly, and grew so ill
He could not sit his mule.
KATHERINE   Alas, poor man.
GRIFFITH   At last, with easy roads,° he came to Leicester,   *stages of a journey*
Lodged in the abbey, where the reverend abbot,
With all his convent,° honourably received him,   *monastery*

---

7. Stokesley was Bishop of London; already secretary to the King, Gardiner also became Bishop of Winchester following Wolsey's demise.
4.2 Location: Katherine's apartments in Kimbolton.

20   To whom he gave these words: 'O father abbot,
An old man broken with the storms of state
Is come to lay his weary bones among ye.
Give him a little earth,° for charity.'   *a resting place*
So went to bed, where eagerly his sickness
25   Pursued him still, and three nights after this,
About the hour of eight, which he himself
Foretold should be his last, full of repentance,
Continual meditations, tears, and sorrows,
He gave his honours to the world again,
30   His blessèd part° to heaven, and slept in peace.   *soul*
KATHERINE   So may he rest, his faults lie gently on him.
Yet thus far, Griffith, give me leave to speak° him,   *describe*
And yet with charity. He was a man
Of an unbounded stomach,° ever ranking   *ambition*
35   Himself with princes; one that by suggestion°   *underhanded dealing*
Tied° all the kingdom. Simony[1] was fair play.   *Shackled*
His own opinion was his law. I'th' presence°   *King's chamber*
He would say untruths, and be ever double°   *duplicitious*
Both in his words and meaning. He was never,
40   But where he meant to ruin, pitiful.°   *merciful*
His promises were, as he then was, mighty;
But his performance, as he is now, nothing.
Of his own body he was ill,° and gave   *sexually immoral*
The clergy ill example.
GRIFFITH   Noble madam,
45   Men's evil manners live in brass, their virtues
We write in water.[2] May it please your highness
To hear me speak his good now?
KATHERINE   Yes, good Griffith,
I were malicious else.
GRIFFITH   This cardinal,
Though from an humble stock, undoubtedly
50   Was fashioned to much honour. From his cradle
He was a scholar, and a ripe and good one,
Exceeding wise, fair-spoken, and persuading;°   *persuasive*
Lofty and sour to them that loved him not,
But to those men that sought him,° sweet as summer.   *befriended him*
55   And though he were unsatisfied° in getting°—   *insatiable / (riches)*
Which was a sin—yet in bestowing, madam,
He was most princely: ever witness for him
Those twins of learning that he raised° in you,   *set up*
Ipswich and Oxford[3]—one of which fell with him,
60   Unwilling to outlive the good that did it;
The other, though unfinished, yet so famous,
So excellent in art,° and still so rising,   *scholarship*
That Christendom shall ever speak his virtue.
His overthrow heaped happiness upon him,
65   For then, and not till then, he felt° himself,   *recognized*
And found the blessèdness of being little.°   *humble*

---

1. Trading, for money or favors, in ecclesiastical offices.
2. *Men's . . . water:* Evil deeds are long remembered, good ones soon forgotten (proverbial).
3. Wolsey founded colleges at Ipswich and Oxford; the latter survives as Christ Church.

And to add greater honours to his age
Than man could give him, he died fearing God.
KATHERINE   After my death I wish no other herald,
70   No other speaker of my living actions
To keep mine honour from corruption
But such an honest chronicler as Griffith.
Whom I most hated living,° thou hast made me,   *while alive*
With thy religious truth and modesty,°   *equanimity*
75   Now in his ashes honour. Peace be with him.
[*To her woman*] Patience, be near me still, and set me lower.
I have not long to trouble thee. Good Griffith,
Cause the musicians play me that sad note°   *melody*
I named my knell, whilst I sit meditating
80   On that celestial harmony I go to.[4]
Sad and solemn music. [KATHERINE *sleeps*]
GRIFFITH [*to the woman*]   She is asleep. Good wench, let's sit down quiet
For fear we wake her. Softly, gentle Patience.
[*They sit*]

THE VISION

*Enter, solemnly tripping one after another, six person-
ages clad in white robes, wearing on their heads garlands of bays, and golden visors on their faces.[5] [They
carry] branches of bays or palm in their hands. They first
congé° unto [KATHERINE], then dance; and, at certain   bow
changes,° the first two hold a spare garland over her   dance movements
head at which the other four make reverent curtsies.
Then the two that held the garland deliver the same to
the other next two, who observe the same order in their
changes and holding the garland over her head. Which
done, they deliver the same garland to the last two who
likewise observe the same order. At which, as it were by
inspiration, she makes in her sleep signs of rejoicing, and
holdeth up her hands to heaven. And so in their dancing
vanish, carrying the garland with them. The music continues*
KATHERINE [*waking*]   Spirits of peace, where are ye? Are ye all gone,
And leave me here in wretchedness behind ye?
[GRIFFITH *and* PATIENCE *rise and come forward*]
GRIFFITH   Madam, we are here.
85   KATHERINE   It is not you I call for.
Saw ye none enter since I slept?
GRIFFITH   None, madam.
KATHERINE   No? Saw you not even now a blessèd troop
Invite me to a banquet, whose bright faces
Cast thousand beams upon me, like the sun?
90   They promised me eternal happiness,
And brought me garlands, Griffith, which I feel
I am not worthy yet to wear. I shall,
Assuredly.

4. After death, the soul supposedly could hear the music of the spheres (the heavenly bodies) as they revolved around the earth.

5. White to signify purity; bay leaves ("bays") to indicate triumph or joy; golden masks ("visors") perhaps to suggest they are spirits.

GRIFFITH   I am most joyful, madam, such good dreams
    Possess your fancy.°   *Fill your imagination*
95 KATHERINE   Bid the music° leave.   *musicians*
    They are harsh and heavy° to me.   *tiresome*
        Music ceases
    PATIENCE [*to* GRIFFITH]   Do you note
    How much her grace is altered on the sudden?
    How long her face is drawn? How pale she looks,
    And of an earthy colour? Mark her eyes?
    GRIFFITH   She is going, wench. Pray, pray.
100 PATIENCE   Heaven comfort her.
        Enter a MESSENGER
    MESSENGER [*to* KATHERINE]
    An't like° your grace—   *If it please*
    KATHERINE   You are a saucy fellow—
    Deserve we no more reverence?
    GRIFFITH [*to the* MESSENGER]   You are to blame,
    Knowing she will not lose her wonted° greatness,   *forgo her usual*
    To use so rude behaviour. Go to, kneel.
    MESSENGER [*kneeling before* KATHERINE]   I humbly do entreat
105   your highness' pardon.
    My haste made me unmannerly. There is staying°   *waiting*
    A gentleman sent from the King to see you.
    KATHERINE   Admit him entrance, Griffith. But this fellow
    Let me ne'er see again.   *Exit* MESSENGER
        Enter Lord CAPUTIUS [*ushered by* GRIFFITH]
                    If my sight fail not,
110 You should be lord ambassador from the Emperor,°   *Charles V*
    My royal nephew, and your name Caputius.
    CAPUTIUS   Madam, the same, [*bowing*] your servant.
    KATHERINE   O, my lord,
    The times and titles now are altered strangely
    With me since first you knew me. But I pray you,
    What is your pleasure with me?
115 CAPUTIUS   Noble lady,
    First mine own service to your grace; the next,
    The King's request that I would visit you,
    Who grieves much for your weakness, and by me
    Sends you his princely commendations,°   *compliments*
120 And heartily entreats you take good comfort.
    KATHERINE   O, my good lord, that comfort comes too late,
    'Tis like a pardon after execution.
    That gentle physic,° given in time, had cured me;   *medicine*
    But now I am past all comforts here but prayers.
    How does his highness?
125 CAPUTIUS   Madam, in good health.
    KATHERINE   So may he ever do, and ever flourish
    When I shall dwell with worms, and my poor name
    Banished the kingdom. [*To her woman*] Patience, is that letter
    I caused you write yet sent away?
    PATIENCE   No, madam.
130 KATHERINE [*to* CAPUTIUS]   Sir, I most humbly pray you to deliver
    This to my lord the King.
        [*The letter is given to* CAPUTIUS]

CAPUTIUS   Most willing,° madam.   *willingly*
KATHERINE   In which I have commended to his goodness
          The model° of our chaste loves, his young daughter[6]—   *image*
          The dews of heaven fall thick in blessings on her—
135   Beseeching him to give her virtuous breeding.°   *raise her virtuously*
          She is young, and of a noble modest nature.
          I hope she will deserve well—and a little
          To love her for her mother's sake, that loved him,
          Heaven knows how dearly. My next poor petition
140   Is that his noble grace would have some pity
          Upon my wretched women, that so long
          Have followed both my fortunes° faithfully;   *(good and bad)*
          Of which there is not one, I dare avow—
          And now I should not lie[7]—but will deserve,
145   For virtue and true beauty of the soul,
          For honesty° and decent carriage,°   *chastity / conduct*
          A right good husband. Let him be a noble,
          And sure those men are happy that shall have 'em.
          The last is for my men—they are the poorest,
150   But poverty could never draw 'em from me—
          That they may have their wages duly paid 'em,
          And something over to remember me by.
          If heaven had pleased to have given me longer life,
          And able° means, we had not parted thus.   *sufficient*
155   These are the whole contents; and, good my lord,
          By that you love the dearest in this world,
          As you wish Christian peace to souls departed,
          Stand these poor people's friend and urge the King
          To do me this last rite.
CAPUTIUS   By heaven I will,
160   Or let me lose the fashion of a man.°   *forfeit my humanity*
KATHERINE   I thank you, honest lord. Remember me
          In all humility unto his highness.
          Say his long trouble now is passing
          Out of this world. Tell him, in death I blessed him,
165   For so I will. Mine eyes grow dim. Farewell,
          My lord. Griffith, farewell.
          [*To her woman*]   Nay, Patience,
          You must not leave me yet. I must to bed.
          Call in more women. When I am dead, good wench,
          Let me be used° with honour. Strew me over   *treated*
170   With maiden° flowers, that all the world may know   *(signifying chastity)*
          I was a chaste wife to my grave. Embalm me,
          Then lay me forth.° Although unqueened, yet like   *prepare me for burial*
          A queen and daughter to a king inter me.
          I can° no more.   *can say or do*
          Exeunt [CAPUTIUS *and* GRIFFITH *at one door;*
          PATIENCE] *leading* KATHERINE [*at another*]

6. Mary was Katherine and Henry's only child who survived infancy (see 2.4.35 and note). She was Queen for five years (1553–58) before Elizabeth, her half sister.

7. Now, on the point of death, I would not (ought not to) lie. It was generally thought that people spoke truth on their deathbeds.

5.1

Enter [at one door] GARDINER, *Bishop of Winchester;*
before him, a PAGE *with a torch*

GARDINER   It's one o'clock, boy, is't not?

PAGE   It hath struck.

GARDINER   These should be hours for necessities,
Not for delights; times to repair° our nature   *restore*
With comforting repose, and not for us
To waste these times.

[Enter at another door] Sir Thomas LOVELL *[meeting*
them]

5   Good hour of night, Sir Thomas!
Whither so late?

LOVELL   Came you from the King, my lord?

GARDINER   I did, Sir Thomas, and left him at primero°   *a card game*
With the Duke of Suffolk.

LOVELL   I must to him too,
Before he go to bed. I'll take my leave.

10   GARDINER   Not yet, Sir Thomas Lovell—what's the matter?
It seems you are in haste. An if there be
No great offence° belongs to't, give your friend   *inappropriateness*
Some touch° of your late business. Affairs that walk,   *hint*
As they say spirits do, at midnight, have
15   In them a wilder nature than the business
That seeks dispatch° by day.   *to be done*

LOVELL   My lord, I love you,
And durst commend° a secret to your ear   *entrust*
Much weightier than this work.° The Queen's in labour—   *my affairs*
They say in great extremity—and feared°   *it is feared that*
She'll with the labour end.

20   GARDINER   The fruit she goes with
I pray for heartily, that it may find
Good time,° and live. But, for the stock,° Sir Thomas,   *Fortune / trunk (Anne)*
I wish it grubbed up° now.   *rooted out*

LOVELL   Methinks I could
Cry the amen,° and yet my conscience says   *Agree*
25   She's a good creature and, sweet lady, does
Deserve our better wishes.

GARDINER   But sir, sir,
Hear me, Sir Thomas. You're a gentleman
Of mine own way.¹ I know you wise, religious.
And let me tell you, it will ne'er be well—
30   'Twill not, Sir Thomas Lovell, take't of me—
Till Cranmer, Cromwell—her two hands—and she,
Sleep in their graves.

LOVELL   Now, sir, you speak of two
The most remarked° i'th' kingdom. As for Cromwell,   *regarded*
Beside that of the Jewel House is made Master
35   O'th' Rolls and the King's secretary. Further, sir,
Stands in the gap and trade° of more preferments   *open road*
With which the time will load him. Th'Archbishop

5.1 Location: London, a gallery at court.
1. Of my religious persuasion (Catholicism, as opposed to Anne's Lutheranism).

Is the King's hand and tongue, and who dare speak
One syllable against him?
GARDINER   Yes, yes, Sir Thomas—
40   There are that dare, and I myself have ventured
To speak my mind of him, and, indeed, this day,
Sir—I may tell it you, I think—I have
Incensed° the lords o'th' Council that he is—   *Angered*
For so I know he is, they know he is—
45   A most arch heretic, a pestilence
That does infect the land; with which they, moved,°   *angered*
Have broken with° the King, who hath so far   *revealed to*
Given ear to our complaint, of his great grace
And princely care, foreseeing those fell mischiefs
50   Our reasons laid before him, hath° commanded   *that he has*
Tomorrow morning to the Council board
He be convented.° He's a rank° weed, Sir Thomas,   *summoned / rotten*
And we must root him out. From your affairs
I hinder you too long. Good night, Sir Thomas.
55 LOVELL   Many good nights, my lord; I rest° your servant.   *remain*
           Exeunt GARDINER *and* PAGE [*at one door*]
       Enter KING [HENRY] *and* SUFFOLK [*at another door*]
KING HENRY [*to* SUFFOLK]   Charles, I will play no more tonight.
My mind's not on't. You are too hard° for me.   *skillful*
SUFFOLK   Sir, I did never win of you before.
KING HENRY   But little, Charles,
60   Nor shall not when my fancy's° on my play.   *attention is*
Now, Lovell, from the Queen what is the news?
LOVELL   I could not personally deliver to her
What you commanded me, but by her woman
I sent your message, who returned her thanks
65   In the great'st humbleness, and desired your highness
Most heartily to pray for her.
KING HENRY   What sayst thou? Ha?
To pray for her? What, is she crying out?
LOVELL   So said her woman, and that her suffrance° made   *suffering*
Almost each pang a death.
KING HENRY   Alas, good lady.
70 SUFFOLK   God safely quit° her of her burden, and   *release*
With gentle travail, to the gladding° of   *making joyful*
Your highness with an heir.
KING HENRY   'Tis midnight, Charles.
Prithee to bed, and in thy prayers remember
Th'estate° of my poor queen. Leave me alone,   *condition*
75   For I must think of that which company
Would not be friendly to.[2]
SUFFOLK   I wish your highness
A quiet night, and my good mistress will°   *I will*
Remember in my prayers.
KING HENRY   Charles, good night. *Exit* SUFFOLK
       Enter Sir Anthony DENNY
Well, sir, what follows?
80 DENNY   Sir, I have brought my lord the Archbishop,
As you commanded me.

---

2. *which . . . to:* which requires privacy.

876 ◆ All Is True 5.1

KING HENRY   Ha, Canterbury?
DENNY   Ay, my good lord.
KING HENRY   'Tis true—where is he, Denny?
DENNY   He attends your highness' pleasure.
KING HENRY   Bring him to us.
                                        [*Exit* DENNY]
LOVELL [*aside*]   This is about that which the Bishop° spake.   *Gardiner*
85   I am happily° come hither.   *fortunately*
              Enter CRANMER [*the Archbishop, ushered by*] DENNY
KING HENRY [*to* LOVELL *and* DENNY]   Avoid° the gallery.   *Quit*
              [DENNY *begins to depart.*] LOVELL *seems to stay*
Ha? I have said. Be gone.
What?   *Exeunt* LOVELL *and* DENNY
CRANMER [*aside*]   I am fearful. Wherefore° frowns he thus?   *Why*
'Tis his aspect° of terror. All's not well.   *countenance*
90   KING HENRY   How now, my lord? You do desire to know
Wherefore I sent for you.
CRANMER [*kneeling*]   It is my duty
T'attend your highness' pleasure.
KING HENRY   Pray you, arise,
My good and gracious Lord of Canterbury.
Come, you and I must walk a turn together.
95   I have news to tell you. Come, come—give me your hand.
              [CRANMER *rises. They walk*]
Ah, my good lord, I grieve at what I speak,
And am right sorry to repeat what follows.
I have, and most unwillingly, of late
Heard many grievous°—I do say, my lord,   *serious*
100 Grievous—complaints of you, which, being considered,
Have moved us and our Council that you shall
This morning come before us, where I know
You cannot with such freedom purge° yourself   *with ease clear*
But that, till further trial in those charges
105 Which will require your answer, you must take
Your patience to you,³ and be well contented
To make your house our Tower. You a brother of us,°   *a fellow-councillor*
It fits we thus proceed, or else no witness
Would come against you.
CRANMER [*kneeling*]   I humbly thank your highness,
110 And am right glad to catch this good occasion
Most throughly to be winnowed, where my chaff
And corn shall fly asunder.⁴ For I know
There's none stands under° more calumnious tongues   *is subject to*
Than I myself, poor man.
KING HENRY   Stand up, good Canterbury.
115 Thy truth and thy integrity is rooted
In us, thy friend. Give me thy hand. Stand up.
Prithee, let's walk.
              [CRANMER *rises. They walk*]
                    Now, by my halidom,°   *by our Lady*
What manner of man are you? My lord, I looked°   *predicted*

---

3. *must . . . you:* must be patient.
4. *And am . . . asunder:* And I am glad to have the occasion thoroughly to see the bad ("chaff") separated from

the good ("corn," or wheat) in my character. See Matthew 3:12 and Luke 3:17.

You would have given me your petition that
120 I should have ta'en some pains to bring together
Yourself and your accusers, and to have heard you
Without indurance° further.   *imprisonment*
CRANMER   Most dread liege,
The good° I stand on is my truth and honesty.   *virtue*
If they shall fail, I with mine enemies
125 Will triumph o'er my person, which I weigh not,
Being of those virtues vacant.⁵ I fear nothing°   *not at all*
What can be said against me.
KING HENRY   Know you not
How your state stands i'th' world, with the whole world?
Your enemies are many, and not small;° their practices   *insignificant*
130 Must bear the same proportion, and not ever
The justice and the truth o'th' question carries
The dew o'th' verdict with it.⁶ At what ease°   *How easily*
Might corrupt minds procure knaves as corrupt
To swear against you? Such things have been done.
135 You are potently° opposed, and with a malice   *powerfully*
Of as great size. Ween you of° better luck,   *Do you anticipate*
I mean in perjured witness,° than your master,°   *evidence / Christ*
Whose minister you are, whiles here he lived
Upon this naughty° earth? Go to, go to.   *wicked*
140 You take a precipice for no leap of danger,
And woo your own destruction.
CRANMER   God and your majesty
Protect mine innocence, or I fall into
The trap is° laid for me.   *that is*
KING HENRY   Be of good cheer.
They shall no more prevail than we give way to.°   *let them*
145 Keep comfort to you, and this morning see
You do appear before them. If they shall chance,
In charging you with matters, to commit° you,   *imprison*
The best persuasions to the contrary
Fail not to use, and with what vehemency
150 Th'occasion shall instruct you. If entreaties
Will render you no remedy, [*giving his ring*] this ring
Deliver them, and your appeal to us
There make before them.
          [CRANMER *weeps*]
                    Look, the good man weeps.
He's honest, on mine honour. God's blest mother,
155 I swear he is true-hearted, and a soul
None better in my kingdom. Get you gone,
And do as I have bid you.   *Exit* CRANMER
                    He has strangled
His language in his tears.
          Enter [*the*] OLD LADY
LOVELL (*within*)   Come back! What mean you?
          [*Enter* LOVELL, *following her*]
OLD LADY   I'll not come back. The tidings that I bring

5. *If . . . vacant*: If I lack truth and honesty, I will agree
with my enemies in condemning myself, whom I do not
value in the absence of truth and honesty.

6. *their . . . it*: their schemes are equally numerous and
powerful, and justice and truth do not always prevail.

160 Will make my boldness manners.° [*To the* KING] Now good angels   *into manners*
    Fly o'er thy royal head, and shade thy person
    Under their blessèd wings.
KING HENRY   Now by thy looks
    I guess thy message. Is the Queen delivered?
    Say, 'Ay, and of a boy.'
OLD LADY   Ay, ay, my liege,
165 And of a lovely boy. The God of heaven
    Both now and ever bless her! 'Tis a girl°   *Anne; Elizabeth*
    Promises boys hereafter. Sir, your queen
    Desires your visitation, and° to be   *and for you*
    Acquainted with this stranger. 'Tis as like you
    As cherry is to cherry.
KING HENRY   Lovell—
170 LOVELL   Sir?
KING HENRY   Give her an hundred marks.° I'll to the Queen.   *roughly 65 pounds*
                                                       Exit
OLD LADY   An hundred marks? By this light, I'll ha' more.
    An ordinary groom is for° such payment.   *deserves*
    I will have more, or scold it out of him.
175 Said I for this the girl was like to him? I'll
    Have more, or else unsay't; and now, while 'tis hot,
    I'll put it to the issue.   *Exeunt*

5.2

Enter [pursuivants,° pages, footboys, and grooms. Then   *messengers*
enter] CRANMER, *Archbishop of Canterbury*
CRANMER   I hope I am not too late, and yet the gentleman
    That was sent to me from the council prayed me
    To make great haste. All fast?° What means this? [*Calling at*   *The doors closed*
       the door] Ho!
    Who waits there?
       Enter [a DOOR]KEEPER
                    Sure you know me?
DOORKEEPER   Yes, my lord,
    But yet I cannot help you.
5 CRANMER   Why?
       Enter Doctor BUTTS [*passing over the stage*]
DOORKEEPER   Your grace must wait till you be called for.
CRANMER   So.
BUTTS [*aside*]   This is a piece of malice. I am glad
    I came this way so happily.° The King   *fortunately*
    Shall understand it presently.°   *Exit*   *immediately*
CRANMER [*aside*]   'Tis Butts,
10 The King's physician. As he passed along
    How earnestly he cast his eyes upon me!
    Pray heaven he sound° not my disgrace. For certain   *fathom; announce*
    This is of purpose laid° by some that hate me—   *carried out*
    God turn their hearts, I never sought their malice—
15 To quench° mine honour. They would shame to make me   *destroy*
    Wait else at door, a fellow Councillor,
    'Mong boys, grooms, and lackeys. But their pleasures
    Must be fulfilled, and I attend with patience.

5.2 Location: Anteroom and council chamber at court.

Enter KING [HENRY] *and* [*Doctor*] BUTTS *at a window,*
above

BUTTS I'll show your grace the strangest sight—
KING HENRY   What's that, Butts?

20 BUTTS I think your highness saw this many a day.
KING HENRY Body o'me, where is it?
BUTTS [*pointing at* CRANMER, *below*] There, my lord.
  The high promotion of his grace of Canterbury,
  Who holds his state° at door, 'mongst pursuivants,   *waits with dignity*
  Pages, and footboys.
KING HENRY   Ha? 'Tis he indeed.
25 Is this the honour they do one another?
  'Tis well there's one above 'em¹ yet. I had thought
  They had parted° so much honesty among 'em—   *shared*
  At least good manners—as not thus to suffer
  A man of his place° and so near our favour   *rank*
30 To dance attendance on their lordships' pleasures,
  And at the door, too, like a post with packets!°   *courier with letters*
  By holy Mary, Butts, there's knavery!
  Let 'em alone, and draw the curtain close.
  We shall hear more anon.

[CRANMER *and the* DOORKEEPER *stand to one side.*
Exeunt the lackeys]
[*Above,* BUTTS *partly draws the curtain close. Below,*]² *a*
council table [*is*] *brought in* [*along*] *with chairs and*
stools, and placed under the [*cloth of*] *state. Enter* [*the*]
LORD CHANCELLOR, [*who*] *places himself at the upper*
end of the table, on the left hand, [*leaving*] *a seat void*
above him [*at the table's head*] *as° for Canterbury's seat.*   *as if*
[*The*] *Duke of* SUFFOLK, [*the*] *Duke of* NORFOLK, [*the*
Earl of] SURREY, [*the*] LORD CHAMBERLAIN, [*and*] GARDI-
NER, [*the Bishop of Winchester,*] *seat themselves in order*
on each side [*of the table*]. CROMWELL [*sits*] *at* [*the*]
lower end, [*and acts*] *as secretary*

35 LORD CHANCELLOR [*to* CROMWELL] Speak to the business, master secretary.
  Why are we met in council?
CROMWELL   Please your honours,
  The chief cause concerns his grace of Canterbury.
GARDINER Has he had° knowledge of it?   *been given*
CROMWELL   Yes.
NORFOLK [*to the* DOORKEEPER]   Who waits there?
DOORKEEPER [*coming forward*]
  Without,° my noble lords?   *Outside*
GARDINER   Yes.
DOORKEEPER   My lord Archbishop;
40 And has done half an hour, to know your pleasures.
LORD CHANCELLOR Let him come in.
DOORKEEPER [*to* CRANMER]   Your grace may enter now.
CRANMER *approaches the Council table*
LORD CHANCELLOR My good lord Archbishop, I'm very sorry
  To sit here at this present° and behold   *moment*

1. Both God and King, here implicitly linked.
2. Some editions begin a new scene here. But Cranmer
should be visible throughout, and the King and Butts stay
sequestered in the gallery above the stage until the King's
abrupt entrance.

That chair stand empty, but we all are men
45 In our own natures frail, and capable°   *prone to failings*
Of our flesh; few are angels; out of which frailty
And want° of wisdom, you, that best should teach us,   *lack*
Have misdemeaned yourself, and not a little,
Toward the King first, then his laws, in filling
50 The whole realm, by your teaching and your chaplains'—
For so we are informed—with new opinions,
Diverse and dangerous, which are heresies,
And, not reformed, may prove pernicious.°   *lethal*

GARDINER   Which reformation must be sudden too,
55 My noble lords; for those that tame wild horses
Pace 'em not in their hands to make 'em gentle,[3]
But stop their mouths with stubborn bits and spur 'em
Till they obey the manège.° If we suffer,°   *training / allow*
Out of our easiness° and childish pity   *leniency*
60 To one man's honour, this contagious sickness,
Farewell all physic°—and what follows then?   *remedies*
Commotions, uproars—with a general taint
Of the whole state, as of late days our neighbours,
The upper Germany, can dearly witness,[4]
65 Yet freshly pitied in our memories.

CRANMER   My good lords, hitherto in all the progress
Both of my life and office, I have laboured,
And with no little study,° that my teaching   *effort*
And the strong course of my authority
70 Might go one way, and safely; and the end
Was ever to do well. Nor is there living—
I speak it with a single° heart, my lords—   *pure*
A man that more detests, more stirs against,°   *actively resists*
Both in his private conscience and his place,°   *office*
75 Defacers° of a public peace than I do.   *Destroyers*
Pray heaven the King may never find a heart
With less allegiance in it. Men that make
Envy and crooked malice nourishment
Dare bite the best. I do beseech your lordships
80 That, in this case of justice, my accusers,
Be what they will,° may stand forth face to face,   *Whoever they are*
And freely urge against° me.   *openly accuse*

SUFFOLK   Nay, my lord,
That cannot be. You are a Councillor,
And by that virtue° no man dare accuse you.   *by virtue of that*

GARDINER [*to* CRANMER]   My lord, because we have business of
85   more moment,°   *import*
We will be short° with you. 'Tis his highness' pleasure   *brief*
And our consent, for better trial of you,
From hence you be committed to the Tower
Where, being but a private man again,
90 You shall know many dare accuse you boldly,
More than, I fear, you are provided for.°   *anticipate*

CRANMER   Ah, my good lord of Winchester, I thank you.
You are always my good friend. If your will pass,°   *is approved*

3. Do not put them through their paces with only a hand
for restraint.
4. Alluding to Protestant sects in Germany who fo-
mented uprisings in urban centers in the 1520s and 1530s
(the Peasants' War, 1524–26, and perhaps the killing of
the Münster Anabaptists in 1535).

I shall both find your lordship judge and juror,[5]
95   You are so merciful. I see your end°—   *aim*
  'Tis my undoing. Love and meekness, lord,
  Become a churchman better than ambition.
  Win straying souls with modesty again;
  Cast none away. That I shall clear myself,
100   Lay all the weight ye can upon my patience,
  I make as little doubt as you do conscience[6]
  In doing daily wrongs. I could say more,
  But reverence to your calling makes me modest.°   *temperate*
GARDINER   My lord, my lord—you are a sectary,°   *Protestant*
105   That's the plain truth. Your painted gloss discovers,
  To men that understand you, words and weakness.[7]
CROMWELL [*to* GARDINER]   My lord of Winchester, you're a little,
  By your good favour,° too sharp. Men so noble,   *If you'll excuse me*
  However faulty, yet should find° respect   *be offered*
110   For what they have been. 'Tis a cruelty
  To load° a falling man.   *burden further*
GARDINER   Good master secretary,
  I cry your honour mercy.[8] You may worst°   *least justifiably*
  Of all this table say so.
CROMWELL   Why, my lord?
GARDINER   Do not I know you for a favourer
  Of this new sect? Ye are not sound.°   *loyal; orthodox*
115 CROMWELL   Not sound?
GARDINER   Not sound, I say.
CROMWELL   Would you were half so honest!
  Men's prayers then would seek you, not their fears.
GARDINER   I shall remember this bold language.
CROMWELL   Do.
  Remember your bold life, too.
LORD CHANCELLOR   This is too much.
  Forbear, for shame, my lords.
GARDINER   I have done.
120 CROMWELL   And I.
LORD CHANCELLOR [*to* CRANMER]   Then thus for you, my lord. It
      stands agreed,
  I take it, by all voices,° that forthwith   *votes*
  You be conveyed to th' Tower a prisoner,
  There to remain till the King's further pleasure
125   Be known unto us. Are you all agreed, lords?
ALL THE COUNCIL   We are.
CRANMER   Is there no other way of mercy,
  But I must needs to° th' Tower, my lords?   *must go to*
GARDINER   What other
  Would you expect? You are strangely° troublesome.   *extraordinarily*
  Let some o'th' guard be ready there.
      Enter the guard
CRANMER   For me?
  Must I go like a traitor thither?
130 GARDINER [*to the guard*]   Receive° him,   *Take*
  And see him safe i'th' Tower.

---

5. Gardiner would both try (as "judge") and pass judgment (as "juror")—to Cranmer, an injustice.
6. I doubt no more than you act ethically.
7. *Your . . . weakness:* Your false exterior (or, perhaps, your

specious language) exposes, to men who can see through
you, empty words and human frailty.
8. I beg your pardon.

CRANMER   Stay, good my lords.
I have a little yet to say. Look there, my lords—
    [*He shows the King's ring*]
By virtue of that ring I take my cause
Out of the grips° of cruel men, and give it   *clutches*
135   To a most noble judge, the King my master.
LORD CHAMBERLAIN   This is the King's ring.
SURREY   'Tis no counterfeit.
SUFFOLK   'Tis the right ring, by heav'n. I told ye all
When we first put this dangerous stone a-rolling
'Twould fall upon ourselves.
NORFOLK   Do you think, my lords,
140   The King will suffer but the little finger
Of this man to be vexed?
LORD CHAMBERLAIN   'Tis now too certain.
How much more is his life in value with him!°   *esteemed by the King*
Would I were fairly out on't.°   *out of (the plot)*
                    [*Exit* KING *with* BUTTS *above*]
CROMWELL   My mind gave me,°   *I suspected*
In seeking tales and informations
145   Against this man, whose honesty the devil
And his disciples only envy at,°   *covet; despise*
Ye blew the fire that burns ye. Now have at ye!°   *on guard*
     Enter [*below,*] KING [HENRY] *frowning on them.* [*He*]
     takes his seat
GARDINER   Dread sovereign, how much are we bound to heaven
In daily thanks, that gave us such a prince,
150   Not only good and wise, but most religious.
One that in all obedience makes the church
The chief aim of his honour, and, to strengthen
That holy duty, out of dear respect,°   *sincere piety*
His royal self in judgement comes to hear
155   The cause betwixt her° and this great offender.   *(the church)*
KING HENRY   You were ever good at sudden commendations,°   *extempore flattery*
Bishop of Winchester. But know I come not
To hear such flattery now; and in my presence
They are too thin and base to hide offences.
160   To me you cannot reach. You play the spaniel,
And think with wagging of your tongue to win me.
But whatsoe'er thou tak'st me for, I'm sure
Thou hast a cruel nature and a bloody.
[*To* CRANMER] Good man, sit down.
     [CRANMER *takes his seat at the head of the Council*
     table]
                     Now let me see the proudest,
165   He° that dares most, but wag his finger at thee.   *The man*
By all that's holy, he had better starve°   *die*
Than but once think this place becomes thee not.
SURREY   May it please your grace—
KING HENRY   No, sir, it does not please me!
I had thought I had had men of some understanding
170   And wisdom of° my Council, but I find none.   *in*
Was it discretion, lords, to let this man,
This good man—few of you deserve that title—
This honest man, wait like a lousy footboy

At chamber door? And one as great as you are?
175 Why, what a shame was this! Did my commission
Bid ye so far forget yourselves? I gave ye
Power as he was a Councillor to try him,
Not as a groom. There's some of ye, I see,
More out of malice than integrity,
180 Would try him to the utmost, had ye mean;°   *the means*
Which ye shall never have while I live.
LORD CHANCELLOR   Thus far,
My most dread sovereign, may it like° your grace   *please*
To let my tongue excuse all. What was purposed°   *intended*
Concerning his imprisonment was rather—
185 If there be faith in men—meant for his trial
And fair purgation° to the world than malice,   *acquittal of suspicion*
I'm sure, in me.
KING HENRY   Well, well, my lords—respect him.
Take him and use him well, he's worthy of it.
I will say thus much for him—if a prince
190 May be beholden to a subject, I
Am for his love and service so to him.
Make me no more ado, but all embrace him.
Be friends, for shame, my lords. *(To* CRANMER*)* My lord of Canterbury,
I have a suit which you must not deny me:
195 That is a fair young maid that yet wants baptism—
You must be godfather, and answer for her.
CRANMER   The greatest monarch now alive may glory
In such an honour; how may I deserve it,
That am a poor and humble subject to you?
200 KING HENRY   Come, come, my lord—you'd spare your spoons.[9]
You shall have two noble partners with you—the old Duchess
of Norfolk and Lady Marquis Dorset. Will these please you?
[To GARDINER*]* Once more, my lord of Winchester, I charge you
Embrace and love this man.
GARDINER   With a true heart
And brother-love I do it.
       *[*GARDINER *and* CRANMER *embrace]*
205 CRANMER *[weeping]*   And let heaven
Witness how dear I hold this confirmation.
KING HENRY   Good man, those joyful tears show thy true heart.
The common voice,° I see, is verified   *opinion*
Of thee which says thus, 'Do my lord of Canterbury
210 A shrewd turn,° and he's your friend for ever.'   *An act of malice*
Come, lords, we trifle time away. I long
To have this young one made a Christian.
As I have made ye one, lords, one remain—
So I grow stronger, you more honour gain.   *Exeunt*

5.3

Noise and tumult within.° Enter PORTER *[with rushes]*   *offstage*
and his MAN *[with a broken cudgel]*
PORTER *[to those within]*   You'll leave° your noise anon, ye rascals.   *stop*
Do you take

---

9. The King teases Cranmer that he hesitates only because he wants to spare himself the expense of christening

spoons, the customary gift from a godparent to a child.
5.3 Location: The palace yard.

The court for Paris Garden,[1] ye rude slaves?
Leave your gaping.°   *yelling*
ONE (*within*)   Good master porter, I belong to th' larder.°   *serve in the pantry*
5   PORTER   Belong to th' gallows, and be hanged, ye rogue!
Is this a place to roar in?
[*To his* MAN] Fetch me a dozen crab-tree staves, and strong ones,
[*Raising his rushes*] These are but switches to 'em.
[*To those within*]   I'll scratch your heads.
You must be seeing christenings? Do you look
10   For ale and cakes here, you rude rascals?
MAN   Pray, sir, be patient. 'Tis as much impossible,
Unless we sweep 'em from the door with cannons,
To scatter 'em as 'tis to make 'em sleep
On May-day morning[2]—which will never be.
15   We may as well push against Paul's° as stir 'em.   *St. Paul's Cathedral*
PORTER   How got they in, and be hanged?
MAN   Alas, I know not. How gets the tide in?
As much as one sound cudgel° of four foot—   *club*
[*He raises his cudgel*]
You see the poor remainder°—could distribute,   *what's left of it*
I made no spare,° sir.   *spared no one*
20   PORTER   You did nothing, sir.
MAN   I am not Samson, nor Sir Guy, nor Colbrand,[3]
To mow 'em down before me; but if I spared any
That had a head to hit, either young or old,
He or she, cuckold or cuckold-maker,
25   Let me ne'er hope to see a chine° again—   *cut of beef*
And that I would not for a cow,° God save her!   *for anything*
ONE (*within*)   Do you hear, master porter?
PORTER   I shall be with you presently,
Good master puppy. [*To his* MAN] Keep the door close, sirra.
MAN   What would you have me do?
30   PORTER   What should you do,
but knock 'em down by th' dozens? Is this Moorfields[4] to muster in? Or have we some strange Indian with the great tool
come to court,[5] the women so besiege us? Bless me, what a fry
of fornication[6] is at door! On my Christian conscience, this one
35   christening will beget a thousand. Here will be father, godfather, and all together.
MAN   The spoons° will be the bigger, sir. There is a fellow some-   *(for christening)*
what near the door, he should be a brazier° by his face, for o'   *brass worker*
my conscience twenty of the dog-days° now reign in's nose. All   *hottest summer days*
40   that stand about him are under the line[7]—they need no other
penance. That fire-drake° did I hit three times on the head, and   *fiery dragon*
three times was his nose discharged against me. He stands there
like a mortar-piece, to blow us.[8] There was a haberdasher's wife
of small wit near him, that railed upon me till her pinked por-

---

1. A park for bear- and bullbaiting located in Southwark,
a London suburb, where the Globe Theatre also stood.
2. On May Day, revelers rose before dawn for festivities to
greet spring.
3. Figures of legendary physical powers. In the Bible,
Samson is renowned for his strength; in the romance tradition, Sir Guy of Warwick, who killed the Danish giant
Colebrand, was also known for his prowess.
4. Parkland outside London's walls where citizen militias

may have trained.
5. Indians brought to England and exhibited at court
excited popular fascination, here about their genitalia.
6. Crowd of would-be fornicators or bastards.
7. All those near him seem to be standing at the equator,
his face is so red.
8. Like a cannon, ready to blow us up; ready to blow his
nose at us.

45 ringer⁹ fell off her head, for kindling such a combustion° in the   *tumult*
state. I missed the meteor° once, and hit that woman, who cried   *brazier*
out 'Clubs!',¹ when I might see from far some forty truncheon-
ers° draw to her succour, which were the hope o'th' Strand,² *men with cudgels*
where she was quartered.° They fell on.° I made good my place. *lived / attacked*
50 At length they came to th' broomstaff to° me. I defied 'em still, *right next to*
when suddenly a file of boys behind 'em, loose shot,³ delivered
such a shower of pebbles that I was fain° to draw mine honour   *obliged*
in and let 'em win the work.° The devil was amongst 'em, I   *fort*
think, surely.
55 PORTER These are the youths° that thunder at a playhouse, and *apprentices*
fight for bitten apples, that no audience but the tribulation of
Tower Hill or the limbs of Limehouse,⁴ their dear brothers, are
able to endure. I have some of 'em in *limbo patrum*,⁵ and there
they are like to dance these three days, besides the running
60 banquet of two beadles that is to come.⁶
     Enter [the] LORD CHAMBERLAIN
LORD CHAMBERLAIN Mercy o' me, what a multitude are here!
They grow still, too—from all parts they are coming,
As if we kept a fair here! Where are these porters,
These lazy knaves? [*To the* PORTER *and his* MAN] You've made
  a fine hand,° fellows!   *nice work (ironic)*
65 There's a trim° rabble let in—are all these   *an elegant (ironic)*
Your faithful friends o'th' suburbs?⁷ We shall have
Great store of room, no doubt, left for the ladies
When they pass back from the christening!
PORTER   An't° please your honour,   *If it*
We are but men, and what so many may do,
70 Not being torn a-pieces, we have done.
An army cannot rule 'em.°   *keep them in order*
LORD CHAMBERLAIN As I live,
If the King blame me for't, I'll lay ye all
By th' heels,° and suddenly—and on your heads   *In the stocks*
Clap round° fines for neglect. You're lazy knaves,   *large*
75 And here ye lie baiting of bombards° when   *you lie drinking*
Ye should do service.
    [*Flourish of trumpets within*]
        Hark, the trumpets sound.
They're come, already, from the christening.
Go break among the press,° and find a way out   *crowd*
To let the troop pass fairly,° or I'll find   *fittingly*
80 A Marshalsea shall hold ye play⁸ these two months.
  [*As they leave, the* PORTER *and his* MAN *call within*]
PORTER Make way there for the Princess!

---

9. Perforated small cap.
1. London apprentices would shout this when about to begin or end a street fight.
2. Fashionable shopping and residential part of London.
3. Marksmen (here, throwers) unattached to a company.
4. The tough crowds at the Tower for executions; or further east in Limehouse, a rough part of London near the docks.
5. In prison (literally, limbo of the fathers). Jewish patriarchs, because they predated Christ, at death went not to Christian heaven but to limbo, near hell, where they remained until Judgment Day. With echoes of "limbs of Limehouse" (line 57).
6. *dance . . . come:* festive celebration ("dance") with dessert ("running banquet"); public whipping of prisoners (like a "running banquet," or dessert) after imprisonment (the main course) by minor law-enforcement officials ("beadles").
7. From the suburbs, areas outside London's city walls, beyond the city's legal jurisdiction, and hence considered lawless.
8. *I'll . . . play:* I'll shut you in the Marshalsea, a prison in Southwark.

MAN   You great fellow,[9]
     Stand close up,° or I'll make your head ache.   *Move aside*
PORTER   You i'th' camlet,° get up o'th' rail—   *rough cloth*
     I'll peck you o'er the pales else.[1]   *Exeunt*

5.4

Enter trumpet[er]s, sounding. Then [enter] two alder-
men, [the] Lord Mayor [of London], GARTER [King-of-
Arms], CRANMER [the Archbishop of Canterbury, the]
Duke of NORFOLK with his marshal's staff, [the] Duke of
SUFFOLK, two noblemen bearing great standing bowls for
the christening gifts; then [enter] four noblemen bearing
a canopy, under which [is] the Duchess of Norfolk, god-
mother, bearing the child [Elizabeth] richly habited in a
mantle, [whose] train [is] borne by a lady. Then follows
the Marchioness Dorset, the other godmother, and
ladies. The troop pass once about the stage and GARTER
speaks

GARTER   Heaven, from thy endless goodness send prosperous
     life, long, and ever happy, to the high and mighty Princess of
     England, Elizabeth.[1]
          Flourish. Enter KING [HENRY] and guard
CRANMER [*kneeling*]   And to your royal grace, and the good Queen!
5   My noble partners° and myself thus pray   *fellow godparents*
     All comfort, joy, in this most gracious lady,
     Heaven ever laid up to make parents happy,
     May hourly fall upon ye.
KING HENRY   Thank you, good lord Archbishop.
     What is her name?
CRANMER   Elizabeth.
KING HENRY   Stand up, lord.
          [CRANMER *rises*]
     [*To the child*] With this kiss take my blessing—
          [*He kisses the child*]
10   God protect thee,
     Into whose hand I give thy life.
CRANMER   Amen.
KING HENRY [*to CRANMER, old Duchess, and Marchioness*]
     My noble gossips,° you've been too prodigal.°   *godparents / generous*
     I thank ye heartily. So shall this lady,
     When she has so much English.
CRANMER   Let me speak, sir,
15   For heaven now bids me, and the words I utter
     Let none think flattery, for they'll find 'em truth.
     This royal infant—heaven still° move about her—   *always*
     Though in her cradle, yet now promises
     Upon this land a thousand thousand blessings
20   Which time shall bring to ripeness. She shall be—
     But few now living can behold that goodness—
     A pattern to all princes living with her,

---

9. Addressed to someone either onstage or in the audience.
1. *get . . . else*: get off the rail (the railing running around
the edge of the stage), or I'll throw you off.
5.4 Location: The court.
1.This formulaic speech is similar to one given at the 1613

wedding of King James I's daughter Elizabeth to Prince
Frederick, the Elector Palatine. This scene parallels the
christening celebration of one Princess Elizabeth, in the
play, to the wedding celebration of another, at the time of
the play's first production.

And all that shall succeed. Saba² was never
More covetous° of wisdom and fair virtue   *desirous*
25   Than this pure soul shall be. All princely graces
That mould up° such a mighty piece° as this is,   *produce / masterpiece*
With all the virtues that attend the good,
Shall still be doubled on her. Truth shall nurse her,
Holy and heavenly thoughts still counsel her.
30   She shall be loved and feared. Her own° shall bless her;   *own people*
Her foes shake like a field of beaten° corn,   *windswept*
And hang their heads with sorrow. Good grows with her.
In her days every man shall eat in safety
Under his own vine what he plants, and sing
35   The merry songs of peace to all his neighbours.
God shall be truly known,° and those about her   *(via Protestantism)*
From her shall read° the perfect ways of honour,   *learn*
And by those claim their greatness, not by blood.
Nor shall this peace sleep with her, but, as when
40   The bird of wonder dies—the maiden phoenix³—
Her ashes new create another heir
As great in admiration° as herself,   *deserving of wonder*
So shall she leave her blessèdness to one,°   *(James I)*
When heaven shall call her from this cloud of darkness,°   *earthly state*
45   Who from the sacred ashes of her honour
Shall star-like rise as great in fame as she was,
And so stand fixed. Peace, plenty, love, truth, terror,
That were the servants to this chosen infant,
Shall then be his, and, like a vine, grow to him.
50   Wherever the bright sun of heaven shall shine,
His honour and the greatness of his name
Shall be, and make new nations.⁴ He shall flourish,
And like a mountain cedar reach his branches
To all the plains about him. Our children's children
Shall see this, and bless heaven.
55   KING HENRY   Thou speakest wonders.
CRANMER   She shall be, to the happiness of England,
An agèd princess. Many days shall see her,
And yet no day without a deed° to crown it.   *an accomplishment*
Would I had known no more. But she must die—
60   She must, the saints must have her—yet a virgin,
A most unspotted lily shall she pass
To th' ground, and all the world shall mourn her.
KING HENRY   O lord Archbishop,
Thou hast made me now a man. Never before
65   This happy child did I get° anything.   *beget; achieve*
This oracle of comfort has so pleased me
That when I am in heaven I shall desire
To see what this child does, and praise my maker.
I thank ye all. To you, my good Lord Mayor,

2. The Queen of Sheba visited Solomon in Jerusalem in order to benefit from his wisdom, and thus became a model for wise (but presumably deferential) women. See 1 Kings 10: 1–10.
3. Mythical Arabian bird, the only one of its kind, who, when it dies after a long life, regenerates itself from its own ashes. James I inherits the spirit of the phoenix, Queen Elizabeth—a spirit now, perhaps, being passed on to his daughter Princess Elizabeth.
4. See Genesis 17:4: "A father of many nations have I made thee." The passage was frequently invoked in relation to Princess Elizabeth's marriage. The play here also compliments James on the "new nation" he has established in America, appropriately named Virginia after the "virgin" Queen Elizabeth (line 60).

70   And your good brethren, I am much beholden.
      I have received much honour by your presence,
      And ye shall find me thankful. Lead the way, lords.
      Ye must all see the Queen, and she must thank ye.
      She will be sick° else. This day, no man think   *unhappy*
75   He's business at his house, for all shall stay°—   *stop work*
      This little one shall make it holiday.   [*Flourish.*] *Exeunt*

Epilogue

      [*Enter* EPILOGUE]
EPILOGUE   'Tis ten to one this play can never please
      All that are here. Some come to take their ease,
      And sleep an act or two; but those, we fear,
      We've frighted with our trumpets; so, 'tis clear,
5   They'll say 'tis naught.° Others to hear the city   *worth nothing*
      Abused extremely, and to cry 'That's witty!'[1]—
      Which we have not done neither; that,° I fear,   *such that*
      All the expected good° we're like to hear   *anticipated praise*
      For this play at this time is only in
10   The merciful construction of° good women,   *interpretation by*
      For such a one we showed 'em. If they smile,
      And say "Twill do', I know within a while
      All the best men are ours—for 'tis ill hap°   *luck*
      If they hold° when their ladies bid 'em clap.   [*Exit*]   *refrain*

TEXTUAL VARIANTS

Control text: F

F: The Folio of 1623

Title: The Famous History of the Life of King HENRY the Eight [main Title] *The Life of King Henry the Eight* [running title; see the Introduction]

s.p. PROLOGUE, EPILOGUE [Though treated in this edition as characters, F's THE PROLOGVE and THE EPILOGVE could be either speech prefixes or section headings.]

s.p. KING HENRY [F's *King* has been expanded throughout.]

s.p. LORD CHAMBERLAIN [F uses *Chamberlain* and *Lord Chamberlain*; standardized throughout.]

s.p. LORD CHANCELLOR [F's *Chancellor* has been expanded throughout.]

s.p. SANDS [F uses *Sands* and *Lord Sands*; standardized throughout. See note to 2.1.54 stage direction.]

s.p. GUILDFORD [F's *Sir Henry Guilford* has been shortened throughout.]

s.p. CARDINAL WOLSEY [F uses *Cardinal* and *Wolsey*. The latter occurs primarily when Cardinal Campeius is also onstage, although even then Cardinal Wolsey is usually referred to in the dialogue as "Cardinal"; standardized throughout.]

s.p. BUCKINGHAM'S SURVEYOR [F's *Surveyor* has been expanded throughout.]

s.p. CARDINAL CAMPEIUS [F uses *Campeius*, presumably in part to distinguish him from Cardinal Wolsey; expanded throughout.]

---

1. "The city," both London and its citizens, was satirized in "city comedies" at the private theaters (as opposed to public playhouses like the Globe, whose leading dramatist here retaliates).

s.p. PAGE [F's *Boy* has been changed throughout.]

s.p. QUEEN KATHERINE, KATHERINE [F uses *Queen* until she becomes the princess dowager (4.2), at which point it switches to *Katherine*. Similarly, this edition switches from "Queen Katherine" to "Katherine" at 4.2.]

s.p. GRIFFITH [F's *Gentleman Usher* (2.4), *Gentleman* (3.1), and *Griffith* have been standardized throughout. See notes below for more information.]

s.p. ANNE Boleyn [F uses *Anne* and *Anne Bullen*; standardized throughout.]

s.p. OLD LADY [F uses *Old Lady* more frequently than *Lady*; standardized throughout.]

s.p. LINCOLN [F uses *Lincoln* and *Bishop of Lincoln*; standardized throughout.]

s.p. GENTLEMEN [F's "1," "2," and "3" have been expanded to "First Gentleman," etc.]

Prologue s.d. / s.p. *Enter* PROLOGUE / PROLOGUE *THE PROLOGVE.* **11 pass, if** *passe: If*
1.1.7 Ardres . . . Guisnes . . . Ardres *Andren . . . Guynes . . . Arde* **23** *mesdames* Madams **42–48 to. All . . . function. s.p.** BUCKINGHAM **Who . . . together, as you guess? s.p.** NORFOLK **too.** / *Buc⟨kingham⟩. All . . . Function: who . . . together? / Nor⟨folk⟩.* As you guesse: [In F, Buckingham begins speaking at "All was Royal" (line 42) and continues through "together" (line 47). Norfolk then begins the following speech with the phrase "As you guesse" (line 47).] **63 web, a** Web. O **116, 117 s.p.** SECRETARY *Secr⟨etary⟩.* [We cannot be certain which secretary speaks which lines, since two enter with Wolsey and they are not distinguished by speech prefix.] **120 venom-mouthed** venom'd-mouth'd **154 July** *Inly* **167 rinsing** wrenching **183 Privily he** Priuily **200 Hereford** Hertford **211 Abergavenny** Aburgany **219 Perk, his chancellor** Pecke, his Councellour. [The emendation derives from Holinshed.] **221 Nicholas** Michaell [The emendation derives from Holinshed.] **227 lord** Lords
1.2.9 s.p. CRIER **(within)** Room . . . Norfolk. *A noyse within crying roome . . . Duke of Norfolke.* [In F, this entire sentence is a stage direction, and there is no speech prefix.] **68 business** basenesse **140 His** This **148, 149 Hopkins** *Henton.* [The emendation derives from Holinshed. At 1.1.221, the name is presented correctly.] **157 feared** feare **165 confession's** Commissions [The emendation derives from Holinshed.] **171 win** [not in F] **181 To** For this to **191 Bulmer** *Blumer* [The emendation derives from Holinshed.] **191 remember** remember of
1.3.13 Or A **21 'messieurs'** Monsieurs **34 'oui'** wee **59 he's** Ha's
1.4.6 feast first
2.1.21 Perk Pecke. **54 s.d.** *William* Walter [The emendation derives from Holinshed.] **79 i'** a **87 mark** make
2.2.1 s.p. LORD CHAMBERLAIN [*reads*] [not in F]
2.3.59 note's notes **61 of you** of you, to you **87 fie, fie** fye, fye, fye
2.4.7, 10 come into the court &c. **11 s.p.** QUEEN KATHERINE [not in F] **124 s.p.** GRIFFITH *Gent⟨leman⟩ Vsh⟨er⟩.* [It seems reasonable to suppose that this gentleman is the same as the *Gentleman* who attends the queen at 3.1.14. s.d. and is referred to as *Gent⟨leman⟩* at 3.1.16, 18 s.p., later identified as *Griffith, her Gentleman Vsher* at 4.2.0 s.d. **171 A** And **188 does yield to th'** does to th' **196 throe** throw
3.1.3 s.p. GENTLEWOMAN [*sings*] SONG. [In F, no speech prefix precedes the song.] **16, 18 s.p.** GRIFFITH *Gent⟨leman⟩.* **60 your** our **118 he's** ha's **123 accursed** a Curse
3.2.58 Has Ha's **143 glad** gald **172 filed** fill'd **340 legantine** Legatiue **344 Chattels** Castles
4.1.20 s.p. SECOND GENTLEMAN **1** **56 s.p.** FIRST GENTLEMAN [not in F, which gives all of lines 55–56 to "2." Here, FIRST GENTLEMAN speaks the beginning of line 56.] **103 Stokesley** *Stokeley* [The emendation derives from Holinshed.] **119 s.p.** FIRST *and* SECOND GENTLEMEN *Both.*
4.2.5 led'st lead'st **7 think** thanke **99 colour** cold **109 s.d.** CAPUTIUS *Capuchius*
5.1.37 time Lime **140 precipice** Precepit **158 s.p.** LOVELL **(within)** *Gent⟨leman⟩ within.*
5.2.7 piece Peere **119, 121 s.p.** LORD CHANCELLOR *⟨Lord⟩ Cham⟨berlain⟩.* **126 s.p.** ALL THE COUNCIL *All.* **167 this** his **207 heart** hearts
5.3.2 Paris Parish **4, 27 s.p.** ONE **(within)** *Within.* **78 a way** away
5.4.37 ways way **70 your** you **75 He's** 'Has
Epilogue s.d. / s.p. *Enter* EPILOGUE / EPILOGUE *THE EPILOGVE.*

APPENDICES

APPENDICES

The Shakespearean Stage
by
ANDREW GURR

Publication by Performance

The curt exchange between the sentries in the first six lines of *Hamlet* tells us that it is very late at night (" 'Tis now struck twelve") and that " 'tis bitter cold." This opening was staged originally at the Globe in London in broad daylight, at 2 o'clock probably on a hot summer's afternoon. The words required the audience, half of them standing on three sides of the stage platform and all of them as visible to one another as the players were, to imagine themselves watching a scene quite the opposite of what they could see and feel around them. The original mode of staging for a Shakespearean play was utterly different from the cinematic realism we are used to now, where the screen gives us close-ups on a simulacrum of reality, an even more privileged view of the actors' facial twitches than we get in ordinary life. Eloquence then was in words, not facial expressions.

The playgoers of Shakespeare's own time knew the plays in forms at which we can only now guess. It is a severe loss. Shakespeare's own primary concept of his plays was as stories "personated" onstage, not as words on a page. He himself never bothered to get his playscripts into print, and more than half of them were not published until seven years after his death, in the First Folio of his plays published as a memorial to him in 1623. His fellow playwright Francis Beaumont called the printing of plays "a second publication"; the first was their showing onstage. Print recorded a set of scripts, written for the original players to teach them what they should speak in the ensemble of the play in production. The only technology then available to record the performances was the written word. If video recordings had existed at that time, our understanding of Shakespeare would be vastly different from what it is today.

Since the texts were composed only to be a record of the words the players were to memorize, we now have to infer how the plays were originally staged largely by guesswork. Shakespeare was himself a player and shareholder in his acting company, and he expected to be present at rehearsals. Consequently, the stage directions in his scripts are distinctly skimpy compared with some of those provided by his fellow playwrights. He was cursory even in noting entrances and exits, let alone how he expected his company to stage the more complex spectacles, such as heaving Antony up to Cleopatra on her monument. There are sometimes hints in the stage directions and more frequently in the words used to describe some of the actions, and knowing what the design of the theater was like is a help as well. Knowing more about how Shakespeare expected his plays to be staged can transform how we think about them. But gaining such knowledge is no easy matter. One of the few certainties is that Shakespeare's plays in modern performance are even more different from the originals than modern printed editions are from the first much-thumbed manuscripts.

The Shakespearean Mindset

The general mindset of the original playgoers, the patterns of thinking and expectation that Tudor culture imposed on Shakespeare's audiences, is not really difficult to identify. It is less easy, though, to pin it down in the sort of detail that tells us what the original concept of staging the plays would have been like. We know that all the original playgoers paid for the privilege of attending the plays and committed themselves willingly to suspend their disbelief in what they were to see. They knew as we do that they were paying to be entertained by fictions. Beyond that, we need reminding today that going to open-air performances in daylight in Shakespeare's time meant being constantly aware that one was in a theater, a place designed to offer illusions. On the one hand, this consciousness of oneself and where one was meant that the players had to do more to hold attention than is needed now, when audiences have nothing but the stage to look at and armchairs to sit in. On the other hand, it made everyone more receptive to extratheatrical tricks, such as Hamlet's reference to "this distracted globe," or Polonius's claim in the same play to have taken the part of Julius Caesar at the university and been killed by Brutus. The regular playgoers at the Globe who recognized Polonius as the man who had played Caesar in Shakespeare's play of the year before, and who recognized Hamlet as the man who had played Brutus, would laugh at this theatrical in-joke. But two scenes later, when Hamlet kills Polonius, they would think of it again, in a different light.

Features of the original mindset such as these are quite readily identifiable. For others, though, we need to look further, into the design of the theaters and into the staging traditions that they housed and that Shakespeare exploited. Invisibility has a part to play in *A Midsummer Night's Dream* that we can easily underrate, for instance. Invisibility onstage is a theatrical in-joke, an obvious privileging of the audience, which is allowed to see what the characters onstage can't. The impresario Philip Henslowe's inventory of costumes used at the Rose theater in 1597, which lists "a robe for to go invisible," indicates a fictional device that openly expects the willing suspension of the audience's disbelief. In *A Midsummer Night's Dream*, the ostensible invisibility of all the visible fairies emphasizes the theatricality of the whole presentation while pandering to the audience's self-indulgent superiority, the feeling that it knows what is going on better than any character, whether he be Bottom or even Duke Theseus. That prepares us for the mockery of stage realism we get later, in the mechanicals' play in Act 5, and even for the doubt we as willing audience might feel over Theseus's own skepticism about the dangers of imagination that he voices in his speech at the beginning of Act 5.

More to the point, though, it throws into question our readiness to be an audience, since we have ourselves been indulging in just the games of suspending disbelief that the play staged by the mechanicals enters into so unsuccessfully. When Theseus disputes with Hippolyta about the credibility of the lovers' story, he voices the very skepticism—about the lover, the lunatic, and the poet—that any sensible realist in the audience would have been feeling for most of the previous three acts in the forest. The play starts and ends at the court in broad daylight, while the scenes of midsummer madness take place at night in a forest. At the early amphitheaters, all the plays were staged in broad daylight, between 2 and 5 o'clock in the afternoon, and without any persuasive scenery: the two stage posts served as trees onstage. So the play, moving as it does from daylight realism to nocturnal fantasy and back again, with a last challenge to credulity in the mechanicals' burlesque of how to stage a play, has already thoroughly challenged the willing suspension of the viewers' disbelief. *A Midsummer Night's Dream* is a play about nocturnal dreams and fictions that are accepted as truths in broad daylight. It was only a small extension of this game to have the women's parts played by boys, as well as plots in which the girls dressed as boys, to the point where in *As You Like It* Rosalind was played by a boy playing a girl pretending to be a boy playing a girl.

The Shakespeare plays were written for a new and unique kind of playhouse, the Elizabethan amphitheater, which had a distinctive design quite different from modern theaters. Elizabethans knew what the standard features in their theaters stood for, and Shakespeare drew on that knowledge for the staging of his plays. The physical features of the playhouses were a potent element in the ways that the plays were designed for the Elizabethan mindset. When Richard III, the archdeceiver and playactor, appears "aloft between two Bishops" to claim the crown in *Richard III* 3.7, his placing on the stage balcony literally above the crowd on the stage would, even without the accompanying priests, have signified his ironic claim to a social and moral superiority that ought to have matched his elevation. When Richard II comes down from the wall of Flint Castle to the "base court" in *Richard II* 3.3, Elizabethans would have seen his descent as a withdrawal from power and status. These theaters were still new when Shakespeare started to write for them, and their novelty meant that the plays were written more tightly to fit their specific design than the plays of later years, when theatergoing had become a more routine social activity and different kinds of theater were available.

London Playgoing and the Law

This heightened sense of theatricality, or "metatheater," in Shakespearean audiences was far from the only difference in their mindset from that of all modern audiences. Regular playgoing in London only started in the 1570s, and through Shakespeare's earlier years it was always a perilous and precarious activity. The Lord Mayor of London and the mayors of most of England's larger towns hated playgoing and tried to suppress it whenever and wherever it appeared. Playgoing was exciting not only because it was new but because it was dangerous. The hostility of so many authorities to plays meant that they were seen almost automatically as subversive of authority. Paradoxically, the first London companies were only able to establish themselves in London through the active support of Queen Elizabeth and her Privy Council, which tried hard, in the face of constant complaints from the lord mayor, to ensure that the best companies would be on hand every Christmas to entertain the queen's leisure hours. Popular support for playgoing depended on royal protection for the leading companies.

London was by far the largest city in England. Within a few years of Shakespeare's death, it became the largest in Europe. It was generally an orderly place to live, especially in the city itself. Even in the suburbs, where the poorer people had to live, there were not many of the riots and other disorders that preachers always associated with the brothels, animal-baiting arenas, and playhouses clustering there. The reputation that the playhouses gained for promoting riots was not well justified. Any crowd of people was seen by the authorities as a potential riot, and playhouses regularly drew some of the largest crowds that London had yet seen. The city's government was not designed to control large crowds of people. There was no paid police force, and the lord mayor was held responsible by the Privy Council, the queen's governing committee, for any disorders that did occur. So the city authorities found that playgoing challenged their control over their people.

The rapid growth of London did not help the situation. Officially, the city was governed by the lord mayor and his council. But he had authority only inside the city, and London now spread through a large suburban area in the adjacent counties of Middlesex to the north and Surrey across the river to the south. Because the court and the national government were housed in London, the Privy Council often intervened in city affairs in its own interests, as well as when orders were needed that covered broader zones than the city itself. The periodic outbreaks of bubonic plague were one clear instance of such a need, because the plague took no notice of parish or city boundaries. The intrusion of the professional companies to play in London provided another. In the early years, they were chronic travelers and London was simply one of many stopovers. But the queen enjoyed seeing plays at Christmas, and her council accordingly supported the best companies so that they could perform for her. It protected the playing companies against the hatred of successive lord mayors, except when a national emergency such as a plague epidemic erupted. The Privy Council took control then by ordering the 126 parishes in and around London to list all deaths from plague separately from ordinary deaths. Each Thursday, the parish totals were added together. When the total number of deaths from plague in these lists rose above thirty in any one week, the Privy Council closed all places of public assembly. This meant especially the playhouses, which created by far the largest gatherings. When the theaters were closed, the playing companies had to revert to their traditional practice of going on tour to play in the towns through the country, provided that the news of plague did not precede them.

Plague was not the only reason for the government to lay its controlling hand on the companies. From the time the post was inaugurated in 1578, the Master of the Revels controlled all playing. He was executive officer to the lord chamberlain, the Privy Council officer responsible for the annual season of royal entertainment and thus by extension for the professional playing companies. The Master of the Revels licensed each company and censored its plays. He was expected to cut out any references to religion or affairs of state, and he tried to prevent other offenses by banning the depiction of any living person on-stage. After 1594, he issued licenses to the approved London playhouses too. Later still, the printing of any playbook was allowed only if he gave authority for it. The companies had to accept this tight control because the government was its only protector against the hostile municipal authorities, who included not only the Lord Mayor of London but also the mayors of most of the major towns in the country.

Most mayors had the commercial interest of keeping local employees at work to justify their hostility to playgoing. But across the country, the hostility went much deeper. A large proportion of the population disliked the very idea of playacting. Their reasons, ostensibly religious, were that for actors to pretend to be characters they were unlike in life was a deception and that for boys to dress as women was contrary to what the Bible said. Some-where beneath this was a more basic fear of pretense and deceit, of people not acting honestly. It put actors into the same category as con men, cheats, and thieves. That was probably one reason why companies of boys acting men's parts were thought rather more tolerable than men pretending to be other kinds of men. The deception involved in boys playing men was more transparent than when men played characters other than them-selves. There was also a strong Puritan suspicion about shows of any kind, which looked too much like the Catholic ceremonial that the new Church of England had renounced. Playgoing found much better favor on the Catholic side of English society than on the Puritan side. Different preachers took different positions over the new phenomenon of playgoing. But few would speak in its favor, and most of them openly disapproved of it. Playgoing was an idle pastime, and the devil finds work for idle hands.

In the 1590s, when *Romeo and Juliet* and Shakespeare's histories and early comedies were exciting audiences, only two playhouses and two companies were officially approved by the queen's Privy Council for the entertainment of London's citizens. The other main forms of paid entertainment were bear- and bullbaiting, which were much harder on the performers than was playing and so could be staged less frequently. The hostility to plays meant that the right to perform was confined to only a few of the most outstanding compa-nies. These few companies were in competition with one another, and this led to a rapid growth in the quality of their offerings. But playacting was always a marginal activity. Paying to enter a specially built theater in order to see professional companies perform plays was still a new phenomenon, and it still met with great opposition from the London authorities. The open-air theaters like the Globe were built out in the suburbs. London as a city had no centrally located playhouses until after the civil war and the restoration of the monarchy, in 1661. And even playing in the city's suburbs, where they were free from the lord mayor's control, the companies had to work under the control of the Privy Coun-cil. All the great amphitheaters were built either in Middlesex, to the north of the city walls, or in Surrey across the river from the city, on the south bank of the Thames. At the height of their success, in the years after Shakespeare's death, the Privy Council never licensed more than four or five playhouses in London.

Playgoing in London was viewed even by the playgoers as an idle occupation. The largest numbers who went to the Globe were apprentices and artisans taking time off work, often surreptitiously, and law students from the Inns of Court doing the same. These fugitives were linked with the wealthier kind of idler, "gallants" or rich gentlemen and other men of property, along with soldiers and sailors on leave from the wars, people visiting London from the country on business or pleasure (usually both), and above all the women of London. Women were not expected to be literate, but one did not need to be able to read and write to enjoy hearing and seeing a play. A respectable woman had to make sure she was escorted by a man. He might be a husband or a friend, or her page if she was rich, or her husband's apprentice if she was a middle-class citizen. She might have

The city of London and its suburbs in 1572.

a mask on, part of standard women's wear outdoors to protect the face against the weather and to assert modesty, and perhaps anonymity. Market women (applewives and fishwives) went to plays in groups. Whores were expected to be there looking for business, especially from the gallants, but they usually had male escorts too.

The social range of playgoers at the two playhouses approved for use in 1594 was almost complete, stretching from the aristocracy to the poorest workmen and boys. Many people disapproved of plays, but at peak times up to 25,000 a week flocked to see the variety of plays being offered. Prices for playgoing remained much the same throughout the decades up to 1642, when the parliamentary government that was fighting the king closed all the theaters for eighteen years. Until then, one could get standing room at an amphitheater for one penny (1/240th of a modern pound, roughly one cent), or a seat on a bench in the roofed galleries for twopence. A seat in a lord's room cost sixpence, which was not much less than a day's wage for a skilled artisan in 1600. The smaller roofed

theaters that opened in 1599 were much more expensive. They were called "private" theaters to distinguish them from the "public" open-air amphitheaters, though the claim to
privacy was mainly a convenient fiction to escape the controls imposed on the "public"
theaters. At the Blackfriars hall theater, sixpence only gained you a seat in the topmost
gallery, while a seat in the pit near the stage cost three times that amount and a seat in a
box five times, or half a skilled worker's weekly wage.

It was not only the plays and players that were the sights at the playhouses. The richest
lords and gallants went to be seen as much as they went to see. At the Globe, the costliest
rooms were positioned alongside the balcony "above," over the stage. They were called
"lords' rooms," and the playgoers who chose to sit there had a limited view of what went
on beneath them. They saw no "discoveries," for instance, such as Portia's three caskets in
The Merchant of Venice, which were uncovered underneath them inside the alcove in the
center of the *frons scenae*, nor anything other than the backs of the players when they
entered. But as audience they were themselves highly visible, and that was what they paid
for. In the hall, or "private," playhouses, with much higher admission prices than at the
Globe, there were boxes flanking the stage for the gentry, which gave them a better view
of the "discoveries." But at these "select" (because costlier) hall playhouses, where unlike
the Globe everyone had a seat, some of the most colorful and exhibitionistic gallants could
go one better. Up to fifteen gallants could pay for a stool to sit and watch the play on the
stage itself, sitting in front of the boxes that flanked the stage. Each would enter from the
players' dressing room (the "tiring-house") with his stool in hand before the play started.
This gave them the best possible view of the play and easily the most conspicuous place in
the audience's eye. Playgoing was a public occasion in which the visibility of audience
members allowed them to play almost as large a part as the players.

Through the 1590s, the only permanent and custom-made playhouses were the large
open-air theaters. Paying sixpence for a ferry across the river, as the richer playgoers did,
or walking across London Bridge to the Rose or the Globe, or else trudging north through
the mud of Shoreditch and Finsbury Fields or Clerkenwell to the Theatre or the Fortune
in order to see a play, did not have great appeal when it was raining. Consequently, the
companies were always trying to secure roofed halls nearer the city center. Up to 1594,
they could use city inns, especially in winter, but the lord mayor's hostility to playing never
made them reliable places for performing. Two constant problems troubled the players
throughout these first years of professional theater in London: the city officials' chronic
hatred of plays and the periodic visitations of the plague, which always led the government
to close the theaters as soon as the number of plague deaths rose to dangerously high
levels.

Playgoing was not firmly established in London until the Privy Council chose to protect it in 1594 and to approve specific playhouses for the two companies that it officially
sanctioned. By then, Shakespeare had already made his mark. He became a player, a
shareholder, and the resident playwright for one of these two companies. That status gained
him a privileged place in the rapidly growing new world of playgoing. From then on,
although his theater was still located only in the suburbs of the city, his work had the law
behind it. That status was amply confirmed in 1603, when the new king made himself the
company's patron. The King's Men held their status until the king himself lost power in
1642.

The Design of the Globe

The Globe was Shakespeare's principal playhouse. He put up part of the money for its
construction and designed his best plays for it. It was built on the south side of the Thames
in 1599, fashioned out of the framing timbers of an older theater. Essentially, it was a
polygonal scaffold of twenty bays or sections, nearly one hundred feet in outside diameter,
making a circle of three levels of galleries that rose to more than thirty feet high, with

The second Globe, from Wenceslas Hollar's engraving of the "Long View" of London (1647).

wooden bench seating and cushions for those who could afford them. This surrounded an open "yard," into which the stage projected.

The yard was over seventy feet in diameter. Nearly half the audience stood on their feet to watch the play from inside this yard, closest to the stage platform. The stage extended out nearly to the middle of the yard, so the actors could stand in the center of the crowd. The uncertain privilege of having standing room in the open air around the stage platform could be bought with the minimal price for admission, one penny (about a cent). It had the advantage of proximity to the stage and the players; its disadvantage was keeping you on your feet for the two or three hours of the play, as well as leaving you subject to the weather. If you wanted a seat, or if it rained and you wanted shelter, you paid twice as much to sit in the three ranks of roofed galleries that circled behind the crowd standing in the yard. With some squeezing, the theater could hold over three thousand people. It was an open-air theater because that gave it a larger capacity than a roofed hall. The drawback of its being open to the weather was more than outweighed by the gain in daylight that shone on stage and spectators alike.

The stage was a great square platform as much as forty feet wide. It had over it a canopied roof, or "heavens," to protect the players and their expensive costumes from rain. This canopy was held up by two pillars rising through the stage. The stage platform was about five feet high, and without any protective rails, so that the eyes of the audience in the yard were at the level of the players' feet. At the back of the stage, a wall, or *frons scenae*, stretched across the front of the players' tiring-house, the attiring or dressing room. It had a door on each flank and a wider curtained space in the center, which was used for major entrances and occasionally for set-piece scenes. Above these entry doors was a gallery or balcony, most of which was partitioned into rooms for the wealthiest spectators. A central room "above" was sometimes used in staging: for example, as Juliet's balcony, as the place for Richard III to stand between the bishops, as the wall of Flint Castle in *Richard II*, and as the wall over the city gates of Harfleur in *Henry V*. After 1608, when Shakespeare's company acquired the Blackfriars consort of musicians, this central gallery room

A photograph of the interior framework of the "new" Globe on the south bank of the Thames in London, showing the general dimensions of the yard and the surrounding galleries.

was turned into a curtained-off music room that could double as an "above" when required. Fewer than half of Shakespeare's plays need an "above."

The Original Staging Techniques

Shakespearean staging was emblematic. The "heavens" that covered the stage was the colorful feature from which gods descended to the earth of the stage platform. When Jupiter made his appearance in *Cymbeline*, in clouds of "sulphurous breath" provided by fireworks, he was mounted on an eagle being lowered through a trapdoor in the heavens. The other trapdoor, set in the stage platform itself, symbolized the opposite, a gateway to hell. The large stage trap was the place where the Gravedigger came to work at the beginning of Act 5 of *Hamlet*. It was the cell where Malvolio was imprisoned in *Twelfth Night*. The Shakespearean mindset accepted such conventions automatically.

Shakespeare inherited from Marlowe a tradition of using the stage trap as the dreaded hell's mouth. Barabbas plunges into it in *The Jew of Malta*, and the demons drag the screaming Faustus down it at the end of *Dr. Faustus*. Hell was not a fiction taken lightly by Elizabethans. Edward Alleyn, by far the most famous player of Faustus in the 1590s, wore a cross on his breast while he played the part, as insurance—just in case the fiction turned serious. Tracking the Elizabethan mindset about the stage trapdoor can give us a few warnings of what we might overlook when we come fresh to the plays today.

In the original staging of *Hamlet* at the Globe, the stage trap had two functions. Besides serving as Ophelia's grave, it was the distinctive entry point, not used by any other character, for the Ghost in Act 1. When he tells his son that he is "for the day confined to fast in fires," the first audiences would have already taken the point that he had come up from the underworld. His voice comes from under the stage, telling the soldiers to swear the oath of secrecy that Hamlet lays upon them. The connection between that original entry by the Ghost through the trap and the trap's later use for Ophelia is one we might easily miss. At the start of Act 5, the macabre discussion between the Gravediggers about whether

The Globe as reconstructed in Southwark near the original site in London.

she committed suicide and is therefore consigned to hell gets its sharpest edge from the association of the trap, here the grave being dug for her, with the Ghost's purgatorial fires. More to the point, though, Hamlet, as he eavesdrops on the curtailed burial ceremony, makes the same connection when he discovers that it is the body of Ophelia being so neglectfully interred. He remembers the other apparition that came up through the trap

The *frons scenae* of the new Globe.

A gesture using the language of hats, as shown by the man attending the brothers Browne.

and springs forward in a grotesque parody of the Ghost, crying, "This is I, Hamlet the Dane!" It is a melodramatic claim to be acting a new role, that of his father the dead King. The first audiences would have remembered the ghost of dead King Hamlet using the stage trap at this point more readily than we do now. Hamlet's private knowledge of the Ghost and the trapdoor sets him, as so often in the play, at odds with his audience. Consequently, centuries of editors, like the characters onstage, have misread this claim as a declaration that young Hamlet ought to be king.

Since his own name is Hamlet, and since he alone could have made the connection between the Ghost and the trapdoor, he was all too likely to be misunderstood. In the next scene, Osric certainly shows that he understands Hamlet's graveside claim that he is his father's ghost to be a claim that he should now be King of Denmark. That explains why Osric insists on keeping his hat in his hand when he comes to invite Hamlet to duel with Laertes. With equals, an Elizabethan gentleman would doff his hat in greeting and then put it back on. Only in the presence of your master, or as a courtier in the presence of the king, did you keep it in your hand. Osric is trying tactfully to acknowledge what he thinks is Hamlet's lunatic claim to be king. He missed the private connection that Hamlet had made with the trapdoor and his father's ghost. Tudor body language, with its wordless gestures and signals that defined human relations, was an aspect of social life so widely understood that it needed no stage direction. The language of hats was a part of the Shakespearean mindset that we now have to register in footnotes.

Other signifiers are necessarily more elusive. We might take heart from the range of the comments made in *Much Ado About Nothing* 4.1 when Hero is accused and is seen to go red. Each of the viewers—Claudio, Leonato, and Friar Francis—gives a different reading (or "noting") of her blush. Different mindsets lead to visual indicators being read in different ways. Each reading tells as much about the observer as about the thing observed. We might add that since the blush is commented on so extensively, Shakespeare must have been concerned to save the boy playing Hero from the necessity of holding his breath long enough to produce the right visual effect.

Costume was a vital element in the plays, a mute and instant signifier of the scene. If a character entered carrying a candle and dressed in a gown with a nightcap on his head, he had evidently just been roused from bed. Characters who entered wearing cloaks and riding boots and possibly holding a whip had just ended a long journey. York, entering in *Richard II* with a gorget (a metal neck plate, the "signs of war about his agèd neck" [2.2.74]), was preparing for battle. Even the women's wigs that the boys wore could be used to indicate the wearer's state of mind. Hair worn loose and unbound meant madness, whether in *Hamlet*'s Ophelia or *Troilus*'s Cassandra.

Comparable audience expectations could be roused by other visual features. Charac-

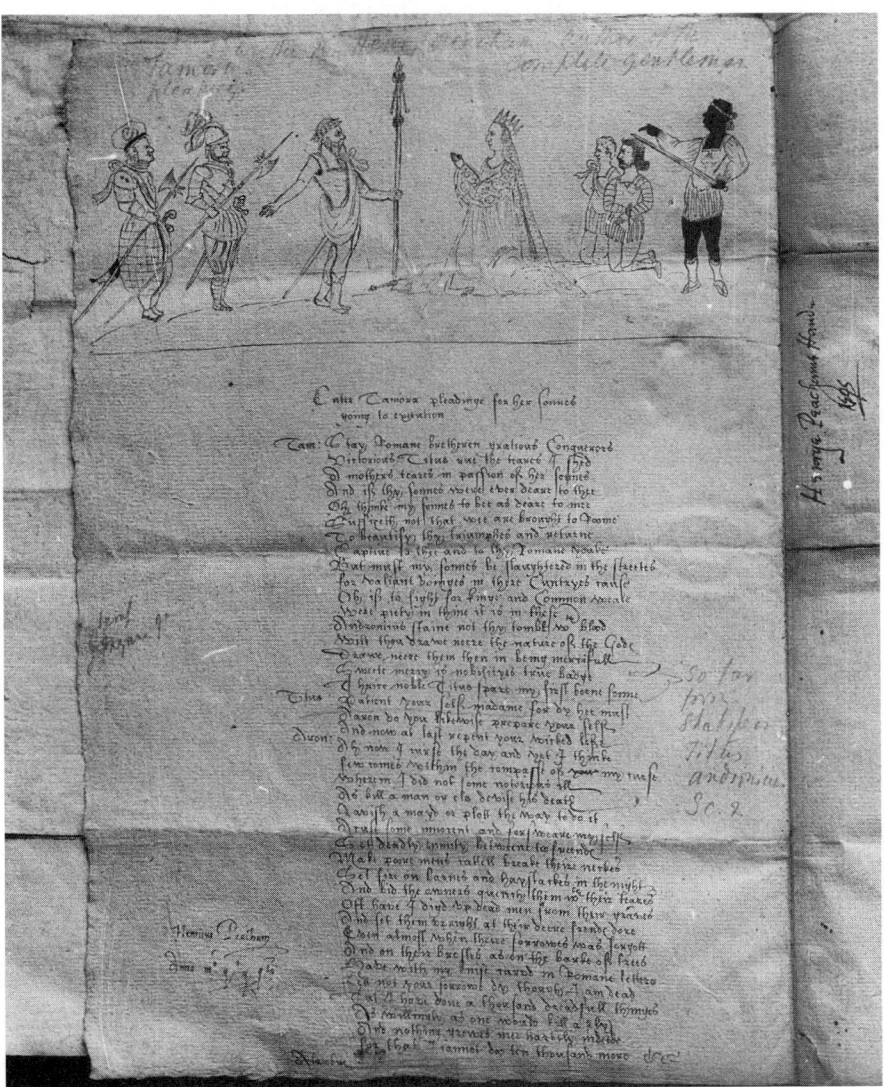

A sketch by Henry Peacham of an early staging of *Titus Andronicus* by Shakespeare's company (1595). Note the attempt at Roman costume for Titus but not for his soldiers, who carry Tudor halberds, and note Aaron's makeup and wig.

ters with faces blackened and wigs of curly black wool were recognized as Moors, alien and dangerous non-Christians. Aaron the Moor in *Titus Andronicus* and the Prince of Morocco in *The Merchant of Venice* acquire that character as soon as they come in view. Othello, by Iago's report and by his own first appearance, takes on the same stereotype. By contrast, Iago is dressed like a simple and honest soldier. Only in the course of Act 1 does it become apparent that it is Othello who is the honest soldier, Iago the un-Christian alien. The play neatly reverses the visual stereotypes of Elizabethan staging. Twentieth-century playgoers miss most of these signals and the ways that the original players used them to

A detail from Johannes De Witt's drawing of the Swan theater in 1596, showing two boys playing women greeted by a chamberlain.

show the discrepancy between outward appearance and inner person. As King Lear said, robes and furred gowns hide all.

For *The Merchant of Venice*, Shylock wore his "Jewish gabardine" and may also have put on a false nose, as Alleyn was said to have done for the title role in *The Jew of Malta*. Other national characteristics were noted by features of dress, such as the Irish "strait strossers" (tight trousers) that Macmorris would have worn in *Henry V*. The dress of the women in the plays, who were usually played by boys with unbroken voices, was always a special expense. The records kept by Philip Henslowe, owner of the Rose playhouse and impresario for the rival company to Shakespeare's, show that he paid the author less for the script of *A Woman Killed with Kindness* than he paid the costumer for the heroine's gown.

Women's clothing and the decorums and signals that women's costume contained were very different from those of men and men's clothing. Men frequently used their hats, doffing them to signal friendship and holding them in their hands while speaking to anyone in authority over them. Women's hats were fixed to their heads and were rarely if ever taken off in public. The forms and the language of women's clothes reflected the silent modesty and the quiet voices that men thought proper for women. Women had other devices to signal with, including handkerchiefs, fans, and face masks, and the boys playing the women's parts in the theaters exploited such accessories to the full. A lady out of doors commonly wore a mask to protect her complexion. When Othello is quizzing Emilia in 4.2 about his wife's behavior while she spoke to Cassio, he asks Emilia, who should have been chaperoning her mistress, whether Desdemona had not sent her away "to fetch her fan, her gloves, her mask nor nothing?" There is little doubt that the boys would have routinely worn masks when they played gentlewomen onstage, and not just at the masked balls in *Romeo and Juliet*, *Love's Labour's Lost*, and *Much Ado About Nothing*.

Other features of the original staging stemmed from the actor–audience relationship, which differs radically in daylight, when both parties can see one another, from what we are used to in modern, darkened, theaters. An eavesdropping scene onstage, for instance, works rather on the same basis as the "invisible" fairies in *A Midsummer Night's Dream*, where the audience agrees to share the pretence. At the Globe, it also entailed adopting the eavesdropper's perspective. In *Much Ado*, the two games of eavesdropping played on Benedict and Beatrice are chiefly done around the two stage posts. In these scenes, the posts that held up the stage cover, or "heavens," near what we now think of as the front of the stage were round, like the whole auditorium, and their function was to allow things to be seen equally by all of the audience, wherever people might be standing or sitting. Members of the audience, sitting in the surrounding galleries or standing around the stage itself at the Globe or its predecessors, had the two tall painted pillars in their sight all the time, wherever they were in the playhouse. And since the audience was in a complete circle all around the stage, if the stage posts were used for concealment there was always a large proportion of the audience who could see the player trying to hide behind a post. It was a three-dimensional game in which the audience might find itself behind any of the game players, victims or eavesdroppers, complicit in either role.

The first of *Much Ado*'s eavesdropping scenes, 2.3, starts as usual in Shakespeare with a verbal indication of the locality. Benedict tells his boy, "Bring it hither to me in the orchard." So we don't need stage trees to tell us where we are supposed to be. He later hides "in the arbour" to listen to what Don Pedro and the others have set for him; this means concealing himself behind a stage post, closer to the audience than the playactors who are talking about him. Don Pedro asks, "See you where Benedict hath hid himself?," a self-contradiction that confirms the game. When it is Beatrice's turn in her arbor scene, 3.1, she slips into a "bower" behind "this alley," which again signals a retreat behind the prominent stage post. These games are played with both of the eavesdroppers hiding behind the post at the stage edge, while the others do their talking at center stage between the two posts.

Such games of eavesdropping, using the same bits of the stage structure, make a strong visual contrast with all that goes on at what we two-dimensional thinkers, used to the pictorial staging of the cinema, call the "back" of the stage, or upstage—where, for instance, the Friar starts the broken-off wedding and where Claudio and Don Pedro later figure at Leonato's monument. These events are more distant from the audience, less obviously comic and intimate. The close proximity of players to audience in such activities as eavesdropping strongly influenced the audience's feeling of kinship with the different groupings of players.

A multitude of other staging differences can be identified. Quite apart from the fact that the language idioms were more familiar to the playgoers at the original Globe than they are now, all playgoers in 1600, many of them illiterate, were practiced listeners. The speed of speech, even in blank verse, was markedly higher then than the recitation of Shakespeare is today. The original performances of *Hamlet*, if the Folio version reflects what was usually acted, would have run for not much more than two and a half hours (the time quoted by Ben Jonson for a play as long as *Hamlet*), compared with the more than four hours that the full Folio or 1605 Quarto text with at least one intermission would take today. Quicker speaking, quicker stage action, no intermissions, and the audience's ability to grasp the language more quickly meant that the plays galloped along. The story, not the verse, carried the thrust of the action. Occasional set speeches, like Hamlet's soliloquies or Gaunt's "sceptred isle" speech in *Richard II*, would be heard, familiar as they already were to many in the audience, like a solo aria in a modern opera. In theory if not in practice, the business of hearing, as "audience" (from the Latin *audire*, "to hear"), was more important than the business of seeing, as "spectators" (from the Latin *spectare*, "to see"). The visual aspects of acting, like scenic staging, are inherently two-dimensional and do not work well when the audience completely surrounds the actors. Most of Shakespeare's fellow writers, notably Jonson, understandably set a higher priority on the audience's hearing their verse than on their seeing what the players did with the lines. The poets wanted listeners, although the players did try to cater to the viewers. Yet for all the games with magic tricks and devils spouting fireworks that were part of the Shakespearean staging tradition, spectacle was a limited resource on the scene-free Elizabethan stage. Shakespeare in this was a poet more than a player. Even in his last and most richly staged plays, *Cymbeline*, *The Winter's Tale*, and *The Tempest*, he made notably less use of such "spectacles" than did his contemporaries.

One piece of internal evidence about the original staging is Hamlet's advice to the visiting players. In 3.2, before they stage the *Mousetrap* play that he has rewritten for them, he lectures them on what a noble student of the theater then considered to be good acting. He objects first to overacting and second to the clown who ad libs with his own jokes and does not keep to the script. How far this may have been Shakespeare's own view it is impossible to say. Hamlet is an amateur lecturing professionals about how they should do their job. His views are what we would expect an amateur playwright with a liking for plays that are "caviar to the general" to hold. His objections to the clown are noteworthy, because once the original performances ended, the clown would conclude the afternoon's entertainment with a comic song-and-dance jig. Thomas Platter, a young German-speaking Swiss student, went to the Globe in 1599 to see *Julius Caesar*. He reported back home that

> on 21 September after lunch I and my party crossed the river, and there in the playhouse with the thatched roof witnessed an excellent performance of the tragedy of the first emperor Julius Caesar with a cast of about fifteen people. When the play was over they danced marvellously and gracefully together as their custom is, two dressed as men and two as women.[1]

The script for one jig survives, probably played by Will Kemp, who was the Shakespeare company clown until he left just before *Hamlet* came to the Globe. Its story is a bawdy knockabout tale of different men trying to seduce a shopkeeper's wife in rhyming couplets, hiding in a chest from her husband, and beating one another up. There is nothing to say

---

1. *Thomas Platter's Travels in England* (1599), rendered into English from the German, and with introductory matter by Clare Williams (London: Cape, 1937), p. 166.

The hall screen in the Middle Temple Hall, built in 1574. Shakespeare's company staged *Twelfth Night* in this hall in February 1602.

what the audience reaction to such a jig might have been after they had seen a performance of *Julius Caesar* or *Hamlet*. It is possible that the Globe players stopped offering that kind of coda when they acquired the clown who played Feste in *Twelfth Night* in 1601. The song with which Feste ends that play might have become an alternative form of closure, replacing the traditional bawdy jig.

Vigorous and rapid staging was inevitable when the half of the audience closest to the stage had to stand throughout the performance. Shakespeare's plays were distinctive among the other plays of the time for their reliance on verbal sparkle over scenes of battle and physical movement, but even the soliloquies raced along. There was little occasion for long pauses and emoting. Dumb shows, like the players' prelude to the *Mousetrap* play in *Hamlet*, were the nearest that the players came to silent acting. There were no intermissions—apples, nuts, and drink were peddled in the auditorium throughout the performance—and the only "comfort stations" were, for the men, the nearest blank wall; for the women, whatever convenient pots or bottles they might be carrying under their long skirts.

Nor were there any pauses to change scenes. There was no static scenery apart from an emblematic candle to signify a night scene, a bed "thrust out" onto the stage, or the canopied chair of state on which the ruler or judge sat for court scenes. Usually any special locality would be signaled in the first words of a new scene, but unlocalized scenes were routine. Each scene ended when all the characters left the stage and another set entered. No act breaks appear in the plays before *The Tempest*. *Henry V* marked each act with a Chorus, but even he entered on the heels of the characters from the previous scene. Blue-coated stagehands were a visibly invisible presence onstage. They would draw back the central hangings on the *frons scenae* for a discovery scene, carry on the chair of state on its dais for courtroom scenes, or push out the bed with Desdemona on it for the last act of *Othello*. They served the stage like the house servants with whom the nobility peopled every room in their great houses, silent machines ready to spring into action when needed.

There has been a great deal of speculation about the tiring-house front at the rear of the stage platform: did it look more like an indoor set or an outdoor one, like the hall screen of a great house or palace or like a house front exterior? In fact, it could easily be either. The upper level of the *frons*, the balconied "above," might equally represent a musicians' gallery, like those in the main hall of a great house, or a city wall under which the central discovery space served as the city gates, as it did for York in *Richard Duke of York (3 Henry VI)* 4.8, or *Henry V*'s Harfleur (3.3.78). The "above" could equally be an indoor gallery or an outdoor balcony. The appearance of the stage was everything and nothing, depending on what the play required. Players and playwrights expected the audience members to use their imagination, as they had to with the opening lines of *Hamlet*, or, as the Prologue to *Henry V* put it, to "piece out our imperfections with your thoughts."

Shakespeare's Companies and Their Playhouses

Shakespeare's plays were written for a variety of staging conditions. Until 1594, when he joined a new company under the patronage of the lord chamberlain, the queen's officer responsible for licensing playing companies, poets had written their plays for any kind of playhouse. The Queen's Men, the largest and best company of the 1580s, is on record as playing at the Bell, the Bel Savage, and the Bull inns inside the city, and at the Theatre and the Curtain playhouses in the suburbs. Early in 1594, it completed this sweep of all the available London venues by playing at the Rose. But in that year, the system of playing changed. The lord mayor had always objected to players using the city's inns, and in May 1594 he succeeded in securing the lord chamberlain's agreement to a total ban. From then on, only the specially built playhouses in the suburbs were available for plays.

The Queen's Men had been set up in 1583, drawn from all the then-existing major companies with the best players. This larger and favored group at first monopolized playing in London. But it was in decline by the early 1590s, and the shortage of companies to perform for the queen at Christmas led the lord chamberlain and his son-in-law, the lord admiral, to set up two new companies in its place as a duopoly in May 1594. Shakespeare became a "sharer," or partner, in one of these companies. As part of the same new establishment, his company, the Lord Chamberlain's Men, was allocated the Theatre to perform in, while its partner company in the duopoly, the Lord Admiral's Men, was assigned to the Rose. This was the first time any playing company secured a playhouse officially authorized for its use alone.

The Theatre, originally built in 1576 by James Burbage, father of the leading player of the Lord Chamberlain's company, was in Shoreditch, a suburb to the north of the city. The Rose, built in 1587 by Philip Henslowe, father-in-law of the Lord Admiral's leading player, Edward Alleyn, was in the suburb of Southwark, on the south bank of the Thames. Henslowe's business papers, his accounts, some lists of costumes and other resources, and his "diary," a day-by-day listing of each day's takings and the plays that brought the money in, have survived for the period from 1592 until well into the next decade. Together they provide an invaluable record of how one of the two major companies of the later 1590s, the only rival to Shakespeare's company, operated through these years.[2] Some of Shakespeare's earlier plays, written before he joined the Lord Chamberlain's Men, including *1 Henry VI* and *Titus Andronicus*, were performed at the Rose. After May 1594, the new company acquired all of his early plays; every Shakespeare play through the next three years was written for the Theatre. Its familiarity supplied one sort of resource to the playwright. But the repertory system laid heavy demands on the company.

Henslowe's papers give a remarkable record of the company repertory for these years. Each afternoon, the same team of fifteen or so players would stage a different play. With

---

2. See *Henslowe's Diary*, ed. R. A. Foakes and R. T. Rickert (Cambridge: Cambridge University Press, 1961).

only two companies operating in London, the demand was for constant change. No play at the Rose was staged more than four or five times in any month, and it was normal to stage a different play on each of the six afternoons of each week that they performed. A new play would be introduced roughly every three weeks—after three weeks of transcribing and learning the new parts; preparing the promptbook, costumes, and properties; and rehearsing in the mornings—while each afternoon, whichever of the established plays had been advertised around town on the playbills would be put on. The leading players had to memorize on average as many as eight hundred lines for each afternoon. Richard Burbage, who played the first Hamlet in 1601, probably had to play Richard III, Orlando in *As You Like It,* and Hamlet on successive afternoons while at the same time learning the part of Duke Orsino and rehearsing the new *Twelfth Night*—and still holding at least a dozen other parts in his head for the rest of the month's program. In the evenings, he might be called on to take the company to perform a different play at court, or at a nobleman's house in the Strand. The best companies made a lot of money, but not without constant effort.

The companies were formed rather like guilds, controlled by their leading "sharers." Each senior player shared the company's profits and losses equally with his fellows. Most of the plays have seven or eight major speaking parts for the men, plus two for the boys playing the women. A normal London company had eight or ten sharers, who collectively chose the repertory of plays to be performed, bought the playbooks from the poets, and put up the money for the main company resource of playbooks and costumes (not to mention the wagon and horses for touring when plague forced the London theaters to close). Shakespeare made most of his fortune from his "share," first in his company and later in its two playhouses.

As a playhouse landlord, Henslowe took half of the takings from the galleries each afternoon for his rent, while the players shared all the yard takings and the other half of the gallery money. From their takings, the sharers paid hired hands to take the walk-on parts and to work as stagehands, musicians, bookkeeper or prompter, and "gatherers" at the different entry gates. The leading players also kept the boys who played the women's parts, housing and feeding them as "apprentices" in an imitation of the London livery companies and trades, which ran apprenticeships to train boys to become skilled artisans, or "journeymen." City apprenticeships ran for seven years from the age of seventeen, but the boy players began much younger, because unbroken voices were needed. They graduated to become adult players at an age when the city apprentices were only beginning their training. Most of the "extras," apart from the playing boys, would be left in London whenever the company had to go on tour.

Because the professional companies of the kind that Shakespeare joined all started as traveling groups rather than as companies settled at a single playhouse in London, the years up to 1594 yielded plays that could be staged anywhere. The company might be summoned to play at court, at private houses, or at the halls of the Inns of Court as readily as at inns or innyards or the custom-built theaters themselves. They traveled the country with their plays, using the great halls of country houses, or town guildhalls and local inns, wherever the town they visited allowed them. Consequently, the plays could not demand elaborate resources for staging. In this highly mobile tradition of traveling companies, they were written in the expectation of the same basic but minimal features being available at each venue. Besides the stage platform itself, the basic features appear to have been two entry doors, usually a trap in the stage floor, a pair of stage pillars, sometimes a discovery space, and very occasionally a heavens with descent machinery. Apart from these fixtures, properties such as chairs and a table, a canopied throne on a dais, and sometimes a bed were also in regular use, though in a pinch these could be as mobile as the players themselves. The only essential traveling properties were players, playbooks, and costumes.

Once the two authorized companies settled permanently at the Theatre and the Rose in 1594, they slowly lost some of this mobility. The demands of versatility and readiness to make rapid changes now had to be switched from the venues to the plays themselves. A traveling company needed very few plays, since the locations and audiences were always changing. When the venues became fixed, it was the plays that had to keep changing. The Henslowe papers record that the Lord Admiral's Men staged an amazingly varied repertory of plays at the Rose. Shakespeare's company must have been equally versatile. The practice of giving popular plays long runs did not begin until the 1630s, by which time the number of London playhouses had grown to as many as five, all offering their plays each afternoon. Shakespeare's company in London had only the one peer from 1594 until 1600; and only two from then until 1608, aside from the once-weekly plays by the two boy companies, the "little eyases" mentioned in *Hamlet*, that started with the new century.

In the years from May 1594 to April 1597 at the Theatre, in addition to all his earlier plays that he brought to his new company, Shakespeare gave them possibly *Romeo and Juliet* and *King John*, and certainly *Richard II, A Midsummer Night's Dream, 1 Henry IV*, and *The Merchant of Venice*. But then they ran into deep trouble, because they lost the Theatre. In April 1597, its original twenty-one-year lease expired, and the landlord, who disliked plays, refused to let them renew it. Anticipating this, the company's impresario James Burbage had built a new theater for them, a roofed place in the Blackfriars near St. Paul's Cathedral. The Blackfriars precinct was a "liberty," free from the lord mayor's jurisdiction. But the plan proved a disaster. The rich residents of Blackfriars objected, and the Privy Council stopped the theater from opening. From April 1597, Shakespeare's company had to rent the Curtain, an old neighbor of their now-silent Theatre, and it was there that the next four of Shakespeare's plays—*2 Henry IV, Much Ado About Nothing, The Merry Wives of Windsor*, and probably *Henry V*—were first staged.

In December 1598, losing hope of a new lease for the old Theatre, the Burbage sons had it pulled down and quietly transported its massive framing timbers across the Thames to make the scaffold for the Globe on the river's south bank, near the Rose. Most of their capital was sunk irretrievably into the Blackfriars theater, and they could afford only half the cost of rebuilding. So they raised money as best they could. Some of the company's more popular playbooks were sold to printers, including *Romeo and Juliet, Richard III, Richard II*, and *1 Henry IV*. More to the point, the Burbage brothers raised capital for the building by cutting in five of the leading players, including Shakespeare, and asking them to put up the other half of its cost. The Globe, its skeleton taken from the old Theatre, thus became the first playhouse to be owned by its players, and, within the limits set by the old frame, the first one built to their own design.

For this theater, one-eighth of which he personally owned, Shakespeare wrote his greatest plays: *Julius Caesar, As You Like It, Hamlet, Twelfth Night, Othello, All's Well That Ends Well, Measure for Measure, King Lear, Macbeth, Pericles, Antony and Cleopatra, Coriolanus, Cymbeline, The Winter's Tale*, and most likely *Troilus and Cressida* and *Timon of Athens*. As the first playhouse to be owned by the players who expected to use it, its fittings must have satisfied all the basic needs of Shakespearean staging. At one time or another, the company staged every one of Shakespeare's plays there.

In 1600, a company consisting entirely of boys started using the Blackfriars playhouse that Richard Burbage's father had tried to open four years before. Companies of boy players had a higher social status than the adult professionals, and, playing only in halls, they commanded a more affluent clientele. The boys performed only once a week, and the relative infrequency of their crowds, plus their skills as trained singers (they were choir-school children turned to making money for their choirmasters), proved less offensive to the local residents than a noisy adult company with its drums and trumpets. Leasing the Blackfriars to the boy company made a minor profit for the Burbages, who took the rent for eight years.

In the longer run, though, this arrangement provided a different means for the Burbage–Shakespeare company to advance its career. The boys' eight years of playing in their rented hall playhouse eventually made it possible for the company of adult players to renew Burbage's old plan of 1596. Shakespeare's company had been made the King's Men when James came to the throne in 1603, and their new patron gave them a status that made it impossible for the residents of Blackfriars to prevent them from implementing the original plan. During a lengthy closure of all the theaters because of a plague epidemic in

A section from Hollar's "Long View" of London. Drawn from a standpoint on the tower of the church that is now Southwark Cathedral, Hollar's view shows the roof of the great hall in which the Blackfriars playhouse was built. It can be seen as the long angled roof with a central turret, below and to the east of St. Bride's Church.

1608, the boys' manager surrendered his lease of the hall playhouse to the Burbages. They then took possession for their own company of the playhouse that their father had built for them twelve years before. They divided the new playhouse property among the leading players as they had done in 1599 with the Globe. They were the King's Men, the leading company in the country, and their status after ten years of playing at the Globe was matched by their wealth. By the time theaters reopened late in 1609, the company had established a new system of playing.

The King's Men now had two playhouses, a large open amphitheater and a much smaller roofed hall. Instead of selling or renting one out and using the other for themselves, they decided to use both in turn, for half of each year. It was a reversion to the old system with the city inns, where through the summer they played in the large open yards and in the winter played at inns with big indoor rooms. This time, though, the company owned both playhouses. Their affluence and their high status are signaled by the fact that they chose to keep one of their playhouses idle while they used the other, despite there now being a shortage of playhouses in London. That affluence was needed in 1613 when the Globe burned down at a performance of *All Is True (Henry VIII)*, and the company chose the much more expensive option of rebuilding it instead of reverting to the Blackfriars for both winter and summer. That decision, in its way, was the ultimate gesture of affection for their original playhouse. It was a costly gesture, but it meant that the Globe continued in use by the company until all the theaters were closed down by Parliament in 1642.

In 1609, when they reopened after the closure for plague, Shakespeare's company had made several changes in their procedures. The restart was at the Blackfriars, and although they offered the same kind of plays, they began to alter their style of staging. Along with the Blackfriars playhouse, they acquired a famous consort of musicians who played on strings and woodwinds in a music room set over the stage. The new consort was a distinct enhancement of the company's musical resources, which until then had been confined to song, the occasional use of recorders or hautboys, and military drums and trumpets for the scenes with soldiery. In 1608, a central room on the Globe's stage balcony was taken over to serve as a music room like the one at the Blackfriars. From this time on, the King's Men's performances began with a lengthy overture or concert of music before the play.

With that change, the plays themselves now had music to back their singers and provide other sorts of atmospheric effects. Some of the songs and music that appear in the plays not printed until the First Folio of 1623, such as the song that Mariana hears in *Measure for Measure* 4.1, may have been added after Shakespeare's time to make use of this new resource. Shakespeare did use songs, sometimes with string accompaniment, quite regularly in the early plays, but instrumental music hardly ever appears. The last play that he wrote alone, *The Tempest*, was the only one in which he made full use of this new resource.

All the plays containing soldiers and battles used the military drums that in war conveyed signals to infantry formations, as well as the trumpets that were used for signaling to cavalry. These were usually employed for offstage noises, sound effects made from "within" (inside the dressing room or tiring-house behind the stage). Soldiers marching in procession, as in the dead march at the close of *Hamlet*, would have the time marked by an onstage drum. Shakespeare never calls for guns to be fired onstage, though other writers did, but he did have other noises at his command. A small cannon or "chamber" might be used, fired from the gable-fronted heavens over the stage, as Claudius demands in *Hamlet* and as the Chorus to Act 3 of *Henry V* notes. It was wadding from a ceremonial cannon shot that set the gallery thatch alight at a performance of *All Is True* in July 1613 and burned the Globe to the ground. Stage battles such as Shrewsbury at the end of *1 Henry IV*, written for the Theatre, were accompanied by sword fights that were not the duels of *Hamlet's* finale but exchanges with broadswords or "foxes" slammed against metal shields or "targets." That action guaranteed emphatic sound effects. The drums and trumpets, with clashes of swords and a great deal of to-ing and fro-ing onto and off the stage, were highlighted in between the shouted dialogue by some hard fighting between the protagonists. The leading players were practiced swordsmen, who knew they were being watched by experts. These were the scenes of "four or five most vile and ragged foils" that the fourth Chorus self-consciously derided in *Henry V* at the Curtain.

The second great reason for noise in the amphitheaters was to mark storm and tempest. Stagehands used the kind of device that Jonson mocked in the Prologue to *Every Man in His Humour*, written for its 1616 publication. His play, wrote Jonson, was free from choruses that wafted you over the seas, "nor rolled bullet heard / To say, it thunders; nor tempestuous drum / Rumbles, to tell you when the storm doth come." For centuries, lead balls rolling down a tin trough were a standard way of making thunder noises in English theaters. The tempest in Act 3 of *King Lear* is heralded several times in the text before a stage direction, "Storm and tempest" (Folio 2.2.450), tells us that it has at last arrived. In 2.2, Cornwall notes its coming twice (Folio 2.2.452, 473). Kent comments on the "Foul weather" in his first line in Act 3, prefaced by the entry stage direction for Act 3, "Storm still," which is repeated for 3.2. Such stage directions appear in both texts (Q has "Storm" for the equivalent Scenes 8, 9, and also at 11, F's 3.4, where F omits any further reference to these noises). These explicit signals indicate that the stagehands provided offstage noises, for all that Lear himself outstorms them with his violent speeches in 3.2.

The main question about the storm scenes in *King Lear* is this: with such consistent emphasis on storm in the language, what was the design behind the stage directions? In the centuries that *Lear* has been restaged, the tempest has been made to roar offstage in a wide variety of ways, often with so much effect that, in the face of complaints that the storm noises made it difficult for the audience to hear the words, some modern productions reduced the storm to solely visual effects, or even left Lear's own raging language to express it unsupported. But the two stage directions indicate that in the original performances the "storm in nature" was not left to Lear himself to convey. The two "Storm still" directions in the Folio suggest a constant rumbling, not the intermittent crashes that might allow Lear to conduct a dialogue with the occasional outbursts of storm noises, as some modern productions have done.

Shakespeare left regrettably few stage directions to indicate the special tricks or properties that he wanted. Curtained beds are called for in *Othello* 5.2 and *Cymbeline* 2.2, and there is the specification "Stocks brought out" in *King Lear* 2.2.132. Small and portable things like papers were a much more common device, from the letters in *The Two Gentlemen of Verona* 1.2.46, 1.3.44, and 2.1.95 to Lear's map at 1.1.35. Across the whole thirty-eight plays, though, there are very few such directions. Shakespeare's economy in preparing his scripts is a major impediment to the modern reader. He hardly ever bothered to note the standard physical gestures, such as kneeling or doffing a hat, and did little more to specify any special effects. Nonetheless, it is important not to imagine elaborate devices or actions where the text does not call for them. On the whole, the demands Shakespeare made of his fellows for staging his plays appear to have been remarkably modest. Since he was a company shareholder, his parsimony may have had a simple commercial motive. Stage properties cost the company money, and one had to be confident of a new play's popularity before investing much in its staging.

There may have been other reasons for avoiding extravagant staging spectacles. Shakespeare made little use of the discovery space until the last plays, for instance, for reasons that we can only guess at. The few definite discoveries in the plays include Portia's caskets in *The Merchant of Venice*, Falstaff sleeping off his sack in *1 Henry IV* 2.5.482, the body of Polonius in *Hamlet*, Hermione's statue in *The Winter's Tale* 5.3.20, and the lovers in *The Tempest* 5.1.173, who are found when discovered to be playing chess. The audience's shock when Hermione moves and comes out of the discovery space onto the main stage is rare in Shakespeare: in every other play, whether comedy or tragedy, the audience knows far more than the characters onstage about what is going on. Shakespeare matched this late innovation in *The Winter's Tale* with his last play, *The Tempest*. After the preliminary and soothing concert by the resident Blackfriars musicians, it opens with a storm at sea so realistic that it includes that peculiarly distinctive stage direction "Enter Mariners, wet" (1.1.46). That startling piece of stage realism turns out straightaway to be not real at all but a piece of stage magic.

Documents

This selection of documents provides a range of contemporary testimony about Shakespeare's character, his work, and the social and institutional conditions under which it was produced. In the absence of newspapers and reviewers, few references to the theater survive. The availability of such hints and fragments as are presented here serves as a mark of Shakespeare's distinction, for the theater was perceived by much of the literate population as ephemeral popular entertainment. The reports of spectators whose accounts we have are more like reviews than any other texts the period has to offer; hence the importance even of brief notes such as Nashe's or Platter's, and the particular value of extended accounts such as those of Simon Forman. The government documents included here offer a vivid glimpse of the institutional procedures by which the theater was regulated. The legal documents—a contract for the construction of a theater modeled on the Globe, and Shakespeare's will—provide the most detailed account available of the material conditions of his life and work. The poems, extracts from criticism, and other literary texts show the diversity of contemporary response to his art.

The source for each text is given at the end of the introductory headnote.

WS: E. K. Chambers, *William Shakespeare: A Study of Facts and Problems.* 2 vols. Oxford: Clarendon Press, 1930.
ES: E. K. Chambers, *The Elizabethan Stage.* 4 vols. Oxford: Clarendon Press, 1923.

Robert Greene on Shakespeare (1592)

[Robert Greene (1560–1592), a prolific author of plays, romances, and pamphlets, attacked Shakespeare in his *Greenes Groats-worth of Wit, bought with a million of Repentaunce.* Greene had studied at Cambridge, and his "M.A." was prominently displayed on his title pages. Shakespeare's lack of a university education is clearly one motive for the professional resentment of the following excerpt. Another is probably that Greene was poor and very ill and felt forsaken while writing the *Groats-worth of Wit*; the preface refers to it as his "Swanne-like song," and the narrative is framed as the repentance of a dying man. (Some scholars have held that the posthumously published work contains fabrications by a publisher attempting to capitalize on Greene's name.) The three colleagues Greene addresses are likely to be Christopher Marlowe, Thomas Nashe, and George Peele. The text is that of 1596, as printed in Alexander B. Grosart's edition of Greene's *Life and Complete Works*, vol. 12 (New York: Russell and Russell).]

> *To those Gentlemen his Quondam acquaintance,*
> *that spend their wits in making Plaies,* R. G.
> *wisheth a better exercise, and wisdome*
> *to prevent his extremities. . . .*

Base minded men al three of you, if by my miserie ye be not warned: for unto none of you (like me) fought those burres to cleave: those Puppits (I meane) that speake from our mouths, those Anticks garnisht in our colours. Is it not strange that I, to whom they al have beene beholding: is it not like that you, to whome they all have beene beholding, shall (were ye in that case that I am now) be both at once of them forsaken? Yes trust them not: for there is an upstart Crow, beautified with our feathers, that with his *Tygers heart wrapt in a Players hide*,[1] *supposes he is as well able to bumbast out a blanke verse as the best of you: and being an absolute Johannes fac totum*,[2] is in his owne conceit the onely Shake-scene in a countrie. O that I might intreate your rare wits to be imployed in more profitable courses: & let those Apes imitate your past excellence, and never more acquaint them with your admired inventions. I know the best husband[3] of you all will never prove an Usurer, and the kindest of them / all will never prooue a kinde nurse: yet whilst you may, seeke you better Maisters; for it is pittie men of such rare wits, should be subject to the pleasures of such rude groomes.

Thomas Nashe on *1 Henry VI* (1592)

[Thomas Nashe (1567–1601), Greene's fellow playwright and pamphleteer, protests the attribution to himself of the *Groats-worth of Wit* in the preface to the 1592 edition of a pamphlet of his own, *Pierce Penilesse his Supplication to the Divell*. The satire of *Pierce Penilesse* is more general and political than that of the *Groats-worth*, attacking the manners of the middle class. The allusion to the Talbot scenes of *1 Henry VI* (4.2–7) comes in a section subtitled "The defence of Playes." Talbot is supposed to have been played by Richard Burbage, later the leading actor of the Lord Chamberlain's and King's Men. The text is from McKerrow's 1904 edition of Nashe's *Works*, vol. 1 (London: Bullen).]

How would it have joyed brave *Talbot* (the terror of the French) to thinke that after he had lyne two hundred yeares in his Tombe, hee should triumphe againe on the Stage, and have his bones newe embalmed with the teares of ten thousand spectators at least (at severall times), who, in the Tragedian that represents his person, imagine they behold him fresh bleeding.

Henry Chettle on Greene and Shakespeare (1592)

[Henry Chettle was involved in publishing Greene's *Groats-worth of Wit* and saw fit several months afterward to offer an apology for Greene's unfavorable treatment of Shakespeare. Chettle's willingness to serve as a kind of character witness for Shakespeare ("the other" playwright of whom he writes) may testify to Shakespeare's growing reputation. The first playwright Chettle mentions, of whom he writes more unfavorably, is Christopher Marlowe. The text is from Chettle's introductory epistle to a literary work of his own, entitled *Kind-Harts Dreame*, as reprinted in WS, vol. 2.]

About three moneths since died M. *Robert Greene*, leaving many papers in sundry Booke sellers hands, among other his Groatsworth of wit, in which a letter written to divers play-makers, is offensively by one or two of them taken; and because on the dead they cannot be avenged, they wilfully forge in their conceites[1] a living Author: and after tossing it to and fro, no remedy, but it must light on me. How I have all the time of my conversing in printing hindered the bitter inveying against schollers, it hath been very well knowne; and how in that I dealt, I can sufficiently proove. With neither of them that take offence was I acquainted, and with one of them I care not if I never be: The other, whome at that time I did not so much spare, as since I wish I had, for that as I have moderated the heate of living writers, and might have usde my owne discretion (especially in such a case) the Author beeing dead, that I did not, I

---

1. A parody of *Richard Duke of York* (*3 Henry VI*) 1.4.138: "O tiger's heart wrapped in a woman's hide!" This obvious allusion and the following pun on Shakespeare's name make it certain that Shakespeare is the

"crow" described here.
2. Jack-of-all-trades. *conceit:* imagination.
3. Steward.
1. Imaginations.

am as sory as if the originall fault had beene my fault, because my selfe have seene his demeanor no lesse civill than he exelent in the qualitie he professes: Besides, divers of worship[2] have reported his uprightnes of dealing, which argues his honesty, and his facetious grace in writting, that aprooves[3] his Art.

Gesta Grayorum on The Comedy of Errors (December 28, 1594)

[Gesta Grayorum is the title of an account of the holiday revels conducted by the law students of Gray's Inn. It was first published in 1688 (hence the modern spelling) from a manuscript that apparently had been handed down since the previous century. The subtitle of the book, "History of the High and mighty Prince, Henry Prince of Purpoole," alludes to the ceremonial ruler chosen for the occasion, the "Prince of State" referred to in the excerpt below. The performance of The Comedy of Errors was evidently part of the entertainment for the second night of revels. The text is from the 1968 reprint of Desmond Bland (Liverpool: Liverpool University Press).]

The next grand Night was intended to be upon Innocents-Day at Night; at which time there was a great Presence of Lords, Ladies, and worshipful Personages, that did expect some notable Performance at that time; which, indeed, had been effected, if the multitude of Beholders had not been so exceeding great, that thereby there was no convenient room for those that were Actors; by reason whereof, very good Inventions and Conceipts could not have opportunity to be applauded, which otherwise would have been great Contentation to the Beholders. Against which time, our Friend, the Inner Temple,[1] determined to send their Ambassador to our Prince of State, as sent from Frederick Templarius, their Emperor, who was then busied in his Wars against the Turk. The Ambassador came very gallantly appointed, and attended by a great number of brave Gentlemen, which arrived at our Court about Nine of the Clock at Night. . . . He was received very kindly of the Prince, and placed in a Chair besides His Highness, to the end that he might be Partaker of the Sports intended. . . .

When the Ambassador was placed, as aforesaid, and that there was something to be performed for the Delight of the Beholders, there arose such a disordered Tumult and Crowd upon the Stage, that there was no Opportunity to effect that which was intended: There came so great a number of worshipful Personages upon the Stage, that might not be displaced; and Gentlewomen, whose Sex did privilege them from Violence, that when the Prince and his Officers had in vain, a good while, expected and endeavoured a Reformation, at length there was no hope of Redress for that present. The Lord Ambassador and his Train thought that they were not so kindly entertained, as was before expected, and thereupon would not stay any longer at that time, but, in a sort,[2] discontented and displeased. After their Departure the Throngs and Tumults did somewhat cease, although so much of them continued, as was able to disorder and confound any good Inventions whatsoever. In regard whereof, as also for that the Sports intended were especially for the gracing of the Templarians, it was thought good not to offer any thing of Account, saving Dancing and Revelling with Gentlewomen; and after such Sports, a Comedy of Errors (like to Plautus his Menechmus) was played by the Players. So that Night was begun, and continued to the end, in nothing but Confusion and Errors; whereupon, it was ever afterwards called, The Night of Errors. . . .

The next Night upon this Occasion, we preferred Judgments thick and threefold, which were read publickly by the Clerk of the Crown, being all against a Sorcerer or Conjurer that was supposed to be the Cause of that confused Inconvenience. Therein

---

2. divers of worship: various men of rank. qualitie he professes: his vocation.
3. Demonstrates. facetious: polished, agreeable.

1. Another of the Inns of Court.
2. Departed.

was contained, How he had caused the Stage to be built, and Scaffolds to be reared to the top of the House, to increase Expectation. Also how he had caused divers Ladies and Gentlewomen, and others of good Condition, to be invited to our Sports; also our dearest Friend, the State of *Templaria*, to be disgraced, and disappointed of their kind Entertainment, deserved and intended. Also that he caused Throngs and Tumults, Crowds and Outrages, to disturb our whole Proceedings. And Lastly, that he had foisted a Company of base and common Fellows,[3] to make up our Disorders with a Play of Errors and Confusions; and that that Night had gained to us Discredit, and it self a Nickname of Errors. All which were against the Crown and Dignity of our Sovereign Lord, the Prince of *Purpoole*. . . .

The next grand Night was upon *Twelfth-day* at Night. . . . First, There came six Knights of the Helmet, with three that they led as Prisoners, and were attired like Monsters and Miscreants. The Knights gave the Prince to understand, that as they were returning from their Adventures out of *Russia*, wherein they aided the Emperor of *Russia*, against the *Tartars*, they surprized these three Persons, which were conspiring against His Highness and Dignity.[4] . . . Which being done, the Trumpets were commanded to sound, and then the King at Arms came in before the Prince, and told His Honour, that there was arrived an Ambassador from the mighty Emperor of *Russia* and *Moscovy*, that had some Matters of Weight to make known to His Highness. So the Prince willed that he should be admitted into his Presence; who came in Attire of *Russia*, accompanied with two of his own Country, in like Habit.

Francis Meres on Shakespeare (1598)

[Francis Meres (1565–1647) was educated at Cambridge and was active in London literary circles in 1597–98, after which he became a rector and schoolmaster in the country. The descriptions of Shakespeare are taken from a section on poetry in *Palladis Tamia, Wits Treasury*, a work largely consisting of translated classical quotations and *exempla*. Unlike the main body of the work, the subsections on poetry, painting, and music include comparisons of English artists to figures of antiquity. Meres goes on after the extract below to list Shakespeare among the best English writers for lyric, tragedy, comedy, elegy, and love poetry. The text is from D. C. Allen's 1933 edition of the section "Poetrie" (Urbana: University of Illinois).]

From XI

As the Greeke tongue is made famous and eloquent by *Homer, Hesiod, Euripedes, Aeschilus, Sophocles, Pindarus, Phocylides* and *Aristophanes*; and the Latine tongue by *Virgill, Ovid, Horace, Silius Italicus, Lucanus, Lucretius, Ausonius* and *Claudianus*: so the English tongue is mightily enriched, and gorgeouslie invested in rare ornaments and resplendent abiliments by Sir *Philip Sidney, Spencer, Daniel, Drayton, Warner, Shakespeare, Marlow* and *Chapman*.

From XIV

As the soule of *Euphorbus* was thought to live in *Pythagoras*: so the sweete wittie soule of Ovid lives in mellifluous & honytongued *Shakespeare*, witnes his *Venus* and *Adonis*, his *Lucrece*, his sugred Sonnets.

From XV

As *Plautus* and *Seneca* are accounted the best for Comedy and Tragedy among the Latines: so *Shakespeare* among ye English is the most excellent in both kinds for

---

3. That is, the actors.
4. This last paragraph has been included because of the theory that this ostensible visit of the Russian ambassa- dor to the court of the Prince of Purpoole provided a model for the masque of Muscovites in *Love's Labour's Lost* 5.2.

the stage; for Comedy, witnes his *Gẽtlemẽ of Verona*, his *Errors*, his *Love labors lost*, his *Love labours wonne*,[1] his *Midsummers night dreame*, & his *Merchant of Venice*: for Tragedy his *Richard the 2. Richard the 3. Henry the 4. King John, Titus Andronicus* and his *Romeo* and *Juliet*.

As *Epius Stolo* said, that the Muses would speake with *Plautus* tongue, if they would speak Latin: so I say that the Muses would speake with *Shakespeares* fine filed phrase, if they would speake English.

Parnassus Plays on Shakespeare (1598–1601)

[The three *Parnassus* plays, *The Pilgrimage to Parnassus* and *The Return from Parnassus*, *Parts 1* and *2*, were performed at Christmastime, probably in 1598, 1599, and 1601, by students of St. John's College, Cambridge. The references to Shakespeare and other contemporary writers are frequently ironic or equivocal. In the excerpts from *The Return, Part 1*, Ingenioso is an aspiring poet and Gullio a fop. In the second excerpt, Ingenioso is presenting the verses requested in the previous excerpt, having begun with examples in the vein or style of Chaucer and Spenser. Ingenioso returns in *Part 2* to discuss the merits of contemporary poets with Judicio (a critic). In the last two excerpts, Richard Burbage and Will Kempe, famous actors and colleagues of Shakespeare, turn up to try recruiting students as actors for their company "at a low rate" of pay. Burbage auditions one of them for the part of Richard III. The text is from J. B. Leishman's edition of 1949 (London: Nicholson and Watson).]

The Return from Parnassus, Part 1
ACT 3, SCENE 1

GULLIO   Suppose also that thou wert my M^ris, as sometime woodden statues represent the goddesses, thus I woulde looke amorously, thus I would pace, thus I woulde salute thee.

INGENIOSO   It will be my lucke to dye noe other death than by hearinge of his follies, I feare this speach thats a cominge will breede a deadly disease in my ears.

GULLIO   Pardon faire lady, thoughe sicke thoughted Gullio maks a maine unto thee, & like a bould faced sutore gins to woo thee.[1]

INGENIOSO   We shall have nothinge but pure Shakspeare, and shreds of poetrie that he hath gathered at the theators.

GULLIO   Pardon mee moy mittressa, ast am a gentleman the moone in comparison of thy bright hue[2] a meere slutt, Anthonies Cleopatra a blacke browde milkmaide, Hellen a dowdie.[3]

INGENIOSO   Marke Romeo and Juliet: o monstrous theft, I thinke he will runn throughe a whole booke of Samuell Daniells.[4]

GULLIO   Thrise fairer than my selfe, thus I began,
The gods faire riches, sweete above compare,
Staine to all Nimphes, [m]ore lovely the[n][5] a man,
More white and red than doves and roses are:
Nature that made thee, with herselfe had strife,
Saith that the worlde hath ending with thy life.[6]

INGENIOSO   Sweete Mr Shakspeare.

GULLIO   As I am a scholler, these arms of mine are long and strong withall:
Thus elms by vines are compast ere they falle.

---

1. The play—or at least the title—has not survived; a bookseller's record of the title does survive, however.
1. *sicke . . . thee*: compare *Venus and Adonis*, lines 5–6. Of the numerous quotations and allusions, only those referring to Shakespeare are identified.
2. *Is. ast*: as I.
3. *Anthonies . . . dowdie*: compare *Romeo and Juliet*

2.3.37.
4. Probably Samuel Daniel's sonnet sequence *Delia*.
5. *more lovely then*: correction is based on *Venus and Adonis*; other slight errors or misquotations are left uncorrected.
6. *Thrise . . . life*: compare *Venus and Adonis*, lines 7–12. *had strife*: the phrase in Shakespeare is "at strife."

INGENIOSO Faith gentleman, youre reading is wonderfull in our English poetts.

GULLIO Sweet M^{ris}, I vouchsafe to take some of there wordes and applie them to mine owne matters by a scholasticall imitation. Report thou upon thy credit, is not my vayne in courtinge gallant & honorable?

INGENIOSO Admirable sanes compare, never was soe mellifluous a witt joynet to so pure a phrase, such comly gesture, suche gentleman like behaviour.

GULLIO But stay, its verie true, good wittes have badd memories: I had almoste forgotten the cheife pointe I cald thee out for: new years day approcheth, and wheras other gallants bestowe Jewells upon there Mistrisses (as I have done whilome), I now count it base to do as the comon people doe; I will bestow upon them the precious stons of my witt, a diamonde of Invention, that shall be above all value & esteeme; therfore, sithens I am employed in some weightie affayrs of the courte, I will have thee, Ingenioso, to make them, and when thou hast done, I will peruse, pollish, and correcte them.

INGENIOSO My pen is youre bounden vassall to comande, but what vayne woulde it please you to have them in?

GULLIO Not in a vaine veine (prettie y faith): make mee them in two or three divers vayns, in Chaucers, Gowers and Spencers, and Mr Shakspeares. Marry I thinke I shall entertaine[7] those verses which run like these:

Even as the sunn with purple coloured face
Had tane his laste leave on the weeping morne,[8] etc.

O sweet Mr Shakspeare, Ile have his picture in my study at the courte.

INGENIOSO Take heede my maisters, hele kill you with tediousness ere I can ridd him of the stage.

ACT 4, SCENE 1

GULLIO Youe schollers are simple felowes, men that never came where Ladies growe; I that have spente my life amonge them knowes best what becometh my pen, and theire Ladishipps ears. Let mee heare Mr Shakspears veyne.

INGENIOSO Faire Venus, queene of beutie and of love,
Thy red doth stayne the blushinge of the morne,
Thy snowie neck shameth the milke white dove,
Thy presence doth this naked worlde adorne;
Gazinge on thee all other nymphes I scorne.
When ere thou dyest slowe shine that Satterday,
Beutie and grace muste sleepe with thee for aye.

GULLIO Noe more, I am one that can judge accordinge to the proverbe *bovem ex unguibus*.[9] Ey marry S^r, these have some life in them: let this duncified worlde esteeme of Spēcer and Chaucer, Ile worshipp sweet Mr Shakspeare, and to honoure him will lay his *Venus and Adonis* under my pillowe, as wee reade of one[1] (I do not well remember his name, but I am sure he was a kinge) slept with Homer under his beds heade. Well, Ile bestowe a Frenche crowne in the faire writinge of them out, and then Ile instructe thee about the delivery of them. Meane while, Ile have thee make an elegant description of my M^{ris}; liken the worste part of her to Cynthia, make also a familiar Dialogue betwixt her and my selfe. Ile now in, and correct these verses.   *Exit.*

INGENIOSO Why, who coulde endure this post put into a sattin sute, this haberdasher of lyes, this Bracchidochio,[2] this Ladye munger, this meere rapier and dagger, this cringer, this foretopp, but a man thats ordayned to miserie?

---

7. Accept; prefer.
8. *Euen . . . morne:* compare *Venus and Adonis*, lines 1–2.
9. [One may know] the bull by his hoof: Gullio's cor-

ruption of the proverb *Leonem ex unguibus æstimare* (The lion is known by his claws).
1. Alexander the Great.
2. Braggart.

The Return from Parnassus, Part 2
ACT 1, SCENE 2

INGENIOSO   *Benjamin Johnson.*
JUDICIO   The wittiest fellow of a Bricklayer in England.
INGENIOSO   A meere Empyrick, one that getts what he hath by observation, and makes onely nature privy to what he endites; so slow an Inventor, that he were better betake himselfe to his old trade of Bricklaying; a bould whorson, as confident now in making of a booke, as he was in times past in laying of a brick.

William Shakespeare.
JUDICIO   Who loves not *Adons* love, or *Lucrece* rape?
His sweeter verse contaynes hart robbing lines,
Could but a graver subject him content,
Without loves foolish lazy languishment.

ACT 4, SCENE 3

KEMPE   Few of the uniuersity [men] pen plaies well, they smell too much of that writer *Ovid,* and that writer *Metamorphoses,*[3] and talke too much of *Proserpina & Juppiter.* Why heres our fellow *Shakespeare* puts them all downe, I and *Ben Jonson* too. O that *Ben Jonson* is a pestilent fellow, he brought up *Horace* giving the Poets a pill, but our fellow *Shakespeare* hath given him a purge that made him beray his credit.[4]
BURBAGE   Its a shrewd fellow indeed. I wonder these schollers stay so long, they appointed to be here presently that we might try them: oh here they come.

ACT 4, SCENE 4

BURBAGE   I like your face and the proportion of your body for *Richard* the 3., I pray [you] M. *Philomusus* let me see you act a little of it.
PHILOMUSUS   Now is the winter of our discontent
Made glorious summer by the sonne of Yorke, [&c.]
BURBAGE   Very well I assure you.

Epilogue to the Queen, possibly by Shakespeare (1599)

[This epilogue was copied into a commonplace book by Henry Stanford, a retainer of the household of the Lord Chamberlain, who was also the official patron of Shakespeare's company. Shakespeare was the chief writer for the company, and the epilogue could have followed a court performance by the Lord Chamberlain's Men recorded for Shrove Tuesday, February 20, 1599, matching the year (1598 by the old calendar) and period (Shrovetide, the three days preceding Lent) specified in the heading and the text, respectively. The scholars who discovered the manuscript argue that the poem matches Shakespeare's style more closely than that of other potential authors. The text is taken from the article in which its discovery was first announced, in *Modern Philology* 70 (1972): 138–39.]

---

3. The title of a work by Ovid, not another "writer." The playwright here mocks the supposed ignorance of a mere player.
4. *he brought . . . credit:* this is a reference to the so-called War of the Theaters, a polemic involving Jonson against fellow playwrights John Marston and Thomas Dekker.

to ye Q. by ye players 1598.

As the diall hand tells ore /
  ye same howers yt had before
still beginning in ye ending /
  circuler account still lending
So most mightie Q. we pray /
  like ye diall day by day
you may lead ye seasons on /
  making new when old are gon.
that the babe wch now is yong /
  & hathe yet no use of tongue
many a shrovetyde here may bow /
  to ye empresse I doe now
that the children of these lordes /
  sitting at your counsell bourdes
may be grave & aeged seene /
  of her ye was ther father Quene
once I wishe this wishe again /
  heaven subscribe yt wth amen.

John Weever on Shakespeare (1599)

[This sonnet, which follows the "Shakespearean" rhyme scheme, was published in a collection entitled *Epigrammes in the oldest Cut, and newest Fashion*. Like many of the other
references to Shakespeare's writings in this period, Weever's poem pays less attention to
the plays than to the narrative poems, which were of higher literary status and (to judge,
for example, from the *Parnassus* plays) popular among young men of fashion. Weever
(1576–1632) was himself a student at Cambridge not long before this poem was published.
The text is from *WS*, vol. 2.]

Ad Gulielmum Shakespeare.

Honie-tongued Shakespeare when I saw thine issue
I swore *Apollo* got them[1] and none other,
Their rosie-tainted features cloth'd in tissue,[2]
Some heaven born goddesse said to be their mother:
Rose-checkt[3] Adonis with his amber tresses,
Faire fire-hot *Venus* charming him to love her,
Chaste *Lucretia* virgine-like her dresses,
Prowd lust-stung *Tarquine* seeking still to prove[4] her:
Romea Richard; more whose names I know not,
Their sugred tongues, and power attractive beuty
Say they are Saints althogh that Sts they shew not
For thousands vowes to them subjective dutie:[5]
They burn in love thy children *Shakespear* het them,
Go, wo thy Muse more Nymphish brood beget them.[6]

1. *when . . . them:* Shakespeare's poetic productions
("issue") are so perfect they seem to have been created
(begotten) by the patron of poets, Apollo, himself. The
identification of Shakespeare's muse as goddess (line 4)
or nymph (line 14) continues the trope of divine inspiration.
2. Rich fabric. *tainted:* tinted.
3. Cheeked.
4. Attempt.
5. *Their . . . dutie:* Shakespeare's characters are so com-

pelling that they have elicited the devotion ordinarily
given to saints. Their actions may not be saintly ("Sts
they show not"), but "thousands" have given to them
the devotion a subject gives a sovereign.
6. *They burn . . . them:* the antecedent for "they" is
"thousands" in line 12; with modern spelling and punctuation, the couplet might read: "They burn in love; thy
children, Shakespeare, het [heated] them. / Go woo thy
muse, more nymphish brood beget them."

Thomas Platter on *Julius Caesar* (September 21, 1599)

[Thomas Platter (b. 1574), a Swiss traveler, recorded his experience at the Globe playhouse in an account of his travels. The German text is printed in WS 2:322.]

Den 21 Septembris nach dem Imbissessen, etwan umb zwey vhren, bin ich mitt meiner geselschaft v̇ber daz wasser gefahren, haben in dem streüwinen Dachhaus die Tragedy vom ersten Keyser Julio Caesare mitt ohngefahr 15 personen sehen gar artlich agieren; zu endt der Comedien dantzeten sie ihrem gebraucht nach gar v̇ber-ausz zierlich, ye zwen in mannes vndt 2 in weiber kleideren angethan, wunderbahr-lich mitt einanderen.

On the 21st of September after lunch, about two o'clock, I crossed the water [the Thames] with my party, and we saw the tragedy of the first emperor Julius Caesar acted very prettily in the house with the thatched roof, with about fifteen characters; at the end of the comedy, according to their custom, they danced with exceeding elegance, two each in men's and two in women's clothes, wonderfully together.

[Translated by Noah Heringman]

Gabriel Harvey on *Hamlet, Venus and Adonis*, and *The Rape of Lucrece* (1598–1603)

[Gabriel Harvey (c. 1550–1631), a scholar perhaps best remembered as the particular friend of Spenser, gave the following account of Shakespeare and other contemporaries in a long manuscript note in his copy of Speght's 1598 edition of Chaucer. The date of the note is uncertain, but internal evidence makes it highly unlikely to be later than 1603. The references to Shakespeare are brief but suggestive, and the note is useful both in providing a context for the appreciation of Shakespeare and for its characteristically keen assessment of the state of modern literature. The text is from G. C. Moore Smith's edition of *Gabriel Harvey's Marginalia* (Stratford-upon-Avon: Shakespeare Head Press, 1913).]

And now translated Petrarch, Ariosto, Tasso, & Bartas himself deserve curious comparison with Chaucer, Lidgate, & owre best Inglish, auncient & moderne. Amongst which, the Countesse of Pembrokes Arcadia, & the Faerie Queene ar now freshest in request: & Astrophil, & Amyntas ar none of the idlest pastimes of sum fine humanists. The Earle of Essex much commendes Albions England:[1] and not unwor-thily for diverse notable pageants, before, & in the Chronicle. Sum Inglish, & other Histories nowhere more sensibly described, or more inwardly discovered. The Lord Mountjoy makes the like account of Daniels peece of the Chronicle,[2] touching the Usurpation of Henrie of Bullingbrooke, which in deede is a fine, sententious, & poli-tique peece of Poetrie: as proffitable, as pleasurable. The younger sort takes much delight in Shakespeares Venus, & Adonis: but his Lucrece, & his tragedie of Hamlet, Prince of Denmarke, have it in them, to please the wiser sort. Or such poets: or better: or none.

Vilia miretur vulgus: mihi flavus Apollo
Pocula Castaliæ plena ministret aquæ:[3]

quoth Sir Edward Dier, betwene jest, & earnest. Whose written devises farr excell most of the sonets, and cantos in print. His Amaryllis, & Sir Walter Raleighs Cynthia,

---

1. By William Warner (1586).
2. *The Civil Wars Between the Two Houses of Lancaster and York* (1595).
3. "Let what is cheap excite the marvel of the crowd;

for me may golden Apollo minister full cups from the Castalian fount" (Ovid, *Amores* 1.15.35–36, Loeb translation). These lines also appear on the title page of Shakespeare's *Venus and Adonis* (1593).

how fine & sweet inventions? Excellent matter of emulation for Spencer, Constable, France, Watson, Daniel, Warner, Chapman, Silvester, Shakespeare, & the rest of owr florishing metricians. I looke for much, aswell in verse, as in prose, from mie two Oxford frends, Doctor Gager, & M. Hackluit: both rarely furnished for the purpose: & I have a phansie to Owens new Epigrams, as pithie as elegant, as plesant as sharp, & sumtime as weightie as breife: & amongst so manie gentle, noble, & royall spirits meethinkes I see sum heroical thing in the clowdes: mie soveraine hope. Axiophilus[4] shall forgett himself, or will remember to leave sum memorials behinde him: & to make an use of so manie rhapsodies, cantos, hymnes, odes, epigrams, sonets, & discourses, as at idle howers, or at flowing fitts he hath compiled. God knowes what is good for the world, & fitting for this age.

Contract for the Building of the Fortune Theatre (1600)

[This contract was drawn up between Philip Henslowe and Edward Alleyn, partners in the venture, and Peter Street, the carpenter (or general contractor) in charge of the construction. In fact, Alleyn seems to have put up all the money, £440 for the work specified in the contract in addition to £80 for decoration and considerable sums to acquire the lot and surrounding properties. Alleyn faced opposition from residents of the neighborhood, but he had secured the favor of key supporters, so that he was able to proceed with the construction. As the new home of the Lord Admiral's Men, the Fortune did in fact become a center of disturbances, with complaints coming to the Middlesex Bench of assaults, petty thefts, and riotous behavior. Alleyn had been the leading actor of the Lord Admiral's Men, chief competitors of the Lord Chamberlain's Men, and the Fortune was conceived to compete with the Globe, meanwhile replacing the decaying and poorly situated Rose Theatre. The contract's descriptions and frequent references to the Globe, given this background, can be seen as providing some of our best evidence on the nature of the Globe itself. The text is reprinted in ES, vol. 2.]

'This Indenture made the Eighte daie of Januarye 1599,[1] and in the Twoe and Fortyth yeare of the Reigne of our sovereigne Ladie Elizabeth, by the grace of god Queene of Englande, Fraunce and Irelande, defender of the Faythe, &c. betwene Phillipp Henslowe and Edwarde Allen of the parishe of Ste Saviours in Southwark in the Countie of Surrey, gentlemen, on thone parte, and Peeter Streete, Cittizen and Carpenter of London, on thother parte witnesseth That whereas the saide Phillipp Henslowe & Edward Allen, the daie of the date hereof, have bargayned, compounded & agreed with the saide Peter Streete ffor the erectinge, buildinge & settinge upp of a new howse and Stadge for a Plaiehouse in and uppon a certeine plott or parcell of grounde appoynted oute for that purpose, scytuate and beinge nere Goldinge lane in the parishe of Ste Giles withoute Cripplegate of London,[2] to be by him the saide Peeter Streete or somme other sufficyent woorkmen of his provideinge and appoyntemente and att his propper costes & chardges, for the consideracion hereafter in theis presentes expressed, made, erected, builded and sett upp in manner & forme followinge (that is to saie); The frame of the saide howse to be sett square[3] and to conteine ffowerscore foote of lawfull assize everye waie square withoutt and fiftie five foote of like assize square everye waie within, with a good suer and stronge foundacion of pyles, brick, lyme and sand bothe without & within, to be wroughte one foote of assize att the leiste above the grounde; And the saide fframe to conteine three Stories in heighth, the first or lower Storie to conteine Twelve foote of lawfull assize in

---

4. Probably Harvey himself.
1. 1600 (New Style).
2. *nere . . . London:* an area then in the northwest suburbs, literally outside Cripplegate and, like the Globe across the water, outside the jurisdiction of a City Coun-

cil often inimical to the theater.
3. This square shape was unusual; the outlines of comparable theaters of the period were round or polygonal (with more than four sides).

heighth, the second Storie Eleaven foote of lawfull assize in heigth, and the third or upper Storie to conteine Nyne foote of lawfull assize in heigth; All which Stories shall conteine Twelve foote and a halfe of lawfull assize in breadth througheoute, besides a juttey forwardes in either of the saide twoe upper Stories of Tenne ynches of lawfull assize, with ffower convenient divisions for gentlemens roomes,[4] and other sufficient and convenient divisions for Twoe pennie roomes, with necessarie seates to be placed and sett, aswell in those roomes as througheoute all the rest of the galleries of the saide howse, and with suchelike steares, conveyances & divisions withoute & within, as are made & contryved in and to the late erected Plaiehowse on the Banck in the saide parishe of Ste Saviours called the Globe; With a Stadge and Tyreinge howse[5] to be made, erected & settupp within the saide fframe, with a shadowe or cover[6] over the saide Stadge, which Stadge shalbe placed & sett, as alsoe the stearecases of the saide fframe, in suche sorte as is prefigured in a plott[7] thereof drawen, and which Stadge shall conteine in length Fortie and Three foote of lawfull assize and in breadth to extende to the middle of the yarde[8] of the saide howse; The same Stadge to be paled in belowe with good, stronge and sufficyent newe oken bourdes, and likewise the lower Storie of the saide fframe withinside, and the same lower storie to be alsoe laide over and fenced with strong yron pykes; And the saide Stadge to be in all other proporcions contryved and fashioned like unto the Stadge of the saide Plaie howse called the Globe; With convenient windowes and lightes glazed to the saide Tyreinge howse; And the saide fframe, Stadge and Stearecases to be covered with Tyle, and to have a sufficient gutter of lead to carrie & convey the water frome the coveringe of the saide Stadge to fall backwardes; And also all the saide fframe and the Staircases thereof to be sufficyently enclosed withoute with lathe, lyme & haire, and the gentlemens roomes and Twoe pennie roomes to be seeled[9] with lathe, lyme & haire, and all the fflowers of the saide Galleries, Stories and Stadge to be bourded with good & sufficyent newe deale bourdes of the whole thicknes, wheare need shalbe; And the saide howse and other thinges beforemencioned to be made & doen to be in all other contrivitions, conveyances, fashions, thinge and thinges effected, finished and doen accordinge to the manner and fashion of the saide howse called the Globe, saveinge only that all the princypall and maine postes of the saide fframe and Stadge forwarde shalbe square and wroughte palasterwise,[1] with carved proporcions called Satiers[2] to be placed & sett on the topp of every of the same postes, and saveinge alsoe that the said Peeter Streete shall not be chardged with anie manner of pay[ntin]ge in or aboute the saide fframe howse or Stadge or anie parte thereof, nor rendringe[3] the walls within, nor seeling anie more or other roomes then the gentlemens roomes, Twoe pennie roomes and Stadge before remembred. Nowe theiruppon the saide Peeter Streete dothe covenant, promise and graunte ffor himself, his executours and administratours, to and with the saide Phillipp Henslowe and Edward Allen and either of them, and thexecutours and administratours of them and either of them, by theis presentes in manner & forme followeinge (that is to saie); That he the saide Peeter Streete, his executours or assignes, shall & will att his or their owne propper costes & chardges well, woorkmanlike & substancyallie make, erect, sett up and fully finishe in and by all thinges, accordinge to the true meaninge of theis presentes, with good, stronge and substancyall newe tymber and other necessarie stuff, all the saide fframe and other woorkes whatsoever in and uppon the saide plott or parcell of grounde (beinge not by anie aucthoretie restrayned, and haveinge ingres, egres & regres to doe the same) before the ffyve & twentith daie of Julie next commeinge after the date hereof; And

---

4. Something like the V.I.P. boxes of the present day.
5. "Attiring house," a dressing room and backstage area extending onto the rear of the stage.
6. A roof (known as "the heavens") partially covering the stage, supported by the pillars that also served as versatile pieces of scenery.
7. Plan.
8. *in breadth . . . yarde*: the stage would then extend

about twenty-seven feet into the yard, specified earlier as fifty-five feet square.
9. Coated both on the "ceiling" (a related word) and the walls.
1. Finished in the form of pilasters, ornamental columns in the classical style.
2. Satyrs. *proporcions*: figures.
3. Plastering.

shall alsoe at his or theire like costes and chardges provide and finde all manner of
woorkmen, tymber, joystes, rafters, boordes, dores, boltes, hinges, brick, tyle, lathe,
lyme, haire, sande, nailes, lade, iron, glasse, woorkmanshipp and other thinges whatsoever, which shalbe needefull, convenyent & necessarie for the saide fframe &
woorkes & everie parte thereof; And shall alsoe make all the saide fframe in every
poynte for Scantlinges[4] lardger and bigger in assize then the Scantlinges of the timber
of the saide newe erected howse called the Globe; And alsoe that he the saide Peeter
Streete shall furthwith, aswell by himself as by suche other and soemanie woorkmen
as shalbe convenient & necessarie, enter into and uppon the saide buildinges and
woorkes, and shall in reasonable manner proceede therein withoute anie wilfull
detraccion untill the same shalbe fully effected and finished. In consideracion of all
which buildinges and of all stuff & woorkemanshipp thereto belonginge, the saide
Phillipp Henslowe & Edward Allen and either of them, ffor themselves, theire, and
either of theire executours & administratours, doe joynctlie & severallie covenante &
graunte to & with the saide Peeter Streete, his executours & administratours by theis
presentes, that they the saide Phillipp Henslowe & Edward Allen or one of them, or
the executours administratours or assignes of them or one of them, shall & will well &
truelie paie or cawse to be paide unto the saide Peeter Streete, his executours or
assignes, att the place aforesaid appoynted for the erectinge of the saide fframe, the
full somme of Fower hundred & Fortie Poundes of lawfull money of Englande in
manner & forme followeinge (that is to saie), att suche tyme and when as the Tymber-
woork of the saide fframe shalbe rayzed & sett upp by the saide Peeter Streete his
executours or assignes, or within seaven daies then next followeinge, Twoe hundred &
Twentie poundes, and att suche time and when as the saide fframe & woorkes shalbe
fullie effected & ffynished as is aforesaide, or within seaven daies then next followeinge, thother Twoe hundred and Twentie poundes, withoute fraude or coven.[5] Provided allwaies, and it is agreed betwene the saide parties, that whatsoever somme or
sommes of money the saide Phillipp Henslowe & Edward Allen or either of them, or
thexecutours or assignes of them or either of them, shall lend or deliver unto the saide
Peter Streete his executours or assignes, or anie other by his appoyntemente or consent, ffor or concerninge the saide woorkes or anie parte thereof or anie stuff thereto
belonginge, before the raizeinge & settinge upp of the saide fframe, shalbe reputed,
accepted, taken & accoumpted in parte of the firste paymente aforesaid of the saide
some of Fower hundred & Fortie poundes, and all suche somme & sommes of
money, as they or anie of them shall as aforesaid lend or deliver betwene the razeinge
of the saide fframe & finishinge thereof and of all the rest of the saide woorkes, shalbe
reputed, accepted, taken & accoumpted in parte of the laste pamente aforesaid of the
same somme of Fower hundred & Fortie poundes, anie thinge abovesaid to the contrary notwithstandinge. In witnes whereof the parties abovesaid to theis presente
Indentures Interchaungeably have sett theire handes and seales. Geoven[6] the daie and
yeare ffirste abovewritten.

P S

Sealed and delivered by the saide Peter Streete in the presence of me William Harris
Pub[lic] Scr[ivener] And me Frauncis Smyth appr[entice] to the said Scr[ivener]
    [*Endorsed:*] Peater Streat ffor The Building of the Fortune.

Augustine Phillips, Francis Bacon, et al. on *Richard II* (1601)

[These extracts from testimony submitted at the Earl of Essex's trial for treason, and related
documents, show that some of Essex's supporters had contracted with the Lord Chamberlain's Men to revive *Richard II*, apparently in order to provide a model for the justified
deposition of a monarch and thus propitiate the coup in which Essex planned to depose

4. Prescribed dimensions of the beams.   6. Given.
5. Deceit.

Elizabeth. The play was performed on February 7, and "it was on the same day," according to E. K. Chambers, "that Essex received a summons to appear before the Privy Council. This interrupted his plans for securing possession of the Queen's person and arresting her ministers, and precipitated his futile outbreak of February 8." Augustine Phillips was one of Shakespeare's colleagues in the Lord Chamberlain's Men. Sir Edward Coke was, for a time, chief justice under King James. The last excerpt is a contemporary record of a conversation between the queen and her archivist several months after Essex was executed. The texts are from WS, vol. 2.]

From the Abstract of Evidence

The Erle of Essex is charged with high Treason, namely, That he plotted and practised with the Pope and king of Spaine for the disposing and settling to himself Aswell the Crowne of England, as of the kingdom of Ireland.

From the Examination of Augustine Phillips, February 18, 1601

The Examination of Augustyne Phillypps servant unto the L Chamberlyne and one of hys players taken the xviij[th] of Februarij 1600 upon hys oth

He sayeth that on Fryday last was sennyght or Thursday S[r] Charles Percy S[r] Josclyne Percy and the L. Montegle with some thre more spak to some of the players in the presans of thys examinate to have the play of the deposyng and kyllyng of Kyng Rychard the second to be played the Saterday next promysyng to gete them xls. more then their ordynary to play yt. Wher thys Examinate and hys fellowes were determyned to have played some other play, holdyng that play of Kyng Richard to be so old & so long out of use as that they shold have small or no Company at yt. But at their request this Examinate and his fellowes were Content to play yt the Saterday and had their xls. more then their ordynary for yt and so played yt accordyngly

Augustine Phillipps

From the speech of Sir Edward Coke at Essex's trial, February 19

I protest upon my soul and conscience I doe beleeve she should not have long lived after she had been in your power. Note but the precedents of former ages, how long lived Richard the Second after he was surprised in the same manner? The pretence was alike for the removing of certain counsellors, but yet shortly after it cost him his life.

From [Francis Bacon's] "A Declaration of the ... Treasons ... by Robert late Earle of Essex"

The afternoone before the rebellion, Merricke,[1] with a great company of others, that afterwards were all in the action, had procured to bee played before them, the play of deposing King Richard the second. Neither was it casuall, but a play bespoken by Merrick. And not so onely, but when it was told him by one of the players, that the play was olde, and they should have losse in playing it, because fewe would come to it: there was fourty shillings extraordinarie given to play it, and so thereupon playd it was. So earnest hee was to satisfie his eyes with the sight of that tragedie which hee thought soone after his lord should bring from the stage to the state, but that God turned it upon their owne heads.

From a Memorandum in the Lambard family manuscript, August 4

... so her Majestie fell upon[2] the reign of King Richard II. saying, 'I am Richard II. know ye not that?'

---

1. Sir Gilly Merrick, one of Essex's supporters, was later tried separately for treason.

2. Came across (in reading). The memorandum describes a scene in which the queen is reading over the

W.L. 'Such a wicked imagination was determined and attempted by a most unkind Gent. the most adorned creature that ever your Majestie made.'

Her Majestie. 'He that will forget God, will also forget his benefactors; this tragedy was played 40[tie] times in open streets and houses.'

John Manningham on *Twelfth Night* and *Richard III* (1602)

[John Manningham (d. 1622) kept a diary during his time as a law student at the Middle Temple, recording the witticisms of his colleagues and a rich variety of anecdotes. The vibrant and boisterous life of the Inns of Court is also illustrated by the *Gesta Grayorum* (see above). The February entry describes the festivities organized for Candlemas Day at the Middle Temple, while the second recounts an anecdote related to Manningham by one Mr. Touse (this name is difficult to read in the manuscript). As with all the documents in this section, any date before March 25 is assigned to the following year according to our calendar, so that 1601 here becomes 1602 (New Style). The text is from the 1976 edition of Robert Sorlien (Hanover, N.H.: University Press of New England).]

Febr. 1601

2. At our feast wee had a play called "Twelve night, or what you will"; much like the commedy of errores, or Menechmi[1] in Plautus, but most like and neere to that in Italian called Inganni.[2] A good practise in it to make the steward beleeve his Lady widdowe[3] was in Love with him, by counterfayting a letter, as from his Lady, in generall termes, telling him what shee liked best in him, and prescribing his gesture in smiling, his apparraile, &c., and then when he came to practise, making him beleeve they tooke him to be mad.

Marche. 1601

13. . . . Upon a tyme when Burbidge played Rich[ard] 3. there was a Citizen grewe soe farr in liking with him, that before shee went from the play shee appointed him to come that night unto hir by the name of Ri[chard] the 3. Shakespeare, overhearing their conclusion, went before, was intertained, and at his game ere Burbidge came. Then message being brought that Richard the 3[d]. was at the dore, Shakespeare caused returne to be made that William the Conquerour was before Rich[ard] the 3. Shakespeare's name William. (Mr. Touse.)

Letters Patent formalizing the adoption of the Lord Chamberlain's Men as the King's Men (May 19, 1603)

[James I issued the warrant ordering this patent shortly after his coronation, enhancing the status of Shakespeare's company. As retainers of the royal household with the title of Grooms of the Chamber, they performed at the court with increasing frequency (177 times between 1603 and 1616) and assisted occasionally with other court functions, but more important, they acted throughout the kingdom under the authority of the royal patent, whose scope the forceful wording below makes clear. The patent, bearing the Great Seal, was issued May 19 as ordered in the warrant of May 17. There is some evidence to suggest that James was particularly taken with Shakespeare's poetry, and the playwright's valorization of James's ancestry (as originating with Banquo) in *Macbeth* certainly suggests that Shakespeare cultivated his esteem. The text is from *ES*, vol. 2.]

---

archives that have been in the keeping of her interlocutor, William Lambard.

1. Source for *The Comedy of Errors.*

2. The two plays with this exact title (1562 and 1592) seem less likely to be "most like" *Twelfth Night* than another Italian play, *Ingannati* (1537), which has char-

acters named Fabio and Malevolti and makes reference to Twelfth Night (Epiphany).

3. Olivia is not a widow in the version of Shakespeare's play that has come down to us, though she is so described in one of Shakespeare's principal sources for the play.

Commissio specialis pro Laurencio Fletcher & Willelmo Shackespeare et aliis[2] James by the grace of god &c. To all Justices, Maiors, Sheriffes, Constables, hedborowes,[1] and other our Officers and lovinge Subjectes greetinge. Knowe yee that Wee of our speciall grace, certeine knowledge, & mere motion[3] have licenced and aucthorized and by theise presentes[4] doe licence and aucthorize theise our Servauntes Lawrence Fletcher, William Shakespeare, Richard Burbage, Augustyne Phillippes, John Heninges, Henrie Condell, William Sly, Robert Armyn, Richard Cowly, and the rest of theire Assosiates freely to use and exercise the Arte and faculty of playinge Comedies, Tragedies, histories, Enterludes, moralls,[5] pastoralls, Stageplaies, and Suche others like as theie have alreadie studied or hereafter shall use or studie, aswell for the recreation of our lovinge Subjectes, as for our Solace and pleasure when wee shall thincke good to see them, duringe our pleasure. And the said Commedies, tragedies, histories, Enterludes, Morralles, Pastoralls, Stageplayes, and suche like to shewe and exercise publiquely to theire best Commoditie,[6] when the infection of the plague shall decrease, aswell within theire nowe usual howse called the Globe within our County of Surrey, as alsoe within anie towne halls or Moute halls[7] or other conveniente places within the liberties and freedome of anie other Cittie, universitie, towne, or Boroughe whatsoever within our said Realmes and domynions. Willinge and Commaundinge you and everie of you, as you tender our pleasure, not onelie to permitt and suffer them herein without anie your lettes hindrances or molestacions during our said pleasure, but alsoe to be aidinge and assistinge to them, yf anie wronge be to them offered, And to allowe them such former Curtesies as hath bene given to men of theire place and quallitie,[8] and alsoe what further favour you shall shewe to theise our Servauntes for our sake wee shall take kindlie at your handes. In wytnesse whereof &c. witnesse our selfe at Westminster the nyntenth day of May

per breve de privato sigillo[9] &c.

Master of the Wardrobe's Account (March 1604)

[This entry offers us a rare glimpse of the players in the entourage of King James, sporting festive regalia in their capacity as Grooms of the Chamber. The royal procession took place March 15, 1604. The text is from WS, vol. 2.]

Red Clothe bought of sondrie persons and given by his Majestie to diverse persons against[1] his Majesties sayd royall proceeding through the Citie of London, viz.:— . . .

The Chamber . . .	
Fawkeners[2] &c. &c.	Red cloth
William Shakespeare	iiii yardes di.
Augustine Phillipps	"
Lawrence Fletcher	"
John Hemminges	"
Richard Burbidge	"
William Slye	"
Robert Armyn	"
Henry Cundell	"
Richard Cowley	"

1. A parish officer similar to a petty constable.
2. *Commissio . . . aliis:* By special commission on behalf of . . . and others.
3. Inclination, desire.
4. The present document.
5. Morality plays.
6. Advantage.
7. Council chambers.

8. Profession.
9. In sum, from the privy seal.
1. For.
2. Obsolete form of "falconers," very likely the men who trained the falcons used for James's fowl-hunting expeditions. The falconers might owe their place in the retinue to James's well-known passion for hunting.

Henry Jackson on *Othello* (September 1610)

[Several excerpts from the letters of Henry Jackson (d. 1662) of Corpus Christi College, Oxford, were made, probably after Jackson's death, by William Fulman, Jackson's successor in the college living of Meysey Hampton. One of these letters reveals that the King's Men played at Oxford in 1610, probably in September when the letter was written (the specific days are not given). After expressing some shock at the "violation" of Holy Scripture occurring in Jonson's *The Alchemist,* also in the repertoire of the King's Men, Jackson proceeds in the excerpt below to a more favorable discussion of the company's "tragedies," singling out *Othello* for special praise. Geoffrey Tillotson reprinted Fulman's transcripts in the *Times Literary Supplement* for July 20, 1933. The original letters do not survive.]

Habuerunt et Tragœdias, quas decorè, et aptè agebant. In quibus non solùm, dicendo, sed etiam faciendo quædam lachrymas movebant.—
—At verò Desdemona illa apud nos a marito occisa, quanquam optimè semper causam egit, interfecta tamen magis movebat; cum in lecto decumbens spectantium misericordiam ipso vultu imploraret.—

Sept. 1610.

They also had some tragedies, which they performed beautifully and with propriety. Among those, a few aroused tears, not only through their words, but even their gestures.—
—But truly Desdemona, having been killed by her husband before our eyes, although she pleaded her cause superbly throughout, nevertheless she moved [us] more after she had been murdered, when, lying upon her bed, her face itself implored pity from the onlookers.

Simon Forman on *Macbeth, Cymbeline,* and *The Winter's Tale* (1611)

[Simon Forman (1552–1611) was a largely self-educated physician and astrologer who rose from humble beginnings to establish a successful London practice. A large parcel of his manuscripts, including scientific and autobiographical material as well as the diary from which this account of the plays is taken, has survived, making his life one of the best-documented Elizabethan lives. These manuscripts provide detailed information about Forman's many sidelines, such as the manufacture of talismans, alchemy, and necromancy, as well about his sex life. The text is from WS, vol. 2.]

The Bocke of Plaies and Notes therof per formane for Common Pollicie[1]

In Mackbeth at the Glob, 1610 ⟨1611⟩, the 20 of Aprill ♄ (Saturday), ther was to be observed, firste, howe Mackbeth and Bancko, 2 noble men of Scotland, Ridinge thorowe a wod, the ⟨r⟩ stode before them 3 women feiries or Nimphes, And saluted Mackbeth, sayinge, 3 tyms unto him, haille Mackbeth, king of Codon;[2] for thou shalt be a kinge, but shalt beget No kinges, &c. Then said Bancko, What all to Mackbeth And nothing to me. Yes, said the nimphes, haille to thee Bancko, thou shalt beget kinges, yet be no kinge. And so they departed & cam to the Courte of Scotland to Dunkin king of Scotes, and yt was in the dais of Edward the Confessor. And Dunkin bad them both kindly wellcome, And made Mackbeth forth with Prince of Northumberland,[3] and sent him hom to his own castell, and appointed Mackbeth to provid for

---

1. *Common Pollicie:* practical use. Forman's title for his notes on plays is not printed in Chambers, but interpolated here from G. Blakemore Evans's transcription in the *Riverside Shakespeare.*

2. Cawdor.
3. Probably Forman's error; Duncan gives Macbeth the title Thane of Cawdor. Duncan's son Malcolm is the Prince of Northumberland.

him, for he would sup with him the next dai at night, & did soe. And Mackebeth contrived to kill Dunkin, & thorowe the persuasion of his wife did that night Murder the kinge in his own Castell, beinge his guest. And ther were many prodigies seen that night & the dai before. And when Mack Beth had murdred the kinge, the blod on his handes could not be washed of by Any meanes, nor from his wives handes, which handled the bloddi daggers in hiding them, By which means they became both moch amazed & Affronted. The murder being knowen, Dunkins 2 sonns fled, the on to England, the ⟨other to⟩ Walles, to save them selves, they being fled, they were supposed guilty of the murder of their father, which was nothinge so. Then was Mack-beth crowned kinge, and then he for feare of Banko, his old companion, that he should beget kinges but be no kinge him selfe, he contrived the death of Banko, and caused him to be Murdred on the way as he Rode. The next night, beinge at supper with his noble men whom he had bid to a feaste to the which also Banco should have com, he began to speake of Noble Banco, and to wish that he wer ther. And as he thus did, standing up to drincke a Carouse to him, the ghoste of Banco came and sate down in his cheier behind him. And he turninge About to sit down Again sawe the goste of Banco, which fronted him so, that he fell into a great passion of fear and fury, Utterynge many wordes about his murder, by which, when they hard that Banco was Murdred they Suspected Mackbet.

Then MackDove fled to England to the kinges sonn, And soe they Raised an Army, And cam into Scotland, and at Dunston Anyse overthrue Mackbet. In the meantyme whille Macdovee was in England, Mackbet slewe Mackdoves wife & chil-dren, and after in the battelle Mackdove slewe Mackbet.

Observe Also howe Mackbetes quen did Rise in the night in her slepe, & walke and talked and confessed all, & the docter noted her wordes.

Of Cimbalin king of England.

Remember also the storri of Cymbalin king of England, in Lucius tyme, howe Lucius Cam from Octavus Cesar for Tribut, and being denied, after sent Lucius with a greate Arme of Souldiars who landed at Milford haven, and Affter wer vanquished by Cim-balin, and Lucius taken prisoner, and all by means of 3 outlawes, of the which 2 of them were the sonns of Cimbalim, stolen from him when they were but 2 yers old by an old man whom Cymbalin banished, and he kept them as his own sonns 20 yers with him in A cave. And howe ⟨one⟩ of them slewe Clotan, that was the quens sonn, goinge to Milford haven to sek the love of Innogen the kinges daughter, whom he had banished also for lovinge his daughter,[4] and howe the Italian that cam from her love conveied him selfe into A Cheste, and said yt was a chest of plate sent from her love & others, to be presented to the kinge. And in the depest of the night, she being aslepe, he opened the cheste, & cam forth of yt, And vewed her in her bed, and the markes of her body, & toke awai her braslet, & after Accused her of adultery to her love, &c. And in thend howe he came with the Romains into England & was taken prisoner, and after Reveled to Innogen, Who had turned her self into mans appar-rell & fled to mete her love at Milford haven, & chanchsed to fall on the Cave in the wodes wher her 2 brothers were, & howe by eating a sleping Dram they thought she had bin deed, & laid her in the wodes, & the body of Cloten by her, in her loves apparrell that he left behind him, & howe she was found by Lucius, &c.

In the Winters Talle at the glob 1611 the 15 of maye ☿ ⟨Wednesday⟩.

Observe ther howe Lyontes the kinge of Cicillia was overcom with Jelosy of his wife with the kinge of Bohemia his frind that came to see him, and howe he contrived his death and wold have had his cup berer to have poisoned, who gave the king of Bohemia warning therof & fled with him to Bohemia.

Remember also howe he sent to the Orakell of Appollo & the Annswer of Apollo,

---

4. Morgan/Belarius is not banished in the version of the play that comes down to us.

that she was giltles and that the king was jelouse &c. and howe Except the child was found Again that was loste the kinge should die without yssue, for the child was caried into Bohemia & ther laid in a forrest & brought up by a sheppard And the kinge of Bohemia his sonn maried that wentch & howe they fled into Cicillia to Leontes, and the sheppard having showed the letter of the nobleman by whom Leontes sent a was ⟨away?⟩ that child and the jewells found about her, she was knowen to be Leontes daughter and was then 16 yers old.

Remember also the Rog⁵ that cam in all tottered like coll pixci⁶ and howe he feyned him sicke & to have bin Robbed of all that he had and howe he cosened the por man of all his money, and after cam to the shep sher⁷ with a pedlers packe & ther cosened them Again of all their money And howe he changed apparrell with the kinge of Bomia his sonn, and then howe he turned Courtier &c. Beware of trustinge feined beggars or fawninge fellouss.

Chamber Account of Performances by the King's Men (May 1613)

[The performances of Shakespeare's company at court are especially well documented, because there were established systems of record keeping for the activities of the royal household. The players, as the King's Men, were officially Grooms of the Chamber, and it was this division of the royal household, under the supervision of the Lord Chamberlain, that organized entertainments, along with many other aspects of the operation of the court. The most significant item to the Treasurer of the Chamber who prepared the accounts was naturally the sum paid to the company on each occasion. In some instances, the titles of the plays given are also preserved, and the list given for May 20, when the company received payment (in two installments) for twenty plays given over the previous weeks, is especially complete. This list indicates the full range of the company's repertoire, which included many plays not by Shakespeare. The amount paid for the first group of plays was 93 pounds, 6 shillings, 8 pence, and for the second, smaller, group, 60 pounds. The text is from the first column of the accounts as reproduced under the heading "Payees" in ES, vol. 4.]

'To him [Hemynges] more'; 'fowerteene severall playes, viz: one playe called ffilaster, One other called the knott of ffooles, One other Much adoe aboute nothinge, The Mayeds Tragedy, The merye dyvell of Edmonton, The Tempest, A kinge and no kinge, The Twins Tragedie, The Winters Tale, Sir John ffalstaffe,¹ The Moore of Venice,² The Nobleman, Caesars Tragedye, And on other called Love lyes a bleedinge'.

'the sayd John Heminges'; 'Sixe severall playes, viz: one play called a badd begininge makes a good endinge, One other called yᵉ Capteyne, One other the Alcumist. One other Cardenno, One other the Hotspur,³ And one other called Benedicte and Betteris'.⁴

Sir Henry Wotton on *All Is True (Henry VIII)* and the Burning of the Globe (1613)

[Sir Henry Wotton (1568–1639), a highly educated poet and essayist, distinguished diplomat, and finally provost of Eton College, wrote to his nephew Sir Edmund Bacon shortly

5. Rogue (Autolycus).
6. Probably "colt-pixie," a mischievous sprite or fairy.
7. Sheep shearing.
1. *1* or *2 Henry IV*, or possibly *The Merry Wives of*
Windsor.
2. *Othello*.
3. *1 Henry IV*.
4. *Much Ado About Nothing*.

after the burning of the Globe. Chambers includes several other accounts of this incident in *The Elizabethan Stage*, vol. 2, pp. 419ff. The event is also recorded in John Stow's chronicles and was lamented by poets, including (several years later) Ben Jonson, and held up by Puritan divines like Prynne as an intimation of God's wrath. The excerpt below is from the earliest extant text, *Letters of Sir Henry Wotton to Sir Edmund Bacon* (London, 1661), p. 29.]

Now, to let matters of State sleep, I will entertain you at the present with what hath happened this week at the banks side. The Kings Players had a new Play, called *All is true*, representing some principall pieces of the raign of *Henry* 8, which was set forth with many extraordinary circumstances of Pomp and Majesty, even to the matting of the stage; the Knights of the Order, with their Georges and Garter, the Guards with their embroidered Coats, and the like: sufficient in truth within a while to make greatness very familiar, if not ridiculous. Now, King *Henry* making a Masque at the Cardinal, *Wolsey*'s house, and certain Chambers[1] being shot off at his entry, some of the paper, or other stuff wherewith one of them was stopped, did light on the thatch, where being thought at first but an idle smoak, and their eyes more attentive to the show, it kindled inwardly, and ran round like a train, consuming within less then an hour the whole house to the very grounds.

This was the fatal period of that vertuous fabrique, wherein yet nothing did perish, but wood and straw, and a few forsaken cloaks; only one man had his breeches set on fire, that would perhaps have broyled him, if he had not by the benefit of a provident wit put it out with bottle Ale. The rest when we meet.

Ballad on the Burning of the Globe (June 30, 1613)

[The ballad reprinted here may be one of the ballads on the burning of the Globe entered in the Stationers' Register on June 30, 1613, the day after the fire occurred. It survives only in a nineteenth-century transcript. The fire was in any case a significant news item, and topical ballads were often turned out rapidly, as a means of disseminating news, and sold cheaply on the streets as single printed sheets, or broadsides. The burning of the Globe had the additional appeal of being a peculiarly literary topic. The text is from *ES*, vol. 2.]

A Sonnett upon the pittiful burneing of the Globe playhowse in London.

Now sitt the downe, Melpomene,[1]
  Wrapt in a sea-cole robe,
And tell the dolefull tragedie,
  That late was playd at Globe;
For noe man that can singe and saye
[But?] was scard on St. Peters daye.[2]
  Oh sorrow, pittifull sorrow, and yett all this is true.[3]

All yow that please to understand,
  Come listen to my storye,
To see Death with his rakeing brand[4]
  Mongst such an auditorye;
Regarding neither Cardinalls might,
Nor yett the rugged face of Henry the Eight.
  Oh sorrow, &c.

1. Small pieces of artillery, used for firing salutes.
1. The muse of tragedy. *the*: thee.
2. June 29, the day of the fire. *scard*: Chambers's emendation; some such word appears to be missing.
3. Reference to the title of the "tragedie" being performed onstage at the time of the fire.
4. Torch; but also, blade—hence the traditional scythe of Death.

This fearfull fire beganne above,
  A wonder strange and true,
And to the stage-howse did remove,
  As round as taylors clewe;[5]
And burnt downe both beame and snagg,
And did not spare the silken flagg.[6]
  Oh sorrow, &c.

Out runne the knightes, out runne the lordes,
  And there was great adoe;
Some lost their hattes, and some their swordes;
  Then out runne Burbidge too;
The reprobates, though druncke on Munday,
Prayd for the Foole and Henry Condye.
  Oh sorrow, &c.

The perrywigges and drumme-heades frye,
  Like to a butter firkin;
A wofull burneing did betide
  To many a good buffe jerkin.
Then with swolne eyes, like druncken Flemminges,
Distressed stood old stuttering Heminges.[7]
  Oh sorrow, &c.

No shower his raine did there downe force
  In all that Sunn-shine weather,
To save that great renowned howse;
  Nor thou, O ale-howse, neither.[8]
Had itt begunne belowe, sans doubte,
Their wives for feare had pissed itt out.
  Oh sorrow, &c.

Bee warned, yow stage-strutters all,
  Least yow againe be catched,
And such a burneing doe befall,
  As to them whose howse was thatched;
Forbeare your whoreing, breeding biles,[9]
And laye up that expence for tiles.[1]
  Oh sorrow, &c.

Goe drawe yow a petition,
  And doe yow not abhorr itt,
And gett, with low submission,
  A licence to begg for itt
In churches, sans churchwardens checkes,
In Surrey and in Midlesex.
  Oh sorrow, pittifull sorrow, and yett all this is true.

---

5. A tailor's ball of thread. Probably a reference to the name "Globe" as well as the shape of the Globe, though not quite round.
6. A flag flying from the top of the theater to indicate that a performance was in progress.
7. John Heminges, Richard Burbadge, and Henry Condell were colleagues of Shakespeare in the King's Men.

8. Another report on the fire indicates that a house adjoining the Globe burned down as well. This house may be the same as the "ale-howse."
9. Boils.
1. Roof tiles, in place of the more flammable thatched roof. The rebuilt Globe, which opened a year after the fire, did in fact have a tile roof.

Ben Jonson on *The Tempest* (and *Titus Andronicus*) (1614)

[This extract from *Bartholomew Fair* contains one of several allusions to Shakespeare in the plays of his associate and sometime rival. The first paragraph alludes to the fashion for revenge plays such as Shakespeare's *Titus Andronicus* and Kyd's *Spanish Tragedy*, at its height roughly twenty-five years before *Bartholomew Fair* was written. The second paragraph refers disapprovingly to *The Tempest* (1613), first produced shortly before *Bartholomew Fair*. The text is that reprinted in WS, vol. 2, from the 1631 edition of Jonson's play (from the play's Induction).]

Hee that will sweare, *Jeronimo*, or *Andronicus* are the best playes, yet, shall passe unexcepted at,[2] heere, as a man whose Judgement shewes it is constant, and hath stood still, these five and twentie, or thirtie yeeres. . . .

If there bee never a *Servant-monster* i' the Fayre; who can helpe it? he[3] sayes; nor a nest of Antiques?[4] Hee is loth to make Nature afraid[5] in his *Playes*, like those that beget *Tales*, *Tempests*, and such like *Drolleries*, to mixe his head with other mens heeles; let the concupisence of *Jigges* and *Dances*, raigne as strong as it will amongst you.[6]

Francis Beaumont (?) on Shakespeare (c. 1615)

[Chambers was the first to print this poem in full, and the attribution to Francis Beaumont, a lawyer (not the playwright) who died in 1616, remains conjectural, though plausible. Not much is known about Beaumont's precise relationship to Jonson, but he had previously written a well-known verse-epistle to the poet, and theatrical allusions in this poem suggest a taste for the theater. The excerpted passage is remarkable as a precursor of the long-dominant view of Shakespeare as an untutored genius whose artistic accomplishment was due to the force of nature's gifts alone. In the lines preceding the excerpt, Beaumont amplifies the claim to authenticity of the love he wishes to express in the epistle by abjuring all stylistic refinement. The text is from WS, vol. 2.]

To Mr. B.J.

heere I would let slippe
(If I had any in mee) schollershippe,
And from all Learninge keepe these lines as ⟨cl⟩eere[7]
as Shakespeares best are, which our heires shall heare
Preachers apte to their auditors to showe
how farr sometimes a mortall man may goe
by the dimme light of Nature.

Shakespeare's Will (March 25, 1616)

[Shakespeare probably dictated this will sometime around January 1616. The first draft seems to have been dated in January, and 1616 is the most likely inference for the year (see note 1). The final revision was certainly made on the date given, but no clean copy was prepared, so the manuscript contains a substantial number of insertions and deletions.

2. Uncriticized.
3. The author.
4. Variant spelling of "antics," grotesque or ludicrous representations, or the actors (such as the clowns in *The Tempest*) playing such parts.
5. Make nature afraid by inexact imitation or too much fantasy.

6. *concupisence . . . you:* a reference to the dance generally incorporated into theatrical performance (see, for example, Platter's account above). Jonson suggests he is refusing to cater to the vulgar taste for more dancing in plays.
7. Chambers's emendation. The manuscript reads "deere," probably a scribal error.

The text here has been silently emended to assist in ease of reading. Deleted passages have been eliminated; the most significant of these is reproduced in the notes, where significant interlineations are also identified. Most of the altered passages, as Chambers writes, simply "correct slips, make the legal terminology more precise, or incorporate afterthoughts." The revision of the will was occasioned chiefly by the February marriage of Shakespeare's daughter Judith. Our text is adapted from E. A. J. Honigmann and Susan Brock, *Playhouse Wills, 1558–1642*. For a facsimile and thorough discussion of the will, see WS 2:169–80.]

Testamentum willelmij Shackspeare
Vicesimo Quinto die martij Anno Regni Domini nostri Jacobi nunc Regis Anglie &c decimo quarto & Scotie xlixo Annoque domini 1616[1]
In the name of god Amen I William Shackspeare of Stratford upon Avon in the countie of warrwick gentleman in perfect health & memorie god be praysed doe make & Ordayne this my last will & testament in manner & forme followeing That ys to saye ffirst I Comend my Soule into the handes of god my Creator hoping & assuredlie beleeving through thonelie merittes of Jesus Christe my Saviour to be made partaker of lyfe everlastinge And my bodye to the Earth whereof yt ys made Item I Gyve & bequeath unto my Daughter Judyth One Hundred & ffyftie poundes of law-full English money to be paied unto her in manner & forme followeing That ys to saye One Hundred Poundes in discharge of her marriage porcion[2] within one yeare after my Deceas with consideracion[3] after the Rate of twoe shillinges in the pound for soe long tyme as the same shalbe unpaied unto her after my deceas & the ffyftie poundes Residewe thereof upon her Surrendring of or gyving of such sufficient securi-tie as the overseers of this my Will shall like of to Surrender or graunnte All her[4] estate & Right that shall discend or come unto her after my deceas or that shee nowe hath of in or to one Copiehold tenemente with thappurtenaunces lyeing & being in Stratford upon Avon aforesaied in the saied countie of warrwick being parcell or holden of the mannour of Rowington unto my Daughter Susanna Hall & her heires for ever Item I Gyve & bequeath unto my saied Daughter Judith One Hundred & ffyftie Poundes more if shee or Anie issue of her bodie be Lyvinge att thend of three Yeares next ensueing the daie of the Date of this my Will during which tyme my executours to paie her consideracion from my deceas according to the Rate afore saied And if she dye within the saied terme without issue of her bodye then my will ys & I doe gyve & bequeath One Hundred Poundes thereof to my Neece Elizabeth Hall & the ffiftie Poundes to be sett fourth by my executours during the lief of my Sister Johane Harte & the use & proffitt thereof Cominge shalbe payed to my saied Sister Jone & after her deceas the saied l li[5] shall Remaine Amongst the children of my saied Sister Equallie to be Devided Amongst them But if my saied Daughter Judith be lyving att thend of the saied three Yeares or anie yssue of her bodye then my Will ys & soe I devise & bequeath the saied Hundred & ffyftie poundes to be sett out by my executours & overseers for the best benefitt of her & her issue & the stock[6] not to be paied unto her soe long as she shalbe marryed & Covert Baron[7] but my will ys that she shall have the consideracon yearelie paied unto her during her lief & after her deceas the saied stock and consideracion to bee paied to her children if she have Anie & if not to her executours or assignes she lyving the saied terme after my deceas Provided that if such husbond as she shall att thend of the saied three Yeares be marryed unto or attaine after doe sufficientle Assure unto her & thissue of her bodie landes Awnswereable to the porcion by this my will gyven unto her & to be adjudged

1. *Testamentum . . . 1616*: The Will of William Shake-speare (marginal heading). On the twenty-fifth day of March, in the fourteenth year of the reign of our lord James now King of England, etc., and of Scotland the forty-ninth, in the year of our Lord 1616. (The abbrevia-tion for "January" is crossed out in the manuscript, "March" having been substituted at the time the will was revised.)

2. The phrase "in discharge of her marriage porcion" was inserted during the course of revision.
3. Compensation, or interest.
4. Susanna Hall's. (The preceding "All" marks the beginning of a new sentence.)
5. *l li:* fifty pounds.
6. Principal.
7. *Covert Baron:* under the protection of a husband.

soe by my executours & overseers then my will ys that the saied Cl li[8] shalbe paied to such husbond as shall make such assurance to his owne use Item I gyve & bequeath unto my saied sister Jone xx li & all my wearing Apparrell to be paied & Delivered within one yeare after my deceas And I doe Will & devise unto her the house with thappurtenaunces in Stratford wherein she dwelleth for her naturall lief under the yearelie Rent of xii d. Itm I gyve & bequeath unto her three sonns William Harte[9] hart & Michaell Harte ffyve poundes A peece to be payed within one Yeare after my deceas[1] Item I gyve & bequeath unto her the saied Elizabeth Hall All my Plate (except my brod silver & gilt bole)[2] that I nowe have att the Date of this my Will Itm I gyve & bequeath unto the Poore of Stratford aforesaied tenn poundes to mr Thomas Combe my Sword to Thomas Russell Esquier ffyve poundes & to ffrauncis Collins of the Borough of Warwick in the countie of Warrwick gentleman thirteene poundes Sixe shillinges & Eight pence to be paied within one Yeare after my Deceas Itm I gyve & bequeath to Hamlett Sadler xxvi s viii d[3] to buy him A Ringe to William Raynoldes gentleman xxvi s viii d to buy him A Ringe to my godson William Walker xx s in gold to Anthonye Nashe gentleman xxvi s viii d & to mr John Nashe xx vi s viii d & to my fellows John Hemynnges Richard Burbage & Henry Cundell xxvi s viii d A peece to buy them Ringes[4] Item I Gyve Will bequeath & Devise unto my Daughter Susanna Hall for better enabling of her to performe this my will & towardes the performans thereof All that Capitall messuage or tenemente[5] with thappurtenaunces in Stratford aforesaied Called the newe place Wherein I nowe Dwell & twoe messuages or tenementes with thappurtenaunces scituat lyeing & being in Henley streete within the borough of Stratford aforesaied And all my barnes stables Orchardes gardens landes tenementes & hereditamentes[6] Whatsoever scituat lyeing & being or to be had Receyved perceyved or taken within the townes Hamlettes villages ffieldes & groundes of Stratford upon Avon Oldstratford Bushopton & Welcombe or in anie of them in the saied countie of warrwick And alsoe All that Messuage or tenemente with thappurtenaunces wherein one John Robinson dwelleth scituat lyeing & being in the blackfriers in London nere the Wardrobe & all other my landes tenementes & hereditamentes Whatsoever To Have & to hold All & singuler the saied premisses with their Appurtenaunces unto the saied Susanna Hall for & During the terme of her naturall lief & after her Deceas to the first sonne of her bodie lawfullie Issueing & to the heires males of the bodie of the saied first Sonne lawfullie Issueinge & for defalt of such issue to the second Sonne of her bodie lawfullie issueinge & to the heires males of the bodie of the saied Second Sonne lawfullie issueinge & for defalt of such heries to the third Sonne of the bodie of the saied Susanna Lawfullie issueing & of the heires males of the bodie of the saied third sonne lawfullie issueing And for defalt of such issue the same soe to be & Remaine to the ffourth ffyfth sixte & Seaventh sonnes of her bodie lawfullie issueing one after Another & to the heires[7] Males of the bodies of the saied ffourth fifth Sixte & Seaventh sonnes lawfullie issueing in such manner as yt ys before Lymitted to be & Remaine to the first second & third Sonns of her bodie & to their heires males And for defalt of such issue the saied premisses to

8. *Cl li:* One hundred fifty pounds.
9. A blank in the manuscript. Shakespeare appears to have forgotten the name of one of his nephews, Thomas.
1. *unto . . . deceas:* this passage was inserted at the top of the second page, probably when the will was revised. The following lines, with which the page originally began, are crossed out in the original: "to be sett out for her within one Yeare after my Deceas by my executours with thadvise & direccions of my overseers for her best proffitt untill her Marriage & then the same with the increase thereof to be paied unto her." These lines evidently referred to Judith Shakespeare as unmarried.
2. This parenthetical clause is an insertion, and has sparked some debate about Shakespeare's opinion of

Judith's marriage.
3. The "s" stands for "shillings," the "d" for "pence."
4. *to my fellows . . . Ringes:* Shakespeare's "fellows," or colleagues, Heminges, Burbage, and Condell, had worked with him in the Lord Chamberlain's Men and King's Men for many years. Many other wills and documents of the period provide evidence of the practice of wearing mourning rings alluded to here.
5. Residence. *messuage:* dwelling house with its outbuildings or adjoining lands.
6. Heritable property.
7. In addition to the signature near the end, Shakespeare signed the will here, in the bottom right-hand corner of the second page.

be & Remaine to my sayed Neece Hall[8] & the heires Males of her bodie Lawfullie yssueing for Defalt of such issue to my Daughter Judith & the heires Males of her bodie lawfullie issueinge And for Defalt of such issue to the Right heires of me the saied William Shackspere for ever Itm I gyve unto my wief my second best bed[9] with the furniture Item I gyve & bequeath to my saied Daughter Judith my broad silver gilt bole All the Rest of my goodes Chattelles Leases plate Jewels & household stuffe Whatsoever after my dettes and Legasies paied & my funerall expences discharged I gyve Devise & bequeath to my Sonne in Lawe John Hall gentleman & my Daughter Susanna his wief Whom I ordaine & make executours of this my Last Will & testa-ment And I doe intreat & Appoint the saied Thomas Russell Esquier & ffrauncis Collins gentleman to be overseers hereof And doe Revoke All former wills & publishe this to be my last Will & testament In Witnes Whereof I have here unto put my hand the Daie & Yeare first above Written. /   By me William Shakespeare witnes to the publishing hereof Fra: Collyns Julyus Shawe John Robinson Hamnet Sadler Robert Whattcott[1]

William Basse's Elegy for Shakespeare (1616–23)

[This highly literary elegy was written sometime between 1616 and 1623 by William Basse (c. 1583–c. 1653), of whom Chambers reports that he "was an Oxford student and a retainer of Lord Wenman of Thame." In numerous manuscript sources, the poem is ascribed to Basse, and in the 1640 *Poems: Written by Wil. Shake-speare, Gent.*, it is sub-scribed "W. B.," but it was also published in the 1633 edition of John Donne's poetry. In one source, "comedian" is substituted for the "Tragœdian" of line 12. The text is from WS, vol. 2.]

On Mr. Wm. Shakespeare
he dyed in Aprill 1616.

Renowned Spencer, lye a thought more nye
To learned Chaucer, and rare Beaumont lye
A little neerer Spenser to make roome
For Shakespeare in your threefold fowerfold Tombe.
To lodge all fowre in one bed make a shift
Untill Doomesdaye, for hardly will a fift
Betwixt this day and that by Fate be slayne
For whom your Curtaines may be drawn againe.
If your precedency in death doth barre
A fourth place in your sacred sepulcher,
Under this carved marble of thine owne
Sleep rare Tragœdian Shakespeare, sleep alone,
Thy unmolested peace, unshared Cave,
Possesse as Lord not Tenant of thy Grave,
    That unto us and others it may be
    Honor hereafter to be layde by thee.

Wm. Basse

8. Susanna Hall's daughter Elizabeth, actually Shake-speare's granddaughter (the sense of "niece" is less restricted in early modern usage). Elizabeth proved to be Susanna's only surviving child, and since Susanna was already thirty-three in 1616, the hypothetical series of seven sons preceding this mention of Elizabeth is doubly remarkable.
9. This bequest to Shakespeare's wife, Anne, was inserted in the course of his revision of the will. She is not mentioned elsewhere in the will at least partly because, as Shakespeare's widow, she would be guaran-teed a certain portion of the estate by law. The appear-ance of this inserted bequest is nevertheless strange enough to have evoked much speculation.
1. After Shakespeare's death, the will was endorsed here at the bottom of the third page with a Latin inscription indicating that the will had gone to probate before a magistrate on June 22, 1616.

Nicholas Richardson on *Romeo and Juliet* (1620)

[The following passage from *Romeo and Juliet*, together with the note describing its spiritual application, is recorded in an early seventeenth-century commonplace book. The recorder had evidently heard the sermons in which Richardson, a Church of England clergyman, used the passage (slightly misquoted here) from Shakespeare, and was impressed by them. Of Richardson it is known that he became a fellow of Magdalen College, Oxford, in 1614. The text is from WS, vol. 2.]

> 'Tis almost morning I would have thee gone
> And yet no farther then a wantons bird,
> That lets it hop a little from his hand,
> Like a poore prisoner, in his twisted gyves,
> Then with a silken thread plucks it back againe
> So jealous loving of his liberty. Tragedy of
> Romeo and Juliet. 40: pag. 84:
>   Said by Juliet: pro eadem.[1]

this Mr Richard^son Coll. Magd: inserted hence into his Sermon, preached it twice a^t St Maries 1620. 1621. applying it to gods love to his Saints either hurt with sinne, or adversity never forsaking thè.[2]

Front Matter from the First Folio of Shakespeare's Plays (1623)

[John Heminges and Henry Condell, friends and colleagues of Shakespeare, organized this first publication of his collected (thirty-six) plays. Eighteen of the plays had not appeared in print before, and for these the First Folio is the sole surviving source. Only *Pericles*, *The Two Noble Kinsmen*, and *Sir Thomas More* are not included in the volume. The first twelve (printed) pages of the Folio are reproduced below in reduced facsimile, with a minimum of explanatory notes. This "front matter" includes Droeshout's portrait of Shakespeare, Jonson's brief address "To the Reader" along with four other commendatory poems, two epistles by Heminges and Condell, a table of contents, and a list of actors, followed by the first page of text from *The Tempest*.]

---

1. On her own behalf.   2. Them.

To the Reader.

This Figure, that thou here seeſt put,
 It vvas for gentle Shakeſpeare cut;
Wherein the Grauer had a ſtrife
 with Nature, to out-doo the life :
O, could he but haue dravvne his vvit
 As vvell in braſſe, as he hath hit
His face ; the Print would then ſurpaſſe
 All, that vvas euer vvrit in braſſe.
But, ſince he cannot, Reader, looke
 Not on his Picture, but his Booke.

B. I.

Mr. WILLIAM

SHAKESPEARES

COMEDIES,
HISTORIES, &
TRAGEDIES.

Published according to the True Originall Copies.

Martin Droeshout ſculpſit London.

LONDON
Printed by Iſaac Iaggard, and Ed. Blount. 1623.

TO THE MOST NOBLE
AND
INCOMPARABLE PAIRE
OF BRETHREN.

WILLIAM
Earle of Pembroke, &c. Lord Chamberlaine to the
Kings most Excellent Maiesty.

AND

PHILIP
Earle of Montgomery, &c. Gentleman of his Maiesties
Bed-Chamber. Both Knights of the most Noble Order
of the Garter, and our singular good
LORDS.

Right Honourable,

*Hilst we studie to be thankful in our particular, for
the many fauors we haue receiued from your L.L
we are falne vpon the ill fortune, to mingle
two the most diuerse things that can bee, feare,
and rashnesse; rashnesse in the enterprize, and
feare of the successe. For, when we valew the places your H.H.
sustaine, we cannot but know their dignity greater, then to descend to
the reading of these trifles: and, vvhile we name them trifles, we haue
depriu'd our selues of the defence of our Dedication. But since your
L.L. haue beene pleas'd to thinke these trifles some-thing, heereto-
fore; and haue prosequuted both them, and their Authour liuing,
vvith so much fauour: we hope, that (they out-liuing him, and he not
hauing the fate, common with some, to be exequutor to his owne writings) you will vse the like indulgence toward them, you haue done*

A 2   *vnto*

Line 2. *L.L.*: Lordships.   Line 11. *prosequuted:* pursued.
Line 6. *places:* rank(s), status. *H.H.*: Highnesses.

The Epiſtle Dedicatorie.

vnto their parent. There is a great difference, vvhether any Booke
chooſe his Patrones, or finde them : This hath done both. For,
ſo much were your L L. likings of the ſeuerall parts, vvhen
they were acted, as before they vvere publiſhed, the Volume ask'd to
be yours. We haue but collected them, and done an office to the
dead, to procure his Orphanes, Guardians; vvithout ambition either of ſelfe-profit, or fame : onely to keepe the memory of ſo worthy
a Friend, & Fellow aliue, as was our SHAKESPEARE, by humble offer of his playes, to your moſt noble patronage. Wherein, as
we haue iuſtly obſerued, no man to come neere your L.L. but vvith
a kind of religious addreſſe; it hath bin the height of our care, vvho
are the Preſenters, to make the preſent worthy of your H.H. by the
perfection. But, there we muſt alſo craue our abilities to be conſiderd,
my Lords. We cannot go beyond our owne powers. Country hands
reach foorth milke, creame, fruites, or what they haue : and many
Nations (we haue heard) that had not gummes & incenſe, obtained their requeſts with a leauened Cake. It vvas no fault to approch
their Gods, by what meanes they could : And the moſt, though
meaneſt, of things are made more precious, when they are dedicated
to Temples. In that name therefore, we moſt humbly conſecrate to
your H.H. theſe remaines of your ſeruant Shakeſpeare; that
what delight is in them, may be euer your L.L. the reputation
his, & the faults ours, if any be committed, by a payre ſo carefull to
ſhew their gratitude both to the liuing, and the dead, as is

Your Lordſhippes moſt bounden,

IOHN HEMINGE.
HENRY CONDELL.

To the great Variety of Readers.

ROM the moſt able, to him that can but ſpell: There you are number'd. We had rather you were weighd. Eſpecially, when the fate of all Bookes depends vpon your capacities : and not of your heads alone, but of your purſes. Well ! It is now publique, & you wil ſtand for your priuiledges wee know : to read, and cenſure. Do ſo, but buy it firſt. That doth beſt commend a Booke, the Stationer ſaies. Then, how odde ſoeuer your braines be, or your wiſedomes, make your licence the ſame, and ſpare not. Iudge your ſixe-pen'orth, your ſhillings worth, your fiue ſhillings worth at a time, or higher, ſo you riſe to the iuſt rates, and welcome. But, what euer you do, Buy. Cenſure will not driue a Trade, or make the Iacke go. And though you be a Magiſtrate of wit, and ſit on the Stage at *Black-Friers*, or the *Cock-pit*, to arraigne Playes dailie, know, theſe Playes haue had their triall alreadie, and ſtood out all Appeales ; and do now come forth quitted rather by a Decree of Court, then any purchas'd Letters of commendation.

It had bene a thing, we confeſſe, worthie to haue bene wiſhed, that the Author himſelfe had liu'd to haue ſet forth, and ouerſeen his owne writings ; But ſince it hath bin ordain'd otherwiſe, and he by death departed from that right, we pray you do not envie his Friends, the office of their care, and paine, to haue collected & publiſh'd them; and ſo to haue publiſh'd them, as where (before) you were abuſ'd with diuerſe ſtolne, and ſurreptitious copies, maimed, and deformed by the frauds and ſtealthes of iniurious impoſtors, that expoſ'd them : euen thoſe, are now offer'd to your view cur'd, and perfect of their limbes; and all the reſt, abſolute in their numbers, as he conceiued thē. Who, as he was a happie imitator of Nature, was a moſt gentle expreſſer of it. His mind and hand went together : And what he thought, he vttered with that eaſineſſe, that wee haue ſcarſe receiued from him a blot in his papers. But it is not our prouince, who onely gather his works, and giue them you, to praiſe him. It is yours that reade him. And there we hope, to your diuers capacities, you will finde enough, both to draw, and hold you : for his wit can no more lie hid, then it could be loſt. Reade him, therefore ; and againe, and againe : And if then you doe not like him, ſurely you are in ſome manifeſt danger, not to vnderſtand him. And ſo we leaue you to other of his Friends, whom if you need, can bee your guides : if you neede them not, you can leade your ſelues, and others. And ſuch Readers we wiſh him.

A 3

Iohn Heminge.
Henrie Condell.

Line 8. *Stationer:* bookseller.

Line 13. *Iacke:* machine.

Lines 13–14. *And though . . . dailie:* addressed in particular to men of fashion who occupied seats onstage so they could be seen while watching the play.

Lines 15–17. *these Playes . . . commendation:* the legal puns that began with "Magistrate of wit" (fashionable playgoer) in line 13 continue here. The "purchas'd Letters of commendation" refer to escaping the conse-

quences of a crime by means of bribery or other undue influence; Shakespeare's plays, by contrast, have been acquitted after a proper and rigorous trial (approved by theater audiences and not insinuated into the public favor by some outside influence).

Line 27. *absolute in their numbers:* correct in their versification. *the:* them.

Line 28. *a happie:* an apt; a successful.

To the memory of my beloued,
The AVTHOR
Mr. William Shakespeare:
And
what he hath left vs.

To draw no enuy (Shakespeare) on thy name,
   Am I thus ample to thy Booke, and Fame :
While I confesse thy writings to be such,
As neither Man, nor Muse, can praise too much.
'Tis true, and all mens suffrage. But these wayes
   Were not the paths I meant vnto thy praise :
For seeliest Ignorance on these may light,
   Which, when it sounds at best, but eccho's right ;
Or blinde Affection, which doth ne're aduance
   The truth, but gropes, and vrgeth all by chance ;
Or crafty Malice, might pretend this praise,
   And thinke to ruine, where it seem'd to raise.
These are, as some infamous Baud, or whore,
   Should praise a Matron. What could hurt her more ?
But thou art proofe against them, and indeed
   Aboue th'ill fortune of them, or the need.
I, therefore will begin. Soule of the Age !
   The applause ! delight ! the wonder of our Stage !
My Shakespeare, rise ; I will not lodge thee by
   Chaucer, or Spenser, or bid Beaumont lye
A little further, to make thee a roome :
   Thou art a Moniment, without a tombe,
And art aliue still, while thy Booke doth liue,
   And we haue wits to read, and praise to giue.
That I not mixe thee so, my braine excuses ;
   I meane with great, but disproportion'd Muses :
For, if I thought my iudgement were of yeeres,
   I should commit thee surely with thy peeres,
And tell, how farre thou didstst our Lily out-shine,
   Or sporting Kid, or Marlowes mighty line.
And though thou hadst small Latine, and lesse Greeke,
   From thence to honour thee, I would not seeke
For names ; but call forth thund'ring Æschilus,
   Euripides, and Sophocles to vs,
Paccuuius, Accius, him of Cordoua dead,
   To life againe, to heare thy Buskin tread,
And shake a Stage : Or, when thy Sockes were on,
   Leaue thee alone, for the comparison

of

Of all, that insolent Greece, *or haughtie* Rome
  sent forth, or since did from their ashes come.
Triumph, my Britaine, *thou hast one to showe,*
  To whom all Scenes of Europe *homage owe.*
He was not of an age, but for all time!
  And all the Muses still were in their prime,
when like Apollo *he came forth to warme*
  Our eares, or like a Mercury *to charme!*
Nature her selfe was proud of his designes,
  And ioy'd to weare the dressing of his lines!
which were so richly spun, and wouen so fit,
  As since, she will vouchsafe no other Wit.
The merry Greeke, *tart* Aristophanes,
  Neat Terence, *witty* Plautus, *now not please;*
But antiquated, and deserted lye
  As they were not of Natures family.
Yet must I not giue Nature all: Thy Art,
  My gentle Shakespeare, *must enioy a part.*
For though the Poets *matter, Nature be,*
  His Art doth giue the fashion. And, that he,
Who casts to write a liuing line, must sweat,
  (such as thine are) and strike the second heat
Vpon the Muses *anuile: turne the same,*
  (And himselfe with it) that he thinkes to frame;
Or for the lawrell, he may gaine a scorne,
  For a good Poet's *made, as well as borne.*
And such wert thou. Looke how the fathers face
  Liues in his issue, euen so, the race
Of Shakespeares *minde, and manners brightly shines*
  In his well torned, and true-filed lines:
In each of which, he seemes to shake a Lance,
  As brandish't at the eyes of Ignorance.
Sweet Swan of Auon! *what a sight it were*
  To see thee in our waters yet appeare,
And make those flights vpon the bankes of Thames,
  That so did take Eliza, *and our* Iames!
But stay, I see thee in the Hemisphere
  Aduanc'd, and made a Constellation there!
Shine forth, thou Starre of Poets, *and with rage,*
  Or influence, chide, or cheere the drooping Stage;
Which, since thy flight frō hence, hath mourn'd like night,
  And despaires day, but for thy Volumes light.

BEN: IONSON.

Vpon the Lines and Life of the Famous
Scenicke Poet, Maſter WILLIAM
SHAKESPEARE.

THoſe hands, which you ſo clapt, go now, and wring
You *Britaines* braue; for done are *Shakeſpeares* dayes :
His dayes are done, that made the dainty Playes,
Which made the Globe of heau'n and earth to ring.
Dry'de is that veine, dry'd is the *Theſpian* Spring,
Turn'd all to teares, and *Phœbus* clouds his rayes :
That corp's, that coffin now beſticke thoſe bayes,
Which crown'd him *Poet* firſt, then *Poets* King.
If *Tragedies* might any *Prologue* haue,
All thoſe he made, would ſcarſe make one to this :
Where *Fame*, now that he gone is to the graue
(Deaths publique tyring-houſe) the *Nuncius* is.
   For though his line of life went ſoone about,
   The life yet of his lines ſhall neuer out.

HVGH HOLLAND.

Line 5. *Thespian*: the Greek poet Thespis was regarded as the originator of tragedy.
Line 6. *Phoebus*: Apollo; the sun.
Line 7. *besticke*: cover; infest. *bayes*: a crown of bay leaves was the traditional prize for the victors of Greek poetry contests.

Line 10. *All those*: All those tragedies. *this*: the great tragedy of Shakespeare's death.
Line 12. *publique tyring-house*: the tiring-house was the actors' dressing room; the grave is a public tiring-house because there every mortal prepares for Judgment Day.
Line 12. *Nuncius*: messenger.

A CATALOGVE
of the seuerall Comedies, Histories, and Tragedies contained in this Volume.

TO THE MEMORIE
of the deceafed Authour Maifter
W. SHAKESPEARE.

*Hake-fpeare, at length thy pious fellowes giue
The world thy Workes : thy Workes,by which,out-liue
Thy Tombe, thy name muft · when that ftone is rent,
And Time diffolues thy Stratford Moniment,
Here we aliue fhall view thee ftill. This Booke,
When Braffe and Marble fade,fhall make thee looke
Frefh to all Ages: when Pofteritie
Shall loath what's new,thinke all is prodegie
That is not Shake-fpeares ; eu'ry Line,each Verfe
Here fhall reuiue,redeeme thee from thy Herfe.
Nor Fire,nor cankring Age,as Nafo faid,
Of his,thy wit-fraught Booke fhall once inuade.
Nor fhall I e're beleeue, or thinke thee dead
(Though mift)vntill our bankrout Stage be fped
(Impofsible) with fome new ftraine t'out-do
Pafsions of Iuliet,and her Romeo ;
Or till I heare a Scene more nobly take,
Then when thy half-Sword parlying Romans fpake.
Till thefe,till any of thy Volumes reft
Shall with more fire,more feeling be expreft,
Be fure,our Shake-fpeare, thou canft neuer dye,
But crown'd with Lawrell,liue eternally.*

L. Digges.

To the memorie of M. W. Shake-fpeare.

*VVEE wondred (Shake-fpeare) that thou went'ft fo foone
From the Worlds-Stage,to the Graues-Tyring-roome.
Wee thought thee dead, but this thy printed worth,
Tels thy Spectators,that thou went'ft but forth
To enter with applaufe. An Actors Art,
Can dye,and liue,to acte a fecond part.
That's but an Exit of Mortalitie ;
This, a Re-entrance to a Plaudite.*

I. M.

Digges
Line 8. *prodegie:* freakish, deformed.
Line 11. *cankring age:* meddlesome or critical period of history. Naso is the Roman poet Ovid.
Line 14. *mist:* missed. *sped:* provided.

Line 15. *straine:* song or verse.
I. M.
Line 2. *Graves-Tyring-roome:* see note to Holland poem, line 12.
Line 8. *Plaudite:* accolade, applause.

The Workes of William Shakespeare,

containing all his Comedies, Histories, and
Tragedies: Truely set forth, according to their first
ORIGINALL.

The Names of the Principall Actors
in all these Playes.

William Shakespeare.

Richard Burbadge.

John Hemmings.

Augustine Phillips.

William Kempt.

Thomas Poope.

George Bryan.

Henry Condell.

William Slye.

Richard Cowly.

John Lowine.

Samuell Crosse.

Alexander Cooke.

Samuel Gilburne.

Robert Armin.

William Ostler.

Nathan Field.

John Underwood.

Nicholas Tooley.

William Ecclestone.

Joseph Taylor.

Robert Benfield.

Robert Goughe.

Richard Robinson.

Iohn Shancke.

Iohn Rice.

THE
TEMPEST.

Actus primus, Scena prima.

A tempestuous noise of Thunder and Lightning heard: Enter a Ship-master, and a Botefwaine.

Mafter.

B Ote-fwaine.

Botef. Heere Mafter: What cheere?

Maft. Good: Speake to th'Mariners: fall too't, yarely, or wee run our felues a ground, beftirre, beftirre. *Exit.*

Enter Mariners.

Botef. Heigh my hearts, cheerely, cheerely my harts: yare, yare: Take in the toppe-fale: Tend to th'Mafters whiftle: Blow till thou burft thy winde, if roome enough.

Enter Alonfo, Sebaftian, Anthonio, Ferdinando, Gonzalo, and others.

Alon. Good Botefwaine haue care: where's the Mafter? Play the men.

Botef. I pray now keepe below.

Anth. Where is the Mafter, Bofon?

Botef. Do you not heare him? you marre our labour, Keepe your Cabines: you do afsift the ftorme.

Gonz. Nay, good be patient.

Botef. When the Sea is: hence, what cares thefe roarers for the name of King? to Cabine; filence: trouble vs not.

Gon. Good, yet remember whom thou haft aboord.

Botef. None that I more loue then my felfe. You are a Counfellor, if you can command thefe Elements to filence, and worke the peace of the prefent, wee will not hand a rope more, vfe your authoritie: If you cannot, giue thankes you haue liu'd fo long, and make your felfe readie in your Cabine for the mifchance of the houre, if it fo hap. Cheerely good hearts: out of our way I fay. *Exit.*

Gon. I haue great comfort from this fellow:methinks he hath no drowning marke vpon him, his complexion is perfect Gallowes: ftand faft good Fate to his hanging, make the rope of his deftiny our cable, for our owne doth little aduantage: If he be not borne to bee hang'd, our cafe is miferable. *Exit.*

Enter Botefwaine.

Botef. Downe with the top-Maft: yare, lower, lower, bring her to Try with Maine-courfe. A plague

A cry within. *Enter Sebaftian, Anthonio & Gonzalo.*

vpon this howling: they are lowder then the weather, or our office: yet againe? What do you heere? Shal we giue ore and drowne, haue you a minde to finke?

Sebaf. A poxe o'your throat, you bawling, blafphemous incharitable Dog.

Botef. Worke you then.

Anth. Hang cur, hang, you whorefon infolent Noyfe-maker, we are leffe afraid to be drownde, then thou art.

Gonz. I'le warrant him for drowning, though the Ship were no ftronger then a Nutt-fhell, and as leaky as an vnftanched wench.

Botef. Lay her a hold, a hold, fet her two courfes off to Sea againe, lay her off.

Enter Mariners wet.

Mari. All loft, to prayers, to prayers, all loft.

Botef. What muft our mouths be cold?

Gonz. The King, and Prince, at prayers, let's affift them, for our cafe is as theirs.

Sebaf. I'am out of patience.

An. We are meerly cheated of our liues by drunkards, This wide-chopt-rafcall, would thou mightft lye drowning the wafhing of ten Tides.

Gonz. Hee'l be hang'd yet,

Though euery drop of water fweare againft it, And gape at widft to glut him. *A confufed noyfe within.* Mercy on vs.

We fplit, we fplit, Farewell my wife, and children, Farewell brother: we fplit, we fplit, we fplit.

Anth. Let's all finke with' King

Seb. Let's take leaue of him. *Exit.*

Gonz. Now would I giue a thoufand furlongs of Sea, for an Acre of barren ground: Long heath, Browne firrs, any thing; the wills aboue be done, but I would faine dye a dry death. *Exit.*

Scena Secunda.

Enter Profpero and Miranda.

Mira. If by your Art (my deereft father) you haue Put the wild waters in this Rore, alay them: The fkye it feemes would powre down ftinking pitch, But that the Sea, mounting to th' welkins cheeke, Dafhes the fire out. Oh! I haue fuffered With thofe that I faw fuffer: A braue veffell

A   (Who

Leonard Digges on Shakespeare (1623–35)

[Leonard Digges (1588–1635) was a scholar apparently associated for most of his adult life with University College, Oxford. According to Chambers, he is remembered primarily as a translator, and G. Blakemore Evans adds that he was a scholar, traveler, and poet. It is impossible to date the following poem exactly, for Digges had been dead five years when it was printed as one of two commendatory poems in the opening pages of a 1640 edition of Shakespeare, *Poems: Written by Wil. Shake-speare, Gent*. He had written a shorter commendatory poem for the First Folio of 1623 (see above). The first forty lines of praise are quite conventional, but the discussion of specific plays and their impact on audiences is almost unique among such records of Shakespeare. The text is from the first edition (1640).]

Upon Master William Shakespeare, the Deceased Authour, and his Poems

Poets are borne not made,[1] when I would prove
This truth, the glad rememberance I must love
Of never dying *Shakespeare*, who alone
Is argument enough to make that one.
First, that he was a Poet none would doubt,
That heard th'applause of what he sees set out
Imprinted; where thou hast (I will not say
Reader his Workes for to contrive a Play:
To him twas none) the patterne of all wit,
Art without Art unparaleld as yet.
Next Nature onely helpt him, for looke thorow
This whole Booke, thou shalt find he doth not borrow,
One phrase from Greekes, nor Latines imitate,
Nor once from vulgar Languages Translate,
Nor Plagiari-like from others gleane,
Nor begges he from each witty friend a Scene
To peece his Acts with, all that he doth write,
Is pure his owne,[2] plot, language exquisite,
But oh! what praise more powerfull can we give
The dead, then that by him the Kings men live,
His Players, which should they but have shar'd the Fate,
All else expir'd within the short Termes date;
How could the Globe have prospered, since through want
Of change, the Plaies and Poems had growne scant.
But happy Verse thou shall be sung and heard,
When hungry quills shall be such honour bard,
Then vanish upstart Writers to each Stage,
You needy Poetasters of this Age,
Where *Shakespeare* liv'd or spake, Vermine forbeare,
Least with your froth you spot them, come not neere;
But if you needs must write, if poverty
So pinch, that otherwise you starve and die,
On Gods name may the Bull or Cockpit[3] have
Your lame blancke Verse, to keepe you from the grave
Or let new Fortunes younger brethren see,

1. A commonplace of the period, based on an anonymous Latin saying.
2. *Art without Art . . . owne:* another, more exaggerated view of Shakespeare's untutored genius and originality (compare Beaumont's poem, above).
3. The Red Bull, the Cockpit, and the Fortune (below) were other public theaters. The Fortune was rebuilt in 1623 after being destroyed by fire.

What they can picke from your leane industry.
I doe not wonder when you offer at
Blacke-Friers,[4] that you suffer; tis the fate
Of richer veines, prime judgements that have far'd
The worse, with this deceased man compar'd.
So have I seene, when Cesar would appeare,
And on the Stage at halfe-sword parley were,
Brutus and *Cassius:*[5] oh how the Audience,
Were ravish'd, with what wonder they went thence,
When some new day they would not brooke a line,
Of tedious (though well laboured) *Catalines*;
Sejanus[6] too was irkesome, they priz'de more
Honest *Iago*, or the jealous Moore.[7]
And though the Fox and subtill alchimist,[8]
Long intermitted could not quite be mist,
Though these have sham'd all the Ancients, and might raise,
Their Authours merit with a crowne of Bayes.
Yet these sometimes, even at a friends desire
Acted, have scarce defrai'd the Seacoale fire
And doore-keepers: when let but *Falstaffe* come,
Hall, Poines,[9] the rest you scarce shall have a roome
All is so pester'd: let but *Beatrice*
And *Benedicke*[1] be seene, loe in a trice
The Cockpit Galleries,[2] Boxes, all are full
To heare *Malvoglio*[3] that crosse garter'd Gull.
Briefe, there is nothing in his wit fraught Booke,
Whose sound we would not heare, on whose worth looke
Like old coynd gold, whose lines, in every page,
Shall passe true currant to succeeding age.
But why do I dread *Shakespeares* praise recite,
Some second *Shakespeare* must of *Shakespeare* write;
For me tis needlesse, since an host of men,
Will pay to clap his praise, to free my Pen.

Richard James on Falstaff (c. 1625)

[The following is one of several surviving discussions of Shakespeare's great comic character and his resemblance to the two actual personages for whom he was successively named,
Sir John Oldcastle and Sir John Falstaff. Richard James studied at Oxford and served as
librarian to Sir Robert Cotton. The text is an excerpt from the *Epistle* to Sir Harry Bour-
chier, as printed in WS, vol. 2.]

A young Gentle Lady of your acquaintance, having read ye works of Shakespeare,
made me this question. How Sr John Falstaffe, or Fastolf, as he is written in ye Statute
book of Maudlin[1] Colledge in Oxford, where everye day that society were bound to
make memorie of his soul, could be dead in ye time of Harrie ye Fift and again live in
ye time of Harrie ye Sixt to be banished for cowardice: Whereto I made answear that

---

4. The indoor, "private" theater acquired by the King's
Men in 1608 and used afterward along with the Globe.
5. See *Julius Caesar* 4.3.
6. Ben Jonson's two poorly received tragedies.
7. In *Othello*.
8. Jonson's comedies *Volpone* and *The Alchemist*.

9. Characters in *1* and *2 Henry IV*.
1. Characters in *Much Ado About Nothing*.
2. Standing room around the stage, more often known
simply as "the pit."
3. Character in *Twelfth Night*.
1. Magdalen.

it was one of those humours[2] and mistakes for which Plato banisht all poets out of his commonwealth.[3] That Sr John Falstaffe was in those times a noble valiant souldier, as apeeres by a book in ye Heralds Office dedicated unto him by a Herald who had binne with him, if I well remember, for the space of 25 yeeres in ye French wars; that he seems also to have binne a man of learning, because, in a Library of Oxford, I find a book of dedicating Churches sent from him for a present unto Bishop Wainflete, and inscribed with his own hand. That in Shakespeares first shew of Harrie the fift, the person with which he undertook to playe a buffone was not Falstaffe, but Sir Jhon Oldcastle, and that offence beinge worthily taken by Personages descended from his title (as peradventure by many others allso whoe ought to have him in honourable memorie) the poet was putt to make an ignorant shifte of abusing Sir Jhon Falstophe, a man not inferior of Vertue, though not so famous in pietie as the other, who gave witnesse unto the truth of our reformation with a constant and resolute Martyrdom, unto which he was pursued by the Priests, Bishops, Moncks, and Friers of those days.

Milton on Shakespeare (1630)

[John Milton (1608–1674) was born in London and as a boy might conceivably have seen Shakespeare's company act. This poem first appeared prefixed to the Second Folio of Shakespeare's works in 1632, and again in the 1640 *Poems* of Shakespeare. The text is from the 1645 edition of Milton's *Poems*, as reprinted in WS, vol. 2, but the title given is from the Second Folio version.]

An Epitaph on the admirable Dramaticke Poet, W. Shakespeare

What needs my *Shakespear* for his honour'd Bones,
The labour of an age in piled Stones,
Or that his hallow'd reliques should be hid
Under a star-ypointing[1] *Pyramid?*
Dear son of memory, great heir of Fame,
What need'st thou such weak witnes of thy name?
Thou in our wonder and astonishment
Hast built thy self a live-long Monument.
For whilst toth' shame of slow-endeavouring art,
They easie numbers flow, and that each heart
Hath from the leaves of thy unvalu'd[2] Book,
Those Delphick[3] lines with deep impression took,
Then thou our fancy of itself bereaving,[4]
Dost make us Marble with too much conceaving;
And so Sepulcher'd in such pomp dost lie,
That Kings for such a Tomb would wish to die.

Ben Jonson on Shakespeare (1623–37)

[In addition to numerous allusions to Shakespeare in his plays, Ben Jonson (1573–1637) writes explicitly about his friend, colleague, and rival in a number of places, most significantly in the two commendatory poems prefixed to the First Folio (see above) and in the

2. Whims.
3. See the *Republic*, Books 2–3.
1. Pointing to the stars.
2. Invaluable.
3. Reference to Apollo, god of poetry, whose most

famous shrine was at Delphi.
4. *our . . . bereaving:* "our imaginations are rapt 'out of ourselves,' leaving behind our soulless bodies like statues"—Isabel MacCaffrey.

published extracts from his notebooks entitled *Timber: or, Discoveries; Made upon Men and Matter,* first published in his *Works* of 1640. It is impossible to date the original entries precisely; Chambers's conjecture is that the following entry on Shakespeare was made after 1630. The text is from the authoritative edition of Herford and Simpson, vol. 8 (Oxford: Clarendon Press, 1952).]

Indeed, the multitude commend Writers, as they doe Fencers, or Wrastlers; who if they come in robustiously, and put for it, with a deale of violence, are received for the *braver-fellowes:* when many times their owne rudenesse is a cause of their disgrace; and a slight touch of their Adversary, gives all that boisterous force the foyle. But in these things, the unskilfull are naturally deceiv'd, and judging wholly by the bulke, thinke rude things greater then polish'd; and scatter'd more numerous, then compos'd: Nor thinke this only to be true in the sordid multitude, but the neater sort of our *Gallants:* for all are the multitude; only they differ in cloaths, not in judgement or understanding.

I remember, the Players have often mentioned it as an honour to *Shakespeare,* that in his writing, (whatsoever he penn'd) hee never blotted out line.[1] My answer hath beene, Would he had blotted a thousand. Which they thought a malevolent speech. [I had not told posterity this,] but for their ignorance, who choose that circumstance to commend their friend by, wherein he most faulted. And to justifie mine owne candor, (for I lov'd the man, and doe honour his memory (on this side Idolatry) as much as any.) Hee was (indeed) honest, and of an open, and free nature: had an excellent *Phantsie*[2]; brave notions, and gentle expressions: wherein hee flow'd with that facility, that sometime it was necessary he should be stop'd: *Sufflaminandus erat;*[3] as *Augustus* said of *Haterius.*[4] His wit was in his owne power; would the rule of it had beene so too. Many times hee fell into those things, could not escape laughter: As when hee said in the person of *Cæsar,* one speaking to him; *Cæsar, thou dost me wrong.* Hee replyed: *Cæsar did never wrong, but with just cause*[5]: and such like; which were ridiculous. But hee redeemed his vices, with his vertues. There was ever more in him to be praysed, then to be pardoned.

John Aubrey on Shakespeare (1681)

[What Chambers calls "the Shakespeare-mythos" was already well under way by the time John Aubrey (1626–1697) collected these anecdotes for the biographies in his *Brief Lives,* first anthologized in 1692. Aubrey's chief sources were prominent figures of the Restoration stage, which had seen increasingly popular revivals and adaptations of *Hamlet, The Tempest,* and many other plays of Shakespeare. Numerous actors and critics in the latter part of the seventeenth century helped to "rehabilitate" Shakespeare; if at the time of the Restoration his plays had seemed terribly musty and old-fashioned, by the 1680s his reputation as an author of lasting value was well established, thanks to the enthusiasm of Restoration playgoers. Aubrey's first source, Christopher Beeston, was the son of a one-time member of Shakespeare's company. William Davenant was a formidable entrepreneur as well as a dramatist, and Thomas Shadwell a prolific playwright perhaps best remembered as Dryden's King of Dullness. The text is from Chambers's transcription (WS, vol. 2), with a few silent emendations for ease of reading. Some of the material is from the published version of *Brief Lives,* and some of it from manuscript notes apparently used in writing the *Lives.*]

---

1. Compare Heminges and Condell's address to the reader in the First Folio: "And what he thought, he uttered with that easinesse, that wee have scarse received from him a blot in his papers."
2. Imagination.

3. "He needed the drag-chain" (adapted from Marcus Seneca's *Controversiae* 4, Preface).
4. Quintus Haterius, Roman rhetorician (d. A.D. 26).
5. See *Julius Caesar* 3.1.47.

the more to be admired q[uia][1] he was not a company keeper[2]
lived in Shoreditch, wouldnt be debauched, & if invited to
writ; he was in paine.[3]

W. Shakespeare.

M[r]. William Shakespear. [*bay-wreath in margin*] was borne at Stratford upon
Avon, in the County of Warwick; his father was a Butcher, & I have been told hereto-
fore by some of the neighbours, that when he was a boy he exercised his father's
Trade, but when he kill'd a Calfe, he would doe it in a *high style*, & make a Speech.
There was at that time another Butcher's son in this Towne, that was held not at all
inferior to him for a naturall witt, his acquaintance & coetanean,[4] but dyed young.
This Wm. being inclined naturally to Poetry and acting, came to London I guesse
about 18. and was an Actor at one of the Play-houses and did act exceedingly well:
now B. Johnson was never a good Actor, but an excellent Instructor. He began early
to make essayes at Dramatique Poetry, which at that time was very lowe; and his
Playes tooke well: He was a handsome well shap't man: very good company, and of
a very readie and pleasant smooth Witt. The Humour[5] of ... the Constable in a
Midsomersnight's Dreame, he happened to take at Grendon [*In margin*, 'I thinke it
was Midsomer night that he happened to lye there'.] in Bucks[6] which is the roade
from London to Stratford, and there was living that Constable about 1642 when I first
came to Oxon.[7] M[r]. Jos. Howe is of that parish and knew him. Ben Johnson and he
did gather Humours of men dayly where ever they came. One time as he was at the
Tavern at Stratford super[8] Avon, one Combes an old rich Usurer was to be buryed,
he makes there this extemporary[9] Epitaph

> Ten in the Hundred[1] the Devill allowes
> But *Combes* will have twelve, he sweares & vowes:
> If any one askes who lies in this Tombe:
> Hoh! quoth the Devill, 'Tis my John o' Combe.

He was wont to goe to his native Country once a yeare. I thinke I have been told that
he left 2 or 300[li] per annum[2] there and therabout: to a sister. [*In margin*, 'V.[3] his
Epitaph in Dugdales Warwickshire'.] I have heard S[r] Wm. Davenant and M[r]. Thomas
Shadwell (who is counted the best Comœdian we have now) say, that he had a most
prodigious Witt, and did admire his naturall parts beyond all other Dramaticall writers. He was wont to say, That he never blotted out a line in his life: sayd Ben: Johnson,
I wish he had blotted out a thousand. [*In margin*, 'B. Johnsons Underwoods'.] His
Comœdies will remaine witt, as long as the English tongue is understood; for that he
handles mores hominum;[4] now our present writers reflect so much upon particular
persons, and coxcombeities, that 20 yeares hence, they will not be understood.
Though as Ben: Johnson sayes of him, that he had but little Latine and lesse Greek,
He understood Latine pretty well: for he had been in his younger yeares a Schoolmas-
ter in the Countrey. [*In margin*, 'from M[r] —— Beeston'.]

S[r] William Davenant Knight Poet Laureate was borne in ____ street in the City of
Oxford, at the Crowne Tavern. His father was John Davenant a Vintner there, a very

---

1. Because.
2. "Company keeper" can mean "libertine" or "rev-
eler"; the general sense of the passage is that Shakespeare is "the more to be admired" for his temperance
and modesty.
3. The embarrassment ("paine") at being asked to write
is presumably due to the same alleged modesty.
4. Contemporary.
5. Character, personality.
6. Buckinghamshire.

7. Oxford.
8. Upon.
9. Extemporaneous.
1. 10 percent interest. (Combe is damned because he
charges 12 percent on his loans, 2 percent above the
maximum allowed for usury not to be a mortal sin.)
2. 300 pounds a year.
3. See.
4. *for that ... hominum:* because he treats of (general)
human manners or customs.

grave and discreet Citizen: his mother was a very beautifull woman, & of a very good witt and of conversation extremely agreable. . . . Mr William Shakespeare was wont to goe into Warwickshire once a yeare, and did commonly in his journey lye at this house in Oxon: where he was exceedingly respected. I have heard parson Robert D[avenant] say that here Mr W. Shakespeare here gave him a hundred kisses. Now S^r Wm. would sometimes when he was pleasant over a glasse of wine with his most intimate friends e.g. Sam: Butler (author of Hudibras) &c. say, that it seemed to him that he writt with the very spirit that Shakespeare,[5] and seemed contented enough to be thought his Son: he would tell them the story as above. in which way his mother had a very light report, whereby she was called a whore.

---

5. A word such as "had" seems to be missing.

A Shakespearean Chronicle
1558–1616

Entries marked by • are from John Stow's *Abridgement of the English Chronicle* (1618). Stow, a member of the Merchant Tailor's Guild, published his first chronicle in 1565 and offered continued, expanded, and abridged versions constantly thereafter, sometimes as often as every year; after his death in 1605, the work was continued by Edmund Howes. Stow's chronicles give us a sense of how "history" was actually experienced from day to day by the citizens of London. Major political events share the page with developments in civic government and portentous signs of all kinds; Stow does not record the date of distant events like the Battle of Lepanto (1571), but he tells us when the news arrived in London and how the citizens responded.

Following Stow, marked by ■, are additional cultural and political details, and then, marked by ♦, information about (probable) first performances of Shakespeare's and others' works, Shakespeare's life and career, and stage history. While some years include all of the categories, most do not. Plays are listed under the year of their first performance; dates in parentheses are (probable) dates of composition, and those in brackets are dates of publication (in the case of Shakespeare's plays, quarto publication).

1558

• The 17 of November 1558 came certain news unto the Parliament house of the death of Queen Mary, whereat many rejoiced, and many lamented, and forthwith her death being generally known, they proclaimed the Lady Elizabeth second daughter to King Henry the eighth Queen of England, France, and Ireland, defender of the faith, &c.

♦ *Translation of Euripides'* Iphigenia in Aulis *by Jane Lumley.*

Mary I (1553–58), by John Master (fl. 1544–45).

1559

• The 20 of January began a Parliament . . . the Queen granted license for a free disputation to be held in Westminster Church, concerning some different points in Religion, but it came to no effect.

The 24 of June the Book of Common Prayer was established, and the Mass clean suppressed in all Churches.

In August following all ancient Church relics and new made Images in Queen Mary's reign, were beaten down and burned in the open streets.

■ **Acts of Uniformity and Supremacy passed. Elizabeth rejects a reluctant offer of marriage from Philip II of Spain.**

♦ *First account of Lord Robert Dudley's Men (later known as the Earl of Leicester's Men).*

Sources: Bentley, *Shakespeare: A Biographical Handbook*; Bullough, *Narrative and Dramatic Sources of Shakespeare*; Chambers, *The Elizabethan Stage* and *William Shakespeare: A Study of Facts and Problems*; Harbage, Schoenbaum, and Wagonheim, eds., *Annals of English Drama, 975–1700*.

1560

- In April the Lord Gray entered Scotland with ten thousand men, and besieged Leith, where between the French and the English were many hot skirmishes, and many slain on either part.

  The 5 of July through shooting of a Gun in a house in crooked lane, a barrel of powder was set on fire, which blew up four houses, shattered divers others, slew twenty persons outright, and hurt as many, besides great damage to houses and goods.

  This year the Queen by consent of her council, made Proclamation for the utter abolishing and suppression of all manner of base copper monies, which until this time had been current through out the Realm in divers Kings' reigns, and after this publication there was not any base metal coined in England.

- **Treaty of Edinburgh: French withdraw from Scotland. Presbyterianism established in Scotland. Publication of the Geneva Bible.**

- *Translation of Seneca's* Thyestes *by Jasper Heywood.*

Title page to the New Testament of the Geneva Bible (1560).

1561

- The 21st of March, the wardens and assistants of the Merchant-Tailors in London, founded the famous free school in the Parish of St. Lawrence Pountenay.

  The 10 of April W. Geffrey was whipped from the Marshalsea unto Bedlam, for publishing that one John Moore was Jesus Christ, which said John Moore after he had been well whipped, confessed himself a cozening knave.

  The 4 of June between 4 and 5 a clock in the afternoon, there chanced a terrible tempest of thunder and lightning, and chiefly about London, where amongst many harms, it fired the lofty spire of Paul's steeple.

- **Silver coinage reformed. Tulips brought to Europe. Rebellion in Ireland.**

- *Translation of pseudo-Seneca's* Hercules Oetaeus *by Elizabeth I.*

1562

- The 14 of May a man child was borne at Chichester in Sussex, the head, arms, and legs whereof, were like an Anatomy, the breast and belly big, from the navel a long string hanging about the neck, a collar of flesh like the ruff of a neckerchief, coming up about the ears.

- **French civil wars begin. Elizabeth sends an English force to occupy Le Havre. First slave-trading voyage of John Hawkins.**

- *Thomas Norton and Thomas Sackville,* The Tragedy of Gorboduc *[1565], the first English play in blank verse; shows strong influence of Seneca.*

1563

- The plague of pestilence being in the town of Newhaven [Le Havre], through the number of soldiers that returned into England, the infection thereof spread into divers parts of this realm, but especially the City of London.

  There was no term kept Michaelmas.

  An earthquake in the month of September, specially in Lincoln and Northhampton shires.

- **Church of England adopts the Thirty-Nine Articles.**

1564

- Peace proclaimed between England and France.

  The second of October was an obsequy at Pauls for Ferdinando late Emperor.

  The seventh of October at night all the North parts of the Element seemed to be covered with flames of fire, proceeding from the Northeast and Northwest toward the midst of the firmament, and descended West.

- *Birth of William, John Shakespeare's eldest son (christened April 26). John Shakespeare listed as a "capital burgess" of Stratford and contributes toward the relief of local plague victims.*

1565

- The third day of February, Henry Stuart Lord Darnley . . . took his journey toward Scotland, and in summer following married Mary Queen of Scotland.

✦ *John Shakespeare is made an alderman of Stratford.*

1566

- The 31 of August the Queen's Majesty in her Progress came to the University of Oxford, and was of all the Students honorably received.

    Charles James, the first of that name, son to Henry Stuart Lord Darnley and Mary, King and Queen of Scots, was born in Edinburgh Castle. . . . The Queen's Majesty of England was the Godmother, who gave a font of gold curiously wrought and enamelled, weighing 333 ounces.

■ **Tobacco brought from the New World around this time.**

✦ *Ariosto's* Il Suppositi, *translated by George Gascoigne [1573]; first English comedy with significant amount of prose.*

1567

- The 10 of February in the morning, H. Stuart Lord of Darnley, before named King of Scots, was traitorously murdered, the revenge whereof remaineth in the mighty hands of God.

    Within the space of ten months last past, died seven Aldermen in London.

    The 29 of July Charles James the young Prince of Scotland, after a sermon made by John Knox, was crowned King of Scots [James VI] at Sterling Church, and at that time the Queen of Scots was prisoner at Loughleven.

■ **Revolt against Spanish rule in the Netherlands. The Irish leader Shane O'Neill defeated by Lord Deputy Sir Henry Sidney and later murdered by "certain wild Scots."**

1568

- The 16 of May, Mary Q. of Scots after her escape made out of Loughleven, where she had been long imprisoned, arrived at Werkington in England . . . where she was stayed, and conveyed to Carlisle, and from thence to Bolton castle.

    The eleventh of October were taken in Suffolk at Downham Bridge, 17 monstrous fishes, some of them 27 foot in length, 2 miles from Ipswich.

    The 22 of December was the first day that the Marchants left their meeting in Lombard street, and came into the Burse in Cornhill, builded for that purpose.

■ **Publication of the Bishops' Bible. Foundation of English College at Douai, to train Jesuits.**

✦ *John Shakespeare elected Bailiff of Stratford, the town's highest office. The Queen's Players and Earl of Worcester's Men perform at Stratford.*

1569

- The 27 of January a Frenchman & two Englishmen were drawn from Newgate to Tiburne, and there hanged, the French man quartered, who had coined gold counterfeit, the Englishmen, the one had clipped silver, the other cast testons of tin.

The 17 of August, an Ambassador from Muscovy, landed at Tower-wharf, and was there received by the Lord Mayor of London.

The 11 of October, Thomas Duke of Norfolk was brought to the Tower prisoner.

The 24 of November the Queen's Majesty caused the Earls of Northumberland and Westmerland, who rebelled in the north, to be proclaimed traitors, and forthwith prepared an Army for their suppression.

Two swordsmen. From "The Norfolke Gentleman," *Roxburghe Ballads*.

1570

- The fourth and fifth of January did suffer [for their part in the Northern Rebellion] at Durham to the number of sixty six Constables and other, amongst whom an Alderman of the towne, and a Priest called Parson Plomtree.

  The Lord Scrope Warden of the West Marches, entered Scotland the 18 of April, burnt and spoiled almost the Dumfries, took many prisoners, and returned safely. . . . There were razed and overthrown and burnt in this journey, above fifty strong Castles and piles, and above 3 thousand towns and villages.

- **Elizabeth excommunicated by Pope Pius V.**

1571

- The 16 of July Rebecca Chambers of Heriettesham, for poisoning T. Chambers her husband, was burnt at Maidstone in Kent.

  The 9 of November great rejoicing was made in London, for the late come news of a marvelous victory obtained against the Turks [The Battle of Lepanto].

1572

- It was enacted that all persons above the age of fourteen years, being taken, vagrant, and wandering misorderly, should be apprehended, whipped, and burnt through the right ear with a hot iron for the first time so taken, the second time to be hanged. [The order includes actors not under the protection of a patron.]

This year 1572, was the [St. Bartholomew's Day] Massacre in Paris.

The 2 of June Thomas Duke of Norfolk was beheaded on Tower Hill.

The 18 of November was seen a star Northward, very bright and clear in the constellation of Cassiopeia, which with three chief fixed stars of the said constellation made a Geometrical figure lozengewise, of the learned men called Rombus. . . . The same star was found to be in place celestial, far above the Moon, otherwise than ever any comet hath been seen, or naturally can appear: therefore it is supposed, that the signification thereof is directed purposely, and specially to some matter not natural but celestial, or rather supercelestial, so strange, as from the beginning of the world never was the like.

✦ *The Earl of Leicester's Men perform at Stratford.*

1573

● The 18 of January William Lord Herbert Earl of Worcester, began his journey toward France, to the christening of the King's daughter there, in stead of the Queen's majesty of England. The said Earl with many of his company, were robbed upon the sea of much of their baggage, and three or four of their men slain.

1574

● The 7 of August, a solemn Obsequy was held in Paul's Church in London, for Charles the 9 King of France.

The 15 of August, being Sunday, Agnes Bridges, a maid about the age of 20 years, and Rachel Pinder, a wench about 12 years old, who both of them had counterfeited to be possessed by the devil, stood at Paul's Cross, where they acknowledged their hypocritical counterfeiting, requiring forgiveness of God, & the world: for they had made the people believe many things.

✦ *The Earl of Warwick's and Earl of Worcester's Men perform at Stratford. The Earl of Leicester's men are issued a patent by Queen Elizabeth permitting them to act in London and the provinces.*

1575

● The 16 of February, between four and five of the clock in the afternoon, great Earthquakes happened in the City of York, Worcester, Gloucester, Bristol, Hereford, and the Countries about, which caused the people to run out of their houses, for fear they should have fallen upon their heads.

On Easter day, the third of April, was disclosed a Congregation of Anabaptists, Dutchmen, in a house without the bars of Algate, at London, whereof 17 were taken, and sent to prison, and four of them bearing faggots, recanted at Paul's cross, on the 15 of May. [The rest were later banished or burned.]

✦ *Gascoigne (?) and Sir Henry Lee (?), The Queen's Entertainment at Woodstock.*

1576

- The 11 of February Anne Averies widow, forswearing herself for a little money, that she should have paid for six pounds of tow [rope] at a Shop in Woodstreet in London, fell immediately down speechless, casting up at her mouth, the same matter, which by Nature's course, should have been voided downwards, till she died.

■ **Spanish sack Antwerp. Dutch provinces unite against Spain (Treaty of Ghent). Martin Frobisher makes his first voyage in search of the Northwest Passage to Asia.**

♦ *James Burbage (father of Richard, the leading actor in Shakespeare's company) builds The Theatre (located in Shoreditch), London's first regular playhouse.*

Burning city under siege. From Raphael Holinshed, *Chronicles of England, Scotland, and Ireland* (1587).

1577

- The 31 of May, Martin Frobisher, with one Ship and two Barks, furnished for that purpose, sailed from Harwich, in Essex, towards Cathay, by the Northwest Seas, and entered his straits, beyond Queen Elizabeth's foreland, about thirty leagues, where he went on shore, and finding store of gold Ore (as he had been informed) fraught his Ship and Bark, caught a man, woman and child of that country, and then on the twenty four of August, returning, arrived at Milford haven on the twentieth of September.

  The stone tower of London Bridge, being decayed, was taken down, and a new foundation drawn.

■ **Sir Francis Drake begins his voyage around the world.**

♦ *Around this time, John Shakespeare begins his decline into debt.*
  The Curtain Theatre (Shoreditch) opens.

1578

- The 3 of February, John Nelson, for denying the Queen's supremacy, was drawn to Tyburn, and there hanged and quartered.

✦ *Mary Shakespeare pawns her estate, Asbyes at Wilmcote, and her lands at Snitterfield.*
   Lord Strange's Men and Lord Essex's Men perform at Stratford. (Performances in Stratford continue at the rate of at least one a year.)

1579

- This year Mark Scaliot, Blacksmith of London, for trial of his workmanship made one hanging lock of Iron, steel and brass of eleven several pieces, and a pipe key, all clean wrought, which weighed but one grain of gold. He also at the same time made a chain of gold of forty-three links, to which chain the lock and key being fastened and put about a fleas neck, she drew the same with ease. All which lock, key, chain, and flea, weighed but one grain and a half: a thing most incredible, but that I myself have seen it.

   This year John Fox of Woodbridge, William Wicnor, Robert Moore Englishmen, having been prisoners in Turkey about the space of thirteen years, with more than 260 other Christians of divers nations, by killing of their keeper, marvelously escaped, and returned to their native countries.

- **Protestant northern provinces of Holland unite (Union of Utrecht). John Stubbs loses his right hand for attacking Elizabeth's proposed marriage to the Duke of Alençon.**

1580

- About the 18 of July, the Lord Gray took his voyage towards Ireland, as Lord Deputy thereof, after whom were sent divers bands of lusty soldiers, both horsemen and footmen, under the leading of expert captains. [In November, Gray massacred several hundred Spanish and Italian mercenaries at Smerwick.]

   The 23 of September at Fennistanton in Huntingtonshire, one Agnes, wife to William Linsey, was delivered of an ugly and strange monster, with a face black, mouth and eyes like a Lion, and both male and female.

- **Jesuit mission established in England. Return of Sir Francis Drake.**

✦ *John Shakespeare unable to redeem Mary Shakespeare's pawned property.*

1581

- About the 11 of January proclamation was published at London, for revocation of sundry of the Queen's Majesty's subjects remaining beyond the seas under color of study, and yet living contrary to the laws of the Realm. And also against the retaining of Jesuits and massing Priests, sowers of sedition, and other treasonable attempts, &c.

   The first of November Monsieur the French King's brother Duke of Anjou, and other Nobles of France having lately arrived in Kent, came to London, and were honorably received and retained at the Court with great banqueting.

   The first of December, Edmund Campion Jesuit, Ralph Sherwin, and Alexander Brian Seminary Priests, having been arraigned and condemned for high treason, were drawn from the tower of London to Tyburn, and there hanged and quartered.

✦ *A new patent is issued to the Master of the Revels authorizing him to "reform, authorize and put down, as shall be thought meet or unmeet unto himself" any play to be performed in England.*

1582

- This year was first founded a public lecture in Surgery, to begin to be read in the College of Physicians in London.
  Peter Morris free denizen, conveyed Thames water in pipes of Lead . . . up to the Northwest corner of Leaden Hall (the highest ground of London) . . . plentifully serving to the commodity of the inhabitants near adjoining in their houses, and also cleansing the kennels of the street towards Bishops gate, Algate, the Bridge, and the Stocks market. But now no such matter, private commodity being preferred, common commodity is neglected, and not reformed as was promised.

- **Alençon departs from England. Plague in London. Pope Gregory XIII reforms calendar; Protestant countries retain old calendar.**

- *Shakespeare marries Anne Hathaway (license issued November 27).*

1583

- This year 1583, William Prince of Orange was slain by John Jowrigny a Walloon Soldier, who notwithstanding sundry extreme torments inflicted upon his body and limbs in prison, as also having his flesh plucked off with hot pincers upon an open stage, yet he neither shrunk, nor craved any favor, neither repented him of the fact, but feared he had not slain him. [In fact, William was assassinated in 1584.]
  This year 1583, the Queen being at Barne Elmes, at the earnest suit of Sir Francis Walsingham, she entertained twelve Players into her service, and allowed them wages and liveries, as Grooms of the Chamber, and until then she had none of her own, but divers Lords had Players [Queen Elizabeth's Men].

- **Galileo discovers the principle governing the motion of the pendulum.**

- *Birth of Shakespeare's older daughter, Susanna.*
  Queen Elizabeth's Men established by royal order.

1584

- On the 10 of January, William Carter was arraigned and condemned of high treason, for printing a seditious and traitorous book, entitled, A Treatise of Schism, and was for the same on the next morrow, drawn from Newgate to Tyburn, and there hanged, boweled and quartered, and forthwith a book was published, entitled, A Declaration of the favorable dealing of her Majesty's Commissioners, &c.

- **Failure of Sir Walter Ralegh's Virginia colony.**

Indians gathering food in their Virginia village. From Thomas Hariot, *A Briefe and True Report of the New Found Land of Virginia* (1590).

1585

- The 26 of June, arrived at London, Deputies for the States of the Netherlands, who were lodged about the Tower street, and had their diet worshipfully appointed at the charges of her Majesty, in the Clothworkers hall. Those on the 29 of June, repaired to the Court then at Greenwich, where they presented to her Majesty the sovereignty of those countries.

- **Elizabeth declines sovereignty of the Netherlands but sends an army to the Low Countries under the Earl of Leicester.**

- *Birth of Shakespeare's twin son and daughter, Hamnet and Judith. John Shakespeare fined for not going to church.*

1586

- A Commission was erected from her Majesty, tending to the ratifying of a firm League of amity, between her Majesty and James King of Scots [confirmed July 1].

  In the month of July, divers traitorous persons were apprehended, and detected of most wicked conspiracy against her Majesty [the Babington Plot], and also of minding to have stirred up a general rebellion throughout the whole Realm. For joy of whose apprehension, the Citizens of London on the 15 of the same month at night, and on the next morrow caused the Bells to be rung, and bonfires to be made, and also banqueted every man according to his ability, some in their houses, some in the streets.

- **Mary, Queen of Scots is implicated in the Babington Plot and sentenced to death. Sir Philip Sidney dies from wounds received at the Battle of Zutphen. Leicester is recalled to England.**

- *Shakespeare may leave Stratford at about this time. A contemporary reports that he became a country schoolmaster. It is certain only that he is in London by 1592.*

1587

- The 8 of February being Wednesday according to sentence lately given by the nobility, Mary Stuart Queen of Scots, about ten of the Clock before noon, was executed and suffered death, by beheading. . . .

  This year was a late spring, and a cold Summer, so that at Midsummer Peas in the cods were sold at London for 8 pence the peck, yet after were plenty, no cherries ripe til Saint James's-tide or Lammas, and then such plenty that they were sold for a penny the pound.

- **Drake defeats Spanish fleet at Cadiz.**

- *Thomas Kyd,* The Spanish Tragedy *[c. 1592]. Christopher Marlowe,* 1 Tamburlaine the Great *[1590].*

  John Shakespeare loses his position as an alderman.

  The Rose Theatre (located at Bankside, on the Thames) built by Philip Henslowe.

1588

- Great provision was made this year both by Land and Sea, for withstanding the invasion by the Spanish Armada against the Realm.

The 19 of July, intelligence was brought to the Lord Admiral by a pirate Pinnace, whose captain was Thomas Fleming, that the Spanish Fleet was seen in the sea.

The 20 of July, the Lord Admiral made toward the Sea, and the same day had sight of the Spanish fleet, in number by estimation 158 sails. The Lord Admiral cast about toward the land to interrupt them from approaching, & having got the wind of them, prosecuted them all that night, and so continually, from place to place, until the second of August, in which space by the power of GOD having wonderfully overcome them, he returned to Margate in Kent.

- **Death of Leicester. Puritan "Martin Marprelate" tracts ridicule the prelacy. African Company receives charter.**

♦ *John Lyly,* Endymion, the Man in the Moon.

Naval battle. From Raphael Holinshed, *Chronicles of England, Scotland, and Ireland* (1587).

1589

- The first of February two soldiers were set on the Pillory at the Leadenhall, whereon they stood by the space of three hours, the one had his ear nailed, the other his tongue pierced with an awl, which awl remained in his tongue till he was taken from the Pillory, for abusing their captains and Governors with bad speeches.

In the month of September, the Citizens of London furnished 1000 men to be sent over into France, to the aiding of Henry late King of Navarre, then challenging the Crown of France.

This year 1589, was devised and perfected, the Art of knitting, or weaving of silk stockings, Wastcotes, Coverlets, and divers other things by engines, or steel Looms, by William Lee, sometime master of St. John's College in Cambridge: and sixteen years after this, he went into France, and taught it to the French, because he was not regarded in England.

- **Henry III of France assassinated by a friar.**

Medal of Henry III of France. From the *Shirburn Ballads*, no. 46.

✦ *Robert Greene*, Friar Bacon and Friar Bungay. *Thomas Kyd*, Hamlet *(1582–89, not extant; likely source of Shakespeare's* Hamlet). *John Lyly*, Midas *[1592]. Christopher Marlowe*, The Jew of Malta. *Anonymous*, The Taming of a Shrew *(c. 1588–93) [1594]; may be a "bad quarto" of Shakespeare's play.*

Shakespeare is probably affiliated with the amalgamated Lord Strange's and Lord Admiral's Men from about this time until 1594.

Master of the Revels obtains authority to censor and license all plays.

1590

● The 21 of September, being the Feast of Saint Matthew in the afternoon, was a great stir at Lincoln's Inn, by Prentices, and others, against young Gentlemen students at Law there, for some rude demeanors, late before by them done, against the inhabitants of Chancery Lane, which had like to have grown to great mischief, had not the same been by wise Magistrates soon appeased: for the uproar grew great and violent, suddenly.

■ **James VI returns to Scotland with his bride, Anne of Denmark. Beginning of witchcraft trials in Scotland.**

✦ *Translation of Garnier's* Tragedy of Antonius *by Mary Herbert, Countess of Pembroke. Anonymous,* Edward III *(the "Countess scenes" in this play have been attributed to Shakespeare). Anonymous,* The True Chronicle History of King Leir, and His Three Daughters.

1591

● The 16 of July, Edmund Coppinger, and Henry Arthington, Gentlemen, came into Cheap, and there in a car, proclaimed news from heaven, (as they said) to wit, that one William Hacket Yeoman, represented Christ, by partaking his glorified body, by his principal spirit, and that they were two Prophets, the one of mercy, the other of Judgment, called and sent of God, to assist him in his great work, &c. [Hacket

Three old witches with familiars. From *The Wonderful Discoverie of the Witchcrafts of Margaret and Phillip Flower* (1619).

was hanged and quartered; Coppinger starved himself to death in prison; Arthington repented and was set free.]

■ **Robert Devereux, Earl of Essex, leads expedition to France in aid of Henry IV. Tea is first drunk in England.**

◆ 2 Henry VI *(1591); quarto,* The First Part of the Contention of the Two Famous Houses of York and Lancaster *[1594].* 3 Henry VI *(1591); octavo,* The True Tragedy of Richard Duke of York and the Good King Henry the Sixth *[1595].*

Acting is restricted on Sundays and Thursdays to provide for sufficient turnout at bearbaitings.

The bull- and bearbaiting arenas. Detail of *Civitas Londinum,* by Ralph Agas.

1592

● The 13 of December, a certain gentlewoman by the Council's commandment was whipped through the City of London, for affirming her self to be the daughter of Philip king of Spain, as she had been persuaded (by some accounted Soothsayers, after proved liars) for she was known to be a Butcher's daughter in Eastcheap.

■ **Plague hits London.**

◆ 1 Henry VI *(1592).* Richard III *(1592–93) [1597].* Venus and Adonis *(1592–93) [1593].* The Comedy of Errors *(1592–94).*

Marlowe, The Tragical History of Dr. Faustus *and* The Troublesome Reign and Lamentable Death of Edward II.

Robert Greene attacks Shakespeare in his Groats-worth of Wit, *the earliest reference to Shakespeare's career in the theater.*

Philip Henslowe's records show a total of 105 performances between February 19 and June 22, 1592, in London by Lord Strange's Men, probably in the Rose Theatre. Of the plays listed, two are possibly by Shakespeare: Harey the vj *(1 Henry VI, 15 performances) and* Titus & Vespacia *(Titus Andronicus?, 7 performances). Other plays include Greene's* Friar Bacon and Friar Bungay *and Marlowe's* Jew of Malta.

Henslowe begins his diary (continued until 1604), an important source on the the-ater. From June 1592 until June 1594, London theaters are shut down because of the plague, and acting companies take to the provinces.

1593

- This year was no Bartholomew fair kept at London, for the avoiding of concourse of people, whereby the infection of the pestilence might have increased.

  The whole number this year buried within the City of London, the suburbs and other places adjoining, as well of the plague, as of the other diseases, from the 29 of December in the year 1592, until the 20 of December, 1593 was as followeth. Within the walls of all diseases, 8598, whereof the plague, 5390, without the walls & in the liberties, 9295, the plague 5285. So that within the City and Liberties, of all diseases 17863 [*sic*]. Whereof the Plague was 10675.

- **Decree requiring church attendance on pain of banishment. Henry of Navarre becomes Catholic.**

- *Sonnets (1593–1603) [1609]. The Rape of Lucrece (1593–94) [1594]. Titus Androni-cus (1592) [1594]. The Taming of the Shrew (1592).*

  Henslowe's records show 29 performances for December 29, 1592, to February 1, 1593, again including 1 Henry VI *and* Titus Andronicus. *Lord Strange's Men are led at this time by Edward Alleyn (from the associated Lord Admiral's Men), and also include Will Kempe and John Heminges, Shakespeare's eventual colleagues in the Lord Chamberlain's Men. (There is no mention of Shakespeare himself, who may have trav-eled with another company or may not have acted at all during the plague years of 1592–94.)*

Woodcut showing the plague in London.

1594

- The last of February, Roderigo Lopez a Portugal (as it was said) professing Physic, was arraigned in the Guild-hall of London, found guilty, and had judgment of high Treason, for conspiring her majesty's destruction by poison.

  The 16 of April Ferdinando Earl of Derby deceased at Latham, in a very strange manner.

- **Henry of Navarre crowned Henry IV of France. Birth of James VI's first son, Henry.**

- ◆ *Shakespeare dedicates* The Rape of Lucrece *to Henry Wriothesley, Earl of Southampton.* The Two Gentlemen of Verona *(1590–91).* Love's Labour's Lost *(1594–95)* *[1598].* Sir Thomas More *(1592–93; parts revised by Shakespeare, 1603–4).*

  Francis Bacon, Thomas Campion, et al., Gesta Grayorum *(1594–95; contains the first surviving formal masque).*

  Henslowe's record for the early part of this winter includes one play probably by Shakespeare, listed as Titus & Ondronicous, *suggesting a possible revision of the previous season's* Titus *play. On June 11,* The Tamynge of a Shrowe *enters the London record; this could be an early version of* The Taming of the Shrew, *similar to the bad quarto of this year bearing the same title. The repertoire of the united Lord Admiral's and Lord Chamberlain's Men at this time also includes* Hamlet *(the "Ur-Hamlet," not Shakespeare's), as well as* The Jew of Malta, Titus Andronicus, *and other plays. After June 15, however, the Lord Chamberlain's company re-forms as a separate entity, no longer involving Edward Alleyn.*

1595

- This year by means of the late transportation of grain into foreign Countries, the same was here grown to an excessive price, as in some parts of this Realm, from fourteen shillings to four marks the quarter.

  On the 29 of June being Sunday in the afternoon, a number of unruly youths on the Tower hill, being blamed by the Warders of Towerstreet-ward to sever themselves and depart from thence, threw at them stones, and drave them back into Tower street, and were heartened thereunto by a late Soldier, sounding of a trumpet, but the trumpeter and many other of them being taken by the sheriffs of London, and committed to prison.

  The two & twenty of July, in presence of the Earl of Essex, and other sent from the Queen, were arraigned in the Guild-hall of London, five of those unruly youths that were on the Tower hill apprehended, they were condemned, and had judgment to be drawn, hanged and quartered.

- **Hugh O'Neill, Earl of Tyrone, rebels in Ireland. Sir Walter Ralegh sails to Guiana. Robert Southwell, Jesuit poet, is executed.**

- ◆ Richard II *(1595) [1597].* Romeo and Juliet *(1595) [1599; "bad quarto," 1597].* A Midsummer Night's Dream *(1594–96) [1600].*

  Shakespeare living in St. Helen's Parish, Bishopsgate, in London. He apparently becomes a sharer in (provides capital for) the newly re-formed Lord Chamberlain's Men.

  Evidence of the activity of the Lord Chamberlain's Men from 1595 to 1599, no longer reflected in Henslowe's records, is scanty. Records of payments in Cambridge and Ipswich indicate at least one provincial tour. Internal evidence suggests that A Midsummer Night's Dream *was the play performed at the court wedding of the Earl of Derby and Lady Elizabeth Vere on January 26, 1595.*

  Swan Theatre (Bankside) built.

1596

- On the 11 of April being Easter day about ten of the clock came a new charge, so that all men being in the parish Churches ready to have received the Communion, the Aldermen, their deputies, and Constables, were fain to close up the Church-doors, till they had pressed so many to be soldiers, that by 12 of the Clock, they had in the whole City 1000 men, and they were forthwith furnished of armor and weapons &c. And they were for the most part that night and the rest on the next morning sent away, to Dover, as the like out of other parts of the Realm, but returned again about a week after, for the French had lost Calais, &c. [The Spanish held Calais until 1598.]

    This year, like as in the months of August, September, October, and November, fell great rains, whereupon high waters followed: wheat in meal was sold at London for ten shillings the bushel, Rye six shillings, and Oatmeal eight shillings.

- **"League of amity" between England and France.**

- ✦ King John *(1596)*. The Merchant of Venice *(1596–97) [1600]*. 1 Henry IV *(1596–97) [1598]*.

John Shakespeare is granted a coat of arms, hence the title of "gentleman." William Shakespeare's son Hamnet dies.

Court records list payments to the Lord Chamberlain's Men for several performances in the winter of 1596 and again a year later. Provincial records indicate extensive touring in 1596–97. Payments during this tour average about 20 shillings.

The Shakespeare coat of arms, drafted October 20, 1596.

1597

- This summer arrived here an Ambassador from the King of Polonia, and had audience the twenty five of July, whose Oration was presently answered by her Majesty in Latin.

    A Parliament began at Westminster, on the 24 of October: on the which day divers people were smuldered and crushed to death, pressing between White-hall, and the College Church, to have seen her Majesty, and Nobility riding in their Robes to the said Parliament.

- ✦ The Merry Wives of Windsor *(1597–98) [1602]*.

    James Burbage builds Second Blackfriars Theatre. Restraint on playing in London forces the Lord Chamberlain's Men to tour the provinces. They perform at the Curtain Theatre from late 1597 to 1599 while the Globe is under construction. The scene showing the deposition of Richard is cut from the First Quarto of Richard II, *as Elizabeth perceives an analogy between Richard and herself.*

1598

- On the third of April, Twiford Town in Devonshire was burnt by casualty of fire, beginning in a poor cottage, a woman there frying pancakes with straw, the same fired the house, and so to the Town, about one of the clock in the afternoon.

    The third of September, died Philip the second of that name, King of Spain.

    In the month of December, great frosts, the Thames nigh over-frozen at London.

■ **Edict of Nantes ends French civil wars, granting toleration to Protestants.**

◆ 2 Henry IV *(1597–98) [1600]*. Much Ado About Nothing *(1598) [1600]*.

    Jonson, Every Man in His Humor.

    Shakespeare's name is first on the list of "principal Comedians" for Every Man in His Humor.

    Court records of 1598 and 1599 again show payments to the Lord Chamberlain's Men in late December, early January, and late February, specifying Shakespeare's colleagues "Thomas Pope and John Heminges servants to the Lord Chamberlain" as recipients.

    Materials from the demolished Theatre (at Shoreditch) are transported across the river and used in building the Globe as the "public," outdoor theater to replace it.

1599

- The 27 of March, about two of the clock in the afternoon, Robert Devereux, Earl of Essex, Lieutenant General, Lord High Marshal, &c. departed from his house in Seding lane, through Fenchurch street, Grace-street, Cornhill, Cheap, &c. toward Iseldone, High-gate, and rode that night to Saint Albans, towards Ireland.

    The City and Citizens kept unusual watch and ward, and all sorts of people were much amazed and frighted, as well by reason of preparation for wars, not knowing any cause, as also by the sudden strange, and terrible rumors and reports of the Spaniards fierce approach.

    On Michaelmas even, Robert, Earl of Essex, Lieutenant General for Ireland, having secretly returned into England, came to the Court at Nonsuch, & spake with the Queen, and on the second of October, was for contempt, &c. committed to the Lord Keeper.

■ **Satires and other offensive books called in and burned by ecclesiastical order. Thomas Nashe and Gabriel Harvey forbidden to publish.**

◆ Henry V *(1598–99) [1600]*. Julius Caesar *(1599)*. As You Like It *(1599–1600)*.

    Drayton et al., The First Part of the True and Honorable History of the Life of Sir John Oldcastle, the Good Lord Cobham *(response to Shakespeare's treatment of Oldcastle-Falstaff in the* Henry IV *plays; falsely attributed to Shakespeare).*

    Globe playhouse opens as home of the Lord Chamberlain's Men. Will Kempe, the most famous comedian of his day, leaves the Lord Chamberlain's Men around the same time that he performs his famous dance from London to Norwich.

1600

- The fifth of June, the Earl of Essex was called before the Lords of the Council, at the Lord Keepers, where for matters laid to his charge, he was supended from use of divers offices, till her Majesty's pleasure to the contrary, to keep his house, as before: whereat the people still murmured.

    The 8 of August, 1600, came Ambassadors from Abdela Wayhetanow, King of

Barbary. . . . They were very bountifully entertained at the Queen's charges, during their five months abode, they were very subtle and unthankful, they abhorred to give any manner of Alms unto any poor Christians, they sold their broken meat unto those who would give most for it, they killed all their own meat in the Ambassador's house, as Lambs, and all kinds of Pullen, &c. which they usually killed, turning their faces toward the East, they used to wash their own feet twice or thrice a day, and sometimes to wash their bodies: they use beads, and pray to Turkish Saints: they diligently observed the manner of our weights and measures, and all things else that might avail their native Merchants, and prejudice the English Nation.

■ **Birth of James VI's second son, Charles. Founding of East India Company.**

◆ Hamlet *(1600–1)* *[1604; "bad quarto," 1603]*.
Jonson, Cynthia's Revels.
A letter of Rowland Whyte to Sir Robert Sidney describes a command performance of one of the Falstaff plays arranged by the lord chamberlain (Lord Hunsdon) to entertain a foreign dignitary on March 6: "Upon Thursday my Lord Chamberlain feasted him, and made him very great, and a delicate Dinner, and there in the Afternoon his Players acted, before Vereiken, Sir John Oldcastle [Falstaff], to his great Contentment."
Edward Alleyn and Philip Henslowe build the Fortune Theatre for the Lord Admiral's Men, competing with the Globe.

Engraving of the Earl of Essex as Lord General.

1601

- Sunday the eight of February, about ten of the clock before noon, Robert Devereux Earl of Essex, assisted by sundry Noblemen and Gentlemen in warlike manner entered the City of London at the Temple Bar, crying for the Queen. [The rising failed, and Essex yielded to arrest the same day.]

  Ash Wednesday, the five and twenty of February, the Earl of Essex was beheaded in the Tower. . . . The Hangman was beaten as he returned thence, so that the Sheriffs of London were sent for, to assist and rescue him from such as would have murdered him.

  The 15 of March, in the night, a new Scaffold was carried from Leaden Hall in London to the Tower hill, and there set up by Torchlight.

  Lightning and thunder often before Christmas, and in the holy days, and an Earthquake at London on Christmas even at noon.

The execution of the Earl of Essex. From the *Shirburn Ballads*, no. 79.

- **New Poor Law places responsibility for relief for the poor on the local parish.**

- ◆ *"The Phoenix and Turtle" (1601) published in Robert Chester's* Loves Martyr. Twelfth Night *(1601).*

  Shakespeare's father, John, dies.

  Essex's followers arrange a staging of Richard II *at the Globe, to incite rebellion. Culmination of the War of the Theaters, with Ben Jonson in opposition to John Marston and Thomas Dekker.*

1602

- In the month of January news came out of Ireland, that on Christmas day the Spaniards and Irish were overcome and slain in great numbers, and the Englishmen were victors.

  The last of June, Atkenson a customer of Hull, was set on the Pillory in Cheap, and with him three other, who had been brought thither on horse back, with their faces toward the horses' tails, and papers on their heads. They were there whipped on the Pillory, and lost their ears by judgment of the Star-Chamber, for slanderous words by them spoken, against the Council.

✦ Troilus and Cressida (1602) [1609].

    Anonymous, Timon *(its relationship to Shakespeare's* Timon of Athens *is unclear).*

    Shakespeare receives a conveyance of land in Old Stratford (127 acres) for £320 and copyhold for a cottage in Stratford.

    Salmon Pavy, a boy player referred to as "the stage's jewel" in his epitaph written by Ben Jonson, dies at the age of thirteen.

    Opening of the Bodleian Library.

Sketch by George Vertue (1737) of Shakespeare's house in Stratford.

1603

• In the month of March, the Queen lying at Richmond, dangerously sick, straight watches were kept in London with warding at the gates, lanthorns with lights hanged out all night, at which news the people were sore perplexed.

    Thursday the four and twenty of March, about two of the clock in the morning, deceased Queen Elizabeth. . . .

    [James VI of Scotland declared King James I of England.] This change was very plausible, and well pleasing to the nobility and the Gentry, and generally to all the Commons of the Realm, among whom the name of a King was then so strange, as few could remember, or had seen a King before, except they were aged persons, considering that the government of the Realm had continued near the space of 50 years under the reign of two Queens, which is the far greater part of an old man's age.

    Against this time of Coronation, the citizens had made wondrous great provision; but through the terrible increase of pestilence in the City and the Suburbs, their sumptuous Pageants, and other triumphant entertainments, stood like ruins, being not yet finished, and the King constrained to omit his former determination in riding through London, as Kings have accustomed, and all Londoners prohibited by Proclamation from coming at Court: there died that week of all diseases, eleven hundred and three: the twenty five of July being Monday, and the feast of St. James the Apostle, King James the first of that name, King of England, and the most noble Lady Queen Anne his wife, were both crowned and anointed at Westminster.

■ Hugh O'Neill surrenders in Ireland.

✦ *Shakespeare's name appears for the last time in Jonson's actors' lists, as a "principal Tragedian" in* Sejanus.

    The average take during a provincial tour of this year by Shakespeare's company,

*now the King's Men, seems to increase relative to earlier tours, approaching 30 shillings.
A letter described by Lady Herbert in 1865 but never subsequently found alludes to a
performance of As You Like It that may have taken place in the fall 1603: "We have a
letter, never printed, from Lady Pembroke to her son, telling him to bring James I from
Salisbury to see As You Like It; 'we have the man Shakespeare with us.'"*

Theaters closed again on account of the plague from mid-1603 until April 1604.

The coronation of Macbeth. From Raphael Holinshed, *Chronicles of England, Scotland, and
Ireland* (1587).

1604

- The 5 of March was Proclamation made, for the authorizing the Book of Common
  Prayer.

  In October, the Customs of Merchandise were raised both inward and outward,
  and then let to farm.

- **Peace with Spain. Tax on tobacco.**

- Measure for Measure *(1603)*. Othello *(1603–4) [1622]*.

  The Malcontent *(possible source for Gloucester's suicide attempt in* King Lear*).*
  Anonymous, The London Prodigal *(possibly influenced Edgar's use of dialect in* King
  Lear*).*

  *Shakespeare's status as a member of the King's Men is recognized in an allowance
  of four yards of red cloth to wear as a participant in James's coronation procession
  through London.*

  *A nobleman's letter of January 15, 1604, states: "On New years night we had a
  play of Robin goodfellow,"* probably *A* Midsummer Night's Dream. *Records of eight
  performances at court during the winter season reflect the growing prominence of the
  King's Men. The first entry in the Revels Accounts, kept under the auspices of Edmund
  Tilney, for the 1604–5 season reads: "Hallowmas Day being the first of November A
  Play in the Banqueting house at Whitehall Called The Moor of Venice [Othello]." The*
  Merry Wives of Windsor *is performed on November 4. Shakespeare is listed several
  times under the category "the poets which made the plays," though in the unusual
  spelling "Shaxberd"; he is credited for the performance of* Measure for Measure *on
  December 26 and of* The Comedy of Errors *two days later.*

1605

- The twenty first of February was a Lion whelped in the Tower, which whelp was taken from the Dam, and brought up by hand, as the King had commanded.

  Upon May day last, Richard Haydocke, a Physician, asked forgiveness of the Lord Archbishop of Canterbury, for deluding the King and many others, under pretense of being inspired, and to preach in his sleep by night with which deceit he had so strongly possessed the vulgar, as it was hard to remove them, although he confessed the abuse.

  [Discovery of Gunpowder Plot] to undermine and blow up the Parliament House, at the instant when the King, Queen, Prince, Peers, and Commons were all assembled. [Guido ("Guy") Fawkes arrested.] The same day in the afternoon, the manner of the treason was by Proclamation made known unto the people, for joy whereof, there was that night as many bonfires as the streets could permit.

- ✦ All's Well That Ends Well *(1604–5)*. King Lear *(1604–5) [1608]*.

  Ben Jonson writes his first masque for the court.

  The Revels Accounts continue into the new year, listing Love's Labour's Lost *for early January,* Henry V *for January 7, and* The Merchant of Venice *for February 10.* The Merchant of Venice *is evidently a hit; the entry for February 12 states, "On Shrove Tuesday A play Called the Merchant of Venice Again Commanded By the Kings Majesty." The company also performs three plays not by Shakespeare, including Jonson's* Every Man in His Humour *(February 2).*

  Red Bull Theatre built.

1606

- A very great Whale came within eight miles of London whose length was divers times seen above the water, and the same was judged to be a great deal longer than the longest ship in the river.

  Friday the 28 of March 1606 in the Guildhall in London was arraigned and condemned Henry Garnet Provincial of the Jesuits in England, for being acquainted with the Gunpowder plot, and concealing the same, for the which he was adjudged to be drawn, hanged & quartered, and his head to be set upon London bridge. [The chief conspirators in the plot had been executed in January.]

  The 15 of July the wife of Richard Homwood of East Grimsted in Sussex without any known cause murdered her own three children, and threw them into a pit, and then cut her own throat likewise.

- ■ **London and Plymouth Companies receive charters to colonize Virginia.**

- ✦ Macbeth *(1606)*. Antony and Cleopatra *(1606)*.

  Jonson, Volpone, *or* The Fox. *Anonymous,* The Revenger's Tragedy.

  Provincial performances of the King's Men continue along with regular London engagements.

  Parliament passes "An Act to Restrain Abuses of Players" in order to purify the language in plays.

1607

- About the middle of May, certain common persons assembled themselves in Northamptonshire, Warwickshire, and Leicestershire: they cut and brake down hedges, filled up ditches, and laid open all such enclosures of commons and other grounds, which of ancient time had been open, and employed to tillage.

About the beginning of September, there fled out of Ireland into the parts beyond the Seas, Hugh Earl of Tyrone, Tyrconnel, Hugh Baron of Dongannon . . . with divers others their servants and followers.

▪ **Captain John Smith settles Jamestown, Virginia.**

◆ Timon of Athens *(1607–8)*. Pericles *(1607–8) [1609]*.
Shakespeare's daughter Susanna married to John Hall. Shakespeare's brother Edmund (described as a player) dies.

1608

● From Sunday the tenth of January, until the fifteenth of the same, the frost grew extreme, so as the Ice [on the Thames] became firm, and removed not, & then all sorts of men, women, and children, went boldly upon the Ice in most parts; some shot at pricks, others bowled and danced, with other variable pastimes; by reason of which concourse of people, there were many that set up booths and standings upon the Ice, as Fruit sellers, Victuallers, that sold beer and wine, Shoemakers, & a Barber's tent, &c. Every of them had fire near their beings.

All the Hartichokes in gardens about London were killed with this frost.

◆ Coriolanus *(1608)*.
William Rowley, The Birth of Merlin *(Shakespeare mistakenly named as a collaborator on the title page). Documents mention performances in London of* Pericles.
Birth of Shakespeare's granddaughter and death of his mother. Shakespeare obtains a one-seventh share in the Second Blackfriars Theatre.
Hamlet *and* Richard II *(not performed by the King's Men) serve as entertainment on board an East India vessel, the* Dragon, *off the coast of Sierra Leone. On March 31, Captain Keeling records in his journal: "I invited Captain Hawkins to a fish dinner, and had Hamlet acted aboard me: which I permit to keep my people from idleness and unlawful games, or sleep."*
The King's Men lease the Second Blackfriars as a second venue, for private indoor performances.

1609

● The last year, and this spring, according to his Majesty's express order, upon apparent reason and great likelihood of future good & utility to the common subjects of this land, there were many thousands of young Mulberry trees brought hither out of France . . . which were likewise by order sent into divers shires, and there planted for the feeding of Silkworms to make silk, like as it is made in France.

The first, second and third of June, the king in person royal heard the differences between the ecclesiastical and the temporal Judges argued, touching prohibitions out of the King's Bench, and Common Pleas.

▪ **Moors expelled from Spain.**

◆ *Publication of the Sonnets.* Cymbeline *(1609–10)*. A Lover's Complaint *(1609)*.

1610

- Thursday the 3 of May, the French Queen, with all solemnity was crowned in Paris, having been ten years before married to the king: and the next day after the King was murdered in his coach as he rode through Paris by a base villain that stabbed him in the body with a long knife twice, that he died instantly, and his body was carried to the Louvre.

  The Triumphs, Trophies, and pleasant devices at this time, in honor of the Lord Mayor and City of London, were extraordinary great, being in a manner twice so much as hath been usual within the City, and so likewise were the stately shows and ingenious devices upon the water, at the charges of the Company of Merchant-Tailors.

- Henry is made Prince of Wales. James dissolves Parliament.

- The Winter's Tale *(1609)*.
  Jonson, The Alchemist.
  Shakespeare probably returns to Stratford and settles there.
  Documents mention performances in London of Othello *(Globe, April 30, 1610).*
  There are also records of five provincial performances.

1611

- The 6 of June the King by Proclamation straightly commanded the oath of Allegiance to be ministered unto all sorts of people, and a true certificate to be made thereof unto the great Lords of the Council.

  At this time was concluded a double match between the young French King and the King of Spain's daughter, and the Prince of Spain and the French King's sister.

- Plantation of Ulster. Publication of the Authorized (King James) Version of the Bible.

Inigo Jones's design for Oberon's palace in Ben Jonson's masque *Oberon, the Fairy Prince* (1611).

♦ *The Revels Accounts are again available for 1611–12. Two of Shakespeare's last plays are given:* The Tempest *(November 1) and "ye winters nightes Tayle" (November 5). The series also includes Francis Beaumont and John Fletcher's* A King and No King.

1612

• Barthelmew Legat an obstinate Arian Heretic was burned in Smithfield. . . . Edward Wightman, an other perverse Heretic, having refused more favor than he could either desire or deserve, was burned at Lichfield, this Heretic would fain have made the people believe, that he himself was the Holy Ghost and immortal, with sundry other most vile opinions, not fit to be mentioned among Christians.

At this time the corpse of Queen Mary late Queen of Scotland, was translated from Peterborough to Westminster . . . and there placed in a vault, upon the South-side whereof the King had made a Royal Tomb for her, where she now resteth.

Friday the sixth of October [actually November] died the most Noble and hopeful Prince Henry Prince of Wales.

■ **Execution of Lancashire Witches.**

♦ Cardenio, *with Fletcher (1612–13, lost).*

John Webster, The White Devil *(1609–12). Anonymous,* Thorney Abbey, *or* The London Maid *(1606–14; influenced by* Macbeth*).*

Henry, Prince of Wales (1610–11), by Isaac Oliver.

1613

• The 17 of April 1613 at Alington in Lancashire was born a maiden child, having four Legs, four Arms, two Bellies joined to one back, one head with two faces, the one before and the other behind, and this year likewise was great Shipwrack, by violent tempests, there happened also sundry Inundations, and strange accidents, and much damage done by fire in divers places, and upon Saint Peter's day the Globe on the bankside was burned.

■ **Princess Elizabeth married to Frederick, Elector Palatine.**

♦ All Is True (Henry VIII), *probably with John Fletcher (1613).* The Two Noble Kinsmen, *with Fletcher (1613–14) [1634].*

Shakespeare purchases Blackfriars Gatehouse.

The Chamber Accounts for 1612–13 indicate that the King's Men had given a total of twenty plays at court by May 20, including revivals of Much Ado About Nothing, 1 and 2 Henry IV, Othello, and Julius Caesar, taking in £60. A further payment is recorded in compensation of a performance before a foreign dignitary in June.

1614

● In September there was a general muster of horse and foot throughout the Land, and therewithal training of soliders, but chiefly in the City of London by the citizens themselves, many whereof by their former voluntary exercise of Armes and Military discipline, were now so ready and expert that they taught others.

■ "Addled" Parliament is summoned and dissolved.

♦ Jonson, Bartholomew Fair. *Webster,* The Duchess of Malfi.

Philip Henslowe and Jacob Meade build the Hope Theatre (Bankside), a combination theater and bear garden. The Globe reopens.

1615

● At this time proclamation was made again, not only to stay, all further increase of buildings, which were daily erected in and about London, contrary to sundry former Edicts, and thereupon this Proclamation ratified and confirmed all former Proclamations, and straightly charged all Commissioners in that behalf, to look and search in to the depth of such offenders, and offenses, and to punish them accordingly. This Proclamation was dated the 16 of July 1615. And yet for all this, there was wondrous new increase of buildings round about London.

♦ Lady Elizabeth's players draw up a series of articles of grievance against Philip Henslowe, concerning their considerable debt to him. The Privy Council orders the eight leading members of four London companies, including Richard Burbage and Christopher Beeston, to come before them for performing during Lent against the orders of the Master of the Revels.

1616

● This Summer, and harvest was so dry, that passengers were annoyed with dust in the highways the 20 of November.

■ William Harvey describes the circulation of blood.

♦ Marriage of Shakespeare's daughter Judith. Shakespeare makes his will on March 25; he dies April 23.

Ben Jonson, The Works of Benjamin Jonson, the first collection of plays by an English author. His Masque of Christmas presented at court.

Christopher Beeston builds the Phoenix Theatre.

James I (1603–25), by Simon de Passe.

1616–23

♦ *The First Folio of Shakespeare's plays is published by members of the King's Men in 1623.*

Records for the years immediately following Shakespeare's death show the continued popularity of Twelfth Night *and* A Winter's Tale, *among other plays. Both are performed at court by the King's Men in April 1618; a performance at court of* A Winter's Tale *is recorded for 1619–20 and of* Twelfth Night *for Candlemas (February 2), 1623. A letter of May 20, 1619, written by Sir Gerrard Herbert describes the entertainment of a visiting French nobleman: "In the kinges great Chamber they went to see the play of*

Pirrocles, Prince of Tyre, which lasted till 2 aclocke. After two actes, the players ceased till the French all refreshed them with sweetmeates brought on Chinay voiders, & wyne & ale in bottells, after the players begann anewe." The new Master of the Revels, Sir Henry Herbert, notes on August 19, 1623: *"For the king's players. An olde playe called Winter's Tale, formerly allowed of by Sir George Bucke, and likewise by mee on Mͬ Hemminges his worde that there was nothing profane added or reformed, thogh the allowed booke was missinge; and therefore I returned it without a fee."*

General Bibliography

There is a huge and ever-expanding scholarly literature about Shakespeare and his culture. This general list and the ten-item lists accompanying the individual plays and poems in this volume are only a small sampling of the available resources. Journals devoted to Shakespeare studies include *Shakespeare Bulletin, Shakespeare Jahrbuch* (Germany), *Shakespeare Newsletter, Shakespeare Quarterly, Shakespeare Studies, Shakespeare Studies* (Tokyo), and *Shakespeare Survey* (England). The categories below are only approximate; many of the texts could properly belong in more than one category.

Shakespeare's World
Social, Political, and Economic History

Archer, Ian W. *The Pursuit of Stability: Social Relations in Elizabethan London.* Cambridge: Cambridge University Press, 1991.

Aries, Philippe, and Georges Duby, eds. A *History of Private Life: Passions of the Renaissance.* Vol. 3. Ed. Roger Chartier. Trans. Arthur Goldhammer. Cambridge: Belknap Press of Harvard University Press, 1989.

Barry, J., ed. *The Tudor and Stuart Town.* London: Longman, 1990.

Barry, Jonathan, and Christopher Brooks. *The Middling Sort of People.* New York: St. Martin's Press, 1994.

Barthelmey, Gerard. *Black Face, Maligned Race.* Baton Rouge: Louisiana State University Press, 1987.

Beier, A. L. *Masterless Men: The Vagrancy Problem in England, 1560–1640.* New York: Methuen, 1987.

———, and Roger Finlay, eds. *London 1500–1700: The Making of a Metropolis.* London: Longman, 1986.

Ben-Amos, Ilana Krausman. *Adolescence and Youth in Early Modern England.* New Haven: Yale University Press, 1994.

Bridenbaugh, Carl. *Vexed and Troubled Englishmen, 1590–1642.* New York: Oxford University Press, 1968.

Camden, Carroll. *The Elizabethan Woman.* Rev. ed. Mamaroneck, N.Y.: Appel, 1975.

Chew, Samuel. *The Crescent and the Rose.* New York: Octagon Books, 1965.

Clark, Alice. *Working Life of Women in the Seventeenth Century.* 1968. London: Routledge, 1992.

Clay, C. G. A. *Economic Expansion and Social Change.* 2 vols. Cambridge: Cambridge University Press, 1984.

Cruickshank, C. G. *Elizabeth's Army.* 2nd ed. Oxford: Clarendon Press, 1966.

Elliot, J. H. *The Old World and the New, 1492–1650.* Cambridge: Cambridge University Press, 1970.

Ellis, Steven G. *Tudor Ireland.* London: Longman, 1985.

Elton, G. R. *The Tudor Revolution in Government.* Cambridge: Cambridge University Press, 1959.

———. *England Under the Tudors.* London: Methuen, 1955.

Emmison, P. G. *Elizabethan Life: Disorder.* Chelmsford: Essex County Council, 1970.

Erickson, Amy Louise. *Women and Property in Early Modern England.* London: Routledge, 1993.

Finlay, Roger. *Population and Metropolis: The Demography of London, 1580–1650.* Cambridge: Cambridge University Press, 1979.

Fletcher, Anthony. *Gender, Sex, and Subordination in England, 1500–1800.* New Haven: Yale University Press, 1995.

——, and John Stevenson, eds. *Order and Disorder in Early Modern England.* Cambridge: Cambridge University Press, 1985.

Gittings, C. *Death, Burial and the Individual in Early Modern England.* London: Croom Helm, 1984.

Helgerson, Richard. *Forms of Nationhood: The Elizabethan Writing of England.* Chicago: University of Chicago Press, 1990.

Hirst, Derek. *Authority and Conflict: England, 1603–1658.* Cambridge: Harvard University Press, 1986.

Ingram, Martin. *Church Courts, Sex, and Marriage in England, 1570–1640.* Cambridge: Cambridge University Press, 1987.

James, Mervyn. *Society, Politics and Culture: Studies in Early Modern England.* Cambridge: Cambridge University Press, 1986.

Kantorowicz, E. H. *The King's Two Bodies.* Princeton: Princeton University Press, 1957.

King, J. N. *Tudor Royal Iconography.* Princeton: Princeton University Press, 1989.

Klein, Joan Larsen. *Daughters, Wives, and Widows: Writings by Men about Women and Marriage in England, 1500–1640.* Urbana: University of Illinois Press, 1992.

Laqueur, Thomas. *Making Sex: Body and Gender from the Greeks to Freud.* Cambridge: Harvard University Press, 1990.

Laslett, Peter. *The World We Have Lost: Further Explored.* 3rd ed. New York: Scribner, 1984.

Levin, Carole. *"The Heart and Stomach of a King": Elizabeth I and the Politics of Sex and Power.* Philadelphia: University of Pennsylvania Press, 1994.

Lockyer, Roger. *The Early Stuarts: A Political History of England.* London: Longman, 1989.

MacCaffrey, Wallace T. *Elizabeth I: War and Politics.* Princeton: Princeton University Press, 1992.

——. *The Shaping of the Elizabethan Regime.* Princeton: Princeton University Press, 1968.

Manning, Roger B. *Village Revolts: Social Protest and Popular Disturbances in England, 1509–1640.* Oxford: Clarendon Press, 1988.

Mattingly, Garrett. *The Armada.* Boston: Houghton Mifflin, 1959.

Mukerji, Chandra. *From Graven Images: Patterns of Modern Materialism.* New York: Columbia University Press, 1983.

Neale, J. E. *Queen Elizabeth I.* London: Cape, 1961.

Neale, John E. *Elizabeth I and Her Parliaments.* 2 vols. New York: St. Martin's Press, 1958.

Nichols, John, ed. *The Progresses and Public Processions of Queen Elizabeth.* 3 vols. London, 1823.

Notestein, Wallace. *The House of Commons, 1604–1610.* New Haven: Yale University Press, 1971.

Palliser, D. M. *The Age of Elizabeth.* 2nd ed. London: Longman, 1992.

Parry, G. *The Age of Reconnaissance: Discovery, Exploration, and Settlement, 1450–1650.* New York: Praeger, 1969.

Pearson, Lu Emily. *Elizabethans at Home.* Stanford: Stanford University Press, 1957.

Peck, Linda Levy. *Court Patronage and Corruption in Early Stuart England.* Boston: Unwin Hyman, 1990.

Pocock, J. G. A. *The Ancient Constitution and the Feudal Law.* Rev. ed. Cambridge: Cambridge University Press, 1987.

Quinn, David B. *The Elizabethans and the Irish.* Ithaca, N.Y.: Cornell University Press, 1966.

Scarisbrick, J. J. *Henry VIII.* Berkeley and Los Angeles: University of California Press, 1968.

Sharpe, J. A. *Crime in Seventeenth-Century England: A Country Study*. Cambridge: Cambridge University Press, 1983.

Slack, Paul. *The Impact of Plague in Tudor and Stuart England*. London: Routledge & Kegan Paul, 1985.

———, ed. *Rebellion, Popular Protest and the Social Order in Early Modern England*. Cambridge: Cambridge University Press, 1984.

Stone, Lawrence. *The Causes of the English Revolution, 1529–1642*. New York: Routledge & Kegan Paul, 1986.

———. *The Family, Sex and Marriage in England, 1500–1800*. New York: Harper & Row, 1977.

———. *The Crisis of the Aristocracy, 1558–1641*. Oxford: Clarendon Press, 1965.

Stow, John. *Survey of London*. Ed. C. L. Kingsford. Oxford: Clarendon Press, 1971.

Tawney, R. H. *Religion and the Rise of Capitalism*. 1926. New York: Peter Smith, 1962.

Thirsk, Joan. *Economic Policy and Projects: The Development of a Consumer Society in Early Modern England*. Oxford: Clarendon Press, 1978.

Thomas, Keith. *Religion and the Decline of Magic*. New York: Scribner, 1971.

Underdown, David. *Revel, Riot, and Rebellion: Popular Politics and Culture in England, 1603–1660*. Oxford: Clarendon Press, 1985.

Walvin, James. *The Black Presence: A Documentary History of the Negro in England, 1555–1860*. London: Orbach & Chambers, 1971.

Willson, David Harris. *King James VI & I*. 1956. London: Cape, 1972.

Wilson, F. P. *Elizabethan and Jacobean*. Oxford: Clarendon Press, 1945.

Yates, Frances. *Astraea: The Imperial Theme in the Sixteenth Century*. London: Routledge & Kegan Paul, 1975.

Zagorin, Perez. *Rebels and Rulers, 1500–1660*. 2 vols. Cambridge: Cambridge University Press, 1982.

———. *The Court and the Country: The Beginnings of the English Revolution*. New York: Atheneum, 1970.

Zeeveld, W. Gordon. *Foundations of Tudor Policy*. Cambridge: Harvard University Press, 1948.

Intellectual and Religious History

Baker, Herschel C. *The Race of Time: Three Lectures on Renaissance Historiography*. Toronto: University of Toronto Press, 1967.

Barkan, Leonard. *Nature's Work of Art: The Human Body as Image of the World*. New Haven: Yale University Press, 1975.

Bouwsma, William J. *John Calvin: A Sixteenth-Century Portrait*. New York: Oxford University Press, 1988.

Brower, Reuben A. *Hero and Saint: Shakespeare and the Graeco-Roman Tradition*. New York: Oxford University Press, 1971.

Cassirer, Ernst. *The Individual and the Cosmos in Renaissance Philosophy*. Trans. Mario Domandi. Philadelphia: University of Pennsylvania Press, 1972.

Collinson, Patrick. *The Elizabethan Puritan Movement*. New York: Oxford University Press, 1989.

———. *The Religion of Protestants: The Church in English Society, 1559–1625*. Oxford: Clarendon Press, 1982.

Dickens, A. G. *The English Reformation*. New York: Schocken Books, 1964.

Haydn, Hiram. *The Counter-Renaissance*. 1950. Gloucester, Mass.: P. Smith, 1966.

Hill, Christopher. *Society and Puritanism in Pre-Revolutionary England*. New York: Schocken Books, 1967.

Kelly, Henry Ansgar. *Divine Providence in the England of Shakespeare's Histories*. Cambridge: Harvard University Press, 1970.

Klaits, Joseph. *Servants of Satan: The Age of the Witch Hunts*. Bloomington: Indiana University Press, 1985.

Kocher, Paul. *Science and Religion in Elizabethan England.* 1953. New York: Octagon Books, 1969.

Kristeller, Paul Oskar. *Renaissance Thought: The Classic, Scholastic, and Humanistic Strains.* New York: Harper, 1961.

Levao, Ronald. *Renaissance Minds and Their Fictions.* Berkeley and Los Angeles: University of California Press, 1985.

Levin, Harry. *The Myth of the Golden Age in the Renaissance.* Bloomington: University of Indiana Press, 1969.

Levy, Fred J. *Tudor Historical Thought.* San Marino, Calif.: Huntington Library Press, 1967.

Lovejoy, A. O. *The Great Chain of Being: A Study of the History of an Idea.* Cambridge: Harvard University Press, 1936.

Mack, Peter, ed. *Renaissance Rhetoric.* New York: St. Martin's Press, 1994.

Popkin, Richard H. *The History of Skepticism from Erasmus to Spinoza.* Berkeley and Los Angeles: University of California Press, 1979.

Rossi, Paolo. *Francis Bacon: From Magic to Science.* London: Routledge & Kegan Paul, 1968.

Shuger, Debora Kuller. *Habits of Thought in the English Renaissance: Religion, Politics, and the Dominant Culture.* Berkeley and Los Angeles: University of California Press, 1990.

Sonnino, Lee A. *A Handbook to Sixteenth-Century Rhetoric.* London: Routledge & Kegan Paul, 1968.

Strong, Roy. *The Cult of Elizabeth.* London: Thames and Hudson, 1977.

——. *The English Icon: Elizabethan and Jacobean Portraiture.* London: Routledge & Kegan Paul, 1969.

Tillyard, E. M. W. *The Elizabethan World Picture.* London: Chatto & Windus, 1943.

Wind, Edgar. *Pagan Mysteries in the Renaissance.* 2nd ed. London: Faber, 1968.

Cultural History

Aers, David, Bob Hodge, and Gunther Kress. *Literature, Language and Society in England, 1589–1680.* Totowa, N.J.: Barnes & Noble, 1981.

Austern, Linda Phyllis. " 'Sing Againe Syren': The Female Musician and Sexual Enchantment in Elizabethan Life and Literature." *Renaissance Quarterly* 42 (1989): 420–48.

Bakhtin, Mikhail. *Rabelais and His World.* Cambridge: MIT Press, 1968.

Barkan, Leonard. *The Gods Made Flesh: Metamorphosis and the Pursuit of Paganism.* New Haven: Yale University Press, 1986.

Barker, Francis. *The Tremulous Private Body.* London: Methuen, 1994.

Beilin, Elaine V. *Redeeming Eve: Women Writers of the English Renaissance.* Princeton: Princeton University Press, 1987.

Bevington, David. *Tudor Drama and Politics: A Critical Approach to Topical Meaning.* Cambridge: Harvard University Press, 1968.

Bray, Alan. *Homosexuality in Renaissance England.* London: Gay Men's Press, 1982.

Briggs, K. M. *Pale Hecate's Team: An Examination of the Beliefs on Witchcraft and Magic among Shakespeare's Contemporaries and His Immediate Successors.* New York: Humanities Press, 1962.

——. *The Anatomy of Puck: An Examination of Fairy Beliefs among Shakespeare's Contemporaries and Successors.* London: Routledge & Kegan Paul, 1959.

Burke, Peter. *Popular Culture in Early Modern Europe.* New York: New York University Press, 1978.

Burt, Richard, and John Michael Archer, eds. *Enclosure Acts: Sexuality, Property, and Culture in Early Modern England.* Ithaca, N.Y.: Cornell University Press, 1994.

Buxton, John. *Elizabethan Taste.* London: Macmillan, 1963.

Caldwell, John. *The Oxford History of English Music.* Vol. 1. Oxford: Clarendon Press, 1991.

Cressy, David. *Literacy and the Social Order: Reading and Writing in Tudor and Stuart England.* Cambridge: Cambridge University Press, 1980.

Dolan, Frances. *Dangerous Familiars: Representations of Domestic Crime in England, 1550–1700.* Ithaca, N.Y.: Cornell University Press, 1994.

Eisenstein, Elizabeth. *The Printing Press as an Agent of Change.* 2 vols. Cambridge: Cambridge University Press, 1979.

Ferguson, Margaret W., Maureen Quilligan, and Nancy J. Vickers, eds. *Rewriting the Renaissance: The Discourses of Sexual Difference in Early Modern Europe.* Chicago: University of Chicago Press, 1986.

Fumerton, Patricia. *Cultural Aesthetics: Renaissance Literature and the Practice of Social Ornament.* Chicago: University of Chicago Press, 1991.

Garber, Marjorie, ed. *Cannibals, Witches, Divorce: Estranging the Renaissance.* Baltimore: Johns Hopkins University Press, 1987.

Gillies, John. *Shakespeare and the Geography of Difference.* New York: Cambridge University Press, 1994.

Goldberg, Jonathan. *Writing Matter: From the Hands of the English Renaissance.* Stanford: Stanford University Press, 1990.

——. *James I and the Politics of Literature: Jonson, Shakespeare, Donne and Their Contemporaries.* Baltimore: Johns Hopkins University Press, 1983.

——, ed. *Queering the Renaissance.* Durham, N.C.: Duke University Press, 1994.

Greenblatt, Stephen. *Learning to Curse: Essays in Early Modern Culture.* New York: Routledge, 1990.

——. *Renaissance Self-Fashioning: From More to Shakespeare.* Chicago: University of Chicago Press, 1980.

——, ed. *New World Encounters.* Berkeley and Los Angeles: University of California Press, 1993.

——, ed. *Representing the English Renaissance.* Berkeley and Los Angeles: University of California Press, 1988.

Grout, Donald Jay. *A Short History of Opera.* New York: Columbia University Press, 1988.

Hall, Kim F. *Things of Darkness: Economies of Race and Gender in Early Modern England.* Ithaca, N.Y.: Cornell University Press, 1996.

Haselkorn, Anne M., and Betty S. Travitsky, eds. *The Renaissance Englishwoman in Print: Counterbalancing the Canon.* Amherst: University of Massachusetts Press, 1990.

Henderson, Katherine Usher, and Barbara F. McManus. *Half Humankind: Contexts and Texts of the Controversy About Women in England, 1540–1640.* Urbana: University of Illinois Press, 1985.

Hendricks, Margo, and Patricia Parker, eds. *Women, "Race," and Writing in the Early Modern Period.* London: Routledge, 1994.

Hoeniger, F. David. *Medicine and Shakespeare in the English Renaissance.* Newark: University of Delaware Press, 1991.

Huizinga, Johan. *The Autumn of the Middle Ages.* Trans. Rodney J. Payton and Ulrich Mammitzsch. Chicago: University of Chicago Press, 1996.

Hull, Suzanne W. *Chaste, Silent and Obedient: English Books for Women, 1475–1640.* San Marino, Calif.: Huntington Library, 1982.

Jardine, Lisa. *Still Harping on Daughters: Women and Drama in the Age of Shakespeare.* 1983. 2nd ed. New York: Columbia University Press, 1989.

Javitch, Daniel. *Poetry and Courtliness in Renaissance England.* Princeton: Princeton University Press, 1978.

Jordan, Constance. *Renaissance Feminism: Literary Texts and Political Models.* Ithaca, N.Y.: Cornell University Press, 1990.

Kelso, Ruth. *Doctrine for the Lady of the Renaissance.* 1956. Urbana: University of Illinois Press, 1978.

——. *The Doctrine of the English Gentleman in the Sixteenth Century.* 1929. Gloucester, Mass.: P. Smith, 1964.

Manley, Lawrence. *Literature and Culture in Early Modern London.* Cambridge: Cambridge University Press, 1995.

Marcus, Leah. *The Politics of Mirth: Jonson, Herrick, Milton, Marvell, and the Defense of Old Holiday Pastimes.* Chicago: University of Chicago Press, 1986.

Miller, David Lee, Sharon O'Dair, and Harold Weber, eds. *The Production of English Renaissance Culture.* Ithaca, N.Y.: Cornell University Press, 1994.

Norbrook, David. *Poetry and Politics in the English Renaissance.* London: Routledge & Kegan Paul, 1984.

Orlin, Lena Cowen. *Private Matters and Public Culture in Post-Reformation England.* Ithaca, N.Y.: Cornell University Press, 1994.

Parry, G. *The Golden Age Restor'd: The Culture of the Stuart Court, 1603–1642.* Manchester: Manchester University Press, 1981.

Patterson, Annabel. *Censorship and Interpretation: The Conditions of Writing and Reading in Early Modern England.* Madison: University of Wisconsin Press, 1984.

Shapiro, James. *Shakespeare and the Jews.* New York: Columbia University Press, 1996.

Sharpe, K., and Lake, P., eds. *Culture and Politics in Early Stuart England,* Stanford: Stanford University Press, 1993.

Simon, Joan. *Education and Society in Tudor England.* Cambridge: Cambridge University Press, 1966.

Sinfield, Alan. *Literature in Protestant England, 1560–1660.* Totowa, N.J.: Barnes & Noble, 1983.

Smith, Bruce. *Homosexual Desire in Shakespeare's England.* Chicago: University of Chicago Press, 1991.

Spufford, Margaret. *Small Books and Pleasant Histories: Popular Fiction and Its Readership in Seventeenth-Century England.* Athens: University of Georgia Press, 1981.

Stallybrass, Peter, and Allon White. *The Politics and Poetics of Transgression.* Ithaca, N.Y.: Cornell University Press, 1986.

Turner, James Grantham, ed. *Sexuality and Gender in Early Modern Europe: Institutions, Texts, Images.* Cambridge: Cambridge University Press, 1993.

Whigham, Frank. *Ambition and Privilege: The Social Tropes of Elizabethan Courtesy Theory.* Berkeley and Los Angeles: University of California Press, 1984.

Woodbridge, Linda. *Women and the English Renaissance: Literature and the Nature of Womankind, 1540–1620.* Urbana: University of Illinois Press, 1986.

Wright, L. B. *Middle-Class Culture in Elizabethan England.* Chapel Hill: University of North Carolina Press, 1935.

Shakespeare's Literary and Theatrical Contexts

Agnew, Jean-Christophe. *Worlds Apart: The Market and the Theatre in Anglo-American Thought, 1550–1750.* Cambridge: Cambridge University Press, 1986.

Alpers, Paul. *What Is Pastoral?* Chicago: University of Chicago Press, 1996.

Altman, Joel. *The Tudor Play of Mind.* Berkeley and Los Angeles: University of California Press, 1978.

Barber, C. L. *Creating Elizabethan Tragedy: The Theater of Kyd and Marlowe.* Chicago: University of Chicago Press, 1988.

Barish, Jonas. *Ben Jonson and the Language of Prose Comedy.* Cambridge: Harvard University Press, 1960.

———. *The Antitheatrical Prejudice.* Berkeley and Los Angeles: University of California Press, 1981.

Bate, Jonathan. *Shakespeare and Ovid.* Oxford: Clarendon Press, 1993.

Bates, Catherine. *The Rhetoric of Courtship in Elizabethan Language and Literature.* Cambridge: Cambridge University Press, 1992.

Belsey, Catherine. *The Subject of Tragedy: Identity and Difference in Renaissance Drama.* London: Methuen, 1985.

Bentley, G. E. *The Profession of Player in Shakespeare's Time, 1590–1642.* Princeton: Princeton University Press, 1984.

———. *The Profession of Dramatist in Shakespeare's Time, 1590–1642.* Princeton: Princeton University Press, 1971.

———. *The Seventeenth-Century Stage: A Collection of Critical Essays.* Chicago: University of Chicago Press, 1968.

———. *The Jacobean and Caroline Stage.* 7 vols. Oxford: Clarendon Press, 1941–68.

Bevington, David. *From "Mankind" to Marlowe: Growth of Structure in the Popular Drama of Tudor England.* Cambridge: Harvard University Press, 1962.

Bowers, Fredson T. *Elizabethan Revenge Tragedy, 1587–1642.* Princeton: Princeton University Press, 1940.

Bradbrook, M. C. *The Rise of the Common Player: A Study of Actor and Society in Shakespeare's England.* London: Chatto & Windus, 1962.

Braden, Gordon. *Renaissance Tragedy and the Senecan Tradition.* New Haven: Yale University Press, 1985.

Briggs, Julia. *This Stage-Play World: English Literature and Its Background, 1580–1625.* Oxford: Oxford University Press, 1983.

Bristol, Michael D. *Carnival and Theater: Plebeian Culture and the Structure of Authority in Renaissance England.* New York: Methuen, 1985.

Bruster, Douglas. *Drama and the Market in the Age of Shakespeare.* Cambridge: Cambridge University Press, 1992.

Bullough, Geoffrey, ed. *Narrative and Dramatic Sources of Shakespeare.* 8 vols. New York: Columbia University Press, 1957–75.

Butler, Martin. *Theatre and Crisis, 1632–1642.* Cambridge: Cambridge University Press, 1984.

Clubb, Louise George. *Italian Drama in Shakespeare's Time.* New Haven: Yale University Press, 1989.

Cohen, Walter. *Drama of a Nation: Public Theater in Renaissance England and Spain.* Ithaca, N.Y.: Cornell University Press, 1985.

Dessen, Alan C. *Recovering Shakespeare's Theatrical Vocabulary.* Cambridge: Cambridge University Press, 1995.

———. *Elizabethan Stage Conventions and Modern Interpreters.* Cambridge: Cambridge University Press, 1984.

———. *Elizabethan Drama and the Viewer's Eye.* Chapel Hill: University of North Carolina Press, 1977.

Doran, Madeleine. *Endeavors of Art: A Study of Form in Elizabethan Drama.* Madison: University of Wisconsin Press, 1954.

Empson, William. *The Structure of Complex Words.* 1951. London: Chatto & Windus, 1970.

Farnham, Willard. *The Medieval Heritage of Elizabethan Tragedy.* 1936. New York: Barnes & Noble, 1956.

Foakes, R. A. *Illustrations of the English Stage, 1580–1642.* Stanford: Stanford University Press, 1985.

Gardiner, H. C. *Mysteries' End.* New Haven: Yale University Press, 1946.

Harbage, Alfred. *Shakespeare and the Rival Traditions.* 1952. New York: Barnes & Noble, 1968.

Hardison, O. B. Jr. *Christian Rite and Christian Drama in the Middle Ages.* Baltimore: Johns Hopkins University Press, 1965.

Hattaway, Michael. *Elizabethan Popular Theatre: Plays in Performance.* London: Routledge & Kegan Paul, 1982.

Heinemann, Margot. *Puritanism and Theatre: Thomas Middleton and Opposition Drama under the Early Stuarts.* Cambridge: Cambridge University Press, 1980.

Homan, Sidney, ed. *Shakespeare's "More Than Words Can Witness."* Lewisburg, Pa.: Bucknell University Press, 1980.

Hosley, Richard, ed. *Shakespeare's Holinshed: An Edition of Holinshed's Chronicles.* New York: Putnam, 1968.

Hunter, G. K. *John Lyly: The Humanist as Courtier.* Cambridge: Harvard University Press, 1962.

Jones, Emrys. *Scenic Form in Shakespeare.* Oxford: Clarendon Press, 1971.

Kernan, Alvin. *The Cankered Muse: Satire of the English Renaissance.* New Haven: Yale University Press, 1959.

Kolve, V. A. *The Play Called Corpus Christi.* Stanford: Stanford University Press, 1966.

Leggatt, Alexander. *Citizen Comedy in the Age of Shakespeare.* Toronto: University of Toronto Press, 1973.

Levin, Harry. *The Overreacher: A Study of Christopher Marlowe.* 1932. Cambridge: Harvard University Press, 1964.

Levin, Richard. *The Multiple Plot in English Renaissance Drama.* Chicago: University of Chicago Press, 1971.

Lomax, Marion. *Stage Images and Traditions: Shakespeare to Ford.* Cambridge: Cambridge University Press, 1987.

McLuskie, Kathleen. *Renaissance Dramatists.* New York: Harvester Wheatsheaf, 1989.

McMillin, Scott. *The Elizabethan Theatre and the Book of Sir Thomas More.* Ithaca, N.Y.: Cornell University Press, 1987.

Montrose, Louis. *The Purpose of Playing: Shakespeare and the Cultural Politics of the Elizabethan Theatre.* Chicago: University of Chicago Press, 1996.

Muir, Kenneth. *Shakespeare's Sources.* 2 vols. London, 1957.

Orgel, Stephen. *The Illusion of Power: Political Theater in the English Renaissance.* Berkeley and Los Angeles: University of California Press, 1975.

Rose, Mark. *Shakespearean Design.* Cambridge: Harvard University Press, 1972.

Rose, Mary Beth. *The Expense of Spirit: Love and Sexuality in English Renaissance Drama.* Ithaca, N.Y.: Cornell University Press, 1988.

Sanders, Wilbur. *The Dramatist and the Received Idea: Studies in the Plays of Marlowe and Shakespeare.* Cambridge: Cambridge University Press, 1968.

Spivack, Bernard. *Shakespeare and the Allegory of Evil.* New York: Columbia University Press, 1958.

Waith, Eugene. *The Herculean Hero in Marlowe, Chapman, Shakespeare, and Dryden.* New York: Columbia University Press, 1962.

Weimann, Robert. *Shakespeare and the Popular Tradition in the Theater: Studies in the Social Dimension of Dramatic Form and Function.* Ed. Robert Schwartz. Baltimore: Johns Hopkins University Press, 1978.

Woolf, Rosemary. *The English Mystery Plays.* Berkeley and Los Angeles: University of California Press, 1972.

The Playing Field: London Theaters and State Regulation

Astington, John H., ed. *The Development of Shakespeare's Theater.* New York: AMS Press, 1992.

Barrol, Leeds. *Politics, Plague, and Shakespeare's Theater: The Stuart Years.* Ithaca, N.Y.: Cornell University Press, 1991.

Beckerman, Bernard. *Shakespeare at the Globe, 1599–1609.* New York: Macmillan, 1962, 1967.

Berry, Herbert. *Shakespeare's Playhouses.* Illustrated by C. Walter Hodges. AMS Studies in the Renaissance 19. New York: AMS Press, 1987.

Chambers, E. K. *The Elizabethan Stage.* 4 vols. Oxford: Clarendon Press, 1923.

——. *The Medieval Stage.* 2 vols. Oxford: Clarendon Press, 1903.

Clare, Janet. *"Art Made Tongue-Tied by Authority": Elizabethan and Jacobean Dramatic Censorship.* New York: St. Martin's Press, 1990.

Cook, Ann Jennalie. *The Privileged Playgoers of Shakespeare's London: 1576–1642.* Princeton: Princeton University Press, 1981.

Gair, W. Reavley. *The Children of Paul's.* Cambridge: Cambridge University Press, 1982.

Gildersleeve, Virginia C. *Government Regulation of the Elizabethan Drama.* Westport, Conn.: Greenwood Press, 1975.

Greg, W. W., ed. *Dramatic Documents from the Elizabethan Playhouses: Stage Plots; Actor's Parts; Prompt Books.* 2 vols. 1931. Oxford: Clarendon Press, 1969.

Gurr, Andrew. *The Shakespearean Stage, 1574–1642.* 3rd ed. Cambridge: Cambridge University Press, 1992.

———. *Playgoing in Shakespeare's London.* Cambridge: Cambridge University Press, 1987.

———, and John Orrell. *Rebuilding Shakespeare's Globe.* London: Weidenfeld and Nicolson, 1989.

Harbage, Alfred. *Shakespeare's Audience.* New York: Columbia University Press, 1941.

Henslowe, Philip. *Henslowe's Diary.* Ed. R. A. Foakes and R. T. Rickert. Cambridge: Cambridge University Press, 1961.

Hodges, C. Walter. *The Globe Restored.* 1953. New York: Norton, 1968, 1973.

Ingram, William. *The Business of Playing: The Beginnings of Adult Professional Theater in Elizabethan London.* Ithaca, N.Y.: Cornell University Press, 1992.

Joseph, Bertram L. *Acting Shakespeare.* London: Routledge & Kegan Paul, 1960.

Kernodle, G. R. *From Art to Theatre: Form and Convention in the Renaissance.* 1944. Chicago: University of Chicago Press, 1965.

King, T. J. *Shakespearean Staging, 1599–1642.* Cambridge: Harvard University Press, 1971.

Knutson, Roslyn L. *The Repertory of Shakespeare's Company, 1594–1613.* Fayetteville: University of Arkansas Press, 1991.

Mullaney, Steven. *The Place of the Stage: License, Play and Power in Renaissance England.* Chicago: University of Chicago Press, 1987.

Orgel, Stephen. *Impersonations: The Performance of Gender in Shakespeare's England.* Cambridge: Cambridge UP, 1996.

Shapiro, Michael. *Children of the Revels: The Boy Companies of Shakespeare's Time and Their Plays.* New York: Columbia University Press, 1977.

Smith, Irwin. *Shakespeare's Blackfriars Playhouse.* New York: New York University Press, 1964.

———. *Shakespeare's Globe Playhouse.* New York: Scribner, 1956.

Wickham, Glynne. *Early English Stages: 1300 to 1660.* 4 vols. New York: Columbia University Press, 1959–81.

Shakespeare's Life

Alexander, Peter. *Shakespeare's Life and Art.* New ed. New York: New York University Press, 1961.

Baldwin, T. W. *William Shakspere's Small Latine and Lesse Greeke.* 2 vols. Urbana: University of Illinois Press, 1944.

Bentley, G. E. *Shakespeare: A Biographical Handbook.* New Haven: Yale University Press, 1961.

Bradbrook, Muriel. *Shakespeare: The Poet in His World.* London: Weidenfeld and Nicolson, 1978.

Burton, S. H. *Shakespeare's Life and Stage.* Edinburgh: W. & R. Chambers, 1989.

Chambers, E. K. *William Shakespeare: A Study of Facts and Problems.* 2 vols. Oxford: Clarendon Press, 1930.

Eccles, Mark. *Shakespeare in Warwickshire.* Madison: University of Wisconsin Press, 1961.

Fraser, Russell. *Shakespeare: The Later Years.* New York: Columbia University Press, 1992.

——. *Young Shakespeare*. New York: Columbia University Press, 1988.

Greer, Germaine. *Shakespeare*. New York: Oxford University Press, 1986.

Honigmann, E. A. J. *Shakespeare: The Lost Years*. Totowa, N.J.: Barnes & Noble, 1985.

——, ed. *Shakespeare and His Contemporaries: Essays in Comparison*. Manchester: Manchester University Press, 1986.

Hotson, Leslie. *Shakespeare Versus Shallow*. London: Nonesuch Press, 1931.

Levi, Peter. *The Life and Times of William Shakespeare*. New York: Holt, 1989.

Matus, Irvin Leigh. *Shakespeare: The Living Record*. New York: St. Martin's Press, 1991.

Reese, M. M. *Shakespeare: His World and His Work*. Rev. ed. New York: St. Martin's Press, 1980.

Rogers, Joyce. *The Second Best Bed: Shakespeare's Will in a New Light*. Westport, Conn.: Greenwood Press, 1993.

Sams, Eric. *The Real Shakespeare: Retrieving the Early Years, 1564–1594*. New Haven: Yale University Press, 1995.

Schmidgall, Gary. *Shakespeare and the Poet's Life*. Lexington: University Press of Kentucky, 1990.

Schoenbaum, Samuel. *Shakespeare's Lives*. New ed. New York: Oxford University Press, 1991.

——. *Shakespeare: His Life, His Language, His Theater*. New York: Signet, 1990.

——. *William Shakespeare: A Compact Documentary Life*. Rev. ed. Oxford: Oxford University Press, 1987.

Thomson, Peter. *Shakespeare's Professional Career*. Cambridge: Cambridge University Press, 1992.

Wells, Stanley. *Shakespeare: A Life in Drama*. New York: Norton, 1995.

Shakespearean Criticism

Founding Figures

Shakespeare: The Critical Heritage. Ed. Brian Vickers. Multiple volumes. London: Routledge & Kegan Paul, 1974–.

Coleridge, S. T. *Coleridge on Shakespeare: The Text of the Lectures of 1811–12*. Ed. R. A Foakes. Charlottesville: University of Virginia Press, 1971.

Coleridge, S. T. *Samuel Taylor Coleridge: Shakespearean Criticism*. 2 vols. 2nd ed. 1960. Ed. T. M. Raysor. Totowa, N.J.: Biblio Distribution Center, 1974, 1980.

Hazlitt, William. *Characters of Shakespear's Plays*. London, 1817.

Johnson, Samuel. *Johnson on Shakespeare*. Ed. Arthur Sherbo. Vol. 7 of The Yale Edition of the Works of Samuel Johnson. New Haven: Yale University Press, 1968.

Morgann, Maurice. *Shakespearean Criticism*. Ed. Daniel Fineman. Oxford: Clarendon Press, 1972.

Language and Style

Baxter, John. *Shakespeare's Poetic Styles*. London: Routledge & Kegan Paul, 1980.

Blake, N. F. *Shakespeare's Language: An Introduction*. New York: St. Martin's Press, 1983.

Cercignani, Fausto. *Shakespeare's Works and Elizabethan Pronunciation*. New York: Oxford University Press, 1981.

Clemen, Wolfgang. *The Development of Shakespeare's Imagery*. London: Methuen, 1951.

Danson, Lawrence. *Tragic Alphabet: Shakespeare's Drama of Language*. New Haven: Yale University Press, 1974.

Donawerth, Jane. *Shakespeare and the Sixteenth-Century Study of Language*. Urbana: University of Illinois Press, 1984.

Edwards, Philip, Inga-Stina Ewbank, and G. K. Hunter, eds. *Shakespeare's Styles*. Cambridge: Cambridge University Press, 1980.

Hussey, S. S. *The Literary Language of Shakespeare*. London: Longman, 1982.

Kökeritz, Helge. *Shakespeare's Pronunciation*. New Haven: Yale University Press, 1959.

Mahood, M. M. *Shakespeare's Wordplay*. London: Methuen, 1957.

Miriam Joseph, Sister. *Shakespeare's Use of the Arts of Language*. New York: Columbia University Press, 1947.

Parker, Patricia. *Shakespeare from the Margins: Language, Culture, Context*. Chicago: University of Chicago Press, 1996.

Partridge, Eric. *Shakespeare's Bawdy: A Literary and Psychological Essay and a Comprehensive Glossary*. 3rd ed. New York: Routledge, 1991.

Spurgeon, Caroline. *Shakespeare's Imagery and What It Tells Us*. 1935. Cambridge: Cambridge University Press, 1968.

Vickers, Brian. *"Shakespeare's Use of Rhetoric." A New Companion to Shakespeare Studies*. Ed. Kenneth Muir and S. Schoenbaum. Cambridge: Cambridge University Press, 1971. 83–98.

——. *The Artistry of Shakespeare's Prose*. London: Methuen, 1968.

Wright, George T. *Shakespeare's Metrical Art*. Berkeley and Los Angeles: University of California Press, 1988.

Critical Approaches

Adelman, Janet. *Suffocating Mothers: Fantasies of Maternal Origin in Shakespeare's Plays*. New York: Routledge, 1992.

Andrews, John F. *William Shakespeare: His World, His Work, His Influence*. 3 vols. New York: Scribner, 1985.

Bamber, Linda. *Comic Women, Tragic Men: A Study of Gender and Genre in Shakespeare*. Stanford: Stanford University Press, 1982.

Barber, C. L. *Shakespeare's Festive Comedy: A Study of Dramatic Form and Its Relation to Social Custom*. Princeton: Princeton University Press, 1959.

——, and Richard P. Wheeler. *The Whole Journey: Shakespeare's Power of Development*. Berkeley and Los Angeles: University of California Press, 1986.

Barker, Deborah E., and Ivo Kamps, eds. *Shakespeare and Gender: A History*. New York: Verso, 1995.

Barton, Anne. *Essays, Mainly Shakespearean*. Cambridge: Cambridge University Press, 1994.

Battenhouse, Roy, ed. *Shakespeare's Christian Dimension: An Anthology of Commentary*. Bloomington: Indiana University Press, 1994.

Berry, Ralph. *Shakespeare and Social Class*. Atlantic Highlands, N.J.: Humanities Press International, 1988.

——. *Shakespeare and the Awareness of the Audience*. New York: St. Martin's Press, 1985.

Boose, Lynda E. *"The Father and the Bride in Shakespeare." PMLA* 97 (1982): 325–47.

Booth, Stephen. *"King Lear," "Macbeth," Indefinition and Tragedy*. New Haven: Yale University Press, 1983.

Bradley, A. C. *Shakespearean Tragedy*. 1904. 3rd ed. New York: St. Martin's Press, 1992.

Bradshaw, Graham. *Misrepresentations: Shakespeare and the Materialists*. Ithaca, N.Y.: Cornell University Press, 1993.

——. *Shakespeare's Skepticism*. New York: St. Martin's Press, 1987.

Brissenden, Alan. *Shakespeare and the Dance*. Atlantic Highlands, N.J.: Humanities Press International, 1981.

Bristol, Michael. *Shakespeare's America, America's Shakespeare*. London: Routledge, 1990.

Burkhardt, Sigurd. *Shakespearean Meanings*. Princeton: Princeton University Press, 1968.

Calderwood, James. *Shakespeare and the Denial of Death*. Amherst: University of Massachusetts Press, 1987.

——. *Shakespearean Metadrama*. Minneapolis: University of Minnesota Press, 1971.

Callaghan, Dympna. *Woman and Gender in Renaissance Tragedy: A Study of "King Lear," "Othello," "The Duchess of Malfi," and "The White Devil."* Atlantic Highlands, N.J.: Humanities Press International, 1989.

Carroll, William C. *The Metamorphoses of Shakespearean Comedy*. Princeton: Princeton University Press, 1985.

Cavell, Stanley. *Disowning Knowledge in Six Plays of Shakespeare*. Cambridge: Cambridge University Press, 1987.

Charnes, Linda. *Notorious Identity: Materializing the Subject in Shakespeare*. Cambridge: Harvard University Press, 1993.

Clemen, Wolfgang H. *Shakespeare's Soliloquies*. Trans. Charity Scott Stokes. London: Methuen, 1987.

Cohen, Derek. *Shakespeare's Culture of Violence*. New York: St. Martin's Press, 1993.

Colie, Rosalie L. *Shakespeare's Living Art*. Princeton: Princeton University Press, 1974.

Colman, E. A. M. *The Dramatic Use of Bawdy in Shakespeare*. London: Longman, 1974.

Cox, John D. *Shakespeare and the Dramaturgy of Power*. Princeton: Princeton University Press, 1989.

Cunningham, J. V. *Woe or Wonder: The Emotional Effect of Shakespearean Tragedy*. Denver: University of Denver Press, 1951.

Dash, Irene. *Wooing, Wedding, and Power: Women in Shakespeare's Plays*. New York: Columbia University Press, 1981.

Dawson, Anthony. *Indirections: Shakespeare and the Art of Illusion*. Toronto: University of Toronto Press, 1978.

De Grazia, Margreta. "Homonyms before and after Lexical Standardization." *Deutsche Shakespeare Gesellschaft West (Jahrbuch)*. Bochum, Germany, 1990. 143–56.

Dollimore, Jonathan, and Alan Sinfield, eds. *Political Shakespeare: Essays in Cultural Materialism*. 2nd ed. Manchester: Manchester University Press, 1994.

——. *Radical Tragedy: Religion, Ideology, and Power in the Drama of Shakespeare and His Contemporaries*. Durham, N.C.: Duke University Press, 1993.

Drakakis, John, ed. *Alternative Shakespeares*. London: Methuen, 1985.

Dubrow, Heather, and Richard Strier. *The Historical Renaissance*. Chicago: University of Chicago Press, 1988.

Dusinberre, Juliet. *Shakespeare and the Nature of Women*. 2nd ed. Houndsmill, Basingstoke: Macmillan, 1996.

Eagleton, Terry. *William Shakespeare*. Oxford: Blackwell, 1987.

Edwards, Philip. *Shakespeare: A Writer's Progress*. Oxford: Oxford University Press, 1986.

Eliot, T. S. "Shakespeare and the Stoicism of Seneca." *Selected Essays, 1917–1932*. 1932. New York: Harcourt Brace Jovanovich, 1950.

Engle, Lars. *Shakespearean Pragmatism: Market of His Time*. Chicago: University of Chicago Press, 1993.

Erickson, Peter. *Patriarchal Structures in Shakespeare's Drama*. Berkeley and Los Angeles: University of California Press, 1985.

——, and Coppèlia Kahn, eds. *Shakespeare's Rough Magic: Essays in Honor of C. L. Barber*. Newark: University of Delaware Press, 1985.

Evans, Malcolm. *Signifying Nothing: Truth's True Contents in Shakespeare's Text*. Athens: University of Georgia Press, 1986.

Farrell, Kirby. *Play, Death, and Heroism in Shakespeare*. Chapel Hill: University of North Carolina Press, 1989.

Felperin, Howard. *Shakespearean Romance*. Princeton: Princeton University Press, 1972.

Fiedler, Leslie. *The Stranger in Shakespeare*. New York: Stein & Day, 1972.

French, Marilyn. *Shakespeare's Division of Experience*. London: Cape, 1981.

Frye, Northrop. *Fools of Time: Studies in Shakespearean Tragedy*. Toronto: University of Toronto Press, 1967.

——. *A Natural Perspective: The Development of Shakespearean Comedy and Romance*. New York: Columbia University Press, 1965.

Garber, Marjorie. *Coming of Age in Shakespeare*. London: Methuen, 1981.
———. *Shakespeare's Ghost Writers: Literature as Uncanny Causality*. New York: Methuen, 1987.
Girard, Rene. *A Theater of Envy: William Shakespeare*. New York: Oxford University Press, 1991.
Goldberg, Jonathan. *Sodometries: Renaissance Texts, Modern Sexualities*. Stanford: Stanford University Press, 1992.
Goldman, Michael. *Shakespeare and the Energies of Drama*. Princeton: Princeton University Press, 1972.
Grady, Hugh. *The Modernist Shakespeare: Critical Texts in a Material World*. Oxford: Clarendon Press, 1991.
Greenblatt, Stephen. *Shakespearean Negotiations: The Circulation of Social Energy in Renaissance England*. Berkeley and Los Angeles: University of California Press, 1988.
Hapgood, Robert. *Shakespeare: The Theatre-Poet*. Oxford: Oxford University Press, 1988.
Hawkes, Terence. *Meaning by Shakespeare*. London: Routledge, 1992.
———. *That Shakespeherian Rag*. London: Methuen, 1986.
Hibbard, G. R. *The Making of Shakespeare's Dramatic Poetry*. Toronto: University of Toronto Press, 1981.
Holderness, Graham, ed. *Shakespeare's History Plays: "Richard II" to "Henry V."* New York: St. Martin's Press, 1992.
———, ed. *The Shakespeare Myth*. Manchester: Manchester University Press, 1988.
Holland, Norman. *Psychoanalysis and Shakespeare*. New York: McGraw-Hill, 1966.
———, et al., eds. *Shakespeare's Personality*. Berkeley and Los Angeles: University of California Press, 1989.
Honigmann, E. A. J. *Myriad-Minded Shakespeare: Essays, Chiefly on the Tragedies and Problem Plays*. New York: St. Martin's Press, 1989.
———, ed. *Shakespeare's Impact on His Contemporaries*. London: Macmillan, 1982.
Hope, Jonathan. *The Authorship of Shakespeare's Plays*. Cambridge: Cambridge University Press, 1994.
Houston, John Porter. *Shakespearean Sentences: A Study in Style and Syntax*. Baton Rouge: Louisiana State University Press, 1988.
Howard, Jean. *The Stage and Social Struggle in Early Modern England*. New York: Routledge, 1994.
———, and Marion F. O'Connor, eds. *Shakespeare Reproduced: The Text in History and Ideology*. New York: Methuen, 1987.
Hughes, Ted. *Shakespeare and the Goddess of Complete Being*. London: Faber, 1992.
Hunt, Maurice. *Shakespeare's Labored Art: Stir, Work, and the Late Plays*. New York: Peter Lang, 1995.
Jones, Emrys. *The Origins of Shakespeare*. Oxford: Clarendon Press, 1977.
Kahn, Coppèlia. *Man's Estate: Masculine Identity in Shakespeare*. Berkeley and Los Angeles: University of California Press, 1981.
Kamps, Ivo, ed. *Materialist Shakespeare: A History*. New York: Verso, 1995.
Kastan, David Scott. *Shakespeare and the Shapes of Time*. Hanover: University Press of New England, 1982.
Kermode, Frank, ed. *Four Centuries of Shakespearean Criticism*. 1965. New York: Avon, 1974.
Kernan, Alvin. *Shakespeare, the King's Playwright: Theater in the Stuart Court, 1603–1613*. New Haven: Yale University Press, 1995.
Kirsch, Arthur. *Shakespeare and the Experience of Love*. Cambridge: Cambridge University Press, 1981.
Knapp, Jeffrey. *An Empire Nowhere: England, America, and Literature from "Utopia" to "The Tempest."* Berkeley and Los Angeles: University of California Press, 1992.
Knapp, Robert S. *Shakespeare—The Theater and the Book*. Princeton: Princeton University Press, 1989.

Knight, G. Wilson. *The Wheel of Fire*. 1930. 5th rev. ed. Cleveland: World Publishing, 1962.

Kott, Jan. *Shakespeare Our Contemporary*. Trans. Boleslaw Taborski. Garden City, N.Y.: Doubleday Anchor, 1966.

Laroque, François. *Shakespeare's Festive World: Elizabethan Seasonal Entertainment and the Professional Stage*. Cambridge: Cambridge University Press, 1993.

Lenz, Carolyn Ruth Swift, Gayle Greene, and Carol Thomas Neely, eds. *The Woman's Part: Feminist Criticism of Shakespeare*. Urbana: University of Illinois Press, 1980.

Levin, Harry. *Shakespeare and the Revolution of the Times*. New York: Oxford University Press, 1976.

Levith, Murray J. *Shakespeare's Italian Settings and Plays*. New York: St. Martin's Press, 1989.

Loomba, Ania. *Gender, Race, Renaissance Drama*. Manchester: Manchester University Press, 1989.

Lukacher, Ned. *Daemonic Figures: Shakespeare and the Question of Conscience*. Ithaca, N.Y.: Cornell University Press, 1994.

Mack, Maynard. *Everybody's Shakespeare: Reflections Chiefly on the Tragedies*. Lincoln: University of Nebraska Press, 1993.

Mahon, John W., and Thomas A. Pendleton, eds. *"Fanned and Winnowed Opinion": Shakespearean Essays Presented to Harold Jenkins*. London: Methuen, 1987.

Mallin, Eric S. *Inscribing the Time: Shakespeare and the End of Elizabethan England*. Berkeley and Los Angeles: University of California Press, 1995.

Marcus, Leah S. *Puzzling Shakespeare: Local Reading and Its Discontents*. Berkeley and Los Angeles: University of California Press, 1988.

Maus, Katharine. *Inwardness and Theater in the English Renaissance*. Chicago: University of Chicago Press, 1995.

McDonald, Russ. *The Bedford Companion to Shakespeare: An Introduction with Documents*. Boston: Bedford Books, 1996.

McMullan, Gordon, and Jonathan Hope, eds. *The Politics of Tragicomedy: Shakespeare and After*. London: Routledge, 1992.

Miola, Robert. *Shakespeare's Rome*. Cambridge: Cambridge University Press, 1983.

Mooney, Michael E. *Shakespeare's Dramatic Transactions*. Durham, N.C.: Duke University Press, 1990.

Mowat, Barbara. *The Dramaturgy of Shakespeare's Romances*. Athens: University of Georgia Press, 1976.

Muir, Kenneth. *The Sources of Shakespeare's Plays*. London: Methuen, 1977.

Neely, Carol Thomas. *Broken Nuptials in Shakespeare's Plays*. New Haven: Yale University Press, 1985.

Nevo, Ruth. *Tragic Form in Shakespeare*. Princeton: Princeton University Press, 1972.

Newman, Karen. *Fashioning Femininity and English Renaissance Drama*. Chicago: University of Chicago Press, 1991.

Novy, Marianne. *Love's Argument: Gender Relations in Shakespeare*. Chapel Hill: University of North Carolina Press, 1984.

——, ed. *Women's Re-Visions of Shakespeare*. Urbana: University of Illinois Press, 1990.

O'Brien, Peggy, ed. *Shakespeare Set Free*. 3 vols. New York: Washington Square, 1993–95.

Orkin, Martin. *Shakespeare against Apartheid*. Craighall, South Africa: Ad. Donker, 1987.

Parker, Patricia, and Geoffrey Hartman, eds. *Shakespeare and the Question of Theory*. London: Routledge & Kegan Paul, 1985.

Paster, Gail Kern. *The Body Embarrassed: Drama and the Disciplines of Shame in Early Modern England*. Ithaca, N.Y.: Cornell University Press, 1993.

Patterson, Annabel. *Shakespeare and the Popular Voice*. Oxford: Blackwell, 1989.

Pechter, Edward. *What Was Shakespeare?: Renaissance Plays and Changing Critical Practice*. Ithaca, N.Y.: Cornell University Press, 1995.

Pitt, Angela. *Shakespeare's Women*. Totowa, N.J.: Barnes & Noble, 1981.

Rabkin, Norman. *Shakespeare and the Problem of Meaning*. Chicago: University of Chicago Press, 1981.

———. *Shakespeare and the Common Understanding*. New York: Free Press, 1967.

Rackin, Phyllis. *Stages of History: Shakespeare's English Chronicles*. Ithaca, N.Y.: Cornell University Press, 1990.

Ranald, Margaret Loftis. *Shakespeare and His Social Context: Essays in Osmotic Knowledge and Literary Interpretation*. New York: AMS Press, 1987.

Ryan, Kiernan. *Shakespeare*. 2nd ed. London: Prentice Hall, 1995.

Salingar, Leo. *Dramatic Form in Shakespeare and the Jacobeans*. Cambridge: Cambridge University Press, 1986.

———. *Shakespeare and the Traditions of Comedy*. London: Cambridge University Press, 1974.

Schwartz, Murray, and Coppélia Kahn, eds. *Representing Shakespeare: New Psychoanalytic Essays*. Baltimore: Johns Hopkins University Press, 1980.

Shapiro, Michael. *Gender in Play on the Shakespearean Stage: Boy Heroines and Female Pages*. Ann Arbor: University of Michigan Press, 1994.

Shepard, Simon. *Amazons and Warrior Women: Varieties of Feminism in Seventeenth-Century Drama*. N.Y.: St. Martin's Press, 1981.

Siemon, James. *Shakespearean Iconoclasm*. Berkeley and Los Angeles: University of California Press, 1985.

Skura, Meredith Anne. *Shakespeare the Actor and the Purposes of Playing*. Chicago: University of Chicago Press, 1993.

———. *The Literary Use of the Psychoanalytic Process*. New Haven: Yale University Press, 1981.

Snyder, Susan. *The Comic Matrix of Shakespeare's Tragedies*. Princeton: Princeton University Press, 1979.

Sprengnether, Madelon, and Shirley Nelson Garner, eds. *Shakespearean Tragedy and Gender*. Bloomington: Indiana University Press, 1996.

Stockholder, Kay. *Dream Works: Lovers and Families in Shakespeare's Plays*. Toronto: University of Toronto Press, 1987.

Summers, Joseph H. *Dreams of Love and Power: On Shakespeare's Plays*. Oxford: Clarendon Press, 1984.

Tennenhouse, Leonard. *Power on Display: The Politics of Shakespeare's Genres*. New York: Methuen, 1986.

Thomas, Vivian. *The Moral Universe of Shakespeare's Problem Plays*. New York: Routledge, 1991.

Traub, Valerie. *Desire and Anxiety: Circulations of Sexuality in Shakespearean Drama*. London: Routledge, 1992.

Trousdale, Marion. *Shakespeare and the Rhetoricians*. Chapel Hill: University of North Carolina Press, 1982.

Watson, Robert. *The Rest Is Silence: Death as Annihilation in the English Renaissance*. Berkeley and Los Angeles: University of California Press, 1994.

———. *Shakespeare and the Hazards of Ambition*. Cambridge: Harvard University Press, 1984.

Wells, Robin Headlam. *Shakespeare: Politics and the State*. London: Macmillan, 1986.

Wheeler, Richard P. *Shakespeare's Problem Comedies: Turn and Counter Turn*. Berkeley and Los Angeles: University of California Press, 1981.

Wilson, Richard. *Will Power: Essays on Shakespearean Authority*. Detroit: Wayne State University Press, 1993.

Woodbridge, Linda, and Edward Berry, eds. *True Rites and Maimed Rites: Ritual and Anti-Ritual in Shakespeare and His Age*. Urbana: University of Illinois Press, 1992.

Young, David. *The Action to the Word: Structure and Style in Shakespearean Tragedy*. New Haven: Yale University Press, 1990.

Zimmerman, Susan, ed. *Erotic Politics: Desire on the Renaissance Stage*. New York: Routledge, 1992.

The Dream of the Master Text

Allen, Michael J. B., and Kenneth Muir, eds. *Shakespeare's Plays in Quarto*. Berkeley and Los Angeles: University of California Press, 1981.

Blayney, Peter W. M. *The First Folio of Shakespeare*. Washington: Folger Library Publications, 1991.

———. *The Texts of "King Lear" and Their Origins*. Vol. 1: *Nicholas Okes and the First Quarto*. Cambridge: Cambridge University Press, 1982.

Bower, Fredson. *On Editing Shakespeare*. Charlottesville: University of Virginia Press, 1966.

Crewe, Jonathan. *Trials of Authorship: Anterior Forms and Poetic Reconstruction from Wyatt to Shakespeare*. Berkeley and Los Angeles: University of California Press, 1990.

De Grazia, Margreta. *Shakespeare Verbatim: The Reproduction of Authenticity and the 1790 Apparatus*. Oxford: Oxford University Press, 1991.

———, and Peter Stallybrass. "The Materiality of the Shakespearean Text." *Shakespeare Quarterly* 44 (1993): 255–83.

Franklin, Colin. *Shakespeare Domesticated: The Eighteenth-Century Editions*. Brookfield, Vt.: Scolar Press, 1991.

Greg, W. W., ed. *The Merry Wives of Windsor, 1602*. Oxford: Clarendon Press, 1910.

Hinman, Charlton. *The Norton Facsimile: The First Folio of Shakespeare*. 2nd ed. New York: Norton, 1996.

———. *The Printing and Proof-Reading of the First Folio of Shakespeare*. 2 vols. Oxford: Clarendon Press, 1963.

Honigmann, E. A. J. *The Stability of Shakespeare's Text*. London: E. Arnold, 1965.

Ioppolo, Grace. *Revising Shakespeare*. Cambridge: Harvard University Press, 1991.

Irace, Kathleen O. *Reforming the "Bad" Quartos: Performance and Provenance of Six Shakespearean First Editions*. Newark: University of Delaware Press, 1994.

Maguire, Laurie E. *Shakespeare's Suspect Texts: The "Bad" Quartos and Their Contexts*. Cambridge: Cambridge University Press, 1996.

McKerrow, R. B. *Prolegomena for the Oxford Shakespeare*. Oxford: Clarendon Press, 1939.

Mcleod, Randall, ed. *Crisis in Editing: Texts of the English Renaissance*. New York: AMS Press, 1994.

Pollard, A. W. *Shakespeare's Fight with the Pirates*. Cambridge: Cambridge University Press, 1920.

———. *Shakespeare's Folios and Quartos*. London: Methuen, 1909.

Seary, Peter. *Lewis Theobald and the Editing of Shakespeare*. Oxford: Clarendon Press, 1990.

Taylor, Gary, and Michael Warren, eds. *The Division of the Kingdoms*. Oxford: Clarendon Press, 1983.

Urkowitz, Steven. *Shakespeare's Revision of "King Lear."* Princeton: Princeton University Press, 1980.

Walker, Alice. *Textual Problems of the First Folio*. Cambridge: Cambridge University Press, 1953.

Wells, Stanley. *Re-Editing Shakespeare for the Modern Reader*. New York: Oxford University Press, 1984.

———, and Gary Taylor. *William Shakespeare: A Textual Companion*. Oxford: Clarendon Press, 1987.

———, and Gary Taylor. *Modernizing Shakespeare's Spelling*. Oxford: Clarendon Press, 1979.

Werstine, Paul. "*Narratives About Printed Shakespeare Texts: 'Foul Papers' and 'Bad' Quartos.*" *Shakespeare Quarterly* 41 (1990): 65–86.

Williams, George Walton. *The Craft of Printing and the Publication of Shakespeare's Works*. Washington: Folger Books, 1985.

Wilson, J. Dover. *The Manuscript of Shakespeare's "Hamlet" and the Problems of Its Transmission.* 2 vols. Cambridge, Eng. 1934.

Shakespeare in Performance

Ball, Robert Hamilton. *Shakespeare on Silent Film.* New York: Theater Art Books, 1968.

Bartholomeusz, Dennis. *Macbeth and the Players.* Cambridge: Cambridge University Press, 1969.

Barton, John. *Playing Shakespeare.* London: Methuen, 1984.

Bate, Jonathan, and Russell Jackson, eds. *Shakespeare: An Illustrated Stage History.* New York: Oxford University Press, 1996.

Berger, Harry Jr. *Imaginary Audition: Shakespeare on Stage and Page.* Berkeley and Los Angeles: University of California Press, 1989.

Berry, Francis. *The Shakespeare Inset: Word and Picture.* London: Routledge & Kegan Paul, 1965.

Berry, Ralph. *Changing Styles in Shakespeare.* Boston: Allen & Unwin, 1981.

Bevington, David. *Action Is Eloquence: Shakespeare's Language of Gesture.* Cambridge: Harvard University Press, 1984.

Branam, George C. *Eighteenth-Century Adaptions of Shakespearean Tragedy.* Berkeley and Los Angeles: University of California Press, 1936, 1956, 1973.

Brennan, Anthony. *Onstage and Offstage Worlds in Shakespeare's Plays.* New York: Routledge, 1989.

———. *Shakespeare's Dramatic Structures.* Boston: Routledge & Kegan Paul, 1986.

Brockbank, Philip, ed. *Players of Shakespeare.* Cambridge: Cambridge University Press, 1985.

Brown, Ivor. *Shakespeare and the Actors.* London: Bodley Head, 1970.

Brown, John Russell. *Shakespeare's Dramatic Style.* London: Heineman, 1970.

———. *Shakespeare's Plays in Performance.* New York: St. Martin's Press, 1967.

Bulman, James C., and H. R. Coursen, eds. *Shakespeare on Television.* Hanover, N.H.: University Press of New England, 1988.

———, J. R. Mulryne, and Margaret Shewring. *Shakespeare in Performance Series.* Manchester: Manchester University Press, 1982.

Carlisle, Carol Jones. *Shakespeare from the Greenroom: Actors' Criticisms of Four Major Tragedies.* Chapel Hill, N.C.: University of North Carolina Press, 1969.

Cohn, Ruby. *Modern Shakespeare Offshoots.* Princeton: Princeton University Press, 1976.

Cook, Judith. *Shakespeare's Players.* London: Harrap, 1983.

Dawson, Anthony B. *Indirections—Shakespeare and the Art of Illusion.* Toronto: University of Toronto Press, 1978.

Dean, Winton. "Shakespeare in the Opera House." *Shakespeare Survey* 18 (1965): 75–93.

Donohue, Joseph W., Jr. *Dramatic Character in the English Romantic Age.* Princeton: Princeton University Press, 1970.

Downer, Alan S. *The Eminent Tragedian, William Charles Macready.* Cambridge: Harvard University Press, 1966.

Eckert, Charles W., ed. *Focus on Shakespearean Films.* Englewood Cliffs, N.J.: Prentice-Hall, 1972.

Goldman, Michael. *Acting and Action in Shakespearean Tragedy.* Princeton: Princeton University Press, 1985.

Hartwig, Joan. *Shakespeare's Analogical Scene: Parody as Structural Syntax.* Lincoln: University of Nebraska Press, 1983.

Hirsch, James F. *The Structures of Shakespearean Scenes.* New Haven: Yale University Press, 1981.

Hogan, Charles B., ed. *Shakespeare in the Theatre, 1701–1800.* 2 vols. Oxford: Clarendon Press, 1952–57.

Homan, Sidney, ed. *When the Theater Turns to Itself: The Aesthetic Metaphor in Shake-speare*. Lewiston, Pa.: Bucknell University Press, 1981.

——, ed. *Shakespeare's "More Than Words Can Witness": Essays on Visual and Nonverbal Enactment in the Plays*. Lewisburg, Pa.: Bucknell University Press, 1980.

Howard, Jean E. *Shakespeare's Art of Orchestration: Stage Technique and Audience Response*. Urbana: University of Illinois Press, 1984.

Jones, Emrys. *Scenic Form in Shakespeare*. Oxford: Clarendon Press, 1971.

Jorgens, Jack L. *Shakespeare on Film*. Bloomington: Indiana University Press, 1976.

Manvell, Roger. *Shakespeare and the Film*. London: Dent, 1971.

McGuire, Philip C. *Speechless Dialect: Shakespeare's Open Silences*. Berkeley and Los Angeles: University of California Press, 1983.

——, and David A. Samuelson. *Shakespeare: The Theatrical Dimension*. New York: AMS Press, 1979.

Odell, George C. D. *Shakespeare from Betterton to Irving*. 2 vols. New York: Scribner, 1920, 1966.

Poel, William. *Shakespeare in the Theatre*. 1913, 1968. New York: AMS Press, 1974.

Rosenberg, Marvin. *The Masks of Lear*. Berkeley and Los Angeles: University of California Press, 1972.

Rutter, Carol, et al. *Clamorous Voices: Shakespeare's Women Today*. London: Women's Press, 1988.

Shattuck, Charles H. *Shakespeare on the American Stage from the Hallams to Edwin Booth*. Washington, D.C.: Folger Shakespeare Library, 1976. . . . *from Booth and Barrett to Sothern and Marlowe*. Washington, D.C.: Folger Shakespeare Library, 1987.

——. *The Shakespeare Promptbooks: A Descriptive Catalogue*. Urbana: University of Illinois Press, 1965.

Slater, Ann Pasternak. *Shakespeare the Director*. Totowa, N.J.: Barnes & Noble, 1982.

Speaight, Robert. *Shakespeare on the Stage: An Illustrated History of Shakespearian Performance*. Boston: Little, Brown, 1973.

——. *William Poel and the Elizabethan Revival*. London: Heineman, 1954.

Spencer, Hazelton. *Shakespeare Improved: The Restoration Versions in Quarto and on the Stage*. Cambridge, Mass., 1927.

Sprague, Arthur Colby. *Shakespearian Players and Performances*. Cambridge: Harvard University Press, 1953.

——. *Shakespeare and the Actors*. Cambridge: Harvard University Press, 1944.

Styan, J. L. "Sight and Space: The Perception of Shakespeare on Stage and Screen." *Shakespeare, Pattern of Excelling Nature*. Ed. David Bevington and Jay L. Halio. Newark: University of Delaware Press, 1978.

——. *Shakespeare's Stagecraft*. Cambridge: Cambridge University Press, 1967.

Thaler, Alwin. *Shakespeare to Sheridan*. Cambridge, Mass.: Arno Press, 1922.

Thompson, Marvin and Ruth, eds. *Shakespeare and the Sense of Performance*. Newark: University of Delaware Press, 1989.

Trewin, J. C. *Shakespeare on the English Stage, 1900–1964*. London: Barrie & Rockliff, 1964.

Van den Berg, Kent. *Playhouse and Cosmos: Shakespearean Theater as Metaphor*. Newark: University of Delaware Press, 1985.

Wells, Stanley. *Royal Shakespeare: Four Major Productions at Stratford-upon-Avon*. Manchester: Manchester University Press, 1977.

Glossary

STAGE TERMS

"Above"   The gallery on the upper level of the *frons scenae*. In open-air theaters, such as the Globe, this space contained the lords' rooms. The central section of the gallery was sometimes used by the players for short scenes. Indoor theaters such as Blackfriars featured a curtained alcove for musicians above the stage.

"Aloft"   See *"Above."*

Amphitheater   An open-air theater, such as the Globe.

Arras   See *Curtain.*

Cellerage   See *Trap.*

Chorus   In the works of Shakespeare and other Elizabethan playwrights, a single individual (not, as in Greek tragedy, a group) who speaks before the play (and often before each act), describing events not shown on stage as well as commenting on the action witnessed by the audience.

Curtain   Curtains, or arras (hanging tapestries), covered a part of the *frons scenae*, thus concealing the discovery space, and may also have been draped around the edge of the stage to conceal the open area underneath.

Discovery space   A central opening or alcove concealed behind a curtain in the center of the *frons scenae*. The curtain could be drawn aside to "discover" tableaux such as Portia's caskets, the body of Polonius, or the statue of Hermione. Shakespeare appears to have used this stage device only sparingly.

Doubling   The common practice of having one actor play multiple roles, so that a play with a large cast of characters might be performed by a relatively small company.

Dumb shows   Mimed scenes performed before a play (or before each act), summarizing or foreshadowing the plot. Dumb shows were popular in early Elizabethan drama, but although they already seemed old-fashioned in Shakespeare's time, they were employed by writers up to the 1640s.

Epilogue   A brief speech or poem addressed to the audience by an actor after the play. In some cases, as in 2 *Henry IV*, the epilogue could be combined with, or could merge into, the jig.

Forestage   The front of the stage, closest to the audience.

Frons scenae   The wall at the back of the stage, behind which lay the players' tiring-house. The *frons scenae* of the Globe featured two doors flanking the central discovery space, with a gallery "above."

Gallery   Covered seating areas surrounding the open yard of the public amphitheaters. There were three levels of galleries at the Globe; admission to these seats cost an extra penny (in addition to the basic admission fee of one penny to the yard), and seating in the higher galleries another penny yet. In indoor theaters such as Blackfriars, where there was no standing room, gallery seating was less expensive than seating in the pit; indeed, seats nearest the stage were the most expensive.

Gatherers Persons employed by the playing company to take money at the entrances to the theater.

Groundlings Audience members who paid the minimum price of admission (one penny) to stand in the yard of the open-air theaters; also referred to as "understanders."

Heavens Canopied roof over the stage in the open-air theaters, protecting the players and their costumes from rain. The "heavens" would be brightly decorated with sun, moon, and stars, and perhaps the signs of the zodiac.

Hut A structure on the top of the cover over the stage, where stagehands produced the effects of thunder and lightning and operated the machinery by which gods, such as Jupiter in *Cymbeline*, descended through the trapdoor in the "heavens."

Jig A song-and-dance performance by the clown and other members of the company at the conclusion of a play. These performances were frequently bawdy and were officially banned in 1612.

Lords' rooms Partitioned sections of the gallery "above," where the most prestigious and expensive seats in the public playhouses were located. These rooms were designed not to provide the best view of the action on the stage below, but to make their privileged occupants conspicuous to the rest of the audience.

Open-air theaters Unroofed public playhouses in the suburbs of London, such as the Theatre, the Rose, and the Globe.

Part The character played by an actor. In Shakespeare's theater, actors were given a roll of paper called a "part" containing all of the speeches and all of the cues belonging to their character. The term "role," synonymous with "part," is derived from such rolls of paper.

Patrons Important nobles and members of the royal family under whose protection the theatrical companies of London operated; players not in the service of patrons were punishable as vagabonds. The companies were referred to as their patrons' "Men" or "Servants." Thus the name of the company to which Shakespeare belonged for most of his career was first the Lord Chamberlain's Men, then was changed to the King's Men in 1603, when James I became their patron.

Pillars The "heavens" were supported by two tall painted pillars or posts near the front of the stage. These occasionally played a role in stage action, allowing a character to "hide" while remaining in full view of the audience.

Pit The area in front of the stage in indoor theaters such as Blackfriars, where the most expensive and prestigious bench seating was to be had.

Posts See *Pillars*.

Proscenium The space of the transparent "fourth wall," which divides the actors from the orchestra and audience in the standard modern theater. The stages on which Shakespeare's plays were first performed had no proscenium.

Rearstage The back of the stage, farthest from the audience.

Repertory The stock of plays a company had ready for performance at a given time. Companies generally performed a different play each day, often more than a dozen plays in a month and more than thirty in the course of the season.

Role See *Part*.

Sharers Senior actors holding shares in a joint-stock theatrical company; they paid for costumes, hired hands, and new plays, and they shared profits and losses equally. Shakespeare was not only a longtime "sharer" of the Lord Chamberlain's Men but, from 1599, a "housekeeper," the holder of a one-eighth share in the Globe playhouse.

Tiring-house The players' dressing (attiring) room, a structure located at the back of the stage and connected to the stage by two or more doors in the *frons scenae*.

Trap A trapdoor near the front of the stage that allowed access to the "cellarage" beneath and was frequently associated with hell's mouth. Another trapdoor in the "heavens" opened for the descent of gods to the stage below.

"Within" The tiring-house, from which offstage sound effects such as shouts, drums, and trumpets were produced.

Yard The central space in open-air theaters such as the Globe, into which the stage projected and in which audience members stood. Admission to the yard in the public theaters cost a penny, the cheapest admission available.

TEXTUAL TERMS

Aside See *Stage direction.*

Autograph Text written in the author's own hand. With the possible exception of a few pages of the collaborative play *Sir Thomas More*, no dramatic works or poems written in Shakespeare's hand are known to survive.

Canonical Of an author, the writings generally accepted as authentic. In the case of Shakespeare's dramatic works, only two plays that are not among the thirty-six plays contained in the First Folio, *Pericles* and *The Two Noble Kinsmen*, have won widespread acceptance into the Shakespearean canon. (This sense of "canonical" should not be confused with the use of "the canon" to denote the entire body of literary works, including but not limited to Shakespeare's, that have traditionally been regarded as fit objects of admiration and study.)

Catchword A word printed below the text at the bottom of a page, matching the first word on the following page. The catchword enabled the printer to keep the pages in their proper sequence. Where the catchword fails to match the word at the top of the next page, there is reason to suspect that something has been lost or misplaced.

Compositor Person employed in a print shop to set type. To speed the printing process, most of Shakespeare's plays were set by more than one compositor. Compositors frequently followed their own standards in spelling and punctuation. They inevitably introduced some errors into the text, often by selecting the wrong piece from the type case or by setting the correct letter upside-down.

Conflation A version of a play created by combining readings from more than one substantive edition. Since the early eighteenth century, for example, most versions of *King Lear* and of several other plays by Shakespeare have been conflations of quarto and First Folio texts.

Control text The text upon which a modern edition is based.

Dramatis personae A list of the characters appearing in the play. In the First Folio such lists were printed at the end of some but not all of the plays. The editor

Nicholas Rowe (1709) first provided lists of dramatis personae for all of Shakespeare's dramatic works.

Exeunt / Exit   See *Stage direction.*

Fair copy   A transcript of the "foul papers" made either by a scribe or by the playwright.

Folio   A book-making format in which each large sheet of paper is folded once, making two leaves (four pages front and back). This format produced large volumes, generally handsome and expensive. The First Folio of Shakespeare's plays was printed in 1623.

Foul papers   An author's first completed draft of a play, typically full of blotted-out passages and revisions. None of Shakespeare's foul papers is known to survive.

Licensing   By an order of 1581, new plays could not be performed until they had received a license from the Master of the Revels. A separate license, granted by the Court of High Commission, was required for publication, though in practice plays were often printed without license. From 1610, the Master of the Revels had the authority to license plays for publication as well as for performance.

Manent / Manet   See *Stage direction.*

Memorial reconstruction   The conjectured practice of reconstructing the text of a play from memory. Companies touring in the provinces without access to promptbooks may have resorted to memorial reconstruction. This practice also provides a plausible explanation for the existence of the so-called bad quartos.

Octavo   A book-making format in which each large sheet of paper is folded three times, making eight leaves (sixteen pages front and back). Only one of Shakespeare's plays, *Richard Duke of York* (*3 Henry VI*, 1595), was published in octavo format.

Playbook   See *Promptbook.*

Press variants   Minor textual variations among books of the same edition, resulting from corrections made in the course of printing or from damaged or slipped type.

Promptbook   A manuscript of a play (either foul papers or fair copy) annotated and adapted for performance by the theatrical company. The promptbook incorporated stage directions, notes on properties and special effects, and revisions, sometimes including those required by the Master of the Revels. Promptbooks are usually identifiable by the replacement of characters' names with actors' names.

Quarto   A book-making format in which each large sheet of paper is folded twice, making four leaves (eight pages front and back). Quarto volumes were smaller and less expensive than books printed in the folio format.

Scribal copy   A transcript of a play produced by a professional scribe (or "scrivener"). Scribes tended to employ their own preferred spellings and abbreviations and could be responsible for introducing a variety of errors.

Speech prefix (s.p.)   The indication of the identity of the speaker of the following line or lines. Early editions of Shakespeare's plays often use different prefixes at different points to designate the same person. On occasion, the name of the actor who was to play the role appears in place of the name of the character.

Stage direction (s.d.)   The part of the text that is not spoken by any character but that indicates actions to be performed onstage. Stage directions in the earliest editions of Shakespeare's plays are sparse and are sometimes grouped together at the beginning of a scene rather than next to the spoken lines they should precede, accompany, or follow. By convention, the most basic stage directions were written in Latin. "Exit" indicates the departure of a single actor from the stage, "exeunt" the departure of more than one. "Manet" indicates that a single actor remains onstage, "manent" that more than one remains. Lines accompanied by the stage direction "aside" are spoken so as not to be heard by the others on stage. This stage direction appeared in some early editions of Shakespeare plays, but other means were also used to indicate such speech (such as placing the words within parentheses), and sometimes no indication was provided.

Stationers' Register   The account books of the Company of Stationers (of which all printers were legally required to be members), recording the fees paid for permission to print new works as well as the fines exacted for printing without permission. The Stationers' Register thus provides a valuable if incomplete record of publication in England.

Substantive text   The text of an edition based upon access to a manuscript, as opposed to a derivative text based only on an earlier edition.

Variorum editions   Comprehensive editions of a work or works in which the various views of previous editors and commentators are compiled.

ILLUSTRATION ACKNOWLEDGMENTS

General Introduction Plague death bill: By permission of the Folger Shakespeare Library • Webbe: By permission of the British Library • Amman: Spencer Collection, The New York Public Library, Astor, Lenox and Tilden Foundation • *Swetnam* title page: By permission of The Huntington Library, San Marino, California • Pope as Antichrist: By permission of the Folger Shakespeare Library • de Heere: The National Museum of Wales • Armada portrait: By kind permission of Marquess of Tavistock and Trustees of the Bedford Estate • Boaistuau: By permission of The Huntington Library, San Marino, California • Mandeville: By permission of the Houghton Library, Harvard University • Funeral procession: Additional Ms. 35324, folio 37v. By permission of the British Library • Gheeraerts: By permission of the Trustees of Dulwich Picture Gallery • van den Broek: Fitzwilliam Museum, University of Cambridge • Swimming: Bodleian Library, University of Oxford, 4°G.17.Art • Panorama of London: By permission of the British Library • Tarleton: Harley 3885, folio 19. By permission of the British Library • Hanging: Pepys Library, Magdalene College, Cambridge • Syphilis victim: By permission of The Huntington Library, San Marino, California • *Spanish Tragedy* title page: By permission of the Folger Shakespeare Library • Stratford-upon-Avon: By permission of City of York Libraries • Cholmondeley sisters: Tate Gallery, London • Alleyn: By permission of the Trustees of Dulwich Picture Library • *If You Know Not Me* title page: By permission of The Huntington Library, San Marino, California • van der Straet: By permission of the Folger Shakespeare Library

The First Part of the Contention (2 Henry VI) Child king: Additional Ms. 48976, Figure 50. By permission of the British Library • Kemp: By permission of the Folger Shakespeare Library • Halle: By permission of the Folger Shakespeare Library

Richard Duke of York (3 Henry VI) Halberd: Reproduced by permission of the Trustees of the Wallace Collection • Edward IV: The Royal Collection. © Her Majesty Queen Elizabeth II • Whitney: By permission of the Folger Shakespeare Library

1 Henry VI Henry VI: By courtesy of the National Portrait Gallery, London • Joan of Arc: Giraudon/Art Resource, NY • Whitney: By permission of the Folger Shakespeare Library

Richard III Richard III: By courtesy of the National Portrait Gallery, London • Sittow: By courtesy of the National Portrait Gallery, London • Vischer: By permission of the Folger Shakespeare Library

Richard II Rastell: C.15.e.6. By permission of the British Library • Holbein: Reproduced by courtesy of the Trustees, The National Gallery, London • Tempesta: © British Museum

King John Coronation: Eton College Ms. 123. Reproduced by permission of the Provost and Fellows of Eton College • Tomb: Reproduced by permission of The Huntington Library, San Marino, California

1 Henry IV Glyn Dwr seal: By permission of The National Museum of Wales • The Wits: By permission of the Folger Shakespeare Library • Peacham: By permission of the Folger Shakespeare Library

2 Henry IV 1600 Quarto page: By permission of the Folger Shakespeare Library • Cartari: By permission of the Folger Shakespeare Library • Rollos: Spencer Collection, The New York Public Library, Astor, Lenox and Tilden Foundations. Photo: Robert D. Rubic

Henry V Rastell: G6030. By permission of the Houghton Library, Harvard University • Renatus: By permission of the Houghton Library, Harvard University • Comenius: By permission of the Folger Shakespeare Library

Sir Thomas Moore From *The Booke of Sir Thomas Moore*: Harley 7368, folio 9. By permission of the British Library

All Is True (Henry VIII) Wotton/Bacon letter: Bodleian Library, University of Oxford, Vet. A 3.f.137 • Cavendish: Bodleian Library, University of Oxford, Douce 363 for. 71R • Matsuys: © British Museum

The Shakespearean Stage Braun and Hogenburg: 8.Tab.c.4. Bk.1.pl.1. By permission of the British Library • Hollar: Guildhall Library, Corporation of London • Interior of the "new" Globe: Courtesy of The International Shakespeare Globe Center Ltd. Photo: John Tramper • Exterior of the "new" Globe: Courtesy of The International Shakespeare Globe Center Ltd. Photo: Richard Kalina • *Frons scenae* of the "new" Globe: Courtesy of The International Shakespeare Globe Center Ltd. Photo: Richard Kalina • Oliver: The Burghley House Collection. Photograph: Courtauld Institute of Art • Peacham: Reproduced by permission of the Marquess of Bath, Longleat House, Warminster, Wiltshire, Great Britain. Photograph: Courtauld Institute of Art • de Witt: University Library, Utrecht, MS 842, f.132r • Middle Temple Hall: The Benchers of the Honorable Society of the Middle Temple, London • Hollar: Guildhall Library, Corporation of London

Contemporary Documents

First Folio front matter: *The Norton Facsimile of the First Folio of Shakespeare*, 2nd ed. (1996)

A Shakespearean Chronicle, 1558–1616

Master John: By courtesy of the National Portrait Gallery, London • Geneva Bible page: Bodleian Library, University of Oxford, Bibl.Eng.1560 • Swordsmen: By permission of the Folger Shakespeare Library • Holinshed (burning city): By permission of the Houghton Library, Harvard University • Holinshed (naval battle): By permission of the Houghton Library, Harvard University • Henri III: By permission of the Folger Shakespeare Library • Witches: C.27.b.35. By permission of the British Library • Agas: Guildhall Library, Corporation of London • Plague woodcut: Ashley 617. By permission of the British Library • Coat of Arms: Shakespeare Drafts (Vincent 157, no. 23). By permission of the College of Arms • Earl of Essex: © British Museum • Execution of Essex: By permission of the Folger Shakespeare Library • Vertue sketch: Additional Ms. 70438, folio 18. By permission of the British Library • Holinshed (Macbeth's coronation): By permission of the Houghton Library, Harvard University • Inigo Jones: Devonshire Collection, Chatsworth. Reproduced by permission of the Duke of Devonshire and the Chatsworth Settlement Trustees. Photo credit: The Courtauld Institute of Art • Henry, Prince of Wales: Fitzwilliam Museum, University of Cambridge • van de Passe (James I): Bodleian Library, University of Oxford, E 14 Th.Seld

THE HOUSE OF LANCASTER

EDWARD III

John of Gaunt, Duke of Lancaster
m. Blanche of Lancaster   m. Katherine Swynford

Henry Bolingbroke (HENRY IV)

Thomas Beaufort, Duke of Exeter

Henry Beaufort, Bishop of Winchester

Joan Beaufort m. Ralph Neville, Earl of Westmoreland

John Beaufort, Earl of Somerset

Richard Neville, Earl of Salisbury

Henry of Monmouth (HENRY V)
m. Catherine of France

Thomas, Duke of Clarence

John of Lancaster, Duke of Bedford

Humphrey, Duke of Gloucester

John Beaufort, Duke of Somerset

Edmund Beaufort, Duke of Somerset

John Neville, Marquess of Montague

Richard Neville, Earl of Warwick

HENRY VI m. Margaret of Anjou

Margaret Beaufort m. Edmund Tudor, Earl of Richmond

Henry Beaufort, Duke of Somerset

Edward, Prince of Wales m. Anne Neville

Henry Tudor, Earl of Richmond (HENRY VII) m. Elizabeth of York

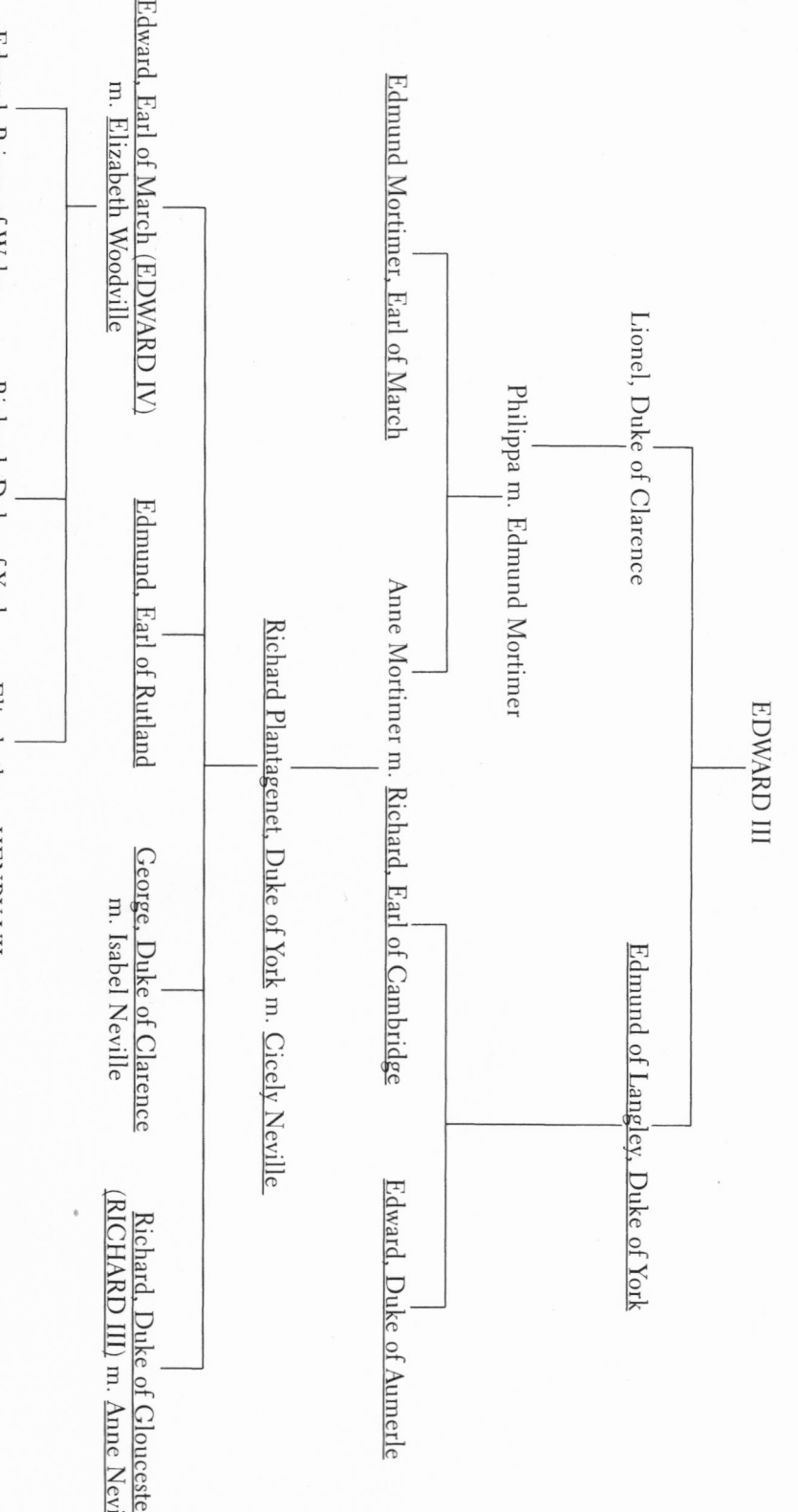

THE HOUSE OF YORK